Praise for

Framing the State in Times of Transition

"Laurel Miller and her colleagues at USIP have produced what will undoubtedly be the definitive study on constitution making in states emerging from conflict. This volume will be an invaluable source to all those interested in how any one of the nineteen constitutions were constructed. It will be of even greater help to those faced with a similar task in the future. The book provides wise guidance as to what approaches to constitution writing have worked in the past, and offers advice to both the international community and local actors in societies emerging from civil strive and governmental collapse on how to approach this task."

—James Dobbins, Director of the International Security and Defense Policy Center at the RAND Corporation, and lead author of *The Beginner's Guide to Nation Building*

"New states face both the challenge of dealing with their often violent past and that of constructing a stable democracy for the future. After the path-breaking volumes on transitional justice, the United States Institute of Peace has now produced an equally indispensable volume on the problems and challenges of constitution making. The breadth and depth of the chapters on individual cases ensure that the book will be a vademecum for both country specialists and comparativists. The country studies are framed by theoretical chapters that will also speak to political theorists. Future framers will have much to learn from the analyses of past mistakes proposed in many of the chapters. It is not too much to say that with this book the study of constitution making has come of age."

—Jon Elster, Columbia University, Robert K. Merton, Professor of Social Science

"Constitution-making in a post-conflict country is fraught with many risks and traps. How can we avoid or find creative solutions to them? In this useful book, scholars and practitioners reflect on the experience of two decades. Framing the State in Times of Transition: Case Studies in Constitution Making *demonstrates the critical importance of the process itself in producing a constitution that provides a solid foundation for peace—a lesson anyone interested in technical assistance and peacekeeping should remember."*

—Jean-Marie Guéhenno, U.N. undersecretary-general for peacekeeping operations

*"*Framing the State *is a rich resource and high quality reference work for academics and practitioners on constitution making. One reason for this is that its nineteen case studies are authored . . . by practitioners who have been close to the constitution making experiences they write about.* Framing the State *is both a product of, and reflects, the renewed interest in constitutionalism and constitution making. The book's special contribution is its geographically diverse and comprehensive treatment of the "new" post-conflict constitutions. These constitutions serve as peace agreements and offer opportunities for a reformulation of a national social compact in a divided society. This volume canvasses*

important considerations and contemporary lessons on process. It also surveys the expanding subject matter treated by these constitutions, which may embrace issues of identity, national values, or a necessary confrontation with history. This book will certainly be in my library."

—Nicholas Haysom, UN Director of Political, Peacekeeping, and Humanitarian Affairs, and former legal counsel for Nelson Mandela

"The enlightening case studies and overview essays in this impressive collection show how modern constitution drafters face common problems and arrive at quite diverse solutions, some successful and others less so, all set in the precise political context the drafters face. The book is sure to be an essential resource for all those interested in constitutional development and regime transitions."

—Mark Tushnet, William Nelson Cromwell Professor of Law, Harvard Law School

Framing the State in Times of Transition

Framing the State in Times of Transition

Case Studies in Constitution Making

Laurel E. Miller, *editor*

with Louis Aucoin

UNITED STATES INSTITUTE OF PEACE PRESS

WASHINGTON, D.C.

The views expressed in this book are those of the authors alone. They do not necessarily reflect views of the United States Institute of Peace.

UNITED STATES INSTITUTE OF PEACE
1200 17th Street NW, Suite 200
Washington, DC 20036-3011
www.usip.org

First published 2010

To request permission to photocopy or reprint materials for course use, contact the Copyright Clearance Center at www.copyright.com. For print, electronic media, and all other subsidiary rights, e-mail permissions@usip.org.

Printed in the United States of America

The paper used in this publication meets the minimum requirements of American National Standards for Information Science—Permanence of Paper for Printed Library Materials, ANSI Z39.48-1984.

Library of Congress Cataloging-in-Publication Data

Framing the state in times of transition : case studies in constitution making / Laurel E. Miller, editor; with Louis Aucoin.
        p. cm.
    Includes index.
    ISBN 978-1-60127-055-9 (pbk.)
    1. Constitutional history.   2. Constitutional conventions.   3. New democracies.
    I. Miller, Laurel (Laurel E.)   II. Aucoin, Louis.
    K3161.F73 2010
    342.02'9—dc22
                                                                    2009032360

Contents

PART III: ASIA AND THE PACIFIC

PART IV: EUROPE

PART V: LATIN AMERICA

PART VI: MIDDLE EAST AND CENTRAL ASIA

PART VII: CONCLUSION

Acknowledgments

This book results from work conducted under the auspices of the Project on Constitution Making, Peace Building, and National Reconciliation of the United States Institute of Peace (USIP). The United Nations Development Programme (UNDP) and USIP cosponsored the study of constitution-making processes presented in this volume. The views expressed herein do not necessarily reflect the views of UNDP, its executive board, or its member states.

The editor gratefully acknowledges the roles of Louis Aucoin, Neil Kritz, and Jamal Benomar in creating the concept for the Project on Constitution Making, initiating this study, and forming and guiding the working group and expert roundtables that contributed to the development of the material in this book.

The editor also wishes to thank the members of the working group, and particularly the group's chairman, Bereket Habte Selassie, for their valuable work in advising on the study's methods and structure, the selection of case studies, and the initial guidance provided to contributing authors. The working group included Andrew Arato, Louis Aucoin, Jamal Benomar, Andrea Bonime-Blanc, Gérard Conac, Francis Deng, Clarence Dias, Jon Elster, Owen Fiss, Vivien Hart, Jerry Hyman, Neil Kritz, Victor LeVine, Makau Mutua, Melanie Beth Oliviero, Herman Schwartz, Ann Seidman, Robert Seidman, Bereket Habte Selassie, Timothy Sisk, Mark Tushnet, Jennifer Widner, and William Zartman.

Finally, the editor appreciates the work of the late Vivien Hart and J Alexander Thier in reviewing portions of this volume, as well as Brian Slattery's excellent copyediting and other editorial help.

While this study was a collaborative one in many ways, the views expressed in the chapters of this book are the individual authors' own.

Foreword

Richard H. Solomon

President of the United States Institute of Peace

Constitutionalism has long been regarded as an essential foundation of the rule of law. In many countries seeking to reconstruct—or construct for the first time—a democratic system of governance based on the rule of law, one of the first steps undertaken is the adoption of a new constitution. This document may articulate a shared vision of the state and society, define the fundamental principles guiding governance of the state, and seek to distribute power equitably on some territorial or social basis. In meeting such objectives, the newly crafted constitution can contribute to building peace and achieving national reconciliation.

The experiences of societies emerging from periods of conflict, authoritarianism, or political upheaval have repeatedly demonstrated the importance of building the rule of law in order to consolidate peace and establish democracy. Countries transitioning from war and despotism cannot maintain peace over time unless the population and former antagonists are confident that their grievances will be addressed through legitimate structures and justice administered fairly. The extent to which a society succeeds in consolidating peace, democracy, and the rule of law depends on myriad factors, including the quality of a constitutional text and the respect accorded to the constitution. *Framing the State in Times of Transition* tests the notion that an additional factor

must be given weight: the manner in which a constitution is constructed and ratified. By examining nineteen cases of constitution-making processes and analyzing international norms that apply to constitution making, this volume demonstrates that well-conducted processes can, indeed, contribute to building stable, peaceful states, whereas poorly conducted processes most certainly undercut such efforts. This volume, which arose from a collaborative project of the United States Institute of Peace and the United Nations Development Program, offers a wealth of information about how countries have faced the challenges of constitution making in vulnerable and unsettled times, suggests ideas about ways to approach the political and technical aspects of constitution making, and gives practical considerations that will be of interest to those responsible for designing future constitution-making processes.

This comparative study also confirms a lesson that has become apparent to those concerned with state building and promotion of the rule of law: There are no one-size-fits-all formulas or models. Rather, each nation must find its own way, and those advising and supporting constitution makers must respect the particular context and the paramount role of national decision makers. In addition, the volume reveals once again that political will—the desire of those who hold power to create democratic societies in earnest and to put public before personal or parochial interests—is an essential ingredient for success.

Framing the State in Times of Transition illuminates the complexity of the process of constitution making. We hope that future constitution makers will draw both knowledge and inspiration from this volume as they seek to secure peace, justice, and democracy for their peoples.

Introduction

Louis Aucoin

At any constitutional moment in a country's history, political actors must make pivotal decisions that affect the country's future, defining the allocation of state power and enshrining in the constitution fundamental principles intended to guide society and the state. When constitution making is undertaken in the aftermath of violent conflict or in the context of a dramatic political transition or institutional crisis, the stability of a society and its prospects for future peaceful resolution of political and social conflict depend at least in part on these decisions. A constitutional text that articulates a new, broadly shared vision of society and organizes the system of governance in a way that respects and protects the interests of diverse groups can play a crucial role in consolidating peace and strengthening democracy. This is particularly true in societies riven by ethnic, religious, or other divisions. This volume explores the ways in which the *process* of arriving at a new constitution under conditions of serious political and social stress also can play—and sometimes fail to play—such a role.

In its focus on process, this book diverges from the bulk of the voluminous literature on constitutions and constitutionalism, which concentrates largely on substantive themes, such as constitutional design, human rights, and decentralization, to name just a few. This book responds to the growing attention that practitioners of constitution making, and

experts, foreign assistance providers, and international organizations supporting their work are paying to the potential advantages and implications of procedural choices in the constitution-making process. It is intended to contribute substantially to the intellectual foundation for designing constitution-making processes that can build a durable consensus on the structure of the state and foundational principles, embed peaceful modes of political competition, and foster reconciliation among diverse elements in society.[1]

This volume uses case studies—nineteen individually selected episodes of constitution making across a broad range of cultures, political contexts, and geographic regions—to advance a detailed understanding of the nature of constitution-making processes. The case studies, along with a concluding chapter that synthesizes and draws lessons from them, illuminate the procedural options available to constitution makers, the effects of employing those options in varying circumstances, and key issues that those designing constitution-making processes should consider. This book also offers analysis of an emerging international norm that constitution-making processes should be democratic, transparent, and participatory; illustrates concrete manifestations of that norm; and demonstrates how those attributes of a constitution-making process are pragmatically desirable.

The overarching point of view of this volume is that process matters, a perspective that developed out of observations of constitution-making processes particularly in countries emerging from conflict. While the term *process* contains a multitude of elements, we use it principally to encompass the methods of negotiating constitutional questions, the character of the institutions used to draft and adopt constitutional texts, the designation of decision makers and the decision-making procedures they use, and the mechanisms for allowing diverse perspectives to be aired and incorporated. Fundamentally, the material in this study explores the ways in which process matters, for good and for ill, depending on the choices made in various contexts. While practical attention to constructing effective constitution-making processes is increasing,[2] a deeper exploration of the nature and implications of process choices has been absent. This book intends to help remedy that deficit.

Development of this Study and Case Study Selection and Structure

The study presented in this volume is a product of the United States Institute of Peace's (USIP) Project on Constitution-Making, Peace-Building, and National Reconciliation. The United Nations Development Program co-sponsored the study, and collaborated in the formulation of its approach. This author designed the study to provide a practical perspective on the process of constitution making, informed by the insights of a group of writers who had direct experience in constitution making, relevant academic expertise, or both. To benefit from a variety of disciplinary viewpoints in developing the study, a working group was formed to advise on the study's methods and structure; the group included experts in comparative constitutional law, conflict resolution, economic development, political science, and sociology, as well as representatives of the foreign assistance community who had experience supporting

constitution making.[3] This working group—chaired by Professor Bereket Habte Selassie of the University of North Carolina, the former chair of the constitutional commission of Eritrea—participated in selecting case studies and preparing the initial guidance for authors. For most of the case studies in this volume, working group members, joined by relevant country and regional experts, also met with each author to review a preliminary draft and discuss key issues.

Several criteria guided the selection of cases. In general, the instances of constitution making included in this volume were chosen because working group experts knew them both to provide rich bases for insights into the nature of constitution-making processes and to be of likely interest to future constitution makers. More specifically, representing a variety of contexts was a key factor in case selection. The USIP project is particularly focused on the role of constitution making during periods in which countries are emerging from conflict, and almost half of the selected cases reflect that focus. But for purposes of comparison and to broaden the reach of the study, the remainder of the selected cases concerns constitution making during periods of transition from autocratic rule to democracy, or during periods of institutional crisis or major governance reform. In addition, diversity of regional, cultural, and economic settings was an important criterion, to ensure that conclusions drawn from the study would be broadly applicable and that the study would contain material that might resonate with the experiences of future constitution makers throughout the world. Cases were selected also to represent a range of time periods, from 1978 to 2005, though the study's focus on contemporary modes of constitution making, given its practical orientation, constrained the range.[4] Some cases were chosen partly because they were expected to offer useful information and analysis concerning public participation procedures, as the working group was aware of growing interest in that aspect of constitution-making processes. Finally, attention was paid to including many of the most prominent recent instances of constitution making that also satisfied the preceding criteria, as it was clear that these would be of great interest to practitioners and scholars; two such cases—Afghanistan and Iraq—were added in the course of the study.

To shape the case studies, the working group prepared a concept paper to serve as a research guide for the authors. This paper grouped a series of research questions into eight categories: general issues pertaining to conflict resolution and constitution making; the structure of the constitution-making process; public participation in the process; democratic representation; the timing and sequencing of the process; the role of the international community; the role of international law; and essential issues of substance. Some of the chapter authors adhered quite closely to these categories in organizing their material. Others drew from the categories the questions most relevant to their particular case and addressed them within a unique structure. The variation among the case studies in the specific questions addressed is unsurprising, considering the diverse experiences of the different countries studied.

The purpose of applying a uniform analytical framework across a broad range of cases was to create a basis for discerning the variables that underlie the different approaches to constitution making, evaluating their respective effects, and deriving common lessons from the varying experiences. The concept paper's questions about general issues pertaining to conflict resolution and constitution making, for example, asked the authors to identify the variables that determined the particular approach to constitution making and to address choices such as referring to a former constitution as a starting point versus beginning with a blank slate. This category also included questions concerning the incorporation of substantive and procedural parameters for constitution making into peace agreements.

The second category of questions, regarding the structure of the process, solicited the detailed information needed to evaluate each case and compare it to others. What were the benefits and detriments, for example, of using a constitutional commission? Was it preferable to use a constituent assembly or an ordinary parliament to adopt a constitution? Who should actually draft the constitution and how should the drafters be selected? And how did the answers to these structural questions pertain to the overarching questions of legitimacy and stability?

The third category of questions focused on public participation. These questions asked authors to consider the benefits and costs of public participation in the constitution-making process, as well as the methods of inviting participation and offering civic education in conjunction with participation. This category included questions concerning the use and timing of plebiscites; the identification of conditions under which a constitution-making process, or some portion of a process, should be more or less participatory; and the relationship between participation and the ultimate legitimacy of the constitution.

The fourth category, dealing with democratic representation, sought in general to find out how and whether the constitution-making process protected a broad range of interests. These questions focused, for example, on the composition of constituent assemblies and issues raised by refusals of particular groups to participate in the processes.

Key questions in the fifth category—the timing and sequencing of the constitution-making process—revolved around the implications of the phasing of the process's steps and the length of the process, including whether a connection could be drawn between the duration of the process and its effectiveness. Questions concerning the use of an interim charter or some other temporary arrangement during the constitution-making period proved particularly pertinent.

Questions in the sixth category, the role of the international community, centered on the variables that determine the appropriate role for outside actors in the process. Authors were asked to consider the potential impact of foreign involvement on the legitimacy of the processes and the helpfulness of different forms and methods of foreign assistance to constitution makers.

The seventh category, dealing with the role of international law, in the end bore little fruit. We sought to discover whether any of the key players in the constitution-making processes felt compelled by any relevant international norms to make particular choices in connection with the process, but such a dynamic turned out not to feature in the case studies.

The final category of questions, essential issues of substance, also did not make a significant impression on the case studies, though some chapters identify substantive issues that were central to the constitutional negotiations.[5]

In addition to the case studies, this volume includes two thematic chapters that explore, from differing angles, emerging ideas in international law and practice regarding a possible legal norm favoring, or even requiring, popular participation in constitution-making. The late Thomas Franck and Arun Thiruvengadam, legal scholars, address the question whether international law has anything to say about the way in which a constitution is negotiated or drafted; they find that it is not yet clear that anything in international law requires a state to adhere to particular practices, but that there is growing acceptance of the norm that constitutions should be prepared through participatory processes with a high degree of transparency. The chapter by the late Vivien Hart, who was a political sci-

entist, sets forth some building blocks of a case for a right to participation, giving attention to the legal, normative, and practical aspects of democratic constitution making. The subject of these two chapters merited close examination in this volume, in light of increasing attention among constitution-making experts to the value and significance of public participation—and, perhaps, growing popular expectations of participation, at least in democracies.

Using This Volume

The material in this book is intended to be of use to policymakers engaged in designing constitution-making processes, constitutional experts advising those policymakers, and interested scholars. The material may be navigated in a variety of ways. A reader seeking to understand how various countries have shaped programs of public participation, and with what effects, for example, will find material on this core theme under an appropriate section heading in each of the case studies in which participation is featured, as well as in the concluding chapter. Selective review across the case studies of other key structural elements of the processes under examination is similarly possible. In addition, as indicated in the preceding discussion, case study authors proceeded from a common analytical framework. While the specific outline of each chapter varies, common thematic threads run, on the whole, throughout the chapters; by scanning section headings in the chapters, readers focused on particular themes—such as democratic representation, for example—will be able to identify pertinent material easily.

Some readers will no doubt wish to narrow their attention to a particular case study, either because of its inherent interest or because it concerns factual circumstances considered analogous to a new instance of constitution making. Readers interested in a particular geographic region will find the case studies ordered in the book on this basis. And readers focused on a particular category of circumstances, such as constitution making in countries emerging from conflict, may find the discussion of the nature of the cases in the concluding chapter, and their categorization in table 2 there, a helpful starting point.

Other readers may find it useful to begin accessing the material in this volume by reading the concluding chapter, which analyzes all the main themes in the case studies and thematic chapters, accompanied by references to cases pertinent to such analysis. Readers can use the conclusion to identify themes of interest and case studies on which they may wish to focus attention. The conclusion also identifies common pitfalls to avoid when undertaking constitution making—of interest to perhaps a broad range of readers—as well as contextual factors that should be assessed when designing a constitution-making process.

* * *

The material in this book presents and assesses an array of options for and approaches to processes that constitution makers and those advising them can use to make informed choices in designing processes intended to contribute to settling conflict, promoting social and political reconciliation, and fostering lasting peace. Moreover, because it is impossible in the present to conceive of all the possible lessons that might be deduced from this study in the future, each of the case studies stands on its own as a valuable historical record of how each particular process responded to a unique set of circumstances. Thus, this volume is a rich resource for those who will face challenges similar to those explored in these pages.

Notes

1. A forthcoming review of the literature on constitution-making processes notes that the impact of procedural choices remains understudied. "More than a decade after [Jon] Elster ... lamented the dearth of theory on constitutional design (and, we would add, systematic empirical evidence), the field retains a frontier quality ... notwithstanding Elster's own valuable contributions. Many of us likely suspect that the conditions and rules under which founders write, deliberate, and ratify will be consequential. We just cannot say how they matter, or to what extent, with any authority." Tom Ginsburg, Zachary Elkins, and Justin Blount, "Does the Process of Constitution-Making Matter?" *Annual Review of Law and Social Science* 2009 (forthcoming) (version of January 15, 2009).

2. USIP has been actively engaged in this type of work. See information regarding its Constitution Making, Peace Building and National Reconciliation project, available at http://www.usip.org/ruleoflaw/projects/constitution.html (accessed April 15, 2009). Other organizations involved in such work include International IDEA and Interpeace. See, respectively, http://www.idea.int/cbp/index.cfm and http://www.interpeace.org/index.php?option=com_content&task=view&id=44&Itemid=105 (accessed April 15, 2009). See also the 1999 recommendations of the Commonwealth Human Rights Initiative to the Commonwealth heads of government, advancing the idea that the process of constitution making is as important as the substantive content of a constitution, available at http://www.humanrightsinitiative.org/publications/const/constitutionalism_booklet_1999.pdf (accessed on April 15, 2009).

3. The working group included Andrew Arato, Louis Aucoin, Jamal Benomar, Andrea Bonime-Blanc, Gérard Conac, Francis Deng, Clarence Dias, Jon Elster, Owen Fiss, Vivien Hart, Jerry Hyman, Neil Kritz, Victor LeVine, Makau Mutua, Melanie Beth Oliviero, Herman Schwartz, Ann Seidman, Robert Seidman, Bereket Habte Selassie, Timothy Sisk, Mark Tushnet, Jennifer Widner, and William Zartman. Working group members were not asked to review this volume, which was independently peer reviewed.

4. The set of cases selected is not intended to suggest that the period since 1978 (the Spain case) should be considered a distinctive era in constitution making. One possibility might have been to include cases covering the period since the end

of World War II, though, given a reasonable limit on the number of cases, this would have stretched the study thin over a long time period. The working group considered 1989 as a possible beginning date for the study's time frame, recognizing that the end of the Cold War was a true milestone of democratic transition. But in the end, Spain, though earlier, was included because the constitution-making process there was an intimate part of the transition from autocratic rule to democracy and the case study was likely to yield valuable lessons regarding constitution making in transitional settings.

5.   One substantive topic that is explored to a limited extent in the study, but which has attracted interest among practitioners and merits further examination, is the incorporation of immutable—or unamendable—principles in constitutional text as a means of definitively securing basic principles and ensuring against the recurrence of past abuses.

PART I

THEORY AND CONCEPTS

1

Norms of International Law Relating to the Constitution-Making Process

Thomas M. Franck and Arun K. Thiruvengadam

Does international law have anything to say about the way in which a constitution is negotiated or drafted? This paper attempts to address this issue by approaching it from several perspectives. After an overview of the general principles of international law (both treaty and customary law) which may be relevant for this purpose, we focus on the provisions of one particular treaty, the International Covenant on Civil and Political Rights (ICCPR), and the manner in which states and the UN Human Rights Committee have interpreted its provisions. We next analyze recent state practice on the issue by seeking to ascertain whether recent exercises in constitutional drafting have followed any general norms.

How to Read the Applicable Law

International law consists of customary law and treaty law. We cannot find persuasive evidence that customary law requires any particular modalities to be followed in the

process of writing a state's constitution.[1] States are presumed by international law to be sovereign and it has been held that this sovereignty cannot be limited without a state's consent.[2] As the Permanent Court of International Justice pointed out in 1927, "the rules of law binding upon States emanate from their own free will as expressed in conventions or usages generally accepted. . . . Restrictions upon the independence of States cannot therefore be presumed."[3]

Nevertheless, in the twenty-first century, sovereignty is not absolute. Treaties are construed to give effect to their general purpose; as the Vienna Convention on the Law of Treaties states, they are to be interpreted "in the light of [the treaty's] object and purposes."[4] It may thus be inferred that even if a human rights treaty pertaining to the governance of states does not specifically apply to constitution drafting, such applicability may still be implied by reference to the object and purposes of the treaty. A treaty's norms and strictures may have a penumbra of necessarily implied additional terms because its provisions are deemed, by the other parties or the organ of treaty interpretation, to have broad objectives and purposes requiring adherence to these implied terms to effectuate its purposes.[5] As the separate opinion of Judge Sir Percy Spender noted in a significant International Court of Justice case,

> a general rule is that words used in a treaty should be read as having the meaning they bore therein when they came into existence. But this meaning must be consistent with the purposes sought to be achieved. Where, as in the case of the [UN] Charter, the purposes are directed to saving succeeding generations in an indefinite future from the scourge of war. . . . the general rule above stated does not mean that the words in the Charter can only comprehend such situations and contingencies and manifestations of subject-matter as were within the minds of the framers.[6]

Customary law, too, may have implications for a state even in the absence of specific consent. Professor Theodor Meron, a former president of the International Criminal Tribunal for the Former Yugoslavia, argues that rules established by treaties to which most states have subscribed may become law of a "customary character" that may also obligate "states that are not parties to the instrument in which the norm is stated."[7]

Thus, the treaty provisions applying more generally to governance may apply to constitution drafting in specific states, either by a broad construction of the object of a treaty on governance to which they are parties or by operation of customary law if they are not parties to the relevant universal instrument. Treaty parties would be bound to observe the general norms applicable to governance by virtue of the binding nature of those treaties as broadly construed in the light of their object and purposes. New states, which may not yet be party to such treaty obligations, might be bound by the universal customary norm that emanates from the fact of near-universal adherence to a treaty on governance. As the International Court of Justice has observed, states which, because of special circumstances, are not bound by the norms set out in a treaty of almost-universal ratification may nevertheless be bound by approximately the same normative requirements as the actual parties by operation of customary law—deriving from states' compliance with the treaty—that reflects the common practice of states.[8]

Not infrequently, the United States has accepted and utilized the tendency of universal treaty law to manifest itself to nonparties as customary law. With respect to at least two universal conventions—the Law of Treaties[9] and the Law of the Sea[10]—the United States has taken the position that until its objections to a particular provision have been met, it will not ratify the convention, but will regard all its other provisions as enunciation of binding international customary law.

With such interpretive considerations in mind, it is possible to consider the international norms applicable to governance. However, because the principal treaty establishing rules pertaining to the lawmaking processes of states—the way legislators are elected, the public right to be consulted—is not specifically directed toward the constitution-drafting process, this can only be done speculatively, as it is far from clear whether the general terms of the normative structure are implicitly applicable to this particular aspect of governance. If the answer to the preceding question is in the affirmative, we may then speculate how the terms of the principal source of such international rules pertaining to governance might apply to the process of constitution drafting.

The principal source of such universal procedural norms is the ICCPR,[11] particularly articles 1(1), 2(1), 3, 25, 26, and 27. While the ensuing discussion focuses on these norms as they might apply to constitution drafting—in either established states that are parties to the ICCPR and in the process of drafting a new constitution, or new states that may not yet be parties to the ICCPR but may nevertheless be bound by the customary law emanating from it—in the jurisprudence of the Human Rights Committee, which is charged with monitoring and implementing the ICCPR, there has so far been little consideration of how the obligations and rights of that treaty apply to the constitution-drafting process. The few instances in which the Human Rights Committee has made observations on this specific aspect will be analyzed in the next section.

The International Covenant on Civil and Political Rights

Article 1(1) of the ICCPR stipulates that "all peoples have the right to self-determination. By virtue of that right they freely determine their political status and freely pursue their economic, social and cultural development." This provision has received a substantial amount of interpretation by the Human Rights Committee, established under the convention and consisting of eighteen experts elected by the UN General Assembly.[12] None of this interpretation, however, has pertained to constitution drafting. Nevertheless, the ICCPR provides for complaints of noncompliance to be heard by the committee when instituted by other state parties and—when the state complained against has declared its acceptance of the requisite optional protocol—by individual persons claiming to be victims of a violation.[13] In addition, the committee makes periodic observations on the meaning of parts of the treaty and reviews periodic reports on compliance, which parties are required to present and to explicate before the committee. It is entirely possible that, in the future, a complaint could allege that a constitution-drafting process has violated the right of self-determination. That this is not fanciful is suggested by the third paragraph of the same article, which specif-

ically obliges states with dependent territories to "promote the realization of the right of self-determination." In the context of decolonization, this requirement evidently envisages that the right of peoples "freely [to] determine their political status" should apply equally to the process of achieving independence, including the design of the new nations' constitutions.

In practice, this is precisely what happened when the transfer of power from colonial authorities was conducted in an orderly fashion under UN supervision.[14] In the thirty-five years following the end of World War II, self-determination transformed the political landscape. Beginning with India, Burma, and West Africa's Gold Coast, Britain led the way in compliance with the norm's requirements, negotiating independence constitutions with elected parliamentary representatives of the colonial populations under the watchful monitoring eye of the UN committee on dependent territories established under Article 73(e) of its charter. As early as May 1956, the UN Trusteeship Council sent monitors to the plebiscite in which British Togoland chose to join Ghana in its move to constitutional governance. Preindependence plebiscites followed in the British Cameroons in November 1959 and in Belgian-administered Ruanda-Urundi. In 1961, the United Nations aided New Zealand, the administering authority, in conducting a plebiscite in Western Samoa that endorsed the draft constitution and a form of association with the former trustee.[15] On June 17, 1975, the United Nations observed the vote in which residents of the Northern Mariana Islands endorsed a loose form of association with the United States,[16] and at various times in the 1980s, it supervised plebiscites in the rest of the U.S. Pacific Islands Trust, which determined the future constitutional status of those several archipelagos.

The monitoring of political progress in trust territories led to a case-by-case enunciation of principles applicable to an implicit emerging democratic entitlement that gradually became more generally applicable. Throughout the 1950s and 1960s, on the basis of reports from visiting missions, the Trusteeship Council and General Assembly recommended to the administering powers specific steps necessary to create democratic participation for the territories' inhabitants in the process of choosing their political future. In the Trusteeship Council's 1959 report concerning Belgian administration of Ruanda-Urundi, it called for the introduction of universal suffrage and an increase in the responsibilities of elected local authorities.[17] Such advice was influential in determining both the rate and direction of a dependent territory's emancipation and in formulating a generally shared expectation as to what the emerging democratic entitlement entailed. The United Nations demanded that every adult should be entitled to vote and that those elected should rule, which colonial systems that had fostered qualified franchises and limited self-government only gradually accepted. It cannot be said that the right to self-determination emerged from this period of practice as a developed code of specified requisites, but it is demonstrable that it was accepted as requiring, at a minimum, the direct and democratic participation of all adult men and women in a parliamentary, plebiscitary, or both a parliamentary and plebiscitary process of constitution drafting.

Against the background of the above developments, the concept of self-determination was cast as a right extending beyond decolonization into the pantheon of universal rights captured in the ICCPR. By the time the United Nations began to administer the transition to independence of Namibia in 1990, deploying more than seven thousand military and civilian personnel at a cost of $373 million, it was considered routine that it would supervise elections in the runup to independence and the drafting of a new consti-

tution.[18] Most recently, this plebiscitary and parliamentary norm was implemented in the UN administration of East Timor leading to independence.

The rights set out in the ICCPR are expressly to be respected in the process of governance without distinction and on the basis of strict equality of persons. Thus, Article 2(1) requires states "to respect and to ensure to all individuals within its territory and subject to its jurisdiction the rights recognized in the present Covenant, without distinction of any kind, such as race, colour, sex, language, religion, political or other opinion, national or social origin, property, birth or other status." The U.S. Constitution, drafted by persons chosen in part in accordance with distinctions of sex and property, would not have accorded with the contemporary requirements established by this provision. This is underscored by Article 3, which states that "the parties to the present Covenant undertake to ensure the equal rights of men and women to the enjoyment of all civil and political rights set forth in the present Covenant." Article 26 reemphasizes the right to strict equality "before the law," and Article 27 reiterates the entitlement to equality as it extends to minorities.

The ICCPR envisages extensive rights of persons to participate in the political process. Article 25 specifies that

> every citizen shall have the right and the opportunity, without any of the distinctions mentioned in article 2 and without unreasonable restrictions: (a) to take part in the conduct of public affairs, directly or through freely chosen representatives; (b) to vote and to be elected at genuine periodic elections which shall be by universal, and equal suffrage and shall be held by secret ballot, guaranteeing the free expression of the will of the electors.

The Human Rights Committee of independent experts has had extensive opportunity, both in its review of obligatory country compliance reports and in hearing individual petitions alleging violations, to develop the jurisprudence of this provision.[19] In deciding upon a complaint filed by the Mikmaq tribal society in Canada, the Human Rights Committee was required to interpret and apply Article 25. The committee appears to have concluded that while the right "to take part in the conduct of public affairs, directly or through freely chosen representatives," applies also to constitution making, it does not provide any particular model for this. In the words of the committee, "it is for the legal and constitutional system of the State party to provide for the modalities of such participation."[20]

The Human Rights Committee also has made a general comment on the matter, indicating that the "right to participate in public affairs" set out in Article 25 is satisfied, inter alia, when citizens "choose or change their constitution or decide public issues through a referendum or other electoral process."[21] This comment, together with the committee's willingness to take jurisdiction in the Mikmaq case, may indicate a tendency to regard constitutional drafting as coming within the purview of the ICCPR.

In sum, all states contemplating the drafting or redrafting of their constitutions are well advised to consider the ICCPR in organizing the framework within which their citizens participate in that process. Whether this is a legal or merely prudential requisite is not yet clear. Possibly it is also not very important, except to theorists. Regional norms may be even more relevant. For African states, attention needs be paid to the Banjul Charter.[22] For European states engaged in constitution drafting, similar consideration is appropriate for the even more extensive and intrusive provisions of the European Convention for the Protection of Human Rights and Fundamental Freedoms.[23] Not only are its terms even more explicit in guaranteeing popular rights of political participation and other democratic entitlements, but the treaty also has sharper teeth. Admission of a state to the Council of Europe and its parliamentary institutions is conditional upon acceptance of the treaty and of the jurisdiction of the European Court of Human Rights, to which access is available to citizens who allege violations of the rights extended to them by the treaty.

Analysis of State Practice: Recent Constitution-Making Experiences for International Normativity

International law derives not only from treaties and international custom but also in part from state practice. When the state practice of many states becomes consciously patterned, these patterns are recognized as evidence of international customary law. "General principles of law recognized by civilized nations" are also considered a source of international law.[24] Therefore, analyzing the practice of states, and the general principles of law that they follow, can help in ascertaining norms of international law.

We examine two distinct phases of constitution making that occurred in the recent past with a view to discerning whether common norms relating to the process of constitution making can be said to have evolved. The first of these is the flurry of constitution drafting that occurred in Africa as its nations sought to legitimize their governance. The second occurred in central and eastern Europe with the end of communist rule.

Constitutional Drafting in Africa in the 1990s

The 1990s witnessed a spate of constitutional reform across Africa. While several states, including Namibia, Malawi, Uganda, South Africa, and Benin, adopted new constitutions, several others, including Tanzania, Kenya, and Zimbabwe, experienced major constitutional reforms. What distinguished this phase from the earlier rounds of constitutional-drafting exercises in the period of and following decolonization was the extraordinary emphasis on public participation in the processes of constitution making.

Postcolonial Africa has witnessed several rounds of constitution making. In what one scholar has termed "the old approach,"[25] in the era after the departure of the colonial powers, constitution-making processes across Africa were largely driven by the elected government or ruling power. The government either appointed or attempted to control the election of a constituent assembly, parliamentary committee, technical committee, or select committee of lawyers and politicians to write a new constitution for the country. Usually, the process of the old approach ensured that there was little or no public debate prior to or during the drafting process, no consultation with ordinary people, and no referendum on the draft constitution before it became law. Even where there was some limited debate, the result was predetermined and manipulated and not informed by the debate's logic or content. African scholars contend that it was largely because of such processes that at the end of the 1980s, constitutionalism across Africa was viewed as a failed project. Nigeria, which became independent from British colonial rule in 1960, has experienced five different attempts at constitution making since then, and all of these processes could be considered as variations on the old approach.

At the beginning of the 1990s, there seemed to be widespread acceptance among Africans that the process of constitution making had to change. This led to the adoption of the "new approach," which emphasizes participation and puts great premium on dialogue, debate, consultation, and participation. It is guided by principles including diversity, inclusivity, participation, transparency and openness, autonomy, accountability, and legitimacy.[26] This focus on processes of constitution making has generated productive and innovative methods as well as a healthy debate on effective modes of public participation. It has also resulted in a number of different approaches being followed. One leading scholar has identified two principal strategies as part of the new approach: first, appointment of a constitutional commission, followed by the election of a constituent assembly to adopt and enact the new constitution (this was the process followed in Uganda and Malawi); and second, establishment of a national (sovereign) conference or convention that leads to the enactment of a new constitution (this process was followed in Benin and later adopted in Mali, Niger, Gabon, and Togo).[27]

To understand the details of the process requirements, we focus on two specific instances of constitution making: the adoption of the Ugandan constitution in 1995 and that of the constitution of South Africa in 1996. Both these processes are now considered landmark events in African constitutional history and have generated an impressive body of scholarly literature.[28] For our purposes, it is not necessary to narrate the entire story of constitution drafting in Uganda and South Africa; much about both cases has already been painstakingly documented and analyzed in the literature cited beforehand, and further analysis of both cases appears in this volume. We must, however, note patterns in the processes that are relevant to our purposes.

In Uganda, the process of drafting the 1995 constitution began in earnest in 1988, when Uganda's constitutional commission was established by a statute.[29] The commission, created to solicit the views of the Ugandan people on the content of the new constitution, was the first step in the constitutional drafting process, followed by the creation of a new constituent assembly, for which fresh elections were held. The newly constituted assembly ultimately drafted the 1995 constitution. The constitutional commission included representatives of various interest groups in Uganda, including those who had opposed the president domestically, giving the commission the required legitimacy.[30] Scholars have commended the lengthy process—nearly four years—employed by the commission for its recognition of the importance of taking whatever time was necessary to truly receive wide citizen input.[31] The commission undertook special efforts to ensure that groups that had traditionally remained outside the consultative process, including women, were consulted and that their views would be taken into account.[32]

The Ugandan constitutional commission adopted a variety of methods to collect views from the public.[33] To consider all submissions equally, each and every one of the 25,000-odd submissions was summarized and translated into English from local languages. All the submissions that the commission received were eventually published, along with the final report. The commission solicited the views of the large community of Ugandans who live abroad, and also traveled to several countries to gain a comparative understanding of constitutional practices and experiences.

Soon after the commission submitted a final report, the Constituent Assembly Bill was enacted. This statute placed great emphasis on building consensus.[34] It dictated that the constituent assembly was to be constituted through fresh elections, though the president had the power to nominate ten members. Special provisions were included to ensure that women were adequately represented.[35] Elections were held in March 1994, supervised by international observers, donor agencies, and local monitors, and were viewed as free and fair. The assembly began its work in May 1994 and completed the draft of the new constitution in August 1995. The assembly's draft was enacted as law by the government on September 22, 1995, and was officially promulgated on October 8, 1995.[36] The assembly's constitution is substantially similar to the commission's draft and appears to give credence to the view that the actual text of the constitution reflects the views of the Ugandan people, as expressed by them in their submissions to the commission.

Because of its unique history, South Africa's constitutional drafting process had several features that were peculiar to it, dictated by the political and social circumstances that existed in South Africa in the late 1980s and early 1990s.[37] Although the negotiations for drafting a new constitution formally began in March 1993, it was only after an interim constitution had been adopted in November 1993, and the constituent assembly elected in May 1994, that attempts to involve the public in the constitutional process were initiated. Although begun late in the process of evolving the constitution, the public participation process was enthusiastically pursued between January 1995, when the assembly launched its media campaign shortly before it began its work, and September 1995, when the first draft of the constitution was produced.

The program developed to achieve the participation of 40 million-odd South African citizens, most of whom were illiterate and did not have access to print or electronic media, was extremely ambitious and multifaceted. The program had three modes: community liaison, media liaison, and advertising.[38] The first component involved participatory workshops; between February and August 1995, twenty-six public meetings were organized in all nine provinces, in which more than two hundred assembly members became involved.[39] As part of the media campaign, the press, radio, television, and Internet were employed to spread the message about the new constitution.[40] In response to all these initiatives, the assembly received nearly 1.7 million submissions from the public, though the bulk of these were more in the nature of petitions. Of these, 11,000 were substantive submissions and canvassed a broad range of issues. After the first draft of the constitution had been finalized in November 1995, it was published and distributed, and the public was asked to respond to the specific provisions of the draft. This time, the assembly received more than 250,000 submissions and attempted to record and reply to each individually.[41] After hectic deliberations, on May 8, 1996, the assembly adopted the final text of the constitution. However, thanks to the peculiar circumstances under which the constitution was negotiated, its text had to be reviewed by the South African constitutional court for certification that the final text was in agreement with the preset constitutional principles. On September 6, 1996, the court rendered its judgment, pointing out that the final text was deficient in certain respects. The assembly reconvened to discuss changes in accordance with the judgment, and on October 11, 1996, tabled the new document before the court. On December 4, 1996, the court approved the final text. President Nelson Mandela signed the final constitution on December 10, 1996, and it came into force on February 4, 1997.[42]

The developments in South Africa seem almost revolutionary in character, but African scholars themselves have added cautionary notes to this discourse. It has been pointed out that though the new approach is far more participatory than earlier experiences, even in South Africa, the participation was largely limited to urban intelligentsia and the middle classes.[43] The process either bypassed rural folk, or they had little interest in what was essentially a middle-class social project. Several commentators criticized the South African public participation process in particular, pointing to the huge volume of submissions and asking if any constitutional draftsman could be reasonably expected to review them all. Several argued that the entire program was an elaborate hoax, designed to hide the fact that even the final constitution was to be a negotiated document and would not be submitted for the general public's approval.[44] Similar criticisms were directed at the 1997 Eritrean constitution, although it too was the product of an elaborate procedure to involve the public in the drafting

process.[45] This has been one of the notable aspects of recent exercises in constitution making in Africa: Though there are attempts to involve the public at various stages of the constitution-drafting process, apart from the recent exception in Rwanda,[46] there have not been attempts to have the general populace approve the final product. The reasoning appears to be that assembly members possess sufficient representative capacity to obviate the need to seek the final nod of approval of the people through a referendum.

In analyzing the recent exercises in constitution drafting in Africa, one has to note the emergence in practice of several similar devices designed to increase public participation. At the same time, however, it must be emphasized that there are no general norms that have been uniformly applied in these countries. Both Uganda and South Africa, while employing several innovative strategies to increase public participation, used them at different stages of the constitution-making process. In Uganda, public participation was sought at the very outset. In South Africa, the public were involved at a fairly late stage, after an interim constitution had been adopted and elections for the new constituent assembly had been held. Another distinction is that in South Africa, the views of the populace were sought on a draft of the constitution; in Uganda, the views of the public were sought to prepare the draft of the constitution without seeking their specific reactions to the actual provisions of the draft of the constitution itself. Based on these trends, one can safely declare that while all African countries currently seem to feel an obligation to involve the public in constitution-making or constitution-reform processes, there seem to be no clear rules for how and when the public are to be involved. Each country appears to feel free to fashion appropriate strategies based on its own internal circumstances.

Constitutional Drafting in Eastern and Central Europe in the 1990s

In the aftermath of the Cold War, starting from the late 1980s, the former Soviet republics as well as the countries of Eastern and Central Europe underwent periods of constitutional reform that saw a number of them either adopting wholly new constitutions or substantially amending their existing constitutions. Due to constraints of space, this paper does not analyze in detail the constitution-making processes in the former Soviet republics, including Estonia, Latvia, Lithuania, Belarus, Moldova, Russia, Ukraine, Azerbaijan, Kyrgyzstan, and Kazakhstan, though nearly all these countries adopted new constitutions in the first half of the 1990s. In general, public participation in the process of drafting new constitutions for the former Soviet republics has been low. However, in some of these countries—specifically, Estonia, Lithuania, and Russia—the newly drafted constitutions were approved in a national referendum before being brought into force.[47]

Unlike African countries in the 1990s, which by then had varying but relatively substantial experiences of constitutionalism, all the countries in Eastern and Central Europe as well as in the former Soviet Union were coming out of a shared past of communism.[48] In transitioning to constitutional democracies, all these countries faced multiple challenges at the same time, in that they had to simultaneously transition to market-based economies while also seeking to fashion themselves into constitutional democracies.[49] As they sought to tackle the various legal, political, social, and economic issues that confronted them, each country adopted different strategies to reconcile its communist past with a democratic future. Although at times the countries used similar strategies, very different results were seen in different cases, depending on the mix of domestic factors that controlled the consequences. Involving the public in constitution-drafting exercises has generally been considered a significant aspect, but it never assumed the importance or the scale that the issue garnered in Africa in the 1990s.

Trying to describe constitution-making processes across Central and Eastern Europe generally is a difficult exercise: Despite some shared characteristics, the constitutional experiences of these nations have been very different. In view of this difficulty, this section offers a broad overview of the processes of constitution making employed in these countries, focusing on the extent of public participation.

In several of Central and Eastern European countries, including Bulgaria, Hungary, Poland, Czechoslovakia, and East Germany, the transition to democracy was negotiated through a process of roundtable talks, whereas different paths were followed in the rest. In countries where roundtable talks were held, they featured the Communist Party—together with various satellites and pseudo-independent organizations—on the one hand and a more or less well-organized opposition on the other.[50] Several countries opted for setting up a constituent assembly to draft a new constitution. In Albania, Bulgaria, and Romania, constituent assemblies were established after holding elections, whereas in Poland, Hungary, and Czechoslovakia, they were self-constituted bodies. It was generally believed that the genesis of the constituent assembly might be crucial for its legitimacy and the legitimacy of the final document produced.[51] In most of these countries, once the constitution was finally adopted, it was subjected to the referendum process to obtain the approval of the people. This was a departure from the trend in Africa, where the participation of the public was sought at earlier stages, but not after the assembly adopted the final draft of the constitution. By contrast, the views of the public in several of these countries were sought only at the final stage, that is, during the referendum.

Albania, described as being "without question, the most problematic of the post-communist states,"[52] experienced major struggles in transitioning to democracy in the 1990s. However, on November 22, 1998, despite calls for a boycott from the former leader, Sali Berisha, and his Democratic Party, Albanians ratified a new constitution in a nationwide referendum. Records showed that more than 50 percent of the total population voted in the referendum despite heavy snow in the north, and almost 90 percent of those who voted affirmed the new constitution. The constitution had been drafted by a constitutional commission, which conducted a robust program of public participation in connection with the production of the draft, finished its work in July 1998, and obtained approval of its work from the Council of Europe's Venice Commission on Law and Democracy in a bid to increase the legitimacy of the draft. Subsequently, on October 21 1998, the Kuvend Popullore (People's Assembly) approved the draft constitution. After ratification by the people of Albania, the new constitution came into effect on November 28, 1998.[53]

Bulgaria and Romania were the first countries in the region to draft new constitutions. In Bulgaria, once elections were held in 1990, the old Communist Party—renamed the Bulgarian Socialist Party—won a majority of seats and exploited the window of opportunity to quickly adopt a new constitution. In view of the fear of the drafters that the people would not approve the new constitution, it was brought into force in July 1991 without a referendum. Public participation in this process was therefore minimal.[54] In Romania, after engineering the fall of the dictator, Nicolae Ceausescu, the National Salvation Front (NSF), comprising communists, dissidents, and intellectuals, won a huge majority in the 1990 elections and swiftly began the constitution-making process. There

is some debate about the exact nature of the NSF. Some scholars have referred to them as the old communists in a new guise, while others have pointed out that by causing the overthrow of Ceausescu and breaking from the past, they constituted a new political force.[55] The NSF appointed a constitutional commission, which involved representatives from the communist-dominated parliament, and completed its work in fifteen months. Though the NSF's methods in the assembly have been described as "dictatorial" and "heavy-handed,"[56] the NSF did seek public approval for the final draft of the constitution. It was only after the constitution was approved in a referendum held in November 1991 that it was brought into force.[57]

Constitutional politics in Czechoslovakia were unusually strained and unpredictable, even by the generally tumultuous standards of Eastern and Central Europe. After the Velvet Revolution—a reference to the bloodless transformation of power—of 1989, the differences between the two main ethnic groups, the Czechs and the Slovaks, began to emerge. As elections were held in the federation and steps were taken to drafting a constitution, the main political parties of the two groups agreed to break up the Czechoslovak federation as of January 1, 1993. This decision has been criticized as being against the popular will. Public polls showed that a majority of people in both parts of the federation opposed it. This, coupled with the fact that no referendum was held on the issue, led to questions about the legitimacy of the decision.[58] Nevertheless, the velvet divorce was effected. The constitutions adopted by Slovakia (on September 1, 1992) and the Czech Republic (on December 16, 1992) before the official date of extinction of the Czechoslovak Federation went on to become the constitutions of the two separate and independent states.[59]

Poland garners interest as the earliest country in the region to start planning for a new constitution and among the last to complete the task.[60] When Solidarity won elections by a landslide in 1989, the popular expectation was that Poland would have a new constitution within a short span of time. However, as Wiktor Osiatynski has noted, one of the main problems with constitution making in Poland in particular was that the process became intertwined with ordinary politics, resulting in long delays.[61] From 1989 to 1991, two separate constitutional committees of the Sejm (lower house) and the Senate prepared different constitutions, neither of which was ultimately accepted. A new parliament, elected in 1991, consisted of representatives from twenty-nine political parties and proved to be too fragmented to form a constitutional majority. It did manage, however, to agree on the so-called Little Constitution, which served as an interim document. Seven draft constitutions were submitted to the national assembly before parliament was dissolved on May 30, 1993. Following a Sejm decision to permit a "citizens' constitutional initiative," various groups submitted several drafts.[62] However, the process kept getting delayed, until finally, on May 25, 1997, a new constitution was adopted by national referendum. This constitution had earlier been adopted by the National Assembly on April 2, 1997, by a vote of 451 to 40. The new constitution was validated by the Supreme Court on July 15, 1997, and came into force on October 17, 1997. However, the long delay in adopting a new constitution has had its negative repercussions. Only about 43 percent of eligible voters participated in the referendum, and polls showed that as many as 46 percent of the population stated that they had no interest in the constitution. Some constitutional scholars have argued that the long gestation period of nearly seven years has severely undermined the legitimacy of constitutionalism in Poland.[63]

Hungary is unique in that it did not adopt a new constitution. Instead, the Hungarians decided to amend their old constitution several times, and later on, crafted a workable constitutional order by a series of special statutes and decisions made by their strong constitutional court. During the roundtable talks between the governing Hungarian Socialist Workers' Party and the democratic opposition in 1989, it was agreed that, though the drafting of a new constitution would be left to the first freely elected parliament, the existing 1949 constitution would be significantly amended. The commonly accepted theoretical reason for not adopting a new constitution in 1989 was the illegitimacy of the parliament elected in 1985.[64] On October 23, 1989, the 1949 constitution was drastically amended, affecting nearly 90 percent of the document. In retrospect, it can be argued that the legality of the entire roundtable itself is questionable, as the parties at the roundtable had not been elected.[65] The preliminary draft of the significant 1989 amendment had in fact been prepared by expert commissions under government directions. Different sections of the draft were then discussed in the working groups and subcommittees of the roundtable talks, when the democratic opposition thoroughly modified its final text. The parliament passed the constitutional amendment with no serious debate. It is therefore clear that the important amendments passed in 1989 were evolved through a very closed, nonparticipatory process. Yet Hungary made its peaceful transition from a communist state to a liberal state largely as a result of this amendment. The 1989 amendment gave all Hungarians open access to the constitutional court, and in later years, that court was instrumental in bringing about monumental changes in the Hungarian legal order. However, the further amendments passed by the new, freely elected legislature served as the express acknowledgment of the revisions in the 1989 amendment, adding legitimacy to the new order. Later, the idea of writing a completely new constitution took a back seat, as it became obvious that the 1989 text was a new, democratic document that had provided the constitutional base for Hungary's smooth transition.[66] By 1997, through a series of constitutional amendments and statutory changes, Hungary had almost completely transformed the legal order established by the constitution of 1949.[67] Yet this process had happened with little direct participation from the masses in the process of constitutional change.

Constitutional scholars from the region have offered explanations for the limited involvement of the masses in the constitution-making processes. Nenad Dimitrijevic argues that it is wrong to point to the mixing of constitutional and normal politics as a flaw in the region's constitution making. According to Dimitrijevic, constitution making in postcommunist Europe was part of a larger process of regime change and the only way to avoid violence. To do this successfully, it became necessary to limit the participation of the public. Dimitrijevic agrees that compared with Africa, the process in Eastern and Central Europe was extremely closed to public participation, but he contends that by keeping the context and political circumstances in Eastern and Central Europe in mind, one cannot but conclude that it was the right approach.[68] Gabor Halmai contends that East Europeans generally are extremely skeptical of the direct approach to constitution making and prefer a more aristocratic approach, which may also partially explain the phenomenon.[69]

Conclusion

A survey of the practice of the international system in the application of treaty law and custom reveals no firm evidence of rules applicable to the process of constitution making. What does appear, however, is a general requirement of public participation in governance. This emerges from the

UN-supervised practice of decolonization, in which the democratic participation of the colonial peoples became a practical prerequisite, and also from the textual requirements of the ICCPR and the interpretation and implementation of those norms by the Human Rights Committee. Moreover, the textual requirements of the ICCPR and the Human Rights Committee's General Comment no. 25 on that text suggest that these norms may well be applicable to processes of constitution drafting whether the countries undergoing them are parties or not; nonparties might be subject to such requirements by operation of customary law.

A quick review of the process of constitution making in the most recent exercises of constitutional drafting—in East Timor,[70] Rwanda,[71] and Afghanistan[72] (see this volume also)—reveals that the drafters were, or are, as the case may be, greatly concerned with involving the public in the actual process of drafting the constitution's final text. It would appear that involving the public in the process is now a universal trend. One can argue that the drafters of all modern constitutions have attempted to increase the legitimacy of the drafting process by adopting different strategies aimed at imparting a representative character to the final text. Moreover, in recent times, these strategies have become extremely innovative and seek to cover a substantial proportion of the target population.

Despite such discernible trends in the practice, the question of whether there are any specific uniform norms to be followed when drafting a constitution must, as yet, be answered in the negative. The survey conducted over the previous pages reveals that, while all recent constitution-drafting experiences have witnessed the use of one or several strategies and devices to involve the public, no two countries have followed precisely the same procedures. Even within Africa, where there is a tendency to adopt open procedures, there is great disparity in the strategies used and the timing of various phases of the consultative process. This is clearly demonstrated by contrasting the working methods by which consultation occurred in the contemporaneous drafting of constitutions for Uganda, South Africa, and Eritrea.

While following the global trend toward openness in the process of constitution making has advantages, and would seem to be both desirable and pragmatic, it is not yet clear that anything in international law requires a state to adhere to uniform practices. Constitutions of nations that have used relatively closed drafting procedures are not considered to violate international law or be less legal than those that have adopted more open procedures. As Hungary's experience seems to demonstrate, sometimes constitutions that have been adopted (or amended) by closed procedures can prove equally adept at promoting democratic ideals within a society. Nevertheless, a high degree of public participation appears to be becoming axiomatic. This does not constrain states' choice as to how, and at what stage, this participation occurs. In the African model, a constitutional assembly's legitimacy may derive from its having been elected at the beginning of the drafting process, there may be widespread public consultation, and the final product may then not require further direct approval. In other situations, notably in Eastern Europe, the drafting may occur in unelected commissions with little public participation, but the final product will be legitimized only by its submission to popular approval. There is no evidence of a requirement for a particular mode of public participation, but there is growing evidence that public participation is required. The elements that make up international law—the treaties, customs, and practice of states—indicate a growing convergence around universal principles of legitimate governance, and these are tending to be applicable also to the process of constitution drafting. It appears,

therefore, that there is growing acceptance of the norm that constitutions should be prepared through participatory processes with a high degree of transparency.

Notes

1. An anonymous reviewer of the manuscript of this chapter offered this reaction to our conclusion on customary international law: "This is not a surprising conclusion insofar as what is sought is a set of specific prescriptions as to mechanisms to be used in constitution making. However, if the matter is viewed somewhat more broadly. . . . If instead of looking for specific, affirmative requirements in the law, one looks for injunctions against certain conduct, then the customary law may well be seen to contain a certain guidance in constitution making. At the very least, peremptory norms of international law forbid a state from acts such as genocide and systematic racial discrimination." The reviewer goes on to suggest that there may be rules in customary international law that would frown upon, say, the exclusion of a segment of a national population from a process of constitution making. We believe that the question we were asked to address was precisely the narrow one identified by the reviewer, namely, whether there are specific prescriptions in international law about the mechanisms to be used in constitution making, and stand by our conclusion expressed in the text accompanying this endnote. We are, however, reproducing the reviewer's concern in this endnote for those who may be interested in the broader issue identified by the reviewer.

2. The "Lotus" Case (*France v. Turkey*), 1927 P.C.I.J. (ser. A) no. 10

3. The "Lotus" Case.

4. U.N.Doc. A/CONF. 39/27 (1969). Entered into force 1980.

5. Advisory Opinion regarding Certain Expenses of the United Nations, 1962 I.C.J. 151.

6. Advisory Opinion regarding Certain Expenses, 182, 186.

7. Theodor Meron, *Human Rights and Humanitarian Norms as Customary Law* (Oxford: Oxford University Press, 1989), pp. 80–81.

8. Military and Paramilitary Activities in and against Nicaragua *(Nicaragua v. United States of America)*, Jurisdiction and Admissibility, Judgment, 1984 I.C.J. 392 424.

9. U.N. Doc. A/CONF. 39/27(1969), entered into force 1980.

10. U.N. Doc. A/CONF. 62/122(1982).

11. 999 UNTS 171, entered into force March 23, 1976.

12. For a discussion of the interpretive jurisprudence, see Thomas M. Franck, *Fairness in International Law and Institutions* (Oxford: Oxford University Press, 1995), pp. 140–72.

13. Some seventy countries have agreed to permit individual citizens to petition the committee under the optional protocol.

14. Franck, *Fairness,* pp. 95–98. For an authoritative analysis of the transfer of power in British colonies, see S.A. de Smith, *The New Commonwealth and Its Constitutions* (London: Stevens & Sons, 1964). For an insightful analysis that relies on recently released Colonial Office records that provides revealing new information on this process, see Charles O.H. Parkinson, *Bills of Rights and Decolonization* (Oxford: Oxford University Press, 2007).

15. G.A. Res. 1579, 1961 and G.A. Res. 1605, 1961.

16. *Report of the United Nations Visiting Mission to Observe the Plebiscite in the Northern Mariana Islands, Trust Territory of the Pacific Islands,* 43 UN TCOR Supp. (no. 2) 24, U.N. DOC. T/1771 (1976).

17. UN TCOR Annex I (Agenda Item 3) 21, U.N. DOC. T/L.928 (1959).

18. "Namibia, Independence at Last," *UN Chronicle,* vol. 27, no. 2 (June 1990), p. 4.

19. See Dominic McGoldrick, *The Human Rights Committee* (Oxford: Oxford University Press, 1991), p. 461ff. See also Franck, *Fairness,* pp. 100–04.

20. Communication no. 205/1986, CCPR/C/43/D/205/1986, *Report of the Human Rights Committee,* U.N.G.A.O.R., 47th sess., Suppl. no. 40. U.N. Doc. A/47/40.

21. General Comment No. 25(57), *Report of the Human Rights Committee,* vol 1., U.N. G.A.O.R., 55th Sess., Suppl. no. 40. U.N. Doc. A/51/40 para. 6 (1996). We are thankful to Professor Vivian Hart for her USIP paper where this aspect has been dealt with in some detail.

22. OAU DOC.CAB/LEG/67/3/Rev. 5, entered into force October 21, 1986.

23. 213 UNTS 221, Europ. T.S. no. 5, entered into force September 3, 1953.

24. Art. 38 (1)(d) of the Statute of the International Court of Justice, June 26, 1945, art. 4, 59 Stat. 1031, T.S. no. 993.

25. Otive Igbuzor, "Constitution-Making in Nigeria: Lessons for Making a People's Constitution," Paper presented at the Conference on Constitutional Development, Kibuye, Rwanda, August 19–24, 2001, p. 6, available online www.cdd.org.uk/cfcr/constitutionlessons.htm (accessed April 19, 2009).

26. Igbuzor, "Constitution-Making in Nigeria," p. 7. For more details on the new approach, see generally Julius Ihonvbere, *Towards a New Constitutionalism in Africa,* CDD Working Paper Series no. 4 (2000), pp. 50–57; Julius Ihonvbere, "Towards Participatory Mechanisms and Principles of Constitution Making in Africa," in *The Path to People's Constitution* (Lagos, Nigeria: Committee for the Defence of Human Rights, 2000); Issa Shivji, ed., *State and Constitutionalism: An African Debate* (Ann Arbor, MI: SAPES and University of Michigan Press, 1991); Owen Sichone, ed., *The State and Constitutionalism in Southern Africa* (Harare, Zimbabwe: SAPES, 1998).

27. Issa Shivji, "Three Generations of Constitutions and Constitution-Making in Africa: An Overview and Assessment in Social and Economic Context," in *Constitutionalism in Transition: Africa and Eastern Europe,* ed. Mihaela Serban Rosen (Warsaw: Helsinki Foundation for Human Rights, 2003), pp. 84–85.

28. For literature on the 1995 Ugandan constitution, see generally David Mukholi, *A Complete Guide to Uganda's Fourth Constitution: History, Politics and the Law* (Kampala: Fountain Publishers, 1995); Sam Moyo and Kayode Fayemi, "Zimbabwe's Constitution-Making Process of 1999/00: A Multi-Dimensional Assessment," in *Constitutionalism in Transition,* pp. 323–49; and Maria Nassali, "Women and the Constitution of Uganda of 1995: Challenges and the Future," in *Constitutionalism in Transition,* pp. 261–79. For literature on the 1996 South African constitution, see generally Hassan Ebrahim, *The Soul of a Nation: Constitution-Making in South Africa* (Oxford: Oxford University Press, 1998), pp. 239–50; Christina Murray, "A Constitutional Beginning: Making South Africa's Final Constitution," *University of Arkansas at Little Rock Law Review,* vol. 23 (2001), p. 809; and D.J. Brand, "Constitutional Reform—The South African Experience," *Cumberland Law Review,* vol. 33, no. 1 (2002–03), pp. 1–14.

29. The three previous postindependent Ugandan constitutions of 1962, 1966, and 1967 were either abrogated or rendered useless and irrelevant by a succession of dictatorial regimes. Mukholi, *A Complete Guide*, p. 82.

30. Moyo and Fayemi, "Zimbabwe's Constitution-Making Process," p. 333.

31. The first phase of the consultation process stretched over one year and focused on determining whether the citizens of Uganda believed a new constitution was required for the country and, if so, what the new document should contain. During this stage, documents were disseminated that explained the context of constitutional reform in both national and vernacular languages.

32. For instance, to ensure that women's interests would be represented before the commission, women leaders were trained in all 167 counties to solicit women's views on the constitution. This resulted in the submission of a common "women's memorandum" to the commission, apart from the fact that views of individual women accounted for nearly one-third of the total of 25,542 submissions that the commission received. For an elaborate analysis of the various methods initiated to ensure that views of Ugandan women were represented in the constitution-making process, see Nassali, *Women and the Constitution of Uganda of 1995*.

33. These included written memoranda, public meetings, oral submissions, newspaper articles, and position papers delivered at seminars of professional bodies, interest groups, and educational institutions. Mukholi, *A Complete Guide*, pp. 29–30.

34. The Constituent Assembly Bill contained a provision which provided that in the absence of a two-thirds majority, contentious issues should be sent back to the citizens for consultation.

35. Out of the 284 members of the constituent assembly, there were a total of 51 women delegates, of which 39 were from affirmative action seats, 9 were directly elected from constituency seats, 2 were presidential nominees, and 1 was a worker's delegate. Nassali, "Women and the Constitution of Uganda of 1995," p. 265.

36. Mukholi, *A Complete Guide*, p. 59.

37. For a brief overview of these circumstances, see Murray, "A Constitutional Beginning," pp. 809–16. For details about the historical background of South Africa and the circumstances leading to the constitutional drafting process, see generally Ebrahim, *The Soul of a Nation*, p. 28.

38. Ebrahim, *The Soul of a Nation*, p. 242.

39. It was estimated that 20,549 people attended these workshops, which also witnessed the participation of 717 organizations. Between May 8 and June 4, 1995, a series of public hearings were organized in which 596 organizations were consulted. Ebrahim, *The Soul of a Nation*, pp. 244–45.

40. Radio was an extremely effective delivery mechanism because it could reach more people in both urban and rural areas. On October 1, 1995, a weekly constitutional education radio talk show was launched, comprising hour-long programs broadcast on eight radio stations in eight languages. These programs were estimated to reach over 10 million South Africans every week. Television programs were launched on April 24, 1995, and continued until October 10, 1995, for a total of twenty-five programs on two channels. The constitutional assembly's official newspaper, *Constitutional Talk*, was produced to provide information to the public by presenting material in a detailed and educative manner. It was usually an eight-page publication produced fortnightly and distributed to 160,000 people. A constitutional talk line was established, allowing callers to leave messages requesting information or to record their suggestions and comments. Over 10,000 people used it. The constituent assembly also made use of an Internet home page that was visited quite regularly by people across the globe. Ebrahim, *The Soul of a Nation*, pp. 242–46.

41. Ibid., p. 248.

42. Ibid., pp. 224–37.

43. Shivji, "Three Generations," p. 86.

44. Murray, "A Constitutional Beginning," pp. 821–22.

45. Richard A. Rosen, "Constitutional Process, Constitutionalism, and the Eritrean Experience," *North Carolina Journal of International Law and Commercial Regulation*, vol. 24 (1999), pp. 307–09. In Eritrea, the members of the commission, though representative of the various divisions of Eritrean society, were appointed by the government and were not democratically elected. Members of other political groupings were consequently excluded from the constitutional commission. These aspects of the constitution-making process also attracted criticism. Rosen, "Constitutional Process," pp. 304–06.

46. In Rwanda, a legal and constitutional commission was set up in 1999 to solicit the views of Rwandan citizens in preparing a draft constitution. In January 2002, the commission began to organize public meetings to involve the public, holding at least two. On April 24, 2003, the parliament of Rwanda adopted the draft constitution, which was later approved by a national referendum on May 26, 2003. Voter turnout at the referendum was 89 percent of the total population, and 93 percent of those voting approved. The new constitution was

promulgated by the president of Rwanda on June 4, 2003. Official Web site of the Legal and Constitutional Commission of the Republic of Rwanda, available at www.cjcr.gov.rw/index.htm (accessed on April 18, 2009).

47. For a recent survey of constitutional developments in several of the former Soviet Republics, see generally Gisbert H. Flanz and Rett R. Ludwikowski, eds., *Comparative Human Rights and Fundamental Freedoms* (New York: Oceana Publications, 2002), describing constitutional developments in Estonia, Latvia, Lithuania, Poland, Belarus, Moldova, Russia, and Ukraine. See also Rett R. Ludwikowski, "Constitutional Culture of the New East-Central European Democracies," *Georgia Journal of International and Comparative Law,* vol. 29, no. 1 (2000); and Rett R. Ludwikowski, "Constitution Making in the Countries of Former Soviet Dominance: Current Developments," *Georgia Journal of International and Comparative Law,* vol. 23 (1993), p. 155.

48. For details of the constitution-making processes employed in these various countries, see generally Jon Elster, "Constitutionalism in Eastern Europe: An Introduction," *University of Chicago Law Review,* vol. 58, no. 2 (Spring 1991), pp. 447–82; Jon Elster, "Forces and Mechanisms in the Constitution-Making Process," *Duke Law Journal,* vol. 45, no. 2 (November 1995), pp. 364–96; Rett R. Ludwikowski, "Constitution Making in the Countries of the Former Soviet Dominance."; Dick Howard, ed., *Constitution Making in Eastern Europe* (Washington, DC: Woodrow Wilson Center, 1993); Ludwikowski, "Constitutional Culture"; Flanz and Ludwikowski, *Comparative Human Rights*; Andrew Arato, *Civil Society, Constitution, and Legitimacy* (Lanham, MD: Rowman and Littlefield Publishers, 2000); "Constitutional 'Refolution' in the Ex-Communist World: Rule of Law," *American University Journal of International Law and Policy* (1997); Eli M. Salzberger and Stefan Voight, "On Constitutional Processes and the Delegation of Power, with Special Emphasis on Israel and Central and Eastern Europe," *Theoretical Inquiries in Law,* vol. 3, no. 1 (2002), p. 207.

49. Some scholars have noted an additional difficulty: Among those participating in the preparations of the new constitutions were representatives of the old regimes, seeking to retain their power. Faced with a dramatic loss of control, these proponents of communism adopted a wide range of tactics, ranging from a willingness to compromise and engage in coalition building to a far more aggressive opposition to constitutional development. Joanna

Regulska, "Self-Governance or Central Control? Rewriting Constitutions in Central and Eastern Europe," in *Constitution Making in Eastern Europe,* p. 150.

50. Elster, "Constitutionalism in Eastern Europe," pp. 455–56. For details of roundtable talks held in Poland, Hungary, the former East Germany, and Czechoslovakia, see Jon Elster, ed., *The Roundtable Talks and the Breakdown of Communism* (Chicago: University of Chicago Press, 1996).

51. The legitimacy of constitutions has been an extremely important issue in the context of Eastern and Central Europe. For literature on this issue, see generally Ulrich K. Preuss, *Constitutional Revolution,* trans. Deborah Lucas Schneider (Amherst, NY: Prometheus Books, 1995); Arato, *Civil Society, Constitution, and Legitimacy,* pp. 129–66; and Andras Sajo, "Preferred Generations: A Paradox of Restoration Constitutions," in *Constitutionalism, Identity, Difference and Legitimacy: Theoretical Perspectives,* ed. Michel Rosenfeld (Durham, NC: Duke University Press, 1994), p. 341.

52. Terence Duffy, "Albania: Beyond the Hoxha Legacy," in *Transformations of Post-Communist States,* ed. Wojciech Kostecki, Katarzyna Zukrowska, and Bogdan J. Goralczyk (New York: Palgrave Macmillan, 2000), p. 73.

53. "Constitution Watch: Albania," *East European Constitutional Review,* vol. 7, no. 4 (1998), p. 1.

54. Salzberger and Voight, "On Constitutional Processes," p. 222.

55. Arato, *Civil Society,* pp. 159–63.

56. Ibid., p. 163.

57. Salzberger and Voight, "On Constitutional Processes," p. 223. See also Regulska, "Self-Governance or Central Control?" p. 150, arguing that the relative urgency in drafting these two constitutions can be attributed to the decisions by members of the old Communist guard—who knew that their days were numbered but were determined to preserve whatever legitimacy possible—to present themselves as progressive founding fathers of a new era.

58. Katarina Mathernova, "Czecho?Slovakia: Constitutional Disappointments," in *Constitution Making in Eastern Europe,* p. 78.

59. See generally Jiri Grospic, "Some Constitutional Problems of the Czech Republic," in *Constitutionalism and Politics,* ed. Irena Gross (Bratislava: Slovak Committee of the European Cultural Foundation, 1993), pp. 220–29; Martin Butora,

"Constitutionalism in Values and Stories," in *Constitutionalism and Politics,* pp. 324–28, arguing that the absence of a referendum renders the division of the Czechoslovak republic illegitimate; Dusan Hendrych, "Constitutionalism and Constitutional Change in Czechoslovakia," in *Constitutional Policy and Change in Europe,* ed. Joachim Jens and Nevil Johnson (Oxford: Oxford University Press, 1995), pp. 278–95.

60. Some scholars have argued that the process of drafting a new constitution for Poland began as far back as in 1982, with a fundamental transformation in the way the Poles viewed their constitution. Salzberger and Voight, "On Constitutional Processes," p. 224.

61. Wiktor Osiatynski, "A Brief History of the Constitution," *East European Constitutional Review,* vol. 6, no. 2–3 (1997).

62. Wiktor Osiatynski, "Rights in New Constitutions of East and Central Europe," *Columbia Human Rights Law Review,* vol. 26, no. 1 (1994), pp. 119–21.

63. Ewa Letowska, "A Constitution of Possibilities," *East European Constitutional Review,* vol. 6, no. 2–3 (1997). For literature on constitutionalism in Poland, see generally Wojceich Sokolewicz, "The Relevance of Western Models for Constitution-Building in Poland," in *Constitutional Policy and Change in Europe,* pp. 243–77; Miroslaw Wyrzykowski, ed., *Constitution-Making Process* (Warsaw: Institute of Public Affairs, 1998); Jacek Kurcewski, "Democracy and the Rule of Law: Poland after 1989," in *Constitutionalism and Politics,* pp. 200–19; and Andrzej Rapaczynski, "Constitutional Politics in Poland: A Report on the Constitutional Committee of the Polish Parliament," in *Constitution Making in Eastern Europe,* pp. 93–132.

64. Peter Paczolay, "The New Hungarian Constitutional State: Challenges and Perspectives," in *Constitution Making in Eastern Europe,* p. 29.

65. It appears that the Hungarian participants at the roundtable talks were aware of this problem and have been described as being "obsessed with their lack of legitimacy." Arato, *Civil Society,* p. 148.

66. Paczolay, "The New Hungarian Constitutional State," pp. 30–31.

67. For literature on constitutionalism in Hungary, see generally Attila Agh, "The Permanent 'Constitutional Crisis' in the Democratic Transition: The Case of Hungary," in *Constitutional Policy and Change in Europe,* pp. 243–77; Gabor Halmai, "Democracy versus Constitutionalism? The Reestablishment of the Rule of Law in Hungary," in *Constitutionalism and Politics,* pp. 301–10; Mate Szabo, "Constitutional Change in Hungary," in *Constitutionalism and Politics,* pp. 288–92.

68. "Comment, Discussion on Reconstructing the State through Constitution-Making," in *Constitutionalism in Transition,* pp. 102–03.

69. *Constitutionalism in Transition,* pp. 103–04.

70. In East Timor, the constituent assembly consisted of elected representatives of the people and was aided by thirteen constitutional commissions established to ascertain the views of the public. These commissions conducted public meetings throughout East Timor involving some 38,000 people. However, the need to draft the new constitution at great speed appears to have cast some doubt on the actual impact of the consultations on the final draft of the constitution of East Timor, which came into force in May 2002. Hillary Charlesworth, "The Constitution of East Timor, May 20, 2002," *International Journal of Constitutional Law,* vol. 1 (2003), pp. 325–34.

71. For details on Rwanda, see note 46.

72. In Afghanistan, the constitution-drafting commission produced a draft constitution in April 2003, which was subject to a public consultation process between May 1, 2003, and June 30, 2003. See chapter in this volume; Amin Tarzi, "Afghanistan's New Constitution: A Sneak Preview," E-Ariana.com, April 24, 2003, e-arianacom/ariana/eariana.nsf/allArticles/EFFC46729FD0C5D387256D1300523C38?OpenDocument (visited on April 18, 2009).

2

Constitution Making and the Right to Take Part in a Public Affair

Vivien Hart

Constitution making is a contest over the distribution, redistribution, and limitation of power. The making or remaking of a constitution is of particular significance in divided and conflicted societies, where the process frequently is part of peacemaking and nation-building endeavors. Traditionally, negotiating a constitution was the province of political leaders who held power or claimed it. Drafting the constitutional text was expert work. The public was, at most, drawn in only to give consent to the final version. In a significant change, it is now widely assumed that whatever the axes of conflict, the constitutional outcome will be more sustainable if those who experienced past injustices are involved in creating new solutions. The widening and deepening of public participation characteristic of many recent processes have involved power sharing with a general public that extends to groups that were previously excluded: women, minorities, the poor, and the otherwise marginalized. The resulting process may on the one

hand seem more just, but on the other be less controlled.

The International Covenant on Civil and Political Rights (ICCPR), which came into force in 1976, declared a right to take part in public affairs. If this general right to democratic governance is taken to extend to constitution making, then the only issue for discussion—no small issue—is how best to implement the right through practices that are fair, efficient, and effective. This chapter explains that the first part of this proposition, that participation is a requirement of a constitution-making process, has only recently gained recognition in international law, and that the law remains in need of further clarification and development in important respects. Legal justifications matter, not least as a resource for disadvantaged members of the polity, and it is therefore worthwhile to substantiate the case for a legal right to participation, as this chapter aims to do. But constitution making is an inherently political as well as legal process. It is not surprising, then, that the emergence of a legal right to participation has been paralleled by the emergence of normative political criteria for participation, along with considerable experimentation with participatory practices. Political practice has reinforced and even run ahead of the development of the law. The discussion that follows gives attention to the legal, normative, and practical aspects of democratic constitution making, all of which are involved in the realization of the high aspirations of the right to participate.

A Continuing Debate

Once the ICCPR came into force, and as legal thinking about the right to democracy developed, constitution making was at first ignored in favor of traditional assumptions about its distinctive nature as a process standing above and apart from the everyday business of governance. The right to democracy acquired a strong interpretation, but only in relation to the day-to-day activities of voting and office holding. In 1992, in his classic article "The emerging right to democratic governance," Thomas M. Franck identified a change in the concept of democracy found in international law, from aspiration to entitlement, political vision to "normative rule of the international system."[1] As a result of this article, much effort has been devoted to defining an applicable standard for what constitutes a democracy. The focus has continued to be on procedure—on, for example: free and fair elections; the rights of candidates, political parties, and other organizations to engage in the political sphere; and activities that allow for codes, remedies, and enforcement as befits a rule of the international system.[2] Progress has allowed Franck, revisiting the topic in this volume with coauthor Arun K. Thiruvengadam, to find the right now established as a clear "general requirement of public participation in governance."[3] Con-

stitution making, however, is still widely assumed to be a prior condition for, rather than a part of, governance, and so may remain beyond the reach of the right to participate in governance.

In parallel with such developments in international law, a philosophical argument has developed favoring a right to participate in constitution making. This has asserted the importance of democratic constitutions in a world of multiple and intersecting nations, cultures, and conflicts. James Tully, a leading exponent of this view, asks why the constitution is seemingly the "one area of modern politics that has not been democratised over the last three hundred years."[4] From his perspective, a dominant tradition defining constitutional matters as outside of and above normal politics, the province of an expert elite, is the fairy-tale emperor with no clothes. Constitution making is the foundation of democratic governance. Why should the people not share in making the constitutions that govern them, and have their moral claim to participate bolstered by a legal right that all are bound to respect?

In the recent unprecedented era of constitution making, political actors also have taken up the issue of participation. Constitution-making processes involving experiments in public participation have multiplied.[5] The 2 million public submissions to South Africa's constitutional assembly have set a standard for constitution makers, unmatched as yet in other nations.[6] Even the 2004 Transitional Administrative Law for Iraq, itself written without public participation, mandated informed public debate in the constitutional process.[7]

No amount of intellectual or practical innovation necessarily creates a "normative rule of the international system," a right in international law to take part in the making of constitutions. But Franck and Thiruvengadam now determine that there is "a growing convergence around universal principles of legitimate governance and these are tending to be applicable also to the process of constitution drafting."[8] This chapter suggests that evidence of various kinds allows us to go further than this cautious conclusion. In legal developments, the right granted in Article 25 of the ICCPR "to take part in the conduct of public affairs" has been interpreted as extending to the making of constitutions.[9] International, regional, and national charters of rights have embodied increasingly expansive guarantees of access to every aspect of democratic governance, leading, by implication or deliberate design, toward including constitution making as governance. The Canadian Supreme Court ruling of 1998 on the *Reference re Secession of Quebec,* influential beyond its borders, has made dialogue over constitutional matters an obligation of the state and citizens.[10] In parallel, political theory and action provide both trenchant arguments and a body of practice that support public involvement as a requisite of democratic constitution making.

Yet both the authority and the merits of the right to participate in constitution making remain contested, unsurprisingly, when the exercise of power and its legitimacy are at stake. How might the issue best be taken forward to contribute constructively to the practice of constitution making? If the legal regime is all, then a more firmly established legal entitlement can serve advocates of participation. Political scientist Tony Evans has argued critically that such a legal approach so dominates the human rights field that inadequacies are naturally taken to require only more lawyerly "refining, polishing, and elaborating accepted norms and standards, in an attempt to make the regime more elegant, sophisticated, imposing, and magisterial."[11] But establishing a firm legal basis would also be a politically significant move, fortifying a moral claim with an applicable right. The present (relative) legal reticence regarding constitu-

tion making does not diminish the significance of holding a legal right, and not just a political desire, to participate in constitution making. Rights are aspirations and resources as well as entitlements.[12] Aspirations will no doubt be pursued by every political means, but political means are mightily reinforced when a defined and potentially enforceable entitlement exists alongside. Thus, this chapter argues for a dual perspective, lawyerly refinement alongside political development as essential counterparts. To clarify the present state of both law and practice, I first review both international and national textual provisions and judicial rulings that clarify both the scope and limits of the ICCPR's promise. Next, the recent practice of participation is discussed. Finally, I conclude that in principle, in law, and in practice, a right indeed exists. The public has a right to take part in the foundational affair of constitution making, and the powerful interests that will always be involved in the process must recognize and respect that right.

Textual Promises

International Instruments

The right to participate in public life was first articulated in UN documents. Article 21 of the declaratory UN Declaration of Human Rights of 1948 and especially Article 25 of the enforceable ICCPR, adopted in 1966 and entered into force in 1976, establish rights to participate in public affairs, vote, and have access to public service.[13] Article 25 declares the rights:

(a) To take part in the conduct of public affairs, directly or through freely chosen representatives;

(b) To vote and to be elected at genuine periodic elections which shall be by universal suffrage and shall be held by secret ballot, guaranteeing the free expression of the will of the electors;

(c) To have access, on general terms of equality, to public service in his country.

This language weights the right to democratic governance toward the "historically-bounded form of governance in modern states (i.e., liberal democracy)"—that is, toward a procedural, representative, electoral model.[14] This was the model of democracy for the post–World War II world, understood to embrace the making of policy but not constitutions. The ICCPR set the stage for the electoral preoccupations of the predominant international human rights approach to the topic, leaving openings to participatory fortune in such open-ended wording as "take part" and "public affairs."

The Council of Europe, formed in 1949, was another early and influential rights-making body.[15] In Europe, according to Henry J. Steiner, a right to participation was controversial. Following a debate about whether "political rights stood outside the tradition of human rights, and hence outside the proper scope of the European Convention," it was decided that the European Convention on Human Rights (ECHR) of 1950 should contain no such right.[16] Even with the addition of the First Protocol to the ECHR in 1952, the limited meaning of participation for the framers of rights regimes in the immediate postwar years was clear. According to the First Protocol, "the High Contracting Parties undertake to hold free elections at reasonable intervals by secret ballot, under conditions which will ensure the free expression of the opinion of the people in the choice of the legislature."[17]

Steiner has compared the drafting discussions of the ECHR protocol with those of ICCPR Article 25. He points out that those negotiating the 1952 protocol could assume a Western European democracy, where "conditions" meant electoral choice through a pluralistic or multiparty system. The ICCPR drafters, on the other hand, had included a good many supporters of one-party states. Pluralism had been a bone of contention, and they failed to make it a requirement for a democratic system. Nevertheless, the protocol "says nothing about non-electoral participation," offering, in this respect, a narrower conception of democracy than that of the potentially expansive "take part" clause of the ICCPR.[18]

Later international conventions show a progressive tendency to develop a broader paradigm, becoming more specific about both the arenas of participation and fair conditions of access.[19] Article 5 (c) of the 1965 Convention on the Elimination of All Forms of Racial Discrimination defines "political rights, in particular the rights to participate in elections—to vote and to stand for election—on the basis of universal and equal suffrage, to take part in the Government as well as in the conduct of public affairs at any level and to have equal access to public service."[20] The Convention on the Elimination of All Forms of Discrimination Against Women of 1979 guarantees the right for women "on equal terms with men" to participate "in the formulation of government policy and the implementation thereof and to hold public office and perform all public functions at all levels of government" and "to participate in non-governmental organizations and associations concerned with the public and political life of the country."[21] The European Framework Convention for the Protection of National Minorities (1995, Articles 15 and 17) further promises that "the Parties shall create the conditions necessary for the effective participation of persons belonging to national minorities in cultural, social and economic life and in public affairs, in particular those affecting them," and that "the Parties undertake not to interfere with the right of persons belonging to national minorities to participate in the activities of non-governmental organisations, both at the national and international levels."[22] While none of these refers specifically to constitution making, they cumulatively create a set of conditions for meaningful participation in any aspect of public and political affairs.

Regional Charters

Recent regional rights instruments have also progressively expanded the definition of participation. Several important examples can be cited. The African Charter on Human and Peoples' Rights of 1981 (the Banjul Charter) repeats the ICCPR Article 25 language with an added emphasis on "strict equality."[23] The Commonwealth's Harare Declaration (1991) recognizes "the individual's inalienable right to participate by means of free and democratic political processes in framing the society in which he or she lives," a form of words surely applicable to constitution making.[24] The Asian Charter of Rights (1998) builds into its text an understanding, which has developed elsewhere in legal and theoretical discussions, that the right to participate depends upon the existence of a panoply of supporting rights such as freedom of speech and assembly:

> The state, which claims to have the primary responsibility for the development and well-being of the people, should be humane, open and accountable. The corollary of the respect for human rights is a tolerant and pluralistic system, in which people are free to express their views and to seek to persuade others and in which the rights of minorities are respected. People must participate in public affairs, through the electoral and other decision-making and implementing processes, free from racial, religious or gender discriminations.[25]

The twenty-eight articles of the Inter-American Democratic Charter (2001) of the Organization of American States (OAS) take the right to participation to new levels of both normative and practical specification.[26] The charter was itself forged by an unprecedentedly participatory process, with the views of civil-society organizations invited and, to their surprise, taken into account.[27] Article 1—"the peoples of the Americas have a right to democracy and their governments have an obligation to promote and defend it"—has been described as lifting

the concept of democracy "to a significantly advanced reciprocal contract of peoples with governments."[28] Section II recognizes a penumbra of civil and political rights that support genuine participation, including workers' rights, and the rights to seek redress, to be free from discrimination, and to enjoy respect for diversity. In language from the UN's Vienna Declaration of 1993, the charter also endorses the "universality, indivisibility and interdependence" of human rights.[29] Section III goes further: Article 11 again echoes the Vienna Declaration in pronouncing that "democracy and social and economic development are interdependent and are mutually reinforcing."[30] Social rights are integrally associated with the right to democracy in this charter. The traditional procedural elements of good electoral practice are also included, with the addition in Article 6 that

> it is the right and responsibility of all citizens to participate in decisions relating to their own development. This is also a necessary condition for the full and effective exercise of democracy. Promoting and fostering diverse forms of participation strengthens democracy.[31]

The OAS charter also contains language concerning the necessary framework of "constitutional order," the "constitutional subordination" of state institutions, and fundamental freedoms and human rights "embodied in the respective constitutions of states" as well as in international instruments.[32] In this respect, the charter reflects the contemporary era of attention to constitutionalism. Indeed, this document may imply, though it does not develop, regional requirements for a constitution-making process in its assertion that "an unconstitutional alteration of the constitutional regime" is a sanctionable offense under the charter.[33]

The effect of the above regional instruments—and of national constitutions, discussed below—may extend beyond their own territorial scope, even to states that are not yet signatories to the relevant treaties. As

Franck and Thiruvengadam observe, their adoption contributes to creating a "universal customary norm" that "reflects the common practice of states."[34] The international circulation of rights and constitutional clauses has been a familiar story since the earliest studies of the influence of the United States Constitution or the Westminster model.[35] In new environments, some have simply gathered dust or their meanings have been transformed, yet, in the shorter or longer term, the formal legal ground they create may equally be a political stimulus and support for the development of new or improved practice.

National Constitutions

Including the right to participate in national constitutions is important for symbolism or for symmetry with international instruments, but also for a practical reason. Scholars have noted that the silences of constitutions as well as their express recognition of values or identities carry a symbolic message about the priorities of regimes.[36] A national right to participation says something about the character of the constitutional regime and about its commitment to meeting international standards. More practically, possession of a national right gives members of the polity faced with resistance to or neglect of their input the best chance of enforcement. Nations may be bound by their ratification of the ICCPR, but enforcing the treaty through the judicial process of the Human Rights Commission is cumbersome and slow and must follow the exhaustion of domestic remedies.[37] When constitutions inscribe the right to participate, they bring enforcement home to channels within the nation.

As noted earlier, a preoccupation with electoral systems and procedures, required by ICCPR Article 25, clauses (b) and (c), has tended to overshadow the ill-defined possibilities of clause (a), contained in the words of "take part" and "public affairs." The rights

to run for office and to vote in free and fair elections fulfilled the definition of democracy dominant through much of the late twentieth century, famously declared by Joseph Schumpeter as an "institutional arrangement for arriving at political decisions in which individuals acquire the power to decide by means of a competitive struggle for the people's vote."[38] Whether the "institutional arrangement," or constitution, preexisted democratic politics, or must be made democratically, became an issue once the concept of democracy came under scrutiny by theorists of "deliberative democracy."[39] Their ideas fit well with the concurrent rise of debate about a "new constitutionalism" that envisaged constitution making as an open-ended and inclusive conversation.[40] It is a natural step from the conjunction of such ideas to the expansion of the democratic content of "taking part" and the logical assumption that constitution making is a "public affair." New national charters and constitutions gradually have built stronger understandings of the terms of Article 25 (a) onto the traditional procedural foundation.

Among the examples mentioned below, some constitutions remain more traditionally procedural, concentrating on electoral systems, while others expand the idea of participation, giving additional substance to the "take part" clause. Illustrating the traditional approach of procedural constitutionalism, South Africa's 1996 constitution lacks the phrase "right to participate," but makes universal suffrage, regular elections, and a multiparty system of government a "Founding Provision."[41] A bill of rights follows the ICCPR, containing the rights to free electoral choice; to form, participate in, and campaign for political parties; to regular, free, and fair elections; and to vote for and stand for public office.[42] Like other recent examples of this procedural approach, East Timor's constitution declares, more expansively than the South African text but without development of the ICCPR promise, that "every citizen has the right to participate in the political life and in the public affairs of the country, either directly or through democratically elected representatives."[43]

Some constitutions, however, offer more specific guarantees. In optimistic experiments, several African states have gone further than South Africa in acknowledging new norms of participation. Among textual promises, the constitution of Angola makes it the "right and duty of all citizens . . . to take an active part in public life," while Ethiopian citizens are assured that their "sovereignty shall be expressed through their representatives elected in accordance with this Constitution and through their direct democratic participation."[44] Imposing a positive duty on the state, the Ugandan constitution declares that "the State shall be based on democratic principles, which empower and encourage the active participation of all citizens at all levels in their own governance."[45] "Direct democratic participation" takes Ethiopia beyond the traditional electoral guarantees, but its promise is probably impossible ever to realize in practice and so vague in any case as to have value only as a rhetorical flag for waving. Angola and Uganda have introduced more substantial ideas of duty and obligation. Citizens with a duty to take part and states with an obligation to empower them to do so enter a relationship much closer than that offered by free and fair elections. Furthermore, when Uganda speaks of "all levels in their own governance," it is possible to read a literal meaning of every structural level from local to national. In a state that had created a process with a rare degree of public involvement, it is plausible that such language could also embrace every level, from micropolicy decisions to macroconstitutional politics.[46]

New constitutions also have elaborated political rights in Central and South America. The 1991 Colombia constitution aspires to "ensure its members . . . a legal, democratic and participatory framework." This text spells out in some detail both electoral provisions and the "people's means of participating in the exercise of their sovereignty: the vote, the plebiscite, the referendum, the popular consultation, the open town council meeting, the legislative initiative and the recall of officials."[47] Colombia had incorporated several of these practices into its constitution-making process. The process was initiated by acts of popular sovereignty: a referendum and election of a constitutional assembly empowered to write a new constitution, which Colombia's Supreme Court deemed to create a legitimate override of the prior constitution.[48] Peru in 1993 placed the right to participate among its "fundamental personal rights."[49] Ecuador (1998) and Venezuela (1999) enumerated political rights, Venezuela echoing decades of debates about the basic criteria for democratic governance by declaring as a fundamental principle that its government "shall always be democratic, participatory, elective, decentralized, alternative, responsible and pluralist."[50]

Too few of the above regimes have lived up to their paper promises. But with or without participatory practices to draft their constitutions—and Venezuela for one was notable for the lack of general public participation—each enumeration of rights to participate in more than periodic elections contributes to defining a more generous norm for "taking part." As and when "public affairs" fully embraces constitution making, this increasingly generous norm sets the standards for participation.

Thomas Franck's original terminology of the "emergence" of a right amply conveys the process of accretion. In neither law nor practice does a single authoritative moment mark the arrival of a right within the field of constitution making, and none of the documents discussed above explicitly declares such a right. These texts do, first, extend the concept of "taking part" as an act and even an obligation of sovereignty and citizenship. They bring the concept directly into national purview rather than leaving it as an obligation at one remove in an international treaty, they require governments to respect and even facilitate participation, and they specify expected practices in addition to elections. Second, with increasing specificity, these texts require the conditions that make authentic participation possible—equality, freedom from discrimination and state interference, tolerance, and civil and social rights. Such ever more idealistic promises build the foundation for claims as of right from within and without the nation, both against regimes that fail in their obligations and for inclusion in the process of nation building. The opportunities offered in all these clauses support both lawyers and political activists and provide openings to further specify and entrench the right. How the texts have been used, and with what success the right to participate in constitution making has been entrenched, is the subject of the remainder of this chapter, which looks first at legal and then political events.

Legal Interpretations

Rights on paper remain fine rhetoric until they are taken up, tested, interpreted, and applied. One route to such development is through challenges in the courts. Whether and on what grounds to litigate can be a highly political decision as rights campaigners choose the moment to make their claim. They hope for affirmative judgments that clarify the sweeping generalizations of conventions and constitutions and build a procedural manual for the application of rights. But even negative judgments may contribute, warning of limitations and suggesting new directions.

The right to participate has been little pursued through legal channels, and then principally with reference to electoral procedures and access to public office.[51] The importance of formal interpretive rulings was noted by a member of the UN Committee on Human Rights (UNCHR) during the drafting of a formal comment on Article 25, with the observation that "a general comment was undeniably stronger when grounded in the Committee's jurisprudence."[52] A handful of cases addressing the right to participate in constitution making conveys a mixed message of both potential and limits.

Marshall v. Canada *(1991)*

Marshall v. Canada—brought in 1986 with a UNCHR ruling in 1991—pitted leaders of the Mikmaq tribal society against the Canadian government.[53] The claim was that the group's exclusion from a series of constitutional conferences on changes to the Canadian constitution "infringed their right to take part in the conduct of public affairs, in violation of article 25(a) of the Covenant [the ICCPR]."[54] In a crucial statement for participation advocates, the UNCHR ruled that

> at issue in the present case is whether the constitutional conferences constituted a 'conduct of public affairs' . . . [and] the Committee cannot but conclude that they do indeed constitute a conduct of public affairs.[55]

For the Mikmaq people, however, this was a Pyrrhic victory. They learned that while they had the right to participate in constitution making, there had been no infringement in their case. Their efforts gained for posterity the most secure—and largely unnoticed[56]—legal interpretation of the right to participate in constitution making, but also established a major limitation on its practical value. The UNCHR ruled that "it is for the legal and constitutional system of the State party to provide for the modalities of such participation" and that

> Article 25(a) of the Covenant cannot be understood as meaning that any directly affected group, large or small, has the unconditional right to choose the modalities of participation in pub-

lic affairs. That, in fact, would be an extrapolation of the right to direct participation by the citizens, far beyond the scope of Article 25(a).[57]

Although the Mikmaq leaders had stated that their submissions through an intermediary body had never even been transmitted to negotiators, the UNCHR found the Canadian provisions for the representation of "approximately 600 aboriginal groups" by "four national associations," and later by "a 'panel' of up to 10 aboriginal leaders," adequate.[58] The record of judicial deference to political authorities to decide how participation shall be carried out remains a difficulty.

The UNCHR General Comment (1996)

In 1996, the UNCHR issued a General Comment parsing the meaning of Article 25 of the ICCPR, of which the committee is the guardian. This comment clarifies in a statement of general application what the Mikmaq people had learned, that constitution making is a public affair under the terms of the ICCPR. The comment first expounds Article 25 as universal and fundamental:

> Article 25 of the Covenant recognizes and protects the right of every citizen to take part in the conduct of public affairs, the right to vote and to be elected, and the right to have access to public service. Whatever form of constitution or government is in force, the Covenant requires States to adopt such legislative and other measures as may be necessary to ensure that citizens have an effective opportunity to enjoy the rights it protects. Article 25 lies at the core of democratic government.[59]

Henry J. Steiner has commented that "for a right regarded as foundational, political participation suffers from serious infirmities."[60] He notes the difference between "the relatively vague and abstract right to take part in the conduct of public affairs or government, and the relatively specific right to vote in elections."[61] The General Comment begins to correct this deficiency. Minutes of a UNCHR meeting drafting the comment confirm that

"the difficult issues had proved to be a definition of the concept of the 'conduct of public affairs' and the extent of citizens' participation in those affairs."[62] No minutes record how the right to participate in constitution making came to be mentioned, but the drafters had a precedent in *Marshall v. Canada*. Regardless of how it came there, however, the assertion of the right is unqualified. As the comment first declares, "Peoples have the right to freely determine their political status and to enjoy the right to choose the form of their constitution or government."[63]

Then, in enumerating forms and forums of participation, lest there be doubt, there is added: "Citizens also participate directly in the conduct of public affairs when they choose or change their constitutions."[64]

Such a statement from the authoritative UNCHR may offer the kind of legal peg, so helpful to marginalized citizens, on which to hang formal claims for participation and complaints about exclusion. Yet this empowering declaration is also very limited in more than one respect. A General Comment is at one remove from a direct treaty right. It clarifies the general right to democratic participation, but not the promulgation of a specific right to participation in the constitutional process. If the only binding text is the convention itself, not the comment, then it is technically the fact, as Franck and Thiruvengadam comment, that

> since the principal treaty establishing rules pertaining to the lawmaking processes of states—the way legislators are elected, the public right to be consulted—is not specifically directed toward the constitution-drafting process, this can only be done speculatively, since it is far from clear whether the general terms of the normative structure are implicitly applicable to this particular aspect of governance.[65]

Politically, the comment's speculative status need not vitiate it for citizens claiming a share in constitution making. Legally, however, the distinction between the treaty and the comment is crucial and potentially a serious limitation for constitution makers seeking a rock-solid foundation for claims for democratic rights.[66] General comments, according to the UNCHR itself, are "intended to make the Committee's experience available for the benefit of all States parties, so as to promote more effective implementation of the Covenant; . . . [and] to stimulate the activities of States parties and international organizations in the promotion and protection of human rights."[67] Nonetheless, minority rights lawyer Marcia Rooker notes the importance in her field of "the General Comments of the Committee, which are quite authoritative and indicate which case law can be expected."[68] As a middle position, the view of Franck and Thiruvengadam on General Comment 25 is that "this comment, though not binding in actual cases before the committee, may indicate a tendency to regard constitutional drafting as coming within the purview of the ICCPR."[69]

The authority of UNCHR comments has been particularly questioned when they expand rather than merely explain the content of clauses of the ICCPR. One type of general comment uncontroversially offers specifications for mandatory reports by states to the UNCHR. A second type has been described as the "restatement, interpretation, and elaboration of provisions for the Covenant."[70] The latter attract the critique that they "amount to a bold elaboration, an emphatic development of ideas in the Covenant itself, to 'legislation by Committee.'"[71] To constitutional traditionalists, including constitution making in the realm of public affairs might seem an unacceptably "bold elaboration." For James Tully, the Mikmaq leaders, and other advocates of participation, the same words would be merely a logical clarification.

Canadian Courts (1994 and 1998)

Taking one step backward and one large step forward, two Canadian decisions also contribute to the scanty jurisprudence concerning participation in constitution making. A case brought by the Native Women's Association of Canada (NWAC) in 1994 clarified that the unresolved issue is no longer whether participation in constitution making is a right,[72] but rather who decides on the modalities of participation, to borrow the UNCHR's terminology, and on their adequacy in any particular instance.

In *Marshall v. Canada*, the UNCHR deferred to state authorities to decide who participates by right in constitutional negotiations, and how such participation occurs. The NWAC complained about the same negotiations. The Canadian government had chosen the four aboriginal associations that represented First Nations and funded them to prepare their submissions. NWAC argued that those organizations were male dominated and represented only one view of constitutional reform, favoring male interests; the denial of equal funding to NWAC further infringed the equality guarantees of the Charter of Rights and Freedoms, requiring that rights, including freedom of expression, be available to women and men without discrimination. NWAC argued that, thus, the constitutional negotiations had failed to meet standards of both symbolic (the presence of women) and substantive (the articulation of the interests of women) representation, as well as guarantees of gender equality.[73]

NWAC won the equality point in the Federal Court of Appeal, which volunteered that it would "paralyze the process to hold that the freedom of expression encompassed a right for everyone to sit at the table."[74] It lost on all counts in the Supreme Court of Canada. In particular, the highest court affirmed that the preparation of constitutional amendments was not governmental activity of a kind that was required to comply with the charter's rights. The tradition of constitution making in Canada was of intergovernmental negotiations, and the court stuck with this, saying that questions "as to whom federal and provincial governments ought to meet with and consult during the development of constitutional amendments" were "political questions for which there are no legal or constitutional principles to guide a court in its decision."[75]

Four years later, the Supreme Court of Canada advised on the legitimacy of a hypothetical unilateral secession by the province of Quebec.[76] In the *Reference re Secession of Quebec,* the court provided a widely noted philosophical underpinning for Canadian constitutionalism.[77] Defining democracy as a core Canadian constitutional principle, it recognized an "obligation to negotiate" over fundamental disagreements. In institutional terms, this required that "the system must be capable of reflecting the aspirations of the people."[78] Because "a functioning democracy required a continuous process of discussion" and because "no one has a monopoly on the truth," there was a duty to listen to "dissenting voices" and to seek "to acknowledge and address those voices." The Canadian constitution, the court concluded, "gives expression to this principle [of democracy] by conferring a right to initiate constitutional change on each participant," and imposing "a corresponding duty . . . to engage in constitutional discussions in order to acknowledge and address democratic expressions of a desire for change."[79]

The *Reference* confirmed that a right to participation in democratic governance includes constitution making. It required that participation be an egalitarian dialogue among citizens and between state and citizens. But the ways in which a legitimate debate should be conducted were left unspecified. Instead, the court relied on the traditional electoral definition of democracy without interrogating its adequacy, stating that "historically, this Court has interpreted democracy to mean the process of representative and responsible government and the right of citizens to par-

ticipate in the political process as voters."[80] Beyond such clarification of the "relevant aspects of the Constitution in their broadest sense," the court could not go: "Within that framework, the workings of the political process are complex and can only be resolved by means of political judgments and evaluations."[81]

The Constitutional Court of South Africa (2006)

The legal sources discussed thus far leave to states and citizens to discover what forms of political practice can meet both normative standards and the requirement of practicality for "taking part." Each defers to existing political powers to determine the form of participation, likely disadvantaging the powerless in crucial early decisions on process. Specifically noting this deficiency, South Africa's Constitutional Court began to develop criteria for "reasonable" opportunities for participation, or at least to set a baseline for unacceptable practice. In *Doctors for Life International v. Speaker of the National Assembly and Others* and *Matatiele Municipality and Others v. President of the Republic and Others,* handed down in August 2006, the court considered the positive constitutional duty of legislative bodies to facilitate public involvement in the lawmaking process, including, in *Matatiele,* in formulating a constitutional amendment.[82] In decisions that give an authoritative judicial imprimatur to the analysis offered in this chapter—thus strengthening the formal status of the right to participate—the court noted "taking part" as a requirement of international law as well as a foundational principle of the South African constitutional regime.[83] South African democracy, drawing on African tradition as well as international norms, was both representative and participatory:[84] "The participation by the public on a continuous basis provides vitality to the functioning of a representative democracy," and the participatory component "is of special importance to those who are relatively disempowered in a country like ours where great disparities of wealth and influence exist."[85]

Given the specific constitutional duty, the court asserted its right to review the legislative process itself, not to specify standardized modes of facilitating participation, but to rule on the reasonableness of those modes employed at the discretion of legislatures in any particular instance.[86] Thus, two of the three pieces of legislation under review in *Doctors for Life* had attracted great public interest.[87] In such circumstances, it was unreasonable to assume that the public could simply approach the legislature as it wished. The obligation to facilitate participation required such positive action as the provision of public meetings and the solicitation of submissions, especially at the most local, and thus most accessible, level.[88] The decision in *Matatiele*, closely following the lengthy reasoning of *Doctors for Life*, showed perhaps an even stronger sensitivity to the context of public participation, to the extent of putting legislatures on notice that mechanisms for aiding the public might on occasion extend to "providing transportation to and from hearings or hosting radio programs in multiple languages on an important bill, and may well go beyond any formulaic requirement of notice or hearing."[89] Finally, *Matatiele* summarized this important development of the doctrine of "taking part":

> The nature and the degree of public participation that is reasonable in a given case will depend on a number of factors. These include the nature and importance of the legislation and the intensity of its impact on the public. The more discrete and identifiable the potentially affected section of the population, and the more intense the possible effect on their interests, the more reasonable it would be to expect the legislature to be astute to ensure that the potentially affected part of the population is given a reasonable opportunity to have a say.[90]

Legal Prospects

International law offers both promise and problems for the development of the right to participate in constitution making. General Comment 25 and *Marshall v. Canada* confirm that the right exists. The Canadian *Reference* adds the moral authority of a respected court to the idea of a dialogic process of constitution making. But in the eyes of lawyers, a general comment carries uncertain authority. And each of these utterances defers to existing political powers to determine the form of participation, disadvantaging the less powerful in crucial early decisions on process. Clarifications in international law may, however, be a long time in coming. After the formulation and pursuit of their case through Canadian channels, the Mikmaq people waited five more years for a UNCHR ruling. No cases addressing the constitution-making process are currently in the UN pipeline. Instead, momentum lies with the development of political norms and political experience. Their wide diffusion through international institutions and networks may throw up further grounds for litigation, as has happened in South Africa. In the meantime, the existing body of law supports the expectation that participation is a normal part of constitution making and increases the body of practical experience that informs new experiments.

Taking Part

A commonsense definition of "public affairs" surely includes constitution making, and this definition now finds support in international law. But we lack an adequate definition of what it means to "take part." Constitution making traditionally has carried an aura of learning and technical expertise that has discouraged inexpert participation. Judges have backed away from expansive ideas about taking part, and international legal scholars have

viewed procedures cautiously. Can requirements of process be broadened to allow even
the most marginal and disadvantaged groups
to be heard and respected, and can standards
be enforced? In considering the phrase "take
part," the complementarity of the legal and
political aspects of rights becomes most
apparent.

Three principal modes of participation
have been used: the election of representatives to constitution-making bodies; referendums on draft constitutions; and education
of, consultation with, and responsiveness to
the public.[91] These are not mutually exclusive,
although each has its own merits and problems. States have chosen to use none, all, or
any combination of the three. For example,
during 1994–95, South Africa used the first
and third; Rwanda in 2001 used the second
and third; and the European Union between
2001 and 2005 gave token attention to the
third, while some EU member states held
ratifying referendums on the completed text.

Electing Representatives

The two most common modalities for giving the public a voice in constitution making, the election of constituent assemblies
and constitutional conventions, and referendums on constitutional texts share all the
strengths and weaknesses of general election
procedures as the prime means of fulfilling
a general democratic right.[92] Voting in any of
these forms does, on the face of it, meet the
requirement of Article 25 of the ICCPR that
citizens have the right to take part "directly
or through freely chosen representatives." A
simple, culturally esteemed act is available
to the public. Good practice can be codified
and monitored. But elections offer citizens
an agenda set from above: structured choices
created by governments, candidates, or, most
commonly, political parties. The classic
political-science definition of the function of
parties is that they order public preferences

into manageable packages. Ideally, they facilitate the stable democracy that has been a
frequently stated goal of both constitutional
and electoral design.[93] But few would claim
that party platforms fully represent political
diversity. More likely, they introduce a systematic bias against people and ideas that
the political elites undervalue, dislike, or
even fear. The effect is to exclude minority or
radical views from electoral decision making,
while simplifying the preferences of those
who do engage.[94]

In contrast, writers on a new, deliberative
constitutionalism expect that constitution
making will occur amid instability and assume that conflict and diversity will be continuing facts of political life.[95] Even if the best
outcome can only be to agree to continue to
debate disagreement, as the Canadian Supreme Court recognized, intransigent critics
must be drawn into dialogue. The tentative
language of new constitutionalism contrasts
with the decisive intent of an election or referendum. For a Chilean observer, creating a
new democracy is "an exercise in optimiza-
tion," the goal of which is to "seek" measures
that are "both feasible and most conducive
to the purpose of contributing to build or reconstruct a just order."[96] James Tully spoke
of the dangerous illusion of attaining a "constitutional settlement in accordance with the
comprehensive theory of justice," suggesting
that "the philosophy and practice of contemporary constitutionalism offers a mediated
peace."[97] In such a world of seeking, contributing to, and mediating, a sole reliance
on participation through elections designed
to create winners and losers appears problematic. To create a constitution that allows
the search for the ideal to continue makes a
tough assignment for a process that codifies
the judgment of one moment.

Despite their limitations, however, elections remain at the heart of conceptions of
democracy. The vote is powerful for its history
and symbolism, and electoral participation

in constitution making is the most concrete indicator of accessibility. Voting may be the only form of participation in politics about which citizens are knowledgeable and experienced. Thus the vote, as a means of consent to the process, its terms, its procedures, or its outcomes, is part of many participatory constitution-making processes. Those who would set standards for taking part must maximize the empowering potential of the vote and minimize its imperfections, enabling the representation of complexity, informed decision making, and continuing accountability to the electorate. Constitutional reformers thus have devoted much attention to the electoral aspects of consociationalism, the varieties of proportional representation, and systems of cross-community and supermajorities.[98]

The drafting of a constitutional text is inevitably the task of some relatively small group. Full-scale direct democracy is never a practical proposition, although many would go much further than the cautious legal rulings. The issues for participation through electoral means are not whether the process will involve representation, but the nature and function of the representative body, the kind and degree of representation, constraints placed upon representatives, and their accountability to the public, specifically for constitution-making decisions.[99] Who is to be represented within the chosen forum of legislature, constitutional assembly, or commission? The choices include, descriptively, demographic groups in the population, geographical regions, or political parties; substantively, the choices include different views of national identity, constitutional purpose and principles, legal traditions, or key structural choices, such as federalism or a unitary state. The choice of electoral system biases the outcome, as no system can accommodate all of these. Even proportional representation—whether with multi- or single-member electoral (national or local) districts, lists, simple party labels or transferable votes, or quotas

and affirmative action—cannot be guaranteed to work as intended, as studies of the high hopes and mixed fortunes of women in proportional elections have shown.[100]

Next, the most balanced system of electoral representation does not, in itself, ensure continuing accountability to the public throughout a drafting process, which can be expected to throw up new problems, solutions, and compromises along the way. The constitution-making body may be entrusted to act as it sees fit, required to return to public scrutiny during its proceedings, or required to subject the draft constitution to parliamentary, judicial, or electoral review before promulgation. Whatever the chosen mechanism, the principle of the accountability of decision makers does require that the "process is made receptive" and that the public be "regularly informed at every reasonable stage about the progress of the constitutional process."[101] As can be seen from recent examples, even the best formal procedures cannot guarantee that a democratic process ensues. Mechanisms for representation and accountability have a habit of inconveniencing powerful interests. In some processes, the mechanisms may be mere facades erected to conceal the exercise of power. For a public ostensibly taking part by right, however, early procedural choices regarding representation and accountability are both an opportunity for involvement and a necessary baseline for expectations of their role.

The incidence of key constitution-making practices has been recorded for 194 instances of nations making or revising constitutions or instituting regime changes between 1975 and 2002. In 83 percent of these processes, there was an electoral element in the selection of constitution makers. In some 17 percent of cases, the executive either comprised or appointed the main deliberative body. Constitution making was in the hands of a legislature in 36.6 percent of cases. Legislatures meeting in special session as constituent assemblies were found in 5.7 percent of cases. Elected constituent assemblies with the sole function either of making or ratifying a constitution appeared in 17.9 percent of cases.[102] In either of the last two modes, the electoral mandate knowingly includes responsibility for constitution making, presumptively enabling the electorate to choose between alternative constitutional visions.

In a recent analysis of peace processes, Catherine Barnes highlights two examples of what she calls "representative participation" in the negotiation of a new constitutional framework in profoundly divided societies.[103] Her examples of South Africa and Northern Ireland illustrate the possibility that while representative participation is likely to privilege organizationally experienced but not necessarily socially inclusive political parties, it can be constructed to mitigate such bias to some degree. South Africa's 1994 election was primarily a multiparty contest favoring existing major parties. But the free hand of parties in the constitution-making assembly was circumscribed by the Constitutional Principles of the interim constitution, which had been negotiated in a process that had given all parties a voice, regardless of size. Representatives of women and minorities also moderated the domination of the partisan electoral victors through procedural rules guaranteeing equal membership on working committees. In Northern Ireland, the 1996 election mandated parties to negotiate at multiparty talks and the Peace Forum. The four sectarian parties, two on each side, dominated decision making. But while "perhaps not designed to do so, this [transferable vote] system also provided opportunities for those outside the political mainstream to participate."[104] The effect was to bring into the talks a small but crucial number of delegates from three minor parties, including the Northern Ireland Women's Coalition, that were unaligned with

the two conflicted communities and extended the bases of representation.

The election of constitution makers cannot guarantee effective representation. But, depending on the circumstances of each polity, elections improve access and can be designed to maximize the likelihood of this beneficial outcome. An elected assembly is undoubtedly better than a self-appointed elite group. Politically, it may be the most that can be won. Especially where the vote is on the single issue of constitution making, elections offer the public a chance to take part and to express broad preferences. However, a special election for a one-off body also exposes a weakness of accountability if there is no chance for the public to punish representatives who fail to fulfill their mandate. In an ideal world, negotiations among diverse political parties or among elected delegates would be responsive and accountable to the public. But these are contests among powerful interests over the future exercise of power. Negotiators develop new ideas and face new challenges. Without means to bind delegates or call them to be accountable, the public can only trust their elected representatives to observe their wishes. In the typical constitution-making process of recent years, trust has often been a commodity in short supply at any stage. Sometimes the process itself has been seen as a means of creating trust, "to clarify issues, grasp and articulate differences, let people speak in their own voice, and ultimately, build trust and recognition."[105] Looking ahead to implementing the constitution, a participatory process is no automatic guarantor of respect. But a process from which trust remains absent must surely work against the longer-term legitimacy and sustainability of constitutionalism. Appropriately constructed from the overflowing toolbox of elections and referendums, the vote will always be an important mode of public participation.

Referendums on Constitutional Texts

Referendums on final texts were held in 41.5 percent of the 194 cases of modern constitution making.[106] An increasing frequency might be expected as a right to participation and a culture of democratic expectations has emerged.[107] For example, it was said of Canada's 1992 referendum on the Charlottetown Accord that "the very fact that the question was put to the Canadian people as a whole represents a new stage in Canadian constitutionalism."[108] But neither numbers of referendums nor their frequency automatically equate to a deepening of the public's ability to "take part" constructively. A referendum may seem as close as the process can come to direct democracy, permitting each voter a public judgement on the outcome. But rather than the voicing of complex desires and criticisms, the voter is faced with an up or down vote.[109] The vote may be seen as an opportunity for partisan comments on current politics; there may be partisan pressure to vote a certain way. Frequently, referendums have been devices "to be used by the executive, on issues, timing, and a question of its choosing."[110] Governments, Arend Lijphart has claimed, tend to use a referendum "only when they expect to win," although in constitution-making processes, this tactic has by no means always succeeded.[111]

As with the constitution-making process itself, the structure of a referendum vote, timing, funding, and accessibility may authenticate or manipulate participation. Acknowledging the potential power of even a nonbinding referendum, such as has been held on constitutional changes in the United Kingdom, it has been noted that a result may be politically obligatory even if not legally so.[112] But details can undermine the authority of the outcome, such as what majority of what group carries the day (e.g., of all registered voters or only those voting), whether there is a minimum threshold for voter turnout, whether there are distribution requirements (e.g., for majorities in each region or province), and finally, whether a referendum was accompanied by an educational campaign or even circulation of the text in all the languages of the electorate.[113] Failing clarity on all these points, as in Zimbabwe in 2000, where official observers reported that "very little preparation seemed to have been made in advance and virtually nothing was done to keep the public informed," a referendum will inevitably be weakened by "suspicion" of plans "to rig the vote."[114]

Rwanda's constitutional process provides a model of a validating referendum. The 2003 referendum was preceded by a two-year program of education and discussion that included women, reached into urban and rural areas, and contended with problems of literacy and multiple languages. Opportunities were given for learning and feedback, and changes in drafts were widely circulated before the final popular vote. As a result, the referendum was the culmination of a prolonged conversation, not the single point of access. The result was a resounding 93 percent vote of approval, with a turnout of at least 87 percent of eligible voters.[115]

The experience of referendums has generally been more ambiguous. Ratification of constitutions by a huge majority in Spain (1978) and a majority in a low turnout in Poland (1997) followed the completion of elite negotiations and parliamentary agreements. Voters who had been relatively uninvolved to that point nonetheless endorsed the outcomes. Both processes might be declared successful in approving the constitution and permitting its implementation. But neither electorate showed much enthusiasm for exercising the democratic right to "take part." The oft-cited function of legitimizing the text, essential if a culture of constitutionalism is to support its implementation, may not be achieved merely by casting a vote.[116] Albania's 1999 referendum resulted in endorsement by 90 percent of those voting. This vote followed efforts to enhance education and participation, both before the constitution was drafted and during the short referendum campaign. But the Albanian public was also conflicted by intense partisan pressure and disinformation campaigns.[117] Political pressure was almost the sole influence in Venezuela's two constitutional referenda of 1999. In April, a majority of those voting authorized a constituent assembly, but upward of 60 percent of the electorate abstained. In December a majority of those voting approved the text, but more than 55 percent of the electorate did not vote. The country was deeply divided over President Chavez's intention to write a new constitution and the referendums did nothing to heal that division.[118]

For the purposes of developing the right to "take part," the most interesting examples of constitutional referendums may be those that reject the proposed text. If a referendum is prime ground for manipulating the public through their timing, wording, and procedures, it is also prime ground for voters to protest marginalization in a constitutional process, vote from different preferences, or manipulate the process themselves and turn it into a vote on another political issue. A referendum can be a tool, in Susan Marks' terms, for "self-rule on a footing of equality among citizens," with the unsettling, critical possibilities that the right to democratic governance can create.[119]

In 1992, a Canadian public that had relatively recently "come to aspire to a more democratic form of constitutionalism than their forebears" voted 54.2 to 44.8 percent to reject the Charlottetown Accord that was the product of prolonged intergovernmental negotiations.[120] It was said of this episode that "the development of constitutional proposals was completely detached from the referendum process," and others as well as the Mikmaq people and NWAC disliked the deals that had been cut.[121] Referendums in France and the Netherlands in April and May 2005 were expected to ratify the proposed Constitution of the European Union. Instead, in voting down the constitution, the referendums were used to protest in one case President Chirac's administration, in the other Dutch immigration policies.[122] In 2000, the Zimbabwe electorate voted by 54 to 46 percent to reject the proposed constitution. This had been drawn up in an ostensibly participatory process that was actually tightly controlled by the regime and procedurally deeply flawed, as noted above. The Zimbabwe electorate had no other means of holding the government accountable. The reason voters most often gave to pollsters for a negative vote was that the draft "did not fully take into account the expressed wishes of the people."[123] The public did express its view by rejecting the government draft. But as an observer mission of the Centre for Democracy and Development concluded,

> The debate about the constitution could have provided an opportunity for Zimbabweans to have taken a deeper look more calmly and soberly into key questions that define their body politic and shape their political configuration. . . . This was a missed opportunity to reach a historic settlement that would constitute the basis on which the way forward would be charted. Unfortunately, up to the day of voting, the debate degenerated into an un-refereed shouting match.[124]

The circumstances differ, but the consistent lesson is that taking part in public affairs only after key decisions have been made is not adequate participation in democratic governance, and the public knows this. A referendum can be a means of holding representatives to account and creating legitimacy for the constitution, but only when it is embedded in a process of continuous and sustained participation.

Consultation and Education

A third cluster of participatory modes—education, consultation, and the free expression of views—may begin to meet criticisms of voting as a sole mode of participation. Uninhibited dialogue and deliberation around the vote can save that act from becoming a purely token or formal assent to constitutional proposals. Education does not, of course, itself constitute participation. But because constitution making, constitutional law, and constitutional practice in older constitutional democracies have been regarded as arcane specialities, and in many newer nations have short or nonexistent histories, broad public education in constitutionalism is often an essential preliminary to effective exercise of the right to "take part." A number of recent constitution-making processes have tried to make direct and sustained participation possible through these modes.[125]

Of the 194 constitution-making processes since 1975 recorded in the USIP-sponsored database, 70 included negotiations with various groups about the constitution-making procedure. Determining the process itself is where public involvement must start, given the propensity of procedures to be exclusionary even before any substantive discussion. Decisions on the time available, selection of representatives, and requirements of balance, transparency, and ratification may include or exclude parts of the public. In nearly a quarter of the cases, all political parties were consulted; in 39.3 percent, only those political parties represented in the legislature were consulted; and in 22 percent, some but not all parties were consulted. Among civil-society categories, in 10.2 percent of these cases, economic groups were consulted, in 8.5 percent, major social groups, and in 10 percent, major identity groups. In 8.3 percent of cases, religious leaders were consulted, while in a mere 4.9 percent of cases did women participate in these conversations as a recognized group.[126]

Who should be considered as part of the public for consultation purposes? Article 25 of the ICCPR is the only article of the convention that limits its scope to citizens.[127] Depending on national citizenship rules, the effect may be to exclude some residents or include absentees in consequential ways.[128] The structure of representation can itself exclude or create bias. For example, negotiations with political parties are the traditional route and remain the most used channel to reach consensus on a new constitutional framework. Representation therefore has often been seen as a matter of accurately reflecting party strengths. Party negotiations input the views of existing power blocs, and party representation is characteristically oligarchic and exclusive. Civil-society organizations may be, but are not necessarily, more inclusive and less elitist. But many of the economic, social, identity, religious, gender, and class groups—or indigenous peoples—that form civil societies are less likely to be organized and experienced than partisan groups, and will often have interests that cut across party lines.[129] Some constitution-making processes have attempted public education and the free expression of views from below through open access channels, setting a broader goal for "taking part" than can be met solely by votes and organization-based debate. Of their nature, such modes are likely to make for a less orderly and less controlled process. In the end, perhaps, it is also a process with greater legitimacy, and certainly one that produces a public that will be better informed when constitution making is succeeded by implementation.[130]

Under the database heading of civic education and popular participation, government-funded civic education campaigns were recorded in 35.5 percent of the 194 cases and civic (non-governmental) initiatives in at least 10 percent. Education initiatives included closed meetings among delegates, staff, and civic leaders in at least 14.5 percent and open meetings with citizens in at least 20 percent of cases in the study. Consultation sometimes meant polling, but most commonly (25 percent of cases) gave citizens and civic groups opportunities to submit written briefs or comments. In at least 18 percent of cases, education and consultation were carried to remote rural areas, crucial in many new nations. In 23.2 percent of cases, there was an opportunity for public comment on a draft before a final text was adopted and ratified.[131]

Media campaigns and ad hoc and independent initiatives may be as significant as those of recognized governmental, partisan, civic, or economic organizations. Can there be operational standards for a process that is by definition open to both formal and informal involvement? The South African process between 1992 and 1996, widely hailed as a model of participatory constitution making, suggests some initial criteria for "taking part."[132] A staged agenda ensured that the stakes were never an all or nothing outcome. An interim constitution operated from 1992. This included a set of "Constitutional Principles,"—general propositions about equality, fairness, and democracy, with which it was hard to disagree and which were binding on the structures and rights negotiated for the next constitution. A parliament elected in 1994 on a new inclusive electoral roll doubled as the constitutional assembly and was bound by the principles. Public submissions were invited. A sequence of committees to work on drafts, expert consultations, public meetings, provisions for second thoughts, and a final surety of vetting by the Constitutional Court created trust that power would not trump the process. Efforts to inform and widen participation included a weekly radio program with 10 million listeners, a weekly assembly newsletter, *Constitutional Talk,* with a circulation of 160,000, colorful ads on buses, talk lines, and an open phone line and Web site.[133] An independent nation-wide survey in April 1996 "found that the [constituent assembly] media campaign had succeeded in reaching 73 percent of all adult South Africans (or 18.5 million people)."[134] Two million public submissions were made. Twelve million free copies of the ratified constitution were circulated with a primer, *You and the Constitution.* Statistics, however, as Christina Murray recalls, "fail to convey the vitality and energy of the public participation program."[135]

Vitality and energy have characterized other recent processes in which creative solutions have been found to the difficulties involved in opening up the process. Inexperience, illiteracy, impoverishment, insecurity, prejudice, and lack of resources challenge many constitution-making processes. Countries may lack accessible channels of communication or channels where all feel able to speak freely: women to speak without the shadow of male authority, employees or estate workers without the oversight of the boss, minorities in their own language, entire populations without the threat of violence. However, populations sharing such disadvantages are demeaned by easy assumptions about their ignorance and incapacity. Effective communication to receptive audiences has proved possible through the inventive use of printed educational materials that are free, in clear prose, and that use pictures; eye-catching advertisements placed on buses; street theaters; and the widely available media of radio, text messaging, and the Internet.[136]

It is considerably more difficult to create a bottom-up process in the insecure circumstances of some recent constitution-making exercises. Ideally, this requires openness to genuine and undirected input by the public, enabling them to create their own agenda, which will not necessarily replicate that of the experts. The principle was well taken by a member of the Uganda Constitutional Commission (UCC) who recalled that whatever was raised was defended by the UCC as having a link with the Constitution-Making exercise. Women raised issues of domestic violence . . . young people raised issues of unemployment and drop-out from schools for failure to pay school fees. Elders raised issues of decay of good morals . . . As some members of the audience wished to silent [sic] them that their concerns were not constitutional, the UCC members were there to defend them that every concern of a Ugandan, every experience, every suggestion for the betterment of life and society was a key concern for the exercise.[137]

In practice, the Ugandan process fell short of this ideal.[138] National Resistance Movement attempts to control the process raised doubts over whether commissioners who were government appointees were as open-minded as this account implies and whether the concerns of local meetings did receive attention in the constitutional text. Many proposals doubtless fell by the wayside. But some, with effective community mobilization, survived. Gender-equity clauses in the Uganda constitution are attributed to women's lobbying, especially to the sustained efforts of the nonpartisan Women's Caucus.[139]

Characteristic of many recent processes is the calling of open meetings, by constitutional commissioners, as in Uganda, Rwanda, Mali, or Kenya; local officials, as in Nicaragua; or civil-society groups outside of the formal process, as with the Citizens' Constitutional Forum in Fiji.[140] International and national women's organizations frequently have tried to tap women's views to compensate for exclusionary processes.[141] Despite these sometimes heroic efforts, the authenticity of the participation achieved must be realistically evaluated in each case. This chapter has been critical of various types of electoral participation as adequate channels for diverse public opinions. Citizen activity, however, often has been problematic as well.

Ethiopia's constitutional commission was "specifically charged with the duty to promote the widest possible opportunities for participation." Even to attempt to fulfill its duty, it had to seek external help, including funds. Its seminars, public assemblies, meetings for women and elders, and guidance sheets were models of their kind, yet in the end there was little open debate, much politicking, a boycott by opposition groups, drafting decisions made under time pressure in private commission meetings, and key final determinations reflecting the power of one party rather than the product of democratic deliberation.[142] The South African process appeared to meet just about every criterion of good practice. Yet reactions ran from those who regarded the entire process as a cover for elite negotiation behind closed doors to sympathizers who were optimistic if modest: "one goal frequently invoked was that the new Constitution should be 'owned' by all South Africans." To African National Congress negotiator Cyril Ramaphosa, Murray reports, "this meant that the Constitution should be one which South Africans 'know' and which they 'feel' belongs to them."[143] Did the immense public relations exercise exist only to create a feeling? Few would go so far as that, but undeniably the process was driven from above, not below. There was no pretense that the public made final decisions on detail, and although at first drafting was undertaken openly, on "the most controversial issues . . . politicians started engaging in closed bilateral or multilateral meetings with their political counterparts."[144] The final word lay with the Constitutional Court to verify compatibility with the 1993 Constitutional Principles. Unlike Rwanda, the safeguards built in throughout were taken to obviate the need for a referendum, and there was none.

From her research in Uganda, Devra Moehler has suggested that the public view for or against constitutional proposals is unlikely to be spontaneous, but will reflect the position of opinion leaders in their communities.[145] Even in more open and multiparty negotiations, including the acclaimed South African process, a fully free and effective system of public participation has yet to be approached. This remains a field of trial and both error and evolution, ripe for further development. But, particularly because the interests of previously disadvantaged, unorganized, or underrepresented groups, such as the poor, indigenous peoples, and women, may be undreamed of or misconstrued by even the most benevolent constitution-making elite, opening the process up is an obligation for democrats. The idea of a constitutional conversation, a dialogue among participants who are equal in standing, equally respected by others, and equally able to contribute regardless of formal education or political experience, may be far from attainment. The potential of dialogue for representing diverse and complex opinions must, however, be greater than that of an electoral system. The dialogue that proponents of participatory constitutionalism envisage remains open to creative methods that have, in the best cases, avoided some of the problems of hierarchy, resources, time limitations, cultural inhibitions, and insecurity that threaten spontaneity and responsiveness. Not the least of reasons for mitigating these problems is that, increasingly, the public expects access to the process. Even a limited participation process or a feeling of ownership sponsored by community leaders is preferable for the future prospects of a new constitution to a process that frustrates and disappoints the population's expectations.

Participation and Change

In an evaluation of the constitution-making process in Ethiopia between 1991 and 1994, James N.C. Paul made an eloquent case for public participation in the "reconstitution" of states: "Participation is necessary to 'legitimate' the new constitutional order, promote awareness, acceptance and assertion of human rights and promote democratic gover-nance at the outset . . . to promote 'human development' . . . to close social and political gaps . . . to promote reconciliation and the amelioration of widely shared grievances . . . [and] to eliminate discrimination."[146] Advocates of participation often assume that such desirable consequences result from participatory processes, as in a recent summary by Clarence J. Dias: "International experience in constitution-making has shown that there is a clear correlation between the degree of *transparency, inclusiveness and participation* and the *sustainability and longevity* of the constitutions that result from these processes."[147]

Radical critics of participatory ideals might at this point bring the discussion back to the issue of power, proposing that, after all, constitution making is about the pursuit of power and constitutions are always instruments of domination. Other critics note that constitutions of long standing were normally made without the kind of participation that is attempted today, and yet have acquired legitimacy and observance from politicians and publics, while a good many of those cited above as models of participation have failed in practice. If South Africa is the success story, then Ethiopia, Eritrea, and other nations challenge easy generalization.

The widening and deepening of public participation imply a substantial redistribution of power to a general public and previously excluded groups. According to democratic ideals, such participation is a value in itself. Advocates of participation must take this value and develop ways of "taking part" that yield positive results. The strongest defense of the difficult enterprise of participatory constitutionalism, and a guard against such activity generating only frustration, must be that it makes a difference.[148] We do not yet have enough systematic research into this connection. But some specific positive outcomes address the questions of whether participation leads to change—in the public, the agenda, or the outcome.

Evidence of change in the public does not appear only in numbers, as in high electoral turnouts in South Africa or Rwanda, but also in a sustained and better-informed interest in politics during and after the constitution-making process. In Uganda, Moehler, whose research is the most systematic in this field, has found that involvement in the constitution-making process had the indirectly positive effect of creating informed citizens, whose enhanced political knowledge and energy carried over into postconstitution-making politics.[149] This confirms the anecdotal observations of a Ugandan parliamentarian who, despite her disappointment at antidemocratic political developments under the new constitution, remarked recently that her country's participative process had been an education in politics, rights, and ethical standards. As a consequence, "the Uganda government is dealing with a very different 'people' now from the early 1980s."[150]

An increasing body of practical experience demonstrates that public participation can change the constitution-making agenda, with potentially the "emancipatory and critical force" that Susan Marks predicted. Canadian women organized to write their interests into the new 1982 Charter of Rights, and in so doing, stimulated other groups to mobilize, changing the previous concentrated focus on Quebec and language issues into a broader agenda of citizenship, gender, and indigenous peoples' concerns.[151] At Brazil's public hearings, "government ministers, environmentalists, human rights activists, feminists, business associations, unions, landlords, Indians, street urchins, prostitutes, homosexuals, and maids" spoke out, and 61,142 amendments to the draft constitution were proposed.[152] In Colombia, 1,580 working groups came up with 100,000 proposals. Open town meetings in Nicaragua raised issues missing in constitutional drafts but subsequently incorporated—women's issues again being an example.[153] In Albania,

as Scott Carlson describes in this volume, a series of modifications to the constitutional text have been attributed to public input.

But how many of the 2 million submissions in South Africa, 61,142 amendments in Brazil, and 100,000 proposals in Colombia found their way into constitutional texts, and how many, left unfulfilled, created new frustrations? There is some evidence of the incorporation of public demands into new constitutional texts. One of the strongest examples is undoubtedly the introduction of constitutional clauses establishing the rights of women in general, including a new right to be free from personal and public violence.[154] The inclusion of previously marginalized women and aboriginal peoples in recent constitutional texts provides one of the best arguments for institutionalizing the right to and practice of participation. Martha I. Morgan reports that even underrepresentation of women in making Colombia's 1991 constitution led to unprecedented "broad tri-generational civil and political, social, and collective rights, including not only provisions specifically addressing gender equality but also several other gender-related provisions."[155] Andrew Reding observes of Nicaragua that the "extent to which the popular input in the *cabildos* [town meetings] has been incorporated is striking," exemplified by women's rights at work and in the family, recognition of minority languages and indigenous communal landholding, and social and citizenship rights.[156] Joyce Green is sure that "without the collective activism of women and of Aboriginal peoples, neither would be explicitly protected in the [Canadian] Constitution," and itemizes crucial clauses unimagined at the start but included in the outcome.[157] The impact of women in Uganda has already been noted, while Cathi Albertyn observes that in South Africa, "what was perhaps unexpected was the extent to which women were written into the heart of the democratic process," attributing this to their early mobilization to gain a voice in a constitution-making process that might have been expected to center on race.[158] More generally, one certain reason recent constitutions have incorporated social rights is the pressure exerted for their inclusion by disproportionately deprived, and even in previous texts "constitutionally stigmatized," groups to whose lives such rights are central.[159]

A handful of examples is enough to indicate the potential of participatory processes to bring previously unconsidered people and issues into the constitutional arena. The benefits of a firmly established right to enter the process, accruing particularly to those who most need support, offer the best hope of proving that constitutions are not necessarily always solely instruments of domination. Legal and practical hurdles remain, however, to achieving genuine and effective exercise of the right to democratic constitution-making processes. For advocates of participation, progress requires not only maintaining the momentum that has built up behind the emerging norm of participation, so that it is ever more widely demanded and expected, but strategizing to clarify and develop the law and build on the lessons of practical experience.

Conclusion

"Public affairs" is now assumed to include the making of a nation's constitution, and "taking part" is an established right. Establishing these fundamentals in international law and political culture may, however, prove to have been the easy part. The developments reviewed in this chapter show that while much has been gained, a huge area of difficulty remains around the issue of what "taking part" means, in law and in practice. The idea of "taking part" is all too easily watered down. In what respects can the law be clarified? Can the right be enforced? Who decides how participation shall be structured?

Is agreement on basic standards of good practice possible, as a guide to processes and a marker for monitors? These are lead issues for any future agenda for securing more firmly the right to participate in constitution making.

Part of the agenda concerns legal procedures and substance. Where exclusion, inequality, insecurity, or manipulation impinges, there is currently little scope for legal redress. Procedurally, courts must be satisfied of the standing of plaintiffs, will develop the law only on a case-by-case basis, and may, as the Mikmaq people found, take years to reach a decision. Each of the handful of judicial rulings discussed above affirmed the right to participate but backed off from guidance on how it should be implemented. As opined in *Marshall v. Canada,* "it is for the legal and constitutional system of the State party to provide for the modalities of such participation."[160] Using existing texts and channels strategically depends in large part on supporting appropriate cases that might clarify, for example, what modes of participation meet the requirements of Article 25, whether leaving fundamental decisions on process to national authorities is adequate in terms of Article 25, and whether redress is possible after the event. As with the handful of cases discussed above, the outcome of such a litigation strategy is liable to be piecemeal and partial. But case law is important both as formal legal confirmation of rights in particular cases and as a political resource demonstrating judicial backing of claims for inclusion, which typically come from those dispossessed of political power.

Developments in the law not only enhance political resources for effectuating change but often are themselves spurred by political developments. Any comprehensive restatement of the right to take part in constitution making will more likely come, as Franck and Thiruvengadam have observed, from the multiplication and elaboration of participation rights in international and national charters, conventions, comments, and indeed, from authoritative writings such as their own, rather than from piecemeal judicial rulings.[161] As noted above, regional charters and national constitutional texts increasingly have broadened and deepened their guarantees of participation and the social and political circumstances that make it effective. Momentum has built as progressively more texts have addressed participation seriously. However, none has yet incorporated the textual affirmations of UN bodies on constitution making.[162]

As discussed earlier, the foundations of the right to participate in constitution making lie in clauses of the UN Declaration of Human Rights and the ICCPR. UN agencies themselves have recently been involved in constitution-making processes, testing the adequacy of their own precepts.[163] No constitution-making equivalent to their election-monitoring apparatus, in structure or code of practice, exists within the organization, however.[164] James Paul reflects that in the early 1990s, Ethiopia was disadvantaged by the absence of international standards for participation to provide a model and source of international pressure on its flawed national process. His challenge that the "international community can—I believe it is now obligated to—create a framework of standards governing the processes of reconstitution that would address not only participation but other necessary subjects as well," remains open.[165] Can process requirements for constitution making be conceived that could provide both political guidance and legal guarantees? Could constitution making be monitored as electoral processes are monitored for their freedom and fairness?[166]

Henry Steiner found that "infirmities" inherent in the idea of a right to participate—its "relatively vague and abstract" nature compared with the clarity of voting—presented an obstacle to securing a firm legal grounding for participation.[167] Several international organizations and projects supported by non-governmental organizations and think tanks have assumed that at least the process, as opposed to the substance, is susceptible to codification by a standard of democratic practice.[168] The code presented by the Commonwealth Human Rights Initiative (CHRI) to Commonwealth heads of government in 1999 was an early attempt to address process issues: "governments must adopt credible processes for constitution making; that is, a process that constructively engages the largest majority of the population." The CHRI code called for good management, responsiveness, accessibility, a positive duty to provide the public with "the necessary tools to participate," respect for dissent, inclusiveness, mediation, and continuous review, evaluation, and feedback.[169] In addition to these principles, it enumerated practices such as ensuring the independence of the drafting commission, giving adequate time and funding, assisting civil society, facilitating access to international experience, using the media to communicate with and report to the public throughout the process, and providing representative means of ratifying the constitution and forward-looking means for regular review thereafter.[170]

Many of these items are now general currency. But no single authoritative set of standards has yet emerged in law or from organizational sources to guide those trying to create participatory processes or monitor their progress. What we have to date perhaps most resembles traditional definitions of the uncodified British constitution, a "curious compound of custom and precedent, law and convention," ("convention" in the British sense of "general agreement . . . about the 'rules of the game' to be borne in mind in the conduct of public affairs").[171] Such a compound may fit with the vague and abstract character asserted by Steiner and allow flexibility and attention to local context. But compared with more formal codes of practice, bundles of miscellaneous advice are difficult for the uninitiated to know or use. Rules designed to be "borne in mind" by persons of goodwill are hard to enforce. Observance of custom and convention depends a great deal on goodwill and a culture of respect for the spirit of constitutionalism that is easily lost in the pursuit of power. The right to participate is legally enforced with difficulty. In politics, an advisory code of sufficient generality to provide a common starting point of principle for constitution-making processes in many different national contexts might at least begin to establish a bottom line that all can work to achieve.

To conclude that a right to participate in constitution making is established—and is, to varying degrees, being further defined by conventions and charters, national constitutions, judicial opinions and decisions, and practical experiments in numerous constitution-making processes—is clearly not to assert that authentic and effective participation always or even often takes place. A serious "participation deficit" still exists, a gap between that right and its implementation. Constitution makers are experimenting with ways to fill that gap. They have been backed on occasion by taking flawed processes to courts and to the UNCHR to test the extent of the right and seek enforcement. They are supported every time another process takes up the experiment and carries on the work. Even as the right is strengthened, however, the hardest task remains for advocates of participatory constitutionalism: how, in practice, to persuade powerful and power-seeking elites to abandon prior possession of the field and admit whole populations to this foundational political process. In an important step on the way, the evidence marshaled in this chapter suggests that the culture of constitution making has come to include the expectation of democratic practice. Only concerted legal and political work can ensure that optimis-

tic experiments in such practice become the binding precedents of an international right that resistant powers are either persuaded or forced to respect.

Notes

1. Thomas M. Franck, "The Emerging Right to Democratic Governance," *American Journal of International Law*, vol. 86 (1992), p. 46.

2. See Gregory H. Fox and Brad R. Roth, eds., *Democratic Governance and International Law* (Cambridge: Cambridge University Press, 2000). In particular, chapter 3 by James Crawford, "Democracy and the Body of International Law," gives the substance of Crawford's 1993 Whewell Inaugural Lecture at the University of Cambridge, published as *Democracy in International Law: Inaugural Lecture* (Cambridge: Cambridge University Press, 1994). This stands with Franck's work as foundational to the debate about the right to democratic governance; to this later version, Crawford has added a reprise of responses to his lecture.

3. See the chapter in this volume by Thomas M. Franck and Arun K. Thiruvengadam.

4. James Tully, *Strange Multiplicity: Constitutionalism in an Age of Diversity* (Cambridge: Cambridge University Press, 1995), p. 28.

5. In 1997, Giovanni Sartori recorded that "Of the 170 or so written documents called constitutions in today's world, more than half have been written since 1974." *Comparative Constitutional Engineering: An Inquiry into Structures, Incentives, and Outcomes*, 2nd ed. (New York: New York University Press, 1997), p. 197. A database compiled under sponsorship of the United States Institute of Peace by Professor Jennifer Widner includes 194 cases of constitution drafting, between 1975 and 2002, that produced new or extensively amended constitutions or changes in regime type (excluding processes where there was no risk of violence). See Jennifer Widner, Princeton University, *Constitution Writing and Conflict Resolution: Data and Summaries*, available at www.wws.princeton.edu/pcwcr/index.html (January 2006; accessed on April 18, 2009). I am grateful to Professor Widner for advance data from this source.

6. Penelope Andrews and Stephen Ellmann, eds., *The Post-Apartheid Constitutions: Perspectives on South Africa's Basic Law* (Johannesburg: Witwatersrand University Press, 2001), and the full discussion of the South African case by Ebrahim and Miller in this volume. Other examples from the United States Institute of Peace Project on Constitution Making, Peacebuilding, and National Reconciliation that highlight experiments in participation include Albania, Brazil, Eritrea, Ethiopia, Nicaragua, Uganda, and Venezuela; the most recent may be Rwanda. In both Afghanistan and Iraq, the rhetoric of participation has been prominent. For examples of a large and scattered literature of books, articles, and reports, see the regional study by Julius O. Ihonvbere, *Towards a New Constitutionalism in Africa* (London: Centre for Democracy and Development, 2000), and studies of particular aspects, such as Yash Ghai, *Public Participation and Minorities* (London: Minority Rights Group, 2001); Alexandra Dobrowolsky and Vivien Hart, eds., *Women Making Constitutions: New Politics and Comparative Perspectives* (Houndmills: Palgrave, 2003); and Helen Irving, *Gender and the Constitution: Equity and Agency in Comparative Constitutional Design* (Cambridge: Cambridge University Press, 2008).

7. Iraqi Governing Council, Law of Administration for the State of Iraq for the Transitional Period, March 2004, arts. 60, 61. Jonathan Morrow discusses the flagrant breach of this mandate in his chapter in this volume.

8. Franck and Thiruvengadam, this volume.

9. *Marshall et al. v. Canada* (Human Rights Committee, CCPR/C/43/D/205/1986), 3 December 1991; Human Rights Committee, "The right to participate in public affairs, voting rights and the right of equal access to public service" (Art. 25): 12/17/96. CCPR General Comment 25, 6(b).

10. Supreme Court of Canada, *Reference re Secession of Quebec*, 2 SCR 217 (1998).

11. Tony Evans, "International Human Rights Law as Power/Knowledge," *Human Rights Quarterly* vol. 27 (August 2005), p. 1048.

12. See, e.g., Owen M. Fiss, "Human Rights as Social Ideals," in *Human Rights in Political Transitions: Gettysburg to Bosnia*, eds. Carla Hesse and Robert Post, 263–76 (New York: Zone Books, 1999); Harold Hongju Koh and Ronald C. Slye, eds., *Deliberative Democracy and Human Rights* (New Haven, CT: Yale University Press, 1999); and a discussion in an American context, Stuart A. Scheingold, *The Politics of Rights: Lawyers, Public Policy, and Political Change* (New Haven, CT: Yale University Press, 1974).

13. The ICCPR was adopted in 1966 and entered into force in 1976 when the required initial number of 35 ratifications or accessions by states

had been filed (art. 49). By June 2003 it had been ratified by 149 states.

14. Robin Luckham, Anne Marie Goetz, Mary Kaldor, *Democratic Institutions and Politics in Contexts of Inequality, Poverty and Conflict*, IDS Working Paper no. 104, Institute of Development Studies, Brighton, 2000, p. 1.

15. The Council of Europe was founded in 1949 with ten western european members: Belgium, Denmark, France, Ireland, Italy, Luxembourg, Netherlands, Norway, Sweden, and the United Kingdom. By 2003, it had grown to forty-five members, including many eastern european and former Soviet Union nations.

16. Henry J. Steiner, "Political Participation as a Human Right," *Harvard Human Rights Yearbook* 1 (1988), p. 94.

17. ECHR, First Protocol to the Convention, 1952, art. 3.

18. Steiner, "Political participation as a Human Right," pp. 94–96, quotations p. 96.

19. See also the review of international provisions in Gregory H. Fox, "The Right to Political Participation in International Law," in *Democratic Governance and International Law*, pp. 50–69. These all refer to political participation in general without mentioning constitution making.

20. Convention on the Elimination of All Forms of Racial Discrimination, 1965, art. 5(c). See also United Nations Declaration on the Rights of Persons Belonging to National or Ethnic, Religious and Linguistic Minorities, 1992, art. 2 (General Assembly Resolution 47/135 of 18 December 1992).

21. Convention on the Elimination of All Forms of Discrimination Against Women, 1979, art. 7.

22. European Framework Convention for the Protection of National Minorities, 1995, arts. 15 and 17.

23. African Charter on Human and Peoples' Rights, 1981, art. 13.1.

24. Commonwealth Heads of Government Meeting, 1991, The Harare Declaration, October 20, 1991, at www.dfaitmaeci.gc.ca/foreign_policy/the commonwealth.org/Internal/20723/34457/harare_commonwealth/imoc310-en.asp (accessed April 18, 2009).

25. Asian Charter of Rights, 1998, art. 5, "The Right to Democracy." See text and a discussion of the drafting process led by the Asian Human Rights Commission, a body without governmental stand-

ing, in *Asia Pacific Journal on Human Rights and the Law,* vol. 1 (2000), pp. 126–66. As this source notes, the Asia Pacific region remains without a formal human rights system. In November 2007, leaders of the Association of South East Asian Nations (ASEAN) signed an ASEAN Charter with weak and nonsanctionable human rights and democracy provisions; the ten member states have yet to ratify it.

26. Organization of American States, *Inter-American Democratic Charter* (Washington: OAS, 2001).

27. See John W. Graham, "A Magna Carta for the Americas: The Inter-American Democratic Charter: Genesis, Challenges and Canadian Connections," Policy Paper FPP-02-09, Canadian Foundation for the Americas, August 2002.

28. Inter-American Democratic Charter, art. 1, Graham, "A Magna Carta for the Americas," p. 7.

29. UN, Vienna Declaration and Programme of Action, 25 June 1993, art. 5.

30. UN, Vienna Declaration, art. 8: "Democracy, development, and respect for human rights and fundamental freedoms are interdependent and mutually reinforcing." See examples linking participation with development in Clarence J. Dias, *Peacebuilding: International Law and Constitution-Making,* Report for the United Nations Development Programme, July 10, 2005.

31. Inter-American Democratic Charter, art. 6.

32. Inter-American Democratic Charter, arts. 2, 4, 7.

33. Inter-American Democratic Charter, art. 19. The idea of sanctions goes against the tradition of noninterference in the affairs of a sovereign state, long a principle of international law and breached by the OAS only after tough intergovernmental debate. Graham, "A Magna Carta for the Americas," p. 2, describes how the protection of national sovereignty was the key issue in the drafting of the charter, responsible for several major setbacks in the process, and perhaps only overcome by acclamation through the coincidence that the final vote took place on the morning of September 11, 2001, with U.S. Secretary of State Colin Powell delaying his return home from the signing ceremony in Peru to endorse this strong version.

34. Franck and Thiruvengadam, this volume.

35. See, e.g., Louis Henkin and Albert Rosenthal, eds., *Constitutionalism and Rights: The Influence of the United States Constitution Abroad* (New York: Columbia University Press, 1990); S.A. de Smith, *The New Commonwealth and Its Constitutions* (London: Stevens, 1964).

36. Michael Foley, *The Silence of Constitutions: Gaps, "Abeyances," and Political Temperament in the Maintenance of Government* (London: Routledge, 1989); Alan C. Cairns, "Constitutional Stigmatization," in Patrick J. Hanafin and Melissa S. Williams, eds., *Identity, Rights, and Constitutional Transformation* (Aldershot: Ashgate, 1999), chap. 2.

37. Alex Conte, Scott Davidson, and Richard Burchill, *Defining Civil and Political Rights: The Jurisprudence of the United Nations Human Rights Committee* (Aldershot: Ashgate, 2004), chap. 2; Bayeksky.com, "How to Complain about Human Rights Treaty Violations: The Covenant on Civil and Political Rights," available at www.bayefsky.com/complain/10_ccpr.php (accessed on April 18, 2009).

38. Joseph A. Schumpeter, *Capitalism, Socialism, and Democracy* (London: Routledge, 1965), p. 269.

39. See John S. Dryzek, *Discursive Democracy* (Cambridge: Cambridge University Press, 1990), defining a collective, social, communicative, and argumentative democracy; also his overview of the considerable debate that developed in the 1990s, *Deliberative Democracy and Beyond: Liberals, Critics, Contestations* (Oxford: Oxford University Press, 2000).

40. See, e.g., Tully, *Strange Multiplicity*; Simone Chambers, "Contract or Conversation: Theoretical Lessons from the Canadian Constitutional Crisis," *Politics and Society,* vol. 26, no. 1 (March 1998), pp. 143–72; Vivien Hart, "Constitution-Making and the Transformation of Conflict," *Peace and Change,* vol. 26, no. 2 (April 2001), pp. 153–76.

41. South Africa, Constitution Act of 1996, chap. 1, s. 1 (d).

42. South Africa, Constitution Act of 1996, chap. 2, s. 19.

43. Constitution of East Timor (2002), s. 46. See other examples across continents, such as the constitutions of Slovakia (1992, art. 30), and Venezuela (1999, art. 62). Like South Africa, the Hong Kong Basic Law (1991, art. 21) spells out under the heading "Right to Participate in Public Life" that freely chosen representatives, genuine periodic elections, equal access to public service are required.

44. Constitution of Angola (1992), art. 28; Constitution of Ethiopia, chap 2, art. 8.

45. Constitution of Uganda (1995), chap. II (i).

46. Macro (or mega) constitutional politics is Peter H. Russell's term to distinguish "efforts at broad constitutional renewal as compared with piecemeal constitutional reform." Peter H. Russell, *Constitutional Odyssey: Can Canadians Become a Sovereign People?* 2nd ed. (Toronto: University of Toronto Press, 1993), p. 275, note 8. Uganda presents an interesting example of a constitution-making process apparently designed in the spirit of inclusion, democratic consultation, and decentralization that theoretically guided the National Resistance Movement's so-called no-party politics. Yet this was systematically subverted by the same NRM in government, in order to control the process. Aili Mari Tripp's chapter in this volume describes the latter process. For the contradictions, see Anne-Marie Goetz, "The Problem with Patronage: Constraints on Women's Political Effectiveness in Uganda," in Anne Marie Goetz and Shireen Hassim, eds., *No Shortcuts to Power: African Women in Politics and Policymaking* (London: Zed Books, 2003), pp. 113–16. Goetz describes the paradoxical conjunction of the offer of openness and its simultaneous subversion as one of "various self-imposed moments of reckoning, each of which has stiffened the executive's resistance to political competition," p. 113.

47. Constitution of Colombia 1991, preamble and art. 103.

48. William C. Banks and Edgar Alvarez, "The New Colombian Constitution: Democratic Victory or Popular Surrender?" *University of Miami Inter-American Law Review,* vol. 23, no. 1 (Fall 1991), esp. pp. 80ff.

49. Constitution of Peru, title 1, chap. I, art. 2: "Every person has the right: (xvi) to participate individually or in association with others in the political, economic, social and cultural life of the nation." Constitutional reform, total or partial, may be subject to a referendum (art. 32).

50. Political Constitution of the Republic of Ecuador 1998, title III, chap. 3. Constitution of the Bolivarian Republic of Venezuela 1999, title I, art. 6; the standard English translation quoted in my text reads in the original: "El gobierno . . . es y será siempre democrático, participativo, electivo, descentralizado, alternativo, responsable, pluralista y de mandatos revocables." Professor Allan R. Brewer-Carias—author of the chapter on Venezuela in this volume—notes that the words *democrático, alternativo* (referring to the possibility for political or partisan alternations in power in the presidency and the legislature), and *responsable* have their origin in the 1830 Venezuelan constitution. Demon-strating the importance of language and of retaining fundamental guarantees against future abuse in constitutional texts, Professor Brewer-Carias recalls that, as a delegate to the 1999 national constituent assembly, faced with the government proposal to delete the traditionally used word *representativo,* he succeeded in substituting the word *electivo* (email to author, January 12, 2006).

51. The summary compilation of cases on political rights at www.bayefsky.com/themes/political_jurisprudence.php lists three decisions on Article 25(a) and nineteen on clauses (b) and (c). Conte et al., *Defining Civil and Political Rights*, pp. 68–77, suggests a similar ratio.

52. Mr. Lallah, in UNCHR, "Summary Record of the 1460th Meeting," 30/10/95. CCPR/C/SER.1460, para. 41.

53. *Marshall et al. v. Canada*; see the documentary history, with an introduction by Sákéj Henderson on the history of litigation by the Mikmaq people, at www.usask.ca/nativelaw/unhrfn/mikmaq.php (accessed May 7, 2009).

54. *Marshall et al. v. Canada*, paras. 3.1 and 3.2. The UNCHR was acting in its judicial capacity to hear individual complaints under Optional Protocol I to the ICCPR. The constitutional conferences promised in art. 35.1 of the Canadian Charter of Rights and Freedoms of 1982 were for negotiations between federal, provincial, and territorial governments and representatives of indigenous peoples on amending the constitution as it affected those peoples. Art. 35.1 (b) promised that "The Prime Minister of Canada will invite representatives of the aboriginal peoples of Canada to participate in the discussions." The Mikmaq case questioned the adequacy of representation in the crucial discussions in the Canada Round between 1982 and 1992 that produced the Charlottetown Accord (*Consensus Report on the Constitution*, August 29, 1992). This proposed sixty changes, including the controversial Canada Clause, which attempted to define basic Canadian values, acknowledged Quebec as a "distinct society" within Canada, and recognized aboriginal governments as "one of the three orders of government in Canada." The public rejected the accord in a referendum in October 1992.

55. *Marshall et al. v. Canada*, paras. 5.2 and 5.3.

56. The case is discussed in Mary Ellen Turpel, "Rights of Political Participation and Self-Determination in Canada," in H. Reynolds and R. Nile, eds., *Indigenous Rights in the Pacific and North America* (London: University of London and Sir

Robert Menzies Centre for Australian Studies, 1992), pp. 95–109. It is occasionally mentioned in recent literature on the general right to participate, e.g., Ghai, *Public Participation and Minorities*, p. 8.

57. *Marshall et al. v. Canada*, para. 5.5.

58. *Marshall et al. v. Canada*, para. 2.2.

59. UN Committee on Human Rights, CCPR General Comment 25, 12 July 1996, para. 1.

60. Steiner, "Political Participation as a Human Right," p. 77.

61. Steiner, "Political Participation as a Human Right," p. 78.

62. UNCHR, Summary Record of the 1399th meeting: 10/04/95. CCPR/C/1399.

63. General Comment 25, paras. 1–2.

64. General Comment 25, para. 6.

65. Franck and Thiruvengadam, this volume.

66. When the UNCHR claimed a determinative status for its own decisions (General Comment 24, 2 November 1994, CCPR/C/21/Rev.1/Add.6., para. 11), there was a speedy counterblast in defense of national sovereignty. The UNCHR asserted: "The Committee's role under the Covenant . . . necessarily entails interpreting the provisions of the Covenant and the development of a jurisprudence." The U.S. government replied that the comment "appears to go much too far" and denied any binding status for the committee's interpretations. The UK government suavely noted that it was "of course aware that the general comments adopted by the Committee are not legally binding. They nevertheless command great respect," and then adapted the language of the committee's assertion above to conclude that "the Committee must necessarily be able to take a view," a subtle shift of tone which negated the UNCHR's authority. See UN, *Report of the Human Rights Committee*, vol. 1, General Assembly, Official Records, Fiftieth Session, Supplement no. 40 (A/50/40), pp. 126, 130.

67. UNCHR, 1994 report, vol. 1, GAOR 49th Sess., Supp. no. 40 (A/49/40), para. 50, quoted in Henry J. Steiner and Philip Alston, eds., *International Human Rights in Context: Law, Politics, Morals* (Oxford: Clarendon Press, 1996), pp. 533–34.

68. Marcia Rooker, "Monitoring Human Rights: The Importance of the Universal Level for Roma and Sinti," *CPRSI Newsletter*, vol. 3, no. 1 (February 1997), p. 9.

69. Franck and Thiruvengadam, this volume.

70. Steiner and Alston, eds., *International Human Rights in Context*, p. 526; see pp. 522–35 for an overview of the functions of General Comments.

71. Steiner and Alston, eds., *International Human Rights in Context*, p. 534.

72. Supreme Court of Canada, *Native Women's Association of Canada v. Canada* [1994], 3 S.C.R.

73. *Native Women's Association of Canada v. Canada*, pp. 634–36.

74. Quoted in the Supreme Court decision, *Native Women's Association of Canada v. Canada*, p. 640.

75. From the initial decision in the Trial Division, *Native Women's Association of Canada v. Canada* (T.D.) T-2238-92 (1993), conclusions, available at http://reports.fja.gc.ca/eng/1992/1993fca0449.html/1993fca0449.html.html (accessed on April 18, 2009).

76. Supreme Court of Canada, *Reference re Secession of Quebec* [1998] 2 S.C.R. For contemporary reactions, see David Schneiderman, ed., *The Quebec Decision: Perspectives on the Supreme Court Ruling on Secession* (Toronto: James Lorimer, 1999), esp. Alan C. Cairns, "The Constitutional Obligation to Negotiate," chap. 14.

77. See, e.g., the attempt to work out how the *Reference* might be applied in the Sri Lankan situation, in Andrew Pilliar, "Canada's Unwritten Constitutional Principles and Their Relevance to Sri Lanka," *Moot Point: Legal Review 2003–2004*, vol. 7 (Colombo: Centre for Policy Alternatives, 2005), pp. 103–11. Ran Hirschl has noted the impact of the *Reference* in "other fragmented polities (Spain, Britain, Belgium, India, France, Cyprus, Sri Lanka, Bolivia)," in "Canada's Contribution to the Comparative Study of Rights and Judicial Review," paper presented at the Canadian Political Science Association, London, Ontario, June 2005, p. 26.

78. *Reference re Secession of Quebec*, para. 67.

79. *Reference re Secession of Quebec*, paras. 68–69.

80. *Reference re Secession of Quebec*, para. 65.

81. *Reference re Secession of Quebec*, para 100.

82. *Doctors for Life International v. Speaker of the National Assembly and Others*, CCT 12/05 (2006), ZACC 11, 17, August 2006; *Matatiele Municipality and Others v. President of the Republic and Others*, CCT 73/05A (2006), ZACC 12, 18, August 2006. I am grateful to Professor Christina Murray for drawing my attention to these decisions.

The duty to facilitate involvement appears in the Constitution of South Africa at art. 59 (National Assembly), art. 72 (National Council of Provinces), and art. 118 (provincial legislatures). The Constitution Twelfth Amendment Act of 2005 redrew provincial boundaries, with the effect of transferring the local municipality of Matatiele from KwaZulu-Natal to the Eastern Cape, which affected the provision of public services to the municipality; art. 97 of the *Matatiele* decision notes that: "While it is true that the people of the province have no right to veto a constitutional amendment that alters provincial boundaries, they are entitled to participate in its consideration in a manner which may influence the decisions of the legislature."

83. *Doctors for Life,* from para. 90. The court had begun to develop arguments about democratic participation in the earlier case of *Minister of Health and Another v. New Clicks South Africa (Pty) Ltd.,* CCT 59/04A (2005), ZACC 25, 30 September, 2005, but with reference to secondary legislation, not to primary legislation as in *Doctors for Life* or constitutional amendment as in *Matatiele.*

84. *Doctors for Life*, para. 101, and the supporting opinion by Justice Albie Sachs, paras. 227–35.

85. *Doctors for Life,* para. 115.

86. *Doctors for Life*, paras. 125–29.

87. Proposals concerning the recognition of traditional health practitioners and facilities for the termination of pregnancies generated wide interest; a bill concerning the licensing of dental technicians did not. The first two were declared invalid, the third allowed to stand.

88. *Doctors for Life*, paras. 159–62.

89. *Matatiele*, para. 67.

90. *Matatiele*, para. 68. Both decisions were written by Justice Ngcobo.

91. Constitutional amending processes, which have not been addressed in this chapter, are analogous but usually may be differentiated from constitution making as concerned with relatively limited adjustments to existing texts rather than creating new regimes. This is the same distinction between mega- and piecemeal constitutional politics made in Russell, *Constitutional Odyssey.* The participation debate has impinged less on discussion of amending processes, which has been more prone to leave the process to legislatures, perhaps requiring supermajorities and only in some places and circumstances requiring referendums for ratification. See essays in Sanford Levinson, ed., *Responding to Imperfection: The Theory and Practice of Constitutional Amendment* (Princeton, NJ: Princeton University Press, 1995), including Akil Reed Amar's observations on the absence of direct public initiative or participation in the U.S. system, and the appendix of "Amending Provisions of Selected New Constitutions in East-

ern Europe" that vary considerably in the degree of citizen involvement.

92. Electoral standards have been the prime focus of discussions of the right to participation. See litigation discussed above, and see also Thomas M. Franck, "Legitimacy and the Democratic Entitlement," and Gregory H. Fox, "The Right to Political Participation in International Law," in Fox and Roth, eds., *Democratic Governance and International Law*, chaps. 1 and 2.

93. See Harry Eckstein, *A Theory of Stable Democracy* (Princeton, NJ: Woodrow Wilson School of Public and International Affairs, Princeton University, 1961), for the classic statement. Giovanni Sartori points out that while stable, in the sense of permanent, democracy must be a good thing, this is often mistakenly construed as meaning stable government. See his *Comparative Constitutional Engineering*, pp. 111–14.

94. In a particularly strong critique of the international law approach to democracy, Susan Marks alleges that "international legal scholars . . . precisely *do not* identify democracy with a concept or ideal of self-rule on a footing of equality among citizens. Rather they largely elide democracy with certain liberal ideas and institutions [and] attenuate the emancipatory and critical force that democracy might have." Susan Marks, "International Law, Democracy and the End of History," in Fox and Roth, eds., *Democratic Governance and International Law*, p. 533; for a similar criticism, see also Brad R. Roth, "Evaluating Democratic Progress," in the same volume, chap. 17. A strong criticism of the American constitutional system on the same lines is by Robert A. Dahl, *How Democratic Is the American Constitution?* (New Haven, CT: Yale University Press, 2001).

95. See, e.g., Edward Said, "The Politics of Partition," *Progressive,* vol. 63 (December 1999), pp. 18–19; Robin Luckham, Anne Marie Goetz, and Mary Kaldor, "Democratic Institutions and Democratic Politics," in Sunil Bastian and Robin Luckham, eds., *Can Democracy Be Designed? The Politics of Institutional Choice in Conflict-Torn Societies* (London: Zed Books, 2003), chap. 1.

96. Interview with José Zalaquett by Naomi Roht-Arriaza, "The Need for Moral Reconstruction in the Wake of Past Human Rights Violations," in Carla Hesse and Robert Post, eds., *Human Rights in Political Transitions: Gettysburg to Bosnia* (New York: Zone Books, 1999), p. 197.

97. Tully, *Strange Multiplicity*, p. 211.

98. See, e.g., the works of Arend Lijphart, recently reviewed by him in "The Wave of Power-Sharing Democracy," in Andrew Reynolds, ed., *The Architecture of Democracy: Constitutional Design, Conflict Management, and Democracy* (Oxford: Oxford University Press, 2002), chap. 2 (see also other essays in this volume); Donald L. Horowitz, "Constitutional Design: An Oxymoron?" in Ian Shapiro and Stephen Macedo, eds., *Designing Democratic Institutions,* Nomos XLII (New York: New York University Press, 2000), chap. 9; Sartori, *Comparative Constitutional Engineering*; and critical essays in Bastian and Luckham, eds., *Can Democracy Be Designed?*

99. See Hanna Fenichel Pitkin, *The Concept of Representation* (Berkeley: University of California Press, 1972).

100. See e.g., Graham Hassall and Cheryl Saunders, *Asia-Pacific Constitutional Systems* (Cambridge: Cambridge University Press, 2002), chap. 5; Shireen Hassim, "Representation, Participation, and Democratic Effectiveness: Feminist Challenges to Representative Democracy in South Africa," in Goetz and Hassim, eds., *No Shortcuts to Power*, pp. 81–109; and Kishali Pinto-Jayawardena, "Proportional Representation, Political Violence, and the Participation of Women in the Political Process in Sri Lanka," and Jon Fraenkel, "Electoral Engineering and the Politicization of Ethnic Friction in Fiji," both in Bastian and Luckham, eds., *Can Democracy Be Designed?*

101. Commonwealth Human Rights Initiative (CHRI), *Constitutionalism: Best Practices of Participatory Constitution-Making*, available at http://www.humanrightsinitiative.org/programs/constitutionalism/practices.htm (accessed January 2003), arts. 4.4, 5.9. For a review of these issues from a gendered perspective, see Anne Marie Goetz, "Gender and Accountability," in Dobrowsky and Hart, eds., *Women Making Constitutions*, chap. 3.

102. Figures provided by the project director, Professor Jennifer Widner, July 2005. The project, designed to support research on constitution making as a mode of conflict transformation, was sponsored by the U.S. Institute of Peace. Data are for 194 cases, between 1975 and 2002, of constitution drafting that produced new constitutions or changes in regime type (except those for which there was no risk of violence). The remaining cases involved transitional legislatures (appointed) at 5.7 percent; national conferences at 3.1 percent; roundtables at 1.5 percent (usually responsible for interim constitutions or design of the process); and peace negotiations or decolonization conferences at 4.2 percent.

103. Catherine Barnes, "Democratizing Peace Processes: Strategies and Dilemmas for Public Participation," in *Owning the Process: Public Participation in Peacemaking*, ed. Catherine Barnes, Accord no. 13 (2002), p. 2.

104. Barnes, "Democratizing Peace Processes," p. 2. See also Kate Fearon, *Women's Work: The Story of the Northern Ireland Women's Coalition* (Belfast: Blackstaff Press, 1999), chaps. 1, 2.

105. Chambers, "Contract or Conversation?" p. 156.

106. Figure provided by the project director, Professor Jennifer Widner, July 2005.

107. See Lawrence LeDuc, "Theoretical and Practical Issues in the Study and Conduct of Initiatives and Referendums," prepared for discussion at the International IDEA Workshop on Direct Democracy, London, March 13–14, 2004, p. 1., available at www.idea.int/news/upload/direct_democracy.pdf (accessed on April 18, 2009).

108. Chambers, "Contract or Conversation," p. 149.

109. A particular problem when the vote is on an entire constitution. Referendums on single constitutional amendments often give a more reliable verdict, e.g., the vote to end the role of the monarchy in Australia (where voting in referendums as in elections is compulsory), rejected by 55 percent (see www.statusquo.org), or the simultaneous votes in Ireland and Northern Ireland to accept the Belfast Agreement, which received a 95 percent yes vote south of the border and a 71.2 percent yes vote with an 81 percent turnout in the north. See Quintin Oliver, "Developing Public Capacities for Participation in Peacemaking," in Barnes, ed., *Owning the Process*.

110. Robert Hazell, "The New Constitutional Settlement," in *Constitutional Futures: A History of the Next Ten Years*, ed. Robert Hazell (Oxford: Oxford University Press, 1999), p. 237.

111. Arend Lijphart, *Democracies: Patterns of Majoritarian and Consensus Government in Twenty-One Countries* (New Haven, CT: Yale University Press, 1984), p. 203; Mads Qvortrup, "Is the Referendum a Constitutional Safeguard?" available at www.iandrinstitute.org (accessed on April 18, 2009).

112. The USIP-sponsored database does not distinguish binding from advisory referendums. The United Kingdom's first ever referendum was held in

1975, on membership in the European Community. A series of subsequent referendums on devolution proposals effectively "make it impossible for the [sovereign] Parliament to abolish those assemblies without their consent," and have begun to establish a precedent that this method should be used "to authorize constitutional change." Hazell, "The New Constitutional Settlement," p. 236.

113. See LeDuc, "Theoretical and Practical Issues in the Study and Conduct of Initiatives and Referendums."

114. *The Zimbabwe Constitutional Referendum, 12–13 February 2000: The Report of the Centre for Democracy and Development Observer Mission* (London and Lagos: CDD, 2000), p. 46. Guidelines and a list of polling stations were only released two days before the vote (p. 46), while the authorities busied themselves with "perfecting the voters roll" (p. 40). The draft constitution was only published in the Ndebele language two weeks beforehand, and the English text "was sold at a price not affordable by many" (p. 39).

115. Figures from BBC News, May 27, 2003; this is the most conservative estimate from news reports. Details of the two-year program are on the Web site of the constitutional commission at www.cjcr.gov.rw/eng/ (accessed on April 18, 2009). Activities included training programs, the residences of constitutional commissioners in the districts, the circulation of drafts in French, English, and Kinyarwanda, and the preparation of visual material. Early in the process, the Inter-Parliamentary Union sponsored a meeting to address the special needs of women; see I-PU, "A New Gender-Sensitive Constitution for Rwanda," www.ipu.org/english/press doc/gen121.htm (accessed May 7, 2009).

116. In Spain, on December 6, 1978, 67.11 percent of eligible voters cast votes, and 87.87 percent of the votes cast were in favor of the constitution; see Andrea Bonime-Blanc, *Spain's Transition to Democracy: The Politics of Constitution-Making* (New York: Studies of the Research Institute of Columbia University, 2003), p. 62. In Poland's 1997 referendum, held on May 25, 1997, after years of elite debate, party division, and Catholic Church opposition, only 42.68 percent of voters cast votes, 52.7 of them voting for the constitution, which was duly promulgated; see Lech Garlicki chapter on Poland in this volume.

117. Scott Carlson, "Politics, Public Participation, and the 1998 Albanian Constitution," *Osteuropa Recht* (December 1999), p. 506.

118. Figures for abstention vary slightly in different sources. Brewer-Carias, in his chapter on Venezuela of this volume, gives 62.2 percent abstaining in April, 57.7 percent in December; the Centre d'études et de documentation sur la démocratie directe, Geneva, has 61 percent in April, 55.6 in December; see http://www.c2d.ch/ (accessed April 18, 2009).

119. Marks, "International Law, Democracy and the End of History," p. 533.

120. Russell, *Constitutional Odyssey*, pp. 219, 227.

121. Ibid., p. 207.

122. The referendums held in France and Netherlands in April and May 2005, occurring between regular elections, offered the opportunity to protest in France against President Chirac's administration, and in the Netherlands against immigration policies. See, e.g., "The French and Dutch say no" and "After the French and Dutch referendums," *Economist*, June 2, 2005.

123. Masipula Sithole and Charles Mangongera, "Why the Referendum Rejected the Draft Constitution: A Public Opinion Survey," *Agenda*, vol. 4, no. 1 (March 2001).

124. *The Zimbabwe Constitutional Referendum*, p. 44. See also the chapter on Zimbabwe by Muna Ndulo in the present volume, which elaborates upon the context and the reality of presidential power sheltered behind a facade of public participation.

125. Experiments in participation range from Nicaragua (1986), Brazil (1988), Colombia (1991), Uganda (1986–95), South Africa (1992–96), and Eritrea (1994–97) to Albania in 1998, and Rwanda in 2002–03. In addition to chapters in this volume, see Bereket Habte Selassie, "The Eritrean Experience in Constitution Making: The Dialectic of Process and Substance," in *The Architecture of Democracy*, ed. Andrew Reynolds (Oxford: Oxford University Press, 2002), chap. 12; and Carlson, "Politics, Public Participation, and the 1998 Albanian Constitution," p. 506. There seems to be no escaping the fact that informed elites are bound to take a lead in devising programs, though there is escape from the worst kinds of external intervention. On the latter, see opposing views from Nicolas Guilhot, *Democracy Makers: Human Rights and International Order* (New York: Columbia University Press, 2005), and Louis Aucoin, "The Role of International Experts in Constitution-Making: Myth and Reality,"

Georgetown Journal of International Affairs, vol. 5, no. 1 (Winter–Spring 2004), pp. 33–49.

126. Figures provided by the project director, Professor Jennifer Widner, July 2005.

127. ICCPR art. 25: "Every *citizen* shall have the right and the opportunity . . . to take part in the conduct of public affairs"; compare the earlier Universal Declaration of Human Rights, Art. 21: "*Everyone* has the right to take part in the government of his country" (emphasis mine). The General Comment on art. 25 notes the contrast to "other rights and freedoms recognized by the Covenant (which are ensured to all individuals within the territory and subject to the jurisdiction of the State)" and proposes that "State reports should outline the legal provisions which define citizenship," which must accord with the nondiscrimination precepts of art. 25; Human Rights Committee, "The Right to Participate in Public Affairs, Voting Rights and the Right of Equal Access to Public Service (Art. 25): 12/17/96," CCPR General Comment 25, para. 3.

128. Whereas possession of a number of rights is now based upon residency, citizenship criteria might, for example, be affected by national boundary disputes; exclude longtime resident aliens, migrant, nomadic, indigenous peoples, or children of noncitizens; or include detached diaspora populations or the beneficiaries of grandfather clauses. See Ghai, *Public Participation and Minorities*, pp. 10–11; Mark Tushnet, "Partial Membership and Liberal Political Theory," in Christina Duffy Burnett and Burke Marshall, eds., *Foreign in a Domestic Sense* (Durham, NC: Duke University Press, 2001), pp. 209–25; David Jacobson, *Rights across Borders: Immigration and the Decline of Citizenship* (Baltimore: Johns Hopkins University Press, 1996); and Hassall and Saunders, *Asia-Pacific Constitutional Systems*, pp. 46, 241–48.

129. A classic example of the consequences of such exclusion is described in Jonathan Morrow, *Iraq's Constitutional Process II: An Opportunity Lost*, Special Report 155 (Washington, DC: U.S. Institute of Peace, 2005), with reference to the Sunni Arabs; on this point, see especially "Imbalanced Negotiating Capacity," pp. 12–13. Morrow elaborates upon this example in his chapter in the present volume.

130. See Devra Coren Moehler, "Participation and Support for the Constitution in Uganda," *Journal of Modern African Studies*, vol. 44 (2006), pp. 275–308, in which she concludes that participation can teach citizens about the constitution even if it does not guarantee popular support. A full account appears in her book, *Distrusting Democrats:*

Outcomes of Participatory Constitution Making (Ann Arbor: University of Michigan Press, 2008).

131. Figures provided by the project director, Professor Jennifer Widner, July 2005. She cautions that these figures are only indicative. In many cases, records are incomplete and certainly underestimate the incidence. They also do not record independent activity by the media.

132. A detailed account and evaluation of the very complex South African process appears in Hassen Ebrahim and Laurel Miller's chapter on South Africa in the present volume.

133. Christina Murray, "Negotiating beyond Deadlock: From the Constitutional Assembly to the Court," in Andrews and Ellmann, eds., *Post-Apartheid Constitutions,* pp. 106–07. See also the detailed account of the process, including the difficulties of dealing with the submissions, by Eldred de Klerk, "South Africa's Negotiated Transition: Context, Analysis, and Evaluation," in *Owning the Process*, pp. 7–8.

134. Murray, "Negotiating beyond Deadlock," p. 107.

135. South Africa Constitutional Assembly, *You and the Constitution* (Cape Town: Constitutional Assembly, 1996). This was a classic piece of civic education, portraying in vivid sketches a representative group of citizens, bags under their eyes from negotiating under the stars, who have made "lots of compromises" to achieve "*a big step* towards a united South Africa!" The same cartoon characters used in *Constitutional Talk* conveyed "a delightful racial ambiguity," and "a sense of joyous excitement about our emerging democracy," according to Murray, "Negotiating beyond Deadlock," p. 108.

136. See, e.g., Bereket Habte Selassie, *The Making of the Eritrean Constitution: The Dialectic of Process and Substance* (Trenton, NJ, and Asmara: Red Sea Press, 2003), pp. 37–44, 58–62, 73–78.

137. John Mary Waliggo, "The Uganda Constitution-Making Process and Implementation: Lessons Learnt, 1986–2001," unpublished paper in the author's possession, for the USIP Project on Constitution-Making, Peace Building, and National Reconciliation, March 28, 2003, p. 19. The review commission for the constitution of Kenya included among its frequently asked questions, "What will the new constitution contain? This will depend on the views of the people." A public consultation in Sri Lanka found similar demands for recognition of social rights. See International Centre for Ethnic Studies, *Final Draft Report: Public Consultations on the Constitution* (Colombo: ICES, 2005).

138. Tripp more fully discusses Uganda's flawed process in the present volume.

139. Goetz, "The Problem with Patronage," p. 117.

140. On Uganda, see Waliggo, "The Uganda Constitution-Making Process," and Tripp in this volume; on Mali, Kåre Lode, "The Regional Concertations Process: Engaging the Public," in *Owning the Process;* on Rwanda, Legal and Constitutional Commission, "Towards a Constitution for Rwanda, Action Plan 2002–2003," April 2002, www.cjcr.gov.rw/eng/ (accessed on April 18, 2009); on Kenya, Constitution of Kenya Review Commission at www.commonlii.org/ke/other/KECKRC/ (accessed April 18, 2009); on Nicaragua, Andrew Reding, "'By the People': Constitution Making in Nicaragua," *Christianity and Crisis*, vol. 46 (December 8, 1986), pp. 434–41; and on Fiji, Jill Cottrell and Yash Ghai in this volume.

141. For example, women's activities reported for Rwanda, "Seminar on the Process of Engendering a New Constitution for Rwanda"; Women for Women International, *Our Constitution, Our Future: Enshrining Women's Rights in the Iraqi Constitution*, Dead Sea, Jordan, June 27–28, 2005, available at www.womenforwomen.org (accessed on April 18, 2009).

142. James N.C. Paul, "The Reconstitution of Ethiopia: 1991–1994: A Procedural History," unpublished paper for USIP Project on Constitution-Making, Peace Building, and National Reconciliation, pp. 33–34, in author's possession. Meetings for women and elders described in "The Making of the Constitution," www.ethiospokes.net/Backgrnd/b1011981.htm (accessed January 2003).

143. Murray, "Negotiating beyond Deadlock," p. 112.

144. Ibid., p. 113.

145. Moehler, "Participation and Support for the Constitution in Uganda."

146. Paul, "The Reconstitution of Ethiopia: 1991–1994: A Procedural History," p. 1.

147. Dias, *Peacebuilding: International Law and Constitution-Making*, p. 6.

148. Some literature implies that public participation will be inherently flawed because the nature of a mass public renders it incapable of the reasoned and moderate input required for effective constitution making. An example of such views is found in postmortems on the inconclusive but prolonged constitutional debate that followed introduction of the Canadian Charter of Rights and Freedoms in 1982; see, e.g., Michael Lusztig, "Constitutional Paralysis: Why Canadian Constitutional Initiatives Are Doomed to Fail," *Canadian Journal of Political Science*, vol. 27 (December 1994), pp. 747–71; Matthew Mendelsohn, "Public Brokerage: Constitutional Reform and the Accommodation of Mass Publics," *Canadian Journal of Political Science*, vol. 33 (June 2000), pp. 245–72. In other cases where participation is viewed critically, the problem is located in the way the process is structured and executed, as in the study of Brazil's constitution making by Keith Rosenn in this volume. Here a solution can in principle be found in improved practice.

149. Moehler, "Participation and Support for the Constitution in Uganda." See also her argument that "participation can create informed distrusting democrats—knowledgeable citizens who possess democratic attitudes but distrust their government institutions," in "Informed Distrusting Democrats: The Effect of Participatory Constitution-Making," unpublished paper, 2005, p. 1, as well as her book, *Distrusting Democrats* (Ann Arbor, MI: University of Michigan Press, 2008). On the valuable role of distrusting democrats, see Vivien Hart, *Distrust and Democracy* (Cambridge: Cambridge University Press, 1978).

150. Moehler, "Participation and Support for the Constitution in Uganda." Miria Matembe, comment at UN International Peace Academy workshop on governance and power after conflict, Greentree, New York, May 27–29, 2005.

151. Briefly summarized in Hart, "Constitution-Making and the Transformation of Conflict," pp. 161–62. See also Beverley Baines, "Using the Canadian Charter of Rights and Freedoms to Constitute Women," in *The Gender of Constitutional Jurisprudence*, eds. Beverley Baines and Ruth Rubio-Marin (Cambridge: Cambridge University Press, 2005), chap. 2.

152. Keith S. Rosenn in this volume.

153. Reding, "'By the People,'" pp. 7–8.

154. Note the UN General Assembly Declaration on the Elimination of Violence Against Women 1993, GA Res 48/104; examples in regional conventions of rights noted in Fareda Banda, *Women, Law and Human Rights: An African Perspective* (Oxford: Hart, 2005), chap. 5, esp. pp. 161–65; cross-community demands for constitutional guarantees as found in Sri Lanka, see International Centre for Ethnic Studies, *Final Draft Report: Public Consultations on the Constitution*, pp. 14–15. See also Kenneth Roth, "Domestic Violence as a

Human Rights Issue," in *Human Rights of Women: National and International Perspectives*, ed. Rebecca Cook (Philadelphia: University of Pennsylvania Press, 1994), chap. 13.

155. Martha I. Morgan, "Gender Jurisprudence under the Colombian Constitution," in Baines and Rubio-Marin, eds., *The Gender of Constitutional Jurisprudence*, pp. 75–76.

156. Reding, "'By the People,'" pp. 7–8.

157. Joyce Green, "Balancing Strategies: Aboriginal Women and Constitutional Rights in Canada," in *Women Making Constitutions*, p. 42.

158. Catherine Albertyn, "Towards Substantive Representation: Women and Politics in South Africa," in *Women Making Constitutions*, p. 99.

159. Margot E. Salomon, ed., *Economic, Social and Cultural Rights: A Guide for Minorities and Indigenous Peoples* (London: Minority Rights Group International, 2005). For a trenchant criticism of constitutions that have stigmatized social groups by ignoring or excluding their identities and needs, see Cairns, "Constitutional Stigmatization," in *Identity, Rights, and Constitutional Transformation*, pp. 13–38.

160. *Marshall et al. v. Canada*, para. 5.

161. Franck and Thiruvengadam in this volume.

162. A place to start might be in the provisions made for amending constitutions (see note 84 above). Whether makers of new constitutions are obligated to follow procedures laid down in texts they seek to replace entirely is a different question; megaconstitutional politics is more likely to make its own rules. A case in point is whether the Colombian constitution of 1991 "was illegally adopted, in violation of the amending clause of the 1886 Constitution," as discussed in Banks and Alvarez, "The New Colombian Constitution," p. 42. In this volume, see Ebrahim and Miller for South African provisions for bridging the transition from one constitutional regime to another, and Ndulo's discussion on amending procedures in Zimbabwe. See also Arato, *Civil Society, Constitution, and Legitimacy*, (Lanham: Rowman & Littlefield Publishers, Inc., 2000), pp. 129–38.

163. See, e.g., Michele Brandt, *Constitutional Assistance in Post-Conflict Countries: The UN Experience: Cambodia, East Timor and Afghanistan*, Report for the UN Development Programme, June 2005; Morrow, *Iraq's Constitutional Process II*, pp. 13–14.

164. UN Electoral Assistance Division, available at www.un.org/Depts/dpa/ead/index.shtml (accessed April 18, 2009).

165. Paul, "The Reconstitution of Ethiopia," p. 40.

166. See details of criteria and activities on Web sites in addition to the United Nations: Inter-Parliamentary Union, "Declaration on Criteria for Free and Fair Elections," 1994, available at www.ipu.org/cnl-e/154-free.htm (accessed April 18, 2009); Organisation for Security and Cooperation in Europe, Office for Democratic Institutions and Human Rights, Denis Petit, "Resolving Election Disputes in the OSCE Area: Towards a Standard Election Dispute Monitoring System," available at www.osce.org/odihr/item_11_13590.html (accessed on April 18, 2009). In addition to many general elections, the OSCE-ODIHR monitored constitutional referendums in Azerbaijan in 1995 and Albania in 1998.

167. Steiner, "Political Participation as a Human Right," pp. 77–78.

168. See, e.g., the USIP project reported in this volume; CHRI, *Constitutionalism: Best Practices of Participatory Constitution-Making*; International IDEA, Constitution Building Programme, December 2005, available at www.idea.int/ (accessed on April 18, 2009).

169. CHRI, *Constitutionalism: Best Practices of Participatory Constitution-Making*, para. 4, listing fourteen requirements.

170. CHRI, *Constitutionalism: Best Practices of Participatory Constitution-Making*, para. 5, listing twelve requirements.

171. Peter Hennessy, *The Hidden Wiring: Unearthing the British Constitution* (London: Gollancz, 1995), p. 3; G.H.L. LeMay, quoted in Hennessy, p. 33.

Part II

Africa

3

Constitution Making in Eritrea

A Process-Driven Approach

Bereket Habte Selassie

Comparative constitution making has become a favored area of academic study in recent years, principally due to Eastern Europe's experience following the fall of the Soviet Union.[1] Once consigned by reductionist ideology to being mere superstructure, constitution making and constitutionalism have achieved the status of paradigms in scholarly discourse, or at least are now regarded as bases for paradigm shifts. In the realm of statecraft, constitutional engineering is increasingly relied upon as a promising enterprise in the search for bridges of understanding among factions in divided societies as well as between civil society and the state, based upon a foundation of consensus. It is assumed that constitution making, with extensive public participation, can be crucial to building such consensus. It is also assumed that constitution making can provide a framework for ongoing conflict resolution in post-conflict situations.

The present essay approaches this subject with a focus on the process of constitution making in Eritrea, a new African country. The emphasis on process, with public participation as the primary element, is based on the belief that a participatory process creates an enabling environment, helping the public to gain a sense of ownership of their country's constitution. This sense of ownership, it is assumed, increases the likelihood that the public seeks to control its government.[2] There is growing agreement on the importance of public participation as a factor in successfully implementing a constitution, as borne out by the literature resulting from several international meetings.[3] Whether such a participatory process can create a proper and effective framework for conflict resolution is a challenging question; this chapter attempts some tentative answers.

The transitional government of Eritrea, which was based on an armed political organization—the Eritrean People's Liberation Front (EPLF)—that had come out of a protracted liberation war, expressed a commitment to democratic transition and constitutional government. Two years after liberating the country from Ethiopian military occupation in 1991, the government decided to hold an internationally observed referendum, in which the Eritrean people were asked whether they wanted independence or some form of association with Ethiopia. The government took this step to dispel any lingering doubt that the liberation war enjoyed the support of the Eritrean people, contrary to Ethiopian propaganda. The referendum consummated the military victory and was also the basis for the government to express its commitment to democracy and the active participation of the public in writing the constitution, which it formalized with Proclamation 37/1993. The Constitutional Commission of Eritrea was established under Proclamation 55/1994, fulfilling the government's commitment.

The commission, which was accountable to the National Assembly, was comprised of a fifty-member council and a ten-member executive committee drawn from the council. It was charged with the duty of organizing and managing "a wide-ranging and all-embracing national debate and education through public seminars and lecture series on constitutional principles and practices."[4] Following public debate, the commission was required to submit a draft of the new constitution to the National Assembly that took into account the views of the public. The approved draft would then be submitted to a constituent assembly for ratification. The public consultation took over two years, and, following a public debate on the draft and approval by the National Assembly, the draft was submitted to the constituent assembly three years to the day after the commission was established. The constituent assembly ratified the constitution on May 23, 1997.

However, this ratified constitution has not been implemented, and this fact has become the most important political issue in the country. As will be discussed below, it has given rise to a serious political crisis that still awaits resolution.

The Relationship Between Process and Substance

In a previous essay on Eritrea's constitution-making experience, I attempted to examine the dialectical relationship between process and substance.[5] This paper focuses on the process of constitution making. The rationale behind this focus is the conviction that the recent approaches to process-driven constitution making are better than previous approaches were. The latter tended to depend on the decisions of a select group of people, be they distinguished statesmen, as were the framers of the U.S. Constitution, or a select committee of the government of the day and its expert legal draftsmen, as was the case for the independence constitutions of much of Africa. The process involved in drafting the constitutions of African countries on the eve of their independence, which I call the Lancaster House model, excluded the public—the African populations—from participating in the making of the basic law by which they would be governed.[6]

However, no analysis devoted to process can avoid reference to substance. The process and product are dialectically linked: The ends prescribe the means and the means impinge on the ends. Involving the public in the process empowers the public, giving its members a sense of ownership of the constitution and allowing them to air their views on a range of critical issues that affect their lives. Thus, public participation in the making of a constitution necessarily raises questions of substance. The contemporary debate on the meaning of democracy underscores this point. The debate has largely focused on two aspects of democracy: its substantive aspect—that is, its source and purpose—and its procedural elements.[7]

The classical approach defined democracy in terms of its source (the will of the people) and purpose (the common good).[8] According to current prevailing thought, however, the central feature of democracy is procedural, concerning the selection of leaders through competitive popular elections. Pioneered by Joseph Schumpeter, procedural democracy, or what may be called the democratic method, is the "institutional arrangement for arriving at political decisions in which individuals acquire the power to decide by means of a competitive struggle for people's vote."[9] Democracy is thus defined in terms of method, according to which a political system is democratic "to the extent that its most powerful collective decision makers are selected through fair, honest, and periodic elections in which candidates freely compete for votes and in which virtually all the adult population is eligible."[10] Two critical elements are posited in this definition: popular participation and the competition of candidates representing different interests or ideologies. Adding another dimension to the debate is Robert Dahl's concept of polyarchy, which underscores the importance of the freedoms of speech and of the press for meaningful pluralist politics.[11] Dahl defines polyarchies as "regimes that have been substantially popularized and liberalized, that is, regimes that are highly inclusive and extensively open to public contestation."[12]

Does the above minimalist procedural conception of democracy embrace other critical requirements for meaningful democratic government? Do elections, per se, constitute the only core element of democracy? Certainly they are a critical part of it, to the extent that national assemblies or parliaments, as representative institutions, are the primary national institutions accountable to the citizens of a country. In theory, these institutions are the principal mediators in the relationship between the governors and the governed. Electoral laws and politics can thus be regarded as prerequisites of democratic (representative) government. But once parliaments are elected, their responsibilities do not end when the election is over. In short, election is a means to an end—the functioning of representative institutions—which constitutes the substantive aspect of democracy. The procedural imperative, though essential, must be analyzed in relation to the role of representative institutions in the totality of a constitutional order. As Jean Bethke Elshtain has put it:

> Democracy is not and has never been primarily a means whereby popular will is tabulated and carried out but, rather, a political world within which citizens negotiate, compromise, engage and hold themselves and those they choose to represent them accountable for action taken. Have we lost this deliberative dimension to democracy? Democracy's enduring promise is that citizens can come to know a good in common that they cannot know alone.[13]

The above general comments about democracy apply with equal force to constitution making, which engages, or should engage, citizens to negotiate and compromise in framing the issues concerning their rights and duties as well as the powers and responsibilities of government defined in the constitution. That process cannot be entirely divorced from substance and must inform any analysis of a constitution-making process, such as the one that occurred in Eritrea.

Background

Eritrea's Constitution Making in Historical Perspective

The present Eritrean constitution was ratified by an elected constituent assembly in May 1997, on the eve of the sixth anniversary of the country's liberation from Ethiopian occupation. The constitution was the first of its kind in Eritrea, as it was created with the participation of the people as citizens of a free and sovereign nation. A very brief historical review offers some perspective on this constitution-making process.

Having been an Italian colony (1890–1941), Eritrea was occupied by the British for a decade (1942–52), pending a disposition of its status by the United Nations. In 1950, a U.S.-sponsored UN resolution joined Eritrea with Ethiopia in a lopsided federation, under which Eritrea was granted local autonomy but not full independence. Ethiopia's emperor, Haile Selassie, gradually destroyed even this limited autonomy. In November 1962, he abolished the federation, declared Eritrea to be simply a province of his empire, and sent an army to occupy the territory. A year earlier, the Eritrean Liberation Front (ELF)[14] had begun an armed struggle that was to last thirty years. During much of its latter phase, the liberation war encompassed a sweeping social revolution that would turn out to be perhaps its most important legacy, with notable achievements in such areas as women's equality, human rights, social justice, and democracy. These values, acquired during the long war of liberation, critically influenced the constitution-making process. As public debates later made clear, Eritreans saw the constitution as fulfilling the goals of the liberation war, thus helping to vindicate their enormous sacrifice.

The Context of Democratic Transition

Following liberation in May 1991, the EPLF, then an armed guerilla organization, declared itself to be a provisional government. To be sure, the EPLF had been exercising quasi-governmental power in the last years of the struggle and had created impressive administrative and technical infrastructure behind enemy lines in its Sahel base area. Formal independence, however, did not arrive until two years later. The delay was due to the EPLF leadership's insistence that an internationally observed referendum be held. The leadership believed that the people would freely choose independence, showing a hitherto skeptical or indifferent world—and especially Africa—that the independence struggle had popular backing. The result of the referendum of April 23–25, 1993, fully justified this confidence. In voting that a UN-observer mission certified as fair, a 99.8 percent majority opted for full independence.[15] Soon after the referendum, Eritrea became a member of the United Nations. Thus began a transition process that culminated in the ratification of the Eritrean constitution, capping three years of intensive and extensive public debate and consultation.

As the EPLF had chosen itself to be the government, it was not elected by the general population. The provisional government was composed of the EPLF's central leadership, which had been elected in the front's organizational congress. That congress elected a thirty-seven-member central committee, which in turn elected a political bureau with a secretary general as the leading figure. At the post-liberation congress held in February 1994 (the Third Congress), the EPLF changed its name to the Peoples Front for Democracy and Justice (PFDJ), the name of the central committee to the Central Council, and the political bureau to the Executive Committee. The chairman of the Executive Committee became the key figure, with a secretary general tasked to administrative matters.

The PFDJ laid down the rules governing the government's actions, as well as newly formulated laws and regulations. The central committee acted as a legislative body until the Third Congress, after which a transitional parliament was formed, composed of the members of the Central Council and an equal number of members chosen by the PFDJ to represent the various regions of the country. The chairman of the PFDJ presided over the transitional parliament and a cabinet of ministers whom he appointed. The provisional government established a constitutional commission in 1994, and three members of the transitional parliament—all members of the PFDJ's Central Council—were among the commission's fifty members. All three also became members of the commission's Executive Committee; two of them had legal training.

The provisional government of Eritrea passed several laws that expressed a commitment to democracy. One such law, adopted in 1993, charged the government, inter alia, with the responsibility of preparing and laying the foundation for a democratic system of government.[16] The Constitutional Commission of Eritrea was established a year later in fulfillment of that duty.[17] In addition, at its Third Congress, the governing party adopted a national charter expressing the vision of the governing party for the future of the country, setting forth democracy, human rights, and social justice as the guiding principles and objectives, together with stability, national unity, and economic development. The commission used this charter as the point of departure for the national debate that followed.

The Constitution-Making Process

Public Participation: The Litmus Test

As is noted above, with some justification, one can use public participation or the lack of it to distinguish between newer and older modes of constitution making. The Canadian scholar James Tully has framed the question of public inclusion in constitution making in a larger historical perspective:

> The question of our age . . . is whether a constitution can give recognition to the legitimate demands of the members of diverse cultures in a manner that renders everyone their due, so that all would freely consent to this form of constitutional association. Let us call this first step towards a solution "mutual recognition" and ask what it entails.[18]

Tully argues that there should be a radical paradigm shift in the manner of constitu-

tion making and constitutionalism. Backed by a historical and critical survey of over three hundred years of European and non-European constitutionalism, his approach seriously challenges the prevailing school of modern western constitutionalism. Sometimes called a postimperial approach to organizing political community, it calls for the conciliation of different claims for recognition over time through constitutional dialogue, in which citizens reach agreement on appropriate forms of accommodation of their cultural differences, guided by constitutional rules.[19]

When the Constitutional Commission of Eritrea embarked on its constitution-making mission in April 1994, none of its members was aware of the new paradigm, which was only then developing. But the commission regarded popular participation in constitution making as a strategic point of reference; it was a point that no one disputed. The commission's understanding of the purpose of popular participation had to do, first and foremost, with the issue of public ownership of the constitution, an issue described above. Moreover, following the revolutionary armed struggle, the Eritrean political and social context was marked by an anti-imperialist and antifeudal bourgeois ideology that was suspicious of any event or process controlled by elites. Such ideology, justifiable in view of Eritrean history and the temper of the times, was actually twisted to serve purposes contrary to the popular interest, as is discussed below. Despite differences in the language, the approach followed in Eritrea's constitution making approximates Tully's postimperial prescription—and aligns with an emergent global postimperial consciousness, according to which the creation of a country's constitutional system must be grounded in popular consent that accommodates all of the component elements of a society.[20]

The members of diverse cultures to which Tully refers, with their complaints, claims of rights, or demands for inclusion, could have no better opportunity to have their day in court than during a constitution-making process. Public consultation or participation should facilitate the airing of grievances or registering of specific claims or demands. The Eritrean experience demonstrates that better understanding among members of different cultural groups can best be achieved when they are exposed to each other in a common effort. Of course, in the Eritrean case, the common purpose was the fight for independence, which brought common bonds to the surface and subordinated group demands or grievances. The experience of armed struggle brought together young men and women from all of Eritrea's ethnic groups, and their experiences fighting alongside one another became a building block for a sense of nationhood.

But nationhood and national unity cannot be taken for granted. Mutual recognition, to use Tully's phrase, above all entails attentiveness to local customary laws and cultures. The national government needs to help groups preserve all of the good parts of their customs, laws, and cultures, while dealing delicately with their harmful aspects with a view to changing them over time. Eritreans' mutual exposure to one another's customs and ways of life has made them receptive to suggestions for change, such as in matters concerning women's rights and the practice of female genital mutilation. One of the provisions of the law establishing the Constitutional Commission of Eritrea aimed to facilitate such a process of gradual change by enabling the commission to appoint advisory boards. Under this provision, the commission established two such boards, one on Eritrean customary laws and the other on the constitutional experiences of other countries. The board of Eritrean customary-law experts advised the commission on the board members' respective customs. There were no grievances regarding the treatment of customary prac-

tices in the constitutional process expressed to this writer or, to his knowledge, to other members of the commission by any member of the advisory board of customary law experts. At the initiative of its chair, Owen Fiss, a professor at Yale University, the board of constitutional experts convened two symposia, to which the members of the commission's executive committee were invited. Contacts continued between individual experts and members of the commission, all to good effect.

The Role of the Constitutional Commission

The period after liberation was a time of transition for Eritrea, from a devastating war and its consequences to peaceful reconstruction and rehabilitation. It was also a transition from a government of military provenance to one of democratic constitutionalism. It is worth reiterating that the EPLF was an armed political organization with the principal aim of freeing the country from foreign occupation. That task having been accomplished, the foundation was laid under Proclamation No. 1 to organize a society that would be ruled by a democratically elected government. To that end, the Eritrean government established a constitutional commission, to both "draft a constitution on the basis of which a democratic order would be established and . . . [which] would be the ultimate point of reference of all the laws of the country," and organize national debate on constitutional principles and practices.[21] As the commission was thus central to the constitution-making process, it is necessary to consider its work and contribution to process-driven constitution making—how and why it was formed, its composition, its structure and organization, and some of the methods it utilized to achieve optimum results.

The law establishing the Constitutional Commission of Eritrea, Proclamation 55/

1994, charged the commission with organizing and managing "a wide-ranging and all-embracing national debate and education through public seminars and lecture series on constitutional principles and practices."[22] The law also provided that following public debate on a constitutional draft and having accounted for the views of the public, the commission would then submit a draft constitution to the National Assembly. The National Assembly-approved draft would then be submitted to a constituent assembly for ratification.[23] Proclamation 55/1994 required that the members of the commission comprise "experts and other citizens with proven ability to make a contribution to the process of constitution making."[24] That the commission was appointed by the National Assembly could be said to have lent it presumptive legitimacy, but the diversity and divisions within Eritrean society had to be accounted for as well, as it contained many ethnic groups and a population more or less equally divided between Christians and Muslims. Wisely, the assembly created a well-balanced, representative commission. Its fifty members included twenty-one women, the majority of whom were veteran liberation fighters. Each of Eritrea's nine ethnic groups was represented, as were the business and professional communities. A ten-member executive committee drawn from the commission's larger membership guided its work.

The commission's mandate ran for three years, and its work followed a four-stage process, at a cost of approximately $4.3 million. First was a logistical phase, which ran through the end of 1994 and involved organizing the commission, raising funds, educating the public, and initial drafting work. The second phase focused on public education regarding the commission's role and basic constitutional concepts, as well as preparation of a full draft and taking public opinion into account where deemed necessary. The third phase involved broad public debate of the commission's draft

and submission of the draft to the National Assembly for its consideration. The fourth phase was designated for public debate and submitting the draft for ratification to the constituent assembly.[25]

The commission's task of organizing wide-ranging public debates and soliciting expert opinion placed an unusually heavy emphasis on direct and active involvement of people outside of government during the drafting phase. Article 12(4) of the proclamation enjoined the chairman of the commission to encourage the participation and contribution of Eritrean and foreign experts and to organize ad hoc committees and advisory boards to help expedite the process of preparing the draft constitution. A fourteen-member board of foreign advisers was established to advise the commission on the experience of other countries in constitution making and provide a multidisciplinary perspective on the debate and analysis of the commission's work. As previously noted, the chair was Professor Owen Fiss of Yale Law School. Other members were scholars and practitioners from the United Sates, Europe, Africa, and Asia. The majority were lawyers, but there were also two historians, three political scientists, and one anthropologist in limited advisory roles. The international community supported the commission's work primarily through financial aid from the United Nations, the United States, and some European countries, as well as several non-governmental organizations.

Historically, the drafting phase of a new constitution has been dominated by a constitutional convention or conference, often held under conditions of secrecy or quasi-secrecy, or else by a specially appointed committee of the legislature, as were the cases in the 1787 convention that drafted the U.S. constitution and the Westminster model, respectively. Constitution making through a commission thus marks a significant stage in the development of democracy. For this new approach to succeed, however, three principal prerequisites must be satisfied. First, the government must be committed to the ideal of constitutional democracy. Second, the public must be aware of this ideal and willing to play a role in its attainment. Third, there must be a body with a clear legal mandate to freely solicit public views through widely held debates and other forms of political consultation; it must then seriously consider these views when drafting the constitution. Needless to say, the members of this body must be selected not only on grounds of regional, ethnic, and religious representativeness but also on those of professional competence.[26] In Eritrea's case, these requirements were in place, as will be seen below.

Regarding the first requirement, the Eritrean government's earlier commitment to constitutional democracy, which included pluralist politics, has been frustrated. The delay in implementing Eritrea's constitution has provoked such public outcry that in September 2000, the National Assembly passed a resolution calling for elections to be held by the end of 2001. To that end, the assembly appointed a committee to draft a law on political-party formation and another committee to draft an electoral law. The fate of the law on party formation and the proper manner of implementing it has been the subject of bitter controversy between the country's president and some of his colleagues in the government and party, including the chairman of the committee that drafted the law.[27]

As noted above, a key issue related to both the principles and politics of constitution making concerns the choice of the entity to be tasked with organizing and managing the drafting process. The choice of entity is a matter of principle in that the entity needs to be representative of the stakeholders—the various interest groups comprising a nation. The choice is also political in that the leaders of a country have the right to decide on the nature of the entity and the appointment of its members only insomuch as their

own power is legitimate. Where the leaders' power is illegitimate, there is bound to be contestation.[28] Assuming legitimate political authority, a political leadership can appoint a commission or committee and assign it the task of drafting a constitution, but based on Eritrea's experience, public participation in its making, through wide-ranging public debate or consultation, is imperative if such a constitution is to be widely supported.

Who should determine the mandate, timetable, and rules of a constitutional commission? The temporal mandate may be determined either by the appointing authority, or left flexible for the commission to determine. The advantage of the latter, which was the case in Eritrea, is that the commission can shorten or lengthen the timetable as circumstances dictate. The Constitutional Commission of Eritrea reported to the National Assembly, both administratively by periodically reporting on the progress of its activities and substantively by submitting the final product of its process, but it alone determined all its rules and operational programs. At the start of its work, the Eritrean constitutional commission had planned to complete its work in two years. This proved impossible, however, and so the commission extended its timetable by another year—a crucial aspect of the commission's autonomy that the government undertook to honor, and did honor, until the commission's mission was accomplished.

In some cases, the question of what type of body should lead the consultation and drafting process has involved some stakeholders in disputes with their governments. In Kenya, there was contestation between the government of President Daniel Arap Moi and organized members of civil society as to whether Kenya's constitution should be reformed through the appointment of a constitutional commission, as several other African countries had done. The government preferred to use a commission, whereas representatives of civil society demanded that a constitutional conference be held embracing all stakeholders. In the end, even though there was agreement in principle in Kenya on the need for public participation, there was disagreement on the modalities of consultation: Though Kenya's parliament had tabled a proposal for constitutional review in 1998, it took several years for the government's position of appointing a commission—under the chairmanship of Professor Yash Ghai and with representatives from civil society—to prevail.

The Kenyan case demonstrates that the means chosen to manage a constitution-making process, including a consultation process, must suit the peculiarities of the politics of individual nations. Such peculiarities determine the nature of consultation, rather than generalizations based on the experience of other countries. That said, the latter can be useful guides; one can insist on certain principles, and perhaps use such principles to help contesting parties, both governments and organized members of civil society, arrive at a suitable compromise.[29]

What principles may be invoked to apply to the commission approach, enabling it to commend itself and be acceptable to both sides of a dispute over the architecture of a constitution-making process? The first principle concerns its independence. If one can guarantee that once appointed, a commission will be permitted to act independently without any pressure from any source, it should be acceptable to all concerned. On its own initiative or at the request of the government, a commission may consult with appropriate government ministers or party leaders to gather information on specific matters or gain insight into them. But this is different from pressure or influence. A commission's independence ensures the integrity of the process and consequent public confidence in the process and its outcome, that is, the constitution itself. The second principle is related to composition. Obviously, a commission's composition is a matter of great interest; on this question, too, each nation's own peculiarities must determine the result. The most that can be said, in principle, is that it must be inclusive, as widely representative of society as possible.

In sum, there are two defining features of the commission mode of constitution making or constitutional reform, the importance of which cannot be overstated. First, a commission must represent a society's stakeholders. Second, once appointed, the commission must be independent. Principles and politics are involved, the former having to do with the integrity of the process and professional competence, and the latter pertaining to the representation of interested parties.

It must be remembered, however, that a commission is not the final deciding authority in a constitution-making process. For the principle of legitimacy to be complete, a commission must submit the draft constitution that it has prepared to an elected body, such as a constituent assembly or national legislature, or alternatively—and sometimes additionally—to the public in a referendum.[30] In many of the recent cases of constitution making in Africa, such as Eritrea, Ethiopia, Namibia, South Africa, and Uganda, final ratification was all done by constituent assemblies.[31]

Question and Answer Method of the Constitutional Commission

Organizing debate on the most fundamental political questions facing a nation is far more than a technical or logistical matter. It involves substantive issues concerning both the most appropriate literature to be translated and distributed and the best way to communicate essential ideas about democracy and constitutional rule. The participation of Eritreans in making their constitution relied on the inherent wisdom of encouraging and organizing people to be involved in decisions affecting their lives. This made sense theoretically and conforms to universal principles of democracy. It also accords with the historically evolved system of village democracy in much of Eritrea, in which village communities govern themselves democratically through periodically elected assemblies. This village democracy forms a central part of Eritrean customary law and was preserved and utilized during the long period of armed struggle.[32]

The constitutional commission in Eritrea strategized and organized research and public consultation based on the conviction that the process was as important as the product. A great deal of attention was paid to preparing the public to contribute as fully and well informed as possible. Equal emphasis was placed on the need to record, collate, and eventually analyze the views that emerged during public debate. This step had twofold importance, for not only might such views be used to draft the constitution, but the very fact of keeping track of them gave people a sense of ownership of the constitution.

The commission began its work by posing a series of questions that it had to answer before launching the public debate and drafting the constitution. The essence of the major questions may be summed up as follows:

1. What lessons, if any, do the historical experiences of other countries offer?
2. Do such experiences yield helpful models or guidelines?
3. Is it desirable or practicable to use models? Are they transferable, like some technology is?
4. What, after all, are the values and goals that a nation needs most emphatically to promote, nurture, and protect? How should these be incorporated in a constitution?
5. Should such values and goals be incorporated into the constitution or should they be determined in the crucible of political

and social interaction, in the daily discourse of culture?
6. What form of government would be best suited for Eritrea?
7. What degree of decentralization should there be? Is federalism appropriate for a small and comparatively cohesive nation?
8. Should there be an official language or languages? If so, which ones should be selected and why?

It was apparent from the outset that some subjects could be left out of the constitution while others could not, making the question of what to include susceptible to debate. There were questions of detail, including some pertaining to technicalities, such as the constitution's size. Should the document be long or short? How detailed should the chapter on the bill of rights be? Should the constitution incorporate international covenants on human rights by reference or by detailed inclusion? In all, the commission listed twenty-three questions for consideration at its earliest meeting.[33] The proposals that were ultimately submitted to the public for debate were based partly on these questions, but also were enriched by research and expert consultation.

From the outset, there was consensus within the commission not to rely on ready-made models, whatever their source or merit. Rather, it was thought better to take stock of the reality and paramount needs of the country. The commission's research and consultation activities were designed with that objective in mind.

The Civic Education and Consultation Process

In July 1994, the commission held a small international conference in Asmara that focused on the eight key questions identified above. Before this meeting, the commission had established four ad hoc research committees—later combined into a single committee—and a standing committee on civic education and public debate, all acting under the guidance of the executive committee. The four ad hoc committees were concerned with government institutions and human rights, economic issues, social and cultural questions, and governance and related issues, respectively. Each committee was authorized to appoint subcommittees and solicit views and research assistance from both Eritrean and foreign experts. At the conference, the four ad hoc committees submitted papers, and commission members heard and discussed presentations by Namibian and Swiss ambassadors to Ethiopia and by the chairman of the constitutional committee of Ethiopia.[34]

The substantive phase of the commission's work continued with a well-attended international symposium in Asmara in January 1995, at which two hundred Eritreans and forty-two invited experts from around the world participated in discussions.[35] The issue-by-issue discussion with which the commission launched its work was now replaced by an approach that aggregated the relevant questions into four themes, focusing on the constitution's relationship to government, human rights, social and economic rights, and democracy. Commission members were assigned to draft issue papers on these themes, including analysis and recommendations. Specific topics addressed in the issue papers included legislative, executive, and judicial powers; electoral systems; decentralization; fundamental rights and freedoms; social, economic, and cultural rights; and equality guarantees. After the January 1995 conference, the commission and its members transformed these issue papers into a series of eight position papers.[36] Among the goals of these efforts, which would prove crucial to the success of the public debate that ensued, was to distill these vital issues

to their essences and, ultimately, frame them as proposals in a way that the average citizen could readily grasp. The proposals prepared for public discussion thus reflected not only the research committee's sophisticated and careful work but also the larger commission's overall focus on concision and accessibility.

The January 1995 conference was followed by an extensive civic education campaign that proved integral to actively engaging the Eritrean population in the constitutional process. Commission members and more than four hundred specially trained instructors conducted public seminars in village and town meetings on constitutional issues and related political and social questions. The commission also established seven provincial offices and seventy-three locally based committees to assist in public education.[37] To this end, the commission prepared pamphlets and translated into Arabic and Tigrinya several international legal instruments, including the Universal Declaration of Human Rights, the Convention on the Rights of the Child, and the international covenants on civil and political rights as well as social, economic, and cultural rights.[38]

A central obstacle to the civic-education campaign was the country's low literacy rate, approximately 20 percent. The commission sought to address this problem using nonprinted means of communication, including songs, poetry, short stories, and plays delivered orally in the various vernaculars. Artists and writers were invited to submit proposals for these projects, which were chosen on a competitive basis. Mobile theater groups and concerts dealing with constitutional themes were designed, and a cartoon comic book entitled *Elements of a Constitution* was published.[39] Special efforts were also made to involve students in the process. Radio was a huge help in this regard, as the commission sponsored contests and debates, many of which were broadcast on radio and television, in schools throughout the country, and at Eritrea's national university.

In all, a great deal of money, skill, and other resources went toward the civic-education campaign, which reached more than five hundred thousand people out of a population of four-and-a-half million, and proved crucial to rallying public opinion behind the constitution-making process.[40] The civic-education efforts also were crucial in preparing people to participate in the public debates on the constitution that were to follow. Civic education not only equipped members of the public with relevant knowledge but also empowered them and made them more confident participants. The public's diffidence was palpable at the start, but by the time full-scale debate on the commission's proposals had begun, people were asking probing questions and making suggestions with great confidence, such as the importance of harnessing the government to the concept of *lugam,* or accountability.

By the summer of 1995, the commission was ready to disseminate a set of proposals to focus attention on and clarify the most important issues to the ensuing public debates. These proposals were divided into two parts. In the first part, the commission outlined principles that related to the basic constitutional framework, stressing the organic link between the people and the government as well as the importance of democracy, diversity, and national unity.[41] The second part proposed specifics to the constitutional order, including a unicameral legislature (the National Assembly) with members elected for five-year terms. The assembly would choose the chief executive—the president—who would be commander-in-chief of the armed forces and limited to two five-year terms. There would be an independent judiciary, with a supreme court having the power of judicial review. Federalism was rejected in favor of a unitary governmental structure, and the commission proposed not to designate

an official language. The proposals offered a guarantee of the right to vote, but without specifying an electoral system. Fundamental rights—including life, privacy, and freedom of belief, expression, and organization—were included, with special emphasis on the equality of women.[42]

From September to December 1995, there were extensive public debates about the proposals, which had been distributed to the public and broadcast over the national radio starting in the last week of August. Before the public debates began, the commission reorganized its implementation machinery, dividing the country into four regions and creating a fifth to include those countries abroad in which Eritreans (about half a million) resided. One member of the commission was put in charge of each region; the rest of the commission's members were assigned to manage and coordinate the discussions and debates. The debates were launched in the regions by members of the Executive Committee, who introduced the subject and explained the salient features of the proposals. Debate sessions included exchanges of questions and answers with the audience.

Extensive efforts were made to record the debates, using note takers and, when possible, tape recorders.[43] The Standing Committee on Civic Education and Public Debates oversaw the documentation and collation of the questions and points raised in all meetings and submitted summary reports to the Executive Committee for consideration at the final drafting stage. The questions raised were analyzed statistically, based on variables including region, age, and gender, to gauge public opinion for drafting purposes and for future reference; the commission's duty was to produce a draft that reflected public opinion as much as possible.[44] The records show that most of what may be called new points not covered by the proposals were in the nature of details that the draft constitution would address; answers were given to that effect.

The points of detail raised at public meetings and the countless questions raised about the issues covered in the proposals demonstrated the seriousness with which Eritreans viewed the process and the time and other resources that people were willing to spend. All in all, public meetings, each lasting about three hours, were held in 157 different places inside Eritrea, involving over 110,000 Eritreans; 11,000 additional Eritreans participated in 16 locations abroad.[45]

As will be explained below, at the end of the year, the commission collected and analyzed the questions raised and opinions expressed during the public debates, and sat down to write the first draft of the constitution, which was released in July 1996. The National Assembly approved the commission's draft with a few amendments, and further public debate ensued in late 1996 and early 1997. The commission then met again to finalize the draft constitution. The final step of the process involved presenting the draft to the constituent assembly for ratification. The assembly discussed the final draft in the city hall of Asmara for three days in May 1997, and after making several minor changes, it unanimously ratified the constitution on May 24, 1997.

It is beyond dispute that the public consultation and debates throughout the constitution-making process were important in instilling a sense of public ownership in the constitution. Whether and to what extent public input actually influenced the text of the constitution is more difficult to discern. The constitutional commission began its work presuming that public debate would influence the draft. When the Executive Committee—which became the drafting committee—reviewed the voluminous materials collected during the debates, its members were clearly inspired by the depth and extent of public comment. Some members were astonished by the clarity, precision, and wisdom of some of the collected sentiments

and views. Age-old constitutional concepts had been encapsulated in proverbs and rhyming couplets, expressing a high sense of public commitment to responsible government, as conveyed by the term *lugam*. The spirit of such public input is reflected in the constitution. Nevertheless, as inspiring and profound as some of the ideas that the public put forward were, they were not susceptible to being explicitly translated into the language of a modern constitution.

That said, the commission accepted and included in the constitution some opinions or proposals offered during the public consultation. One example concerns the concept of secular government. As Eritrea is a society evenly divided between Christians and Muslims, the commission was encouraged to soften its stance in declaring the state to be secular. Another example concerns the oath of office. The commission's original draft contained language requiring office holders to swear in the name of the martyrs of the independence struggle. The objections of religious people, ably expressed by a young Muslim man, compelled the commission to change this to give office holders a choice in forming their own oaths.[46] However, the commission did not accept the view or proposal of a minority in the public and a couple of its own members concerning capital punishment. Despite the impassioned arguments of two members, the commission's text reflected widespread public opinion in favor of capital punishment.

In sum, the commission's initial hypothesis that public participation would influence the text of the constitution crucially cannot be said to have been proven. However, the value of the sense of ownership created by the public participation process is certain. It is the view of this author and other observers that during the tragic Ethiopian-Eritrean War of 1998–2000, the constitution became an important rallying point, causing the Eritrean people to close ranks behind their government. Equally certain is that the public was profoundly disappointed when the government went back on its word and refused to implement the constitution.

Constitution Making and Conflict Resolution

If the contention is accepted that public participation in constitution making creates, among the general public, a sense of ownership of a constitution, it follows that such a participatory process could also be used to facilitate conflict resolution. Such a process can create auspicious conditions for parties in conflict to bury the hatchet. What makes this plausible is an engaged public seeking to redefine its basic charter, a public that, conceivably, could pressure contesting elite leaders to compose their differences for the sake of a higher purpose. But how should those involved in the constitution-making process determine the issues that are appropriate for resolution through the process rather than through political negotiation? Some issues are hard to avoid by their very nature, as they force themselves on any entity mandated to organize and manage a constitution-making exercise; examples include grievances of certain sectors of societies, such as ethnic and religious minorities; the distribution of power between the national government and regions making up a country; the distribution of resources; electoral systems; the place of religion and language in the constitutional scheme; and the role of defense and security services.

The principle of inclusion requires that serious grievances must be heard during the constitution-making process. To begin with, minorities must be represented in constitutional commissions. Moreover, organized groups of such minorities should be given a chance to air their views in structured meetings and have their views debated, recorded, and submitted as part of the data that the drafting entity takes into account. This exercise in itself opens avenues to resolve conflicts related to such issues. In the Eritrean experience, there were no ethnic- or religious-based grievances expressed or complaints submitted to the commission, although the issue of language was debated extensively, as will be further explained below. The question of whether certain sectors of society and institutions, such as churches, mosques, and the military, should be formally represented in or excluded from the official process of constitution making is a subject that different countries have answered in different ways. In Eritrea's case, the constitution makers meticulously separated religious institutions and the state, due to their desire to establish a secular state in a country evenly divided between Christians and Muslims. But members of different churches and Muslim clerics participated in the debate in their individual capacities. They made significant contributions, being among the better educated in their respective communities.[47]

As for the military, at the time of constitution making, the members of the Eritrean armed forces occupied (and still occupy) a special place in Eritrea's history of armed struggle, having been crucial to the country's liberation. At that time, the military was composed almost entirely of former guerilla fighters who saw the constitution-making process as both a continuation of the liberation struggle and its consummation. Some military leaders expressed this sentiment repeatedly. The commission thus considered members of the military to be crucial to the process in their own right, as well as being a base of support for constitutional government in the future. Accordingly, the commission paid special attention to military figures in terms of their representation in organized seminars and debates, and they were receptive to the military's views on a range of issues. The commission sent some of its members to conduct seminars in many units of the armed forces, as well as in the national service training camp at Sawa, to record the proceedings of those meetings.

Among the questions listed above with which the Eritrean commission started its work, there was no controversy over the fundamental values that should be incorporated in the constitution, such as democracy, the rule of law, and social justice. There were, however, debates as to whether Eritrea should have an official language and how much power the national government should delegate to the country's various regions. The controlling principle in finding solutions to contentious issues through the constitution-making process should be respect for the will of the public and the strength of the feelings expressed regarding the issue concerned. This principle was applied in Eritrea.

The two issues of language and decentralization of power provide useful examples of the commission's approach to handling controversial issues. Language is one of those sensitive issues that interest groups can politicize easily, particularly in countries in which language is associated with national identity or religious sentiments. A constitution-making process, however, provides an opportunity to bring people together for mutual education on their differing perspectives and sentiments. Such an exercise can go a long way, as it did in Eritrea, toward minimizing politically motivated manipulation. In Eritrea's experience, the different views expressed on the language question may be grouped into four camps. The first camp was composed of people who insisted that Arabic and Tigrinya should be declared official languages. The second argued that Arabic, Tigrinya, and Tigre should be made official languages. The third argued that Tigrinya and Tigre should be official languages, as they were spoken by over 80 percent of the Eritrean population. The fourth camp accepted the commission's position, which simply declared the equality of all Eritrean languages—a principle espoused and practiced during the armed struggle, supported by the PFDJ, and generally accepted by the public.

The majority of Eritreans who participated in the public debates during the process of constitution making were persuaded by the argument that it was better to leave the question of official language open and instead declare the equality of languages, and the commission felt justified in writing the essence of that argument into the draft constitution.[48] When the principle of equality became the controlling factor, instead of providing for one or more official languages, what should have been given constitutional backing was what had already been a government policy, that of developing all languages. The commission's proposals expressed it thusly:

> We must handle the issue of language in a way that serves and strengthens our basic goal of building a unified and strong nation. The equality of all Eritrean languages, the cultural and psychological importance of starting education with the mother tongue, the need for a common medium of instruction from the middle to higher levels of education, the right of every citizen to use in government activities any language he/she chooses, are important considerations.[49]

However, the commission duly noted the continued use of Arabic and Tigrinya as working languages, a practice that had started during the armed struggle, while leaving the matter open for possible future amendment in the event of demands to adopt a different language policy.[50] Ultimately, the commission's approach in this regard was adopted in the constitution's final text, an outcome that was largely due to the views expressed by a majority of the public.

As for the other main issue of contention, the division of power between the national government and the regional governments, the experiences of many African countries show that this subject must be handled carefully and has to be among the principal issues considered in the constitution-making process. The Constitutional Commission of

Eritrea decided to recommend the adoption of a unitary structure, with details on the degree of devolution of power to the regions to be settled by legislation. The commission offered the subject for public debate, indicating the small size of the country, the resource endowment of the various regions, the history of national unity, and the country's ethnic makeup as the major factors favoring a unitary rather than federal system.

Another issue related to conflict resolution and constitution making concerned traditional methods of conflict resolution. In much of Africa, traditionally evolved mechanisms resolve conflict through the mediation of elders; traditional African societies extolled the virtue of harmony and encouraged "out of court" settlement of disputes. Eritrea is no exception in this respect, and the constitutional commission constantly referred to this tradition and to the role of elders in conflict resolution, eventually incorporating the spirit of the tradition in the preamble to the constitution as follows: "Appreciating the fact that for the development and health of our society, it is necessary that we inherit and improve upon the traditional community-based assistance and fraternity, love for family, respect for elders, mutual respect and consideration."

The Commission's Approach to the Drafting Process

Constitution makers must address two principal and related questions: What should be included in a constitution and how long should it be? These questions logically raise another one: How does one determine what should or should not be included in a constitution? Is there a set of universally applicable criteria, or is each country's choice determined by specific historical conditions?

The answer to the last question must be both. From the writing of the U.S. constitution onward, modern constitutions have been based on preceding models or experiences. At the same time, the historical conditions of a given country—its culture, social structure, and government policies—inevitably modify the outcome. How much this modification affects the universal principles differs from case to case. Scholars and statesmen have wrestled with the question and some have attempted to provide general rules for good constitution writing. Lord Brice, the British scholar, affirms the rule of brevity in writing a constitution, adding simplicity of language and precision as essential requirements. He ranks the U.S. constitution above all other hitherto written constitutions "for the intrinsic excellence of its scheme, its adaptation to the circumstances of the people, the simplicity, brevity, and precision of its language, its judicious mixture of definiteness in principle with elasticity in details."[51]

Drafting a constitution can thus be likened to both a work of art and an engineering exercise. It can test the writing skill of the best draftsman in choice of language, precision, and clarity, while at the same time requiring craftsmanship in building the edifice of state institutions. An edifice is built to last, and in the case of a constitutional edifice, it has to be built to weather the storms of changing political fortunes. Abbe Sieyes, who influenced constitution making in post-revolutionary France, counseled to "keep the constitution neutral," or at least open-ended in political and ideological terms—particularly for the bill of rights provisions, one might add, as otherwise, they may be too closely identified with "the transient fortunes of a particular party or pressure group, and rise and fall with them."[52] This counsel justifies and explains the need for a core of professional legal personnel to lead the drafting of a constitution. Neutrality may be disputed as a controlling concept in this respect, but not objectivity. Even a partisan of a ruling party or group can see objectively the rationale behind Sieyes' counsel if the partisan is forward-looking and also can see the perils of being wrapped in only present or parochial concerns.

In Eritrea's constitution-making experience, the commission met the above questions head-on. It insisted that the contents of the constitution "must reflect present realities as well as be mindful of future developments of the society." As the concluding paragraph of Part 1 of the commission's proposals states,

> Our constitution has to be concise, clear and forward-looking, it has to be written in a general way rather than in detail, such that it will be amenable for future developments through a process of interpretation in response to future events. Its detailed implementation should be left to ordinary legislation.[53]

With these general considerations in mind, the commission's Executive Committee reviewed the mass of documents that were the product of over two years of research, seminars, conferences, and public debate before writing the first draft. The draft that came out of the committee's discussions and was submitted for the commission's approval reflected the outcome of the previous two years' debate and the thinking of commission members.

Approval and Ratification of the Constitution

Approval

There were three steps in approving the draft constitution. The first concerned approval by the entire membership of the constitutional commission of the draft prepared by the Executive Committee. The latter was designated as a drafting committee at the commission's fifth regular meeting in August 1995. The second step in the process was approval by the National Assembly, which met July 2–4, 1996, and approved the draft with a few amendments.[54] The law establishing the commission provided that following the National Assembly's approval of the draft constitution, the commission would distribute it to and receive comments from regional assemblies, localities, and members of professional, business, and civic organizations, as well as individual citizens.[55]

Accordingly, the public debate on the approved draft was launched in mid-August 1996. The draft was published in Tigrinya, Arabic, and English, and widely distributed throughout Eritrea and shipped abroad for distribution among Eritrea's diaspora communities before debates began. The draft was also published in the weekly newspapers in the three languages and broadcast on the radio. As with the commission's proposals, the introductory meetings were launched by members of the Executive Committee in Eritrea's main urban centers.

It is out of the purview of this paper to discuss in detail the substance of the questions raised and changes introduced, but suffice it to say that several points were taken into account as a result of the debates. Moreover, the commission members who took part in the conduct of the public meetings were invited to introduce any suggestions for change on the basis of their experience in conducting the meetings. Similarly, the Executive Committee thoroughly reviewed the opinions of the External Panel of Advisors; several points were found to be helpful.

Ratification

The concept of ratification is not new to any people with a long history of organized life. What may be new is the form of ratification and the type of ratifying entity. In Eritrea, prescribing the ratifying entity meant providing for a constituent assembly.[56]

The constituent assembly was composed of the seventy-five members of the National Assembly from the PFDJ, seventy-five members of the six regional assemblies, and seventy-five representatives of Eritreans living abroad, elected by their respective communities.[57] Seen in comparative perspective with the practice of other countries, the composition of the constituent assembly was an interesting combination of national representatives. In Namibia, the first parliament, elected on the eve of independence, turned itself into a constituent assembly. In Ethiopia and Uganda, the respective constituent assemblies were formed by special national elections.

The Eritrean case had two novel features. The first was the representation of Eritreans living abroad, who were included in the process of constitution making through their participation in both the debates and the constituent assembly. These Eritreans were included in the process because of the critical role they played during the armed struggle in providing intellectual, diplomatic, and financial resources.[58] The second novel feature was the inclusion of elected members of the six regional assemblies along with the members of the National Assembly.

Why was it seen as necessary to have a constituent assembly approve the draft after the National Assembly approved it? This question is connected to the issue of legitimacy, with its theoretical and practical significance. The underlying assumption of the concept of legitimacy is that government is established by and on behalf of the people. Thus, the nation as a whole must be represented in the approval of its fundamental charter, and the election of an entity—a constituent assembly—to perform this supreme act of legitimization is a common practice, which the National Assembly adopted. In the Eritrean case, only the seventy-five representatives from abroad were elected specifically to ratify the constitution, thus arguably weakening the constituent assembly's value as a body in representing the public's interests in constitution making. Nevertheless, the law establishing the constituent assembly gave it power to ratify the draft con-

stitution "having conducted debates thereon and making all necessary amendments,"[59] and it did make a few useful amendments. It was not a mere ritual. The unusual use of two elected bodies to approve the constitution was related to political realities as well. The governing party, the PFDJ, wanted to maximize its control over the constitution-making process. As the PFDJ had complete political control of the National Assembly but not the constituent assembly, it envisioned the former as a filtering entity.

Problems of Promulgation and Implementation

Eritrean constitution makers chose to develop a concise constitution with built-in flexibility to facilitate constitutional development. This approach gave enormous power to the principal institutions of the state, especially the judiciary. The constitution also made no reference to transitional provisions, a regrettable omission, as it turned out. There are two ways to effect a transition in the practice of constitution making. One way is to write relevant requirements into the constitution itself, invariably under a section entitled "transitional provisions," with details providing for the manner or timing of the transfer of power from the old to the newly elected government. The other way is to enact an enabling law that facilitates a transfer of power.[60] In the Eritrean case, the decision not to address the transition in the constitution was based on trust that the governing party would do what was necessary to fulfill the constitution's requirements and live up to popular expectations in implementing the document speedily and electing a new government based on the constitution. The decision was made because it was thought to allow flexibility.

Certain legal steps are required, however, to ensure the smooth transfer of power and help avoid confusion or conflicts in the law. Consequently, the constituent assembly was given a key role in putting in place the legal measures necessary to facilitate the transition.[61] The constituent assembly was given legislative powers to play that role, exclusively related to and effective until the constitution's implementation. Its intended function, in other words—in addition to ratification—was to act as a transitional parliament, facilitating a smooth transfer of power to a new National Assembly elected in accordance with constitutional requirements. In the meantime, the existing National Assembly was not disbanded; it continued to perform its normal functions. In reality, except for its role in ratifying the constitution, the constituent assembly has been dysfunctional and disregarded by the PFDJ. It did not take any of the legal steps required of it with respect to transferring power, thus contributing to the constitutional crisis that has prevailed to the present day.

Among the steps that the constituent assembly was supposed to take were those necessary to elect a new government. This requires passing an electoral law and establishing an electoral commission to organize such an election. It also may require passing a law authorizing the existing government to continue in power, pending the election of a government on the basis of the new constitution. There can be no power vacuum, not only for theoretical reasons that may seem esoteric, but also and above all for practical reasons. Furthermore, the constituent assembly's mandate necessitated enacting laws that create institutions, in addition to an electoral commission, necessary for the constitution to come into force and effect. Again, none of these necessary steps has been taken.

In addition to excluding transitional provisions, the constitution also did not provide for an effective date, further complicating the transition and implementation process. The question of an effective date, like the transition process generally, was left to be dealt with by the constituent assembly under Proclamation 92/1996, which gave the constituent assembly the power "to take, or cause to be taken, all the necessary legal steps for the coming into force and effect of the constitution."[62] This approach was due, first, to the reality that a number of existing laws and institutions within Eritrea at the time, if left unchanged, would have violated provisions of the new constitution. The commission was persuaded that the government needed time to change these, and that imposing a deadline or specific time limit for doing so would create unnecessary problems, including legal confusion to the detriment of an already traumatized population upon whom four different legal systems had been foisted: Italian, British, Ethiopian, and now that of the fledgling PFDJ. In such circumstances, why not give the government flexibility to clear the deck of old laws and institutions and prepare the ground for the new constitutional order?

The second and related reason not to include an effective date was trust in the government, which only in retrospect was misplaced. It is easy to criticize the commission with the benefit of hindsight, but at the time, the commission had little reason to believe that President Isaias Afwerki would renege on his promises. By all appearances, the president and his PFDJ comrades were committed to a democratic transition to constitutional government and the rule of law. Many of his closest colleagues were shocked by his breach of faith.

What remains now is for the necessary institutions of the state to be created and elections to be held to fulfill the constitution's promise. The principal institutions are the top organs of the state, namely the legislature—the National Assembly—an independent judiciary to be the guardian of the law, and a dynamic executive branch with an efficient bureaucracy to execute the policies of the government. These institutions need to be created, or where they exist, streamlined to accord with the constitution. Thus, everything depends on the constitution's implementation.

Conclusion

As the foregoing discussion demonstrated, the Eritrean constitution was created with the government's complete support. Accordingly, all expectation was that it would be implemented very soon after it was ratified. This author had not imagined that a constitution created with so much government care and support would be shelved by the same government. Indeed, the care and support—themselves based on the promise of democracy and rule of law endorsed at two congresses of the ruling party—were such that, far from expecting the shelving of the constitution, the constitutional commission had every reason to believe that the government would implement it within a year of its ratification. The reason that the government gave for the delay was the 1998–2000 War with Ethiopia.

At the time of this writing, it has been eleven years since the constitution was ratified and eight years since the war ended, and the constitution remains shelved, gathering dust. This fact gives the lie to the government's reason for not implementing the constitution. Since the war ended, all demands for its implementation have been ignored. The issue has become a litmus test of the legitimacy of the ruling party and its leader, Isaias Afwerki, who has been ruling by decree.

In 2000, some high-ranking members of the ruling party, including several ministers and army generals, formally called on the president to implement the constitution, actually challenging him to abide by democratic principles of governance. As has already been noted, the president agreed to establish two committees with a view to implementing the constitution, one committee to draft an electoral law and another to regulate politi-

cal parties. Mahmud Sherifo, minister of regional government (who also acted as deputy president), was appointed to head the committee on political parties. It soon became clear, however, that the president had no intention of implementing the constitution. He dismissed Sherifo from his chairmanship of the committee and his ministerial post, short-circuiting the making of the law on regulating political parties. Sherifo and his comrades persisted in their demand to implement the constitution, publicizing it first to the members of the National Assembly, then to all members of the ruling party and the nation at large. The president sent threatening letters in response to their demand. Then, following the events of September 11, 2001, when the attention of the world community was focused on New York and Washington, he ordered the arrest of Sherifo and fourteen other ministers and generals. He also ordered the arrest of all of the editors and lead writers of the private newspapers in the country, which he ordered shut. All of the people thus arrested remain in detention, incommunicado, without being charged in a court of law. Partly as a result of such disrespect for the rule of law, and partly due to the general condition of economic hardship, several opposition political parties have sprouted in the diaspora, vowing to bring about constitutional democracy.

In view of all of the above, two related questions have been raised consistently regarding the issue of the constitution's implementation. First, could the constitutional commission have adopted a different approach in implementing the constitution? Second, can the ratified constitution, in whole or in part, have force and effect by the fact of its ratification?

Regarding the first question, the commission considered inserting a provision fixing an effective date. But because there were several statutes and other laws that contained provisions inconsistent with the constitution, the commission thought it wise to give the government time and flexibility to bring such laws in line with the constitution. This necessarily implied the trust that the commission had in the government, on the strength of its record of supporting the constitution-making process and the resolutions of two-party congresses. Who would have thought that the PFDJ would go against its own resolution and promise?

Opinions are divided on the second question. One school of thought holds that the constitution must be considered as having come into effect, in its entirety, upon its ratification. The other school takes the position that the bill of rights chapter must be considered as having come into force, whereas the provisions dealing with establishing government institutions, in particular the legislative branch and executive that comes out of the legislature, must, by their very nature, await the constitution's implementation. The constituent assembly was supposed to deal with all of this.

The detained members of the ruling party were heading toward the above ends. But a president who was unwilling to be held accountable in a democratic system defeated their efforts. Thus, a process that was participatory and earned general admiration has been defeated by a willful president who hijacked the democratic process. As the saying goes, the operation was brilliant, but the patient is dead.

Eritrea's promising start was thus frustrated. After the foundation for democratic government was laid, an autocratic man sprung a surprise on the nation, violating past promises and popular expectations. Because dictators use some of the problems associated with democracy as excuses for the delay or denial of constitutional government, it is worth making two points in this respect. First, democracy is a worldwide phenomenon, and thoughtful people everywhere are convinced that there is no better alternative

to it. Nonetheless, no nation can afford to throw caution to the wind and push blindly for overnight democratization at any cost. This leads to the second point, namely that, once launched, constitutional government needs time to take root and flourish. However, this caution is no reason to block the road to democratic transition.

Notes

1. See, e.g., Jon Elster, "Constitutionalism in Eastern Europe: An Introduction," *University of Chicago Law Review,* vol. 58, no. 2 (1991), p. 447; Rett R. Ludwikowski, "Constitution Making in the Countries of Former Soviet Dominion: Current Development," *Georgia Journal of International and Comparative Law,* vol. 23 (1993), p. 155. See also Richard A. Rosen, "Constitutional Process, Constitutionalism, and the Eritrean Experience," *North Carolina Journal of International and Commercial Regulation,* vol. 24, no. 2 (Winter 1999).

2. The above argument is based partly on my own personal experience in Eritrea's constitution making. It is hoped that such specific experience will contribute additional insight to the usual methodology.

3. Such meetings include the Conference on Constitutionalism in Africa, held at Makerere University in October 1999, and the Conference on Constitutional Design in the 21st Century, held at Notre Dame University in December 1999. Two volumes coming out of these conferences are edited, respectively, by Joseph Oloka-Onyango and Andrew Reynolds. See Joseph Oloka-Onyango, ed., *Constitutionalism in Africa: Creating Opportunities, Facing Challenges* (Kampala: Fountain Publishers, 2001); and Andrew Reynolds, ed., *The Architecture of Democracy: Constitutional Design, Conflict Management, and Democracy* (Oxford: Oxford University Press, 2002).

4. Art. 4(4), Proclamation no. 55/1994.

5. See Bereket Habte Selassie, "The Eritrean Experience in Constitution Making: The Dialectic of Process and Substance," in Reynolds, *Architecture of Democracy.*

6. Lancaster House is the government building in London in which most of the independence constitutions of former British colonies were negotiated on the basis of drafts prepared by legal experts and bureaucrats of the departing colonial power.

7. See Samuel Huntington, *The Third Wave: Democratization in the Late Twentieth Century* (Norman, OK: University of Oklahoma Press, 1991), p. 6.

8. See Joseph Schumpeter, *Capitalism, Socialism, and Democracy,* 2nd ed. (New York: Harper Collins, 1947), p. 269.

9. Ibid.

10. Ibid.

11. See Robert Dahl, *Polyarchy: Participation and Opposition* (New Haven, CT: Yale University Press, 1971).

12. Ibid., p. 8.

13. "Democracy at Century's End," keynote address delivered at the National Humanities Center's third annual America Issues Forum. See *IDEAS,* vol. 4., no. 2 (1996), pp. 26–33.

14. Although it was the ELF that started the armed struggle in 1961, the EPLF emerged as a splinter group in 1970, eventually displacing the ELF and becoming the dominant front to defeat the Ethiopian army of occupation. After 1981, the ELF collapsed and left the field of armed struggle.

15. Bereket Habte Selassie, "Field Report: Creating a Constitution for Eritrea," *Journal of Democracy,* vol. 9, no. 2 (April 1998), p. 164.

16. Proclamation no. 37/1993.

17. Proclamation no. 55/1994.

18. James Tully, *Strange Multiplicities: Constitutionalism in an Age of Diversity* (Cambridge: Cambridge University Press, 1995), p. 7.

19. See Bereket Habte Selassie, *The Making of the Eritrean Constitution: The Dialectic of Process and Substance* (Lawrenceville, NJ: Red Sea Press, 2003), p. 20, citing Tully, *Strange Multiplicities*, p. 7.

20. Selassie, *The Making of the Eritrean Constitution*, p. 7

21. Ibid., p. 14.

22. Proclamation no. 55/1994, art. 4(2).

23. Art. 4(4) of Proclamation no. 55/1994.

24. Preamble to Proclamation no. 55/1994.

25. Art. 4(4) of Proclamation no. 5/1994. See Rosen, "Constitutional Process," p. 284.

26. Selassie, "Creating a Constitution for Eritrea," p. 167.

27. The chairman of the committee, Mahmud Sherifo, who at the time was minister of regional government and who deputized for the president in his absence, insisted on sharing his committee's findings and the draft law with members of the National Assembly and then with the public at large. The president, on the other hand, required that the draft should be submitted to him and not distributed to members of the assembly. Sherifo would not budge, whereupon the president summarily dismissed him from his post as minister. Sherifo and other reformist assembly members then requested a meeting of the Central Council of the party and of the assembly to discuss this and other issues of contention, including the matter of formation of multiparties before the December 2001 elections. The president did not see this with favor, and the rift has continued to widen between him and the reformist group, which includes some of the heroes of the armed struggle.

28. The resolution of the Organization of African Unity summit held in Algiers in July 1999—demanding that, henceforth, no government formed as a result of a military coup should be recognized—is a hopeful sign that governments in the Africa of the twenty-first century will be sensitive to the question of legitimacy.

29. The author's recent experience as a consultant to the presidential committee on the 1999 constitution of Nigeria confirms the importance of process-driven constitution making or review. The committee adopted the commission model and convened several public meetings in various regions of the country, with generally satisfactory results. Some contentious issues were not resolved as a result of these meetings, but at least a beginning was made to thrash them out in future meetings. One such issue is the role of *sharia* in Nigeria's constitutional dispensation. Another is revenue sharing and its associated derivation principle, i.e., the share in revenue of the areas where resources such as oil are located.

30. Spain, Venezuela, and Zimbabwe provide three examples (examined in this volume) of constitution-making processes that involved both parliamentary or constituent assembly approval as well as a public referendum.

31. In the recent Nigerian review process, the presidential review committee did not accept the popular referendum that some elements of civil society demanded. In its report, dated February 2001, the committee explains its rejection of the referendum option by pointing out that referendums are better used in instances in which there is a single issue, or a few simple issues, requiring a yes-or-no answer.

32. On the customary laws of Eritrea, see Carlo Conti Rossini, *Principi di Diritto Consuetu-diario dell'Eritrea* (Rome: Topografia dell'Unione, 1916).

33. These questions dealt with such issues as separation of powers; presidential or parliamentary (or mixed) government; limiting government powers; appointing government officials; powers, terms, and election of the executive branch; foreign relations leadership; the legislature (unicameral or bicameral, election, role, etc.); the judiciary; emergency suspension of the constitution; decentralization; the military's role; religion; basic rights guarantees; guarding minority rights; political parties and their roles; control of the economy; school curricula; mass media; nationality; the connection between international and national law; amending the constitution; and ratification of the constitution.

34. Rosen, "Constitutional Process," p. 285.

35. International Symposium on the Making of the Eritrean Constitution, Asmara, January 6–12, 1995.

36. These eight papers were: 1) *The Electoral System*; 2) *The Legislative Branch*; 3) *Women and the Constitution*; 4) *Decentralization*; 5) *Chapter on Fundamental Rights and Freedom in the Constitution*; 6) *The Executive Branch and the Structure of Government—Which System is Appropriate for Eritrea?*; 7) *The Judiciary*; and 8) *Defense and Security Institutions*. See Rosen, "Constitutional Process," p. 286, n. 128.

37. Rosen, "Constitutional Process," pp. 291–92.

38. Dec. 1966, 99 U.N.T.S. 171, and 993 U.N.T.S. 3. Article 1 of each covenant provides: "All peoples have the right of self-determination. By virtue of this right, they freely determine their political status and freely pursue their economic, social, and cultural development."

39. Rosen, "Constitutional Process," p. 292.

40. Ibid., p. 292.

41. Ibid., p. 286.

42. Ibid., pp. 285–88.

43. Rosen, "Constitutional Process," p. 293.

44. Selassie, *The Making of the Eritrean Constitution*, 31–32.

45. See Report on Civic Education, Constitutional Commission of Eritrea, February 1996.

46. The young man put it this way: "The constitution proclaims freedom of religion as a fundamental right. I am a devout Muslim, and according to my religion any swearing of an oath must be done in the name of Allah. If you force the draft's version, you would be violating my religious right."

47. Soon after the start of the process, as chairman of the commission, I invited the heads of the various religious bodies—the mufti of the Muslim community, the archbishop (later patriarch) of the Eritrean Orthodox Church, and the heads of the Catholic and Protestant communities of Eritrea—for a meeting in my office. At that meeting, I explained to them the commission's position on religion: that religion is a fundamental human right and freedom of worship would be one of the cardinal principles of the constitution's bill of rights, and that the commission was dedicated to the principle of the separation of church/mosque and state. Each of the participants expressed support for this. Throughout the process, I maintained contact with these leaders in various capacities, and they graced the commission with their presence.

48. Language persists as a contentious issue, principally centered around the demand by Muslim intellectuals that Arabic be an official language together with Tigrinya. Referring to the fact that the two languages were made official languages under the UN-imposed constitution of 1952, the intellectuals argue that this represents the aspirations of the Muslim segment of the Eritrean population, which comprises approximately 50 percent of the whole population, and that such aspirations must be given due weight in the constitutional scheme. An additional consideration is that Arabic is the language of the Holy Quran, which every Muslim child is expected to study in the Quranic schools. Opposing the idea of making any language official, the commission replied by pointing out that Arabic and Tigrinya are working languages of the state and are both taught at government schools. To insist on officializing language, apart from derogating from the principle of equality of languages, would unduly politicize the issue. It is possible that when the time comes to amend any of the articles of the constitution, this issue will be among the first to be tabled.

49. See Proclamation no. 86/1996, p. 24.

50. In fact, there is a strong movement among Muslim intellectual elites (who depend on Arabic for their own careers) demanding an amendment of the article on language.

51. See Edward McWhinney, *Constitution-Making Principles, Process, Practice* (Toronto: University of Toronto Press, 1981), quoting Russell F.

Moore, *Modern Constitutions* (Ames, IA: Littlefield, Adams, 1957), p. 12.

52. McWhinney, *Constitution-Making Principles*, p. 134.

53. See Commission's Proposal.

54. Pursuant to art. 4(4) of Proclamation no. 55/1994.

55. See art. 5 of Proclamation no. 55/1994.

56. Proclamation no. 92/1996.

57. The seventy-five seats assigned to Eritreans living abroad were distributed in accordance with the number of residents, divided into Ethiopia, Sudan, the Arabian peninsula, Europe, and North America, comprising the United States and Canada.

58. Again, during the 1998–2000 so-called border war with Ethiopia, Eritreans in the diaspora played a crucial role in providing similar resources.

59. Proclamation no. 92/1996, art. 3(1).

60. Constitutions of countries that have a legacy of numerous laws and a complex history and society, such as South Africa and Nigeria, follow the first method. The South African constitution is perhaps the world's most detailed constitution. Eritrea followed the second method; its constitution is one of the world's shortest.

61. Proclamation no. 92/1996, art. 3(2).

62. Proclamation no. 92/1996, art. 3(2).

4

Namibia's Long Walk to Freedom

The Role of Constitution Making in the Creation of an Independent Namibia

Marinus Wiechers

For almost two decades, constitution making lay at the heart of Namibia's peacebuilding and national reconciliation initiatives. In many other countries ravaged by internal and external strife, or harassed by a prolonged struggle for independence from colonial or foreign rule, constitution making came almost as an appendix to the final peace agreement and settlement of a date for independence. In Namibia, however, constitution making was a means to stimulate active politics and focus minds on the future of the country for more than fifteen years. In this regard, Gretchen Carpenter aptly remarks that "the Namibian Constitution did not fall out of the sky; it is the product of many years of negotiation and political growth."[1] To understand the pivotal role of constitution making in the Namibian peace process, it is necessary to summarize the genesis of Namibian independence.

From mandated territory to independent state

Namibia, the League of Nations, and the United Nations

After World War I and Germany's defeat, the allied powers established the erstwhile German colony of South West Africa as a mandate under the supervision of the League of Nations.[2] South Africa was given the sacred trust of promoting the material and moral well-being of the less than two million people in the territory. To fulfill this mandate, South Africa was allowed to administer the territory as an integral part of itself and required to report periodically to the League's Mandate Commission. South Africa made such reports, but stopped when the League fell into disarray shortly before World War II. After the war, although the newly established United Nations was not the successor in law to the League of Nations, South Africa approached it in 1945, asking to have the mandated territory officially incorporated into South Africa. The request was denied, and South Africa was instructed to place the territory under the supervision of the General Assembly and its Trusteeship Council. South Africa refused, leading to a prolonged feud in the United Nations and one of the most protracted legal battles in the International Court of Justice (the World Court).

The South West Africa/Namibia Cases in the World Court

A full explanation of the weighty legal issues raised in the South West Africa/Namibia cases is beyond the scope of this chapter. Suffice it to say that in many respects, the advisory opinions, judgments, and separate opinions of individual judges of the World Court regarding the case influenced and shaped international law on such fundamental issues as the succession and powers of international organizations, international peacekeeping, the jurisdiction of the court, and the international protection of human rights. Since the court's involvement supplied the legal justification for the UN's actions, it is necessary to give an overview of these opinions and judgments. The General Assembly approached the court for advisory opinions on three occasions. In 1950, the court advised that the General Assembly had the competence to request South Africa to place the territory under its trusteeship, although it lacked the power to compel the mandatory to do so. It also advised that the obligations of the mandatory under the new trusteeship agreement should not be more burdensome than the obligations that existed previously. In 1955, the court gave an opinion on the voting procedure in the Trusteeship Council as opposed to the procedure of the former Mandate Commission of the League of Nations. In 1956, a court opinion gave the green light to the Trusteeship Council to receive petitions directly from the inhabitants of the territory. The court's opinions, although of great persuasive authority, had no binding force, and South Africa refused to give effect to them.

In 1960, Liberia and Ethiopia, two former members of the League of Nations, instituted action against South Africa, requesting the court to declare the forfeiture of the mandate on the grounds that South Africa, by applying its apartheid policies in the territory, had betrayed its sacred trust of promoting the material and moral well-being of the territory's inhabitants. It was hoped that, this time, a court judgment with binding force would compel South Africa to relinquish its claims to the territory, or at least comply with UN demands.[3] In 1962, the court judged the preliminary issues and found that it had competence to hear the case. But in 1966, with its president casting the deciding vote, the court held that the applicants had failed to prove a legal right and interest in the matter and declined to give judgment. The result of the judgment was far-reaching. Whereas South Africa hailed the outcome of the case as a legal victory and immediately went ahead with its plans to administer South West Africa as its own province, member states of the General Assembly condemned it vehemently. This led the General Assembly to revoke the mandate in 1966, perhaps more an act of political offense and outrage than a legally sound decision.[4] In the ensuing years, however, the mandate's revocation not only received Security Council support, but was also finally endorsed by the World Court in its opinion of June 21, 1971. Nevertheless, South Africa completely ignored the revocation.

The Revocation of the Mandate and Growing Internal and International Pressure

Resistance to South Africa's continued presence in the territory grew throughout the

1950s and 1960s, not only internationally but also in the territory itself. The South West African People's Organization (SWAPO), the Ovambo-based liberation force in the territory, started with military operations on the northern borders; with Cuban support, this led to a low-intensity war that continued almost to the end of the peace process.[5]

In the mid-1970s, South Africa realized that with growing international pressure and a multitude of UN resolutions calling for its withdrawal from the territory, as well as the insurgency on the northern borders, the time had come to prepare the territory for independence. However, South Africa still hoped that the territory would adopt a kind of apartheid system of government that would ensure the white population a predominant position by assigning black and colored population groups to ethnic homelands, where they would enjoy the benefits, albeit limited in some important respects, of citizenship without being able to exercise direct power in the central government.[6] This no doubt explains why the South African government frequently interfered in the Namibian constitutional processes in the years before independence, especially when it perceived that political developments in the territory would cast doubts on the tenability and feasibility of its apartheid policies, not only in Namibia, but in South Africa as well. Stated in very simple terms, what chance did apartheid have to succeed in South Africa if it proved to have failed in Namibia?

The Turnhalle Constitutional Conference and the Democratic Turnhalle Alliance

On September 1, 1975, the Turnhalle Constitutional Conference was convened by the ruling white authority in the territory with the support of the South African government.[7] The Turnhalle conference was a unique experience with decisive political influence. For the first time in Namibia's history, leaders of the various ethnic groups were convened to debate the constitutional future of their country. SWAPO refused to participate, however, and the United Nations—both the Security Council and the General Assembly—condemned this exercise in constitution making as an unauthorized act of unilateral independence. Notwithstanding the fierce opposition it provoked, the Turnhalle conference constituted a landmark in the processes of Namibian constitutional development and political emancipation. Conference leaders were taken to the United States, United Kingdom, and Europe, where they met unofficially with members of government and leaders of political parties. In the territory itself, as well as in South Africa, the conference and its deliberations received much publicity and exposure. Mainly through the leadership, charisma, and foresightedness of Clemens Kapuuo, chief of the Hereros, and Dirk Mudge, member of the white delegation and chairman of the conference, a new political alliance of eleven ethnic political parties was formed; it was called the Democratic Turnhalle Alliance (DTA).[8] Toward the beginning of 1978, the Turnhalle conference adopted a constitution for an interim government,[9] which was promulgated as law by the South African parliament. The elections that followed were conducted on the basis of proportional representation. Although the interim constitution did not include general principles of good government, it provided for a justiciable bill of rights, a parliamentary regime, and decentralized government in the form of ethnic authorities with certain exclusive competences.

The ethnic component of the interim constitution—which was very much in line with the ideologies of the South African government and the white authorities in Namibia—was a compromise that no doubt discredited the constitution and the Turnhalle conference in the eyes of SWAPO and the United Nations. Both summarily rejected this constitutional draft, but it received overwhelming support in the countrywide elections held later in that same year. Seventy-eight percent of voters supported the constitution for the interim government, which was soon after installed by an act of the South African parliament.[10] Needless to say, neither the United Nations nor SWAPO recognized the interim government.

A South African Administrator-General

With the installation of the interim government in Namibia, the South African government abolished white representation for Namibians in its own parliament and appointed an administrator-general with wide-ranging legislative and administrative powers to prepare Namibia for eventual independence. The newly appointed administrator immediately abolished some of the most offensive apartheid legislation applicable in the territory[11] and remained in Namibia until independence. As representative of his government, he played a most important role in preparing the transition. It was with him that the special representative of the United Nations, Martti Ahtisaari, concluded the agreements of the final phases of the peacekeeping and electoral processes in 1989. The administrator-general also assumed full legislative and administrative functions for the territory when the South African government, in 1983, dissolved the interim government.[12] He promulgated Proclamation AG 8, which retained the ethnic authorities of the interim constitution. In the ensuing year, a multiparty conference with a broader political party representation—still without SWAPO participation—was convened to reach consensus on a new permanent constitution.

Security Council Resolution 435 (1978)

In the years of internal political development and turmoil leading to independence,

and especially because of the activities of the Turnhalle conference and the DTA, there was a growing awareness among some Security Council members that South Africa, after all, was not as intransigent as it previously seemed to be, and that a negotiated settlement on Namibia could well be attempted. This awareness led to the formation of the so-called Western contact group, an unofficial body of representatives of the governments of the United States, France, the United Kingdom, Canada, and West Germany. In 1978, the contact group managed to win the support of the South African government and all the Namibian political parties, including SWAPO, for a comprehensive peace and independence process. The Western contact group's negotiated agreement was endorsed by the Security Council as Resolution 435 (1978); in the ensuing years, this resolution would form the basis for the entire political transition up to the elections and independence. However, South Africa (backed by the United States) refused to have Resolution 435 implemented as long as the Cubans maintained their presence in Angola. At that time, the fear of communist intrusion into Africa was not farfetched, and on these grounds, the reluctance to implement Resolution 435 can be appreciated to a certain extent. The dispute concerning the Cuban presence in Angola dragged on for a full ten years and was resolved only in 1988, when South Africa, Angola, and Cuba entered into a trilateral agreement. Under the terms of that agreement, Resolution 435 was to be implemented and Cuban forces withdrawn in accordance with an agreed timetable.

The 1982 Constitutional Principles

Resolution 435 prescribed the peace process, the conducting of free and fair elections under UN supervision, and the formation of a constituent assembly to draw up and adopt a constitution for an independent Namibia. The resolution did not, however, indicate at all what the nature and content of such a constitution should be. The internal political parties perceived this as a serious shortcoming. In early 1981, an all-party conference in Geneva tried to reach agreement on this matter but did not succeed. The conference, however, did succeed in the sense that leaders of all the political parties and formations formally came together for the first time to express their views on a future constitution. Through vigorous U.S. initiative, the Western contact group managed to reach an agreement with all the interested parties, including the so-called frontline states—the African states that shared borders with Namibia— the Organization for African Unity, South Africa, SWAPO, and the internal political parties, on the principles concerning the constituent assembly and the constitution for an independent Namibia. In July 1981, these principles, which came to be known as the 1982 constitutional principles, were submitted by the Western contact group in a letter to the secretary-general of the United Nations with the request that both the letter and principles be treated as a document of the Security Council. From the ensuing Security Council resolutions as well as further negotiations between the Council and South Africa, it can be deduced that the principles, although not formally adopted and incorporated into Resolution 435, were effectively considered as part of it. At the constituent assembly's first meeting after the elections on November 21, 1989, it resolved to adopt the 1982 constitutional principles as a "framework to draw up a constitution for South West Africa/Namibia."[13]

Resolution 435 was a remarkable exercise in international strategy and diplomacy insofar as it not only provided the parameters for the conduct of the peace and independence processes but also settled the difficult prob-

lem of a transitional authority. In this respect, the resolution made it clear that transitional authority would remain with the South African administrator-general, who would exercise his powers and functions in conjunction with the UN special representative. Thus, a breach in the transition was avoided and the need for interim governing authorities before independence rendered moot.[14] The abandoning of South African authority during the transitional period also would have created considerable political tension and certainly would have jeopardized the electoral processes. However, although the general political situation during the transitional period improved and, as a result of the administrator-general's abolition of the most offensive apartheid laws, human relations also became more relaxed, there still were mistrust and tensions. These existed not only among the ethnic groups that feared Ovambo domination but also among whites, a large number of whom strongly resented the idea of an independent Namibia and were prepared to express their sentiments by violent means.

The United Nations Transition Assistance Group (UNTAG)

On April 1, 1989, Resolution 435 entered into force. Under it, South Africa would continue to administer the Namibian territory and the administrator-general would organize elections, but UNTAG would supervise and control all aspects of government to the extent required to ensure that the central objective—the creation of conditions for free and fair elections of a constituent assembly— was achieved.

UNTAG, for most of its mission, had about 4,300 military, 1,500 police, and up to 2,000 civilian personnel. At the time of the elections in 1989, UNTAG personnel reached a total of 7,900 with 109 nationalities represented. Total UNTAG outposts, including military, were almost 200. UNTAG's task was of a considerable magnitude and is described by Martii Ahtisaari, the Special Representative of the UN Secretary-General, as follows:[15]

> The [peace] process would move step-by-step, from a cease-fire in a long and bitter war, to the final moment of transition, that of independence. Each aspect—cease-fire, confinement to the base, demobilization, withdrawal of troops, the continuous process of supervising the conduct of the local police, the release of political prisoners,[16] the repeal of discriminatory laws, the adoption of the general amnesty and the return of many thousands of Namibian refugees; then the process of registration for elections, the political campaign, the voting itself—all had to be completed to my satisfaction, as the Representative of the Secretary-General of the United Nations, and in accordance with the Security Council's mandate.[17]

The 1989 Elections

Elections for the constituent assembly were held from November 7 to November 11, 1989.[18] Altogether, 701,483 voters registered for the election and 670,830—just over 97 percent—cast their votes. During the elections, on November 9 and 10, 1989, a momentous occurrence took place in Eastern Europe that would directly affect the constitution-making process in Namibia: The Berlin Wall fell, marking the beginning of the demise of communist hegemony. SWAPO emerged as the winner in the Namibian election, with nearly 60 percent of the vote and almost total support by the Ovambo; the DTA polled almost 30 percent, whereas the remaining votes were distributed amongst the smaller parties. In accordance with Resolution 435, the elections were run on a proportional basis, but because the territory, for election purposes, was divided into electoral districts, it was more than evident that SWAPO gained its major support in the northern parts of the territory that were inhabited by the Ovambo.

The DTA defeated SWAPO in many southern districts.

Immediately after the elections, the UN special representative declared them to be free and fair in accordance with Resolution 435, and a seventy-two-member constituent assembly convened for its first session on November 21, 1989. According to principles of proportional representation and based on the outcome of the elections, SWAPO held forty-one seats, the DTA twenty-one seats, and the other five smaller parties ten seats.

The Constituent Assembly and Constitutional Proposals of the Political Parties

Before describing constitutional developments after the elections, it is important to note preceding events that relate to the role of the constitutional council established in 1985. In November 1983, six political parties—excluding SWAPO, the Damara council, and other minor parties—assembled as a multiparty conference to draft a so-called permanent constitution. On April 18, 1984, the multiparty conference reached agreement on a bill of fundamental rights and objectives, which, together with other constitutional proposals, was presented to the South African government along with a call for an interim government of national unity. In 1985, the administrator-general instituted by proclamation the second interim government, following the first interim government that the South African government had installed in 1978. The proposed bill of fundamental rights and objectives was included in the proclamation as an integral part of the constitution of the interim government.

Although instituting an interim government—and especially adopting a bill of fundamental rights and objectives—raised vehement opposition from SWAPO and other political parties, it did serve an immeasurably important purpose in helping to create a human rights culture. Because transgressions of the bill were made justiciable, a number of major human rights judgments resulted, both in the Namibian courts and the South African appellate division, which remained the final court of appeal for Namibia at that time. The task laid upon the South African court to judge human rights issues was extremely challenging and certainly presented a most important learning experience, especially in light of things to come in South Africa itself. At that stage, South Africa had no justiciable bill of rights and the measuring of laws and governmental acts against the provisions of a bill of rights, was completely foreign to South African law and experience. It is remarkable that the South African human rights decisions that emanated from appeals from Namibia proved, in some cases, to be of major significance, serving as precedents for post-1994 South African legal practice as well as judgments for the situation at hand. The distinction between the legal treatment of human rights in Namibia and South Africa was partly a result of UN oversight in Namibia, but also largely a result of South Africa's realization that the protection of minorities and individuals in Namibia—especially whites, most of whom also had South African citizenship—would depend on a bill of rights.

One of the most important steps that the newly established second interim government undertook was to request the white legislative Council of South West Africa to institute a constitutional council responsible for drafting a national constitution that would ultimately be submitted to the electorate for approval. Some four months after the installation of the second interim government, in 1985, such a council was established to draw up a constitution for an independent Namibia. SWAPO refused to participate, but eighteen other political parties were represented in the body. The council worked for almost two years on a draft constitution. In June 1987, the council's chairman had to report to the cabinet of the interim government that it had failed to

achieve unanimous support for its draft, as four of the eighteen participant parties refused to give their assent. With its clear rejection of any form of institutionalized ethnic categories, the draft constitution also failed to meet the South African government's approval, and was therefore never implemented. The administrator-general abolished the second interim government shortly after that, when the DTA withdrew.

After convening in November 1989, the newly elected constituent assembly immediately invited the participant political parties—that is, all parties that had gained seats in the seventy-two-member assembly—to submit constitutional proposals. The parties all submitted more or less complete constitutional drafts. The proposals of two of the minority parties, the United Democratic Front and the National Patriotic Front, expressly referred to the binding nature and applicability of the 1982 constitutional principles. The DTA proposals were virtually the same as the draft constitution developed by the previous constitutional council, and, as the council kept to the 1982 principles, the DTA proposal conformed to them as well.[19] The constitutional proposals of the two predominantly white minority parties, the National Party and the Action Christian National (which together garnered about 3 percent of the vote), included executive and legislative organs specifically organized on ethnic and racial lines.

The SWAPO proposals were of major significance. In August 1989, the party had circulated its draft proposals in a working document prepared at their Lusaka Institute.[20] These proposals reflected East European ideology and constitutional thinking insofar as they emphasized the idea of a party state with party leaders exercising strong influence in both legislative and executive spheres.[21] A wide range of state and government principles was included without extending binding force or judicial review to them. The original draft provided for the judicial protection of some basic human rights, but with strong qualifications and extensive governmental powers of derogation and limitation.

Officially, the original SWAPO proposals never saw the light of day; with the fall of the Berlin Wall and the overwhelming signs of a crumbling communist empire, the East European inspiration for these proposals suddenly became extremely suspect. SWAPO then hastily had to convene a drafting committee to draw up new proposals. The proposals eventually submitted to the constituent assembly were contained in a rather untidy document that included almost verbatim many of the proposals of the other participant parties, especially those of the DTA. SWAPO's proposed bill of rights almost literally conformed to the 1984 bill of fundamental rights and objectives of the previous multiparty conference, which drew its inspiration from the UN Universal Declaration of Human Rights and the European Convention for the Protection of Human Rights and Fundamental Freedoms. The only element of the original SWAPO proposals that remained related to the rather extensive list of nonjusticiable government principles on socioeconomic and environmental affairs.[22]

When the constituent assembly met on November 21, 1989, it was faced with the seemingly insurmountable task of drawing up a constitution from a multitude of proposals. Two breakthroughs of major significance occurred. First, the assembly decided unanimously to adopt the 1982 constitutional principles as a "framework to draw up a constitution for South West Africa/Namibia."[23] Second, Dirk Mudge of the DTA proposed, and the assembly unanimously agreed, that the SWAPO proposals be accepted not as SWAPO proposals, but as a working document that would serve as the basis for the drafting of the constitution. The reason for this unanimous acceptance was obvious.[24] All the parties recognized elements of their own proposals in the SWAPO draft and were quite content to treat the document as a working paper without having to accept it as emanating from SWAPO alone. Ironically, this meant that SWAPO, although the victorious political party with support from 60 percent of the voters, officially had no constitutional proposals on the table. The SWAPO initiative was no doubt a most valuable contribution to the assembly's work, as it consolidated elements of most of the other proposals, albeit in a somewhat crude and untidy form. Moreover, general awareness that the working document emanated from SWAPO produced among SWAPO supporters a perception of credibility and legitimacy for the assembly's work.

Having lived through an extremely stressful year, and having been engaged in a hard election campaign, assembly members were not in the mood to tackle the working document immediately and undertake the arduous task of thrashing out the particulars of a new constitution. The December holidays gave them time to absorb the outcome and effect of the elections, especially among those population groups, such as Herero traditionalists and whites, who found it emotionally difficult to cope with the idea of a mainly Ovambo majority.[25]

The Drafting Panel of Constitutional Experts

Instead of immediately tackling the working document itself, the constituent assembly appointed a three-member drafting panel of experts charged with presenting to the assembly a constitutional draft early in 1990. Three South African lawyers were appointed: Arthur Chaskalson, Professor Gerhard Erasmus of the University of Stellenbosch, and this author.[26] In the assembly, these three members were jokingly referred to as the "men from heaven" who, with celestial wisdom, would have the almost impossible task of preparing the constitutional draft.

It is an intriguing question why the constituent assembly, notwithstanding the fact that an abundance of constitutional expertise was offered to it from all parts of the world, decided to appoint three South African lawyers of whom two were Afrikaners—the Afrikaners being popularly perceived as the original perpetrators of apartheid. On a purely practical level, the answer to this question was quite simple: Assembly members knew that a future Namibian constitution would have its roots in the South African legal system since the common law of the two countries remained the same. Also, the constitutional law and traditions of both countries were similar. On a deeper level, the choice of South African lawyers might well have been the result of rather strong suspicions toward the "outside world." In particular, the turmoil in Eastern Europe after the fall of the Berlin Wall created the sentiment that the Namibian constitution should not be the product of some foreign experiment. Assembly members conveyed to this author the view that "we should rather have some of our own people, and South Africans and we are family." It should also not be forgotten that Afrikaans was and still is the lingua franca of Namibia and is well understood by most members of the population, although all the proceedings of the constituent assembly and constitutional committee were conducted in English. Moreover, the assembly realized that appointing South African lawyers would go a long way toward dispelling mistrust in the entire constitution-making process, especially among white members of the population.

The drafters met in Johannesburg toward the end of December 1989 and the beginning of January 1990, drawing up a draft of the complete constitution based on the working paper. Because the working paper, in certain respects, was incomplete and lacking in detail, the drafters had to augment it in their drafting. These lacunae in the working paper related mainly to states of emergency and national defense, powers of the president, and, particularly, matters concerning local and regional government. An entire chapter on the second house of parliament, the national council, its composition, and its powers of review also had to be drawn up. In addition, and apart from necessary transitional provisions regarding the application of existing laws and regulations, provision had to be made for implementing the new constitution, especially as far as election of the national assembly and the president was concerned. In the latter regard, the drafters proposed that the members of the constituent assembly become the members of the new national assembly, which should elect the first head of state. After the first term of office, the president would be elected directly by popular vote. In conjunction with the constitutional draft, the drafters compiled a memorandum to explain precisely the scope and meaning of each article and provision of their draft. This memorandum was submitted to the assembly together with the draft constitution.

The Constitutional Committee

In mid-January 1990, the draft constitution was submitted to the constituent assembly and immediately referred to a specialist constitutional committee for scrutiny, discussion, and preparation of a final draft.[27] The twelve-member committee was proportionally composed of representatives of the political parties in the assembly. The committee began its work on January 16, 1990, in closed sessions to debate the draft with the panel of drafters. Hage Geingob, who was to become the first prime minister of independent Namibia, was elected the committee's chairperson.

On January 22, 1990, the constitutional committee unanimously adopted the full draft constitution and referred it to the constituent assembly for deliberation and adoption. The assembly unanimously adopted the draft on February 9, 1990. The work of the constitutional committee was carried out in camera without any direct press coverage. The reason for this secrecy, no doubt, was to aid the members in reaching consensus. Wide-ranging behind-the-scenes negotiations took place during the committee's deliberations, as it was felt that public exposure at such a sensitive stage could jeopardize the process. However, there was extensive press coverage of the debates in the constituent assembly, and the proceedings were open to the public. Given that all the political parties were repre-sented in the constitutional committee, very little debate and certainly no major disagree-ment occurred in the assembly; unanimous support for the draft was reached without any difficulty.[28] When the constituent assembly met in February 1990 for the final adoption of the constitution, it had no fixed timetable. However, because consensus was reached in the constitutional committee, it took little more than a week for the assembly to adopt the final constitution. More important was that the assembly already had decided on the day for Namibia's independence—March 21, 1990—which assuredly made drawn-out de-bates in the assembly impossible.

Discussions in the constitutional commit-tee were generally of a high standard and the atmosphere most cordial.[29] Approved amend-ments were referred to the drafters, who, dur-ing the same night, would reformulate new provisions and present them to the commit-tee.[30] Very few modifications of substance were made; the most important concerned the position of the president vis-à-vis parliament. The draft suggested that the president should also be a member of parliament, but the com-mittee decided on a nonparliamentary head of state. Most of the other modifications were of a technical or editorial nature.

Another noteworthy aspect of the com-mittee's deliberations was that SWAPO members constantly expressed individual opinions and convictions and were not afraid to contradict their other SWAPO colleagues. It was apparent that SWAPO members were not burdened with fixed party directives, which lent much openness to the discussions. In only one matter the SWAPO members expressed their views in concert and clearly under a party directive, namely that the fu-ture president should not be a member of the national assembly.

Having discussed and approved every article and provision of the draft constitu-tion, on January 22, 1990, the constitutional committee unanimously approved the draft as a whole and referred it to the constituent assembly.[31]

Adoption of the Constitution and Independence

After a discussion of the constitutional com-mittee's draft constitution, the constituent as-sembly unanimously approved Namibia's con-stitution on February 9. Amendments to the draft in the assembly related mainly to gram-matical and editorial matters and did not in any way alter the substance. With the new constitution meticulously tested against the 1982 constitutional principles, the secretary-general of the United Nations reported to the Security Council on March 16, 1990: "The Constitution is to enter into force on Inde-pendence Day. As the fundamental law of the sovereign and independent Republic of Na-mibia, the Constitution reflects the 'Principles for a Constituent Assembly and for a Consti-tution for an Independent Namibia' adopted by all parties concerned in 1982."[32]

On March 21, 1990, Namibia became inde-pendent; the constitution entered into force; the newly elected president, Sam Njoma, was sworn in by the UN secretary-general[33]; and the new government assumed office after having been sworn in by President Njoma. The constitution provided for a justiciable bill of rights and freedoms as well as a non-justiciable set of principles of state policy. It is noteworthy that under the constitution, the fundamental freedoms may not be diminished or detracted from. An electoral system of proportional representation underpinned the universally elected executive presidency as well as the national assembly. A prime minister became elected by the national assembly from its own members, and a cabinet of ministers was appointed by the president from members of parliament. Decentralized government was instituted in the form of regional councils, the members of which were also elected proportionally within defined constituencies. A national council, elected by members of the regional councils, would in the future form the upper house of parliament. Other important institutions created by the constitution were the ombudsman, a public service commission, and a security commission. Finally, the constitution safeguarded the independence of the judiciary. On the strength of the November 1989 elections, SWAPO gained 62 percent of the seats in parliament. President Njoma became the first head of state, also elected by the national assembly. The transitional provisions of the constitution that converted the constituent assembly into the first national assembly (the number of seats in both assemblies being the same) and provided for the first president to be elected by a majority in the national assembly were necessary to have the major institutions in place by independence. It was quite correctly realized that fresh elections for the newly instituted organs of state would amount simply to a repetition of the November elections; also, at that stage, they would have been infeasible and totally unnecessary.

The extremely successful outcome of the Namibian constitution-making process proved beyond doubt that constitution making could be a potent element in reducing conflict and building peace and national reconciliation. But what were the salient features of the Namibian constitution-making process? Does it hold any lessons for other countries and especially African countries? Did it influence South Africa's own constitution-making and peace-building processes?

The Central Role of Constitution Making in Conflict Resolution in Namibia

The effect of the Namibian constitution-making process in resolving both internal and external conflict and in facilitating a peaceful transition to independence must be viewed in its particular Namibian context of past systems of government, the land, and its people.

In colonial times, the entire country fell directly under the authority and powers of a German governor. German administration, however, did not extend fully over the territory; the northern parts of Ovambo, Kovango, and Caprivi fell above the so-called red line, which meant that there were no settler farms and very little colonial administration in those parts. When South Africa took up its mandate in 1919, more or less the same administrative arrangement was retained. In 1924, the territory was given a constitution, drawn up and passed by the South African parliament, which provided for limited self-rule under the overall sovereignty of the South African parliament. This self-rule was given to the white part of the population only, with no provisions for power sharing with other population groups. In 1968, acting under the erroneous belief that it had won the South West Africa/Namibia case in the World Court, the South African parliament adopted a new constitution for the territory, under which Namibia virtually became a fifth province of South Africa. Again, whatever vestiges of the former self-rule remained were left in the hands of Namibia's white population. This direct takeover of the Namibian government certainly was also inspired by the policy of dividing Namibia into various ethnic homelands on the same lines as the apartheid policies in South Africa.[34] However, the constitutional situation changed drastically in 1978 when, in preparation for eventual independence, the 1968 constitution was repealed, the administrator-general was appointed to take direct control, and Namibian representation in the South African parliament was terminated.

In short, it can be deduced that apart from its unofficial constitutional processes, Namibia had its fair share of constitutional vicissitudes. However, population groups other than the whites had little or no experience of these constitutional arrangements and manipulations since, for the most part, their homeland governments were under the direct authority of commissioners-general who were South African-appointed officials. Although some members of the homeland governments were elected,[35] most of these members were traditional leaders. It could be said that until the advent of the Turnhalle conference, formal political life among the peoples of the territory was extremely underdeveloped, except, of course, among the white population.

On the other hand, informal political organization in the territory was alive and well. These political organizations and activities were, in the main, directed against the South African administration and the application of apartheid policies. In earlier years, under the League of Nations and more so when the United Nations asked for a trusteeship agreement, the Hereros played a major role under the leadership of the famous chief Hosea Kotako and later under the leadership of chief Clemens Kapuuo.[36] In later years, when the Hereros and chief Kapuuo took a more conciliatory attitude and declared themselves willing to participate in internal political and peace processes,[37] SWAPO increasingly took over active resistance; in the beginning of the 1970s, it started a campaign of military operations and incursions, operating mainly on the Angolan side of Namibia's northern borders.[38]

To grasp the impact of the Namibian constitution-making processes, a few explanatory remarks on the land and its peoples should also be added. Namibia is a vast, largely arid and desert country. It is sparsely populated, with fewer than two million people.[39] The majority of its inhabitants live in the northern parts of Ovambo, Kavango, and the Caprivi—the regions that fell outside the original field of German government administration and to this day consist of tribal land with no commercial farming. For many years, Ovambo workers moved to the south as laborers on farms and in the fishing industry under former migrant worker regulations. The Hereros constitute another dominant traditional group, mainly in the central parts of Namibia; they are fiercely traditional and led the war against the Germans, who severely reduced their numbers in these military clashes. The Damara, probably one of the oldest groups in the territory, were subjugated mainly by the Hereros, and in the process lost their original language. Interestingly enough, they form a heterogeneous group that had much contact with and an understanding of most of the other groups. The Tswana are a small group who originally migrated from neighboring Botswana. The Bushmen are Khoi-San people and certainly the original inhabitants of the territory; they led a nomadic life and were the most marginalized of all the groups. The white population is mainly comprised of descendants of German settlers and South Africans who came to live in the territory after the conquest of Namibia by South African forces in 1915.[40] In many respects, the various Namibian ethnic groups have some deep ethnic and other cleavages among them. On the other hand, through the development of advanced transport and communication systems in the country,[41] there was a widespread mutual understanding not only of their differences, but also of the common ground they shared.

In the context of Namibia's history, politics, peoples, and progress to independence, the process of conflict resolution and peacebuilding in that country went hand in hand with constitutional reform and constitution making; the latter processes were the means and, in essence, the vehicles for conflict resolution, peacebuilding and national reconciliation. Of course, some issues could not be resolved by constitution making alone and had to be dealt with conjunctively to sustain and strengthen the peacebuilding process. The termination of the border war and the conclusion of a peace agreement were of vital importance, and the abovementioned trilateral agreement among Angola, Cuba, and South Africa to withdraw Cuban forces created the necessary conditions for constitution-making to proceed. The creation of these conditions for peace, although not directly related to constitution making, was not entirely divorced from it; the political parties engaged in the making of the constitution were constantly informed of these developments and indeed attended some of the meetings at which the termination of the war was discussed.

Another issue that could not have been resolved by constitution making alone was the matter of the South African government's presence and role during the period of transition to independence. This depended on an agreement concluded among Namibia's de facto government, South Africa, and the United Nations. As mentioned above, this agreement, which materialized in the form of Resolution 435, was negotiated with all the interested political parties as well as the Organization for African Unity and the so-called frontline states. Some of these transitional arrangements eventually found application in the constitution, but they were not part of the constitution making itself.

The Namibian experience teaches that participants in a constitution-making process must agree and believe that constitution making is a valid and important means of achieving peace and creating conditions for stability and national reconciliation. From this, it flows naturally that such participants must know what a constitution and its impact on the affairs of state are. This does not mean that members of constitution-making bodies should all be constitutional experts; it is important to have trusted constitutional advisers and expert committees to support and guide the constitution-making process and also formulate agreements and decisions in constitutional terms, without forcing their ideas on the constitution-making body or manipulating the process. In this respect, the Turnhalle Constitutional conference of 1975–78 provided valuable lessons. In that conference, excepting the members of the white legislative assembly, who through their training and experience in that body had considerable knowledge of constitutions, almost all the other members were from ethnic authorities with little or no knowledge of constitutions and constitution making, as their homeland constitutions had been drawn up for them by the South African government. The Bushmen delegates had absolutely no experience because there was no homeland authority for them at all; the delegates themselves were mostly illiterate and had little experience of modern towns and life. Similarly, the Tswana also did not come from a tribal authority, but were members of a small fledgling political party. The Damara ethnic authority, the Damara Council, refused to participate. To have Damara representation at the conference, members of a small Damara opposition party were invited. All the delegations had constitutional advisers, mainly South African lawyers and academics, assigned to them—or, more precisely, the South African government told the homeland authorities whom to appoint as their advisers.[42] This author was approached by the Damara and Tswana delegations themselves, admittedly, in the beginning, with the tacit consent of the conference conveners, the white legislative assembly.[43] The constitutional advisers had regular meetings with their respective delegations and drew up proposals for them. They did not participate directly in conference deliberations, but followed the proceedings through microphones in an adjoining venue.

A major breakthrough occurred in the Turnhalle conference's first week, when it adopted a declaration of intent in which the delegations declared themselves to be the true representatives of the Namibian people and took it upon themselves to exercise their right of self-determination by adopting a constitution for their country. A constitutional committee of representatives of all the delegations was elected under the chairmanship of Dirk Mudge. In the following two years, however, the full conference assembled only sporadically, and the constitutional committee carried out the main work and deliberations.

There is every reason to believe that the Pretoria government and some members of the host body, the white legislative assembly of South-West Africa, had previously drawn up a draft constitution. This constitution, drafted on classic apartheid lines, was to create a United States of South-West Africa with self-ruling homeland governments and a rather weak central authority to look after matters of common interest. In this federation of states, the white second-tier government would be assured of a dominant position. The South African government, no doubt, thought that by presenting the United Nations with a homeland-based constitution endorsed by the constitutional conference, it would satisfy the demands that the peoples of the territory must themselves exercise their right of self-determination.[44]

The South African government's original scheme for a Turnhalle constitution—a federation with ethnic state components—never saw the light of day, mainly due to the initiatives of the Damara and Tswana delegations. Soon after the constitutional committee's work commenced, these delegations presented the conference with a draft constitution for an independent Namibia, comprising a bill of rights and providing for universal franchise and judicial review of all governmental laws and practices. Instead of ethnic governments, it proposed a federation of northern and southern regions with two autonomous legislatures and governments for each of these two regions, as well as a central government composed of representatives of the two regional legislatures and governments. The Damara and Tswana proposals met with outrage on the part of some of the white delegates,[45] but had the overall effect of diverting plans for a federation based on ethnic systems of government.

Eventually, when the Turnhalle constitution was adopted in 1978, it contained the Tswana and Damara proposal for a bill of rights, but found a compromise in proposing second-tier governments, not to be exclusively territorially based, for the various ethnic groups. These governments would have exclusive jurisdiction over the so-called special affairs of each ethnic group. What constituted special affairs for each group became the bone of contention that eventually led Dirk Mudge and his followers to break away from the white ruling party. The latter's insistence that matters such as agriculture and transport should remain special affairs, even though these matters were clearly geographically defined, proved that at the end of the day, the ruling white party was not prepared to engage in meaningful power sharing with other groups. The other fundamental point of divergence between the ruling white party and Mudge and his followers was the ruling party's refusal to enter into alliance politics with the other groups.

What is of paramount importance, however, is that the Tswana and Damara delegations, at the time of the Turnhalle conference and also in later years, engaged in serious debate among themselves and other delegations on the meaning and importance of a democratic constitution. Evening lectures, seminars, discussions, and workshops were held on a wide range of topics pertaining to constitutions and constitution making, as well as many substantive issues such as the opinions and judgments of the World Court, systems of government, the role of political parties in a multiparty democracy, the international protection of human rights, the role of the United Nations in Namibian affairs, and many other subjects. As a result, in the conference debates, members of these delegations expertly discussed constitutional matters, even when some members of the white delegation wanted to exasperate them with seemingly superior knowledge of these matters. When the Tswana and Damara delegations released their constitutional draft, they held an international press conference at which they discussed and explained their proposals, on their own, with considerable knowledge, understanding, and insight. The infusion of constitutional expertise into the debates tremendously enhanced the level of discussion. It was most encouraging and indeed heartwarming that even the Bushmen delegation started to participate on its own.[46]

At the time of the DTA's formation, a parallel process of unofficial constitution making, albeit of a more political nature, was also taking place. As was mentioned above, the delegations other than the whites were mostly representatives of ethnic authorities and did not represent political parties. Even the Damara and Tswana delegates, who formally represented political parties, had a very rudimentary form of party organization. The DTA was founded as an alliance of political parties, however, which necessitated the drawing up of the political parties' constitutions and their adoption by the party leaderships and annual congresses. Constitutions for all the alliance parties were negotiated and

adopted, including for Dirk Mudge's Republican Party. This parallel process of developing party charters was of significance to the later official constitution-making process because it emphasized the normative and overriding force of constitutions in regulating matters of governance. In addition, the charters required the creation of political party manifestos, in which participation in the official constitution making for a future democracy was contained as a clear goal. In other words, all the political party charters prepared the parties for the constitution-making process.

In the years following Turnhalle, constitutional debate pervaded the political scene and influenced all political developments. The place and importance of a constitution in a democratic system, as well as the vital elements for its protection, were constant themes in the 1978 elections and all the political campaigns leading to the final elections in 1989. In the debates and decisions of the 1985 constitutional council, constitution making was the central issue, and the local press regularly reported on constitution making and constitutional issues.[47]

In the DTA's election campaigns and party propaganda, it as well as most other internal political parties insisted that a constitution had to be written in the hearts and minds of people to become a living document. Events in Namibia before the advent of the final constitution making certainly fostered this conviction.

Another lesson to be learned from the Namibian constitution-making process is that a future constitution must be inspired by an abiding ideology, or more ideally, a clear definition of the nature of the state that the constitution is to govern. For Namibia, this clear definition was provided by the 1982 constitutional principles, which laid down that "Namibia will be a unitary, sovereign, and democratic state." Over and above the other specific instructions of the 1982 principles that relate to the binding force of the constitution, the organization and powers of all levels of government, the electoral system, the protection of human rights, and the structuring of public services and local and regional government,[48] the constituent assembly had to ask itself constantly whether a specific proposal would serve the goal of founding a democratic state. This constant questioning found practical application, for instance, when the tenure of the head of state was discussed and it was unanimously agreed that a life presidency or a presidency for more than two terms of office would be contrary to the tenets of democracy. The 1982 constitutional principles were the guiding star of the assembly's deliberations. They came to be known as the "holy cow" in the deliberations of both the assembly and the constitutional committee. Each time it was perceived that a proposal would offend the "holy cow," the chairperson would immediately rule the proposal out of order.

Another rather obvious but essential element of the success of the Namibian constitution-making process was that all participants expected the process to benefit their parties and themselves in some way. Stated differently, all participants, for some reason or other, assumed ownership of the process. Except perhaps for the three white members of the erstwhile ruling National Party,[49] who still harbored nostalgia for the continuation of a constitutional connection with South Africa, all the other parties were fiercely patriotic and adamant about eventual Namibian sovereignty. By their total rejection of any kind of ethnic divisions of the country, they fully supported and indeed strongly propagated the concept of a unitary state. It can be said safely that these parties all entered the elections as true freedom parties: All of them realized that the foundation of a sovereign, unitary, and democratic Namibia would depend on the outcome of the constitution-making process, and were therefore bent

on making the process successful. SWAPO not only supported the constitution-making process wholeheartedly, but simultaneously pushed for its timely conclusion because it knew that the coming into operation of an independence constitution was a prerequisite for SWAPO's entry into government. Once a date for independence was set, a prolonged and protracted process of constitution making would have been extremely perilous, as it would have been perceived as a means of deliberately obstructing SWAPO's accession to power. The minority parties also understood the benefits that successful constitution making would hold for them, namely, a system of government under which political freedom would be assured. Adopting a binding and justiciable bill of rights would safeguard the personal liberty and security of all the minority parties' supporters in the face of possible abuse of power by the majority.[50]

The constitution contained two other elements that attracted support for it from most citizens and assured its legitimacy among the broad population; these elements made the population feel that it was their constitution. The first was the constitution's express affirmative action article, which provided that, notwithstanding the constitutional prohibition on different forms of discrimination, the parliament could enact laws that provided directly or indirectly for the advancement of persons who had been socially, economically, or educationally disadvantaged by past discriminatory laws and practices. In this respect, the position of women was explicitly mentioned. The second element that assured broad popularity was a chapter on so-called principles of state policy. Although not enforceable in a court of law, these principles gave the constitution a definite programmatic character and enjoined the government to promote the welfare of the people as well as take care of a broad range of other matters, such as foreign relations and the country's economic order.

Structure of the Process

In Namibia, the 1982 constitutional principles simply provided that "in accordance with UN Security Council resolution 435(1978), elections will be held to select a Constituent Assembly which will adopt a Constitution for an independent Namibia" and that "the Constitution will determine the organization and powers of all levels of government." Nothing further was added about the way the constituent assembly would go about drafting the constitution, setting a timetable, or implementing the document—nor were any such provisions really necessary. There was a general realization that the parties in the assembly, as a result of the considerable constitutional expertise and acumen gained in the years leading up to the elections, would know how to proceed and reach agreement on these matters. Moreover, it was apparent that the time was ripe for Namibian independence and that most parties would press for the constitution's expeditious drafting and adoption. The way that the constituent assembly dealt with the rather vexed questions of installing the new government, applying the new constitution, and declaring independence bore ample witness to the assembly's astuteness and readiness to assume ownership of its own constitution-making process.

Other countries, as a result of their particular circumstances and preceding events, had to initiate and further strengthen their constitution-making processes, first by appointing a constitutional commission, then by electing an interim authority. Namibia, however, as a result of the experiences of the preceding years and especially through the internal constitutional and political developments that took place, was geared for the structuring of a relatively simple and efficient constitution-making process: the straightforward election of a constituent assembly, which, it was realized, would be well equipped to proceed with the process on its own.

Public Participation in the Process

There was little direct public participation in the process in either the years preceding the final constitution-making phase in Namibia or the final phase itself. Referendums and plebiscites were not part of the Namibian constitution-making process, except a plebiscite organized for white voters in May 1977 to ask them whether they favored the installation of an interim government and independence of the territory on the basis of a constitution to be adopted by the Turnhalle Constitutional Conference. Some 95 percent of the white voters answered in the affirmative. A referendum was held at that time because the leaders of the white legislative assembly wanted to give force to the deliberations and decisions of the Turnhalle conference but on their conditions, namely, the adoption of an interim constitution drawn up on the lines of ethnic governmental structures. Mudge and his followers were strongly opposed to the idea of a referendum for the white electorate only. The plebiscite's effect was largely overtaken by subsequent events, especially the adoption of Resolution 435, but, importantly, it conditioned white voters' minds by preparing them to accept the idea of eventual Namibian independence.

However, indirect public participation in the Namibian constitution-making process was intense and stretched over many years, reaching its climax in the 1989 elections. This indirect public participation underpinned the elections of 1978 and 1989, as elections and election campaigns clearly would be meaningless without public participation. Election campaigns in Namibia were extensive, and party political meetings and rallies drew thousands of people, even in the remotest parts of the country. Political rallies and meetings—especially those of the DTA—were huge social events, with food, song, and dance. The border war made some of the rallies in the northern areas rather perilous at times, but on the whole, these political events infused the country with social activity never before experienced on that scale. In addition, advanced communication systems spread political messages over the whole land. In pre-independence days, SWAPO conducted a network of radio services from outside Namibia's borders. SWAPO was never banned formally in the years leading up to the 1989 elections, but its leaders were constantly harassed and even imprisoned, making political life and open participation extremely difficult, if not impossible. Overall, the Namibian population was saturated with political propaganda and information, much of the latter relating to constitutional matters and the content of a future constitution for an independent Namibia.

The process of constitution making must be driven by elites. It cannot be conducted and successfully concluded solely by popular initiative and mass movements. Elites have to plan, conduct, and conclude the process of constitution making, although, admittedly, this process must, for its ultimate legitimacy, be continuously sustained by popular support. Because political parties in Namibia were the major actors in planning and conducting the constitution-making process, while at the same time vying for popular support, a word should be added about the political party leadership in that country. For a long time, the white population supplied the strongest political party leadership, and largely because of their dominant position, its leaders constituted the elites of Namibian society. Most of the SWAPO leadership and elites had to flee the country during the years of transition, and some of them were imprisoned. This created a gap among the elites of the country. Among the other population groups, there were very few political elites, except for some traditional leaders such as chief Clemens Kapuuo and a few others, who as a result of their political engagement and personal qualities of mod-

ern leadership, transcended pure traditional leadership and achieved elite political stature. The DTA—and more particularly, the white alliance party of Dirk Mudge, the Republican Party—was the major factor in broadening the basis of the Namibian elite among the other population groups by drawing their leaderships into the alliance. Without this broadening of the Namibian elite, the final phase of the constitution-making process would not have had its successful outcome. Though it might have become politically incorrect to acknowledge the crucial role of some of the white elite, the success of the Namibian constitution-making process must to a large measure also be ascribed to Mudge and his followers, who not only wholeheartedly immersed themselves in the liberation movement, but also created the opportunities for many other political leaders to join in the class of Namibian elites.

Receiving information surely also constitutes a form of public participation, albeit a more passive one. The Namibian media and particularly its press played an important role in this regard. Over the years, Namibia had a well-developed radio system, and radio stations operated in the languages of the various population groups. In the preindependence years, SWAPO's radio station, the Voice of Namibia, broadcasted extensively from Zambia. Namibia always had a relatively large number of newspapers, given its small population numbers. Apart from the Afrikaans press, there were also newspapers in English and German as well as newspapers in some of the indigenous languages, though these were mainly supplements of the Afrikaans and English press. In 1978, the newly formed DTA started its own party mouthpiece, the Republican Press, which in later years took over the German and one of the English newspapers to become the strongest press company in the country. Understandably, the Republican Press of the DTA, in its early years, was fiercely partisan, but after independence, it became more neutral without entirely losing its character of being, if not in direct opposition, then rather critical of government. Television service became available in the country toward the end of the 1970s and was a forceful instrument in informing the population about political developments.

In the period leading up to the elections of 1989 and during the time of implementing Resolution 435, UNTAG also provided extensive information services. A total of forty-two regional and district centers were established and provided the necessary information network to assist in the process of reconciliation. In addition, the UNTAG information service produced 32 television programs and 201 radio programs in thirteen languages; it also distributed 600,000 UNTAG shirts, buttons, stickers, pamphlets, and posters. UNTAG regional and district officials spoke to local opinion formers, political parties, churches, and farmers, and directly contacted the people. Admittedly, the UNTAG information campaign was not about constitution making, but it reinforced the constitution-making process tremendously in that it propagated the idea of free and fair elections for all. Such elections, of course, were an absolute prerequisite for the constitution-making process that was to follow.

At least in indirect forms, public participation in the overall constitution-making processes was so wide-ranging and intense that additional ratification of the final constitutional draft by means of a plebiscite or referendum was seen as unnecessary. It can safely be said that public education in Namibia on constitutional matters, including the contents of the final constitution as well as future public participation in political affairs, was so effective that the legitimacy of the final independence constitution was ensured by the time the constituent assembly adopted it. Moreover, the nature and composition of the assembly and public respect for that body made an additional act of ratification seem superfluous.

One proposal, considered by the committee and rejected, has some potential relationship with public participation: that the constitution be subjected to a periodic review process. Some authorities have suggested that such a procedure could be the occasion for public participation on an ongoing basis, which in some cases could offer opportunities for participation over and above that associated with adopting the final text. The proposal was rejected because the committee feared that such a procedure would create the impression that the constitution was a precarious document that needed to be amended and changed. The committee feared that the creation of such an impression might encroach on the fundamental character of the text.

Democratic Representation

In Namibia, the question of democratic representation in the constituent assembly was not a bone of contention. It was simply agreed during the peace negotiations that the various political parties would be represented in the constitution-making body. This longstanding agreement eventually found its place in Resolution 435 and the 1982 constitutional principles. The elections for the constituent assembly established the distribution of power among the political parties and could not be contested, as the UN special representative certified the elections to have been free and fair.[51]

At the commencement of the UNTAG operations, the relationship between the UN special representative and the interim authority, the South African administrator-general, was somewhat strained. Over time, however, the relationship became increasingly cooperative.[52] The constitution contains a remarkable provision regarding the administration of the administrator-general as well as the previous South African administration, stating[53] that "nothing contained in this Constitution shall be construed as recognizing in any way the validity of the Administration of Namibia by the Government of the Republic of South Africa or by the Administrator-General appointed by the Government of the Republic of South Africa to administer Namibia." This was a rather clever legal device to solve (or sidestep) the vexed problem of, on the one hand, accepting the continuation of existing laws and regulations and not creating a break in the evolutionary development, and on the other hand, acknowledging the idea, which SWAPO held very strongly, that the South African administration was illegal after the mandate had been revoked. In law, the provision did not affect the actual application of the relevant laws and regulations because it did not declare them invalid, but merely refused to recognize them as valid. In legal theoretical terms, this provision is a textbook example of the so-called *Normative Kraft des Faktischen*—the normative force of an existing factual state of affairs.

The Namibian constituent assembly made no provision for any kind of representation on the basis of ethnic origin. This did not mean, as explained above, that there were not marked ethnic divisions in Namibia. Active party politics to a large measure resolved this difficult and potentially explosive element. SWAPO, although predominantly Ovambo, included in its voting list many members of other ethnic origins, and some of these members held important positions in the party and later government.[54] Whereas SWAPO's voting list basically was composed on the strength of candidates' rank and position in the party, the DTA's list, in accordance with its alliance nature, allotted an equal number of candidates to the respective alliance parties. In this manner, equal ethnic representation in the constituent assembly was assured. The political party solution to the vexed

question of ethnic representation certainly relieved the assembly of a massive burden; the matter presented no hurdle in deliberations about the future constitution. With respect to the DTA in particular, affording the various ethnically based political parties an equal status in the alliance defused any possible ethnic conflict within its ranks.

The Namibian experience also offers a lesson for dealing with a political party or group that refuses to join in the constitution-making process. With the support of the UN General Assembly, SWAPO refused to be part of the internal constitutional processes until the final stages, once Resolution 435 was implemented. This refusal by SWAPO, however, did not deter the other parties from proceeding with their constitution-making efforts. In the end, these efforts bore fruit and certainly contributed to the ultimate success of the country's final constitution making. The lesson to be learned is that where groups and parties are prepared to engage themselves in constitution-making processes for a future democracy, such initiatives should be encouraged. Eventually, it becomes almost inevitable that recalcitrant groups and parties, especially with the encouragement and even coercion of the international community, will follow the course of events and join in the process. Admittedly, this approach can prolong the constitution-making process, but it will help ensure its ultimate legitimacy.[55]

The Timing and Sequencing of the Constitution-Making Process

Timing issues have been addressed above and need only be summarized. First, in Namibia, the conclusion of a peace agreement and the Cuban withdrawal of its presence in Angola were preconditions for applying Resolution 435 and certainly created a propitious climate for the country's final phases of constitution making. The fortuitous crumbling of the Soviet and communist hegemony was a factor that saved the Namibian constitution from many complications and burdens of political ideology.

Second, the prolonged process of Namibian constitution making no doubt gave internal parties much opportunity to activate political life and strengthen and position themselves. It must be emphatically stated that a multiparty democracy in Namibia would have been impossible if internal parties were not afforded these opportunities, as a political culture of multiparty democracy does not come easily, especially in African countries.

Third, the final phase of constitution making in Namibia was remarkably quick. The speed with which the process was concluded must be ascribed to the host of internal and external factors described above, and was not achieved merely because, at a given point, interested parties agreed to draft a constitution for an independent Namibia.

Fourth, the final Namibian constitution emanated from a single draft, drawn from the constitutional proposals of the various parties—which was possible because the proposals contained considerable points of convergence. In a very real sense, the elections for the constituent assembly served three purposes: first, to elect an assembly; second, to inform the electorate what would be the content of the future constitution; and third, to elect a future government. This explains why the assembly had the legitimacy necessary to form the new independence government. When the constituent assembly was convened in November 1989, voters and political leaders already knew who, from a political point of view, would be the future government; the constitution was needed to legalize this future government. This was certainly a factor that serves to explain why the process moved so smoothly and expeditiously from that point.

Fifth, Resolution 435, which underpinned the peace process in Namibia, was also the guiding light in the constitution-making process. This is understandable, as Resolution 435 was the concrete outcome of a long and complex process of peacebuilding, international diplomacy, negotiation, and agreement. Put very succinctly, it could be said that a country in transition, for its constitution making, ideally should have some type of road map such as Resolution 435.

Sixth, Namibia had its fair share of interim constitutions and notwithstanding their imperfections and lack of acceptance, they were crucial in all the phases leading up to the final constitution making. The effect and overall value of these interim arrangements speak from the above.

Finally, the role of the internal parties in Namibia during the time when the conflict was still raging and the international disputes continued unabated proved to have been of the utmost importance. Attempts at constitution making in the 1970s were initial efforts that exercised a beneficial influence in the final phase. The Namibian case demonstrates the potential benefits for a country in transition of beginning the process of constitution making as early as possible, even though such early constitution making may be rather hesitant and rudimentary.

The Role of the International Community

From the end of World War I, the organized international community's part in Namibia's journey toward independence was all-pervasive and encompassing, culminating in the implementation of Resolution 435 and the deployment of UNTAG. The international community's involvement in Namibia's affairs was, of course, a direct consequence of the territory's international status.

Namibia's international status flowed from the mandate system, and although South Africa fiercely denied it for a long time, this system was the justifying and determining factor for international preoccupation with the territory. What should not be forgotten is that, before independence, Namibia represented the last vestige of colonial rule in Africa. This raised much emotion among Third World countries in the UN General Assembly, especially among African members. To them, what was infinitely worse was South Africa's continued occupation of Namibia, widely labeled as illegal after the revocation of the mandate. The South African government itself became branded as "colonialism of a special kind." Also, the buildup of the Cold War after World War II increased and intensified the Namibian conflict. Support for the Namibian cause became the yardstick against which East and West identification with anticolonial movements and causes was measured.

In those years, and especially in General Assembly debates, South Africa's presence in the territory and obduracy in the matter were constantly branded as threats to world peace. This was certainly far-fetched, but it has to be understood in the context of the United Nations. The UN's peacekeeping powers are well defined in its Charter and mainly reserved for the Security Council. Over the years, however, the General Assembly became more and more anxious to exercise peacekeeping competences and to bypass the hurdle of a Security Council endorsement. When, in the 1960s, the Third World members of the General Assembly became dominant, these new members understandably tried to assume more and more peacekeeping powers on behalf of the Assembly. Their identification of threats to world peace raised the expectation that the Security Council would become operative and discard its lethargy. In the case of Namibia, the matter was extremely sensitive. Neglect of the General Assembly's demands to have the Namibian conflict treated as a threat or potential threat to world peace subjected the Western members of the Security Council to severe censure for supporting the white racist South African regime. This, of necessity, could severely damage relations with the Third World and nonaligned countries. All these reasons explain why the Western contact group was so concerned to have Resolution 435 accepted by all interested parties and be put into operation. Namibia, certainly, was not a country of major importance, but the political implications of the dispute there were immense and had international dimensions.

Fortunately for Namibia, the involvement of the organized international community ultimately was spearheaded not by the General Assembly—with its at times disproportionate political emotions—but by the Security Council and, more particularly, the Western contact group. The Contact Group's evenhanded and diplomatic treatment of the Namibian problem was to a large measure the reason for its successful outcome. Similarly, the role of the then secretary-general of the United Nations and his balanced way of dealing with the obstacles as they arose deserve credit. Namibia's former international status as a dependent territory was terminated at the time of independence when the country acceded to its new international status, that of a sovereign independent state and full member of the family of nations. Recognition of Namibia's independence on the basis of Resolution 435 immediately assured the country of de jure recognition by the international community.

However, even as all Namibian parties recognized the international community's crucial role in Namibian independence, they were set on the idea of preserving the autochthony of their constitution-making process. There is little doubt that the 1982 constitutional principles that gave instructions about the nature and contents of the future Namibian constitution would not have gained the political parties' acceptance had these principles emanated from an outside source or been imposed on them by the international community. The constituent assembly's appointment of three South African lawyers to write the draft constitution for them could be explained in the same way.

The Role of International Law

In the Namibian experience, with all its international ramifications, the importance of international law does not need to be emphasized. For years, the Namibian dispute dominated the jurisprudence of the World Court. Other pertinent international law issues also pervaded the peace process, such as the competences of the United Nations and its secretary-general, the Security Council's peacekeeping powers, the status of political prisoners, and the status of the Walvis Bay enclave.[56]

What is of overriding importance is that the Namibian dispute, apart from having been regulated by international law, also contributed to the progressive development of general principles of international law as well as customary international law on such matters as international protection of human rights, the elimination of racial discrimination, and the succession of international organizations. This development came about mainly as a result of the World Court's jurisprudence in the Namibia disputes and played a considerable role in the court's later decisions.

Given the immense impact of international law in Namibian affairs, it is little wonder that the Namibian constitution expressly provided that unless otherwise provided in the constitution or an act of parliament, general rules of international law and treaties binding upon Namibia under the constitution were to form part of the law of Namibia.[57]

Essential Issues of Substance

In Namibia, essential issues of substance—such as the protection of human rights, the elimination of racial and other forms of dis-

crimination, socioeconomic development, regionalism, and democratic representation—all had to be considered in assuring the constitution-making process's success. It can safely be said that the formal process of constitution making was never divorced from matters of substance. If it were not so, the process would have become hollow and would not have contributed to peacebuilding and national reconciliation.

Of special interest is the question of the legal force of the 1982 constitutional principles after the conclusion of the constitution-making process. Many would probably argue that these principles, after having been complied with, lost their binding force and effect; in other words, according to this reasoning, the principles were mainly directed to the constitution-making process and, once absorbed into the constitution's provisions, ceased to exert any legal force, except insofar as they assisted in constitutional interpretation in the future. This author's (more contested) opinion is that the principles were preconstitutional inasmuch as they defined the democratic foundations of the future Namibian state. According to this reasoning, if a future government were to amend the constitution and discard these principles, the nature of a democratic Namibia would be violated. Given that the principles constituted the conditions for Namibian statehood, rejecting them arguably would constitute such a fundamental encroachment that the international recognition of Namibia as an independent democratic state could be affected.[58]

Conclusion

The Namibian constitution-making process was an unqualified success. It gave Namibians a modern constitution in which the protection of human rights, the independence of the judiciary, the accountability of government, the decentralization of government, and the conducting of free and fair elections were all constitutionally ensured and safeguarded. Most important, it laid the foundations for a multiparty democracy. In this respect, the people themselves, probably for the first time in Africa, totally rejected the concept of a one-party state. Namibians are proud of their constitution and the values it contains. What is more, the Namibian constitution-making process, in many respects, gave invaluable guidance and provided some important lessons for South Africa's constitution making in the 1990s. Perhaps the most important lesson was that a rigid apartheid regime could peacefully evolve into a fully democratic system. On a practical level, Namibian constitution making taught South Africa the importance of having a set of constitutional principles in the making of a constitution. The South African constitutional principles, adopted at the time of the drafting of the interim constitution, were accepted by all the parties as a solemn pact and provided the basic tenets of the final constitution.

Yet there are disconcerting elements in the evolution of the Namibian constitutional practice. A democracy should constantly be vigilant and guard against unconstitutional tendencies and developments. In Namibia, a large part of the population, perhaps out of complacency based on the fact that they adopted a model constitution, lost interest in practical politics. This apathy has led to increased political maneuvering and abuse of power on the part of government. Presently, opposition parties lack effective leadership, and the alliance parties of the DTA have lost their organization and coherence. Concentration of power in the hands of central government and the neglect of regional and local institutions suggest a disturbing *jacobinisme*. The exaltation of Ovambo nationalism does not augur well for national unity and reconciliation. The vital issue of necessary land reform is addressed more to gain short-term political advantages than to

resolve acute economic and social malaise. A third term of office for the president in 2000 was manifestly unconstitutional and calls up the horrifying threat of an African life presidency.[59] It is said all is well that ends well. This is surely true as far as the Namibian constitution-making process was concerned; whether it is true for the continued application and role of the constitution itself remains to be seen.

After more than sixteen years of independence, the Namibian Constitution still holds good. Notwithstanding the misgivings expressed, political party life is still active. A small but vibrant opposition party—the Namibia Democratic Party, which emerged from SWAPO ranks—and other political parties still enjoy all their constitutional rights and freedoms. Most comforting, there are no signs of the constitution being sidestepped or parts of it being suspended. In its years of independence, Namibia has not known any state of emergency or undergone any serious political upheavals.

The final word here belongs to Bryan O'Linn, staunch opponent of apartheid, seasoned politician, and esteemed judge of the Namibian High Court:

> The question whether or not all the ideals of the sacred trust of civilization have been realized can not be answered convincingly at this point in time. The ideal of the self-determination of the Namibian people has been achieved. However, it still has to be seen whether the ideal will be realized of a lasting and enlightened democracy and compassionate society with substantial economic and social benefits to all its people, which not only ensures the protection of their human rights and freedoms, but enjoins them to meet their responsibilities.[60]

Notes

1. Gretchen Carpenter, "The Namibian Constitution: Ex Africa Aliquid Novi After All?" *South African Yearbook of International Law*, vol. 15 (1989–90), p. 63.

2. There is a wealth of literature on Namibia, its history, geography, peoples, politics, etc. Probably one of the most comprehensive and authoritative works remains John Dugard's *The SWA/Namibia Dispute* (Lansdowne: Juta, 1973).

3. At the same time, the court's condemnation of South Africa's apartheid policies in the territory would have had the much broader effect of giving the United Nations a legal basis for attacking the application of these policies in South Africa as well. As it speaks for itself that should the court have declared apartheid policies detrimental to the material and moral well-being of the inhabitants of the territory, the same argument would hold against South Africa, where identical policies were in place. A clear condemnation of its governmental policies could have led to a questioning of the legitimacy of the South African regime, as happened in the ensuing years when the South African regime became branded as "colonialism of a special kind."

4. For a criticism of the legal grounds for the revocation of the Mandate, see Marinus Wiechers, "South West Africa: The Background, Content, and Significance of the Opinion of the World Court of 21 June 1971," *South Africa Journal of Foreign and Comparative Law,* vol. 5 (1975), pp. 123–70.

5. SWAPO, although not exclusively Ovambo, draws its main support from that population group. The Ovambo, who constitute more than half of the Namibian population, live mainly in the northern part of the territory. The colonial border between South West Africa and Angola, as happened in many parts of Africa, divided the various Ovambo tribes, although their ethnic ties and sympathies remained. This explains why SWAPO could maintain its military operations on the northern borders for so many years: They were assured of the support of the local populations on both sides of the border. The Angolan government supported SWAPO from the outset. Jonas Savimbi's insurgency against the Angolan government made him a natural ally of the South African forces, and this alliance remained until the end of the struggle for independence. In South Africa, the border war was justified as a war against communist expansion; the Cuban presence lent credibility to this conviction. The restriction of the border war to the northern confines of the territory allowed political parties and groupings other than SWAPO to develop their constitutional experiences and political organization in a relatively peaceful manner.

6. In 1962, the South African government appointed a commission for South West Africa that recommended that the territory should be divided into homelands for the various ethnic groups and be governed on exactly the same apartheid lines as in South Africa. After that, the recommendations of the commission were vigorously applied in the territory.

7. The Turnhalle is an old historical building in Windhoek that was a gymnasium in German colonial times.

8. Chief Clemens Kapuuo was assassinated on March 27, 1978. To this day, his murder is unsolved. After independence, President Sam Njoma acknowledged Dirk Mudge, a white farmer and member of the ruling white legislative assembly, to have been one of two white leaders who contributed most to the peace process in Namibia. Mudge, a leading member of the ruling white Nationalist Party—in all respects an offspring of the ruling Nationalist Party in South Africa—realized that his party would never win broad support among the other population groups, and decided on March 18, 1977, to break away and form the Republican Party, founded on the express premise of joining the other ethnic parties and forming the Democratic Turnhalle Alliance (DTA). The breakaway by Mudge and his followers created deep animosities among the Afrikaner community; it is only recently, years after independence, that these rifts have closed. For an excellent account of the life and political career of Dirk Mudge, see At van Wyk, *Dirk Mudge Reënmaker van die Namib* (Pretoria: JL van Schaik Publishers, 1999) (in Afrikaans).

9. The making of the 1978 interim constitution adopted by the Turnhalle conference had a history of its own. At the end of 1977, deliberations in the conference did not go well, especially as a result of the formation of the DTA and the clash of opinions between Mudge and his followers on the one side and the members of the white legislative assembly on the other side. Members of other groups also increasingly felt that the conference was just a ploy of the white government to have a kind of homeland constitution adopted. To assuage feelings, the legal advisers were asked to find some common ground and to draw up a working document for further discussion. In December 1977, the legal advisers met in Pretoria and this author was asked to draw up such a working document. Instead, a draft interim constitution was drawn up and laid before the conference. The prompt drafting of an interim constitution aroused considerable emotions among the members of the ruling white party and the South African government, especially as the draft constitution proposed that South West

Africa's name should be changed to Namibia. In the minds of these members, the name Namibia was synonymous with UN interference and implied support for SWAPO, as during those years, the UN General Assembly (but not the Security Council), came to regard SWAPO as the "sole and true representatives of the people of Namibia." Eventually, the conflict was resolved when the conference opted for the name South West Africa/Namibia. This name remained until independence.

10. The elections, which gave the vote to all adult Namibians, were hurriedly organized without proper voter registration and other necessary safeguards. There is every reason to believe that the 78 percent was inflated and even manipulated. However, the elections were important in that influential religious leaders supported them and that all Namibians, for the first time in history, were given the opportunity to have a voice in their own destiny. The result was that the masses flocked to the voting polls notwithstanding the opposition by the United Nations and SWAPO.

11. For instance, the laws prohibiting mixed marriages and sexual relations between the races.

12. The dissolution of the interim government was a result of deep-seated differences between Dirk Mudge, the chairman of the interim cabinet, and the then–South African president P.W. Botha. Whereas Mudge wanted more autonomy for his interim government, Botha insisted on a definite entrenchment of the rights of the white population. In those years, especially with the rise of white right-wing opposition, Botha and his government were extremely wary of being seen to sell the white man out in South West Africa.

13. For a full account of the background, content, and application of the 1982 constitutional principles, see Marinus Wiechers, "Namibia: The 1982 Constitutional Principles and Their Legal Significance," *South African Yearbook of International Law*, vol. 15 (1989–90), pp. 1–21. Immediately after the elections, there were some misgivings among some of the internal political parties that the 1982 principles were not binding and constituted mere guidelines. The South African administrator-general tried to assuage these fears by incorporating the principles in his proclamation governing the constitution-making process. The UN special representative strongly opposed this, quite correctly contending that such an incorporation would have made the principles seem to be South African prescriptions, depriving them of their legitimacy. Fortunately, all doubt concerning the principles' binding

force was removed when the constituent assembly, at its first meeting, took it upon itself to adopt them.

14. That the South African parliament adopted the Recognition of the Independence of Namibia Act 34 of 1990 is proof, constitutionally speaking, of the evolutionary nature of Namibian independence and the transfer of sovereignty. In international law, transfer of sovereignty to an independent Namibia posed a problem. As a result of the revocation of the mandate in 1966, South Africa ceased to exercise legal authority over the territory. Thus, strictly speaking, South Africa's emancipatory power to confer sovereignty to an independent Namibia also ended. The United Nations also did not have such authority under its charter. This problem was solved by Resolution 435, under which it was agreed that South Africa's de facto administration of the territory would be recognized for the purpose of transferring sovereignty. However, it was also agreed that the Namibian constitution would not mention South Africa's bestowing of sovereignty and independence. Looking at the process from a constitutional law perspective, it can well be described as evolutionary rather than revolutionary.

15. Martii Ahtisaari, "Foreword," *South African Yearbook of International Law*, vol. 15 (1989–90), p. ix.

16. The administrator-general released all but sixteen political prisoners; after reconsideration by an independent arbiter, Professor Norgaard, another nine were released. See Gerhard Erasmus, "Namibian Independence and the Release of Political Prisoners," *South African Yearbook of International Law*, vol. 14 (1988–90), p. 137.

17. To quote Ahtisaari, "Foreword": "The Namibian exiles repatriated by the UN High Commissioner for Refugees were 43,332, and they came from forty countries of exile. The discriminatory laws repealed in whole or in part were fifty-six. The political prisoners released under the UN required amnesty were thirty."

18. Notably, the UN secretary-general, during his visit to Namibia in July 1989, negotiated a code of conduct for political parties that was adopted by the ten parties that registered for the election.

19. Bryan O'Linn, *Namibia: The Sacred Trust of Civilization, Ideal and Reality* (Gamsberg: Macmillan Press, 2004), p. 357.

20. The Lusaka Institute was a SWAPO research institute, predominantly funded by East European governments, which in the 1980s drew up political plans and formulated constitutional proposals for a postindependent Namibia. The institute also gathered and disseminated valuable information regarding exiles, political prisoners, and socio-economic conditions in Namibia generally.

21. For instance, in these original proposals, it was foreseen that political parties would have the authority to recall their disobedient members in the legislature. Such a proposal was dropped from the final SWAPO proposals.

22. On matters such as emergency powers as well as the powers of the executive, regional, and local governments, the SWAPO proposals were very cursory, no doubt because the proposals had to be produced in such a very short time.

23. Constituent Assembly Resolution of November 21, 1989.

24. The only members with serious misgivings about the SWAPO proposals and the decision to use them as a working document were the representatives of the two white minority parties. On the other hand, they realized that their objection would have no effect, as resolutions of the constituent assembly, in accordance with Resolution 435, were to be taken with a two-thirds majority.

25. In fact, on November 20, 1989, the Herero council issued a statement that it was not prepared to accept an Ovambo government.

26. Justice Chaskalson is one of South Africa's most prominent and respected lawyers; for years he excelled as a human rights lawyer and was a leader in the field of legal aid movements. He gained a reputation as one of the country's staunchest opponents of apartheid, and in the 1950s and 1960s was a legal counsel in the Mandela trials. In the 1993 Kempton Park conference for a new South Africa constitution, he played a leading role in the constitutional technical committee and later, after the first democratic elections in 1994, was appointed president of the first South African constitutional court. Professor Gerhard Erasmus, a native of South West Africa, was a well-known academic writer on matters of international law and also a known opponent to apartheid policies. This author's own involvement in Namibian politics went back to the Turnhalle conference and the ensuing political and constitutional development within Namibia. In South Africa, I had the reputation of being a constitutional activist and, although I was mainly involved in governmental and other informal processes, my personal conviction, during those years, was that constitution making on various levels could break up monolithic apartheid structures. For this reason, I drafted constitutions for the independent homelands of Bophuthatswana and Ciskei, each with

their own justiciable bills of rights. During my years of active participation, I drew up several charters of human rights for implementation by the business communities and other organizations. During these years, I also had frequent informal contact with SWAPO and ANC leaders; because I was a teacher of constitutional law at the University of South Africa, the world's pioneering university for distance teaching, it happened that SWAPO and ANC leaders in exile or prison knew my writings and teachings, as many of them, including Nelson Mandela, were my students.

27. It was rumored at that time that some members of the constituent assembly felt that the panel of drafters, in drafting a complete constitution, went beyond the limits of their mandate. This author, however, could never discover the grounds for their objections. It is presumed that some members—especially those of the minority opposition parties who previously had positions of power and influence—hoped that the constitution-making process would take much longer so that they could settle their affairs under the existing regime. The promptness with which the panel of drafters presented them with a fully-fledged constitutional draft certainly took them by surprise.

28. During its first meeting in November 1989, the constituent assembly resolved to have the constitution adopted by a two-thirds majority. However, since complete consensus was reached, applying this resolution became unnecessary.

29. This was most remarkable, as at the committee table were members who suffered personally under apartheid, and also opposition members who as former dissidents of SWAPO in previous years suffered severely in SWAPO punishment camps. It was also most encouraging that the apprehensions of the representative of the white minority party were addressed sympathetically and with understanding.

30. Differences and serious clashes of opinion were often diverted to the panel of drafters by blaming them for not having considered all aspects of a particular matter sufficiently. It was sometimes jokingly said that the lack of wisdom on the part of the "men from heaven" was perhaps proof that they were not from heaven, but from the other place. The drafters understood this as a necessary diversion to avoid open conflict or acrimony. At the close of deliberations, the drafters received effusive praise and words of thanks from all members.

31. Close scrutiny of the constitution reveals many idiosyncrasies on the part of individual members. For instance, Article 10(2) reads: "No persons may be discriminated against on the grounds of *sex,* race, colour, ethnic origin, religion, creed or social or economic status." Discrimination on the ground of sex was mentioned first and foremost because the only woman member of the committee felt strongly that discrimination on the ground of sex was worse than any other kind of discrimination. The other members of the committee, all males, agreed. In the committee, individual personalities were significant, and again, it was Dirk Mudge who gave direction and guidance in many respects. It was clear that no proposal would get full support, not even among all SWAPO members, if Mudge himself did not support it.

32. S/20967/add 2. SC Document.

33. It was considered inappropriate and politically incorrect that the new president should be sworn in by the South African head of state, as such an act would have created the impression that Namibia was a former colony of South Africa.

34. The 1968 constitution was also an act of defiance in the face of the UN General Assembly, which unilaterally revoked the mandate in 1966.

35. The elections for homeland governments were poorly supported, especially when resistance to the application of these South African apartheid policies grew. The political formations that participated in these homeland elections were generally very rudimentary and, for the most part, organized and funded by the South African government in Pretoria.

36. In those earlier years, the Herero regularly petitioned the Mandate Commission and later the UN General Assembly; this practice led the General Assembly to seek a World Court opinion in 1956.

37. The fact that chief Kapuuo was prepared to participate in the Turnhalle Constitutional Conference was of tremendous importance and was, to a large extent, the result of the personal friendship and trust between him and Dirk Mudge. To this day, Mudge is still regarded by members of the traditional Herero Council as "the brother of chief Kapuuo."

38. SWAPO was founded in Cape Town in 1960. The founding leaders were Herman Toivo ya Toivo, who, following many years of incarceration, became a member of the Namibian cabinet after independence; Murumba Kerina, who returned to Namibia from exile in the 1970s by invitation of the South African government, founded his own political party, and won a seat in the Namibian national assembly; and Sam Njoma, who was in exile from the 1960s to 1989 and was elected by the assembly as Namibia's first head of state.

39. There are eleven ethnic groups in Namibia: the Ovambo, Kovango, Caprivians, Hereros, Damara, Tswana, Nama, Coloureds, the Basters (a small group of mixed European and indigenous origin), the Bushmen, and the Whites. Being such a small population, Namibians were familiar with the leadership of the various groups. It was amazing at the time of constitution making how well those leaders knew each other, even though some of them spent years in exile.

40. Whites in Namibia became greatly attached to their new country over the years, which explains why, after independence, there was no significant exodus of whites from the country. Moreover, many of the white leaders, especially those who joined the DTA, regarded themselves as very much part of the independence processes. This, however, does not deny that for many years, the majority of whites in Namibia strongly supported the National Party of South Africa and were loyal members of the National Party of South West Africa, which was in all respects a daughter party of the South African party. This also explains why the rift in the party that occurred when the DTA was formed was such a traumatic and bitter experience for many whites.

41. As a result of South Africa's war efforts on the northern borders, the transport and communication systems in the northern outreaches became very advanced. This factor, namely the development of an excellent infrastructure, served the election campaigns and eventual peace processes admirably and was crucial to UNTAG's peacekeeping task.

42. Except for the Herero, chief Kapuuo, in the beginning, was rather distrustful and appointed two American lawyers, but as all the proceedings of the Turnhalle conference were conducted in Afrikaans, the lawyers found it very difficult to follow the process. Eventually, Fanuel Kosanguisi, a returned Herero exile and London barrister, became the Hereros' adviser. After independence, he was appointed as the country's first ombudsman.

43. The constitutional advisers were handsomely rewarded for their services by the South African government, through the various ethnic authorities. This author was an exception: When it soon became apparent that the Damara and Tswana were to take up an independent line of thinking, the South African government refused any kind of remuneration or payment for expenses on the pretext that the appointment had not been ratified by any ethnic authority. Private funding for expenses was arranged. This is mentioned to demonstrate concretely that not all the conference participants were paid puppets of the South African government, as SWAPO averred in the years to come.

44. The direct inspiration for this political move was the 1974 report of the special UN delegate, Dr. Esscher, and his recommendation that future independence of the territory should be worked out by the people themselves in the exercise of their right to self-determination. See O'Linn, *Namibia*, p. 82. The South African government always insisted that their apartheid and homeland policies were intended to afford other ethnic groups the opportunity to give effect to their right to self-determination.

45. When open conflict between members occurred and it seemed that the conference itself was in jeopardy, recourse would be had to prayer. After praying, members were more pacified and the debate could continue on a more conciliatory note. Traditionally in Namibia, all official meetings as well as party political rallies, gatherings, and proceedings were opened by prayer. The Namibian population is overwhelmingly Christian, and the churches wielded much influence in political affairs, with church leaders often assuming party political roles. Pastor Cornelis Njoba, who was assassinated in 1985, was president of the DTA.

46. Bushmen members of the DTA remained in politics, and two of them eventually became members of the independent Namibian legislature. The history of the Bushmen's role in the Namibian constitutional process proves how strongly emancipating the experience of participation in constitution making can be on a human level.

47. This author became a regular writer of articles on constitutional issues in the local press and addressed numerous church, school, business, and agricultural associations. Speeches written by this author for many of the DTA leaders concentrated on constitutional matters as central themes. At the initial report-back meetings of the Turnhalle conference and later, after the formation of the DTA when it became engaged in various election campaigns, this author accompanied political campaigners, often to the remotest parts of the country, to give addresses on the constitution and constitutional issues.

48. The exact wording of these instructions read as follows:

The Constitution will be the supreme law of the state. It may be amended only by a designated process involving the legislature and/or votes cast in a popular referendum.

The Constitution will determine the organization and powers of all levels of government. It will provide for a system of government with three branches: a legislative branch to be elected by universal and equal suffrage which will be responsible for the passage of all laws; and an independent judicial branch which will be responsible for the interpretation of the Constitution and for ensuring its supremacy and the authority of the law. The executive and legislative branches will be constituted by periodic and genuine elections which will be held by secret vote.

The electoral system will seek to ensure fair representation in the Constituent Assembly to different political parties which gain substantial support in the election.

There will be a declaration of fundamental rights, which will include the rights to life, personal liberty and freedom of movement; to freedom of conscience; to freedom of expression, including freedom of speech and a free press; to freedom of assembly and association, including political parties and trade unions; to due process and equality before the law; to protection of arbitrary deprivation of property or deprivation of private property without just compensation; and to freedom from racial, ethnic, religious or sexual discrimination. The declaration of rights will be consistent with the provisions of the Universal Declaration of Human Rights. Aggrieved individuals will be entitled to have the courts adjudicate and enforce these rights.

It will be forbidden to create criminal offences with retrospective effect or to provide for increased penalties with retrospective effect.

Provision will be made for the balanced structuring of the public service, the police service and defence services and for equal access by all to recruitment of these services. The fair administration of personnel policy in relation to these services will be assured by appropriate independent bodies.

Provision will be made for the establishment of elected councils for local and/or regional administration (S/15287).

49. In the 1989 elections, the old National Party was renamed Action Christian National, which then belatedly and without any real success preached alliance politics with other parties and groups.

50. This is in essence the integrating and emancipating force of a bill of rights, namely that it not only empowers every individual against state authority and power but also integrates individuals into the operation and application of the constitution, as the constitution finally ensures that the bill of rights is safeguarded. The protection that a future bill of rights would afford to them convinced the former National Party members of the constitutional assembly to vote for adopting the constitution, notwithstanding the severe reservations they had in many other respects. As it turned out, these very same members, after independence, fulfilled valuable roles as part of the opposition to the government, and were—and still are—held in high government and public regard.

51. Immediately after the elections, there were rumors of malpractices and election fraud. This was to be expected, as the elections evoked much fervor and raised many expectations. However, the special representative's certification ended these rumors, and during the process of actual constitution making, the distribution of power among the parties that resulted from the elections was never contested.

52. See Ahtisaari, "Foreword," p. xi: "As for South-African co-operation, mutual suspicion was prevalent at the beginning, but there was a steady relaxation, especially, I believe, as the objectivity and professionalism of UNTAG became accepted. At a number of levels, the co-operation was excellent."

53. Art. 145(2) of the constitution.

54. For instance, Captain Hendrik Witbooi of the Namas was vice-president of SWAPO, and both the later prime minister (Mr. Geingob) and minister of foreign affairs (Mr. Ben-Guriab) were Damara.

55. In a real sense, this is what happened in the South African constitution-making process when the right-wing white parties and Zulu-based Inkatha Freedom Party initially refused to join or later threatened to withdraw from the process.

56. South Africa, perhaps justifiably, maintained that Walvis Bay was never included in the mandated territory and therefore fell outside UN jurisdiction. The constitution, in a sense, preempted the whole matter, including in art. 1(4) the Walvis Bay enclave in its identification of Namibian state territory. After independence, South Africa and Namibia, through agreement and international convention, settled the matter and the Walvis Bay enclave was incorporated into Namibia.

57. Art. 144 of the constitution, therefore, does away with the requirement of express incorporation by act of parliament. See Gerhard Erasmus, "The Namibian Constitution and the Application of International Law," *South African Yearbook of International Law,* vol. 15 (1989–90), p. 90.

58. See Wiechers, "Namibia," p. 17.

59. This clear breach of the constitution was justified on the ground that the president's first election was not by direct popular suffrage, but by the new national assembly, whereas the constitution prescribed two terms of office by virtue of direct, popular suffrage. This clearly goes against the original intent. Surely, a presidential term of office is a term of office, notwithstanding the method of election.

60. O'Linn, *Namibia,* p. 390.

5

Creating the Birth Certificate of a New South Africa

Constitution Making after Apartheid[1]

Hassen Ebrahim and Laurel E. Miller

South Africa's first democratic constitution came into effect on February 4, 1997, bringing to a close a long series of events that defined the country's astonishing transition from oppressive minority rule and violent civil conflict to nonracial democracy. This constitution—the result of negotiations among political enemies at war not long before they joined together to chart the country's future—is both the symbol of South Africa's seemingly miraculous transformation and the anchor of its new order.

Albie Sachs, a justice of South Africa's first constitutional court, eloquently summarized the immensity of the challenge facing the country's constitution makers in looking back at the start of preliminary talks in 1990:

> [South Africa] at that time was the epitome of division, repression, and injustice, a point of reference for anybody who wanted to condemn anything in the world. . . . It was a country that sent death squads across its borders to hurt and to torture people to death and that had an organized system of repression that extended into every village and into every nook and cranny

of society. It was a country that was racist, authoritarian, and narrow. This very South Africa had to be converted into a country—with the same people, the same physical terrain, the same resources, and the same buildings—into a country that was democratic and respected human rights. It had to be a country where people of widely different backgrounds would respect each other, where everybody could live in dignity, and where social peace prevailed. This was not a small task.[2]

The task also was not sure to be accomplished. The issues facing the constitution makers were extremely complex, the stakes were high for both the privileged minority and the disenfranchised majority, and the parties' positions had been hardened by years of conflict. Not surprisingly, both the basic principles for the foundation of a transformed democratic state, as well as the process for translating those principles into a final, fully ratified constitution, were highly contested.[3]

Nevertheless, despite tremendous obstacles, the parties found enough common ground to enable them to agree on a new constitution—

one that is widely regarded as being among the most substantively advanced constitutions in the world.[4] Remarkably, South Africa also has become the paradigm for a well-designed, successful constitution-making process intended to facilitate national dialogue and reconciliation and largely accomplishing these objectives. The South African process has become the reference point for many subsequent constitution-making exercises and has undergone extensive evaluation by constitutional scholars and practitioners.[5]

An examination of the South African experience is essential to a study of the significance of the process of constitution making, in part because an unusual degree of attention was paid to the process's design, and because the leading participants explicitly recognized the importance of process to a successful constitution-making exercise. The constitution makers saw a link between the nature of the process and the legitimacy of the outcome, and perceived that, at least for the final constitution, circumstances in South Africa demanded a transparent, inclusive, and participatory process. The emphasis on process was at least partly due to a typically South African obsession with consultation; South Africans tend to be suspicious of any process about which they have not been consulted. Consensus on the precise design of the process was not easily achieved, however. The history of the negotiations reveals that more time and energy were spent on negotiating the process of arriving at the final constitution than on negotiating the substance of it. Moreover, the most vigorous oppositions, disruptions, and disturbances took place in support of process-related demands.

The story of the South African constitution-making process cannot be separated from the larger story of the negotiated transition to democracy. Constitutional issues were integral to the set of substantive issues on the agenda in the transition negotiations, and indeed, the question how a new constitution would be crafted and adopted was a principal item of debate. Moreover, the package of agreements produced by the multiparty transition negotiations included the first post-apartheid constitution: the interim constitution of 1993, which both prefigured much of the substance of the final constitution and defined the process for creating it.

Thus, while this chapter focuses mostly on the final constitution-making process, conducted by an elected constitutional assembly, it begins by looking at the historical context from which the transition process emerged and the transition negotiations themselves.[6] The seminal agreement concerning the architecture of the transition was that it would proceed in two stages: first, closed-door negotiations, in which all participating parties ostensibly would have an equal voice, would produce an interim constitution and arrangements for a transitional government of national unity; and second, an elected, proportionally representative body would create and adopt a final constitution. A feature of this design that was critical to drawing a wide range of parties into the process was the incorporation in the negotiated interim constitution of binding principles that would fetter the discretion of the democratically elected constitution-making body. This chapter discusses each of these architectural elements: the two-stage approach, the role of the interim constitution, and the use of constitutional principles. It then turns to a detailed discussion of the work of the constitutional assembly in drafting and adopting the final constitution, and the extensive and (from a comparative perspective) pathbreaking public consultation process undertaken by the assembly. The unique role of the constitutional court in certifying the final document's compliance with the constitutional principles, as required by the interim constitution, is then explored, as is the limited contribution of international players to the constitution-making process. The chapter concludes by assessing the ways in which the constitution-making process can be regarded as a success, and the factors that contributed to that outcome.

Background and Early Stages of Negotiation

Historical Context

The demand for a democratic constitutional dispensation, finally met with the adoption of the new constitution in 1996, was as old as South Africa itself. Many of the constitution's provisions were the result of years of struggle and are imbued with historical significance. The first South African constitution—made by a whites-only national convention and then approved by the British parliament—took effect in 1910, and its legal entrenchment of racialism catalyzed the unification of black leadership and helped to shape the struggle of the majority for a system free of discrimination. The birth of the African National Congress (ANC) in 1912 provided the African majority with a united leadership that articulated their plight and led their resistance, but more important, it offered a vision of a better life.[7] Almost invariably, the Africans' struggles were against a constitutional dispensation that provided the legal basis for their oppression. Accordingly, their vision included a just and democratic constitutional order.

Throughout the first half of the twentieth century, nationalism rose on both sides of the racial divide. Along with industrialization and the development of the economy in this period came urbanization, greater segregationist laws, and a growing militancy among workers. In August 1941, Franklin D. Roosevelt and Winston Churchill signed the Atlantic Charter, containing eight principles that included self-government and freedom from fear and want. These principles inspired the emerging African nationalists of South Africa, for they raised the issue of basic rights

and the idea of self-determination in particular. Drawing from the Atlantic Charter, the ANC drafted its own African Claims, which demanded full citizenship, the right to land, and an end to all discriminatory legislation. This was the first time that the concepts of fundamental rights and self-determination became demands. In 1948, however, the National Party (NP) came to power, introduced the policy of apartheid, and enacted notoriously discriminatory laws.[8] Apartheid provoked resistance. In response to these laws, the African, colored,[9] and Indian peoples of South Africa found cause to unite in action and launched a defiance campaign in 1952.

By 1955, the historical antecedents of the constitution-making process that was to unfold at the end of the century had already emerged: the Congress of the People took place in that year, a meeting to which all political parties were invited. After nationwide consultation, several thousand delegates met in Johannesburg to draft the Freedom Charter, which was, in effect, the first draft of a new constitution for South Africa.[10] The political movement of the oppressed majority was maturing, and the charter it produced sketched a vision of the country's political landscape that was to become deeply etched in the thinking of several generations of leaders. Moreover, consultation and participation were already hallmarks of the movement's style.[11]

The vision of a democratic constitution as a vehicle for solving the problems of deep inequality and rising violence, as well as the touchstone for a new political order, thus developed long before the first tentative steps toward a negotiated transition in the mid-1980s. In 1961, the All-in Conference explicitly called for a national convention of elected representatives to adopt a new, nonracial democratic constitution for South Africa. The conference, which was attended by 1,400 delegates from all over the country, representing 150 different religious, social, cultural, and political bodies, directed ANC leader Nelson Mandela to draw Prime Minister Hendrik Verwoerd's attention to its resolution. In a letter to the prime minister, Mandela referred to the rising tide of unrest in many parts of the country, stating that "it was the earnest opinion of Conference that this dangerous situation could be averted only by the calling of a sovereign national convention representative of all South Africans, to draw up a new non-racial and democratic Constitution."[12] In a letter to the leader of the parliamentary opposition, Mandela stated, "the alternatives appear to be these: talk it out, or shoot it out."[13]

Instead of heeding the call of the All-in Conference, the government banned the ANC and other organizations, leaving the majority of the population with no legal avenue to pursue its interests. By 1964, most of the ANC's leaders, including Mandela, were in jail, and others had fled into exile. As the ANC transformed from a nonviolent African nationalist organization into a revolutionary liberation movement, the country slid into thirty years of armed conflict.

By the late 1970s, with mounting resistance and increasing international condemnation of apartheid, the government was obliged to show some willingness to reform. Upon coming to power in 1978, Pieter Willem Botha—first as prime minister and later as president—began reorganizing the state. One of the significant developments at this time was the creation of a new government entity, the Department of Constitutional Development and Planning, mandated to introduce reforms while the security establishment took over the major strategic decision-making responsibilities of the state. Botha's strategy included, on one hand, modest constitutional reform intended to co-opt elements of the opposition, and, on the other, stepped-up repression to fend off real change. In 1983, the constitution was changed to divide the parliament into three houses: the white House of Assembly, the colored House of Representatives, and the Indian House of Delegates; blacks were excluded. At the same time, the NP began to focus on cleavages that could be exploited within the black community. The reform packages of the 1980s aimed to create a small privileged African elite that could act as a buffer against the majority of black South Africans.

The "reform and repression" strategy had only limited success.[14] Armed resistance intensified, and by 1984, armed actions had risen to an average of fifty operations per year. In 1985, the ANC first deployed land mines and began to develop a presence in rural areas. As alternative township structures, street committees, and people's courts began functioning in many areas, the state struggled to govern much of the country. From 1986 onward, the number of attacks rose to between 250 and 300 per year.

The Negotiated Transition

Beginning the Search for Constitutional Solutions

It was against this background that in 1985 Nelson Mandela, imprisoned since 1962, initiated the first secret exploratory discussions in the search for a negotiated solution with representatives of P.W. Botha's government. Botha had begun to realize that the crisis in South Africa was becoming unmanageable and that drastic political changes would have to be made, including constitutional changes. Botha's government floated constitutional proposals intended to resolve the crisis on its own terms and in cooperation with black leaders of its own choosing, but these went nowhere. Botha was not bold enough to launch genuine negotiations with representatives of the black majority, though following four years of secret talks between Mandela and other officials, Botha did meet directly, albeit inconclusively, with Mandela in July 1989.[15]

The environment for serious talks began to ripen when Frederik Willem de Klerk assumed the presidency in 1989. Soon after taking over, de Klerk committed himself to seeking a new constitution that would eliminate the domination of any one group by another. He recognized the need for inclusive negotiation among political party leaders, but—illustrating how far his party had yet to go—he remained implacably opposed to a one-person one-vote system, which, he argued, would lead to domination by the majority. In the last whites-only general election of September 1989, voters gave de Klerk's government a mandate to proceed with new constitutional proposals. The demand for constitutional negotiations was developing momentum, spurred in part by contemporary events in eastern Europe surrounding the collapse of communism. At the same time, the Department of Constitutional Development and Planning began looking at various constitutional models, and all major government speeches now spoke of a "new South Africa."

The accumulated pressure of South Africa's political crisis, right-wing resistance, economic concerns, the changing political situation in eastern Europe, and the international community's demands for change led de Klerk to the inescapable conclusion that clinging to power would only lead to increasingly bloody conflict. While the liberation movements could not defeat the government by armed force, the government also could not continue to govern as it had.[16] Thus, in November 1989, de Klerk called for an accord among all peoples of the country that would offer full political rights to everyone. The government had no choice but to accede to the demand to create a climate conducive to negotiation. Momentum toward a constitutional negotiation was further intensified by the Conference for a Democratic Future in December 1989, organized by the Mass Democratic Movement and attended by more than 6,000 delegates representing 2,000 organizations throughout the country.

Meanwhile, the secret talks to explore the feasibility of negotiation that Mandela had initiated in 1985 continued, through as many as forty-seven meetings between Mandela and government leaders.[17] These meetings allowed both sides to see that the option of negotiation was real and could offer both the opportunity to realize their objectives. But as there was no guarantee of the outcome of the discussions, both sides saw secrecy as necessary to ensure that the talks did not appear as a sign of weakness.

Under Oliver Tambo's leadership in exile, the ANC sought to prepare itself for negotiation by successfully lobbying African governments in 1989 to adopt the Harare Declaration of the Organization of African Unity.[18] Tambo was keen to seize the initiative, for he knew that if the ANC did not, the international community would, and the ANC would lose control of the negotiating agenda. The Harare Declaration contained the first real vision of a transition to democracy. It called for creating a climate for negotiations by, among other things, lifting the state of emergency, releasing political prisoners, lifting the bans on organizations, and repealing repressive legislation. Once a conducive climate was created, the representatives of all parties could negotiate a new constitution.

In October 1989, the government unconditionally released an initial group of political prisoners—the first tangible result of Mandela's endeavors. The following month, Mandela met with de Klerk, who had recently taken office, and the government publicly reported the meeting. The pace of change, particularly in the government's posture, quickened from there, and 1990 opened with high expectations. A major milestone of the entire transition process was reached at the opening of parliament on February 2, 1990, when de Klerk made a dramatic speech—his so-called crossing the Rubicon speech—announcing the unbanning of liberation movements, the release of political prisoners, and a series of measures intended to address obstacles to the process of negotiation.[19] By positively responding to a number of the demands in the Harare Declaration, and going further than any other minority party leader had ever been prepared to go, de Klerk signaled his commitment to negotiate and established his bona fides. Mandela was released the following week.

Talks about Talks

Though the stage was set, the process of creating the conditions for substantive negotiations was lengthy; the parties entered into so-called talks about talks that lasted throughout 1990 and 1991. Political violence flared up regularly throughout this period of both hope and uncertainty, and the talks proceeded in fits and starts, with Mandela and de Klerk often needing to meet to put negotiations back on track. Both sides courted international opinion and support. De Klerk lobbied for lifting trade restrictions on the basis of the reforms and policy shifts instituted thus far, while Mandela urged countries to maintain sanctions until there was proof that the process of transformation was irreversible. But progress was made. The formal agreements reached in this phase—including the Groote Schuur Minute, the Pretoria Minute, and the D.F. Malan Accord—were the first to be signed by the government and the ANC. Mistrust remained high at this stage, however, and support for the process was not unanimous on either side.

The breakthrough agreements reached in this period, and the repeals of discriminatory legislation that followed, constituted a step-by-step dismantling of apartheid and lifting of repressive measures. In addition, the agreements addressed the release of political prisoners, return of exiles, and immunity from prosecution for political offenses. For its part, the ANC agreed to suspend armed struggle. The agreements were not always implemented smoothly and quickly, but they cleared the way for constitutional negotiations by removing obstacles, and the personal contacts among former enemies that produced them had a tremendous confidence-building effect.

Nonetheless, vigorous debate arose over the central procedural issues concerning how a new constitution would be created, including whether an interim government was necessary to oversee an election before the drafting of a constitution, and whether the new constitution should be drafted by a constituent assembly. While these questions would not be resolved for some time, the battle lines had already been drawn. The NP view was that the present government should remain in place while political parties negotiated a constitutional pact, which would then be brought into effect by the white-dominated parliament. The ANC insisted that a new constitution be drafted by an elected body after the installation of an interim government. (In the end, as discussed below, the making of the interim constitution looked much like the process the NP proposed, while the making of the final constitution followed closely the ANC's preferred model.)

The challenge of dealing with potential spoilers, which dogged the negotiations until the final constitution was adopted, was already evident in the early stages. On the right, the Conservative Party, and on the left, the Pan Africanist Congress (PAC) and Azanian Peoples Organization, a radical liberation movement, rejected agreements reached by the ANC and NP. More concerning, Mangosuthu Buthelezi, the leader of the Inkatha Freedom Party (IFP), threatened that the escalating violence would not end until there was agreement between himself and Mandela; it seemed he felt that he was not being respected as a key player.[20] Mandela met with Buthelezi in early 1991, but IFP disruptions and on-again, off-again boycotts continued throughout the process, despite repeated ANC and NP attempts to bring the party along.

By February 1991, formal talks had successfully removed obstacles to multiparty negotiations, but a further ten months of preparation followed before substantive negotiations finally commenced. The major stakeholders used the time to develop their negotiating positions, and as the ANC, NP, and Democratic Party unveiled constitutional proposals, it became apparent that some convergence was developing among the different parties' perspectives. This marked a historic shift in the country's politics, from conflict among competing forces to competing constitutional visions. But at the same time, the parties faced threats to and delays in the negotiating process emanating from the unrelenting spiral of violence, as well as complications caused by the government's effort to be both negotiating participant and process referee. These difficulties reinforced ANC insistence on an interim government as part of the transitional arrangements. In addition, major disagreement remained over questions concerning the process that would lead to a new constitutional order, particularly who would manage the transitional period and how. These questions of process and the framework for a transition—including whether an interim authority should be elected, what power it should have, and within what constitutional framework it should operate—dominated the agenda during the next phase of negotiation.

CODESA I and II

The first attempt at multiparty transition negotiations, the Convention for a Democratic South Africa (CODESA), was ultimately a failed one, but it produced progress on some substantive issues, as parties on both sides gradually shifted their positions, and it of-fered procedural lessons for the successful effort that followed. Nineteen organizations and political parties plus the government, in a delegation separate from the NP, attended the first plenary (CODESA I), which convened in late December 1991. The agenda included, among other issues, general constitutional principles, a constitution-making body or process, and transitional arrangements.

On the procedure for making decisions, the forum agreed that where consensus failed, a principle of so-called sufficient consensus would be applied, a rule that carried over into subsequent negotiations. This approach proved to be controversial yet useful. Because parties were not mandated by an electorate and the process was designed to be as inclusive as possible—no matter how small a party may have been—it was agreed in principle that no decision would be made on any matter unless the government and the ANC, at the very least, agreed. This implied, however, that agreement by the ANC and government alone would not be enough for a decision to be made. The IFP felt so aggrieved by this procedure that the party challenged it in court; the Supreme Court ruled against its claim that all decisions arrived at on the basis of sufficient consensus be invalidated.

CODESA I adopted a declaration of intent that firmly committed all parties to the basic principles of genuine, nonracial, multiparty democracy, in which the constitution was supreme and regular elections were guaranteed. In the South African context, the statement was revolutionary, in a sense representing the preamble to the first democratic constitution.[21] The first plenary also established five working groups[22] and a management committee—a steering committee and full-time secretariat had already been created in preparation for the plenary—and resolved that the second plenary session, CODESA II, would take place in March 1992 (this was later postponed).

The negotiating structure was large and complex. Each party was entitled to two delegates and two advisers in each working group and one delegate and one adviser each in the management committee. Also, a daily management committee and a secretariat were mandated to assist the management committee and ensure implementation of its decisions. In all, CODESA involved more than 400 negotiators representing nineteen parties, administrations, organizations, and governments. Each working group had a steering committee that attended to its agenda and program of work. Also, each working group tabled its reports through its steering committee and was directly accountable to the management committee. Agreements concluded in this manner were then to be tabled at the CODESA plenary for approval and ratification. It became apparent, in hindsight, that this structure was flawed in several respects: There were no technical bodies to provide legal and constitutional advice, each party had to include its own technical experts in its delegation of advisers, the working groups were large and therefore cumbersome, and the negotiations occurred behind closed doors. The five working groups commenced discussions in January 1992, and CODESA soon became the most important locus of the country's political activity. The public was invited to submit views on constitutional proposals at this stage, but CODESA made little attempt either to educate the public about its work or to solicit seriously the views of important interest groups.[23]

In March 1992, the government held an all-white referendum to confirm the support of the white electorate for the negotiating process. The ANC opposed the referendum, but supported the CODESA management committee's decision to call on whites to take part and vote affirmatively.[24] The result was an overwhelming victory for the NP[25] and confirmation that the majority of white people favored a negotiated settlement. The result had the unfortunate consequence, however, of encouraging the NP to overplay its hand and hold back on some necessary compromises.

At the same time, progress stalled in the CODESA working groups, as tensions developed over a number of issues related to leveling the playing field for elections as well as determining the shape and role of an interim government. In addition, continuing countrywide violence dampened the climate for political activity. The ANC's proposals in February 1992 for interim constitutional arrangements and a final constitution-making process resembled in many respects the result finally agreed upon twenty-one months later, but lengthy negotiations still were required to reach that end and fill in all the necessary details. Bilateral meetings between the ANC and NP were stepped up, and an eleven-member technical committee was established to push the CODESA process forward.

Once substantive agreements on some fronts concerning the interim government and the nature of the constitution-making body were achieved, the management committee set a date in May 1992 for the second plenary, CODESA II, to pressure the parties to wrap up other matters. The period leading up to CODESA II saw a cycle of deadlocks followed by breakthroughs followed by new deadlocks. With a mixture of tension and anticipation—and tremendous public and media attention—the two-day meeting went forward, but quickly reached an impasse on issues concerning the final constitution-making process, in particular the required majority for the constituent assembly to adopt the constitution. CODESA II adjourned without ratifying any agreements, but with the expectation of a further plenary.

The Multiparty Negotiating Process

After the failure of CODESA, the parties spent the better part of a year negotiating an end to the deadlock and preparing the ground for a new round of multiparty talks. The months following CODESA were tumultuous. A massacre of forty persons prompted the ANC to break off all talks for a time,[26] and business and international interests applied pressure to put the talks back on track. This was followed by bilateral efforts to find compromises and, in August 1992, the biggest mass protests seen in the country since the 1950s. The latter mobilized the black population around the ANC's demands. At the same time, the ANC mandated Cyril Ramaphosa (later the chairperson of the constitutional assembly) and the NP mandated Roelf Meyer to establish a channel of communication with the purpose of maintaining some form of dialogue. In what came to be known as the channel bilateral, these two continued to serve as key interlocutors for the two sides through the end of the constitution-making process, even talking behind the scenes during periods in which talks were suspended.[27]

The deteriorating security climate and tumbling economy motivated the negotiators to move forward. The channel bilateral produced results, and, after last-minute bargaining between the two leaders, Mandela and de Klerk met in September 1992 to sign the Record of Understanding. This agreement, which represented a turning point in the negotiations, addressed major areas of deadlock and laid the foundation for restarting multiparty talks.[28] It also established important principles concerning constitutional arrangements, discussed further below.

The following month, the ANC adopted a position paper titled "Strategic Perspectives" that guided its negotiating strategy. The document laid out proposed phases to attain majority rule that ultimately came to be agreed upon and implemented: the establishment of a transitional executive council, the election of a constituent assembly, the establishment of an interim government of national unity, the drafting and adoption of the new constitution, the phasing-in of the new constitution, and the period of consolidation of the new democracy.

To prepare for the resumption of talks, ANC and NP negotiators held a private meeting over several days at a nature reserve. In the two years since the ANC had been unbanned, this was the first opportunity that these individuals had to interact on a social level, and the rapport they developed later proved invaluable. In further bilateral meetings, the two parties resolved many outstanding issues, putting them in a good position to jointly drive multiparty negotiations forward.

The next round of formal multiparty talks—named the Negotiation Planning Conference—convened at the beginning of March 1993. To set parties on an equal footing, the conference was called on the basis of each party inviting one another. This two-day meeting called for negotiations to resume and resolved that a new forum—the Multi-party Negotiating Process (MPNP)—would begin meeting the next month. Establishing a new forum, involving twenty-six participating parties and organizations, enabled the parties to create a more efficient structure than CODESA and to look for ways to accommodate right-wing objections to CODESA.

The MPNP structure was more efficient than CODESA because, instead of negotiating issues in different working groups, a single negotiating council, composed of four delegates and two advisers per party, became the effective bargaining forum. Compared to the fragmented negotiations in CODESA's five working groups, this was an important improvement that contributed to the MPNP's better result.[29] The negotiating council initially reported to a negotiating forum, but this soon fell away, and all agreements reached in the council were ratified by the plenary, composed of ten delegates per party. Due to concern regarding the lack of female participants at CODESA, each party was required to have at least one female delegate at every level.[30]

Another innovation was the establishment of five- to six-member technical committees, consisting of experts who had the confidence of the major parties, but who were not political party representatives.[31] In addition, instead of orally presenting their views in the negotiating council, parties made written submissions that were considered by the technical committees. This was a major improvement because these committees' reports accounted for everyone's views and the committees could serve as compromise-seeking and deadlock-breaking mechanisms. A ten-person planning committee played the same role as CODESA's management committee, and a subcommittee to the planning committee acted as secretariat. To deal with specialized issues, the council established two nonpartisan commissions to deal with demarcation of regions and with national symbols.

Despite the process's sound footing, circumstances were to severely test the parties' commitment to negotiation. On April 10, 1993, Chris Hani, one of the ANC's most popular leaders and general secretary of the Communist Party, was assassinated by a Polish immigrant with right-wing ties. This event prompted a violent backlash, a national strike involving 90 percent of the workforce, and further deepening of the economic crisis. An appeal for calm by Mandela, broadcast live on television on the night of Hani's murder, averted a national crisis.[32] In response to the demonstration of impatience unleashed by the assassination, the ANC and its allies resolved to speed up the negotiating process and to seek early announcement of an election date and other concrete measures. The NP, too, saw a need to instill the process with a new sense of urgency. Two immediate measures were thus agreed: a date for the country's first nonracial democratic election—and therefore a deadline for the conclusion of multiparty talks[33]—and the establishment of the transitional executive council.

With the same types of setbacks[34] and breakthroughs that had characterized the negotiating process until this point, the MPNP then proceeded over the subsequent months to agree, before the end of 1993, on an interim constitution and the terms of a final constitution-making process. The MPNP's role in producing these results is considered further below in the discussion of the interim constitution.

The Constitution-Making Process

Overview of the Structure of the Process

The principal structural feature of the South African constitution-making process was its division into two phases. This division concretized a fundamental compromise between those who sought a swift transition to majority rule and those who sought to preserve some governmental influence and group privileges for the constituencies of the ancien régime.[35]

The first phase involved the adoption of the interim constitution, negotiated and agreed by the participants in the MPNP March to November 1993. The negotiations took place in a roundtable format and produced a pact among the key political parties that was then enacted by the last apartheid-era parliament. The interim constitution provided a framework for governing South Africa until the adoption of the final constitution, specified the process for writing the final document, and imposed certain substantive requirements for that document by including thirty-four "constitutional principles." A new constitutional court was created as well, which, in addition to being assigned the usual duties of such a body, was tapped to be the guarantor of the principles; it would have to certify that the final constitution complied with the principles for the constitution to come into effect.

In the second phase, a democratically elected (in April 1994) constitutional assembly wrote the final constitution, which it adopted in May 1996. While the first phase consisted only of closed-door negotiations, the second phase saw the implementation of an extensive public education and consultation process that opened the making of the new constitution to civil society and ordinary citizens. The constitutional assembly emphasized transparency and inclusiveness in its work. This phase concluded with a first certification decision by the constitutional court that sent the document back to the assembly for several modifications in line with the constitutional principles, and then a second certification decision approving the text.

Elaborate formal negotiation and technical support structures were constructed for both phases of constitution making, particularly the second, which had a larger number of players and more complex management needs. Parallel to the work of these structures, behind-the-scenes deal making—generally on a bilateral basis between the ANC and NP, sometimes in a multilateral format—occurred in both phases as well. The agreements reached out of the public eye, which would then be tabled in and ratified by the formal structures, pushed the process forward at numerous critical junctures.

The sections that follow describe in more detail the two-phase approach and the role of the interim constitution, the outcome of the 1994 elections, the work of the constitutional assembly in preparing the final constitution, the certification role of the constitutional court, and the (limited) foreign contribution to constitution making in South Africa.

The Two-Phase Approach and the Role of the Interim Constitution

In the history of the South African transition, the creation of the interim constitution of 1993 was as important a milestone as the adoption of the final constitution.[36] The interim constitution—the culmination of almost four years of concerted effort to reach a negotiated settlement—was effectively a peace treaty. It established transition mechanisms, specified the process for crafting the final constitution, and substantively constrained the final document through its embrace of thirty-four binding constitutional principles. While its operative effect was short-lived, its influence was peremptory due to the mandatory impact of the constitutional principles on the parameters within which the final constitution was written; also, the constitutional assembly used the interim constitution as the basis for its drafting work.[37]

The interim constitution was the practical embodiment of the transition from minority rule to democracy, adopted at the conclusion of a negotiating process in which political parties and homeland governments from across the political spectrum participated. It was the fruit of the first stage of constitution making and provided the basis for organizing government and regulating society during the transitional period from the April 1994 elections to the promulgation of the final constitution two years later.[38] Though a time-limited framework, it was a fully elaborated constitution that created the basic institutions of democracy.[39]

On a more theoretical level, the interim constitution also helped to bridge the illegitimacy of the apartheid regime and the legitimacy of the new constitutional system inaugurated in 1996. As Richard Spitz and Matthew Chaskalson have observed, the two-stage constitution-making process, of which the interim constitution was a central feature, resolved the traditional dilemma of whether the power of the day, the "constituted power," has the legitimacy to serve as the "constituent power" by putting in place a new constitutional arrangement. If not, a new body must be created with the legitimacy to write and adopt a new constitution. In South Africa, the constituted power was a minority regime lacking democratic legitimacy. In addition, the MPNP, the forum negotiating the transition, was unelected, and thus also lacked the democratic legitimacy to serve as the constituent power. These facts raised the question of how to ensure unimpeachable legitimacy for the new constitutional dispensation.[40]

The ANC and NP devised the answer of the interim constitution, which the existing parliament would approve.[41] This document would provide a link between the act of the constituted power in dissolving the existing order and the act of a newly elected constitutional assembly in adopting a final constitution.[42] To this, they added an important device unique to South Africa: constitutional principles, agreed in the MPNP and enshrined in the interim constitution, which circumscribed the power of the elected constitutional assembly. This approach "corrupted the notion of a constituent power creating a new order from nothing, but did so in a way that gave any party which willingly participated in the process a stake in its final outcome."[43] The bilaterally agreed approach, subsequently adopted by the MPNP negotiating council, included a period of power sharing under the interim constitution before the transition to full majority rule, once the final constitution was adopted. This approach provided for an immediate political settlement, in the form of elections, the institution of a transitional government, and a new though temporary constitution. At the same time, it provided controls on the transition to democracy, which included a period of power sharing, binding constitutional principles, and a role for political parties in the final constitution making. In this way, the two-stage framework and the interim constitution "reconciled the ANC's desire for a swift transfer to majority rule with the NP and other parties' concerns for structural guarantees and long-term influence in the constitution-making process."[44]

As the product of a political negotiation and an enactment of the apartheid regime's parliament, the interim constitution's democratic credentials can be seen as weak, as is often the case with interim measures in transitional and postconflict settings. Given the control the interim constitution exercised over the final constitution through the constitutional principles, that weakness is not insignificant. More important in the circumstances, however, was that the document embodied a deal that ended apartheid; drew a range of parties into the constitution-making process; ensured that the final constitution would be created by a democratically elected body; and, by providing legal continuity, prevented the emergence of legal or administrative uncertainty.[45] Substantively, the interim constitution had to satisfy the distinct imperatives of laying a foundation for democracy and accommodating those parties whose cooperation was necessary for a smooth transition. In doing so, as Cyril Ramaphosa later observed, the document "created the conditions which allowed the final Constitution to be written in a less volatile climate and far more considered manner."[46]

The interim constitution itself characterized its role as "a historic bridge between the past of a deeply divided society characterized by strife, conflict, untold suffering and injustice, and a future founded on the recognition of human rights, democracy, and peaceful coexistence and development opportunities for all South Africans, irrespective of color, race, class, belief or sex."[47] The most important building blocks in the construction of that bridge were the constitutional principles, the idea of which was agreed between the ANC and NP in the September 1992 Record of Understanding.[48] The first eleven of the principles were developed during the CODESA phase of the transition negotiations; during the MPNP process, the number of principles grew to thirty-four.[49] The basic purpose of the principles was to guarantee the protection of certain fundamental interests of minority groups, thereby gaining those groups' acceptance of a process in which the final constitution would be adopted by a democratically elected assembly.[50] The principles' binding nature was assured by giving the constitutional court the role of certifying the final constitution's adherence to them before the document could come into effect (discussed further below). Neither the principles nor the certification requirement in the interim constitution could be repealed or amended.[51]

Albie Sachs later observed that it was not difficult for the ANC to agree, in principle, to binding constitutional principles: It wanted language, cultural, and religious rights to be protected, and it wanted everyone "to feel at home in this new South Africa."[52] Reaching agreement on the content of the principles, however, was more challenging. Those who stood to lose power wanted to "pack as much as possible into the principles," while those who clearly would gain power after elections wanted to leave as much as possible to the discretion of a legitimately elected body.[53]

More than any other issue, the substance of the constitutional principles concerned the allocation of powers between the national and provincial levels of government.[54] One legal adviser involved in the constitution-making process calculated that the thirty-four numbered principles actually included fifty-one principles and subprinciples, of which twenty-three dealt with the division of powers. By comparison, only one prescribed, in very general terms, the content of a bill of fundamental rights.[55]

Another key feature of the interim constitution was the establishment of a framework for a government of national unity to exercise power during a transitional period following elections. (For the period between the interim constitution's adoption and the elections, a transitional executive council was established to oversee the existing government and provide for a level electoral playing field.[56])

The text provided that cabinet posts—up to twenty-seven of them—would be allocated proportionally on the basis of the election results to political parties garnering at least 5 percent of the vote. The purpose of this procedure was to produce a broad governing coalition to facilitate national reconciliation.[57] After much debate, not only over the form of power sharing, but over its duration, it was agreed—at first bilaterally between the ANC and NP and then in the MPNP—that coalition government could continue for five years until 1999.[58] (In the event, the NP exited the government of national unity in 1996.)

The story of the negotiation of the interim constitution illustrates many of the dynamics of the overall transition negotiations and final constitution-making process, including the parallel use of formal multiparty procedures and informal bilateral talks between the main parties, the use of deadlines to maintain momentum, and the main parties' persistence in trying to keep potential spoilers involved in the process. One aspect of the first phase of constitution making that differed significantly from the second phase, however, was the secrecy of the process. Closed-door meetings were essential at certain junctures of the final constitution making, especially toward the end of the process,[59] but the entire process in the first phase was closed to the public.[60]

A brief summary of the negotiating history of the interim constitution during the MPNP reveals these similarities and differences. In June 1993, the negotiating council of the MPNP, which had commenced two months earlier, determined that sufficient progress had been made for it to set April 27, 1994, as the date for South Africa's first ever nonracial elections. To proceed with elections, the council instructed the technical committee on constitutional issues to prepare a draft of a transitional constitution. At the same time, on the basis of a previous agreement between the ANC and NP, as noted above, the council agreed that the constitution-making body for the final document would be bound by constitutional principles negotiated in the MPNP.[61]

Having set a date for elections before agreeing on the text of an interim constitution, the parties effectively set a tough deadline for themselves: Agreement would have to be reached by the middle of November to leave sufficient time for a special session of the parliament before the end of the year to enact the necessary legal changes, and then for elections preparations.[62] The rush meant little rest: While parties were negotiating outstanding issues, technical experts were drafting proposals and the administration was preparing for the plenary. The atmosphere at the World Trade Centre, the site of the MPNP, was electric.

The first draft of the interim constitution was published in July 1993. In it, the technical committee recommended establishing both a constitution-making body, made up of the joint sitting of a national assembly and a senate, and a constitutional court. The interim constitution would be the supreme law, and the elected constitution-making body would be sovereign and entitled to draft and adopt a new constitution subject only to the constitutional principles. The final constitution would have to be adopted within two years and by a two-thirds majority.

By late October 1993, the ANC and the NP were ready to finalize the interim constitution. Jointly, in the MPNP's technical committee on constitutional issues, the parties tabled agreements on the text that they had reached on a bilateral basis. Their agreements included arrangements for a government of national unity. The main compromise in these agreements lay in the powers of provinces; the ANC had shifted its position to accommodate the federalist demands of the NP, IFP, and others. Both the IFP and the right-wing Freedom Alliance remained intransigent despite the compromises in-

tended to bring them on board, but the ANC and NP resolved to proceed with the interim constitution despite this, leaving the door open for others to join the process later.[63]

The main parties' resolve to keep the constitution-making process moving forward was manifest also in the decision-making procedure used in the MPNP. Under the rules of procedure, all decisions in the plenary, negotiating forum, and negotiating council were to be reached by consensus, but if this could not be achieved, sufficient consensus (described above) would do. The rotating chairperson would rule on whether consensus or sufficient consensus had been obtained. Not surprisingly, this procedure was controversial in the MPNP, as smaller parties frequently were frustrated by their inability to gain concessions; nevertheless, this highly subjective decision-making rule enabled the negotiators to reach a historic political settlement.[64]

By November 16, 1993, the outstanding issues were narrowed to a handful, and Mandela and de Klerk met to resolve them in a crucial bilateral meeting. Mandela persuaded de Klerk to shift from insisting on a minority veto on government decisions and an enforced coalition to voluntary co-rule. The outcome showed that de Klerk had come to accept that he would have to rely on the ANC's commitment to national unity. In the four-hour meeting, the two leaders, assisted by their chief negotiators, Cyril Ramaphosa and Roelf Meyer, agreed in principle on all the outstanding issues. The NP agreed to decisions being taken by a simple majority in the cabinet. The ANC compromised on the deadlock-breaking mechanisms for adopting the final constitution, agreeing that if a referendum failed, a newly elected constitutional assembly would be able to adopt a final constitution by a reduced, 60 percent, majority. It also agreed to provisions protecting the powers of the provinces, and—in a concession to the Democratic Party—agreed that six of the ten constitutional court judges would be appointed from among ten nominated by the judicial services commission.[65] The ANC made a further concession by agreeing to guarantee the white minority a substantial share of power in local government. The agreement called for local government elections within two years, and guaranteed whites at least 30 percent of seats on each council, as well as an effective veto for budget decisions.

The final political agreement on the text of the interim constitution was reached in the early hours of November 18; nineteen of the twenty-one parties still participating in the MPNP (the IFP and others had previously walked out) voted in favor; the left-wing PAC and right-wing Afrikaner Volksunie voted against.[66] Party leaders signed the agreement, bringing about the single most dramatic political and constitutional change ever experienced in South Africa, which would take effect on the date of the elections.

The document that the MPNP plenary passed was not quite complete, however. The plenary thus instructed the negotiating council to finalize outstanding technical issues and refer the document to the parliament for its formal passage into law. On December 22, the debate on the interim constitution in the last white parliament completed its course. The NP had firmly demanded that the existing parliament adopt the interim constitution; this procedure represented a significant concession on the part of the ANC, which until then had resolutely denied the legitimacy of the organs of the apartheid regime.[67] Once adopted, the Department of Constitutional Affairs and Planning initiated a campaign to promote the new constitution, including advertisements in a variety of media and the distribution of booklets about the constitution. As further confirmation of South Africa's burgeoning democracy, an independent electoral commission and independent media commission were established in January 1994 to prepare the ground for elections.

The ANC and NP later supported amendments to the interim constitution, in February 1994, in a bid to draw the right wing into the process and, in particular, to secure full participation in the upcoming elections.[68] All mention of concurrent powers was removed and the provinces were granted powers that would prevail over those of the national government in all areas within their competency. The Electoral Act, which had been adopted just after the interim constitution, also was amended to extend the date for registration of political parties. Ultimately, the right-wing Freedom Front participated in the elections.

Changes to the interim constitution, including guaranteeing the position of the Zulu king, also were made in an effort to overcome the objections of the IFP, the greatest potential spoiler of the election process.[69] While the IFP sought more, on the basis of a tripartite agreement reached among the ANC, NP, and the IFP only a few days before April 27, it finally agreed to participate in the election. In the end, all major political stakeholders and parties took part in the elections, held on April 27–29, 1994; only the white ultraright wing did not participate.[70] The inclusiveness of the elections was the product of tremendous perseverance by the parties committed to a peaceful transition in their efforts to bring the more extreme elements of South Africa's polity into the process.

South Africa's First Democratic Elections

South Africa's first nonracial elections were an overwhelming success, confounding the prophets of doom. Though violence spiked before the polls—hundreds of people were killed each month in politically related violence and there were several bombings in the final days intended to scare people away from polling stations[71]—the elections themselves proceeded without any major incidents.[72] An overwhelming majority of eligible voters

Table 5.1 Constitutional Assembly Election Results

Party	Number of seats	Leader
African National Congress	312	Nelson Mandela
National Party	99	F.W. de Klerk
Inkatha Freedom Party	48	Mangosuthu Buthelezi
Freedom Front	14	Constand Viljoen
Democratic Party	10	Tony Leon
Pan Africanist Congress	5	Clarence Makwetu
African Christian Democratic Party	2	Kenneth Meshoe

Note: This table is drawn from Ebrahim, *Soul of a Nation,* 181. For detailed data on the results of the 1994 elections, see the Web site of the Independent Electoral Commission, http://www.elections.org.za/Elections94.asp (accessed April 25, 2009).

came out, standing patiently in long lines to cast their votes.[73] Despite enormous logistical problems, some occasioned by the IFP's late decision to participate, as well as ordinary election squabbles, the Independent Electoral Commission, a new body established during the transition process, judged the election substantially free and fair.[74] That judgment was, of course, important to the credibility of the resulting constitution-making body.[75]

The election handed the new leaders two separate and distinct mandates: to govern a newly democratic society and to draft the final constitution. These were not entirely compatible tasks, as a political leader's engagement in one of them was often a detriment to the other. The major problem was one of available time. On the one hand, political leaders were expected to establish a functioning democratic government, for which there was neither precedent in South Africa nor experience. On the other, they were expected to engage in extended negotiations with many different stakeholders to draft the final constitution.

The election produced 490 political leaders at the national level: 400 in the national assembly, elected by proportional representation using national and provincial candidate lists, and 90 in the Senate (ten from each of the nine provinces). In accordance with the interim constitution, a joint sitting of these parliamentary bodies made up the constitutional assembly. In addition, the interim constitution gave parliament the function of choosing the president, who in turn was required to select cabinet members from the ranks of parliament, in accordance with the formula for the government of national unity described earlier. An indirectly elected president was settled upon to avoid potential gridlock between competing centers of power and to break with South Africa's history of highly centralized rule, experienced through colonial structures, traditional leadership, and in the underground resistance.[76] The president chosen, of course, was Nelson Mandela (see Table 5.1).

The successful elections and wide acceptance of the results set the stage for the second phase of constitution making, to be conducted by the constitutional assembly.

The Constitutional Assembly and Creation of the Final Constitution

Structural Framework for Negotiations

In drafting the final constitution, the constitutional assembly had to work within both political and legal parameters. These shaped the process and determined the document's content. In the main, the assembly sought to produce a constitution that would be both legitimate and enduring. Legitimacy was seen to depend on the extent to which the drafting exercise was considered credible. It was also seen as important that the final text be as widely accepted as possible.

Three politically imperative fundamental principles guided the way in which the assembly designed the final constitution-making process to ensure its credibility. First was inclusiveness. The constitution had to integrate the ideas of all the major players, including the political parties represented in the assembly, organized civil society, and political parties outside the assembly, as well as individual citizens. The second principle was accessibility. The assembly invested a great deal of energy and resources in ensuring that the process was as open as possible. This principle suggested that it was not good enough merely to invite submissions; it was necessary to reach out and solicit views deliberately. To this end, an elaborate media campaign was devised to reach as many South Africans as possible. Accessibility also was seen as relating to both the nature of the language of the text and the ability of ordinary citizens to obtain physical copies of it. The argument was that the ordinary citizen should be able to read and understand the document. The third principle was transparency. All meetings of the assembly and its sub-bodies were open to the public, though a large number of bilateral and multilateral meetings took place in private, with no media or public access. The closed nature of these meetings raised objections, especially from certain civil-society groups.[77]

Several important requirements set out in the interim constitution helped to define the process as well: a two-thirds majority for adoption of the text, complete adoption of the document within two years of the first sitting of the national assembly, and compliance with the thirty-four constitutional principles. The supermajority requirement meant that the dominant party, the ANC, did not have enough votes to adopt the final text on its own.

The strict deadline was imposed to ensure that the final constitution would be drafted within a reasonable period of time. To deter parties from withholding their support for the new constitutional text within the tight time frame, the interim constitution contained elaborate deadlock-breaking measures, including the possibility of sending a completed draft text to a referendum if the assembly failed to adopt it.[78] Negotiators on both sides considered the prospect of a referendum undesirable, as it would signal their political and personal failures to reach agreement, entail an inevitably adversarial campaign, and possibly reopen contentious issues.[79] At the start of the assembly's work, some raised concerns that there might not be sufficient time to complete the task, but, because an extension would have required amending the interim constitution, agreement was reached to complete the work within the time allocated.

The use of the constitutional principles was novel. Namibia provided a precedent, in which a set of principles determined the parameters for drafting a new constitution, though in Namibia the principles were guidelines.[80] In South Africa, they were binding on the negotiators, and, as noted above, the constitutional court would assure their adherence to the principles. The principles had emerged from the negotiating process as a compromise; thus, they were sufficiently precise to guarantee that the constitution-making body did not stray from certain fundamental, agreed-upon notions, but not so detailed as to preempt the work of that body. The constitutional principles guided both the structure and the substance of the assembly's debates. As discussed further below, six theme committees were established to facilitate the assembly's work, and these were given terms of reference based on a division of the thirty-four principles.

The formal organizational structure used for the negotiation and drafting process in the assembly was complex. At the highest level was the constitutional assembly, which, as mentioned, consisted of the 490 members of the two houses of the parliament. These members represented seven political parties in proportion to the results of the 1994 elections. Cyril Ramaphosa of the ANC served as chairperson of the assembly and Leon Wessels of the NP as deputy chairperson.[81]

Within the assembly, and reporting directly to it, the constitutional committee was the main negotiating and coordinating structure. It consisted of forty-four members, appointed by parties on a proportional basis. The committee met at first on a weekly basis to receive reports from the theme committees (described below), but met less frequently after the establishment of its subcommittee. It continued to function, however, as the decision-making structure.

The subcommittee of the constitutional committee was established in June 1995 to better facilitate negotiations. With Ramaphosa as its chairperson and Wessels as its deputy chairperson, the subcommittee proved to be extremely effective and important because of its small size and ability to meet frequently and more easily than the full constitutional committee. Though it was not a decision-making forum, the subcommittee improved the efficiency of the constitutional committee, and unlike the latter, could meet at the same time as the national assembly without affecting the quorum. At any one time, the subcommittee consisted of about twenty members, some of these were permanent members, and others were nominated by parties from time to time to deal with specialized matters. Its membership, therefore, depended on the issue at hand.

The constitutional assembly also established a management committee to deal with the day-to-day management of the negotiations and matters of process rather than substance. The twelve-member management committee met once a week throughout the proceedings. One of its specific responsibilities was to ensure that the constitutional assembly worked according to an agreed schedule. While not as glamorous as the issues of political debate, timekeeping was essential for all the structures to adhere to the overall plan and meet the May 8, 1996, deadline.

The aforementioned theme committees were established to work on different parts of the constitution[82] and to ensure the involvement of as many members of the assembly as possible. Each theme committee consisted of thirty members nominated by political parties in proportion to their representation. However, due to the difference in numbers between the largest and smallest parties, a bias in favor of the smaller parties was agreed upon. Each committee's members elected three chairpersons to ensure that no single party chaired meetings of all the committees. Together with a core group of seven or eight members, the chairpersons were responsible for managing and coordinating the committee's work.

In addition to ensuring that the constitution-making process was as inclusive as possible of the members of the large constitutional assembly, the theme committees functioned to ensure inclusiveness in a broader sense. They were the assembly's initial interface with the public and were used to receive views from the public and civil society (discussed further below in the section on public participation). The work of these committees also had the beneficial effect of giving politicians who had not been involved in the first phase of constitution making the equivalent of an intensive course in constitutional issues.[83] A technical committee, consisting of three or four experts in particular fields, supported each theme committee, and some theme committees were assigned additional technical advisers to deal with specialized matters, such as local government, self-determination, and the role of traditional leaders. Some committee members also participated in workshops with international experts, though this was not a major feature.

To illustrate the nature of the theme committees' work, Theme Committee 1, which dealt with the character of the democratic state, held fifty-six meetings from September 19, 1994, to September 11, 1995, and processed 3,000 submissions from the public. It held six orientation workshops to facilitate the preparation of submissions. And it held public hearings on the seat of government, languages, names and symbols, the secular state, equality and affirmative action, and the character of the state.[84] Overall, the theme committees began producing reports in February 1995 and tabled their final reports, accompanied by draft constitutional texts, in September 1995.

In addition to the various committees just described, three other structures established in accordance with the requirements of the interim constitution supported the constitutional assembly's work. First was an independent panel of constitutional experts, which advised the constitutional assembly through its chairperson.[85] The panel, composed of two practicing and five academic lawyers, also had a deadlock-breaking function under the terms of the interim constitution, but was not called upon to perform this role.[86] Second was a commission on provincial government, the main task of which was to help formulate new arrangements for provincial government. This commission also advised the constitutional assembly on provisions in the new constitution regarding boundaries, structures, powers, functions, and transitional measures for the provinces.

Finally, a *volkstaat* council was established to enable proponents of the idea of a volkstaat (that is, an Afrikaner homeland) to pursue this option constitutionally. The provision in the interim constitution calling for the council was a compromise that helped convince right-wingers to participate in the 1994 elections and seek to advance their interests within the framework of the constitution.[87] The council gathered information and reported to both the constitutional assembly and the commission on provincial government. In short, the volkstaat council was principally a mechanism to ensure the greatest possible consensus and inclusiveness; it provided a back door to participation for the right wing and served as a face-saving device.

Negotiating and Drafting the Final Constitution

At the outset, the constitutional committee settled on a work program that envisaged three broad phases. The first phase would involve a public participation program and the development of a draft text. The second phase would include the publication of the first draft and further solicitation of public comment. In the third phase, the constitutional assembly would finally negotiate and adopt the constitution.

During the first phase, the assembly struggled with the question of how much detail to include in the constitution. The invitation to the public to submit comments and ideas elicited a wish list of provisions to include in the text. Smaller political parties and lobby groups as well as the broader public were naturally inclined to seek to secure particular interests by addressing them in the constitution. The technical committees organized all the submissions and prepared reports based on them for consideration by the theme committees, which, in turn, produced reports for the constitutional committee reflecting the major trends in the submissions and whether they demonstrated consensus or considerable differences of opinion. Often these reports were supported by a set of draft formulations, but invariably, the reports begged the question of how much detail should be included.

To address the question, the chairperson of the constitutional assembly asked the independent panel of constitutional experts to draft a document setting out criteria that should be applied when considering issues for inclusion in the constitution. Nevertheless, the debates in the theme committees were repeated in the constitutional committee, often without any progress. The sometimes cumbersome and redundant proceedings were part of the price that had to be paid for trying to involve as many of the 490 members of the assembly as possible in negotiating the constitutional text. Regardless, however, at this early stage, parties were not yet ready to make the necessary compromises.

As these debates progressed, the management committee appointed a team of experts, including law advisers, language experts, and the members of the panel of constitutional experts, to prepare the first working draft of the constitution. The draft was essentially to serve as a report on how the constitutional assembly had addressed the submissions made, and the format was intended to draw attention to areas that remained contentious or were outstanding. This document, referred to as the Refined Working Draft, was produced for discussion by the constitutional committee in October 1995. It provided the first glimpse of what the final text might look like and clearly set out the agenda for further negotiation. After a year of meeting to consider different views and submissions, political parties were sufficiently primed and ready to plunge into closing negotiations. The constitutional committee addressed a vast number of issues and reached many agreements at this stage, reflected in the version of the draft that was ultimately published in November 1995. To solicit a second round of public comment, more than 4.5 million copies of the draft were distributed in tabloid form throughout the country. Meanwhile, guided by the discussions of the constitutional committee, and after further research (including some consultation with foreign experts), the drafters prepared a further edi-

tion of the working draft in December; revised drafts were then produced at regular intervals to reflect the latest agreements.

While the second broad phase of the work program—the solicitation of comment on the Refined Working Draft—proceeded, the subcommittee of the constitutional committee continued to negotiate outstanding issues. As would occur at critical junctures throughout the negotiations (as intermediate deadlines approached, or as stumbling blocks were reached), the parties engaged in bilateral and multilateral meetings behind closed doors to seek agreement on a next edition of the draft. While the parties themselves privately arranged the bilateral meetings, multilateral meetings among parties were facilitated by the constitutional assembly's administration. These meetings held behind closed doors did not sit well with members of civil society or the media, but they were important vehicles for enabling the parties to make compromises gracefully without appearing publicly to have betrayed their constituencies. The meetings also allowed for very frank discussions without negotiators having to make statements purely for the media's benefit.

The major issues requiring resolution at this stage related to the bill of rights, the council of provinces, national and provincial competencies, courts and the administration of justice, and local government. By mid-March 1996, there were deadlocks on five issues: the death penalty, whether the right to strike should be balanced by a right to lockout, the right to education in single-language schools, the appointment of judges, and the appointment of the attorney general. Fifty-four further issues remained in contention, and twenty-five matters required technical attention.

Rounding out the second phase, the constitutional assembly produced a further edition (the fourth) of the working draft on March 20, 1996, which contained a detailed study of the submissions made in response to the publication of the Refined Working Draft. This document included endnotes intended to facilitate consideration of the public submissions. The fourth edition of the text was published in limited quantities and distributed to those who had made submissions. In part, the publication was an attempt to prove that the assembly was giving due consideration to the views of the public.

In the third phase of the work program, during March 1996, it became clear that it would be extremely difficult to adopt the constitution by the May 8 deadline. To expedite the process, the negotiators accepted a proposal mooted by the assembly's administration to hold a multilateral meeting in an isolated area over several days. This would allow parties, with the benefit of experts being present, to hold intensive negotiations without the disruptions occasioned by remaining in close proximity to their work environments. The meeting, held in Arniston at the beginning of April 1996, proved extremely successful, as most of the outstanding issues were resolved. Important issues remained in contention, however, including the death penalty, education, and lockout provisions; formulations on the preamble and local government were still in progress as well. Nevertheless, for the first time, negotiators began to see the light at the end of the tunnel.

As it turned out, the issues on which the parties were deadlocked proved to be serious enough to throw into question the adoption of the final constitution by general consensus, as the NP and Democratic Party felt strongly enough about them to consider voting against the entire constitution. Most extraordinary, however, was that none of the major political debates that had raged among parties for several years—namely, the question of a government of national unity, whether to establish a senate, and national and provincial competences—were among these issues.[88]

Based on the progress achieved at Arniston, a fifth edition of the working draft was produced, together with the first draft of transitional arrangements, by the middle of April 1996. At this point, the negotiation process intensified as pressure mounted on the parliament. Despite a full regular legislative agenda, it was agreed that the work of the constitutional assembly would take priority, and a hectic series of bilateral, multilateral, and subcommittee meetings ensued. Party caucuses and meetings of the policy-making structures were regularly convened to renew or obtain fresh negotiating mandates. Generally, meetings took place at all hours, even stretching late into the night. During this period, the Ramaphosa and Meyer–led "channel bilateral" was resumed as well.

Mixed into the intense activity was a great deal of lobbying by interest groups, particularly those of business and labor. Adding to the pressure on the side of labor, thousands of workers marched to support their demands. Consultations were held with the Congress of Traditional Leaders as well regarding their concerns about the treatment of their authority and of customary law in the new constitution.

By April 18, negotiators entered the final stretch. In a marathon meeting of the constitutional committee that started that day, the basic text of the constitution was agreed upon. This meeting heralded some of the most dramatic breakthroughs in all the negotiations, including agreement among the ANC, NP, and right-wing Freedom Front that the new constitution would feature a commission to promote and protect the rights of cultural, religious, and language groups. In addition, a clause was added acknowledging the principle of collective rights for cultural, religious, and linguistic communities. This was vitally important to bringing the right-wing constituency on board. Major issues unresolved at Arniston remained unresolved,[89] but the text was rapidly polished with respect to all agreed matters and published in bill form on April 22.

A milestone in the process was reached on April 23, when the draft constitution was tabled in the constitutional assembly and a two-day plenary debate began. In tabling the draft, assembly chairperson Ramaphosa observed that the country had come a long way since 1909, when the first Union constitution was passed in the British House of Commons; in his opinion, the new constitution would be the birth certificate of the new South African nation.

The procedures at this stage focused on amendments to the constitution bill tabled by parties in the plenary. The constitutional committee began meeting on April 25 to consider 298 proposed amendments tabled by various parties, including twenty-eight that were jointly tabled by the ANC and NP, reflecting agreements reached between them. In the main, the amendments were of a technical nature; others were no more than a restatement of well-known party positions that had been asserted in the previous two years. The constitutional committee agreed to move the debate on amendments into various subcommittees, but unfortunately, even the subcommittees failed to make much progress on the unresolved issues and the parties remained deadlocked. Ultimately, the formal public procedures in the constitutional committee were insufficient on their own to overcome the final obstacles, though the committee and its subcommittees continued to meet to resolve the issues that they could and to record progress in the negotiations overall. Bilateral discussions between the ANC and NP were critical from this point to the end of the process, as the parties worked to bridge their outstanding differences. For example, an important series of deadlock-breaking meetings took place on Sunday, April 28, when President Mandela and de Klerk met at Mandela's official residence in Pretoria. Overshadowing these particular side talks was a threat of a national strike on April 30, and the fact that the rand was at an all-time

low. Delegations of labor and business leaders joined the talks, and significant agreements in principle on some issues, including the lockout clause, were reached, though the parties remained deadlocked on the property clause.

As the May 8 deadline loomed, the intensification of the negotiation process began to take its toll. After mid-April, negotiators found themselves involved in a hectic round of bilateral talks, subcommittee meetings, extensive consultations, and continuous reporting to policymaking bodies of their parties. Signs of physical strain and stress emerged. The smaller parties were particularly disadvantaged, as they did not have sufficient members to field in the various meetings or to engage other parties in lobbying for support. Thus, they often found themselves led by agreements between the ANC and NP. Despite some irritation this dynamic produced, and even though it was necessary ultimately to arrive at agreements multilaterally, the important deadlocks were, in fact, essentially between the two largest parties.

By May 1, the constitution-making process was effectively into overtime. The delay in finalizing the text was beginning to cause significant problems for the administration and drafters. For example, language experts were recruited from different parts of the country to carry out the translations in the hope that the final text would be presented to the constitutional assembly for adoption in all eleven official languages, but the continuous amendments completely frustrated their efforts. As time ran short with no agreement in sight on deadlocked issues,[90] the tension reached a fever pitch.

Though consensus remained the goal, as the constitutional committee completed its work, the ANC found it necessary to assert itself as the majority party to determine formulations on the final issues, and its preferences prevailed on several points. Thus an amended constitutional bill was drafted by

May 4. It was still not clear, however, how the political parties would vote on the text, as not all provisions of the draft were fully agreed. Bilateral meetings continued over the next two days to iron out differences, and on Monday, May 6, the constitutional assembly sat in plenary to debate the amended bill.

The opening of the final plenary irreversibly set in motion a process that would oblige parties to either adopt the text or allow the deadlock-breaking mechanisms to come into effect. As noted earlier, these included the possibility of the independent panel of constitutional experts taking thirty days to develop compromise formulations to which the parties might agree, and the possibility of resorting to a referendum on the draft text.[91] The implications of the latter, which would jettison the process of multiparty constitution writing and thus jeopardize the compromises that had been reached, were a source of considerable concern to the negotiators.

Both the plenary session and bilateral meetings continued through May 7, interspersed with meetings of the constitutional committee to consider new amendments; an eleventh-hour modification of the assembly's rules was needed to allow further amendment procedures. When the committee members assembled at 10:45 p.m. that day, an incredible air of excitement ran through the room. By this time, many of the assembly members who were attending the plenary debate had squeezed into the old assembly chamber to hear the parties report on the outcome of the bilateral discussions. Though reluctantly in some cases, final compromises were reached on the right to education in languages of choice, the exclusion of a constitutional right to lockout, the nature of the right to collective bargaining, the property clause (balancing land reform with property rights), and several more minor matters. At 11:30 p.m., the committee adjourned to allow the constitutional assembly to complete its debate. Several hours later, sufficient support for

adopting the constitution was confirmed, and the constitutional assembly went on by a vote of 87 percent in favor[92] to adopt the resolution containing amendments reflecting the final agreements. Around 11:00 a.m. on May 8, the new constitution was adopted.

The Public Participation Process

One of the most distinguishing—and from a comparative constitutionalist perspective, precedent-setting—aspects of the South African process was the intensive effort the constitution makers made to solicit and reflect on a wide range of citizens' views about the document being produced. A guiding principle, upheld throughout the drafting process, was that the development of a new constitution must involve the greatest possible number of South Africans representing the broadest possible range of views. This approach was intended to give real effect to the notion of participatory democracy. Though the constitutional assembly's mandate entitled it to draft the final constitution on its own, its members believed that broader involvement was needed to ensure the popular legitimacy of the outcome.

One of the assembly's stated objectives was to make the constitution-making process transparent, open, and credible.[93] Moreover, the final constitution had to enjoy the enduring support of all South Africans, regardless of ideological differences. Credibility was an important aim for a document born out of a history of political conflict and mistrust. Achieving that aim was thought to depend on a process through which people could claim ownership of the constitution. Not only did the South African people have to feel a part of the process, but the content of the final constitution had to represent their views. In addition, the process had to be *seen* to be transparent and open.

The assembly's main challenge was to find ways to enter into effective dialogue and consultation with a population of more than forty million people. South Africa had a large rural population, most of which was illiterate and without access to print or electronic media. Moreover, South Africa had never had a culture of constitutionalism or human rights, which made it difficult to consult with people who did not recognize the importance of a constitution. Meeting this challenge thus had to include raising awareness to empower people to be able to participate meaningfully in the process.

The timing of the public participation program heightened the challenge. First, the time available for the project was short. It was not until the second quarter of 1995—well into the constitutional negotiations—that the full complement of necessary staff was in place to implement the program. Second, the constitutional drafting exercise followed closely after South Africa's "liberation" election. Therefore, the program of public participation had to compete for public attention with the broader process of transformation. In particular, the program overlapped with two local government elections and various government campaigns aimed at involving communities in reconstruction and development programs. In addition, it was difficult to make clear to the general public the distinction between, on the one hand, constitutional dialogue, and on the other hand, articulation of growing demands on government for delivery of basic services and other results promised in elections.

The participation program was conducted at two stages in the process. The first occurred during the negotiations leading up to the constitutional assembly's production of the Refined Working Draft. The second followed and was focused on that draft. Public education about constitutions and the constitution-making process was an integral—and simultaneously undertaken—element of both phases of public participation. This two-stage process avoided the usual

dilemma of whether to consult the public before a draft is prepared, at which point the solicitation of input may be, and may be *perceived* to be, wide open, or whether to consult after preparation of a draft, at which point the range of solicited input may be more constrained but also more constructively focused.

The first phase, which ran from January to November 1995, involved a wide variety of means to communicate and interact with the general public and organized interest groups. To create awareness of the constitution-making process and constitutional issues, and to stimulate public interest in participation, a media campaign was launched in January 1995. As part of the outreach strategy, a national advertising campaign included messages such as "you've made your mark"—a reference to voting in the 1994 elections—"now have your say," and "it's your right to decide your constitutional rights." Advertisements were run on television, on radio, in local newspapers, and on outdoor billboards. The constitutional assembly commissioned a national survey to assess the penetration and impact of this media campaign as well as ascertain public attitudes on key constitutional issues.[94] The results revealed that the assembly's media campaign reached 65 percent of all adult South Africans in the three months between January 15 and April 19, 1995. However, the survey also revealed that the public was clearly skeptical about the seriousness of the assembly in calling for their involvement and the treatment their submissions would receive. The credibility of the process obviously needed some attention. In addition, the survey made clear that the public still needed education about the nature and function of a constitution, as well as information about the assembly and the constitution-making process.

To communicate with the public throughout the entire constitution-making process—in other words, not limited to the two phases of the public participation program, but overlapping with them—the constitutional assembly also employed a newsletter, and television and radio programs, all bearing the title Constitutional Talk; a telephone talk line; and an Internet Web site. The newsletter, usually published every two weeks in an eight-page format, provided detailed information about the constitution-making process. One hundred thousand copies were distributed through taxi ranks, and another 60,000 were sent to subscribers. A series of twenty-five television programs ran from April to October 1995, and a series of twelve ran from February to May 1996. The format allowed representatives of civil-society groups to engage a multiparty panel of assembly members on topics including the bill of rights, separation of powers, the national anthem and flag, freedom of expression, traditional authorities, and the death penalty.

Radio was a particularly effective information delivery mechanism because it could reach large numbers of people in both rural and urban areas. In collaboration with the South African Broadcasting Corporation's (SABC) educational directorate, the constitutional assembly launched a weekly radio talk show in October 1995. The hour-long programs were broadcast on eight SABC stations in eight languages, with constitutional experts appearing as studio guests. These programs reached over ten million South Africans each week.

The constitutional talk line enabled people with access to a telephone to obtain a briefing on political discussions and to leave messages requesting information or to record comments. The service was available in several languages. While over 10,000 callers used the talk line, the effectiveness of this mechanism was limited. With insufficient time to prepare for the talk line's use, the system to update information and monitor responses was not very efficient. The assembly's Web site, established in conjunction with the University of Cape Town, which maintained it, included a database of information containing minutes, drafts, opinions, and submissions. More than 6,600 users from forty-six countries accessed the site during the period from January 1 to April 17, 1996.

To engage the public directly in the process in the first phase of the participation program, the constitutional assembly solicited submissions and held public meetings, participatory workshops, and public hearings. These procedures were publicized through the public outreach mechanisms described above. Between February and August 1995, twenty-six public meetings were held in all nine provinces, focused mostly on rural and disadvantaged communities, which had limited access to other means of following the process. The meetings involved a total of more than 200 assembly members in face-to-face interactions with the public. The meetings served two functions: Political actors in the assembly reported on various issues in the negotiations, and members of the public were invited to voice their views on those issues. Each oral submission of views was recorded and transcribed for consideration by the structures within the assembly. Public meetings were preceded by smaller participatory workshops with an educational orientation, mostly involving non-governmental organization (NGO) and other civil-society representatives, to equip participants to contribute substantively to the public meetings. In all, 20,549 people and representatives of 717 civil-society organizations attended the public meetings.

For most participants, the meetings were the first occasion on which they could interact directly with their elected representatives. More important, this was the first time in South Africa that public events were held involving politicians who were previously at war with one another, talking jointly to the people. The meetings were extremely successful: Discussions were lively, ideas original, and the exchange of views appreciated.

In addition to the public meetings, a national-sector public hearing program was conducted to enable the theme committees (discussed above) to consult civil-society groups on particular issues, such as certain rights to be included in the bill of rights. In an effort to ensure broad representation at the hearings, the assembly sought to prepare for the hearings in partnership with civil-society organizations. The partnership was not entirely successful, however, as few organizations—with the notable exception of the trade union movement—made a concerted effort to draw their members into discussions about the constitution-making process. Most of the hearings took place within four weeks during May and June 1995. Despite the limited time available for this element of the participation program, 596 organizations were consulted. In addition, theme committees hosted many seminars and workshops, at which expert opinion was sought on particular issues. Many of these workshops included international experts.

Numerical data indicates the huge scale of the assembly's effort to engage the public in the first phase of consultation, as well as the swell of popular interest in participation. Altogether, this phase of the public participation program involved direct interaction with 117,184 people; 807 public events; regular liaison with 1,588 civil-society organizations; twenty-six public meetings, which 20,549 people attended and in which 717 organizations were represented; thirteen public hearings involving 1,508 representatives from 596 organizations; 486 constitutional education-oriented participatory workshops preceding public meetings; and 259 briefings by politicians reporting to their constituencies on progress in the constitution-making process. In terms of percentages of South Africans, the participation numbers are not huge—a survey indicated that only 13 percent of the population was even aware that meetings on the constitution had taken place[95]—but as a sampling of the public's views, the numbers are significant and reveal a serious effort to involve the public.

The success of the effort to solicit public input can be seen in the number of submissions made: Close to two million were received. The bulk of these were signatures on petitions promoted by various civil-society structures, however, rather than original written submissions presenting individuals' views, though the latter also arrived in large numbers. The petitions dealt with a wide variety, though limited number, of issues, among them language rights, animal rights, abortion, the death penalty, and the location of the seat of parliament.[96] Of the submissions received, just over 11,000 were substantive rather than petitions. The substantive submissions ranged in length from a few handwritten lines to printed reports over 100 pages long.[97] These were often wide-ranging wish lists that arrived at an early stage in the process, when the political parties were still developing their thinking on many issues. Many people discussed issues that confronted them in everyday life, such as spousal abuse or problems with cattle.[98] In whatever form, though, the submissions reflected the views of a large number of people.

The overwhelming number of submissions made in the first phase led to concern, especially among civil-society organizations, about whether the views expressed would be seriously considered.[99] There was some doubt on this score among the public at large as well.[100] As a result of this concern, civil society sustained pressure for openness in the constitutional assembly to the end of the constitution-making process.

In hindsight, the figures regarding the extent of participation obscure both the "vitality and energy of the public participation program" as well as the fact that the program's goals and "concrete results" were not entirely clear.[101] Some critics argued that the program was designed to hide the reality that like the interim constitution, the final constitution would be a negotiated document. The huge number of submissions—too many to be reviewed by any of the politicians—and the vagueness of many of them appear to support the critics to some extent.[102] However, such criticisms miss the fundamental significance of the submissions as responses to the first invitation that many previously disenfranchised people had received to voice their aspirations. Even vague requests to address poverty represented expressions of a desire for the constitution to ensure a better future. As Christina Murray, a member of the panel of constitutional experts, has pointed out, the participation program had broader, less instrumental goals than providing a list of matters that should be included in the document, such as fostering a sense of ownership of the new constitution by all South Africans, and facilitating communication between politicians and the citizens they represented.[103]

The second phase of public participation, which ran from November 1995 to February 1996, centered on the Refined Working Draft, a complete set of textual formulations produced at the end of the theme committees' work. The draft provided alternative options for contentious formulations, as well as supporting notes explaining the options, and was effectively a progress report on the negotiation of the final constitution. It also reflected the ways in which the ideas and submissions put forward during the first phase of public consultation were addressed.

Over four and a half million copies of the working draft, printed in user-friendly tabloid form, were distributed throughout the country on November 22, 1995. The distribution means included newspaper inserts, door-to-door delivery, and supply of copies to taxi kiosks at major centers. A survey conducted a couple of months after the draft was released found that, by then, 8 percent of all South African adults had seen the document, while 5 percent had read some or all of it. The

public education effort in this phase utilized posters, the Constitutional Talk newsletter, a booklet titled *You and Building the New Constitution,* and a pamphlet titled *Constitutions, Democracy, and a Summary of the Working Draft* to provide information about constitutions and the constitution-making process.

A supporting media campaign was launched with the publication of the working draft and ran through the period of public debate to February 20, 1996. Through this campaign, the public was invited to make further submissions and was asked to comment specifically on the provisions of the draft. As a result, the 250,000 submissions received in the second phase were much more focused than those received in the first phase, though the vast bulk were again ordinary petitions rather than substantive submissions. The petitions dealt with many of the same issues as they did in the first phase—the death penalty, sexual orientation, and animal rights, in particular. Some of the submissions expressed skepticism about the assembly's invitation to the public for written comments, wondering whether the politicians would take them seriously.

After considering the views contained in the submissions,[104] the assembly produced a further edition of the working draft. This edition recorded where the submissions came from and the formulations that were affected, as well as reports by the experts who had processed the submissions. A copy of this new draft was sent to each person or party that had made a submission.

The participation program was not without practical imperfections. For example, in distributing the copies of the revised working draft to those who had made submissions in the second phase, many complained that they did not make any submissions and could not understand why they had been identified as having done so. Upon investigation, it became apparent that a number of submissions had been sent under names from the congregation lists of churches. In addition, some schoolteachers encouraged students to make submissions by dictating one to them.

The degree to which the text was modified solely in response to public submissions is difficult to measure, as the issues that were the subject of popular debate were generally the same as those pursued by the contesting political parties, and the views of the parties and elements of the public often coincided. Some submissions from civil society did directly affect the text, including the constitution's recognition of religious personal law, as well as its recognition of certain languages such as Gujarati. But ultimately, the textual formulations were in the hands of the elected officials who were legitimately mandated to negotiate the final constitution.[105]

Nevertheless, the consultation program had a strong effect on the public's perception of being included in the constitution making. Survey data revealed that within one year of the process of public participation, just less than half (48 percent) of all adult South Africans felt part of the assembly's process, while just over a quarter (28 percent) did not. Notably, positive feeling about the assembly process was expressed nearly evenly across formal metropolitan areas (48 percent) and formal urban areas (49 percent),[106] as well as more disadvantaged areas, including rural areas (46 percent) and informal metropolitan and urban areas, such as shantytowns (43 percent). The legacy of these perceptions can be seen in the South African experience since the adoption of the constitution. In that period, there have been no political or legal challenges to the legitimacy of the constitution. Though public political debate may be vigorous, it has not encroached on the fundamental tenets and principles set out in the constitutional framework. The inclusiveness, legitimacy, and ownership engendered by the public participation program can be credited for this.

After the second phase of the public participation program came the period, discussed earlier in this chapter, in which the issues threatening deadlock began to crystallize. This development constrained the openness of the process. To facilitate resolving the contentious issues, parties held various bilateral and multilateral meetings behind closed doors, which did not sit well with the media or civil society. Consultations with affected interest groups during this period were limited to areas of deadlock only, and when these consultations took place, they occurred with very little time to plan or prepare. The assembly had prided itself throughout on excellent relationships with civil-society groups. However, several of these saw themselves as being outside the process, particularly when political parties found it necessary to hold closed bilateral or multilateral meetings.[107]

The assembly continued its public outreach effort even after adopting the final constitution. In keeping with the assembly's focus on the educational aspect of its communications with the public, as well as with the principle of accessibility, the final project the assembly carried out was to distribute seven million copies of the final constitution in all eleven official languages. This took place during the week of March 17–21, 1997, which was dubbed national constitution week. The project was intended to help ensure that the constitution would become a reference point for all South Africans, to create a sense of ownership of the document, and to engender enduring respect for it.

The distribution strategy for this final project emphasized accessibility, particularly for historically disadvantaged sectors of society. Four million copies were distributed to secondary schools; two million were made available at post offices countrywide; 500,000 were distributed to all members of the South African police service and national defense force, as well as all members of the Department of Correctional Services and prisoners; and 500,000 were distributed through civil-society organizations. Each copy of the constitution was accompanied by an illustrated guide in the same language, highlighting key aspects of the document and explaining many of the legal concepts. Other related publications included one million copies of a human rights comic, which was distributed to all schools and adult literacy organizations, and a teacher's aid to introduce the constitution to students, which was provided to all secondary schools. In addition, taped and Braille versions of the constitution and guide were available for visually impaired persons.

Given its scale and publicity, the assembly's public participation program understandably has been the principal focus of attention by those considering the role of participation in the South African constitution-making process. But other types of outreach occurred at earlier stages of negotiation as well. In particular, though consultation with key members is not unusual for political parties engaged in negotiations,[108] the ANC at times sought wide-ranging involvement by its constituency in developing its constitutional proposals. For example, in 1990, during the period of talks about talks, the ANC's constitutional committee launched a public debate on the party's constitutional proposals and proposed bill of rights. Between 1990 and 1993, the committee held a series of about ten broadly inclusive conferences to discuss the proposals in detail in a format that invited participation. Participants included ANC and Communist Party members, trade union activists, NGO and community-based organization representatives, and foreign and local academics.[109] This mediated form of participation was important to bringing ideas into the process.[110]

In addition, a wholly different type of participation—or at least popular influence—was evident during the negotiation of the interim constitution, even though the negotiations themselves involved rather undemocratic elite bargaining. Mass action, demonstrations, and petitions supported the efforts of the ANC and its allies to shape the transition, and "various forms of public display of claims, outrage, and strength continued to be employed by groups on all sides, trying to ensure that their concerns or demands be placed on the agenda at the multiparty talks."[111] The interim constitution ultimately accommodated many of these claims.[112]

Special Role of the Constitutional Court

As noted earlier, the agreement during the multiparty negotiations to give the constitutional court—a new body established during the transition—the role of certifying the constitution was a compromise essential for reaching the goal of a consensus-based settlement.[113] The specific task handed to the court was to certify that the text adopted by the constitutional assembly complied in all respects with the constitutional principles. In other words, the court in effect had to determine the constitutionality of the new constitution.[114] The interim constitution that both incorporated the constitutional principles and established the constitutional court gave the court absolute discretion in interpreting the principles and deciding on the validity of the final text: "A decision of the Constitutional Court . . . certifying that the provisions of the new constitutional text comply with the Constitutional Principles, shall be final and binding, and no Court of law shall have jurisdiction to enquire into or pronounce upon the validity of such text or any provision thereof."[115] Compared with most other constitution-making processes, in which either a popular referendum or the vote of an elected body constitutes the final validating act of a new constitution (an executive signature may be required as well), the South

African process, which substituted judicial affirmation of compliance with a political agreement for final democratic authorization, was unusual. Indeed, using a judicial body for such a purpose appears to be unprecedented.[116]

The court that undertook this role was "different from any other South Africa had seen," with members chosen through a transparent process intended to reflect the ideals of the new democracy, and with regard to the interim constitution's prescription that the court be representative in terms of race and gender.[117] In accordance with the interim constitution, the court's president, Arthur Chaskalson, was chosen directly by the president of South Africa; four judges were drawn from the existing judiciary; and six more were chosen after being publicly interviewed by a new judicial service commission, subject to the president's final decision. The resulting bench was still overwhelmingly male and white, yet it was the most mixed court then sitting in the country.[118] In political terms, the court was not as broad-based as the government of national unity; from the start of the selection process, it was clear that no candidate whose "background was in any way touched by too close an association with apartheid or discredited views or institutions would be seriously considered."[119]

The constitutional court was intent on dealing with the certification process expeditiously and also on ensuring that the process of testing the adopted text was handled in the same open manner as the drafting. It was, however, in a difficult position, as the constitutional principles were essentially political agreements among parties bringing an end to conflict. To make matters worse, a fair number of the thirty-four principles could be interpreted in various ways. Moreover, the court had to undertake its task against the background of the text already having been adopted by an overwhelming majority of a democratically elected body. Whichever way

it decided, the court risked jeopardizing the credibility it had established as well as public acceptance of the outcome.[120] The stakes were extremely high.

To the court's credit, the process adopted in the directions issued by the judge president assured openness and transparency.[121] The directions allowed about six weeks for submitting written arguments, to be followed by oral arguments commencing on July 1, 1996. They provided for written argument on behalf of the constitutional assembly to be lodged with the court and invited the political parties represented in the assembly to present written grounds of objection and oral argument if they wished. The directions also invited any other body or person wishing to oppose certification to submit a written objection. With the help of the constitutional assembly, the court published notices in all official languages inviting objections and explaining the procedure. Objectors were required to specify the grounds of objection and indicate the constitutional principles allegedly contravened. The court then invited detailed written argument with respect to those objections that raised new issues germane to the certification.

Five political parties tabled objections to certification: the African Christian Democratic Party, the Democratic Party, the IFP (joined by KwaZulu/Natal province), the NP, and the Conservative Party. Eighty-four private parties lodged objections as well.[122] The assembly, the political parties, and twenty-seven of the private parties were afforded a right to present oral arguments. In the court's words, "in deciding whom to invite to present oral argument, we were guided by the nature, novelty, cogency and importance of the points raised in the written submissions. . . . The underlying principle was to hear the widest possible spectrum of potentially relevant views."[123] The court's hearings, which ran from July 1 to July 11, were open to the press and public and were summarized each day on television, together with visual footage of the proceedings.[124]

The novelty and the burden of the court's task were at times apparent in the course of the proceedings. According to one first-hand observer, "during the hearing, the judges occasionally gave the impression of being uncertain about the role in which they had been cast. Their questions about the approach they should adopt, the nature of the task they were carrying out, and the extent of their latitude to check the will of the Constitutional Assembly combined to convey a sense of the stress under which they were working."[125] One of the judges, Albie Sachs, later commented on the complexity of the issues presented to the court, which included "the entire ground of what a constitution is, what it can be, what it ought to be, what international practice is, what the principles require, and how to interpret this text of over two hundred articles that comprised the new constitution."[126]

Two months after the hearing, the court delivered its judgment. The judges found that the text adopted on May 8 did not comply with the constitutional principles in nine respects.[127] The court was mindful, however, not to cast too dark a shadow on the text. The judgment concluded with two observations: "The first is to reiterate that the Constitutional Assembly has drafted a constitutional text which complies with the overwhelming majority of the requirements of the Constitutional Principles. The second is that the instances of non-compliance which we have listed . . . although singly and collectively important, should present no significant obstacle to the formulation of a text which complies fully with those requirements."[128] The court deliberately said as little as possible in its judgment. According to Sachs, the judges were "very aware of the fact that our decisions would be binding in the future, and that here we were, most unusually, interpreting a constitution from beginning to end and already

establishing perspectives and fundamental interpretations. So we were reluctant to go beyond the absolute minimum necessary to answer the questions that were asked."[129]

The judgment did not spark any controversy; instead, it was hailed as a victory for constitutional democracy. The court's ability to assert itself in this manner, barely eighteen months after it had heard its first case, indicates that most political actors during the transition period had come to accept constitutional supremacy, the rule of law, and the subordination of parliamentary sovereignty to the principles of a constitutional state.[130] The court's decision to invite the general public, rather than just the political parties, to participate in the certification process may partly explain the widespread support for the outcome.[131] Also, during the life span of the interim constitution, South Africans had begun to take for granted constitutional democracy in general and the institutional role of the constitutional court in particular.[132]

Ironically, the return of the text presented the constitutional assembly with some valuable opportunities: Principally, it was possible to attempt once again to bring the IFP on board. One of the more serious flaws the court found in the adopted text was that the powers of the provinces were substantially reduced compared with those in the interim constitution; this was an issue of particular interest to the regionally based IFP. In addition, the drafters had a chance to clean up the text, as continual amendment of the document during the pressure-filled two weeks preceding May 8 had introduced a number of inconsistencies.

Within days of the court's judgment, the assembly's management committee met to decide on a way forward. The committee members sensed that it was necessary to finalize the constitution as soon as possible to allow assembly members to redirect their time to the crucial demands of governance and transformation. The management committee therefore agreed that the constitutional committee should be convened to negotiate the amendments and table its report with the assembly for adoption at its earliest possible convenience. The management committee proposed the formation of two subcommittees of the constitutional committee to handle the actual negotiation of the amendments; these divided the work along subject matter lines. To save time, when the subcommittees began their work on September 25, technical experts supporting them tabled two sets of draft formulations. One suggested amendments to address the defects that the court had identified, and the other proposed a technical refinement of the text.

Agreement on some amendments, such as the addition of special procedures for constitutional amendment, was not difficult to achieve, given the court's clear guidance and the relatively straightforward changes needed. The most critical and challenging issue that had to be addressed at this stage concerned provincial powers. The court found that in several respects, the provinces' powers were substantially less than and inferior to the powers they had enjoyed under the interim constitution and that the revised scheme thus violated the constitutional principles. The court's guidance made it immediately apparent which amendments ought to be made, though negotiating some of the needed revisions, particularly concerning the structural design of local government, proved difficult. Nevertheless, the process moved swiftly at this stage.

The IFP toyed with joining in the amendment process; its members attended a number of meetings and participated in bilateral and multilateral discussions with the ANC and other parties. But when the IFP insisted that meetings renegotiate matters long settled that did not offend any constitutional principle, these requests were rejected. Thus, shortly before the completion of the amendment exercise, the IFP for the last time abruptly withdrew its participation.

The constitutional committee approved for adoption the amendments tabled by the subcommittees, and the constitutional assembly met at its last sitting on October 11, 1996, to pass the amended text. The text was adopted with the same overwhelming majority as on May 8, and then immediately tabled before the constitutional court. The interim constitution required the court to examine afresh whether the text complied with the constitutional principles. Nevertheless, the judges had to approach the second-round certification exercise in the context of their previous judgment.

The court issued directions similar to those given for the first certification exercise, and ordered the assembly to publish the directions as widely as possible and to make copies of the amended text freely available. Hearings were scheduled for November 18. While any objector could raise any issue, whether previously considered or not, the court made it clear that because of the extensive written and oral submissions in the first round, it believed it was unlikely that any important issues had been overlooked.

By this point, the opposition parties had clearly won as much ground as they could.[133] Only two political parties represented in the constitutional assembly lodged objections, the Democratic Party and IFP; the NP formally announced that it did not intend to object to the amended text. The province of KwaZulu/Natal and eighteen private individuals and interest groups also lodged objections, while the assembly in turn filed submissions supporting certification. The hearing lasted two and a half days, and on December 4, 1996, the court delivered its unanimous judgment certifying the amended text.[134] The court noted that the amended text bore every sign that the assembly took the court's previous judgment, which had carefully spelled out the reasons for its finding of noncompliance, as the blueprint for modifying the text.

Handed a historically significant and politically charged task, the constitutional court performed its role with transparency, extreme care, and scrupulous fairness. A less well-executed performance might have made the court's decisions more difficult to accept. Moreover, the certification procedure may have been accepted as valid at least in part because the function was given to a court with a "growing reputation for independence," and because the final result was seen as a legal rather than political decision.[135]

The International Dimension

Unlike the constitution-making experiences in various other countries in transition from authoritarianism or conflict after the Cold War,[136] the international community—in the form of international or regional organizations or even individual constitutional experts—played a relatively insignificant role in the constitution-making process in South Africa. Some limited consultations with foreign experts occurred[137] and parties used comparative research and knowledge in preparing their proposals,[138] but both the design and substantive outcome of the process were homegrown. One particular foreign experience that the South African constitution makers looked to for lessons was that of Namibia; in Albie Sachs' words, "it was like a trial run." In particular, Namibia's use of fundamental principles that served as the foundation of the final settlement, the use of proportional representation, and the structure of the constitution served as positive models.[139]

The international community neither directly catalyzed nor mediated in the negotiated transition. The 1989 Harare Declaration of the Organization of African Unity had envisioned a prominent role for the international community and the PAC supported a prominent place for it in the process, but in the event, such a role never materialized.[140] Early on, when both sides were developing a commitment to negotiation, the ANC recognized that unless it seized the initiative in preparing for negotiation, the international community would play this role. To lose this initiative would have meant losing the ability to determine the agenda of the process, as happened in Zimbabwe and Namibia. The NP likewise opposed international involvement, having found the experience of U.S. and British pressure in the Namibian negotiations humiliating.[141]

However, the international community did help to shape the broader environment in which the negotiated transition was launched. Apartheid South Africa had been treated as an international pariah in many quarters for decades and was subjected to various sanctions, even as Cold War priorities, combined with South Africa's profitable investment environment for international business interests, encouraged many Western governments to treat the NP government as an ally.[142] But as the Cold War ended, Western allies, encouraged by the ANC,[143] began to intensify pressure for change, thus helping to weaken the regime's untenable grip on power after de Klerk took the helm. For example, by October 1989, British prime minister Margaret Thatcher looked to the South African government to provide her with sufficient grounds to stave off demands by Commonwealth leaders for tougher sanctions. And in the United States, the State Department demanded that the South African government unban political parties, lift the state of emergency, allow for the return of exiles, remove all discriminatory legislation, and begin negotiating with credible black leaders on a new constitutional order by June 1990.[144] Weeks later, the government unconditionally released several senior political prisoners.

Conclusion: The Impact of the Constitution-Making Process and Factors Contributing to Success

The signing ceremony for the final constitution was infused with symbolism. The event was held on December 10, International Human Rights Day; the venue chosen was Sharpeville, in Vereeniging, where on May 31, 1902, the Treaty of Vereeniging between the Boers and British was signed, ending a bitter anti-imperialist war and allowing South Africa to be united as one sovereign territory from four independent states. The treaty had paved the way for the first constitutional dispensation, one that sealed the disenfranchisement of the black majority. Signing the final constitution in this location provided a bookend to a history that started in division and conflict and ended in reconciliation. Vereeniging also represented more recent South African history: It had been the scene of much political conflict and strife, gaining international notoriety after the Sharpeville massacre on June 16, 1960.

President Mandela's signing of the new constitution—the birth certificate of a new South Africa—was undoubtedly a remarkable moment. What were the key characteristics of the negotiating process and the conditions in the country that enabled this moment to come about? And what, so far, has been the constitution-making process's lasting impact?

Impact of the Constitution-Making Process

The constitution-making process produced both a document of unquestioned legitimacy and high substantive quality and a form of democracy that has become increasingly stable and institutionalized. The 1996 constitution has been implemented and respected in actual practice. Moreover, the constitution making was an integral part of the broader process of dismantling the abhorrent apartheid system, and, in effect, concluding a peace treaty between black and white South Africans. The constitution-making process was the heart of a transition that, against the odds, was essentially peaceful, despite extremist-instigated political violence during the multiparty negotiating process. While the country today suffers many social woes associated with the legacy of colonialism and apartheid, including severe economic disparities and very high crime rates, political violence is largely absent.[145] In these important and enduring respects, the outcome of the process must be regarded as a success.

The nature of the process—its qualities, on the whole, of inclusiveness, transparency, and participation—was clearly instrumental in producing the outcome. Indeed, the process and the substantive outcome were two sides of the same coin. A high degree of consensus was achieved among parties representing a wide range of ideological perspectives both because the design of the process emphasized the necessity of consensus and because the parties crafted substantive compromises that they could actually agree upon. In other words, reconciliation between the black majority and white minority—in the sense of creating a political system that both could accept and use to settle differences peacefully—was achieved, and in tracing the source of that achievement, process and substance cannot be distinguished. The process was structured and conducted in a way that enabled both sides to achieve important objectives and to create a South Africa that all could live in; the substantive agreements reached through the process were the concrete manifestation of those satisfied objectives. The process and substance were of a piece in another sense as well. As Heinz Klug observes, the parties' substantive goals shaped their procedural preferences,[146] and thus, the agreements negotiated with respect to the design of the constitution-making process automatically implicated certain substantive ends.

However, the constitution-making process did not achieve reconciliation between the ANC and IFP, and the country suffered subsequent violence between supporters of these two groups. These parties could not find common ground through the process, despite ANC as well as NP negotiators' persistent efforts to bring the IFP on board. It may be that the IFP's positions were not reconcilable with the consensus achieved among other parties; or perhaps IFP leader Buthelezi was simply too obstreperous. The IFP showed that it felt alienated by elements of the process, including the sufficient consensus procedure and the use of parallel bilateral meetings. The party's own orientation may have been to blame for this alienation, or it may be that it is difficult in any situation for a constitution-making process to satisfy relatively minor players with outlying positions. The IFP's lesser negotiating skill also might have been a factor in the failure to make the party part of the process. More than any other party, during the interim constitution negotiations, the IFP "locked itself into positions which were out of the mainstream negotiating process."[147]

While the impact of the nature of the process on its immediate result may be clear, assessing precisely how the process has, in a lasting way, affected the nature of politics and governance in South Africa is more difficult. In particular, what impact has the inclusiveness and participatory quality of the constitution-making process had on the political process in South Africa?[148] One concrete effect is that the success of the public participation program influenced the constitution makers to insert a constitutional requirement that all new legislation be accompanied by a process of public participation and public hearings. More broadly, the continuing political stability in South Africa—despite a history of conflict—surely reflects the legitimacy of the constitutional system, which, in turn, is a consequence of the nature of the process.

Ingredients of Success

A confluence of conducive conditions, key events, and wise choices explains the successful outcome of the constitution-making process. It is impossible to do more than catalogue the factors contributing to success, as their relative importance cannot be ascertained objectively. Regardless, such a catalogue can be a highly useful resource for those wishing to assess whether the techniques applied in South Africa can be translated into other contexts.

The relevant factors may be organized into three somewhat overlapping general categories: political, practical, and personal. Regarding political circumstances, the parties' commitment to negotiating a transition and a new constitutional dispensation was born of a stalemate. The ANC recognized that it could not defeat the government by force,[149] and the NP recognized that it could no longer rule the country as it had without entirely ruining it. This factor combined to good effect with other factors, such as the presence of wise leaders on both sides of the divide who perceived the need for negotiation in these circumstances, and who understood that negotiations could deliver results that each side could live with. Pressure from the international community, especially trade partners, contributed as well to the NP's appreciation of the need to negotiate.

A strong sense of South African identity on both sides contributed as well. Especially after the 1994 elections, negotiators across the spectrum espoused a common nationalism. This removed from the agenda the issue of national identity, which has bedeviled other constitution-making processes, and facilitated the finding of common ground. In addition, a strong legal tradition in South Africa—which, surprisingly, both the oppressed and oppressor respected—helped the constitutional engineers to resolve many serious divergences of interests through legal formulation and provisions calling for resort to legal institutions, such as the constitutional court.[150]

Finally, the presence of two dominant players on the political scene facilitated agreement. The ANC and NP drove the negotiating process through their bilateral contacts and worked in concert to broaden consensus to include other players.[151] For the most part, they successfully performed a difficult balancing act between forging agreements between themselves and keeping the more peripheral, and often more ideologically extreme, players on board to prevent spoiling.

As for practical factors, including both the procedural choices the participants made and the technical arrangements they put in place, the priority given to achieving consensus was critical. For example, while the ANC did not have sufficient votes in the constitutional assembly to adopt the constitution on its own, its relative strength—63.7 percent of members—weighed heavily on its negotiating partners. Nevertheless, it repeatedly demonstrated willingness to compromise to gain wider support for particular provisions. Closely related to the focus on consensus was the parties' emphasis on inclusiveness as a means of clothing the constitution in legitimacy. In the constitutional assembly phase, the principle of inclusion produced a cumbersome process in some respects because it meant involving a large number of people. The assembly had 490 members, many of whom were directly engaged in negotiation and drafting. But any inefficiencies that resulted from this approach were a fair price for the legitimacy of the final document, and the commitment to inclusiveness was not permitted to derail progress. While one

objective of this commitment was to draw potential spoilers into the process, the main parties moved ahead when necessary, even when the IFP and others walked out.

Furthermore, though some of the most important aspects of the process were the least open and democratic—specifically, the negotiation of the constitutional principles, the extensive use of private bilateral meetings, and the constitutional court's certification of the final result—the public's involvement in other aspects seems to have contributed to the respect that the final document enjoys. One analyst of the process has observed a feeling of loyalty to the constitution spanning political ideologies that seems connected to the sense of ownership that emerged from the process, including from the lack of international mediation.[152] Participation enabled ordinary people to begin to realize that they could influence laws and the government. In the course of the process, there was a groundswell of interest among citizens in matters that were previously the exclusive preserve of those in power. In this way, the process may have helped to foster a culture of constitutionalism in South Africa.

The parties' decision to establish a two-stage structure for the process was of perhaps paramount importance to the realization of the fundamental compromise between the interest of the majority in a swift transition to democracy and the interests of the minority in a guaranteed role in the transition and in certain lasting protections. This structure proved to be an effective conflict management device. The graduated nature of the approach created the opportunity to bring potential spoilers into the constitution-writing process and transitional governance arrangements, as well as to build the confidence of minorities in the prospect of an ANC-led government before that eventuality occurred.

Another practical factor was the very long lead-up to adopting the final constitution. The preliminary negotiation stages, CODESA, and the MPNP all resolved many procedural and substantive obstacles to final agreement, with the consequence that the final constitution-making process was not overburdened with issues. The slate was cleaned as much as possible, in effect, before the assembly ever started its work. The length of the overall process also enabled parties to hone their negotiating skills and fully develop their substantive positions. Moreover, direct contacts throughout the slow buildup to substantive negotiation gave interlocutors the opportunity, on the Afrikaner side, to shed their demonized perceptions of the ANC, and on the ANC side, to become sensitized to white fears.[153]

In addition, the generally efficient negotiating structures that the parties created played a positive role. The use of lessons learned at CODESA to build better structures for the MPNP, and the care taken in devising the assembly structures, enabled those forums to translate disparate positions into agreed-upon results.

The contribution of personal factors, it is widely agreed, cannot be overstated. There is no question that the right people were on the scene at the right historical moment, and that those individuals exercised mature and effective leadership. The quality of leadership shown by Mandela and de Klerk, as well as Ramaphosa, Meyer, and others, has rarely been matched in such difficult circumstances. The maturity of the top leaders was evidenced in part by their recognition that they had to tolerate a certain amount of crowing by the other side about successes achieved at the negotiating table, even if exaggerated; each side realized that they needed the other to be able to deliver the support of its constituency.[154] Exceptional personal qualities were exhibited by the members of the constitutional court as well. If they had been any less skillful and scrupulously fair in playing their unusual role, the result of their work might not have been as well accepted as it was.

Furthermore, the personal chemistry that developed among negotiators, and their willingness to develop personal relationships across the divide, facilitated their ability to find compromises.[155] The length of the process, noted as a contributing practical factor above, helped create opportunities for these relationships to develop. Over the course of negotiations, key participants spent a great deal of time together and came to know one another personally. This shared time humanized political opponents, and negotiators began to learn to separate their political differences from their growing respect for each other as people. In a sense, the long process enabled reconciliation between the leaderships of the parties.

The essentially equal sophistication of the main actors on both sides contributed significantly as well.[156] Both sides had skilled negotiators and well-developed positions and proposals. The depth of expertise and organizational experience on the ANC's part was born of years of operation in exile as well as the participation of highly skilled individuals. The NP had the experience of running the country for almost half a century. Without this depth of political and technical expertise on both sides, it might not have been possible for the complex negotiating and drafting structures put in place to have operated as effectively as they did.

Finally, a sine qua non of South Africa's success was the commitment of both sides to negotiating a solution to the country's need for a new constitutional dispensation. This factor is a personal one because it required a commitment to negotiation on the part of individual participants, as well as the capacity of those individuals to transcend their past experiences as oppressed and oppressor, and to work patiently and persistently over a long period of time to reach the desired end. But it is also a factor resulting from those individuals' appreciation of political realities. The commitment to negotiation, and concomitant willingness to compromise, constitutes the necessary condition for any successful negotiation: political will. That condition was manifest in South Africa in the fact, for example, that parties on both sides moved their positions during the process, realizing that they had to recognize and respect the diversity of interests involved. The presence of political will to see the process through to a conclusive end was supported by the parties' shared belief that they could achieve their main objectives through negotiation, and, in turn, supported the parties' efforts to overcome the many obstacles that South Africa faced in moving from apartheid to democracy.

* * *

Whether or not the South African experience can be a model for future constitution-making exercises depends at least partly on whether the conditions contributing to success in this case can be created elsewhere, and whether those future circumstances are ripe for the constructive procedural choices made in South Africa. Certainly, the South African case offers practical ideas regarding procedural design that can inform and inspire future constitution makers. Perhaps above all, the South African constitution-making experience can serve as a source of hope for others seeking to bridge seemingly unbridgeable divides.

Glossary of Acronyms

ANC   African National Congress (main party opposing the apartheid regime; ruling party postapartheid)

CODESA   Convention for a Democratic South Africa (first attempt at multiparty talks)

IFP   Inkatha Freedom Party (led by Mangosuthu Buthelezi, opposed to unitary state and to use of elected constitutional assembly)

MPNP   Multi-Party Negotiating Process (multiparty talks that culminated in adoption of the interim constitution and other transitional measures)

NP   National Party (ruling party of the apartheid regime)

PAC   Pan-Africanist Congress (left-wing extremist party, formed by ex-ANC members)

Notes

1. Significant portions of this chapter are adapted from Hassen Ebrahim, *The Soul of a Nation: Constitution-making in South Africa* (Cape Town: Oxford University Press, 1998). Hassen Ebrahim served as the executive director of the South African constitutional assembly and previously as national coordinator for the African National Congress's negotiations commission.

2. Albie Sachs, "The Creation of South Africa's Constitution," *New York Law School Law Review,* vol. 41 (1997), pp. 669–70.

3. Nico Steytler, "Constitution-Making: In Search of a Democratic South Africa," in *Negotiating Justice: A New Constitution for South Africa,* ed. Mervyn Bennum and Marilyn D. Newitt (Exeter: University of Exeter Press, 1995), pp. 62–63.

4. Fink Haysom, "Special Features and Mechanisms in Negotiating the South African Constitution," in *Constitution-Making and Democratisation in Africa,* ed. Goran Hyden and Denis Venter (Pretoria: Africa Institute of South Africa, 2001), p. 93.

5. The body of literature on the South African constitution is large; many of the texts pertinent to the process of making the interim and final constitutions are cited herein.

6. For a detailed and fascinating telling of the history of the transition negotiations, see Allister Sparks, *Tomorrow Is Another Country: The Inside Story of South Africa's Road to Change* (New York: Hill and Wang, 1995).

7. The racial and ethnic landscape of South Africa is, of course, more complex than black and white. For reasons of economy and confinement to the scope of this chapter, such complexities are not explored here.

8. Like the racial landscape, the political landscape and history of South Africa are more complex than the treatment in this chapter reveals.

As the ANC and NP were the main actors in the constitution-making process, their roles and perspectives are given the lion's share of attention here.

9. This is a term used in South Africa to refer to persons of mixed race.

10. The consultation involved thousands of volunteers, who "went from door to door to document people's grievances and aspirations." Cyril Ramaphosa, "Negotiating a New Nation: Reflections of the Development of South Africa's Constitution," in *The Post-Apartheid Constitutions: Perspectives on South Africa's Basic Law*, ed. Penelope Andrews and Stephen Ellmann (Johannesburg: Witwatersrand University Press, 2001), p. 81.

11. See Eldred de Klerk, "South Africa's Negotiated Transition: Context, Analysis and Evaluation," *Accord*, no. 13 (2002), pp. 14–19. De Klerk observes that the Congress of the People "was a unique experience of mass participation in a political visioning process amidst hostile political circumstances and shaped the implicit expectation for public participation in creating a new South Africa." See also Sparks, *Tomorrow Is Another Country*, p. 61, pointing out that consultation was "an obsessive requirement within the internal resistance movement."

12. This letter is reproduced in Ebrahim, *Soul of a Nation*, Document 9, p. 429.

13. This letter is reproduced in Ebrahim, *Soul of a Nation*, Document 10, p. 433.

14. Regarding Botha's half-hearted reforms and the intensified resistance they provoked, see Sparks, *Tomorrow Is Another Country*, pp. 68–75.

15. See Sparks, *Tomorrow Is Another Country*, pp. 53–56.

16. See Ramaphosa, "Negotiating a New Nation," p. 72.

17. See Sparks, *Tomorrow Is Another Country*, p. 36. Toward the end of this period, ANC leaders in exile and government officials also held secret talks in Switzerland. Sparks, *Tomorrow Is Another Country*, chap. 9.

18. The Organization for African Unity declaration adopted August 21, 1989, at the suggestion of the ANC, is available at www.anc.org.za/ancdocs/history/oau/harare.html (accessed April 25, 2009).

19. For a discussion of de Klerk's speech and its context and significance, see Sparks, *Tomorrow Is Another Country*, pp. 5–14.

20. Despite their rejection of the homeland system, ANC leaders approved of Buthelezi's acceptance of the position of chief minister of KwaZulu, the Zulu tribal homeland, in the hope that he would establish "an internal political platform for their outlawed movement. But the relationship soured and Buthelezi turned Inkatha into a Zulu ethnonationalist party opposed to the ANC." Sparks, *Tomorrow Is Another Country*, p. 125. Regarding government complicity in Inkatha-instigated violence, see, e.g., Sparks, *Tomorrow Is Another Country*, pp. 163–78.

21. See "Planning a New Nation," *Star*, December 21, 1991.

22. The first working group considered the creation of a climate for free political participation and the role of the international community, the second was mandated to explore constitutional principles and the constitution-making body, the third dealt with an interim government, the fourth was to debate the future of the homelands, and the fifth was to deal with time frames.

23. See "Codesa to Call for Submissions on New Constitution," *Citizen*, February 5, 1992.

24. "Support for Talks is Vital—Codesa," *Business Day*, February 26, 1992.

25. Of more than 2.8 million voters, 68.7 percent endorsed the reform program. John Hatchard and Peter Slinn, "The Path towards a New Order in South Africa," *International Relations*, vol. 12, no. 4 (1995), p. 7.

26. Regarding the Boipatong massacre of June 1992 and other violence committed by IFP supporters after the collapse of CODESA, as well as government complicity, see Sparks, *Tomorrow Is Another Country*, pp. 140–47.

27. See Roelf Meyer (as told to Hennie Marais), "From Parliamentary Sovereignty to Constitutionality: The Democratization of South Africa, 1990–1994," in *The Post-Apartheid Constitutions*, p. 56.

28. Haysom notes that this was arguably the most important of the accords reached in the period leading up to substantive constitutional negotiations, because it reflected both major parties' acceptance that the basic preconditions for substantive talks had been met, as well as their agreement on the fundamentals of the process ahead. "Special Features and Mechanisms," p. 101. Regarding the significance of the Record of Understanding, see also Meyer, "From Parliamentary Sovereignty to Constitutionality," pp. 56–58.

29. Meyer, "From Parliamentary Sovereignty to Constitutionality," p. 63.

30. Hatchard and Slinn, "Path towards a New Order," p. 8.

31. See Haysom, "Special Features and Mechanisms," pp. 104–05. Haysom notes that substantive negotiations were conducted "under the guise of a technical umbrella" to avoid the public posturing that had characterized CODESA. See also Richard Spitz with Matthew Chaskalson, *The Politics of Transition: A Hidden History of South Africa's Negotiated Settlement* (Oxford: Hart Publishing, 2000), p. 48. In remarking on the importance of the technical committees, these authors note, "One of Codesa's legacies was the lesson that working groups comprising 76 politicians were singularly incapable of discussing and settling core issues on a rational, technical basis."

32. Ramaphosa, "Negotiating a New Nation," p. 78. According to Ramaphosa, the broadcast of Mandela's appeal "signaled for many people that the balance of forces in South Africa had changed irrevocably. Nothing could illustrate more clearly that Mandela had become the *de facto* head of state in South Africa."

33. Ramaphosa ("Negotiating a New Nation," p. 78) points out that there was no such deadline until this moment.

34. In one particularly dramatic event, several hundred armed right-wingers stormed the site of the MPNP and invaded the negotiating chamber. Several people were injured, and a great deal of property was damaged. See Meyer, "From Parliamentary Sovereignty to Constitutionality," pp. 63–64, regarding violence during the MPNP.

35. Sachs explains that during the debates over the design of the constitution-making process, one group of parties sought a roundtable style format for negotiating and drafting the constitution, followed by a popular referendum to confer legitimacy on the negotiated document. The other group, led by the ANC, "argued that the basic problem all along in South Africa had been the complete failure of self-determination." Thus, a small, self-appointed set of negotiators could not produce a legitimate document. Legitimacy was "a fundamental element of the psychological, cultural, and historical transformation that the country needed," and making a constitution by dealing around a table "could result in a precarious situation, for the new constitutional order, leaving it without the sense of destiny and historical evolution, intensity, or drama that one needs for an event of this kind." Sachs, "Creation of South Africa's Constitution," pp. 671–72.

36. The opinion page of the *Sunday Times* on November 21, 1993, just after political party leaders signed the interim constitution, captured the moment: "We, the people of South Africa, have wrought a miracle. We have accomplished what few people anywhere in the world thought we could do: we have freed ourselves, and made a democracy, and we have done so without war or revolution."

37. See Nicholas Haysom, "Federal Features of the Final Constitution," in *The Post-Apartheid Constitutions*, p. 511 ("The final constitution in most respects constitutes a refinement of the interim text."); and Haysom, "Special Features and Mechanisms," p. 109 (the main innovations in the final constitution were the National Council of Provinces, the chapter on cooperative governance, and, to some extent, the elevation of local government to a level or sphere of government).

38. Spitz, *Politics of Transition*, pp. 2–3.

39. Sachs, "Creation of South Africa's Constitution," p. 673.

40. Spitz, *Politics of Transition*, pp. 3 and 74, the latter explaining the theory underlying the two-stage approach.

41. Haysom points out that the ANC had, in fact, prepared a full draft of the constitution, as well as supporting research and submissions on supplementary legislation, prior to the MPNP. This gave the ANC an advantage in establishing the terms and direction of the debate. Haysom, "Special Features and Mechanisms," p. 103.

42. The ANC and NP agreed upon the two-phase framework for the transition in the September 1992 Record of Understanding. Spitz, *Politics of Transition*, p. 69.

43. Spitz, *Politics of Transition*, p. 3.

44. Ibid., p. 69. Other parties envisioned the two stages differently, while the right-wing Concerned South Africans Group alliance insisted on a one-stage transition, with a new constitution negotiated by an unelected convention of political parties. See Spitz, *Politics of Transition*, pp. 69–72. Ultimately, as with many other issues, ANC-NP agreements held sway. More to the point, it was the moderate camp in both parties that prevailed, as neither the ANC nor the NP leaderships were unanimous in their views on the negotiating and transition processes. See Spitz, *Politics of Transition*, p. 77.

45. See Spitz, *Politics of Transition*, p. 416: "Although neither of South Africa's post-apartheid Constitutions would be the product of a perfectly legitimate, democratic and unfettered process, a two-stage process afforded enough continuity, enough democracy, and enough legitimacy to satisfy the main political forces."

46. Ramaphosa, "Negotiating a New Nation," p. 80. See also Siri Gloppen, *South Africa: The Battle over the Constitution* (Aldershot: Dartmouth/ Ashgate, 1997), p. 269, noting that an advantage of the two-stage process is that it delinked, to some extent, the final constitution from the transition negotiations, in which the creation of a well-functioning constitutional framework was secondary to reaching a deal to achieve peaceful change.

47. Chapter 15, Constitution of the Republic of South Africa, Act 200 of 1993, available at www.concourt.gov.za/site/constitution/english-web/interim/ch15.html (accessed April 25, 2009).

48. Agreement on the device of the constitutional principles resolved an impasse between the ANC, which wanted a democratically elected body to draft the constitution, and political and racial minority groups, which sought a process in which all existing political parties would agree unanimously on a new constitution. Haysom, "Federal Features," p. 509.

49. Meyer, "From Parliamentary Sovereignty to Constitutionality," p. 66.

50. Haysom, "Federal Features," p. 509.

51. Sec. 74, Constitution of the Republic of South Africa, Act 200 of 1993, available at www.concourt.gov.za/site/constitution/english-web/interim/ch5.html (accessed April 25, 2009).

52. Sachs, "Creation of South Africa's Constitution," p. 672.

53. Ibid., pp. 672–73.

54. The principles are contained in Schedule 4 of the Constitution of the Republic of South Africa, Act 200 of 1993, available at http://www.concourt.gov.za/site/constitution/english-web/interim/index.html (accessed April 25, 2009). For a general description of each of the principles, see Spitz, *Politics of Transition*, pp. 81–82.

55. Haysom, "Federal Features," pp. 509–10. See also Haysom, "Special Features and Mechanisms," p. 102, in which he notes that, surprisingly, principles concerning the issues that had divided South Africans for 300 years were brief and universally accepted, while the issue of the status and powers of provincial governments overwhelmingly dominated the principles and attracted the sharpest contestation.

56. Regarding the role of the transitional executive council, see Hatchard and Slinn, "Path towards a New Order," pp. 9–12.

57. See Spitz, *Politics of Transition*, pp. 87–89.

58. Spitz notes that power sharing in South Africa was not consociational, as it was not a system for the representation of various ethnic groups. The election results revealed that only Inkatha was an ethnically based political power: "The power-sharing arrangement had little if anything to do with South Africa's ethnic and racial diversity, and all to do with the pact negotiated between the key political forces at that moment." Spitz, *Politics of Transition*, p. 99. Heinz Klug also makes the point that, compared to a consociational arrangement, the proportional participation scheme for the government of national unity was "less static and more representative." Heinz Klug, "Participating in the Design: Constitution-Making in South Africa," *Review of Constitutional Studies*, vol. 3, no. 1 (1996), p. 40.

59. Christina Murray, "Negotiating beyond Deadlock: From the Constitutional Assembly to the Court," in *The Post-Apartheid Constitutions*, pp. 113–14.

60. See Spitz, *Politics of Transition*, p. 55: "It may be that the secrecy during the MPNP was necessary because at Kempton Park [the location of the talks] the very future of the negotiating process was tenuous, partly because of the mutual suspicions but principally because there was no formal political framework that guaranteed that negotiations would continue to completion."

61. See Meyer, "From Parliamentary Sovereignty to Constitutionality," p. 65.

62. Scheduling the election also had the effect of slowing progress in reaching compromises, because parties began to try to score political points. Meyer, "From Parliamentary Sovereignty to Constitutionality," p. 66.

63. While the IFP's walkouts throughout the process were problematic in certain respects, they did have the salutary effect of enabling agreements to be reached more quickly than might have been the case had they participated, given their positions. See Haysom, "Special Features and Mechanisms," pp. 109–10.

64. See Spitz, *Politics of Transition*, pp. 56–61, and Haysom, "Special Features and Mechanisms," p. 105.

65. The Democratic Party had insisted that the appointment of judges involve the judiciary and legal profession; the opposing argument was that neither the judiciary nor legal profession were representative of the country's population, since their members were overwhelmingly male and white.

66. Meyer, "From Parliamentary Sovereignty to Constitutionality," p. 69.

67. Hatchard and Slinn, "Path towards a New Order," p. 9.

68. Ramaphosa explains that the ANC continued after the MPNP to engage right-wing groupings and encourage them to participate in the election process in order to defuse the threat to stability that they posed. Ramaphosa, "Negotiating a New Nation," p. 79.

69. See Ramaphosa, "Negotiating a New Nation," p. 79.

70. Hatchard and Slinn, "Path towards a New Order," p. 14.

71. See Sparks, *Tomorrow Is Another Country*, p. 226.

72. Jessica Piombo, "Politics in a Stabilizing Democracy: South Africa's 2004 Elections," *Strategic Insights*, vol. 3, no. 5 (May 2004), available at www.ccc.nps.navy.mil/si/2004/may/piombo May04.asp (accessed April 25, 2009). Piombo notes that the highest number of pre-election violent incidents occurred between members of the ANC and IFP. In the runup to the election, violence also broke out over the status of the Bophuthatswana homeland, illustrating the alliance of convenience between the white right-wing and certain black homeland leaders. See Sparks, *Tomorrow Is Another Country*, pp. 206–19.

73. Eighty-six percent of eligible voters turned out. For these elections, all South Africans over the age of eighteen could vote, without any registration requirement (the 1996 Constitution required a voters' roll for future elections). Piombo, "Politics in a Stabilizing Democracy."

74. See International Republican Institute, "South Africa: Campaign and Election Report, April 26–29, 1994" (October 1994), available at www.iri.org/africa/southafrica/pdfs/South%20 Africa's%201994%20Presidential%20and%20 Parliamentary%20Elections.pdf (accessed April 25, 2009); and Haysom, "Special Features and Mechanisms," p. 108.

75. See Steytler, "Constitution-Making," pp. 71–77. Steytler notes that the questions of how the elections should be managed and who should administer them had been highly contested.

76. Sachs, "Creation of South Africa's Constitution," pp. 673–74.

77. For example, the Human Rights Commission, the Gender Project, and the South African Council of Churches. The media voiced strong objections to being excluded from multilateral meetings.

78. The full panoply of deadlock-breaking procedures provided in Section 73 of the interim constitution can be summarized as follows:

(a) If the constitutional assembly failed to adopt the draft text by a two-thirds majority of all members, but a simple majority supported the draft, the panel of constitutional experts would have thirty days to propose amendments;

(b) An amended draft unanimously recommended by the panel would be sent to the constitutional assembly, which would have fourteen days to approve it by a two-thirds majority;

(c) If the panel could not make a unanimous recommendation, of if the two-thirds majority vote requirement was not met for a recommended amended draft, the constitutional assembly could adopt any proposed draft before it by simple majority; however, in this case, after certification of the adopted text by the constitutional court, the text would have to be submitted to popular referendum;

(d) A referendum would have to be held within ninety days of being called, and 60 percent of votes cast would be needed to approve the draft constitution;

(e) If none of the above measures produced a final approved constitution, the president would have to dissolve parliament; in this situation, a newly elected constitutional assembly would have one year to adopt a final constitution by a 60 percent majority of all members.

Sec. 73, Constitution of the Republic of South Africa, Act 200 of 1993, available at www.concourt.gov.za/site/constitution/english-web/interim/ch5.html (accessed April 25, 2009).

79. Murray, "Negotiating beyond Deadlock," 118–19.

80. As described in the chapter on Namibia in this volume, the constituent assembly there in November 1989 formally adopted UN Security Council Resolution 435, which incorporated a set of constitutional principles laid down in 1982 by the Western contact group.

81. In the constitutional assembly's decision-making procedures, a vote was called only when the terms of the rules or the interim constitution required one. Otherwise, all matters were decided by consensus. However, whenever a vote was called, the resolution concerned was passed unanimously.

82. Theme committees each were assigned to deal with the issues implicated by specific constitutional principles. In general terms, the topics covered by each numbered committee were as follows: 1—character of the democratic state (preamble, representative government, state name and symbols, separation of powers, etc.); 2—structure of government; 3—relationship between levels of government; 4—fundamental rights; 5—judiciary and legal systems; and 6—specialized structures of government (i.e., public administration, financial institutions and public enterprises, transformation and monitoring, and security services). See Ebrahim, *Soul of a Nation,* pp. 183–86 for a detailed list of the subject matter mandate of each committee.

83. Murray, "Negotiating beyond Deadlock," p. 113.

84. For data on the work of the other theme committees, see Ebrahim, *Soul of a Nation,* notes 26, 28, 30, 32, and 34–37, pp. 338–43.

85. For an example of substantive advice from the panel concerning rights of noncitizens, see Jonathan Klaaren, "Contested Citizenship in South Africa," in *The Post-Apartheid Constitutions,* pp. 308–09.

86. Murray, "Negotiating beyond Deadlock," p. 118. Christina Murray was a member of the panel.

87. See Ramaphosa, "Negotiating a New Nation," p. 74.

88. As Ramaphosa explains, though the final obstacles may seem minor compared to the broader issues already resolved, they "lay at the heart of what the ANC was trying to achieve, and what the NP was trying to prevent. The question of single-medium instruction in schools, property rights and the employer's right to lock out, all represented in some way the National Party's desire to maintain through the Constitution some of the privileges and inequalities that had characterized apartheid. . . . These were not matters on which the ANC was prepared to compromise." Ramaphosa, "Negotiating a New Nation," p. 82.

89. These included the lockout clause, the property clause, the death penalty, the appointment of judges, the attorney general, language, local government, the question of proportional representation, and the bar against members of parliament crossing the floor.

90. At this point, deadlock remained on the lockout, property, and education clauses. Specifically, the NP continued to demand a right for employers to lock out striking workers (ultimately dropped at the eleventh hour), a guaranteed right to property in the Bill of Rights (in the end, settled with a compromise limiting the circumstances in which property could be expropriated), and a right to education in one's own language (resolved by providing a right to education in the language of one's choice, with single-medium schools being one option for the government to consider). See Ramaphosa, "Negotiating a New Nation," pp. 83–84.

91. See note 78 laying out the full set of deadlock-breaking mechanisms.

92. The other 13 percent comprised the members from the IFP, who had boycotted the negotiations since April 1995; the Freedom Front members, who abstained; and the two African Christian Democratic Party members, who voted against the constitution because it failed to subject all government and law to the law of God. See Spitz, *Politics of Transition,* p. 425, and Murray, "Negotiating beyond Deadlock," p. 119, note 35.

93. Constitutional assembly resolution, October 11, 1995.

94. The survey, designed and analyzed by the Community Agency for Social Enquiry (CASE), was carried out in April 1995. Later surveys were conducted throughout the process. The results of the CASE survey appear in an unpublished volume titled *Taking the Constitution to the People: Evaluating the Constitutional Assembly,* compiled by David Everett (Johannesburg: CASE, 1997).

95. Community Agency for Social Enquiry, "A New Constitution for a New South Africa," (Johannesburg: CASE, 1996), cited in Heather Deegan, "A Critical Examination of the Democratic Transition in South Africa: The Question of Public Participation," *Commonwealth & Comparative Politics,* vol. 40, no. 1 (March 2002), p. 47. To the question "Have there been any meetings?" 13 percent answered yes, 63 percent answered no, and 24 percent did not know.

96. About half the submissions (1,001,246) petitioned for Afrikaans as an official language, 650,000 to keep the parliament in Cape Town, 186,376 in favor of the death penalty, 42,069 against South Africa as a secular state, 19,854 against the legalization of abortion, 17,209 against including sexual orientation in the antidiscrimination clause, 17,778 for constitutional protection of animal rights, and 14,475 for the right to own firearms. Gloppen, *Battle over the Constitution*, pp. 257–58.

97. Catherine Barnes and Eldred de Klerk, "South Africa's Multi-Party Constitutional Negotiation Process," *Accord*, no. 13 (2002), pp. 26–33. The authors note that about 10 percent of submissions came from organizations, about 0.6 percent from political parties, and the vast majority from individuals.

98. Remark by Heinz Klug at working group session of the U.S. Institute of Peace/UN Development Program Project on Constitution Making, Peacebuilding, and National Reconciliation, September 28, 2001, p. 143 of transcript (on file with the U.S. Institute of Peace). See also Deegan, "A Critical Examination," pp. 49–51, noting that the issues most South Africans wished to see addressed in the constitution concerned practical matters, such as the need for more jobs, more housing, better schools, and crime control.

99. Barnes and de Klerk state that submissions from organizations with links to parties or with specialized knowledge were seriously considered, but the drafters did not use submissions from individual citizens systematically in the first phase, in part because of the huge volume of submissions and in part because some of the issues raised seemed unrelated to the negotiating agenda. Barnes and de Klerk, "South Africa's Multi-Party Constitutional Negotiation Process."

100. According to the CASE opinion survey (1996), only 38 percent of the population over the age of fifty, but 57 percent of the population ages eighteen to twenty-four, believed that the government genuinely sought participation. Cited in Deegan, "A Critical Examination," p. 48.

101. Murray, "Negotiating beyond Deadlock," pp. 107–11.

102. Ibid., p. 112.

103. Murray asserts that it was always clear that the constitutional assembly would mediate the public's views rather than directly incorporate them in the constitution. In Murray, "Negotiating beyond Deadlock," p. 112.

104. The procedure for processing the submissions was improved in the second phase over the first, making their consideration more manageable. These submissions were summarized, organized according to the relevant section, and presented as endnotes to the working draft. Gloppen, *Battle over the Constitution*, p. 261.

105. One analyst finds very few signs that the public submissions directly influenced the text of the constitution. For example, of the major subjects of the petitions, only one—in favor of Afrikaans as an official language—is consistent with the final text, though it is unlikely that this result is attributable to the petitions. Gloppen, *Battle over the Constitution*, pp. 260–62. In comparison, Ramaphosa writes: "Clearly not every submission had an impact on the final product, nor did they substantially influence some of the positions taken by the various parties. But they did highlight some of the key concerns shared by ordinary South Africans, and allowed South Africans to engage directly with the process of shaping their future." Ramaphosa, "Negotiating a New Nation," p. 81.

106. Metropolitan areas are urban areas that include commercial zones; urban areas are generally residential in nature.

107. For example, Professor Jeremy Sarkin of the Human Rights Committee, in a letter to the president of the constitutional court dated April 18, 1996 (on file), argued that "the final stages of the constitution-making process have been characterised by closed political party negotiation (referred to as bi- or multilaterals), and it is in these forums where political agreement on contentious issues has been reached. . . . Thus civil society has been effectively excluded from the last and crucial phases of the process. This is particularly true of more marginalized groups. Moreover, civil society has not been afforded the opportunity to comment on whether the final package complies with the principles which underlie a democratic nation." Ironically, the Human Rights Committee, despite having filed an objection to the certification of the constitution, failed to appear at the court to argue its case.

108. In the South African case, many of the parties participating in the multiparty talks that led to the interim constitution "used their membership structures to consult with their constituencies on key issues in the negotiations and to 'bring them along' in the process, thus involving them indirectly in the negotiations." Barnes and de Klerk, "South Africa's Multi-Party Constitutional Negotiation Process."

109. Klug, "Participating in the Design," pp. 34–36. Klug observes that the debates and discussions initiated by the constitutional committee contributed significantly to the development of the ANC's constitutional vision.

110. Remark by Heinz Klug at working group session of the U.S. Institute of Peace/UN Development Program Project on Constitution Making, Peacebuilding, and National Reconciliation, September 28, 2001, pp. 178–79 of transcript (on file with the U.S. Institute of Peace).

111. Klug, "Participating in the Design," p. 42.

112. Klug, "Participating in the Design," pp. 42–43.

113. See Carmel Rickard, "The Certification of the Constitution of South Africa," in *The Post-Apartheid Constitutions*, p. 224. Carmel Rickard was responsible for reports on the certification process as legal editor of the *Sunday Times.*

114. See Sachs, "Creation of South Africa's Constitution," p. 676.

115. Constitution of the Republic of South Africa, Act 200 of 1993, sec. 71(3).

116. Samuel Issacharoff, "Constitutionalizing Democracy in Fractured Societies," *Journal of International Affairs,* vol. 58, no. 1 (Fall 2004), p. 83; Spitz, *Politics of Transition*, p. 427.

117. Rickard, "Certification of the Constitution," pp. 224–25.

118. Ibid., p. 225.

119. Rickard, "Certification of the Constitution," pp. 225–26, also p. 209, note 7: "Initially, some concern was voiced by those disappointed in the make-up of the Court that it might be a lackey of the ruling African National Congress. However, even before the certification case was heard, the Court had handed down judgments indicating that these criticisms and concerns were misplaced."

120. See Rickard, "Certification of the Constitution," p. 285.

121. As the interim constitution gave no details of the procedures to be followed, the court had to define its own approach to its task. Gloppen, *Battle over the Constitution*, p. 210.

122. Submissions from the IFP and a cluster of white right-wing groups including the Conservative Party and various religious, farming, and other organizations was particularly significant because they "might have been expected to stay aloof from the process." Rickard, "Certification of the Constitution," p. 286.

123. Judgment of the Constitutional Court, CCT 23/96, September 6, 1996. *In re: Certification of the Constitution of the Republic of South Africa, 1996*, 1996 (10) BCLR 1253 (CC) (First Certification judgment).

124. Sachs, "Creation of South Africa's Constitution," p. 676. Sachs also notes that the voice-over summary approach to televising the proceedings was a compromise between banning television altogether and allowing what some feared would be play-acting for the cameras.

125. Rickard, "Certification of the Constitution," p. 285.

126. Sachs, "Creation of South Africa's Constitution," p. 677.

127. Several elements of the text, in the court's judgment, failed to comply with the principles. First, the right of individual employers to engage in collective bargaining was not recognized and protected. Second, the text failed to provide that constitutional amendments require special procedures involving special majorities and did not ensure that the fundamental rights, freedoms, and civil liberties protected in the constitution were entrenched by giving the relevant provisions enhanced protection from amendment. Third, the text did not adequately provide for and safeguard the independence and impartiality of the public protector and the auditor general. Fourth, the failure to specify the public service commission's powers and functions rendered it impossible to certify that the commission could exercise its powers independently. Fifth, chapter 7 of the text failed to provide a "framework for the structures" of local government, did not provide for appropriate fiscal powers and functions for local government, and did not provide for formal legislative procedures to be adhered to by legislatures at local government level. Sixth, the text did not provide for "appropriate fiscal powers and functions for different categories of local government." Seventh, the text purported to place the Labor Relations Act beyond constitutional scrutiny, but did not incorporate the act's provisions, thus impermissibly shielding those provisions from constitutional review. Eighth, the text similarly and impermissibly purported to place the Truth and Reconciliation Act beyond constitutional scrutiny. Finally, the powers and functions given to the provinces were substantially less than or inferior to those which the provinces enjoyed under the interim constitution. See summary of the September 6, 1996, judgment of the court in Ebrahim, *Soul of a Nation*, Document 36, pp. 627–30, and Spitz, *Politics of Transition*, pp. 426–27.

128. Judgment of the Constitutional Court, CCT 23/96, September 6, 1996, para. 31.

129. Sachs, "Creation of South Africa's Constitution," p. 677.

130. Spitz, *Politics of Transition,* p. 427.

131. Rickard, "Certification of the Constitution," p. 286.

132. Spitz, *Politics of Transition*, p. 425. Regarding the important role of the constitutional court, particularly during its first eight years, in settling questions concerning the transition to democracy, see Ran Hirschl, *Towards Juristocracy: The Origins and Consequences of the New Constitutionalism* (Cambridge, MA: Harvard University Press, 2004), pp. 29–30.

133. See Rickard, "Certification of the Constitution," p. 288.

134. On the critical issue of provincial powers, the court found that "the powers and functions of the provinces in terms of the amended text are still less than or inferior to those accorded to the provinces in terms of the interim Constitution, but not substantially so." Judgment of the Constitutional Court, CCT 37/96, December 4, 1996.

135. Rickard, "Certification of the Constitution," pp. 288–89.

136. See, e.g., the chapters on Namibia, Albania, Bosnia, Cambodia, East Timor, Afghanistan, and Iraq in this volume.

137. For example, the panel of constitutional experts traveled to Europe in November 1996 to attend workshops in Britain and Germany in order to exchange ideas with international experts on technical issues in the new constitution. Other examples are provided elsewhere in this chapter.

138. Haysom, "Special Features and Mechanisms," p. 106.

139. Sachs, "Creation of South Africa's Constitution," p. 689.

140. Over the years, there were several failed attempts at international mediation, including an effort proposed by the Commonwealth Eminent Persons Group in 1986. See Hatchard and Slinn, "Path towards a New Order," p. 2.

141. De Klerk, "South Africa's Negotiated Transition."

142. Ibid.

143. Haysom notes that the ANC used its international credibility to leverage international resolutions and declarations on the route negotiations should follow from the Organization for African Unity, the United Nations, and the Commonwealth. See Hayson, "Special Features and Mechanisms," p. 95. See also Ramaphosa, "Negotiating a New Nation," p. 75, noting that the ANC successfully pressured the international community to maintain sanctions against the South African regime in the period leading up to multiparty negotiations on the transition.

144. "Deadline for Big Changes June—U.S.," *Star*, October 4, 1989.

145. One observer has commented, "It is safe to say that the dialogue processes at the heart of the transition helped to establish a culture of peaceful negotiations entrenching and affirming a habit of constructive cooperation and coexistence, politically as well as economically." De Klerk, "South Africa's Negotiated Transition."

146. Klug, "Participating in the Design," pp. 31–33.

147. Spitz, *Politics of Transition*, p. 419.

148. See Heather Deegan, "A Critical Examination of the Democratic Transition in South Africa: The Question of Public Participation," *Commonwealth and Comparative Politics*, vol. 40, no. 1 (March 2002), pp. 43–60. Deegan observes that the South African government since the transition in 1994 has stressed participatory democracy, but she finds uneven results.

149. Moreover, Haysom observes that "the liberation movements recognized the futility of inheriting a wasteland, of capturing the bank only to find the safe empty. The members of the liberation movements in exile had seen at first hand how neighbors such as Angola and Mozambique had been reduced to extreme poverty as a result of a flight of capital and skills, and a long and debilitating civil war." See Hayson, "Special Features and Mechanisms," p. 93.

150. Remark by Nicholas (Fink) Haysom at working group session of the U.S. Institute of Peace/UN Development Program Project on Constitution Making, Peacebuilding, and National Reconciliation, September 28, 2001, pp. 162–63 of transcript (on file with the U.S. Institute of Peace).

151. Remark by Haysom at working group session, pp. 174–75 of transcript (on file with the U.S. Institute of Peace).

152. Ibid., pp. 163–64 of transcript (on file with the U.S. Institute of Peace).

153. See, e.g., Sparks, *Tomorrow Is Another Country,* pp. 81–84.

154. Remark by Haysom at working group session, pp. 181–82 of transcript (on file with the U.S. Institute of Peace).

155. A number of participants in the process have commented on the importance of personal encounters across the political divide to the success of the process. See, e.g., Leon Wessels, "The End of an Era: The Liberation and Confession of an Afrikaner," in *The Post-Apartheid Constitutions.* See also Meyer, "From Parliamentary Sovereignty to Constitutionality," p. 69, in which Roelf Meyer comments that "you must create personal interactions with your opponents," and that "it was important to build a relationship of trust with [the ANC]. It was therefore essential that I should establish such a relationship with Cyril Ramaphosa." Meyer and Ramaphosa were their respective parties' chief negotiators.

156. See, for comparison, the chapter on Iraq in this volume, in which the author identifies problems associated with the Sunni negotiators' lesser negotiating skill and preparation than their counterpart Shia and Kurds.

6

The Politics of Constitution Making in Uganda

Aili Mari Tripp

Since 1990, thirty-eight African constitutions have been rewritten, and eight involved major revisions. Uganda rewrote its constitution in 1995. Many of the constitutional changes witnessed throughout Africa have to do with individual rights and liberties, the rights of traditional authorities, the protection of customary rights, issues of land rights, and the rights of women. These issues were central to the constitution-making process in Uganda; however, the undemocratic outcomes in that country demonstrate the ways in which these processes have often been politicized to serve the interests of those in power.

Since the 1995 constitution was adopted, Uganda has slid backward precipitously in respecting civil and political liberties. The government increasingly has restricted the freedom of association, harassed and intimidated opposition members and media workers, attempted to ram through undemocratic legislation in Parliament without a quorum, and narrowed political control from what once was a broad-based government to a much smaller circle of individuals. As Ann Mugisha, a member of the opposition, wrote in a 2004 *Journal of Democracy* article, "The real transition taking place there is from a relatively enlightened and benevolent authoritarian regime . . . to a textbook case of entrenched one-man rule."[1] A decade after its passage, 119 amendments to the 1995 constitution had been made, some of them key changes to the earlier constitution. It was widely acknowledged that 70 percent of parliamentarians were openly bribed to give President Yoweri Museveni the two-thirds vote needed to alter the constitution to allow him a third term.[2]

How did such undemocratic outcomes emerge from a constitution-making process that was touted as unprecedented in its participatory character? To understand the problems with Uganda's constitution, one needs to examine the broader context within which it was drafted, debated, and voted on. It is especially important to look at the relationship between the process and the outcomes because the constituent assembly elections in 1994 marked the end of the broad-based coalition that had characterized the ruling National Resistance Movement (NRM) and the beginning of the NRM acting as a de facto single party under an increasingly authoritarian regime. President Museveni, who came to power in 1986, had envisioned that the NRM—or the Movement, as it is referred to—would encompass all political interests and parties in Uganda, suppressing sectarian tendencies in the country and garnering legitimacy for himself. By the mid-1990s, however, rather than ushering in a period of greater inclusiveness in the political process as was purported, the constitution-making process signaled the shrinking of political space, as Museveni eliminated the non-NRM multipartyists from his cabinet and other key positions. Later, in the early 2000s, the circle was to close even further, as Museveni purged some of his staunchest NRM supporters from the cabinet, military, and security agencies when they opposed his bid for a third term. Meanwhile, Museveni has strengthened his reliance on Uganda's military.

Continuities from Past Constitution-Making Efforts

Many of the problems encountered in making the 1995 constitution have their origins in earlier constitution-making efforts and events. Oliver Furley and James Katalikawe have argued that the prevalent view of drafting constitutions in Uganda has been that if one could come up with an adequate constitution, it would provide a basis for good and democratic governance.[3] But political, historical, and social conditions have conspired to create undemocratic and exclusionary processes for Uganda's experience with constitution making, which in turn has contributed

to the creation of autocratic and unstable regimes, highly polarized polities, and decades of civil strife. In other words, Uganda's substantive problems with its constitutions have been related to the procedural frailties of constitution making.

Uganda's first constitution—the 1962 independence constitution—was established in the context of a newly formed alliance between Milton Obote's Protestant-led Uganda People's Congress (UPC) and the Baganda Kabaka Yekka party (KY, or King Alone). The Baganda are the largest ethnic group in Uganda, constituting 18 percent of the population, and Buganda, their area of origin, has always been regarded as the largest, wealthiest, and best educated of the country's kingdoms. The two parties had come together in an unlikely and ultimately untenable coalition to challenge the Catholic-led Democratic Party (DP). The DP's leader, Benedicto Kiwanuka, had become chief minister of Uganda in 1961. KY was focused on the fate of Buganda and the kingship, rather than the entire nation, and its members believed that the DP, though led by a Muganda, was not interested in the kingship. KY-UPC members outnumbered the DP in the new 1962 parliament, ensuring that Obote could form a government to oversee the transition to independence that same year.

The first constitution, negotiated in London among various parties and interests, provided for a Westminster form of government. Executive powers were vested in the prime minister, who, with his cabinet, was head of government. The British Queen remained head of state and appointed a governor until 1963, when the constitution was to be amended to install a president. Under this constitution, Uganda instituted a unitary system, with Buganda enjoying autonomous status—referred to as federal status in Uganda—with greater rights and privileges than other districts in Uganda. The country's other three kingdoms, Ankole, Bunyoro, and Toro, enjoyed only quasi-autonomous status. Buganda's Lukiiko (parliament) served as an electoral college for its representatives to the Ugandan national assembly.

Buganda's special status became a source of tension after independence, especially after Buganda's *kabaka* (king), Edward Mutesa, became the president of Uganda in 1963, while the UPC head, Milton Obote, served as prime minister. The kabaka's dual loyalties to Buganda and Uganda led to a constitutional crisis in 1966.[4]

The matter came to a head when Uganda was to decide on the so-called Lost Counties in a 1965 referendum. The issue of the Lost Counties arose from the animosity between the Bunyoro and Baganda, who had been enemies throughout much of the nineteenth century. The British had used Buganda to conquer Bunyoro and rewarded Buganda by giving it six counties of Bunyoro territory that had particular cultural and historical significance to Bunyoro. The British preferential treatment of Buganda created tension among Ugandan citizens living outside of Buganda[5]; in the referendum, which allowed the residents of the Lost Counties to choose between remaining part of Buganda or returning to Bunyoro, the counties voted to join Bunyoro, leading to a split between the Baganda leadership and Obote. The ill-fated anti-DP alliance between Buganda's (KY) party and Milton Obote's UPC was already frayed, but after the referendum, it crumbled. KY fell apart, and many of its members joined UPC to support the Buganda faction of the UPC that had opposed Obote, who was a Langi from northern Uganda. Mutesa, Buganda's king, sought military assistance from the British, but before he and the Buganda faction of UPC could make a move, Obote arrested five ministers and charged their faction with plans to have Buganda secede from the rest of Uganda.

The developments regarding the Lost Counties led to the constitutional crisis of 1966, in which Obote assumed full executive powers and suspended the 1962 constitution, in direct violation of that document. The king sought Buganda's secession, demanding that the central government remove itself from Bugandan soil and appealing to the United Nations for support. Obote's forces marched on the Buganda stronghold in Mengo and brutally suppressed the royalists, killing at least two thousand civilians. Mutesa fled to exile in Britain and Obote seized the presidency. On April 15, 1966, parliamentarians found a new draft constitution in their pigeonholes (mail compartments), and Obote, who came to Parliament surrounded by troops, forced the members of Parliament to adopt what came to be known as the pigeonhole constitution. He also ordered the national assembly to become a constituent assembly; it debated the constitution for three months before its adoption in September 1967 in a controlled process. Obote then imposed the adoption of the new constitution and declared himself president without elections.

The new constitution established a unitary and highly centralized state. It abolished the position of the prime minister, placing all executive powers in the hands of the president. Moreover, the executive powers were expanded at the expense of the judiciary and legislature. The constitution also abolished all kingdoms in Uganda, and Buganda's special status was eliminated. Buganda was divided into four districts, wiping its name from the political map, and its parliament building (the Bulange) was transformed into the headquarters of Uganda's Ministry of Defense. The kabaka's palace at Bamunanika outside Kampala became an army barracks. This enraged the Baganda; even though many were not enamored with the king himself, they were loyal to the idea of the kingship and the traditions it represented. The new constitution paved the way for further consolidation of the UPC as the single ruling party, now that the Buganda monarchy and the DP were out of the way. These events set the stage for the reign of terror experienced under Idi Amin (1971–79) and Obote's second government (1980–85). This period of Uganda's history produced the abolition of parties in 1969 and, as the rule of law was abandoned, the use of security forces to suppress opposition.

After the NRM took power in 1986, its leaders felt a need to break with the previous regime of Obote and create a new basis of legitimacy for the party by drafting a new constitution. The new constitution was meant to delegitimize both the old political parties (i.e., the UPC and DP) as well as the idea of multiparty democracy. Simultaneously, the new constitution was intended to advance the goal of bringing about a no-party democracy based on popular consensus.[6] The NRM embarked on a constitution-writing process in 1989, having formed a ministry for constitutional affairs in 1986. Opponents of the new constitution-writing exercise included those who wanted to reinstate the model of Buganda autonomy and federalism embodied in the 1962 independence constitution as well as UPC supporters who wanted simply to amend the 1967 constitution.

The process of constitution making was expensive, long, and drawn out. It was originally planned to take two years, beginning in 1989; instead, it took six years to produce a constitution. Some say the NRM extended the length of the process as a delaying tactic to give it more time in power. The entire constitution-making exercise cost $20 million, 42 percent of which came from the government of Uganda and 58 percent from foreign donors. The European Union, the United States, the United Kingdom, Japan, Denmark, and the United Nations Development Programme were among the largest contributors to the exercise.[7]

With 287 articles and seven schedules, the 1995 Ugandan constitution is one of the longest in the world, several times longer than most European constitutions and ten times the length of the U.S. constitution.[8] This is partly because the Ugandan constitution addresses many policy issues that generally are not included in constitutions, as they encumber legislators dealing with new situations and contingencies.

Political Context of Constitution Making

The 1989–95 constitution-making process took place against the backdrop of a number of NRM initiatives designed to ensure that its objectives were met in the exercise. The first such initiative was a ban on the activities of political parties. When the NRM first came to power in 1986, it had not taken an antiparty line; it brought the leaders of opposition parties into its leadership coalition and used them to legitimate itself as a broad-based movement representing the interests of all, and to promote itself as a movement opposed to sectarianism. In a bid to consolidate the NRM's power, however, in 1992 the Parliament adopted a resolution suspending political activity. By 1993, the constituent assembly statute prohibited parties from running candidates in the elections for the assembly established to adopt a new constitution. This kept the playing field tilted in favor of the NRM.

Critics believe that the constitution-making process was flawed from the outset because political parties could not mobilize freely. Parties could exist and issue press releases, but they could not hold workshops, conferences, or party congresses. Rallies that were organized were forcibly stopped. Political candidates were forbidden from running on a party ticket in elections, and had to run as individuals. Parties could have national offices, but they were not permitted to open branch offices. The NRM justified the ban based on a purported need to unify the country through building a no-party movement that would represent all interests. The UPC had been responsible for massive atrocities during the second Obote government and was sufficiently discredited by its past record to allow the NRM to suppress all party activity without risk of serious public backlash. But the ban not only curtailed the activities of the UPC; it prevented other parties from forming and weakened existing parties, most of which were in disarray.

Second, the NRM sought to ensure that the politically and numerically important Baganda—one-fifth of the population—supported the new constitution. Museveni permitted the restoration of the Ugandan monarchies and traditional rulers—Buganda, Ankole, Toro, and Bunyoro—as cultural though not political entities, and returned properties and lands to the kabaka and Baganda royals.

Third, the NRM initiated a decentralization program through the 1993 Local Government Statute. The stated goal was to devolve planning and budgetary decisions and deliver services to the districts and their subunits. However, the law was used later to invalidate Baganda appeals for federalism because decentralization was said to have already succeeded in bringing services and accountability to the people.[9]

Finally, the NRM capitalized on the existence of continued fighting and instability in the north to remind the southerners, who enjoyed relative peace, what a return to the UPC-Obote days would bring. Most of the constituent assembly delegates from the north were opposed to the NRM and supported multiparty politics. The government had been working toward a settlement in the north but abruptly halted peace negotiations in 1994 for no apparent reason. Critics have long charged that the lack of settlement in

the north has been part of a cynical and concerted propaganda effort to remind the south of the ills that would befall the rest of the country should it fall into non-NRM hands, as well as a way to keep the north from becoming a more cohesive political bloc capable of opposing the NRM.[10] It has also given the government a pretext for keeping its defense budget high.

The Role of the Constitutional Commission

The Selection of Constitutional Commission Members

Many of the undemocratic characteristics of the 1995 constitution can be traced back to undemocratic aspects of the constitution-making process itself. Plans to create a new constitution under NRM leadership dated back to the establishment of a Ministry of Constitutional Affairs in 1986. The ministry did very little until 1989, when a constitutional commission was formed.[11] The selection of members of the constitutional commission was ad hoc and done in batches. Some members who were appointed by the minister for constitutional affairs were not approved by the president, and some were appointed by the president without approval of the minister, as the Uganda Constitutional Commission Act of 1988 required. There was no nomination process allowing anyone else to suggest names.[12]

Even though the commission's composition was regionally balanced and one DP member sat on the commission, almost to a person, the body was made up of strong supporters of the Movement system.[13] It included both the political commissar of the NRM and his counterpart in the National Resistance Army (NRA). Not one member of the commission openly opposed the Movement system. This left the commission open to criticism that the process of selecting members was not carried out in a sufficiently democratic fashion.[14] The commission was headed by Justice Ben Odoki, under the direction of the minister of constitutional affairs, and was financed by the government, which gave the executive additional leverage in running the commission.

Activities of the Constitutional Commission

With few exceptions, rarely in Africa has one seen the level of popular engagement in education seminars, debates, media discussions, and submission of opinion memoranda that was evident in the Ugandan constitution-making process. At least 25,547 separate submissions of views were sent to the commission.[15] That there was such wide consultation with the public through formalized methods may itself be seen as a major achievement. The submissions to the commission included local council memoranda (10,134); essay competitions (5,844); seminar reports from district, subcounty, and various other institutions (899); newspaper opinion articles (2,763); individual memoranda (2,553); group memoranda (839); and position papers (290).[16] The level of involvement of women in the process was unprecedented in Africa and perhaps worldwide. No other sector of society sent as many memoranda to the commission as did women's groups.

Commission members also toured the country, holding seminars and gathering the views of opinion leaders and representatives of key organizations in each district. A draft constitution in the form of guidelines and guiding questions was prepared to elicit further commentary. Massive numbers of people attended the seminars and participated in debates. John Waliggo, one of the commission members, indicates that about 30,000 community leaders were engaged in seminars regarding the constitution.[17] This was followed by seminars in 870 subcounties around the country, in which commissioners introduced and explained the constitution-making process and let people air their views. These seminars were followed by the solicitation of memoranda.[18]

The constitutional commission claimed that the draft constitution it produced was based on people's views. Critics have been skeptical about how much of the constitution reflected popular views, however, especially because the commission's tour emphasized educating people about the constitution rather than consulting with them. Opposition leaders accused the commission of ignoring memoranda that raised contentious issues. Moreover, NRM leaders vetted memoranda written at the subcounty level before submitting them to the commission. Critics also have argued that the commission was part of NRM designs to persuade the public to support the NRM: While the guiding questions that set the framework for the debate allowed for either a multiparty, one-party, or no-party system, the advantages and disadvantages of the multiparty system were listed, while only the advantages of the other two options were presented.

Non-Governmental Civic Education

The controlled nature of the civic education associated with the constitution-making process was underscored by the difficulties that independent non-governmental organizations (NGOs) faced in carrying out civic education activities. Two bodies attempted to supplement the educational activities of the commission: the Uganda Joint Christian Council and the National Organisation for Civic Education and Election Monitoring (NOCEM). NOCEM's experiences exemplify some of the ways in which limits on freedom of association for independent organizations framed the constitution-making process.

NOCEM was made up of fourteen human rights, religious, media, and legal rights associations, in addition to several women's organizations, including Action for Development (ACFODE), the Uganda Federation of Business and Professional Women, and the Association of Uganda Women Lawyers (FIDA). They aimed to carry out civic education and monitor the constituent assembly elections, which they did along with other national and international observers. Even though the organization was nonpartisan and included members with past and present affiliations with the NRM, UPC, DP, and Conservative Party, the organization was banned. Prior to this, the president had attacked NOCEM on January 26, 1994, accusing it of being a partisan organization. The announcement that NOCEM's accreditation as an NGO had been withdrawn gave no reason for this disqualification.[19] Additionally, NOCEM faced harassment by the parliamentary representative in Mukono and was banned by both the district executive secretary in Bushenyi and the district administrator in Mpigi.

In an interview at the time with the chairperson of NOCEM and president of the Uganda Law Society—later to become a High Court judge and a judge of the International Criminal Tribunal for Rwanda—Salome Bossa pointed out that NOCEM was a new organization and faced both internal and external problems.[20] Internally, the organization made a few innocent mistakes with some individuals who had not been screened properly. Those who were found to be asserting partisan positions were expelled immediately.[21] One member who was expelled, Amos Muhindo, had been working in Kasese and was identified as a former UPC Youth Winger who had an allegedly controversial political record in the early 1980s; UPC Youth Wingers were associated with inflicting random terror on communities under Obote's post-1980 government. NOCEM argued that the problem was partly a result of the NRM's inexperience in dealing with such

an independent body. It also argued that in some cases, the complaints against NOCEM had been launched by government officials who were attempting to rig elections in favor of Movement politics by delegitimizing NOCEM's nonpartisan activities. Eventually, NOCEM was allowed to operate, but the experience showed the limits of autonomous organizations within the process and the government's fear of alternative views regarding the role of political parties.

Key Issues Considered by the Constitutional Commission

The substantive issue at the heart of the constitution-making process regarded the nature of the political system in Uganda: Would it be a multiparty democracy or a no-party Movement system? In its report and in draft proposals on the political system, the commission set the framework for the debate over multipartyism in the constituent assembly. The most contentious specific issues that the commission addressed concerned, first, the form of government suitable for a democratic Uganda (i.e., multiparty versus no-party Movement system), second, the role of political parties, and third, the position of traditional rulers.

The commission originated the idea of maintaining the Movement system in the new constitution, but holding a referendum on the political system (Movement versus multipartyism) five years after promulgation of the constitution. The commission, however, did not address issues relating to the context in which the referendum would be held. Its proposals did nothing to ensure that supporters of a multiparty system could articulate their views freely. Instead, party activities that were defined in the commission's draft constitution as incompatible with the Movement system were to remain suspended during the period the system was in place—that is, in the period leading up to the referendum. This left an unlevel playing field for those who did not want a Movement system.

The Constituent Assembly Elections

Constituent Assembly Election Act of 1993

The constituent assembly was the most important body in the constitution-making process. The NRM's original intent was to have the national assembly serve as the constituent assembly, as had been the case in the 1967 constitutional deliberations. However, many questioned the representativeness of the existing Parliament, given its large number of historicals—NRM members who were given parliamentary seats in recognition of their role in the guerrilla war that brought Museveni into power—as well as presidential nominees, army representatives, and women elected by an electoral college that was closely associated with the NRM. None of these members was seen as having the mandate of the people.[22] As a result of pressure from political parties to have delegates elected freely from all parts of the country, the idea of using the national assembly was dropped. But other crucial efforts to keep the playing field unlevel succeeded.

The constituent assembly statute of 1993 provided for the special selection of 74 of the delegates in addition to the 214 directly elected from the districts. Of the 74, ten were to be appointed by the president, ten by the NRA, two by the National Organisation of Trade Unions, two by each of the four political parties, four by a National Youth Council, and one by the National Union of Disabled Persons of Uganda. In addition, 39 women were elected by an electoral college of subcounty counselors and members of the subcounty Women's Councils within the district. The actual number of special delegates seated in the assembly was only 70, as the UPC refused to send its two delegates in protest against the ban on party activities. The Uganda Patriotic Movement (UPM), which Museveni had formed in 1980, also did not send delegates because it argued that the NRM was already representing its views.[23] This meant that at least 66 of the assembly's delegates were institutionally beholden to the NRM for their positions. Although they were not a majority, they formed a major block of NRM supporters that could be counted on to adopt pro-NRM positions in addition to the chair and vice chair, who were to be elected from among five presidential nominees. Despite the insistence of political parties that they be consulted on these five nominations, no such consultations took place. Movementist James Wapakhabulo became the assembly's chair, and the vice-chair went to Professor Victoria Mwaka, who mobilized the support of women and the Baganda. Three of the four committees established within the assembly also were headed by Movementists.[24]

The Constituent Assembly Election Act of 1993 was the first opportunity for the NRM government to translate its implicit ban on political party activity into a legal ban, with the effects mentioned above. Under the act, candidates could not use a political party affiliation in running for the assembly. They also could only participate in campaign rallies or meetings organized by the government; no other rallies or any forms of public demonstration in support of or against a candidate were allowed.[25] Political party membership recruitment, establishment of branch offices, party member conferences, and campaigning under party banners were all forbidden. Candidates simply had to run as individuals. These provisions of the act violated the 1967 constitution's guarantees of freedom of association and of assembly. They also suppressed public debate, especially on the draft constitution's more controversial aspects.

Meanwhile, NRM candidates continued to use the media to assert their views, an opportunity not as available to non-NRM candidates. Candidates participated in the assembly elections as though they were contestants in a struggle for political power rather than as participants in a constitutional debate, as evidenced by Museveni's proclamation after the assembly elections that "we have won!" Who was to win if everyone was simply running as an individual? By directly and openly supporting Movement candidates, the NRM in effect behaved as a political party while not allowing others to operate in the same fashion. As a result, the assembly elections became a turning point, out of which the Movement emerged as a de facto single ruling party.

The 1993 assembly statute adopted by the national assembly was challenged in the Constitutional Court by a petition from the UPC, which argued, first, that the ban on party activity suppressed constitutionally guaranteed rights of free assembly and association, and second, that the provisions governing campaigning adversely affected the right to free expression. In a blatantly political decision, the court dismissed the petition on the grounds that the suspension of party activity was a temporary measure and that such a measure was necessary to prevent a reversion to the chaos of the past.

The effect of the regulations governing the assembly elections was to drive parts of the electoral process underground, with campaign events held at funeral meetings, in churches, and at fund-raising events with limited impact. It also shifted the debate from a focus on the issues to a focus on personalities and their relationships to the president. Not surprisingly, Museveni won the 1996 and subsequent 2001 and 2006 presidential elections in sweeping victories over opposition candidates. In light of the restrictions on campaigning and organized political activity, the electorate could not consider viewpoints that were effectively excluded from the public debate. As a result, the election process suffered, as the differing positions on issues that lay at the heart of Uganda's political conflicts were not represented effectively.

The Election Process and Results

All in all, the elections gave every advantage to the NRM. The fairness of the elections largely depended on the impartiality and integrity of the commissioner running the elections. Museveni appointed his friend Steven Akabway as commissioner; many regarded him as a political flunky and were critical of his appointment.[26]

There were complaints that government ministers were holding public rallies before the date set for campaigning to begin, on the pretext that they were conducting government business. Police were called in, but no one was prosecuted for holding such events. In many cases, government ministers standing as candidates used so-called official tours to donate large sums of money and goods to local schools and hospitals before and during the election campaign. This was just one way that ministers employed the trappings of state power for their campaigns to gain undue advantage over their rivals. Almost every minister was accompanied by convoys of ministerial vehicles, which they used to transport themselves and their supporters to polling stations. One even traveled from his home less than half a mile from the polling place in an official helicopter.

In some cases, NRM candidates initiated the giving of gifts, money, alcohol, food, and promises of future gains to voters. In other instances, the electorate became extortionists.[27] Adoko Nekyon, a long-time member of Parliament, said that in the forty-three years since the national assembly was formed, he had never seen such extensive buying of votes as he witnessed in the constituent assembly elections.[28] Such charges are hard to prove or disprove, but there was ample anecdotal evidence to support them.

Voter turnout in the constituent assembly election was very high, ranging from 66 percent in Karamoja to 97 percent in Kabale.[29] In the election, 84 percent of the national assembly members ran in the constituent assembly elections, and despite the NRM's many advantages, 51 percent of the parliamentary candidates who ran for the constituent assembly lost. The largest number who lost overall were in the east (60 percent of parliamentary candidates) and the north (67 percent). There were also significant losses for the NRM in the north and east—areas of opposition where citizens were frustrated by continued conflict and lack of development in their regions. Thus, the NRM remained the dominant political force in the western and central regions, while multiparty advocates held sway in the eastern and northern regions.[30]

Because political parties could not field candidates or carry out campaigns, it is difficult to know to what extent the outcome of the elections reflected real political sentiments rather than the capacity of candidates to hand out material inducements. Ethnic allegiances were an additional factor in many of the races. But in many ways, the elections also tested the strength of existing political organizations. Finally, the elections reflected support for the NRM among the Baganda in the south, who by this point had been persuaded to endorse the Movement after the restoration of their kingship in 1993.[31]

Constituent Assembly Deliberations

Several caucuses formed in the process of deliberation on the draft constitution produced by the constitutional commission: the National Resistance Movement Caucus; the Buganda Caucus, to promote the idea of a federal system, in which the kabaka would serve as the constitutional leader of Buganda; the National Caucus for Democracy to promote multipartyism, political pluralism, and freedom of association; and the Women's Caucus, which cut across party and NRM lines and promoted the cause of women's rights. These caucuses formed around key controversial issues being debated and thus featured prominently in the constituent assembly's deliberations.

Future of the Political System

One of the most controversial issues addressed in the assembly deliberations was the future of the political system, that is, whether the country should adopt a no-party Movement system, a multiparty system, or some other type of democratic and representative system. There were several dramatic standoffs between the Movementists and supporters of a multiparty system around this issue.

The multipartyists wanted the constitution to provide for freedom of association and the creation of an interim government composed of all political parties that would govern the country for three years until the new constitution would come into force. The Movementists felt that the country was not ready for multipartyism and that it would fracture the country irreparably. In the end, the assembly's decisions reinforced the recommendations of the constitutional commission that the Movement system should continue in power for another five years, after which a referendum should be held to determine whether or not to transition to a multiparty political system. Its advocates deemed the Movement system to be broad-based, inclusive of all people, nonsectarian, and hence, nonpartisan. Using a referendum was seen as enhancing democracy and popular participation, allowing people to have a say in deciding on which political system should govern them.

Ultimately, the constituent assembly reaffirmed the monopoly on political power held by the NRM and banned "any activities" that might "interfere with the movement political system"(Article 269 of the 1995 constitution). The crucial debate over the future of multipartyism in the constituent assembly was resolved in July 1995 after four days of deliberations and a walkout by multiparty forces. The NRM prevailed with 199 votes in favor of continued no-party rule, 68 opposed, and 2 abstentions. Multipartyists argued against enshrining the Movement political system in the constitution because it would constrain Ugandans' ability to alter their own political system. Multipartyists also argued that using periodic referendums to change the political system would create instability and could be easily manipulated by whoever was in power. The constituent assembly rejected these arguments and voted down the multipartyists' proposals.

The no-party Movement system not only circumscribed the activity of opposition parties, it also gave the NRM—because it was theoretically to be a movement representing the entire citizenry—a rationale not to institutionalize itself as an internally democratic political party. This left key elements of political control highly centralized within the NRM. Power within the NRM continues to be concentrated at the top. The NRM has never held elections for any of its leaders, nor has it convened any popularly elected body to vote on policies.[32] This has led to disaffection within the Movement, although signs of such dissatisfaction were already evident during the assembly deliberations.

At one point in the constituent assembly discussions, Major-General Tinyefuza, a high-ranking army delegate, ignored Movement discipline and openly criticized the extension of the Movement system through the period leading up to the referendum. He

called for a rapid return to multiparty politics, saying that "it is almost immoral to want another free extension of five years to make it twenty" years of NRM rule.[33] The NRM forced him to apologize, retract his comments, and promise to seek guidance from the army before expressing an opinion on the constitution.

Multipartyists and Movementists clashed on other points as well. Dick Nyai, a UPC assembly member, wanted presidential and parliamentary elections to be held on the same day, on the grounds of expense, logistics, and practicality. This proposal was rejected, even though it seemed reasonable to many, purely because a multipartyist had presented it. Many observers were incredulous that this move was defeated. Many multipartyists felt that if the elections were split and the presidential elections held first, a large Museveni victory would demoralize multipartyist supporters and convince some of those who were wavering to join the Movementists. Similarly, the Movementists reasoned that a successful presidential victory would guarantee them a victory in the upcoming parliamentary elections as well.

Federalism and the Status of Buganda

Another major conflict erupted over federalism and the governance of Buganda. Bugandan royalists had sought to reestablish Buganda's pre-1966 autonomous status, under which all districts in the kingdom paid taxes to the Mengo government rather than central government. The royalists proposed that the kabaka should administer Buganda while serving primarily as a titular head. Some wanted the name Republic of Uganda changed to Sovereign State of Uganda. The constituent assembly resolved this by calling Uganda a sovereign state and a republic.

The Buganda parliament (the Lukiiko) promoted the creation of fourteen federal states in Uganda to gain greater acceptance for a federal structure. Within the constituent assembly, however, the Baganda representatives had mixed feelings about federalism and, while many supported the recognition of Baganda culture, they were not ready to give up Uganda's republican identity. Many also feared that Buganda's federalism was the first step toward secession. They were wary of the Lukiiko's authority and of attempts to undermine their legitimacy as elected representatives of districts within Buganda.

Prior to the constituent assembly, the UPC and DP both endorsed Buganda's demands for federalism. This was a dramatic change from their earlier positions. As explained above, the UPC abolished Buganda's special status when it replaced the 1962 constitution. The NRM sought to preempt the assembly's debate on the subject by passing a Traditional Rulers Statute in 1993, which allowed for the restoration of traditional rulers as cultural leaders.[34] In addition, fearing an alliance among the opposition parties and the Buganda leadership in Mengo, the NRM met with the Mengo government and agreed that Buganda would form a regional government under the new constitution.

In the end, Mengo gambled and lost its bid for federalism. It agreed to support NRM positions on antidemocratic aspects of the constitution in exchange for federalism. But the NRM reneged on its end of this perceived bargain. The majority of the assembly delegates took the view that federalism would undermine the unity of the country. They agreed to recognize Buganda as a distinct entity, but instead of federalism, they opted for decentralization and devolution of power from the center to the district level, a policy that was already in place before the assembly convened. The constituent assembly rejected the NRM's agreement on federalism and other promises made to Mengo before the assembly's deliberations. Opportunism by Mengo and the multiparty caucus

ended up hurting both as they tried to use one another.[35]

The issue of federalism continued to dog Ugandan politics in the years after the constitution's enactment. Continuing pressure for a federal system from Buganda resulted in a government proposal for regional parliaments in a federal system for Buganda, Busoga, Toro, and Bunyoro. With waning political backing nationwide, Museveni was eager to shore up his support among the kingdoms, especially Buganda, before the 2006 presidential elections. Having been granted symbolic cultural recognition in the 1995 constitution, the kingdoms continued to press for greater political power and a more public role. In 2005, a constitutional amendment was passed to create regional tiers throughout the country as a layer of administration above the existing district system funded by the central government. Regional leaders would be unable to tax the population, yet they were to be accountable to them. The regional bodies were to be in charge of secondary education, referral hospitals, cultural matters, interdistrict roads, water and sanitation, and agriculture monitoring. A few days before the 2006 presidential elections, the Buganda leadership in Mengo rejected the regional tier arrangement, opting instead for their own version of autonomy, referred to commonly as *federo*.

Outcomes of the Constitution-Making Process

Overall, the constituent assembly's deliberations lasted twenty-nine months from the time the assembly opened in February 16, 1993, to its conclusion on August 25, 1995, when the 284-member assembly adopted the new constitution in toto. The constitution was enacted on September 22 and promulgated on October 8, 1995, by the president. The NRM tried to use the constitution-making process to give its Movement system greater legitimacy and entrench its control. This may have worked in the short run, but it soon began to cost the NRM politically as it became apparent that the Movement was not interested in furthering the democratization process. All democratization measures have been controlled by the regime, which has been limiting political space and centralizing power since the mid-1990s, both within the Movement itself and within the country. The resulting system has kept one person in power for over twenty years with limited possibilities for the development of a truly competitive electoral system and loyal opposition.

The early broad-based NRM government that had sought to incorporate a wide spectrum of political, ethnic, religious, and other interests through political appointments and processes of consensus building was replaced by the time the constitution was adopted by a smaller clique of loyalists, whose activities are cloaked in secrecy. The internal division that emerged within the Movement after the adoption of the 1995 constitution was one of the most striking developments. Some of the sharpest criticisms of the lack of democracy have come from within the Movement itself, including some of Museveni's closest confidantes and political appointees: Colonel Kiiza Besigye, Miria Matembe, Jaberi Bidandi Ssali, Eriya Kategaya, Mugisha Muntu, and Augustine Ruzindana.

A series of legislative acts since the constitution was adopted entrenched Movement dominance, transforming what was to be a no-party system into one-party hegemony. Some of these bills were passed without the required quorum or were speedily pushed through under pressure from the executive. The new constitution gave the Parliament the power to create the organs of the Movement political system and required that the system be democratic, accountable, and transparent, and give all citizens access to positions of leadership. In 1997, however, the Parliament passed a highly controversial Movement Act, requiring all adult Ugandans to belong to the Movement system, even those who opposed it. Multipartyists and many prodemocracy advocates opposed the bill on the grounds that it was unconstitutional. They feared it would destroy freedom of association by making membership in the Movement mandatory. It was seen as enhancing the authority of the executive and reducing the already limited powers of the legislature. It was also seen as a ploy to turn the five-tiered local governance system into branches of the Movement.[36] An earlier version of the bill, promoted by the NRM leadership, was even more undemocratic. It declared the president of Uganda to be the chair of the Movement, making the election of the NRM leader unnecessary. It also made all members of Parliament ex officio members of the NRM national conference, whether they chose to join or not. Although a majority of the Parliament were Movement supporters, they rejected this version of the bill in favor of a modified one. When the first national Movement conference was finally held in July 1998, unsurprisingly, Museveni ran unopposed and was elected chair of the Movement; similarly, the vice chair and the national political commissar were elected unopposed.

At the eleventh hour, the NRM brought the referendum bill to the Parliament in 1999 with little time for debate. The passage of the act paved the way for a constitutionally mandated referendum that was held in 2000. The referendum was meant to determine whether Uganda would have a Movement, multiparty, or some other kind of political system. The bill was steamrolled through Parliament, and Museveni signed it even though the required ninety-member quorum was not reached, as only fifty members of Parliament voted on the bill. The referendum was held on July 1, 2000; the Movement system won with 94.3 percent of the vote. However, turnout for the referendum was exceptionally low by Ugandan standards: Only about 50 percent of registered voters turned out. In some areas, the turnout was as low as 11 percent. This contrasted sharply with the 1996 presidential elections, in which 73 percent of registered voters participated.[37] The major opposition parties, the Uganda People's Congress (UPC) and the Democratic Party (DP), boycotted the referendum, refusing to lend legitimacy to the process.

Yet another controversial piece of legislation—the Political Parties and Organisations Bill—was introduced and withdrawn numerous times in Parliament as a result of sharp disagreements over its content. After many years of debate, the act was finally passed on June 7, 2002. The resulting act did not allow parties to operate at the local level, prohibited them from holding more than one national conference a year, banned public meetings of parties except for national meetings, and provided for the imprisonment of party leaders should the act be violated. Legislation such as this could be directly traced back to the constitution-making process's failure to achieve a genuine popular consensus regarding Uganda's political system.

Many of the above controversial acts were challenged in the Constitutional Court. In March 2003, in *Ssemogerere and Others v. Attorney-General Constitutional Petition No. 5*, the court struck down sections of the Political Parties and Organisations Act that suppressed activities of opposition political parties. In *Ssemogerere and Others v. Attorney-General Constitutional Appeal No. 1* of 2000, the court supported the contention that the Referendum Act in 1999 was unconstitutional; a third ruling in *Ssemogerere and Olum v. Attorney-General Constitutional Petition No. 3* of 2000 found that the Referendum Act of 2000 was unconstitutional and that the referendum itself, which sanctioned the continuation of the Movement system, was invalid. The supreme court, however, overturned this latter ruling.[38]

In an about-face in 2005, multipartyism suddenly became acceptable in a quid pro quo arrangement that allowed Museveni to stay in power. In December 2004, the government presented Parliament with 119 constitutional amendments, including amendments that would lift limits on the president's service of two terms (Article 105.2), lift the restriction on political parties (Article 269), change the political system to a multiparty system (Articles 69–74), and impose sanctions on cultural leaders (kings and chiefs) who violated the constitution. At the same time, Museveni openly bribed 213 of the 305 (70 percent) members of Parliament with 5 million shillings ($3,000) each in exchange for supporting his attempt to remove term limits on the presidency. Ten others signed up to receive the funds. The government needs two-thirds of Parliament to approve amendments to the constitution, such as an amendment to remove term limits on the presidency.[39] The constitutional commission had incorporated the provision of two five-year term limits on the presidency because of the fear of unrestrained power that has had such detrimental effects on postcolonial politics in Africa.[40] In recent years, civil societies and legislatures have fought bitterly over attempts to lift executive term limits and succeeded in keeping them in Nigeria, Zambia, and Malawi, but failed in Togo, Burkina Faso, Gabon, Guinea, Chad, Tunisia, and Uganda. Term limits were removed in Uganda in June 2005, paving the way for Museveni to run for president in 2006.

In the 2006 elections, Museveni won by a 22 percent margin over his opponent, Kizza Besigye; however, the opposition contested the 59 percent of the votes that he claimed. Even Uganda's supreme court found evidence of irregularities, intimidation, and violence, but a 4–3 majority of judges narrowly rejected Besigye's request for a recount on grounds that it was unlikely to overturn the final outcome.

The opposition has come under increasing repression since 2000. It has not been uncommon for treason and sedition charges to be brought against people who voice opposition to the government through the media or in other fora. Often such charges have been used as a pretext to detain people without bail indefinitely, only later to have the charges dropped. Political prisoners have numbered in the thousands, extralegal killings of opposition party members have been reported, and torture has been carried out and widely acknowledged, even by the Parliament and government-appointed commissions. Preelection harassment and intimidation of the opposition were widespread in the 2001 and 2006 elections.[41]

The more recent move toward multipartyism thus needs to be understood in light of Museveni's bid for a third term. Popular discontent with the Movement system made it untenable as a political system, but the way in which multipartyism was introduced—and in particular, its link to Museveni's quest for a third term—raises questions about the Movement's interest in fundamental change. Moreover, the harassment, intimidation, and violence directed at opposition parties in the 2006 election raises serious doubts about the government's commitment to democratization and multipartyism. On November 16, 2005, Kizza Besigye—the key opposition leader of the Forum for Democratic Change (FDC)—was arrested on charges of treason and rape. The day he was to be brought to the High Court to be released on bail, a Black Mamba armed security squad had been deployed at the court to rearrest him in an extralegal action. This prompted protests from the High Court judges, Chief Justice Odoki (who had been the head of the constitutional commission), the inspector general of government, leaders of the Uganda Law Society, the government's human rights commission,

and many others, who condemned the siege of the courts as undermining the rule of law. Over three hundred lawyers went on strike to protest the military's interference in the judiciary's independence.

Lessons of Uganda's Constitution-Making Experiences

The 1995 constitution needs to be understood in light of the broader context within which it was written, including the NRM's bargaining with the Bugandan leadership and the recognition given the kingdoms before the adoption of the constitution; the restrictions on party and associational activities; control over appointments to the constitutional commission and constituent assembly; bribing of voters during the constituent assembly elections; and, more generally, the role of patronage and corruption in the political process.

At no time was Uganda's constitution-making exercise a neutral and open process, free of manipulation; the entire exercise was part of a broader political agenda of those in power who sought to use the new constitution to remain in power at all costs. From the outset, this limited what could be accomplished through the process of adopting a new constitution. Though the level of popular engagement in the process was unprecedented, that engagement had little impact on the substance of the constitution and may have lent unwarranted legitimacy to the more undemocratic aspects of the process and the resulting constitution, giving the Movement more time to entrench itself.

It is important to look at which constituencies were appeased in the process and to what end. Was there a quid pro quo negotiated through the constitution-making process that led to undemocratic outcomes? Women, for example, were very pleased with the extensive constitutional recognition of women's rights and gave the Movement considerable electoral support in subsequent elections. Women also were very active in the entire process of the constituent assembly, carrying out civic education programs and submitting memoranda to the constitutional commission. Yet when it came to legislation that would have concretely advanced women's rights, such as key amendments to the 1998 Land Act, Museveni refused support. Similarly, the promised equal opportunities commission, which, according to the constitution, was to oversee the enforcement of women's rights, never materialized. A decade later, the very same supporters of the positive constitutional measures regarding women have joined forces under the rubric of the advocacy and lobbying coalition Uganda Women's Network (UWONET) to protest the proposed lifting of presidential term limits. In a very brave initiative, given the levels of repression in the country, eighteen high-profile women activists went to Parliament in December 2004 to express their opposition to the constitutional amendment pertaining to presidential terms, referred to in Uganda as *kisanja* (dry banana leaves).[42] *Kisanja* is also the Kiganda word for giving someone a second chance.

All the controversial issues in which the majority voted down the minority opposition in the constituent assembly have come back to haunt Uganda's political leaders in subsequent years and have been fought out politically in the legislature. But the executive has more direct control over the process in the legislature than it did in the assembly, and the possibilities for real change are even more limited.

Uganda's experience also shows that donor support for constitution-making processes needs to be considered carefully. Many citizens interpreted international donor support for the process in Uganda as support for Museveni and his agenda. Donors believed they were supporting a neutral process in which the outcome was contingent on open

and free deliberations. They underestimated the extent to which the entire exercise was subject to political manipulation and the ways in which an unlevel playing field would influence the outcomes. Museveni used continued donor support for his government to justify the continuation of NRM dominance. This became even more evident after September 11, 2001, when Museveni could more easily get away with characterizing political opposition, especially the widespread opposition to him in the northern part of Uganda, as linked to terrorist activity.

The situation in Uganda today is fraught with contradictions. Uganda has a constitution that provides for the protection of political and civil rights. Yet there has been increased repression of the opposition and greater limits on civil and political liberties since the constitution was adopted. The 1995 constitution expands the powers of Parliament and potentially allows it to check executive excesses. Parliament is to approve presidential appointments of the vice president, cabinet ministers, judges of the High Court, justices of the Court of Appeal and Supreme Court, and heads of key commissions. Yet the executive has been able to push undemocratic legislation through Parliament without a quorum, despite constitutional limitations on executive powers. During the debate over term limits, Museveni threatened to weaken Parliament further by eliminating its powers of censure and dissolving it altogether if it disagreed with him. Although the constitutional review committee rejected Museveni's efforts to abolish the two-term limit on the presidency, he openly bribed members of Parliament to vote for lifting the limit and won the 2006 presidential elections. This means that by 2011, when his term ends, he will have been president for twenty-five years. To fully understand what happened in the 1995 constitution-making exercise in Uganda, it is necessary to account for the political dimensions of constitution making and consider the broader political agendas at work within the country.

Notes

1. A. Mugisha, "Museveni's Machinations," *Journal of Democracy,* vol. 15, no. 2 (2004), p. 140.

2. "A new element was introduced into our parliamentary methods of work, whereby the legislators of a particular persuasion, namely the NRM, were given large sums of money outside their normal remuneration in order to 'facilitate' their voting for some proposals, particularly the removal of presidential term limits." See "Constitution Has Become a Temporary Document!" editorial, *New Vision,* August 23, 2005; "When the Loan Shark Comes Knocking, Even MPs Have a Price," *The East African,* August 15, 2005.

3. See O. Furley and J. Katalikawe, "Constitutional Reform in Uganda: The New Approach," *African Affairs,* vol. 96, no. 383 (April 1997), pp. 243–61.

4. P. Mutibwa, *Uganda since Independence: A Story of Unfulfilled Hopes* (Trenton: Africa World Press, 1992), p. 58.

5. See generally M. Doornbos and F. Mwesigye, "The New Politics of Kingmaking," in *From Chaos to Order: The Politics of Constitution-Making in Uganda,* ed. H.B. Hansen and M. Twaddle (Kampala and Oxford: Fountain Publishers and James Currey, 1995); D. Mukholi, *A Complete Guide to Uganda's Fourth Constitution: History, Politics, and the Law* (Kampala: Fountain Publishers, 1995); Mutibwa, *Uganda Since Independence.*

6. Uganda Constitutional Commission, *The Report of the Uganda Constitutional Commission* (Kampala: Uganda Constitutional Commission, 1993); J.J. Barya, *The Making of Uganda's 1995 Constitution: Achieving Consensus by Law* (Kampala: Centre for Basic Research, 2000), p. 46.

7. Mukholi, *A Complete Guide,* pp. 42, 99.

8. Furley and Katalikawe, "Constitutional Reform in Uganda," p. 257.

9. Barya, J.J., *The Making of Uganda's 1995 Constitution,* Working Paper no. 57 (Kampala: Centre for Basic Research, 2000), p. 42.

10. Barya, *The Making of Uganda's 1995 Constitution,* pp. 14–15.

11. J. Katorobo, "Electoral Choices in the Constituent Assembly Elections," in *From Chaos to Order,* p. 117.

12. Furley and Katalikawe, "Constitutional Reform in Uganda," pp. 247–51.

13. J. Oloka-Onyango, "New Wine or New Bottles? Movement Politics and One-Partyism in Uganda," in *No-Party Democracy in Uganda: Myths and Realities,* ed. J. Mugaju and J. Oloka-Onyango (Kampala: Fountain Publishers, 2000), p. 45.

14. Barya, *The Making of Uganda's 1995 Constitution,* p. 17.

15. Republic of Uganda, *Constituent Assembly Proceedings.*

16. Mukholi, *A Complete Guide,* 30.

17. J.M. Waliggo, "Constitution-Making and the Politics of Democratisation in Uganda," in *From Chaos to Order,* pp. 18–40.

18. Waliggo, "Constitution-Making," pp. 26–27.

19. Ofwono Opondo, "Akabway Rejects NOCEM," *New Vision,* February 13, 1994.

20. Salome Bossa, interview by the author, July 4, 1995.

21. John Nzinjah, "NOCEM Man Sacked," *New Vision,* February 24, 1994.

22. Mukholi, *A Complete Guide,* p. 35.

23. Ibid., p. 37.

24. The business committee was responsible for organizing and managing the schedule of the assembly. It was headed by the chair, James Wapakhabulo, together with his deputy Victoria Mwaka, both Movementists. The legal and drafting committee was charged with overseeing the content and wording of the constitution. The rules and orders committee was to advise the chairman on the order of business. The privileges, discipline, and welfare committee was charged with handling matters pertaining to the welfare of the delegates and general discipline.

25. Barya, *The Making of Uganda's 1995 Constitution,* p. 22.

26. Furley and Katalikawe, "Constitutional Reform in Uganda," p. 252.

27. J. Geist, "Political Significance of the Constituent Assembly elections," in *From Chaos to Order,* p. 97.

28. "Museveni Rigging Worse than Obote, says Nekyon," *The Monitor,* March 21, 2001.

29. Katorobo, "Electoral Choices," p. 131; and Geist, "Political Significance," p. 99.

30. Katorobo, "Electoral Choices," p. 121.

31. N. Kasfir, "Ugandan Politics and the Constituent Assembly Elections," in *From Chaos to Order*, pp. 171–76.

32. Ibid., p. 61.

33. Robert Kabushenga, "Tinyefuze Owes Ugandans an Explanation," *New Vision*, November 7, 1999.

34. Mukholi, *A Complete Guide*, p. 33.

35. Barya, *The Making of Uganda's 1995 Constitution*, p. 42.

36. "Critics Tear Up NRM Bill," *The Monitor*, February 15, 1997; "Prof. Mujaju Slams Museveni's Praise Singers," *The Monitor*, February 8, 1997; "Fireworks Expected as NRM Bill Moves to House," *The Monitor*, February 13, 1997.

37. Okello Jabweli, Felix Osike, and Simon Kaheru, "Movement in Big Lead," *New Vision*, July 1, 2000.

38. Erica Bussey, "Constitutional Dialogue in Uganda," *Journal of African Law*, vol. 49, no. 1 (2005), pp. 2–23.

39. "223 MPs Got Shs5m Cash," *The Monitor*, November 16, 2004.

40. Odoki Commission Report 1993, available at www.federo.com/pages/odoki_report_1993.htm (accessed July 18, 2009).

41. "Observers Declare Poll Peaceful Despite Vote-Buying and Violence," *The East African*, February 28, 2006; Patrick Onyango, "Poll Violence Team Lines Up Museveni," *The Monitor*, March 2, 2002.

42. "Women Activists Say No to Kisanja," *New Vision*, December 2, 2004.

7

Zimbabwe's Unfulfilled Struggle for a Legitimate Constitutional Order

Muna Ndulo

This chapter is primarily focused on the need to examine the extent to which the process of constitution making can become a vehicle for national dialogue and the consolidation of peace, allowing competing perspectives and claims within a postwar society to be aired and incorporated. A number of issues affect the development of a country's constitution, especially when the country has undergone some degree of political turbulence. Nevertheless, most scholars would agree that one issue that stands out, and often bedevils post-conflict societies, is how to establish nation states with institutions that promote reconciliation, economic development, and good governance; facilitate political harmony and stability; manage diversity; process disputes between state and citizens and among citizens; and minimize the possibility of conflicts through enfranchisement of the people.[1] This chapter seeks to examine the experience of Zimbabwe in its efforts to develop a constitutional order that not only addresses the issues raised above

but also enjoys the allegiance and support of most Zimbabweans. It examines broadly the constitutional history of Zimbabwe and details the numerous efforts to develop an enduring constitution for that country, paying particular attention to the structures of the processes that have been employed; the scope, nature, and effectiveness of public participation in the constitution-making processes; the relevance of international human rights norms in the process; and the role the international community can or should play in constitution-making processes in post-conflict societies.

Who should initiate a constitution-making process? For how long should the process run? What kind of forum offers the best framework for the process? What are the mechanisms for maximizing citizen participation? How should the final adoption of the constitution be organized? We address these questions and also highlight the main issues, context, and substance regarding the Zimbabwe constitutional process. While recognizing the uniqueness of the Zimbabwean experience, we also attempt to draw common lessons learned from the process with respect to achieving an acceptable and durable constitution that can foster peace, stability, and prosperity for post-conflict societies.

This chapter is organized as follows: First, it will provide an overview of the most pressing challenges confronting Zimbabwe in terms of constitution making; second, it will assess the relevance of international human rights norms to the constitution-making process in post-conflict societies; third, it will summarize Zimbabwe's colonial history as it bears on current governance; fourth, it will assess the crisis of legitimacy surrounding the 1980 Lancaster House Constitution; fifth, it will assess the failure of the 1999 constitutional process, its impact on national reconciliation and the ongoing crisis which has resulted in the 2000 and 2008 elections' producing a government which lacks both national and international legitimacy; and sixth, it will make observations regarding the international community's role vis-à-vis an individual nation's constitution-making process. The chapter will conclude with a discussion of the lessons learned from the Zimbabwe experience.

The Colonial Period

The colonial history of what is today Zimbabwe bears directly on the political, economic, and social development of the country and many of its current obstacles to effective democracy. Zimbabwe, formerly Southern Rhodesia, was originally inhabited by descendants of the great southern migration that populated most of present-day Zimbabwe and Central Africa. A highly organized Shona-speaking state developed with a tradition of self-government and independence going back to the kingdom of Monomotapa and centered on Great Zimbabwe. In ap-

proximately 1830, the Matebele ethnic group, an offshoot of the Zulu nation, established a centralized state in the southwestern part of modern day Zimbabwe, with Bulawayo as its capital. By 1888, Lobengula, the Ndebele king, claimed sovereignty over all the territory that now forms Zimbabwe, including what was known at the time as Matebeleland and Mashonaland.[2]

In October 1889, Cecil Rhodes obtained a royal charter of incorporation setting up the British South Africa Company[3] (BSA). Under the charter, the BSA was authorized and empowered to hold, use, and retain for its purposes the full benefit of the concessions and agreements it had already acquired from African chiefs insofar as they were valid. It was further empowered, subject to the approval of one of the principal secretaries of state, from time to time to acquire any powers of any kind or nature whatever, including powers necessary to govern and preserve public order.[4] In 1890, the Mashonaland part of present-day Zimbabwe was occupied by British South Africa forces, which founded the capital in Salisbury (now Harare); in the following year, the territory was declared a British protectorate. In 1893, hostilities between the BSA and the Ndebele led to the occupation of present-day Matebeleland.[5] Lobengula was forced to flee, the British declared the Matebeleland kingdom to be ended, and the company seized land and cattle. In 1895, the entire territory was named Southern Rhodesia. The establishment of BSA and British rule over the territory was fiercely resisted by the African population.[6] Nevertheless, until 1923, Southern Rhodesia was administered by the BSA.[7]

In 1922, when the BSA's mandate was about to end, a referendum was held regarding a new constitutional structure and the question of whether Rhodesia would become part of the union of South Africa. The majority of white settler voters opted for responsible government rather than incorporation into the Union of South Africa, and Southern Rhodesia became a British colony. Accordingly, under letters patent (1923), the country became a self-governing colony. However, the constitution provided for such a high degree of internal autonomy that Southern Rhodesia held a special position among British dependencies. From 1923, the head of the government was called prime minister. Britain retained the power to veto legislation as a safeguard of African rights, but never exercised it, though the British government did exercise, in theory, a limited restraining influence. Thus, the overwhelming black majority found themselves governed under the loosest of imperial supervision by ministers responsible to a legislature elected by the white settlers and under the day-to-day control of an administration staffed by locally recruited whites. In 1953, Britain formed a federation of Southern Rhodesia, with the two northern territories of Northern Rhodesia and Nyasaland, both of which, unlike Southern Rhodesia, were administered as colonial protectorates. The federation failed as a consequence of the conflict between the growing African nationalism in the north and the hesitant white reformism of the South. In 1963, the federation was dissolved. The two northern territories soon became the independent states of Zambia and Malawi. Southern Rhodesia remained a self-governing colony and was not to become independent until after a protracted liberation war.

The issue of land ownership, which remains a matter of bitter dispute, has its roots in the BSA's expropriation of 39 million hectares of land from indigenous people, without compensation.[8] In 1930, the Land Apportionment Act formally introduced the principle of racial discrimination into land allocation by, among other things, assigning 50.8 percent of the land to the sole occupation of whites, who comprised less than 25 percent of the population.[9] This meant that

at independence in 1980, the most productive land remained in the hands of whites, whose interests were protected by complex provisions against compulsory land acquisition for a minimum of ten years contained in the 1979 independence constitution.[10]

In 1961, a new constitution provided for considerable internal sovereignty and, for the first time, included a justiciable declaration of rights.[11] Under the 1961 constitution, Britain relinquished virtually all its powers in return for a declaration of rights and a multiracial constitutional council that was charged with reviewing subsequent legislation in light of the declaration and assurances that Southern Rhodesia would enter a new phase in political and social development. The 1961 constitution was to be the first step toward ultimate majority rule, while the newly entrenched declaration of rights was to ensure the elimination of discrimination, equality before the law, and the protection of the rights and liberties of the individual.[12]

However, the declaration of rights suffered two notable omissions from the traditional list of human rights: the right to freedom of movement and the right to free choice of employment. Even the protections that the declaration granted were rendered largely illusory by a number of careful and far-reaching exceptions and qualifications. In several sections, the legislature was given the power to derogate in normal times from the rights and liberties for stated purposes, such as the exercise of police powers.[13] A major weakness of the 1961 constitution was that it exempted all preexisting laws from the need to comply with the declaration of rights.[14] Consequently, all the existing machinery of repression and discrimination was safeguarded. The constitution was fatally flawed, however, in that its franchise provisions supposedly enshrined the principle of unimpeded progress to majority rule, but in practice, the educational and economic requirements for voting all but guaranteed a permanently subordinate role for Africans.[15] During this period, the Southern Rhodesian government enacted and used increasingly repressive security legislation.[16] In particular, the government extensively used the 1960 Law and Order Maintenance Act, which provided for preventive detention.[17]

On November 11, 1965, the Rhodesian government, led by Ian Smith, declared unilateral independence against the British government and adopted the 1965 constitution.[18] The British government responded by making drastic changes to the 1961 constitution and declaring null and void and of no effect any law passed or promulgated by the illegal Smith regime.[19] It also revoked the legislative power of Southern Rhodesia's legislative assembly, enabled the British parliament to legislate for Rhodesia, and conferred executive power in Rhodesia upon the British secretary of state for commonwealth relations.[20] The Southern Rhodesian courts, however, recognized the Smith regime as valid. In 1966 and 1968, Southern Rhodesia's high court ruled that although the unilateral declaration of independence and the 1965 constitution were illegal, the revolution had achieved internal success and the Smith regime was the only effective government in Southern Rhodesia; therefore, necessity demanded that the de facto government be endowed with all the power of its predecessors under the 1961 constitution. In another decision in 1968, the high court finally gave the regime de jure recognition based on the argument that not only was the government in effective control, but there were no prospects that any actions by the mother country would alter that condition.[21] Matters came to a head in *Madzimbamuto v. Lardner-Burke*.[22] Here, the judicial committee of the privy council upheld the right of the UK parliament to exercise unfettered legislative power over Southern Rhodesia and to deny all legal validity to the actions of the Smith regime.

The majority of the Southern Rhodesian judiciary continued to recognize the legality of the Smith regime and ignored the privy council decision. The unilateral declaration of independence succeeded and lasted fifteen years. It did so largely because while the international community condemned Smith's unilateral declaration of independence, it did not take any positive action to end the rebellion.[23]

In 1970, the Smith regime purported to adopt a republican constitution, which precluded any prospect of majority rule.[24] The constitution had a declaration of rights, but rendered it ineffective by providing that "no court shall inquire into or pronounce upon the validity of any law on the ground that it is inconsistent with the Declaration of Rights."[25] Further, the bill of rights did not outlaw discrimination.[26] From 1970 to 1979, the Smith regime's violation of human rights was systematic and widespread: Captured and suspected guerrillas—as well as their supporters—were mercilessly tortured to extract confessions and information. The violation of human rights was a deliberate tactic aimed at intimidation and deterrence.[27]

Organized African resistance to white rule began around 1947 with the establishment of the African Workers Voice Association, which was an important forerunner to the African nationalist groups.[28] The organization was banned in 1952, but in 1957, the first African nationalist party, the African National Congress (ANC), was formed with Joshua Nkomo as president. The ANC was likewise later banned, as were its successors, the National Democratic Party (NDP) and the Zimbabwe African Peoples Union (ZAPU). In 1963, a split emerged in the nationalist movement with the founding of the Zimbabwe African National Union (ZANU). Both ZAPU and ZANU launched armed struggles, but it was not until 1980 that this finally led to independence.[29] In the 1970s, both ZAPU and ZANU forces intensified the armed struggle within the country.[30] With the continuing success of the struggle and international pressure, in 1978, the Smith regime was forced to seek an internal settlement with a number of compliant African leaders.[31] As a result, a new constitution for the renamed Zimbabwe-Rhodesia was introduced.[32] The internal settlement failed largely because it lacked legitimacy and did not end the war, which was clearly intensifying, and it equally failed to receive any international recognition.

Thus, in 1979 an all-party constitutional conference was held at Lancaster House in London from September 10 to December 21, at which an independence constitution was agreed.[33] The conference followed a commonwealth heads of government meeting in Lusaka, at which it was agreed that Britain was responsible for granting legal independence to Zimbabwe. The conference was attended by delegations from ZANU led by Robert Mugabe, ZAPU, led by Nkomo, and the Zimbabwe-Rhodesia government, which included Ian Smith's Rhodesian Front and Muzorewa's United African National Congress. The conference was organized and negotiations mediated by the British government under the leadership of Lord Carrington. The constitutional negotiations did not provide for public participation.

The new constitution provided for a ceremonial president, a prime minister, and a bicameral legislature consisting of elected members of parliament and an indirectly elected senate. The legislative chambers were to be elected on two race-based rolls. Executive power was to reside in the prime minister, assisted by a cabinet chosen by the prime minister.[34] The liberation movements (ZANU and ZAPU) were virtually forced to accept its terms, including the restrictive land acquisition provisions.[35] Lord Carrington's strategy was to push for an agreement; he warned that if there was no agreement, the British government would recognize the Mu-

zorewa regime, which Ian Smith had installed in Zimbabwe, and call for the lifting of sanctions against Zimbabwe. The British government was aware that the frontline states could not provide the kind of support the liberation movements needed to continue the liberation war. Further, the states were unhappy with the provisions relating to the nature and extent of executive powers, the organization of the legislature and the judiciary, and the general protection of racial interests in the bill of rights, including guaranteeing a voter roll for the white population.[36] Even so, the most remarkable feature of the Lancaster House conference was that it produced a settlement that led to a peaceful transition to majority rule. Southern Rhodesia reverted to being a British colony, and a British governor was installed to run the country until independence.[37] ZANU won the elections that followed, and Zimbabwe became an independent state on April 19, 1980.

The new majority government adopted a policy of reconciliation toward the white population and its black rivals. However, it retained the state of emergency, which the Smith regime had announced in 1965 before the declaration of unilateral independence; this continued until 1990, along with all the repressive security laws inherited from the previous regime.[38] Shortly after independence, violence erupted in Matebeleland. Emergency powers were widely used to quell the violence, including both preventive detention laws and restrictions on movement. A special unit sent to the area, known as the fifth brigade, was responsible for perpetrating widespread human rights violations. The problem was ended in 1987 by a unity agreement that led to ZAPU being merged[39] into ZANU, giving the ruling party an overwhelming parliamentary majority.[40] Not until the late 1990s did a viable new political party, Movement for Democratic Change (MDC), appear on the scene to seriously challenge ZANU's dominance. However, as the economy has declined, opposition to government has increased. From the 1990s to date, Zimbabwe has experienced a total collapse of its economy and widespread human rights abuses as the government has sought to remain in power by any means.[41] By 2009, Zimbabwe had the highest inflation rate in the world, and its economy had shrunk by almost a third.[42] Two recent examples that highlight the human rights abuses and the regime's determination to stay in power are the breach of electoral laws by the government in the 2008 elections and the manner in which ZANU PF has continuously violated the Global Political Agreement to further its interests. The mediation between ZANU PF and MDC under the supervision of President Thabo Mbeki led, among other things, to the amendments of the Electoral Act in Zimbabwe.[43] Section 110 of the Electoral Act provided for a runoff election within twenty-one days of the announcement of the results if no single candidate managed to obtain 50.1 percent of the total votes cast in a presidential poll. When ZANU PF realized that they had lost the 2008 election and that there was a high probability of losing the runoff election as well, they delayed announcing the presidential election results by more than three weeks and, instead of holding elections within the stipulated twenty-one days, held the election three months later. The delay was designed to allow ZANU PF to purge the electorate of opposition support. Massive violence and killings were inflicted on opposition supporters, forcing the MDC to withdraw from the elections.[44] On the current government of national unity, ZANU PF has acted in bad faith before and after signing the Unity Agreement. President Mugabe went on to appoint permanent secretaries unilaterally, without consulting the other parties that are members of the government, in contravention of the Global Political Agreement.[45] In addition, the president unilaterally appointed the reserve bank governor, the attorney general, and all the provincial governors without consulting the other parties that are members of the Unity Government.[46]

Constitution Making: The Challenges in Zimbabwe

In 1980, after ninety years of colonial rule and decades of armed struggle against a white minority government regime, modern Zimbabwe inherited a constitution, which was a result of a negotiated settlement at Lancaster House in London.[47] The Lancaster House constitution-making process was dominated by the British government, which was associated at the time with the minority government of Southern Rhodesia.[48] A majority of the liberation movements perceived the constitution as unsatisfactory, as it lacked popular participation and contained unsavory provisions. The liberation groups believed that a new constitution was needed to consolidate a democratic state in Zimbabwe once independence was achieved. In significant respects, Zimbabwe's 1980 constitution continued the colonial legacy in the sense that some of its provisions maintained the economic status quo. Immediately after the Lancaster House constitution was adopted, elections were held and a populist government led by ZANU was elected to power: ZANU won fifty-seven seats, ZAPU twenty seats, ANC three seats, and the Rhodesian Front all the twenty seats reserved for whites.

Although a constitution is primarily a legal document, it is at the same time a political charter, particularly when it is expected to enact far-reaching change in the political and economic structure of society. Unfortunately, the Lancaster House Constitution did not create the potential for the necessary institutional change—not merely the institutions in the political realm, but also the institutions that govern the way the economy functions and influence productivity and equity. The Lancaster House Constitution itself failed to serve as a framework for local political and economic actors to negotiate the transformation from a colonial state with great economic disparities to a more equitable Zimbabwe, largely because it contained entrenched provisions, which ensured certain policies could not be changed until a specified time.[49] As a result, the basic structure of Zimbabwean society, especially as it related to land ownership, remained the same. As protests mounted regarding the government's corruption and failure to improve the quality of life for the majority of Zimbabweans, the government became undemocratic and authoritarian, increasingly centralizing power in its attempt to stay in office. The attributes of the Zimbabwean state thus include the following: a highly centralized system of governance; excessive state control of all aspects of human endeavor, coupled with limited capacity to govern; excessive regulation of civil society; weak institutions of state and civil society; few countervailing forces to the power of the executive branch; limited participation in governance by the general citizenry; and preferential access to power and resources, often determined by religious, ethnic, and geographical considerations. The result has been unprecedented economic decline and increasing poverty among ordinary Zimbabweans.

Clearly, the Lancaster House Constitution failed to gain legitimacy or provide a framework for the democratic governance of Zimbabwe. The challenge for Zimbabwe remains how to achieve a stable political and constitutional order that promotes development and good governance and guarantees citizens government under the rule of law regardless of their gender, color, sexual orientation, sex, or ethnic origin. This calls for the development of political, economic, and administrative institutions for the proper governance of the state. The aim should be to achieve a constitutional order that is legitimate, credible, enduring, and structurally accessible to the people without compromising the integrity and effectiveness of the process.

In Zimbabwe, a serious search for viable constitutional arrangements must begin with the frank recognition of the specific problems confronting the country. Foremost is the need for sufficient national unity or cohesion to generate social and political power strong enough to enable the diverse peoples that make up Zimbabwe to achieve a level of well-being and development beyond their reach as separate units. Any constitutional structure adopted in Zimbabwe likewise needs to accommodate the ethnic diversity of the country. The issue of ethnicity could potentially destabilize the democratic process; democracy could magnify the adverse effects of ethnicity. At the same time, there is the need to accommodate the racial minorities that exist in the country. The constitution-making process must deal with all these facts sensitively, consciously assuming the fears and apprehensions of minority groups, meeting their legitimate demands, and involving them in meaningful ways in the political system and nation building. Zimbabwe cannot ignore the disproportionate economic and social importance of public office to individuals in the midst of widespread poverty and ignorance. A serious search for a viable constitutional arrangement must respond to the need to decentralize power. It must find the means to eradicate the pervasive inequality of the sexes perpetuated by traditional roles assigned to women. The constitution-making process must also address the question of peaceful transfer of power from one leader to another. Several of its neighbors—Zambia,[50] Malawi,[51] and South Africa,[52]—have adopted term limits for presidents to ensure a change of leadership from time to time. The essence of government is power, and power, lodged as it must be in human hands, is always liable to abuse. Limits are therefore essential to minimize the danger of dictatorship and the development of an oligarchy in a presidential system.

Constitution-Making and International Human Rights Norms

It is important to ensure that a constitution-making process relies on international standards. This acts as a check on government and empowers minorities and other stakeholders. Democracy involves three central rights: the right to take part in government, the right to vote and to be elected, and the right to equal access to services. The Universal Declaration of Human Rights (UDHR) states that the will of the people shall be the basis for the authority of government.[53] A number of international instruments reflect the principal concerns underlying governance, including the right of peoples freely to determine their political status,[54] the right of all elements of society to participate actively in defining and achieving developmental goals,[55] and the right of all people to participate in the political life of their country. Thus, international instruments for promoting and protecting human rights within the UN system are replete with admonitions that popular political participation must be free.[56] While such instruments do not describe a particular methodology for ensuring such freedom, their essence is clear: To be free, participation in the political processes of a country must be conducted in an atmosphere characterized by the absence of intimidation and the presence of a wide range of fundamental human rights.[57]

While the UDHR enunciates the rights, the Covenants elaborate upon each of the rights, and regional conventions contribute to their protection. Some rights take on additional importance for political participation purposes, such as the rights to free opinion,[58] free expression,[59] information,[60] assembly and association,[61] independent judicial procedure,[62] and protection from discrimination.[63] The Human Rights Committee states that the right to hold opinions without interference permits no exception or restriction.[64] The committee also states that the right to freedom of expression includes not only freedom to impart information and ideas but also the freedom to seek and receive them.[65] To ensure the full participation of the people in a constitution-making process, all obstacles to individual participation in the affairs of the state must be removed. Public participation not only ensures that the development of basic law goes through a process of popularization and legitimization but facilitates consensus building. Only under such an atmosphere will participation be effective and contribute to the development of a durable and widely acceptable constitution. To that end, as Thomas Franck has argued, the idea that only democracy validates governance is an emerging norm.[66] A corollary norm may also be emerging that only a democratic constitution-making process validates a constitution. Governments increasingly recognize that their legitimacy depends on meeting the normative expectations of the international community and their own citizens.

The Postindependence Constitution-Making Process in Zimbabwe

The 1979 constitution is commonly referred to as the Lancaster House Constitution. It contains a justiciable bill of rights, which recognizes a range of rights, including the rights to freedom of expression, association, and assembly.[67] Beginning in 1980, however, the government amended the Lancaster House Constitution repeatedly, on the pretext that it needed to be made more relevant to Zimbabwe's particular situation. In reality, the amendments concentrated more and more power in the executive.[68] By the 1990s, the Zimbabwe constitution, in important respects, bore little relationship to the original 1980 document. Sixteen separate amendments, all of which made multiple constitutional changes, entirely reshaped the document. Given the circumstances of its birth, some amendments were inevitable and entirely desirable,[69] but the same cannot be said of the majority of the amendments.[70] In 1989, the constitution was amended to shield the president from questioning by and accountability to parliament.[71] Some provisions of the amendment placed the president above the judiciary, in that the judiciary was denied the right to question the substance of or the process through which presidential decisions were reached.[72] The constitution furthermore provides for presidential powers (i.e., temporary measures) that essentially give the president rule-making ability equal to that of the legislature.[73] The constitutional amendments have sought to limit the jurisdiction of the courts,[74] prevented the Supreme Court from hearing a particular case relating to fundamental rights provisions, and overturned the court's decisions regarding that case.[75] In 1990, in *S. v. Chileya*, the Supreme Court asked for full argument on the issue of whether the use of hanging in the administering of the death penalty constituted inhuman or degrading treatment or punishment contrary to Section 15 (1) of the constitution. A date was set for the hearing. The government's response was immediate: Shortly before the hearing, a constitutional amendment bill was published that included a provision specifically upholding the constitutionality of execution by hanging. The minister of justice, legal, and parliamentary affairs informed parliament that any holding to the contrary would be untenable to government, which held the correct and firm view that parliament made the laws and the courts interpreted them. He added that abolishing the death sentence was a matter for the executive and legislature, and that the government could and would not countenance the death penalty's de facto abolition through a legal back door.[76]

In addition to amending the constitution, the government has resorted to legislative measures to overrule court decisions without any hesitation when it disagrees with those decisions. When the Supreme Court ruled in *S. v. Juvenile*[77] to outlaw judicial corporal punishment of juveniles and, in an *obiter dicta*, reached a similar conclusion regarding corporal punishment of school pupils, the legislative response of the government was to amend the constitution to permit corporal punishment to be imposed on children by their parents, guardians, and persons in loco parentis, and on male juveniles convicted of criminal offenses.[78] In September 2000, the government intervened in the case of *Capital Radio (Pvt) Ltd. v. Minister of Information & Others*,[79] in which a private radio station, Capital Radio, filed suit in the Supreme Court against Section 27 of the Broadcasting Act. Capital Radio argued that Section 27, which prohibited the unauthorized possession, establishment, and operation of signal transmitting stations, contravened Section 20 of the Zimbabwean constitution, which guarantees freedom of expression and information. The section effectively prohibited privately owned radio stations in Zimbabwe. The Supreme Court ruled in favor of Capital Radio,[80] enabling it to begin broadcasting as a radio station. In response, in October 2000, the government promulgated the Presidential Powers (Temporary Measures) Broadcasting Regulations, arguing that the Supreme Court's decision created a regulatory vacuum. Under the regulations, the government created a board consisting of members appointed by the minister of information, which was tasked with issuing licenses. The board declared independent radio stations illegal, ordered them switched off, and had their broadcasting equipment confiscated. The board promptly proceeded to revoke the license that had been issued to Capital Radio as a result of its Supreme Court case, reversing its victory.[81]

Yet another example of the government's defiance of the judiciary was its reaction to the Supreme Court's decision in *Rattigan and Others v. Chief Immigration Officer and Others*.[82] The court declared that a female citizen of Zimbabwe who was married to an alien was entitled, by virtue of the right to freedom of movement—protected under Section 22 (1) of the constitution—to reside permanently with her husband in any part of Zimbabwe.[83] The decision held that to prohibit the alien husband of a marriage genuinely entered into with the shared intention of establishing a matrimonial abode in Zimbabwe from residing in Zimbabwe would place the wife in the dilemma of having to decide whether to accompany her husband to a country other than Zimbabwe and live together there or to exercise her constitutional right to continue to reside in Zimbabwe without him. Within a matter of months, the ruling was extended in *Salem v. Chief Immigration Officer and Others*[84] to embrace the mobility rights of the citizen wife and the right of the alien husband to lawfully engage in employment or other gainful activity in any part of Zimbabwe. On December 6, 1996, the Constitution of Zimbabwe Amendment (No. 14) Act was promulgated.[85] The amended paragraph provided that

> nothing contained in or done under the authority of any law shall be held to be in contravention of sub section (1) to the extent that the law in question makes provision for (i) the imposition of restrictions on the movement or residence within Zimbabwe of any person who is neither a citizen of Zimbabwe nor regarded by virtue of a written law as permanently resident in Zimbabwe, whether or not he is married or related to another person who is a citizen or permanent resident in Zimbabwe.

However, the effort to undo the court's decisions proved unsuccessful, as a subsequent Supreme Court case ruled that the new wording did not diminish the rights of the citizen wife.[86]

The Zimbabwean experience highlights the problem of centering the amendment procedure of the constitution solely in the legislature, even with special majorities, as opposed to providing checks such as requiring constitutional amendments to be approved in a referendum or by a high percentage of provincial legislatures where they exist. As one political party has dominated the first twenty years of independence, a two-thirds parliamentary majority has proved of no practical value to check retrogressive constitutional amendments. It is arguable that the ruling party's overwhelming parliamentary majority demonstrated that it enjoyed the popular support necessary to pass such amendments. However, this overlooks the reality of a dominant one-party state in which the party seeks to exercise complete control over voting in parliament: The result is that parliament rubber-stamps all constitutional amendments. Further, it is questionable that all members of parliament are able or prepared to undertake a critical and informed view of proposed constitutional changes, especially as such amendments are more often than not rushed through parliament.

Zimbabweans' desire in the 1990s for the elaboration and adoption of a new constitution arose not only because of the need to right the inequities of the 1980 constitution but also because, as mentioned above, the 1980 constitution had been made increasingly less democratic through numerous government amendments. As the Zimbabwe Council of Churches (ZCC) succinctly stated: "A just system is based on a just constitution." Agitation for a new democratic constitution was spearheaded by the nongovernmental organization (NGO) community, which set up the National Constitutional Assembly (NCA), an NGO-driven constitution-making process comprised of a number of civil-society organizations, with the collective mission of developing a new democratic constitution for Zimbabwe.[87]

Clearly wishing to control the process, the government responded by establishing its own constitutional commission, with the majority of members being its own supporters.[88]

The main body of the commission was a plenary made up of about five hundred commissioners. The substantive work of the commission was to be carried out through nine thematic committees, each with about forty-three commissioners. The commission adopted nine themes: the nature of the executive organs of state; citizenship, fundamental, and directive rights; separation of levels of governments; public finance and management; customary law; independent commissions; separation of powers among the three branches of government; transitional arrangements; and legal matters.[89] The thematic committees were formed into one hundred provincial teams that held meetings in which they received submissions from the public. The provincial teams each had nine members, representing each of the nine major themes examined by the committee. While the commission's secretariat provided logistical support, the commission's coordinating committee, made up of about twenty-five commissioners, did the substantive organization and management of the commission's thematic work.

With the launching of the government's constitutional commission—and the NGO-sponsored NCA's decision to boycott it—two parallel processes were under way. The NCA concentrated on both providing civic education on the constitution throughout the country and gathering views on the constitution. Initially, the NCA spent most of its energy on the process of constitutional reform. Later, it turned to the problems of constitutional content, discussing in great depth the kind of constitution the people wanted. It sought to develop an alternative constitution to the document that the constitutional commission was developing. The NGO community and opposition parties rejected any participation in the commission's process on the grounds that, first, the constitution should be developed by a constituent assembly along the lines of the South African model[90]; second, not all stakeholders agreed to the commission as an appropriate method to make the national constitution; third, the exercise of national consensus building on the values and provisions of a national constitution could not be done through a process that was exclusive, partisan, divisive, conflict ridden, and contested; fourth, the commission's appointment under the Commissions of Inquiry Act meant that the process and results were entirely subject to the president's powers to reject or modify the will of the people; fifth, the commission was dominated by members of one political party and was therefore not national in character; sixth, the fixed period of six months to complete the exercise was too short and inhibited full public participation; and seventh, there should have been legally binding guarantees that the commission's constitutional recommendations, as arrived at through public participation, would be final. The commission's opponents considered the legal framework of the Commissions of Inquiry Act[91] to be inadequate for constitution making, as it gave sweeping powers to the president to alter, revoke, or stop the process, and therefore, did not guarantee the effective participation of all stakeholders. Further, while the act provided for the commission to report to the president,[92] opponents noted the act's failure to oblige the president to publish the commission's findings. This undermined the constitution-making process by placing the president in a dominant and determinative role rather than a facilitative one.[93] Critics also objected to the commission's gender imbalance.[94]

In its work, the constitutional commission developed a program for public participation. The commission noted that getting the views of the public on the kind of constitution that Zimbabweans wanted should be done in a manner that was both politically and scientifically credible.[95] It was mindful that how it gathered information would ultimately determine whether the public and the international community had confidence in the commission's process and results.[96] In its program, the commission used several sources of information, including written submissions, views of constitutional experts,[97] views by individuals and interest groups giving oral submissions before the commission, and academic publications relating to governance. The coordinating committee used two methods—an open-meetings approach and a scientific approach—to gather information from the public. The open-meetings approach took three forms: public hearings by the commission's thematic committees at various provincial locations, written submissions to the commission by members of the public, and submissions to the commission's Web site. The commission held well over five thousand meetings in all fifty-seven districts in Zimbabwe.[98] The scientific method consisted of a nationwide opinion poll and the administration of a questionnaire to people throughout the country.

Clearly, as a result of pressure from civil society, the constitutional commission attempted to ensure public participation in the process. But its efforts were defective: That the participation mechanism was set up under the Inquiry Act[99] implied that there was no obligation, if the president so wished, to actually publish what came out of it. In the end, in November 1999, the commission adopted a draft constitution, which was submitted to a referendum. On the whole, the draft constitution contained major improvements over the 1980 constitution. It recommended limiting a president to two five-year terms in office; a division of executive powers between the president and a prime minister; proportional representation; an independent electoral commission; and no land seizures without compensation. Despite a vigorous government

campaign to approve the constitution, it was rejected by 54 percent of the voters. This sparked a furious reaction from the government. Within days, large-scale invasions of white-owned farms began, headed by so-called war veterans who were fanatically loyal to Mugabe, as well as vitriolic attacks on the MDC and white farmers. The constitution-making project was abandoned. In September 2007, a ZANU PF-dominated parliament voted to pass constitutional amendments, paving the way for the holding of joint parliamentary and presidential elections in March 2008. The elections were held under increased levels of violence and human rights violations. Following these elections, the MDC became the largest party in the House of Assembly.[100] Both Mugabe and Tsvangirai claimed victory in the presidential elections. The results were not released for three weeks. On May 2, the presidential elections were finally announced. Neither candidate passed the 50 percent threshold to be elected in the first round. Violence increased before the scheduled June 27, 2008, runoff election. On June 22, Morgan Tsvangirai, MDC president, withdrew from the runoff, blaming violence and fraud.[101] On September 15, ZANU PF and the MDC signed a power-sharing agreement under the mediation of the South African president, Thabo Mbeki.[102] As part of the 2008 Unity Government Agreement, the parties agreed to come up with a new constitution in 2009. Once a new constitution is in place, the power-sharing government is expected to call fresh parliamentary, presidential, and local government elections. Already, differences are emerging on how the process of drafting a new constitution should proceed. The Congress of Trade Unions, student groups, and civil society are calling for an independent commission to lead the drafting of a new constitution for the country, rejecting plans by the government for parliament to spearhead the writing of the new constitution.[103] They argue that issues of national importance will be lost in the corridors of power if parliament controls the process. On the other hand, the speaker of parliament has appointed a twenty-five-member committee of legislators drawn from ZANU PF and MDC that will oversee the drafting of the country's new constitution.[104] The speaker insists that parliament will drive the writing of the new constitution, as outlined in the power-sharing agreement signed by the three main political parties in 2008. The 1990 Zimbabwe experience illustrates how a government can use a commission to ostensibly consult with the people on constitutional reform while in reality ensuring that the government controls the process. The president's establishment of a commission in 1999, using his powers under the Commission of Inquiries Act, had two significant consequences. First, because the president appointed the commission's members, he could determine the commission's size and composition. As a result, the great majority of its five hundred members supported the ruling party. Second, establishing the commission enabled the president to pick and choose from among the commission's recommendations, as he was under no obligation to accept any or all of them. He rejected a number of recommendations, including the one prohibiting land seizures without compensation. The work of the hugely expensive commission was also seriously hampered by its ridiculously unwieldy size, a fact seemingly admitted even by the commission's chairman.[105] Why Mugabe deemed it necessary to appoint such a large number of commissioners is not clear. Seemingly, it was some kind of presidential overkill, designed to ensure a favorable report.

The commission's final draft was never put to a vote, but was instead forced through at a plenary session in which the chair declared the draft constitution adopted "by acclamation," despite a number of dissenting voices.[106] Although the commission undertook an impressive and wide-ranging consultation exercise throughout the country, its work and report were undoubtedly tainted by the public's perception that it was a government-oriented body. Nonetheless, its draft constitution did not satisfy the president.[107] Despite prior assurances to the contrary, the government gazette a few weeks later published what were termed "corrections and clarifications" to the document.[108] Despite the rhetoric, these "corrections and clarifications" made several significant changes of substance to the draft constitution submitted with the constitutional commission's report explaining how it conducted its work. Both the draft constitution and the commission's report were available to the public. The president's power to place before the electorate whatever proposed constitution he wished was made clear following a legal challenge to the referendum, brought by some commission members on the grounds that the draft constitution had not been properly adopted. In rejecting the submission, Justice Bartlett in the Zimbabwe High Court stated:

> The president is not in my view required to put before the voters a constitution approved by the Constitutional Commission. He is entitled to put forward any draft constitution he so wishes to ascertain the views of the voters. It may or may not be considered unwise to make changes to a document produced by a body specifically set up to produce a draft constitution but it is certainly not unlawful.[109]

The Failure of the 1999 Constitutional Process and Its Impact on National Reconciliation

Zimbabwe has acceded to a number of international instruments, including the International Covenant on Civil and Political Rights (ICCPR), the International Covenant on Economic, Social, and Cultural Rights (ICESCR), the Convention on the Elimination of All Forms of Discrimination (CEAFD), the Convention on the Elimination of All Forms of Discrimination Against Women (CEDAW), and the African Charter on Human and People's Rights (ACHPR). A number of other specific commonwealth declarations and principles were until recently applicable to Zimbabwe.[110] Under these treaties, the government must guarantee equal protection of the law to all persons without discrimination and prosecute serious violations of the rights enumerated, including when the perpetrator is a private citizen. The independence of the judiciary is a cornerstone of these international provisions. The Zimbabwean constitution provides similar guarantees. Notwithstanding these frameworks for human rights, however, the unprecedented defeat of the government in the February 2000 referendum regarding whether to accept the government's draft constitution ushered in a rapid deterioration of the human rights situation in Zimbabwe[111] and ended all government efforts to replace the Lancaster House Constitution of 1980.

Since 2000, state-sponsored intimidation, arbitrary arrest, torture, and attacks on the political opposition, independent media, and human rights organizations have escalated.[112] The government has used its supporters as well as state agents—namely, so-called war veterans, youth militia, police, and the army—to wage a targeted campaign of repression in a bid to retain control. Parliamentary and presidential elections held in 2000 and 2002, respectively, were marred by politically motivated violence.[113] The government initiated a controversial land reform program that sparked illegal occupations of commercial farms by the veterans and other settlers, resulting in the forced evictions of hundreds of thousands of farm workers, farmers, and their families.[114] Human rights violations have become commonplace. A 2003 report of the Observatory of the Protection of

Human Rights Defenders, entitled *Human Rights,* highlighted the abuses suffered by human rights defenders in Zimbabwe.[115] It noted that since the 2002 presidential elections, the pressure on human rights defenders has not only significantly increased but also developed more subtle and sophisticated forms of oppression. The report stated that human rights defenders, including members of NGOs, lawyers, magistrates, journalists, and trade unionists, are constantly harassed and subjected to violence, arbitrary arrest, detention, fiscal pressure, or administrative sanctions. In 2005, in a move condemned by the United Nations and the international community, the government demolished the homes of 700,000 Zimbabwean city dwellers.[116] President Mugabe claimed that Operation Murambatsvina (Drive Out Rubbish) was needed to restore sanity to Zimbabwe's cities, which he claimed had been overrun by criminals. Human rights activists pointed out that it was no coincidence that opposition to his rule is strongest in urban areas—and that in the March 2005 elections, the MDC won almost all urban seats.[117] As in all previous elections in Zimbabwe, the March 2008 elections were marred by violence. In the period leading to the June 2008 runoff elections, political rallies by the opposition parties were virtually not permitted, and in rural areas and high-density areas, attendance at ruling-party rallies was compulsory. Opposition party supporters were subjected to beatings and had to flee their homes for safety. As mentioned above, this forced Tsvangirai to withdraw from the election. The elections went ahead with only Mugabe as the contestant.[118]

The United Nations Human Rights Committee, charged with monitoring member-state compliance with the ICCPR, noted in 2001 of Zimbabwe

> that not all of the rights in the covenant have been made part of domestic law and cannot be invoked directly before domestic courts. Not-

withstanding the state party's policy of thorough legislative review in order to ensure compatibility of domestic legislation with the Covenant, the Committee notes the absence of effective institutional mechanisms to ensure systematic implementation and monitoring of its provisions.

The Human Rights Committee expressed concern about the increasing trend to enact parliamentary legislation and constitutional amendments intended to frustrate Supreme Court decisions that uphold rights protected under the ICCPR and overturn certain laws incompatible with it.[119] Similarly, the African Commission on Human Rights and Peoples' Rights has criticized the Zimbabwean government. It has stated that, through the use of legislation curtailing the rights to freedom of expression, association, and assembly, the Zimbabwean government has violated the provisions of the African Charter on Human and Peoples' Rights, under which these rights are guaranteed.[120] Further criticism of the government has come from the International Labor Organization (ILO) Committee on Freedom of Association, which in November 2002 cited Zimbabwe for serious infringements of the principle of freedom of association and violations of trade union rights, asking the government to ensure that the principles of noninterference by the authorities in the meetings and internal affairs of trade unions are respected.[121]

With respect to the land issue, Zimbabwean human rights groups have observed that, although land ownership reforms are needed to address stark inequalities in land distribution and wealth, the crisis in Zimbabwe is not due to the land problem, but has been induced by bad governance and serious misuse of power.[122] As stated in the African Charter on Human and Peoples' Rights and reinforced by the ICCPR and other binding international treaties, the rules providing for compulsory purchase should be clearly set out in law, and those affected should have the right to voice their opposition to the acquisi-

tion and to challenge it before a competent and impartial court. In addition, the security forces and criminal justice system must provide equal protection to all those who are victims of violence, and the law should take its course without interference from political authorities. UN Secretary General Kofi Annan has questioned the Zimbabwean government's approach to land reform, noting that such reform must be credible and legal and entail adequate compensation to those whose land is being expropriated.[123] Nonetheless, the Mugabe regime continues to rule Zimbabwe and violate the rights of its people for the same reasons that led to the survival of Ian Smith's rebellious regime from 1965 to 1980. There has not been concerted international pressure on the regime. To begin to effect meaningful change, the international community must insist that the government abide by its constitution and international human rights norms. However, attempts to censure Zimbabwe have been blocked by African states whose response has been strongly shaped by the history of southern Africa and the long struggle to end colonial rule; except for Botswana and Zambia, the strong criticism of Zimbabwe by the United States, Britain, and the Commonwealth[124] has not been matched by similar statements from Zimbabwe's African neighbors. The situation is almost a complete replay of the failure of the international community to deal with Ian Smith after he declared independence in 1965.

Constitution Making and the International Community

Although it is important that a constitution-making process be a local product driven by local stakeholders, the international community can play an important role.[125] It can encourage the observance of international standards as reflected in international human rights instruments and ensure that the standards are well articulated; provide requisite expertise and resources for a successful constitution-making process; and help in capacity building, knowledge networking, and sharing of best practices. The international community should, however, remain mindful that its role is to support the process; it should refrain from being prescriptive. This avoids the danger of importing institutions without regard for local conditions. For there to be genuine ownership of a constitution, its making must be geared to the social, political, and economic conditions of the people that the constitution is intended to serve. The process should therefore be in the hands of those who live with the result. The influence of the international community is less likely to be resented when the international community focuses on the process rather than on results, in other words, ensuring that the process is inclusive and ensures the participation of all stakeholders rather than advocating a particular result.

In Zimbabwe's 1999 constitution-making process, experts from Africa, the United States, Asia, and Europe were invited to participate in the constitutional commission's plenary session, termed an "international conference on the Making of Zimbabwe New Democratic Constitution."[126] The experts gave advice but did not get involved in the process itself. At the time of the conference, the commission had completed its collection of views from the public and the various theme committees were considering their recommendations to the commission's drafting committee. The experts presented papers on areas of their expertise to a full commission meeting and participated in the discussions of the various theme committees. They also participated in various meetings scheduled by NGOs. Access to the experience of comparative constitution-making exercises is particularly useful during a constitution-making process, as it provides a wide range of information on possible options and les-

sons on what to do and what not to do, and the commission's chairperson acknowledges the value of the experts' comparative experience.[127] The international community has to be mindful, however, that in some situations, foreign experts are brought in to legitimize a flawed process. When this is clearly the intention, international experts should refrain from participating. This was, however, not the case in Zimbabwe; despite the president's heavy hand in the process, there was a genuine effort on the part of the commission to draw on comparative experience.

Lessons from the Failure of the Zimbabwean Constitutional Process

Developing an effective procedure to prevent those in power from manipulating a constitution-making process is a considerable challenge—one that would be helped by articulating the principles and mechanisms that govern the process. Such articulation would enhance the process's quality and increase the possibility of its success. The conditions under which a constitution-making process is initiated are important. The process leading up to the 1980 Lancaster House Constitution would have benefited from separating the constitution-making process from the process of securing a cease-fire, as this would have helped prevent the dominant and belligerent groups from having an overwhelming influence on producing the country's constitution. Such a separation also enables or simply gives time for public participation where possible, or where there is willingness to develop a vision for a future society. The 1999 Zimbabwean constitution-making process failed partly because it came about as a government attempt to undercut while appearing to satisfy civil-society as well as opposition demands. It was not part of a larger political renewal process. The government also lacked the credibility to spearhead the process, in that civil-society's demands for constitutional reform in 1999 coincided with the emergence of the first very strong opposition party in Zimbabwe. Zimbabwe's experience demonstrated that when leadership resists change and openly engages in repressive practices to prevent public discussion of reforms, it has already squandered the public's goodwill toward believing that constitutional change is genuine.

A central lesson of the Zimbabwean case is that before any post-conflict society launches a constitution-making process, the society must debate and come to an understanding about what kind of society it wants to create. The constitution must be an exercise in building national consensus on the values and provisions to be included in the document. One of Zimbabwe's continuing constitutional problems involved the question of who was and was not a Zimbabwean and whether or not Zimbabwe was to be a nonracial society, with all its citizens having equal rights and protection under the law regardless of racial identity[128]—a problem not discussed at Lancaster. By contrast, part of South Africa's constitution-making process was devoted to debating the kind of society South Africa was to create.[129] One can argue that the African National Congress (ANC) was clearly dedicated to establishing a nonracial society as long ago as 1955 through the adoption of the Freedom Charter,[130] and some of the discussions in the 1993 Multi-Party Negotiating Forum focused on identifying institutions and legislation that needed to be changed to create a nonracial and democratic South Africa.[131] Consideration of the type of society to be created enables the process to look at conditions in the country and the types of institutions and legislation required to bring about the change envisioned.

Zimbabwe's failed constitution-making process under Mugabe also reveals that a constitutional commission must be fully representative of society and account for the concerns of the widest possible segment of the population. Moreover, the work of the commission must be transparent toward the population and the international community; the commission must make public and expert consultations meaningful and properly structure its methods to ensure effective participation by all stakeholders in the country. These factors are important to maintain the process's integrity. In addition, participation of the people in the process is good civic education for the populace. Citizens begin not only to understand the process but to understand and appreciate its importance to their lives and communities. They also begin to see the values that the constitution seeks to protect and promote, and such values are better protected when they have become entrenched in the culture of the society. Another lesson learned is that a commission that reports to the president can be susceptible to manipulation by the party in power, resulting in the government imposing its preferred constitutional model. Matters are made worse by the common perception that such commissions are often filled by people sympathetic to the ruling party.

Furthermore, the report and draft constitution developed by a constitutional commission must not be subject to unilateral executive interference and must be guided by a reasonable time frame. The Zimbabwean constitutional commission was given six months to complete its work.[132] Although the commission met its deadline, the time frame was clearly unrealistic; the deadline was met at the expense of adequate public consultation. It is possible that if the commission had been given more time to do its work, it could have organized more consultations, perhaps resolved existing disagreements with groups that opposed the process, and gained legitimacy. As it stood, civil society in Zimbabwe was clearly opposed to the process. The NCA argued that "a defective process will lead to a defective constitution which does not reflect the wishes of the people."[133] Time does not always guarantee quality, but there is no doubt that a truly participatory and consultative approach in pluralist developing countries requires sufficient time to give meaning to the process and bring alienated interests and communities into it. A rushed process often leaves many issues unresolved and leads to quick compromises that do not stand the test of time. The 1979 Lancaster House constitutional negotiations had only three months to complete their work, leaving unresolved several important issues, such as property rights and land reform, past human rights violations perpetrated in the long and brutal liberation wars, and ensuring the economic empowerment of the black majority after decades of discrimination that left them landless and poor. Finally, rushed processes often tend to compromise opportunities to engage in mass education to build ownership around the final constitution.

A third lesson from the Zimbabwean experience is that the process of adopting a constitution is as important as the substance of it. A defective process is unlikely to lead to a constitution that reflects the wishes of the people. Clearly, a constitution that is perceived as being imposed on a large segment of the population, or having been adopted through manipulation of the process by one of the stakeholders, is unlikely to gain sufficient popularity or legitimacy to endure. In the Lancaster House Constitution process, there was no public participation in developing the terms and conditions set therein to govern the people's relationship with their rulers. The constitution-making process remained the preserve of politicians, with the people as bystanders. The Mugabe government has perpetuated the status quo, with parliament enacting sixteen amendments with no participation of the people.[134] The people have to feel that they own a document before they can respect, defend, or obey it. In this regard, the 1999 constitution, which was put to the 2000 referendum, had several ma-

jor improvements in substance over the 1980 Lancaster House Constitution. First, it significantly reduced the power of the executive to avoid abuse and the concentration of power in a single person or institution and adopted a two-term limit for the presidency.[135] Second, it recommended two houses in parliament, a lower house and an upper house, with the upper house acting as a house of review over the functions and actions of the lower house. Third, it recommended a mixed proportional representation and constituency-based electoral system. Fourth, it recommended several measures, such as the ratification of constitutional office holders by parliament, to ensure that parliament was the center of power rather than the president. Fifth, it adopted provisions guaranteeing the independence of the judiciary and security of tenure. However, all these improvements were lost in the dispute over the process.

A fourth lesson from the commission approach is that, on practical grounds, using a commission with a broad and unregimented agenda is inappropriate for elaborating a document as complex as a constitution. With thousands of submissions to the commission, it is possible to write any number of versions of a constitution and find justification for each in the submissions made to the commission. The Zimbabwean government's so-called clarifications and corrections to the 1999 commission report illustrate this point. A further point, learned from the manner in which Mugabe changed provisions adopted in the 1999 constitution, is that it must be agreed at the start of the constitution-making process how decisions are going to be made, and once made, that those decisions should be final. Again, the South African process is instructive, as it was based on an agreement that all decisions of the constituent assembly were to be by consensus, and once the draft constitution was adopted, all stakeholders would support the enactment of the constitution in parliament and would not seek to amend the text. In the South African process, the African National Congress (ANC) did not dictate the process and had no power whatsoever over its results.

In Zimbabwe, because the 1999 constitutional process was bogged down by disagreements over the process, exclusive attention was directed at the land issue and questions of executive power, overlooking other equally important constitutional issues. The need to deal with gender inequality and adopt measures to ensure its elimination in Zimbabwean society did not receive as much attention as it deserved.[136] This was true of the 1980 Lancaster House constitutional conference as well, at which there were only two women among the sixty-five delegates. Even though women form 52 percent of the population, are the main providers of labor for farming (approximately 70 percent), and are the primary managers of homes in communal areas,[137] they suffer from pervasive inequality perpetuated by the traditional roles assigned to them. On the land, women are treated as dependants of men, not as landholders or farmers in their own right. Section 23 of the Lancaster House constitution prohibits discrimination, but recognizes exceptions to this general principle in issues relating to, among other things, the application of African customary law.[138] In 1999, the Supreme Court, basing its judgment on this exception, ruled in *Magaya v. Magaya*[139] that a woman could not inherit land from her deceased father. The Administration of Estates Act of 1997, which passed after the *Magaya* case, has changed this position in relation to inheritance specifically, but only for deaths that occurred after November 1, 1997. Under this law, a widow retains rights to land upon the death of her husband. But in reality, women still occupy a subordinate position in communal areas and generally only have access to land through their husbands. In another 1999 Supreme Court case, *Mahlangu v. Khumalo*,[140] the court ruled that

Section 23 of the constitution still exempted African customary law from the principles of nondiscrimination; in addition, other legislation still discriminates on gender grounds. Only equality between men and women can create the proper conditions to transform Zimbabwean society, and any future constitution-making process ought to pay particular attention to this.

The South African constitution was subject to judicial certification before presentation to parliament. The constitutional court was responsible for examining the text and deciding whether it conformed to the agreed constitutional principles.[141] No precedent exists elsewhere in the world for certification of a constitutional text by a court. This approach, though attractive, would not have worked in Zimbabwe, where the judiciary is not perceived as independent. South Africa was fortunate in that the constitutional court was new, having only been established in 1994. All its judges were selected and appointed through a process adopted after the end of apartheid.

After the elaboration of a draft constitution, the next important issue is how to adopt the constitution and ensure maximum legitimacy. The supreme law of the land should not be adopted using procedures that apply to ordinary legislation. Two methods of adopting constitutions are common: adoption through a two-thirds majority in parliament or through a constituent assembly or national referendum. A constituent assembly could take a variety of paths. In Namibia and South Africa, the constituent assemblies were elected; in Uganda, it was a collection of all stakeholders defined as inclusively as possible. With respect to parliament adopting the constitution, the important issue is not so much whether parliament has power to adopt and enact a constitution; rather, it is how to ensure that the sovereign will of the people on which the edifice of democracy rests is expressed in producing a legitimate, credible, and enduring constitution. If any-thing, the process of consulting the people strengthens parliament, as it implies parlia-ment's unequivocal acceptance that its pow-ers are delegated to it by the people. The rela-tionship between parliament and the people can endure only if this is recognized. Thus, in matters of great national importance, such as adopting a new constitution, parliament must consult and defer to the wishes of the people. Adopting a constitution through a referendum is one of the most transparent ways to further the culture of consultation. Popular democracy demands the institution-alization of a culture of consultation, recip-rocal control in lawmaking, and the use of power and privilege. It should be entrenched in a constitution as a mechanism for obtain-ing the mandate of the people on constitu-tional matters and as a deterrent to amend-ments. The two-thirds majority requirement is often within reach of the largest party in parliament, making it little different in prac-tice from the simple majority required for ordinary lawmaking. To safeguard democ-racy, much more should be required to effect a constitutional amendment than the will of the majority party in parliament. Approving a constitution through a national referen-dum encourages the full participation of the people, who can give it their formal seal of approval. The process can also generate wide publicity and engender full public debate and education of the people on the substantive is-sues that the constitution covers. It increases the chances of the document receiving the sort of critical and objective consideration that it deserves. Finally, a referendum can counterbalance a president- or government-inspired document being approved by a com-plaint parliament.

However, the February 2000 referendum on the draft constitution in Zimbabwe illus-trates some of the pitfalls associated with the process. The referendum was merely a con-sultative exercise, as the president was under no obligation to abide by its result. Govern-ment manipulation of the process quickly became apparent, as in the weeks leading up to the referendum, the state-controlled media launched an intensive publicity cam-paign in support of the constitution and was seemingly less prepared to allow airtime to those campaigning against it. Referendums inevitably have their own drawbacks. In par-ticular, the actual wording of the questions may greatly influence the result; they are expensive and time-consuming and could be considered to be too formal and static. The success of the NGO's campaign against adopting the constitution amply demon-strates that NGOs can be key to ensuring that the wishes of the president and government remain subordinate to those of the people. The Zimbabwean process also demonstrated the crucial role of NGOs and other civil-society groups in bringing the issue of a just constitution to the fore and helping to defeat a bad product. If not for their mobilization, the referendum on the flawed draft constitu-tion in 2000 would have passed, given the government's unparalleled use of state media to campaign for it.

Conclusions

There are two root causes of the so-called cultural problem of constitutionalism in Af-rica: the colonial experience overlaid with the postcolonial imposition of a one- or domi-nant-party system. The legacy of colonialism is offered frequently as an explanation for Af-rica's current failures in governance. Western criticism of bad governance, as in the case of Zimbabwe, is often branded as neocolonial-ist. Undoubtedly, colonial governments were not conducive to developing a culture of the rule of law in a Diceyan sense, notwithstand-ing hasty and belated attempts to create a framework for constitutional government in the last years of colonial rule. Indeed, for most of its history, colonial government was by nature authoritarian, and its legacy provided a temptation for similar conduct by successive rulers of the new states. The time has come, however, for Africans to take responsibility for transforming their own societies. Zimbabweans must realize that economic recovery and political stability begin by recovering those values that are acknowledged to be the true foundation of every human society. These values are, in turn, the foundation of social creativity and democratic governance. Zimbabwe must establish a stable political order that promotes development and aids the eradication of poverty, hunger, disease, and ignorance while guaranteeing citizens the rule of law, as opposed to rule by law, and equal protection under the law regardless of a citizen's gender, sexual orientation, age, religion, color, or ethnic origin.

Such a stable political order can only be achieved by establishing a constitutional order that is legitimate, credible, enduring, and accessible to the people, without compromising the integrity and effectiveness of the process of governance. The stark lessons learned from Zimbabwe's failure in its 1999 constitutional process are that the process of adopting the constitution is as important as its substance, and that the process must be legitimate if all stakeholders are to accept it. In turn, for the process to be legitimate, it must be inclusive. No party, including the government, should control it. A constitution should be the product of the integration of ideas from all stakeholders in a country, including political parties both within and outside parliament, organized civil society, and individuals in society. The question of developing a durable constitution for Zimbabwe remains a matter of priority. There is an urgent need for the nation to be engaged constructively in finding positive approaches to nation building for a just and sustainable society in Zimbabwe. As the Zimbabwe Council of Churches (ZCC) stated in a pastoral letter, the rejection of the

constitution in 1999 clearly did not imply the continued acceptance of the amended Lancaster House Constitution. Producing a homegrown constitution remains a national priority.[142] A new constitution for Zimbabwe could be the common platform through which Zimbabweans promote national reconciliation, build a national identity, promote national reconstruction, and engage in nation building.

Notes

1. See, generally, Patrick McAuslan, "Good Governance and Aid in Africa," *Journal of African Law,* vol. 40, no. 2 (1996), p. 168.

2. C. Palley, *The Constitutional History and Law of Southern Rhodesia, 1888–1965 with Special Reference to Imperial Control* (Oxford: Clarendon Press, 1966); see also Colin Leys, *European Politics in Southern Rhodesia* (Oxford: Oxford University Press, 1959).

3. Royal Charter of Incorporation of the British South Africa Company, October 29, 1889. Cecil Rhodes approached the British government with a request for a royal charter. His reasons were set out in the royal warrant and were mainly that, first, the existence of a powerful British company would be advantageous to the commercial and other interests of the United Kingdom and her colonies; second, the company would carry into effect diverse concessions and agreements that had been made by chiefs in the region and such other concessions and treaties as the petitioners should obtain; and third, that if the concessions obtained could be carried out, the conditions of the natives could be improved and their civilization advanced.

4. Royal Charter of Incorporation, 1889.

5. Hugh Marshall Hole, *The Making of Rhodesia* (London: Macmillan, 1926).

6. In 1918 the African chiefs mounted a legal challenge to the BSA Company claims of land ownership. See In re Southern Rhodesia, 1919, A.C. 211.

7. By the early 1920s, BSA Company officials had become convinced that Rhodesia was too costly to administer, and the Crown in turn was satisfied that company administration could be improved upon. The Crown assumed responsibility for administration of Rhodesia. Southern Rhodesia Order in Council, 1924.

8. *Report of the Constitutional Commission 1968* (Harare: Government Printer, 1968). See chap. 16, p. 143, on land tenure and economic development.

9. Claire Palley, *The Constitutional History and Law of Southern Rhodesia, 1888–1965 with Special Refrence to Imperial Control* (Oxford: Clarendon Press, 1966), p. 265.

10. Constitution of Zimbabwe, 1979, art. 52 (4).

11. Constitution of Rhodesia, 1961.

12. Leo Baron discusses the impact of the 1961 constitution in detail in "The Rhodesian Saga," *Zambia Law Journal,* vol. 1, no. 1 (1969), p. 43.

13. Baron, "The Rhodesian Saga."

14. Constitution of Southern Rhodesia, 1961, art. 70. See also Baron, "The Rhodesian Saga," p. 44.

15. Ibid., p. 45.

16. *Racial Discrimination and Repression in Southern Rhodesia,* International Commission of Jurists (ICJ) report (undated). See also Reg. Austin, *The Character of the Rhodesian Front since UDI,* Africa Bureau, 1968. See also Law and Order (Maintenance) Amendment Act 50 of 1967.

17. Law and Order (Maintenace) Amendment Act 50 of 1967.

18. There are several good accounts of Rhodesia's Unilateral Declaration of Independence, such as Douglas Anglin, *Zambian Crisis Bahavior: Confronting Rhodesia's Unilateral Declaration of Independence, 1965–1966* (Montreal: McGill-Queen's University Press, 1994).

19. Southern Rhodesia Order 1965 no. 1952, (S.I. 1965/1952). Article 2 (1) states: "It is hereby declared for the avoidance of doubt that any instrument made or other act done in purported promulgation of any Constitution for Southern Rhodesia except as authorized by Act of Parliament is void and of no effect. . . . (2) This section shall come into operation forthwith and shall then be deemed to have had effect from 11th November 1965."

20. Southern Rhodesia Order 1965 no. 1952.

21. *Madzimbamuto v. Ladner-Burke and Baron v. Ayre N.O. and Others,* GD/Civ/23/66 and AD 1/68.

22. (1969) AC 645.

23. Sanctions were imposed, but were largely ineffectual. General Assembly Resolution 2012 (XX) 12 October 1965; General Assembly Resolution 2151 (XXI) 17 November 1965; Security Council Resolution 216, 12 November 1965, and Security Council Resolution 217, 20 November 1965. For a critical analysis of the international response, see Baron, "The Rhodesian Saga," p. 37.

24. The Constitution of Rhodesia, 1969, Act no. 54. The adoption of the constitution followed a referendum held on June 20, 1969, which approved a Republican status. The 1969 constitution continued to entrench the prevailing land ownership. Article 8 (1) (b) stated: "any provision of the law relating to tenure of land, including Tribal Trust Land, which is specified in that law to be a specially entrenched provision for the purposes of this section shall, subject to the provisions of sub section (4) be subject to the same procedure in all respects as if it were a constitutional Bill to amend a specially entrenched provision of this constitution specified in the Third Schedule."

25. Constitution of Rhodesia, 1969, Act no. 54, art. 92 (schedule 2) provided for a bill of rights. Article 84 excluded the courts jurisdiction from hearing any allegations of the violation of the rights.

26. Constitution of Rhodesia, 1969. Article 10 provides that "(1) Every person is entitled to the enjoyment of the rights and freedoms set forth in this schedule without unjust discrimination on the grounds of race, tribe, political opinion, color or creed; (2) For the purposes of subparagraph (1) of this paragraph, a law shall not be construed to discriminate unjustly to the extent that it permits different treatment of persons or communities if such treatment is fair and will promote harmonious relations between such persons or communities by making due allowance for economic, social or cultural differences between them; (3) No law shall be construed to be inconsistent with any of the following provisions, that is to say, paragraphs 2, 5, 6, 7 (other than subparagraphs (a) and (b) of subparagraph (3) thereof), 8 and 9 of this schedule to the extent that the law in question provides for: (a) the application in the case of Africans of African customary law; or (b) the exercise by tribal courts of their jurisdiction; or (c) restrictions on the ownership, occupation or use of land."

27. The injustices and suffering caused during the ninety years of colonial rule that began in 1899, in particular during the last fifteen years of colonialism (the UDI period), have been well documented, especially the abuses of the 1970s. The Catholic Commission for Justice and Peace (CCJP) in the country was an important part of the documentation process. CCJP facilitated the international publication of several reports, including *The Man in the Middle* (1975), *Civil War in Rhodesia* (1976), and *Rhodesia, the Propaganda War* (1977). See also *Racial Discrimination and Repression in Southern Rhodesia*.

28. A.J. Hanna, *The Story of the Rhodesias and Nyasaland* (London: Faber and Faber, 1960), and Thomas Franck, *Race and Nationalism: The Struggle for Power in Rhodesia-Nyasaland* (Santa Barbara, CA: Greenwood Press, 1960).

29. Terence Ranger, *Peasant Consciousness and Guerrilla War in Zimbabwe: A Comparative Study* (London: James Currey, 1985).

30. For an excellent account of the liberation war in Zimbabwe, see Ranger, *Peasant Consciousness*.

31. Ibid.

32. Constitution of Zimbabwe Rhodesia, 1979.

33. Southern Rhodesia Act, 1979, chap. 52. It provided for the bringing into effect a new constitution for Zimbabwe and the revocation of the 1961 constitution. See articles 1 (1), (2), (3). The constitution was brought into force by the Southern Rhodesia Constitution (Interim Provisions) Order 1979 (S.I.1979/1571). It provided that the constitution was to come into force on December 4, 1979. See art. 1 (1), (2), (3), (4), (5).

34. Constitution of Zimbabwe, 1979.

35. Constitution of Zimbabwe Amendment no. 4, 1979, art. 16 (1) provided: "No property of any description or interest or right therein shall be compulsorily acquired except under the authority of a law that—(a) requires the acquiring authority to give reasonable notice of the intention to acquire the property, interest or right to any person owning the property or having any other interest or right therein that would be affected by such acquisition; (b) requires that the acquisition is reasonably necessary in the interests of defense, public safety, public order, public morality, public health, town and country planning, the utilization of that or any other property for a purpose beneficial to the public generally or to any section thereof or, in the case of land that is under-utilized, the settlement of land for agricultural purposes; (c) requires the acquiring authority to pay promptly adequate compensation for the acquisition; (d) requires the acquiring authority, if the acquisition is contested, to apply to the General Division or some other court before, or not later than thirty days after, the acquisition for an order confirming the acquisition; and (e) enables any claimant for compensation to apply to the General Division or some other court for the prompt return of the property if the court does not con-

firm the acquisition and for the determination of any question relating to compensation, and appeal to the Appellate Division."

36. Constitution of Zimbabwe, Act no. 4, 1979. Article 38 (1) provided that "the House of Assembly shall consist of one hundred members qualified in accordance with schedule 3 for election to the House of Assembly, of whom: (a) eighty shall be elected by voters registered on the common roll for eighty common roll constituencies; (b) twenty shall be elected by voters registered on the white roll for twenty white roll constituencies."

37. The Constitution of Zimbabwe Rhodesia, Act no. 12, 1979. Article 2 (b) provided that "Zimbabwe Rhodesia shall cease to be an independent state and shall become part of her Majesty's dominions."

38. The state of emergency gave power to legislate by regulation, rather than through parliament. Regulations included the Emergency Powers (Maintenance of Law and Order) Regulations, which gave sweeping powers of arrest and detention without trial, the right to control meetings, and so on.

39. Jason Beaubien, "Government Policies Lead to Collapse of Zimbabwe Economy," available at www.npr.org/templates/story/story.php?storyId=5446596 (accessed May 26, 2009).

40. Constitution of Zimbabwe Amendment no. 7 Act no. 23, 1987.

41. Amnesty International, *Zimbabwe: Terror Tactics in the Run-up to the Parliamentary Elections, June 2000*, AFR 46/014/2000, available at www.unhcr.org/refworld/docid/3b83b70ce.html (accessed April 27, 2009).

42. Beaubien, "Government Policies Lead to Collapse."

43. Section 110 (3), Electoral Act, 2008.

44. "Mugabe Rival Quits Election Race," *BBC News*, June 22, 2008, http://news.bbc.co.uk/2/hi/africa/7467990.stm (accessed May 28, 2009).

45. Article 20.1.7 of the eighth schedule of the Global Political Agreement.

46. Southern African Development Communique, issued in Pretoria on January 27, 2009.

47. The Constitution of Zimbabwe Rhodesia Amendment no. 4 Act 1979. It was published as a schedule to the Zimbabwe Constitution Order, 1979 (SI 1979/1600), United Kingdom.

48. The Lancaster Talks were held at Lancaster House London in 1979 under the auspices of the British government. These negotiations led to a cease-fire in the guerrilla war that the black liberation movements had been waging against the Unilateral Declaration of Independence regime. The movements were Zimbabwe African National Union (ZANU-PF) and the Zimbabwe African Peoples Union Party (ZAPU-PF). The armed wing of ZANU-PF was called Zimbabwe National Liberation Army (ZANLA) and that of ZAPU-PF was called Zimbabwe Peoples Liberation Army (ZIPLA).

49. Constitution of Zimbabwe, 1979, art. 52(4).

50. See Constitution of Zambia as amended by Act no. 18 of 1996, Article 35 (1): "Every president shall hold office for a period of five years; (2) notwithstanding anything to the contrary contained in this constitution or any other law no person who has twice been elected as President shall be eligible for re-election to that office."

51. See Constitution of Malawi, 1996, art. 83(2): "The President or Vice President may serve a maximum of two consecutive terms."

52. See South African Constitution, 1996, art. 88(2): "No person may hold the office as president for more than two terms, but when a person is elected to fill a vacancy in the office of the president, the period between that election and the next election of a president is not regarded as a term."

53. Universal Declaration of Human Rights, U.N. GAOR, 3rd sess., U.N. Doc. A/810 pmb. (1948), art. 21(3): "the will of the people shall be the basis of the authority of government; this shall be expressed in periodic and genuine elections."

54. Universal Declaration of Human Rights, art. 20: "(1) everyone has the right to freedom of peaceful assembly and association. (2) No one may be compelled to belong to an association."); American Declaration of the Rights of Man, May 2, 1948, art. XXV (right to peaceful assembly), XXI (right to associate) "to promote, exercise and protect... legitimate interests of a political, economic, religious, social, cultural, professional, labor union or other nature," OEA/Ser.L. V/II/71, Doc. 6 rev. 1, 18 (1988).

55. See, e.g., Universal Declaration of Human Rights, art. 21(1): "Everyone has the right to take part in the government of his country, directly or through freely chosen representatives," International Covenant on Civil and Political Rights, December 19, 1966, art. 25 (a), 999 U.N.T.S. 171, echoing art. 21 (1) of the Universal Declaration of Human Rights.

56. See, e.g., International Covenant on Civil and Political Rights, art. 25: "Every citizen shall have the right and the opportunity without any of the distinctions mentioned in article 2 and without unreasonable restrictions: (a) to take part in the conduct of public affairs, directly or through freely chosen representatives; (b) to vote and to be elected at genuine periodic elections which shall be by universal and equal suffrage and shall be held by secret ballot, guaranteeing the free expression of the will of the electors; (c) To have access, on general terms of equality, to public service in his country"; American Convention on Human Rights, July 18, 1978, art. 23, 1144 U.N.T.S. art. 123: "(1) Every citizen shall enjoy the following rights and opportunities: (a) to take part in the conduct of public affairs, directly or through freely chosen representatives; (b) to vote and to be elected in genuine periodic elections, which shall be by universal and equal suffrage and by secret ballot that guarantees the free expression of the will of the voters; and (c) to have access, under general conditions of equality, to the public service of his country"; African Charter on Human and Peoples' Rights, art. 13: "(1) Every citizen shall have the right to participate freely in the government of his country, either directly or through freely chosen representatives in accordance, either directly or through freely chosen representatives in accordance with the provisions of the law. (2) Every citizen shall have the right of equal access to the public service of his country."

57. The International Covenant on Civil and Political Rights preamble states: "Recognizing that, in accordance with the Universal Declaration of Human Rights, the ideal of free human being enjoying civil and political freedom and freedom from fear and want can only be achieved if conditions are created whereby everyone may enjoy his civil and political rights, as well as his economic, social and cultural rights."

58. See Universal Declaration of Human Rights, art. 2 (1); see also International Covenant on Economic, Social, and Cultural Rights, art. 2; International Covenant on Civil and Political Rights, art. 19 (right to freedom of thought, conscience and religion and art) and art. 20 (prohibiting war propaganda and incitements to discrimination); African Charter on Human and Peoples' Rights, art. 8.

59. See Universal Declaration of Human Rights, art. 19; International Covenant on Civil and Political Rights, art. 19; see also African Charter on Human and Peoples' Rights, art. 9.

60. See International Covenant on Civil and Political Rights, art. 20. See also African Charter on Human and Peoples' Rights, art. 9.

61. See Universal Declaration of Human Rights, arts. 20 (10) and 23 (4) (right to form and join trade unions); see also International Covenant on Civil and Political Rights, arts. 21, 22 (right of freedom of association including trade unions); African Charter on Human and Peoples' Rights, arts. 10, 11.

62. See Universal Declaration of Human Rights, arts. 6–11; see also International Covenant on Civil and Political Rights, art. 2(3), 14–16, and African Charter on Human and Peoples' Rights, art. 7.

63. See Universal Declaration of Human Rights, arts. 2, 23 (1); see also International Covenant on Civil and Political Rights, arts. 2, 26.

64. United Nations Human Rights Committee, art. 19, June 29, 1983, general comment 10.

65. United Nations Human Rights Committee, art. 19, general comment 10.

66. Thomas Franck, "The Emerging Right to Democratic Governance," *American Journal of International Law*, vol. 86, no. 1 (1992), p. 46.

67. Constitution of Zimbabwe, 1979, chap. 111, arts. 11–26.

68. Constitution Amendment no. 7, 1987.

69. For example, one of the earlier changes was the removal (by the expiry date of the provision) of the twenty seats reserved for whites in parliament's Constitution Amendment Act no. 15 of 1987. Related changes were the substitution of a ceremonial presidency and premier for an executive president, as well as the abolition of the Senate to create a 150-member unicameral legislature, Act 23 of 1987.

70. Constitution of Zimbabwe Amendment Act no. 30, 1990. Article 15 (4) provided that "the execution of a person who has been sentenced to death by a competent court in respect of a criminal offence of which he has been convicted shall not be held to be in contravention of subsection (1) solely on the ground that the execution is carried out in the manner prescribed in section 315 (2) of the criminal Procedure and Evidence Act as that section existed on the 1st October, 1990." The amendment was passed as the Supreme Court was hearing the case *S. V. Chileya*. The appellants in the case argued that hanging was a cruel and unusual form of punishment. The Government did not wait for the case to be concluded.

71. Constitutional Amendment no. 7, 1987.

72. Constitutional Amendment no. 7, 1987.

73. Constitutional Amendment no. 7, 1987.

74. This is the case even though the Zimbabwe constitution guarantees the independence of the judiciary and vests judicial authority in the courts (art. 79 [1]) and declares: "the constitution is the Supreme law of Zimbabwe and if any other law is inconsistent with this constitution that other law shall, to the extent of the inconsistency, be void." See Zimbabwe Constitution, art. 3.

75. Constitution of Zimbabwe Amendment no. 12 Act of 1993, sec. 2, which amended section 16(1) (e) of the constitution.

76. Parliamentary debates, December 6, 1990. (Harare, Zimbabwe: Government Printer). The Supreme Court was progressive on the death penalty; in *Catholic Commission for Justice and Peace v. Attorney General* 1993, (1) ZLR 242, the Supreme Court passed an order to set aside and substitute the sentences of death with sentences of life imprisonment because of undue delays in executing four prisoners. The delay had been declared to be inhumane.

77. Bulletin of Zimbabwe Law no. 1, 1991, p. 19.

78. Constitution of Zimbabwe Amendment no. 11 Act of 1990, sec. 5.

79. 2000 (2) ZLR 243.

80. Supreme Court of Zimbabwe, 2000.

81. Amnesty International, *Zimbabwe: Rights under Siege*, AFR 46/012/2003, available at http://www.unhcr.org/refworld/docid/3f12edab4.html (accessed on April 27, 2009), p. 14.

82. 1994 (2) ZLR 54.

83. 1994 (2) ZLR 54.

84. 1994 (2) ZLR 54.

85. Constitution of Zimbabwe Amendment no. 14 Act of 1996. Paragraph (d) to section 22 (3) of the constitution was repealed.

86. In *Kohlhasas v. Chief Immigration Officer*, 1997 (2) ZLR 441, the court held that the amendment did not in any way impact upon, interfere with, or diminish the mobility rights of a citizen wife, in particular the right to have her alien husband reside with her permanently in Zimbabwe.

87. See National Constitutional Assembly, *AGENDA: Building a Peoples' Constitution*, vol. 2, no. 2 (October 1999). The National Constitutional Assembly was a voluntary and inclusive association of civil-society organizations and individuals, including civic groups, political parties, churches and other religious organizations, youth organizations, women's organizations, and pressure groups.

88. *Constitution Commission of Inquiry into the Establishment of a New Democratic Constitution* (Harare: Government Printer, 1999), a publication of the constitutional commission. The commission was established under Proclamation no. 6, 1999, issued under the Commission of Inquiry Act.

89. *Constitutional Commission of Inquiry.*

90. Lovemore Madhuku, "How Independent Is the Constitutional Commission?" *AGENDA: Building a People's Constitution,* vol. 2, no. 2 (October 1999).

91. Presidential Commissions of Inquiry Act.

92. Presidential Commissions of Inquiry Act, p. 10.

93. National Constitutional Assembly, *Why the NCA Says No to a Partisan Constitution-Making Process* (Harare: Government Printer, 1999), pp. 5, 6.

94. National Constitutional Assembly, *Why the NCA Says No,* p. 7. The commission had 13 women out of 500 commissioners.

95. *Constitution Commission of Inquiry.*

96. Ibid.

97. The coordinating committee developed a comprehensive roster of key individual opinion leaders in Zimbabwe from all walks of life, notably politics, business, education, religion, media, and civil society.

98. Justice G. Chidyausiku, constitutional commission chairperson, speech delivered at the International Conference, November 17, 1999 (on file with the author).

99. On April 28, 1999, Mugabe set up a commission of inquiry under the Commission of Inquiry Act (chap. 10:07) in terms of Proclamation no. 6 of 1999 (SI 138/99).

100. Inter-Parliamentary Union (IPU), Parline database: Zimbabwe, Last Elections, available at www.ipu.org/parline/reports/2383_e.htm (accessed May 27, 2009).

101. Inter-Parliamentary Union (IPU) Parline database: Zimbabwe, Last Elections.

102. Inter-Parliamentary Union (IPU), Parline database: Zimbabwe, Last Elections.

103. Tichaona Sibanda, "Zimbabwe: Who Should Write Country's Constitution?" AllAfrica.com, available at http://allafrica.com/stories/printable/200904290850.htm1 (accessed July 18, 2009).

104. Sibanda, "Zimbabwe: Who Should Write Country's Constitution?"

105. See John Hatchard, Muna Ndulo, and Peter Slinn, *Comparative Constitutionalism and Good Governance: An Eastern and Southern African Perspective* (New York: Cambridge University Press, 2004), p. 32.

106. Hatchard, Ndulo, and Slinn, *Comparative Constitutionalism.*

107. Contrary to expectations, the final draft did not permit the state to acquire land from white farmers without compensation.

108. The reasons advanced by the government in the government gazette were as follows: "It is common knowledge that any draft is by definition subject to improvement by way of grammatical and factual corrections as well as linguistic clarifications in order to avoid any doubt about the meaning of what is in the draft. The corrections and clarifications below were done based on the records of the Commission as contained in the commission's Committee minutes and published in the Commission's 1,437 page report. It is all there for the asking and there is nothing new because the record is public and therefore speaks for itself. Only people with literacy problems or hidden political agendas will find it difficult to tell the otherwise clear difference between corrections and clarifications on the one hand and amendments on the other. Don't be misled." See Hatchard, Ndulo, and Slinn, *Comparative Constitutionalism,* p. 33.

109. *Mushayakarara v. Chidyausiku* no. 2000 (1) ZLR 248, p. 252.

110. E.g., the Harare Commonwealth Declaration, signed October 20, 1991, by heads of government of the member countries of the Commonwealth, which reaffirms member countries' commitment to the primacy of equal rights under law and includes a specific pledge by member countries to concentrate, with renewed vigor, on established national systems based on the rule of law and independence of the judiciary; see The Harare Declaration, 1991. Zimbabwe withdrew from the Commonwealth in 2003.

111. Human Rights Watch, "Fast Track Land Reform in Zimbabwe," March 2002, vol. 14, no. 1 (A); Amnesty International, *Zimbabwe: Rights under Siege.* See also International Bar Association, "International Human Rights Day," December 10, 2004; the association marked the day by publishing a collection of personal accounts, opinions, and images about human rights in Zimbabwe. See Human Rights Institute, "International Human Rights Day," December 10, 2004, London.

112. See previous note.

113. Commonwealth Observer Group to the Zimbabwe Presidential Elections, Preliminary Report of the Commonwealth Observer Group to the Zimbabwe Presidential Elections March 9–10, 2002, (Harare, Zimbabwe) March 14, 2002, concluded that although the actual polling and counting process were peaceful and secrecy of the ballot was assured, the conditions in Zimbabwe did not adequately allow for a free expression of will by the electors. See also SADC Parliamentary Forum (SADCPF) Observer Mission, Report on Zimbabwe Elections, March 13, 2002, Harare, Zimbabwe. which concluded that the election process could not be said to adequately comply with the norm and standards for elections in the SADC region (on file with the author).

114. Human Rights Watch, *Under the Shadow: Civil and Political Rights in Zimbabwe,* Human Rights Briefing Paper, June 6, 2003, New York.

115. Human Rights Defenders Report, "Evaluation Mission 2003: Systematic Repression of Human Rights Defenders in Zimbabwe," February 18, 2004, Paris.

116. Joseph Winter, "What Is Behind the Zimbabwe Demolitions?" *BBC News,* July 26, 2005.

117. Winter, "What Is Behind the Zimbabwe Demolitions?"

118. Inter-Parliamentary Union, Parline database: Zimbabwe, Last Elections.

119. UN Human Rights Committee, Initial Report on Zimbabwe (CCPR/C/SR.1664) para. 4.

120. African Commission on Human and Peoples' Rights, Resolution on the Rights to Freedom of Association, Gambia, December 2002.

121. International Labor Organization, "Latest Report of ILO Committee on Freedom of Association Cites Belarus, Colombia, Zimbabwe, Others," November 21, 2002 (ILO/02/51).

122. See Human Rights NGO Forum, "Complying with the Abuja Agreement: Two Months Report," Harare, December 2001, p. 4.

123. Human Rights Watch, *Under the Shadow,* p. 40.

124. Meeting in Abuja, Nigeria, the Commonwealth heads of state and government voted to renew Zimbabwe's suspension, which was in place in March 2002 following the country's flawed presidential election. Zimbabwe called the Commonwealth decision unacceptable and announced that Zimbabwe would withdraw from the organization immediately. See Human Rights First Media Alert, "Zimbabwe Suspended Indefinitely from Commonwealth," available at www.humanrightsfirst.org/media/2003_alerts/1208.htm (accessed on April 27, 2009).

125. Hatchard, Ndulo, and Slinn, *Comparative Constitutionalism,* p. 33.

126. The author was one of the experts who participated in the conference. He did so as an Intitute for Democracy and Electoral Assistance (IDEA) consultant.

127. In his welcome remarks at the International Conference on the Making of Zimbabwe's New Democratic Constitution, November 17, 1999, G. Chidyausiku stated: "A homegrown constitution can and needs to be enriched by drawing on the experiences of other countries. Indeed there is no country in the modern world including Zimbabwe that can escape the imperative of a global society."

128. One of the justifications for the seizure of land from the white population has been on the grounds that it was being transferred to Zimbabweans.

129. See Katherine Savage, "Negotiating South Africa's New Constitution: An Overview of the Key Players and the Negotiating Process," p. 1,664, in Penelope Andrews and Stephen Ellman, eds., *The Post-Apartheid Constitutions: Perspectives on South Africa's Basic Law* (Athens, OH: Ohio University Press, 2001).

130. Freedom Charter, 1954. See Anthony Sampson, *Mandela: The Authorized Biography* (New York: Vintage, 1999), pp. 93–95.

131. Andrews and Ellman, *The Post-Apartheid Constitutions.*

132. The commission was appointed on May 21, 1999. It was directed to complete its work by November 30, 1999.

133. See NCA, *Why We Say No.*

134. Constitution of Zimbabwe Amendment Act of 1981; Constitution of Zimbabwe Amendment no. 2 Act of 1981; Constitution of Zimbabwe Amendment no. 3 Act of 1983; Constitution of Zimbabwe Amendment no. 4 Act of 1984; Constitution of Zimbabwe Amendment no. 5 Act of 1985; Constitution of Zimbabwe Amendment no. 6 Act of 1987; Constitution of Zimbabwe Amendment no. 7 Act of 1987; Constitution Amendment no. 8 Act of 1989; Constitution Amendment no. 9 Act of 1989; Constitution Amendment no. 10 Act of 1990; Constitution Amendment no. 11 Act of 1990; Constitution Amendment no. 12 Act of 1990; Constitution Amendment no. 13 Act of 1993.

135. *Report of the Constitutional Commission* 1968.

136. Other constitutional issues not suffi-ciently attended to included administrative struc-tures and issues of decentralization, rights of farm workers, the relationship between church and state, and minority rights.

137. Women and Land Lobby Group, *Report on WLLG Workshop on Women's Land Rights, Held 27–28 November, 2000* (Harare: WLLG, 2001). Many men are migrant workers in the cities or in other areas away from their homes.

138. The Zimbabwe Constitution, sec. 33: "No law or public officer shall discriminate against any person on the grounds of that person's tribe, race, and place of origin, political views, color, religion or sex. It shall be lawful to discriminate on any of the above grounds in the areas of family law (including marriage, divorce and inheritance), customary law, rights/privileges relating to communal lands, quali-fications for serving under the civil service or the armed forces, or the spending of public funds."

139. Supreme Court of Zimbabwe, 1999.

140. Supreme Court of Zimbabwe, 1999.

141. Savage, "Negotiating South Africa's New Constitution," p. 184. The constitutional court in September 1996 refused to certify the first draft submitted to the court on the grounds that a num-ber of provisions of the constitutional text were not in compliance with the relevant constitutional principles. Finally, in December 1996, the constitu-tional court certified the new constitution. See In re: Certification of the Constitution of the Republic of South Africa Act May 1996, CCT 23/96.

142. Zimbabwe Christian Council Pastoral letter, Victoria Falls, August 2001.

PART III

ASIA AND THE PACIFIC

8

The Process of Creating a New Constitution in Cambodia

Stephen P. Marks

The process of drafting the constitution of the Kingdom of Cambodia, which entered into force on September 24, 1993, was a striking case of peacebuilding and national reconciliation and was a major feature of Cambodia's transition from civil war to fragile democracy. It was the culmination of a transitional period during which Cambodia was under the authority of the United Nations. Cambodia's mandate was, first, to elect a constituent assembly, which it did in May 1993; that body was to transform itself into a new national assembly, in accordance with articles 1 and 12 of the Paris Agreements, which had settled Cambodia's twenty-year conflict.[1] Cambodia is one of the most extraordinary cases in international efforts to promote democratic transitions in the post–Cold War era.[2] The country's democratic transition ended one of the most brutal chapters of twentieth-century barbarity, during which over a million people out of a population of some eight million perished through civil war, mass murder, starvation,

and repression, especially while the country was under the control of the Party of Democratic Kampuchea (PDK or DK, the latter acronym being used throughout this chapter), popularly known as the Khmer Rouge.[3]

The transition from civil war to a fragile democracy resulted from the implementation, under UN supervision, of an international treaty by which the four contending Cambodian parties[4] and eighteen other countries, including the five permanent members of the Security Council and the principal regional powers,[5] agreed to detailed conditions for a "comprehensive political settlement of the Cambodia conflict," the terms used in the Paris Agreements.[6] The agreements and the UN Transitional Authority in Cambodia (UNTAC), established pursuant to the agreements, did much to lay the groundwork for such a settlement. However, they did not and could not achieve their goals completely. The agreements' implementation was particularly unsuccessful in disarming, demobilizing, and cantoning forces; preventing cease-fire violations; accessing all territories; and maintaining a neutral political environment. This failure to implement the military provisions of the agreements was the result of a calculated risk by the United Nations, which sought to proceed with the elections. This calculation was not unwarranted, as the Cambodian people did participate massively in free and fair elections. However, though the May 1993 elections were a defining moment of the mission, they were not an end in themselves, but rather a means to drafting and adopting a new national constitution as a precondition to setting up a democratic government.

It is most accurate to describe the essence of the Cambodian process as an exercise in political self-determination through a UN-managed transition to a democratic form of government. The new system was based on a constitution that both acknowledges Cambodian tradition and current political forces, and establishes a parliamentary form of government under a relatively powerless monarchy, with a relatively robust bill of rights but weak mechanisms for protecting those rights. UNTAC would have failed if the elections, however free and fair, had not resulted in the adoption of a constitution and the transfer of sovereignty to the new government under that constitution.[7] The process leading to the constitution's adoption and the installation of a new government has been analyzed from the perspective of post-conflict nation building[8]; however, few works have addressed the constitutional process itself or the legal system.[9]

Despite a disappointing process, the final product of the constituent assembly's work contains a reasonable blueprint for democratic governance. Nevertheless, the path to Cambodian democracy has not been smooth. The secession of several provinces under Prince Chakrapong following the election immediately threatened the entire process and re-

quired the creation of a provisional national government. An unstable power-sharing arrangement between the Cambodian People's Party (CPP) and the royalist National United Front for an Independent, Neutral, Peaceful, and Cooperative Cambodia (FUNCINPEC by its French acronym) and the continued military confrontation with the DK weakened the application of the constitution in the mid-1990s. These developments culminated in a coup in July 1997 and the consolidation of power around Hun Sen, followed by the troubled election of 1998 and the suspension of foreign aid, and the difficulty in forming a government after the 2003 election. The constitution has not functioned as initially drafted, with unacceptable delays in creating a constitutional court and Supreme Council of the Magistracy and in adopting amendments to establish a senate. Violence and corruption mar the democratic process. Yet the essential structures of Cambodian democracy are in place, civil society continues to be vigorous and courageous, and the economy is improving.

This chapter reviews the historical background leading up to the process of conflict resolution and addresses the structure of the constitution-making process, public participation in the process, the post-conflict role of the political parties, the timing and duration of the constitution-making process, the role of the international community, the role of international law, and key substantive issues dealt with in the process. The conclusion draws attention to negative outcomes, such as the lack of transparency at critical moments, manipulation of the process by Prince Norodom Sihanouk (who was restored to the throne), and the consolidation of authoritarian personal power by Hun Sen. Those outcomes are then weighed against the positive achievements of putting in place the legal and institutional basis for democratic governance—the constitution and the separate branches of government—and providing a degree of democratic empowerment of civil society.

Historical Background

Influence of Cambodia's History on the Constitution-Making Process

Cambodia's ancient, colonial, and recent history all influenced the constitution, and to dwell exclusively on the impact of the civil war overlooks the two other major historical influences. Like many countries in Southeast Asia, Cambodia's political traditions derive primarily from Indian culture and the absolute rule of god-kings, as well as from Buddhist beliefs.[10] A legal system and formal constitution defining the functions and powers of national institutions only arrived with French colonialism and the realization of independence. Attitudes toward the constitution and law in general continue, nevertheless, to be affected by past traditions, which date from the age of the Khmer empire that ruled from Angkor from the ninth to the fifteenth centuries. As an eminent historian of Cambodia, David Chandler, explains, "a Cambodian king, like most Chinese emperors, could rule only by extending networks of patronage and mutual obligations outward from his palace, at first through close associates and family members but becoming diffuse—and more dependent on local powerholders—at the edges of the kingdom."[11] The king was distant from the people, who rarely saw him. Even in the nineteenth century, villagers had only a vague idea of the king, generally believing him to have the power to influence the weather, to "dispense true justice," and to be "the only political source of hope among peasants."[12] François Ponchaud explains that

> in the traditional mindset, the king, at the national and even universal planes was the key for the "preservation of harmony with the ele-

> ments" . . . it was incumbent upon him to have the power and duty to rule over the broad universal expanses, and even "to master the earth spirits" . . . the absence of a sovereign implied the lack of effective communication between the celestial powers and the world of men; without him you have complete chaos.[13]

Patronage and clientship at the village level remained an essential part of the social structure up to the nineteenth century, as the "rectitude and permanence of these relationships had been drummed into people from birth."[14] Chandler cites Cambodian proverbs and didactic literature that "are filled with references to the helplessness of the individual and to the importance of accepting power relationships as they are." In addition to the king, his high-ranking officials (*okya*), and the village leaders (*chaovay sruk*), members of the royal family were an influential connection between the people and their king.[15]

Justice in Angkor appears to have been a matter of royal prerogative, with particularly brutal forms of determining responsibility and meting out punishment.[16] Reminiscent of practices in medieval Europe, it does not appear to provide much of a model for human rights. More generally, the social structures of the past and the place of the individual in the Khmer cosmology were adapted under modern ideas of government but not entirely eliminated by the introduction of constitutions in the mid-twentieth century.

The Angkor tradition is reflected in three features of the 1993 constitution. First, in paragraphs 1, 2, and 3 of the preamble, the constitution refers to Cambodia's "grand civilization of a prosperous, powerful, and glorious nation whose prestige radiates like a diamond" and to "the prestige of Angkor civilization." Second are the constitutional provisions, particularly in articles 68–71, concerning the preservation, dissemination, and teaching of Khmer languages and culture. The third dimension of Cambodia's ancient past is the restoration of monarchy. As one constitutional scholar has observed, "monarchy has witnessed the most glorious moments of Khmer civilization. Its millennial embedding makes it the principal feature of the political tradition that still prevails among the peasant masses."[17]

The colonial period also strongly influenced the constitution, providing the model on which the drafters drew most heavily. The struggle for independence, which Cambodia gained on November 9, 1949, resulted in both a strong influence of French legal tradition and a firm commitment to national sovereignty and nonalignment. Thus, the 1993 constitution contains many elements of the 1947 constitution as well as a reaffirmation of the kingdom's position, already in the constitutions of Democratic Kampuchea and the People's Republic of Kampuchea, as an "independent, sovereign, peaceful, permanently neutral and non-aligned country."[18]

Beyond historical and colonial influences, the termination of the conflict was a precondition for the constitution-making process. Cambodia had been in a civil war virtually since 1970, when Lon Nol came to power following a coup, only to be overthrown in 1975 by the DK, who destroyed economy and society until the Vietnamese invaded in 1978 and installed the People's Republic of Kampuchea in 1979. The latter was resisted by FUNCINPEC, the Buddhist party Khmer People's National Liberation Front (KPLNF), and the Maoist movement (DK) for a decade until the Paris Conference on Cambodia was convened and eventually succeeded in getting all four factions to agree to a peace process centering around an election.

Impact of the Civil War

Twenty years of civil war created hardened and virtually irreconcilable ideological and political postures among the U.S.-supported anticommunist resistance, the Soviet Union–supported pro-Vietnamese government, and the China-supported DK. After years of deadly warfare and high stakes geopolitics, it seemed very unlikely that the groups' leaders would engage on their own initiative in a process of reconciliation and construction of national institutions for power sharing. The end of the Cold War severely weakened the political support each faction received from the outside, but the divides among them showed no signs of narrowing.

The impact of the civil war and its resolution on the constitution begins with the mutually hurting stalemate that led all four factions to recognize that none could win militarily, that they could no longer rely on outside support, and that they had to work something out. The earlier initiatives in the 1980s for a negotiated settlement by Vietnam, the Soviet Union, the Coalition Government of Democratic Kampuchea (CGDK), Indonesia (the Jakarta Informal Meeting, or JIM and JIM2), and the Paris International Conference on Cambodia (PICC) were unsuccessful because the situation was not ripe, but the efforts did create a decade of proposals on a wide range of issues. By the time of Gareth Evans's Australian Plan in 1989, picking up on proposals by U.S. Congressman Stephen Solarz, the parties were more convinced that they had to accept a settlement,[19] though the Cambodian factions and other concerned parties focused more on withdrawal of Vietnamese forces and delineating the transitional powers of the UN and the Supreme National Council (SNC)—the interim representative body created by the Paris Agreement—than on the role of a constitution or the preferred process for producing one. The shape of the constitutional arrangement was not really agreed upon until the fourth SNC meeting in New York in September 1991, at which it was decided that the peace process would lead to an electoral system of proportional representation by province and a permanent system of liberal democracy.[20] When the PICC reconvened at the end of October 1991, it adopted four final agreements, including an annex containing constitutional principles.[21]

The Influence of the Paris Agreements

The Paris Agreements required the constituent assembly to produce a constitution that "shall declare that Cambodia will apply a liberal democracy, based on pluralism."[22] The term "liberal democracy" has been attributed to Prince Sihanouk, who had called for Cambodia to be a liberal democratic state during earlier negotiations.[23] It seems likely that he used this term in the context of the negotiations because he assumed it was what the U.S. representatives and other key participants in the Paris Conference wanted to hear. The concept certainly does not reflect the principles of government he applied when he was king or prime minister in the 1950s,[24] and questions remain regarding the adaptability of the western political theory of liberalism to the conditions of a Buddhist, extremely poor, and agrarian society such as Cambodia. The Paris Agreements do not define the term, although they enumerate eight elements of an electoral process that the constitution must mention and that, presumably, are part of the definition of liberal democracy. First, elections must take place regularly, which one can assume to mean that the terms of national assembly members must be limited and that members must either be re-elected or a new candidate elected to occupy a seat in the assembly after the term expires. Second, elections must be "genuine," presumably meaning that the process must be free of manipulation. This criterion is close to the concept of fairness in an election. Third and fourth are the rights to vote and to be elected. Fifth, suffrage must be universal. Sixth, and closely related to universality, is the concept of equal suffrage, meaning that every vote has the same value. Equal and universal suffrage supposes nondiscrimination. Seventh, ballots must be secret. Finally, Annex 5 requires that the constitution provide for full and fair possibilities to organize in order to participate in the electoral process. This requirement relates to the formation and functioning of political parties, the essential feature of pluralism, and the possibility of conducting a campaign to attract voters. The eight elements cover the formal aspects of what is understood by "liberal democracy, on the basis of pluralism."

The Paris Agreements properly dealt with all of the main post-conflict issues—ceasefire, repatriation, restored sovereignty and unity, transitional arrangements, and rehabilitation and reconstruction—except for the issue of responsibility for past abuses. The unwillingness to address the latter issue went so far as to exclude the word "genocide"[25] from the text of the Paris Agreements, which referred instead to ensuring that "the policies and practices of the past shall never be allowed to return." Moreover, none of the various drafts of the constitution referred to prosecutions or truth and reconciliation; they did not even mention the policies and practices of the past.[26] The need to include the DK and China in the agreement and the Buddhist belief in reconciliation and love without retribution are strong arguments in favor of such silence, but impunity continues to be a major concern of Cambodian justice. Perhaps alienating the DK during the PICC was not an option and the Chinese vote was needed in the UN Security Council. But DK refusal to respect the Paris Agreements and continued violence would have justified a harder line at the time of the constitution's drafting.

In any event, the product of the constitution-making process in 1993 was essentially a reversion to previous constitutions—combining elements of the 1947 and 1989 constitutions, with some liberalizing improvements—rather than a newly structured constitution built on Annex 5. This illustrates how Cambodian politics tended to outweigh the United Nations' role as guarantor of the integrity of the Paris Agreements. Mixing the 1947 and 1989 constitutions, that is, combining the royalist electoral victors' conception of stable government with CPP and State of Cambodia (SOC) habits as de facto government, makes sense in Cambodian politics. However, the starting point of the agreements was an internationally agreed-upon definition of what was meant constitutionally by a liberal democracy on the basis of pluralism. UNTAC judged unwisely that it should respect Cambodian ways by allowing, first, the DK to behave contrary to the letter and the spirit of the agreements, and second, FUNCINPEC and the CPP to resolve a disputed election through pure politics. Its merits notwithstanding, the constitution was a victim of that politicization.

One can argue that the constitution is better grounded in Cambodian culture than would have been the case if the United Nations had succeeded in making the parties comply strictly with the ideas of constitutionalism agreed to in Paris, or provided more guidance on constitution making beyond the guidelines for an electoral process that were contained in the Paris Agreements. However, restoring politics as usual allowed for much political violence, extreme delays in creating the Supreme Council of the Magistracy, continued impunity for the DK and other politically protected perpetrators of abuse, restrictions on press freedoms, and the lack of an independent judiciary. These problems would not have been eliminated merely by adopting a constitution that met the overly optimistic claim of Chem Sngoun, former minister of justice, who died in 1999, that it was "neither monarchical, nor republican, but a democratic constitution."[27] But a constitution-making process and constitution that were closer to what was achieved in South Africa might have encouraged less brute politics and more democracy.

Structure of the Process

During Cambodia's transition in 1992–93, though the constitution-making process was guided by the United Nations, sovereignty remained theoretically vested in the representatives of the Cambodian people. For this purpose, the Paris Agreements created the SNC as an interim representative body. Headed by Prince Sihanouk, the council consisted of six members from the SOC—controlled entirely by the CPP—and two members from each of the three other factions. The Paris Agreements characterized this body as the "unique legitimate body and source of authority in which, throughout the transitional period, the sovereignty, independence and unity of Cambodia are enshrined."[28] For its part, the SNC delegated "all powers necessary" to the United Nations to implement the agreement.[29] This delegation of powers placed an extraordinary amount of authority in UN hands. In practice, however, the United Nations did not exercise all of the authority that Article 6 granted to it; rather, it used the SNC as a sounding board, and the SNC met regularly (usually monthly) to endorse UNTAC proposals.

Prince Sihanouk could be a dynamic chair of these meetings, but he usually deferred to the special representative of the secretary-general (SRSG) and head of UNTAC, Yasushi Akashi. A particularly significant example of Sihanouk's ultimate influence on the process, however, could be seen at the SNC meeting in Sihanouk's palace in Siem Reap on September 10, 1992. Wanting to help the SNC prepare for the tasks that the constituent assembly would face, Akashi placed an item relating to the draft constitution on the agenda of the SNC and distributed a brief, factual analysis prepared by Professor Reginald Austin, the head of the electoral component and himself a professor of law and former dean of the law school of the University of Zimbabwe. The Austin paper deliberately avoided any suggestion that UNTAC intended to write the constitution or propose draft texts; it merely set out generally the issues that must be addressed when drafting a constitution, such as name, flag, delimitation of territory, and form of government. The SRSG intended to suggest an SNC task force that would consider the issues and prepare the ground for the constituent assembly. Following Professor Austin's presentation, Prince Sihanouk expressed his warmest congratulations, then proceeded to formulate his preferences through a section-by-section review of what the future Cambodian constitution should contain. He would punctuate each point by addressing the SRSG with words to the effect of "that's what we should do, isn't it, Mr. Akashi?"[30] In this manner, he stated his positions on the name, flag, national anthem, borders, type of government, institutions of government, independence of the judiciary, requirements for the presidency, and so forth. He even proposed a senate ("for men with white hair, like on *Dallas*"),[31] which was eventually created in 1999. Though anticipating the outcome of the work of the constituent assembly, formally Sihanouk was merely endorsing the idea of creating an SNC task force to study these issues, the importance of which was so great, he felt, that both he and Akashi should participate.

As explained above, the constitution-making process was structured around a constituent assembly. The overall transition process, of which the constitution-making process was a part, took place in seven phases:

- Cease-fire, demobilization, and creation of a neutral political environment.
- Election of the constituent assembly through a UN-run election, the outcome of which was declared free and fair by the SRSG and Security Council.
- Selection of a drafting committee from among the members of the constituent assembly.
- Adoption by the assembly of the committee's draft.
- Proclamation by the king of the constitution.
- Transformation of the constituent assembly into the national assembly.
- Winding down of the process and the departure of UNTAC.

In retrospect, although the structure of the political process set out in the Paris Agreements may have been adequate for bringing peace to the territory, perhaps more thought should have been given to the structure of the constitution-making process itself. Had the Paris Agreements provided for the appointment of an inclusive and independent constitutional commission to direct a constitution-making process that included a comprehensive program of public participation, the process itself may have been more transparent and democratic. In turn, perhaps a more democratic and transparent process would have contributed to more transparent and democratic political processes than those that exist in Cambodia today.

The Election and Functioning of the Constituent Assembly

The 120 members of the constituent assembly were elected in accordance with the Paris Agreements, Article 12 of which reads as follows:

> The Cambodian people shall have the right to determine their own political future through the free and fair election of a constituent assembly, which will draft and approve a new Cambodian Constitution in accordance with Article 23 and transform itself into a legislative assembly, which will create the new Cambodian Government. This election will be held under United Nations auspices in a neutral political environment with full respect for the national sovereignty of Cambodia.

An annex set out UNTAC's mandate regarding the organization and conduct of the election, including the adoption of an electoral law and code of conduct, abrogation of existing laws where necessary, voter education, voter registration, registration of parties and candidates, fair access to the media, monitoring the campaign and balloting procedures, conducting balloting and polling, facilitating foreign observers, investigation of complaints and taking corrective action, and, in the end, "determining whether or not the election was free and fair and, if so, certification of the list of persons duly elected."[32]

The election was conducted pursuant to the electoral law drafted by UNTAC and submitted to the SNC on April 1, 1992, but not adopted until August 5, 1992. The law was promulgated on August 12; registration of parties began on August 15. By January 27, 1993, twenty out of the twenty-two provisionally registered political parties applied for official registration. Voter registration began on October 5, 1992, for three months, and then was extended to January 31, 1993. In that time, 4.6 million Cambodians registered, representing nearly all estimated eligible voters in zones to which UNTAC had access. The DK did not give access to areas under its control, although hundreds of voters from those areas managed to reach polling stations and vote.

Voting took place from May 23 to May 28, 1993, in all twenty-one provinces. From May 23 to May 25, 1,400 fixed polling stations and 200 mobile teams were in operation. Some fixed stations were converted to mobile units for the final three days (May 26–28). Despite DK disruption of voting in some places and intensified political violence, 4,267,192 voters turned out—89.56 percent of those that registered—and a total of 4,011,631 valid ballots were cast. The royalist FUNCINPEC won 45.47 percent of the votes and, according to a complicated

formula of the electoral law, was accorded fifty-eight seats in the constituent assembly. The CPP, then the governing party, ran second with 38.23 percent of the votes, receiving fifty-one seats. Next was the Buddhist Liberal Democratic Party (BLDP), the party of the KPLNF, with 3.81 percent and ten seats. Finally, Mouvement de Liberation Nationale du Kampuchea (MOLINAKA), the only party elected that did not represent one of the SNC factions, came in with 1.37 percent, receiving one seat.[33]

At the SNC meeting of June 10, 1993, Special Representative Akashi, on behalf of the secretary-general, declared that the election had been on the whole free and fair. On June 15, 1993, the Security Council endorsed the results.[34] Prince Sihanouk convened the constituent assembly on June 14 and, following tradition, chose its eldest member, Son Sann, head of the BLDP, as president. Co-prime ministers Hun Sen of the CPP and Prince Ranariddh of FUNCINPEC headed the interim government.

On June 30, 1993, the constituent assembly appointed a twelve-member drafting committee, with six members from FUNCINPEC, five from the CPP, and one from BLDP. The committee was headed by Chem Sngoun, former head of the legislative commission of the SOC national assembly, who had been designated minister of justice by the interim government. This committee developed a draft of the constitution over the course of that summer; its draft was kept secret from the 108 other assembly members, as well as from interested non-governmental organizations (NGOs), although its contents were leaked. The secrecy of the procedure was in accordance with assembly rules, which had been adopted without debate or discussion at the meeting on June 30. It has been reported that the vote on these rules was secret and not even tallied.[35] In the second week of September 1993, the drafting committee released its draft, about the same time as FUNCINPEC made available its monarchical draft.

Although the drafting committee apparently worked hard and independently, the assembly as a whole did not show much independence from the two dominant parties, the CPP and FUNCINPEC, or their leaders, Hun Sen and Prince Ranariddh. Rather than present a single draft prepared by the committee to Sihanouk, who had once again removed himself to Pyongyang, the two leaders traveled to the North Korean capital carrying two constitutions, a republican version, most likely containing language proposed by the CPP, and another restoring the monarchy, drafted by FUNCINPEC. Milton Osborne describes what happened as follows: "Sihanouk commented publicly that the decision as to whether he once again became king was the Cambodian assembly's, but there was no doubt in the minds of those who had seen him that he expected to become king again. And, indeed, he is reported to have made many handwritten amendments to the monarchical constitution shown to him for his approval." He then describes how, after plans to restore monarchy were known in Phnom Penh, "Sihanouk called for the population to renounce the monarchy and his projected role as king. To further compound confusion, the prince also announced he was ending his presidency of the SNC." Osborne concludes that this "was all very much of a piece with Sihanouk's behaviour in the past. Once the members of the assembly begged him to change his mind, he graciously did so. He had shown that he was truly wanted."[36]

Completely sidelining its own drafting committee, the assembly examined the FUNCINPEC draft edited by Sihanouk for five days, finally adopting the text on September 21, 1993, by a vote of 113 to 5, with two abstentions. On September 24, 1993, Prince Sihanouk ratified the new constitution during an elaborate ceremony in the ornate Royal Palace. Akashi's voice broke with emotion when he announced at the airport as he left two days later, "Cambodia has made a giant step on September 24 when it promulgated the new Constitution" and gave UNTAC a grade of "nine out of ten."[37] Other countries also gave UNTAC considerable credit for the outcome.[38] Charles Twining, head of the U.S. mission to the SNC and afterward appointed ambassador to Cambodia, remarked that the adoption of the constitution "carries out completely the designs of those Cambodians and non-Cambodians who drafted the Paris Agreements."[39]

A few days after the proclamation of the constitution, the Security Council welcomed the accession to the throne of His Majesty Samdech Preah Norodom Sihanouk and "the formation of the new Government of all Cambodia, established in accordance with the constitution and based on the recent election."[40]

Control over the Process

The election of the constituent assembly appears to have been a wise precondition to the constitution-drafting process, even though the members ultimately did not exercise independent control of that process. None of the previous constitutions could be regarded as politically neutral; simply giving new life to one of them would have been unacceptable to one or more of the parties. Furthermore, each had defects unacceptable for a transition involving the United Nations, in light of the organization's standard-setting role regarding democratization and human rights. That parts of the 1947 constitution were included in the end is a result of peculiarities from Sihanouk's last-minute jockeying and shifting. It could not have been the public basis for committee deliberation, as the committee's mandate was to implement

Annex 5 of the Paris Agreement. Nevertheless, the secrecy of the process made it possible for the most influential political leaders to draw on whichever of the two earlier constitutions—1947 or 1989—reflected their political interests most, rather than allowing the drafting committee to draw on the various models and principles introduced during the transition period.

It was quite appropriate for the Paris Agreements and the electoral law to emphasize freeness and fairness in the election process and to provide for registration of all citizens, exiles, and refugees. These aspects were clearly set out in the Paris Agreements. The agreements also gave responsibility to UNTAC to draft the electoral law and to run the elections. The electoral law was thorough but perhaps excessively detailed, more in the mode of Anglo-American legal drafting than the French mode. Its qualities derive from the director of the electoral component, Reginald Austin, who drew heavily on experience with Namibian elections.[41] Only a few people in UNTAC, especially in the electoral component, and some advisers to the major parties understood this fifty-six-page law thoroughly. The most disputed provision related to defining who is Cambodian for the purposes of voting eligibility. It took four months to resolve the matter, with the United Nations partially acceding to alter the language from the Paris Agreements in order to exclude ethnic Vietnamese.

The provisions of the law relating to settling disputes called for a panel of outside judges, which the SRSG refused to convene. This was unfortunate, as the disputes led to violence and loss of credibility for the United Nations, which was unable to control Prince Chakrapong's attempted secession. It is expected that losing parties challenge the procedure and that irregularities occur. Fair and impartial procedures to settle disputes, such as the ones provided for in the UNTAC

electoral law, should be applied vigorously. This was not done.

However, there was nothing basically wrong with the electoral system, nor with the fact that UNTAC was completely in charge. The United Nations failed to translate the fiction of "existing administrative structures"—a concept that was supposed to treat all four factions in the same way—into fact. Under those circumstances, the de facto government, in this case the SOC/CPP, was positioned to influence the process unduly. The situation would have been worse had UNTAC not been in charge, as illustrated by the difficulties of the Cambodian-run election in 1998.

As mentioned above, the transition process called for the constituent assembly to become the national assembly. In Cambodia's case, this appears to have been wise. This was the first free election for almost all Cambodians, who tended to believe they were voting for peace. Had the process required them to vote twice, once for a constitutional assembly and again for parliamentary representatives, the risks would have been high that ordinary people would not understand and that the opportunities for political manipulation would multiply. The more difficult question about the process is whether an inclusive and independent constitutional commission could have been appointed to direct the nation through a phased process of constitution making. A commission of this nature could have moved the process from one that was secretive, elite driven, and opaque to one involving the public participation and transparency that has characterized other constitution-making processes. The drafting committee's sincere and independent efforts suggest that there was some potential for such an approach. However, the near-complete absence of competent jurists, to say nothing of constitutional experts, would have made selecting a commission for this purpose challenging, to say the least.

Thus, in the end, although the mandate, timetable, and rules for the election of the constituent assembly were controlled by the United Nations, UN control over the transition as a whole and the constitutional process in particular was in fact more formal than real. Constitution drafting is a fundamental act of sovereignty and should, therefore, be as free of foreign influence as possible. However, in Cambodia, effective control by political factions weakened both the sense among the population that the constitution was theirs and the constituent assembly's compliance with the requirements of the Paris Agreements. The United Nations might have exercised more influence to ensure that both the spirit and the letter of the Paris Agreements were respected, and that some degree of opportunity for public participation in the process was provided. Such a role of active referee would not have meant foreign control over how people draft their constitution—and hence a questionable interference in political self-determination—but rather an effective and efficient approach to carrying out the functions that the Cambodian parties, along with other signatories, assigned to UNTAC in the Paris Agreements.

The way the constitution-making process turned out was logical. FUNCINPEC did win the election and, in the end and with Sihanouk as ultimate arbiter, got its way regarding the constitution's content. However, it was a confused process, and the confusion occurred because the United Nations did not exercise its assigned functions and was too sensitive to the sovereignty issue.

Public Participation in the Process

Pre- and Post-Constitution Public Education and Participation

Efforts to engage the public in the constitutional process mainly consisted of information dissemination and education. The popular engagement with the constitution-making process grew out of the human rights education effort of UNTAC and its partners among indigenous NGOs. The mandate for human rights education, which was broadened to include education about constitutional principles, was extensive. The Paris Agreements obligated Cambodia "to support the right of all Cambodian citizens to undertake activities which would promote and protect human rights and fundamental freedoms."[42] Annex 3 referred to the rights, freedoms, and opportunities of all Cambodians to take part in the electoral process; such rights included freedoms of speech, assembly, and movement, as well as fair access to the media for registered political parties. The secretary-general's report to the Security Council on Cambodia stated that "the development and dissemination of a human rights education program is foreseen as the cornerstone of UNTAC's activities in fostering respect for human rights."[43] To fulfill its human rights education mandate, the education, training, and information unit of UNTAC's human rights component developed a strategy and plan of action.[44] After determining that the mandate included all levels and types of education, the next step was to plan and implement a strategy of identifying target groups, establishing goals for each group, specifying the requisite financial resources, setting a timetable, and carrying out and evaluating the activities.

UNTAC's education and information efforts were directed at formal education at all levels and at informal education for the emerging civil society. The secretary-general's report called for UNTAC "to collaborate with non-governmental organizations (NGOs) operating in Cambodia for this purpose as well as to encourage the establishment of indigenous human rights associations."[45] The human rights component's strategy was to work with existing human rights and women's groups to enhance their capacity to act effectively as NGOs, and to train their trainers, who could then conduct human rights education activities throughout the provinces. The mandate stated that "UNTAC would also work closely with . . . special groups, [including] those individuals best placed to be further disseminators of information, such as teachers and community leaders."[46] The Buddhist clergy was a particularly effective vehicle to reach the public at large, especially in remote areas. The experience with human rights education for each of the targeted constituencies—law enforcement, teachers, civil servants, judges, human rights associations, monks, health professionals, and women's groups—paved the way for the shift to constitutional literacy as the election approached.

The component's strategy for NGOs was implemented in part through a trust fund project called the Human Rights Task Force for the Cambodian Elections. The task force prepared human rights activists from each of the main indigenous human rights associations to monitor human rights during the election. As a rule, these associations provided by far the largest numbers of election observers registered by the electoral component. The task force facilitated the planning and coordination of activities for these groups; it was so successful that the entity continued after the elections as the Cambodian Human Rights Task Force with additional funding from the trust fund. This project was an example of how indigenous human rights associations and women's organizations were both partners and learners in the component's human rights education effort. The component's education strategy focused particularly on women's associations because, even more than in most other countries, women are the bedrock of Cambodian society, comprising a disproportionately high 63 percent of the population. Taken together with their dependent children, the figure rises to 75 per-

cent. The component taught human rights courses in Phnom Penh and in the provinces, providing both basic education (introduction to concepts) and in-depth training of trainers for these associations. They were also provided with trust-fund grants to conduct their own human rights education activities.

It is fair to estimate that the component's education and training directly reached approximately 120,000 people. The figure for mass communication is in the millions, through the dissemination of hundreds of thousands of leaflets, brochures, stickers, balloons, comic books, and posters, as well as the broadcasting of highly popular radio and television programs.[47] The mass-communication messages disseminated through radio and television were simple, focusing on basic awareness of the significance of the constitution and its importance for the human rights of the population. Meanwhile, Cambodian human rights associations were a visible presence in virtually every province, proactively seeking to inform the population about the significance of the new constitution. The population's receptiveness to the civic education that the international community undertook in fulfilling UNTAC's human rights education mandate, including constitutional literacy efforts, demonstrated that the population would likely have been receptive to broad direct participation in the constitution-making process if it had been made available.

NGOs, the Clergy, and the Press in the Constitution-Making Process

The civic education of the population described above served concurrently to foster the development of a vibrant civil society, which eventually came to demand a role in the constitution-making process. NGOs concerned with human rights, women's issues, and economic development, organizations representing the Buddhist clergy, and journalists were courageous and significant in both creating a popular awareness of the constitution-making process and monitoring the freeness and fairness of the constituent assembly elections.

The proliferation of NGOs independent of state and party structures has been described as the "first step towards a civil society in Cambodia after its destruction between 1975 and 1978."[48] During the transitional period, UNTAC registered associations and was quite liberal in approving applications. Human rights NGOs were the most influential of the groups in the constitution-making process. Five human rights groups were functioning in Cambodia during the transitional period with a combined claimed membership of over 150,000. After UNTAC's departure, seven more human rights NGOs emerged. Today, an estimated forty NGOs are active in human rights. The period of constitution making saw the founding of a coalition of fourteen Cambodian NGOs called Ponleu Khmer (Cambodian Illumination), which defined a strategy for lobbying the constituent assembly to press for strong human rights provisions, especially regarding the rights of women. The strategy was implemented with a remarkable degree of courage, initiative, and perseverance. As the election of the constituent assembly drew near, a women's movement emerged in Cambodia, demanding a role in crafting the new constitution. During a National Women's Summit on March 5–8, 1993, 109 women from eight provinces spoke out on this issue. Socua Mu Leiper, one of the organizers and also a founder of Ponleu Khmer, said, "We want to participate at all levels of policy-making, including drafting the new constitution."[49]

The NGOs favored detailed human rights provisions based on international standards, with effective enforcement procedures, but in the end, they were disappointed. Nevertheless, after the proclamation of the constitution and UNTAC's departure, Ponleu Khmer continued to educate the population about participatory democracy and push for a sense of accountability on the part of elected officials and civil servants. In June 1994, nine human rights NGOs founded the Cambodian Human Rights Coordination Committee to strengthen links and improve information exchange. In July, August, and September 1994, the Cambodian Institute of Human Rights organized four month-long constitutional workshops for professors at the law school, government leaders, members of the assembly, persons trained in law, and judges, in an effort to help them better understand the constitution and take it more seriously.

Buddhism and Buddhist monks were severely victimized under the Khmer Rouge. According to a leading authority on the period, "Khmer Rouge policy toward Buddhism constituted one of the most brutal and thoroughgoing attacks on religion in modern history."[50] The population of monks was reduced from about 60,000 to less than 1,000.[51] Under the PRK and SOC, monks were tolerated, although supervised by the National Front for Construction and Defense, an organ of the party.[52] Buddhism flourished again after the arrival of the United Nations, and several monks who returned from exile became leaders in the human rights movement. The Venerable Maha Ghosananda, the supreme patriarch and cofounder of the Inter-Religious Mission for Peace in Cambodia, became head of Ponleu Khmer at its founding in December 1993. During this period, Buddhist clergy organized marches and teach-ins, lobbied governmental and parliamentary leaders, and provided spiritual guidance to the population, which is 90 to 95 percent Buddhist. The clergy were the principal vehicle for popularizing constitutionalism and human rights in remote areas.

Freedom of expression was generally respected during the transitional period, and there was hope that it would continue to thrive under the new constitution, which guarantees freedom to express opinions and to publish.[53] By the time the constitution was adopted, some twenty newspapers were published in Khmer, English, French, and Chinese, some of which criticized the government and its leaders freely.[54] Throughout the drafting of the constitution, the media covered the issue, although most of the Khmer-language press was partisan. The United Nations Education, Scientific, and Cultural Organization (UNESCO) ran a Danish-funded program to upgrade the skills of journalists, frequently introducing human rights and constitutional themes in the training. The English-language *Phnom Penh Post* was particularly active in analyzing the background of the constitution-drafting process and reporting on otherwise secret negotiations. Soon after the election, the paper published an article by Raoul Jennar, author of the *Cambodian Chronicles*, detailing the constitutional decisions the assembly would have to make regarding a republican or monarchical system, a unicameral or bicameral parliament, the separation of powers, and similar matters.[55] The *Phnom Penh Post* also voiced concern over the secrecy of the constitution-drafting process and echoed NGO claims that certain elements, such as human rights provisions, had not been drafted by August.[56] It reported the timetable for consideration of the final draft by the drafting committee and the entire constituent assembly, and revealed that two drafts had been sent to Prince Sihanouk[57] and that Prince Ranariddh had disagreed with the committee's draft and planned to resurrect the 1947 monarchical constitution.[58]

Impact of Civil Society on the Constitution-Drafting Process

Ponleu Khmer found the draft prepared in secret by the drafting committee contradictory in that it

specifies human rights fairly clearly and stipulates that there should be a separation of powers, but on the other hand it concentrates the decision-making power of the state in the hands of a few people. While the principles stipulated in the constitution are good, for example that "the power comes from the people," there is no check on the power of the president. . . . When power is concentrated in the hands of only a few people, how can human rights be protected?

Ponleu Khmer also denounced the secrecy of the drafting process as a denial of participatory democracy. In a letter to the provisional government and to Akashi, the organization complained,

> We have the right to ask all the elected representatives about what they are going to include in the constitution. They should let us know openly what their intentions are. The drawing up of the constitution is not a secret thing. All citizens have the right to know about what will be written in the constitution. The people have the right to oppose what they think is inappropriate or should not be in the constitution.[59]

In the end, however, there was precious little participation from either NGOs or members of the assembly in the formulation of the constitution.

Given the limited opportunities for participation, most human rights organizations focused on popular education about the constitution. The Cambodian League for the Promotion and Protection of Human Rights (LICADHO) used cartoons and presentations by monks to educate Cambodians about human rights and the constitution, and assisted other independent and nonpolitical bodies in efforts to advise the population and government on constitutional issues.[60] The Khmer Institute of Democracy, established by a former aide to Prince Sihanouk with funding from Australian and North American sources, held public seminars, workshops, and debates about democratic ideals and principles.[61]

NGOs such as Vigilance and Ponleu Khmer gathered the views of citizens in the provinces through public workshops, constituent meetings with elected members of the constituent assembly, and public open houses, creating an open dialogue among Cambodians.[62] These expressions of public attitudes were disseminated by the media and NGOs that organized the events, but do not appear to have influenced the drafters of the constitution very much. As the drafting process neared completion, word got out about the possible restoration of the monarchy, and several Khmer prodemocracy organizations opined that the draft constitution was "dangerous." They were also concerned about reports that it might be set aside in favor of the 1947 version. In general, they felt that the constitution granted too much power to the government.[63]

The freedom of action of NGOs and the clergy, protected by UNTAC, and the freedom of expression of the media created a high degree of public expectation that there would be opportunities to influence the drafting of the constitution. However, with only a few exceptions, the elected members of the constituent assembly took their cues from their respective parties rather than their constituents. In the end, the two issues on which NGOs were particularly vocal—strong human rights provisions and no return to the 1947 constitution—were lost causes.

One way citizen involvement could have been handled differently would have been for UNTAC to insist on a public process with verbatim records and public access to deliberations. UNTAC had proposed such practices, and several sources offered technical support, including the Inter-Parliamentary Union (IPU). The problem was that UNTAC was in complete control of the election but not of the drafting process. Without a clear mandate, Sihanouk and the parties made a good case for a hands-off approach by UNTAC, especially because that was Akashi's inclination in any case. The Cambodian people

had, after all, elected legitimate representatives, and real sovereignty was being restored to the nation. The idea that public access to the deliberations and the creation of a public record could be invaluable to the people's sense of their national history had little or no effect on the political class in Cambodia, despite indigenous NGO support for such transparency. Public scrutiny was simply not a feature of political behavior.

The public's failure to gain access to the drafting sessions and influence the text is only part of the picture, however. The process of reading and hearing about the constitution, and of learning that something so significant to their future was being decided in secret may well have influenced the population's long-term expectations. Despite subsequent consolidation of one-party domination under Hun Sen, the population and the opposition Sam Rainsy Party (SRP) have been remarkably persistent in calling for greater transparency and accountability of government. Even the role of Sihanouk, whose ultimate decisions his subjects tend to support, may not have discouraged people from believing that the political leadership should respond to their aspirations. This is much more true for educated activists than for ordinary citizens, however.

The transitional authority partially opened the constitution-making process to popular participation, but it was less successful in convincing the political parties to establish detailed records of drafts, amendments, debates, and votes. The secrecy of the Cambodian process and its final distortion were not conducive to public participation or responsible constitution making. In the end, however, the ultimate legitimacy of the constitution arguably depends on the freeness and fairness of the process that selected the constitution's drafters and the quality of the final text, not the extent to which those entrusted with the drafting benefited from popular consultations.

In other words, as an elected body, the constituent assembly embodied a democratic process in Cambodia but, once entrusted with the responsibility of drafting the constitution, it should have provided transparency, including public access to official records, to ensure the credibility of the process. Despite this deficiency, three factors seem to have made the constitution legitimate in the eyes of the Cambodian people: the endorsement from Sihanouk, the revered national leader; the international community's recognition that the assembly election was relatively free and fair and the successful transition process; and the intrinsic merit of the constitution's provisions on human rights and the separation of powers.

From the constituent assembly's inaugural session on June 14, 1993, to the constitution's adoption on September 24, 1993, the political leadership showed no inclination to delay the drafting to allow the public to learn or participate more. Constitutional literacy projects began well before June, and NGOs, the press, and Buddhist monks kept the public informed and raised awareness of the issues. A long process of consultations with all major elements of the population may have been useful in other situations, but in Cambodia, the political violence in the runup to the election, during the voting, and especially before the interim government could be formed justified finishing the job fairly quickly—but not doing it in secrecy and without a public record.

With the benefit of hindsight and knowledge of other constitution-making processes that included comprehensive public participation programs, it would have been preferable for the Paris Agreements to set out the basic structure of the process of citizen involvement and transparency. Without unduly extending the process, the agreements could have required transcriptions of the deliberations as well as some degree of popular consultation. Such requirements might have helped transform a closed and opaque process into a more open and democratic one.

Democratic Representation

In a democratic process, the interests of the people are advanced by elected representatives participating in government. The Paris Agreements' emphasis on pluralism and UNTAC's encouraging both the four factions to register as political parties and other politically ambitious individuals to form and register political parties were clearly openings for democratic representation in the constituent assembly. However, these openings could not wipe out the legacy of control of the state apparatus by a single party.

Communist Legacy

Superficially, the opening of political space for democratic representation in the constitution-making process was a remarkable success. However, the ultimate impact of this opening was severely limited by Cambodia's inability to cast off its communist legacy of conflating the party and the state. Although officially UNTAC was cooperating with "existing administrative structures" of all factions, throughout the transitional period, the CPP maintained the advantage of controlling the SOC—the state administration—and effectively running the government.[64] Early on, the DK criticized UNTAC for failing to exercise direct control over foreign affairs, national defense, finance, public security, and information as the Paris Agreements required[65]; it stressed that there should be "no government" in Cambodia and that the SOC, which it called the Phnom Penh party, should be dismantled and the SNC given more power under UNTAC supervision.[66] While this position was a pretext to avoid compliance with the cease-fire and cantonment phase of the peace process, the DK was correct that UNTAC was allowing the CPP to function as a government through the SOC. This situation continued throughout the electoral process. The only reason that the CPP allowed FUNCINPEC to share power after the 1993 election is that it came in second in the elections. As soon as the CPP could reassert complete power, after a few years of coalition government, it did so. No new political formation could enter the political arena, with the exception of the Sam Rainsy Party, an offshoot of FUNCINPEC, which constitutes the only real opposition today. The political compromise that the CPP was forced to make with FUNCINPEC did, however, give the latter bargaining power during the drafting of the constitution.

Participation of Political Parties

Of the twenty-two parties that registered to present candidates, twenty participated in the election.[67] However, only three really counted: the CPP, FUNCINPEC, and the BLDP, founded in 1992 by the KPNLF to contest the elections. Of those, FUNCINPEC and the CPP dominated. FUNCINPEC won fifty-eight seats to the CPP's fifty-one seats; the BDLP won ten seats; and the National Liberation Movement of Kampuchea, an offshoot of FUNCINPEC, won one seat. Surprised by the outcome, the CPP at first called for a revote in four provinces and threatened violence if their demands were not met. Prince Chakrapong, Ranariddh's half brother but nevertheless a CPP politician, left the SOC government, where he was deputy prime minister, and rallied seven provinces in the east to secede. The constituent assembly convened under this unstable situation and selected Prince Sihanouk as head of state, in charge of forming an interim government. Sihanouk appointed himself as prime minister.

Attempted Reconciliation with the Khmer Rouge

From the perspective of national reconciliation, the evolving power arrangement appears to have successfully transformed warring factions into political parties. However, the transformation was incomplete, as violent conflict continued. In particular, the DK withdrew from elections and, although still technically a member of the SNC, was not involved in the constitution-making process, despite Sihanouk's efforts to bring them in.[68] Moreover, UNTAC could not prevent the DK and other factions from violating the cease-fire and continue operations of armed forces. As Human Rights Watch explained,

> UNTAC's inability to bring about the peace it had promised made the other components of the mission exponentially harder to achieve. A "neutral political environment" for the elections could not be established; in the absence of cantonment, the country continued to be rife with heavy weaponry, and armed gangs, party gunmen, common criminals and off-duty police all freely committed murders and other acts of violence.[69]

There is a link between the failure of the military phase and the failure to leverage the election and constitution drafting to bring the DK into the peacebuilding process. The DK's continued war against the newly created Royal Cambodian Armed Forces (RCAF) was clearly a failure of the peace process, attributable to Akashi's calculated risk that by not confronting the DK, he could preserve the essential goal of holding the election. He was able to hold the election, but the price for Cambodians was another six years of military confrontation.

The Timing and Sequencing of the Constitution-Making Process

The timing as established in the Paris Agreements was politically wise in light of UN peacekeeping goals. Because the parties had reached a sufficient degree of mutually painful stalemate and concluded that none could take power by military means, by the time of the Paris Conference, Sihanouk and the political parties appeared ready to accept whatever process made sense to the international community. Given Cambodia's constitutional history, incorporating into the peace agreement the formal and substantive requirements regarding constitution drafting was extremely sensible. Even with the unanticipated restoration of the monarchy, the reassertion of power politics, and domination by one party, the timing of the constitution drafting ensured for the Cambodian people a basis for the eventual consolidation of democracy, however slow and uneven that process might be.

Similar comments can be made about the sequencing of the political steps set out in the peace agreements. The constitution drafting had to come after an opportunity for political self-determination through the election of the assembly, in which Cambodians residing in the territory, refugees in camps, and exiles living abroad participated. It also had to come before the full restoration of governmental powers by any political force, and therefore had to precede the formation of a government and take place while UNTAC was asserting its transitional administrative powers. Therefore, the sequencing of the main phases of the transition laid out in the Paris Agreements—demobilization, creation of a secure environment, election of a constituent assembly, adoption of a constitution, transformation of the constituent assembly into the national assembly, and formation of a legitimate government—was logical and necessary from a peacemaking perspective. However, as noted above, the Paris Agreements failed to provide for the specific elements and sequencing of the constitution-making process itself, leaving that to the constituent assembly.

In light of the tendency of warring parties to distrust one another, there can only be an advantage to defining clear sequencing in a peace agreement. Any adjustment of the sequencing requires a high degree of diplomatic skill, by someone such as a UN mission head, as any party that sees another party gaining advantage will protest furiously. The peacemaking phase does not end when the peacebuilding and peacekeeping processes begin.

UNTAC assigned high priority to convening the constituent assembly rapidly after the 1993 election. The timing of UNTAC's mandate was limited to the period from the entry into force of the Paris Agreements to the approval of the constitution and the transformation of the constituent assembly into a legislative assembly and the creation of a government.[70] The election itself was required to be held within nine months from the commencement of voter registration.[71] Work on the constitution began soon after the constituent assembly appointed the drafting committee on June 30, 1993. The committee's work was essentially completed by the second week of September 1993, when it released its draft and FUNCINPEC made available its draft based on the 1947 text. After Hun Sen and Prince Ranariddh returned from Pyongyang, with Sihanouk's decision to approve the FUNCINPEC draft, the assembly took only five days to adopt it, on September 21, 1993. Sihanouk ratified it on September 24, 1993. Akashi needed the process to be completed quickly so that the UN mission could end by autumn 1993. The five permanent Security Council members had expressed concern that the mission end quickly, as new challenges for peacekeeping were arising in El Salvador and Bosnia and donor fatigue was setting in.

In retrospect, despite the very real time pressures, it is clear that more time should have been allotted for the constitution-making process. Certainly, more time would have had to be allotted if the process had included more civic education focused specifically on constitutional issues, followed by a phase of popular consultation—particularly in light of the time that has been required for constitution making in those countries that have appointed a constitutional commission to direct distinct phases of civic education and popular consultation.

The Role of the International Community

The transition was in large part the work of the international community, in the form of the contact group, the regional powers, the permanent members of the Security Council, the cochairs of the Paris Conference, and the UN secretariat. The SNC, especially Prince Sihanouk, its president, represented Cambodian sovereignty. Because the SNC was only the nominal seat of sovereignty, the peace process was primarily in the hands of the international community, but the constitution-making phase was primarily the work of Cambodian political leaders. However, the United Nations and specific governments had roles to play in both the peace process and the constitution-making effort.

The United Nations

UNTAC's role in the overall transition was defined in the secretary-general's report of February 19, 1992, to the Security Council,[72] which the council approved on February 28.[73] The report set out detailed guidelines for the seven components of the mission, especially regarding demobilization and cease-fire, assuring public security, organizing elections, and promoting and monitoring human rights. But it did not specify any particular role for UNTAC in the constitution-drafting process. This, once again, is regrettable, as it offered little or no guidance to Cambodians regarding process design and did not secure for the United Nations a firm basis for assisting with design or managing the process.

Nevertheless, the electoral component, headed by highly experienced constitutional lawyer Reginald Austin, consulted widely with experts in constitution drafting and compiled significant amounts of information on the style and content of constitutions for the Cambodian parties to use. He presented these materials in various settings, including at the SNC meeting described above.[74] The electoral component convened several working sessions on constitutional matters with party representatives and a few outside experts, but without the participation of either Sihanouk or Akashi. The most significant event of this type was the constitutional seminar held from March 29 to April 3, 1993. All Cambodian parties and many Cambodian NGOs were invited to participate in discussions centered on presentations made by UNTAC staff and several Cambodian and outside experts. These efforts all focused exclusively on substantive constitutional issues. While helpful in deepening participants' awareness of comparative approaches to key issues of governance and constitutional structure, the seminar did not appear to have much influence on the persons who actually drafted the text.

UNTAC's human rights component redirected its human rights education program during the postelection period toward constitutional literacy, to inform Cambodian NGOs and the general public about popular participation in constitution drafting, drawing upon other Asian examples, and a basic understanding of constitutional concepts. Audiovisual materials were prepared and disseminated, discussion groups set up with NGOs, and a constitutional forum organized, during which three Cambodian activists—a monk, a representative of women's organizations, and a head of an indigenous human-rights organization—participated in a panel with three Asian experts who had been active with popular organizations during the drafting of other constitutions in the region. The audience of over one hundred activists engaged in an animated discussion, showing an intense interest in political participation and in strong human rights provisions in the constitution. The Cambodian groups requested the UN meeting room for closed sessions the following day. At the conclusion of a full day's efforts, they formed Ponleu Khmer, the abovementioned coalition of fourteen groups.

When UNTAC arrived, Cambodians held an exaggerated expectation that the United Nations would bring peace. They were bound to be let down, and they were. Akashi tended to leave the constitution-making process to the Cambodians, but Sihanouk's shifting attitude undermined the effectiveness of the process and UN ability to contribute positively to it. On August 31, 1993, Sihanouk wrote from North Korea that he would agree to be king if the assembly insisted, but four days later, he asked not to be considered, saying, "We have already found the ideal formula: Cambodia is an independent, neutral and non-aligned state, neither a Kingdom nor a Monarchy. It is simply a Cambodian Cambodia."[75] It was in this context that he became furious at the United Nations, alleging that UNTAC told the BBC that he wanted the restoration of monarchy. On September 4, 1993, he wrote to Akashi that he was breaking off all relations with UNTAC and asked Akashi not to make a scheduled trip to Beijing. He subsequently tempered his furor against UNTAC, but remained suspicious of perceived UN meddling in the constitution-drafting process.

In hindsight, the Cambodian leadership might have been less sensitive to the issue of UN meddling had UN efforts focused more on process than substance. In this way, the international community could have been perceived as a more neutral and supportive agent in designing a process that would

have allowed the Cambodians themselves to make key substantive choices. This is true particularly given that, as noted in the previous section, the Cambodians appeared to be open to whatever process the international community might suggest.

The final assessment of the role of the United Nations in the transition overall must certainly be positive for having held the election and repatriated refugees, even though the United Nations can be faulted for having failed the military phase of the process. As an exercise in peacemaking, it must certainly be seen as a success. However, while UN efforts enabled the constitution to be drafted, the organization's direct role in that element of the process was negligible.

Foreign Experts

Several foreign experts, some sponsored by governments and foundations, sought to assist the drafting committee of the constituent assembly. A French lawyer was seconded from UNTAC's civil administration component—itself headed by a French administrative judge—to the French-educated chair of the drafting committee and given an office in the Ministry of Justice. Her influence appears to have been negligible, however. Claude Gille Goure, a law professor from the University of Toulouse, was more influential; he "had an important role in drafting the version that was the closest to the one that was adopted."[76] Brown and Zasloff describe his role:

Sihanouk, through his son Ranariddh, himself a former professor of law at the University of Aix-en-Provence in France, had engaged Goure following the election to prepare a draft constitution. Goure worked in Phnom Penh until sometime in July 1993, and left the draft with Ranariddh before returning to France. One might assume that the draft conformed to the positions of Prince Sihanouk and Ranariddh. According to a source who was closely following the drafting process in late July 1993,

Ranariddh came before the drafting committee and said, in effect, "Here's the constitution. My father has agreed to it and so do I." It was substantially Goure's draft. According to this account, Ranariddh expected that a draft endorsed by Prince Sihanouk and himself would be immediately accepted. Instead, the chairman of the committee calmly thanked Ranariddh and noted that the committee would consider it, along with the draft that it had been working hard to develop.[77]

This version of events is credible. The CPP clearly expected to control the constitution-drafting process and introduce language from the 1989 SOC constitution. However, FUNCINPEC's electoral victory and the high regard everyone, including Hun Sen and Chem Sngoun, had for Sihanouk resulted in the drafting of one text based on the 1989 SOC constitution and another based on the 1947 monarchical constitution, rather than the formulation of a new constitution based on Annex 5 and the advice of foreign experts. Even though Ranariddh is a law professor, it is unlikely that he could have come up with a complete text without assistance. It is also unlikely that Professor Goure relied on the 1947 text without the French government favoring this approach. The French government and experts assisting the Ministry of Justice and FUNCINPEC displayed a good deal of political realism by acknowledging Sihanouk's special role and placing themselves in a position to influence both the once and future king and the leader of the victorious party by supporting a version of the constitution favorable to the royalists.

The U.S. government was not directly involved, although it did fund expert advice from Americans through the Asia Foundation, the National Democratic Institute for International Affairs (NDI), and the International Republican Institute (IRI), the latter two organizations created under congressional mandate through the National Endowment for Democracy. Both the NDI and IRI established presences in Phnom Penh. Among their activities was to invite the members of the new constituent assembly to a workshop they sponsored, at which elected representatives from the United States and Bangladesh advised their guests regarding what works and what does not work in constitutional drafting in democratic societies.[78] The NDI and IRI also offered information on political party training, voter education, and use of media.[79] At another seminar for the parties, they distributed the U.S. constitution in Khmer and brought in a U.S. constitutional law professor who spoke about the relevance of U.S. constitutional principles to Cambodia.

More useful was the role of two other U.S. law professors, Louis Aucoin and Dolores Donavan, who visited on behalf of the Asia Foundation. According to an interview Aucoin gave to Joseph Zasloff in April 1993, the two professors were welcomed by Chem Sngoun, the chair of the drafting committee, who gave them a desk near his office in the Ministry of Justice. Chem Sngoun "recommended to committee members that they consult the professors with questions about comparative constitutions."[80] After providing information and suggestions on certain sections of the constitution, "during the second week of August, the two professors were abruptly cut out of the advisory process, apparently due to an order from Prince Sihanouk that no foreigners (presumably other than those from whom he was drawing assistance) were to be involved in the constitution-writing process."[81] This author's personal recollections of Aucoin's and Donavan's role was that unlike the French, who wanted to restore the French language and legal system in the country, they used a healthy comparative law approach, drawing on whatever legal traditions Cambodia had and the most useful elements of other Asian legal systems, as well as U.S. law, to assist in developing a legal system adapted to the needs of post-conflict Cambodia.

In retrospect, the involvement of foreign experts in Cambodia raises significant questions as to the role, ethics, and methodology that should be exercised by the international community and experts providing advice. When their efforts strengthen the hand of an already dominant political party, there is danger that their work shrinks the political space available to all political forces in society and the population at large, rendering the process less democratic.

The Role of International Law

Both the role that international law played in the constitution-making process and the role that it did not play where it might have been expected to are of interest in the Cambodian case. International law provided a foundation for the constitution's provisions on democratic governance and human rights, and could have done the same—but did not—for the issue of accountability for the Khmer Rouge's past crimes.

Legal Obligation to Establish Democratic Governance

Broad principles of democratic governance, which began to be considered in the early 1990s an entitlement under international law,[82] were contained in the mandate to prepare for a constitution in the Paris Agreements and in Security Council Resolution 745 (1992) of February 28, 1992. According to Article 23 of the Paris Agreements, the new constitution was required to contain "basic principles, including those regarding human rights and fundamental freedoms" as set out in Annex 5, entitled Principles for a New Constitution for Cambodia. This text is drawn from a 1982 proposal of the five-state contact group that prepared recommendations for Namibia's transition to independence. A member of the U.S. delegation to the Paris Conference on Cambodia and

the negotiations on Cambodia among the permanent five Security Council members describes this text as follows:

> Like the constitutional principles prepared for Namibia, these provisions of the Agreement transcend existing international human rights instruments. They go beyond recognizing free elections as the sole process for choosing a government after internal strife, and beyond committing the elected regime to guaranteeing the human rights of its people, by identifying the path—labeled "liberal democracy, on the basis of pluralism"—it is to follow. The Agreement thereby establishes the political foundation of a government able to protect human freedom. Moreover, it incorporates this principle for internal governance in an agreement resolving a regional conflict, and thus places an international obligation on Cambodia to observe it and on other signatories to respect it.[83]

International Law of Human Rights

The second aspect of international law relevant to the Cambodian constitution-making experience of 1993 is the set of international norms of human rights. Including a bill of rights in the constitution stems not only from Annex 5 of the Paris Agreements referred to above, but also from Article 15 (2a) of the Paris Agreements, according to which "Cambodia undertakes to take effective measures to ensure that the policies and practices of the past shall never be allowed to return." This wording suggests that the drafters expected the new constitution to affirm human rights as a testimony to the break with the past and as an important preventive measure for the future.

The chapter of the constitution entitled The Rights and Obligations of Khmer Citizens covers twenty articles (Articles 31–50), seventeen of which relate to rights and three to duties. This chapter constitutes the declaration of fundamental rights required by Annex 5 of the Paris Agreements. At a minimum, the declaration had to contain the twelve rights enumerated in Annex 5, namely "the rights to [1] life, [2] personal liberty, [3] security, [4] freedom of movement, [5] freedom of religion, [6] assembly and [7] association including political parties and trade unions, [8] due process and [9] equality before the law, [10] protection from arbitrary deprivation of property or deprivation of private property without just compensation, and [11] freedom from racial, ethnic, religious or sexual discrimination. It will prohibit the [12] retroactive application of criminal law." The text basically meets these requirements, though by borrowing from older constitutions, it often protects the rights to a lesser degree than do the international texts.[84] Clearly, the drafters did not choose to draw from the language or normative richness of relevant international instruments. It is a sad commentary on the entire process that most of the rights and duties are expressed in wording similar to that of the SOC constitution of 1989. In some cases, the constitutional and international standards are both quite general and differ only in drafting. On the whole, the new constitution enumerates the same rights and duties as the 1989 constitution, with minor adjustments—and without having taken advantage of the extensive drafting suggestions from NGOs and various advisers nor given due consideration to the requirements of the Paris Agreements or international treaties to which Cambodia is a party.

International Law Relating to Impunity

The third dimension of international law relevant to the constitution-making process in Cambodia concerns norms of accountability for the past. In recent years, numerous countries have faced the need to balance reconciliation and stability with responsibility for gross violations of human rights.[85] Given the magnitude of the crimes that the Khmer Rouge committed, the fact that Cambodia is a party to the Genocide Convention, and the

degree of the international community's involvement in Cambodia's affairs, one might have expected the constitution to deal with the issue. After all, the principal explanation for the reference to human rights in the Paris Agreements is universal condemnation of the atrocities of the Khmer Rouge. Nevertheless, the Paris Agreements did not go as far as the peace agreement in El Salvador, which explicitly called for prosecutions for past abuses.[86] The absence of a similar reference may be explained by the diplomatic necessity of keeping China and the DK in the process. In this sense, the Cambodian case is an example of how the nature of a constitution-making process and the participants in it affect the content of the constitution, even for issues on which international law provides clear guidance.

The human rights provisions of the 1993 constitution contain no explicit references to genocide,[87] the Genocide Convention, the actions of the DK, or prosecutions for gross violations of human rights. There are also no references to such prosecutions in the eight articles on the judicial power.[88] One of the provisions in the section on political regime stipulates that "the Royal Government of Cambodia is committed to . . . implement the policy of national reconciliation."[89] Conceivably, this article could be invoked to avoid prosecutions for genocide, but such an interpretation would contradict the principle that unless the text expressly stipulates otherwise, it should be construed so as not to conflict with Cambodia's international obligations, including its obligations under the Genocide Convention. Therefore, while the constitution does not address the issue of accountability or criminal responsibility for acts of genocide and crimes against humanity, it does not cast any doubt on Cambodia's obligations under Articles IV, V, and VI of the Genocide Convention to "punish," "provide effective penalties," and "try" persons charged with genocide.

The prevailing impunity for genocidal crimes in Cambodia has been denounced from various quarters[90] and was the object of intense negotiations over ten years between the Royal Government and the United Nations, leading the national assembly to adopt a Law on the Establishment of Extraordinary Chambers in the Courts of Cambodia for the Prosecution of Crimes Committed During the Period of Democratic Kampuchea, which was promulgated in October 2004.[91] In June 2007, the Extraordinary Chambers in the Courts of Cambodia (ECCC) held its inaugural session. On July 18, 2007, the co-prosecutors filed introductory submissions with the coinvestigating judges for five unnamed individuals. On July 31, 2007, charges were laid against Kaing Guek Eav, otherwise known as Duch, the former head of Toul Sleng, and later in 2007, four other individuals were arrested and placed in the ECCC's custody.[92] In 2008, the ECCC held pretrial proceedings for all five defendants. The prosecution of Duch began in March 2009. The entire process is expected to end in early 2011. Among the ECCC's major challenges are the independence and impartiality of the judiciary and other organs of the court, especially from government pressure and interference; compliance with due process and fair-trial standards; transparency and public access to documents; and resources to ensure the capacity and effectiveness of the court's operations.[93] One observer explained that "questions of corruption have already slowed the proceedings, as have restrictions on investigations and procedures that other courts would have never have accepted," concluding that it "is dubious that the tribunal can really set the historical record straight."[94] NGOs, especially the Documentation Center of Cambodia (DC-Cam), have been providing detailed documentation and analysis and reaching out to young Cambodians to know this dark period of their nation's history.[95]

Essential Issues of Substance

Several substantive issues were crucial to the development of the final constitutional text. Without a record of the deliberations of the drafting committee, and given the lack of transparency in the ultimate decision-making process, we can review only in general terms the restoration of monarchy, structure of government, and provisions for promoting and protecting human rights.

The Restoration of Monarchy and Structure of Government

Monarchy in Asia (as elsewhere) tends to be autocratic, and considering Cambodia's previous experience, one might wonder whether the constitutional provisions on the monarchical nature of the government diminish its liberal democratic character or the prospects for implementing constitutionally guaranteed human rights. During the drafting of the Paris Agreements and the transitional period, there was no hint that the task of establishing a "liberal democracy, on the basis of pluralism" would entail the restoration of the king. During the SNC session described above, when Prince Sihanouk outlined his vision of the constitution, he noted that the name of the country as set out in the constitution could be neither the Kingdom of Cambodia ("which would not please certain parties") nor the Khmer Republic ("which would not please my son [Prince Ranariddh, head of the royalist FUNCINPEC] and, in truth, would not please me either"). He suggested that the country simply be called Cambodia.[96] He did see a special role for himself, but not as king; he felt that the "president" should be someone who is above parties and brings the nation together. Using the example of François Mitterrand (and, oddly, Danielle Mitterrand), he said that their affiliation with the Socialist Party exemplified a partisan type of presidency that would not work in Cambodia.[97] He said that the Cambodian president could be a man or a woman, but there is little doubt that the person above parties whom he had in mind was none other than himself. He may have been deliberately misleading the members of the SNC, the senior staff of UNTAC, and the diplomatic corps in the room, intending all along that the process lead to restoration of the Kingdom of Cambodia with his return to the throne. It may also have been his view at the time that the surest road to power for him was to be elected under a constitution with a strong presidential regime. Alternatively, the relative victory of his son's FUNCINPEC party may have opened the way for a restoration of the monarchy that Sihanouk had not envisaged before the constituent assembly began meeting.

Whatever may have been the expectations of the palace or of FUNCINPEC, the United Nations did not seriously consider that the Kingdom of Cambodia would be the framework for the liberal democracy it was mandated to help establish. From a historical and sociological perspective, however, one might doubt whether any other form of government than monarchy could have emerged in Cambodia from a process of political self-determination, in which opposing factions needed to compromise and the general population obviously supported the royal family and monarchical tradition. In traditional Khmer society, the king occupies an exalted position, and Sihanouk's personality fit that traditional model. Popular support, for FUNCINPEC, reflecting veneration for Sihanouk, proved greater than that for the CPP, despite the latter's control over the propaganda and security apparatus.

Politically, influential foreign governments and the United Nations had always recognized that Sihanouk was the only person capable of holding the SNC and the peace process together, however capricious he might be. No one doubted that he would be

accorded a special place in the constitution to allow him to continue to play his unique role. Restoring him to the throne was not the expected way of maintaining his supreme authority, but it was consistent with what all perceived as a political necessity. It was also the result of the "idealization of the pre-1970 past the defect of which had been erased by subsequent atrocities."[98]

Despite the short-term imperative to accord Sihanouk a special role, the question remains whether the provisions of the 1993 constitution relating to the status, powers, and duties of the king are compatible with the functioning of a liberal democracy that safeguards human rights. Akashi and his staff were well aware that constitutional monarchy need not be incompatible with liberal democracy and respect for human rights, considering the examples of the United Kingdom, Denmark, the Netherlands, Spain, and Sweden. The essential characteristic of those constitutional systems is that power is legally and effectively exercised by duly elected representatives of the people who are accountable to their constituents and respectful of the rule of law and separation of powers. On its face, the 1993 constitution of Cambodia provides that "all powers belong to the people. The people exercise these powers through the National Assembly, the Royal Government and the Judiciary."[99] The same article stipulates that the three branches of government shall be separate. Democracy is reconciled with monarchy in the first article of the constitution, which reads, "Cambodia is a kingdom with a King who shall rule according to the Constitution and to the principles of liberal democracy and pluralism." If one accepts that a constitutional monarchy can establish a liberal democracy—which seems acceptable—then this provision contains the essential guarantees of it by subordinating the king to the constitution and the principles of liberal democracy and pluralism. Article 1 also constitutes formal compliance with a clear requirement of Annex 5.[100] The formal limitations on the king are reinforced by Article 7, according to which "the king of Cambodia shall reign but shall not govern."[101] The members of the constituent assembly attached particular importance to this limitation because they added that it "absolutely shall not be amended."[102]

Nevertheless, the king is given considerable authority and a few real powers. He "shall assume the august role of arbitrator to ensure the faithful execution of public powers"[103], and he appoints the prime minister.[104] He also appoints, transfers, and removes high officials, ambassadors, and judges, the last group on the advice of the Supreme Council of the Magistracy.[105] He can declare war,[106] proclaim a national emergency,[107] and sign and ratify international treaties.[108] He also must sign royal acts and decrees to promulgate the constitution and laws.[109] Finally, the king is the supreme commander of the Royal Khmer Armed Forces[110] and president of the Supreme Council of National Defense.[111] Vesting these powers in the ailing father of modern Cambodia, who spent most of his time in Beijing and Pyongyang and was revered by most of the population, may have been appropriate for the prestige of the office and insignificant in practice. However, full use of them by his successor could easily jeopardize the democratic institutions provided for elsewhere. The king cannot appoint his successor[112]; the Royal Council of the Throne—consisting of the president of the assembly, the prime minister, two head monks, and the first and second vice presidents of the assembly—must elect a new king from among the royal family members.[113] Sihanouk abdicated in 2004, and his eldest son, Norodom Sihamoni, was named by the nine-member throne council to become the next king.

Democracy is doubly fragile under Cambodia's political system. First, the impoverished population has too little education and experience with democracy to influence party platforms and the choice of party candidates. Second, the constitution does not provide for other levels of democratic participation apart from electing members of the assembly, such as directly voting candidates into offices in the local and provincial governments. Rather than belonging to the people, real powers belong to the king and the politicians who control the royal government, consisting of the Council of Ministers, normally headed by one prime minister assisted by two deputy prime ministers.[114] The prime minister is appointed by the king from the representatives of the winning party in the assembly, on the recommendation of the president and with the assent of the two vice presidents of the assembly.[115] The executive continues to be the dominant political force, with the king having considerably more than ceremonial functions. These are the structures of government that are supposed to establish democracy—that is, empower the people and their representatives to decide on behalf of the people. Despite constitutional incantations of the supremacy of the people and the king's frequent reference to it, in practice, the parliament appears weak.

Constitutional Provisions for Promoting and Protecting Human Rights

In large part, the constitution's liberal character is a function of the bill of rights and related enforcement procedures set out in it. Incorporating human rights provisions was a critical element of compliance with the Paris Agreements in the constitution-making process, although it is uncertain whether and to what extent the drafters focused on this aspect of the constitution. In addition to affirming human rights consistent with the Universal Declaration of Human Rights and other relevant instruments, Annex 5 required the constituent assembly to provide that "aggrieved individuals will be entitled to have the courts adjudicate and enforce these rights"[116]; as the annex states, "An independent judiciary will be established, empowered to enforce the rights provided under the constitution."[117] Formal declarations of rights are of little value unless the law and political culture permit an effective remedy against abuses, as required by Article 8 of the Universal Declaration and Article 2(3)(a) of the International Covenant on Civil and Political Rights, to which Cambodia is a party.[118] An effective remedy assumes that the rule of law and trained judicial and administrative officials are in place. Cambodia has neither. Nevertheless, the constitution does stipulate that

> Khmer citizens shall have the right to denounce, make complaints or file claims against any breach of the law by State and social organs or by members of such organs committed during the course of their duties. The settlement of complaints and claims shall reside under the competence of the courts.[119]

Regarding the existence of effective remedies under the new constitution, Justice Michael Kirby, the first special representative of the secretary-general for human rights in Cambodia, did not hesitate to conclude that the above-quoted provision notwithstanding, "no effective criminal or civil remedies exist in law for the prosecution of persons who engage in violations of rights recognized in the Constitution."[120] The constitution could not declare such prerequisites of justice into existence. It could, however, establish in law an array of organs and procedures that would make it difficult if not impossible for the new government to deny an effective remedy to aggrieved individuals without disregarding the constitution. However, the constituent assembly only provided the most superficial guarantees of such remedies. It was, therefore, a wise precaution to provide, in Article 17 of the Paris Agreements, for the ongoing UN supervision,[121] which has been exercised by the Commission on Human Rights and

the Human Rights Council since February 1993,[122] through the SRSGs.[123]

The principal mechanism for promoting and protecting human rights that a constitution can appropriately establish is an independent judiciary, which the Paris Agreements stress as the privileged means to enforce human rights. Due to a paucity of people with any legal training at all, however, it has not yet been possible to establish a fully trained judiciary. A court system is meaningless if judges and prosecutors lack even a minimal degree of training and independence. Before the constitution was drafted, the head of the investigation unit of the Human Rights Component of UNTAC wrote that under new constitutional provisions on independence of the judiciary, "it would be necessary to abolish the judiciary as it exists now, completely."[124] He also found that for Cambodian judges with whom he had discussed the matter, "the whole concept of independence of the judiciary was alien to them."[125]

Constitutionally requiring the independence of the judiciary was a necessary but insufficient step to allow the justice system to function as an effective means of enforcing constitutional rights and protections. While the constitutional affirmation of an independent judiciary and provision for a Supreme Council of the Magistracy are welcome, it is illusory to think that the constitution will produce, in the near term, anything approaching effective means of adjudicating and enforcing rights through the courts, as the Paris Agreements require.

Conclusion

Adopting Cambodia's 1993 constitution was the defining event in implementing the Paris Agreements' commitment to establish a "liberal democracy on the basis of pluralism." The United Nations deployed over twenty thousand civilian and military personnel and spent $2 billion to assist Cambodia through a transitional period, the end of which was defined as the adoption of the constitution and the establishment of the first government pursuant to it. Without the constitution, UNTAC would have failed in an essential aspect of its mission, although its role in the actual drafting process was minor. The Cambodian operation made constitutional reform an integral part of the comprehensive political settlement, with the United Nations keeping the process on course. The ultimate question addressed in this chapter is whether and to what extent the process of constitution drafting contributed to national reconciliation and establishment of the foundations for a stable and peaceful society. The constitution-making process can best be assessed as an element of intervention from above rather than intervention from below.[126]

Political and military arrangements among fighting factions are the most visible elements of UN peacemaking, peacekeeping, and post-conflict peacebuilding, and require high-level intervention from above by the international community. Such intervention and the resultant political arrangements are accepted by those who seek political power only as long as they have no choice. Once they feel empowered enough, they will exclude the international community and dismantle those aspects of the political arrangements that do not suit them. In Cambodia, this has meant the concentration of power in the CPP and in the person of Hun Sen. Support for civil society, human rights, democratic participation, and community-based development efforts tends to be a less visible form of intervention from below. Intervention from below involves a partnership among human rights and development components of the international community, interacting with elements of the population in a process of societal transformation through democratic empowerment, enhancing citizens' capacity to participate effectively in society and government. Such

participation requires a vibrant civil society benefiting from freedom of expression and association. Political parties, trade unions, religious organizations, public interest, and similar groups must function free of undue government control. Democratic empowerment requires that democratic laws, policies, and institutions be in place, including electoral laws and commissions, genuine and periodic elections, an independent judiciary and bar, a professional police separate from the military, and accountability and transparency in public service. Working to put these elements in place during a transition holds the potential for long-term social transformation as the population, made aware of its rights to democratic governance, constantly seeks to occupy and expand the political space available to it.

The constitution-drafting process falls in between interventions from above and below. It is an essential component of elite-level arrangements, standing on the fragile ground of a formal agreement by previously warring parties, who would have preferred military victory but have had to settle for a political role under the constitution. But it can also be a feature of democratic empowerment, both as a process and foundation for future expansion. The massive participation in the Cambodian election of the constituent assembly in 1993 clearly contributed to democratic empowerment. People's expectations of what a peaceful Cambodia could be like were altered, probably irrevocably. To the extent that the population is informed and feels its views are reflected in the constitution-drafting phase, democratic participation is enhanced. However, in Cambodia, that phase was to a large extent a manifestation of intervention from above because the drafting process was not transparent and civil society was given few opportunities to be heard. At the same time, the demands of the Paris Agreements and the governments that sought to influence the process, as well as the minimal expectations of the parties represented on the drafting committee, resulted in the constitution's adoption of many essential features of a liberal democracy. Such a legal basis for human rights and democratic governance contributes to democratic empowerment.

In other words, national dialogue and consolidation of peace receive a necessary but temporary boost from the military and political aspects of intervention from above, but their longer-term prospects depend on democratic empowerment, to which constitution drafting may contribute. In Cambodia, the drafting process belonged more to the power struggle among the political factions than it did to the democratic empowerment function of UNTAC's peacebuilding mandate. That is why it is necessary to monitor carefully how the subsequent societal development and application of the constitution have filled the empowerment gap created by the politicization of the constitution-drafting process.

It should be clear that formally including in the constitution the key language of the Paris Agreement and its Annex 5 regarding liberal democracy and human rights did not change Cambodia's power structure. It is evident that "the provisions of the formal constitution concerning the selection of members of the ruling group and the right to individual liberties are not the ultimate determinants of the distribution of effective power in the political system, much less in the political society as a whole."[127] Cambodia is an example of Nelson Kasfir's sharp observation that "no matter how careful the constitutional drafting process reestablishing democratic rule, and no matter how bitter the memory of past experience, the dependent political economies and swollen states characteristic of the Third World raise profound structural challenges to the success of democratic constitutions."[128] According to Shahid

Qadir, this democratization at the top is a "game élites play to manage the granting of very carefully selected concessions. It is a cosmetic exercise and does not install the fundamentals of democratization."[129]

The question that arises, however—and that will remain unanswered here—is whether a more democratic and transparent constitution-making process might have fostered a more genuinely democratic result. The question leads to speculation as to what might have happened had the demands for participation by the vibrant civil society that took shape in the course of the process actually been met. If so, perhaps the process itself would have been a capacity-building exercise, strengthening the role of civil society and the population at large in the political destiny of the country. As it stands, the new constitution is democratic to the extent that the people's interests were genuinely reflected by their elected representatives in the constituent assembly. That a coalition of human rights and development NGOs attempted to pressure the assembly during the drafting phase is a promising sign of the potential for deeper democratization, as is the continued effort of these activists to see in the constitution a source of protection of their human rights, which they could not have expected under the previous regime.

The liberal character of Cambodia's new constitution is a function of the clarity and thoroughness with which rights and procedures for their implementation are set out. We have seen that the drafters did little more that graft the monarchical provisions of the 1947 constitution onto a liberalized version of the 1989 constitution, without incorporating international standards except for a general—and potentially significant—reference to them. Nevertheless, the continuing applicability of those portions of the transitional provisions that have not been replaced and the legal authority for interpreting the constitutional declaration of rights by reference to international standards expand considerably the scope of the enumerated rights. The constitutionally established procedures for effective remedies are particularly weak, however. The constitution's text is disappointing in this regard, but gives a legal basis for a broad program of reform. The Cambodia Office of the High Commissioner for Human Rights, and the constant vigilance of the successive special representatives for human rights in Cambodia (Michael Kirby, Thomas Hammarberg, Peter Leuprecht, Yash Ghai, and Surya Subedi) as well as key bilateral donors, all contribute to consolidating adherence to constitutional rights and freedoms.

Thus, Cambodia's constitution established a weak democratic structure with limited liberalization. This result must not be judged too harshly, however, considering the devastation of the country and the intensity of the conflict from which it has yet to emerge entirely. The end of the Cold War removed Cambodia's significance as a strategic zone of conflict, by which the United States sought to contain and push back Soviet influence through the latter's Vietnamese proxy. That strategic interest was seen to be so great that the United States bombed Cambodia during the Vietnam War and supported the Khmer Rouge diplomatically after the Vietnamese invasion. Without these strategic interests, stability and democracy in Cambodia are desirable but not vital: to the West, Cambodia is now another poor country that deserves aid but is unlikely to turn against Western interests. Under these circumstances, the concern of powerful nations during transition was to complete the mission on time and within budget, even if the constitution—its principal product—was not as good as it might have been.

The CPP today, as heir to a communist-type party and state structure but without the Marxist ideology, continues to dominate political and administrative life despite a constitution purporting to establish a liberal democracy based on pluralism. As one member of the constituent assembly remarked when the constitution was adopted, the public and near-unanimous voting on limited matters in the assembly was "just like under communism."[130] Nevertheless, the constitution has provided the legal basis for power sharing between the previously warring FUNCINPEC (and KPLNF) and the CPP; it has also allowed the Sam Rainsy Party to emerge as genuine opposition, frequently harassed by the government but persevering.

The constitutional text makes it the policy of the royal government of Cambodia to advocate "a national reconciliation policy in defense of national unity."[131] At the ceremony following the constitution's promulgation, Akashi was perhaps a bit too optimistic in declaring that "Cambodia has proved to the world that an insoluble conflict can be settled and that apparently irreconcilable points of view can be reconciled."[132] The king's preference for accommodation with the DK to achieve reconciliation seemed at first to hold promise, especially when, soon after the constitution's adoption, Khieu Samphan, nominal head of the DK, came to Phnom Penh to pay homage to King Sihanouk and declare his group's support for the new constitution[133] even as defections multiplied among the ranks of the Khmer Rouge armed forces (NADK).[134] The prospects for reconciliation as conceived by the king changed, however, with the 1994 assembly vote to outlaw the DK, with the support of the first prime minister, Prince Ranariddh, who had originally supported his father's policy of accommodation, and the DK's establishment of a so-called Provisional Government of National Union and National Salvation. Eventually, the NADK defections and Pol Pot's death ended the threat to reconciliation that the DK represented, and Khieu Samphan sits today (May 2009) in the docket of the ECCC. The constitution-making process did not achieve reconciliation among the four Cambodian parties to the Paris Agreements, but it was a critical first step toward that end.

The long-term viability of a constitution depends not so much on how it is drafted as on conditions that allow for the consolidation of democracy, including overcoming the lack of historical experience with democracy, sustaining a growing economy, avoiding political violence, and ensuring separation of powers and a professional and independent civil service and judiciary. Cambodia has had virtually no previous experience with democratic governance, although there is no doubt about the enthusiasm with which Cambodians participated in the elections and aspire to enjoy human rights and honest government. Cambodia's poverty[135] is slowly being offset by substantial aid,[136] some international investment,[137] and modest economic growth.[138] Regarding a peaceful transition to democracy, political and ethnic violence continued during the 1993, 1998, 2002, and 2003 elections, but all were relatively free and fair under the circumstances. Commune elections were held in April 2007 and National Assembly elections in July 2008, but with less violence than the 2002 and 2003 elections. The Cambodian People's Party emerged victorious, with the Sam Rainsy Party (SRP) increasing its representation in the assembly as the main opposition party. The armed conflict with the DK did not end until 1998. But since transition began, the scale of political violence has not threatened democracy fatally. Progress in maintaining the separation of powers and independence of the civil service and judiciary is painfully slow but the constant vigilance and denunciation of backsliding by the SRSGs, local and international NGOs, and the political opposition have sustained pressure on the regime. Thus, judging by the presence of these four con-

ditions, consolidation of democracy appears difficult in Cambodia, but not hopeless.

The current CPP, FUNCINPEC, and SRP leaderships and the relatively weak king, Norodom Sihamoni (who replaced the ailing and absentee Sihanouk in October 2004), do not possess the requisite qualities to breathe life from the top into the potentially democratic provisions of the constitution. But prospects may be brighter for the long-term advance toward democratization from below, through the empowerment of people to participate in government. Democratization requires unfettered development of civil society, through genuine freedom of association and expression, political space being given to diverse segments of the community, respect for privacy, and development of independent media; periodic elections, especially at the local level with voter education; meaningful recourse and effective redress through judicial and administrative remedies, open to ordinary people, both citizens and noncitizens; and access to official information, members of parliament, and public officials. At least limited popular involvement in politics first appeared during the May 1993 elections and the constitutional-drafting process, and continued during the five more recent elections. Democratization has thus had a spectacular beginning, but will take generations to become embedded in Cambodia's political culture.

Cambodia has emerged from chaos and destruction with many unsolved problems. In the final analysis, the 1993 constitution is not much better than previous communist, monarchical, or republican versions on which it is largely based. Power is beginning to be exercised more broadly through the political opposition and civil society, and certain checks are being placed on the dominant leadership. Cambodia has not yet entirely emerged from civil strife, and its democratic foundations are fragile. But the 1993 constitution, for all its defects, has cemented that foundation.

Acronyms

BLDP — Buddhist Liberal Democratic Party.

CGDK — the Coalition Government of Democratic Kampuchea.

CPP — the Cambodian People's Party, the pro-Vietnam faction. Previously named the PRPK. Controlled the PRK, renamed SOC in 1989.

DK — the Party of Democratic Kampuchea, also called PDK. Popularly known as Khmer Rouge.

FUNCINPEC — National United Front for an Independent, Neutral, Peaceful, and Cooperative Cambodia, the royalist faction headed by Prince Norodom Ranariddh.

IRI — International Republican Institute, U.S.-based democratization assistance organization.

KPLNF — Khmer People's National Liberation Front, also known as the BLDP — Buddhist Liberal Democratic Party.

KR — Khmer Rouge, name given to the DK (also called PDK) by Sihanouk and generally used by the media.

LICADHO — Cambodian League for the Promotion and Protection of Human Rights.

MOLINAKA — Mouvement de Liberation Nationale du Kampuchea (National Liberation Movement of Kampuchea).

NDI — National Democratic Institute for International Affairs, U.S.-based democratization assistance organization.

PICC — the Paris International Conference on Cambodia.

PRK — People's Republic of Kampuchea, controlled by the PRPK (later renamed the CPP).

PRPK — People's Revolutionary Party of Kampuchea, previous name of the CPP.

SNC — Supreme National Council, the interim representative body created in the Paris Agreements.

SOC — State of Cambodia, name of PRK since 1989, controlled by the CPP.

SRP — Sam Rainsy Party.

SRSG — Special Representative of the Secretary-General of the United Nations (during the Cambodian transition, Yasushi Akashi held this position). Since the UNTAC period, it refers to the Special Representative of the Secretary-General for human rights in Cambodia.

UNTAC — United Nations Transitional Authority in Cambodia.

Notes

1. Agreements on a Comprehensive Political Settlement of the Cambodian Conflict, signed in Paris on October 23, 1991, at the final meeting of the Paris Conference on Cambodia. The comprehensive settlement comprises four documents: the Final Act of the Paris Conference; the Agreement on a Comprehensive Political Settlement of the Cambodian Conflict, with five annexes (Annex 5 contains constitutional principles); the Agreement Concerning the Sovereignty, Independence, Territorial Integrity and Inviolability, Neutrality and National Unity of Cambodia; and the Declaration on the Rehabilitation and Reconstruction of Cambodia. Reprinted in 31 I.L.M. 174 (1992). This compilation will be referred to below in the plural as the Paris Agreements; the singular Paris Agreement will refer to the second of the four documents.

2. Among the books written about the Cambodian transition are Grant Curtis, *Cambodia Reborn? The Transition to Democracy and Development* (Washington, DC: Brookings Institution Press, and Geneva: The United Nations Research Institute for Social Development, 1998); M.H. Lao, *The Unfinished Settlement of the Cambodia Conflict* (Phnom Penh: Khmer Institute of Democracy, 1994); William Shawcross, *Cambodia's New Deal* (Washington, DC: Carnegie Endowment for International Peace, 1994); Janet E. Heininger, *Peacekeeping in Transition: The United Nations in Cambodia* (New York: The Twentieth-Century Fund Press, 1994); Steve R. Heder and Judy Ledgerwood, eds., *Propaganda, Politics, and Violence in Cambodia: Democratic Transition under United Nations Peace-Keeping* (Armonk, NY: M.E. Sharpe, 1996); Henry Kamm, *Cambodia: Report from a Stricken Land* (New York: Arcade Publishing, 1998); MacAlister Brown and Joseph J. Zasloff, *Cambodia Confounds the Peacemakers: 1979–1998* (Ithaca, NY: Cornell University Press, 1998); David W. Roberts, *Political Transition in Cambodia: Power, Elitism, and Democracy* (New York: St. Martin's Press, 2001).

3. Among the numerous books about this period, see Elizabeth Becker, *When the War Was Over: The Voices of Cambodia's Revolution and Its People* (New York: Simon and Schuster, 1986); Michael Vickery, *Cambodia 1975–1982* (Cambridge, MA: South End Press, 1984); David Chandler and Ben Kiernan, eds., *Revolution and Its Aftermath in Kampuchea: Eight Essays,* Yale University Southeast Asia Studies, Monograph Series no. 25, 1983; Ben Kiernan, ed., *Genocide and Democracy in Cambodia: The Khmer Rouge, the United Nations, and the International Community*, Yale University Southeast Asia Studies, Monograph Series no. 41, 1993; Karl D. Jackson, ed., *Cambodia 1975–1978: Rendezvous with Death* (Princeton, NJ: Princeton University Press, 1989).

4. These four parties were the Cambodian People's Party (CPP), previously known as the People's Revolutionary Party of Kampuchea (PRPK), which headed the People's Republic of Kampuchea (PRK), since 1989 called State of Cambodia (SOC); the National United Front for an Independent, Neutral, Peaceful, and Cooperative Cambodia (FUNCINPEC); the Khmer People's National Liberation Front (KPLNF), also known as the Buddhist Liberal Democratic Party (BLDP) since May 1992; and the Party of Democratic Kampuchea (PDK) or Khmer Rouge (KR). It is important to keep in mind that the distinction between SOC and the functioning government structure and CPP as a political party was more of a fiction than a reality, as the party controlled the state.

5. The eighteen other signatories are Australia, Brunei, Canada, China, France, India, Indonesia, Japan, Laos, Malaysia, the Philippines, Singapore, Thailand, the USSR, the United Kingdom, the United States, Vietnam, and Yugoslavia.

6. On the background of the agreements, see Steven R. Ratner, "The Cambodia Settlement Agreements," *American Journal of International Law,* vol. 87, no. 1, pp. 2–8. See also Steven R. Ratner, "The United Nations in Cambodia: A Model for Resolution of Internal Conflicts?" in *Enforcing Restraint: Collective Intervention in Internal Conflicts*, ed. Lori Damrosch (New York: Council on Foreign Relations Press, 1993), p. 241.

7. Technically, this outcome was a condition precedent for the termination of the transition period of UN authority. Article 1 of the Paris Agreement provides that the transitional period shall "terminate when the constituent assembly elected through free and fair elections, organized and certified by the United Nations, has approved the constitution and transformed itself into a legislative assembly, and thereafter a new government has been created."

8. See note 2.

9. See Maurice Gaillard, *Démocratie Cambodgienne. La Constitution du 24 septembre 1993* (Paris: L'Harmattan, 1994); Siphana Sok and Denora Sarin, *Legal System of Cambodia* (Phnom Penh: Cambodian Legal Resources Development Center, 1998); Koy Neam, *Introduction to the Cambodian Judicial Process* (Washington, DC: The Asia Foundation, 1998); Stephen P. Marks, "The New Cambodian Constitution: From Civil War to a Fragile Democracy," *Columbia Human Rights Law Review*, vol. 26, no. 1 (Fall 1994), pp. 45–110.

10. George Coedès, *The Indianized States of Southeast Asia* (Honolulu: University of Hawaii Press, 1986), English edition.

11. David Chandler, *A History of Cambodia*, 2nd ed. (Chiang Mai, Thailand: Silkworm Books, 1993), p. 48. See also Mahesh Kumar Sharan, *Political History of Ancient Cambodia, from 1st Cent. A.D. to 15th Cent. A.D.* (New Delhi: Vishwavidya Publishers, 1986); Michael Vickery, *Kampuchea: Politics, Economics, and Society* (Boulder, CO: Lynne Rienner, 1986).

12. Chandler, *History*, p. 107. Chandler also notes that the "Cambodian king, at the pinnacle of society, was remote from his subjects. Scholars have argued that this remoteness was expected of an Asian king; he was to rule by his largely invisible example, just as the sun shone, and he was to act as the custodian of a fund of merit and power—viewed perhaps as an interlocking, expendable commodity—that he had accumulated in previous existences en route to the throne" (112).

13. François Ponchaud, "Social Change in the Vortex of Revolution," in *Rendezvous with Death*, p. 176, quoting Alain Forest, *Le Cambodge et la colonisation française: Histoire d'une colonisation sans heurts (1897–1920)* (Paris: L'Harmattan, 1980).

14. Chandler, *History*, p. 105. See also Marie-Alexandrine Martin, "La paysannerie Khmère et le processus démocratique," in *Les Cambodgiens face à eux-mêmes, Dossier pour un débat*, Fondation pour le progrès de l'homme, no. 4, 1993, pp. 127–142, quoted in Gaillard, *Démocratie Cambodgienne*, p. 25.

15. Chandler, *History,* p. 111.

16. The practice of justice is included in the account of customs in Angkor in the last days of the Khmer Empire, written around 1312 by a Chinese embassy official who had spent a year in Angkor. In determining rights and obligations in civil matters, "points of dispute, however trifling, are taken to the ruler." When two men have a dispute over a matter,

"each of the contestants is forced to be seated in one of the [twelve little stone towers in front of the palace] with his relatives standing guard over him. They remain imprisoned two, three, or four days. When allowed to emerge, one of them will be found to be suffering some illness—ulcers, or catarrh, or malignant fever. The other man will be in perfect health. Thus is right or wrong determined by what is called 'celestial judgement.' Thus is shown supernatural strength of the God of this country." In criminal matters, an accused thief who denies the charge is forced to plunge his hand in boiling oil. "If he is truly guilty, the hand is cooked to shreds; if not, skin and bones are unharmed. Such is the amazing way of these barbarians." Other criminal punishments included, for serious crimes, placing the criminal in a ditch and "earth and stones are thrown back and heaped high, and all is over. . . . Lesser crimes are dealt with by cutting off feet or hands, or by amputation of the nose." Chou Ta-Kuan (Zhou Daguan), *The Customs of Cambodia,* 2nd ed. (Bangkok: The Siam Society, 1992), p. 33.

17. Gaillard, *Démocratie Cambodgienne,* p. 25.

18. Constitution of September 23, 1993, art. 1, para. 2.

19. Lao, *The Unfinished Settlement,* pp. 169–97.

20. Ibid., pp. 203–04.

21. See note 1.

22. Paris Agreement, annex 5, para. 4.

23. Nayan Chanda, quoted by Ratner, "The Cambodia Settlement Agreements," p. 27, note 163.

24. For example, Milton Osborne reports that "time and again Sihanouk had made clear his distrust of radical politics within Cambodia and his readiness to sanction the repressive measures used by his security services." Milton Osborne, *Sihanouk: Prince of Light, Prince of Darkness* (Honolulu: University of Hawaii Press, 1994), p. 121.

25. Lao Mong Hay affirms, "At the PICC the Khmer Rouge had fought hard to remove that word from all conference documents, and had succeeded." Lao, *The Unfinished Settlement,* p. 199.

26. Stephen P. Marks, "Forgetting 'The Policies and Practices of the Past': Impunity in Cambodia," *Fletcher Forum,* vol. 8, no. 2 (1994), pp. 25–26, 28–30, 36–38.

27. Text on file with the author.

28. Paris Agreement, art. 3.

29. Paris Agreement, art. 6.

30. Personal recollection of the author.

31. Personal recollection of the author.

32. Paris Agreements, annex 1, section D.

33. Formed by armed groups on the Thai-Cambodian border in August 1979, the Mouvement de Liberation Nationale du Kampuchea (National Liberation Movement of Kampuchea, or MOLINAKA) was supported mainly by French-based Cambodian exiles. The party under the MOLINAKA name that won a seat in the 1993 elections was formed in 1992 from members of FUNCINPEC and was dissolved in 1998.

34. UN Security Council Resolution 840 (1993).

35. John C. Brown, "Khmer Democracy: Where's the Participation?" *Phnom Penh Post,* August 27–September 9, 1993, p. 8.

36. Osborne, *Sihanouk,* pp. 261–62.

37. Isabelle Hourcade, "M. Akashi 'profondément satisfait' de la mission de l'ONU au Cambodge," Agence France Presse, September 26, 1993 (LEXIS-NEXIS, September 27, 1993).

38. Francis Curta, "La France salue l'adoption de la nouvelle constitution," Agence France Presse, September 21, 1993 (LEXIS-NEXIS, September 21, 1993). See also "EC Welcomes New Constitution in Cambodia," European Report, European Information Service, October 6, 1993, section I, Institutions and Policy Coordinationn no. 1891 (LEXIS-NEXIS, October 6, 1993).

39. Associated Press, AP Online, VO155, September 24, 1993.

40. UN Security Council Resolution 880 (1993).

41. Brown and Zasloff, *Cambodia Confounds the Peacemakers,* pp. 132–33.

42. Paris Agreement, art. 15(2)(a). See also the Agreement Concerning the Sovereignty, Independence, Territorial Integrity and Inviolability, Neutrality and National Unity of Cambodia, art. 3(2).

43. *Report of the Secretary-General,* UN Document S/23613, para. 12. This document is the principal source, after the text of the Paris Agreements, of UNTAC's mandate.

44. Stephen P. Marks, "Human Rights Education in UN Peace-Building: From Theory to Practice," in *Human Rights Education for the Twenty-First Century,* ed. George J. Andreopoulos and Richard Pierre Claude (Philadelphia: University of Pennsylvania Press, 1997), pp. 36–39.

45. UN Document S/23613, para. 13.

46. UN Document S/23613, para. 13.

47. Marks, "Human Rights Education in UN Peace-Building," p. 47.

48. *Report of the Special Representative of the Secretary-General, Mr. Michael Kirby (Australia), on the Situation of Human Rights in Cambodia, Submitted in Accordance with Commission Resolution 1993/6,* UN Doc. E/CN.4/1994/73, February 24, 1994, para. 165, p. 42.

49. "Women's Rights Movement Starts," *Cambodia Times,* March 15–21, 1993, p. 11.

50. David Hawk, "The Photographic Record," in *Rendezvous with Death,* p. 212.

51. Ibid., p. 212.

52. Eva Mysliwiec, *Punishing the Poor: The International Isolation of Kampuchea* (Oxford: Oxfam, 1988), p. 47.

53. 1993 Constitution, art 41.

54. *Report of the Special Representative of the Secretary-General, Mr. Michael Kirby,* para. 159, p. 41.

55. "Monarchy or Republic?" *Phnom Penh Post,* June 18–July 1, 1993, p. 8.

56. "The U.N. Says It Is Not Worried at This Point. Charter: Out of Sight, Out of Mind," *Phnom Penh Post,* August 13–26, 1993, p. 1.

57. "Sihanouk Backs Royalist Charter," *Phnom Penh Post,* September 10–23, 1993, p. 1.

58. John C. Brown, "NGOs Express Concern over Draft Constitution," *Phnom Penh Post,* August 27–September 9, 1993, p. 1.

59. Brown, "Khmer Democracy: Where's the Participation?" at p. 7. In Akashi's reply, he supported their "democratic right to lobby the members of the Constituent Assembly and the political parties to which they belong, on any matters of concern relating to the Constitution," but noted that the process was the responsibility and prerogative of the assembly.

60. "Comics, Monks Spread Human Rights Message," *Phnom Penh Post,* September 25, 1992, p. 8.

61. "Former Royal Aide Opens Think Tank," *Phnom Penh Post,* November 20–December 3, 1992.

62. "Taking It to the People," *Phnom Penh Post,* September 10–23, 1993, p. 7. "What Do You Think of the Constitution?" *Phnom Penh Post,* September 24–October 7, 1993, p. 6.

63. "NGOs Express Concern over Draft Constitution," *Phnom Penh Post,* August 27–September 9, 1993, p. 1.

64. See note 4.

65. Paris Agreements, annex 1, section B, para. 1, and S/23613, February 19, 1992, para. 94.

66. Letter dated June 27, 1992, from Mr. Khieu Samphan, transmitting proposal of the Party of Democratic Kampuchea (PDK) on cooperation between UNTAC and the Supreme National Council, in United Nations, *The United Nations and Cambodia, 1991–1994,* document 38, pp. 198–99; and proposal dated July 12, 1992, of the Party of Democratic Kampuchea on the implementation of phase II of the cease-fire and the regroupment and cantonment of the forces of the PDK, United Nations, *The United Nations and Cambodia,* document 40, pp. 200–01.

67. A description of nine of the twenty parties was published in Phnom Penh on the eve of the election. "Party Profiles," *Phnom Penh Post,* May 21–June 3, 1993, p. 10.

68. During his brief attempt to form a coalition government, Sihanouk had invited the DK to join in "national reconciliation and national union" and offered Khieu Samphan and Son Sen, the nominal leaders of the DK, "official recognition." Brown and Zasloff, *Cambodia Confounds the Peacemakers.*

69. Human Rights Watch, *The Lost Agenda: Human Rights and UN Field Operations* (New York: Human Rights Watch, 1993), p. 46. The reference to a "neutral political environment" is from the requirement of Article 12 of the Paris Agreement that such an environment exist for the elections.

70. Paris Agreement, art. 1.

71. Paris Agreement, annex 1, sec. D, para. 5.

72. Report of the Secretary-General on Cambodia, containing his proposed implementation plan for UNTAC, S/23613 of February 19, 1992.

73. S/RES/745 (1992) of February 28, 1992.

74. See note 32 and accompanying text.

75. Shawcross, *Cambodia's New Deal,* p. 33.

76. Brown and Zasloff, *Cambodia Confounds the Peacemakers,* p. 195.

77. Ibid., pp. 195–96.

78. "Assemblymen in Workshop," *Phnom Penh Post,* July 2–15, 1993, p. 5.

79. Later in 1993, NDI and IRI brought experts from Bangladesh, Thailand, the Philippines, and the United States to share experiences on lawmaking, policy development, public accountability, parliamentary procedures, and the role of political parties. "Parliamentary Training for MPs," *Phnom Penh Post*, Oct. 8–21, 1993, p. 2.

80. Brown and Zasloff, *Cambodia Confounds the Peacemakers*, p. 195.

81. Ibid., p. 195.

82. See Gregory H. Fox and Brad R. Roth, eds., *Democratic Governance and International Law* (Cambridge: Cambridge University Press, 2000); Thomas M. Franck, "The Emerging Right to Democratic Governance," *American Journal of International Law,* vol. 86 (1992), pp. 46–91.

83. Ratner, "The Cambodia Settlement Agreements," pp. 27–28. Footnotes omitted.

84. See Stephen P. Marks, "The New Cambodian Constitution: From Civil War to a Fragile Democracy," *Columbia Human Rights Law Review*, vol. 26, no. 1 (Fall 1994), pp. 74–76.

85. Among the growing literature on this topic, see Diane Orentlicher, "Settling Accounts: The Duty to Prosecute Human Rights Violations of a Prior Regime," *Yale Law Journal,* vol. 100 (1991), p. 2537; Martha Minow, *Between Vengeance and Forgiveness: Facing History after Genocide and Mass Violence* (Boston: Beacon Press, 1998); Geoffrey Robertson, *Crimes against Humanity. The Struggle for Global Justice* (New York: The New Press, 1999); "Seeking International Justice: The Role of Institutions," *Journal of International Affairs,* vol. 52, no. 2 (Spring 1999).

86. The peace agreement of January 16, 1992, provides as follows: "5. End to Impunity. The Parties recognize the need to clarify and put an end to any indication of impunity on the part of officers of the armed forces, particularly in cases where respect for human rights is jeopardized. To that end, the Parties refer this issue to the Commission on the Truth for consideration and resolution. All of this shall be without prejudice to the principle, which the Parties also recognize, that acts of this nature, regardless of the sector to which their perpetrators belong, must be the object of exemplary action by the law courts so that the punishment prescribed by law is meted out to those found responsible."

87. The term *genocide* was deliberately avoided to keep the DK in the peace process but was clearly understood by the references to "policies and practices of the past." In his testimony before the House Foreign Affairs Subcommittee on Asian and Pacific Affairs, Assistant Secretary of State Richard H. Solomon stated, in the view of the administration,

"the bottom line is that the peace process is the one promising way of bringing security and justice to the Cambodian people. Its successful completion cannot be held back over the issue of including or not including the word 'genocide.' The Khmer Rouge would be the only beneficiary if discord over this issue blocks moving forward to conclude a political settlement." 102nd Congress, Subcommittee on Asian and Pacific Affairs of the Committee on Foreign Affairs, House of Representatives, *Review of Proposed Economic and Security Assistance Requests for Asia and the Pacific*, March 6, 7, 22, and April 10, 17, 1991, p. 391 (1992).

88. Constitution of September 21, 1993, arts. 109–16.

89. Constitution of September 21, 1993, art. 52.

90. See Marks, "Forgetting 'The Policies and Practices of the Past,'" pp. 37–38; Stephen P. Marks, "Elusive Justice for the Victims of the Khmer Rouge," *Journal of International Affairs*, vol. 52, no. 2 (Spring 1999), pp. 691–718. The 1994 law outlawing the DK refers to "crimes of murder, rape, robbery of private property, destruction of public and private property," as well as "acts of secession" and "incitement of the population to take up arms against the state authority," but does not refer to international crimes of genocide or crimes against humanity. The problem has been regularly raised by the special representatives of the secretary-general for human rights in Cambodia. See *Situation of Human Rights in Cambodia. Report of the Special Representative of the Secretary-General for Human Rights in Cambodia, Peter Leuprecht*, UN Doc. E/CN.4/2005/116, December 20, 2004, para. 36; *Report of the Special Representative of the Secretary-General for Human Rights in Cambodia, Yash Ghai*, UN Doc. E/CN.4/2006/110, January 24, 2006, para. 26.

91. Law on the Establishment of Extraordinary Chambers in the Courts of Cambodia for the Prosecution of Crimes Committed During the Period of Democratic Kampuchea with amendments as promulgated on October 27, 2004 (NS/RKM/1004/006).

92. These defendants are: Khieu Samphan, Nuon Chea, Ieng Sary, and Ieng Thirith. Official information is provided on the Cambodian government's Web site for the ECCC, available at http://www.eccc.gov.kh/english/default.aspx (accessed May 21, 2009). The Open Society Justice Initiative maintains an ongoing monitoring of progress, priorities, and challenges at the ECCC, with monthly updates available at http://www.justiceinitiative.org/db/resource2?res_id=103899./.

93. The Open Society Justice Initiative, *Progress and Challenges at the Extraordinary Chambers in the Courts of Cambodia* (New York: Open Society Institute, 2007). See also Open Society Justice Initiative, *The Extraordinary Chambers* (New York: Open Society Institute, 2006); Open Society Justice Initiative, *Recent Developments at the Extraordinary Chambers in the Courts of Cambodia: October 2008 Update* (New York: Open Society Institute, 2008), and monthly updates cited *supra* note 93.

94. Elizabeth Becker, "When justice is delayed," *International Herald Tribune*, March 13, 2009.

95. DC-Cam's Web site is at http://www.dccam.org/.

96. Personal recollections of the author.

97. Personal recollections of the author.

98. Gaillard, *Démocratie Cambodgienne*, p. 25.

99. Constitution, art. 51.

100. Annex 5 of the Paris Agreements requires that the words "liberal democracy and pluralism" appear in the constitution. In addition to the provision of Article 1 noted above, Article 51 of the constitution satisfies this requirement by providing that "The Kingdom of Cambodia adopts a policy of Liberal Democracy and Pluralism."

101. The second sentence of this article reads "The king shall be the Head of State for life." Sihanouk's propensity for reigning rather than ruling has been identified as a reason for his failures in the 1950s. Michael Leifer wrote that Sihanouk's record "suggests a greater facility for reigning than for ruling. He is more at home with the pomp and circumstances of government than with its good practice. His neglect of the latter when in power is part of the tragedy of modern Cambodia." Quoted by Osborne, *Sihanouk*, p. 268.

102. Constitution, art. 17.

103. Constitution, art. 9.

104. Constitution, art. 19.

105. Constitution, art. 21.

106. Constitution, art. 24. The consent of the parliament is required before he can declare war.

107. Constitution, art. 22.

108. Constitution, art. 26. Treaties must first be adopted by the national assembly.

109. Constitution, art. 28.

110. Constitution, art. 23.

111. Constitution, art. 24.

112. Constitution, art. 10.

113. Constitution, art. 123.

114. Constitution, art. 99.

115. Constitution, art. 100.

116. Paris Agreement, annex 5, para. 2.

117. Paris Agreement, annex 5, para. 5.

118. Cambodia acceded to the International Covenant on Civil and Political Rights on August 26, 1992, as one of the human rights treaties ratified by the SNC during the administration of UNTAC.

119. Constitution of September 21, 1993, art. 39.

120. *Report of the Special Representative of the Secretary-General, Mr. Michael Kirby,* para. 137, p. 36. Louis Aucoin has informed the author that the drafters intended to adopt the German model of judicial review in Article 39, allowing the court to refer any constitutional challenge to the constitutional court. Communication of January 24, 2002.

121. "After the end of the transitional period, the United Nations Commission on Human Rights should continue to monitor closely the human rights situation in Cambodia, including, if necessary, by the appointment of a special Rapporteur who would report his findings annually to the Commission and to the General Assembly."

122. Commission on Human Rights Resolution 1993/6, adopted on February 19, 1993.

123. Twenty-seven reports had been issued by the SRSGs between February 1994 and February 2008. See http://cambodia.ohchr.org/EN/report_srsg.htm.

124. J. Basil Fernando, *The Inability to Prosecute: Courts and Human Rights in Cambodia and Sri Lanka* (Hong Kong: Future Asia Link, 1993), p. 9.

125. Fernando, *The Inability to Prosecute*, p. 10.

126. This distinction was suggested to the author by Professor Richard Falk.

127. Gene Sharp, *Social Power and Political Freedom* (Boston: Porter Sargent Publishers, 1980), p. 322.

128. Nelson Kasfir, "Popular Sovereignty and Popular Participation: Mixed Constitutional Democracy in the Third World," *Third World Quarterly,* vol. 13, no. 4 (1992), p. 595.

129. Shahid Qadir, Christopher Clapham, and Barry Gills, "Sustainable Democracy: Formalism vs. Substance," *Third World Quarterly,* vol. 14, no. 3 (1993), p. 416.

130. Osborne, *Sihanouk,* p. 8.

131. Constitution of September 21, 1993, art. 52.

132. Quoted by Christian Chaise in "Le prince Sihanouk promulgue la Constitution 'la plus démocratique qui soit,'" Agence France Presse, September 24, 1993 (LEXIS-NEXIS, September 24, 1993) (this author's translation from the French).

133. Sheila McNulty, "Khmer Rouge 'for King and Country,'" *The Independent*, October 2, 1993, p. 13.

134. Jean-Claude Pomonti, "Cambodge: Les Khmer Rouge connaissent de nombreuses défections," *Le Monde,* September 20, 1993 (LEXIS-NEXIS, September 21, 1993).

135. Cambodia ranks 131 out of 177 in UNDP's Human Development Index and 85 out of 108 developing countries on the Human Poverty Index. UNDP, *Human Development Report 2007/08*, pp. 231 and 240.

136. Cambodia received $537.8 million in foreign aid in 2005, which is 8.7 percent of its GDP. These figures show an increase in aid received compared to 2003 ($508 million, or 12 percent of GDP) and 2004 ($478 million, or 9.8 percent of GDP). UNDP, *Human Development Report 2007/08*, p. 292; UNDP, *Human Development Report 2006*, p. 345; and UNDP, *Human Development Report 2005*, p. 282.

137. Net foreign direct investment was 6.1 percent of GDP in 2005 (up from 2.7 percent of GDP in 2004, 2.1 percent in 2003, and 3.3 percent in 2001). UNDP, *Human Development Report 2007/08*, p. 292, UNDP, *Human Development Report 2006*, p. 345, UNDP, *Human Development Report 2005*, p. 282, and UNDP, *Human Development Report 2003*, p. 293.

138. The Economic Institute of Cambodia (EIC), which is supported by the World Bank, calculated Cambodia's 2008 economic growth rate at 5.2 percent in 2008, down from a growth rate of 10.2 percent in 2007. The global economic crisis is expected to bring Cambodia's economic growth rate down to about 2 percent in 2009. Economic Institute of Cambodia, *Cambodia Economic Watch—April 2009* (Phnom Penh, 2009), p. vii.

9

East Timor's Constitutional Passage to Independence

Louis Aucoin and Michele Brandt

In a post-conflict environment, a constitution-making process has great potential to serve as a peacebuilding and nation-building tool if it is designed to promote, when appropriate, the values of inclusion, representation, transparency, participation, and national ownership. How these values should be promoted in any given situation is context specific. There is no one way to design a constitution-making process.

However, in cases where the international community is supporting a constitution-making exercise, it should seek to support, to the extent appropriate, a process that gives life to these values. National actors should also seek to promote these values because such a process has the potential to

- facilitate conflict resolution by providing a mechanism within which a wide range of interest groups can develop consensus on how to address the past and current causes of conflict and on an appropriate framework for governance;

- address and reflect the concerns and rights of women, minorities, key stakeholders, and other marginalized members of society;

- lay the foundation for more democratic practices and public participation in governance;

- foster a more informed citizenry that respects the rule of law, questions unconstitutional governmental actions, has a sense of ownership over the constitution, and is more likely to defend the constitution.

The East Timor constitution-making process is a lesson for the international community as well as national actors designing or supporting their own constitution-building process about creating a process that fails to place these values front and center and instead focuses primarily on producing a constitution. Although there is no guarantee that a representative, inclusive, transparent, participatory, and nationally owned and led constitution-making process will achieve the above results, the international community and national actors leading the process should strive to capitalize on the peace-building and nation-building opportunities that this unique moment in history affords or risk creating a document that fuels conflict rather than resolves it.

This chapter discusses in depth why East Timor's constitution-making process was largely a missed opportunity to contribute to a sustainable peace in East Timor; deliberative processes that promote national reconciliation, conflict resolution, and consensus building take time, a commitment to public participation, and a representative body to deliberate and adopt the constitution. The process in East Timor was rushed, did not create the conditions necessary to include the public in the process, and emphasized an electoral process that in the East Timorese context led to single-party domination of the constituent assembly and a resulting constitution that largely reflected the desires of one party rather than the aspirations of the country as a whole and even of other key elite power bases.

This chapter, first, provides a background to the constitution-making process; second, discusses why the legal framework established a foundation for a flawed process; third, reflects on how democratic representation may have been achieved through a different type of selection and election process from constitution makers; fourth, underscores the demand for public participation in the process, but ultimately the lack of commitment, time, and effective mechanisms to adequately address this demand; fifth, examines the diverse role of the international community, including the key role of the United Nations, which contributed to the rushed timetable of the process; sixth, reflects on the technical assistance to the process, which, given the structure and composition of the constituent assembly, could ultimately have little real impact on improving the process or the resulting constitution; and, finally, highlights the lessons learned from the process.

Background

East Timor became the first independent state of the new millennium when its constitution came into force and independence was declared on May 20, 2002. It was a momentous occasion for the Maubere people, who have inhabited the eastern half of the island of Timor for more than five hundred years. During that long history, the Maubere had always lived under the yoke of one colonial power or another, with the exception of one brief period, beginning on November 28, 1975, when the popular resistance movement Frente Revolucionária de Timor-Leste Independente (Fretilin) declared East Timor's independence after four hundred years as a Portuguese colony.[1] Very shortly thereafter, on December 7, 1975, Indonesian troops invaded East Timor in a move that had received prior sanction from the United States.[2]

The invasion marked the beginning of East Timor's long and arduous struggle for independence, in which the East Timorese people endured enormous suffering and sacrifice. During the period of resistance to Indonesian rule, it is estimated that more than two hundred thousand East Timorese lost their lives. It was a struggle fought against horrendous odds, pitting a small and poor[3] population of seven hundred thousand, inhabiting a small half-island with few resources, against the Indonesian Goliath, with a population of 130 million and the advantage of being viewed as geopolitically important. International attention to the East Timorese cause during most of this period was either absent or marked by duplicity.[4] For most of the major powers in the world, East Timor is a remote island, and its remoteness was a factor in both the neglect that characterized Portuguese colonization and the abuse that characterized Indonesian occupation.

East Timor's first brief experience with independence was preceded by a United Nations General Assembly declaration in 1960 that the Timorese territories under Portuguese control were "non-self governing" within the meaning of Chapter XI of the United Nations Charter, creating a basis for East Timor's right to self-determination.[5] Until that point, Portugal had long considered East Timor to be one of its overseas provinces. However, in the aftermath of Portugal's overthrow of its authoritarian regime in April 1974, it adopted a constitutional law that set the course for the self-determination of its colonies and provided for a transitional administration in East Timor.[6]

In the meantime, the East Timorese had begun forming their own political parties. Three parties were formed; the first was the Uniao Democrática Timorense (UDT), which was closely aligned with Portugal and favored the Portuguese proposal for gradual transition toward independence.[7] Subsequently, the Associaçao Social Democrata Timorense (ASDT) was formed; the predecessor to Fretilin, it advocated the reconstruction of East Timorese society on the basis of indigenous customs and kinship alliances.[8] The third party formed was the Associaçao Popular Democrata Timorense (Apodeti), which advocated integration with Indonesia. After the ASDT became Fretilin in 1972, it undertook an ambitious program tackling such issues as health and illiteracy throughout the provinces. Its well-developed program and focus on indigenous identity earned it a wide popularity, along with its association with indigenous pride.

The months between Portugal's Carnation Revolution in April 1974 and the Indonesian invasion of East Timor in December 1975 were characterized by great political instabil-

ity. In the early part of the period, UDT and Fretilin formed a coalition, but it soon collapsed. By the end of the period, hostilities had escalated to civil war between Fretilin, which favored independence from Portugal, and a realigned coalition comprising UDT and Apodeti, which favored integration with Indonesia. On November 28, 1975, Fretilin declared East Timor's independence and the establishment of the new Democratic Republic of East Timor. Two days later, the UDT-Apodeti coalition declared independence and integration with Indonesia.[9] These same parties would later take part in the election of East Timor's constituent assembly in 2001.

Indonesia justified its 1975 invasion as an attempt to pacify the territory. However, it later annexed the territory as its twenty-seventh province in May 1976.[10] The United Nations Security Council's Resolution 384 in 1975 and Resolution 389 in 1976 called upon Indonesia to withdraw its forces immediately; from then through 1981, the General Assembly adopted resolutions annually reaffirming the right of the East Timorese people to self-determination. Though the illegal annexation was otherwise universally condemned by the international community, in 1978, Australia became the only country in the world to officially recognize it, a decision grounded in perceived geopolitical interests.

From the moment of its invasion to the end of its occupation in 1999, Indonesia maintained a heavy military presence. The military imposed brutal rule on the territory while Fretilin maintained an almost uninterrupted armed resistance.[11] Given the disparity of size and power between Fretilin and the Indonesian military, and the latter's persistence in its attempt to annihilate the former, the Fretilin fighters' bravery and tenacity were extraordinary. The resistance could not have been maintained, however, without the equally extraordinary protection of the populace, which often went to great lengths to conceal Fretilin members and members of its armed wing, called the Forças Armadas de Libertaçao Nacional de Timor Leste (FALANTIL).[12] The leader of these forces, Kay Rala Xanana Gusmão, became the beloved hero of the nationalist movement, and the power of his popularity would be significant in the unfolding of the constitutional process and the country's independence. Ultimately, he was elected as the country's first president.

The Indonesian military's abuses of the East Timorese population during the occupation have been well documented.[13] Indonesian values were imposed and East Timorese culture circumscribed. The military undertook an intensive program of forced migration and engaged in sexual slavery and forced sterilization. In its attempt to crush the armed resistance, Indonesian forces conducted saturation bombing and massacred entire villages.

During the long struggle for independence, a number of proindependence groups emerged.[14] In 1986, Gusmão formed an umbrella organization called the Conselho Nacional da Resistência Maubere (CNRM), which acted as a shadow government with him as its leader. By then, several leading figures of the various political parties were in exile, and they also joined this umbrella organization. In 1998, the organization changed its name to the Conselho Nacional da Resistência Timorense (CNRT).

The grave and systematic abuses of human rights committed during the Indonesian occupation went almost unnoticed in the international community until 1991, when, on November 12, Indonesian forces opened fire on an unarmed crowd that was peacefully demonstrating at the burial of a slain independence fighter. Two hundred East Timorese were slaughtered while foreign journalists filmed the incident.[15] That event

raised the international profile of the suffering of the East Timorese people.

In the following years, several of the independence movement's leading figures gained international attention. In 1992, Gusmão was captured and imprisoned by the Indonesians, who forced him to denounce his fight for independence in a televised appearance. Two others achieved notoriety in repeated appeals to the international community for support. One was Jose Ramos Horta, a vocal proponent of independence since 1974. The other was Bishop Carlos Filipo Ximenes Belo, a vocal opponent of the Indonesian occupation throughout the 1980s. In 1996, these two leaders were jointly awarded the Nobel Prize for Peace, bringing increased international attention to East Timorese pleas for independence. Nevertheless, Indonesian authorities under President Suharto remained intransigent before these appeals.

In 1998, the Asian economic crisis led to the fall of Suharto and the appointment of B.J. Habibie to replace him. Shortly after assuming office, Habibie announced that he was prepared to accord wide-ranging autonomy to East Timor. In the course of that year, under the auspices of Ambassador Jamsheed Marker of Pakistan, UN Secretary-General Kofi Annan's personal representative for East Timor, the United Nations led negotiations on the evolution toward East Timor's autonomy.[16] A tripartite agreement among Indonesia, Portugal, and the United Nations was reached on May 5, 1999. Under that watershed agreement, the United Nations would supervise a "popular consultation" in East Timor, in which the East Timorese people would be given the opportunity to accept or reject the status of autonomy within Indonesia. The agreement also provided that if the people rejected autonomy, then the United Nations would assume responsibility for the territory during a transition to independence.[17]

On June 11, 1999, the United Nations Mission in East Timor (UNAMET) was established by Security Council Resolution 1246, in accordance with the May 5 agreement. UNAMET immediately set up operations in East Timor to prepare for the referendum on autonomy, which, according to Resolution 1246, was to take place in August. However, even before UNAMET became operational, the security situation in the territory began deteriorating. Although Habibie had consulted with the Indonesian generals in connection with the May 5 agreement, factions of the military, as well as prointegrationist East Timorese militia, were violently opposed to independence.

In spite of the sporadic violence and increasing security problems, UNAMET proceeded with its planning and supervision of the referendum after Indonesian General Wiranto presided over the signing of an agreement to cease hostilities. Violence nevertheless continued up through the day of the referendum on August 30, 1999. On that day, 432,287 East Timorese—98.4 percent of the eligible voters—went to the polls amid the violence and intimidation and cast their votes;[18] 78.5 percent of them favored independence.

Prointegrationist militias supported by Indonesian forces immediately responded with a scorched-earth campaign of destruction. More than one thousand people were killed, vast portions of the population were forced to flee into the mountains and across the border into West Timor, and the UNAMET headquarters in Dili was forced to evacuate its personnel.[19] In the ensuing weeks, at least 80 percent of the country's infrastructure was pillaged and burned in a carefully orchestrated program of devastation.

In early September 1999, United States president Bill Clinton severed military ties with Indonesia and insisted that President Habibie invite international intervention. In response to a mounting wave of international pressure, Habibie agreed, and on September 15, the United Nations Security Council adopted Resolution 1264, establishing a multinational force to quell the destruction in East Timor. The International Forces in East Timor (INTERFET), acting under the direction of Australian Major General Peter Cosgrove, commenced operations on September 20. By the end of October, INTERFET had established security and was acting as a de facto administration in the territory. It remained in East Timor through February, when it transferred its authority to peacekeeping forces under the United Nations Transitional Authority in East Timor (UNTAET), established by Security Council Resolution 1272, adopted on October 25.

Under its mandate, the broadest in the history of the United Nations, UNTAET acted as the de jure transitional government of the territory, with executive, legislative, and judicial authority. Because one of the key components of the UNTAET mandate was to "consult and cooperate closely with the East Timorese people,"[20] one of its first steps was to consult the political leadership of the country under the umbrella of the CNRT. Gusmão took up leadership of the CNRT after his release from prison in Indonesia and return to East Timor in October 1999.[21]

UNTAET did not have a plan for devolving power to the East Timorese. Instead, the UN transitional administrator, Sergio Vieira de Mello, developed ad hoc approaches to devolution as he implemented and interpreted UNTAET's mandate. Initially, UNTAET acted as a caretaker government and did not bring East Timorese into the transitional administration to share governing authority. Rather, the transitional administrator governed the territory with the policy advice of a fifteen-member National Consultative Council (NCC), composed of both East Timorese, largely from the CNRT, and foreign UN mission staff. The transitional administrator chose not to promulgate a regulation or endorse a policy unless it had been agreed upon by the NCC, giving this body practical veto power for its key members, including Gusmão.

Responding to the need to further devolve power, as well as to popular criticism of the slow pace of reconstruction, about seven months into the mission the transitional administrator dissolved the NCC and established a thirty-six-member National Council (NC) composed solely of East Timorese. The NC, with Gusmão as its speaker, was a quasi-legislature, with the power to initiate, recommend, and amend transitional regulations as well as call cabinet members to answer questions about their respective policies and programs.[22] The transitional administrator created additional structures in which East Timorese leaders shared power with UN personnel, including an eight-member (half East Timorese) Cabinet of the Transitional Government[23] and a transitional administration responsible for public administration. Some functions remained directly under UNTAET's control, however, including the peacekeeping force, foreign affairs, and the implementation of the transitional process, in particular the elections and constitution making.

After national elections for a constituent assembly in August 2001, the transitional administrator retained executive authority but delegated responsibility for day-to-day governance to the transitional administration, now under the control of a fully East Timorese cabinet. Mari Alkatiri, a Fretilin member who had returned from exile in Mozambique, was chosen as prime minister.

UNTAET's final tasks were to organize the election of the country's first president and support the elaboration of the country's independence constitution. That constitution was adopted on March 22, 2002, and took effect on May 20 of that year. On that date, chosen to coincide with the founding of Fretilin's predecessor, UNTAET brought its mission to a close and fully transferred authority to the newly created state.

Structure of the Constitution-Making Process

Debates on the Legal Framework

In establishing UNTAET, Security Council Resolution 1272 did not specify how the shift from a UN transitional administration to an independent East Timor would take place. Unlike the peace processes in Cambodia or Afghanistan (see Chapters 8 and 20), there was no peace agreement specifying that a constitution would be a component of the state-building effort. In April 2000, de Mello briefed the Security Council and underscored that UNTAET was formulating a detailed strategic plan, including benchmarks, that would lead to the phasing out of UNTAET, devolution of power to East Timorese authorities, and establishment of an independent East Timor. One of the key benchmarks in this plan was the drafting of an independence constitution.[24]

CNRT's diverse membership met several times, in part to discuss how East Timor's hoped-for independence constitution would be created. In August 1998, CNRT members gathered to develop a set of policies for the development of the country in every sector, including constitutional, health, education, judicial, etc. Two more conferences were held in April 1999 in Melbourne and May 2000 in Tibar, East Timor. CNRT also held a National Congress in August 2000 to review its structure and vote on policy recommendations that had emerged from the conferences. Throughout these policy-planning meetings, the preferred model for drafting East Timor's independence constitution was a constitutional convention.

Over three hundred participants gathered at the CNRT conference in Melbourne, held April 5 to April 9, 1999. They recommended that a special convention be established, comprised of all social and political groups; this convention, in turn, should appoint a commission of legal professionals to assist with the drafting process. The CNRT participants at the Melbourne conference did not foresee that Indonesian armed forces and East Timorese militia would launch a scorched-earth campaign after the results of the 1999 referendum were announced. They assumed that existing structures would be in place when they began the difficult task of reconstructing East Timor. When it became clear, following the postreferendum violence and destruction, that reconstruction had to begin from nearly the ground up, the Melbourne conference recommendations needed to be reviewed in light of the new circumstances. Nearly three hundred people again gathered for the meeting in Tibar, East Timor, from May 29 to June 2, 2000, under the auspices of the CNRT to attend a conference entitled "Reconstructing East Timor: Analysis of the Past and Perspectives for the Future."

The participants restated the strategic plan to draft a constitution agreed upon in Melbourne but added that a constitutional working committee should be formed to draft the constitution, and that this committee should establish a mechanism to ensure full public consultation and participation in the process.[25] The CNRT and civil society stressed the importance of public participation in the making of the constitution, regardless of the model of constitution making chosen.

However, at the Tibar meeting, the Political, Constitutional, and Electoral Affairs Department of UNTAET (Political Affairs Department) announced the following model of constitution making, which did not provide for an independent commission or stress the role of public participation:

The defining events of the political transition are the adoption of a constitution and the holding of free elections. Elections will choose a Constituent Assembly which in turn will write, debate and adopt a constitution. Following its adoption, the Constituent Assembly will become the Parliament (or legislative assembly) of the new country.[26]

This was markedly different from the model proposed by CNRT. In August 2000, participants from every district in East Timor attended the CNRT National Congress and there agreed that a constitutional commission, in consultation with the East Timorese people, would first draft the independence constitution. The draft constitution would then be submitted to an elected constituent assembly for approval and adoption. The constituent assembly would also be tasked with conducting further consultations and making any necessary amendments to the draft. These recommendations were adopted by a vote of 290 delegates in favor, 8 against, and 42 abstaining.

At the same congress, the transitional administrator addressed the CNRT delegates and suggested two different options for adopting the constitution. The first model he presented was to select a representative constitutional commission to prepare a draft constitution, with the possibility of a referendum on the draft being held at the same time as the national elections for the members of the constituent assembly. If the draft constitution were approved in the referendum, a provisional government would be formed on the basis of the system of government outlined in the approved draft. The elected constituent assembly would then serve as the interim legislature until preparation and adoption of the final constitution.

The second alternative proposed was that offered by the Political Affairs Department of UNTAET a few months earlier at the Tibar conference: to elect an assembly that would both draft and adopt a constitution. The transitional administrator stressed the need for widespread participation in the drafting of the constitution regardless of the model chosen, noting that "[t]he constitution will stand the test of time if it has been drafted in a participatory manner and has emerged from the real lives and aspirations of people."[27]

Approximately one month after UNTAET officials presented constitution-making options to the CNRT National Congress, the transitional administrator briefed the Security Council on September 29, 2000, describing the political transition process that would take place in East Timor. He outlined the same constitution-making approach that the director of the Political Affairs Department, Peter Galbraith, had presented at the earlier Tibar conference. Transitional administrator de Mello stated that

> [t]he major elements of political transition are clear. As things currently stand, our plan is to hold national elections in the second half of next year with a view to establishing a Constituent Assembly. This Assembly will be tasked with drafting the Constitution, choosing the members of the new transitional government and serving as an interim legislature. Upon completion of the Constitution, the Assembly would become the new National Assembly of an independent East Timor.[28]

No mention was made of a representative commission or of public consultations.

In November 2000, Gusmão, as president of CNRT, provided the transitional administrator with a political calendar outlining suggested steps towards independence. The broad framework followed the model that the transitional administrator had discussed with the Security Council at the end of September.

In addition to serving as the president of CNRT, Gusmão was also the presiding speaker of the National Council and the presiding member of its Standing Committee on Political Affairs (Standing Committee),

tasked with examining the electoral and constitutional processes for East Timor. On December 12, 2000, he submitted the political transition calendar to the National Council. It was entitled "Broad Timeline for the Process Leading to East Timor's Declaration of Independence." The calendar proposed that the constitution should be debated, drafted, and adopted in a period of ninety days. After a few hours of debate, the National Council determined that it did not have enough information to decide the matter and requested that the Standing Committee hold hearings and provide the council with a set of recommendations on the subject.

On December 23, in his role as presiding member of the Standing Committee, Gusmão drafted a letter to representatives of political parties, civil society, the church, and academia; he attached a copy of CNRT's political transition calendar and requested comments on the plan. Gusmão highlighted the questions that for him remained outstanding, such as how many representatives the constituent assembly should have and the appropriate process to elect its members. It did not seek alternative views on the approach to constitution making.

From January 18 to January 23, 2001, the Standing Committee invited some of those who had received the letter to comment on the calendar at public hearings. Throughout the five-day period, the committee heard or received written testimonies from approximately twenty-six East Timorese, including representatives of political parties, civil-society organizations, the Catholic Church, and the University of East Timor, as well as two CNRT members, an UNTAET cabinet minister, and a District Advisory Council member from Liquica.

During the hearings, most of those who testified preferred that an unelected body, such as a constitutional convention or commission, consult with the population and draft the constitution, in keeping with the earlier CNRT positions. Only five of the political parties represented agreed that an elected body, such as a constituent assembly, should draft the constitution. However, most also preferred that a constituent assembly should adopt the draft constitution. Many underscored that this two-stage process would allow for broad participation from diverse sectors of society, including technical experts. Some of those testifying were familiar with constitution-making processes that had taken place in Africa, such as the South Africa process, which had prioritized widespread public participation in the preparation of the constitution.

Aderito Soares, speaking on behalf of the Jurists Association and as a CNRT member, expressed grave concern about the proposed political transition process. He underscored that the CNRT National Congress had agreed to a constitutional convention that would consult widely with the public. He also expressed concern about the proposed structure and the short time given to complete the process. Joaquim Fonseca of Yayasan Hak, a human rights group, also noted that the process under discussion was inconsistent with the consensus reached at the National Congress. The NGO Forum, an umbrella group for non-governmental organizations (NGOs) in East Timor, raised the same issue and asked what had happened to the National Congress's recommendations.

In his role as a cabinet member, the director of UNTAET's Department of Political Affairs, Peter Galbraith, also gave his views about the process. Similar to his speech in May 2000 at the Tibar conference, he again explained that "the final phase of the Political Transition begins with the election of a constituent assembly with a mandate to prepare the Constitution for an independent East Timor." However, he also described his views about why it was important that an elected body draft the constitution. He stated that creating a constitution involves

making hundreds of decisions, and those decisions should not be made by appointed officials, but by elected representatives. He pointed out that a constituent assembly would have power to decide how it would draft the constitution, what type of constitution it would be, how it would be ratified, and how much debate should be involved in its adoption. This opinion did not reflect the history of constitution making, whereby unelected although representative bodies had often prepared or debated the constitution, as in constitutional conferences in West Africa or the two-stage processes that began with a constitutional commission preparing the draft prior to submitting to an elected body. Moreover, constitution-making bodies were often mandated to ensure widespread public participation in the process, including providing comments and suggestions on drafts of the constitution.

The director of political affairs' position also failed to account for the dominance of the Fretilin party, which was virtually assured of a landslide victory in the elections. This was a key factor in the views expressed by those favoring a more participatory and representative model of constitution making, which would have more reflected the trends and international standards of constitution making at the time. Civil society as well as other leaders in Timorese society wanted the process to be an opportunity for consensus building by allowing all of the various political voices in East Timor to be heard. They saw this as preferable to a process that would, in effect, allow one political group to decide all of the key constitutional issues for the entire country, which could lead to an illegitimate constitution that was not owned by all citizens.

After the hearings, the Standing Committee of the National Council reported back to the council and made a series of recommendations for the electoral law; their recommendations only slightly revised the political transition calendar. Few of the suggestions made by the East Timorese who testified before the Standing Committee were incorporated, and the suggestion by most—that an unelected body draft the constitution and that sufficient time be allocated for the process—was not among them.

Although the Standing Committee had held public hearings on how the process should be structured, ultimately it was a few political elites and key UN officials who decided that an elected body should not only debate and adopt the constitution but also draft the constitution in a period of ninety days. On March 16, 2001, the National Council adopted UNTAET Regulation 2001/2 on the Election of the Constituent Assembly.[29]

The Legal Framework

Regulation 2001/2 called for the election of an eighty-eight-member constituent assembly, seventy-five members of which would be nationally elected on the basis of proportional representation and thirteen of which would be elected on a first-past-the-post basis in each of East Timor's thirteen districts. The regulation provided that the constituent assembly should adopt the draft constitution within ninety days from its first sitting by an affirmative vote of at least sixty of its eighty-eight members.

Regulation 2001/2 also gave the assembly the option of choosing to transform itself into the nation's first parliament. That an assembly dominated by Fretilin—a foregone conclusion—would choose to do so was certain. This provision incorporated an inherent conflict of interest because the assembly would be deciding the parameters of its future powers.

The ninety-day time frame was also certain to exclude widespread public consultations on the draft constitution or a process of careful deliberations within the assembly itself. The preparation of a constitutional

process that educates the public on the role of a constitution and constitutional issues as well as carefully consults the public on constitutional issues requires time.

Even though the time frame was short, Regulation 2001/2 was skeletal; it did not contain constitutional principles, rules of procedure, or guidance on a work plan or require public participation in the process. This led to confusion throughout the process, as the East Timorese rushed to prepare a draft yet had little or no experience regarding how to go about doing so.

The Deliberations in the Assembly: Single-Party Domination

On September 15, 2001, Vieira de Mello swore in East Timor's first constituent assembly. The members faced a daunting task. Although time was very limited, the assembly spent three weeks drafting and debating the internal rules of procedure. In the end, it roughly adopted the rules of procedure of the Portuguese Assembly, but these were ill-suited to a body that should have been attempting to create a constitution by consensus rather than majority rule.

The rules established a forty-two-member systemization and harmonization committee (SHC) to agree upon the structure of the constitution, establish thematic committees, and integrate the individual articles developed and approved by the committees into the body of the constitution. Although Asia Foundation consultants who were providing technical advice suggested that the assembly take time to prepare a constitutional agenda and agree upon constitutional principles to guide the process, this suggestion was sidestepped in the rush to prepare a draft. The SHC created four thematic committees. Committee I focused on fundamental rights, freedoms, and duties, as well as national defense and security; Committee II focused on the organization of the state and political power; Committee III focused on economic, social, and financial organization; and Committee IV focused on fundamental principles, control of constitutionality, amendment of the constitution, and final and transitional provisions.

The president of the assembly, Francisco Guterres ("Lú-Olo"), told the members that they should agree upon draft provisions for their respective subject areas by referring to the few drafts of the constitution submitted by political parties. The Fretilin draft constitution had been prepared in 1998, well in advance of independence. It was largely inspired by the constitutions of Portugal and Mozambique.[30] The committees were also to call experts to testify on their specific subject matter at public hearings. The committees were initially given only ten days to review the parties' draft constitutions, hold public hearings, and provide their recommendations to the SHC.

The thematic committees began meeting on October 17 and immediately began preparations for public hearings. They invited representatives of civil-society groups, international organizations, UNTAET, the East Timor Public Administration (ETPA), and the Church to prepare submissions and scheduled their appearances. In addition, the Asia Foundation provided constitutional experts to each of the committees.

All of the Asia Foundation experts noted that though many groups provided useful submissions, the committees rarely referred to them in their deliberations. Instead, the committees focused on reviewing the Fretilin draft, and by taking that draft as their point of departure, the committees failed to develop the constitution from the ground up, examining and discussing which options would be most suitable for East Timor. Also, because the focus was on the Fretilin draft rather than an agreed set of principles and goals for the nation, the discussions occasionally focused on issues that had no relevance to East Timor.

By November 30, 2001, the SHC had harmonized the recommendations submitted by the thematic committees and the plenary had agreed upon a draft constitution on which to debate. Consequently, even though the assembly had begun deliberating on the day it was sworn in, when the ninety-day period set for adopting the constitution expired on December 15, 2001, it still had over one thousand pending votes on proposed constitutional provisions. As a result, the process was extended from December 15, 2001, to March 22, 2002.

Throughout the process, the assembly's plenary sessions and thematic committee hearings were made accessible to the public. However, the general public had little awareness of the contents of the draft. The debates in the assembly were broadcast live over the radio, but they were often difficult to follow and it was not always easy to determine what had been concluded.

For those members of the public attending the sessions, simultaneous translation was provided in English, Tetum, Portuguese, and Bahasa. Initially, it was difficult for members of the media to obtain information about developments and the agenda. In response to requests, the secretariat assisted the assembly in developing daily press briefings and posted the agenda at the entrance to the assembly. These were positive steps in making the process more accessible and open. Indeed, as the process evolved, the leaders in the assembly began to be more and more open about sharing their early drafts with the public and allowing the public to be present in nearly all its discussions and deliberations. Indeed, it was rare that a session would be closed; this only occurred if small groups were meeting to try to reach consensus on sticking points.

On February 9, 2002, the assembly approved the first draft of the constitution. Sixty-five members of the assembly voted to approve the draft, thirteen members abstained, and ten members were absent. In the end, that document very closely resembled the original Fretilin draft. Due to the clamor for effective popular consultation, members of the assembly then engaged in one week of popular consultation during February, reviewing the recently approved draft with the population. Subsequently, the assembly made minor changes to the February 9 draft, and on March 22, 2002, the assembly adopted the new constitution by a vote of seventy-two members in favor and fourteen against, with one abstention and one absence due to illness.[31]

By its own terms, the constitution would take effect and East Timor would achieve its independence on May 20, 2002.[32] The assembly chose that date because it marked the twenty-eighth anniversary of the founding of ASDT, the predecessor of the Fretilin party.[33]

Democratic Representation

In the early part of 2001, the NC organized consultations to determine the structure of the constitution-making process. The results of the consultations were summarized in a document entitled "The Report on the Political Transitional Calendar compiled by the Standing Committee of Political Affairs of the National Council," referred to as the PAC report. Most all of the PAC recommendations relating to the election of the constituent assembly were incorporated into UNTAET Regulation 2001/2. That regulation set out the basic electoral rules, which included a determination of the electoral system; the issue had been discussed during the consultations that formed the basis of the PAC report. Three options were considered: a majority/plurality option, a proportional list option, and a hybrid of the two. Some advantages of each of the systems were considered. The majority/plurality option was viewed as offering the advantage of the personalization of the candidates and assuring their ac-

countability before the electorate. One disadvantage was that it would likely lead to a two-party system, which would discourage plurality. The proportional system offered the advantage of placing all voters on an equal footing and encouraging plurality. A disadvantage was the lack of accountability to constituencies. Though a preference for the proportional system was expressed because it was the system used in the continental tradition with which the East Timorese were most familiar, in the end, the regulation put in place a hybrid system.

For the national elections, parties were allowed to submit lists of up to seventy-five names; these candidates were to be elected according to a somewhat complex formula set out in Section 37.1 of Regulation 2001/2. Independent candidates, who were allowed to run for both national- and district-level seats, had to gather five hundred signatures for registration on the national level and one hundred signatures for registration for the district elections. In calculating election results at the national level, independent candidates were to be treated as belonging to a political party that only entered a single candidate.

One key recommendation in the PAC report that was not incorporated into UNTAET Regulation 2001/2 was that 30 percent of the seats in the constituent assembly should be reserved for women. The issue proved to be hotly contested; UNTAET's director of political affairs and the chief electoral officer were strongly opposed to the quota and lobbied against it; Gusmão, however, expressed strong support for it. In the end, the proposal failed to garner enough support in the NC and was rejected.[34]

In addition to determining the nature of the electoral system and establishing rules for party registration, Regulation 2001/2 set August 30, 2001, as the date for the election and provided for the creation of an independent electoral commission, composed of three international electoral experts and two

East Timorese. The electoral commission was given broad authority over the conduct of the election, including the power to implement the rules established under Regulation 2001/2, resolve disputes arising under them, and establish rules of its own. Among the rules established by the electoral commission was that requiring parties to confine their campaigning to the period between July 15 and August 28, 2001. Some saw the rule as offering too little opportunity for new parties to develop and promote their programs. This failing was seen in turn as reinforcing Fretilin's advantage, which everyone involved in the process acknowledged as significant.

The election was held on August 30, 2001, with sixteen political parties having registered.[35] These parties represented a variety of interests, such as Christian values, rejection of communism, protection of landowners, economic liberalism, protection of local custom and tradition, alignment with Portugal, alignment with Indonesia, securing of reparations from Portugal, and promotion of youth and labor. Several of the parties were new, appearing for the first time in East Timorese politics specifically to compete in this election.

By June 22, 2001, near the cut-off date for voter registration, 775,602 voters had registered, and on August 30, 2001, 91 percent of the eligible voters cast ballots.[36] In accordance with the election results, twelve political parties and one independent member gained seats in the assembly. Fretilin won fifty-five seats. The remaining seats were divided among the others, with no other party gaining more than seven seats. The leaders of the constituent assembly included Francisco Guterres from Fretilin as president, Arlindo Francisco Marçal from PDC as a vice president, and Francisco Xavier do Amaral from ASDT[37] as another vice president.

Clearly, UNTAET Regulation 2001/2 provided for democratic representation in the constitution-making process. However, this seemingly positive aspect of the process must be assessed as part of the process as a whole. The regulation established a system whereby only elected officials would be allowed to take part in the constitutional drafting process. In a post-conflict context, this type of system often advantages political elites, who are better prepared to participate in an election. Determining who drafts the constitution through an election may not lead to a representative body in all cases that ensures that all voices of the people are heard, in particular those of women or rural poor.

Because it was a foregone conclusion that Fretilin would win any election by a significant margin, structuring the process as the regulation did precluded the formation of a diverse body, without perhaps strong political ties, to consult with the public about what should be included in a draft constitution and share this with an elected body. To avoid a constitution-making process representing merely the division of spoils by elites, an emerging trend in constitution making is to have a two-phase approach to the process: the formation of an appointed, broadly representative constitutional commission to develop a draft constitutional text and adoption of a final constitution by an elected body or a body that is both selected and elected to ensure the diversity of the nation is represented.

An independent commission or technical drafting body has often been used to prepare a draft constitution because it tends to be more distanced from political agendas and may allow for greater diversity of views, improved opportunities for consensus building, input of experts, and greater public participation. Nonetheless, establishing an effective constitutional commission has been very challenging in recent constitution-making processes. In processes directed by a constitutional commission, the goal is to choose an independent and diverse group that is small enough to manage the tasks of drafting the constitution efficiently and assuring public buy-in of the process. To achieve such ends, a commission often includes professionals, youth, women, the disabled, veterans, minorities, and other relevant groups in society who often may not have access to the formal political party system.

This observation obviously raises the question of how the commission should be selected. This is a difficult question because the answer is so closely related to the desired end, which is to create a commission that assures buy-in by the population and reflects as broad a range of political, ethnic, religious, and other groupings as possible. In most recent cases, the protagonists of the process have agreed on the general nature of the desired composition and, in some cases, have achieved it through a selection process in accordance with these principles. This, however, does not mean that the same result cannot be achieved through a carefully designed electoral process. The point here is that the emphasis is not on the mode of the selection or election, but on the desired composition and having a flexible mode of selection or election to best achieve that result. In many post-conflict contexts, where nascent political parties do not have a strong representational basis, democratically elected representation may not lead to representation of the aspirations of the people as well as the political elite.

In East Timor, the constitution-making process did not lead to a broadly based representative body either to consult with the public or prepare the constitution. With fifty-five of the eighty-eight seats in the assembly, Fretilin was just short of the two-thirds majority required under Regulation 2001/2 to adopt the new constitution, but with its close links to a few small parties, it effectively controlled the necessary votes. This meant that Fretilin did not need to build consensus or compromise for the constitution to be adopted. This factor contributed to the resulting institutional arrangements set out in the final constitution, including a weak pres-

idency and a dominant parliament—hardly the result that the population had sought during the abortive period of popular consultation (described in the next section).

In addition, the process failed to create the political space for minority voices to be heard. This state of affairs set the stage for the president, who enjoyed wide support among the population, to exercise powers beyond the narrow strictures of the constitution; it also planted seeds for future conflict. This scenario did not bode well for the nation-building process or the constitution's sustainability.

Public Participation

Debates on the Framework for Public Participation

Of all the issues that were debated in early 2001, the two most controversial were the role of public participation in constitution making and the time frame of the process. During the consultations that formed the basis of the PAC report, those testifying widely agreed that an independent constitutional commission should conduct a program of civic education and public consultation, and that the views expressed during such a process should be integrated into the draft submitted for debate and ratification by the constituent assembly. Catholic bishops advocated the adoption of an interim constitution, to be followed by the establishment of a constitutional commission that would prepare the final constitution for adoption by an elected body.[38] These views coincided with those put forward in earlier policy recommendations by CNRT.

UNTAET Regulation 2001/2 did not incorporate the above views, but a young East Timorese lawyer who represented Yayasan Hak, East Timor's leading human rights NGO, attempted to remedy the situation. He presented a draft regulation to the National Council proposing the appointment of an independent constitutional commission. It would be composed of twenty-six East Timorese who had no official affiliation with the Transitional Administration of East Timor (ETTA) or with UNTAET, nor were they active members of any political party or group. The commission would be selected from diverse sectors of the society, including "representatives of the academic institutions, youth groups, representatives of religious denominations, a representative of the National Council, and the NGO forum." Two commissioners—one man and one woman—would head an office in each of the country's thirteen districts. Each office would be responsible for conducting consultations in their district. The commission would be assisted by a national planning team composed of nationals and foreign experts, who would coordinate the work of the commission. They would have expertise in "constitutional processes, including experience in the consultation and drafting of a recent constitution, political science, anthropology, education, particularly experience in mass education in a developing country, economics, legal drafting, human rights law, and gender."

Section 3.2 of the proposed regulation provided the following:

The work of the Commission will be divided into the following successive phases:

(a) *Public Information Phase*, which will include mass dissemination of information on the Nature of a Constitution and the decisions needed to be taken for its adoption;

(b) *Debating Phase*, during which members of the public will be assisted in discussing the key issues under the Constitution through debates, workshops or group discussions from the national to the community level;

(c) *Consultation Phase*, during which members of the public will be able to

formally submit their views at public hearings held at the Sub-Districts level;

(d) *Reporting Phase*, during which members of the Commission compile the views expressed during the Consultation process and draw recommendations for submission to the constituent assembly;

(e) *Drafting Phase*, during which members of the Commission assist the constituent assembly with the drafting of the Constitution.[39]

The commission's work was to be carried out over twelve months, nine of which would be spent on the first three phases with three months devoted to the last two.

Though the proposal received wide support from civil society, it proved to be one of the most contentious events in the development of the constitution-making process. Notably, the proposed regulation was inconsistent with Regulation 2001/2, which had already been adopted. The UNTAET Political Affairs Department and Fretilin opposed it on the grounds that it required an expanded time frame to draft the constitution, it was overly complex and cumbersome, and it provided that an unelected commission would draft the constitution.

Had the proposed regulation been adopted, it may have been viewed by the UN as requiring the extension of the UNTAET mandate—a difficult proposition given that some member states in the Security Council were already questioning the enormous expense entailed in the United Nations' administration of a country so small.[40] The resource issue should not have been a stumbling block, however, as the Security Council had already agreed to a UN support mission after the conclusion of UNTAET's mandate. Nevertheless, it was clear that for UNTAET, early adoption of a new constitution would be a benchmark of success for the mission, which needed to illustrate results to justify its huge costs.

The proposal was the subject of heated debate in the NC. Gusmão supported the proposal, as did the NGO community. This was a significant reversal, given that Gusmão had proposed the political calendar that called for a ninety-day time frame for the constitution-making process. Aderito Jesus de Soares, who was then a representative of the East Timor Jurists Association (he would later chair the systemization and harmonization committee of the constituent assembly), appeared before the NC and pleaded for an extended time frame for consultation. He stated: "Isn't this a process for us to teach the people of the importance of the constitution for the country?"[41] When one Fretilin member of the NC characterized the proposal as political maneuvering, an angry exchange ensued, in which the ever-deepening tensions between Gusmão and the Fretilin party were apparent. The author of the proposed regulation defended his submission, arguing that democracy entails more than elections, and explained that he had submitted the proposal to empower people, not parties.[42]

During the debates over the issue, the NGO Forum submitted a letter to the Security Council stating its case. Endorsed by twenty-eight NGOs, the letter stated:

A Constitution is a complex document embodying fundamental choices about the type of country an independent East Timor will be. This Constitution has to be a living document, which reflects how the East Timorese as a people see themselves, relate to each other, and finally, after many centuries, govern themselves.

So, how are the East Timorese people to make those fundamental decisions? By ensuring that a legitimate constitutional process established. [sic]

To achieve this legitimacy, we need to establish a process that will provide the East Timorese people with a real opportunity to have their views on the key issues reflected in the draft-

ing of the Constitution. This process will need to balance the urgency of East Timor becoming an independent country with the essential need for the Constitution to be a document reflecting the aspirations of the East Timorese people.

For this to happen, the East Timorese people have to be provided with the information on the choices that have to be made, information on what a Constitution is, information on the options available to them on the fundamental issues. They will then need time to consider and debate so that they are able to form opinions, time to hold discussions in order to seek consensus where opinions are divided, and finally time to officially record their views. None of this can happen in three months.

The proposed timeframe being pushed by UNTAET and some East Timorese leaders would only allow consultation on the constitutional process to take place over a period of approximately three months due to the rush to hold the election on the 30th of August. This is forgetting that the very purpose of the election is to establish a Constituent Assembly that will draft the Constitution. The Constituent Assembly will not be in a position to carry out any further consultation on the Constitution with the East Timorese people. It will be under enormous pressure to deliver the document that will declare the independence of East Timor. The Constituent Assembly will have 90 days within which to prepare and adopt the Constitution.

All the legitimate constitutional processes that have taken place in recent years were carried out over a period of three to four years. The consultation process for the South African Constitution lasted over three years. A three-month process would rob the East Timorese of their right to contribute to the future of their country and it will alienate them from the very document that should voice their aspirations.[43]

Although the pleas of civil society were compelling, the proposed regulation was ultimately defeated. Gusmão resigned as NC president because Fretilin refused to accept the regulation, which would have ensured that the process incorporate public consultation. He complained to UNTAET that the NC no longer reflected the aspirations of the people.

Civic Education and Consultation Prior to the Constituent Assembly

The debate made it clear that there was demand for popular consultation, and UNTAET felt constrained to respond. It soon issued Directive 2001/13, which established thirteen constitutional commissions to engage in civic education and conduct popular consultations in East Timor's thirteen districts.[44] The key differences between this approach and that advocated by civil-society representatives and others was that these commissions did not have a mandate to prepare a draft of the constitution and they would receive heavy guidance from UNTAET. The UNTAET directive also did not address the concerns of civil society and Gusmão (after he reversed his position) that there be adequate time to first educate the people on constitutional issues before consulting them. In addition, one of the important elements of a consultation process is that those preparing the draft of the constitution are able to travel throughout the country and hear the voices and concerns directly from citizens. This process has been very transformative for the constitutional drafters and helps set a precedent for law makers consulting the people.

Nonetheless, the transitional administrator, Sergio Vieira de Mello, announced the process, stating:

> A national civic education framework has been developed in close consultation with major civil society groups. . . . This framework provides for widespread civic education through training of trainers, mass information, and multiple civil society initiatives, including village-level discussion and other interactive activities. The main themes—the basic principles of a stable democracy, constitutional issues, and voter education—will provide the foundation for an informed public engagement in the process.[45]

UNTAET appointed seventy-seven commissioners under the directive. The commissions' work was undertaken between June 18 and July 14, 2001, with the active support of the Political Affairs Department.[46] Groups of five commissioners conducted consultations in the districts and groups of three held sessions in the subdistricts. The commissions held 205 open hearings throughout the country, which 38,000 people attended.[47] The populace responded enthusiastically; a single hearing would sometimes bring as many as 1,000 people. At each hearing, the commissioners presented the public with basic information on a number of constitutional issues, such as systems of government, official languages, electoral systems, national symbols (the flag and anthem), defense and security, the economy, the legal system, nationality, religion, health, the environment, human rights, education, customary law, gender, and amendment of the constitution. Sometimes information on all of these topics would be conveyed in a single day. The civic education and popular consultation were conflated in a single process that sometimes occurred in a single day. After a presentation on the issues, the commissioners would consult those present about their views on these subjects.

This consultation process was not preceded by a separate, well-developed program of civic education designed to ensure the public's understanding of the role of a constitution, how the constitution would be prepared, and the role of the public. Given that so few attending understood the above, they largely spoke about issues that affected their daily lives.

In accordance with the directive's terms, a rapporteur recorded the results of the sessions, which later formed the basis of thirteen reports, one for each district. No formal procedure or questionnaire was used to ensure an accurate recording of the views; the public had to rely solely on the rapporteur for this purpose. This was problematic because the rapporteurs had received minimal training to undertake such an important task.

In the resulting reports, it was recorded that a clear majority of the participants in the consultations had expressed a preference for either a presidential or a semipresidential system of government. Those participants wanted a strong president who would act as commander in chief of the armed forces and direct the country's foreign policy. It was clear that they envisaged Gusmão in this role. They also expressed a preference for a proportional electoral system, although some opted for a mixed proportional/majority system. Participants demonstrated a good understanding of human rights norms and strongly advocated their incorporation into the constitution. They also insisted that amending the constitution should require some form of popular consultation, such as a referendum.

As noted, the responses related very much to the concerns of the everyday lives of the people. Participants were very concerned about preserving customary cultural traditions, especially those relating to marriage and family. They wanted to preserve and reform their dowry practices and sought to abolish polygamy. They wanted to regulate gambling and cock fighting. They wanted the government's assistance in providing housing, clean water, health facilities, education, and farm equipment. They thought that the constitution should protect people's rights with respect to land and they wanted measures to protect against deforestation. They also wanted measures to prevent foreign ownership of the country's natural resources, mentioning gas and oil in particular. Finally, they thought the constitution should require reparations from Portugal and Indonesia for the destruction and abuse that occurred during their respective periods of colonization and occupation.

While UNTAET engaged in its consultation process, civil society held its own independent consultations with the public as well. The human rights community as well as Feto Timor Loro Sae Timorese Women's Network (Women's Network) conducted consultations and provided reports, and in the case of the Women's Network, it provided a charter for the constituent assembly to consider.

Critics of the UNTAET consultation process expressed the view that the process was ineffective, in part, because it 1) attempted to conduct civic education and popular consultation at the same time and too quickly (during a one-month period), 2) was not conducted by an independent commission or elected assembly of Timorese that was tasked with preparing a draft constitution and therefore lacked national ownership, credibility, and the important purpose of connecting the drafters to the people, 3) was viewed as foreign influenced, and 4) did not have a well prepared and cohesive system for gathering, collating, and analyzing the views of the public.

In the end, it was clear that the process UNTAET designed in response to the demand for popular consultation was a far cry from the civil-society proposal offered during the debates, which was based on participatory processes that had already occurred in places they had learned about, such as South Africa, Thailand, and Eritrea.

Unlike these processes whereby the constitutional drafters had committed to an extensive process of public participation and ownership by the people of their new constitution, neither Fretilin nor the United Nations had prioritized a participatory constitution-making exercise. Only one month was devoted to civic education and popular consultation, and the two activities were conflated.

De Mello presented the thirteen reports to the constituent assembly on its opening day.[48] Section 2.4 of UNTAET Regulation 2001/2 provided that the "Constituent Assembly should give due consideration to any duly constituted Constitutional Commission or Commissions." Nonetheless, the constituent assembly, as a whole, ignored the reports, which were viewed as an UNTAET product. Constituent assembly members stated publicly during the discussions in the assembly that they had never opened the report for this reason.[49] However, the independent reports from the human rights community were read by some of the members.

When the four political parties submitted draft constitutions to the assembly's systemization and harmonization committee at the beginning of the process, it was clear that they, too, had ignored the results of UNTAET's popular consultation.[50]

Civil Society Pressure for the Constituent Assembly to Consult with the Public

Throughout the assembly's mandate, its members rarely traveled to the districts to inform the public about what was happening, even though some were selected to represent districts. The U.S.-based National Democratic Institute for International Affairs (NDI), through its Civic Forum Program, established groups in each district that discussed the draft constitution and repeatedly attempted to set up meetings with assembly members to have them brief their constituencies. Members were rarely responsive to these requests. In part, the fast pace of the process allowed them little time to travel and meet with the people. Also, because the legal framework for the constitution-making process did not stress consultations with the public as an important element of creating the new constitution, they were not a priority for many assembly members. Some members expressed the view that because they knew the views of their constituencies, there was no need for popular consultation. They felt that public participation was sufficiently assured through the electoral process.

Nevertheless, pressure developed for the constituent assembly to share a draft constitution with the public and engage in a consultation process of its own. The Asia Foundation supported an assembly monitoring group called Assembly Watch, which, together with other members of civil society, journalists, and some assembly members, pressed the president of the assembly to be publicly forthcoming with the draft. After much discussion within the assembly about whether members should gather and debate public comments to use as the basis for further revisions and amendments, a decision was finally made to leave open this possibility. Members then decided that a popular consultation focused on the draft constitution would be held in the last week in February.

During a weekly press conference in mid-February held by assembly leadership, Arlindo Marçal, vice president of the assembly, told journalists that the main task of the members was to "listen to the people." He also explained how the views of the public would be considered during the consultations, which were set to begin on February 25. In his view, if a certain issue was raised in all districts, then it would certainly be discussed in the assembly plenary, but if only one person raised it, then it would not be considered.

Not all the members agreed with Marçal's point of view. On February 13, 2002, the assembly members discussed the methodology for the public consultations. The proposed plan was to release copies of the draft constitution at least one week in advance of the meetings, conduct public consultations for six days, and then return to the capital to write up the results. The SHC would analyze the reports and consolidate them into one document.

The one-week public consultation process was held from February 25 to March 1, 2002, when thirteen groups of assembly members traveled to each district to gather the views of the people. Thousands of copies of the draft constitution and a magazine summarizing the drafting process and the main articles of the constitution were widely distributed and produced in four languages.

However, because the process was rushed, the documents were often received the same day as the consultations or not at all. Also, because of the ad hoc approach to consultations, there was no plan to ensure that the 60 percent of the population who were illiterate could participate. Some districts received copies of the draft constitution only in Portuguese. Because the overwhelming majority of East Timorese citizens under the age of forty do not read Portuguese, this oversight excluded many youth from participating in the consultations.

Asia Foundation personnel observed many consultations around the country and the foundation supported Assembly Watch to travel to all thirteen districts and report on the proceedings. It was widely reported that women were rarely seen with copies of the constitution, and at some of the consultations, they were simply not present. At one consultation process in the district of Lautem, in the far east of the country, the consultation was held on market day when the women were not available to attend. Again, because of the rushed planning for the process, an effective gender strategy was not considered and so the largest constituency was largely sidelined.

Because distribution of the draft constitution and magazine was so tardy, some of the assembly consultation teams decided to explain the draft. This could have been useful to promote greater participation, but it left very little time for the public to provide comments. Some participants became bored and went home; others felt cheated out of their opportunity to have a say.

Selective Consideration of the Views of the Public

On March 8, 2002, the president of the assembly, Lú-Olo, officially submitted the reports on the public consultations to the SHC. The reports summarized the main recommendations on the draft constitution.

The SHC then met with each of the thirteen consultation teams and came up with proposed recommendations for amendments, to which all the political parties had to agree. This meant that only carefully selected views would come before the assembly. The proposals were then to be considered in the plenary and voted upon. On March 15, 2002, the SHC provided its provisional report to the assembly president.

In the plenary debate on the SHC report, some political parties complained that the report did not reflect the aspirations of the people. The president explained that the report was drafted after discussion with all parties and was an attempt at consensus and negotiation. Although there was some feeling that not all views were represented, the SHC did facilitate consensus, as eighty-two assembly members approved the provisional report.

However, it was also evident that sensitive issues raised by the public in nearly every district were negotiated behind closed doors and not raised in the plenary. Eight of the districts proposed that Tetum be the official language of East Timor and Portuguese be an official language for only a limited period of time. Because of Fretilin's strong position on using Portuguese as an official language, the views of many of the youth, who generally do not speak Portuguese, did not get an airing in the plenary.

Based upon a review of the changes made to the draft constitution after the public consultation process and comments by international experts, it is clear that the SHC revised the draft based more on comments from UN officials, experts in the technical secretariat, and the Asia Foundation consultants than on the views of the public.

The Role of International Law

There is no indication that the protagonists, national or international, of the constitution-making process in East Timor felt bound by international norms relating to the process. They did, however, devote considerable attention to the role of international law in East Timor's legal system. After careful consideration of the subject, they decided to incorporate the international norms contained in international agreements to which East Timor is a party,[51] thus opting for the monist approach to the subject, in keeping with many continental constitutions.[52]

Customary international law was not so incorporated, and the approach taken with respect to these norms creates some ambiguity. Section 9 of the constitution provides that "the legal system of East Timor shall adopt the general or customary principles of international law." It does not make them superior to domestic law, however, thus leaving the question of how conflicts between customary international norms and domestic law might be resolved somewhat ambiguous.

There is no doubt that the human rights provisions of the constitution have been inspired by international law, as all internationally recognized civil and political rights and many of the economic, social, and cultural rights have been included. In addition, Section 23 provides that all human rights embodied in the constitution shall be interpreted in light of the Universal Declaration of Human Rights.

Role of the International Community

The Role of the United Nations in the Constitution-Making Process

When UNTAET was established in October 1999, it was faced with an enormous challenge. Because of Indonesia's scorched-earth policy and the inevitable loss of Indonesian civil servants who had largely run East Timor's government, UNTAET, with only a few staff in place, had to reinstate basic services, such as health care and educa-

tion; rebuild infrastructure and sustainable institutions; and establish the rule of law. The immensity of the tasks that had to be undertaken to begin the reconstruction process often appeared insurmountable.

In the face of daunting challenges and the fact that there was no blueprint for how to rebuild a nation, UNTAET responded with robust efforts and invested significant resources. UNTAET's leadership was willing to be flexible as the mission evolved, and it often rethought strategies. This was particularly true regarding the devolvement of power to the East Timorese. The road map for the political transition process emerged by trial and error and with some creativity. In the early days of the mission, the transitional administrator ruled with the advice of a fifteen-member National Consultative Council, but later determined that the East Timorese should take more political responsibility in decisionmaking and policymaking. It established a mixed East Timorese and international cabinet, along with the thirty-six-member NC, which served as a quasi-legislature. The overriding policy was to devolve more power as independence neared, and accordingly, a fully Timorese council of ministers governed the day-to-day administration of East Timor following the constituent assembly elections.

UNTAET's determinative role, and in particular that of the Department of Political Affairs, in the development of the legal framework for establishing the constituent assembly and constitutional commissions has been addressed above. However, during the drafting of the constitution, UNTAET adopted an overtly hands-off policy, to ensure that the constituent assembly did not view the United Nations as interfering in the creation of the independence constitution and to promote a homegrown constitution. UNTAET's official distancing from the process during the actual drafting was wise. Although there were accusations from the public that the final constitution was more Portuguese than Timorese, no one saw it as having been prescribed by UNTAET.

The transitional administrator did ensure, however, that the assembly had the necessary material and human resources to complete its task. The office oversaw the budgeting and funding for the process and provided translation services, one technical adviser, and other UNTAET staff to assist with the administration of the secretariat. This support was crucial to the success of the drafting process. For example, the constituent assembly had a newly refurbished assembly hall with a modern speaker system in place from the first day of their sitting. Although the Australian government financially supported this, UNTAET staff ensured that the resources needed to run the constituent assembly and the secretariat were provided, including the provision of computers, paper, cars, and support staff.

Some of the members could not have followed the discussion without the benefit of the simultaneous translation in the four working languages of the constituent assembly, which was supported by UNTAET and the Asia Foundation. UNTAET also facilitated the public consultation process in February by photocopying copies of the draft constitution and providing transportation and security. It is a common assumption that a constitution-making process in any country would occupy a preeminent position in the nation-building process. However, in a postconflict setting, in which many nation-building tasks compete for attention, crucial funding or material support can be overlooked or delayed because of a lack of timely planning.

Despite the positive aspects of UNTAET's role, however, UNTAET was responsible for a significant failure. The mission should have supported a legislative framework for a constitution-making process that followed

what most East Timorese leaders outside of Fretilin were calling for, and which would have led to, first, the drafting of the constitution by an independent and diverse body of East Timorese, including professionals; second, a constituent assembly that would have been more representative of the diversity of the nation; and third, space for the East Timorese people to participate and feel more ownership of the constitution as a document that reflected the aspirations of the people as a whole and not largely Fretilin's political aspirations. Instead, the Department of Political Affairs pushed for a process that led to the dominance of the process by Fretilin and precluded genuine popular participation.

Provision of International Technical Advisers

The secretariat coordinated international and local technical advice and support to the constituent assembly, establishing a technical staff with five foreign parliamentary experts to assist with advice on rules and procedures, legal drafting, and substantive issues. Four of these advisers were Portuguese and one was Canadian. None of them had experience in constitution making, but they had crucial experience in parliament and parliamentary procedures; previous experience supporting the NC, East Timor's quasi-legislature; and four of them could assist with drafting provisions in Portuguese. These advisers were provided by a variety of sources: UNTAET, the Portuguese Parliament, the United Nations Development Programme (UNDP), and the Inter-Parliamentary Union (IPU). During the first week of the assembly's deliberations, UNDP and the IPU jointly organized a seminar to provide an overview of comparative constitutional processes and content.

An Asia Foundation (TAF) program also provided technical support to the process. TAF had a full-time program manager and resident adviser and local program officer to assist the process. The TAF program was initiated through a one-week consultation process to identify the most critical needs and determine the most suitable forms of technical assistance during the constitutional drafting process. TAF met with the president and vice presidents of the constituent assembly, political party leaders in the assembly, the secretariat, members of UNTAET (including the transitional administrator), the minister of foreign affairs, and key donors, such as UNDP. During these discussions, TAF emphasized that its technical assistance was to enhance the assembly's capacity to fulfill its all-important role of drafting the constitution in the most inclusive and transparent way possible; responsibility for preparing, adopting, and implementing the constitution remained solely with the people and the assembly.

Many of the consultative meetings with assembly members were at least two hours long because before members could articulate what types of assistance they wanted, they had many questions about how the process in general would or should proceed. The president of the assembly specifically requested that TAF organize a workshop on the issue of public consultations. Some of the members also requested an immediate options paper on the constitution-making exercise, which could assist with defining the goals and strategy of the process. Following this one-week consultation period, and based on members' specific requests and suggestions, TAF provided the members with a paper on suggested methods of assistance to the assembly. The assembly welcomed these methods and, throughout the process, continued to make specific requests to the TAF resident adviser as additional needs arose, such as the provision of translators.

The consultation process was very important in gaining assembly members' trust. TAF's philosophy was not to impose a program of assistance on the assembly but to develop it with them, and TAF remained flexible in meeting the CA's needs. TAF provided nine technical constitutional advisers, both generalists and specialists (e.g., a land and property specialist), during twelve separate visits in the seven-month constitutional drafting program. TAF experts provided constitutional advice directly to the committees and the plenary, held weekly meetings with all political parties in the assembly who requested advice, and produced over a dozen options papers on constitutional issues, such as customary law, international law, independence of the judiciary, transitional provisions, human rights, and public participation. Some of these papers were discussed during lunchtime dialogues on specific constitutional issues. TAF also supported a seminar for members on measures to increase public dialogue and plan the public consultation process for the draft constitution. Lastly, it provided substantive revisions or corrections to the draft constitution, some of which were incorporated into the final draft by the assembly.

Objectives of Technical Assistance

To provide effective technical assistance in a constitution-making process, all advisers must understand their role and work cooperatively to provide the types and frequency of technical assistance that are needed to produce a homegrown constitution. The level of technical assistance needed varies, particularly in a postconflict context in which there may be few nationals with legal experience, as was the case in East Timor; the Timorese were rarely allowed to practice law or participate in governance during the Indonesian occupation. The technical advice should always promote local ownership over the content and process of the constitution-making exercise.

In East Timor, most assembly members welcomed the technical assistance, and as they gained trust that the advisers to the process were respectful of the members' roles, the requests for advice and discussions increased. In-country advisers from both the technical secretariat and TAF were available to all members and parties. Although some parties had private technical advisers, the advisers openly assisting the process did not favor one party over another.

Close coordination between the technical secretariat advisers and TAF advisers contributed to providing effective technical advice. Some of the advisers met regularly to share information and discuss options for the constitution. Comparative constitutional experts learned more about the specifics of the East Timorese context, and Portuguese legal experts learned more about innovative constitutional provisions and procedures from other countries. Technical advisers commented on the draft constitution, as did representatives of international organizations, including Mary Robinson, the UN high commissioner for human rights, and UNTAET's transitional administrator. The assembly's harmonization committee largely welcomed the input and revised portions of the draft based on advice from foreign commentators. Nearly all of the advisers raised the problem in the draft constitution of rights being afforded only to citizens. The appropriate provisions were revised to adhere to international human rights standards, thus affording rights protection to all persons in East Timor.

The technical advice and support affected not only the substance, but also the process. Internews, TAF, and staff from UNTAET worked together to help the secretariat produce materials for the public consultation process. UNTAET provided a graphic artist and Internews oversaw the publishing process. A technical adviser as well as a local adviser from TAF assisted in the development of a constitutional magazine to explain the draft constitution to the people in clear and simple terms; 50,000 copies of this magazine were distributed. NDI also developed easy-to-understand descriptions of the draft constitution in Tetum and distributed these through its civic forum program. All of these activities contributed to a greater emphasis on public participation in the process. In the end, the technical assistance relating to the process served to increase the receptivity to public participation of many members of the assembly who initially resisted it. However, this could not overcome a rushed process or lead to the desired objective of public participation, which is to promote ownership and legitimacy of the constitution.

Conclusion

The process of developing, drafting, and adopting a constitution is beyond a doubt a critical phase in any political transition, requiring careful planning to ensure that it is done in a representative, inclusive, participatory, transparent, and nationally owned and led manner. This is especially true in a post-conflict context. The process of how the constitution is prepared is as important as the content of the resulting constitution because it can lead to a more legitimate constitution, as well as a social contract reflecting the aspirations of the people. In East Timor, despite the clear demand from diverse leaders in civil society for public participation and a representative and inclusive process, pressure from the international community and a few elite actors who wanted to take power quickly resulted in a process that focused on hastily producing a constitution and not on establishing democratic practices and precedents.

Although each constitution-making process is unique and lessons learned from one process are not always transferable to another, there are a few key lessons from the East Timorese process that may prove useful to future constitution makers, other national actors, and those within the international community who support and contribute to the process. This conclusion does not summarize all lessons learned and good or poor practices highlighted throughout the paper, but focuses on a few key flaws that should be avoided in future processes.

The Legal Framework

The legal framework in East Timor was skeletal. Skeletal frameworks can be useful when there is not broad agreement by key stakeholders on the objectives of the process, when key actors are still outside of peace processes, or where the situation remains volatile. However, East Timor was a fairly stable society at the time and a more detailed framework would have better served the process. The framework in East Timor created a very rushed timetable (ninety days to draft, debate, and adopt the constitution), did not mandate public participation in the process, and created a structure for the process that precluded a broadly representative group of constitution makers.

The legal framework should be carefully prepared to promote the principles and values discussed above. It should allow sufficient time to plan and implement a participatory process that includes nationwide civic education before, during, and after the adoption of the constitution. This should be combined with a genuine and inclusive consultation process that may also occur during several different phases, including before and after the draft of the constitution is produced. It should establish mechanisms for electing or selecting a group of constitution makers that does not merely represent elite political interests (which are important) but also includes broader societal interests.

Public Participation

For the East Timorese, who had largely been excluded from the political life of the country during the Indonesian occupation,

to have participated meaningfully in a nationwide and inclusive civic education process would have served several purposes. It would have facilitated an understanding of the process by which the new constitution was to be made, of the role of a constitution in a society, of key constitutional issues, and of democratic practices and principles. It also would have allowed citizens to reflect upon what they wanted in the constitution. The one-month UNTAET-led civic-education and -consultation process was not sufficient; it was mere window dressing for what these types of civic-education components in a constitution-making process typically are designed to achieve. It conflated civic education and consultation, sometimes in a single day, and this did not provide the time needed to achieve any of the purposes civil society had been requesting throughout the consultations on the structure of the process.

Moreover, the structure of the UNTAET-managed public consultation process lacked legitimacy and impact because it was seen as an UNTAET process rather than a nationally owned and led campaign. The constitution makers themselves were not required to travel to all areas of the country and hear firsthand from the public about their concerns and aspirations. This was a major flaw in the process. The constitution makers also had little contact with the public, outside of some civil-society groups that presented papers at committee hearings. Consultation processes are often very transformative for constitution makers because they hear concerns from everyday people, and often this leads to more focus on issues that may not have received attention otherwise. It also sets up an important democratic precedent for representative democratic practices, whereby representatives meet with their constituents and are accountable. In East Timor, the constitution makers, the delegates of the constituent assembly, were simply handed the reports of the constitutional commissions, but members were skeptical of the methodology and the contents and rarely, if ever, referred to the documents. The consultations may have boasted tens of thousands of participants, but the consultations had little impact on the content of the constitution, and the assembly was not required to consider the views or report back to the public how the views were taken into account.

After the draft was prepared, both the media and civil society demanded that the assembly engage the public in a meaningful consultation process, and the leaders, including the assembly's president, felt compelled to respond. However, it was too little, too late. Few of the members of the public could read or learn about the contents of the draft constitution before the consultations. Some members of the public did not get a chance to speak because a few consultation teams wanted to speak rather than to listen. There was no uniform methodology for the process, and even when views were gathered in the process, it was unclear what weight to give those views. In the end, the process was rushed and few of the views were debated and discussed by the assembly. It became readily apparent that only the views that did not require any kind of compromise from Fretilin would be incorporated.

The lesson learned from the East Timor process is that public participation is not merely an exercise in public relations. It serves very important purposes and carrying it out takes time, adequate resources, and direct engagement by the constitution makers. It should be carried out at several phases of the process.

Democratic Representation

As noted in this chapter, the political transition period witnessed ever-deepening tensions between Fretilin and Gusmão. In a move designed to check Gusmão's burgeon-ing de facto power and capitalize on its own organizational strength and popular legitimacy as a resistance party, Fretilin put forward a constitution that limited presidential powers. Immediately preceding the presidential elections under UNTAET, Gusmão expressed reluctance to run because, as he explained to reporters, the only powers accorded the president under the draft constitution were the powers "to eat and sleep." In the end, Gusmão ran for the office nonetheless and won as predicted.

In short, East Timor's independence constitution reflects the political power that Fretilin enjoyed as the preeminent political organization left in the wake of Indonesia's withdrawal. Thus, the constitution's shape was heavily influenced by Fretilin's significant popular support because of its primary role in the previous liberation struggle.

It may be that the split between Fretilin and Gusmão was not widely recognized, and those who voted for Fretilin did not expect that these votes would assist Fretilin to limit Gusmão's power in his expected role as the future president. That most people who voted for Fretilin also voted for Gusmão for president and that the consultation process raised public aspirations for a strong president indicate some of the contradictions in the process. Using an elected constituent assembly ensured that the constitution reflected the interests of the most powerful political party, but the lack of a competing political organization that reflected the public's desire for Gusmão as a strong president meant that the constitution-making system could not balance or lead to negotiations between the main power bases in the country.

Because Fretilin dominated the elected constituent assembly, and the assembly was tasked with drafting, debating, and adopting the constitution, the constitution largely reflected the views of this single political party and was not seen as a consensus-based constitution. Because the process was rushed, other stakeholders had little time to push for more inclusion in the process or to even prepare to do so.

Fretilin leaders were not inclined to consult the public on the draft because they felt they had garnered such a high percentage of the votes during the elections that they had a mandate to represent the people and could make decisions on the constitution without public consultation. Indeed, they arrived at the constituent assembly with a draft in hand, modeled after the Portuguese constitution, and the final text did not stray far from this initial draft. Although the public may not have been initially aware of the origins of the initial draft, the foreign flavor of the constitution is one of the rallying points of its critics, which has detracted from the constitution's legitimacy.[53]

Certain UN actors and political elites argued that a constitution should only be prepared by a democratically elected body. However, it is common for drafts of a constitution to be prepared by a group of selected members, who then carry out broad consultations with the public and have an elected body debate and adopt the text. This was the process civil society had demanded but did not get.

In a post-conflict context, where nascent political parties are weak, rarely put forward fully articulated constitutional platforms, and do not have strong representational bases for their positions, certain parties or individuals thrive based on their past roles during the conflict and not what they claim to achieve in the future. Elections in and of themselves may not necessarily be a sufficient conduit for the expression of the people's constitutional aspirations. These aspirations, however, must inform not just the choices about who should govern for one term but the blueprint for society itself. Hence, a strictly democratic electoral model dependent on representation through the ballot is usually insufficient to capture public preferences in post-conflict constitution-making exercises. Groups that have been marginalized or did not participate in the conflict may be excluded from participating. While elected bodies do in some cases contribute to legitimacy, other mechanisms also can be used to ensure that the constitution is a product of consensus building and that the concerns of the diversity of the nation are represented.

Impact of the Process on Conflict in East Timor

With the passage of time, some of the events that have unfolded reflect the effects of the failings of the constitution-making process. The violence of 2006[54] and the divide between the president and prime minister have shown that the constitution has not facilitated a unified sense of national identity or provided the means for effective and nonviolent resolution of political conflict. The weaknesses of the process and the charter that resulted from it have led many to call for constitutional reform; since the adoption of the constitution, the public has grown increasingly critical of Fretilin's role in drafting it and of the flaws in the constitution itself. This has tarnished both Fretilin and Gusmão. As a result, the failings of the constitution have emerged as a favorite rallying point for whatever political forces are trying to gain favor among the population, and the charter appears to be sorely lacking in legitimacy.

Nevertheless, even though the constitution called for a review process in 2008, the moment came and went with a great deal of rhetoric and debate but no reform. Meanwhile, the institutions of government have evolved much more in response to political realities than to the strictures of the constitution. The country has seen two presidencies since the adoption of the constitution, that of Gusmão and that of Jose Ramos Horta, and many critics assert that each of them have exercised powers above and beyond those which the constitution has granted to them.

These observations underscore the dangers of a failed constitution-making process and clarify that that process was a missed opportunity. Although the East Timorese rejoice that at long last, they have achieved the freedom and independence that they had struggled for, the creation of the constitution as part of that process has failed to contribute to the peace and stability that they hoped for. As a result, the future is marked with uncertainty on many levels, and many questions remain unanswered. Will those who serve as president and prime minister eventually conform to the demands of the constitution, or will the powers they exercise continue to be more likely determined by the politics of the moment? Will new conflicts emerge that will be resolved by force rather than by law? Will there be the momentum and political will required to clearly identify the weaknesses of the constitution and address them, or will the issue of constitutional reform continue to be a pawn in the game of politics? Will a constitutional reform process be developed that leads all key stakeholders and society to feel that the constitution belongs to them and encourages them to defend it? These questions remain unanswered for the present, but if the project of constitutional reform moves forward, the missed opportunity of 2002 will be a stark reminder of the need to afford the time to ensure a process that is inclusive, transparent, representative, and participatory, so that the constitution as amended will benefit from consensus building and from the legitimacy it currently lacks. Perhaps then the people of East Timor will finally have a government that offers them the peace and stability they have known too rarely.

Notes

1. Peter Carey and Carter Bentley, eds., *East Timor at the Crossroads: The Forging of a Nation* (Honolulu, HI: University of Hawaii Press, 1995), pp. 3, 33.

2. U.S. embassy cables have shown that "Suharto was given the green light" prior to the invasion. In fact, hours before the invasion, President Suharto had been entertaining President Gerald Ford and Secretary of State Henry Kissinger at an official state visit in Jakarta. Noam Chomsky, "Introduction," in Matthew Jardine, *East Timor: Genocide in Paradise* (Cambridge, MA: Odonian Press, 1995), pp. 6, 10.

3. East Timor ranks among the poorest countries in the world, with an annual per capita GDP of an estimated $800 in 2005. *CIA World Factbook*, available at www.cia.gov/cia/publications/factbook/geos/tt.html#Econ.

4. One of the best-known histories of this period is James Dunn, *A People Betrayed* (San Jose, CA: The Jacaranda Press, 1983).

5. Ian Martin, *Self Determination in East Timor: The United Nations, the Ballot, and International Intervention* (London: Lynne Rienner Publishers, 2001), p. 15.

6. Martin, *Self Determination*, p. 15.

7. Carey and Bentley, *East Timor at the Crossroads*, p. 33.

8. Carey and Bentley, *East Timor at the Crossroads*, p. 33.

9. Martin, *Self Determination*, p. 16.

10. Irena Cristalis, *Bitter Dawn: East Timor, a People's Story* (London: Zed Books, 2002), p. 286.

11. Prior to 1978, Fretilin had been able to maintain control over certain areas of the territory. It lost that control when it incurred devastating losses in 1978, but it managed to regroup by 1981. See Carey and Bentley, *East Timor at the Crossroads*, p. 36.

12. Cristalis, *Bitter Dawn*, p. xi.

13. See, e.g., Carey and Bentley, *East Timor at the Crossroads*, p. 38.

14. Carey and Bentley, *East Timor at the Crossroads*, p. 8.

15. ETAN/US, "The Santa Cruz Massacre: November 12, 1991," East Timor and Indonesia Action Network, http://etan.org/timor/SntaCRUZ.htm (accessed April 16, 2009).

16. Although the United Nations had been brokering talks between Portugal and Indonesia since 1983, little progress was made in the talks prior to 1998. Moreen Dee and Michael Smith, *Peacekeeping in East Timor: The Path to Independence* (London: Lynne Rienner Publishers, 2003), p. 39.

17. Dee and Smith, *Peacekeeping in East Timor*, p. 43.

18. Cristalis, *Bitter Dawn,* p. 288.

19. Dee and Smith, *Peacekeeping in East Timor,* p. 18.

20. United Nations Security Council Resolution 1272 (1999), UN Doc S/RES/1272, para 8.

21. Dee and Smith, *Peacekeeping in East Timor,* p. 66; Cristalis, *Bitter Dawn,* p. 288.

22. See generally, UNTAET Regulation 2000/24, "On the Establishment of a National Council," July 14, 2000, available at www.un.org/peace/etimor/untaetR/Reg2400E.pdf (accessed on April 16, 2009).

23. See generally, UNTAET Regulation 2000/23, "On the Establishment of the Cabinet of the Transitional Government of East Timor," July 14, 2000, available at www.un.org/peace/etimor/untaetR/Reg2300E.pdf (accessed on April 16, 2009).

24. *Security Council Briefed by Sergio Vieira de Mello, Special Representative of the Secretary General for East Timor,* UN Doc SC/6850, April 27, 2000.

25. "Reconstructing East Timor: Analysis of the Past and Perspectives for the Future Conference," Final Report (Tibar Document), Tibar, East Timor, May 29–June 2, 2000, p. 23 (unpublished paper on file with the authors).

26. Remarks by Peter Galbraith, Director, Office of Political, Constitutional and Electoral Affairs for UNTAET, at the Conference on Reconstructing East Timor: Analysis of the Past and Perspectives for the Future, May 29, 2000 (on file with the authors).

27. Address by Sergio Vieira de Mello, Special Representative of the Secretary General and Transitional Administrator, August 21, 2000, First CNRT Congress, Dili (on file with the authors).

28. *Militias Root Cause of Problems for UNTAET and Indonesia in East Timor,* Sergio Vieira de Mello, Special Representative of the Secretary General to East Timor and Transitional Administrator, UN DOC SC/6928, September 29, 2000.

29. For a description of the major features of this regulation, see the section of this chapter on democratic representation.

30. Jim Della-Giacoma, "Results Over Process, Analysis of the Creation of the East Timor Constituent Assembly," p. 12 (unpublished paper on file with the author).

31. See KITLV, Royal Netherlands Institute of Southeast Asian and Caribbean Studies, "East Timor: Constitution OK'd But Ramos Horta Critical of Dissenters," press release, March 22, 2002, available at www.etan.org/et2002a/march/24–31/22consti.htm (accessed on April 16, 2009).

32. Constitution of the Democratic Republic of East Timor, preamble.

33. See "East Timor: Assembly Slates 20 May 2002 for UN to Hand Over Sovereignty," United Nations UNTAET Report, www.un.org/peace/etimor/news/01oct22.htm (October 22, 2001).

34. Della-Giacoma, "Results Over Process."

35. These parties included the following: Partido Democratica Cristao (PDC); Uniao Democrática Timorense (UDT); Partido Democratico (PD); Associaçao Popular Democratica Timorense (Apodeti); Frente Revolucionarea de Timor Leste Independente (Fretilin); Klibur Oan Timor Asuwain (Kota); Partido Republika Nacional Timor Leste (PARENTIL); Partido Nasionalista Timorense (PNT); Partido Trabalhist Timorense (PTT); Partai Demokratik Maubere (PDM); Partido Social Democratica (PSD); Partido Democratica-Cristao de Timor (UDC/PDC); Partido do Povo de Timor (PPT); Partido Socialista de Timor (PST); Associaçao Social-Democratica Timorense (ASDT); and Partai Liberal (PL).

36. See United Nations UNTAET Report, "Nearly 96% of East Timorese Registered in Advance of August Elections," press release, June 22, 2001, available at www.un.org/peace/etimor/news/01jun22.htm (accessed on April 16, 2009); see also United Nations UNTAET Report, "Following First-Ever Elections, East Timor Begins to Count Ballots: UN Mission," press release, August 22, 2001, available at www.un.org/peace/etimor/news/01aug31a.htm (accessed on April 16, 2009).

37. As noted above, ASDT was the original name of the Fretilin party. However, during the UNTAET period, a new party bearing the same name was constituted apparently in an attempt to signify a harkening back to the values espoused when the original Fretilin party bore the name.

38. Della-Giacoma, "Results Over Process," p. 13.

39. See Aniceto Gutierrez, "Proposed UNTAET Regulation," 2001 (unpublished proposal on file with the authors).

40. The International Policy Institute, *A Review of Peace Operations: A Case for Change* (London: King's College, 2002).

41. Della-Giacoma, "Results Over Process," p. 13.

42. Ibid., p. 13.

43. East Timor NGO Forum, "Letter to Members of United Nations Security Council," March 17, 2001, available at www.pcug.org.au~wildwood/01marushed.htm.

44. See UNTAET Directive 2001/13, available at www.eastimorlawjournal.org/UNTAET-Law/Directives/Index.html (accessed July 18, 2009).

45. See "Strategy to Promote Public Participation in the Constitutional Development Process," Statement by Sergio Vieira de Mello, Special Representative of the Secretary General and Transitional Administrator, March 29, 2001.

46. See *UNTAET: A Report of the National Constitutional Consultation in East Timor, June–July 2001,* Constitutional Affairs Branch, Department of Political Affairs and Timor Sea, p. 4.

47. *UNTAET: A Report of the National Constitutional Consultation,* p. 4.

48. Della-Giacoma, "Results Over Process," p. 15.

49. Telephone interview with Aderito Jesus de Soares, former chair of the systemization and harmonization committee, fall 2002.

50. Telephone interview with Aderito Jesus de Soares, former chair of the systemization and harmonization committee, fall 2002.

51. Constitution of the Democratic Republic of East Timor, sec. 9.

52. Graham Nicholson, "Observations on the East Timor Constitution," *Alternative Law Journal,* vol. 27, no. 5 (October 2002), p. 206.

53. Interview of June 1, 2009, with Edward Rees of Peace Dividend, an NGO doing business in East Timor since the adoption of the constitution.

54. See "East Timor Conflict," available at www.reliefweb.int/rw/rwb.nsf/db900sid/EKOI-6-QS3AJ?OpenDocument (accessed July 18, 2009).

10

Between Coups

Constitution Making in Fiji

Jill Cottrell and Yash Ghai

In 1874, the principal chiefs of Fiji signed a deed of cession of their islands to the British crown in the hope of securing, as they put it, "civilization and Christianity." In 1970, the country became independent under a newly prepared constitution. In 1997, Fiji adopted a new constitution by a process that is the focus of this paper. In 1999, the constitution came into force and there was a general election in which the two parties that had been the protagonists of constitutional change were decisively rejected. A year later, there was a curious civil coup, during which the government was held captive in the parliament building by a group of indigenous Fijians led by a failed and dishonest businessman;[1] this movement was superseded by a military takeover, which resulted first in its suspension and then in its abrogation, with the military ruling by decree.[2] The seesaw history of the constitution continued with its restoration following a court ruling;[3] its suspension following, oddly, a proconsti-

tution coup in 2006; and its abrogation after a similar court ruling in 2009.[4]

Had this paper been written in April 1999 or even 2000, we would undoubtedly have said that the constitution-making process was a great success, and that the 1997 constitution, though not flawless, was a considerable achievement. Inevitably, we are compelled to address the question of whether the events of 1999, 2000, and after indicate that the constitution or the process that made it was gravely flawed, even a failure. To understand the process, however, it is necessary to have some understanding of the social and economic structures of Fiji society and of the constitution-making enterprises that had preceded that of the early to mid-1990s.

Since Fiji's inception as a political entity, its politics and political and administrative structures have been obsessed with race and ethnicity, thanks to colonial policies. Every other issue—human rights, trade unionism, land, economy, education, even religion—

has been subordinated to it. Constitutional debates have been fundamentally about ethnic allocations of power; they have not been about national unity or identity, social justice, the appropriate scope of the public sphere, Fiji's place in the world, or the myriad other issues that define people's daily experience. As happens with such an obsession with race, there is a great distortion of reality. The complexity of Fijian society, with its ethnic divisions and class structures, is obscured so that a regional chiefly class assumes the leadership of the entire community. Such obfuscation, prevalent in other communities as well, is the handmaiden of injustice. The 1997 constitution tried to move to a new paradigm, motivated by newer thinking on ethnic differences and celebrating diversity as a source of enrichment and social justice through national unity and integration. Its own checkered career shows the difficulties of its project. But there is little doubt that in the course of time, its vision will win greater acceptance, even if posthumously. A constitution charting a new path does not necessarily achieve its objectives immediately, especially if it operates in a context in which power is fluid and dispersed, with the constitution registering no particular class or ethnic victory. What then matters is the persuasive power of its vision and goals. The Reeves Report on the constitution, a watershed in Fiji, provided that vision, however incompletely and contradictorily the 1997 constitution conveyed it into law and practice.

Background

Society and Economy

In the decade following Fiji's cession to the British crown in 1874, the foundations of a sugar industry were laid, and in 1879, the first of 60,000 Indian indentured laborers arrived to work on the sugar plantations to help respond to Colonial Office insistence that Fiji pay its own way.[5] The colonial government

Table 10.1   Population by Ethnicity

Year	Fijians[1]	Indians	Others	Total
1966	202,176	240,960	33,591	476,727
1976	259,932	292,896	35,240	588,068
1986	329,305	348,708	37,366	715,375
1996	394,999	336,579	41,077	772,655

1. Until 1997, Fiji was the official name of the country, but Fijians were the original inhabitants, whose dominant language is Fijian. In this paper, the word *Fijian* is used to refer to an indigenous Fijian, or the language; the Indian population is referred to as variously *Indian* or *Indo-Fijian*; Fiji is used adjectively, as in the Fiji constitution.

instituted a system of indirect rule—applicable to indigenous Fijians—involving the entrenchment and sometimes distortion of Fiji's chief system and a reinforcement verging on creation of a system of communal land holding.

By the time Fiji became independent in 1970, indenture was a thing of the past, but large numbers of Indo-Fijians were leasing land from Fijians for cane farming, while others were running businesses and entering the professions. Most indigenous Fijians were still engaged in subsistence farming, on land that was, even then, largely communally owned. Table 10.1 shows the breakdown of population over the years.

While other countries have ethnic compositions not dissimilar to that in Fiji, some, such as Trinidad and Guyana, differ in that the two major communities—ignoring the small indigenous Indian population in the latter, which is constantly its fate—are nonindigenous. With a majority of Malays but large ethnic minorities, Malaysia is most similar to Fiji. But in Fiji, by the mid-twentieth century, the largest community was nonindigenous Indian, though it lacked an overall majority. The other large community was indigenous Fijian. This meant that the debate could be conducted in terms of those who belonged versus those who did not, and the Fijians—or at least politicians and other advocates on their behalf—could couch their arguments in terms of the rights of indigenous people, even though their situation was very different from that of peoples like the Maori, Australian Aborigines, Canadian First Nations, or the Sami, who had been swamped, marginalized, and driven from their lands by incomers. Despite the incomers' numerical dominance, indigenous Fijians were not driven off their land or marginalized, but they did have a minority complex that continues today, even though they are now a majority. For their part, Indians also have a minority mindset that comes from their exclusion from control of land, the sense that they have not been accepted as part of the nation, and their vulnerability to racist abuse and physical attacks.

The two communities have remained very separate in many ways. Though not unknown, intermarriage is uncommon. The groups' lifestyles are different. In rural areas, most Indians live in individual farmhouses, whereas Fijians live in villages. Most Indians are Hindu (a small proportion are Muslim and an even smaller proportion Christian), whereas Fijians are overwhelmingly Christian. To a considerable extent, the two communities are educated in different schools and do not learn each other's languages in any systematic fashion.

The ethnic situation in Fiji has been made more acute because almost every aspect of life is affected by it or reflects it: religion, language, and lifestyle. Particularly problematic is land. As mentioned above, large numbers of Indians have been small-scale farmers, mainly of cane, who lease their farms for thirty years at a time from Fijians. There is a small amount of freehold land (about 8 percent of the total) held mostly by Europeans and part-Europeans and some government land. However, it is not only the Fijian-Indian relationship that is rooted in land, but also relationships within the indigenous community. Most of the indigenously held land (over 80 percent) is owned on a custom-ary, communal basis, and not by individuals. It is linked to lineage, or *mataqali*. Revenues from the land are allocated on a hierarchical basis: The chief of the *mataqali* receives the largest share and receipts diminish down through the structure. Most members of the community thus receive only very small benefits from the land, and the land-holding system reinforces the chiefs' dominance. For some commentators, the resentment that is felt toward the cane farmers would be more appropriately directed at the clan and land nexus.

As with immigrant communities in many contexts, there is a perception—and not entirely only a perception—that the Indians are better off than the indigenous people. Until recently, few Fijians went into business. Meanwhile, some Indian businessmen are very wealthy, and even small shopkeepers can seem wealthy to the poor Fijians who come to towns to try their luck, perhaps because they are landless. Far higher proportions of Indians than Fijians tend to be in business. But studies on poverty in Fiji have also shown that the very poorest are actually Indian.[6] This, however, is lost on those who are convinced that the benefits of the ethnic structure all favor the Indo-Fijian community. Living standards in Fiji are by no means as grindingly poor as in some developing countries, but a study in 1997 estimated that overall, the share of poor households was around 25 percent.[7]

There is no denying that the two communities could have done more to diminish the tensions between them. Nor was colonial policy directed towards any such result. "Divide and rule" applied in Fiji as elsewhere. There was no encouragement in colonial times for Indians and Fijians to integrate or learn each other's languages. Since independence, far too little has been done to redress the situation. Neither community has had a leader of stature who has been prepared to reach out in a sustained way to the other, though crucial transitions—especially independence and the 1990s constitution-making process discussed in this paper—have been greatly facilitated by relationships built up between leaders of the communities, such as that between Ratu Kamisese Mara and Siddiq Koya at independence and Sitiveni Rabuka and Jai Ram Reddy in 1995–97.[8]

There are other communities: Europeans, other Pacific Islanders, Chinese, and those of mixed race, some of whom are part-Europeans but others of whom are mixed Fijian–Indo-Fijian or other combinations. The wholly or partly Europeans have tended to be associated with, and to have given support to, the indigenous Fijian population, in political contexts at least. In official terminology, all are sometimes grouped under the rather exclusionary label of "others," or in voting contexts, as "general voters." There is even a General Voters Party.

Political Developments

Fiji at Independence and the 1970 Constitution

The army at independence was and remains overwhelmingly Fijian, a legacy partly of Indian lack of enthusiasm for fighting for the British empire, partly of their reluctance to accept that terms of service for Europeans did not apply to all, and partly of the authorities' disinclination to accept Indo-Fijian soldiers in World War II.[9] The civil service, on the other hand, was more Indo-Fijian than Fijian, though not as greatly so as myth would have it. Political parties were forming with a strong ethnic focus. Seats in the Legislative Council were racially allocated, as they had been ever since the council came into existence. In 1904, only Europeans could elect their representatives. In 1937, there were fifteen members—five Europeans, five Fijians, and five Indians. By the 1960s, the number of members increased to eighteen, six from each race.

A general election was held shortly after Fiji became independent on the basis of a constitution that allocated parliamentary seats ethnically, though some seats were chosen through a common roll of the voters of all communities. 82.6 percent of Fijians voted for the mainly Fijian Alliance Party (AP) and 74.2 percent of the Indo-Fijians for the essentially Indo-Fijian National Federation Party (NFP). The AP had a number of prominent Indo-Fijian leaders, which explains the 24 percent support that party obtained from the Indo-Fijian community. There was also a senate with twenty-two members, of whom eight were nominated by the Great Council of Chiefs (GCC),[10] seven by the prime minister, six by the leader of the opposition, and one by the Council of Rotuma.

Overall, the 1970 constitution fashioned a fairly orthodox Westminster model: a parliamentary system with the queen as head of state, represented by a governor-general who was to act on the advice of the government, except in certain circumstances, such as choosing a head of government. There was a bill of rights on a familiar Nigerian model.[11] However, Fiji's ethnic factor marked this constitution out and affected a number of aspects of it. The ethnic voting setup was particularly unusual, though ethnic representation was not uncommon in colonies with settler populations or that were otherwise ethnically diverse. The constitution also entrenched a number of pieces of legislation protecting the interests of indigenous Fijians, in the sense that enhanced majorities, including the consent of a certain number of GCC Senate nominees, were required to change the laws.[12]

Fiji's process of negotiating and adopting the constitution was also one that had become standard in colonies moving first to self-government and then to full independence. In 1965, Britain called a conference in London, to which all members of the Legislative Assembly were invited. The important decisions to be made at this conference were not discussed widely in Fiji before the meeting. The next stage comprised secret discussions between the two major parties in 1969. Only four active members from each party were involved; the papers and minutes were kept confidential. There is little evidence that the participants consulted even with members of their own parties. The Fijian Council of Chiefs and the back-benchers of both parties complained about this; the secrecy was also criticized by Lord Shepherd, the British minister invited to review progress, with a view to the third stage of the final constitutional conference in London. Lord Shepherd met with the participants and subsequently, at his suggestion, a meeting of the Legislative Assembly was convened to report on the progress of the talks. A report was issued before Lord Shepherd left Fiji.

When the final conference took place in April 1970, there was considerable confusion as to what had been agreed upon in the preceding stages. There had been little public discussion of the issues before the delegates left for London,[13] where, again, Britain's intercession was required before all outstanding issues could be disposed of.[14] Later Pacific constitutions were generally drawn up in a far more participatory fashion; even before Fiji's constitution, there were South Pacific precedents of somewhat open and participatory processes in Western Samoa and Nauru.[15] After the constitution was agreed, there was no referendum, not even so much as an election.[16] One factor was the fear of violence, fear inspired by recent riots in Mauritius, a country that was deemed to bear strong resemblance to Fiji.

The one issue that the various negotiations did not succeed in resolving, it seemed, was that of the electoral system. The system outlined earlier was only for the first postindependence election. In 1975, in accordance with the independence settlement, a royal commission under the chairmanship of Professor Harry Street was appointed to look at the electoral system; it recommended a partial move away from ethnic representation.[17] Although the original understanding—at least in some quarters, though Prime Minister Ratu Mara denied it[18]—had been that the commission's proposals would be binding on the parties, once delivered, they fell like the proverbial lead balloon. The AP had no interest in becoming less communal, and although the NFP accused the government of breach of faith, it has been suggested that the NFP cynically thought that keeping the existing system would be in the interest of the Indo-Fijians as their numbers declined to perhaps less than the indigenous Fijians. As Brij Lal comments,

> The Indo-Fijian leaders had succumbed to the political considerations of the moment, with only myopic visions of the long-term interests of their own people and the nation at large. For this, they and their people would pay a terrible price a decade later.[19]

Although the royal commission sat in Fiji, Lal suggests that it elicited little interest there.

The Ethnicization of Politics, the 1987 Coups, and the Falvey Committee

Fijian politics after independence was distinguished by intensification of ethnicization. Government policies designed to advance the indigenous community and an element of virulent racism that entered politics in the mid-1970s led the Indo-Fijian community to come together in an electoral sense, with the stunning result that in 1977, the NFP was the largest single party, with precisely half the seats in the House. The governor-general (GG) did the right thing and offered the prime ministership to the NFP leader. As the party dithered for a few days, the GG decided to invite the AP leader to form a government. Perhaps if he had done otherwise, Fiji would have had its first coup ten years earlier than it did.

In the mid-1980s, a party emerged based less on ethnicity and more on class interests: the Fiji Labour Party (FLP). It was headed by a Fijian doctor and retired civil servant, Timothy Bavadra, and its secretary was an Indo-Fijian. As the new party realized that it could simply split the anti-AP vote, it entered into a coalition agreement with the NFP to fight the 1987 election under Bavadra's leadership.[20] Within the Fijian community, the new alignment reflected the distinction between the traditionalists, who were happy to uphold communal traditions and the role of chiefs in politics, and those who saw the communal lifestyle as holding back the development of the Fijian community and thought that chieftaincy should be kept separate from modern politics. It also reflected the gap between the Fijians of the western division—more modernizing, less clan and chief bound, with a sense of having been marginalized by the dominant east—and the rest. In response to this coalition, the AP entered into its own coalition agreement with the general electors, a category consisting of all citizens other than indigenous Fijians and Indo-Fijians, dominated by Europeans and part-Europeans.

The FLP-NFP coalition won the April 1987 elections, though voting was still largely along ethnic lines.[21] Bavadra was invited to form a government, which consisted of seven Fijian and seven Indo-Fijian cabinet ministers, the latter holding portfolios that had very often gone to Indo-Fijians in Alliance governments. One month later, Lieutenant Colonel Sitiveni Rabuka led a military takeover.

Fijian chauvinists, shaken traditionalists, and disappointed aspirants to government office or other lucrative benefits of an AP victory had refused to accept the decision of the voters—and along with the victors in the election, the constitution itself was the target of attack. Soon after the election and before the coup, a meeting of two thousand Fijians—the emerging Taukei Movement, *taukei* being the indigenous Fijians—prepared a petition to the GG demanding that the constitution be changed to provide that the indigenous people "must always control the government to safeguard their special status and rights."[22] As soon as a degree of public order was restored to Suva and a government headed by Rabuka was installed, the GG set up a constitution review committee in which the FLP-NFP coalition reluctantly agreed to take part, though they were heavily outnumbered by AP and GCC members. This was the first time that the people of Fiji were seriously asked what they wanted in a constitutional structure.

The committee was chaired by Sir John Falvey, a former attorney general close to indigenous Fijians. The other members of the committee were four nominees each of the GG, GCC, the FLP-NFP coalition, and the AP.[23] Its terms of reference were originally

> to review the Constitution of Fiji with the view to proposing to the Governor-General amendments which will guarantee indigenous Fijian political interests and in so doing bear in mind the best interests of other people in Fiji.

After the coalition members objected, the words after 'interests' were changed to:

> with full regard to the interests of other people in Fiji.[24]

The phrase "in Fiji" rather than "of Fiji" is telling. The committee held hearings in Fiji's four major towns and received 800 written and 160 oral submissions. But the atmosphere in which these consultations took place was hardly conducive to any conciliatory recommendations. The committee did produce a report:[25] By a majority (indigenous Fijians and one general voter) it proposed a single legislative chamber comprising eight nominees of the GCC, twenty-eight Fijian, twenty-two Indo-Fijian, and eight general voter members (plus one Rotuman and up to four nominees of the prime minister). All voting was to be communal, held and voted for by members of the relevant community. The prime minister was to be Fijian. The nominees of the FLP/NFP coalition (two Fijian and two Indo-Fijians) opposed any change to the 1970 constitution, with which the two Indo-Fijian nominees of the GG largely agreed).

The process was leading nowhere. There had already been violence after the coup, and political and economic stability were clearly under threat. The GG instituted a series of meetings between the political parties, resulting in the Deuba Accord, which was to be announced on September 25. An interim government with members drawn equally from the two main parties was to be set up and a new constitution review committee to be established under a foreign expert to propose a constitution acceptable to all, taking into account the aspirations of not only the indigenous community, but of the others as well.

Rabuka's response was rapid: On September 25, he carried out the second 1987 coup. Unable to get the coalition to accept the GCC model constitution, which had a built-in Fijian majority and allowed only Fijians to hold various offices, including that of prime minister, Rabuka declared Fiji a republic and set up a Taukei Movement–dominated government, headed by himself. The GG resigned a month later. By the end of the year, Rabuka had left the position of prime minister, though he remained in the cabinet, and the former GG had become president. The latter then invited former prime minister Ratu Mara to resume that post—he had served from independence until the 1987 election—thus returning the country to civilian if not constitutional rule.

The cabinet then put forward a draft constitution[26] that owed a good deal to the GCC proposals of 1987. It was prepared by a committee comprising nine Fijians, two Indo-Fijians, and one general elector. The Fijians

included Rabuka, Apisai Tora (a Fijian nationalist, even chauvinist), Tomasi Vakatora (later to be on the Reeves Commission), and the moderate Josefata Kamikamica. The Indians were "marginal and discredited" within their own community, Brij Lal observes.[27] This draft was translated into Fijian and Fiji Hindi.

The Manueli Committee and the 1990 Constitution

The government then established the Constitution Inquiry and Advisory Committee, chaired not by a foreign expert but by a retired colonel, Paul Manueli, from the small island community of Rotuma. The committee included six Fijians, five Indo-Fijians, and four general voters.[28] Its terms of reference related strictly to public reaction to the draft, and to making proposals based on that reaction. Ratu Mara observed: "Citizens throughout the country were given the opportunity of making their views known, and eminent legal experts were called on for advice."[29] Yash Ghai had a different view:

> The Interim Government claims that [the Constitution] is a reflection of the will of the people, when no real opportunity was given to them to participate in its making and they were denied the right to vote on it. The various committees which have made recommendations on its provisions were handpicked by the interim regime and enjoyed neither popular support nor public credibility. The views they presented were not those of the majority of Fiji's citizens. Even the most ardent supporters of the regime have not understood the terms of the Constitution.[30]

Brij Lal's evaluation of the process was a little less harsh:[31]

> The Committee conducted 32 hearings at 14 centres in the first half of 1989 and received oral and written submissions reflecting many perspectives.

The committee itself reported that at first, it received few submissions because the Internal Security Decree remained in full force.[32]

Delay in distributing the Fijian and Hindi versions of the draft constitution reduced the number of submissions from non-English speakers, and it seems that Fijians tended to rely on their provincial representatives. The result was that the committee received verbal submissions from 174 groups and 175 individuals, in addition to written submissions from 104 individuals and 105 groups. While 82 Fijians made individual submissions, only 39 Indo-Fijians did so, along with 22 Fijian groups and 141 Indian groups.

Among the submissions the committee received was one from the military that can hardly have failed to have a profound effect, in view of the two still recent coups. Theirs was a vision of a country in which Fijians enjoyed "absolute political dominance," where the press was controlled, judges appointed who would "accept the reality of the situation," workers unable to form trade unions, and the church cut off from what were viewed as subversive foreign influences, while the nation was subject to discipline and deprived of constitutional rule for 15 years. The military also called for a state religion. And in order to ensure that the military could carry out its "monitoring role," it should be "given executive authority."[33]

One of Ratu Mara's experts was the late Albert Blaustein, who was engaged as a draftsman of the 1990 constitution and found himself in a delicate position, trying to persuade the government to moderate some of the worst elements of the draft while being employed to deliver a document with a racist foundation. On the proposal to require that the prime minister must be Fijian, he commented: "With an indigenous Fijian majority in the House, this guarantee may be considered superfluous and will only lead to further criticism." Arguing for the abandonment of communal rolls, he wrote, "Rolls based on race—especially a special roll for voters who are neither Fijian, Indian, or Ro-

tuman—sounds much too South African. . . . But while we know the difference, you can be sure that the South African label will be attached to such proposals."[34] On both counts, his efforts failed.[35]

The Manueli report and the 1990 constitution based on it were both racially based and racially biased documents. The report has been described as enshrining "the exploitative ideology of indigenous Fijian paramountcy."[36] The committee rejected, however, the idea that Fiji should be declared a Christian state, as well as the proposal that the commander of the military forces be a member of the lower House of Parliament, a view with which the military had concurred. Under the committee's approach, all voting would be on an ethnic basis. Thirty-seven of the seventy seats in the lower house would go to Fijians and twenty-seven to Indo-Fijians. An appointed upper house would be over two-thirds Fijian. The constitution mandated affirmative action in favor of Fijians, elevated the status of Fijian customary law, barred access to the ordinary courts in cases involving Fijian customary land law, and provided for human rights provisions to be superseded by a two-thirds majority vote of both houses in a wide range of circumstances. Only an indigenous Fijian could be prime minister, and the president was to be appointed by the GCC.

But Fijian elite views were dominated not only by the question of the Indo-Fijian bogeyman but also an outdated perception of Fijian society as rural, land-linked, chief-dominated, and cohesive. The 1990 constitution was biased toward rural Fijians: The 33 percent of Fijians who lived in urban areas had only 13.5 percent of the parliamentary seats, and the document gave far more prominence to the GCC than that organization had had the past. Events since 1987 have involved the exploitation of tradition, and of religion, and reinforcement of militarism, by the Fijian elite to the detriment of the ordinary Fijian.[37]

Elections were held under the 1990 constitution in 1992. After a good deal of soul searching, the coalition parties participated in them, though differences over whether to do so actually broke the coalition. The election led to Rabuka becoming prime minister as an elected politician rather than as a coup maker. By this time Bavadra had died. We cannot know how the history of Fiji might have been different if this statesman had not died then. He was a key Fijian politician totally committed to the vision of a nonracial and just Fiji, and with his passing, there was no one of his stature who could carry Fijians with him on this platform.

It seemed that the Fijians had won everything they wanted. Writing not long after the constitution came into force, an Indo-Fijian wrote that, for his community, the constitution

> does not lay to rest the ghost of the *girmit* [indenture] experience, but raises the spectre of a new one, a life of subservience, lived as a *vulagi* "foreigner" on the sufferance of the Fijian people. While the original *girmit* lasted only five years, this one, they feel, is intended as a permanent arrangement.[38]

Yet five years after these words were published, Fiji had a new name and a new constitution that was firmly within the tradition of modern constitutions: It recognized human rights, and its electoral system, while not purged totally of racial elements, was designed to counteract ethnic tensions. The commission that prepared the constitution included the same Indo-Fijian who wrote the above despondent words. Most remarkably—but perhaps fatally—eighteen months further on, the country had an Indo-Fijian prime minister. How was all this possible? First, how was the idea of a process even capable of producing such a constitution acceptable to the apparent victors of the events of 1987? Second,

which influences led to the proposals taking the form they did? Third, how could the proposals be enacted by a parliament formed under the 1990 constitution?

The Reform Process

Why More Reform at All?

The 1990 constitution itself provided that it should be reviewed within seven years (the army's view on this did not prevail). In the second reading debate in parliament on the bill for the 1997 constitution, Colonel Manueli said:

> At the time I believed that the 1990 Constitution was the best we could achieve given the circumstances prevailing then. Those of us who were involved were very much aware of its shortcomings. This was the reason why we made it mandatory for the Review of the Constitution at the end of seven years.[39]

The prime minister, Ratu Mara, in a report to the president in May 1992, observed:

> The document you finally promulgated in 1990 was not perfect.... It is the centre of controversy during the current election campaign.... I am confident that negotiations between the two communities will be possible if goodwill and trust can be established among the political leaders.[40]

The Labour Party, which won thirteen seats in the 1992 election, supported the largest party: the newly founded Soqosoqo ni Vakavulewa ni Taukei (SVT),[41] set up by the GCC specifically to champion Fijian interests. One condition of support was that the government should pursue constitutional reform as a priority. Rabuka agreed, though with no evident enthusiasm,[42] and once in power, he dragged his feet on the issue.

However, Rabuka raised an issue with important constitutional implications when he suggested in late 1992 that there should be discussion on the possibility of forming a government of national unity (GNU). But the GNU idea was designed as sugar for the bitter pill of the 1990 constitution, something to make the existing setup palatable to the Indian community and more acceptable overseas. The government's expectation seemed to be that the fundamentals of the constitution would not change. Even Mara described it as "a realistic framework for taking the country back to constitutional government."[43]

However, by mid-1993 the Fijian political elite was beginning to talk openly about a constitutional review, and in June, Rabuka met with the leaders of the opposition parties—the FLP and the NFP—after which he expanded the membership of an existing cabinet committee on constitutional review to include them. In August 1993, the NFP produced a paper exploring issues of reform that foreshadowed many of the points that were to be at issue when the formal review process got under way. The following month, the parliament agreed to set up a review commission.

A number of factors worked together to lead to the government being prepared to embark on a serious reform exercise. First, leaders realized that Fiji's economy suffered when a large sector of the domestic population was alienated and the outside world viewed Fiji with suspicion; private investment as a percentage of GDP dropped markedly after 1987. Second, there was active pressure from the outside to reform (touched on below). Third, Rabuka's government was unable to sustain its credibility. There were some scandals involving corruption and incompetence, and the 1993 budget was defeated as some dissident Fijian members of parliament voted with the opposition, though Rabuka was returned to power in the consequent election. To be fair to the SVT, discussion about constitutional reform began before the budget defeat.

The 1990 constitution was leading to the political fragmentation of the Fijian community, as demonstrated by the rise of provincialism, disintegration of the AP, and the rise of several new Fijian parties. The fragmentation meant that any Fijian faction seeking to form a government would need the parliamentary support of at least some Indo-Fijian members, prompting the realization among Fijians that a majority of Fijian seats in the House of Representatives was insufficient for Fijian domination. Moreover, some elements of the fear felt by Fijians over the risk of Indian dominance were moderated when it was realized that the population balance was shifting, largely as a result of Indian migration and their lower birth rate (see Table 10.1).

Structure of the Process

Once the Fijian political leadership decided that there would be a commission to review the constitution, it was some time before agreement was reached on the commission's structure, size, and membership. At least four basic models were floated (see Table 10.2).

The commission chair ultimately appointed was Sir Paul Reeves, a Maori, former archbishop and former governor-general of New Zealand. The other members of the commission were a Fijian politician, Tomasi Vakatora (nominated by the government), and an Indo-Fijian academic historian, Brij Lal (nominated by the opposition). Counsel to the commission were a New Zealand woman who was familiar with other Pacific island states and a Fiji general vote, a part-European. The commission's secretary was a Rotuman lawyer. The small size of the body made it impossible to have a wide range of interests directly represented within the commission. It is unsurprising that there was no woman on the commission itself, and the presence of one foreign woman as counsel was no answer to this shortcoming, however important that function was.[44]

Table 10.2   Proposed Models for Fijian Constitutional Commission

	Proposed by Cabinet	Proposed by SVT	Proposed by NFP	Actual commission
Size	8	11	6–7	3
Makeup (apart from chair)	3 Fijian 2 Indo-Fijian 1 Rotuman 1 general voter	Deputy chair Indo-Fijian 2 nominees of SVT 1 general voter 1 NFP 1 Fijian Association 1 All National Congress 1 Rotuman 1 state services	1–2 foreign constitutional lawyers or distinguished political scientists with relevant knowledge 1 eminent economist 3 local, chosen for knowledge of law and other relevant fields	1 Fijian 1 Indo-Fijian
Chair	Foreigner (preferably from Malaysia)	Fijian	Not specified	Foreigner (New Zealand)

It took nearly two years from the time when the government began to think about such a commission until the Reeves Commission came into existence. The negotiations over the identity of the chair alone, which happened within the cabinet committee, took about six months. The opposition was determined to reject the SVT government scheme to have a Fijian chair the commission—especially the proposal to designate as chair the chief justice at the time.[45] The opposition was equally adamant that the chair should be a non-Fiji person. Sir Paul Reeves was chosen because of his ethnic and religious background and because he was perceived to be fair-minded.[46]

The commission's terms of reference, crucial to the nature of the enterprise, were the subject of extremely tough negotiations between the government and opposition in the cabinet constitution committee. The government wanted the starting point of review to be the 1990 constitution, and Fijian interests to have pride of place. The opposition wanted the entire constitutional structure to be up for grabs, with the terms of reference reflecting fairness to all communities and the necessity of national unity. The terms of ref-

erence as adopted bear the hallmarks of the ultimate compromise:

The Commission shall review the Constitution promoting racial harmony and national unity and the economic and social advancement of all communities and bearing in mind internationally recognised principles and standards of individual and group rights. Towards these ends, the Commission shall:

(1) Take into account that the Constitution shall guarantee full protection and promotion of the rights, interests and concerns of the indigenous Fijian and Rotuman people.

(2) Scrutinise and consider the extent to which the Constitution of Fiji meets the present and future constitutional needs of the people of Fiji, having full regard to the rights, interests and concerns of all ethnic groups of people in Fiji.

(3) Facilitate the widest possible debate throughout Fiji on the terms of the Constitution of Fiji and to enquire into and ascertain the variety of views and opinions that may exist in Fiji as to how the provisions of the Fiji Constitution can be improved upon in the context of Fiji's needs as a multi-ethnic and multi-cultural society.

(4) Report fully on all the above matters and, in particular, to recommend constitutional arrangements likely to achieve the objectives of the Constitutional Review as set out above.

They set the scene not for a tinkering with the 1990 constitution but for a total overhaul, though the emphasis on "rights, interests and concerns of the indigenous Fijian and Rotuman people" went further than the opposition would have wanted in giving specific protection to sectional interests. In the end, the opposition accepted the compromise to get the process started; it also believed that an independent and just commission would recommend provisions fair to its community.

Brij Lal[47] and Tomasi Vakatora[48] have written about the modus operandi of the commission, which, due to its size, depended very much on the personalities of its members. Initial auguries were not encouraging. Lal was very clearly identified as an NFP sympathizer and had written in fairly strong terms about developments in Fiji up to the early 1990s. Vakatora was a fairly hardline Fijian politician; the first edition of his autobiography indicated few positive feelings toward the Indian community.[49] His appointment initially filled opposition leaders with despair. However, being on the commission wrought a remarkable change in both men. They ended as friends[50] and the report they produced was unanimous. It seems that the experience of traveling around the country listening to the views of ordinary citizens brought them together. They realized the reality of life for the ordinary person, the fact that ethnic rivalries did not dominate their lives, and that there was a genuine willingness to work together for the common benefit. The very burden of responsibility exercises its own influence as well. The chair took the view that the main responsibility lay with the two Fiji citizens. Lal quotes him as saying, "If you two agree among yourselves, I won't stand in your way."[51] As Vakatora wrote,[52]

> Brij and I were able to iron our differences, sometimes after long and tense talks. . . . This was possible because of the mutual trust we had built between ourselves and the confidence and trust placed on us by our Chairman.

The commission ultimately produced a document that essentially contained drafting instructions for an entirely new constitution. Especially in the rather complex drafting tradition of the common law, experience suggests that a very important degree of momentum toward change can be achieved by presenting not just the ideas but the actual formulations required to achieve the recommended result. The commission did not do this, except in some specific instances. But the proposals it made were framed in very precise terms, which was, to a substantial degree, the work of the counsel, especially Alison Quentin-Baxter, as no member of the commission was a lawyer.[53] That said, it is clear that Vakatora and Lal were thoroughly involved in every aspect of the work, and that the commission and not its technical staff made the decisions. Vakatora says that he read the final report at least seven times.[54]

Timing and Sequencing

Table 10.3 shows the timeline from the appointment of the Reeves Commission until the passing of the Amendment Act.

The process involved neither a referendum nor an election before the constitution was adopted. The task of preparing a draft was given entirely to the commission, and enactment was a matter for parliament, as regularly constituted.

The Commission Phase

The commission was originally given just over one year to complete its work, but this was extended by three months. Even so, producing the nearly eight-hundred-page report was a remarkable achievement in the time allotted. This is not just a pleasantry. Timing can be crucial to constitutional reform.

Table 10.3 Timing of Reform Process in Fiji

Date/period	Specific events	Ongoing processes						
		Public hearings	Foreign travel	Developing ideas	Background papers	Public debate	Report writing	Parliament
March 1995	March 15 commission appointed.					█		
April						█		
May						█		
June	Beginning: met for first time. Prepared mission statement. June 16 commission met joint parliamentary committee for briefing. Program of work prepared					█		
July		█				█		
August		█				█		
September		█	█			█		
October	Last submission October 10 (SVT).		█			█		
November	Private meetings with high officers of state, judges, etc.		█			█		
December						█		
January 1996				█		█		
February	Visited Wellington; met electoral commission and others.			█		█		
March				█		█	█
April	Official of Australian electoral commission visited Fiji.			█		█	█
May				█		█	█
June						█	█
July						█	█
August						█	█
September	Reports submitted to president and parliament and then published. Commission winds up.					█	█	█
October						█		█
November						█		█
December						█		█
January–July 1997	July 3 bill passed.					█		█

A constitution that is produced under excessive time pressures—whether internally linked to electoral or conflict resolution factors, or deadlines imposed from outside, as in East Timor and Afghanistan—may not only be defective in a technical sense but also lack the commitment of the public, or "sense of ownership," to use the currently fashionable phrase. Developing that commitment requires time to educate and consult the people. On the other hand, a long, drawn-out process runs the risk, on one hand, of losing the interest of the public, and on the other, of missing the bus in that the factors that made the political context receptive to new possibilities may no longer exist.

The commission's own account of its work shows that in terms of timing, it gave high priority to public hearings.[55] It did not simply present a draft to the people and ask them what they thought of it. This was perhaps less necessary, as the 1990 constitution could have been used as the basis for discussion, though the commission appears not to have provided or facilitated any public education about its contents.[56] Appointed in May 1995, the commission spent most of July, August, and September holding public and occasionally private hearings around the country. These hearings were followed by visits to Malaysia, Mauritius, South Africa, and the United States, despite government reluctance to sanction the trip, which was financed by outside donations. Parallel to these information-gathering exercises, the commission had asked a number of people to prepare research papers and institutions and individuals to supply specific information. These research papers were used during deliberations, solely for the purposes of the commission and not to inform public debate; they were only published after the report itself.

The report was presented to President Mara and then published at the beginning of September 1996. It was submitted not to official popular debate but to parliament, where the main work was done by a select committee.

From Report to Law

The report was published only in English—not surprising for such a voluminous document, but unfortunate. There was no officially sponsored public debate on the report. Only the Citizens' Constitutional Forum (see below) tried to inform the public about the implications of the report. The report itself, and the stages that led to its ultimate enactment as a constitution, disappeared from public view to emerge only as a constitutional amendment bill.

The primary responsibility for hammering out the final decisions lay with an all-party Joint Parliamentary Select Committee (JPSC), which worked in secrecy without assistance from the parties' legal advisers. The parliamentary phase lasted from the completion of the report to the enactment of the amendment bill, and itself comprised two elements: the work of the JPSC and that of the full parliament. The main work of the committee took about six months and produced an agreement dated April 14, 1997, on the most important issues, including the electoral system.[57]

The committee's final report is a poor guide to its discussions and mode of reaching consensus, which they did, but the consensus was colored by their experience and predilections as politicians. The JPSC proceedings were very much a matter of negotiation. More important, the negotiations took place between Sitiveni Rabuka and Jai Ram Reddy, the leaders of the government and opposition, or the SVT and the NFP, respectively. The coup leader of 1987 and the Indian leader seemed to have achieved a quite remarkable working relationship. If the JPSC could not work out an agreement on a particular issue, they would turn it over to the party leaders, a practice reminiscent of the South African process by which Mandela and de Klerk broke deadlocks.

The negotiations in the committee involved a good deal of compromise. The Fijian members did not really want to change the 1990 constitution; the Indo-Fijians wanted radical change. Each in the end accepted things that were basically unpalatable to them. Politicians were more reluctant to move away as emphatically from the older Fiji constitutional assumptions than was the Reeves Commission. They stuck to communal seats for the most part, hoping that an alternative-vote electoral system, which probably most did not understand, would do the trick. They also chose to retain a senate, the membership of which had become a form of patronage for the leaders of the major parties. This having been done, the leaders committed their parties to support the resulting agreed bill, which then went to the draftsmen, who put their peculiar stamp on it. Apparently, in possession of the South African constitution, they managed to sneak in an idea or two of their own. It seems that the drafters included sexual orientation as a prohibited ground for discrimination; certainly it is not in the Reeves Report.

The GCC's support of the bill was a very important element in the negotiation stage. Jai Ram Reddy was invited to address the GCC, the first time such a thing had ever happened; he responded with a much-praised speech, which he began in Fijian.[58] During the parliamentary debates, repeated tribute was paid to the GCC and its role in ensuring acceptance of the constitution.

Not all members of parliament were happy about the way the decision making had been done. V.S. Tunidau objected:

> Using the Joint Parliamentary Select Committee, then lobbied through the Great Council of Chiefs, and formulating the passage of the JSPC Report straight into a Bill form is to me a very clever ploy denying us the fundamental process of parliamentary democracy.[59]

K.R. Bulewa commented that

> the negotiations process from my Party's perspective left a lot of room for improvement. Communications between caucus and the Party's representatives on the Joint Parliamentary Select Committee were haphazard at the best of times and sometimes non-existent. Negotiating strategies were non-existent and were regularly overridden by decisions reached at the top.... The fact that our party was able to reach agreement on issues under discussion is a tribute to the strong leadership of our leader, the Prime Minister, the fair mindedness of the Opposition and the statesmanship-like qualities of my colleagues.[60]

The bill, technically an amendment bill for the 1990 constitution, was introduced by the prime minister on June 23.[61] It produced a new document: the Constitution of the Fiji Islands, the new name intended to solve the problem of nomenclature (see note 1 in Table 10.1). In the debate in the House, there was a great deal of rhetoric about tolerance, the greatest acrimony being reserved for exchanges between the FLP and the NFP. Many Fijians spoke against aspects of the bill, most notably arguing for Fiji to be a Christian state, or generally regretting the loss of Fijian dominance in the 1990 constitution.

There were very few amendments to the bill; most of them were proposed by the prime minister and emanated from the JPSC, which was still sitting as the debate in the full house went on. Among the amendments at this stage were the introduction of compulsory voting (section 56 in the final constitution) and the requirement that the House have at least five sectoral committees (section 74[3]). Both amendments were agreed to without debate or division. The major proposal from the other side came from the Labour Party: Chaudhry wanted an extra Indian communal seat, which was rejected by a vote of fifty-nine to five.

Every member of parliament, save for two absentees, voted for the constitution. Apparently, Rabuka had told his ministers that if they did not support it, they would lose their portfolios.

Public Participation

The Commission's Consultations

The Reeves Commission had no structure outside its members and supporting staff, and no local organization.[62] It simply announced that on a certain day, it would sit in a certain place—a court room, a civic building, a school—to receive views. The commission visited far more places than any other previous commission, though interestingly, this did not generate a significantly larger number of submissions than the Manueli Committee had in 1989.

A quick count of individual submissions (relying on names)[63] indicates the following breakdown: 114 Fijians, 88 Indo-Fijians—of whom 10 seem to be probably Muslim—and 21 others. This is itself interesting, for in some other contexts, the Indian community is more likely to express its views than is the Fijian community, which one might expect in view of the higher average level of education among the former, though the breakdown of submissions to the Manueli Committee was similar. Among the organizations that made submissions, local churches clearly predominated. Many of the views presented were clearly orchestrated. Like an Amnesty International campaign, political parties and other groups made standard forms of presentation available for their members to sign

and submit. Lal wrote of a submission by the Arya Samaj "which will be repeated—worse, read word for word—countless times in the days and weeks ahead."[64] But by no means were all of this type.

The speed with which the commission embarked on tours around the country and overseas was only possible because it made no attempt to undertake any form of civic education. Fiji's literacy level is relatively high and the previous few years had been very political, so there was probably a high degree of awareness of the broad concept of a constitution. However, the population at large was almost certainly uninformed about the details of the constitutions that had prevailed in the country, and even more certainly uninformed about the options available to them. Indeed, the events of the previous six to eight years would very likely have led the ordinary person to think about constitutional issues merely in terms of the system of government and electoral systems—in other words, of the question of how the constitution could prevent (for Fijians) or not obstruct (for Indo-Fijians) the coming to power of another Indian-dominated government.

How far it is either possible or desirable to go in the area of civic education is debatable. While a little learning may indeed be a dangerous thing, there is evidently room for people at large to be given some basic information about what a constitution might do before they are approached for their views. And there is rather more room for specific interest groups to be educated in the devices and institutions that could improve their own situation; women and people with disabilities are only two of the obvious groups that could benefit from such information. But in Fiji, the commission made no attempt and had no mandate to carry out any education of this sort.

That said, the considerable publicity attached to the commission's work, especially the public hearings, was an education tool.

Describing the newspaper, radio, and television coverage, Lal notes that "the words, the gestures, the emotions of the presenters and the audience [were] dissected in minute detail."[65]

Civil Society

Civil society began a dialogue on constitutional reform early in the 1990s. In December 1993, a consultation on reform led to the establishment of the Citizens' Constitutional Forum (CCF), which was to become the principal non-politically aligned group discussing the issue. To a considerable extent, the CCF was the brainchild of Yash Ghai, working closely with Claire Slatter and Satendra Prasad of the University of the South Pacific (USP), academics active in politics. While in Fiji in 1992–93 to advise the coalition parties in the context of the impending issue of a review of the constitution, Ghai realized that there was really no forum for public debate and education on the matter. He therefore met with a number of academics and religious, gender, and trade-union organizations to propose that they consider setting up a civil-society group for just this purpose. The suggestions having been received with enthusiasm, Ghai obtained financial assistance from International Alert, the organization founded by human rights activist Martin Ennals. International Alert funded the initial consultations; later, Conciliation Resources, a breakaway organization of International Alert, provided financial assistance and some help in the form of international linkages.

The organization began in a very small way. At a meeting in Nadi (western Fiji) in 1995—one of the first held outside the capital, Suva—very few people came who were not in some way associated with CCF already, and the meetings never grew to be large public affairs. But they attracted a remarkable cross section of Fijian society. People from all po-

litical parties and religious groups attended, returning to their own organizations and contexts affected in some way by the event. The atmosphere of these events remained almost uniformly positive and without acrimony. The organization had a commendable record of printing the proceedings of its meetings, and thus, the meetings received wider publicity. The organization also produced its own submission to the Reeves Commission; many of the points in the submission were similar to those expressed in the FLP-NFP submission, but they were simpler and more direct.[66] Finally, the organization remained very multiracial, which was itself a valuable contribution. Without the CCF, the issue of constitutional reform might have remained much less visible than it was. That the prime minister, Rabuka, having shunned all CCF activities during the early stages of the process, asked to be permitted to launch its civic education materials on the new constitution, which were deemed to be much superior to the government's efforts, was a measure of CCF's growing impact.

From 1993 until the constitution was adopted, the CCF held a series of consultations that brought together a very wide spectrum of people from within and outside Fiji to discuss constitutional issues. These involved a mixture of information papers—on conditions in and possibilities for Fiji itself and on experience elsewhere in the world—as well as proposals for specific institutions in the constitution, which were published frequently in Fijian and Hindi. It also helped to draft legislation to implement the constitution, particularly a freedom of information bill. The consultations were designed to perform a number of functions, not only to inform and make specific suggestions, but to build bridges between communities and lay the groundwork for a consensual approach to constitution and nation building. What the CCF could do was limited. But it managed to place, and keep, the idea of constitution making on the agenda of at least the press and the middle classes, and not just as a matter for propaganda. Today, the CCF is the most effective and influential organization devoted to constitutionalism, national unity, and racial amity.[67]

The flavor of the contribution that the CCF made to the debate can be gathered from the topics of one of the consultations held in 1994. The topics involved the electoral system, Fijian interests, Indo-Fijian and minority concerns, rights and religious issues, land, power sharing, affirmative action, and state and civil society. Speakers at that event included leaders of the Labour Party, SVT, Fijian Association Party, NFP, and one other Fijian party; a Fijian senator; a Fijian high chief; an Indo-Fijian academic; a Fijian academic; the director of research of the Fiji Council of Churches; and a speaker from Interfaith Search. Various foreign experts spoke as well: an academic from New Zealand, Nigel Roberts; Helmut Steinberger from the University of Heidelberg, who discussed Belgium and Bosnia; Jomo K. Sundaram, who spoke on Malaysia; and Yash Ghai, who addressed power sharing.

The Religious Input

Religion, and for the most part mainstream religion, plays a large part in Fijian social and political life. Most Fijians are Methodist, but whereas in the United Kingdom the Methodist Church has a reputation for a degree of broad-mindedness, the Fiji Methodist Church has been very rigid and at times somewhat racist in its views. After the first coup, the government passed a Sunday observance law that imposed a Victorian notion on the community, including the prohibition of any public transport. This was partly directed at the Indian community. The church has sometimes backed attitudes and policies that have driven the wedges between the communities deeper.

On the other hand, religious organizations have sometimes led efforts to reconcile the differences between communities and worked toward a constitution that respects human rights and all communities. After the 1987 coups, Interfaith Search and Fiji-I-Care came into existence with the specific object of healing rifts, and they have worked with nonreligious organizations, especially the CCF. Early in the 1990s, the Fiji Council of Churches initiated dialogues on constitutional reform, and meetings of this sort were an important catalyst.

The Reeves Commission report shows that of 632 submissions from groups and organizations, roughly 341 came from specifically religious and mostly Christian groupings but included 47 Hindu or Sikh congregations or organizations. This may overestimate Christian input in the sense that in many villages, the church would be the only forum for aggregating views, and those views might well have little religious content.

International Input and the Role of the International Community

International factors were important in various ways. There might never have been a review in the 1990s at all if not for international influence. The World Bank put a great deal of pressure on the constitution-making process, with several of its reports taking the position that unless there was a constitution acceptable to all communities, the prospects for economic growth would remain dim. Individual governments, notably those of the United Kingdom, Australia, and New Zealand, pressured Fiji to reform the 1990 constitution. These three states were not only closely associated with Fiji historically but also were among its largest aid donors, with extensive commercial and educational links. The U.S. ambassador at the time seems to have made constitutional reform his personal agenda, hosting lunches to bring Rabuka and

Reddy together in an informal setting to begin to develop a consensus.

Finally, there was the question of the Commonwealth. Indigenous Fijians were among the most loyal of the Queen's subjects. Fiji's membership in the Commonwealth automatically lapsed when it became a republic, and the racist nature of the state at the time led to restoration of membership—automatic when a country becomes a republic in normal circumstances—being denied. Many Fijians hoped that Fiji might again become a monarchy, part of the Queen's dominions. They viewed return to the Commonwealth as associated with this—indeed, many probably did not understand the distinction between the two issues.[68] John Wilson, a lawyer with experience of legal drafting in various Commonwealth countries, was asked to peruse the draft constitution to see if it would satisfy the Commonwealth's conditions for re-entry, and he endorsed it.

The commission members, especially the Fijian members, naturally brought their own knowledge, expectations, and fears to bear on the process, and almost certainly the input of the lawyers associated with the commission was considerable, but it is clear that the bulk of the particular ideas that found their way into the ultimate draft came from outside the commission. Those ideas came from individuals and groups within Fiji, political parties, visits to other countries undertaken by the commission, and academics.

Experts and Academics: Local and Foreign

Fiji is a country of only seven to eight hundred thousand people, yet contributions to the making of its constitution came from some of the leading constitutional experts in the world. They came from all directions. The commission itself commissioned research papers from academics and practitioners of politics locally and overseas.[69]

It visited other countries and held discussions with both academics and politicians. It met Arend Lijphart, a theorist of consociationalism,[70] and Donald Horowitz, author of *Ethnic Groups in Conflict* and a leading expert on institutional approaches to accommodating ethnicity. In South Africa, it met Albie Sachs, Cyril Ramaphosa, and Desmond Tutu. In Malaysia, it met Jomo K. Sundaram and Kirpal Singh; in the United Kingdom, Vernon Bogdanor, David Butler, and James Crawford; in the United States, Michael Reisman; and in Australia, Cheryl Saunders—to mention only the best known. Non-governmental organizations (NGOs), notably the CCF, invited foreign and local academics, experts, and politicians to participate in consultations. Academics from the USP wrote papers and drafted submissions.

Political parties used foreign and local input from outside the parties. The FLP invited an Australian politician, Don Dunstan, to advise on its submission, though much of the work on the actual document—which was a joint submission with the NFP—was done by Yash Ghai. The SVT had the benefit of the advice of a retired Malaysian judge.

Research papers for the commission itself were written by some of the people mentioned earlier, as well as by local academics and people involved in Fiji affairs in a practical way. Authors of the papers were from the Pacific, Australia, India, Sri Lanka, Malaysia, the United States, Mauritius, the United Kingdom, and New Zealand. One group of papers dealt with specifically Fijian issues: ethnicity, economy, religion, education, and land. Another group dealt with constitutional issues generally: preambles, electoral systems, chiefs and kings and constitutions, antidefection provisions, upper houses, accountability institutions, power sharing, directive principles of state policy, and national and international human rights.[71] Few constitutions have such respectable academic credentials.

How did such extensive foreign-expert involvement come about? No doubt it helped that one of the commission members was himself an academic. Seeking the views of scholars would not necessarily come naturally to politicians, or even archbishops. In addition, Fiji houses the main campus of the USP, an institution that at that time was very respectable in academic terms, with a number of academics in the social sciences who were committed to Fiji. Suva is a small city, Fiji staff at the university are linked to the society, and it seemed perfectly natural for religious and secular organizations to work closely with academics. Personal and accidental factors also play their part. Notably, Yash Ghai could contribute directly to the debate through his involvement with the CCF and by advising the FLP-NFP coalition. He also contributed indirectly by introducing the individuals from overseas who came to CCF consultations—and very much more discreetly, by feeding suitable names for research papers to the Reeves Commission. Other names were suggested by the United Nations.

Finance

Reviewing a constitution is not a cheap enterprise; one elderly, conservative, and European resident of Fiji described the commission as a "million dollar farce."[72] The main costs of the enterprise in Fiji were borne by the national exchequer, though the United Nations (Electoral Assistance Division of the Political Affairs Department) paid for five issue papers on electoral systems[73] and facilitated commission meetings in the United States. The Australian government paid for foreign visits by the commission and for the draftsman of the constitution. The CCF raised money from or through International Alert, Conciliation Resources, the governments of

Australia and the United Kingdom, and the World Council of Churches.

Foreign Experience

Why were Malaysia, Mauritius, and South Africa examined? South Africa is easy: Nelson Mandela was released from prison in 1990, the interim South African constitution was enacted in 1993, and the final constitution was adopted in 1996. In South Africa, race was the dominant political issue—and though blacks are by far the largest group, there is also a significant Indian minority. Perhaps South Africa also appealed to indigenous Fijians because some of their myths of origin suggest that Fijians came from Africa. Most observers agreed that South Africa's experience (see the chapter in this volume) offered a model of constitution making and racial rapprochement that was very worthy of study and perhaps emulation.

Mauritius is less well known. That country has a very large Indian community (now about 68 percent of the entire population) and a smaller black one (now 27 percent). Another parallel is the importance of sugar, as cane cultivation is an important part of Fiji's economy and its social structure is so bound up with the crop, though the Mauritius sugar industry is more technically advanced than that of Fiji.

Malaysia is the most interesting example. Fijian politicians have long admired the Bumiputra policies of the Malaysian government restricting admission quotas to local universities for Chinese and Indians, favoring treatment to indigenous inhabitants in the realms of business, and so on. There was very little recognition in Fiji of the government's heavy-handed treatment of political dissidents, or even of the way in which these policies of racial preference have negatively affected the Indian and Chinese communities. After the 1987 coups, Mahathir Mohammed, prime minister of Malaysia, visited

Fiji to offer support, as did Lee Kwan Yew of Singapore.[74] Various Malaysians had come to Fiji to advise, and a retired judge advised the government and SVT when the constitution was being negotiated. But when the commission visited Malaysia, the effect was rather the opposite of what one might have anticipated. Far from appealing to Sir Paul Reeves and Brij Lal as a model of racial justice that Fiji might emulate, it appeared to the Fijian member of the commission that the Malaysian system should not be emulated. He did not like what he saw as a system biased in favor of Muslims and did not want something similarly biased in favor of Christians.[75]

International Law

Appeals to international law in the reform process took three main forms. First, there was a general awareness of international human rights norms, a consequence perhaps of the general international input already mentioned, and the terms of reference of the commission required it to bear in mind "internationally recognized principles and standards of individual and group rights." The submission of the NFP and FLP referred considerably to international human rights norms, and other writings around the theme of reform did the same. This is reflected in the Reeves Report, which discusses relevant norms, at some length.[76] Section 3(b) of the final constitution provides that in interpreting the constitution, regard must be had for "developments in the understanding of the content of particular human rights; and developments in the promotion of particular human rights," which requires reference to international as well as foreign law. This formulation was apparently added at the drafting stage.

Second, the Indo-Fijian community had appealed to international norms, the con-

cept of equal citizenship, and the rights of the individual as basic building blocks of the constitutional and political system. It had also, ever since the promulgation of the 1990 constitution, relied on the Convention on the Elimination of All Forms of Racial Discrimination (CERD), which Britain had applied to Fiji during the colonial period. At one point, there had been talk of persuading another country to make a formal complaint against Fiji to the international committee supervising the CERD. Mauritius had already agreed to bring the matter to the committee, since the convention has no optional protocol authorizing individuals or political parties to complain to the committee. Only when Rabuka agreed to set up a process for constitution review were plans to approach the committee dropped.[77]

Third, indigenous Fijians were powerfully attracted to the concept of indigenous peoples having group rights. Though only a small part of the land has been alienated on the basis of freehold, or permanent ownership, many Fijians have felt that the leasehold system has taken the control and benefits of cane-growing land away from them; they also feel that they have lost power over their own political destiny. In the SVT submission to the Reeves Commission,[78] of which the chief craftsman is believed to have been a Muslim Indo-Fijian,[79] considerable reference is made to the Draft Declaration on the Rights of Indigenous Peoples and the concept of self-determination, though it also recognizes that the position of indigenous Fijians is not precisely that of indigenous peoples as envisaged in the UN Draft Declaration.[80] The last point was brought out by various contributions to the constitutional debate, including that of an official of the World Council of Indigenous Peoples.[81] The Reeves Commission was unconvinced that the international principles were applicable in the way that the SVT suggested, stating that Fiji's situation is very different from that of countries such as New Zealand. It also thought that the Draft Declaration did not justify discrimination against other communities.[82]

The Issues

Ethnicity

The issues that confronted the commission mainly related to ethnicity. This was inevitable in view of the background—and the composition of the commission, while it responded to the element of ethnicity, also ensured that it remained central. Nonetheless, at least some of the political parties and NGOs that participated in the process responded to the challenge of a comprehensive review in a comprehensive way. The document itself was a blueprint for a fundamental shake-up of the entire system. The range of submissions is dramatized in this section by drawing especially on the submissions of the SVT and the FLP-NFP, though particularly the former submission rather distorts the nature of the debate. It should not be thought that all submissions from Fijians insisted on maintaining the 1990 constitutional status quo.

The SVT submission to the commission sought, in essence, the continued dominance of the Fijian people. It described the process thusly:

> The basic premise of the review is that the 1990 Constitution is here to stay, but that what is desirable in the interests of all communities in Fiji, and to help promote multi-racial harmony and national unity in Fiji, is to make its provisions more considerate of the position and sensitivities of all communities in Fiji's multi-ethnic and multi-cultural society.[83]

Its submission placed emphasis on the non-Fijians as *vulagi,* and the way in which Fijian tradition expected *vulagi* to be humble and to know their place; it contained extended quotations from the work of a Fijian nationalist academic, which included the following:[84]

> All is well if the *vulagi* is humble, respectful, tolerant and cooperative.

The submission of the FLP-NFP,[85] by way of contrast, reads:

> We have not sought to promote the interests of our supporters at the expense of other people of Fiji for we do not think that that approach is fruitful. We believe that all the people of Fiji share a common destiny, and that the country will not progress unless there is a tolerance and accommodation of different views and interests.

The submission goes on to deal with every element one would expect to find in a constitution, right up to the amendment process. The SVT submission viewed that of the FLP-NFP as a further manifestation of Indian hypocrisy, hiding intentions of dominance that it traced back to Jawaharlal Nehru.[86]

Fundamentally different approaches to the ethnic issue motivate the two submissions. The SVT document accepts, and even glorifies and justifies, difference but it is a difference mediated under the hegemony of one ethnic group. Its proposals tended to reinforce and harden those differences and perhaps were designed to do so. They hoped to get the Indo-Fijians to accept their subordinate social position gracefully, in return for a settlement of economic issues, especially those relating to land. The submission also justified the 1990 constitution in terms of constitutional law, legal theory,[87] and national need. For its part, the FLP-NFP submission does not ignore difference by any means, but it looks forward to a future in which races work together and proposes institutions and structures that are positively designed to encourage cross-ethnic collaboration.

Political Control

Political control involved two main issues: the number of parliamentary seats that the two main ethnic groups would hold and the ethnic identity of the prime minister. The commission did not recommend any limitation on the latter. The former involves mainly the question of ethnic seats, and also whether there would be a first-past-the-post, or majoritarian, electoral system or some form of proportional representation. The lines were clearly drawn: The SVT and many other Fijian organizations wanted the retention of a system that ensured that Fijians maintained political control, rejecting a common roll and formal provisions for power sharing, mentioned below. The opposition parties were prepared to accept that the GCC would nominate the president, almost certainly ensuring that he would always be a Fijian. They were also prepared to accept the retention of some seats elected on a communal basis, but wanted to move further away from ethnic voting. The final decision departed from the Reeves recommendations and was an area in which Rabuka and Reddy reached a compromise that they managed to sell to their respective parties. The commission recommended forty-five open seats, twelve Fijian seats, and ten Indo-Fijian seats. The constitution prescribes twenty-five open seats, twenty-three Fijian seats, and nineteen Indo-Fijian seats.

The system of voting for the seats received particular attention, though the SVT did not address it. Other groups focused on encouraging cross-ethnic cooperation, or in other words, diluting ethnic control. The CCF urged a system of proportional representation. It had held a number of meetings on the issue of electoral systems, inviting various overseas experts; one very active member, Father David Arms, a Catholic priest, produced various models of possible systems. The FLP-NFP proposed a preferential voting system for communal seats and a nationwide party list system of proportional representation for the national seats. As it turned out, the system chosen was crucial for the control issue in the

first general election after the new constitution was enacted.

The system adopted in section 54(1) of the constitution is the alternative-vote system—known as AV for short—proposed by Donald Horowitz and accepted by the commission.[88] Under the system, each elector indicates first choice of candidate, second choice, and so on. When first preferences are counted, if no candidate obtains over 50 percent of the votes cast, the candidate with the fewest first preferences is eliminated and the second preferences of that candidate's voters are distributed among the remaining candidates. In open (noncommunal) seats especially, the hope was that parties would plan second preferences to be given according to party strategy, which would involve cross-ethnic cooperation. The system was incorporated into electoral law, dividing ballot papers so that voters who wanted to exercise their individual choice could do so by numbering individual candidates on the list on the bottom segment of the ballot paper. But voters could leave the choice to their party and just tick the name of their party above the line, on the top of the ballot paper.

The other structural issue related to the senate. The commission recommended a mainly elected body, though the final version involves appointed members, fourteen selected by the GCC, nine by the prime minister, and eight by the leader of the opposition.

Fijian Interests

There was much talk in the negotiations about the "paramountcy" of Fijian interests. The rationale lay in the concept of indigenousness, with much being made in some quarters of the history and myths of the Fijian people. The corollary was argued that Fijians should maintain political control, as well as traditional forms of social organization. But for some commentators on the constitutional debate, including some Fijians, the real issue lay in the tension between tradition—or imagined tradition, some might say—and change, and between the chiefly elites and the ordinary person. The traditionalists insisted that once primacy of the Fijian interests was recognized, the foundation would be laid for a harmonious existence for all. In fact, neither the Indo-Fijians nor other communities challenged the Fijians' key legitimate interests. The Indo-Fijians had argued for equality and rights of individuals but were prepared to accept a very significant degree of group rights for indigenous Fijians. The Indo-Fijians even recommended that legislation protecting Fijians—including their land rights, which greatly disadvantaged Indo-Fijians—should remain entrenched, a national role for the GCC should be acknowledged, and effectively the president should always be an indigenous Fijian, to symbolize indigenous Fijians' special status.

The commission rejected notions of a right to Fijian paramountcy but did propose what they described as a "protective principle" of the paramountcy of Fijian interests, the idea of which was to ensure that these interests were not subordinated to those of other ethnic groups.[89]

Religion

Some churches argued that Fiji should actually be designated a Christian state, though precisely what this might mean was not clearly articulated, and it was as much political as religious. A speaker at a CCF consultation said of a leader who would like Sunday observance written into the Constitution:

> I said "How do you justify this, from our teachings from the Bible?" He said "This is not biblical or theological, this is political. This is for Fijians."[90]

The Reeves Commission recommended maintaining the separation of church and state. This issue resurfaced as late as the debate on the constitution amendment bill, when a number of Fijian members emphasized that the GCC attached importance to Fiji being a Christian state. In fact, one of the amendments that was made at a very late stage was moved by the prime minister, presumably to take some of the heat out of the issue; it elaborated the preambular reference to adopting Christianity, with specific reference to conversion from heathenism—no doubt viewed by many Hindus as a dig at their religion.[91]

Land

As mentioned earlier, land was a key issue that has proven remarkably difficult to deal with. Even the CCF, which tackled so many contentious issues, tended to shy away from it. The CCF's own submission to the Reeves Commission makes no specific suggestions on land. The FLP-NFP proposed that the legislation protecting Fijian interests, including those in land, should continue to have special protection. It also proposed a requirement of affirmative action to provide land to the landless. Although all parties and communities realized that land was a major issue requiring constitutional settlement—especially as the leases of many farms that Indo-Fijians rented from indigenous Fijians were to expire shortly—they also felt that putting the issue on the current agenda would overburden it, and that a settlement might be easier once a power-sharing system was in place. Rabuka certainly took this view, and he persuaded a reluctant Reddy.[92]

Human Rights

The 1970 constitution contained a bill of rights of its time, with no recognition of economic, social, and cultural rights. The 1990 constitution also contained a wide provision for suspension of its broadly similar rights.

The SVT conceived of rights as a group matter, but other political parties and civil society laid greater emphasis on individual rights. As mentioned earlier, everyone resorted to international law to support their positions. The SVT referred to the Draft Declaration on Indigenous Peoples and the UN Declaration on the Elimination of All Forms of Intolerance and Discrimination Based on Religion and Belief; others relied on the International Covenant on Civil and Political Rights and the International Covenant on Economic, Social, and Cultural Rights.

Human rights can be profoundly subversive of accepted institutions or perceived as so, and in Fiji, human rights not only affected the relations between the two major communities but potentially challenged the current Fijian social organization. Even in the past, notions of human rights had affected traditional structures: Many of the provisions of the Native Regulations imposing restrictions on commoners had been removed shortly before independence. There was also general unease among the chiefly class regarding notions of liberal individual rights.

The bill of rights ultimately adopted includes full versions of familiar rights, such as those of free speech, association, and assembly, as well as freedom from discrimination. There are also more modern rights, such as the right to privacy and to basic education, though there is no mention of rights to health, housing, and food, such as one finds in the South African and some other recent constitutions. Noting that the Reeves report incorporated some rights from the legislation of New Zealand and Canada, Vakatora concluded, "I believe that the Bill of Rights we have recommended is one of the best in the world."[93]

Affirmative Action

Since 1987, the government had embarked on a major program of affirmative action to benefit the Fijian community, mainly in education and economic opportunity. There were far more scholarships for Fijians and special loan programs, as well as a Fijian holding company designed to hold commercial assets on behalf of the Fijian community. After 1987, the balance in the civil service had radically shifted. The SVT wanted the pro-Fijian programs to continue, while the coalition submission argued that affirmative action should not be restricted to one community.

The Reeves Commission proposed the inclusion of a provision about social justice, targeted at those in need rather than one ethnic group specifically. This was to impose a duty on the state to institute programs, by legislation, particularly in the areas of housing, education, and participation in commerce and in public service. Programs were to have clearly established criteria for participation and measuring success. Such programs would also expire after ten years, though they could be reinstated.[94] The final constitution largely enacts these proposals.[95]

Reconciliation

It was the almost universal hope that a new constitution would lead to a more harmonious relationship between the ethnic communities in Fiji, though visions differed regarding how this was to be achieved, especially if one contrasts the SVT submission with those of the FLP-NFP and CCF.

The CCF proposed that power sharing should be a feature of the constitution, at all levels of government, based essentially upon electoral support for political parties.[96] The FLP-NFP submission also proposed a system under which any party that obtained more than 20 percent of the parliamentary seats should be represented in the cabinet, which should be racially balanced. The principle of ethnic proportionality extended to public office and the use of national resources.

The Reeves Commission itself did not accept the proposal for power sharing in the cabinet; its choice of the AV voting system was directed at encouraging interethnic cooperation of a different sort. However, when the matter came to the JPSC, politicians opted for a model of compulsory power sharing at the cabinet level. Under section 99 of the constitution, any party that has won at least 10 percent of the seats in the House of Representatives has the right to a seat or seats in the cabinet proportional to the number of seats in the House.

The Aftermath

The 2000 Coup and Abrogation of the Constitution

There was a brief period of euphoria after the constitution was passed, not restricted to the Indo-Fijian community. Most people were happy to return to a situation in which the constitution had legitimacy at home and overseas. Few wanted to live at odds with their neighbors. The constitution became law in 1997 but came into effect with the dissolution of parliament in 1999. Various institutions were set up under it, including a human rights commission. The first elections under the new electoral system in 1999 produced results more remarkable even than those in 1987: Rabuka's SVT obtained only seven seats and Reddy's NFP not one. The Fiji Labour Party—no longer in coalition with the NFP, but working to some extent with the Fijian Association—won; Mahendra Chaudhry had to be invited to form a government. Chaudhry seemed to begin well, appointing a cabinet in which a majority of the members were Fijian, including his deputy prime minister. But a year later, there was another coup.

The suspension of the constitution was challenged in court, and the government relied on the successful coup doctrine that the

SVT had invoked in its submission to Reeves, as well as on the doctrine of necessity. Both the court of first instance and the Court of Appeal rejected these arguments. The Court of Appeal held, first, that even if necessity could justify temporary exceptional measures in an emergency, the temporary measures must be directed toward restoring constitutionality. Second, the court held that there was insufficient evidence of a new legal order having been effectively established. The 1997 constitution remained in force.[97] However, Chaudhry's government was not restored. A new election brought to power a Fijian government headed by Laisenia Qarase, who had led the interim military-backed government between 2000 and 2001.

Interpreting the Aftermath

Should we view the results of the 1999 election as a verdict on the constitution? Is the coup of 2000 damning evidence that the constitution was a failure?

To view the 1999 election as a popular vote against the constitution is to oversimplify. Such a view ignores the possibility that the vote reflected not only a rejection of the constitution makers, at least on the part of the Indo-Fijian community, but also a hope that the FLP could deliver in terms of policies.[98] There may have been some element of Rabuka and Reddy taking victory for granted, as they let the campaigning initiative pass to others. And Labour also seems to have latched on to the possibilities created by the new electoral system with more success than any other party.

However, clearly both major communities were worried about the constitution at some level and even harbored a sense that they had been betrayed. At pre-election meetings, Reddy tried to persuade NFP members to see things to some extent from Fijian perspectives, in some eyes thereby dooming himself to lose the election.[99] It was all too easy for those who wanted to stir up strife to portray the constitution to both sides as a sellout.[100]

Of course, it is impossible to tell what would have happened if the FLP had not won the elections in 1999. That said, if Rabuka had won and the NFP had made a good showing, there is some reason to suppose that they could have worked together harmoniously in a power-sharing arrangement. Various factors contributed to the coup: Chaudhry's personality and political miscalculations; the personal circumstances of George Speight, who led the civil coup; and the Fijian elite's fears and ability to play on those of the ordinary Fijian, combined with the fact that most people did not understand the constitution and thus could readily believe that it disadvantaged them.

The two main parties and, ultimately, the nation seem to have paid a price for the rather secretive way in which the constitution-making process was carried out. The Reeves Commission itself offered no options on content to the people. The people and the parties fed their ideas into the machine that was the commission and ultimately out popped a complete report. When it came to formulating the actual document for enactment, the draft again disappeared into a black box, to be adjusted in view of the prejudices and interests of members of parliament and the two main parties. The people were again presented with a *fait accompli*. True, it may all have been better than earlier constitution-making exercises—which is perhaps why it was deemed acceptable—but in terms of true popular participation it left a good deal to be desired. The failure to carry out any form of civic education in advance may also have contributed.

There was also insufficient popular education after the Reeves Report or the final constitution was produced, though there was some donor-funded education for parliamentarians and the public service. The report was not translated into Fijian or Hindi—understandable given that it was over seven hundred pages long, but it thus remained largely unknown to a majority of the people,[101] including the army.[102] The problem continued with the actual constitution, which was supposed to be translated into the two main local languages but never was. As a consequence, the constitution that people criticized, and which disaffected parties used as a rallying cry—especially on the Fijian side, which said that Fijian interests had been sacrificed—was not the real document at all, but a figment of people's fears and imaginations. When the CCF, undaunted by the coup, continued to introduce people to the constitution's ideas and contents, they were repeatedly met with comments along the lines of "It is a good constitution—we did not know!" Much of the myth and manipulation was deliberate, but was much easier to accomplish because people had no real way of knowing the truth of what they were being told. For these various reasons, important groups, such as the military and the people generally, did not understand the constitution or feel that it was theirs.

Ignorance of the constitution perhaps contributed to fears of what an Indian victory—as the result of the election was regarded—meant for the Fijian community. People felt that their land was going to be taken away, a perception that some politicians were only too happy to encourage. In fact, the constitution retained the existing land system and the entrenched status of land legislation.

The introduction of the new constitution was bound to be a delicate moment. Perhaps there was not enough realization of this. Especially since 1987, certain sections of the Fijian community had formed vested interests in the current system, involving an amalgam of chiefly tradition, commercial enterprise, land, and military force. These would all be threatened by a genuinely democratic system and more so by a transition that placed political power in the hands of Indo-Fijians as well as ordinary Fijians. It was evidently in elites' interest to resist the change of government even more than a change in the constitution. An attack on a new constitution is often no more than tactical, as perhaps was the case in the coup after the 1999 general elections. The moment was especially delicate in Fiji, where the coup taboo had been broken: It was not unthinkable that the military could take over.

Yet it must be acknowledged that the constitution itself had contradictions. Perhaps they were not, in the short term, the cause of its misfortunes. But they are likely to affect its full implementation. Drawing upon its sparse terms of reference, the Reeves Commission advanced a vision of Fiji that did not suit all key groups. It embraced an image of a nonracial, multicultural Fiji, with full respect for human rights and social justice. It rejected both the consociationalist assumptions of the independence constitution and the racial hegemonic assumptions of the 1990 constitution. However, its long-term goals were not always consistent with some specific recommendations.

The independence Fiji constitution, built primarily on the idea of racial communities, was an imperfect reflection of consociationalism. It sought to give all communities fair representation but deliberately overrepresented the general electors to ensure Fijian domination. It did not provide for power sharing at the executive level, nor the principle of proportionality in state services. It did nothing to disturb indigenous Fijians' monopoly of the armed forces. It provided various forms of self-government and autonomy for Fijians through the Provincial Councils, Fijian Administration, and the GCC, as well as a qualified veto for them, but it gave little to other communities. These were not merely protective provisions; they were at the heart of a distinctive Fijian paramountcy. Yet there were strong impulses of democracy and

rights, and the vision of a more integrated political community was hinted at in the agreement to review the electoral system to provide a nonracial element. The 1990 constitution was explicitly racist. Its assumptions were the further reinforcement of the separate markers of indigenous Fijians by resurrecting elements of their customary laws and judicial tribunals as well as their hegemony over other communities.

Rejecting the racial hegemonic model, the 1997 constitution moved further toward the consociation model, principally in providing for executive power sharing while flagging a more nonracial, even liberal, model. However, it was unprepared—or perhaps more accurately, unable—to dismantle the laws and institutions that separated the indigenous Fijians from others, such as the GCC, the Provincial Councils, and the Fijian Administration, though it did claw back some of the 1990 provisions on customary law and tribunals. The Fijian institutions provided a powerful base for ethnic identity and mobilization, and a source of legitimacy that often competed with constitutional values and allocations of authority. Moreover, nobody dared to touch the question of Fijian land rights and fairness to Indo-Fijians in lease arrangements, although most leases were about to expire—perhaps the most contentious public issue of all. The qualified veto, to be exercised in the senate, was preserved, although the senate would move away from domination by political parties. The concept of citizenship that emerges from the constitution's provisions does not conform to the universal and equal citizenship of liberalism. Despite Reeves's correct analysis of indigenous rights, group rights may clash with individual rights. The advance to nonracialism and liberalism was signaled by reforms to the electoral system, allocating a majority of parliamentary seats to common roll voting; a stronger system of human rights, substantively and institutionally; and social justice for the disadvantaged of all communities, instead of exclusively for one community.

The problems of the constitution-making process were not all the fault of the Reeves Commission, as we have seen. The commission did not support the same degree of consociationalism as is found in the constitution. It proposed a much higher proportion of nonracial seats than was finally adopted. And it explicitly rejected the model of executive power sharing. By retaining the Reeves system of AV voting and providing for multiparty executive coalitions, the constitution contains two somewhat contradictory methods to reach the same objectives and allows the logic of adversarial politics and voting to prevail over interethnic cooperation. Political leaders saw the route to government under the coalition formula as building up enough support in their own community to secure sufficient parliamentary seats, severely straining multiparty government.

This brings us to the effect of context and procedure. In terms of institutions, the constitution could perhaps only be interim, marking a departure from old orthodoxies but postponing some of the goals of the new vision. An abrupt shift would have generated tensions and anxieties jeopardizing the entire project. These constraints operated on the Reeves Commission as they did on numerous groups and individuals who presented their views to it. The procedure for making and adopting the constitution imposed its own constraints. The commission's composition, restricted to two local members representing parties of competing ethnic groups, was not propitious for defining national goals and identity, though on this point the commissioners confounded the critics and gave us a wonderful and powerful vision of Fiji and a host of sensible recommendations. However, the last word was not with the commission, unfortunately, but with politicians—and more important, with the parliament under the 1990 constitution, which was slated to be reformed in a way that would do away with the assumptions of its own foundation. In other words, the future constitutional order depended on members of parliament, many of whom had a vested personal and ethnic interest in preserving the current constitution. The requirement of enhanced majorities for passing the amending bill meant that each major ethnic group had a veto, which was of more value to the Fijian community than to the Indo-Fijian. The negotiations in the JPSC, the party submissions, and the proceedings of the commission itself had to be carried out in the shadow of this fact.

Conclusion

Some commentators have concluded that the constitution was fundamentally flawed because it permitted the emergence of an Indo-Fijian prime minister, which was unacceptable to the Fijian community. We find this to be a simplistic analysis. It is true that the prime minister was perhaps particularly hard for the other community to swallow. But the result of the 1999 election also made it much easier for those sections of society that really did not want any change in the constitutionally sanctioned reinforcement of Fijian paramountcy—meaning the paramountcy of a particular class and a particular structure for society—to portray the entire constitutional settlement as a disaster for Fijians. It was easier to do this because so few people really understood the document. How much could have been done by way of public education within the time frame is unclear. But we have shown that the process was far less transparent and participatory than it might have been, and we have also tried to show why this was so. The experience of other countries has shown that in the final analysis, what matters may be more the views of community leaders than the participation of the people themselves. And though Rabuka and Reddy may have tried to lead in one direction, other leaders were marching determinedly in another.

The content of the constitution itself may share some of the blame. The electoral system, which hardly anyone understood, was somewhat responsible for the 1999 election results. A power-sharing arrangement that is technically clumsy and politically unworkable with the current players gave the Qarase government a good reason to press for constitutional amendment. And we have noted the constitution's awkward marriage of the liberal and the consociational that retained many ambiguities of the past.

A constitution is not established in a vacuum. For a new and just constitutional system to take root in Fiji, a great deal of damage from the past must be undone. Much of that damage can be traced to the colonial experience; other elements originate in the post-1987 period. The Reeves Commission aimed for a radical restructuring of the values and institutions of the state, and though the people may have been ready for such fundamental change, politicians clearly were not. Experience shows that if politicians, who have a special purchase on state institutions, are not committed to a constitution, its prospects remain dim. In trying to please many groups, the thrust of the constitution was blunted. One critical factor was the reversal of the Reeves Commission's proportion of racial to nonracial seats, with the result that ethnic politics remained dominant. Constitutions that aim for fundamental change need much more care and nourishment than this one got. Had its principal proponents, Rabuka and Reddy, won the elections, more concerted efforts might have been made to observe its spirit and implement its provisions. Certainly little was done to prepare the public, in terms of information and persuasion, for the new constitution and the radical changes that it was intended to promote. The new constitution remained hostage to contingencies it could not control: The election of a prime minister with little respect for the aspirations and conciliatory procedures embodied in the new constitution, an unsuccessful businessman cut off from the largesse of the state who capitalized on ethnic fears, and the easing of external pressures on constitutionalism all damaged the fortunes of the constitution.

In an earlier draft of this paper we concluded that "the constitution survives, and there remains considerable support for it among sections of the population. The vision of Fiji on which the constitution rests still has its admirers. It is too early to write it off." This is not the place to explore the reasons behind the 2006 and 2009 coups (the first military and the second presidential, but both at the behest of the commander of Fiji's military forces). The latter insisted that he supported the 1997 constitution (except for its electoral system); he acted in 2006 to prevent the government from subverting the spirit of that constitution with laws designed to benefit Fijian land owners, and to give amnesties to the 2000 civil coup leaders. However, faced with the decision of the Court of Appeal that his government was illegal, he seems to have jettisoned both the constitution and the judiciary readily, insisting that this is all in the interests of achieving the radical reforms that his government is set on.[103] All this says much more about personalities than it does about the 1997 constitution.[104] Indeed, the 2006 coup prematurely ended the first government to be constituted in a multiparty way as directed by the constitution, though Jon Fraenkel suggests that this government was already falling apart, and had it held together, there would have been no 2006 coup.[105] How much of the spirit of the 1997 constitution will survive into the next constitutional phase can be a matter of conjecture only.

Notes

1. George Speight was dismissed soon after the 1999 election as chair of the Fiji Hardwood Corporation and prosecuted for offenses connected with foreign exchange and extortion. See Michael Field, Tupeni Baba, and Unaisi Nabobo-Baba, *Speight of Violence: Inside Fiji's 2000 Coup* (Auckland: Reid Publishing, 2005), especially chap. 7, "Speight, Son of Sam: Failed Businessman."

2. Fiji Constitution Amendment Act 1997 Revocation Decree 2000, followed by Constitution Abrogation—Interim Military Government and Finance Decree.

3. *Republic of Fiji v. Chandrika Prasad* ABU0078/2000S, reported (2001) 2 *Law Reports of the Commonwealth* 743. The Court of Appeal consisted for the purposes of this case of three Australian judges (Sir Maurice Casey, Sir Ian Barker, and Mr. Justice Handley), Sir Mari Kapi from Papua New Guinea, and Mr. Justice Gordon Ward, then of the Tongan judiciary though appointed in 2004 to head the Fiji Court of Appeal.

4. The new case is *Qarase v. Bainimarama* (2009) FJCA 10 April 9 2009 (available at the Pacific Island Legal Information Institution Web site at www.paclii.org/fj/cases/FJCA/2009/10.html), reversing the decision of the High Court on October 9, 2008. That case was strongly criticized, including by George Williams, Graham Leung, Anthony Regan, and Jon Fraenkel in *Courts and Coups in Fiji: The High Court Judgment in Qarase v. Bainimarama* (Research School of Pacific and Asian Studies, Australian National University, "State, Society and Governance in Melanesia" Discussion Paper 10 of 2008).

5. Adrian C. Mayer, *Indians in Fiji* (London: Oxford University Press, 1963), p. 11.

6. Around the time of the constitutional debate, the main source was the UN Development Programme's (UNDP) *Fiji Poverty Report,* available at www.undp.org.fj/index.cfm?si=main.resources&cmd=forumview&cbegin=0&uid=publications&cid=117.

7. See UNDP, *Fiji Poverty Report.*

8. Robert Norton, "Reconciling Ethnicity and Nation: Contending Discourses in Constitutional Reform," *The Contemporary Pacific,* vol. 12, no. 1 (2000), pp. 83–122.

9. Brij Lal, *Broken Waves: A History of Fiji in the Twentieth Century* (Hawaii: University of Hawaii Press, Pacific Islands Monograph Series, no. 11,

1992). The background section of this chapter relies heavily on this book.

10. The Council of Chiefs was originally set up by the first colonial governor, Sir Arthur Gordon. It is now known as the Great Council of Chiefs (GCC), or Bose Levu Vakataranga (BLV), and has taken on an aura of antiquity and acquired various forms of status and power. It has been used to legitimize events such as the 1987 coup that have little or nothing to do with chiefly traditions.

11. That was based (though with some differences) on the European Convention on Human Rights, to which the United Kingdom had adhered in 1954, and was copied in many colonies. See Stanley de Smith, *The New Commonwealth and Its Constitutions* (London: Stevens & Sons, 1964), chap. 5.

12. The laws were the Fijian Affairs Act; the Fijian Development Fund Act; the Native Land Act; the Native Land Trust Act; the Rotuma Act; the Rotuma Land Act; the Banaban Land Act; and the Banaban Settlement Act, and other laws which affect Fijian land, customs or customary right.

13. The narrow range of consultation and discussion in Fiji is clear from Kamisese Mara, *The Pacific Way: A Memoir* (Honolulu: Center for Pacific Studies, University of Hawaii, 1977), chap. 11.

14. For an account of the attitudes of the two communities, especially the Fijian community, see Mara, *The Pacific Way.* Mara states that at the 1970 constitutional conference, he would have preferred to keep people in Fiji better informed, but it did not seem to be the practice at such conferences where difficult issues were to be resolved (p. 102).

15. For an overview of constitution-making processes in the South Pacific, see Yash Ghai, "Constitution Making and Decolonization," in *Law, Politics and Government in the Pacific Island States,* ed. Yash Ghai (Suva: Institute of Pacific Studies, USP, 1988), p. 1; and J.W. Davidson, *Samoa Mo Samoa* (Melbourne: Melbourne University Press, 1987).

16. According to Mara, it was the leader of the Indian Party, Siddiq Koya, who proposed that there should be no election. See *The Pacific Way,* p. 97.

17. The Street Report was Parliamentary Paper no. 24 of 1975.

18. Mara, *The Pacific Way,* p. 126, pointing to the fact that the constitution said "if Parliament subsequently makes any alteration"—a somewhat weak argument, for presumably Street might have recommended no change.

19. Lal, *Broken Waves,* p. 224.

20. Pronounced *bavanda.* In Fijian, *d* is pronounced *nd* and *b* is pronounced *mb*; hence, Rabuka is *rambuka.* Further, *g* is pronounced as a soft *ng* and *q* as a hard *ng*; hence, the prime minister, Qarase, is *ngarase.* Finally, *c* is pronounced *th,* so Timoci is *Timothy.*

21. For an account of the election see Brij Lal, "Before the Storm: An Analysis of the Fiji General Election of 1987," *Pacific Studies,* vol. 12, no. 1 (1988), pp. 71–96.

22. Lal, *Broken Waves,* p. 272.

23. The committee had available the services of a retired professor of law from the United Kingdom, Keith Patchett.

24. Interestingly, the Manueli Report—of the body that followed the failure of the Falvey Committee—used the original phrase in quoting its predecessor's terms of reference (para. 1.3).

25. *Report of the Constitution Review Committee July/August 1987,* Parliamentary paper No. 21 (1987) (Suva: Parliament of Fiji, 1987). See Lal, *Broken Waves,* 286–9, for an account of the commission, including of some of the submissions to it.

26. Draft Constitution for the Republic of Fiji, September 1988.

27. Brij Lal, *Another Way: The Politics of Constitutional Reform in Post-Coup Fiji* (Canberra: Australian National University, National Centre for Development Studies, 1998), p. 10.

28. *Report of the Fiji Constitution Inquiry and Advisory Committee,* August 1989 (personal files of authors).

29. Mara, *The Pacific Way,* p. 223.

30. *The Fiji Constitution of 1990: A Fraud on the Nation* (A Report by the Fiji Labour Party and the National Federation Party) (Nadi: Sunrise Press, 1991), p. 2. Written by Yash Ghai on behalf of the NFP-FLP Coalition.

31. Lal, *Another Way,* p. 12.

32. Tomasi Vakatora, *From the Mangrove Swamps,* 2nd ed. (Suva: Government Printer, 1998), p. 97, comments that the public was "afraid to speak their minds" to both the Falvey and Manueli committees.

33. See Lal, *Another Way,* p. 14.

34. On file with the authors.

35. Blaustein was reported as distancing himself from the constitution once it was passed, saying that he had wanted a "multi-racial and proportional system." See *Fiji Voice,* no. 15 (September–October

1990), p. 15. *Fiji Voice* was published by the Fiji Independent News Service, PO Box 106, Roseville NSW 2069, Australia.

36. Winston Halapua, *Tradition, Lotu, and Militarism in Fiji* (Lautoka, Fiji: Fiji Institute of Applied Studies, 2003), p. 196. Halapua, a Fiji citizen of Tongan origin, is now Anglican Bishop for the Diocese of Polynesia in Aotearoa, New Zealand.

37. Argued in Halapua, *Tradition, Lotu, and Militarism.*

38. Lal, *Broken Waves,* p. 328.

39. Fiji, *Parliamentary Debates,* House of Representatives, June 30, 1997, p. 569 of published parliamentary debates.

40. Mara, *The Pacific Way,* p. 223.

41. Soqosoqo ni Vakavulewa ni Taukei, roughly translated as Fijian Political Party.

42. In Mahendra Chaudhry, "Why We Backed Rabuka," *Fiji Voice,* no. 22 (July–August 1992), p. 3, and the following article; the correspondence between the FLP and the SVT is reproduced.

43. Mara, *The Pacific Way,* p. 223.

44. Lal, *Another Way,* p. 173, relates the complaint of women in Labasa about the absence of any woman on the commission and suggests they were silenced by Vakatora's pointing out the presence of Quentin-Baxter.

45. The chief justice was a Fijian, Sir Timoci Tuivaga, whom the Indo-Fijian parties to the negotiations viewed with some distrust. Though the judges, including the chief justice, told the government in 1987 that the coups were unlawful, in 2000 Sir Timoci was viewed in some quarters as having been too ready to embrace the coup.

46. His name was put forward by Yash Ghai. Several other names were being bandied about, but in the end Reeves and one other, a former colonial civil servant, were interviewed by Filipe Bole, chair of the Joint Parliamentary Select Committee.

47. Especially in Lal, *Another Way.*

48. Vakatora, *Mangrove Swamps.*

49. Ibid.

50. Lal, *Another Way,* especially pp. 174–75.

51. Ibid., p. 174.

52. Vakatora, *Mangrove Swamps,* p. 114.

53. This was a deliberate decision of the government, according to Brij Lal in a discussion with the authors.

54. Vakatora, *Mangrove Swamps,* p. 117.

55. Fiji, *The Fiji Islands: Towards a United Future*, Parliamentary Paper no. 34 (1996) ("Reeves Report"), chap. 4, "How the Commission Went about Its Task."

56. In Kenya, the chair of the constitution review commission—Yash Ghai—prepared a book reviewing the structure of the existing constitution and suggesting alternative approaches, without advocating any. See *Reviewing the Constitution* (Nairobi: CKRC, 2001). The commission also produced a set of questions, titled "Issues and Questions," perhaps rather too detailed and tending to focus the attention of citizens on minutiae rather than on fundamentals.

57. This document is reproduced in Ganesh Chand and Vijay Naidu, eds., *Fiji: Coups, Crises, and Reconciliation 1987–1997* (Suva: Fiji Institute of Applied Studies, 1997), p. 176.

58. Reproduced in Lal, *Another Way*, p. 138 ff.

59. Parliamentary Debates (HR), June 26, 1997, p. 403.

60. Parliamentary Debates (HR), June 26, 1997, p. 414.

61. The resultant act was the Constitution (Amendment) Act 1997 of the Republic of the Fiji Islands, Act no. 13 of 1997.

62. This is in marked contrast to the Kenyan Commission, which had district coordinators for each of seventy districts and a system of constituency committees. These were all designed to provide a basis for civic education and also for organizing the people in the locality for the visits of the commissioners, whether for civic education, collection of views, or information sessions on the draft constitution once prepared.

63. *The Fiji Islands: Towards a United Future*, appendix D.

64. Lal, *Another Way*, p. 167.

65. Ibid., p. 168.

66. Citizens Constitutional Forum, *One Nation, Diverse Peoples: Building a Just and Democratic Fiji* (Suva: CCF, 1995).

67. Its Web site is at www.ccf.org.fj.

68. The same may well be true of some readers. The Queen is head of the Commonwealth. She is head of state of only about seventeen member countries. There is no necessary connection between membership in the Commonwealth and being a monarchy with the Queen as head of state, though it would be highly unlikely for a country to leave the Commonwealth but remain a monarchy.

69. The papers were subsequently published in two volumes, the first dealing with the socioeconomic situation in Fiji and the other presenting foreign experiences. See Brij Lal and Tomasi Vakatora, eds., *Fiji in Transition* Suva: School of Social and Economic Development of the University of the South Pacific, 1997); Lal and Vakatora, eds., *Fiji and the World* Suva: School of Social and Economic Development of the University of the South Pacific, 1997).

70. See, e.g., Arend Lijphart, *Democracy in Plural Societies:* A Comparative Exploration (New Haven, CT: Yale University Press, 1977).

71. Authors included Guy Powles, Cheryl Saunders, Anthony J. Regan (Australia), Alex Frame (New Zealand), Rohan Edrisinha (Sri Lanka), M.P. Singh (India), MP Jain, Cyrus Das (Malaysia), Daniel Elazar (Israel), John Darby (United Kingdom), Timothy Sisk (United States), and Michael Reisman (United States).

72. The individual was presumably Sir Len Usher. Lal, who mentions this comment, does not give the name, but knights of the realm with newspaper columns are rare anywhere. See Lal, *Another Way*, p. 165. The Fiji dollar is currently worth about forty-six U.S cents.

73. *The Fiji Islands: Towards a United Future*, para. 4.13.

74. At least in Lee Kwan Yew, the Fiji government got more than it bargained for. He actually criticized the government's racist policies and told them that Fiji would not progress without the Indians. Yash Ghai was told that he said this in a public talk that was being broadcast live. The government ordered the rest of the broadcast of the speech to be blocked.

75. Personal information.

76. See especially *The Fiji Islands: Towards a United Future*, chap. 2.

77. Personal knowledge of Yash Ghai, who negotiated the arrangement with Mauritius.

78. *Respect and Understanding: Fijian Sovereignty, The Recipe for Peace, Stability and Progress* (Suva: SVT, 1995).

79. Dr. Ahmed Ali, who had been a minister in the Alliance Party Government and was author of a leading book on the *girmit* experience.

80. The Declaration in its final form was adopted in 2007, see www.un.org/esa/socdev/unpfii/en/declaration.html.

81. Roderigo Contreras, "Indigenous Interests: The Global Picture," in *Protecting Fijian In-*

terests and Building a Democratic Fiji: A Consulta-tion on Fiji's Constitution Review (Suva: Citizens Constitutional Forum and Conciliation Resources, 1995), p. 47. The NFP sought the views of the lead-ing authority on indigenous people's rights at the UN Center on Human Rights when preparing its submission.

82. See *The Fiji Islands: Towards a United Fu-ture,* chap. 3, especially paras. 3.89–3.100. On the role of human rights, including the dialectics be-tween individual and group rights, in constitution making in India, South Africa, Canada, and Fiji, see Yash Ghai, "Universalism and Relativism: Human Rights as a Framework for Negotiating Interethnic Claims," *Cardozo Law Review,* vol, 21, no. 4 (2000), pp. 1095–1140.

83. *Respect and Understanding,* para. 3.1; ex-cerpts are printed in Lal, *Another Way,* p. 143.

84. From Asesela Ravuvu, *The Facade of De-mocracy: Fijian Struggle for Political Control, 1830–1987* (Suva: Reader Publishing House, 1991). Pro-fessor Ravuvu is writing of the concepts of *taukei* and *vulagi* in relation to any village or place, but using the concepts to make a point about incomers generally and specifically Indians (the passage ap-pears in a chapter that covers, among other things, the 1987 coup). The SVT clearly used the concept of *vulagi* in relation to Indians (the next section of the submission being "Fijians' attitudes towards Indians").

85. *Towards Racial Harmony and National Unity.*

86. Ibid., p. 59.

87. For this they cited Yash Ghai and Jill Cottrell, *Heads of State in the Pacific* (Suva: Institute of Pacific Studies of the University of the South Pa-cific, 1990) on the successful coup doctrine.

88. See Brij Lal and Peter Larmour, eds., *Electoral Systems in Divided Societies: The Fiji Con-stitution Review* (Canberra and Stockholm: NCDS, Australian National University and IDEA, 1977), which contains articles by, among others, Horowitz, Lal, and Arms.

89. Especially paras. 3.113–19.

90. Rev. Paula Niukula, research director of the Fiji Council of Churches in *Report on Consulta-tion on Fiji's Constitution Review, University of the South Pacific, Suva, Fiji 21–23 April 1994.* (Suva: International Alert and School of Social and Eco-nomic Development, 1994), p. 101.

91. Interestingly, when Rabuka introduced the bill he indicated that the JPSC had reached agree-ment on the request of the GCC (Parliamentary Debates (HR) June 23, 1997, p. 312); one would read that as saying that they had agreed with it. But in the event, what was introduced was weaker.

92. Personal information.

93. Vakatora, *Mangrove Swamps,* p. 114.

94. Ibid., chap. 8.

95. Ibid., chap. 5 (sec. 44).

96. CCF, *One Nation, Diverse Peoples,* p. 43.

97. *Republic of Fiji v. Chandrika Prasad.*

98. The latter was suggested by Krishna Datt (who is, as a Labour politician, not disinterested) in a recent CCF-sponsored discussion following a lec-ture by Andrew Ladley on multiparty government.

99. Personal comment made to Yash Ghai.

100. See Lal, *Another Way,* pp. 81–82, for early and hostile reactions in some quarters.

101. One of the reasons that the draft con-stitution and short report of the Constitution of Kenya Review Commission was warmly received in general was that the report was short and written in accessible language, and it and the actual draft con-stitution were translated into Swahili and published as pullout sections of the daily newspapers.

102. As Yash Ghai relates, "When I was in Fiji in October 2000, the head of the armed forces invited me for consultations, particularly in view of the impending Court of Appeal decision on the le-gality of the coup. All senior officers were carrying copies of the constitution. During our conversation, I was told that the army had only begun to study it and, to their surprise, found it was an excellent constitution and a better one could not be imagined. But they had not known this when they more or less supported the coup!"

103. See speeches of the prime minister and the attorney general in the aftermath of the 2009 events, available on the government Web site at www.fiji.gov.fj/publish/cat_speeches.shtml.

104. Jon Fraenkel, "Addendum" to Jon Fraen-kel and Stewart Firth, *From Election to Coup in Fiji: The 2006 Campaign and Its Aftermath,* (Canberra: ANU e-Press and Asia Pacific Press, 2007), p. 420. Available at epress.anu.edu.au/fiji_citation.html.

105. Fraenkel, "Addendum," p. 442.

PART IV

EUROPE

11

The Drafting Process for the 1998 Albanian Constitution

Scott N. Carlson

When the Republic of Albania adopted a new constitution in 1998, it joined the ranks of other Central and Eastern European countries that have moved to democratic forms of government. For Albania, the new constitution provides a historic foundation upon which to forge an independent and democratic future. Throughout its recent history, Albania has endured domination and rigid control at the hands of regional powers. Even when independent, the country has suffered under autocracy, most egregiously so under Stalinist dictator Enver Hoxha, who led post–World War II Albania into forty-five years of exile from the international community. Albania's adoption of a democratic constitution was a significant step toward solidifying its democracy and joining the community of countries that rely on constitutions to structure and safeguard their democratic systems of government.

Albania's history of domination and isolation does not fully explain its delay in adopting a new constitution, but it does shape the context in which constitutional reform developed. It helps to explain the lack of constitutional materials in the Albanian language, lack of familiarity and experience with modern democratic institutions and human rights, and both international and local agreement on the need for extensive foreign input.

Introducing a new constitutional system or structure is unavoidably challenging. Even a completely tried and tested system or structure may fail when applied to a new environment. The process of legal transplantation is delicate, as the host state can reject foreign legal concepts for a variety of reasons. Legal and political traditions can be both foundations upon which to graft new structures and obstacles to implementing them. Albania's efforts to develop a democratic constitution provide a classic illustration of the challenges that legal, political, and social traditions pose to persons advocating substantial systemic change. The tumultuous events before and during the 1997–98 drafting process challenged local and international actors to devise new methods to engage politicians and the public, and the drafting and approval of the 1998 constitution represents a novel and sustained effort to incorporate public participation, both local and international, in all aspects of the process.

Albania was introduced to constitutionalism before World War II, but the period concluded with the self-proclaimed King Zog ceding power to occupying Italian fascist forces. During the war, the constitution was suspended and Albania administered by Italian appointees. Immediately after World War II, Enver Hoxha and his partisans secured control of Albania. On January 11, 1946, a constitutional assembly declared Albania to be a "people's republic," and two months later, on March 14, 1946, the assembly adopted a new constitution.[1] This constitution, as amended, provided the structure of the socialist state for the next thirty years.

In 1972, the Sixth Congress of the Albanian Party of Labor issued the directive that a new constitution should be formed, an effort that culminated on December 28, 1976, with the promulgation of a new constitution. In the words of Enver Hoxha, the new constitution was necessary to "complete the construction of socialism and the further development of our state of the dictatorship of the proletariat."[2] According to official state pronouncements, the new constitution was drafted with the benefit of public consultations: Over the course of "several months," the draft was "submitted for study to the working masses all over the country."[3] Suggestions emerging from these consultations with the public were "recorded and studied," and "all suggestions improving on the document" were adopted.[4] Despite this encouraging rhetoric, the 1976 constitution did not recognize the institutions of pluralist democracy nor permit the formation of a market

economy. Party dogma dictated that pluralism in the Western sense simply reflected "the multiplicity of groups with opposing interests in the ranks of the bourgeoisie."[5] The constitution provided for a highly centralized state that emphasized collectivism in all aspects. The constitution nominally permitted some personal property, but state involvement in all aspects of economic and political life was so extensive that taxes and levies were abolished.[6] In general, modern concepts of individual civil and political rights and the separation of powers were considered irrelevant. The will of the masses—as expressed through the monolithic Party of Labor—was to direct all organs and functions of the state "for the purpose of defend ing the victories of the revolution and strengthening of the socialist order."[7]

In 1990–91, the Party of Labor began to acknowledge that their vision of a monolithic socialist state was no longer viable, and gradually, party officials began work on drafting laws that would implement radical reforms in the system of government, introducing political pluralism and modern democratic institutions to protect basic human rights. The result of this process was a set of laws commonly referred to as the Major Constitutional Provisions.[8] Collectively, these laws established the basic framework for a modern democratic state and protections of individual human rights.

The provisions were a dramatic change from the past, but there remained a need and political commitment to develop a permanent constitution. Acknowledging this fact, Albanian legal professionals opened a dialogue with the Venice Commission of the Council of Europe in November 1991, seeking to benefit from their diverse pool of constitutional-law experts.[9] The Major Constitutional Provisions suffered from shortcomings and lacked clarity in certain areas, and Albanian legal professionals were interested in addressing these issues in a manner consistent with international best practices. One area of political concern was the ease with which the provisions could be amended, as a simple two-thirds vote of parliament could amend any and all of them.[10] Such a standard was not unacceptable per se, but a more deliberative process, perhaps including a referendum, would have been more open and less subject to manipulation by political supermajorities. In any case, the provisions were only intended to be temporary, as they called upon the parliament to establish a constitutional commission to control the drafting process. During 1993 and 1994, such a commission worked on a draft text and developed various versions of it. Generally speaking, the various texts all contained the basic provisions for establishing a fully functional parliamentary democracy.[11]

In the summer of 1994, President Sali Berisha and his confidantes handpicked a select group of draftsmen and encouraged them to finalize a draft that would be put to a popular vote in a referendum. Those excluded from the drafting process, such as opposition parties, considered President Berisha's initiative to have placed political considerations above the established drafting process. Of particular concern was the proposed ratification process. Lacking the necessary two-thirds majority to approve a replacement text under the Major Constitutional Provisions, the governing coalition passed a referendum law with a simple majority on October 6, 1994, providing an alternate method of approving a permanent constitution.[12] The opposition Socialist Party protested publicly, challenging the constitutionality of the referendum law in the constitutional court.

As the November 6, 1994, referendum approached, there was concern that the constitutional court had not yet heard the case. When pressed for a response, the court announced that the Socialist Party complaint had been misplaced, causing a delay. Directly before the referendum, three of nine members of the court resigned in protest.[13] Given the court's *sua sponte* review authority[14] and the gravity of the complaint, failure to review the matter before the referendum created the distinct appearance of further political interference.

Nonetheless, the referendum proceeded without the benefit of a court review. Voting was relatively calm and uneventful, and the final tally resulted in an unequivocal defeat for the proposed draft,[15] surprising many in the local and international communities. The Venice Commission had completed its review of the proposed draft the week before, finding it "unfortunate that the protection of human rights ... [does] not form part of the fundamental principles of the Constitution."[16] However, the commission's role was not widely understood and it is unlikely that its evaluation had any impact on the outcome of the referendum. The issue of a permanent constitution languished thereafter for several years.

The next national election was the parliamentary election of 1996. In contrast to the 1994 referendum, this election was fraught with manipulation and intimidation. International criticism followed, and the landslide reelection of the ruling majority was understood to be of questionable legitimacy at best.[17] The government further jeopardized its dubious position when it refused to take legal action to halt Albania's rapidly expanding pyramid schemes later in 1996.[18] Allegations were made that the governing majority was involved in the schemes, and tensions within the country increased as the year ended and the schemes began to fold. From November 1996 through March 1997, the majority of the pyramid schemes collapsed; in some cases, their leaders disappeared. Slowly, thousands of citizens began to realize they had lost much if not all of their life savings. Government institutions reacted clumsily, sometimes curtailing rather than protecting citizens' rights. In a particularly outrageous example, the president of the Tirana District Court rejected all civil actions against the pyramid scheme operators.[19] The government's impotence, combined with an ongoing refusal to fully address the crisis, enraged large segments of the population. Street protests against the government emerged. Most corrective actions were viewed as too little too late, and the governing coalition sought to reassert public confidence and order through coercive tactics.

In a style reminiscent of Albania's communist period, the government derided the protesters, imposed martial law, denied responsibility for the crisis, and reelected Berisha as president.[20] Meanwhile, the largest pyramid scheme remained untouched, reminding the general public of its powerful position on a daily basis through its private, extralegal television station,[21] and the ruling coalition seemed to be emboldened. Public outrage mounted and widespread unrest emerged outside the capital of Tirana. The institutions of government buckled and civil order disappeared. As chaos descended over much of the country, faith in the constitutional order evaporated. People began to flee the country or lock themselves indoors, fearing loss of property and life. Looting occurred, particularly in establishments owned and operated by the pyramid schemes.[22] After days of upheaval, the government finally conceded its inability to govern. On March 6, 1997, leaders of the majority party reached an agreement with opposition leaders and formed a technical government, anticipating new elections in summer 1997.[23] To support a stable transition and avert a humanitarian crisis, the Italian government volunteered to organize and lead Operation Alba, resulting in the rapid deployment of troops from North At-

lantic Treaty Organization (NATO) countries throughout Albania.[24]

Structure of the Process

Complementing Operation Alba's security forces was the international political commitment of the Organization for Security and Cooperation in Europe (OSCE). On March 4, 1997, the OSCE chairman in office appointed Dr. Franz Vranitzky as a personal representative to Albania; on March 27, 1997, the OSCE's Permanent Council established the OSCE Presence in Albania. The OSCE mandate was broad, including "assistance in democratization" and serving as a "coordinating framework for the work of other international organizations."[25] With this commitment in mind, the OSCE Presence in Albania rapidly began to work with a variety of domestic, multilateral, and bilateral actors to prepare for new parliamentary elections.

April to June 1997 saw an intensive period of negotiations, leading ultimately to a political compromise and revision of the electoral law, permitting the elections to proceed in June and July. The elections resulted in a clear defeat for Berisha's Democratic Party, which received approximately 25 percent of the vote. The Socialist Party received over 50 percent of the vote, and with this majority, it joined several center-left parties to form a governing coalition.[26]

A major concern of the 1997 elections was the need to reestablish civil order, and politicians focused on restoring public confidence in the institutions of government—in particular, adopting a new constitution as a symbolic step to instill faith in Albania's future as a modern Western democracy. Within two months of its formation, Albania's new parliament approved Decision 339, which provided a general framework for the process of drafting a new constitution.[27] This decision established a twenty-one-member parliamentary commission and a set of guiding parameters, in which the decision defined public participation, both local and international, as a clear priority.[28] Decision 339 also set forth five substantive groupings around which the parliament expected the drafting process to be organized:

- *Legislative*: The composition, formulation, and administration of legislative powers.
- *Judicial*: The composition, formulation, and administration of judicial powers.
- *Executive*: The composition, formulation, and administration of central executive powers.
- *Local Government*: The composition, formulation, and administration of local government powers.
- *Human Rights*: The definition and protection of human rights.[29]

Primary responsibility for organizing the process was assigned to the newly created Ministry of Institutional Reform and Relations with the Parliament, or Ministry of Institutional Reform. Pursuant to this mandate, the minister invited three lawyers outside of government to develop a proposal for coordinating assistance and public participation in the constitution-drafting process. These lawyers, two Albanian and one foreign, had a number of years of experience designing legal reform initiatives in Albania. After a short period of negotiation, the lawyers obtained sponsorship from the United States Agency for International Development (USAID), the German Technical Cooperation Agency (GTZ), and the OSCE.

Public Participation in the Process

On October 15, 1997, the Administrative Center for the Coordination of Assistance and Public Participation (ACCAPP) opened in offices provided by the OSCE Presence in Tirana.[30] The team of lawyers assembled by the Ministry of Institutional Reform designed ACCAPP[31] as a "quasi non-governmental organization," administered by its directors and financially supported by various other non-governmental organizations (NGOs) and foreign governments, though it enjoyed the cooperation and support of both the ministry and the OSCE as well. ACCAPP operated independently of both the OSCE and Albanian Ministry of Institutional Reform; it worked with Albanians and the international community to facilitate technical assistance, collect and distribute information, provide training, and organize polls and civic-education initiatives. Throughout its existence, ACCAPP remained independent and did not represent the interests of any particular party or government.

ACCAPP was primarily a liaison between and among Albanian and international participants in the constitution-drafting process. The goal of this process was to ensure that all interested parties could participate fully and avoid duplicative and conflicting initiatives. ACCAPP actively solicited assistance from Albanian NGOs and international donors to provide materials, training for constitutional commissioners and interested citizens, and other assistance. It also held working sessions with NGOs and international donors to develop strategies and action plans for organizing assistance and promoting public participation in the constitution-drafting process. To ensure increased coordination, an ACCAPP newsletter regularly reported on its activities, in English and Albanian.[32]

Among Albanian participants in the constitution-making process, NGO and citizen involvement was considered essential to promote informed citizen participation in the drafting of a new constitution and citizen ownership in the final product. As described below, ACCAPP worked with the ministry to ensure that NGOs and citizens took part in commenting on all of the basic categories described in Decision 339.

Development of a National Program of Public Participation

From December 1997 to September 1998, the constitutional commission of the Albanian parliament, the Ministry of Institutional Reform, and ACCAPP worked together to implement a national program of public participation. The program was designed to collect input into the drafting of the constitution (Phase I) and submit draft provisions to the public for review and comment (Phase II).

Phase I consisted of more than a dozen forums and symposia in which constitutional issues were discussed and public input gathered. The results of these forums provided commission members and their technical staff with a basic outline of the issues that the public considered important. International donors and local NGOs organized the Phase I meetings. The initial stage called for a series of meetings consisting of NGO forums, followed by focused discussion groups.

The three national NGO forums brought together various NGO representatives to discuss the five basic categories specified in Decision 339: legislative power, executive power, judicial power, human rights, and local government. At these forums, NGO representatives worked in small groups, brainstorming to produce recommendations and identify issues requiring further discussion. Albania has a relatively vibrant NGO community and invitations to the forums were essentially open, asking each interested organization to designate one or two representatives to participate. In the early phase of the process, NGO participation was used as a proxy for full public participation because of the desire to commence drafting quickly with some sense of the public's concerns; participation in the later public hearings was more broadly citizen based.

After each forum, donors and local NGOs organized a total of four focused discussion groups designed to review in greater detail the issues identified in the NGO forums and to gather more specific recommendations and suggestions. A combination of legal experts, NGO representatives, government officials, and politicians attended the various discussion groups. The results of all the forums and discussion groups were recorded, and detailed written summaries of the main points, including recommendations, were prepared and provided to all commission members.[33]

In May 1998, the results of the NGO input process were used as a basis for a broader discussion at the Three Powers Symposium, sponsored and organized by the American Bar Association Central East European Law Initiative (ABA/CEELI) and GTZ, in coordination with ACCAPP. As the name indicates, the symposium focused on the three classic constitutional themes of legislative, executive, and judicial powers.

The symposium provided an opportunity for Albanian leaders involved in the constitution-drafting process to hear the comments and suggestions of Albanian and foreign experts on the issues that Albanian NGOs identified. Symposium participation included members of the opposition Democratic Party as well as individual citizens. Following the symposium, ABA/CEELI, ACCAPP, and Albanian state television produced a three-part prime-time television series summarizing the discussions for Albanian viewers nationwide.

While Phase I was in progress, the commission began drafting a text; it finished a complete draft in June 1998 and approved a revised text in its entirety on August 5. Phase II was then initiated, consisting of a broad review of the August 5 text by individuals and organizations within and outside of Albania. This public review of the draft text was in addition to foreign experts' drafting consultations. Throughout all phases of the drafting process, foreign constitutional experts were consulted for independent analysis of the technical substance of the various provisions. In this regard, the Venice Commission was the dominant foreign-expert influence. However, extensive consultations also took place with other U.S. and European constitutional experts, and the constitutional commission maintained an inclusive and open approach to foreign advice.[34] ACCAPP facilitated the process wherever possible, providing up-to-the-moment translations of new provisions and coordinating consultations. Consequently, the participation of international experts became an integral component of the drafting process, extending public participation and input beyond the national context.

Domestically, for the Phase II public review, the constitutional drafting commission, ACCAPP, and international assistance providers organized a series of public hearings to solicit public comments on the proposed draft, open to anyone who wished to attend and involving several hundred participants. The public-hearing schedule covered major population centers throughout the country.[35] A diverse cross section of Albanian experts, citizens, politicians, and NGO representatives attended the meetings, and ACCAPP collected suggestions and comments that were then submitted to the commission for consideration. The draft also was published, with public comment invited.

Despite repeated attempts to bring Democratic Party members into the hearing process, participation remained low generally. On a number of occasions, Democratic Party leadership told interested members that they could not participate. However, there were notable exceptions, such as the contribution of the former head of the Central Election Commission.[36] When these persons intervened, they were treated with respect and their comments were incorporated fully into the process.

ACCAPP indexed and organized all the public comments according to subject matter to assist the commission and its technical staff in the review process. Hundreds of suggested changes to the draft were considered and more than 50 proposed changes, affecting more than 45 of 183 total articles, were accepted. Altogether, the commission amended approximately 25 percent of the draft articles based on specific public suggestions. The nature of these amendments varied widely and touched on some high-profile subjects, such as property restitution. Most important, each change was important to a broad range of individuals and interest groups and, once accepted, bolstered the legitimacy of the social contract. On September 30, 1998, the commission approved the constitution's final text.

From October 5 to October 20, the Albanian parliament reviewed the text proposed by the constitutional commission. This review consisted of an intense mixture of committee review and plenary session debates. Each of the following committees reviewed the draft: public order and national information service; industry, public affairs, and trade; agriculture and food; foreign affairs; health and environmental protection; economy, finance, and privatization; and human rights and minorities. These review sessions were open, with journalists, local experts, and a representative of the Venice Commission participating freely. The final draft, approved on October 21, 1998, included virtually all the public suggestions that the constitutional commission incorporated in their final September 30 draft.

Civic Education Initiatives

Given the public's anticipated involvement in the drafting process, Albanian leaders considered it important to provide civic education on constitutional issues before the public consultation phases. ACCAPP worked with a host of local NGOs, the constitutional commission, and citizens to develop these types of activities. The list of contributors and participants is extensive, but certain Albanian NGOs, such as the Society for Democratic Culture,[37] took standout leadership roles: Not only did they educate the public on substantive constitutional issues, but they also demonstrated civil society's important role in the democratic process. As a result, the educational process itself became an example of the processes that must underlie the establishment of a successful constitutional democracy. Throughout the drafting process, ACCAPP, NGOs, and the constitutional commission developed and executed a variety of civic-education initiatives, including issue forums, such as television broadcasts and telephone call-ins; radio programs with telephone call-ins; pamphlets on particular constitutional issues, processes, and definitions; newspaper serials on constitutional issues; constitutional papers prepared by experts for study and review by citizens; and essay writing contests.

The international community recognized the need for education on constitutional issues before the referendum, and international representatives agreed that it should remain a priority for the foreseeable future to encourage understanding of the constitution and ownership in the social contract. After the conclusion of the constitution-making process, ACCAPP's local staff was absorbed by the OSCE Presence with the understanding that they would continue to devote time and resources to education on constitutional issues. In the years since, the OSCE Presence's legal unit has continued to do significant work in rule-of-law education and promotion, publishing a two-volume transcription of the constitutional commission debates.

Democratic Representation

With its adoption of Decision 339, the Albanian parliament decided to use the vehicle originally envisaged in the Major Constitutional Provisions, a constitutional commission, as the official body to produce a draft constitution and receive public comment. The parliament concluded that the commission should be composed of parliamentary representatives from all parties and that the distribution of seats should reflect generally the proportionate voting blocks extant in the parliament. While this distribution gave somewhat disproportionate influence to smaller parties, it was nevertheless endorsed, ensuring that certain minorities, ethnic and otherwise, were officially represented.

Overall, Decision 339 provided a one-seat majority for the Socialist Party and its coalition partners. This slim majority provoked an aggressive and militant response from the Democratic Party and, for the most part, their allies. In autumn 1997, the Democratic Party and its Union for Democracy—the Democratic Party and a group of center-right satellite parties that owed their parliamentary seats in many cases to the Democratic Party's efforts—initiated a boycott campaign that lasted throughout the majority of the constitution-drafting process. The international community immediately tried to calm political tensions and reengage the Democratic Party in the political process. Common sense dictated that a new constitution should be forged with the consensus of all political parties. Initially, the Democratic Party mainly objected to the constitution-drafting process because the parliament had excluded them from the chairmanship of the constitutional commission, giving it to two minority parties instead, the Republican Party and the Democratic Alliance Party.[38] The governing coalition countered that excluding both major parties, the Socialist Party and the Democratic Party, fostered an open and inclusive approach toward minority parties. Furthermore, the coalition and the United Right invited the Democratic Party and its affiliated Union for Democracy to take their seats on the commission to discuss this and other issues. The offer was refused, and the Union for Democracy called for a constitutional convention to handle all constitution-drafting issues. Under their proposal, new elections would be organized immediately to select delegates to the convention. The Democratic Party maintained that it enjoyed the support of the majority of the population, and the elections, if free and fair, would vindicate their position. They later relinquished their call for a convention but insisted on having a blocking minority, or veto power, within the constitutional commission. While the Democratic Party had pledged to accept the results of the 1997 election,[39] they focused on the language in the OSCE election monitoring report that referred to the election results as "acceptable, given the prevailing circumstances."[40] They maintained that this marginal result, combined with new "attacks" on their membership and "democracy,"[41] justified their boycott.

The political atmosphere was particularly supercharged after a couple of controversial constitutional court decisions. On November 13, 1997, the court struck down a legal provision that permitted government-appointed administrators to take charge of pyramid-scheme assets.[42] The provision had been drafted with International Monetary Fund (IMF) consultation, and its invalidation raised concerns about the new government's ability to finish the closing and liquidation of the pyramid schemes. The parliament reacted immediately, amending a constitutional provision and reenacting the contested provision.[43] In an openly confrontational manner, the constitutional court *sua sponte* issued a decision rejecting this parliamentary remedy.[44]

Asserting supremacy in constitutional matters, the constitutional court in effect denied the parliament's authority to amend constitutional provisions in response to court decisions. This contravened the Major Constitutional Provisions, which allowed for amendments with relative ease and a pau-

city of public dialogue; the parliament was clearly acting under their collective authority. Domestic and international criticism of the constitutional court followed. The Venice Commission unequivocally condemned the action, stating: "The Constitutional Court therefore overstepped the limit of its authority and entered into a political dispute with the People's Assembly, which can only be to the detriment of the functioning of both organs."[45] The parliament further politicized tense relations with the constitutional court by issuing a decision requiring the court to execute its constitutionally required rotation of membership. The Democratic Party decried the act, claiming that the constitutional court, consisting of members appointed by the prior Democratic-controlled parliament, was simply exercising its independent constitutional function.

In the midst of the turmoil, the constitutional commission commenced its work cautiously. At the end of 1997, several official meetings were convened, and in each instance, the seven members of the Union for Democracy boycotted. Though work proceeded on a draft of the commission's internal operating rules, cochairmen Sabri Godo and Arben Imami prudently avoided moving substantive decisions to a final vote, noting that final decisions should be postponed until later meetings that might include all members.

The initial meetings were substantively limited, but they did provide both planned and unplanned benefits. Among the planned benefits, ACCAPP enjoyed an adequate opportunity to work with the commission on a realistic public participation program. The specter of a boycott actually increased the influence of public participation, as the commission would need to reach out to the public in a direct and demonstrable manner if it were to proceed with broad public legitimacy. Also, by demonstrating that genuine local efforts had been tried and exhausted, the repeated good-faith attempts by the commissioners who had taken their seats to bring in the Union for Democracy substantially bolstered the case for international assistance to mediate the political dispute. This assistance, in turn, set the stage for the ongoing international involvement that characterized the bulk of the drafting process throughout 1998.

Timing and Sequencing of the Constitution-Making Process

With the chaos of early 1997 as the backdrop, a number of influential Albanian leaders considered a permanent constitution to be an urgent priority for restoring order. Initially, Decision 339 proposed an expedited timeline, with a completion date in late winter to early spring 1998. However, this date soon became unlikely at best and at worst, unwise.[46] The immediate and persistent objections of the Union for Democracy made it clear that more time was needed to explore their concerns fully, not to mention the concerns of the public at large. To maximize the participation of the Union for Democracy and the general public, both local politicians and international actors comprehended the need for a deliberate, inclusive process, characterized by public outreach.

Central to this outreach effort was the full participation of the relevant actors in the international community. The tensions between the two major political blocks were evident, and both looked to international actors to broker various disputes. In the media, the citizenry frequently was confronted with polarized political charges. Given that the press was heavily structured around party affiliations, it was often difficult to discern the underlying facts and issues. This situation gave further weight to the pronouncements of the international community communicated to the grassroots level via local media, in the form of formal declarations, statements to the press, and interviews.

The domestic political conflict and the international community's substantial role in assuaging it necessitated a substantial revision of the original target date. The president, Rexhep Meidani, eventually settled on November 22, 1998, for the popular referendum.[47] This date gave the constitutional commission, ACCAPP, and others in the drafting process enough time to develop viable schedules and allocate the necessary resources. Though the timing remained tight—particularly given the ongoing political disagreements—the drafting process could nevertheless proceed in a considered, professional manner.

However, the process of ratification via referendum proved to be a more significant challenge in resources, logistics, and timing. Upon completing the drafting process at the end of October, the administrators engaged in the referendum process faced additional obstacles, including civic education of the voters regarding the referendum process and the draft text along with the actual technicalities involved in referendum administration. Complicating these inherent difficulties was the Democratic Party's decision to encourage voters to boycott voting in the referendum.

Voter lists historically have been problematic in Albania. Consistently, the OSCE Office for Democratic Institutions and Human Rights (ODIHR) has cited the Albanian government for inadequate voter lists,[48] and government officials were particularly concerned that the Democratic Party might capitalize on voter-list problems to defeat the approval of the constitution in the national referendum. The 1994 Referendum Law requires an absolute majority of registered voters to pass a measure.[49] However, if the voter lists are not accurate, it becomes difficult, if not impossible, to calculate accurately what constitutes such a majority. Given the large number of Albanians working outside Albania, the registration issue posed a logistical problem and a potential source of continuing dispute. With these and other considerations in mind, the ruling coalition amended the law to allow a measure to pass if it received a majority of those voting.[50] The Democratic Party protested, decrying the amendment as politically motivated. The ruling coalition responded that either approach to tallying referendums is acceptable in a democratic system.[51]

With the constitution's final passage in the People's Assembly on October 30 and the referendum date of November 22, preparations were forced into a very tight timeline.[52] The Ministry of Local Government and the Central Election Commission (CEC), with the assistance of the OSCE, ACCAPP, International Foundation for Election Systems (IFES), and European Union, engaged in a nationwide effort to distribute information to voters on registering to vote, voting, the provisions of the constitution, and the constitution-drafting process. Information was distributed through written materials, television, and radio. With this international support, thousands of pages of materials, posters, and copies of the draft constitution were distributed nationwide, and educational television spots, developed in conjunction with the CEC, were aired.

Typically, a referendum campaign focuses on the issues involved in the referendum, with different politicians taking different positions. Parties frequently do not take party positions, leaving members to vote their consciences. Certain issues draw broad coalitions from across political spectrums, and campaigning for or against an issue may unite traditional political opponents in common cause. However, the political polarization that characterized Albanian politics before the referendum campaign intensified during it, limiting the debate and further destabilizing the fragile democratic process. Both the majority and minority spent a relatively limited amount of time on substantive issues. The minority Democratic Party sought to make the referendum a rerun of the elections, discussing personalities more than issues.

The Democratic Party's decision to boycott the referendum and the manner in which it conducted its campaign presented several substantive problems. First, the boycott itself raised the specter of intimidation. With the recent political violence fresh in mind, there was fear that Democratic Party personnel would note who had entered polling stations and target them for later reprisals, intimidating people from freely going to the polls. Second, the Democratic Party construed all voter education to be political campaigning. Because the Democratic Party favored boycott, they argued that encouraging voter participation amounted to a vote in favor of the constitution.[53] Democratic Party personnel attacked all efforts to encourage citizens to exercise their right to vote, and their representatives at the CEC even suggested that the CEC should educate citizens in their right not to vote. Finally, in November, when the Democratic Party engaged in a debate on the substance of the constitutional draft, its approach consisted of a distorted campaign of misinformation reminiscent of the communist period.[54] The distortions were so severe in some cases that international groups were compelled to issue corrective pronouncements.[55]

In contrast, the campaign of the ruling coalition was relatively innocuous and limited in scope. Efforts from ruling-coalition members were generally reactive, focused mostly on responding to various extreme accusations that issued from the Democratic Party. To the extent that the ruling coalition proactively campaigned on substantive issues, it was limited generally to modest, peaceful campaign rallies and basic video spots.

Throughout the campaign period, CEC meetings were acrimonious and polarized along political lines. Democratic Party members made numerous complaints concerning referendum administration. Many complaints were minor, but some involved major issues.[56] Consistent with its previous practice in Albania, the OSCE mediated CEC impasses. Particularly significant were Democratic Party challenges to television programming, as Democratic Party CEC members argued that Albanian law required that, first, only political parties could engage in constitutional programming, to the exclusion of NGOs and the state itself; second, CEC had the right to censor all programming; and third, any news segment involving a government official was by definition campaigning. The OSCE examined these legal issues in great detail and determined that such positions were not mandated under existing law and not required to keep with generally accepted democratic principles.[57] However, the OSCE did assist the disputing parties in arriving at a code of conduct for state television programming on the constitution. The principles agreed upon directed state television to develop balanced programming on the topic.

The OSCE was called upon to mediate in a variety of circumstances. In the final two weeks leading up to the referendum, attempts to mediate became progressively more difficult as the Democratic Party deputy chairman of the CEC took more extreme positions. During the final period, the deputy chairman issued physical threats to the chairman of the CEC and the OSCE ambassador, threatened walkouts, and was generally disruptive.[58]

Responsibility for preparing to administer the referendum was assigned to the Ministry of Local Government.[59] The ministry was ideally suited for the task because it had a nationwide network of offices and an experienced professional staff.[60] Nevertheless, given the tight timeline for preparation and the scarcity of resources, the Ministry of Local Government turned to the OSCE and ACCAPP for assistance; these organi-

zations identified and secured funding for ballots, training, and other logistical needs, produced election-official training materials, and assisted in other aspects of preparation. Within two months, all basic preparations had been completed.

The day of the constitutional referendum, November 22, 1999, the weather was unusually poor. Ballots had to be helicoptered into remote snowbound areas. Despite the poor weather and the boycott, the actual administration of the referendum was relatively smooth. By the close of the polls, the vote was overwhelmingly in favor of the constitution, with approximately 90 percent in support of it. A broad team of international observers from the Council of Europe, European Union, and OSCE issued a joint statement on November 23, 1999, that concluded: "The observers found on 22 November the voting procedures of the referendum were carried out in a correct manner, for which the voters and election officials should be commended."[61]

The observation missions also commented on the drafting process and the Democratic Party's political campaign. Regarding the former, they noted, "The referendum followed an open and transparent process where advice on the constitution was taken from many sources, domestically as well as internationally."[62] Regarding the latter, the observation team commented critically: "The disinformation on the contents of the constitution, the misrepresentation of international representatives and unfounded allegations against the constitutional process by the Democratic Party are to be regretted."[63]

The Role of the International Community

Several organizations and bilateral actors took leadership roles in the constitution-drafting process. Overall, the OSCE was the most influential multilateral actor, positioning itself as an information clearinghouse and general facilitator, which the Albanian government accepted. The government's own lack of capacity to conduct the constitution-making process was one reason for this acceptance. The country was on the verge of all-out civil war at the time, and the high level of instability concerned a broad range of actors. In the circumstances, domestic political actors had proven unable to deal with the situation peacefully and efficiently. The OSCE role complemented that of the Council of Europe and European Union, which emphasized their respective capacities to marshal legal and political expertise. As for bilateral actors, the United States predominated with substantial assistance from EU counterparts, most notably Germany. While the sustained engagement of any one of these actors would have been remarkable, the constitution-drafting process benefited from the engagement of all of them, bearing witness to an extraordinary level of interest, cooperation, and support. Moreover, the involvement of the international community was unusually well coordinated at both a high diplomatic level and an on-the-ground project level throughout the entire eighteen months of activity. The multilateral engagement was most notable on several distinct occasions during the visits of parliamentary delegations and a coup attempt.

Parliamentary Delegations

The OSCE, in collaboration with ACCAPP, undertook an ambitious plan to bring political forces together at both the national and international levels to forge a sense of common purpose and commitment to work together for Albania's common good. The OSCE recognized that the Democratic Party's antagonistic posture bordered on a rejection of the 1997 election results, which would constitute a substantial impediment to consolidating democratic institutions. Further-

more, the domestic political scene was very sensitive to international opinion because the international community had brought them back from the brink of civil war, and the OSCE saw a need to ensure that all international actors viewed and analyzed the local situation objectively. Given the political nature of the issues involved, the OSCE chose to involve experienced politicians.

In mid-January 1998, the OSCE Presence, in cooperation with ACCAPP, organized an international parliamentary delegation to evaluate and counsel Albanian politicians on the political situation with a view to instilling a spirit of compromise and moderation. Local politicians had claimed international support for a variety of their positions, and the international community was interested in clarifying their positions on a number of these issues, in particular efforts to draft a new constitution. To ensure a broad, representative range of international views, the OSCE invited parliamentarians from the OSCE, Council of Europe, and European Union to participate. In the last week of January, a senior group of these parliamentarians, representing a range of political viewpoints, traveled to Albania.[64] This so-called Tri-Parliamentary Delegation met with the entire spectrum of local politicians and diplomats and openly discussed the situation. At the conclusion of their meetings, they adopted and issued a declaration, the first Tri-Parliamentary Declaration,[65] which urged the government to increase efforts to promote democratic institutions, procedures, and values,[66] and at the same time rejected the Democratic Party boycott tactics.[67] The declaration focused on the constitution-drafting process, endorsing the legality of the current parliament and constitutional commission and the need for a constitution and public referendum on that document.[68] Both the governing coalition and the Union for Democracy responded favorably to this counsel: The Union for Democracy returned to parliament and the governing coalition adopted new rules of parliamentary procedure, improved actual parliamentary practice, enhanced the legal framework, and developed the new Magistrates School.[69]

However, political turmoil affecting the constitution-making process subsequently resurfaced. Most notably, the governing coalition summarily removed the president of the constitutional court, Rustem Gjata. After an investigation under the Union for Democracy–authored lustration laws,[70] it was determined that Gjata had committed objectionable acts under the Hoxha regime. Pursuant to the provisions of the lustration laws, the parliament removed the president, stating that the removal had "nothing to do" with the issue of judicial immunity.[71] This action, along with other alleged provocations, led to the resumption of the Democratic Party boycott.

Political forces made some progress, with limited dialogue occurring behind the scenes in the wake of the first Tri-Parliamentary mission, but the international community remained concerned that progress was insufficient, particularly regarding the ongoing Democratic Party boycott of the constitution-drafting process. Though some Union for Democracy members appeared at select events, the Democratic Party had failed to officially engage.

In the last week of June 1998, a second senior group of parliamentarians, including some from the previous mission, traveled to Albania to reevaluate the situation and urge compromise. As before, the delegation met a full range of local politicians and diplomats and openly discussed the situation. At the conclusion of their meetings, they issued a second Tri-Parliamentary Declaration, which again attempted to provide a balanced set of recommendations addressed to all sides. However, regarding the constitution-drafting process, the declaration generally applauded the constitutional commission's efforts, citing its transparency and commitment to public participation; it also rejected Union for Democracy demands for veto powers on the commission.[72] The Union for Democracy, which had refused to participate in a meaningful way, was called upon to do so.[73]

Over the next week, a quiet dialogue with members of the Democratic Party leadership indicated their willingness to join the process. However, in a surprise move, on July 7, 1998, Democratic Party chairman Sali Berisha announced a new "indefinite" boycott of the parliament. Multiple statements from the OSCE, European Union, and Council of Europe condemned the move immediately.[74] Despite continuous urgings, the Democratic Party maintained its boycott position for the remainder of the drafting process.

In August 1998, there appeared to be some possibility that the Democratic Party would participate in a roundtable with coalition politicians. However, the arrest of some former Democratic Party officials for alleged criminal activity in the 1997 civil unrest angered Democratic Party officials and disrupted the roundtable.[75] The constitutional commission and international community continued their efforts to bring the Democratic Party into the process, but without success.

Attempted Coup d'Etat

On September 12, 1998, a high-level leader of the Democratic Party, Azem Hajdari, was assassinated directly after leaving Democratic Party headquarters. Hajdari was a leader of the original student movement and Albanians widely regarded him as one of the instrumental figures in the struggle for democracy in Albania. Within a couple of hours of his murder, the Democratic Party assigned responsibility for his death to the Socialist prime minister, Fatos Nano.[76]

Berisha immediately seized upon the assassination to justify dissolving the current government. The Democratic Party, along with its satellite parties in the Union for Democracy, issued public demands for a technical government in which they would share power. By noon the following day, their supporters had stormed several government buildings and destroyed substantial property.[77] On the afternoon of September 13, using highly inflammatory rhetoric, Berisha gave Nano an ultimatum to relinquish power within twenty-four hours—a period corresponding to the twenty-four hours of truce provided in Albanian customary law to a murderer before blood revenge is exacted.[78] This unstated threat was not lost on Democratic Party supporters, who began streaming into Tirana, particularly from the mountainous north. Preparations were then made to conduct a public funeral protest in the middle of the main square.[79]

On September 14, the twenty-four-hour period elapsed as the funeral procession left the main square heading for government office buildings. A substantial number of the mourners were heavily armed with automatic weapons, and they broke into the Council of Ministers.[80] Union for Democracy supporters claimed government security forces fired upon them at that time. However, trained Western military observers who were present saw no evidence of this, and there were no confirmed injuries. Directly thereafter, Union for Democracy supporters commandeered tanks and took over the state television and several government buildings.

In the following days, intense diplomatic pressure was brought to bear from both multilateral and bilateral actors. Through diplomatic channels, the international community gave the armed insurgents a clear signal that it would not recognize a government installed by force. Moreover, the established position of the OSCE Presence allowed it to lead and coordinate negotiations among various domestic factions. Because the OSCE enjoyed the respect and trust of all involved

and could serve as an honest broker, it successfully created a dialogue among the various parties, stabilizing the situation at several key junctures.[81] Once the armed insurgents relinquished their hold on state institutions, Prime Minister Nano, who had been notably absent during the crisis, resigned, and the ruling coalition chose a new leader. Taken collectively, these factors contained the situation and defused tensions. Within a couple of weeks, street life returned to normal.[82]

While mercifully brief and relatively limited in casualties, the attempted coup was a defining moment in the final stage of the constitution-drafting process. From that point through the referendum, few people expected any significant progress in political dialogue, and many anticipated that Democratic Party supporters would continue to agitate publicly. This factor was an overarching concern for all involved in the preparations for the referendum itself. Many feared that without continued international support, the situation could decay once again, leading to further violence and disorder. However, the coup's failure demonstrated vividly that the Democratic Party and its supporters did not enjoy widespread popular support for their aggressive tactics, and it may well have cast support for the constitution-drafting process in a more inherently favorable light.

Role of International Law

From the outset, the constitutional commission asserted its commitment to securing a full review of the constitution's final draft from a panel of international experts. The commission considered international approval important to ensure both technical quality and political support. As the debate during the referendum process demonstrated, both of these suppositions proved wise. When opposition critics attempted to mischaracterize the human rights provisions as restrictive and out of touch with international standards, the full record of international consultations proved otherwise.

As Albania had joined the Council of Europe, the Albanian drafters were cognizant of their accompanying legal responsibilities. They were anxious to avoid any potential inconsistencies with the European Convention of Human Rights, which would prove embarrassing both internationally and domestically. Since 1991, Albanian constitutional experts had been engaged with experts on the Venice Commission, and as early as 1993, the Venice Commission had submitted formal written comments on draft human rights provisions, analyzing their compatibility with the European convention.[83] Given that the 1994 draft that was put to a referendum had some infirmities in this regard, it is unsurprising that the Venice Commission was highly interested in the process. While other international experts also played significant roles, the Venice Commission convened a special task force and took the unusual step of posting a representative in Albania.[84] This investment of additional resources greatly enhanced the role of the Venice Commission throughout the final stages of the process, providing the infrastructure to coordinate a rapid review of draft provisions.

The rapid review became particularly critical as large segments of the draft text were completed in summer 1998. The constitutional commission's June draft received extensive Venice Commission review at a series of meetings in Rome,[85] and the comments were incorporated into the revised final draft of August 5. For the final stages of parliamentary review in autumn 1998, a member of the Venice Commission's Task Force Albania, Professor Matthew Russell, was sent to Albania to follow up on prior dialogue. Professor Russell was permitted to participate freely throughout the parliamentary committee debates.[86] Following these debates, the Venice Commission stated unequivocally that "the draft [constitution], in particular the human rights chapter, is in line conformity with European and international standards."[87]

Conclusion

On November 28, 1998, the president of Albania signed Decree 2260, formally promulgating Albania's first postcommunist constitution.[88] In 183 articles, the constitution sets forth all the basic institutions and principles of a democratic state and establishes respect for human rights as a clear priority. The drafters ultimately settled on a unicameral parliamentary republic for the general framework. Over the course of the drafting process, discussions and debate addressed dramatically different alternatives, such as a federal or presidential system. However, given the size and relative homogeneity of the population, the drafters concluded that the various alternatives would have introduced an additional degree of complexity without clear offsetting benefits.

The drafting of the 1998 constitution was remarkable in a number of respects. Born out of political turmoil that approached civil war, the process was intended to bring together persons from across the political spectrum. It no doubt fell short of this laudable goal, but it did bring civil society and individual citizens into the drafting and approval process in a manner previously unheard of in Albania. A wide range of NGOs and individual citizens participated in the process and actually affected the final product. While the process failed to bring political unity, it nevertheless was instructive for the Albanian political class in how to run—and how not to run—a democratic political process.

The transparent and open nature of the drafting process made it very difficult for politicians to base their positions on distorted facts and false charges. Both Albanian and foreign participants could identify false charges and react accordingly. Possibly for the first time, the Albanian general public was given a detailed demonstration of the power of free speech and public debate. Though it would have been advantageous if the debate had focused more on substantive constitutional issues than on partisan political disputes, it nevertheless provided lessons in the power of transparency, openness, and citizen participation in the political process.

Furthermore, the 1998 constitution-drafting process demonstrated the efficacy of coordinating logistical support for the process at both local and international levels. Despite the politically polarized domestic environment and the diverse agendas of foreign assistance providers, ACCAPP, in conjunction with the OSCE, could provide a framework for effective coordination throughout the constitution-drafting process. Consequently, precious technical assistance and financial support was brought into an overall scheme that allowed for its efficient use and distribution. The result was that international assistance providers were more responsive to local needs and aid recipients better served. In short, the process lowered the transaction costs of public participation; citizens participated in the process because access was made readily available to them.

While Western democracies share common concepts of democracy and the rule of law, institutional and national differences sometimes result in divergent priorities and create artificial rivalries among foreign assistance providers. The result is that efforts to promote democracy and the rule of law become diluted. ACCAPP demonstrated that a coordinating structure reflecting local needs and international input can be important in organizing sustained and effective multilateral support for democracy and rule-of-law development programs. With such coordination, organizations and bilateral donors in Albania could address issues from their own unique

perspectives while at the same time exchanging lessons learned and endorsing shared principles of democracy and rule of law.

The constitution-drafting process and ACCAPP show that shared democratic values may be expressed across cultural and legal traditions. However, it is not as clear how the diverse Western community can institutionalize the ACCAPP example. ACCAPP arose under relatively special circumstances. In Albania, the government gave the OSCE an overall coordinating role to assist the constitution-making process, and ACCAPP was therefore a logical initiative for the OSCE to support. Natural parochial interests typically compromise efforts to coordinate technical assistance, and the challenge facing the Western community is how to replicate the ACCAPP example without creating a new competing institution.

In the years since its adoption, the 1998 Albanian constitution has successfully shepherded the consolidation of this fledgling democracy. Even those who originally vehemently opposed its adoption have now fully accepted it, and the entire political class of the country operates within the parameters it sets forth. Highlights of the intervening years include successfully electing a new nonpartisan president and the nonviolent transition of power between opposing political groupings. Furthermore, external ratings of Albania's progress in rule-of-law and democratic reforms show positive trends. Freedom House's *Nations in Transit* has posted consistent progress in Albania since the constitution was ratified. While a participatory constitutional process may not be enough to guarantee this type of result, the absence of one certainly reduces the prospects for such growth. The Albanians have an expression that, paraphrased, states that a good start makes for a good result. That certainly appears to have proven true in the case of the Albanian constitution.

Notes

1. Government of Albania, *Portrait of Albania*, (Tirana, Albania: Government Printing House, 1981), pp. 99–101.

2. Ibid., p. 101.

3. Ibid., p. 102.

4. Ibid., p. 102.

5. Ibid., p. 108.

6. Ibid., p. 115.

7. 1976 Constitution, art. 10.

8. Law no. 7491, *On the Major Constitutional Provisions,* approved on April 29, 1991, *Flet. Zyrt.,* 1991, vol. 4, p. 145, as amended (hereinafter ICP).

9. Venice Commission, *Working Party on the Draft Albanian Constitution,* December 16, 1991, CDL(91)37.

10. Venice Commission, *Working Party on the Draft Albanian Constitution,* chap. IV, art. 43.

11. See ABA/CEELI, *Compilation of Albanian Draft Constitutions,* July 1997. The work was fraught with stoppages in the politically charged atmosphere. The prime minister, who chaired the commission, was called upon to explain the delays. See "Constitution Watch," *East European Constitutional Review,* vol. 3, no. 3 (Summer–Fall 1994), pp. 2–3.

12. Law no. 7866, "For Referenda," approved on October 6, 1994, *Flet. Zyrt.,* vol. 10, p. 2.

13. "Constitution Watch," *East European Constitutional Review,* vol. 4, no. 1 (Winter 1995), pp. 2–3.

14. ICP, chap. IIIA, art. 25 ("The Constitutional Court starts action on a complaint of its own initiative").

15. "Constitution Watch," Winter 1995, p 3. A clear majority voted against adoption of the proposed constitution.

16. Venice Commission, *Commentary on the Draft Albanian Constitution as Submitted for Popular Approval on 6 November 1994,* Constitution, January 16, 1995, CDL(95)5.

17. Office for Democratic Institutions and Human Rights, *1996 ODIHR Final Report on Parliamentary Elections of 26 May and 2 June 1996* (in author's personal records). The conclusions cited numerous violations of local and international legal provisions.

18. The one exception was the Central Bank of Albania, which tried to introduce corrective measures in 1996 but was ignored by the central government. See remarks of the president of the Central Bank, Kris Luniku, at the Center for Strategic and International Studies Albanian Conference Series, March 25, 1997.

19. *Gazeta Shqiptare,* January 31, 1997.

20. "Constitution Watch," *East European Constitutional Review,* vol. 6, no. 1 (Winter 1997), pp. 2–5; *Albanian Daily News,* March 5, 1997. President Berisha placed the army under the head of the secret service with instructions to quell the unrest in the south, a state of emergency was declared, and President Berisha was reelected by the parliament.

21. Vefa, the most established pyramid scheme, ran television shows on their pirate television station. Many shows featured propaganda seeking to legitimize Vefa's business image.

22. "Constitution Watch," Winter 1997; *Albanian Daily News,* March 5, 1997.

23. Agreement for the Government of National Reconciliation, March 9, 1997.

24. "Italy in the Balkans," *NATO Review,* vol. 28, no. 2 (Summer/Autumn 2000), pp. 6–7, available at www.nato.int/docu/review/2000/0002-02.htm (accessed on April 10, 2009). Operation Alba comprised 7,000 troops drawn from Denmark, France, Greece, Italy (3,000), Romania, Spain, and Turkey.

25. OSCE, *Annual Report 1997 on OSCE Activities 2.2.3,* December 18, 1997, available at www.osce.org.

26. The Socialist Party, led by Fatos Nano, won 690,000 votes, or 52.5 percent, and its governing coalition won a total of 62 percent. The other coalition members were the Human Rights Party, led by Vasil Melo; the Democratic Alliance Party, led by Neritan Ceka; the Social Democratic Party, led by Skender Gjinushi; the Agrarian Party, led by Lefter Xhuveli, and the National Unity Party, led by Idajet Beqiri.

The Democratic Party, led by former President Sali Berisha, won 336,000 votes, or 25.7 percent of the total, and in conjunction with its affiliated parties in the Union for Democracy, represented approximately 32 percent of the total. The other members of the Union for Democracy were the Legality Party, led by Guri Durollari; Christian Democrats, led by Zef Bushati, the Democratic Union Party, led by Remzi Ndreu; and the Social Democratic Union Party, led by Teodor Laço.

A third, nonaligned center-right parliamentary grouping, the United Right, won 76,000 votes, or 6 percent. The United Right consisted of the Republican Party, led by Fatmir Mediu; the National Front Party, led by Hysen Selfo; Right Democratic Party, led by Petrit Kalakula; and the Movement for Democracy Party, led by Dashimir Shehi.

27. Decision 339, dated September 3, 1997.

28. For example, the commission was instructed to "have a drafting process for the Constitution outside of the narrow political debate and to test it with public opinion" and "cooperate with foreign experts of international institutions." See Decision 339.

29. See Decision 339.

30. OSCE Press Release of October 15, 1997. The May 29, 1997, memorandum of understanding between the OSCE and the government of Albania specifically provided that the OSCE would "provide the framework within which other international organizations can play their part in their respective areas of competence, in support of coherent international strategy, and in facilitating improvements in the protection of human rights and basic elements of civil society."

31. The three lawyers were Ardita Abdiu (Albania), Erinda Ballanca (Albania), and Scott Carlson (United States).

32. These newsletters were available online at the ACCAPP Web site in English and Albanian.

33. These recorded results were also accessible online at the ACCAPP Web site in English and Albanian.

34. GTZ, USAID, and certain universities provided support for additional German and American constitutional scholars to assist in the process.

35. The plan was truncated due to the attempted coup d'etat (discussed later in the text). Nevertheless, the major population centers were covered, including Tirana, Durres, Shkodra, Lezhe, Gjirokastra, Elbasan, Vlore, and Fier.

36. Chairman Kristaq Kume.

37. The Society for Democratic Culture (*Shoqata per Kulture Demokratike*) organized a series of public fora on constitutional issues, at which experts discussed a variety of constitutional issues, including televised debates in Korça, Shkoder, Elbasan, Vlora, and Tirana. In addition, the society conducted public opinion polls to measure citizen understanding and awareness and to test public opinion on particular constitutional issues, e.g., the death penalty.

38. Sabri Godo of the Republican Party and Arben Imami of the Democratic Alliance Party.

39. The Political Contract of May 9, 1997, signed by all the major political parties and referring to the prior agreement of March 9, 1997, forming the technical government.

40. *Final Report on the Parliamentary Elections in Albania, 29 June–6 July 1997,* p. 5. The Democratic Party ignored the language in the report, which stated, "The results of these elections should be the foundation for a strong, democratic system, which Albanians want and deserve."

41. These claims were heard personally by the author.

42. Constitutional Court Decision no. 53.

43. Law no. 8256, November 19, 1997, *Flet. Zyrt.,* vol. 18, p. 433, "'For an Addition to Law no. 8227, Dated 30.7.1997, 'For Some Additions and Changes to Law no. 8215,' Dated 9.5.1997, 'For Financial Audit of Nonbanking Legal Entities which Have Borrowed Money from the Public.'"

44. Constitutional Court Decision no. 57.

45. Venice Commission, *Opinion on Recent Amendments to the Law on Main Constitutional Provisions of the Republic of Albania,* adopted by the Sub-Commission on Constitutional Reform, April 15, 1998, CDL-INF(98)P, p. 11.

46. "Constitution Watch," *East European Constitutional Review,* vol. 6, no. 4 (Fall 1997), p. 5, available at www1.law.nyu.edu/eecr/vol6num4/constitutionwatch/albania.html (accessed April 10, 2009).

47. This date was selected in part because it would allow for promulgation on November 28, the eighty-six-year anniversary of independence from the Ottoman Empire. "Constitution Watch," *East European Constitutional Review,* vol. 7, no. 2 (Spring 1998), p. 1, available at www1.law.nyu.edu/eecr/vol7num2/constitutionwatch/albania.html (accessed April 10, 2009).

48. Statement on OSCE/ODIHR Activities, 12–25 March 1992; OSCE/ODIHR Report on the Referendum on the Draft Constitution. OSCE issued both the statement and the report on November 6, 1994.

49. "The constitutional amendments or any other issue, which the referendum is held for, shall be considered as approved when the option received more than 50 percent of the valid 'Yes' votes." Law no. 7866, "For Referenda," approved on October 6, 1994, *Flet. Zyrt.,* vol. 10, p. 2, art. 36.

50. Law no. 8416, "For Some Changes to Law 7866, dated 6.10.94," approved October 12, 1998, *Flet. Zyrt.,* vol. 9, p. 995.

51. See, e.g., Constitution of Ireland, at art. 47; Constitution of Slovenia, art. 90; and Constitution of Switzerland, art. 123.

52. Voters' lists had to be posted near each polling station by November 7, 1998.

53. This position was maintained despite strong international pressure. See, e.g., Declaration of the European Union, dated November 9, 1999 ("The international community will isolate those groups and individuals who polarise the country and undermine democratic institutions. The EU therefore calls upon the Democratic Party, its leaders and followers to participate in the Referendum on the Constitution on 22 November 1998. Boycott is not a constructive instrument of democracy."); Voice of America interview with Deputy Assistant Secretary of State Eileen Malloy, November 13, 1998 ("The boycott, in reality, closes the doors of democracy. If a political party calls for the boycott of the vote, in fact it goes against the fundamental expression of freedom of speech, something which is of critical importance for a democratic society.").

54. One Democratic Party television spot showed old film footage of Albanians being executed by firing squads, religious buildings being destroyed, and property under collectivist, communist control. The chairman of the European Parliament delegation, Doris Pack, declared this spot "unacceptable." European Parliament press release, November 30, 1998.

Another egregious example of Democratic Party disinformation was their attack on Article 18, which bans arbitrary discrimination. Democratic Party propaganda stated that this article demonstrated the constitutional commission's malicious intent, and the article would be used to affirmatively restrict the individual liberties of people. According to the Democratic Party, it was "in complete violation" of the European Convention on Human Rights. The original text of this article was actually suggested by the president of the Venice Commission, Antonio La Pergola, in a letter of June 13, 1998, to the constitutional commission. When locals and internationals publicly disputed the Democratic Party's accusations, the party reiterated the false charges immediately and continued to do so thereafter. See, e.g., Democratic Party press release of November 8, 1999 (discussing vice-president of the Democratic Party, Genc Pollo, meeting the electorate in Ballsh and Patos).

55. Venice Commission–OSCE press release, November 7, 1998; Council of Europe press release, October 20, 1998.

56. The OSCE conducted a detailed legal analysis of the underlying issues to ensure that proper process was respected. OSCE, *Report no. 1 on the Constitutional Referendum Process: Voting and Appeal Mechanisms under the Law for Referenda*, November 18, 1998.

57. As with the prior allegations, the OSCE conducted a detailed legal analysis of the underlying issues to ensure that proper process was respected. See OSCE, *Report No. 2 on the Constitutional Referendum Process: TV Broadcasts on the Constitution*, November 19, 1998.

58. The deputy-chairman threatened to set the chairman on fire; he stated that if the OSCE Ambassador did not intervene to force television spots to be removed, then he would not be able to leave Tirana "even with a helicopter"; and he staged a temporary walkout on November 6 and refused to join in various substantive meetings.

59. Council of Ministers, Dec. no. 639, October 19, 1998.

60. A demonstrable example of this fact can be found in how quickly the ministry developed an operational outline of the issues involved. Within two days, the minister of local government, Arben Demeti, had circulated his first pronouncement, breaking the task down into component parts. See Ministry of Local Government Internal Memo 3525, October 21, 1998 (in author's personal records).

61. OSCE, EU, and COE Joint Preliminary Statement, issued November 23, 1998, p. 2 (in author's personal records).

62. OSCE, EU, and COE Joint Preliminary Statement, p. 1.

63. OSCE, EU, and COE Joint Preliminary Statement, p. 2.

64. Leni Fischer (Germany), president of the Council of Europe Parliamentary Assembly; Frank Swaelen (Belgium), president emeritus of the OSCE Parliamentary Assembly and president of the Belgian Senate; Renzo Imbeni (Italy), European Parliament vice president; Tana De Zulueta (Italy), rapporteur on economic affairs of the OSCE Parliamentary Assembly General Committee; Doris Pack (Germany), chairman of the European Parliament Commission for Relations with the Southeast; Rene van der Linden, (Netherlands), rapporteur of the Council of Europe Parliamentary Assembly on Albania; and Jordi Sole Tura (Spain), rapporteur of the Council of Europe Parliamentary Assembly on Albania.

65. Declaration by the Tri-Parliamentary Mission to Albania, January 23, 1998 (in author's personal records).

66. The Declaration by the Tri-Parliamentary Mission to Albania "urged safeguarding of the independence of the judiciary."

67. The Declaration by the Tri-Parliamentary Mission to Albania "called on the Union for Democracy to promptly end their boycott of the parliament and to participate in drafting the new Constitution."

68. Declaration by the Tri-Parliamentary Mission to Albania, January 23, 1998.

69. Declaration by the Tri-Parliamentary Mission to Albania, June 30, 1998 (in author's personal records).

70. Law no. 8001, "For Genocide and Crimes Against Humanity Committed in Albania during the Communist Regime for Political, Ideological, and Religious Reasons," *Flet. Zyrt.*, 1995, vol. 21, p. 923; Law no. 8043, "For Checking the Integrity of Officials and Other Persons Who Are Completely within the Protection of the Democratic Government," *Flet. Zyrt.*, vol. 10, p. 2.

71. Notice of Release from Duty of the Member of the Constitutional Court Z. Gjata, March 18, 1998 (in author's personal records).

72. Declaration by the Tri-Parliamentary Mission to Albania, June 30, 1998.

73. Declaration by the Tri-Parliamentary Mission to Albania, June 30, 1998.

74. Joint Statement of the OSCE Presence in Albania and the Office of the Council of Europe Special Representative, July 8, 1998; Joint Statement of the Parliamentary Assembly of the OSCE, Parliamentary Assembly of the Council of Europe, and the European Parliament, July 10, 1998 (in author's personal records).

75. "Constitution Watch," *East European Constitutional Review*, vol. 7, no. 4 (Fall 1998), pp. 2–3.

76. "The Democratic Party Declares that the Death Is Organized Completely from the Chief Criminal of Albania, Fatos Nano," Democratic Party press release, September 12, 1998.

77. "Constitution Watch," Fall 1998, pp. 3–5.

78. See *Code of Lekë Dukagjini*, ed. Shtjefen Gjeçov, trans. Leonard Fox (New York: Gjonlekaj Publishing Co., 1989), art. 854–63. Article 854 provides that "the truce is a period of freedom and security ... suspending pursuit of vengeance in the blood-feud until the end of the specified term [initially, twenty-four hours]."

79. "Constitution Watch," Fall 1998, pp. 3–4.

80. Looting of government buildings in this section of town was substantial. Large quantities of computers and furniture were stolen.

81. This diplomatic pressure helped avoid a number of potentially disastrous situations. Ambassador Everts of the OSCE was instrumental in resolving the armed standoff with the Democratic Party supporters and government forces. On a September 15, 1998, radio broadcast, he pleaded with Berisha to intervene so that supporters would return commandeered tanks, which they did.

82. Political dealings remained tumultuous. Parliamentarians ascribed responsibility for the coup to President Berisha and his parliamentary immunity was lifted. However, further prosecution was not forthcoming.

83. Venice Commission, *Working Party on the Chapter of the Revised Albanian Constitution Relating to Fundamental Rights*, March 8, 1993, CDL(93)13.

84. See Giovanni Favilli, *Report on the Mission to Tirana as a Liaison for the Venice Commission*, February 12, 1998, CDL(98)3.

85. Venice Commission, *Meeting of the Sub-Commission on Constitutional Reform together with Task Force Albania*, June 17, 1998, CDL-CR(98) PV 3.

86. "The Draft Constitution Is in Full Conformity with European Democratic Standards," COE-Tirana press release, October 16, 1998.

87. Council of Europe press release, October 20, 1998 (Ref. 696–98).

88. Decree no. 2260, November 28, 1999 (author's personal records).

12

The Dayton Constitution of Bosnia and Herzegovina

James C. O'Brien

Bosnia and Herzegovina's peace arrived in November 1995 after nearly four years of devastating warfare, the loss of a quarter million lives, and the displacement of a million people. A key feature of the peace agreement that settled the conflict was a new constitution for the new country, drafted by international mediators and negotiated by a handful of wartime leaders in the conference rooms of a U.S. Air Force base in Dayton, Ohio.

The Dayton Constitution bears the scars of the process that produced it. It was part of a compromise that reconciled the competing interests of wartime factions while trying to establish a representative democracy in a state that had not yet completed its transition from socialism. As a compromise, it both enabled and constrained Bosnia's transition toward democracy, and the tensions within the document remain central to Bosnia's experience with state building.

The Bosnian constitution-making process provides four important lessons:

1. A constitution drafted as part of an effort to end a conflict reflects the tensions that fueled the conflict.

2. When negotiating parties represent narrow interests, international mediators should press broader interests, including democratic governance and the constitution's capacity to evolve beyond the immediate purposes of the negotiating parties.

3. International leverage may be at its greatest when conflicts are being resolved. It may be better to address governance issues at that point, rather than deferring them by adopting broad principles or interim governing arrangements.

4. For a constitution crafted in a peace agreement, implementation requires ongoing negotiation and effort, just as the peace agreement does overall. The Dayton negotiations did not produce a clear mandate or plan to address lingering obstacles to implementation. An arbitrarily short and unrealistic deadline to implement the peace agreement fully, imposed by the interna-

tional community, prevented the international community from engaging on implementation as creatively and strategically as it could have. This failure meant that each step toward implementation required continual renegotiation, both within the international community and with Bosnian actors. Implementation was thus awkward, compromised, and hesitant.

Background

Even before the war in Bosnia, the Yugoslav political system had been under strain for years due to ethnic differences, economic inequities, and weak political structures. While the Party and the country's paramount leader, Josip Broz Tito, held the system together in reality, a convoluted constitutional structure held it together in theory. In response to discontent among the republics in the federal system—especially Slovenia and Croatia, which resented the perceived Serb domination of the federal government—the 1974 federal constitution overhauled the system and devolved tremendous authority to the republics. Under the 1974 constitution, each of the six republics of Slovenia, Croatia, Bosnia and Herzegovina, Serbia, Montenegro, and Macedonia, as well as the two autonomous provinces of Kosovo and Vojvodina, which remained within Serbia in that constitution, was represented in an eight-member collective presidency. The collective presidency, in turn, selected a prime minister. Though the system survived Tito's death in 1980, it was wired to produce confusion and deadlock.[1]

As economic troubles mounted during the 1980s, canny politicians such as Slobodan Milosevic in Serbia and Franjo Tudjman in Croatia promoted ethnic nationalism, from opportunism or belief. Given the threat that nationalism posed to Yugoslav cohesion, ethnicity had been a taboo subject, and it proved to be a potent factor in the disintegration of the state and the onset of civil war.[2] In a now infamous speech to a massive crowd of Serbs in Kosovo on June 28, 1989—the six hundredth anniversary of an epic Serbian defeat that marked the beginning of Ottoman rule in the region—Milosevic invoked that historic event to suggest that the Serb nation was once again under threat and might need to employ force.[3] Milosevic's nationalist rhetoric and agenda provoked equal and opposite reactions from Yugoslavia's other ethnic groups, particularly Croats.

Also throughout the 1980s, the Serbian government sought increasingly to dominate the federal institutions, while Slovenia and Croatia increasingly pursued a separatist trend. Among other moves, in March 1989, Serbia effectively gained control of half the votes in the collective presidency, first, by pushing constitutional amendments through the system that virtually eliminated the autonomy of Kosovo and Vojvodina, and second, by co-opting Montenegro. By mid-1991, the Yugoslav People's Army (JNA) was the last fully functioning federal institution.[4]

Though precipitated by the efforts of Milosevic's Serbian government to dominate the federal system and the unwillingness of key figures to negotiate a peaceful dissolution, Yugoslavia's actual death spiral began with Slovenia's and Croatia's declarations of independence on June 25, 1991. Prompted by international recognition of Croatian independence in January 1992, Bosnia followed suit in March 1992. While Slovenia, the westernmost republic, successfully extricated itself from the impending morass after a low-intensity ten-day conflict with JNA forces, Croatia's and Bosnia's independence moves prompted their large Serbian minorities—and in Bosnia, the Croat minority—to seek a major realignment of borders. In Croatia, rebellious Serbs declared their own so-called Republika Srpska Krajina, which they sought to keep within the rump Yugoslavia. In Bosnia, the nationalist Serb political party, the Serb Democratic Party (SDS), declared the creation of the "Republika Srpska," which they also sought to keep within Yugoslavia, while nationalist Croats created their own putative mini-state of Herceg-Bosna. The drive to carve ethnically defined states out of territories with ethnically mixed populations, and the support that the breakaway nationalist groups received from Milosevic (who controlled the JNA) and Tudjman in Croatia, scuttled any possibility of a peaceful transition to independence for Bosnia and Croatia.

The war in Croatia began in summer 1991 and lasted until summer 1995, when Croatian forces defeated the Serbian Krajina republic; in the end, its backers in Belgrade abandoned it.[5] In Bosnia, the war erupted in 1992 and continued until autumn 1995, when new North Atlantic Treaty Organization (NATO) military activity, a newly vigorous U.S. diplomatic effort, and, above all, a coordinated Croat and Bosniac offensive combined to reverse Serb gains.

By 1995, after more than three years of fighting, there was an opening for peace in Bosnia. All sides had good reason to fear another winter at war. As a result of diplomatic initiatives in 1994, Bosnia's Croats and Bosniacs—a multiethnic but predominantly Muslim group that supported the central government—were fighting and negotiating primarily in concert. Bosnia's Serbs for the first time faced Croatian and Bosnian forces that could take and hold territory; were without their buffer sister entity in Croatia, the Republika Srpska Krajina, which Zagreb had defeated in August 1995; and were bent by pressure from their former sponsor in Belgrade. For their parts, Bosniacs were concerned about cities incapable of breaking Serb blockades, and Croatia and Yugoslavia saw more benefit to supporting peace than war. Yugoslavia would see economic sanctions end and Croatia would finish its task of reuniting its territory for the first time since independence. Finally, the international community was willing to impose a settlement if necessary, as it had been horrified by atrocities committed by Serb forces when they overran the UN-protected enclave of Srebrenica in July 1995 and worried about the war's expansion.

The Dayton Agreement

From August through October 1995, U.S. Assistant Secretary of State Richard Holbrooke led a team of U.S. negotiators in multiple rounds of shuttle diplomacy in Balkan capitals and elsewhere. This process led to the November 1–21 peace conference at Wright-Patterson Air Force Base in Dayton, Ohio, at which the final peace agreement was negotiated and initialed. It was signed the following month in Paris.

The Dayton Agreement—formally, the General Framework Agreement for Peace in Bosnia and Herzegovina—comprised an overarching framework agreement and eleven annexes, one of which, Annex 4, was the new constitution. Signed by the Republic of Croatia, the Federal Republic of Yugoslavia (now Serbia and Montenegro), and the Republic of Bosnia and Herzegovina (the government of which, by this time, was dominated by the Bosnian Muslims), the framework agreement provided for the mutual recognition of the sovereignty of the three now-separate states and acknowledgment of the territorial integrity and political independence of Bosnia and Herzegovina. The signatories also committed themselves to respecting and promoting fulfillment of the provisions of the annexes. Different constellations of parties signed the various annexes: in some cases, only the Federation of Bosnia and Herzegovina (Federation)[6] and the Republika Srpska (RS); in other cases, those parties as well as the signatories of the framework agreement. The annexes covered a range of issues, from the military aspects of the settlement to elections to refugees and displaced persons.

The Dayton Agreement resulted in a Bosnia based on the two "Entities," the RS and the Federation, which already de facto existed on Bosnian territory but did not recognize each other's legitimacy. The Entities comprised a unitary state under the new constitution of Bosnia and Herzegovina, which provided for direct elections, international personality, and a set of powers and institutions for the central government adequate to carry out the responsibilities of statehood. The governing structure was strongly decentralized, however, with most government powers held at the Entity level or below.[7]

Structure of the Negotiating Process

Structure of the Peace Negotiations: Proximity Talks

The structure of negotiations is a complicated question for any negotiation. There are essentially three options: shuttle diplomacy; proximity talks; and face-to-face negotiations, as in a constitutional assembly.

By November 1995, shuttle diplomacy had done what it was likely to do. From August to October 1995, an intense shuttle conducted by U.S. diplomats had produced a stable cease-fire, introduced strong NATO military action, won agreement to some basic principles for a peace agreement and constitution, and identified the key players who would participate in final peace negotiations. Continued shuttling, however, would have been less effective. It was difficult and dangerous; three U.S. diplomats died on the shuttle in August. It would have left the parties at home, open to influences and under pressure to disclose details that could damage the peace talks. Bosnia remained at war in the time before Dayton. A cease-fire was held together by exhaustion after months of intense fighting and expectations of a strong international military response to any breach. It is uncertain that the cease-fire would have

survived if the parties had rested over the winter, with the international community's willingness to commit to pursuing a peace agreement declining.

By ending shuttle talks, the United States also added an element of drama to the choreography of its late entry into peacemaking in Bosnia. Business as usual—and after three years of shuttle talks of more or less intensity, they were business as usual—would not be accepted. The call to a peace conference was an element in preparing the environment for a push to concluding a deal. The location of the talks—in the United States, at a military base, after years of U.S. reluctance to become involved in Bosnia's war—heightened the sense of drama. The Dayton talks were set up to close the peace deal or to fail clearly and dramatically; they were not intended to be yet another stage in an ongoing peace process. Finally, conducting a peace conference far from the region allowed the United States to control participation. Prior peace negotiations failed in large part because the array of parties participating could manipulate the process, confident that another side would reject a peace agreement. By having each side present, the U.S. negotiators could tamp down these kinds of manipulations.

Well into summer 1995, Bosnian Serb leaders gave no sign of their willingness to negotiate peace. In July 1995, the International Criminal Tribunal in The Hague indicted Radovan Karadzic and Ratko Mladic, the civilian and military leaders of the Bosnian Serbs. In August 1995, Holbrooke, the lead U.S. negotiator, announced that the United States would not negotiate with Karadzic and Mladic. Soon afterward, the patriarch of the Serbian Orthodox Church arbitrated an agreement under which Serbian President Milosevic would effectively represent Bosnian Serbs. Milosevic sought an end to economic sanctions on the Federal Republic of Yugoslavia; he was not very interested in the details of Bosnia's governance. Given just enough to satisfy Bosnian Serb demands, he would accept a peace agreement that Bosnian Serb leaders would reject.

Similarly, Bosnian Croats were represented by Zagreb. Bosnian Serbs and Bosnian Croats present at Dayton participated in some negotiating sessions, but each group was excluded whenever their patrons from Belgrade or Zagreb requested it. Both of these Bosnian groups rejected elements of the settlement. The head of the Bosnian Croat group resigned and the Bosnian Serb leadership allegedly "fainted" when shown the final territorial arrangement; neither group's leader initialed the agreement at Dayton or signed it in Paris several weeks later. If shuttle diplomacy had continued, these groups would have remained separate voices, speaking from their own capitals through tame media.

One technical advantage of the Dayton negotiations has faded and possibly disappeared forever: Participants agreed to negotiate under news blackout, a feat that would have been impossible in the later age of ubiquitous cell phones. Thirty-six months after Dayton, Israeli-Palestinian talks were located at the Wye Plantation in rural Maryland in part because of poor cell-phone coverage there; five months after Wye, the Rambouillet negotiations outside Paris that sought to avert the NATO-Yugoslavia conflict over Kosovo sprouted cell phones like mushrooms, with damaging leaks prejudicing the negotiations.

The international negotiators entered Dayton with the flexibility to choose proximity or face-to-face talks. Other than a ceremonial plenary session, the parties stayed separate for the first days, with negotiators arranging separate sessions. One senior face-to-face session was arranged; it produced maximal demands and harsh recriminations. Talks thereafter proceeded mostly as proximity discussions. During negotiations, parties made proposals to the negotiators, not to the other side. With few exceptions, this arrangement was at the request of the party leaders.

This allowed the international negotiators to control the pace and heat of proposals. No side knew another's reaction to the proposals, or even whether negotiators would present them, which reduced posturing. When face-to-face negotiations took place, they were private and focused on core issues at the end of negotiations.

The Dayton environment, in short, was tailored to end a war. It did not resemble a constitutional assembly or roundtable either in involving representative elements of Bosnian society (and excluding meddling outsiders) or in permitting time for reasoned deliberation. The negotiators were painfully aware of these defects. I discuss below how they were addressed within the constraints of the situation and may arguably have produced a set of governing arrangements more democratic—and certainly more durable—than Bosnians could have produced themselves by the end of the war.

International Control of the Process

Formally, negotiators Holbrooke and former Swedish prime minister Carl Bildt convened the conference together. Holbrooke represented the Contact Group: at the time, the United States, United Kingdom, Russia, France, and Germany, with Italy first as an informal and later a formal member. Bildt represented both the United Nations and the European Union. However, the U.S. government had decided on its policy concerning the desired substantive outcome of the peace conference while the other international actors decided theirs. The international negotiators consulted among themselves before and during Dayton until they reached agreement on proposals to offer to the parties.

The United States was the driving force of the negotiation, generally preparing papers, controlling the drafting process, and deciding the timing for presenting proposed compromises and written drafts to the parties. Nevertheless, consultations among international negotiators shaped the agreement to a large extent, and the process often was extensive and contentious. On the military, civilian implementation, and police annexes in particular, discussions among the Contact Group consumed much of the time at Dayton, with the parties receiving texts late in the talks. On the constitution, the Contact Group reached broad agreement in the first days of Dayton, though negotiations continued until the final day of the talks (see below).

Each side had talented legal advisers, with Bosnian Croats and Serbs represented often by lawyers from Croatia and Yugoslavia. The Bosniacs had a team of international experts who could work in the style of the international negotiators. The cultural differences among lawyers—public international lawyers and constitutional experts, U.S. and British lawyers used to working with ambiguous texts built to evolve, Europeans split among British and continental lawyers, Yugoslavs most closely tied to a strict interpretation of texts—slowed drafting but also allowed ideas to be examined carefully and provided for cross-fertilization among traditions while keeping Yugoslav notions foremost.

The significance of cultural differences was apparent in debates over the role of the new Bosnian presidency. Negotiators from a Yugoslav tradition wanted a presidential system, and lawyers from that culture expected the powers to be extensive, with little room for interpretation. European lawyers and negotiators maintained constant support for a strong government, headed by a prime minister and relatively autonomous from the presidency; they made the point that a Bosnia seeking to join Europe should have a modern European style of governance. Ultimately, the constitution created a government centered on a presidency comprising three members, one from each of the three main ethnic groups, with the chair rotating among the presidency's members. The presi-

dency generally was to decide by consensus, but on a limited set of issues, it could decide by majority.

The international community ruled Dayton by the sheer number of its participants. A sizable U.S. contingent comprised representatives from the State Department, National Security Council, Office of the Secretary of Defense, Joint Chiefs of Staff, office of the U.S. Permanent Representative to the United Nations, and other agencies. The European Union had its envoy, his staff, and national delegations from the Contact Group. These delegations included senior political representatives (political-director level), lawyers, technical experts, and support staff.

With these resources on site, international negotiators could cover every aspect of the talks. Drafts of each portion of the text were developed by international lawyers, agreed among the senior representatives of the Contact Group, and finally presented to the parties. U.S. and European lawyers developed separate draft constitutions over a period of weeks before Dayton, but a unified draft was agreed upon as the conference opened.

The first U.S. outline of a peace agreement was prepared in late August 1995. The draft drew heavily on previous peace efforts, including in particular the so-called Invincible draft agreement (named after the British carrier *HMS Invincible*, on which peace negotiations took place in September 1993) and the Washington Agreement establishing the Bosniac-Croat Federation.[8] It took organizational lessons from contemporary international practice, including agreements concerning Afghanistan, Ethiopia-Eritrea, and Namibia. It suggested a set of broad principles to support an end to the war, to be included in a general framework agreement, and a series of annexes on issues of specific importance to the parties and the international community. These included governance, elections, human rights, return of persons displaced by the war, and other issues. The suggested outline was largely ignored for several weeks while shuttle talks focused on obtaining a cease-fire.

At several points in September 1995, U.S. negotiators discussed among themselves the framework of a peace agreement. Most attention was devoted to security concerns, though there was a general consensus that the parties would require a peace agreement to include arrangements for governing Bosnia. A more complete U.S. draft peace agreement, including the core elements of a constitution, was prepared at the end of the first week of October. In the last week before the peace conference opened, European experts presented to the U.S. team a set of proposals, and the two were synthesized in Washington. Most of the work was done over the weekend before the talks began.

At Dayton, Milosevic reportedly greeted Holbrooke by saying, "So, I hear that you are going to present us with an encyclopedia." In fact, the peace agreement was presented to the parties piece by piece; the negotiators were trying to establish a steady pace of work and a constructive environment. In the first two weeks, relatively little attention was paid to the constitution, as the bulk of work focused on issues tangential to the final agreement, including the release of a U.S. journalist being held by Bosnian Serbs, the resolution of a territorial dispute between Croatia and the Federal Republic of Yugoslavia, and the strengthening of the Federation.

Substance of the Constitution

The process by which the Dayton Constitution was negotiated raised the real possibility of locking in nationalist control of the country. The international negotiators here faced a dilemma. Nationalists already controlled the country's resources, military might, and fate, so they had to make the peace. It was clear from the start of negotiations that nationalists wanted to convert their wartime power into political authority. This was ap-

parent in negotiations of the substance of the constitution. For example, some positions asserted on the structure of the government reflected the aspirations of particular individuals for particular offices. In the final week of the Dayton talks—roughly November 14 to 21, 1995—attention turned to governing arrangements. Several themes ran through these talks, which took place at both the technical and the principals' level.

First, human rights guarantees were easily accepted. The agreement enumerates a comprehensive list of human rights instruments and standards to be upheld in Bosnia; lawyers could hardly write the provisions quickly enough to stay ahead of the parties' agreement. The agreement as a whole reinforces the primacy of human rights by including annexes on several human rights issues, such as the rights of refugees and displaced persons (Annex 7), rights and avenues for redress for victims of human rights abuses (Annex 6), and police monitoring and reform (Annex 11). The provisions are to be enforced by the international community, witnessing states, and Bosnian authorities. Moreover, the agreement requires cooperation with the International Criminal Tribunal for the Former Yugoslavia and forbids fugitives from the tribunal from engaging in political life. The Dayton Constitution forbids any amendment that would "eliminate or diminish" the human rights standards that it requires, including European human rights law (see Article X[2]). The constitution also provides that European human rights law—that is, the European Convention for the Protection of Human Rights and Fundamental Freedoms—"shall apply directly" in Bosnia and "have priority over all other law" (see Article II[2]). These simple sentences were little noticed, except as an unexceptional statement of Bosnia's desire to be part of Europe.

Second, the governing institutions and their composition received extensive attention from the parties. Two issues in particular were controversial: the authority of the central government, including mechanisms to enforce individual rights; and the ethnic distribution of key positions in the government. As a general matter, the Serb side, with support from the Bosnian Croats, wanted a decentralized state, with each ethnicity largely responsible for governing areas in which its ethnic group held a majority. There would be little if any intrusion by other governing bodies, including the central authorities. This produced a core compromise in the constitution. The central government—itself not called a government, but simply "institutions of Bosnia and Herzegovina"—was given jurisdiction mostly over areas agreed to be necessary to carry out the responsibilities of statehood. It was acknowledged that only central authorities could represent the country in international organizations such as the United Nations.

It was more difficult, however, to address subject matters in which central authority was desired by one of the parties (usually the Bosniacs) or could be efficient or helpful rather than logically necessary. One agreed solution was to provide the central institutions with broad authority, but generally phrased in terms of policy—as in "customs policy"—with the expectation that implementation might be left to the two Entities or to some special body established for a particular purpose. In the document, the line between policy and implementation is not addressed, but left to give-and-take among those responsible for implementing Bosnia's constitution.

The result of a compromise, the delineation of the scope of the central government's authority remains controversial. To some, the central government has limited authority expressly set forth in the constitution, particularly in the specific subject matter listed in Article III(1). Additional specific authorities are allocated to central institutions, including the parliamentary assembly (Article IV[4]), the presidency (Article V[3]), and the council of ministers (Article V[4]), and the document grants other express powers to central institutions as well. From this point of view, the key sentence in the constitution is Article III(3a), which provides that "all governmental functions and powers not expressly assigned in this Constitution to the institutions of Bosnia and Herzegovina shall be those of the Entities."

At Dayton, Bosnian Serbs and Croats pressed this position most often, as they sought to preserve their authority over those parts of Bosnia where they expected to retain political power. The Bosniacs opposed this interpretation. They sought a more powerful central government, in which they expected to have a majority. Also, the international community wanted to ensure that Bosnia's central institutions could follow through on legal obligations and political commitments that would arise during the country's postwar reconstruction as well as its eventual entry into European institutions.

Both the language and the structure of the constitution reflect the resulting compromise. Essentially, the central government is given broad authority to ensure that Bosnia meets its legal obligations; those obligations are framed in open-ended terms. Responsibility for implementing obligations lies initially with the Entities or lower levels of government; with the sentence granting them authority to carry out all "governmental functions and powers" not described in the constitution (quoted above), the drafters intended to ensure that they had the authority necessary to accomplish this. The drafters wanted to ensure that Entity governments, reluctant to enforce guarantees that might reduce their power, could not excuse their nonperformance by claiming that their own Entity constitutions were limiting them. Under this interpretation, the possibility remains for the central institutions to take on responsibilities not fulfilled by the Entities, provided that their doing so is necessary and appropriate to seeing that Bosnia meets its legal obligations under international law and under the Constitutional Court's particular approach to interpreting Bosnia's constitution.

The issue of who decides whether the central institutions can act was left largely unresolved. It is clear that the central judiciary has extensive authority over Entity and lower levels of government. The Entity and other substate levels of government are subject to decisions of the Constitutional Court, a central government institution empowered to act on referrals by central authorities and to hear appeals from courts in either Entity. The establishment of the Constitutional Court and the judicial system as a whole struck at a central assertion from earlier in the negotiations, made most often by Bosnian Serbs, that the Entities were to be the final arbiters of questions about whether international or domestic legal obligations were being met.[9]

Still, as mentioned above, the authority of the political institutions—the presidency, council of ministers, and parliamentary assembly—remains controversial. As Bosnia's international commitments become more intrusive in the society, taking on, for example, Council of Europe rules on education, a subject not addressed in the constitution, the reach of the central government can be expected to grow, at least insofar as it ensures that the Entities are implementing the international commitments appropriately. This authority can be interpreted narrowly, as related only to issues needed to protect Bosnia's international personality, or more expansively, as related to political decisions made in the exercise of Bosnia's sovereignty. The Constitutional Court has endorsed the latter approach, declaring that the central government has a role beyond its enumerated powers, as part of its broad responsibility for taking actions "necessary to preserve the sovereignty, territorial integrity, political independence, and international personality of

Bosnia and Herzegovina." This gives the central institutions responsibility beyond Bosnia's legal personality, inferring a structural role in ensuring that the broad objectives of the peace agreement—reconciliation—and of the constitution itself are implemented. The Court has carried the central government's authorities beyond those enumerated, into areas such as language (paragraph 34 of Partial Decision II) and protection of private property (paragraph 12).

The court properly has refrained from spelling out the circumstances under which the central institutions can act. The constitution deferred questions of central-government authority to the political judgment of the people governing Bosnia. This is an area that cannot be defined prospectively; probably it never can be defined entirely through judicial decisions. It will be a political negotiation among international, state, and substate political players. It seems likely that, as the tensions surrounding the war end, the political authorities can decide on the basis of efficiency and structure to give ever more responsibilities to the central government. But the process is not a ratchet; responsibilities can also be taken away.

Architecture of the Central Institutions

The structure of the central institutions resulted in a cumbersome system. Drawing from their experience under the Yugoslav system, the parties agreed from the start on a multiperson presidency. But when Dayton negotiations started, they had not yet debated the extent to which a government should be constituted as the administration of the country, or whether executive powers would be subordinate to the presidency. The Serb delegation strongly opposed establishing a central government by name, so the "Council of Ministers" was established instead, with a "chair," rather than a prime minister. This body had the authority to implement all functions of the central government, and it survived the negotiations with no clear limitations on its power, which ultimately rests on how little text is devoted to it.

Unfortunately, the absence of an international consensus in favor of a strong governmental system that might make up for the weakness of a multiheaded presidency created problems within weeks after Dayton. The High Representative agreed to have the chair position rotated on an ethnic basis, even though the constitution deliberately omitted such a requirement (the weakness of the High Representative is discussed below). Human rights enforcement was an especially contentious area. All parties readily accepted the human rights principles, but they were unwilling to sign on to any governmental arrangement that would have the authority to intervene in the affairs of the decentralized government bodies they preferred. For example, the Dayton Constitution provides that all government institutions would apply European human rights law to Bosnia; this provision was acceptable to all. The constitution goes further, however, by granting jurisdiction to a central court, unforeseen in the parties' negotiating positions, to order Entity governments into compliance. An ombudsman was given authority to require specific actions of government authorities; individuals were given the ability to reach above Entity governments by invoking domestic administrative and judicial remedies or complaining directly to international civilian officials.

Why were such provisions accepted? At Dayton, their voices muffled by Milosevic's representation, Bosnian Serbs could not argue that the entire peace agreement should be jeopardized for the sake of their Entity's primacy, and Zagreb's representatives were not motivated to hold the line for Bosnian Croats on this issue. In this respect, the bundling of governance arrangements with a peace agreement, which the larger regional powers desired, provided leverage that the international community would have lacked otherwise.

The parties also paid enormous attention to ethnic aspects of governmental arrangements, in both voting procedures and guaranteed spots in government.[10] Throughout the series of Yugoslav peace negotiations up to and including Dayton, the parties had insisted on special voting rights in legislative bodies for ethnic groups. These usually took the form of ethnic vetoes, whereby representatives from one of the three major groups could block any action by majority vote among themselves. In addition, the parties paid close attention to who would get which government jobs. Public administration at all levels was to be representative of the population, and seats in legislative bodies were allocated at least in part by ethnicity. In the last days of negotiation, the parties insisted on adding a second legislative chamber called the House of Peoples, in which Serbs, Croats, and Bosniacs were equally represented. Election to the House of Peoples was governed by Entity-level bodies controlled by the dominant political parties.

The presidency of Bosnia and Herzegovina was created to involve three people, one Serb, one Bosniac, and one Croat. Each was elected directly, a setback for the dominant parties, which sought control over the nominating and selection process. But ethnic guarantees ran deep. The Serb member of the presidency was to be elected only from the territory of the Republika Srpska, and the Bosniac and Croat members elected only from the Federation. This prevented anyone not a member of one of those three groups from holding a seat in the presidency and reinforced the Entities' ethnic character. The rule was designed to protect the dominant political parties, as representatives from the three delegations met jointly to discuss the rules for presidential and legislative elections. It was one of the few times that

Bosnian Serbs represented themselves in negotiations. The Bosnian Serbs calculated that the Republika Srpska would remain Serb-controlled, leaving Bosniacs and Croats to vote in the Federation. Moreover, the Bosnian Croats were concerned that Croats from the Republika Srpska would be less nationalistic than those from the territory of the self-proclaimed rump state of Herceg-Bosna, which lay inside the Federation and had little interest in including more moderate Croats within their electorate.

Various parties sought additional guarantees, including a demand that each member of the presidency be selected by a caucus of the largest party connected with each ethnic group; given the dominance of the nationalist parties and the few nonnationalist parties' rejection of explicit ethnic group affiliation, this arrangement would have locked the presidency into nationalist control. International negotiators, however, rejected this last proposal as incompatible with an agreement negotiated under international auspices and purporting to establish a democracy. The parties apparently knew this, as their more far-reaching proposals were not made in the presence of their own international advisers.

The Dayton Agreement embedded in Bosnian law obligations toward the International Criminal Tribunal for the Former Yugoslavia. Persons indicted by the Tribunal were forbidden from participating in negotiations or holding public office.[11] This requirement followed from the U.S. decision leading to Dayton that persons indicted by the Tribunal would not be allowed to participate in the negotiations. Beneficially, this principle removed from talks Bosnian Serb leaders Radovan Karadzic and Ratko Mladic, who had shown themselves unwilling to conclude peace agreements. It provides an example of how the pursuit of justice can promote peace. Holbrooke has said that without the Tribunal, it would have been much more difficult to conclude an agreement.

Under the terms of the constitution, all Bosnian authorities were required to cooperate with the Tribunal and fugitives from it were forbidden from holding public office, a stipulation enforced by checking electoral lists and lists of persons holding such offices. This process was ineffective at first. Karadzic retained his title as president of the Republika Srpska until July 1996, seven months after Dayton, and war-crime suspects—a broadening of the constitutional requirement—held public office at lower levels for more than a year. But the mechanism became more effective over time, as the High Representative, the Organization for Security and Cooperation in Europe (OSCE), and international police monitors vetted appointees and candidates for public office with the Tribunal.

The Tension at the Heart of the Dayton Constitution

In fact, however, the human rights provisions in the constitution are at odds with the ethnically based provisions that the parties insisted upon: Key provisions that nationalists relied on in deciding to accept the constitution and the broader peace agreement are inconsistent with contemporary European and international human-rights norms regarding individual rights and equality of citizens. The ethnically based provisions in the constitution, which reflect a notion of ethnic group rights, not protection of minority rights, may be vulnerable to legal attack.

The ways in which the parties sought to protect themselves against political competition at the Entity level—such as by declaring the Entities in their constitutions to be "constituted" by some but not all ethnic groups in Bosnia, and by limiting eligibility for key offices to citizens from specified ethnic groups—has already begun to unravel. In 2000, the Constitutional Court established pursuant to the Dayton Constitution decided that because the constitution of Bosnia and Herzegovina recognizes the equality of all three "constituent peoples" it names—Bosniacs, Croats, and Serbs—so too must the constitutions of both Entities recognize all three groups as "constituent peoples."[12] The decision declared unconstitutional several provisions in each Entity's constitution, including a provision in the RS constitution that "Republika Srpska shall be a State of the Serb people and all of its citizens" and one in the Federation constitution that excluded Serbs from "constituent people" status.[13] More generally, the Court found that provisions reserving public office for members of particular groups, or those granting a veto to one or two groups, are a serious breach of the Convention on Racial Discrimination and of the constitutional principle of equality of peoples.[14]

While the Court decision was a step forward in enhancing the rights and opportunities of Bosniacs and Croats in the RS and Serbs in the Federation, like the Dayton Constitution itself, it failed to advance the interests of citizens who were not members of any of the three groups, or who chose not to identify themselves by ethnicity. The Court felt constrained by the constitution's ethnic architecture, and its decision, as well as a subsequent implementing agreement, therefore maintains the principle of ethnic division of power that is at the heart of the Dayton compromise.[15] Nevertheless, the parties almost certainly would not have accepted such a result had they foreseen it. The Bosnian Serbs in particular expected the Dayton Constitution to protect the status of the RS as a Serb enclave, not to be a basis for insisting on the equality within it of the three "constituent peoples" of the state.

Perceived Need for a Complete Constitution

Would it have been better to postpone the drafting of detailed constitutional arrangements until after a peace agreement was secured? In the run-up to Dayton, negotiators discussed alternatives to a full constitution, including an interim arrangement; a decision to extend the Federation to incorporate Republika Srpska; and even the adoption of simple governing principles to serve for an interim period until permanent arrangements could be struck. None of the alternatives received lengthy consideration, however. Simply put, the interests of all of those in the talks argued for a full constitution. Each of the warring factions wanted lasting governing arrangements to lock in what they had gained by fighting and what they hoped to gain at peace talks. The Bosniacs insisted that Bosnia be a single state, with no provision for any group or territorial area to withdraw. The Croats insisted on being an equal partner in governance, even though they were the smallest of the three groups. The Serbs demanded a decentralized state, in which their self-proclaimed Republika Srpska could govern with little interference from the national capital. Finally, international negotiators, weary of the strains that the war in Bosnia imposed on transatlantic relations and eager to move the Bosnia crisis off the front pages, were looking for a final peace settlement, rather than a step in a process. An interim solution would have deferred these issues when the parties asked for them to be resolved.

Moreover, the parties' negotiators would not have agreed to the broad outlines of the peace without assurances that their influence would continue in peacetime Bosnia. In some instances, this was a very personal struggle, as individual negotiators eyed the jobs they wanted and tried to shape the governing arrangements favorably to their future positions. Representatives of all three dominant and nationalist Bosnian political parties watched the details of negotiations carefully to ensure that any arrangement maintained, or even improved, the privileges of their party and ethnic group.

The pattern of Bosnian negotiations reflects the parties' preference for durable governing arrangements. In the Carrington plan of late 1991, the Vance-Owen plan in spring 1993, the Washington Agreement of February 1994, and the Contact Group plan in summer 1994, the parties paid close attention to governing arrangements. Each contained specific principles and even full constitutions. By the time the Dayton talks opened in autumn 1995, the parties expected a peace agreement to include durable constitutional arrangements.

The international community also had little interest in an intrusive civilian presence that could govern Bosnia without full arrangements for Bosnian self-rule. The international military presence was limited initially to one year, and without military force, the civilian international authority would be unable to prevent wartime factions either from returning to war or achieving their ends by other means. In that environment—driven by an arbitrary deadline—the maximum international leverage to decide governance was during the peace negotiations, at the start of the international presence, rather than in the face of a self-imposed, arbitrary deadline.

In addition, a full constitution allowed the introduction of more intrusive human rights provisions as well as provisions allowing the constitution to evolve as Bosnia and its region moved toward EU membership. None of the parties would allow itself to be seen as rejecting clear-cut European norms. The postwar European institutions are heavily lawyered, and the web of norms, standards, and organizations relate to one another in the nuanced, cross-referenced, and oblique language of the law. By importing that language into the constitution, international negotiators insulated these European norms—and the aspirational aspect of the constitution—from direct challenge.

Indeed, the full constitution reflects a substantial advance from the preliminary texts negotiated in the weeks leading to Dayton. As negotiators shuttled around the region, they arrived at two sets of principles, agreed upon in September 1995. These short documents, examined minutely by the parties, set the parameters for the Dayton Agreement. They display an intention, especially from the Bosnian Serbs, to create a weak government with vague and unenforceable commitments to European norms; coercive power would rest not in representative governments but in the hands of executives at the head of each Entity. For example, the principles did not provide for a judiciary but instead provided that the Entities would seek to resolve disputes through arbitration. This would have left citizens in one Entity without practical recourse in the other and, in fact, would have left a central government without the ability to enforce constitutional requirements on either Entity. It was a proposal for a union from a feudal age, not a modern European state.

The principles constrained negotiations at Dayton, as negotiators promised that the principles would be respected in any final negotiation. As events unfolded, the international negotiators' leverage increased as a peace agreement neared, so that it became possible late in the talks to include items—such as a Constitutional Court—that had been impossible when the principles were discussed.

Public Participation

There was no public involvement in Dayton negotiations. Negotiations took place under a blackout, with neither informal public consultation during negotiations—unlike the Good Friday accord negotiations in Ireland—nor formal public or democratic approval thereafter. Upon the peace agreement's signature in Paris, the constitution took effect without any provision for approval by legislatures or popular votes. At Dayton, the parties signed an agreement in which they acknowledged that by initiating the text at Dayton, they agreed to be bound by the peace agreement. The constitutions of the two Entities, which had been adopted through democratic processes, albeit of questionable legitimacy and under wartime pressure, were required to be conformed to the Dayton Constitution. International negotiators were not entirely comfortable with the approach, which seemed less than perfectly democratic. Still, without much controversy, the lawyers proposed and the Contact Group accepted that the new constitution would enter into force once its was signed. The reason was simple: It would end the war. Parties had manipulated previous peace negotiations by pleading incapacity to conclude an arrangement without consultations or democratic approval at home.

Still, the democratic deficit was not as great as it might have been. The parties were encouraged to seek approval of the constitution from their relevant legislative bodies. They were warned, however, that they should not find themselves unable to deliver approval. Ultimately, both Entity legislatures approved the constitution. The process of conforming Entity constitutions to Dayton, which took several months, allowed them to invoke the constitutional mechanisms for amendment. However, the process worked badly if at all. The High Representative was forced to direct the RS authorities to amend their constitution, and the amendments proposed were minimal, leaving a document still largely nationalistic in character. In 2003, nearly eight years after Dayton, the High Representative again ordered amendments to the RS constitution. The process of amending Entity constitutions was theoretically adequate but in practice unsatisfactory.

The Dayton Agreement also called for elections no later than nine months after the agreement's entry into force. These elections were intended to remedy the lack of popular engagement in the negotiation or ratification of the agreement, open the possibility that new leaders might emerge, and demonstrate that conditions in Bosnia had improved, to cement international approval for the intervention there. The elections did reduce nationalist percentages in the governments of each Entity, but nevertheless, the elections were conducted quickly in an environment insufficiently recovered from wartime hatreds. There was substantial risk that elections would convey a sense of legitimacy on wartime leaders, without there having been a electoral process robust enough to test their leadership.

The international community designed a set of safeguards that were incorporated into the Dayton Agreement. Most important, the OSCE organized and conducted elections and did not allow nationalist parties to do so.[16] Terms of office resulting from the first elections were kept short. The OSCE set a pattern of extensive regulation of political parties, including codes of conduct and financial requirements. These became important tools for sidelining obstructionists over the next few years.

The Role of the International Community after the Dayton Peace Talks

Recognizing that the Dayton constitution would not be implemented well immediately upon signature, international negotiators decided to put in place an interim international administrator who could provide broad political guidance and also serve as the civilian interlocutor for the powerful international military force entering Bosnia. Annex 10 of the Dayton Agreement therefore establishes a High Representative who is "the final authority in theater regarding interpretation of this Agreement on the civilian implementation" of the peace settlement. This mandate deliberately tracks that of the commander of the international military force, who is the final authority with regard to military aspects of the agreement.

However, the negotiations at Dayton did not address basic questions about the High Representative. What body would provide political oversight of the office? A peace implementation council (PIC) comprised of donor states was formed to serve this role, but not until several weeks after Dayton concluded. More direct guidance was provided by a steering board of the PIC, again composed of major donors. The High Representative had neither staff nor budget for some time after Dayton; staff was loaned from interested states and organizations, but this process took weeks, even months.

More important, there was little agreement within the international community on how the High Representative should carry out his mandate and how intrusive his authority should be vis-à-vis Bosnian institutions and officials. Initially, civilian implementation was hamstrung by a mistaken pledge that military implementation would end twelve months after the operation began. That year would be taken up by basic reconstruction and cease-fire implementation, leaving little space for the High Representative to assume a direct governing role.

The inattention to civilian implementation had direct consequences for Bosnia's political settlement, including efforts to breathe life into the new constitution. International governance—such as was later put in place under UN authority in Kosovo and East Timor in 1999—can be a powerful interim device for stabilizing a post-conflict political environment and preparing the transition to local self-rule. It can allow wartime emotions to cool, remove obstructionist elites from the scene, and permit reasoned deliberations for a permanent constitution. In Bosnia, however, the international civilian mechanism was structurally weak and without a strong mandate.[17]

The problem was particularly acute regarding civilian international bodies. For the High Representative to carry out his mandate, he would need to be able to set priorities and enforce them, including through instructions to civilian agencies. The Dayton Agreement did not give him this authority. Instead, although he can "coordinate" their activities, he is required to "respect their autonomy within their spheres of operation" while providing "general guidance." The agencies themselves were "requested to assist" the High Representative by providing information, but nothing more (see Annex 10, Article II[1c]). The High Representative had no authority over military commanders, which was appropriate for security purposes but left the High Representative as just about the only official in Bosnia without armed force to back up his decisions. A proposal by the High Representative to seek line authority over international agencies met fierce opposition from the international organizations affected and was rejected by the informal group of states supervising the office. As a consequence, even when the High Representative attempted an initiative, he had to negotiate extensively with an array of ad hoc and institutional international actors. The cost in time and attention—let alone the difficulties of obtaining political support—reduced the High Representative's ability to act.

The problem was rooted partly in the process by which the constitution was negotiated. The World Bank, specialized agencies of the UN system, the European Commission, the OSCE, and other multilateral groups were invited to attend the peace conference but not promised specific roles. Some did appear at Dayton, but their actual involvement was very limited. With few exceptions, they provided advice to international negotiators rather than directly to a negotiating party. This limited participation made sense strictly in terms of ending Bosnia's war. None of the groups could drive the negotiations to conclusion, and several were controversial in Bosnia, particularly the United Nations; their overt, active participation would have complicated efforts to reach peace. Their marginal role had consequences for the agreement, however. Negotiators and parties did not have the benefit of their expertise, and this hurt, especially on economic issues such as establishing a central bank (required by the agreement but still renegotiated until 1997) and reducing public control over the economy, both through privatization (begun haltingly in 1998) and lessened government expenditures. The government structure established in the Dayton Constitution, combined with the 1994 Bosniac-Croat Federation government and the residual Republika Srpska government, left Bosnia with a bloated public sector and an absurd ratio of public to private expenditures.

In addition, the marginality of specialized international agencies deferred negotiations among the international community about both the road map for implementation and the desired end state. There was little talk at Dayton itself about priorities for starting civilian implementation quickly. This discussion began several weeks after Dayton, when the specialized agencies were focused mostly on carrying out their own mandates and unwilling to consider whether they should cede control to others. These bodies did not agree to submit to the authority of the High Representative. Instead, each agency prepared its own approach without the central authority having the ability to set priorities and enforce them, either on the international agencies or on the parties.

Conclusion

The Dayton Constitution set up an ongoing political struggle between central and Entity control over Bosnia's economic and political life. It did not dictate strict rules on these matters, but it did set individual rights and international security issues outside Entity control and it restricted the possibility of amendment. Moreover, today the constitution remains as Bosnia's founding document. Bosnians themselves accept it as the basis for the country's political system, even those who want to see it amended.

In short, the Dayton Agreement was an ambitious and historic achievement. In Bosnia, it stopped a brutal war. It also healed a breach in the United States' relationship with Europe that had been opened by several years of disagreement and lack of cooperation over how to handle the crisis. But the achievement came at a price. The agreement bought off wartime leaders, and the constitution was the price tag. The constitution allocates political positions by ethnicity and allows for a huge governmental structure so that there are enough seats for each faction's followers. It fails to take on the roots of nationalist control over the country's resources, employment, culture, and political agenda. It also leaves untouched the assumption—put starkly by participants in the negotiations—that Bosnia's future would be determined by the people who led it during the war. The continued influence of these wartime partisans required an international presence in Bosnia that was larger, more intrusive, and longer lasting than was expected or agreed upon at Dayton.[18]

Subsequent peace negotiations in the Balkans and elsewhere have reacted to Dayton's nationalist hangover. In Kosovo, East Timor, and parts of Africa, international mediators deferred constitutional negotiations until after conflicts have ended. The attraction of insulating constitutions from the pressures of conflict resolution are inarguable, and it is healthy to allow a constitutional process to mature into one that is less confrontational, more inclusive, and more deeply rooted in postwar realities.

But delay and separation are narrow inferences that omit key lessons of the Dayton experience. The constitution builds into it human and civil-rights standards and enforcement mechanisms far stronger than the parties would have accepted on their own, even after a few years. International leverage to incorporate these standards might have been much less several years after the end of Bosnia's bloody war. Paradoxically, therefore, the Bosnia example shows that there are circumstances in which it is possible to achieve more—eventually—only by addressing governance prematurely.

The process of implementing the constitution has encountered difficulties in making real the ideals it contains. This is true partly because these aspects, even though they are contained in the final text, were not agreed fully among the parties or the international community at Dayton, a function of limited time and the importance of other objectives. The difficulties also arose because the more aspirational aspects of the constitution only gradually became realistic in the years following Dayton, as the states in the region established themselves as credible members of a European neighborhood built on democracy and respect for individual rights, and the international community became willing to include them in the post–World War II European institutions.[19]

The text of the constitution contained certain fundamental principles that did not mean much in practice at first, and in fact were barely noticed, but which could be built upon later as the political situation stabilized and matured. A constructive procedural lesson from the open-ended nature of the text is the importance of implementation: the need for a process that could interpret the norms in the document broadly, in a way that compelled political compromises along with a strong international presence on the ground authorized to support the forging of those compromises. A negative procedural lesson is that failure to agree at the start on the desired end state requires continual renegotiation, among international representa-

tatives and with the parties, at each stage of implementation.

Notes

1. Central Intelligence Agency (CIA), Office of Russian and European Analysis, *Balkan Battlegrounds: A Military History of the Yugoslav Conflict, 1990–1995* (Washington, DC: CIA, 2002), p. 43.

2. CIA, *Balkan Battlegrounds*, p. 44.

3. Laura Silber and Allen Little, *The Death of Yugoslavia* (New York: Penguin Books, 1995), p. 72.

4. CIA, *Balkan Battlegrounds*, p. 45.

5. Silber and Little, *The Death of Yugoslavia*, p. 386.

6. The Federation, which joined the territories of the Bosnian Muslims (Bosniacs) and the Bosnian Croats, was created pursuant to the U.S.-brokered Washington Agreement in February 1994. Prior to that agreement, those two groups were engaged in a conflict with each other separate from the conflict between both groups and Serb forces. The agreement gave rise to military coordination that greatly improved Bosnian Muslim and Bosnian Croat fortunes versus the Serbs, but political integration within the Federation continues to be a challenge to this day.

7. A nicely nuanced description of the context and the agreement by one of the participants appeared soon after Dayton was concluded. See Ivan Simonovic, "Dayton: The State, the Law, and Interests in International Relations," *West-Ost Journal*, vol. 1–2 (1996), pp. 13–14 (copy on file with author). Ambassador Simonovic was legal adviser to the Croatian delegation at Dayton and later Croatia's permanent representative to the United Nations. In different jobs he played important roles in both negotiating and implementing Balkan peace agreements throughout the 1990s.

8. Paul C. Szasz, "The Quest for a Bosnian Constitution: Legal Aspects of Constitutional Proposals Relating to Bosnia," *Fordham International Law Journal*, vol. 19, no. 2 (December 1995), pp. 363, 370–73.

9. This Serb position was the genesis of Annex 5, the Agreement on Arbitration. In September 1995, the Serbs insisted that all disputes would be resolved between the Entity governments, and this proposal was included in the principles for the negotiations announced in Geneva and New York. Once the parties agreed at Dayton on a judicial system in which individuals could bring cases directly against governments, and in which a central court system would have the authority to review Entity decisions, the proposal lost most of its purpose.

10. The word *ethnic* is used because that is how the parties referred to their own group identity. There is no ethnic difference among Serbs, Croats, and Bosniacs, but appeals to national origin were abused throughout the Yugoslav conflict.

11. Article IX(1) of the constitution provides that "no person who is serving a sentence imposed by the International [Criminal] Tribunal for the Former Yugoslavia, and no person who is under indictment by the Tribunal and who has failed to comply with an order to appear before the Tribunal, may stand as a candidate or hold any appointive, elective, or other public office in the territory of Bosnia and Herzegovina."

12. For an analysis of this Court decision, see Anna Morawiec Mansfield, "Ethnic but Equal: The Quest for a New Democratic Order in Bosnia and Herzegovina," *Columbia Law Review,* vol. 103, no. 8 (2003), p. 2052.

13. Office of the High Representative (OHR) and EU Special Representative, *Constituent Peoples' Decision of the BiH Constitutional Court,* September 14, 2000, available at www.ohr.int/ohr-dept/legal/const/ (accessed April 12, 2009).

14. OHR, *Constituent Peoples' Decision,* Partial Decision III at paragraph 116. For a sophisticated analysis of how European human rights law can affect the ethnic participation and voting schemes of Dayton, see G. Nystuen, "Conflicts of Norms Regarding Ethnic Discrimination in the Dayton Peace Agreement," doctoral thesis, University of Oslo, 2003 (copy on file with author).

15. See OHR, *Agreement on the Implementation of the Constituent Peoples' Decision of the Constitutional Court of Bosnia and Herzegovina,* March 27, 2002, available at www.ohr.int/ohr-dept/legal/const/ (accessed April 12, 2009).

16. Serb opposition to OSCE conduct of the elections was intense and lasted until late in the negotiation, most likely because of Yugoslavia's suspension from the OSCE. Instead, the OSCE's responsibility was supervision, a term unprecedented in this context but interpreted, publicly and clearly by negotiators, as requiring that the OSCE assume all responsibility for the elections.

17. It was not until 1997, in a meeting in Bonn, Germany, that the Peace Implementation Council approved an expansive interpretation of the High Representative's authority to include powers to order the promulgation of laws, remove officials from office, and make other binding decisions to "facilitate the resolution of difficulties" in implementation and ensure the "smooth running" of the government. These are commonly referred to as the High Representative's "Bonn powers." See OHR, *Peace Implementation Council Bonn Conclusions,* December 10, 1997, section XI, available at www.ohr.int/pic/archive.asp?sa=on (accessed April 12, 2009).

18. David Kanin sees this as part of a general pattern in which external actors impose political goals and related legal structures on Balkan societies, which he argues are built around "Big Men"—figures whose influence and economic power exist outside these externally generated structures and survive changes in them. See David Kanin, "Big Men, Corruption, and Crime," *International Politics,* vol. 40, no. 4 (December 2003), pp. 491–526. Kanin knows the region well and I subscribe to much of his analysis. His near-fatalism about the dominance of these big men is itself a policy choice, however, and one that would deny people of the Balkans a chance to create their own alternative power structures. Even if one accepts that there will be big men in the Balkans, however, it still seems to matter who they are; those in the 1990s were spectacularly destructive. Even more, societies may flourish if the big men remain but are driven to the margins of political and legitimate economic life. Effective public policy may attack the syndicates that connect big men to political, economic, and criminal power in well-coordinated, homeostatic networks of big men. See Council on Foreign Relations, *Balkans 2010: A Center for Preventive Action Report* (New York: Council on Foreign Relations, 2003). I was a member of the task force that produced that report.

19. The Council of Europe has admitted Bosnia and Herzegovina (April 2002), Croatia (November 1996), and Serbia and Montenegro (April 2003) as members. Croatia has joined NATO's Partnership for Peace (PfP) (May 2000) and is negotiating full NATO membership. Both Bosnia and Herzegovina and Serbia and Montenegro are negotiating PfP membership. Croatia also is currently negotiating accession to the European Union.

13

Constitution Making and Transitional Politics in Hungary

Andrew Arato and Zoltán Miklósi

More than a dozen years and five general elections after the end of its old regime, Hungary has a liberal democratic constitution that established a foundation for its relatively well-functioning parliamentary political system. The process of constitution making was entirely peaceful, was within established legality, and never involved the danger of dual power, civil war, or state or popular violence. As one political regime, a Soviet-type dictatorship, was fully replaced by another, liberal democracy, the destructive logic of friend and enemy well known from the history of revolutions—purges, proscription, massive denial of rights, and terror—was avoided. Since 1989, the main political antagonists under the old regime have functioned on the political if not always the rhetorical level as opponents within a competitive multiparty democracy.

In the strict legal sense, the method of constitution making that achieved this result was one of parliamentary constitution making through legal continuity, utilizing the amendment rule of the old regime, a rule that survives to this day.[1] More important, it was a product of a process, in common with five other countries—Poland, Czechoslovakia, the German Democratic Republic, Bulgaria, and the Republic of South Africa[2]—in which the terms of the political transition from forms of authoritarian rule were developed through roundtable negotiations. On a comparative and theoretical level, the Hungarian case represents an incomplete model of democratic constitution making; it could be characterized as postsovereign with respect to the ideals of the American and French revolutions. Characteristically, in this model, constitutions are drafted in a process of several stages, during which no institution or representative body can claim to represent fully, in an unlimited fashion, the sovereign people. What makes the model democratic is the drafting of the final constitutional product by an assembly, one that is elected, at least ideally, primarily for that purpose, even if it does not become a sovereign constituent assembly of the past. Hungary did not complete this last stage. An ordinary parliament elected in 1996 assumed the task of second-stage constitution drafting but failed to accomplish it, making the interim constitution of 1989–90 ultimately a work of elite agreements, de facto permanent. The only democratic participation that Hungarian constitution making involved—the referendum of November 1989 that decided the question of the country becoming a parliamentary rather than a presidential republic—produced this result because of a rejection of communist attempts to preserve and convert old forms of power. Paradoxically, on the constitutional issue of that referendum, the majority would have always preferred, though not particularly passionately, direct elections of the head of state, probably with greater powers than the current system allows.

The merits of the constitution-making method that Hungarian political actors adopted concern both what it avoids and what it contributes positively to future democratic developments. The significance of round-table negotiations, aside from the great strategic advantage of avoiding violence and civil strife, is to help find an alternative to two forms of imposition that tend to lead to pseudo-democracy and pseudo-constitutionalism: by the forces of an old regime and by new, revolutionary actors. Historically, the former has generally taken the form of imposed constitutions or reformist, top-down constitution making. The preferred form of the latter has been revolutionary and sovereign constituent assemblies with the plenitude of power. In opposition to these models, from a theoretical point of view, the interim constitution tends to impose constitutionalism on the process of constitution making that in traditional European democratic models is under the dominance of potentially dictatorial provisional governments and all-powerful assemblies.[3] Here, the advantage of the method is best seen in what it avoids,

namely renewed authoritarianism or a new form of dictatorship. But positive benefits can be claimed for the approach as well. The many-stage process allows the generation of different modes of legitimacy[4] as well as the institutionalization of learning between the stages. The former advantage implies a solution to the hitherto intractable problem of beginning democratically where there is no democracy by substituting initial pluralist for democratic legitimacy through inclusion of as many relevant actors as possible and having them come to agreement through consensus or fair compromise. The latter advantage means that with or without appropriate sunset clauses, initial power-sharing arrangements or concessions to old regime forces can be adopted without incorporating them in the final constitutional product.

The comparatively important question in the case of Hungarian constitution making is whether the incomplete version of the model of postsovereign constitution making, which we fully present here, allowed Hungary to anticipate and take advantage of the paradigm more completely developed elsewhere, above all in South Africa. There is little question that it did in what it helped to avoid: the danger of authoritarian imposition or relapse to dictatorship during the critical period of constitution making. If we consider the relevant period to be 1989 to 1997, between the meeting of the National Round Table (NKA) and the definitive failure of the new constitution-making effort, it is clear that constitutionalism has been successfully applied in this period, to both constitutional and normal politics through an allegedly interim basic law. There was never constitutional imposition in Hungary during this time by merely one political force.

In positively contributing to democratic developments, the picture is more differentiated. It is clear to us that little democratic legitimacy was generated for the process, or for the interim constitution that became permanent, one reason being that there was no attempt to promote public participation or education during the failed effort of 1996–97. At the same time, constitutional learning proceeded dramatically between 1989 and 1990, the dates of the two main elite agreements concerning the interim text, resulting in the removal of consociational devices in a fashion parallel to developments elsewhere. After 1990, and especially with the failure to produce a new and permanent constitution in 1994–96, constitutional learning became almost exclusively the domain of the very powerful Constitutional Court, immediately raising suspicions about whether such judicial activism or constitution making could be sustained in view of Hungary's "soft" constitutional background, that is, the weak democratic legitimacy of the constitution.[5] For a while, the answer was that it could, as the Constitutional Court imposed important limits on parliamentary actions that endangered constitutionalism, such as attempts to change the constitution through simple statutes. Eventually, however, judicial activism could not be sustained. With the Constitutional Court much more quiescent under new leadership, from 1998 to 2002, a new right-wing coalition adopted a significant number of measures constraining parliamentary democracy that were arguably incompatible with the constitution. Public interest in resisting these measures was minimal. Was this because of the relatively low legitimacy of the constitution or because of the shift of interest to economic performance and joining the European Union? Probably both played a role. In all countries, issues like the latter occupy public interest and the understanding of constitutional and political questions is low. It is up to institutions such as constitutional courts, professional groups such as lawyers, and elites such as liberal parties to raise normative and constitutional issues and mobilize around them. They can do so only if there are latent significant meanings

and available historical narratives to which they can refer, such as the plausible claim that the constitution belongs to the people, or that it was partly the people's work in a great historical period, or that it was made in the people's name by persons in whom the people have or had confidence and who have been entrusted to that purpose. In Hungary, not all of these claims could be made, and even those that could, regarding the dramatic historical events of 1988–89, have not been made successfully. This is what we mean by the constitution's legitimacy problem, which does not mean that constitutional or democratic government is in crisis in Hungary. What they face is a long-term and already ongoing erosion of interest and support, which may or may not matter for stability and the quality of political life depending on historical circumstances.

Both the achievements and the failures of the new Hungarian constitution are best interpreted in terms of the procedural history of its making, which in turn is related to the character of the country's transition from communist rule. Before the transition, Hungary was a partially reformed postcommunist regime.[6] The country's negotiated path of transition, hardly the only type possible, was favored by this particular regime type. On one hand, despite many an earlier dream, there was little chance of a revolutionary overthrow of the system. The memories of the failed revolution of 1956 and the partial successes of communist economic reform[7] more or less guaranteed that there was no possibility in Hungary of a popular uprising, even in the late 1980s. The high level of civil privatism in this period, linked to the development of the second—that is, private—economy, made the emergence and development of even a Solidarity-type non-revolutionary mass movement unlikely. Unlike other governments in Eastern and Central Europe, Hungary's was ready throughout the age of Mikhail Gorbachev to experiment with further economic reforms and even tightly managed political liberalization.

On the other hand, a top-down process of reiterated reforms slowing down the process of eventual system change, as in Mexico or Chile, also turned out to be impossible. The regime's weakness, the existence of a small but well-organized and articulate democratic opposition since the late 1970s, and the activism of a variety of small movements and initiatives in the 1980s, along with the increasing rapidity of change in the whole region, made the top-down option, not to speak of a conservative one, impossible.[8]

Thus, a fully negotiated transition with unbroken legal continuity occurred in Hungary, one resembling the slightly earlier process in Poland and, to an extent, the later processes in the German Democratic Republic and Bulgaria. As in all these cases, the central institution of change in Hungary was a roundtable, the NKA. Unlike in the other transition countries, in Hungary, all democratic forces had been organized as proto-parties before unification in the so-called Round Table of the Opposition (EKA). Though both were weak, the respective strengths of government and opposition at the negotiations were relatively well matched. Undoubtedly, the unexpected pace of prior change in Poland reinforced the strength of the united Hungarian opposition.

Until the South African transition, Hungary's NKA was the only such body that produced a new, detailed, and fully enacted constitution,[9] even if it was technically an amendment of the Stalinist constitution of 1949 and was stated to be an interim document.[10] The constitution was supposed to serve a double purpose: to provide the framework for political institutions as well as political guarantees for all the actors, persons, and groups to be able to continue in the process. A suitable set of rules was to be provided for a unique and one-time event—the democratic transition itself—and for an undetermined

period, for the functioning of a liberal democratic regime. Many of the compromises that were required to make the task in the first period viable were, however, obvious liabilities from the point of view of the second.

Thus, immediately after the Round Table agreements, including the new interim constitution, were signed on September 18, 1989, a process of constitutional reform and adjustment began.[11] The referendum of November 26, 1989, which established the priority of parliamentary elections and provided for parliamentary selection of the president of the republic, set off this process. The parliament of the old regime, which technically had to enact the Round Table constitution and retained the right to amend it by a simple two-thirds majority, was a key institution; its role was not limited to the formal legal one, either before or after the interim constitution was enacted. The new constitutional court set up by the Round Table constitution was another important actor. However, the most important institution after the Round Table that was involved in molding the new parliamentary regime was the first freely elected parliament in 1990. Behind its significant revisions of the Round Table constitution stood a temporary pact between the two major parties during the change of regimes—the nationalist, right-of-center Magyar Demokrata Fórum (MDF), or Hungarian Democratic Forum, and the liberal, left-of-center Szabad Demokraták Szövetsége (SZDSZ), or Alliance of Free Democrats—that together easily formed the required two-thirds parliamentary majority (for a list and description of the parties, see the glossary appended to this chapter). Avoiding the writing of a new constitution, the new parliament's revisions rationalized and completed the development toward a pure parliamentary regime; a few later amendments and many relevant judicial decisions only modified some details.

The constitution-making project was taken up only one more time after the efforts of the late 1980s, during the 1994–98 coalition government of the Magyar Szocialista Párt (MSZP), or Hungarian Socialist Party, and the SZDSZ.[12] This was the only time since 1990 that a governmental coalition had the required votes to change the constitution. Aside from addressing a few substantive deficiencies, the coalition hoped to generate greater political legitimacy by putting in place a democratic constitution no longer laboring under the interim label or its technical continuity with the 1949 constitution. The effort failed, however, and it remains an open question whether it could have succeeded given the piecemeal process of evolutionary development already in motion. To be sure, the workings of the political process sufficiently explain the failure of 1996–97, when adequate political support was not available for any new constitutional alternative, whether a relegitimated and rationalized parliamentary constitution, a more presidential one, or possibly an option with corporatist elements. More generally, in contrast to the much more successful two-stage Polish and South African efforts, the Hungarian failure draws attention to the importance of time, sequence, political opportunity, and procedural learning in processes of constitution making.

The Process

Prehistory: The Development of a Transition Strategy

When political change is widely anticipated in a country and especially in a region, generally only the most rigid authoritarian regimes, such as those in Czechoslovakia and Romania in 1988–89, decide or feel compelled to avoid all preemptive reforms from above. The majority of authoritarian regimes undertake some liberalizing reforms. As Adam Przeworski[13] argued, liberalization tends to release a dynamic that eventually leads to societal polarization and a stark choice between repres-

sion and transition—stark because moderate agents of reform tend to lose power either way. According to Przeworski, if liberalizing elites understood what they were doing, they would not opt for liberalization. The argument, however, works only if we confine the target of liberalization to the sphere outside of politics. As Bolivar Lamounier[14] first noticed in the case of Brazil, liberalization—when not rigidly counterposed to democratization—can involve carefully controlled reform of the political order itself. Such reforms, even when reiterated, may protect the power positions of ruling elites in the context of a gradual change in the very identity of a regime. In our view, there are in principle two fundamental but combinable ways of achieving the goals of transition preservation through reform. One is the purely electoral road Lamounier has in mind, which was most successfully practiced in Mexico. The other is the path of institutionalizing from above a partially authoritarian, partially democratic constitution, as was accomplished in Chile around 1980,[15] which may or may not be coupled with an electoral strategy. The first of these options involves organizing from above *partially* competitive elections, which lead to either "soft" dictatorships or "hard" democracies that can nevertheless appeal to democratic legitimacy. Though we cannot demonstrate it here, we strongly believe that the precondition of this version of reformism is a viable claim of legitimacy, whether it draws on older revolutionary ideologies, newer nationalist ideologies, or their eclectic combination. The method can work because free elections are highly sensitive targets for political intervention even without electoral fraud; they can be influenced on the level of electoral rules, finances, and timetables, as well as through controlling access to the media.[16]

We encounter the model of authoritarian electoral reform in a wide variety of contexts, not only in Latin America, but in South Africa (reforms of 1983) and the old Soviet

Union (reforms of the late 1980s). In Hungary, the policy was tried in 1985 when, as a result of a reform allowing multiple candidacies on all levels, in many electoral districts (about 71 out of 352), competitive elections occurred that led to the loss of 35 parliamentary seats by the ruling party.[17] The hitherto merely paper powers of parliament were not increased in this reform, no independent new parties were allowed to nominate candidates or even organize themselves, and in most districts, the authorities informally blocked truly independent candidates from running. Nevertheless, the turmoil associated with some of the nomination struggles in which dissidents tried to run, and the loss of face involved in the loss of seats, must have convinced the ruling party of the dangers of this road in isolation. In retrospect, the Hungarian communists did not have either the self-confidence or the legitimacy of the Partido Revolucionario Institucional (PRI) in Mexico, or even Gorbachev in the Soviet Union, to seriously try to impose or exploit a controlled electoral transition path.[18]

Nevertheless, in the epoch of Gorbachev, given the significant changes occurring in the Soviet Union and the reformist self-understanding of the Hungarian communist party, the Hungarian Socialist Workers Party (MSZMP, precursor to the MSZP), as well as the intensification of a variety of pressures from below, political reforms had to be tried. In late 1988, after organizing a series of public discussions under the heading of "social discussion," these efforts took the form of enacting a variety of liberalizing reforms targeting civil society, the rights of association and assembly and the right to strike being the most important.[19] In these cases, however, the MSZMP had the unfortunate experience of being forced to enact much more radical measures than it initially envisaged because of the unexpectedly lively character of the social discussions and even parliamentary debates, in which a few unof-

ficial deputies could participate.[20] The idea of producing civil society from above turned out to be as contradictory in Hungary as it was in the Soviet Union.[21]

Thus, the alternative notion of enacting an entirely new, partially liberal, and even democratic constitution came to be advocated by a variety of forces within the ruling party. Initially—around the time that the relevant work group in the Ministry of Justice was formed in May 1988—these forces hoped to use a new constitution to relegitimate a reformed version of the one-party system. Though they were probably unaware of the example, the relative success and stability at that time of the Pinochet constitution of 1980 indicated that the effort was by no means unthinkable or impossible.[22] Differing from the Chilean option, which envisaged elections only much later, the Hungarian variant in all its forms sought to link the project of authoritarian constitution making to a quick move to general elections that the MSZMP would win one way or another. More important for the drafters than the Chilean experience were the results of the Polish Round Table agreements. Concluded in April 1989, these agreements did not create even a provisional new constitution, but rather transitional arrangements defined by a strong executive and partially competitive elections, with the expectation at the time that both the presidency and the parliamentary majority would wind up in the hands of the communist party.[23]

More or less in the Polish spirit, after examining a variety of options, the Hungarian Ministry of Justice came up with two draft conceptions and one proposal for extensive constitutional revisions in November 1988, January 1989, and May 1989. The last two were presented to parliament in March and May, respectively. The first of these latter documents envisaged neither open multiparty competition and fully free elections nor an executive responsible to or even checked by parliament. The proposal brought to parliament in March 1989 sought to imitate the Polish arrangements rather closely, providing for parliamentary elections in which the party shares were divided in advance; as an option, a bicameral legislature, but without a freely elected chamber; a strong presidency; and a relatively weak constitutional court.[24] The discussion of this proposal in the political bureau of the MSZMP foresaw a subsequent election in 1995 that would be free, though under rather unspecified conditions. The final proposal submitted to parliament in May seemed to reduce the power of the president somewhat, at a time when the ruling party was obviously gearing up for projected negotiations. But it still provided for full presidential control over foreign policy, the military forces, and, rather strikingly, states of emergency.[25] Clearly, the political bureau at this time was no longer thinking in terms of formally distributing parliamentary seats in advance, as in the Polish model, but it is less clear that they abandoned the idea of a two-stage process with some kind of electoral restriction in the first of these. In their own words, they sought to reduce the competitive character of the next elections, either by a prior coalition agreement with a part of the opposition or, at the very least, an early timing that would not allow the opposition to organize and campaign adequately.[26] None of the three proposals established parliamentary responsibility for the executive; to somewhat different degrees, each concentrated executive power in a strong or medium-strong directly elected presidency.[27]

Even if many individual parts of the last constitutional draft that the Ministry of Justice produced found their way into the eventual compromise,[28] it is clear that the system-defining features of the two original draft presidential constitutions were quite different in spirit and structure from any fully democratic document. They were semidemocratic and semiauthoritarian constitutions, with important nondemocratic preserves for the old ruling power, both in parliament and the executive.[29] The sponsors may not have believed in the permanence of such a constitution even if it were to be enacted. What they sought was to institutionalize an elaborate, electorally centered transition, in which political power would not be risked for a considerable period—an arrangement that a reformist, partially democratic system of the rule of law was to legitimize.[30] Crucial in this context was not as much the various constitutional contents, of which only a relatively strong presidency seems to have been a constant, but the political timetables involved. The opposition in Hungary—poorly organized, with relatively few members and resources, its leaders hardly known—could not have competed effectively if any of the top-down variants were enacted in early 1989 and elections soon followed, as was planned.

Thus, there was significant danger from the democratic point of view in another set of proposals calling for the early election of a constituent assembly, made variously early in 1989 by groupings within the Hungarian Democratic Forum, already the dominant and best-organized force in the moderate part of the opposition,[31] and somewhat later by some of the most reformist elements of the ruling party, the only group well-enough organized to win such an election (i.e., by Mihaly Bihari and the New March Front). The idea of a constituent assembly was strongly associated with revolutionary democratic ruptures in the European tradition. In principle, such an assembly could have enacted an entirely democratic constitution and organized free, competitive elections. In practice, however, the formula in Hungary also could have very possibly produced yet another variant of the Ministry of Justice proposal: Early elections for such a body, organized by the government in office, were likely to result in a communist majority, which then could enact a reformist, regime-conservative option with greater formal legitimacy than the sitting parliament had. For this reason, the radical part of the opposition rejected this formula, which, after its adoption by the reform socialist New March Front, became unacceptable to the moderate opposition as well.

It was, however, not clear that rhetorically rejecting all of the options could block one of them from being imposed from above. As a series of constitutional amendments enacted in early 1989[32] indicated, the danger of new legislation was constant,[33] and the opposition was divided into a variety of rather weak groupings, or proto-parties. The ruling party could easily exploit political party fragmentation, with the cooperation of some but not all oppositional groups, to stage less than fully competitive elections. Only if united could the opposition force the regime into an alternative procedural mode that favored the opposition—namely, full-scale negotiations. It was quite important, therefore, to block any significant part of the opposition from agreeing to participate in any formula imposed from above, no matter how superficially attractive. This was the main though not the only function of the Round Table of the Opposition that, in March 1989, brought together seven parties or proto-parties and two nonparty associations in a single organization with the purpose of pushing for and engaging in negotiations with the ruling power.

Rejecting the election of a constituent assembly—the classical European democratic formula—as understandable as it was in the circumstances, had unfortunate results. The formula came to be associated with top-down, authoritarian regime–dominated forms of constitution making and was not considered as a model to be combinable with creating an interim constitution by roundtable negotiations. However, this very combination later proved to be successful in Bulgaria and South Africa, in the latter powerfully enhancing the legitimacy of the final constitution, even as the constitutional principles agreed upon in roundtable negotiations were preserved

and adhered to. In Hungary, however, the option was not even raised. As a result, it became clear, if by default, that ordinary parliaments—in the end, two of them—would play significant roles in constitution making. This was a procedure inherited from the communist past and undesirable from the point of view of the heightened legitimacy needed for democratic constitution making, under which voters need to know that the assembly that they elect is about to undertake a constitution-making role. Monistic, parliamentary constitution making is also not conducive to creating the two-track structure needed for constitutionalism.[34]

The Opposition Round Table and the Beginning of Negotiations

Apart from a brief period of increasing repression in the early 1980s after the introduction of martial law and the banning of Solidarity in Poland, the situation in Hungary was characterized by the old regime's growing awareness that it could best contain future pressure from the population by continuing some reform policies. Liberalization in Hungary was not restricted to measures targeting the political system; it also involved making concessions to, or at least tolerating the existence of, dissident or other extrainstitutional groups. Most relevant was the emergence in the 1980s of three distinctive groups of intellectuals who opposed the regime in one form or another. The first and second were a group of democratic dissidents and a circle of so-called populist writers. The third group, soon called the Fiatal Demokraták Szövetsége (FIDESZ), or Alliance of Young Democrats, emerged from various student associations to reach some level of permanence in early 1988. The democratic dissidents consisted of intellectuals who openly opposed the system by publishing declarations (e.g., condemning the arrest of Vaclav Havel in Czechoslovakia) and illegal magazines, and who, as a consequence, were subject to frequent persecution and official abuse. The populist writers for the most part remained within the confines of the official public sphere; their primary concerns focused on social issues, such as declining birth rates or the situation of ethnic Hungarians in neighboring countries, rather than on explicitly political causes. The liberal SZDSZ grew from the first group; the nationalist, populist MDF grew from the second.[35] These groups had a clear view of their own identities and those of the others, and as the process leading to the opening of negotiations about the transition was evolutionary rather than dramatic, there was no point in that evolution at which they would have felt compelled to unite forces altogether and renounce their independence. This did not exclude rather extensive cooperation among these groups and those that emerged later, when the time for negotiations had finally come.

A crucial moment in all negotiated transitions occurs when representatives of the old regime unequivocally announce the need for a general overhaul of the system. The manner and pace of a transition depends on whether such a proclamation was forced by an open and general disintegration of existing power structures or irresistible popular pressure, as in the German Democratic Republic and Czechoslovakia, or was made when the old regime could still claim a vital role in the transformation, or even take charge of it altogether, as in Poland and Hungary. The latter case is much more likely to lead to a real bargaining situation, as the rules of the new regime are neither imposed on society by the old regime nor formulated exclusively by agents representing the would-be new regime, with old institutions and leaders being reduced to placing the official stamp on the new rules. In other words, a real bargaining situation is characterized by the fact that all main parties to the deal see themselves and the others as having a lot to gain as well as a

lot to lose. In Hungary, pronouncements by highest-level leaders of the old regime that the fundamentals of state socialism were to be abandoned came at such an early point that it arguably surprised even many of the dissidents. In May 1988, an impromptu conference of the MSZMP ended the thirty-two-year rule of General Secretary János Kádár. In November, Prime Minister Miklós Németh declared that the Hungarian reforms should eventually lead to a Western-style parliamentary regime.

The proclamations said next to nothing about the pace of transition, the precise character of the new regime to be built, or the prerogatives that the still-ruling party would preserve under the new rules, not to mention the role of opposition groups in devising the new system. The idea of a negotiated transition clearly came into view as a consequence of parallel events in Poland. After months of preparation, the Polish government conducted negotiations with Solidarity between February and April 1989, reaching a compromise solution whereby, in exchange for the relegalization of Solidarity, the opposition conceded partially free elections and a strong presidency to the ruling party. The beginning of Polish negotiations triggered a similar chain of events in Hungary, albeit with altogether different outcomes.

In mid-February 1989, the central committee of the MSZMP announced that it would conduct bilateral and multilateral discussions about the new ways of exercising power. In response, a joint declaration of the most important independent organizations—most notably, the MDF, the SZDSZ, and FIDESZ—urged roundtable talks with the participation of the government and the democratic political organizations. Yet there was no agreement as to the terms and objectives of the proposed negotiations. The government wanted discussions of new constitutional drafts under preparation by the Ministry of Justice. The independent groups wanted merely to work out the legal frame-work needed to freely elect a democratic legislature that would, in turn, adopt a new constitution of its own making. At the same time, preparation of a new electoral law was well under way by the government; apparently, the bilateral and multilateral discussions that the government urged were meant, at least at this point, to do little more than give an air of popular consent to a new regime that the government could impose on the people. The danger was especially great that the government would gain as its partners one or more of the new so-called historical parties that were recently formed: the Független Kisgazda Párt (FKgP), or Independent Small Holders Party; the Kereszteny Demokrata Nep Part (KDNP), or Christian Democratic People's Party; the Magyar Szociáldemokrata Párt (MSZDP), or Hungarian Social Democratic Party; and the Néppart, or People's Party.[36]

The ambiguities of the government's proposal notwithstanding, the prospect of negotiations created a new situation on the opposition side. In Hungary, there was no single unified opposition movement comparable to Solidarity with demonstrable popular support, unquestioned authority, and nationally known leaders. The months preceding the beginning of negotiations in July 1989 were characterized by a rapid proliferation of independent groups, and in the multitude of voices, the general public could hardly perceive the difference between groups with a decade of prehistory and significant intellectual background and newly emerging formations with no discernible substance. With negotiations approaching, the question of political agency was bound to surface with unusual urgency for the opposition. Who would participate in the negotiations? The issue was settled in a more or less ad hoc manner: On March 22, 1989, eight organizations, comprising all of the important independent groups,[37] formed the EKA, which became a coordinating body between them and the single negotiating partner of the government.[38] The EKA delegates, rather than their respective organizations, were to represent the entire opposition at the NKA, the scene of negotiations. As a logical consequence, the EKA had to adopt the consensus principle as its own way of proceeding. Each organization had the right to veto any EKA resolution. Nevertheless, the opposition's groups emphatically retained their ideological as well as organizational independence.

The political agents belonging to the opposition EKA, whatever their previous views as parties, were driven to favor the model of constitution making by a new legislature, which some interpreted as a constituent assembly, for two distinct yet interrelated reasons. Both stemmed from the weakness of the opposition agents. First, agents rightly perceived that being unelected with small memberships, they lacked the popular support necessary for them to claim the authority to devise the rules of the new regime by themselves. Second, opposition groups were divided among themselves on crucial constitutional issues yet, at the same time, were forced by circumstances to act in a coordinated manner; therefore, on pain of losing influence over the transition process altogether, they were left with the single option of postponing decisions on all constitutional issues that separated them until an undefined later point—at the very least, until the election of a new legislature or constituent assembly. Thus, their initial position was that the agenda of the NKA talks should be confined to establishing the conditions for a disciplined transition, in the restricted sense of a transfer of power. The agenda, in their view, should have been limited to adopting a new electoral law and removing or at least neutralizing the MSZMP's strategic organizational and financial advantages, leaving open questions regarding the new regime's features.[39]

The crucial question then turned out to be whether the government might be persuaded to adopt the EKA's terms for the discussions. In this respect, the decisive move came in early June 1989, when—sensing the growing influence of the opposition as well as its own progressive disintegration—the MSZMP agreed to limit negotiations to the conditions of the transition and to abandon its own draft constitution, which it had completed in May.[40] This concession, together with the earlier formation of the EKA, finally created the conditions for a real bargaining situation. But it was sustainable only as long as the MSZMP could keep its promises to avoid entering into the substantive issues of the design of the new regime and to provide fair conditions for the transition, and only as long as the EKA could retain a sufficient level of unity. Given the substantial differences among the opposition groups, the second condition could be met only if the first condition was met. As it happened, the MSZMP kept neither of its two promises, but by that time, it only disturbed the transition process rather than spoiling it altogether.

The most important period of classical bargaining occurred between June and August 1989, when all the essential prerequisites of bargaining between two autonomous parties were present in a particularly clear form. First of all, by this time it was a more or less common understanding that the Soviet Union would not intervene should the outcome of the negotiations lead to adopting an entirely new type of regime. Thus, the single most important strategic advantage of the communist party was removed. Second, the reburial of Imre Nagy, the executed prime minister of the 1956 uprising, on June 16, 1989, altogether shattered the ideological as well as symbolic self-understanding and legitimacy of the old regime. After some initial hesitancy, the reform-minded leaders of the party decided to support preparations for the reburial and even attended the ceremony, which became from a psychological point of view the turning point of the sequence of events. After June 16, there simply was to be no returning to attempts to impose a new regime by the government; the old regime's pretensions to representing the people were given a final blow. Third, the most important opposition groups stabilized their status as the negotiating partners of the government, and some of them—most notably the MDF—even demonstrated substantial popular support in by-elections. Therefore, the opposition realized that it had a direct stake in concluding the negotiations in a timely fashion. Fourth, the relative reversal of perceived strengths notwithstanding, the outcome of any popular elections, either presidential or legislative, was vastly unpredictable, especially for the legislature. In all, the major external constraints on the bargaining process were removed, there was to be no return to the old ways, and neither of the major political agents was strong enough to set the terms of the process all by itself.

The NKA talks had a rather sophisticated structure that facilitated the overcoming of major obstacles yet had little to recommend itself in the way of public accessibility, let alone popular participation.[41] The negotiations were conducted at three levels: one plenary, one medium political level, and one expert level. The two lower levels were divided into various thematic committees. The government insisted, and the opposition reluctantly agreed, on making only the plenary level accessible to the media, the level that, for the most part, was confined to being the public stage for declarations and the forum for striking the final deals on various details.[42] The main bargaining was carried out in the committees and subcommittees of the medium level, with the participation of the most prominent figures of both sides. Minor adjustments and differences were ironed out at the expert level. This structure, combined with informal background talks among various agents as well as the EKA sessions, provided sufficient flexibility and fallback opportunities to retain the unity and continuity of the negotiating process even in the face of serious disagreements. However, the structure also meant that devising the crucial details of the new regime was insulated from the general public, which was hardly aware of either the major issues of the negotiations or the alternative positions and choices. Admittedly, a more open bargaining process could have had undesirable consequences; it is easy to see how greater public involvement could have led to more plebiscitary alternatives, particularly a popularly elected strong presidency. As we argue, the sophisticated bargaining structures made for favorable institutional outcomes but little transparency. There was an important cost for this: Because the population was given little opportunity to see the emerging institutions as their own work, the new constitution was to have much less legitimacy than was generally thought desirable.[43]

From Round Table to Referendum

At a rather late point in the negotiations, in late July 1989, when there was already remarkable progress in almost all areas, the MSZMP delegates changed their stance on both the issue of the agenda of the negotiations and the issue of providing for fair conditions of transition. First, they announced that the party would not abolish its organizations at workplaces or publish accounts of its property, nor would it dissolve the Workers' Guard, the party's own paramilitary organization. All of these were seen as providing unfair electoral organizational advantage to the communists, contrary to any acceptable notion of a fair transition. Second, the party urged that the president of the republic should be elected by the population at large before the new legislative assembly was elected; this was intended to secure this position for the party and its then-popular candidate Imre Pozsgay. The first set of positions could have obstructed the fair conditions of

transition, whereas the position on presidential elections forced the EKA to enter into many of the substantive issues of the new constitutional design. To be sure, the opposition groups had already agreed before this episode to discuss some of the key elements of the new regime, such as the constitutional court, the ombudsmen, and even the presidency itself. It was, however, the question of the timing and manner of presidential elections that was to lead to the (partial) breakdown of the negotiation process.

Arguably, the communist party's change of strategy was due to its perception that its chances of retaining at least some of its powers in popular elections were deteriorating further. The summer of 1989 witnessed the landslide victory of Solidarity for all contested seats (one-third of Sejm, 99 out of 100 of the Senate) in Poland's general legislative elections, as well as the victory of opposition candidates in three by-elections in Hungary. While perceiving its relative weakness had forced the government to accept the EKA's terms of debate early in the summer, the premonition of its possible defeat in popular elections pushed it to tighten its grip on power and seek to retain it by other means. At that moment, the party's only relative asset that could have been mobilized in popular elections was the popularity of one of its nationally known leaders, Imre Pozsgay, who had been up to that point in the forefront of reforms. The only way the party could have cashed in on this advantage was through a popular presidential election with Pozsgay as the party's candidate. After Pozsgay's election as president, the outlook for parliamentary elections could very well change.

The dramatic change of perceptions on the part of the MSZMP leadership transformed the entire bargaining process. Previously, as all parties of the NKA agreed to postpone discussing the substantive issues of the new regime, the opposition parties could also avoid a Polish-type outcome of a previously arranged parliamentary chamber and the division of the executive between a president and a prime minister. It was assumed both that the election of the new legislature would be entirely free and that there would be no division of the executive power. Both assumptions were plausible because the two sides not only felt themselves weak but also perceived their relative weaknesses as being in balance. Because both could hope to win fair but not overwhelming representation in a popular legislative election, they could agree on holding entirely free elections without Polish-type restrictions. According to János Kis, the SZDSZ's most important leader, the weakness of opposition agents paradoxically led to their radicalization; unlike Solidarity, the independent Hungarian organizations lacked the authority they would have needed to persuade society that concessions to the old regime were necessary. Thus, instead of dividing executive and legislative powers, they focused on imposing constitutional constraints on them, such as through establishing the constitutional court and the ombudsman's office.[44] Arguably, the negotiating process was smooth only as long as the self-perceived weaknesses of the bargaining parties were relatively balanced. The moment one of the sides perceived its chances as being considerably better or worse than those of the other party, the bargaining process was bound to face difficulties. Of course, there is an asymmetry here. Had it been the case that the communist party sensed its position to be dramatically improving rather than deteriorating, it could have left the bargaining table altogether instead of changing its strategy.

The change in dynamics between the two sides of the NKA entailed a change in the dynamics within the EKA. The moderate wing, led by MDF, was ready to sign the final agreement and thus for all practical purposes to concede the presidency, albeit with very limited powers, to the MSZMP. The more radical wing, represented by the SZDSZ

and FIDESZ, saw no reason to grant such a concession to the government in the changing circumstances. However, if they used the right of veto given to them by the rules of the EKA, they would risk all the results that were achieved at the round table, possibly spoiling the entire process of transition. Therefore, they decided to neither sign nor veto the final agreement but called for a referendum on the four contested issues of the presidency, the communist party's property, its organizations at workplaces, and the Workers' Guard.[45] On September 18, 1989, the majority of the EKA organizations signed the final agreement and the rest initiated a referendum. FIDESZ and the SZDSZ gathered far more than the necessary 100,000 signatures to support their referendum initiative. As a result, the last communist legislature still in office adopted the agreement reached at the round table and thus amended the constitution on October 17–20; a few days later, a referendum was officially called for November 26 on the four contested questions. The answers favored by the radical wing carried the day on all four questions, although on the presidency issue, the margin was only six thousand votes. Thus, the presidential elections were postponed until after the new legislature was elected and conditions of relative equality for the upcoming competition secured.[46]

To sum up, through the agency of the generally obedient old one-party parliament, the NKA had been without a doubt the chief organ of making the new democratic constitution of Hungary. In institutional terms, its most important products included a new electoral system, a regulation of the relationship between the executive and the legislature—leaving the issue of the presidency unresolved until the referendum—and the introduction of significant constitutional constraints on the government, such as the Constitutional Court and the Ombudsman's office. More specifically, the NKA adopted a mixed proportional-majority electoral system, in which 45 percent of the seats were filled through the majority-plurality system and 55 percent were elected through the proportional representation method, though with peculiarly disproportional consequences due to the relatively low average district size. Regarding executive-legislative relations, the arrangement reached at the NKA was for a mostly parliamentary system, with executive power exercised by a parliament-elected government dependent on legislative confidence. In subsequent steps of constitutional amendments and Constitutional Court rulings, this arrangement was further shifted in the direction of pure parliamentarianism. Regarding constitutional constraints on the executive and the legislature, the restrictions imposed on the government by the arrangements arrived at by the NKA gave the Hungarian democratic regime a truly constitutionalist character. Not only did the constitution emphatically recognize a list of fundamental human rights and other constitutional principles that the government was obliged to respect, but it also provided for effective institutions to enforce these rights and principles. In particular, the Constitutional Court introduced by the NKA was given such extensive powers that until the later creation of the South African Court, it was regarded as the most powerful institution of its kind around the world. In the early 1990s, the Constitutional Court played a crucial role in protecting fundamental rights from invasions by the government and in clarifying the relationship between various branches of government.

In hindsight, one can argue that both the moderate and the radical wings of the opposition were crucial to preparing the way for a peaceful and disciplined transition. By signing the agreement, the moderate organizations helped secure the vital achievements reached at the NKA; by initiating and subsequently winning a referendum, the more

radical organizations helped remove a possibly damaging compromise from the structure of the new constitution. Finally, the government and the MSZMP chose to accept these outcomes rather than block the process altogether.

With the referendum, the most important phase of constitution making was over. It had two long-run effects. First, the referendum turned what was until then a purely elite affair into one involving popular initiative and participation. Whatever legitimacy and popular acceptance the constitution was to have in the beginning certainly benefited from this element of politics from below. Second, the referendum was not strictly about constitutional issues but also about the timing of the elections. On the issue of the presidency, the population probably did not agree with its own decision to avoid direct election of the president; it voted the way it did by a very slim majority only because of the dubious circumstances of the NKA agreement on this issue, which the radical opposition exploited. Certainly linking the issue of the presidency with three additional questions on which there was vast popular agreement facilitated the outcome. Thus, what was gained for the legitimacy of the NKA arrangements was probably limited and certainly unmeasurable, although the party most associated with the referendum, the SZDSZ, definitely gained much new support in this process.

Ironically, the referendum—the single popular moment in any of the phases of the making of the Hungarian constitution—intensified the already existing cleavages among the opposition organizations. When the making of a definitive new constitution required their unity, the major parties of regime change, the MDF and SZDSZ, became bitterly divided, even though the interim constitution more or less satisfied their top negotiators' basic ideals concerning a parliamentary republic. The division of the opposition and of the EKA itself, always one of the aims of the negotiators of the ruling party, finally occurred, even if only at the very end of the process of successfully drawing up the interim constitution. As a result, the new constitution itself was not looked upon even by the new political elite—not to speak of the population in general—as of its own common making. Given that the document itself was in most respects acceptable, it was first and foremost its relatively weak legitimacy that inspired a variety of actors to seek further constitution making.

A Plurality of Constitution-Making Agents

The Old Parliament

The Hungarian model of transition was based equally on comprehensive negotiations and the maintenance of legal continuity. A remarkable feature of this process was the legalism of all the actors, who scrupulously adhered to the letter of the law even when it was to their disadvantage. The ruling party, for example, accepted the validity of the petition campaign and subsequent referendum and was not tempted to manipulate the result concerning the presidency, even when its position lost by a mere six thousand votes. The opposition was equally defenseless when the sitting parliament, the last communist one, enacted the provisions agreed upon by the NKA. It was a technical requirement of the 1949 constitution, then in effect, that parliament had to enact all constitutional changes by a two-thirds majority as well any new electoral rule. The opposition at the NKA had assumed that parliamentary consent would be achieved on all issues in "the usual way," that is, according to the unwritten material constitution of all communist regimes: by the political pressure of the Political Bureau—the party to the agreements—on the government and the parliament. But during the rapid developments of 1988 and 1989, this unwritten constitution, too, was changing. Government

achieved a measure of independence from the party; and parliament, in smaller measure, from both.[47] From a more skeptical point of view, the necessary public role of government and parliament gave a legal opportunity to the ruling party to modify agreements in a retroactive and one-sided way by appealing to the still-fictitious independence of other communist actors. Whatever the truth, the last communist parliament managed to play an independent role in the making of the new constitution twice: once in October during the enactment of the interim constitution and once under the rules of this new basic law.

The electoral rules agreed upon at the NKA were an obvious compromise, mixing directly elected seats (152), seats attained in provincial lists (152), and seats attained from a national compensational list (70), the function of which was to make the overall electoral result more proportional. In discussing this particular proposal, the parliament staged a veritable rebellion, demanding a dramatic expansion of individual seats. It is impossible to know whether this was done to fight for the original bargaining position of the ruling party that the MSZP itself had to modify or to protect the personal interests (however mistakenly interpreted) of deputies who were elected in individual districts in which they were well known.[48] In any case, the result was a compromise that increased the directly elected seats to 176, at the expense of the national compensational list, which was reduced to 58. This produced a much less proportional system than the one agreed upon by the NKA, which survives to this day.[49] That parliament was operating under something like a veil of ignorance about actual voter preferences is shown by the outcome of the first free elections, however. The ex-state party, the renamed MSZP, won only one seat in individual districts in March 1990. The action probably cost at least a few deputies their jobs and political careers.

Modifying the electoral law did not formally require constitutional revision. The same is not true of basic rights. In another example of its exercise of independence, before fully enacting the package agreed upon at the NKA, the old parliament rewrote the paragraph concerning the impossibility of limiting the rights identified in the package by providing a set of classical conservative limits rooted in the requirements of public order, public security, public health, and public morality. More significant and more lasting, parliament also added the right to social security in the table of basic rights.

The same parliament failed, but only temporarily, to establish the direct election of the president of the republic, rejecting the parliamentary solution of the NKA negotiations.[50] The NKA, confusingly, originally established a relatively weak presidency elected by parliament, and it was only for the first free elections that a direct popular election of the president was provided for—if it took place before parliamentary elections. This one-time feature was reversed by the November 1989 referendum, which, in the view of the Constitutional Court, did not deal with the constitutional issue of the mode of electing the president, but only the question of its timing.[51] When the court ruled on the matter, it allowed the old parliament under the new constitution's purely parliamentary amendment rule (two-thirds of an absolute majority) to revise the constitution and provide for a popular election of the president after the first parliamentary elections.[52] This the parliament actually did on the initiative of Deputy Zoltan Kiraly, the most famous independent member elected in 1985, who himself was a candidate for the presidency.[53] What mattered was not the institutional interest of parliament but the strong preference of the now renamed MSZP, still smarting from its defeat in the referendum, for a directly elected presidency. Nevertheless, they did not know what they were doing. As

the MSZP received only 10 percent of the votes in the first parliamentary elections in March 1990, the party was certainly going to lose the presidency in a popular election if it took place any time in 1990 (i.e., after the parliamentary elections).

The New Parliament: the MDF-SZDSZ Pact

That the last communist parliament did not fully adhere to the NKA agreements was an important reason for further constitutional change. However, it was most certainly not the only one. The agreements incorporated features that were important for both sides from the point of view of guarantees of a significant political role in case of severe electoral defeat. These guarantees can themselves be grouped under two headings: consensus democracy and constitutionalism. As in South Africa, coming to agreement by two relatively equal sides was very much facilitated by using both types of guarantees. In both countries, however, it was soon recognized that while constitutionalism enforced by a court could somewhat narrow the framework of possible policy making, strong consensus requirements could interfere with policy making, directly resulting in political deadlock that a new democracy did not need. Such requirements, moreover, could imply that there was only one effective form of government formation, a grand coalition of the largest parties irrespective of their ideological orientation. This approach minimizes the constructive government-opposition relationship of parliamentary democracy and interferes with the accountability of government that is so important for countries extricating themselves from authoritarian regimes. Admittedly, consensus requirements, including qualified majorities required for constitutional amendment, do have an important purpose, namely, stopping temporary majorities from modifying the rules of the game to benefit incumbents. Some consensus democracy is thus required also for constitutionalism. But in Hungary as well South Africa, the initial drafters went much too far in requiring that ordinary legislative (Hungary) and executive (South Africa) acts be consensual. Making ordinary policy making dependent upon reaching consensus among parties with vastly divergent political views substantially increases the risk of failure in the political process, which is particularly dangerous in newly established democracies with mounting economic problems. In Hungary, the last undemocratic parliament added to the NKA agreements further consensual requirements for legislation, to the point that governability itself became a problem.

The most important form that consensus democracy took in Hungary was the very large number of laws that would be modifiable only by two-thirds relative majorities—the vote of two-thirds of those present and voting, almost as difficult to achieve as constitutional amendments that required two-thirds of all members, present and absent. Because the new government formed in 1990 chose not to create a grand coalition, it had an immediate interest in reducing the number of two-thirds laws. Given potential parliamentary volatility, the government also was very interested in measures guaranteeing stability, such as the constructive no-confidence vote and the elimination of the individual responsibility of ministers. The new center-right nationalist Christian coalition, dominated by the MDF, did not, however, have the two-thirds vote necessary to amend the constitution. Of its opponents at that time, the MSZP and FIDESZ strongly defended consensus democracy and opposed the strengthening of the executive at the expense of parliament. So the only plausible partner for change was the liberal, culturally left-of-center SZDSZ, at that time the MDF's toughest competitor and a strong runner-up in the general elections. Because the SZDSZ was thought to have the best chance of the Christian coali-

tion's opponents to take political power from the MDF, it was the most interested in the type of changes that the MDF government favored. The SZDSZ was not ideologically inclined to consensus democracy; the main sponsor of the 1989 referendum, it was deeply committed to reestablishing a purely parliamentary presidency. In return for elements of chancellor democracy providing for a strong parliamentary executive, and the drastic reduction of the number of two-thirds laws to an enumerated group of twenty,[54] the MDF could easily offer the concession concerning the election of the president—which the prime minister, József Antall, in any case favored—along with the nomination of Arpád Göncz as the first president. Göncz was an SZDSZ founding member and veteran of 1956, whom Antall thought (wrongly) he could control. With this concession came a slight strengthening of presidential powers, presumably to offer further guarantees to the SZDSZ that the government would not abuse the new powers of the executive.[55] Thus was born the MDF-SZDSZ pact, easily ratified by parliament as the law 1990: XL.[56] It was the second general agreement that, together with the first (the NKA compromise), established the new Hungarian constitution.

The occasion for enacting the pact seemed to motivate the other parties and individual members of parliament to offer a variety of amendments. Some of these proposals actually passed, and some even helped to improve the rule-of-law dimension of the new constitution. The term of the president was extended from four to five years, and in case of impeachment proceedings, the Constitutional Court had the responsibility to try him. A habeas corpus provision was established, and parliament reversed the limits on rights that the last undemocratic parliament inserted into the NKA package.[57]

These additional amendments show that there was at the time strong latent parliamentary interest in constitution making. Why not then move toward a comprehensive agreement on a new constitution, especially as the Round Table constitution defined itself as an interim one? We do not believe that this option was seriously raised at the time, though the relevant leaders must have considered it. To begin with, the SZDSZ and MDF were by then bitter ideological opponents with an extremely divisive election campaign behind them. It was not clear that they could agree on a wide range of questions for which worldview mattered first of all. Their militants and members were quite hostile to one another; cooperation was not popular among their rank-and-file members. Had there been an all-party constitution-making effort instead of a two-party one, consensus might have been achievable. But the preferences of the MDF's allies and the MSZP for direct election of the president, and even presidentialism, made them impossible partners for the SZDSZ, which cared about this issue most of all. Moreover, the attachment of FIDESZ and the MSZP to consensus democracy made them difficult partners for the MDF government. It is possible that a comprehensive bargaining framework could have ironed out the differences through compromise. But there was no guarantee that from the point of view of the SZDSZ or MDF or both, such a result would not have produced a substantively worse constitution than what they could arrive at through their pact.

What the parties neglected, however—aside from several serious remaining flaws of the constitutional setup, such as the highly disproportional electoral rule and the much-too-easy constitutional amendment rule—was the issue of legitimacy. They did not even try to explore what kind of constitution could be produced through extensive discussion and consultation. It is very likely that if attempted, MDF, SZDSZ, and FIDESZ cooperation could have produced a solid constitution expressing the new public-law ideas of 1989. We have reason to believe that such

a collective effort could also have moderated the destructive ideological and institutional struggles from 1990 to 1994 that helped to weaken decisively the two important parties to the pact. We have even better reason to think that despite the passing of some constitutional amendments between 1990 and 1998, probably the best chance was missed in 1990 to establish the definitive constitution of the new liberal democratic parliamentary republic. This is so because the 1990–94 period was the only and last time when the three parties that were the true motors of the regime change—the MDF, the SZDSZ, and FIDESZ—had overwhelming majority.[58]

As for the procedural aspects of the second major round of constitutional amendments, it was, if anything, even less participatory than the Round Table process itself. The preparations were restricted to secret talks between top leaders of the MDF and SZDSZ, completely excluding all other parties, the media, and the general public. The secretive nature of the preparatory talks, and the fact that the outcome was presented as an accomplished fact, infuriated many of the leaders and ranks of the two participating parties themselves, leading to lasting ruptures within the MDF. The agreements made by the two parties were presented as a fait accompli to the other parliamentary parties and the public as well; hence, the slightly denunciatory term "pact" attached to the whole process. The proposals had been submitted to the legislature jointly by MDF and SZDSZ and were subsequently passed without any substantial alteration, despite the stark criticism of FIDESZ and MSZP, the two opposition parties. MDF secured the support, albeit not without certain misgivings, of the two junior partners of the governing coalition. There is no indication whatever that the chief agents behind this second round of amendments—the MDF and SZDSZ—ever seriously considered that popular participation or citizens' groups should be brought into the process. To be sure, because the agreement, in addition to constitutional amendments concerning governability and the number of two-thirds laws, involved several ad hoc deals to nominate particular persons for offices including the presidency, the governor of the central bank, and the chairmen of the national public television and radio stations, the exclusion of public participation was inevitable. Clearly, citizens could not have been brought into what was to a great extent a self-interested compromise between the two largest parties.

This is not to say that the MDF-SZDSZ pact as a whole was not beneficial for the nation's constitutional arrangement. As was often the case in Hungary's process of negotiated transition, substantively desirable outcomes were reached by less-than-desirable procedural routes. And while the pact left the nation with a much-improved constitutional situation, the act itself—a rare feat of imagination, foresight, and mutual self-restraint in Hungary's extremely divisive post-1989 constitutional politics—was and has been widely perceived as yet another instance in a long series of elite bargains conducted over the heads of ordinary citizens. Therefore, its welcome consequences notwithstanding, the second round of major constitutional amendments did little to refurbish the legitimacy of the new regime.

The Constitutional Court

Political conditions that favor negotiated transitions also increase the likelihood that the constitution-making process will be discontinuous, more extended over time, and the work of different primary agents in different phases of constitutional consolidation. It was argued above that the pure form of negotiated transitions is likely to take place when political agents on both sides perceive themselves as weak; furthermore, it was argued that the weakness of political agents is

likely to produce a constitution with a perceived legitimacy deficiency. It may be added at this point that the outcome of such a process of constitution making is likely to have a provisional, patchwork character. Weak agents may be tempted, by an awareness of a lack of democratic authorization, to resort to amending and revising the existing constitutional document rather than devising an entirely new constitution. Thus, it is also more likely that in subsequent periods, the actors of the new regime will be more prone to engage in amending and revising the resulting document than they might for a constitution with uncontested legitimacy. Also, the patchwork character of the document likely makes it more susceptible to having significantly diverging interpretations. As there is no single unified constitution-making process with uncontroversial democratic authorization, the original intention of the framers, too, is even more obscure than is the case generally, and the room for judicial interpretation greater. Thus, a role for the Constitutional Court would seem to be unusually important in consolidating the new constitutional arrangement—though this logical requirement, inherent in the negotiated transition method of constitution making, has been fully realized among the important cases only in Hungary and South Africa.

For Hungary's 1989–90 constitution, both the creation and the judicial practice of the Constitutional Court to a large extent reflect the circumstances characteristic of negotiated transitions. Although the agreements made at the NKA—modified by the referendum of November 1989—and by the two largest parties after the 1990 elections represented an entirely new constitutional arrangement in substantive terms, the document formally still retained an air of temporariness. The paradoxes of the negotiating process, originally intended merely to provide for the conditions of a disciplined transition but resulting in a new constitution, are well illustrated in the preamble of the document it-self. The preamble claims that the document merely intends to "promote the transition to the rule of law"[59] until the adoption of a new constitution, which has yet to happen as of this writing. Thus, the Constitutional Court established by the new constitution was confronted with the task of exercising constitutional review on the basis of a patch-work document; in this situation, quite a lot depended on how the court understood its function as the constitution's guardian.

The extensive powers granted to the court were certainly necessary conditions for the very active role that the court was to assume in consolidating the new constitutional or-der. But such powers would not have been sufficient to perform this role were it not for the specific circumstances characteristic of negotiated transitions. The usual dilemmas of popular sovereignty versus judicial review surfaced in a special context, in which the constitution not only lacked uncontested le-gitimacy but also was the outcome of a se-ries of substantial revisions and amendments, containing unsettled issues and possible in-consistencies. Thus, an opportunity was pre-sented for the court to act as the constitu-tion's maker as well as its guardian.[60]

In addition, as the law on the Consti-tutional Court was the product of a last-minute compromise, it displays all the traces of a temporary character. Among other things, it leaves a number of questions un-settled, such as the procedural rules and the so-called rules of order of the court. It is nat-ural that the judges interpreted these provi-sions broadly, giving themselves the largest possible freedom.

The specifically activist period of the court stretched from 1990 to around 1993. Although the court's decisions in this period concerned chiefly the evolution of funda-mental rights, they were also consequential for defining the function of the presidency within the structure of the republican consti-tution, as well as for deciding contested issues related to retroactive justice that emerged as a consequence of regime change. In one of his early opinions, the chief justice of the court, László Sólyom (at the time of this writing the president of Hungary) argued that

> the Constitutional Court must continue to … articulate the theoretical bases of the Consti-tution and the rights incorporated in it, and to formulate a coherent system that will serve, as *an invisible constitution*, as a safe guideline of constitutionalism above the existing constitu-tion that is currently still being amended out of fleeting daily purposes.[61]

Thus, initially, the court explicitly asserted the right to revise the constitution itself where it judged necessary. In some instances, the court revised existing constitutional pro-visions.[62] Between 1990 and 1993, Constitu-tional Court rulings provided a very robust interpretation of the freedom of speech, abolished the death penalty, authoritatively settled conflicts of competence between the president of the republic and the prime min-ister (establishing that the role of the presi-dent within the executive branch was merely formal),[63] and prohibited punishment of crimes committed by the previous regime once the term of limitation had expired.[64] In this period, the court had a decisive but am-biguous role in defining the function of vari-ous institutional agents as well as in making different political agents realize the limits of their powers in the new constitutional arrangement. Unsurprisingly, in the same period, the charge of usurping the constitu-ent sovereignty vested in the legislature was most frequently made against the court.

As the consolidation of the new regime progressed and major interpretive decisions were made (which are binding in future rul-ings of the court itself), the coherence of the new regime was stabilized and the room for judicial activism with respect to questions of state organization was reduced to a mini-mum. Since then, the main focus of judicial activism has shifted to such areas as welfare rights.

As with the NKA talks and other phases of the Hungarian constitution-making process, it may be claimed that the court's activity exhibits a characteristic ambiguity vis-à-vis the symbolic and substantive aspects of its outcome. While the court has performed an essential and, in substantive terms, beneficial function in consolidating the republican constitution, judicial constitution making (or consolidation) as a general rule is not the most adequate means to enhance the legitimacy of a constitutional arrangement. As the major interpretive decisions and formulation of rules were carried out by a body insulated from the democratic political process rather than by popular representatives, the experience of constitution making was again lost for the general public. Nevertheless, as the major political agents in subsequent legislative terms were, for the most part and either formally or in terms of legitimacy, too weak to make fundamental constitutional resolutions, not to mention a new constitution, it was left for the court to make such decisions after 1990.

Failure of the Effort to Produce a New Constitution in 1996–97

All acts of constitutional review between 1989 and 1995 were based materially on the supposedly interim Round Table constitution of 1989, which was formally an amendment of the Communist constitution of 1949.[65] Thus the idea of producing a definitive constitution survived on the political back burner, waiting for a time when there was political power and will to accomplish the task. That it took six years to get to that point was not unusual in the history of constitutions. The United States waited six years between the ratification of the Articles of Confederation in 1781 and the drafting of the federal constitution in Philadelphia.

Closer to our context, it took the Poles eight years and the South Africans three to move from interim to definitive constitutions. In principle, the intervening time is quite useful, allowing the accumulation of learning experiences concerning an interim constitution, the weaknesses and difficulties of which become apparent only over a sufficiently long period.[66] It can also happen, however, that the window of opportunity for legitimate and consensual constitution making closes before there is sufficient interest and political support to attempt the task of full-scale redrafting and enactment. That is what seems to have happened in Hungary.[67]

In 1994, a left-of-center coalition of the ex–state party MSZP and the SZDSZ came to power after four years of a national Christian center-right coalition. The new government easily commanded a constitution-amending majority (over 70 percent of the seats when only two-thirds were required), and its intention to draft and enact a constitution was a powerful spur for the other three (eventually four) parliamentary parties to cooperate. On the advice of several experts (including one of the authors), the coalition offered parliament an elaborate constitution-making procedure that was to involve a high level of consensus before any draft could finally be approved. First, it would require the agreement of 80 percent of the deputies to approve a constitution-making procedure; that majority was successfully achieved. Second, the procedure included a formula that gave each of the six parliamentary parties four seats on the drafting committee. Third, it provided that committee decisions required five out of six parties and two-thirds of the members of the committee. To protect the project from the dangers of such high consensus requirements, the procedure also provided that whenever no agreement on a constitutional provision was possible, the corresponding provision of the 1989 constitution would be maintained and integrated in the new draft. Finally, as the biggest party, with 54 percent of the seats, the MSZP had the additional guarantee that as always, the final draft would have to be approved by two-thirds of parliament, which would be impossible without the strong support of that party. This feature was important because the project was not easy to accept for the ex-state party, whose minister of justice, exactly like his predecessor in 1989, continued to play with the idea of producing a constitutional draft by his own experts in the ministry.[68]

Because no constitution actually emerged from the process, it would take us too far afield to discuss the details. It is enough to note that despite exemplary cooperation on the level of the committee, the draft that emerged did not deal with some of the greatest structural problems of the 1989 constitution—the highly disproportionate electoral law and the deep tension between a simple parliamentary amendment procedure and an extremely powerful constitutional court. But a draft did emerge even with the forbidding consensus requirements. What then occurred, however, was extremely peculiar. Though the SZDSZ, the MDF, and FIDESZ voted for the draft, the right-wing Small Holders and Christian Democrats did not. More strikingly, enough members of the governing MSZP, including most government ministers, voted against the draft—for which their own party's committee chairman bore the main responsibility—thus depriving it of the necessary two-thirds majority. In effect, a red-black coalition, present in Hungary only for that moment, brought the effort down. After that fiasco, there were attempts to save the draft by satisfying some of the critics, by including some mildly social corporatist elements, but new defections and the final failure of the project were unavoidable.[69] The comparison with Poland, where, under the leadership of President Kwasniewski, the Poles got rid of most of the presidentialist features of their own interim constitution, is strik-

ing. The Poles, unlike the Hungarians, faced serious structural and legitimation problems with respect to their presidency, which was a forced concession to the Communists at the time of the Round Table and mixed poorly, as President Walesa's tenure showed so well, with parliamentary institutions. There were no problems of this magnitude in Hungary. Moreover, unlike in South Africa, the makers of the interim Hungarian constitution neither constructed a timetable to produce a definitive version nor put in place sufficient rewards and sanctions for the parties to stay loyal to the task.

Several factors militated against success in Hungary in 1996. Having come out from under the empirical veil of ignorance, parties sought not conversion of present into future power or guarantees against future persecution or marginalization but rather the realization of the needs of their new political identities. The ideological field in Hungary, much more than the field of real choices, had become extremely polarized.[70] Around issues of diverging identities, no full consensus was possible. The expert drafting committee only had to reconcile interests, and that turned out to be easy enough. There was no political majority, however, and certainly not a two-thirds one, behind any ideological vision of the constitution, including the 1989 constitution's liberal democratic parliamentary-constitutionalist model. Admittedly, that very constitution was the default for any new provisions that could not be agreed—that was the clever ploy of the liberal leaders of the committee. But a sufficient number of members of parliament, waiting for another day to establish their vague constitutional dreams, could and did choose not to relegitimate the system they were living and acting under.

How could a temporary red-black linkage get away with such sabotage in the face of the majority of the committee and even that of parliament? First, unlike in Poland, no popular participation or discussion was organized, and the government did not have to fear any popular pressure. This state of affairs characterizes the entire constitution-making process in Hungary, where, with the exception of the referendum campaign of the fall of 1989, there was no popular participation at all. There were very few people (including one of the authors) who advised, in 1994, a popular, participatory, and educational process on the model of South Africa, but the legal experts of the coalition parties tended to consider such an approach irrelevant or even dangerous. The liberal party feared that popular participation would lead to a directly elected president, possibly to a strengthened executive. They may have been right about this, but on the other hand, the absence of public attention to the process made it much easier for members of the government, along with unlikely right-wing allies, to sabotage the project of their own coalition.

Second, even the liberal SZDSZ and its lawyers did not care about the issue sufficiently to make cooperation of the MSZP leaders with their own committee a condition of their own continued participation in the governmental coalition, which they should have left when the sabotage of the draft took place. Third, public opinion as well as the liberal party leaders had become accustomed to an evolutionary pattern of constitutional learning and change, of which the Constitutional Court was the main protagonist. They did not fully realize the paradoxical nature of court activism in the context of a soft constitutional background;[71] the likely future reticence of a court eventually attacked from all sides could mean that other political branches could grab the power to mold the material constitution even without formal amendments. That last outcome has been realized under the government cycle of 1998–2002 by the right wing FIDESZ government, putting Hungary's constitutional future temporarily in doubt. However, the lack of popular

attachment to the constitution never allowed authoritarian deformations to emerge as an issue around which the opposition of that particular period could mobilize.

The Constitution as a Product of Models and Bargains

Innovation and Models

During the epoch of the reconstruction of civil society in Eastern Europe, many involved in that process recalled the famous saying *ex oriente lux*. Intellectual innovation was a striking feature of the crumbling Soviet empire in Eastern and Central Europe, and brilliant political projects were organized around the reconstruction of civil society by activist intellectuals such as Adam Michnik, Jacek Kuron, Vaclav Havel, and János Kis.[72] This innovation did not extend to the constitution-making sphere, however. With respect to Western models, the Eastern European innovators felt they had nothing new to offer on the level of constitutional and institutional design. It was the common sense of Hungarian institutional designers that they must take their institutional option from the best that was available. But what was that best?

In Eastern and Central Europe, democratic constitution makers had low regard for the U.S. version of the separation of powers as well as British parliamentary sovereignty. To the extent that elements of either of these appeared, they were in the form of semi-authoritarian strategies of old ruling parties (the U.S. presidency, majoritarian elections) or new nationalist groupings with a parliamentary majority (either the U.S. presidency or British cabinet government). In countries with negotiated transitions (with the temporary exception of the first, Poland), these options were unsuccessful, and we see their lasting influence only where options were imposed from above. From the point of view of professional opinion in the Round Table countries, which was generally echoed by liberal and democratic forces, the constitutions and electoral arrangements of the German Federal Republic and the French Fifth Republic were considered close to the best available. As it turned out, even federal states in the region chose one or another version of parliamentary government or semipresidentialism, with governments headed by prime ministers (supposedly) responsible to parliament. Among parliamentary republics, none chose to operate without a written constitution, insulated amendment rule, and some kind of constitutional review. No country chose a single-district, first-past-the-post, one-round plurality electoral rule, nor was the idea of electing the president through an electoral college ever seriously entertained anywhere. The model of constitutional jurisprudence chosen was invariably the European Kelsen type, fluctuating between weak French and strong German prototypes. But the choice among mostly French, German, and other options—the last including a given country's own earlier constitutional heritage—was filtered through the political party interests as well as legitimating needs faced by the major actors.

As against other countries, especially further east, outside experts and advisers were not significant in the Hungarian constitution-making process, even if the constitutional solutions of other countries were broadly influential.[73] The most direct influence on the Hungarian drafters was the European Convention on Human Rights, the first fourteen articles of which provided the structure and much of the content of the twelfth chapter of the Hungarian constitution on fundamental rights and duties. As far as we can tell, adopting these provisions at the Round Table on the proposal of the ministry of justice was entirely uncontroversial, even if just a few months before, agreement concerning statutory freedoms of association and assembly, as well as the right to strike, was reached only after intense conflict and debate.

Bargaining for an Electoral Rule and the Conversion of Power

The electoral formula for the constituent assembly negotiated at the Round Table was acceptable to all sides. Claims for both proportional and direct individual mandates were satisfied in a combination the high level of disproportionality of which was not yet clear to anyone, least of all to the historical parties that significantly contributed to it by insisting on county lists. The 4 percent cutoff agreed upon seemed relatively unthreatening to the parties of the EKA, many of which had no idea how weak they actually were. This feature would ultimately be an important part of manufacturing a majority out of a minority. Even the parliament's unilateral raising of the number of seats to 176, which was a third source of the high disproportionality of the system, involved a 45 percent–55 percent ratio of direct to proportional representation mandates, which was closer to the EKA formula of 50–50 than the Round Table compromise itself.

What emerged, then, as a result of bargaining over the electoral system, was a set of rules that gave something to all the main forces, and therefore unavoidably a unique set of extremely complex, mixed rules that had some features (two ballots) of the German model that it superficially resembled and some important elements (two rounds) of French elections. Those who hoped that this would be the model only for the first elections were deeply mistaken. The very early freezing of the model confirms the expectation of most political scientists: Despite the embarrassing disproportionality of the system, its inhospitability to small and new parties, and the dangers of super-large majorities, it is unrealistic to ask parties that have just won an election to change the rules

Table 13.1   1990 Elections

Party	Percent of Votes for Party Lists	Number (Percent) of Seats (total: 386)
MDF	24.73	165 (42.7)
SZDSZ	21.39	92 (23.8)
FKgP	11.73	44 (11.3)
MSZP	10.89	34 (8.8)
FIDESZ	8.95	23 (5.9)
KDNP	6.46	21 (5.44)
Independent		7 (1.8)

that led to their success. Close to the next election, however, polls would indicate the beneficiaries of any change with clarity, thus making any tinkering with the rules appear self-serving (see Table 13.1).[74]

Bargaining and the Nature of the Presidency

A similar compromise model was impossible in the case of the presidency, in part because the MSZMP proposal was already a mixed one, putting together, in the French style, a directly elected presidency with a prime minister with parliamentary responsibility. More important than this formal point was the determined opposition of the radical opposition and even many moderates to presidential government that, in the context of Hungarian tradition,[75] seemed like a foreign import. Whereas some of the minor groups in the EKA always favored a directly elected presidency, the radical opposition saw a conversion strategy for what it was and feared the authoritarian possibilities of a plebiscitary presidency more than the potential weaknesses of a model involving problems of divided government, as in the United States, or cohabitation, as in France. The compromise engineered by Antall, but never accepted by the radical SZDSZ and FIDESZ, involved a partial return to the two-stage schemes of the reform Communists. While the constitution would generally affirm a fully parliamentary structure, with a rather weak president elected by parliament,[76] it mandated during the first electoral period the direct election of the president if it took place before parliamentary elections.[77] Ordinary legislation was then to order that the election of the president would occur before parliamentary elections.[78] Thus, it was possible to sell the model to some who opposed it with the idea that direct elections would involve only a one-time, exceptional compromise of their positions.[79]

There is a question whether those who changed their position at the Round Table—in particular the MDF, which always thought in terms of the model of the 1946 weak, parliamentary presidency—were actually naïve concerning the potential meaning of the concession. There has been significant speculation about a private or secret agreement between Imre Pozsgay of the MSZMP and József Antall of the MDF concerning this compromise, which would supposedly lead to a Hungarian version of the Polish "your president, our prime minister" formula. Though there is some evidence of this,[80] it is possible and more charitable to take Antall's remarks at the last plenary at face value, according to which he was still uncertain about the possibility of Soviet intervention and civil war when making the concession. With over ten years' hindsight, it is also possible to say that there was a highly functional division of labor between moderate and radical oppositions, with the former making the then-possible deal with regime reformers, while the radicals who rightly chose not to veto the agreements as a whole chose instead to turn to the electorate in the petition-referendum campaign to get rid of its one objectionable feature.[81] It is easy to see why the radicals won in the referendum, and only won slightly. Whether there was a deal or not, many Hungarians tended to believe that there was, an idea reinforced by the very low level of publicity for what was going on at the Round Table negotiations. Making a deal, however, that shattered the unity of the main opposition parties seemed like sacrificing a great deal at that moment for private party advantage. It would have meant leaving the veil of ignorance and genuine public-regarding argumentation behind. The referendum was won by only 6,000 votes because the actual preference of the majority in a plebiscite was, logically enough, for the plebiscitary election of a president. The dangers of a plebiscitary president concerned only relatively few intellectuals.

Veil of Ignorance and Guarantees

Though they acted as if they knew the future, the parties were under what could be called an empirical veil of ignorance regarding the outcomes of rules for both projected presidential and parliamentary elections. The solid expectations of many were frustrated. The MSZMP did poorly in the single-member districts it originally fought for so hard; many of the small parties were not particularly concerned about the 4 percent threshold, which then led to their elimination; the MDF would have done much worse under the balanced mixed system it advocated than under the more disproportionate system that emerged; and the SZDSZ would have done worse under the system of more direct seats that it wanted. In the end, the acceptance of a mixed formula speaks for the parties hedging their bets in the context of uncertainty.[82] The same is even more true for those parts of the bargain involving guarantees of a continuing political role for losers in the first free elections. While the MSZMP sought to convert part of its powers, it also sought, in case of failure, guarantees that belong to two categories: constitutionalism and consociationalism. Not having anything to convert, the opposition was also interested in guarantees of constitutionalism, but this interest had to be factored in with the concern that

the other side was using guarantees to preserve power.[83]

The most important case in point was the agreement concerning the Constitutional Court. From the beginning of making reform proposals, such a court was on the MSZP/MSZMP's list of innovations. The idea was consistent with the project of controlled liberalization, in which partially free elections and an increased sway of the rule of law would relegitimate a partially authoritarian system. The importance of models in this case is clear: There was never a moment when the Hungarian discussion entertained a U.S.-type judicial review, and all the options were conceived in terms of a Kelsen-type independent tribunal outside the judicial system proper. This type, however, allowed strong (German) and weak (French) variants. In its original version, the plan included a relatively weak court, with no standing for anyone outside the political system, possibly with the option of parliamentary overrule of decisions that in any case would be easy given the existing constitutional amendment rule. Judges, of course, would have been selected through the Ministry of Justice or a combination of actors that the party would control. It was still a variant of this project—allowing only a suspension of unconstitutional laws and including the feature of parliamentary overrule—on which parliament voted in a preliminary version in March 1989, in a "putsch like fashion" in the eyes of the opposition,[84] and that the MSZMP brought to the Round Table. This version restricted standing, in the French pattern, to public law authorities such as the president of the republic, the president of parliament, and large parliamentary minorities. Whereas the existing oppositional political manifestos were for a strong constitutional court, interestingly the EKA did not support its immediate establishment.[85] The EKA sought originally only the enactment of a few organic laws necessary for free elections, and, due to the Round Table's lack of democratic legitimacy, it was against producing a full constitutional synthesis.[86] A new constitutional court in their view presupposed a legitimate constitution, one that Hungary could not have until after the first free elections. Moreover, a court might tend to freeze transitional arrangements that are still based on an old constitution not thought worthy of preservation even if reformed.[87] Nevertheless, using public-regarding reasons, it was difficult to oppose the establishment of a body internationally considered to be the very organ of constitutionalism and the rule of law.

When it turned out that, piece by piece, the EKA had to reverse its position and agree to a massive effort of constitutional rewriting, there was suddenly the prospect of having a constitution worthy of preservation and protection. Thus, the opposition shifted its strategy by accepting the setting up of the Constitutional Court before free elections, but in return demanding, first, that the court be given greater powers, specifically allowing the annihilation and not just suspension of unconstitutional legislation, and that, outside of constitutional amendments, the decisions of the court be regarded as final, without any kind of parliamentary override; second, that the court should be also open to suits emerging outside the political system, and specifically the *actio popularis* that would allow anyone and not just interested persons to challenge the constitutionality of legislation; third, that the judges be elected in part by the new parliament, and even those elected immediately would be elected consensually; and fourth, that former officials of the Ministry of Justice be excluded from serving as constitutional court judges.[88] The resulting compromise wound up producing an even stronger version of the German court than in Germany itself. The opposition very much favored the model, as it had to drop only the last of its demands and concede in effect that the vice-minister negotiating

this very issue would become a Constitutional Court judge.[89] More certain of itself in the beginning of negotiations, the MSZP sought a court that was no more than what was needed for the purposes of legitimation. Less certain toward the end, it became more interested in—or less opposed to—constitutional guarantees.

Once guarantees were sought, it would have been sensible to entrench them, but this did not occur. A massive electoral victory by one of the sides could have led to the abolition or weakening of any guarantee whatsoever by constitutional amendment. The Constitutional Court, in other words, represented no protection against a force controlling two-thirds of the legislature; its powers themselves could be amended. Thus, to be consistent and secure, the MSZMP and some of the parties less certain of their future should have tried to change the easy amendment rule of the inherited constitution, but they did not do so. They were certainly not stopped from doing this by theoretical arguments, such as those of Carl Schmitt and Alf Ross, that amending an amendment rule by its own use was either impossible or invalid. It is unlikely—though possible—that no participant was aware of the logical link between a relatively difficult amendment rule and the possibility of constitutional review, and the theoretical inconsistency involved in establishing one but not the other.

In a potentially multiparty setting, it was rightly thought that no party could obtain a majority, certainly not the two-thirds of parliament needed for amendments. But it should have been noticed that the same multiparty system necessitated coalitions, and there was no obvious limit to how large they could be. Even this argument does not explain why smaller parties and even the SZDSZ—which feared an MDF-MSZMP coalition that certainly would have the power to amend—did not raise the issue of changing the amendment rule. The real explanation is that the opposition especially took for granted the lack of legitimacy of the Round Table and the last communist parliament. They were conscious that the massive constitution making they were engaging in was an elite affair, without genuine publicity or any popular participation. Thus, in Hungary, the problem of generations appeared especially intractable. It made no sense to allow an illegitimate or nonlegitimate set of actors to bind the hands of future, more legitimate actors. By insisting on the interim character of the Round Table constitution, its authors deprived themselves of the right or the rationale to enshrine their work.

The peculiar feature of the interim constitutional settlement was that while the constitution was insulated only by a relatively easy parliamentary amendment rule, much ordinary lawmaking was to have consensus requirements almost as high (two-thirds of present members versus two-thirds of all members). While this feature can be interpreted as a guarantee against unilateral legislation or against the marginalization of a sufficiently large party such as the MSZP, it was one in terms of consociational or consensus rather than constitutional democracy.[90] It seems that the idea of proposing a set of organic laws that can be modified by parliament only by two-thirds majority originated in reform socialist constitutional proposals brought before parliament before Round Table negotiations began.[91] Originally, the idea was part of a conception that limited parliamentary sovereignty, for the benefit of a strong presidency also in the same plan. It is unclear whether or not there was any Round Table discussion of this issue, and it may be that the original justification consisted of the need to protect the organic laws required for the transition toward free elections from easy modification by the communist-era parliament still in place. It may be that an argument subsequently referred to by the Constitutional Court also played a role, namely

that the text of the constitution should be relieved from being inundated with legislative elements.[92] Clearly, with the weakening of the presidency model in the same negotiations, the restriction on legislative powers pointed less and less to an instrument of authoritarian conversion and more and more to a guarantee for all parties, though with the risk of ungovernability.

In any case, it seems that it was the MSZMP—which, because of its built-in advantages in expertise and staff resources, could dominate the formulation of all that was not deemed particularly important at the Round Table—that was primarily responsible for incorporating this feature. The other parties did not oppose the feature, as they were mainly concerned with the risks of the transition period posed by the old parliament, and they probably also wanted to hedge their bets in case of an electoral victory by the ruling party. What then happened was therefore curious. The same old parliament, dominated by the MSZMP, not only willingly established the category of constitutional laws that would tie its own hands and those of its successors but also added a formulation according to which all rules regulating fundamental rights and duties would have to take the form of constitutional laws.[93] Next, the Constitutional Court, when it was still dominated by an MSZP majority, proceeded to interpret this broad premise in a particularly expansive way that implied that any law touching on matters affecting basic rights would have to be passed by a two-thirds majority.[94] Undoubtedly, the more extreme interpretations followed a time sequence that corresponded to a more and more realistic and therefore pessimistic evaluation by the MSZP of its electoral chances.

The MSZP turned out to be right in their pessimism, but the two-thirds requirement could not protect a party that garnered only 10 percent of the vote and 8 percent of the mandates in 1990. The authors of the MDF-

SZDSZ pact of 1990 considered the vast extension of the scope of constitutional laws beyond the Round Table agreements one of the illegitimate acts of the old parliament. They therefore proceeded to abolish the plastic and expandable notion of constitutional law and restricted the number of two-thirds laws to an enumerated twenty.[95] It was a peculiarity of the time that the only party that really fought for preserving more consensual legislation was FIDESZ, which was too small to put the government past the two-thirds threshold and not needed if either of the two other parties were available.[96] Thus, we can presume that their motivation was a principled support for consensus democracy that did not last by the time FIDESZ itself came to power in 1998.

What FIDESZ did not understand, at least in 1990, was the change of function of consensual guarantees from the period of a democratic transition to a time afterward when the institutions of a working democracy should be operating. The kind of protections needed by erstwhile enemies are different from those required by political opponents in a democratic system. While consociational arrangements need not hamper a country getting ready for general elections, they potentially threaten later governability and accountability. Only in radically divided societies should they be resorted to, and there, too, hopefully only within time limits. As the South African constitution makers confirm, the best path is one that moves from a transitional consensus democracy to one whose protections and guarantees are recast in terms of constitutionalism.[97] But FIDESZ's brief for consensus democracy in 1990 could be strengthened by pointing to a difference between South African developments and the earlier Hungarian ones. The South African constitution makers moved beyond consensual features present in their interim constitution only in their definitive constitutional document. In Hungary,

the MDF-SZDSZ pact, eschewing full and open drafting and enactment of a new constitution, did the same without moving beyond the supposedly interim arrangements. The question, therefore, is whether it could be legitimate to move to majoritarianism by mere majority rule (together MDF-SZDSZ had 66 percent of the mandates, but only 45 percent of the popular vote), or whether constitution making presupposes higher conditions of legitimacy, including consensus, than ordinary legislation. To be sure, this argument would not justify the expansive institution of constitutional laws, but it raises questions concerning the method of their abolition in 1990. It also points to the fundamental problem of an otherwise successful process of Hungarian constitutional design: legitimacy.

Conclusions: Achievements and Failures

This chapter began with the achievements of the Hungarian process of constitution making. To that list we can now add the creation of a basic law that establishes a liberal democratic blueprint for a parliamentary republic drawing on the best available European (mainly German but also French) sources. The same blueprint also sets up a system of viable and active judicial protections of constitutionalism, understood as limitations on all branches of power by a system of the rule of law, which enshrines constitutional rules against easy change by temporary majorities, as long as these remain under the two-thirds threshold, which is unfortunately not out of the question for coalition governments.[98] This chapter also noted failures, linked to the problem of democratic legitimacy, that inhibited the emergence of constitutional patriotism—in other words, a political culture oriented to constitutionalism. To this list, too, we can add a variety of unsolved problems. The Hungarian constitution makers could not successfully address structural problems in the constitution—most significantly, in our view, the potentially dangerous combination of an extremely powerful Constitutional Court, a purely and under some possible circumstances easy parliamentary amendment rule, and an electoral framework that tends to produce a high level of disproportionality between votes and seats, to the benefit of the largest parties. On the symbolic level, there is a deep contradiction between a substantively new basic law and the formal state of affairs in which this institutional design represents only a set of amendments of the 1949 Stalinist constitution. Even more important, while the constitution announces its merely temporary status in its very preamble, the chances of producing a definitive new document have by now disappeared. These symbolic failures move some to speak about a revolution stolen by the makers of the Round Table constitution.[99]

In our view, both the achievements and failures can be traced back to the long, drawn-out set of procedures that produced the constitution. The question is whether they necessarily imply one another. If that were so, the Hungarian pattern of constitution making would provide only highly ambiguous lessons for future designers of institutions in democratic transitions and reconstructions. But we believe that the advantages could have been achieved at a much lower set of costs. A summary of what went right in the Hungarian process, what went wrong, and the paradoxical relationship between the two supports this conclusion.

What Went Right: Legal Continuity

The Hungarian model of transition or regime change has been defined by its best participant-interpreter, János Kis, as the unlikely combination of a break in legitimacy and legal continuity. By legal continuity or continuous legality, we mean a fairly unusual requirement in the context of a change of regimes,

namely, that the new constitution is adopted by a body that is formally authorized to amend the constitution, and the outcome establishes the rule of law. Given that this condition would formally empower in a country like Hungary in 1989 a nondemocratic body unaccustomed to the rule of law, namely, the inherited parliament of the old regime, it required the invention of the Round Table and comprehensive negotiations to make the rules of regime change under the condition of legal continuity. The Round Table, however, was not in a position to fully dictate rules to the sitting parliament, especially to force it to violate the existing amendment rule. Legal continuity involved relying on this parliament using the existing amendment rule to formally enact all (or most) changes agreed upon at the Round Table.

Though legal continuity rested on the fiction of the rule of law under a lawless old regime,[100] its value was considerable. An *ex lex* condition of legal rupture or legal state of nature so strongly criticized by Hannah Arendt[101] was thereby avoided, and along with it, the legal insecurity and nihilism characterizing so many of the great modern revolutions. The Round Table, playing the role of a quasi-constitutional convention but without formal powers, could gain its influence only through consensual decision making, which in turn was possible only if all the parties received the required guarantees in case they turned out to be the political losers of the process. These guarantees were the foundation of consensual and constitutional features of the transition and had importance beyond the circle of the negotiating partners. It is certainly true that these features of transition helped to stabilize it and keep it on a peaceful and nonviolent path. Since the Round Table constitution was not imposed by or on any of the sides and was, in effect, their common work—whatever they later came to believe concerning this subject— even one-sided acts, such as the legislation of the old parliament, the referendum of 1989, and the MDF-SZDSZ pact of 1990, did not lead to its violent abrogation, or the defection of any of the sides.

The consensus, to be sure, had an elite character. The parties of the EKA chose one another as partners. The ruling party, itself without democratic authorization, chose as partners those represented in the EKA, who also were not selected democratically. Not only popular participation but also the public sphere was more or less excluded from the Round Table negotiations. Only the plenary sessions, where nothing really happened, were open to the press and the electronic media. There was only one short weekly opinion program on television that dealt with the negotiations. Thus, not surprisingly, the population experienced almost nothing from the momentous changes. Coupled with the absence of a legal rupture was the absence of political rupture. There was no great political novelty, in fact, until the free voting on the referendum of 1989. But even that vote could not compensate for the common experience that old and new elites were managing the entire regime change over the heads of the inert population.[102]

In retrospect, many liberals came to believe, even if they fought for greater openness initially, that the absence of popular pressures made the job of creating a liberal democratic constitution easier. Popular participation and public pressure implied the danger of the intrusion of plebiscitary democratic forms that would leave their institutional traces in the outcome. The result, in their view, could have been a directly elected, strong presidency and a weak constitutional court. In actual fact, the establishment of a strong constitutional court was opposed in the end by only very small segments of society. Even if a large majority would have always preferred a directly elected presidency in principle, the public was certainly educable regarding its dangers in the transition period. The narrow

SZDSZ-FIDESZ victory in the referendum of 1989 proves that even direct democratic instruments could serve the interest of parliamentary democracy, given a sufficiently informative and well-designed campaign. By avoiding such participation in general, along with its very real risks, the Round Table participants endangered the democratic legitimacy of their work. The democratic forces kept their own work hidden, with the consequence that most of these parties themselves did not construct their identity around their own achievements of 1989.

What Went Wrong: the Deficit of Democratic Legitimacy

A constitution-making process might purport to meet the requirements of legitimacy if the political agents who participate in the making of the new constitution are authorized to do so in a relevant sociological rather than in a merely formal legal sense. That is, the constitution makers should be able to demonstrate sufficient popular backing—or better, popular belief in the justification—for their claim that they are giving a constitution to the people in the name of the people.[103]

Certainly, the very idea of popular sovereignty implies that some form of noninstitutional action should at least be involved at some point in the process of making a constitution. On the other hand, the empirically available "people," as a mere multitude of individuals, is incapable of being drawn into the making of a constitution otherwise than ratifying it through a referendum, which may not be a very good way to organize participation or articulate a majority opinion. It follows, therefore, that the noninstitutional agents whose inclusion in constitution making is normatively required by the idea of popular sovereignty will typically be some spontaneously emerging political movements or organizations—voluntary but partial associations of citizens. This inevitably raises the question of democratic authorization. Are these noninstitutional political agents justified in claiming to represent the people? This question cannot be decided by abstract argument.

The existence or lack of such a popular mandate is in a crucial sense an extralegal reality. There is no general rule that would furnish the criteria for deciding whether or not, in a particular case, a popular mandate is obtained.[104] In a similar vein, although the demands of legitimacy with respect to the process of constitution making—primarily, transparency and open access for a variety of agents—may be articulated generally, there are no exact criteria to decide whether these conditions obtain in any one particular instance. These are, to a large extent, questions of political judgment and are open to contestation. There are a variety of ways to achieve the legitimacy of a constitution-making process. In a revolution involving legal rupture, the accomplishment of liberation from a hated old regime and the project of building a better future society together add up to what has been called revolutionary legitimacy. Revolutionary legitimation was in principle excluded, however, in the Hungarian context of legal continuity and a fully negotiated transition. But so was full democratic legitimacy for the makers of the interim arrangements that were the framework for the first free elections—agents who, logically, were not elected to perform that task. Thus, the EKA unsuccessfully fought against the project of creating a detailed interim constitution. When this fight was lost, the opposition had no interest in enshrining through democratic legitimacy based on participation, publicity, or popular ratification an interim instrument that they wished to replace after the first free elections. The political constellation developed, however, in such a way that there was opportunity only for yet another elite bargain, in 1990, concerning a package of constitutional amendments.

Thus, the absence of genuine political legitimacy carried over from the Round Table to all its successors, of which there were many, as they did not have to meet an established hurdle of a high degree of political legitimacy to change the constitution. The fragmentation of the process made its completion in the formal sense less and less likely. In principle, however, a many-stage constitution-making process allows for learning from what does not work to perfect the constitutional product.[105] This is what happened in the case of consensus democracy not only in South Africa but in Hungary even earlier.

For obvious reasons, negotiated transitions are likely to impose certain constraints on majority rule. There are two fundamental types of such constraints, one being a sharing of power among different agents, independently of the outcome of elections. This was the case in Poland and may be interpreted as a form of consensus democracy, where the different agents are forced to reach agreements on matters of policy. The other type might be characterized as imposing limits on what can be made a matter of policy to begin with—that is, on the scope of the legislative and executive powers in general. This version of restricting the rule of the majority is usually referred to as constitutionalism. Much of the Hungarian constitution-making process in its later phases may be described as a movement away from power sharing (or consensus democracy) toward constitutionalism. The movement was already discernible during the months of the national Round Table talks when, perceiving the changes in strength of the different agents, the ruling party gradually came to focus not so much on converting its power in institutional forms as on securing the institutional guarantees of the integrity of the persons and property of its members—that is, on the rule of law. One lingering element of power sharing was nevertheless retained in the MDF and MSZMP's compromise about the presidency, though this compromise was removed by the referendum of November 1989, which represented a further step toward a unified yet constitutionally limited executive power. The agreement between the MDF and SZDSZ, the two largest parties in April 1990, then eliminated the vast majority of two-thirds laws, the single largest element of consensus in the new regime. The last important element of power sharing was removed from the constitutional order in 1992, when the Constitutional Court, arbitrating the conflict of competence between the prime minister and the president, ruled that such rights of the president as granted by the MDF-SZDSZ pact were against the constitution. Mainly due to the activity of the Constitutional Court, the normative and procedural constraints on the executive and the legislature became political realities of the new regime, to be reckoned with by all political agents.

Even though direct democracy, parliament, and the Constitutional Court all played their roles in a many-step process of constitutional learning, it does not follow that leaving a process open-ended and relying on the normal political process to eventually produce the material constitution has much promise in the long run. Empirically, such an approach tends to require reliance on the Constitutional Court as almost the exclusive method of self-improvement. An unelected Constitutional Court acting as "a constituent assembly in permanent session" may work in a country like the United States, which has made its constitutional tradition part of a civil religion.[106] In Hungary, where that tradition has little normative force, such a court only embodies and continually reexpresses the initial legitimation problems. Bruce Ackerman was right to warn that the activist practice of the Hungarian Constitutional Court was untenable in light of its "soft constitutional background."[107] After the retirement of its great first chief justice, László Sólyom, the Hungarian court decisively retreated from

its activist role.[108] In its absence, learning is in the unreliable hands of parliamentarians, who without strong review cannot be stopped from unconstitutional constitutional revision in the form of ordinary legislation.[109]

Beyond the Paradoxes of Hungarian Constitution Making?

Did what went right inevitably imply what went wrong? Would generating greater democratic legitimacy imply substantive losses with respect to the constitutional outcome? Was legal continuity and negotiated transition incompatible with a process that would produce democratic legitimacy?

Most certainly, proponents of constitutionalism in the sense of imposing procedural and normative constraints on the executive and the legislative branches of power—that is, the SZDSZ, FIDESZ, and some leaders of the MDF—were not strong enough during the summer of 1989 to shape the outcome to such an extent as is reflected by the liberal-democratic character of the finished product. That the Hungarian constitution-making process, despite its lack of democratic legitimacy, produced a liberal-democratic outcome can best be explained by the dynamics of negotiated transitions. More accurately, it is not so much some necessary internal dynamics of negotiated transitions as the material conditions that give rise to such a form of transition—primarily, the perceived weakness of agents and a relative veil of ignorance—that lead to outcomes that are truly liberal-democratic. On the other hand, the same material conditions usually lead to a sense of lack of legitimacy regarding the new regime. Such a legitimacy deficit runs through the entire twelve years of Hungarian constitution making.[110]

But was it inevitable that conditions in Hungary in 1989 could not have tolerated a more democratically legitimate process? We believe not. The distinction between up-

stream and downstream publicity that Elster describes allows us to see that while the
presence of public pressure could have led to
undesirable consequences for constitution
drafting, the same would not have been true
for a ratification process afterward, one that
never took place. Granted, even during ratification, a substantively desirable constitution
could be lost as it almost was in the United
States in 1787–89, and as did in fact happen
in France in 1946, and in referendums on a
new European Union constitution in 2005.
Nevertheless, democracy must imply taking
a chance with uncertainty, even in constitution making. When coupled with a massive
education effort as in South Africa, the degree of uncertainty can be greatly reduced.

The problem becomes more difficult,
however, when one is dealing with an interim constitution that the relevant agents
do not want to enshrine. The reasons for not
engaging in an extended ratification process
for extensive amendments to an authoritarian constitution—an inevitable artifact of
legal continuity—are cogent. But it should
be realized after the Hungarian experience
that a constitution, even an interim one,
can be enshrined de facto by pursuing a process of piecemeal constitutional engineering,
as well as by the closing of the window of
political opportunity for constitution making. While it may in principle be desirable
to leave room for an extended learning period, that window may close fully before
that period is over. In this respect, it would
be important for future constitution makers
operating within a similar set of procedures
and constraints to avoid the mistake of Hungarian constitution makers, who postulated
the interim nature of their constitution but
provided neither a democratically enhanced
procedure for making the permanent constitution nor a timetable armed with relevant
sanctions for the production of the definitive
document. While we cannot speak today of
a definitive formula of constitution making

in fully negotiated transitions involving legal continuity, we should readily admit that
the South African constitution makers sur-
passed all their Central European predecessors in elaborating such a project.

One point should be added about the
connection between the procedural history
of the making of the Hungarian constitution
and the regrettable fact that none of the major agents of today's Hungarian politics construct their ideological identities around their
role in the constitution making, even though
the roles of the MDF, the SZDSZ, FIDESZ,
and the Communists were, though different,
very significant. Because of the rather protracted and multistaged character of the constitutional process, there was no single point
that could be identified as the moment of the
coming-to-be of the new constitution, when
all the major actors gave their clear backing to the constitutional state of affairs. The
October 1989 amendment that amounted
to a substantively new constitution is the
most plausible candidate, but at least some
of the important agents did not endorse
the arrangement that led to it. Similarly, at
every other significant juncture—the referendum, the MDF-SZDSZ pact—at least
some of the main participants felt alienated
from the process. The October 1989 constitution, ratifying the Round Table's final
agreement, left the SZDSZ and FIDESZ
feeling betrayed and excluded. In turn, the
outcome of the referendum in November
1989 left the MDF and MSZP feeling hu-
miliated and deceived; more specifically, they
claimed that the Hungarian people had been
deceived by the tendentious grouping of the
questions on the ballot. Finally, the MDF-
SZDSZ pact estranged all those left out
from the outcome. Therefore, even though
over the years that have elapsed since 1990,
all of these parties have pledged allegiance
to the emerging arrangement, at least at the
general rhetorical level, at no point during
the long process of its coming to existence

could the new constitution claim the simultaneous support of all the actors that had a share in its making. Quite independently of the almost total absence of popular participation in the constitution-making process, this must have contributed to the fact that the symbolic political self-understanding of the new democratic republic does not center around the constitution—which, it is widely agreed among experts at least, is worthy of protection and respect.

Glossary

EKA — Ellenzéki Kerekasztal; Round Table of the Opposition. Formed in March 1989, to bring together six parties, one circle, and one independent union for purposes of negotiation with the ruling party.

FIDESZ — Fiatal Demokraták Szövetsége; Alliance of Young Democrats. Formed in March 1988 as a social-political organization of young activists. A political party after the negotiations. In parliament since 1990. Leading party of coalition 1998–2002. Most important early leaders: Viktor Orbán, László Kövér, and Gábor Fodor.

FKgP — Független Kisgazda Párt; Independent Small Holders Party. "Historical" party of middle peasantry. Biggest party of 1945–1948 coalitions. Recreated around old members in November 1988. In government 1990–1994; 1998–2002. Failed to win seats in parliament in 2002. Best known leaders: Imre Boross and József Torgyán.

KDNP — Keresztény Demokrata Nép Párt; Christian Democrat Peoples Party. Formed by mostly older activists of a variety of Catholic organizations (and lively Catholic subculture) in late 1989. In governmental coalition of 1990–1994. Failed to win seats in parliament in 1998.

MDF — Magyar Demokrata Fórum; Hungarian Democratic Forum. Formed by populist writers, and intellectuals and their supporters in 1987. Largest opposition (center-right) party in 1989, at which time won three by-elections. Winner of first free elections in 1990, and leading force of government 1990–1994. Failed to win seats in parliament as an independent party in 1998 and 2002, though several members entered with support of FIDESZ. István Csurka's MIEP (Hungarian Truth and Life Party) is a right-wing offshoot that entered parliament between 1998 and

2002. Most important leader was József Antall, at least during the period of the Round Table.

MSZDP — Magyar Szociáldemokrata Párt; "historical" social democratic party, absorbed into the MDP (renamed Communists) in 1948. Recreated in January 1989, and since troubled by splits and scandals. Failed to win seats in parliament in 1990.

MSZMP/MSZP — Magyar Szocialista Munkás Párt, renamed in October 1989 as Magyar Szocialista Párt; Hungarian Socialist Workers Party, renamed in October 1989 as Hungarian Socialist Party. Successor to KMP, MKP, and MDP (different names of the Hungarian Communist Party). Ruling state party from 1948 to 1989. In parliament since 1990; leading party of government 1994–1998; 2002–present. Best known leaders in 1989: Karoly Grosz, Imre Pozsgay, Miklós Németh, and Gyula Horn.

Néppárt — People's Party. Successor to the "historical" party of the peasantry, the Nemzeti Parasztpart (National Peasants Party). Recreated by officials active in the Patriotic People's Front, the Communist electoral front organization. Has failed to win any seats in parliament.

NKA — Nemzeti Kerekasztal; National Round Table. Met June 1989 to September 1989, and produced Round Table constitution.

SZDSZ — Szabad Demokraták Szövetsége; Alliance of Free Democrats. Inheritor of the democratic opposition of the late 1970s and 1980s. First formed as the Network of Free Initiatives in 1988. A liberal political party since November 1988. Main early leaders were János Kis, Bálint Magyar, Péter Tölgyessy, and Iván Peto.

Notes

1.   Andrew Arato, *Civil Society, Constitution, and Legitimacy* (Lanham, MD: Rowman and Littlefield, 2000), chaps. 5 and 7.

2.   Jon Elster, ed., *The Roundtable Talks and the Breakdown of Communism* (Chicago: University of Chicago Press, 1996); A. Bozoki, ed., *The Roundtable Talks of 1989: The Genesis of Hungarian Democracy* (Budapest: CEU Press, 2002); S. Friedman and D. Atkinson, eds., *The Small Miracle: South Africa's Negotiated Settlement* (Johnnesburg: Raven Press, 1994); and Hassen Ebrahim, *The Soul of a Nation: Constitution-Making in South Africa* (Capetown: Oxford University Press, 1998).

3. See Carl Schmitt, *Verfassungslehre,* 7th ed. (Berlin: Duncker and Humblot, 1989), chaps. 6 and 8.

4. We are ultimately concerned with the sociological sense of the term *legitimacy* as established by Max Weber, having to do with a significant part of a population—at the very least, the main political and social elites (his "administrative staff")—considering a political order as a whole or the government based on it (two different matters) justified or valid. This sociological meaning of the term is related but not identical to legal and moral philosophical meanings. We assume, ceteris paribus, that political orders and governments that can be justified by valid normative (moral and legal) assumptions shared by a political community will be legitimate in the sociological sense as well. But there is no one-to-one relation, and all things are rarely equal. Legitimacy in the sociological sense is undoubtedly also affected by performance as well the presence and effectiveness of delegitimating ideologies. In the present study, not concerned with broader social and political matters, we have to assume a rough identity of legitimacy in the sociological sense with legitimacy in the normative sense. It is primarily in the latter area, however, that we detect a legitimacy deficit, and it is well worth asking for comparative purposes how this deficit came about, even if the translation into empirical legitimation problems has either not occurred or if these phenomena have been neutralized by factors such as relatively successful economic performance and joining the European Union. Such sources of compensation are evidently not always and everywhere available.

5. Bruce Ackerman, *The Future of the Liberal Revolution* (New Haven, CT: Yale University Press, 1992), chap. 6; Andrew Arato, "Constitutional Learning," in *Theoria* 52, no. 106 (April 2005), pp. 1–36.

6. Juan Linz and Alfred Stepan, *Problems of Democratic Transition and Consolidation* (Baltimore, MD: Johns Hopkins Press, 1996), chap. 17.

7. Janos Kornai, "The Hungarian Reform Process: Visions, Hopes and Reality," in *Crisis and Reform in Eastern Europe,* eds. F. Feher and A. Arato (New Brunswick, NJ: Transaction Publishers, 1991).

8. Arato, *Civil Society,* chap. 2.

9. The GDR Round Table produced a draft, but the Volkskammer did not enact it, either before or after free elections. Thus the Hungarian interim constitution was the first of the new genre. It did not, like that of South Africa, contain a procedure for final constitution making. Thus it did not posit itself consistently and insistently enough as interim.

10. The preamble to the constitution states: "In order to facilitate a peaceful transition to a rule of law state that actualizes a multi-party system, parliamentary democracy, and a social market economy, the National Assembly—until the ratification of our country's new Constitution—establishes the text of Hungary's Constitution as the following." *A Magyar Köztársaság Alkotmánya* (Budapest: 1990). Available at net.jogtar.hu/jr/gen/getdoc.cgi?docid= 94900020.tv (accessed July 14, 2009).

11. The parliament fully enacted the interim constitution on October 23, 1989, on the anniversary of the uprising of 1956.

12. MSZMP (Hungarian Socialist Workers Party), the Communist Party, changed its name and identity to MSZP (Hungarian Socialist Party) on October 7, 1989, a social democratic party in terms of its intentions. The old name was kept by a small communist party that plays no role in this story. We will refer to the party before October 6–9 as the MSZMP and after as the MSZP.

13. Adam Przeworski, *Democracy and Market* (Cambridge: Cambridge University Press, 1991), pp. 54–66.

14. Bolivar Lamounier, "Authoritarian Brazil Revisited: The Impact of Elections on the Abertura," in *Democratizing Brazil,* ed. A. Stepan (New York: Oxford University Press, 1989).

15. Przeworski might point out that today all three countries—Brazil, Chile, and Mexico—are democracies. But, first, we do not maintain that the reformist road, when tried, must succeed, only that it need not necessarily fail. Second, the time gained in these relatively slow transitions (ten years in Brazil and Chile, twenty years or more in Mexico) may be the functional equivalent of success for the relevant elites. And third, in all such cases, important preserves are won for the relevant elites that survive democratization.

16. Arato, *Civil Society,* chap. 1.

17. Rudolf Tokés, *Hungary's Negotiated Revolution* (Cambridge: Cambridge University Press, 1996), pp. 189–90; István Kukorelli, *Igy választottunk* (Budapest: ELTE Állam- és Jogtudományi Kar, 1988).

18. Further research is necessary on this point. When a new round of reformism was decided on in Hungary, it took the much broader form of a reform package presented in terms of preemptive constitution making from above.

19. Laws 1989 II, III, and VII. See Jutasi in *Magyarország Politikai Évkönyve 1990* (Budapest: Országgyűlési Napló, 1990), 372; G. Halmai in *Magyarország Politikai Évkönyve 1988* (Budapest: Országgyűlési Napló, 1989).

20. Laszlo Bruszt, "1989: The Negotiated Revolution in Hungary," in *Social Research*, vol. 57, no. 2 (1990), p. 366.

21. "Social Movements and Civil Society in the Soviet Union," in *From Neo-Marxism to Democratic Theory* (Armonk: M.E. Sharpe, 1993), chap. 14.

22. M.A. Garreton, *The Chilean Political Process* (Boston: Unwin Hyman, 1989), pp. 132–45.

23. High-level Political Bureau delegations, including Imre Pozsgay, the leader of the reform faction, traveled to Warsaw to discuss the consequences of the Polish Round Table and their possible applicability to Hungary. See M. Kalmár, "Modellváltástól a rendszerváltásig az MSZMP taktikájának a metamorfózisa a demokratikus átmenetben," in *A rendszerváltás forgatókönyve*, vol. 7, ed. A. Bozoki (Budapest: Magvető and Uj Mandátum presses, 1999 and 2000); *Alkotmányos forradalom*, pp. 287–88.

24. Csaba Tordai, "A harmadik köztársaság alkotmánya születése," in *A rendszerváltás forgatókönyve*, vol. 7, p. 482; K. Kulcsár, *Két világ között: Rendszerváltás Magyarországon 1988–1990* (Budapest: Akademia, 1994). Kulcsár was the last minister of justice before the free elections and his memoirs make for highly interesting reading. It should remind those like ourselves who disagree with his evaluation of top-down reform that there is an important case to be made for the positive role of such efforts.

25. Tordai, "A harmadik köztársaság alkotmánya születése," pp. 483–84.

26. Kalmár, "Modellváltástól a rendszerváltásig az MSZMP taktikájának a metamorfózisa a demokratikus átmenetben," pp. 288–89, versus Kulcsár, *Két világ között*.

27. This is true even of the last of the three constitutional proposals, which, however, was probably more a first statement of a negotiating position than an actual attempt at imposition.

28. Rudolf Tokés speaks of an implausible three-fourths of contents, though he admits that it was probably the new one-fourth that defined the character of the Round Table constitution. Later, however, he resumes treating that constitution as primarily the work of the Ministry of Justice. See "Intézményalkotás Magyarországon elemzésiszem-pontok és alkotmányos modellek," *A rendszerváltás forgatókönyve*, vol. 7, p. 167.

29. See Samuel Valenzuela, "Democratic Consolidation in Post-Transitional Settings," in *Issues in Democratic Consolidation*, eds. Scott Mainwaring, Guillermo O'Donnell, and Samuel Valenzuela (South Bend, IN: University of Notre Dame Press, 1992), pp. 57–105.

30. Most clearly put by Kalmár, "Modellváltástól a rendszerváltásig az MSZMP taktikájának a metamorfózisa a demokratikus átmenetben," p. 287ff.

31. See remarks by József Antall in A. Richter, ed., *Ellenzéki kerekasztal* (Budapest: Ötlet Kiadó, 1990), pp. 160–61; L. Lengyel, "A kerekesztal hosei" in *A rendszerváltás forgatókönyve*.

32. 1989: Amendment I on rights and on a constitutional court; 1989: Amendments VIII and IX on the possibility of a modified parliamentary vote of confidence; 1989: Amendment XVII on popular petition and referendums. These amendments presented needed democratic change but generally were poorly or incompletely formulated. Only the referendum amendment came to have real importance during 1989. The problem with the series of amendments was, however, even more procedural than substantive; they involved the danger of establishing an uncontrollable and mutable, top-down, gradual model of change. Thus the ruling party was forced to agree to a moratorium on further one-sided constitutional legislation at the start of the Round Table negotiations. See I. Kukorelli, "Az országgyülés a többpártredszer elso évében," in *Magyarország Politikai Évkönyve* (Budapest: Aula-Omikk Press, 1990), p. 195, lamenting that the move interfered with the decision-making process of government and the normal working order of parliament.

33. The threat of new legislation was used as a club also during the Round Table negotiations, after the MSZMP formally agreed to suspend such unilateral efforts. See Kilényi at the July 27 meeting of the Middle Level Political Coordinating Council of the National Round Table in *A Rendszerváltás forgatókönve. Kerekasztal-tárgyalások 1989-ben.* II (Budapest: Magveto, 1999), pp. 645–47.

34. See Bruce Ackerman, *We the People, Vol. 1: Foundations* (Cambridge, MA: Harvard University Press, 1991).

35. On the origins of these parties, see Tokés, *Hungary's Negotiated Revolution*, as well as the various writings of Bozóki and Körösényi.

36. These parties were called historical because their forerunners were important in pre–World War II Hungarian history, especially in the coalition governments between 1945 and 1948. While old members played a role in their reorganization, it is generally assumed that so did various factions of the ruling party, the MSZMP, which wished to compete with Imre Pozsgay, who was involved in the formation of the MDF. For this reason, they were obvious targets for overtures from the ruling party at least until the Round Table agreements were concluded. None of this is meant to suggest that significant members of these parties did not at all times seek to play an honorable and independent role.

37. These were the three new orgnizations (MDF, SZDSZ, and FIDESZ), the four historical parties (FKgP, KDNP, MSZDP, and Néppárt), and one association (Bajcsy Zsilinszky Endre Baráti Társaság). The League of Independent Trade Unions (Liga) received only observer status.

38. For the best study by far of the negotiations, see András Bozóki in *Lawful Revolution in Hungary*, eds. Bela Király and András Bozóki (Boulder, CO: Social Sciences Monographs, 1995). Also see Tokés, *Hungary's Negotiated Revolution.*

39. See *A Rendszerváltás Forgatókönyve*, vol. 1, especially Bozóki's own essay.

40. Ibid., pp. 599–607; compare to pp. 88–90.

41. We are neglecting here that the Hungarian Round Table was, on the insistence of the MSZMP, "triangular." The ruling party did not wish to see negotiations as a confrontation of the power and society or even as regime and opposition. See *A Rendszervaltas Forgatókönyve*, vol. 1, pp. 91–92. Thus a third negotiating partner, representing established official and semiofficial organizations, was insisted on. The opposition, however, managed to insist upon consensual decision making; thus, the so-called third side could not team up with the MSZMP to put through proposals. Their only significance was in floating trial balloons that deviated from the MSZMP line that it did not wish to immediately modify. This happened, e.g., when county lists (demanded by the historical parties of the EKA) were accepted first by the third side when the MSZMP still insisted on unified national lists for parties in elections. See *A Rendszerváltás Forgatókönyve*, vol. 3.

42. The reluctance of particular actors depended on party and professional affiliation. It seems to us that the SZDSZ and nonlawyers were most amenable to publicity on any level, while the MSZMP and the lawyers on both sides most insisted on excluding it. See debates in *A Rendszervál-*

tás Forgatókönyve, vols. I, II, and III; M. Vásárhelyi. Eventually the discussion moved on to the type and frequency of television coverage that would be provided. The overall contrast with Poland was obvious, although in Poland some important agreements were made privately at the Magdalenka Castle by a small group around Jaruzelski and Walesa. In Hungary, the existence of primarily nonpublic negotiating sessions also did not prevent most likely important additional private contacts between ruling party officials and important members of opposition parties.

43. See Bruce Ackerman, *The Future of the Liberal Revolution* (New Haven, CT; Yale University Press, 1992), chap. 6, "Judges as Founders"; Arato, *Civil Society*, chaps. 3 and 4.

44. János Kis, "1989: A víg esztendo," *Beszélo*, vol. 4, no. 10 (1999), pp. 22–46.

45. *A Rendszerváltás Forgatókönyve*, vol. 4; see Bozóki and Tokés for two different views.

46. On the referendum see Kis, "1989"; Tokés, *Hungary's Negotiated Revolution*; Tordai, "A harmadik köztársaság alkotmánya születése"; L. Bruszt and D. Stark, "Remaking the Political Field in Hungary," in *Eastern Europe in Revolution*, ed. Ivo Banac (Ithaca, NY: Cornell University Press, 1992); as well as the interviews with Antall and Tölgyessy in Richter, *Ellenzéki kerekasztal.*

47. Many ex-ministers and their expert advisers maintain that the process would have developed more smoothly if the opposition agreed to negotiate with the leaders of the government and not the party. We remain skeptical about the difference this would have made, and the noninclusion of those who controlled sovereign powers for such a long time would not have been or seemed safe in an epoch still marked by uncertainties. See Kulcsár, *Két világ között.*

48. In the latter case confirming Elster's position on the question of the institutional interests of constituted powers that participate in constitution making, against Tokés (*Hungary's Negotiated Revolution*), who is certainly mistaken in his belief that it was the hidden institutional interests of the Ministry of Justice that dominated in the process.

49. J. Schiemann, "A választási törvény megalkotása," in *A rendszerváltás forgatókönyve*, vol 7; Halmai Az, "1949 Alkotmány jogállamositása," in *A rendszerváltás forgatókönyve*, vol 7.; See Arato on the negative aspects of electoral system in *Civil Society*, chaps. 5 and 6.

50. Tordai, "A harmadik köztársaság alkotmánya születése," pp. 494–95.

51. 1/1990 Constitutional Court Ruling.

52. The court was arguably wrong to do this; the referendum covered the first selection of a president, and only careless phrasing that left out reference to the parliamentary election that was already in the constitution (Article 29/A[1]) allowed the interpretation that the issue was merely that of timing and not mode of election. Of course, mode was as important as timing, or even more so, from the point of view of the petitioners. Parliamentary modification of the results of referendums was possible, but only after two years. An interesting feature of this decision was that the court ruled on the constitutional validity, to be sure only in the procedural sense, of a constitutional amendment.

53. Tordai, "A harmadik köztársaság alkotmánya születése," p. 495.

54. The twenty laws that remained subject to the two-thirds requirement fall into two main groups. Some of them concern fundamental liberties, such as the freedom of assembly and the freedom of religion, or they regulate the functions and powers of basic constitutional institutions, such as the judiciary, the prosecutor's office, and the electoral system. In actual fact, many of them have been subject to change since 1990. Neither did the number of two-thirds laws remain constant, as a few have been added to the list.

55. One especially unfortunate aspect of these, which had no significance for the 1990–94 positions of the parties, allows the president to dissolve parliament in forty days if his candidate for prime minister is rejected. The 1989 formulation, requiring at least four attempts, was obviously better, as we found out in 2002, when there was speculation that the current president could offer the office of prime minister to the largest party, which in fact could not form government, thereby forcing new elections in extremely polarized circumstances.

56. For the text of the pact, see *Magyarország Politikai Évkönyve* 1991.

57. See Tordai, "A harmadik köztársaság alkotmánya születése," and Szalay in *Magyarország Politikai Évkönyve* 1991.

58. Seventy-two percent of the mandates. It is thus probably true that József Antall made the gravest error when, on the basis of old-fashioned cultural nostalgia, he chose the Independent Small Holders (FKgP) and the Christian Democrats (KDNP) and not the SZDSZ and FIDESZ as his coalition

partners, an option that János Kis, the leader of the SZDSZ was quite inclined to, as was the FIDESZ leadership.

59. Magyar Köztársaság Alkotmánya (1949/XX), preamble.

60. This was further accentuated by the fact that László Sólyom, the first chief justice of the court, who all but dominated the first years of the court and shaped its self-understanding, had also been a prominent figure of the Round Table discussions on the opposition side. Thus, he might have felt doubly justified in spelling out rulings that substantively shaped the unfinished constitution-making project.

61. 23/1990 Constitutional Court Ruling.

62. This occurred in the case of abolishing the death penalty (23/1990). For an analysis of this ruling, see János Kis, *Alkotmányos demokrácia* (Budapest: INDOK, 2000), pp. 204–11.

63. On the role of the court in defining the presidency, see Andrew Arato, "Az Alkotmánybíróság a médiaháborúban," in *Civil Társadalom, Forradalom és Alkotmány,* ed. Andrew Arato (Budapest: Uj Mandátum, 1999).

64. On these formative years of the court, see András Sajó, "A 'láthatatlan alkotmány apróbetűi,'" *Állam- és Jogtudomány,* vol. 1–2 (1993), pp. 37–96; and János Kis, "Alkotmánybíráskodás a mérlegen," in *Alkotmányos demokrácia,* esp. pp. 200–57.

65. For the important distinction between material and formal constitutions, see H. Kelsen, *The General Theory of State and Law* (Cambridge, MA: Harvard University Press, 1945), pp. 124 ff, 258–60. We do not, however, accept Kelsen's idea that using a constitution's own amendment rule even to completely replace it would leave in place the same constitution, an idea that disregards his own distinction between formal and material.

66. S. Holmes, "Back to the Drawing Board," in *East European Constitutional Review,* vol. 2 (1993/1), pp. 21–25.

67. Ackerman, *The Future of the Liberal Revolution*; Arato, "Constitutional Learning."

68. Arato, "Refurbishing the Legitimacy of the New Regime: Constitution-Making Endgame in Hungary and Poland," in *Civil Society,* pp. 199–228.

69. Halmai, *Magyarország Politikai Évkönyve*; Arato, *Civil Society,* chap. 7.

70. Hungarian politics is increasingly shaped by the hardening of two major blocks, which are themselves internally heterogeneous. The socialist-liberal side is emphatically pro-Western, favors privatization and integration into the international economy, and draws support mostly from the urban, professional middle classes, the elderly, and the ranks of the former Communist party and bureaucracy. The right-of-center block is more open to economic protectionism, less enthusiastic about international integration, and draws support from the rural, agricultural population, small to mid-size entrepreneurs, religious voters, and the younger generation of voters.

71. Ackerman, *The Future of the Liberal Revolution*.

72. For the Hungarian case see Kis, Haraszti, and Solt, *The Social Contract*, samizdat 1987, that involved a creative constitutional package as well as the first open declaration that "Kadar Must Go!"

73. One of the authors of this case study, Andrew Arato, played a very occasional role as an expert of the SZDSZ, in constitutional matters, as well as a more formal role submitting drafts to the parliamentary drafting committee (in 1995–96) concerning the electoral law and the constitutional amendment rule. In both cases, however, Arato was asked to participate as a Hungarian rather than foreign expert.

74. Nevertheless, the latter was done once, in 1993, when the government, with the tacit consent of the largest opposition party, raised the electoral threshold from 4 to 5 percent.

75. Hungary was a monarchy until 1945, in theory with a responsible parliament, a parliamentary republic from 1945 to 1948, and formally even after. See, e.g., Antall's remarks at the last plenary session of the National Round Table, in *A Rendszerváltás forgatókönyve. Kerekasztal-tárgyalások 1989-ben*, vol. 4 (Budapest: Új Mandátum, 2000) pp. 499–500.

76. Constitution of the Republic of Hungary, art. 29(A).

77. Constitution of the Republic of Hungary, 1989 text, art. 40(1).

78. See also the text of the last plenary session of the National Round Table in *A Rendszerváltás forgatókönyve*, vol. 4, pp. 499–507 and note 18.

79. See Antall in Richter, *Ellenzéki kerekasztal*, p. 163.

80. See Kulcsár, *Két világ között*, who, however, mentions no quid pro quo, and most recently Lengyel, "A kerekesztal hosei," who denies a special deal by affirming in effect an even wider and more pervasive collaboration between Pozsgay and Antall.

81. This eventually became Antall's position; see remark attributed to Tölgyessy by Lengyel, but see Antall's denial of explicit coordination with the radical opposition in *Ellenzéki kerekasztal*, pp. 164–65.

82. See Przeworski, *Democracy and Market*; Schiemann, "A választási törvény megalkotása," and Halmai, *Magyarország Politikai Évkönyve*.

83. See Halmai, *Magyarország Politikai Évkönyve*.

84. *A Rendszerváltás forgatókönyve*, vol. 3, p. 649; see *Magyarország politikai évkönyve 1990* for the legislation.

85. SZDSZ, *Rendszerváltás programja* (Budapest: SZDSZ, 1989).

86. For the formal position of the EKA, see Arato, "Az Alkotmánybíróság a médiaháborúban," p. 612. For a vigorous debate on this position see remarks by Tölgyessy and Kilényi in *Ellenzéki kerekasztal*, pp. 649–50.

87. See the September 15, 1989, Middle Level Political Coordinating Council of the National Round Table in *A Rendszerváltás forgatókönyve*, vol. 4, pp. 410–13.

88. Undoubtedly many of the elements of the eventual design for the constitutional court came from reform communist drafts. But Kulcsár's argument that he and vice minister Kilenyi actually wished for the stronger model, did not introduce it for tactical reasons, and were happy when the opposition forced through its points is unconvincing and unverifiable. See *Két világ között*, pp. 252–53. Ultimately what matters is not what these politicians believed but what they proposed. Kulcsár omits from his list the expansion of standing in front of the court, successfully demanded by the opposition.

89. September 18, 1989, session of the EKA; September 18, 1989, Middle Level session of the National Round Table, *A Rendszerváltás forgatókönyve*, vol. 4, pp. 450–51, 472–79.

90. The distinction is papered over by Arend Lijphart in *Democracies*, in which he treats constitutionalism as a dimension of consensus democracy.

91. Kulcsár implies, but supplies no proof, that the conception originated with Tölgyessy, who claimed that it was the MSZMP. See *Két világ között*, p. 261. In any case, the idea of constitutional laws that can be changed only by qualified majorities seems to have been in the draft conception of a new constitution brought to parliament by the

Ministry of Justice in April–May 1989. See Tokés, *Hungary's Negotiated Revolution,* p. 163, who cites the text *Igazságügy Minisztérium—Magyarország Alkotmánya—Szabályozási Koncepció.* We do not see, however, why he claims that parliament received some kind of veto right thereby, in a conception that otherwise sought to limit parliamentary sovereignty in a variety of ways. See also Tordai, "A harmadik köztársaság alkotmánya születése."

92. 4/1990 Constitutional Court Ruling.

93. Jutasi, *Magyarország Politikai Évkönyve 1990.*

94. 4/1990 Constitutional Court Ruling.

95. Jutasi, *Magyarország politikai évkönyve 1990.*

96. Tordai, "A harmadik köztársaság alkotmánya születése."

97. See D. Atkinson, "Principle Born of Pragmatism? Central Government in the Transition," in *A Small Miracle,* eds. S. Friedman and D. Atkinson (Pretoria: Raven Press, 1994); R. Schrire "The President and the Executive," as well as the other essays in *South Africa: Designing New Political Institutions,* eds. M. Faure and J.-E. Lane (London: Sage, 1996).

98. Bruce Ackerman, *We the People,* vol. 1 (Cambridge, MA; Harvard University Press, 1991), chap. 1.

99. Istvan Csurka, "Meg nem történt forradalom" in *Csendes, Forradalom, Volt,* ed. András Bozóki (Budapest: Twins, 1992); "Az alkotmánybiróság döntéséhez," in *Magyar Fórum,* March 12, 1992.

100. Arato, *Civil Society,* p. 3.

101. See Hannah Arendt, *On Revolution* (New York: Penguin Classics, 1990).

102. See Mária Vásárhelyi, "A tárgyalások nyilvánossága, a nyilvánosság tárgyalása," in *A rendszerváltás forgatókönyve,* vol. 7, p. 575 ff.

103. Arato, *Civil Society,* pp. 69, 124–25; Kis, "Between Reform and Revolution," *Constellations* (January 1995), p. 405.

104. Schmitt, *Verfassungslehre.*

105. Holmes, "Back to the Drawing Board."

106. Woodrow Wilson in Arendt, *On Revolution.*

107. Ackerman, *The Future of the Liberal Revolution.*

108. Halmai, *Magyarország Politikai Évkönyve.*

109. Kelsen, *General Theory,* p. 155 ff.

110. The material structure of the Hungarian negotiations based on two weak sides was first stressed by Bruszt and Stark, "Remaking the Political Field."

14

Constitution Making, Peace Building, and National Reconciliation

The Experience of Poland

Lech Garlicki and Zofia A. Garlicka

The history of the Polish parliament dates back to the fifteenth century. Poland's first written constitution—the first constitutional instrument in Europe—was adopted on May 3, 1791, but unfortunately, it was never implemented due to the collapse of the Polish state in 1795. Nevertheless, it became a symbol of independence and progress referred to by historians as well as politicians.

It was the rebirth of a fully independent Poland after World War I that allowed the creation of a modern constitution. The so-called March Constitution, adopted on March 17, 1921, was inspired by concepts underlying the constitution of the Third French Republic. It provided for a system of government based on the preeminent position of the parliament, especially its first chamber, traditionally referred to as the Sejm. The parliamentary system failed, however, to secure proper functioning of the state machinery. A coup d'etat in 1926 was followed by the so-called April Constitution, adopted on

May 23, 1935. It established the supremacy of the presidency over the other branches of government, leaving only residual powers to the parliament. World War II broke out four years later, and Poland lost its independence once again.

After World War II, effective control over the Polish territory passed to the Soviet-controlled government, which imposed a Soviet-style constitution on July 22, 1952. Theoretically, it granted quite formidable powers to the unicameral parliament (the Sejm), but in reality, the Communist Party (Polish United Workers Party) monopolized power. The party's totalitarian grip on Poland relaxed after the social unrest of 1956, but the 1952 constitution remained intact. It was significantly amended in 1976, but even then, its Soviet-oriented nature was preserved. In summer 1980, the Solidarity movement, led by Lech Walesa, started the final decline of the communist system, but another seventeen years passed before the first democratic constitution in two centuries was adopted.

1989: Round Table Agreement and April Amendment

Poland's democratic constitution entered into life on October 17, 1997, but the real beginning of the end of the communist system began in 1980. The shipyard strikes in summer 1980 found their conclusion in so-called agreements signed between the workers' representatives and the government. The Porozumienie Gdanskie (Gdansk Agreement) is the best-known example. This agreement provided not only for social and economic changes but, at least to some extent, intervention in the very essence of the structure of government: While it confirmed the "leading role of the Communist Party," it allowed the establishment of independent trade unions. None of the agreements ever found a translation into constitutional law, but they exemplified conflict resolution through peaceful means. In effect, the opposition—centered around the Catholic Church and the Solidarity trade union—gained sixteen precious months of legal existence. Even if the imposition of martial law in December 1981 disrupted attempts at compromise and reconciliation, the idea of political dialogue had not been discredited and would be revived toward the end of the 1980s, in a completely different international and domestic setting.

With the idea of political dialogue intact, the idea of a roundtable, gathering both the quasi-illegal opposition and representatives of the official regime, found understanding and acceptance on both ends of the political spectrum in summer 1988, even though there was no sign of economic recovery in sight and strikes were sweeping the country. The economic crisis led the moderate wing within the Communist Party, led by General Wojciech Jaruzelski and General Czeslaw Kiszczak, to seek cooperation with the opposition. The parties then spent six months negotiating organizational aspects of the Round Table. These negotiations were held in secret, with the Catholic Church mediating talks involv-

ing some of the most sensitive issues. Finally, the Round Table was convened in February and early April 1989, and a compromise on most issues was reached and formulated into what became colloquially known as the Round Table Agreement.[1] The Round Table as such met only a few times; the real work was conducted in smaller committees (so-called subtables) and working groups, and the most important decisions were made by agreement of the leaders of both camps.

The April agreement provided for several important political changes. First, the existing parliament, the Sejm, would be dissolved and new partly democratic[2] elections would be held in June 1989. Second, the 1952 constitution would be amended to create the second chamber of parliament, the Senate, as well as a new and powerful office of the president. Because it was assumed that General Jaruzelski would hold that office, the Communist Party felt assured that it would preserve control over the executive branch. Thus, the president was given important independent state powers at the expense of parliament, which the party no longer regarded as reliable.

In implementing the agreement, the first step was for the Sejm, still in its old composition, to amend the constitution. On April 7, 1989, the so-called April Amendment transformed the structure of both political branches of government.[3] While the Sejm formally adopted it, the amendment was the product of political compromises concluded at the Round Table; the role of the members of parliament was limited to voting for what was submitted to them. The amendment was designed to satisfy both sides, and for this reason, it was much easier to see it as a temporary compromise mechanism than it was to appreciate its later role in restoring democratic constitutionalism in Poland. Most people in April 1989 anticipated a long period of cohabitation between the old regime and new political forces. Only a few could sense that the entire communist system in Eastern Europe would collapse within the next nine months.

1989–91: Transitory Parliament and Constitution Writing

The Round Table Agreement and April Amendment, as originally conceived, functioned only for a very short time. By summer 1989, it was clear that the Communist Party could no longer maintain control over the newly elected Sejm, and consequently, Tadeusz Mazowiecki, one of the Solidarity leaders, became the prime minister. Six months later, the Communist Party ceased to exist[4] and the amended constitution began to operate in a completely new setting. Political parties used the democratic potential of the April Agreement to construct rules of parliamentary government. While Jaruzelski kept the presidency until the end of 1990, he never attempted to use his constitutional prerogatives. Thus, the April Agreement ceased to guarantee the political distribution of power, its originally intended principal function.

At the same time, it became clear that the old constitution had to be replaced with a new document.[5] The existing constitution was adopted in 1952, at the peak of the Stalinist regime in Poland. It was drafted in language redolent with communist slogans and lacked sufficient guarantees and procedures to be judicially enforceable. While some important improvements were introduced in the 1980s—particularly the 1982 amendment providing for the establishment of a constitutional court—there was no way to adjust the old text to new conditions and no reason to keep the old constitution alive.

Already in autumn 1989, both chambers of parliament separately appointed constitutional committees and entrusted them with the task of preparing full drafts of the new constitution. Both committees were composed of members of the respective houses,

and each of the committees established several subcommittees and working groups, inviting the advice of numerous Polish and foreign experts. The idea was to adopt a new constitution on May 3, 1991, to commemorate the anniversary of Poland's first democratic constitution, voted on May 3, 1791.

But the parallel existence of two constitutional committees resulted in a political struggle. As Wiktor Osiatynski relates,

> political ambitions and institutional rivalries surfaced at this point and have remained central to the entire constitution-making process ... Initially, the Senate committee was willing to cooperate with the freely elected 35 percent of the Sejm committee, but as the relationship between the two houses gradually deteriorated, cooperation between the two committees ceased. The Sejm and the Senate eventually produced two different drafts. The versions were basically irreconcilable and no arbiter existed who could decide which draft should be submitted to a referendum. Constitutional momentum was thus dissipated even before the first transitory Parliament dissolved itself in the Fall of 1991.[6]

Nevertheless, the process of constitution writing had begun, and the drafts prepared and published by both committees delivered a starting point for further discussion. At the same time, several political parties and private persons submitted their own drafts or theses for the new constitution.[7]

Already in autumn 1989, political elites as well as most scholars realized that some changes should be introduced immediately into the existing constitution. Therefore, another method of constitution writing emerged: fragmented amendments that removed most of the obsolete provisions of the 1952 constitution and introduced new institutions and concepts into its text.[8] Toward the end of 1989, the so-called December Amendment deleted the first two chapters of the constitution and introduced new principles of constitutional order, mainly following Western concepts of the rule of law, political pluralism, and protection of property.

This time, the constitutional amendment was meant as an instrument of change and not of compromise. This courageous attempt to re-write the axiological foundations of the constitution proved to be successful, as it encouraged the constitutional court to look at its role in a new light and develop several new concepts and ideas. During the following years, the December Amendment—particularly its rule-of-law provision—served as a vehicle for several key judicial decisions that filled gaps in the existing constitutional texts.[9] Another amendment adopted in March 1990 provided for a new system of local government, and within the next two years, parliament adopted three less important amendments.

All amendments were elaborated within parliament, where the Sejm political elite was the real center of decisions, but all were understood as temporary solutions to the most pressing problems. Therefore, not much attention was given to the amendments' coherence with the original text. Implementing and interpreting such a constitutional patchwork soon became a major challenge.

1991–93: Parliamentary Elections and the Small Constitution

The first stage of the political transition was completed in autumn 1991, when new parliamentary elections took place (Walesa had assumed the presidency of Poland earlier, at the end of 1990). The new parliament was elected by undoubtedly democratic rules,[10] but more than twenty political parties were represented in the first chamber, and the parliament's political fragmentation did not allow too much optimism for the constitution-making process. Thus, the parallelism of constitutional preparations had been maintained: On one hand, the writing of the full constitution had continued; on the other hand, some most pressing changes had to be introduced into the old constitution for the government to function.

The most important amendment was labeled the Small Constitution: On October 17, 1992, a new set of rules concerning the legislative and executive branches was adopted, replacing most provisions of the 1989 April Amendment.[11] The main idea was to eliminate ambiguities in the April Amendment and to limit the powers of the president of the republic. President Walesa had presented first drafts in autumn 1991. The Council of Ministers and some political parties presented drafts later. In spring 1992, a special Sejm committee was created with the task of preparing a final draft of new rules for the separation of powers between the legislative and the executive branches. The committee's final discussions took place after the fall of Olszewski's cabinet[12] and were marked by an open clash between representatives of the president, who was not ready to allow limitations of his powers, and the parliamentary majority, centered around the Democratic Union (UD) and the Alliance of Democratic Left (SLD). In effect, a compromised version of so-called rationalized parliamentarism was adopted, but the president maintained several important portfolios, particularly the armed forces and foreign policy.[13] Parliament, meanwhile, was too fragmented to survive the full term; in May 1993, a vote of no confidence in the Suchocka cabinet prompted Walesa to dissolve both houses. But the left won the new elections held in September, making a confrontation with Walesa unavoidable.

At the same time, the 1991 parliament continued preparations for the full constitution. Having learned that the parallel existence of two constitutional committees in the Sejm and Senate was counterproductive, parliament members agreed to establish a joint committee. On April 23, 1992, the Constitutional Law on the Procedure for Preparing and Enacting of the Constitution was adopted. The law provided for the establishment of a constitutional committee composed of forty-six Sejm members and ten Senate members—10 percent of the parliament's entire composition. Representatives of the president, cabinet, and constitutional court were included in the committee, but without the right to vote. The right to submit drafts of the constitution was given to the committee itself, to the president, and to any group of at least fifty-six parliamentary members. Drafts had to be submitted within six months of the committee's inauguration. After all drafts were submitted, the Sejm would hold a general debate on the principal constitutional issues, as suggested by the committee. Then the committee would prepare the consolidated draft of the constitution and submit it for a first reading in a national assembly—that is, the Sejm and the Senate convened as one body. The assembly had a choice between rejecting the draft and directing it back to the committee to prepare a final version. Once such a version had been completed, a second reading in the national assembly would take place. At this stage, individual deputies could propose amendments to the committee's draft. Then the vote would take place. Incorporating individual amendments and enacting the constitution would require a two-thirds majority of votes and the presence of at least 50 percent of the members of the national assembly. The president could submit his amendments within sixty days; in such a case, a third reading would take place. After debate, the assembly would first vote on each of the presidential amendments (an absolute majority being sufficient to incorporate them into the final text) and then on the final version of the constitution (a two-thirds majority of votes needed and a quorum of at least 50 percent required). The last stage in the proceedings would be a referendum, to take place within four months of the final national assembly vote. The constitution would then be accepted by more than 50 percent of voters participating in the referendum. No participation minimum was required.

Professor Osiatynski—who at that time was one of the experts of the constitutional committee—indicated later that

> this constitution-making procedure was the result of a heated debate and compromise between Parliament and the president. The procedure's purpose was to prevent solutions from being imposed by a temporary majority and then over-turned when a new majority emerged. The constitutional status of the 1992 Law (it could be changed only by a two-thirds majority in both houses of Parliament) was meant to guarantee the durability of rules governing the constitution-making process. Unfortunately, these rules did not prove adequate to overcoming the formidable obstacles to the creation of the new Constitution.[14]

The members of the constitutional committee were elected separately by both houses. The committee inaugurated its proceedings on October 30, 1992. The deadline for submitting drafts of the constitution ended on April 30, 1993. Thus, parliamentary drafting of the constitution was suspended for more than a year. Until the end of April 1993, the committee met seven times. On January 13, the committee adopted a standing order providing for the establishment of a coordinating council, composed of representatives of all parliamentary groups and acting as advisory body for the chairmen of the committee. Further, the standing order provided for six standing subcommittees on drafting, general matters, and introductory provisions; foundations of the political and socioeconomic system; sources of law; the legislative and executive branches and local government; protection of law and administration of justice; and rights and duties of citizens. The committee, as well as all subcommittees, could appoint permanent experts and also invite other state agencies or nongovernmental bodies to prepare opinions and participate in the proceedings. On March 24, the committee appointed all six standing subcommittees and their chairpersons from among its members.

The constitutional committee accepted seven drafts: the so-called Senate draft of March 24, 1993, submitted by fifty-eight members of parliament and repeating most of the draft prepared by the Senate constitutional committee of the former parliament; the SLD draft of April 28, submitted by members representing the Alliance of the Democratic Left; the UD draft of April 29, submitted by members representing the Democratic Union; the Peasant Party (PSL)-Union of Labour (UP) draft of April 30, submitted mostly by members of those parties; the presidential draft of April 30; the Confederation of Independent Poland (KPN) draft of April 30, submitted by members representing the Confederation of Independent Poland; and the Center Alliance (PC) draft of April 30, submitted by members mostly representing the Center Alliance. Four further drafts were submitted by parties and organizations that did not have sufficient parliamentary representation. They could not be officially accepted by the committee and were regarded as sources of information.

In May, the committee decided first to discuss all drafts. It managed to discuss four before the president dissolved parliament on May 29, 1993.

1993–97: Drafting the New Constitution

New elections were held on September 19, 1993.[15] In the Sejm, the SLD-PSL coalition gathered a clear majority. Thus, it became obvious that the speed and substance of constitutional drafting would now depend on the postcommunist wing of the parliament.

Immediately after the parliament's inauguration on October 14, 1993, both houses appointed their members of the constitutional committee. On November 9, the new committee was inaugurated, conferring the chairmanship to Aleksander Kwasniewski, who at the time was the leader of the SLD parliamentary group and later (December 1995) became the president of Poland. On January 18, 1994, the committee adopted its new standing order, identical in most provisions to the standing order of 1993. During the same meeting, the committee appointed all six permanent subcommittees and their chairpersons.

However, because the 1992 constitutional law provided that constitutional drafts could be submitted within six months of the inauguration, no substantive discussion would start before May 9, 1994. At the same time, the new coalition agreed that the 1992 constitutional law should be amended. The political background of this decision was the realization that several center and right parties had lost elections and were not represented in parliament. Thus, new procedures were proposed to gain more legitimacy for the parliamentary decisions. The amendment was finally adopted on April 22, 1994. It allowed the possibility to submit popular drafts of the constitution, if they were signed by at least 500,000 voters; continuous validity of the drafts submitted to the former parliament; and the possibility to conduct a prereferendum on principles of the future constitution.[16]

Three new drafts were submitted to the constitutional committee before May 9, 1994: the presidential draft of May 6, the UD draft of May 9, and the SLD draft also of May 9. All these replaced drafts submitted in spring 1993. Four other 1993 drafts retained their validity, but the authors of the PC draft decided to withdraw it from further proceedings. In June, the committee attempted to discuss all drafts[17] but could not go beyond that because of the April 22 amendment, which established a deadline of September 5 to submit popular drafts to the committee. Only one draft was submitted, signed by almost one million voters and politically sponsored by the Solidarity trade union and its leader, Marian Krzaklewski.[18]

In the meantime, the committee decided on the list of organizations and groups to be invited to participate permanently in its deliberations. The standing order gave the right to participate to the authors of all drafts submitted to the committee or inherited from the former term of parliament. Beyond that, it was agreed that invitations would be sent to all political parties that presented national lists in the last elections, independently of their electoral results.[19] Furthermore, invitations were sent to twelve trade unions and professional organizations and to eleven churches and religious groups.[20] There was no separate representation of the military.[21] The committee agreed also on a list of permanent experts: Five law professors were appointed and participated actively in all committee meetings as well as the work of subcommittees. Initially, in June 1994, the group of experts was composed of professors: Kazimierz Dzialocha (chairman), Osiatynski, Pawel Sarnecki, Piotr Winczorek, and Leszek Wisniewski. In March 1996, due to the resignation of Osiatynski and the election of Dzialocha to the Senate, two other professors—Maria Kruk and Marian Grzybowski—joined the expert group, and Winczorek became its chair. Together with representatives of the president, the council of ministers, and the constitutional court, the participation of which was mandated by the 1992 constitutional law, this was a group of about twenty outside persons actively participating in writing the constitution and enlarging the political spectrum of discussions.

Having received all drafts of the constitution, the committee sought to act promptly and, according to the declarations of Kwasniewski, its chairman, hoped to have the consolidated version ready by December 1994. On September 21–23, 1994, the national assembly convened for the first reading of all submitted drafts. The debate did not move far beyond mere formal presentation of all drafts. In conclusion, the assembly preliminarily accepted all drafts, not using its power to reject any of the drafts at this time. It was then a matter for the constitutional committee to produce a final draft of its own.

But creating the draft proved quite difficult for the committee. Already in autumn 1994, it became clear that the constitution would be an important issue in the coming elections, for president in autumn 1995 and parliament in autumn 1997. The SLD-PSL coalition had a safe majority in both the constitutional committee and the national assembly, but it still needed support from at least two other parliamentary groups to build the two-thirds majority necessary in the assembly for the final enactment of the constitution. The UP and the UD—later renamed the Union of Liberty (UW)—were two potential allies, but their support would require several compromises, and particularly for the UW, some compromises could be rather costly. At the same time, the constitution had to be accepted by popular referendum, and this was the stage at which the right wing of the political scene hoped to play an important role. It was also clear to the SLD that no referendum could be won if the Catholic Church openly disapproved of the new constitution. Thus, the role of some opposition groups, particularly the Church, went far beyond their formal positions in the constitutional committee.

At first, the committee tried to clarify some of the more difficult issues before writing the final version of the constitution. In the beginning of October 1994, the commission selected several problems to be discussed by the Sejm, as the 1992 constitutional law provided that after all drafts had been submitted, the Sejm would hold a general debate on the principal constitutional issues.[22] Deputies also received a large publication, *Basic Constitutional Dilemmas,* prepared by committee experts. The Sejm debate took place on October 21, but was mostly limited to declarations supporting particular drafts.

In the end, no resolutions or conclusions were adopted. Thus, the debate was of no help to the committee. Politicians were simply not ready to discuss constitutional questions; most of the questions that the committee submitted seemed too technical for most Sejm members.

At the same time, two procedural controversies already indicated that it would not be easy to get the opposition to accept the constitution. The first was related to the prereferendum provided by the 1994 amendment to the 1992 constitutional law. The opposition demanded such prereferendums on several major issues, hoping to gain an opportunity to obtain political support among the voters. For exactly the same reason, the majority did not want any prereferendum campaign. From a more technical perspective, it was determined that it would be extremely difficult to draft short questions to be submitted to the people. Thus, no prereferendum was held under the pretense that the constitution's final draft was too advanced to return to basic questions.[23]

The second controversy was related to the question of how the so-called popular draft of the constitution should be treated. Already in autumn 1994, Krzaklewski demanded that this draft be submitted to a national referendum as an alternative to the draft prepared by parliament. This would require amending the 1992 constitutional law, as it would place the Solidarity draft at a higher level than all remaining drafts and would transform constitutional discussion into a political confrontation between the current majority and the emerging extraparliamentary opposition.

Nevertheless, the constitutional committee managed to conclude the first stage of its proceedings with only a brief delay. On January 26, 1995, the committee adopted the "Uniform Draft of the Constitution." The draft prepared by the subcommittee for drafting, general matters, and introductory provisions on January 20 was discussed, revised, and adopted by the committee on that day. Meant to merge the seven submitted drafts into one, the draft was composed of 215 articles and eleven chapters. Further committee proceedings would concentrate on this unified draft. Thus, it was clear that the committee did not want to accept Solidarity's idea to grant special treatment to the popular draft. The Uniform Draft did not solve all problems, however; in almost all controversial matters, the committee presented alternative proposals. Thus, it was clear that the constitution-writing process would not end in the immediate future. Nor had the general political situation suggested any compromises.

In the beginning of 1995, the conflict between President Walesa and the parliamentary majority reached its climax. A shaky compromise was finally reached in April.[24] Leading politicians had neither time nor interest to think about the new constitution, and the constitutional committee remained inactive during the four months of crisis. In late spring, politicians began to focus on the upcoming presidential elections and did not want to open debates by presenting a final draft of the constitution. Aleksander Kwasniewski—then chairman of the constitutional committee—won the presidential election, but the losing side undertook a last attempt to launch espionage accusations against the prime minister and, indirectly, other leading SLD politicians. It took another two months before the political situation stabilized and the new cabinet, led by Wlodzimierz Cimoszewicz, was formed.

The presidential election and the subsequent crisis affected the constitutional committee in a double sense. Kwasniewski had to devote most of his time to the presidential campaign and, after his election, had to be replaced. In December 1995, his position was taken by Cimoszewicz, but two months later, Cimoszewicz accepted the position of prime minister and the committee again had to find a new chairman. In February 1996, Marek Mazurkiewicz, a professor of law, was elected to chair the committee until the end of its existence. In the meantime, leading politicians were so occupied with current political problems that they neglected their committee duties. Thus, there were problems obtaining a quorum, which often made it impossible to make any decisions. Nevertheless, the committee tried to do its best. It was difficult to reach a political consensus, but still possible to work on detailed problems. This allowed more room for experts, who played an important role in this period of constitution writing.

The constitution-writing process finally accelerated in spring 1996, as the coalition—particularly the SLD—understood that successfully completing the constitution might increase its chances in parliamentary elections. Over the next three months, the committee managed to conclude preparation on subsequent chapters of the document. On June 19, 1996, the committee adopted the Uniform Draft, now composed of 221 articles and thirteen chapters.[25] This time the committee decided not to include any alternative proposals in the text. According to Ryszard Chrusciak,

> the period between January 26, 1995 and June 19, 1966 constituted the most important part of the constitutional preparations. . . . It would not be an exaggeration, if we assume that active participation in the constitution writing had been undertaken only by a dozen members of the Committee. They were supported, in a competent and effective way, by the Committee's experts who prepared proposals of subsequent articles and delivered the necessary information. They were also real authors or co-authors of many amendments submitted by the Committee members.[26]

The Uniform Draft was submitted to another group of experts who were asked to edit it technically for language coherence and other editorial matters. On August 27, 1996, the subcommittee for drafting, general matters, and introductory provisions adopted a new version of the Uniform Draft, accepting most of the experts' suggestions. This material was submitted to the constitutional committee for final preparation. Over the next five months, the committee discussed all the constitution's chapters again. This time, there was no possibility of adjourning decisions on controversial matters, and the committee—or rather, the politicians who led its work—had to make final decisions. A constitutional coalition of four parliamentary parties, the SLD, PSL, UP, and UW, emerged; the two smaller partners, the UP and UW, knew quite well that without their support, it would be impossible to obtain a two-thirds majority. Thus, they sought more concessions than their numerical strength suggested they could.[27] On the other hand, it was clear that other parliamentary parties and, more important, Krzaklewski's Solidarity group, which was about to form Electoral Action Solidarity (AWS), had already chosen confrontation and would not support anything short of the full acceptance of the 1999 popular draft. Thus, for the constitutional coalition, the position of the Catholic Church was crucial: Without at least friendly neutrality, the referendum would be lost. Several amendments introduced to the Uniform Draft at the end of 1996 and beginning of 1997 were intended to give necessary concessions to the Church and divert it from supporting the so-called anticonstitutional coalition led by the AWS.[28]

The committee intended to conclude its debates on December 19, 1996. But at the last moment, the PSL—technically still a coalition partner of the SLD—submitted still more amendments and declared that it would not support the new constitution unless these amendments were included in the final version. After one month of discussion, a compromise was reached, and on January 16, 1997, the committee adopted its ultimate version of the new constitution, now 237 articles in thirteen chapters. One of the most important last-minute changes was to introduce a preamble referring to God, adopted to soften the Catholic Church's criticism of the constitution. The committee also submitted forty-seven so-called minority motions to be voted by the national assembly.[29]

January–April 1997: Conclusion of the Parliamentary Procedure

On January 24, the national assembly began its second reading of the constitution. As chairman of the constitutional committee, Mazurkiewicz presented the draft. Later, representatives of the parliamentary groups expressed their positions. While the constitutional coalition—the SLD, PSL, UP, and UW—supported the draft, the parties on the right declared their opposition to the proposed version of the constitution. The floor was also given to Krzaklewski, who was not a member of parliament, on behalf of the popular draft. He criticized the committee's draft proposal and asked to conduct an alternative referendum on both drafts. It became open season for constitutional amendments. In further discussions held February 25–28, over two hundred members took the floor and submitted almost five hundred amendments, some of a quite substantial character.

The constitutional committee discussed the amendments together with the minority motions that committee members had submitted in March. Because some amendments had been withdrawn by their authors, the committee decided on 362 amendments, recommending 113 amendments for adoption.

The second assembly reading continued on March 21. The assembly adopted almost one hundred amendments (i.e., not all the amendments that the committee recommended) and two minority motions. Aside from the preamble, 70 articles were amended and 5 new articles added to the constitution. The constitutional committee checked

the final text yet again, submitting another 5 amendments). On March 22, the assembly adopted the constitution—now 242 articles in thirteen chapters. Out of 560 members, 497 took part in the vote: 461 voted for it, 31 against it, and 5 abstained.

The president then had sixty days to submit his amendments to the constitution. However, because time was running out,[30] on March 24, the president submitted amendments relating to forty-one articles of the constitution. Most of the important amendments dealt with church-state relations, presidential powers to appoint the highest judicial officers, and military appointments. On March 26, the constitutional committee examined the amendments and recommended that the assembly adopt thirty-one of them.

The national assembly's third reading took place on April 2, 1997. It first voted on the presidential amendments and later took the final vote on the constitution. Out of 497 members who took part, 451 voted for it, 40 against it, and 6 abstained. Thus the constitution was adopted: Its final version had 243 articles in thirteen chapters. The parliamentary stage of the proceedings was now complete, and the constitution faced a national referendum.

May 1997: Constitutional Referendum

The 1992 constitutional law provided that the president should set the date for a referendum on the constitution within fourteen days of the national assembly adopting it. The referendum also had to take place within four months of the constitution's passage in parliament. To seize the moment, Kwasniewski issued the referendum order on April 2, setting the referendum for May 25. Each voter had a choice between voting for or against the entire text of the constitution.

The referendum offered the AWS-led anticonstitutional coalition a last chance. While the AWS had no chance at all to win any votes within the national assembly, it could still convince the majority of voters to reject the constitution. The AWS had no alternative but to condemn the constitution and ask Poles to vote against it. The referendum was preceded by an extensive information campaign, sponsored and coordinated mainly by the state electoral commission,[31] intended to acquaint the public with the substance of the new constitution and the main arguments for and against it. This effort largely descended into an electoral campaign in the nature of propaganda rather than education. Opponents of the constitution used rather unsophisticated arguments against its authors.[32]

The state electoral committee strictly regulated television coverage of the campaign and decided that two deputies and two senators, representing views for and against the constitution, would host programs. In addition to public television programs, private radio and television stations, newspapers, and periodicals presented discussions and debates. President Kwasniewski's staunch support of the new constitution and active promotion of it, not only during the television programs stipulated by the electoral commission, but also during his extensive travels around the country, provoked the greatest controversy.[33] On April 23, the AWS filed a formal complaint with the state electoral commission, claiming that the president should discuss the constitution neutrally without stating his opinion. On April 30, the commission issued a reply in favor of the president.[34]

The debate's tone largely ignored substantive constitutional issues. Opponents of the constitution accused its authors of intending to deprive Poland of its sovereignty, because Article 90 provided for the possibility of a transfer of powers of the national government in certain areas to an international organization or an international agency; of intending to take children away from their parents, because Article 48 stipulated that parents should consider their children's ma-

turity as well as their freedom of conscience and beliefs; and of giving state finances to a powerful agency beyond anyone's control, because Article 227 established the Monetary Policy Council, which was to determine annual monetary policy guidelines. Opponents also criticized the preamble for failing to condemn communist rule and for promoting a New Age god rather than the Catholic god. The debate also had a more serious dimension, though it was significantly less prominent. Most constitutional and legal experts pointed out that the new constitution represented important progress in rights and liberties, that most of its provisions met European standards, and that, whatever its shortcomings, it would serve its purpose very well.[35]

The Catholic Church's position on the constitution was not fully clear. While initially the Church refused to follow AWS invitations to condemn the new constitution, the final statement of the Episcopate of Poland was reserved[36]; it could be interpreted as a suggestion to vote against the constitution.

The referendum took place on May 25, 1997. The campaign's intensity did not convince voters to mass participation: Only 42.86 percent (i.e., 12,137,136) of eligible voters decided to cast a ballot. Thus, the constitution had to gather at least 6,068,569 affirmative votes. It received 6,396,641 supporting votes, or 52.7 percent. This was enough to have the constitution confirmed, but the result demonstrated the mounting support for the AWS.[37]

On July 15, 1997, after having examined 433 challenges, the Supreme Court decided that the referendum had been valid, and on July 16, the president ceremonially signed the constitution. It was published in the *Journal of Laws* on the same day. According to Article 243, the constitution became effective three months later, on October 17, 1997. Thus, almost eight years after the Sejm and Senate had appointed the first constitutional committees, the constitution-writing process in Poland came to a successful conclusion.

Constitution Writing and the Reconciliation Process

General Issues

The Function of the Constitution-Writing Process

To a large extent, a constitution-writing process depends on the nature, duration, and intensity of the political conflict, and on the role that a constitutional amendment or new constitution should play in solving that conflict. Sometimes, a new constitution is understood as a vehicle of transformation; such was the intent of those who wrote Poland's 1791 constitution, though in the existing political circumstances and international setting, this constitution had to fail. To a lesser extent, those who wrote the 1921 constitution also had transformation in mind, and they used it quite successfully to breathe new life into the Polish state. The aims of the three constitutional documents that emerged between 1989 and 1997, however, were less ambitious.

The 1989 April Agreement was the best example of a constitutional change that was closely related to the "peace negotiations"— that is, the Round Table talks—and was understood as one of the implementation tools of the agreement concluded between the ancien regime and new revolutionary movement. But the connection between political agreement and constitutional amendment was so close that the constitution-writing process lost its authenticity. As most of the amendment was agreed to and even written during the Round Table negotiations, parliamentary participation in the proceedings was rather formal and did not leave any room for discussion or change. The real decisions were made elsewhere. This was easily explained by the limited level of legitimacy of the existing Sejm. It not only subordinated constitu-

tion writing to political negotiations but also agreed to numerous compromises that could hardly coexist in one constitutional document. The April Amendment played a very important role during the first months of transformation—it paved the way for democratic elections and allowed the opposition to enter the parliament—but by autumn 1989, the whole structure of the Round Table agreement had disintegrated and the amendment, with its strong presidency, became an obstacle to the normalization process.

The 1992 Small Constitution thus emerged as a type of peace instrument, but the dimension of the conflict was completely different than in 1989. While the 1989 amendment was included in a resolution fundamental to the future of Poland, the 1992 Small Constitution was intended to end a conflict within the ruling elites and to create the possibility of cohabitation between President Walesa and the parliamentary majority. Thus, the constitution-writing process was concentrated within parliamentary committees that served as forums for reaching compromises. But the process of transformation was already advanced in Poland, and it was not crucial whether the Small Constitution would come into life at all, nor what its content would be.

The 1997 constitution was understood as an instrument of normalization, but the conclusion of its writing process was not intended to solve any immediate crisis. A new constitution was necessary to give the transformation process a modern framework, but probably nothing would have changed if the constitution had been adopted in 1996 or 1998. Of course, enacting the new constitution was regarded as a success, particularly for the SLD. The SLD understood, however, that because the new constitution would significantly weaken the presidency—held at that time by Kwasniewski—it could better help the AWS in case the party won parliamentary elections. Thus, the SLD attempted to rewrite presidential powers at the last mo-ment and rather unsuccessfully. In sum, the long-term effects of the 1997 constitution were understood as prevailing over short-term effects. At the same time, the last stage of constitution writing opened the floor for a serious political conflict between the consti-tutional coalition, which was identified with 1989 Round Table partners, and the new AWS movement, which represented a more radical approach to the past. Thus, in the short term (summer 1996 to spring 1997), the constitution-writing process not only failed to resolve existing conflict, but was used as a pretext to mount a political conflict of major dimensions. This conflict was resolved once the AWS won parliamentary election. Only a few months later, both sides understood that some degree of cohabitation would be nec-essary and that it could be done within the rules that the new constitution provided.

Enacting the 1997 constitution was de-tached, in time and political context, from concluding the "peace agreement" at the 1989 Round Table. The constitution-writing process incorporated into the peace agree-ment had been clearly visible in drafting the April Amendment, but it was absent in the second half of the 1990s, when the 1997 con-stitution was drafted. That time, the drafting process was concentrated within parliament and mostly interested only a small group of politicians and experts, and there was no ex-ternal peace agreement to be incorporated into the constitution.

Constitution Writing and the Old Constitution

From the very beginning of the transforma-tion process, it was clear that the 1952 con-stitution could not survive the fall of com-munism; a new constitution was required. In late autumn 1989, it also became clear that the new constitution would follow Western examples, departing sharply from the tradi-tion of socialist constitutionalism. Therefore,

there was an almost immediate opening of the constitution-writing process. The initial idea, supported mainly by Mazowiecki and Bronislaw Geremek, was to enact the new constitution promptly, preferably for the two-hundredth anniversary of the 1791 con-stitution. But political developments, in par-ticular the so-called war at the top,[38] made it impossible to agree on the constitution.

Hence, parallel paths of constitutional change evolved, including the writing of a new "full" constitution and an effort to revise fragments of the old constitution through an amendment process. Such an approach meant that the old constitution would con-tinue its existence, at least for the immedi-ate future. Some portions of the constitution had been revised already in the 1980s (the establishment of the constitutional court was the most important change), and it was simply impossible to ignore its existence. At the same time, the problem of the old law was much broader and had to be solved for all statutes and regulations adopted under the communist system. Some supported a so-called zero option—that is, declaring the total invalidity of communist laws—but it was obvious that such a move would produce legal chaos and the population would not ac-cept it. The zero-option would have invali-dated most of the social entitlements legis-lation in place and affected the structure of agricultural private property, a major concern in Poland. Thus, old laws had to be regarded as valid. It was the task of the parliament and cabinet to replace them as soon as necessary. In the meantime, it was the task of the judi-ciary to reinterpret old laws according to a new situation.

The same approach applied to the con-stitution. Some of its provisions had already been revised by April 1989, but several re-mained unchanged. Amendments modified mainly structural parts of the constitution; only the 1989 December amendment enu-merated new constitutional principles. The courts also did not enforce some of the old constitutional provisions. Instead, judges, particularly in the constitutional court, referred to the new constitutional principles, mainly the Rechtsstaat principle, and in some cases, rewrote them using both new constitutional principles and provisions of the European Convention on Human Rights. In this way, the judicial branch civilized and modernized the old constitution and prepared a relatively smooth transition to the post-1997 constitutional order.

Structure of the Process

There are numerous possibilities regarding the authority that can be given constitution-making power. In Poland, theoretically, the constitution could have been drafted by a specially elected constitutional convention or by the parliament itself. Another possibility would have been a combination of executive-branch drafting and popular referendum confirming the draft; such a procedure was used in France in 1958 and Russia in 1993. However, the latter procedure would have bypassed the parliament and contradicted the Polish constitutional tradition. Also, a constitutional convention would not have been practicable in the specific conditions of Polish political developments. It would have been premature to establish such a convention in spring 1989. Later, it was the timing and manner of parliamentary elections that became the main political issue. Once a new, democratically elected parliament emerged in 1991, it had full legitimacy and competence to write the constitution. Because all Polish constitutions in the past had been drafted within the legislative branch, another way could hardly be regarded as legitimate.

The choice between parliament and constitutional convention did not exist in spring 1989, when the April Amendment was drafted. There was no time to convene any

conventions and no possibility of having a democratically elected convention before establishing a constitutional foundation for democratic elections. Besides, the amendment was regarded only as a temporary solution: As already mentioned, it was drafted within the Round Table structure and with the assistance of Round Table experts. The role of the (old) parliament was limited to its formal approval and enactment. From 1991 on, when full democratic elections came into being, new parliaments enjoyed a sufficient level of legitimacy to draft the constitution. Hence, no serious proposals concerning separate constitutional conventions were ever submitted.

After the unfortunate experience of parallel constitutional committees in the Sejm and Senate (1989–91), it was agreed that the only way to conclude constitutional preparations successfully would be to fix rigid procedural rules and create a joint parliamentary committee. This explains how the 1992 constitutional law and the constitutional committee of the national assembly came into being. Although the committee was formally subordinated to the parliament, it enjoyed a considerable degree of autonomy; most of Poland's leading politicians became committee members, and members of the committee were designated by all parliamentary groups, according to their strength. It was clear that the new constitution would be drafted mainly within the committee.

Committee membership was a mix of pure and expert politicians. As mentioned before, at least a dozen members were active in the actual writing process. Most of the writing was done in subcommittees, usually with considerable participation by committee experts, all leading scholars in constitutional law, none of them directly involved in political activity.[39]

There were no specific provisions regarding judicial review of the actions of the constitution-making bodies, and it remains an open question as to what extent the constitutional court has jurisdiction over constitutional laws and amendments. As none of the Polish constitutions has ever had any unchangeable provisions (e.g., Article 79, Section 3 of the 1949 German basic law or Article 89, Section 5 of the 1958 French constitution), no substantive review of constitutional amendments is permitted. But it is not impossible that the court would accept its jurisdiction with regard to procedural review if the procedure to enact a constitutional amendment were not followed. No challenges have been raised to the drafting process of the 1997 constitution.[40]

Public Participation in the Process

In Poland, constitution writing took place in parliament (1992 and 1997) or within the Round Table talks (1989). The level of democratic representation in deciding or co-deciding actual content was crucial for legitimizing the process (see next section). At the same time, direct and indirect participants in the drafting process had to maintain at least some contact with the general public. Thus, public participation played an input and an output role. The input role invited the general public to influence the writing process by communicating suggestions and demands to the political decision makers and parliamentary drafters (active input) as well as forcing the drafters to calculate in advance whether their decisions would be accepted in the referendum. The real chance that different groups' and organizations' suggestions and proposals would be adopted depended on the political strength of their authors. In this respect, the crucial role belonged to the Catholic Church. The output role permitted the use of drafting discussions to educate the general public in constitutional matters, encourage the active return of comments and

suggestions, and gain votes for the next parliamentary elections.

Public participation requires a certain degree of transparency and information about the drafting process. This was the role of the drafting body, but it could not be reasonably achieved without the press and electronic media. An independent media was one of the crucial prerequisites for genuine participation in the constitutional deliberation. Generally speaking, public participation further requires certain avenues of bottom-to-top communication that are the purview of not only an independent media but also political parties and other interest groups. A genuine constitutional discussion can take place only after civil society has reached a certain level of maturity. In Poland, modern civil society began to emerge during the first Solidarity era (1980–81) and the period of martial law. By 1988–89, both an organized opposition and an active general public were in place when the Round Table ideas were prepared and discussed. The following years completed the initial stage of shaping an emerging civil society. When constitutional discussions entered their final stage (1996–97), all the necessary components of a civil society were in place.

A distinction should be made between the constitutional education of the general public and constitutional advocacy. The latter resulted from the necessity to have the constitution confirmed in the popular referendum. That was why all political decision makers became very interested not only in informing the general public about the constitution but also to convince it to vote for or against the draft. Another distinction relates to education (advocacy) and participation. The general public had only one formal avenue of participation: the referendum. Participation in the drafting process had to be exercised through different bodies, in which active members of the public were organized: political parties, including those not represented in parliament; trade unions; and many other similar organizations.

The April 1989 amendment was written during closed sessions of the Round Table's subcommittees, and agreement on the most important parts was reserved for a small group of leaders acting outside the Round Table structure. Except for regular press and television information on the progress of talks, the general public was never formally involved. At that time, all media were still controlled by the Communist Party and the public did not trust them. Solidarity politicians demanded and received certain access to radio and television, but their access remained limited and controlled by the government. However, this represented enormous progress compared to the situation in the past. For most people who had an interest in politics, there were other ways to keep informed, as the Polish general public has always been quite smart in receiving and passing on information by word of mouth.

In 1992, the situation changed. On one hand, drafting of the Small Constitution remained in the hands of a small group of politicians and experts, and unlike in 1989, the general public did not perceive the process as crucial for the future of Poland. Thus, there was relatively limited interest in it. On the other hand, free media had already emerged in Poland by that time, and again unlike in 1989, there was no problem in communicating or obtaining information. Nevertheless, the writing process remained concentrated within parliament, and public input was limited.

Public participation gained importance during the drafting process of the 1997 constitution. There were three contributing factors. The first was time, as the drafting process lasted long enough for public discussions to take place. The second was the referendum, as the requirement to have the constitution confirmed by a popular vote made the general public a necessary partner in enacting the document. Therefore, both proponents and opponents of the constitution had an interest in communicating with the general public. The third was politics, as the drafting process became closely connected with parliamentary elections in its final stage. The constitution thus played an important role in electoral campaigns. The constitutional coalition tried to use enacting the constitution as an asset in its preelection propaganda. The anticonstitutional opposition did its best to criticize the constitution and especially those who had drafted it.

For the above reasons, constitutional problems were constantly present in political discussions and mass media at least until the May 1997 referendum. While the constitutional committee as such had no responsibilities for public education, the task was undertaken partly by President Kwasniewski and partly by political parties and other groups. Thus, it was not regarded as necessary to organize any formalized constitutional discussion, led by the committee.[41] Nevertheless, every household received a copy of the constitution, mailed by the president's office, with an encouragement to read and support it in the referendum. Political actors did their best to attract the general public and convince voters of their ideas and proposals. This did not mean, however, that their attempts were successful. Low participation in the referendum (42.86 percent) demonstrated that the majority of the general public was neither interested in the constitutional discussions nor attracted by the political controversies surrounding them. While there was a general trend of political passivity in Poland, it was not accidental that participation in the constitutional referendum was lower than in the parliamentary elections of 1997 (47.93 percent) and 2001 (46.29 percent).[42]

Generally speaking, public participation in the constitution-drafting process has had different levels and dimensions. While its effect was not particularly evident between

1992 and 1996, the situation changed once political parties understood that they could use constitutional discussions to rally citizens around their programs. Unfortunately, in many cases, constitutional discussions were a tool to achieving other political goals and were not intended to modify the constitution meaningfully.

Regarding the usefulness of the referendum requirement, three remarks should be made. First, the referendum was conducted only after the final text of the constitution had been adopted. Thus, there was no possibility of modifying its text; the only choice was to approve or reject it. Because most voters had been unwilling or unable to study the entire text, their decisions were influenced mainly by political sympathies. Second, the drafters well understood the necessity of winning the referendum. Thus, the (passive) effect of public opinion was that the drafters had to concede to powerful social groups and avoid solutions that could provoke public opposition. This was also well understood by some social partners of the drafting process, especially trade unions and the Catholic Church. Third, the constitution's confirmation in the referendum legitimized the document and contributed to the public's accepting it.[43]

The question remains whether a prereferendum, conducted in the early stages of the drafting process, would enrich public participation in the drafting process. We do not know the answer, but given the political realities of the mid-1990s, it is very probable that such a referendum would soon have been transformed into another political campaign, in which constitutional problems would be used only as a pretext for political confrontation.

Democratic Representation

A legitimate constitution can only be the product of a democratically legitimate assembly. Thus, the easiest way to legitimize a constitution is to start with democratic elections and draft a new constitution afterward. But who should create the rules to conduct the first democratic election if no truly representative institutions existed under the departing regime? Poland had to answer this question in spring 1989. As the existing Sejm, "elected" in 1986, was not sufficiently legitimate, it was necessary to create an extraparliamentary body—the Round Table—to launch the transition process. The Round Table had a bipolar structure of representatives of the existing government versus representatives of the opposition because it resulted from a peaceful agreement, not a revolution. There was no problem in defining who should represent the opposition. As the illegal Solidarity trade union had survived martial law, it was clear that Walesa and his advisers would appoint the oppositional representation. Finally, the Church's representative officially sat at the Round Table, and several key decisions resulted from Church-arranged political mediation. This gave some legitimacy to the Round Table agreement and, consequently, to the April Amendment and June parliamentary election. But it was very clear that this legitimacy was temporary, and by autumn 1989, a legitimacy conflict erupted between both houses that prevented the 1989 parliament from adopting a new constitution.

The 1991 and 1993 parliamentary elections produced democratic legislatures. Hence, the legitimacy problem ceased to exist. There was no doubt that constitution drafting could take place within the existing parliament—that is, that the task should be given to political parties represented in parliament. This was finally decided in the 1992 constitutional law providing for establishment of the national assembly's constitutional committee. The committee was composed exclusively of members of parliament, as all parliamentary groups had proportional representation. The choice of the parliamentary process—a process controlled by political parties—resulted from the sufficient legitimacy of the existing parliament; the relative strength of the existing political parties, as at least the partners of the constitutional coalition have managed to survive to this day; and the relative homogeneity of Polish society. With no major ethnic, religious, or regional conflicts, it was possible to link the constitution-drafting process almost exclusively to the political preferences of Polish voters.

Since 1993, the constitutional committee has been controlled by postcommunist parties, the SLD and PSL, whereas the political right has had very weak parliamentary representation. It could not negate the legitimacy of the 1993 Sejm because the underrepresentation of the right had resulted from its inability to attract voters as well as from the operation of the 1993 electoral law[44]—a law was adopted by the 1991 parliament, in which the majority belonged to those center-right parties that were to lose the next elections and disappear from the 1993 parliament. However, it still produced a certain feeling of uneasiness among the majority parties. Thus, several efforts were made to enlarge the representative character of the constitutional committee. The new committee accepted drafts submitted to the former committee, even if the drafts' authors were no longer represented in parliament. Permanent invitations to participate in committee proceedings were issued to extraparliamentary parties, particularly Solidarity and its political emanation, the AWS. The possibility of submitting popular drafts was opened to large groups of citizens. Also, the committee recognized the specific role of the Catholic Church, as its representatives received a permanent invitation to participate. The Church accepted this invitation, and played a significant role in drafting the constitution. Thus, the decision-making process led to establishing compromises on three levels: first, within the SLD-PSL majority (and the

PSL was not an easy partner), which was strong enough to control committee decisions; second, within the constitutional coalition, in which two other parties—the UP and UW—were necessary to reach the two-thirds majority required in the national assembly); and third, outside the coalition, to win the referendum.[45]

Of course, not all minority interests found full access to the constitutional coalition. For many of them, the supermajority requirement in the national assembly and the subsequent referendum constituted sufficient guarantees to be heard, but other interests remained too weak to attract the support of political parties. Additional guarantees, however, were provided by international law, particularly from the European Human Rights Convention.

The lustration (vetting) problem surfaced in Poland in summer 1992, but necessary statutes were not adopted before spring 1997. Thus, the constitution had been drafted and adopted before the lustration process started. The lack of a prior lustration process did not affect the substance or the quality of the constitution. The later experience with the lustration process in Poland could hardly be evaluated as positive. Had it started earlier, it would have only provided another field of political controversy.

The Timing and Sequencing of the Constitution-Making Process

Constitution writing in Poland took a relatively long time—nearly eight years. There were three separate stages to this process: enactment of the April Amendment (February–April 1989), writing of the Small Constitution (December 1991–October 1992), and writing of the final constitution (October 1992–April 1997). In the first stage, a provisional regulation was adopted quickly. It allowed parliamentary elections to be held in June 1989 and a constitutional dimension to the transition process to begin. Once Solidarity had built a majority coalition within the Sejm, in August 1989, its initial idea was to proceed fast and adopt a new constitution on May 3, 1991. Political developments in 1990 made this impossible, and the constitutional moment was lost. Another provisional regulation was thus adopted—the Small Constitution—while preparations for the full constitution continued with deliberate speed.

The longevity of the constitution-drafting process was due to several circumstances. First, it was impossible to predict the political dynamics affecting developments in Poland and Europe. The April Amendment originally intended to allow a peaceful cohabitation of the Communist Party and Solidarity political forces. In spring 1989, no one could have known that six months later, the Warsaw Pact would disintegrate and communist rule in Poland would cease. Also, in fall 1989, no one could have known how fast Solidarity would split into new political groups or how fast postcommunist parties would be able to win democratic elections. Thus, no time limits could have been set in the beginning, and the target date of May 3, 1991, became completely unrealistic.

Most of the constitution writing took place in the 1993 parliament, with the legislature setting the time limit of completion by September 1997. The parliament managed to beat the deadline by several months, but the new constitution entered into effect only two days before the inauguration of the next parliament.

The longevity of the constitution-writing process had some clear advantages as well as some disadvantages. Of course, the process looks different from today's perspective than it appeared in 1991 or 1993. Many authors regretted then that the "constitutional moment" had been definitely lost.[46] The absence of a full constitution caused several problems. However, all these problems were solved under various interim constitutional provisions,

and at the same time, important experiences were gathered and lessons learned. It was particularly important that the Walesa presidency demonstrated the need for very precise regulation of the relations between the executive and legislative branches. But what became clear in 1996 and 1997 was not clear at all in 1990 and 1991. Therefore, gradual writing of the constitution allowed Poland to introduce significant institutional and procedural guarantees that checked the power of the political branches of government.

A similar observation relates to Poland's bill of rights. The 1997 constitution was drafted after Poland had ratified the European Convention on Human Rights and other important international documents. The constitution drafters had no alternative than to accept and repeat the convention's provisions on personal and political freedoms. In the area of social and economic rights, the authors of the 1997 constitution knew that the social cost of transition could be much higher than predicted in 1990. They also knew that the constitutional court could not be expected to ignore constitutional provisions concerning social and economic rights. Thus, the 1997 constitution was careful in promising those rights. The 1997 constitution also had been drafted after the Concordat treaty with the Vatican had been signed.[47] While the SLD-PSL majority postponed the Concordat's ratification, it was clear that new constitutional provisions had to be adjusted to the treaty. Finally, the 1997 constitution was drafted in an international situation that allowed Poland to integrate into the North Atlantic Treaty Organization (NATO) as well as with the European Union. Accordingly, appropriate provisions were inserted into the constitution's text.

Generally speaking, the eight years of transition allowed the 1997 constitution to be drafted in a more mature way than would have been the case in 1990–91. The experience of the following years (1997–2002) demonstrated that this constitution could function as both a vehicle for the peaceful change of parliamentary majorities and Poland's advancement toward integration into the Western world.

It would be difficult to draw any general lessons from the time and sequencing of constitution writing in Poland. But at least three conclusions can be made. First, at the beginning of the transition process, it was necessary to promptly produce an interim constitutional document allowing democratic elections. This document could be considered a peace agreement. Second, it is usually impossible to predict the dynamics of any future transition process; setting time limits and target dates might not be productive. Third, it may be risky to live under an interim constitution, particularly if the executive branch tries to expand its powers. However, if a country and its democracy are lucky enough to survive a longer period of interim constitutions, it becomes easier to draft a constitution for the twenty-first century. Such a constitution could be regarded not as a peace agreement, but an instrument of normalization and stabilization, allowing for a robust political, social, and economic climate. Hungary's experience suggests similar conclusions.

There is always the danger that a prolonged process of constitution writing would allow some factions—in Poland, the postcommunist faction—to gain an unfair advantage and consolidate power before a democratic constitution can be adopted. Poland managed to avoid this danger. Even if the 1997 constitution had been adopted by a parliament dominated by postcommunist parties, its enactment did not save those parties from losing parliamentary elections in 1997 and did not help the center-right parties not to lose the 2001 elections. In short, the constitution has allowed a smooth trading of places of parliamentary majority and opposition. Given

Poland's turbulent history during the past century, this is no small achievement.

The Role of the International Community

The international community played a crucial role in supporting the first Solidarity movement (1980–81) and in encouraging the Round Table talks in 1988–89, as well as in helping to organize the process of transition. Foreign experts have been present constantly in the parliament, significantly contributing to the process of rewriting communist legislation. They also participated in the constitution-drafting process, particularly in the 1989 parliament. At the same time, however, some factors limited the foreign experts' role. First was the language problem. Only a few foreign experts spoke Polish well enough to be able to take part in the meetings and discussions. Only a few of them were experts in constitutional law. Second, because most of the experts were invited personally (or at least confirmed) by the administration of the parliament or directly by political parties, many experts were associated with definite political sympathies. Nevertheless, the participation of foreign experts in drafting the constitution was very useful. Most of them did their best not to show political sympathies and acted as neutral advisers, providing comparative information. The number of foreign experts began to diminish in the mid-1990s, perhaps due to limited financial resources. Once Poland became recognized as a stabilized country, most of the foreign aid was shifted further to the East. Finally, there was also a considerably large group of Polish scholars who could deliver the necessary information on comparative law and foreign constitutions. Liberalization of academic contacts with Western universities had already begun in Poland in the 1970s. Thus, the pool of Polish experts with considerable Western experience was deeper than in many other emerging democracies. In fact, international organizations frequently included Polish constitutionalists in consultative missions to countries of the former Soviet Union seeking constitutional change.

Essential Issues of Substance

The concept of immutable principles has never been adopted in Poland, and there were no serious proposals to include such principles in the 1997 constitution. However, international standards relating to the substance of the constitution, particularly its human rights standards, act as quasi-immutable principles because it would be extremely difficult to ignore or reject them. But care must be taken in developing a list of immutable principles beyond that. Declaring too many principles untouchable could soon produce a conflict with changing social and political context and a document that risks becoming quickly obsolete.

Conclusion

At this point in time, the longevity of the 1997 constitution allows for three general conclusions. First, the constitution has proven to be particularly stable. Its 1997 text has never been amended, and there was no serious attempt to do so until 2006. In spring 2006, the president introduced a proposal to amend Article 55, Section 1 of the constitution to harmonize it with European Union legislation on the so-called European Arrest Warrant.[48] Parliament adopted the amendment on September 8, 2006; it entered into life on November 7 of the same year.

Second, the constitution's stability resulted not only from the stability of Poland's internal and foreign position but also from numerous judicial decisions, particularly those of the constitutional court, which has developed and reinforced the constitution's written text.

Finally, the constitution has proven to be effective as a framework for political change. After the constitution was adopted, on April 2, 1997, three parliamentary elections took place. Each time, the former majority became a minority, and each time, that change was conducted smoothly, in full respect of constitutional rules. On two other occasions, in 2000 and 2004, the parliamentary majority disintegrated and the cabinet lost clear parliamentary support. Despite the inability to create a new majority in the House, the (now minority) governments managed to survive until the end of the parliament's four-year term. Constitutional provisions on relations between the legislative and the executive contributed to resolving the crises peacefully. Also, the next crisis, in 2007, was solved peacefully and entirely within the framework provided by the 1997 constitution. This time, the disintegration of the parliamentary majority prompted Prime Minister Jarosław Kaczyński to dissolve the 2005 parliament. The November 2007 elections shifted Kaczyński's party into the opposition benches, and the new cabinet was formed by a coalition led by Donald Tusk.

Thus, the 1997 constitution can be regarded as a success and a demonstration that the long time spent on its drafting was not wasted. It can be said that the constitution contributed to developing a stable democracy, or at least to the recognition that there are certain rules of political process and change. However, that assessment, generally shared among scholars and (less unanimously) among politicians, remains restricted to Poland's political and intellectual elites. The constitution is still too young to become a symbol of national reconciliation, and the storminess of Polish politics may prevent it from becoming such a symbol in the future.

Notes

1. See Mark F. Brzezinski and Lech Garlicki, "Polish Constitutional Law," in *Legal Reform in Post-Communist Europe: The View from Within*, eds. S. Frankowski and P.B. Stephan III (London: Kluwer, 1995), pp. 29–30.

2. It was agreed that while the Senate seats would be open to free election, the Sejm seats would be preassigned, so the opposition could gain no more than 35 percent of seats in the First House.

3. See Brzezinski and Garlicki, "Polish Constitutional Law," pp. 30–32; L. Garlicki, "The Development of the Presidency in Poland: Wrong Institutions or Wrong Persons?" in *Poland in a World in Change: Constitutions, Presidents, and Politics*, ed. K.W. Thompson (Lanham, MD: University Press of America, 1992), pp. 80–91.

4. One of the first challenges of the transition process was to establish political parties capable of functioning in the new political environment.

The Solidarity trade union could not be transformed into a political party, but its politicians organized at first the Democratic Union (Unia Demokratyczna, or UD), led by the first non-Communist prime minister, Mazowiecki, that later was transformed into Union of Freedom (Unia Wolnosci, or UW). Later, the liberal wing of that group organized the Civic Platform Party (PO) that won the parliamentary elections in 2007. Another group of Solidarity activists established, in 1990, the Center Alliance (Porozumienie Centrum, or PC), led by the brothers Kaczynskis. In 1996, the Center Alliance and several other political organizations formed the Electoral Action Solidarity (AWS), and this organization won the 1997 parliamentary elections but disintegrated four years later, giving way to the creation of the Law and Justice Party (PiS), led by the Kaczynskis, that won the 2005 parliamentary elections. Another party that emerged from the opposition movement was the Confederation of Independent Poland (KPN), more to the right in the political spectrum.

In the beginning of the 1990s, the more liberally oriented group of former Communist Party activists organized the Alliance of the Democratic Left (SLD), the party led initially by Kwasniewski (from 1995–2005, the president of Poland) that won parliamentary elections in 1993 and 2001. Another smaller political party of the left was the Union of Labour (UP), cooperating with the SLD in the second half of the 1990s.

Finally, there was the Peasant Party (PSL), situated more in the center and participating in the parliamentary majority on several occasions.

5. See Andrzej Balaban, "Developing a New Constitution for Poland," *Cleveland State Law Review*, vol. 41, no. 3 (Summer 1993), pp. 503–09.

6. Wiktor Osiatynski, "Poland's Constitutional Ordeal," *East European Constitutional Review*, vol. 3, no. 2 (Spring 1994), p. 30.

7. The total number of drafts reached eleven (for all texts see *Projekty konstytucyjne 1989–1991*, ed. M. Kallas (Warsaw: Wydawnictwo Sejmowe, 1992).

8. It was too early to have any comprehensive view on the constitutional issues that had to be handled immediately; the first priority was economic reform (later known as Balcerowicz's Plan). To avoid conflicts with the Communist Party, reforms of relations between the parliament and the executive branch had to be put off. Therefore, the first priority was rewriting the general principles of the constitution; its symbolic expression was the restoration of the crown on the head of the Polish white eagle.

9. See M.F. Brzezinski and L. Garlicki, "Judicial Review in Post-Communist Poland: The Emergence of a Rechtstaat?" *Stanford Journal of International Law*, vol. 31 (1995), p. 35; H. Schwartz, *The Struggle for Constitutional Justice in Post-Communist Europe* (Chicago: University of Chicago Press, 2000), p. 49.

10. The 1991 Sejm Electoral Act introduced the proportional system: Political parties and other organizations submitted lists of candidates for about fifty multiseat constituencies. The seats were allocated within each constituency following the Saint Lague method (slightly modified). In addition, sixty-nine seats were allocated on the national level, proportionally to the electoral results of competing parties. This system gave preference to small and medium-size parties and led to political fragmentation of the parliament. See M.T. Grzybowski, *Electoral Systems of Central Europe* (Krakow: Kielce, 1996), p. 43.

11. The Small Constitution did not contain any bill of rights; appropriate provisions of the 1952 constitution still remained in force. They clearly did not fit to the new system of government, and the task of adjusting them to new realities had been undertaken by the judicial branch, particularly by the constitutional court. By the end of 1992, Poland ratified the European Convention for the Protection of Human Rights and Fundamental Freedoms. At the same time, President Walesa submitted a draft bill of rights proposed as a constitutional law, supplementing gaps in the Small Constitution. See W. Osiatynski, "A Bill of Rights for Poland," *East*

European Constitutional Review, vol. 1, no. 4 (Fall 1992), p. 29. An interesting discussion developed among scholars, but the politicians were not particularly interested in supporting presidential initiatives, and the dissolution of the parliament in June 1993 ended the life of the presidential draft as well.

12. In May 1992, the Olszewski cabinet sought to disclose some alleged secret service files, demonstrating that many current politicians had ties with the Communist political police. It provoked a serious political crisis. Olszewski was dismissed by the Sejm (upon the motion of Walesa), and a new cabinet, led by Suchocka, was appointed in late July. See L. Garlicki, "The Polish Interim Constitution of 17 October 1992," in *The Presidency and Governance in Poland: Yesterday and Today,* ed. K.W. Thompson (Lanham, MD: University Press of America, 1984), pp. 68–69.

13. See Brzezinski and Garlicki, "Polish Constitutional Law," pp. 39–45.

14. Osiatynski, "Poland's Constitutional Ordeal," p. 29.

15. The old parliament managed, in May 1993, to adopt the new Sejm Electoral Act. The principle of proportional representation was maintained, but one of the goals of the new act was to prevent an excessive fragmentation of the chamber. The Saint Lague method of allocating seats was thus replaced by the d'Hondt method and a so-called electoral threshold, by which seats could be allocated only among parties that obtained at least 5 percent of the votes at the national level. In effect, only six parties were able to obtain seats in the Sejm—see Grzybowski, *Electoral Systems,* p. 49.

16. Writing the amendment was surrounded by sharp political controversies. Two drafts were submitted initially (by the KPN and the UP); later President Walesa made another proposal. "The president proposed to extend the right to submit drafts of the constitutions to groups of 100,000 citizens, who would thereby have the "public initiative." Representatives of the citizens' groups could participate actively in the work of the constitutional committee and would have the right to submit motions. The presidential proposal stirred severe criticism among the deputies, and on the motion of the UP, the Sejm rejected the presidential draft amendment on the first reading. After the draft was rejected, the president said that he would now "stop cooperating with Parliament in the creation of the Constitution." Subsequently, he also withdrew his representative from the constitutional committee. See "Constitution Watch: Poland," *East European Constitutional Review,* vol. 3, no. 2 (Spring 1994),

p. 15. The SLD politicians, however, did not want an open confrontation with Walesa. They proposed another version of the "public initiative," raising the threshold to 500,000 citizens' signatures. President Walesa unwillingly accepted, and his representatives returned to the committee.

17. "Unfortunately . . . only 16 of 56 Committee members bothered to attend the presentation ceremony. Absent a quorum, the Committee could not dispose of even the formalities and preliminary items of business" See "Constitution Watch: Poland," p. 15.

18. For the English translation of the draft, see *Constitution-Making Process,* ed. M. Wyrzykowski (Warsaw: Institute of Public Affairs, 1998), pp. 143–90.

19. Invitations were sent to eight parties, but none of them actually participated in the committee proceedings. See R. Chrusciak, *Przygotowanie Konstytucji RP z dnia 2 kwietnia 1997 r. Przebieg prac parlamentarnych* (Warsaw: Dom Wydawniczy Elipsa, 1997), p. 25.

20. As far as trade unions were concerned, they systematically participated through representatives of two major unions: OPZZ and Solidarnosc. More sporadic was attendance by representatives of the Solidarnosc 80 trade union, Confederation of Polish Employers, and the Central Council of Physicians. As far as the churches were concerned, representatives of the Catholic Church (as well as of two smaller churches) attended regularly, and the representatives of two other churches attended sporadically (Chrusciak, *Przygotowanie Konstytucji,* p. 25).

21. The Polish military had been important in preparing and executing martial law in the 1980s. Even if General Jaruzelski had been prime minister (1981–86) and chairman of the Council of State (1986–89), mainly his fellow generals ran the country. Generals like Jaruzelski and Kiszczak, supported by the liberal wing of the Communist Party, were also architects of the Round Table talks in 1989. But from 1990 on, the role of the military returned to its normal dimension, and there was no suggestion to include the military in either political decision making or the constitution-writing process.

22. The committee submitted questions related to three general areas. First was the political system: what version of the separation of powers should be adopted; whether the parliament should be composed of one or two chambers; what the position of local government should be; and how relations between the state and churches should be regulated. Second was social rights: whether the constitution should focus on individual rights or state goals; and whether social rights should be guaranteed at the constitutional or statutory level. Third was sources of law: what the fundamental sources of law should be and what the place of international law in the domestic legal order should be.

23. The motion to conduct a prereferendum was submitted by the UP members of the committee on September 27, 1995, and discussed in the constitutional committee during the fall of 1995. Initially, it seemed that it would gain support of the main political forces in the committee. In October, the committee appointed a subcommittee to examine the motion. On December 6, 1995, the subcommittee supported the motion and proposed four questions related to the structure of parliament (one or two chambers); the structure of local government; the mode of presidential elections (popular vote or parliamentary appointment); and church-state relations. As another referendum, related to property matters, had already been scheduled for the spring of 1996, the idea was to conduct both referendums simultaneously. On December 20, the constitutional committee accepted the subcommittee's proposals, but decided to limit its recommendation to general support of the prereferendum and abstained from submitting concrete questions to the national assembly. This suggests that not all committee members were fully convinced of the political usefulness of the prereferendum. The assembly discussed the matter twice—on December 22, 1995, and January 19, 1996—when the discussion was rather unexpectedly adjourned. Two days later, the assembly voted to reject the committee's proposal to conduct the prereferendum (222 members voted to reject, 131 to accept, and 18 abstained). The main argument, raised by the SLD, was that because the constitutional committee had already prepared the uniform draft of the constitution, it was too late to return to basic choices. See Chrusciak, *Przygotowanie Konstytucji*, p. 91.

24. Osiatynski, "A Letter from Poland," *East European Constitutional Review*, vol. 4, no. 2 (Spring 1995), p. 35.

25. M. Mazurkiewicz, "The Draft of the Constitution of the Republic of Poland (1996)," in *Constitution-Making Process*, p. 115. For the English translation of the draft, see pp. 191–250.

26. Chrusciak, *Przygotowanie Konstytucji*, pp. 89, 91.

27. One example relates to the role of the new presidency. Until the end of 1995, all parties of the constitutional coalition were of the opinion that presidential powers should be substantially reduced. There were frequent conflicts with Walesa, and the possibility that he would be elected for a second term was quite real. This convinced the parliamentary parties that the future constitution should strengthen the position of the prime minister at the presidency's expense. After Kwasniewski's victory in December 1995, the SLD, realizing that it might not win parliamentary elections in 1997, quickly rediscovered the virtues of a strong presidency. But the UW and the UP, as well as the PSL, did not share this view and successfully defended the original draft of the constitution.

28. At the time, there was no alternative to the constitution adopted within the assembly and the AWS draft. The Church leadership realized that if the new constitution were rejected in the referendum, no new draft would emerge in the foreseeable future. Thus, the real alternative was either to accept the new constitution as submitted by the constitutional committee or to live with the old 1952 constitutional provisions, which were not particularly friendly toward religion.

29. Among them were the so-called Senate's draft and the so-called popular draft.

30. Two important events should be considered. On one hand, parliamentary elections had to take place in September, and it would be impossible to hold the electoral and the referendum campaigns simultaneously. On the other hand, the Pope's visit to Poland was scheduled to begin in the end of May, and it would be highly improper to carry out the referendum campaign during his stay. Thus, the referendum had to take place before the Pope's visit. The electoral campaign would start immediately after his departure.

31. This body is composed of nine members, appointed in panels of three by the chief justice of the Supreme Court, chief justice of the High Administrative Court, and president of the constitutional court from among judges of each court.

32. "Constitution Watch: Poland," *East European Constitutional Review*, vol. 6, nos. 2–3 (Spring–Summer 1997), p. 26.

33. It should not be forgotten that Kwasniewski was instrumental in the constitution-writing process, as both the chairman of the constitutional committee and the president later. Thus, his degree of identification with the new constitution seemed to be more visible than in the case of some other SLD leaders.

34. "Constitution Watch: Poland" (Spring–Summer 1997), p. 26.

35. Ibid., p. 26.

36. "We call on everyone to make in their conscience a decision expressing their responsibility before God and nature, because the text of the Constitution rouses serious moral reservations." See "Constitution Watch: Poland" (Spring–Summer 1997), p. 26.

37. The success of the May referendum did not save the SLD-PSL coalition from losing the September parliamentary elections. The AWS emerged as a big winner and, together with the UW, constructed the Sejm majority and the cabinet. However, because Kwasniewski held the presidency, some kind of cohabitation had to be adopted. This was the moment in which the AWS understood some virtues of the new constitution. Had the 1997 constitution been rejected in the referendum, the AWS would have had to confront a more powerful president, as shaped by the 1992 Small Constitution. The 1997 constitution, with its strong prime minister and weaker president, offered more to the parliamentary majority. Ironically, the AWS did not regret acting under the new constitution, which it had attacked so sharply before the referendum. Hence, criticism of the constitution was soon abandoned, and the AWS never made any serious attempt to revise the constitution thereafter.

38. This was the slang term for the conflict between Walesa and Mazowiecki, which meant the end of the unity of the Solidarity movement.

39. That said, it was easy to detect the political sympathies of most experts. Only the first chairman of the expert group, Dzialocha, a former justice of the constitutional court, later entered the political field, becoming a member of parliament. Another expert, Grzybowski, became a justice of the constitutional court four years after the constitution had been enacted.

40. However, in 1992, when the Small Constitution was enacted, it had been preceded by an amendment to the Sejm Standing Order. The amendment changed the rules of voting on the Senate's amendments to constitutional laws, making it easier for the Sejm to reject such amendments. It was challenged before the constitutional court, but, in a judgment on November 17, 1992, the court decided that the amendment to the Standing Order was constitutional. Thus, indirectly, the court declared that the Small Constitution had been correctly enacted.

In 1997, the validity of the constitutional referendum was challenged on the grounds that the participation in the referendum did not exceed 50 percent. Because no minimum participation had been required by the 1992 Constitutional Law, the Supreme Court did not have any problems dismissing the challenge (judgment of June 15, 1997).

41. Any formalized discussion could also evoke unpleasant associations with the past. It should be remembered that such discussions were typical in the process of constitution writing in Communist countries. In Poland, "constitutional discussions" took place in 1952. According to the official data, more than 11 million citizens took part in more than 200,000 meetings within nine weeks. Needless to say, there was no room for any criticism, and the whole campaign had a purely decorative character. That was why, forty-five years later, any attempt to copy such a procedure would produce more distrust than support among the electorate. Poland's general public has always been very sensitive to historical comparisons, particularly in the negative sense.

42. But participation was much higher than in the property restitution referendum held on February 18, 1996, when only 32.4 percent of voters participated.

43. See J. Wawrzyniak, "Aksjologia referendum konstytucyjnego," in *Referendum konstytucyjne w Polsce*, ed. M.T. Staszewski (Warsaw: Friedrich Ebert Stiftung, 1997), pp. 189–93.

44. The Sejm Electoral Law provided for a proportional system with threshold requirements of 5 percent for parties and 8 percent for coalitions. Since the parties on the right had been fragmented, they did not manage to form sufficiently strong coalitions and most of their lists did not reach required thresholds. In effect, more than 30 percent of the votes were lost.

45. See Osiatynski's distinction between internal and external compromises in "Kilka uwag na temat trybu uchwalania Konstytucji III Rzeczypospolitej," in *Tryby uchwalania polskich konstytucji*, ed. M. Wyrzykowski (Warsaw: Instytut Spraw Publicznych, 1998), p. 91.

46. See, e.g., R. Chrusciak and W. Osiatynski, *Tworzenie konstytucji w Poskce w latach 1989–1997* (Warsaw: Instytut Spraw Publicznych, 2001), p. 62; Osiatynski, "Poland's Constitutional Ordeal," p. 30.

47. The Concordat is an international treaty, concluded with the Holy See, that regulates the position of the Catholic Church in a given country. In Poland, the Concordat was already signed in 1993 by the Suchocka cabinet, but the subsequent change in parliamentary majority delayed the ratification process (ratification of treaties is made by the president upon a consenting statute adopted by parliament), and formal ratification took place much later, in December 1997. Nevertheless, it was clear to the constitutional committee that any attempt to negate the Concordat provisions would be suicidal, as it would prompt the Catholic Church to join the anticonstitutional opposition and to suggest to Poles to vote no in the referendum.

48. Art. 55, sec. 1 provides that "the extradition of a Polish citizen shall be forbidden." The procedure of the European Arrest Warrant, adopted in the beginning of the current decade, requires all EU member states to deliver their citizens if so requested by judicial authorities of any other EU member. In Poland, the parliament decided initially that delivery did not equal extradition and, hence, was not covered by the constitutional prohibition. However, in April 2005, the constitutional court held this interpretation to be unconstitutional and invalidated portions of the code of the criminal procedure on the European Arrest Warrant implementation. The court indicated that to comply with EU obligations, Poland's constitution had to be amended within eighteen months.

15

Constitution Making and Democratization

The Spanish Paradigm[1]

Andrea Bonime-Blanc

As a type of political change, a transition from authoritarianism to democracy is on par, in its consequences, with a revolution, civil war, or coup d'etat. To understand transitions, one must first understand the nature of the regimes that the transition is evolving away from and toward. Spain in the 1970s was evolving away from an authoritarian regime, which Juan Linz defines as follows:

> Authoritarian regimes are political systems with limited, not responsible, political pluralism; without elaborate and guiding ideology (but with distinctive mentalities); without intensive or extensive political mobilization ... and in which a leader (or occasionally a small group) exercises power within ill-defined limits but actually quite predictable ones.[2]

By utilizing contrasting concepts, one can turn Linz's definition of authoritarian regimes into a useful definition of democratic regimes:

> Democratic regimes are political systems with mostly unrestricted and responsible political pluralism; with a variety of political ideologies and mentalities; with some political mobilization and participation possible through political parties; and in which a leader exercises power within formally well-defined limits (constitutional ones) that are normally quite predictable.[3]

While an authoritarian leader may be characterized as aconstitutional or abusive of constitutional limits (if there are any), a democratic leader usually has well-defined powers limited not only by constitutionally sanctioned powers—the judiciary and the legislature—but also by constitutionally predictable limits.

If an authoritarian regime is the starting point and a democratic regime the end point of a transition, the transition itself may be defined as an evolutionary period of reform coupled with regime change. Such a period of reform and regime change may contain two or more of the following developments: the pluralization and mobilization of society from below; the liberalization of socioeconomic policies; the constitutionalization of

417

political activity; and the liberalization and possible democratization of the bureaucracy.

This chapter focuses on one aspect of one transition to democracy: the constitution-making period during Spain's transition to democracy in the late 1970s. The constitutionalization of political activity consists of the democratic reordering and restructuring of political rules and institutions. Such democratic mainstays as regular elections, freedom of association, the separation of governmental powers, and guarantees of individual liberties are integrated or reintegrated into the mainstream of the polity. Such reorganization of political rules and institutions requires both an elite decision-making phase and an implementation phase. The decision-making phase is the constitution-making process itself, during which the constitution makers hammer out the shape of the document. The implementation phase follows the approval and adoption of the new constitution and consists of the practical translation of constitutional theory into political action.

Preconditions to Constitution Making

A Brief Review of Franco's Record on Reform[4]

Francisco Franco y Bahamonde and his ministers first recognized the need to institute economic reforms in the early 1950s, when the consequences of Franco's post–civil war policies of economic autarky and isolationism proved too costly. While such policies recognized the need to improve Spain's then-desperate economic conditions, they were initiated solely at the governmental level and were not prompted by widespread or well-organized sociopolitical pressures.

Over the next decade, from the mid-1950s to the mid-1960s, some pluralization evolved through the formation of illegal labor movements and political, student, and liberal Catholic groups. The authoritarian regime, especially in the area of labor pol-

icy, began to feel increasing social pressure and demands. Its responses throughout the 1960s were a mix of piecemeal policy reform and overall repression.

In the mid-1960s, however, new political factors began to emerge within Spain's authoritarian regime. A limited number of governmental elites became interested in reforming the political system. The extent of this interest neither became clear nor did it translate into regularized effective action. But politicians did emerge from the ranks of the pro-reform Francoists who would compete in post-Franco democratic politics. Among those who would span both authoritarian and democratic politics were Manuel Fraga Iribarne, a minister under Franco and the leader of the Popular Alliance, a right-wing party founded in 1976, and Adolfo Suarez, a Franco bureaucrat and the first democratically elected prime minister of post-Franco Spain.

As Franco grew older, even he realized the need for some reform. His ideas of reform, however, were intended to perpetuate the system he created, not change it. In Linz's terminology, an authoritarian regime is one that has ill-defined limits. Franco's ill-defined limits were embodied in his Leyes Fundamentales, or Fundamental Laws. Six of these laws were promulgated over a period of twenty years. Franco tried to impose a quasi-constitutional structure on these unrelated laws in 1967 by passing the Seventh Fundamental Law. He also sought to cloak his system with democratic legitimacy by designating his system one of "organic democracy." The result, as one author has aptly put it, was one of "façade democracy."[5]

Important developments with a profound impact on the demise of the authoritarian system followed Franco's 1967 reforms. When Franco designated Prince Juan Carlos de Borbon y Borbon his successor as head of state and Admiral Luis Carrero Blanco his first head of government in 1973—until then

Franco had held both titles—he did not suspect that he had planted the crucial seeds for a legal transition to democracy. Franco had personally supervised the education and rearing of the prince and trusted him implicitly as an ideal successor. The future king, however, turned out to be the opposite of Franco's dreams: a man profoundly dedicated to democracy. Terrorism thwarted Franco's plans for Carrero Blanco, who was assassinated by the Basque terrorist organization Euzkadi ta Azkatasuna (ETA) in 1973, six months after becoming prime minister. Carrero Blanco's death was a severe blow to Franco's plans; he had been one of Franco's most loyal and hard-line supporters, a man who would have stopped at very little to maintain authoritarianism in Spain. His death left the doors for leadership succession for the post of head of government wide open.

Sociopolitical Preconditions for Democratization[6]

In Spain, a phenomenon best described as the pluralization of society had begun under Franco's regime some years before his death. Using Juan Linz's typology of oppositions to and under an authoritarian regime, one can distinguish between opponents within and outside of the system. In doing so, one comes up with a "semiopposition": "groups that are not dominant or represented in the governing group but are willing to participate in power without fundamentally challenging the regime." The monarchist Carlists and the far-right political quasi-party Fuerza Nueva (New Force) were among these groups in Spain. Linz also distinguishes an "a legal opposition which aims at basic change in the regime and its political institutions and to a large extent basic change in the social and economic structure." Many such groups existed in Spain by the early 1970s. Among these were university student groups, liberal clergy, and informal prodemocratic political groups. Finally, Linz also differentiates an "il-

legal opposition," which includes groups that the authoritarian regime officially bans or persecutes and which, in authoritarian Spain, included the communist and socialist parties and their respective labor unions, the Comisiones Obreras (Workers Commissions, or CCOO) and the Union General del Trabajo (General Workers Union, or UGT).[7]

How does an authoritarian regime react to such social and political pluralization? Can it stem the tide of social demand for reform? Or does it try to satisfy some of these demands? The regime has several options. It can refuse to recognize pluralization and choose to suppress it actively. It can also ignore the demands by neither suppressing nor responding to them. The regime may react, however, by liberalizing specific policies without implementing general reform or officially recognizing social or political groups. Finally, the authoritarian regime may do the unexpected and implement an overall policy of reform and democratization. In the latter years of his rule, Franco made a somewhat feeble attempt at the third option of piecemeal reform. Carlos Arias Navarro, the first prime minister of the post-Franco era, tried to maintain this course. King Juan Carlos, however, took the first decisive step toward generalized reform and democratization when he dismissed Arias Navarro and appointed Adolfo Suarez as prime minister.

Post-Franco Reform Attempts, Failures, and Successes[8]

Franco died in November 1975; Arias announced a program of political reform on January 28, 1976. The reform package included small concessions to allow most political groups, except the communists, to hold private political meetings. He also made some minor changes to the composition of Spain's parliament, the Cortes. He did nothing to change the status of the Sindicato Vertical, the official and only labor union. This reform

Table 15.1   Results of the 1976 Referendum

Total electoral census	Number of votes	Votes for	Votes against	Abstentions	Blank ballots	Voided ballots
22.6 million	17.6 million (77.72 percent of electorate)	16.6 million (94.2 percent of voters)	450,102 (2.6 percent of voters)	22,270 or (0.12 percent of voters)	523,457 (3.0 percent of voters)	52,823 (0.3 percent of voters)

Source: Bonime-Blanc, *Spain's Transition,* p. 26.

package was met with general disappointment throughout Spanish political circles. After only a few months of Arias Navarro's halfhearted reform, King Juan Carlos dismissed him and chose Adolfo Suarez, a relative unknown, to succeed him. Together, the king and Suarez would become the major engineers of Spain's transition to democracy.

In September 1976, Suarez presented what would become the first quasi-democratic reform package for Spain. Cleverly disguising it as the Eighth Fundamental Law, he subtitled it "Ley para la Reforma Politica" (law for political reform). The law was the result of a broad political discourse between government and opposition politicians over a period of months. Among its most important provisions were changes in authoritarian institutions. The Cortes was to be democratized, becoming a bicameral body with a lower house, or Congress of Deputies, with 350 directly elected members, and a upper house, or Senate, with 207 members, some of them appointed by the king. The monarchy would retain most powers that Franco conferred upon it. The king would nominate the prime minister, appoint one fifth of the Senate, and submit political questions to national referendum; he could also dissolve the Cortes and call for new elections at will. Key provisions of the law also included statements of democratic principles, affirming popular sovereignty, the supremacy of law, the inviolability of fundamental rights, universal suffrage, and implicit recognition of political plural-

ism. This reform package was submitted to a popular referendum in December 1976. The results, as Table 15.1 demonstrates, overwhelmingly favored the new law. The significance of this double-edged law was that it allowed for the beginning of a balanced transitional period, which effectively neutralized the political extremes (see Table 15.1).

In 1977, Suarez undertook further reforms, the most significant of which were the elaboration of an electoral law, the scheduling of elections, the legalization of political parties, a broader amnesty for political prisoners, and a preliminary recognition of some regional demands from the Basque Country and Catalonia. These events culminated in the first free elections in Spain in over four decades, on June 15, 1977.

Suarez, the king, and the political opposition had achieved a new form of political engagement in Spain: They successfully implemented a peaceful turning point toward democratization by dialogue, compromise, principle, and action. They used the old rules to implement radical yet peaceful change. They used—and abused—Franco's framework of fundamental laws to break out of the authoritarian system legally. Simultaneously, they used democratic devices, such as elections and freedom of the press, to usher in democracy. This process of combining the illusion of authoritarian legality with the reality of democratic practice without risking stability may best be described as *autoruptura.*[9]

The International Background

International factors also were crucial in bringing about change. The Spanish population and its leaders, especially in the business community, felt an increasing need and desire to become integrated into European economic structures. For their part, European Economic Community and North Atlantic Treaty Organization nations applied sometimes subtle and other times direct pressure on Spain to integrate into Western economic and military structures. Other foreign influences—more subtle at first, but later fairly blatant—had a cumulative effect on Spain, its youth, and other sectors over a longer period of time. These influences took the various forms of tourism, newspapers, magazines, music, radio, and other media (despite censorship); foreign economic investment; and the return of immigrant workers from northern Europe. Over time, all these influences had a major effect on modernizing aspects of Spanish life as well as creating a set of broader and greater expectations among key sectors of Spanish society, especially among university students, informal political groups, and businesspeople.

Conflict and Conflict Resolution

In Spain at the time of Franco's death and the beginning of the country's transition to democracy, conflict or potential conflict centered on the following issues: regional autonomy; regional secessionism; military disaffection; the role of the Catholic Church; left-wing disaffection (communists, socialists, trade unions); and right-wing disaffection (Francoists, Falangists, monarchists). How did these issues fare under the political change taking place? Except for a very small yet vocal minority, the vast majority of people concerned with these issues chose to play ball and participate in the process rather than abstain from or throw up obstacles to it. All parties appeared to be willing gen-erally to move closer to the center to make the political changes that were taking place evolve into a more democratic and free societal paradigm.

Thus, the coming together of various key factors over time—long-term pluralization, foreign influence, piecemeal authoritarian reforms, and the potential for serious and perhaps violent civil conflicts—provided compelling reasons for the authoritarian elite to consider and even embrace dramatic political change. If certain key authoritarian leaders had not favored democratization in and of itself, other, perhaps more violent, forms of political change could have followed Franco's death. The elite might have attempted to continue authoritarianism. Mounting social tensions would be met by severe repression, which, in turn, could fuel a military coup, revolution, or civil war. The results in Spain, however, were a peaceful transition to democracy, albeit with a very elaborate, intense, and prolonged constitution-making process.

The Constitution-Making Process: Theory, Participants, and Phases

Theory[10]

A constitution-making process is one of the most intense undertakings of a transition to democracy. No political group, party, or figure can fully avoid personal or ideological involvement in the issues raised during such a period. Everyone—politicians and the public—knows that a constitution legitimizes a democracy. It is the democratic prerequisite without which no democracy fully exists.

Constitution making is at once the most varied and the most concentrated form of political activity during a regime transition. In it, political maneuvering, bargaining, and negotiating take place, and the political positions, agreements, and disagreements of groups and leaders come to the fore. How the constitution makers handle these issues may tell us crucial things about the transition and the regime it leads up to. The discrepancy between the words agreed to in the constitution and the political reality that emerges may point to potentially serious future conflicts. The general character of both the process and the outcome may reveal clues about the regime's potential for stability or instability.

If a constitution is a set of norms and principles limiting political power and protecting individual rights, what is constitution making? It is a policy-making process in which political elites decide on the limits and practices of the new government and regime (the political formula) and on the rights and duties of its citizens (the sociogovernmental formula). Constitution making at its best is a comprehensive attempt at social and political problem solving and conflict resolution. During a transition to democracy, it consists of a momentous set of decisions that may very well affect the viability of the emerging regime. The form that constitution making takes may also reveal the shape of future domestic political relations.

Three types of constitution making may be distinguished: the consensual, the dissensual, and the stillborn. Consensual constitution making takes place when most if not all major political groups participate in drafting the constitution. Agreements are reached through compromise, avoiding dogmatic solutions, and upholding the notion of political responsibility throughout the process. Because of this compromise, the constitutional text often contains ambiguity. While this ambiguity often irritates one or more political parties, none of them fully opposes the entire text and most of them support it. Spain in the 1970s is a prime example of this kind of constitution-making process.

Dissensual constitution making is a process in which not all political actors participate, dogmatic solutions prevail, and prob-

lems are often left unresolved or resolved irresponsibly. Agreements are difficult to reach, and if reached, frequently exclude the views of one or more major political parties. The resulting constitutional text potentially threatens the stability of the new political system. Such a dissensually created constitution contains solutions satisfactory only to the dominant political force. Spain in the 1930s exemplified this type of constitution-making process.

Stillborn constitution making fails even before approval and implementation of the document. An example of such a case was the stillborn French constitution rejected by the French electorate on May 5, 1946. Polarized political coalitions contributed to the unacceptable constitutional results of that process. The French constitution makers regrouped and drafted a second constitution, which the electorate accepted on October 13, 1946.[11]

Immediately preceding a constitution-making process, existing political elites must consider and perhaps agree upon an agenda for political action. Setting such an agenda means recognizing and addressing the crucial national problems of the day and then including some of them in constitutional talks. It also means prioritizing these issues properly, giving the most urgent ones precedence over the less critical ones. If it is inappropriate to include a particular issue in the constitutional talks or in the resulting constitution, suitable arrangements must be made for the extra- or postconstitutional handling of the issue.

The Participants: From One Party to Hundreds[12]

Although there was a wide variety of illegal and extralegal political groups in Spain at the time of Franco's death, the only legal party in the country was Franco's official party, the forty-year old Movimiento Nacional (National Movement). The authoritarian rather

Table 15.2   Spanish National Elections, 1977

Party or coalition	Percentage of votes	Number of seats
Union del Centro Democratico	34.7	165
Partido Socialista Espanol Obrero	29.2	118
Partido Comunista Espanol	9.2	20
Alianza Popular	8.4	16
Convergencia Catalana	4.0	13
Partido Nacional Vasco	2.0	8
Other parties	13.0	10

Note: Information from various periodical sources and the Central Electoral Board as reported in *El Pais* and ABC, June and July 1977.

than totalitarian quality of Franco's rule had allowed for a semblance of semipluralism within that party, with moderate elite conflict taking place within its ranks.

Shortly after Franco's death in November 1975, more than two hundred groups came out of the woodwork claiming to be political parties. Among these were associations historically recognized as parties—such as the communists (Partido Comunista Español, or PCE) and socialists (Partido Socialista Obrero Espanol, or PSOE)—and embryonic party forms that would compete as real parties for the first time in June 1977. Among the newly born parties were the Alianza Popular (AP) and Union del Centro Democratico (UCD).

The Spanish political picture was very diverse, with parties on the far right, right, center-right, center, center-left, left, and far left. Emerging at this time were also key new democratic leaders, among them Felipe Gonzalez, new leader of the PSOE and future prime minister of Spain in the 1980s and 1990s, and Santiago Carrillo, seasoned leader of the communists in exile and the newly legalized PCE.

The June 15, 1977, elections were preceded by a short three-week campaign. The UCD's appeal increased over this period, while other parties had little time to organize or get exposure on television or radio, still controlled by the government. While blatant abuses of their relative position of power were not evident, clearly the prime minister's party, the UCD, had greater access and influence than did the other parties.

Table 15.2 shows the election results. To no one's surprise, the UCD received most of the votes (35 percent of the total popular vote) and seats in the Cortes (165 out of 350). Although not a majority, the result allowed Suarez to form a minority government through a coalition with other centrist and regional parties. Closely trailing the UCD with 29 percent of the popular vote was the PSOE, which received 118 seats in the Cortes. Both parties on the extremes—the rightist AP and the leftist PCE—had disappointing results. The AP received 8 percent of the vote and 16 seats, and the PCE received 9 percent of the vote and 20 seats (see Table 15.2).

Although the results were not unexpected and no major improprieties were evident, one of the major issues emerging from the election was the fairness of the electoral system—mainly, the dubious proportionality of the new system, tailored after the d'Hondt system. Several technicalities favored the party with both the most votes and the most centrist or moderate position, that is, the UCD. Among these favorable technicalities was that each province (50) received two senators regardless of proportionality.

This allowed for equal representation from both rural and urban centers, the latter being more densely populated and liberal. Members of the lower house were chosen through proportional representation. Each province, however, no matter how small or sparsely populated, received a minimum of three representatives. Thus representation once again favored the inland, rural, and conservative Castilian provinces.[13] The electoral bottom line spoke for itself. With 34.7 percent of the vote, the UCD received 47.1 percent of the seats; with 29.2 percent of the vote, the PSOE received 33.7 percent of the seats; with 8.4 percent of the vote, the AP received 4.6 percent of the seats; and with 9.2 percent of the vote, the PCE received 5.7 percent of the seats.

The Formal Phases of Constitution Making[14]

A handful of critical decisions need to be made before a constitution-making process can begin. Among the most important are: How do the transitionary elites decide which constitution-making route to take? What entity initiates the first draft? Should the body be elected or appointed? Should it be elected as part of a general election or as a constituent assembly strictly tasked to draft a constitution?

There are three basic routes that can be taken to constitution making. The caretaker government, under the aegis of the executive branch, can appoint a commission of experts to draft the constitution. Once written, the document can be submitted to a national referendum. Another option involves electing a body, such as a constituent assembly, with the sole mandate of writing a constitution. Finally, the caretaker government can call for general elections (governed by temporary electoral laws) for a new legislature that, in addition to its general duties, will draft a constitution. Arguably the most democratic

form of constitution making is through the creation of a constituent assembly. In Spain, it was not clear at the outset which of these paths would be taken. In the period leading up to the June 15, 1977, elections, it was unclear to the electorate whether the election results would yield a regularly elected Cortes or an extraordinarily created constituent assembly. There was division over this issue among the political parties, with liberal and left-leaning parties favoring the constituent assembly option and the center-right and right favoring a regularly elected Cortes. The latter view prevailed.

The next important question involved who would write the first draft of the constitution. Would the government initiate the draft or would this job be the exclusive domain of the legislature? After some pressure from the PSOE, the government agreed to allow for a parliamentary process. This promise was later broken, but the decision allowed for the momentum of the process to proceed uninterrupted and peacefully. By late July 1977, it was clear that the winning coalition's strength in the Cortes would dictate the shape of the process; it also translated directly into committee representation throughout the process.

Shortly before the beginning of the constitution-making process, the parties all announced constitutional platforms or positions. Felipe Gonzalez of the PSOE urged the need for a "compacted constitution." Santiago Carrillo of the PCE suggested a "government of national democratic concentration." Leopoldo Calvo Sotelo of the UCD emphasized the three immediate objectives of "a constitution, autonomies and economic measures." Fraga Iribarne of the AP was not shy in professing his "loyalty to the past." The Catalan representative, Jordi Pujol, emphasized the paramount importance of regional autonomies. Finally, Xabier Arzallus, the Basque spokesman, stressed the need for the "Basque Country [to] recover its political personality."[15] After these initial declarations were made, the parties worked out a timetable and a set of rules for elaborating the constitution. After much haggling and maneuvering, the parliamentarians finally agreed that the constitution making should occur in seven phases.

Phase One: Congressional Constitutional Subcommittee

The initial phase was perhaps the most important. In it, the framework of the new constitution was created, and seven of the most prominent political leaders participated. The congressional constitutional subcommittee was comprised of three UCD representatives and one representative each from the PSOE, AP, PCE, and Catalan Coalition. This group worked in strict secrecy, but several months into their labors, press leaks occurred, followed by intense public debate. The subcommittee produced the Ante-Proyecto, or first draft of the constitution, on April 10, 1978.

Phase Two: Congressional Constitutional Committee

During this phase, which ran from May to June 1978, the thirty-six members of the Congressional Committee on Constitutional Affairs and Public Liberties studied the preliminary draft, reviewed countless proposed amendments, and came up with their version of the new text: the Proyecto Constitucional.

Phase Three: The Congressional Approval Phase

In early July 1978, the Proyecto Constitucional was presented to the full Congress of Deputies. Another month of speeches and debates followed, culminating in an overwhelming vote in favor of the draft: 258 deputies voted for it, 2 against it, and 14 abstained.

Phase Four: Senate Constitutional Committee

From August to September 1978, an intense review took place within the Senate constitutional committee, the first senatorial body to deal with the constitutional draft. Over 1,250 amendments were considered. Their work ended in September when they turned over the draft to the full senate.

Phase Five: Senate Approval

Lasting less than two weeks, this formal phase encountered some difficulties but ended with an approved Senate version of the constitutional draft on October 5, 1978.

Phase Six: Joint Constitutional Committee

A sixth phase was necessary to reconcile the congressional and senatorial versions of the constitutional draft. Composed of a group of eleven members drawn from both houses, their talks were conducted in secret and efficiently. After two intense weeks, their approved text became the Spanish constitution of 1978.

Phase Seven: National Approval

Both houses overwhelmingly approved the constitution on October 31, 1978. After an intense political campaign, dominated by proconstitutional forces but not entirely free of anticonstitutional and proabstention interests, the Spanish people enthusiastically approved the constitution in a national referendum held on December 6, 1978 (see Table 15.3).

Of a total electorate of approximately 26 million, almost 18 million, or 67 percent, cast a vote. Of those who voted, an overwhelming

Table 15.3   **Results of Spain's Constitutional Referendum,
               December 6, 1978**

Voted	Number of votes	Percentage of votes cast	Percentage of electorate
Yes	15,706,078	87.87	58.97
No	1,400,505	7.83	5.25
Blank	632,902	3.55	2.37
Void	133,786	0.75	0.50

Source: Bonime-Blanc, *Spain's Transition,* p. 42. The total electorate in Spain at the time consisted of over 26 million voters, with 67 percent casting a vote at the referendum.

majority—87 percent—voted in favor of the constitution, while 8 percent rejected it and the remainder cast blank or voided ballots.[16] King Juan Carlos ratified and sanctioned the new fundamental democratic law of the land on December 27, 1978, in a joint session of the Cortes. The Spanish constitution-making process had lasted a total of eighteen months and resulted in a text containing more than 160 hotly debated articles. The Spanish constitution-making process had become one of the lengthiest, most elaborate, and ultimately successful of the twentieth century up until that point.

The Political Phases of Constitution Making: Coalitional Strategies and Political Tactics[17]

By examining the relative political strength of each political party and the various coalitional strategies and tactics deployed during the constitution-making process, a somewhat more analytical and useful view of the process emerges. Unlike analyzing the prescribed technical phases of constitution making, examining the political phases of constitution making captures the distinct coalitional maneuvers that took place. By examining the political phases, one gleans insights into the overall nature of the process and why it succeeded in Spain. The factors to be considered in this analysis of political phases are the fol-

lowing: the relative openness or secrecy of the process; the parliamentary or extraparliamentary nature of discussions (i.e., including nonparliamentary elites); the accommodating versus confrontational nature of debates; the protracted or swift nature of discussions; and the breadth or narrowness of particular issues. When several of these factors change discernibly, it is possible to distinguish a new phase emerging (see Table 15.4).

Thus, the following six political phases of constitution making can be distinguished in Spain's example.

Phase One: Consensual Agenda Setting

This phase lasted from August to November 1977. It was characterized by largely secret parliamentary discussions, carried out in a deliberate, painstaking, but largely consensual manner. The principal task was to identify and prioritize the most crucial issues that the constitution should address and hopefully resolve. The core issues for the constitution makers included the parameters of the new political system, the territorial organization of Spain, the guarantee of fundamental political freedoms, and the elimination or apoliticization of Franco's political institutions.

The dominant coalition of this period—and the entire constitution-making process—emerged at this time. The coalition included

Table 15.4   Coalitional Strategies in the Cortes during the Constitution-Making Process

Political phase	Dominant coalition	Other unsuccessful coalition(s)	Noncoalesced parties
Consensual agenda-setting phase and publicizing and mobilizing phase	Consensual Coalition UCD/AP	PSOE/MC/PCE	PNV
Dissensual precongressional phase	UCD/AP UCD/MC/PCE		PNV PSOE
Consensual parliamentary phase	Consensual Coalition UCD/AP	PSOE/MC/PCE (+ PNV)	PNV AP
Constrained parliamentary phase	Consensual Coalition PSOE/PCE/MC/PNV and three senators appointed by the king	PSOE/MC/PCE (+ PNV)	PNV AP

Note: The Consensual Coalition consisted of the UCD, PSOE, PCE, and MC.

Source: Bonime-Blanc, *Spain's Transition*, pp. 52–53.

such diverse interests as those representing the left (the PSOE), the center-right (the UCD), the far left (the PCE), and the regions (the MC). It came to be known as the Consensual Coalition, and while it did not prevail at all stages of the constitution-making process, it did become the dominant political force behind the constitution-making process and outcome in Spain.

Phase Two: Publicizing and Mobilizing

This phase began with the leaking to the press of the first draft constitution, which blew the cover under which the constitution makers had been secretly operating. An intense public debate followed in all quarters. Even such lower-profile actors as the Catholic Church and the military began to speak up. Other disturbing extraconstitutional events took place during this period: large-scale rioting and vandalism, regional demonstrations throughout Spain, and virulent political debates in the Cortes between the two extremes of the political spectrum, the AP

and the communists. Toward the end of this period—March 1978—the debate became even more antagonistic, although it had not yet succumbed to full-scale dissensual discourse. However, that was about to change.

Phase Three: Dissensual Precongressional

What seemed to be a trend toward consensus abruptly changed. A prominent member of the PSOE, Gregorio Peces-Barba, noisily withdrew from the proceedings, accusing the UCD of breaking a number of key compromises. Simultaneously, a large segment of Suarez's cabinet resigned and a new, distinctly more conservative group of ministers was appointed. The press construed these changes as a turn to the right. Suarez and Felipe Gonzalez held a summit to restore discussion on the draft constitution. Further disarray developed within the membership of the congressional constitutional subcommittee. As one prominent member of the committee said at the time, "the only consensus that exists is that we must finish the work."[18]

The largest thorn in everyone's side was the topic of regionalism. Even with the absence of the socialists and with further objections from the right-wing AP, the remainder of the constitutional committee hammered out a tenuous compromise draft. Surprisingly and still under protest, all members of the committee, including Peces-Barba, signed the proposed draft constitution. The third political phase of the process was the first purely dissensual one. In it, a key player—the PSOE—removed itself from participation, and the specter of a purely right-wing coalition (AP/UCD) emerged but did not fully realize itself. If it had, it could have been the harbinger of a right-leaning constitution.

Phase Four: Consensual Parliamentary

All thirty-six members of the congressional constitutional committee made public and conscious efforts to return to consensus-seeking debate. By early May, they had reached a new plateau of mutual accommodation and deliberation. Almost simultaneously, Felipe Gonzalez declared that the PSOE was a social democratic party rather than a Marxist socialist one. While the UCD often threatened to take the discussions back to a more right-leaning slant, it stopped short of that and conducted a rapprochement with the PSOE. Concomitant with this emerging better understanding between the UCD and PSOE was the increasing marginalization of the extremes, namely, the AP and the Basques, both of which continued to espouse more radical (although very different) views. The AP's inflexible conservatism and the Basques' extreme regionalism increasingly distanced them from the process. Their self-marginalization also antagonized the consensual partners, who often expressed views that were sympathetic to these groups. With some notable exceptions, the UCD, PSOE, PCE, and MC formed a tenuous but steady coalition of views.

Phase Five: Constrained Parliamentary

The key ingredients to the changed atmosphere had to do with the Basque problem and the reawakening of the tensions between the PSOE and UCD in the Senate. While the Consensual Coalition never quite broke down during this period, its endurance was seriously tested, though at the end of the phase, the coalition was at its peak. The main tensions stemmed from regional issues. The UCD introduced broad new proposals to limit regional autonomy as set forth in the congressional draft of the constitution. This set off a major outcry from the regional and PSOE forces. The logjam was cleared with the unexpected help of royally appointed senators, who sided with regionalists and socialists to win the day. Tensions shifted between the PSOE and regional parties shortly thereafter when Basques accused the socialists of abandoning them. A fortuitous side effect of the spat was to strengthen the PSOE/UCD coalition at a time when it was weak. But this was an important phase, as it led up to the approval of the entire new constitution.

Phase Five: Consensual Approval

Almost entirely dominated by accommodations and expressions of goodwill, the approval phase consisted of four stages. The first stage took place within the joint committee of the houses, where eleven representatives swiftly, secretly, and consensually put the final touches on the constitutional draft. The second stage took place on October 31, 1978, when each house separately voted on the adoption of the new constitution; both overwhelmingly supported it. The distribution of the vote clearly reflected the diversity of the consensual coalition: UCD, PSOE, PCE, and MC members voted in favor of the constitution, while members of the AP and Basque parties voted against or abstained. The third stage of approval consisted of an intense political campaign geared toward the anticipated constitutional referendum scheduled for December 6, 1978. Again, the divisions between the consensual coalition partners, on the one hand, and the AP and certain more extreme regional interests, on the other hand, were clear. The fourth and final stage of approval culminated in the actual referendum on the constitution held on December 6, 1978. A little over 67 percent of the eligible electorate voted, with more than 87 percent of those favoring the adoption of the constitution (see Table 15.3). The entire constitution-making process thus ended on a high note. The king signed the Spanish constitution of 1978 on December 27, making Spain finally and officially a democracy.

By tracking the phases of the coalitional dynamics in the constitution-making process, one can obtain a useful analytical overview of the process. This history, in turn, yields lessons on how constitution making may succeed. In this examination of the Spanish case, several important points emerge.

First, by the standards of the time, the process was lengthy and sometimes torturous, often characterized by protracted negotiations and the possibility of a breakdown. Second, secret negotiations were used often to get the talks back on track: Off-the-record discussions took place during some of the most critical political phases of the process. These discussions, far from the limelight, helped the often feuding parties to blow off steam concerning their major disagreements and forge closer positions on some of the most hotly debated topics of the day, such as the shape of territorial regionalization, the relationship of church and state, and the role of the military, to name a few.

Third, nonparliamentary elites were included in certain secret negotiations frequently and successfully. Especially during the difficult dissensual phases mentioned above, while the constitution-making elites were secretly discussing solutions away from media attention, they sought out (and were sought out by) a broad variety of academic, religious, military, regional, and even illegal political groups in their efforts to forge the compromise positions that eventually became part of the new constitution.

Fourth, participants who were unwilling or unable to compromise on constitutional issues—some of the far-right Francoist parties and some of the more extreme nationalistic regional groups, for example—were marginalized and eventually ignored. The pressure to achieve consensus seemed to overwhelm and eventually diffuse the forces on the political extremes. Even those who could have been construed as possible extremists—for example, the PCE—were centripetal rather than centrifugal forces, contributing to the achievement of consensual solutions.

Fifth, while popular participation in the process was never direct, the Spanish political atmosphere was charged and often affected the process. Demonstrations and public expressions of opinion on the issues being debated in the constitutional talks were frequent, sometimes daily, and were voiced by a broad variety of political, regional, and other more issue-specific groups—religious, moral, or rights-related. The public participation, as well as media attention given to such public expressions, helped to pressure the constitution makers to move forward on achieving solutions and compromises that would allow for a new constitution to be adopted sooner rather than later.

Sixth, the foresight and political steady hand of most constitution makers in the face of adverse circumstances—some political, some involving terrorism—were perhaps the greatest assets in the process. The single most important development of the constitution-making process in Spain may have been the emergence of a heterogeneous yet pragmatic coalition: the Consensual Coalition, which represented the nation's *consenso* (consensus) on a broadly based democracy, with a constitution containing solutions for a nation filled with social, economic, and regional diversity.

Constitution Making and Democratization: Some Conclusions

Comparing the Spanish case to others, one can derive several overall conclusions concerning constitution making within a transition to democracy.[19]

Turning Points toward Democratization

The Spanish case illustrates that there are four possible turning points toward democratization from authoritarianism: *ruptura*, reform, *autoruptura*, and external defeat. The key factors determining how that turning point occurs are whether there is an authoritarian decline preceding such a period and whether there is short-term or long-term sociopolitical pluralization taking place in society. The turning points are defined according to the strengths or weaknesses of these factors.

Ruptura occurs when the opposition elite is able to replace the authoritarian elite with a clean, relatively quick, and potentially violent break with the past. Portugal in the early 1970s and Spain in the 1930s are examples.

Reform occurs when, in the face of growing opposition, the authoritarian elite chooses gradual liberalization. The beginning of the long Brazilian transition to democracy, beginning in the 1970s and culminating over a decade later, is a good example of this type of turning point.

In *autoruptura*, the authoritarian elite causes a liberalization crisis by choosing to break with the past in the face of mounting sociopolitical pluralization. This is the type of turning point Spain exhibited in the mid 1970s.

Finally, an authoritarian elite's military defeat or inept handling of a military crisis may bring about an external defeat-turning point. Germany and Italy after World War II are classic examples of this type of turning point.

The Preconstitutional Period

Spain's experience also shows that another key factor in the process of democratization is understanding what happened, if anything, during the period immediately preceding the constitution-making period—namely, whether there was limited or comprehensive preconstitutional reform. The latter took place in Spain and involved the implementation by transitionary elites of political and sociogovernmental reforms necessary for the proper preliminary democratic functioning of the state. Among the key trends that need to occur to attain comprehensive preconstitutional reform are three processes: first, a process of sociopolitical legalization, in which authoritarian controls on fundamental freedoms—such as freedom of the press, association, and speech—are lifted; second, a process of authoritarian illegalization, in which, at a minimum, certain constraints and prohibitions are placed upon the most potentially threatening authoritarian sectors, such as special police forces and the military; and third, the democratization of essential preconstitutional practices, such as legalizing a broad spectrum of political parties, drafting a temporary but fair electoral law, allowing open campaigning, and holding nationwide legislative elections.

The Constitution-Making Process and Outcome

Based on a comparison of several constitution-making processes, including the Spanish case of the late 1970s,[20] four types of processes may be distinguished. The two key factors in determining these processes are the type of coalitional strategies pursued by the constitution makers (nonideological and multilateral versus ideological and unilateral) and the mode of negotiation used in the process (accommodating versus confrontational). A matrix accounting for these two factors yields the following results.

In a consensual constitution-making process, nonideological and multilateral coalitional strategies prevail among the constitution makers who pursue mostly accommodating negotiating tactics. Germany and Italy in the postwar period as well as Spain in the 1970s exhibited this type of constitution making.

A passively dissensual constitution-making process consists of ideological and unilateral coalitional strategies with fairly accommodating behavior. Portugal in the early 1970s exhibited this type of process.

In an actively dissensual constitution-making process, ideological and unilateralist constitution makers either negotiate confrontationally most of the time, or if they do not, they are unable to pursue a successful process. A variant of this type of process is the abovementioned stillborn process, in which no constitutional results are produced. The constitution rejected by the French electorate on May 5, 1946, is an example of such a stillborn constitution. In that case, polarized political groupings could not forge lasting or valid coalitions or consensus on the main issues of the day, resulting in another attempt that succeeded six months later.

The Constitutional Outcome

Depending on whether the constitution resulting from the process contains mostly dogmatic or ideological language, on the one hand, or compromise, consensual language, on the other hand, and whether the language itself is mostly ambiguous or relatively clear and pragmatic, it is possible to distinguish four types of constitutional outcome: a dogmatic guideline constitution (Spain 1931), containing clear but ideological provisions; a dogmatic ambiguous constitution (Portugal), containing vague and ideological language; a compromise guideline constitution (Germany) with clear and nonideological provisions; and a compromise ambiguous constitution (Spain 1978 and Italy), containing nonideological provisions but ambiguous language.

In Spain in 1978, a highly negotiated constitution contained mostly nonideological language, but also ambiguity in many cases. Such ambiguity made implementing some of the constitution's provisions difficult in some instances, as such implementation required further political negotiation and the adoption of further amendments and clarifying legislation.

The Constitution-Making Process in Spain in the Late 1970s: Final Thoughts

Spain in the late 1970s represents a shining example of a political process leading a country from an authoritarian past into a solidly democratic future. Spain exhibited a constitution-making pattern that is best described as a consensual compromise, in which consensus politics and coalitional strategies dominated the process and the outcome—the constitution itself—exhibited a compromising, nonideological quality. The significance of what came to be known as *el consenso* during Spain's constitution-making process cannot be underestimated, especially in a country with the potential to open serious and potentially violent old wounds. *Consenso* was not merely a form of negotiation; it represented the coming together of very diverse political forces of the center-right, left, far left, and regional. Given Spain's sociopolitical and regional composition at the time, no other coalitional force could have carried the weight and legitimacy that the consensual coalition carried.

Spain in the 1970s is an extraordinary example of how the political will of responsible elites, influenced strongly by the sociopolitical climate in the nation, can drive most of those elites to behave broadly and responsibly instead of ideologically and narrow-mindedly to produce a constitution that is widely accepted and adaptable; it has now weathered the test of more than thirty years. The way the Spanish constitution makers and political elites of the late 1970s conducted themselves through the constitution-making process provided a microcosmic look into what the future of democracy would look like, in what has become one of the world's most vibrant democracies.

Glossary of Terms

AP — Popular Alliance/*Alianza Popular*
CC — Catalan Convergence/*Convergencia Catalana*
CCOO — Workers Commissions/*Comisiones Obreras*
EE — Basque Left/*Euskadi Esquerra/Euzkadiko Ezkerra*
ETA — *Euzkadi ta Azkatasuna*
MC — Catalan Minority/*Minoria Catalana*
PCE — Spanish Communist Party/*Partido Comunista Español*
PNV — Basque National Party/*Partido Nacional Vasco*
PSOE — Spanish Socialist Workers Party/*Partido Socialista Obrero Espanol*
UCD — Union of the Democratic Center/*Union del Centro Democratico*
UGT — General Workers Union/*Union General del Trabajo*

Notes

1. This chapter draws heavily on the author's book, Andrea Bonime-Blanc, *Spain's Transition to Democracy: The Politics of Constitution Making* (Boulder, CO: Westview Press, 1987), and makes extensive use and quotation of several sections and chapters of that book.

2. Juan J. Linz, "An Authoritarian Regime: Spain," in *Mass Politics,* ed., Erik Allardt and Stein Rokkan (New York: Free Press, 1970), p. 255.

3. Bonime-Blanc, *Spain's Transition,* p. 6.

4. Ibid., pp. 18–20.

5. Jose Amodia, *Franco's Political Legacy: From Dictatorship to Façade Democracy* (London: Allen Lane, 1977), pp. 92–96.

6. Bonime-Blanc, *Spain's Transition,* pp. 17–18.

7. Juan J. Linz, "Opposition in and under an Authoritarian Regime: The Case of Spain," in *Regimes and Oppositions,* ed. Robert A. Dahl (New Haven, CT: Yale University Press, 1973), pp. 171–259.

8. Bonime-Blanc, *Spain's Transition,* pp. 22–26.

9. See discussion in this chapter.

10. Bonime-Blanc, *Spain's Transition,* pp. 11–14.

11. Ibid., p. 14.

12. Ibid., pp. 27–31.

13. See Bonime-Blanc, *Spain's Transition,* pp. 30–31 for more information concerning the electoral system.

14. Ibid., pp. 36–40.

15. See *El Pais* and ABC, July 28, 1977, author's translation.

16. *El Pais,* December 22, 1978.

17. Bonime-Blanc, *Spain's Transition,* pp. 53–64.

18. Miguel Roca Junyent, the representative from MC. Bonime-Blanc, *Spain's Transition,* p. 57.

19. This section draws on the research and information in chapters 7 and 8 of Bonime-Blanc, *Spain's Transition,* in which a comparative theory of transitions from authoritarianism to democracy is set forth including the cases of Spain in the 1930s, Germany and Italy in the postwar period, and Portugal in the early 1970s. Bonime-Blanc, *Spain's Transition,* pp. 113–61.

20. Ibid., pp. 113–61.

PART V

LATIN AMERICA

16

Conflict Resolution
and Constitutionalism

The Making of the Brazilian Constitution of 1988

Keith S. Rosenn

Brazil's historical experience with conflict resolution contrasts sharply with that of its Latin American neighbors. While the former Spanish colonies fought prolonged and bloody wars to achieve independence, Brazil achieved independence peacefully. This was largely the result of the unusual response of the Portuguese monarch—Prince Regent João, the future King João VI—to Napoleon's invasion of Iberia in 1807: He decided to move the Portuguese court to Rio de Janeiro, where it remained even after Napoleon's fall. In 1815, he declared the United Kingdom of Portugal and Brazil. Only when liberal revolutionaries in Lisbon convened a parliament in 1820 and threatened revolt did João return to Portugal, leaving behind his son Pedro as Prince Regent. In 1822, Pedro declared Brazilian independence. In no position to contest the issue, Portugal peacefully accepted the loss of its former colony in return for a small indemnity.

From 1822 to 1889, Brazil was the only country in Latin America governed by a constitutional hereditary monarchy. In 1889, a military coup d'état overthrew the monarchy, leading to a short experience with pseudo-democratic government. The era of Brazilian history known as the Old Republic (1891–1930) operated with a constitution that created the trappings of democracy, but single-party machines, controlled by the landed oligarchy, rigged the elections. The electorate averaged less than 3 percent of the population. Winning candidates received more than 90 percent of the vote in six of eleven presidential elections and more than 70 percent of the vote in the others. As Kenneth P. Erickson has observed, "For most Brazilians, therefore, the democracy of the Old Republic was only a sham."[1]

In 1930, the Old Republic was overthrown by another military coup d'état. From 1930 to 1945, Brazil was ruled by the dictatorial regime of Getúlio Vargas, who in turn was overthrown by a military coup d'état in 1945. An ensuing democratic interlude was interrupted in 1964, when President João Goulart was ousted by yet another military coup. Brazil was ruled by a series of military regimes from 1964 until 1985. The Brazilian electorate did not have a chance to vote directly for a president until 1989. Disregarding the sham democracy of the Old Republic, Brazil's actual experience with democratic government before adopting the 1988 Constitution was limited to only sixteen years of its 166 years of existence as an independent nation.

A Brief Overview of Prior Brazilian Constitutions

The 1824 Constitution

Dom Pedro, son of João VI, convoked a constituent assembly to draft Brazil's first constitution. One of the assembly's first acts was to crown Dom Pedro I as Emperor and Perpetual Defender of Brazil. Dissatisfied with the limitations on his power in the constitutional draft, Dom Pedro forcibly dissolved the assembly and replaced it with a ten-member commission over which he presided personally. In December 1823, his commission completed a draft constitution satisfactory to Dom Pedro. After municipal councils approved the draft, the Emperor promulgated it on March 25, 1824.

Brazil's first constitution was, to date, also its most enduring, lasting sixty-five years with only one amendment.[2] It was modeled on the French constitution of 1814, establishing a hereditary Catholic monarchy headed by the Emperor. The monarchy spared Brazil the constant coups and political turmoil that characterized the early experiments of its Spanish-speaking neighbors, but the abolition of slavery in 1888 led disgruntled former slave holders to support a military coup that ousted the monarchy in 1889.

The 1891 Constitution and the First Republic

The 1891 Constitution, which was heavily influenced by the U.S. constitution, thoroughly changed Brazil's form of government. The monarchy became a democracy, the unitary state became a federation of twenty states called the United States of Brazil, and the quasi-parliamentary system became a presidential system. The states promulgated their own constitutions, elected their own governors and legislative assemblies, and organized their own systems of courts and public administration. The municipalities had virtual autonomy on subjects of particular interest to them.

The 1891 Constitution was a well-written and liberal document that worked badly. Considerable political instability marked its initial period. Shortly after promulgation of the constitution, Brazil's first elected president, Deodoro da Fonseca, staged an *autogolpe*, dissolving the Congress and declaring a state of siege. Twenty days later, the autogolpe fizzled. The president resigned and his vice president, Floriano Peixoto, assumed the presidency. Although he promised to convoke new elections, Peixoto did not do so. The political crisis was aggravated by a financial crisis that led to many bankruptcies and a series of rebellions.

The First Republic was characterized by widespread electoral fraud and monopolization of political power by the states of São Paulo and Minas Gerais. Resentment over the election returns of 1930—which replaced the incumbent Paulista president, Washington Luís, with another Paulista, Júlio Prestes—coupled with the economic crisis of the Great Depression ultimately led to a successful military revolt.

The Vargas Dictatorship and Constitutions of 1934 and 1937

The Constitution of 1891 was a casualty of the 1930 military revolt that brought Getúlio Vargas to power. Although theoretically in force, the 1891 Constitution was modified by a series of acts of the provisional government, which replaced it with a new constitution in 1934.

Modeled after the Weimar constitution of 1919 and the Spanish constitution of 1931, Brazil's 1934 Constitution substituted social democracy for liberal democracy. It enfranchised women and introduced secret voting. For the first time, all Brazilians over the age of eighteen, regardless of sex, became eligible to vote, provided that they were not illiterate, beggars, or enlisted military. Optional during the Old Republic, voting became compulsory for all eligible males and female civil servants.

The 1934 Constitution lasted only three years. In 1937, under the pretext of putting down a communist takeover plot, Getúlio Vargas staged an *autogolpe* and proclaimed a dictatorship called the New State (*Estado Novo*). Vargas replaced the 1934 Constitution with a shadow constitution, nicknamed the *Polaca* because of its resemblance to Poland's 1935 constitution.[3] Under it, the president was the supreme authority of the state. The provisions for democratic institutions and representative elections were merely window dressing. Vargas dissolved all political parties and dispensed with elections. Even though Article 187 of the 1937 Constitution required ratification by a plebiscite before entering into force, no plebiscite was ever held. Consequently, the Vargas government was actually a de facto regime. Because Congress never met, Vargas simply legislated by decree, issuing more than eight thousand decree-laws between 1937 and 1945; some of these are still in force. During the entire period that the 1937 Constitution was nominally in force, a state of emergency suspended individual rights and guarantees. This state of emergency lasted until November 30, 1945, a month after Vargas was overthrown by the military.

Restoration of Democracy and the 1946 Constitution

The 1946 Constitution reestablished a democratic system of government. Like the 1891 Constitution, it reflected the influence of the U.S. constitution regarding federalism and individual rights. It also reflected the influence of the Weimar constitution regarding socioeconomic rights and structures.

The demise of the 1946 Constitution began in 1961 with the enigmatic resignation of the popularly elected president, Jânio Quadros, who indicated that he had renounced the presidency because the country was "ungovernable" under the existing constitutional regime. Widespread political opposition to leftist vice president João Goulart led to the enactment of Constitutional Amendment 4 of September 2, 1961, which permitted Goulart to assume the presidency, but only under a parliamentary regime that deprived him of most presidential powers. This parliamentary system functioned poorly. After a plebiscite, a constitutional amendment of January 23, 1963, restored presidentialism. But Goulart was neither a popular nor a competent president. Inflation reached a record high after a failed stabilization program that alienated his supporters. Badly miscalculating his tenuous political support, Goulart attempted to move the country sharply to the left. The result was a military coup that ousted Goulart in April 1964.

The Constitutions of 1967 and 1969

The military maintained the Congress and the 1946 Constitution but quickly modified it by a series of institutional acts. These were unconstitutional decrees signed by members of the military high command, who claimed to be exercising the constituent power in the name of the revolution. Thus, the military high command became a self-designated and self-legitimating ambulatory constituent assembly. Military leaders used institutional acts to select presidents, remove opposition members of Congress, and deprive many Brazilians of their political and civil rights for a ten-year period. The Second Institutional Act permitted the president to pack the Supreme Court and issue decree-laws in matters involving national security, a power soon expanded by the Fourth Institutional Act to include all financial and administrative matters.

The 1967 Constitution was designed to lend a greater semblance of legitimacy and permanence to the military regimes running Brazil. Formally ratified by a Congress from which most political opposition had been purged, this constitution incorporated key provisions of the four institutional acts passed between April 1964 and December 1966. Its tenor resembled the 1937 Constitution that institutionalized the Vargas dictatorship. An electoral college consisting of members of Congress and delegates nominated by the state legislative assemblies formally elected the president for a four-year term. In practice, however, only a general could be a candidate.

The 1967 Constitution was followed by a period of constant crisis due to widespread popular opposition to the military government. The military command responded by issuing another series of twelve institutional acts that continuously modified the constitution in accordance with the military's assessment of the needs of the moment. Institutional Act 5 of December 13, 1968, thoroughly eviscerated the constitution, as it authorized President Arturo da Costa e Silva to suspend all legislators and exercise total legislative powers himself. It also gave the president the power to deprive citizens of their political rights for ten years, quash legislative mandates summarily, declare and prolong states of siege, suspend freedom of association, impose censorship, and dismiss or retire any government employee or office-holder. Article 10 suspended habeas corpus

for crimes against national security, the popular economy, and the social and economic order. The president used the act to launch a witch hunt against his opponents and force early retirement of three prominent members of the Supreme Court.

The Constitution of 1969

In August 1969, President da Costa e Silva suffered a stroke. Rather than permit the civilian vice president, Pedro Aleixo, to succeed to the presidency in accordance with the constitution, the armed forces issued Institutional Act 12, authorizing the military leaders to assume executive power in the form of a junta. A few months later Institutional Act 17 of October 17, 1969, authorized the military junta to issue constitutional amendments. The junta promptly issued Constitutional Amendment 1, which rewrote and renumbered the entire text of the 1967 Constitution. Despite its label, most Brazilian constitutional scholars treat Amendment 1 as the 1969 Constitution.

The 1969 Constitution strengthened the powers of the executive. It increased the presidential term of office from four to five years and expanded the ambit of the president's decree-law power to include taxation, creation of public employment, and determination of salaries for civil servants. The greatest expansion of executive power came from a provision allowing the president to send bills to Congress on any subject, but giving each house only forty-five days to consider such bills. If labeled urgent, both houses had only forty days to consider such bills jointly. Any bill not considered or rejected during that period was deemed automatically approved.

The 1969 Constitution sharply reduced the nominal protection previously accorded to individual rights. Publications contrary to good morals were prohibited. The government could impose the sanctions of death, perpetual imprisonment, banishment, and confiscation. Even those individual rights that were theoretically guaranteed remained suspended until October 13, 1978, when the institutional acts were revoked.

The 1969 Constitution, like the 1967 and 1937 Constitutions, institutionalized de facto military regimes. All three constitutions shared the basic feature of heavy centralization of power. All transferred power to the federal government from the states and municipalities, leaving Brazilian federalism a shadow of its former self. All transferred powers from the legislature to the executive. In practice, none actually provided minimally adequate protection for individual rights. All lacked legitimacy, for none was adopted by the people or their democratically elected representatives. None of the regimes they institutionalized had any serious commitment to constitutionalism.

The Process of Adopting the 1988 Constitution

The Long Transition to Democracy

Unlike transitions from military rule in many countries, the Brazilian transition was not initiated by pressure from civil society. Instead, it was initiated by the military. In 1974, President Ernesto Geisel and his chief of cabinet, General Golbery de Couto e Silva, started an eleven-year gradual relaxation of dictatorial measures that eventually resulted in redemocratizing the nation. Their motives for beginning the long transitional process are complex and to some extent remain enigmatic. Alfred Stepan, who conducted interviews on the subject with both Geisel and Golbery, reports that the decision to reach out to civil society for allies was motivated in large part by concern about the growing autonomy of the security apparatus, both in the state and within the military itself. Because Brazil's leftist guerrilla movements had long been destroyed, the security apparatus

was no longer needed and constituted a serious danger to the military as an institution.[4] In 1978, at the end of Geisel's term, Congress enacted Constitutional Amendment 11, which revoked the institutional acts and their complementary measures to the extent they conflicted with the 1969 Constitution.[5] Also in 1978, a massive strike in the auto industry on the outskirts of São Paulo marked the beginning of a period of substantial labor unrest and dissatisfaction with government-dominated labor relations.

General João Baptista de Oliveira Figueiredo, who assumed the presidency in 1979, permitted the enactment of an amnesty law that applied not only to members of the security forces who had committed human rights violations but also to political prisoners and exiles.[6] This double-sided amnesty law—which, unlike similar laws in Argentina and Uruguay, has never been overturned—facilitated widespread acceptance of redemocratization by the military and its most vociferous opponents. A new law on political parties permitted the resumption of a much more vigorous and diverse political life. In 1980, the National Conference of Lawyers approved the Declaration of Manaus, calling for a return of the constituent power to the people. Distinguished jurists, such as Raymundo Faoro and Miguel Seabra Fagundes, began to call publicly for convocation of an assembly to draft a new constitution.[7]

In 1982, concerned about losing its control over constitutional amendments, the military government increased the number of votes required in Congress to adopt a constitutional amendment from an absolute majority to two-thirds.[8] This change proved critical two years later, when the Partido do Movimento Democrático Brasileiro (Party of the Brazilian Democratic Movement, or PMDB), the principal opposition party with 200 seats in the Chamber of Deputies, proposed a constitutional amendment to restore popular election of the president. All opposition parties joined in mobilizing popular support for the measure. Millions of Brazilians attended rallies and took to the streets in the principal cities to demand *diretas-já*, direct presidential elections, immediately. On April 25, 1984, a majority of Congress voted for a constitutional amendment to restore direct elections but fell twenty-two votes short of the two-thirds majority needed for enactment.

As the military government changed the rules for amending the constitution, it decided also to change the rules for the next presidential election, which was moved forward from October 1984 to January 1985. Constitutional Amendment 22, which the military pushed through Congress in 1982, modified the Electoral College that indirectly selected the president. The Electoral College had been composed of the entire National Congress, plus an additional group of electors selected by the state legislatures in proportion to each state's population.[9] Amendment 22 eliminated proportional representation for the additional group of electors; instead, each state selected six additional electors, chosen by the majority party in a winner-take-all vote.[10] Nevertheless, this strategy failed to prevent the Electoral College, which met in January 1985, from ending twenty-one years of military rule by electing as president Tancredo Neves, the head of the PMDB and a principal leader of civilian opposition to military rule.

Shortly thereafter, fate seriously undermined the Brazilian redemocratization process. Neves died shortly before assuming office. The vice president, José Sarney, was a lackluster traditional politician from Maranhão, a backward northeastern state. Until shortly before the 1985 election, he had been president of the Partido Democrático Social (Social Democratic Party, or PDS), the promilitary regime party. The PDS had split, and its dissidents, including Sarney, joined

the Partido a Frente Liberal (Liberal Front Party, or PFL). The PFL then formed a coalition with the PMDB called the Democratic Alliance, which produced the Neves–Sarney ticket. Although many PMDB politicians had wanted Ulysses Guimarães, popular leader of the PMDB, to succeed Neves, the military insisted that Sarney be sworn in as Brazil's transitional president on March 15, 1985.[11] Two months later, Congress adopted Constitutional Amendment No. 25, which not only restored direct elections for all levels of government but also totally liberalized the rules governing political parties by legalizing Marxist parties, abolishing the requirement of party discipline, eliminating obstacles to party formation, and permitting multiparty alliances.

With Constitutional Amendment No. 25, the path of Brazilian constitutionalism reached a critical juncture. Because most of its authoritarian features had been relaxed by subsequent constitutional amendments, the 1969 Constitution could have been maintained. Alternatively, the democratic 1946 Constitution could have been restored. But Neves had promised a new constitution, and after his untimely death, his successor was determined to fulfill that promise.

The Utilization of Congress as a Constituent Assembly

In 1985, Brazil made a critical decision that seriously undermined the democratic character of the constitution-making process. Instead of popularly electing delegates to a constituent assembly, an idea that had substantial popular support,[12] President Sarney proposed and Congress adopted a constitutional amendment empowering the next Congress—elected on November 15, 1986—to double as the constituent assembly.[13] The condition that Congress serve as the constituent assembly appears to have been imposed secretly by the military high command, on the theory that Congress would be more responsive to military demands than would a specially elected constituent assembly.[14] While many countries have used their legislatures as constituent assemblies successfully, in the Brazilian context, the procedure was fundamentally flawed. First, the degree to which Brazilians were democratically represented in Congress was severely attenuated. Brazil's electoral legislation badly underrepresented the most populous states. States from the north, northeast, and center-west, with about 40 percent of the population, had 52 percent of the delegates to the assembly. Using two different models, Barry Ames has calculated that about one-fifth of the crucial votes in the constituent assembly would have been different if its membership had been elected proportionally to population.[15] Second, the 1986 Congress included senators elected indirectly by an electoral college in 1982, under the prior authoritarian electoral legislation. These twenty-three senators had no specific mandate from the electorate to serve as part of a constituent assembly.[16] Third, voters knew virtually nothing about the candidates' views on elaborating a new constitution.[17] Fourth, Congress had—and still has—a ravenous appetite for pork-barrel benefits, that is, government jobs for supporters and geographically specific public works projects. Votes of members of Congress in the constituent assembly were purchased, or at least rented, in exchange for pork-barrel programs.[18] While specially elected members of a constituent assembly also might have been susceptible to the blandishments of pork, their lack of concern for reelection should have made their appetites much smaller than those of members of Congress.

Another element of unfairness resulted from the Sarney administration's success in concealing the ineffectiveness of its eco-nomic stabilization plan from the electorate. Sarney deliberately delayed until just after the November 1986 congressional elections a desperately needed adjustment to his Cruzado Plan, a wage increase coupled with a freeze on prices and the exchange rate that created the illusion of monetary stability and relative prosperity while exacerbating the underlying causes of the galloping inflation it had temporarily suppressed.[19] Had voters realized that the Cruzado Plan was a huge fiasco, and that the country was actually in the grip of the worst inflationary crisis in Brazilian history, the number of members of Congress elected from the PMDB would have been far fewer.[20]

Apart from political fairness, combining legislative and constitution-making functions in Congress had other drawbacks. Drafting a new constitution dragged on for nineteen months, partly because Congress was forced to divide its time, meeting unicamerally in the mornings as the constituent assembly and bicamerally in the afternoons as the legislature. Ideally, constitutions should endure without revision rather than be constantly rewritten.[21] This means that they should be elaborated by statesmen with long-term national perspectives. Brazil's Congress is a highly political body with a short-term perspective and agenda, elected primarily to represent state and local interests rather than the interests of the nation. President Sarney successfully exploited congressional local interests to influence the constitution-making process.[22] Moreover, as a basic political player, Congress had a clear conflict of interest. It is not surprising that the constitutional document that Congress drafted aggrandizes congressional power and confers numerous favors and entitlements upon states, counties, and special-interest groups. Congress also has been the primary beneficiary of frequent constitutional amendments, each of which provides two occasions to open the pork barrel to secure the needed extraordinary majorities in two voting rounds.

The Composition of the Assembly

At the start of the constitutional assembly's deliberations in early 1987, the majority (298 out of 559) of its delegates were members of the PMDB. But Brazilian party affiliations are frequently transient, and many of those elected under the eclectic PMDB label came from other parties. David Fleischer's analysis shows that 82 members of the PMDB in 1987 were former members of the PDS or ARENA (National Renovating Alliance), parties that supported the military government, and that only 212 (40 percent) members were authentic PMDB members in the sense that they either came to the PMDB from the MDB (Brazilian Democratic Movement), the party that opposed the military government, or joined the PMDB directly. But even the so-called authentic PMDB was ideologically quite heterogeneous. Fleischer's research also reveals that the largest group in the assembly consisted of the 217 delegates who were former members of ARENA. The *Folha* of São Paulo, one of Brazil's leading newspapers, estimated the ideological breakdown of the assembly as 9 percent leftist, 23 percent center-leftist, 32 percent centrist, 24 percent center-rightist, and 12 percent rightist. Although 257 (46 percent) of the delegates had law degrees, only 51 (9.1 percent) actually practiced law. In socioeconomic terms, the largest group of delegates was made up of 211 (37.7 percent) delegates whose primary income came from invested capital. Another 133 (23.8 percent) of the delegates were rural property owners.[23]

Adopting the Assembly's Internal Rules

The constitutional assembly convened on February 1, 1987, with a largely undefined agenda. Its first tasks were election of its president and executive committee (Mesa) and the drafting of its internal rules. The constitutional amendment that convoked the assembly mandated only three rules: that the Chamber of Deputies and the Senate meet as a single chamber on February 1, 1987; that the president of the Supreme Court install the constituent assembly and supervise the election of its president; and that the text of the constitution be approved in two rounds of voting by an absolute majority. Ulysses Guimarães, the leader of the PMDB, was easily elected president of the assembly, and he appointed Senator Fernando Henrique Cardoso, a member of the liberal wing of the PMDB from São Paulo, to formulate the internal rules in collaboration with the leadership of the political parties. Cardoso's draft of the internal rules, presented on February 16, 1987, generated controversy on two critical issues: the assembly's sovereign powers to enact measures that would take effect immediately and the process by which the new constitution would be drafted.

The Cardoso draft gave the assembly the power to issue decisional measures (*projetos de decisão*) with immediate effect on any matter deemed relevant. Such measures would have allowed the assembly to amend the existing 1969 Constitution at any time by vote of an absolute majority, rather than the two-thirds majority that the 1969 Constitution required. The center-right elements vehemently opposed this proposal, arguing that the sovereign powers of the assembly were limited to drafting a new constitution rather than governing the country. Eventually, Cardoso worked out a compromise, in which decisional measures could be issued only against acts that threatened the assembly's sovereignty. Although several such measures were proposed, none was ever adopted.[24]

The second issue was whether to start the drafting process with or without a draft prepared by constitutional scholars. The assembly opted to draw up a new constitution without starting from a draft on the theory that this would make the process as open and democratic as possible. The assembly emphatically rejected the idea of commissioning a draft as a "dangerous instrument of control over the assembly."[25]

The No Architect/No Blueprint Approach to Constitution Building

The constitutional assembly's decision to proceed without a draft seriously complicated the assembly's principal task. Had it started with a coherent draft, the assembly could have shortened the drafting process enormously and probably would not have produced a document with such serious conceptual and organizational flaws. In July 1985, President Sarney appointed a blue-ribbon committee, headed by Afonso Arinos, a distinguished jurist and politician, to prepare a draft constitution for submission to the constituent assembly. The extensive Arinos Draft, issued in September 1986, contained 451 articles with many commendable features.[26] It proposed a type of parliamentarism similar to the French Fifth Republic, with a congressionally chosen prime minister and a popularly elected president. It also proposed a badly needed German-style reorganization of the party system with proportional representation and a threshold of 3 percent of the national vote for party representation in Congress. But President Sarney refused to submit the Arinos Draft to the constituent assembly because he disagreed with many of its provisions, particularly the creation of a mixed parliamentary-presidential system of government. Nevertheless, a strikingly similar proposal surfaced in the assembly's draft constitution.

Though the entire 559-member assembly drafted the constitution from scratch, the draft itself was patched together; delegates borrowed many provisions from previous Brazilian constitutions and the Arinos Draft. PRODASEN (Center for Informatics and Data-Processing of the Federal Senate) not only assembled and compared all prior Brazilian constitutions but also collected Portuguese translations of the constitutions of more than thirty-six countries, including Germany, Italy, Japan, Spain, and the United States. These translations, along with the Portuguese constitution, were made available to members of the assembly.[27] The assembly also held seminars on constitution writing for its members with experts from various countries. The strongest outside influence on the assembly members was the Portuguese constitution of 1976 and the doctrinal writings of the distinguished Portuguese constitutional scholar, Professor José Joaquim Gomes Canotilho of the Law School of the University of Coimbra.[28]

Thematic Committees and Subcommittees

The assembly's internal rules, approved on March 24, 1987, adopted a decentralized system of drafting, to be done initially by the members themselves rather than hired experts or a special committee. The rules called for all assembly members to divide themselves into eight thematic committees, each made up of sixty-three regular members and a similar number of substitutes, who were also assembly members. Each committee, in turn, was divided into three thematic subcommittees, each with twenty-one members. At every phase, decisions were made by absolute majority vote. The thematic committees and subcommittees consisted of the following:

I. **Committee on Sovereignty and the Rights and Guarantees of Men and Women**
   (a) Nationality, Sovereignty, and International Relations
   (b) Political Rights, Collective Rights, and Guarantees
   (c) Individual Rights and Guarantees

II. **Committee on Organization of the State**
   (a) Federal Government, Federal District, and Territories
   (b) States
   (c) Counties and Regions
III. **Committee on Organization of the Branches and System of Government**
   (a) Legislative Branch
   (b) Executive Branch
   (c) Judicial Branch
IV. **Committee on Electoral and Party Organization and Institutional Guarantees**
   (a) Election System and Political Parties
   (b) Defense of the State and Society and their Security
   (c) Guarantee of the Constitution, its Reform, and Amendment
V. **Committee on the Tax System, Budget, and Finance**
   (a) Taxation and Revenue Participation and Sharing
   (b) Budget and Financial Oversight
   (c) Financial System
VI. **Committee on the Economic Order**
   (a) General Principles, State Intervention, and Regimes of Property to the Subsoil and Economic Activity
   (b) Urban Questions and Transportation
   (c) Agricultural Policy, Land Tenure, and Land Reform
VII. **Committee on Social Order**
   (a) Rights of Workers and Civil Servants
   (b) Health, Security, and the Environment
   (c) Blacks, Indians, Disabled, and Minorities
VIII. **Committee on Family, Education, Culture, Sports, Communication, Science, and Technology**
   (a) Education, Culture, and Sports
   (b) Science, Technology, and Communication
   (c) Family, Minors, and Elderly

In June 1987, the assembly created a special systematization committee, the function of which was to integrate the final reports of the eight thematic committees into an organic draft for presentation to the entire assembly. The critical role of this committee and its rapporteur is discussed below.

The PMDB had by far the largest representation on each committee and subcommittee because membership on all committees was proportional to each party's representation in the assembly. The PMDB allowed its members to designate the committees on which they wished to serve. Each committee and subcommittee was headed by a president, two vice presidents, and a general rapporteur. These leadership positions were allocated on the basis of negotiations among the leaders of the various parties. The liberal wing of the PMDB took advantage of the internal divisions within the conservative wing of its party to elect Mário Covas, a liberal senator from São Paulo, as floor leader of the PMDB in an internal election on March 18, 1987. Covas made sure that all nine of the committee rapporteurs, who played critical roles in the initial drafting process,[29] were PMDB members, and that eight were drawn from the liberal wing of that party. Eight committee presidents were members of the second largest party, the PFL, and one presidency went to the much smaller PDS. The great bulk of the vice-presidential positions also went to the PMDB. While leadership of the subcommittees was more evenly divided among the parties, Covas secured the bulk of the leadership positions for the more liberal members of the PMDB.[30]

The internal rules permitted civic associations, private citizens, and members of the assembly to submit suggestions to each subcommittee. The first sessions were devoted to collecting and reviewing 11,989 suggestions from civic associations and individuals that had been organized by PRODASEN. The subcommittees then held 182 public hearings and heard testimony from individuals and organizations regarding the public suggestions. Each subcommittee then drafted its respective part of the principal committee's theme, which was then forwarded to the principal committee for integration into that committee's draft. In May 1987, after forwarding their twenty-four drafts to their respective parent-committee rapporteurs, the subcommittees were dissolved.

Between May 25 and June 15, 1987, the eight thematic committee rapporteurs integrated their subcommittee drafts into a single document, which they submitted to the entire committee for amendment and discussion. In this first round, a total of 7,727 amendments were proposed to the eight committee drafts. The rapporteurs then redrafted the documents for further discussion and amendment. Another 7,184 amendments were proposed in the second round. Finally, the proposed text was submitted to a vote of the entire committee. Despite the barrage of proposed amendments, surprisingly few modifications were made at the thematic committee level.[31]

Popular Participation

Unlike the assembly that drafted the U.S. constitution, which operated in complete secrecy, Brazil's constitutional assembly made a concerted effort to make its proceedings as public as possible. The assembly strongly encouraged popular participation from all sectors of civil society. The internal rules created the so-called popular amendment, which enabled citizens' groups to present constitutional proposals that the entire assembly had to consider. Popular amendments required the signatures of at least 30,000 voters and

had to be organized by at least three legally constituted associative entities responsible for the authenticity of the signatures. For each popular amendment, one signatory had the right to make a twenty-minute presentation to the full assembly. One hundred twenty-two popular amendments, some with more than one million signatures, were actually submitted to the assembly in the month following the systematization committee's presentation of its initial draft.

The assembly's internal rules also required that each subcommittee devote five to eight sessions to hearing from entities representing various sectors of Brazilian civil society. Virtually all interest groups—including government ministers, environmentalists, human rights activists, feminists, business associations, unions, landlords, Indians, street urchins, prostitutes, homosexuals, and maids—sought to protect their interests and to include their demands in the new constitution. Proposals from any civic organization were automatically submitted to subcommittees, who were required to hold public hearings on them. PRODASEN sent out more than five million questionnaires to voters and civic groups soliciting suggestions on what they believed should be in the new constitution. PRODASEN also set up a computerized data bank containing the results of the 72,719 popular suggestions received in return.[32]

Television and newspapers kept the work of the assembly in constant public view. O Globo, Brazil's largest television network, carried the entire initial session of the assembly in a live broadcast. The congressional staff set up a media center to ensure that news outlets disseminated and explained the assembly's acts to the general public. This center produced 716 television programs, 700 radio programs, 3,000 hours of video, and 4,871 interviews with members of the assembly. Five-minute radio and television segments on the assembly's work were aired twice a day. The center's weekly journal on the assembly's proceedings was distributed to more than seventy thousand government officials, universities, and research institutions.[33] The press, the Roman Catholic Church, unions, human rights groups, and civic groups repeatedly urged the public to become involved in the process of drafting the new constitution. During the seemingly interminable deliberations, virtually all aspects of Brazilian society were debated. Both in principle and in final result, nothing was deemed too trivial for possible inclusion in the new constitutional text. Some 61,142 amendments were proposed; some 21,000 speeches were delivered. The annals of the constituent assembly fill one hundred volumes.[34] As president of the assembly, Ulysses Guimarães dubbed Brazil's new charter "The Citizens' Constitution" for good reason.

Because the political parties were weakly organized and political forces badly divided, the assembly was unusually susceptible to pressures from societal interest groups.[35] Seven of the most influential societal interest groups were organized labor, business groups, rural landowners, the military, the Church, peasants, and the so-called popular movement.

Organized Labor

Since labor unions had difficulty agreeing upon specific proposals, a lobbying organization called the Inter-Union Department for Parliamentary Action (DIAP) had the task of articulating organized labor's interests before the constituent assembly. Organized in 1983 by a group of labor unions, DIAP was a voluntary organization run by a group of labor lawyers.[36] The interests of the labor movement were also promoted by the Workers' Party (PT), founded in 1980 by Luis Inácio Lula da Silva. Sixteen PT representatives were elected to the 1986 Congress.

The labor movement lobbied hard and effectively for autonomy from the Ministry of Labor and a series of specific labor benefits, such as reducing the number of hours in the workweek from forty-eight to forty-four, extending the right to strike to all workers, extending maternity leave and creating paternity leave, and increasing the compensation rate for overtime. They also lobbied hard for restoration of job tenure, which the military had replaced with the Fund for the Guarantee of the Time of Service (FGTS).[37] Business groups' strong opposition to restoring job tenure in the private sector ultimately resulted in its defeat after bitter debate. However, civil servants successfully lobbied for job security and extending tenure to all government employees with five years of service irrespective of whether they had passed the entrance exams, as well as generous retirement benefits. Maids' organizations, formed specifically to lobby the assembly, successfully inserted a provision that extended to domestic workers the benefits of the minimum wage, a month's paid vacation, one day off a week, a month's notice before dismissal, four months of paid maternity leave, and retirement. The labor movement also supported land reform, albeit much less effectively. The labor movement sought to influence the assembly directly through its PT representatives by sending delegations to lobby, mobilizing the rank and file, and holding rallies to support prolabor candidates.

Business Groups

The business sector was much more diverse than the labor sector and consequently had even greater difficulty in articulating a set of policies for which to lobby. The Federation of Industries of São Paulo (FIESP) set up a special committee to prepare constitutional proposals, which in 1986 produced a neoliberal document called *Contribution to the Fu-*

ture Brazilian Constitution. In March 1986, industrial leaders organized the Union of Brazilian Businessmen (UBE) in Brasília as an umbrella organization for diverse business groups to formulate constitutional proposals for the business community. In November 1987, a similar umbrella organization, the National Front for Free Enterprise (FNLI), was organized to mobilize business interests to defend free enterprise against the constitutional draft emerging from the assembly; it ran a fifteen-day television campaign in favor of free enterprise. Industrial business groups lobbied hard in favor of free enterprise, restriction of governmental enterprises, and neoliberalism. They also lobbied against labor demands for absolute job security and an extension of the right to strike. But some business groups diverged from neoliberalism to support market protection, special privileges for firms of national capital, and extensive restrictions on foreign investment. Perhaps the most effective technique that business groups used to influence the outcome of the constitutional drafting process was to elect 211 of their members to the assembly. Business groups also generated numerous documents articulating and explaining their positions.

Rural Landowners

Rural landowners vigorously and effectively opposed peasant demands for land reform. Membership in its lobbying organization, the Rural Democratic Union (UDR), organized in 1985 in reaction to a land-reform program, grew from 50,000 to 230,000 between 1986 and 1987. In October 1986, several rural agro-business organizations, such as the Confederation of Agriculture (CNA) and the Brazilian Rural Society (SRB), joined the UDR to form an umbrella organization called the Ample Front for Agriculture (FAA) to lobby the constituent assem-

bly. Landowners raised substantial funds by auctioning off cattle, using the funds to mobilize mass demonstrations and buy media time urging rejection of constitutional provisions on land reform.[38] They also had eighty of their members elected to the constituent assembly.

The Military

The military lobbied the assembly very effectively through thirteen superior officers assigned as liaisons to Congress and through its longtime ally, President Sarney. It also strongly pressured—even intimidated—members of the assembly through public threats of another coup d'état by military ministers. The military successfully sought to protect its corporative privileges, retain its historic position as the guardian of domestic order and protector of the constitutional order, increase military appropriations, and maintain its contingent of six cabinet positions. It also successfully opposed civilian control over the military, an attempt to create a ministry of defense, a parliamentary form of government, attempts to dismantle the National Security Council (CSN) and the National Information Service (SNI), land reform, and extension of the right to strike to essential public services. The military's influence on the assembly's deliberations was so great that Alfred Stepan and Juan Linz have placed the 1988 Brazilian constitution in the category of constitutions "created under highly constraining circumstances reflecting de facto power of non-democratic institutions and forces."[39]

The Church

The Roman Catholic Church had been a significant moral force in opposing the military regime, particularly in criticizing its human rights violations and in promoting social justice for the poor through grassroots church committees (CEBs). It eschewed covert lobbying of assembly members; instead, the National Conference of the Bishops of Brazil (CNBB) tried to set the agenda for the assembly by publishing a document in 1986 entitled *For a New Constitutional Order*, which called for protection of human rights, income redistribution for the poor, agrarian reform, reduction in media monopolization, and more active citizen participation in government. Rather than endorse specific candidates for the assembly, the Church urged its members to vote for candidates dedicated to social justice and human rights. The Church did play an active role, however, in promoting popular amendments and organizing public meetings with assembly members. It also organized a special commission to record and disseminate the assembly's work.[40] The bishops successfully included a provision in the constitution that made religious education optional during normal school hours in public elementary schools; they also successfully blocked feminist attempts to legalize abortion. The Church was less successful, however, in preventing expansion of the right to divorce and artificial birth control.

Peasant Groups

With millions of members, the National Confederation of Agricultural Workers (CONTAG) was one of the leading organizations pressing for agrarian reform. In 1985, CONTAG prepared a document for the Arinos Commission setting forth its constitutional agenda for land reform. In 1985, the CNBB formed the Pastoral Commission for Land to support peasant lobbying for land reform. The Movement of the Landless Rural Workers (MST), formed in 1980, also pushed hard for land reform. The agenda of these groups was specific constitutional provisions permitting expropriation of productive land and payment of compensation for land taken for agrarian reform at less than fair market value and in bonds. They urged that 5 percent of governmental revenues be set aside solely for agrarian-reform purposes. They also demanded limits on the size of land holdings by both Brazilians and foreigners, as well as severe constraints on the ability of property owners to resist the expropriation of their lands in the courts. The peasant groups' principal lobbying technique was mass mobilization. Lacking the financial resources of the rural landowners, the peasant groups managed to have only one of their members elected to the assembly. Intense political maneuvering by rural landowners ultimately led to rejection of most of the peasants' demands in the assembly.[41]

The Popular Movement

The popular movement consisted of a diverse group of civic and professional organizations, as well as a broad array of grassroots organizations and technical institutions, that began as a lobby for a popular constituent assembly. It was led by the Brazilian Bar Association (OAB), the CNBB, and the PT. Achieving their initial goal, the groups began lobbying the constituent assembly to make the drafting process transparent and accessible to the public. They succeeded in having the assembly adopt the popular amendment process, which they then used to propose detailed and programmatic measures to make Brazilian society more just. Their lobbying efforts consisted of rallies, leaflets, demonstrations, books, posters, and popular amendments.

The Role of the Systematization Committee

The thematic committee rapporteurs were responsible for forwarding the draft articles to the systematization committee.[42] This committee—the composition of which was decidedly more progressive or liberal than the entire constituent assembly—had the difficult task of trying to mold the twenty-four thematic subcommittees' uncoordinated and often inconsistent articles, plus the thousands of amendments suggested by assembly members and outside groups, into a more or less coherent document. The PMDB leadership designated Bernardo Cabral, a PMDB deputy and former president of the Brazilian Bar Association, as rapporteur for the systematization committee. Cabral and his assistant rapporteurs[43] arranged the thematic committee reports into a single text known as Cabral Zero. In June 1987, Cabral presented this text to the assembly without changing the contents of the committee reports.

Cabral Zero was a 501-article monstrosity quickly nicknamed "the Frankenstein draft."[44] In July 1987, after assembly members presented 5,615 amendments, Cabral submitted his own 496-article draft (Cabral I), incorporating a number of the proposed amendments. This draft pleased none of the major political forces, particularly President Sarney and the military. Because the rapporteur was free to include or reject any proposed amendments, intensive lobbying efforts by assembly members, the executive, and organized societal groups focused upon Cabral to try to persuade him to change the draft to their liking. Assembly members presented Cabral with another 20,790 amendments, and popular groups submitted an additional eighty-three amendments.

In September 1987, Cabral presented his second draft (Cabral II) to the systematization committee. Cabral II reduced the number of articles from 496 to 264, plus 72 transitional provisions. In this second draft, Cabral sought to resolve many constitutional controversies by postponing them to future enactment of complementary or ordinary legislation, deleting them, or attempting compromise solutions. For example, he excluded the direct democracy features of plebiscites, referendums, and popular initiatives. He maintained the concept of Brazilian firms of national capital, which were to be favored by law, but prohibited discrimination against foreign firms. He left the question of expropriability of land for agrarian reform to ordinary legislation. To try to placate President Sarney, Cabral extended the president's mandate from five to six years. The president would be elected by direct elections, but if no candidate received a majority, Congress would select the winner from among the candidates who received the most votes.[45]

The systematization committee made substantial changes to Cabral II, undoing many of Cabral's compromises. The committee took two months to vote out its modified version of Cabral II, known as *Projeto A* (Draft A), released for consideration by the entire assembly on November 18, 1987. At that point, the systematization committee was dissolved, leaving only its rapporteur to continue his crucial role in the redrafting process. The committee's Draft A was a critical document, for the internal rules mandated that an absolute majority (280 votes) was necessary to amend or remove any item. Draft A reflected the center-left agenda: a parliamentary system, significant restrictions on foreign investment, substantial government interference in the economy, mechanisms for direct democracy, reduction of the term of the president to five years, limiting Sarney's mandate to four years, highly protective labor provisions, decentralization, substantial transference of tax authority and revenue to the states and municipalities, agrarian reform, expropriation of productive land, liberal human rights protection, and broad amnesty provisions. Draft A produced a strong backlash from business groups and rural landowners. The military and President Sarney reacted even more negatively, warning that its approval might lead to a military coup.

The Centrão Coalition and the Change in Internal Rules

Initially, conservatives were badly divided, which allowed the forces of the center-left to dominate the early rounds of constitutional bargaining. Reactions to Draft A galvanized the formation of a broad, diverse coalition of constituent assembly members from the center and right known as the Centrão (the big center). This loose-knit group, which cut across party lines, initially coalesced around the strategy of changing the assembly's internal rules.[46] The Centrão accomplished this goal through a petition signed by 290 assembly members; their signatures were collected through intensive lobbying by large landowners and business elites, increasing threats from the military, and President Sarney's generous distribution of blandishments from the government's pork barrel. The petition ultimately changed the rule requiring 280 votes to remove or amend an item in the systematization committee draft to one that required 280 votes either to keep an item in the draft or to remove or amend it. This rule change significantly reduced the power of the progressive-leftist group that dominated the systematization committee, but it made the voting process even more convoluted.

Voting Procedure on the Final Drafts

Amendments were considered in two rounds by roll-call votes. The voting order was to consider first any amendment with at least 280 signatures to the basic text of each chapter and title in the systematization committee's Draft A. Because the Centrão had prepared its own competing draft constitution, its draft was voted upon first. The Centrão's amendments had two chances for success. Approval of an amendment, either when initially pre-

sented or twenty-four hours later, definitively eliminated the corresponding original text from Draft A. Only if the Centrão's substitute provision failed to win the necessary 280 votes in two tries did the assembly vote upon the corresponding provision in Draft A. If the original Chapter A provision also failed to receive the necessary 280 votes, Cabral had forty-eight hours to revise the text. If his proposed revision also failed to win 280 votes, the provision was excluded from the constitution. Each chapter and title of the draft was considered in order, starting with the preamble and ending with the Transitory Constitutional Provisions Act. Each amendment was read aloud by Ulysses Guimarães, opined on by Bernardo Cabral, and debated by assembly members.

Once an absolute majority approved the basic text of a chapter, the assembly moved to the next voting phase. This was consideration of redactive amendments called *destaques*, designed to add, modify, or delete words, phrases, or articles in the approved text. The process also included a mechanism called the *destaque para votação em separado*, used to vote on provisions that were previously excluded from the basic text. The destaques had to be presented previously to the rapporteur for screening and organization.

Lack of Political Domination in the Assembly

No single political group or figure dominated the constituent assembly. Even though the PMDB initially had an overwhelming majority of assembly members, the political party contained deep ideological divisions and no party loyalty or discipline.[47] During the constituent assembly, many of the PMDB's left-wing members deserted it to form the Partido da Social-Democracia Brasileira (Brazilian Social Democratic Party, or PSDB), but "even before the split the PMDB had ceased to enjoy any sort of programmatic coherence or legislative discipline."[48] The PMDB was not alone in this regard. None of the major parties had a coherent party line for drafting the new constitution, and only the PT had some semblance of party discipline.

Lack of political direction and the Byzantine voting procedure meant that majority votes on virtually every issue depended on protracted negotiations and bargaining. Faced with a realistic prospect of stalemate, party leaders created an institution called the Leaders' Council (*Colégio de Líderes*), which has since become a permanent feature of Congress, to accelerate the voting process. Prior to voting sessions, party leaders began meeting to organize the voting, determining in advance official party positions and the areas of agreement and disagreement.[49] The Leaders' Council usually removed the most contentious provisions from the basic texts, leaving them for the destaques. These destaques frequently became the focus of heated debate that was often resolved by compromise after informal negotiations among party leaders.[50] Some of these compromises had to be renegotiated if party leaders could not deliver the necessary votes. Even if the votes were there, often the voters were not: In a constitution-making process that dragged out for nineteen months, absenteeism became a significant problem, particularly for assembly members with business or professional interests in other cities.

The Substantial Revision of Draft A

The constituent assembly made critical changes to Draft A that resulted from the Centrão's internal rule change (described above). In March 1988, by a vote of 344 to 212, presidentialism replaced parliamentarism. By a vote of 304 to 223, Sarney was granted another year in the presidency. On the other hand, because of absenteeism and ideological divisions, the Centrão failed to prevent many leftist provisions in Draft A from remaining in Draft B.

The rules under which Brazilian constitution making was conducted forced assembly members to negotiate hotly contested issues. No side could claim a clear victory and no side was clearly defeated. The process resulted in a series of compromises that allowed conservative forces to prevail on certain issues, such as permitting the military to intervene on the invitation of any branch of government to protect law and order, or prohibiting agrarian reform expropriations of productive land and small- to medium-sized properties. Job security for workers was eliminated in the private sector but retained for the public sector. On other issues, the center-left prevailed, restricting foreign investment, prohibiting usury, granting labor unions greater autonomy, and implementing a broad array of human rights.[51] Political moderation, protracted negotiations, and substantial compromises—all hallmarks of Brazil's lengthy transition to democracy—ultimately also became the hallmarks of the process of drafting the new constitution.

The first round required delegates to vote on 732 occasions and finally concluded, five months later, at the end of June 1988. After a July recess, the same process was repeated, albeit more quickly, with each chapter and title of Draft B. The second round required delegates to vote only 289 times and took a little more than one month.

On July 26, 1988, President Sarney made a last-ditch effort to sabotage the assembly's work, claiming in a televised address that adopting Draft B would leave the country bankrupt and ungovernable. The next day, Draft B was submitted to the entire assembly for a second round of suppressive and corrective amendments. The assembly eventually approved the final draft by a majority of 403 to 13.

The approved text was then sent to an editing committee of thirty people appointed by Ulysses Guimarães. After a final edit for style, the assembly approved the constitution on September 22 and promulgated it on October 5, 1988, twenty months after the assembly began its work. Neither a plebiscite nor any other ratification procedure was held, thereby reducing the constitution's legitimacy and eliminating any chance for further changes dictated by citizen input.

Despite the complex legalistic rules governing the proceedings, at least three articles were adopted by resort to the ubiquitous Brazilian *jeito*.[52] In October 2003, fifteen years after the constitution's adoption, Nelson Jobim, then vice president of the Supreme Court, publicly revealed that with Guimarães's complicity, he had slipped two articles into the final draft of the constitution, bypassing the assembly's rules for submission and voting on amendments.[53] Shortly thereafter, Jarbas Passarinho, then president of the committee on electoral and party organization and institutional guarantees and member of the systematization committee, publicly disclosed that he too had slipped in a last-minute amendment at Guimarães's suggestion.[54] After a group of jurists called for his impeachment,[55] Jobim rationalized his action by opining that his amendments had been ratified by the final vote of the assembly, which he deemed a kind of third round.[56] The effort to impeach Jobim went nowhere.

The Results of Brazil's Constitution-Making Process

The 1988 Constitution reflects the intense political mobilization of interest groups and lobbies for inclusion of their demands and protection of their interests. It contains a host of unwieldy entitlements that often embed traditional Brazilian corporatism and clientelism. The convoluted drafting process virtually assured that the new constitution would lack organic unity and a coherent vision for a democratic Brazil. The end product is a mélange of progressive, conservative, liberal, radical, and moderate provisions, all rather uncomfortably ensconced side by side in a complex, detailed document containing 245 articles and 70 transitional provisions, many of which contain numerous elliptical sections and subparagraphs.

The constitution is *dirigiste* and programmatic, setting out ambitious goals for reforming Brazilian society and attempting to determine the political course of action for future governments. Rather than emphasizing fundamental principles and basic procedural rules for future resolution of societal problems, Brazil's charter sets out detailed substantive rules that belong either in ordinary legislation or administrative regulations rather than in a constitution. The result is a constitutional straightjacket that has been a serious obstacle to effective democratic governance and socioeconomic modernization.

Despite the great detail in which many subjects have been regulated, the constitution requires a great many complementary and ordinary laws to fill in missing elements or permit implementation of its provisions. A principal reason for this constitutional style is the polemical nature of many provisions. Many measures were so divisive that the constituent assembly could finish its task only by leaving aside the details for future legislation.[57]

Moreover, the assembly made a calculated decision to defer rather than resolve constitutional conflicts permanently. It postponed for five years the ultimate resolution of the shape of the constitution that it had just adopted. Given the serious constraints that the military and its ally, President Sarney, placed upon the constitution-making process, as well as the political unfairness associated with the way in which its members were selected, the assembly's decision to make Brazil's 1988 Constitution provisional arguably was a sensible strategy.[58] Two transitional provisions provided for revisiting basic constitutional questions after five years, by plebiscite and a facilitated revision procedure.

Plebiscite after Five Years

The framers deferred ultimate resolution of their bitter fight about whether to adopt a presidential or parliamentary form of government for five years, at which time the issue would be resolved by plebiscite.[59] Initially, supporters of presidentialism proposed to resolve the issue by plebiscite when they were losing in the deliberations of the systematization committee. Thereafter, supporters of parliamentarism embraced the idea after losing to presidentialism in the plenary vote. As the time to introduce new amendments had already passed, the vanquished supporters of parliamentarism hitched a ride on a bizarre amendment by Deputy Cunha Bueno that was awaiting floor consideration. Bueno's amendment proposed holding a plebiscite in five years to decide whether to restore the monarchy or retain a republican form of government.[60] The amendment was passed with the support of the unsuccessful advocates of a parliamentary system, who successfully added a subamendment calling for an additional vote on whether to adopt a presidential or parliamentary system of government.

Both questions were ultimately resolved by a plebiscite held in 1993. In an election marred by significant absenteeism and spoiled ballots, 66 percent of the votes were cast in favor of retaining a republican form of government, against 10.2 percent for restoring the monarchy; 55.4 percent were cast for presidentialism, against 24.6 percent for parliamentarism.[61]

Streamlined Total Revision after Five Years

Article 3 of the Transitional Constitutional Provisions Act provided that the constitution could be revised in 1993 by an absolute majority of Congress in a unicameral session. Some of the constitution's critics cynically observed, only partly tongue-in-cheek, that this was the only sensible provision in the entire constitution, for it allowed Congress to amend the document by a process simpler than enacting an ordinary statute. The president had no veto power, and the unicameral vote facilitated overriding obstructionism from the smaller, more conservative Senate. This was obviously a risky proposition with the potential for scuttling a basic purpose of a written constitution—the preservation of a particular vision of structuring and limiting power and protecting that vision from being easily overthrown by future generations.[62] It also created five years of institutional uncertainty. However, it had the potential to revisit a badly flawed constitutional document during a period in which the president would be popularly elected and the military would be much less likely to intervene.

Unfortunately, the wholesale constitutional revision envisaged for October 1993 never materialized. Important nongovernmental organizations challenged the legitimacy of revising the constitution by a single vote of a bare majority of Congress. Leftist politicians and social groups, fearful that they would lose gains made in 1988, formed an antirevisionist bloc that temporarily succeeded in preventing the revision, initially by litigation and later by parliamentary obstructionism. By this time, congressional attention was diverted toward a major corruption scandal, nicknamed Budgetgate, in which twenty-nine of its members were charged with diverting huge sums from the treasury into their own bank accounts through a budget-rigging scheme. Budgetgate forced postponement of constitutional revision until March 1994. By then, most congressmen were focused on the upcoming elections.

Although more than 17,000 amendments were presented for congressional consideration, only six were enacted, and of these, only two had any real significance. Revision Amendment 1 of March 1, 1994, temporarily changed the revenue-sharing rules, placing 15 percent of the revenues that were to be transferred from the federal government to state and local governments for fiscal years 1994 and 1995 into an emergency social fund. This transfer of an estimated nine billion dollars was critical to the success of the Plano Real, the stabilization plan that successfully lowered the inflation rate from about 50 percent per month to less than 10 percent per year. The other significant revision amendment was Amendment 5 of June 7, 1994, which increased the presidential term from four to five years.

Conflict Resolution via Inflation

Forty years ago, Albert Hirschman, in discussing Chilean society, theorized that inflation could be regarded as "a substitute for civil war."[63] Conflicts over the percentage of national income to which different groups are entitled are resolved by inflating the size of the economic pie so that each group receives an apparently larger slice. Inflation permits governments to temporize and gain additional room for social maneuvering during disruptive periods.

Brazil has been a chronically inflationary society. One of the reasons for the 1964 military takeover was the Goulart regime's inability to control inflation, which reached a record high of 91.7 percent in 1964. Unfortunately, the return of civilian government in 1985 produced unprecedented levels of hyperinflation that made the Goulart era look monetarily stable.[64]

The 1988 Constitution exacerbated Brazil's inflationary problems. Assembly members simply acquiesced to the demands of various socioeconomic groups with little or no concern about whether Brazil could afford to fund the constitutional mandates and entitlements. Even worse, they drafted a straitjacket upon the powers to tax and spend that made it virtually impossible to control the federal government's huge budgetary deficits. The constitution has hindered the reduction of major sources of expenditures,

such as cutting bloated government payrolls and overly generous retirement benefits or privatizing public-sector monopolies. It also forced major increases in fiscal transfers to the state and local governments and mandated significant increases in governmental expenditures. It forgave monetary correction payments of small private firms and farmers on loans from banks and financial institutions contracted between 1986 and 1987. President Sarney warned the assembly for good reason that adopting the proposed constitution would aggravate Brazil's desperate fiscal crisis, but his warning was ignored.

By the end of Sarney's presidential term in early 1990, Brazil was in the middle of the worst inflationary crisis in its history. The domestic debt doubled between 1988 and 1989. By the time Fernando Collor de Mello assumed the presidency, the inflation rate had reached an astonishing monthly rate of 84 percent. Collor reduced inflation drastically by a draconian and hare-brained plan of freezing all bank accounts for eighteen months, which threw the country into a severe recession, but the accumulated inflation for 1990 still reached 1,447 percent. The Collor Plan rapidly collapsed because it failed to address the underlying causes of inflation, and by 1992, the annual inflation rate had climbed back to 1,158 percent. Collor had hoped to persuade Congress to enact a huge constitutional reform package dealing with administrative, fiscal, and civil service reform. But he was ultimately frustrated by a Congress with strong ties "to well-organized groups with vested interests in preserving aspects of the constitution that institutionalized fiscal chaos."[65]

Itamar Franco, Collor's successor, also attempted several times—unsuccessfully—to control inflation. The inflation rate reached 2,489 percent in 1993. Brazil was unable to control inflation successfully until July 1994, when then–finance minister Fernando Henrique Cardoso introduced the Plano Real. At that time, inflation was running at 50 percent a month and the country was in serious economic crisis. Chile's impressive success with a free-market economy, as well as Argentina's successful stabilization and privatization programs, contrasted sharply with Brazil's track record of spiraling inflation, economic stagnation, and growing urban violence. Congress finally relented and enacted a critical constitutional amendment that created an emergency fund to reallocate tax funds to the federal government. The success of the Plano Real propelled Cardoso to the presidency in the 1994 elections.

A Steady Stream of Constitutional Amendments

Amending the constitution is only moderately difficult in Brazil. Approval requires two successive votes by at least three-fifths of each house of Congress. No further ratification is required by the states or the people.[66]

Unlike his predecessors, President Cardoso had considerable success in negotiating with Congress to enact a series of amendments that dismantled important features of the 1988 Constitution. As of April 2009, Congress has enacted sixty-three amendments, and many proposed amendments are presently in the pipeline. Congress has become an ambulatory constituent assembly. From time to time, it appears to recognize that certain fiscal features of the constitution make Brazil ungovernable. Rather than permanently amend those provisions, however, Congress prefers to make temporary changes. Thus, the Emergency Fund, which enabled the federal government to reduce the tax revenues it had to transfer to state and local governments, has been extended for brief periods by a series of constitutional amendments.[67] Four constitutional amendments extended the tax on financial transactions, formerly called the Provisional Assessment on the Movement or Transfer of Securities, Credits, or Rights of a Financial Nature.[68] A

constitutional amendment adopted in 2000 resolved a budgetary crisis by unlinking mandated spending with respect to one-fifth of budgetary resources, but only until 2003. Another amendment extended the period to 2007, and still another amendment extended the period to 2011.[69]

From 1992 to 2005, Congress also enacted amendments removing significant constitutional obstacles to reducing budgetary deficits by reforming social security, eliminating expensive retirement benefits, capping the compensation of all governmental employees, permitting the firing of tenured civil servants, and eliminating certain government monopolies and most restrictions on foreign investment.[70] As a consequence, many of the inflationary, statist, and nationalist features of the constitution have been dismantled. Moreover, much fiscal chaos has been avoided, at least temporarily. Timothy Power has noted the supreme irony: "Most of the political capital in 1987–1988 was spent in the making of a new constitution: In the 1990s, most of the political capital was spent trying to unmake the same document."[71]

The Provisional Measure: The Antidemocratic Drafting Blunder that Facilitated Governability

The constitution's framers sought to concentrate law-making powers in Congress. Because the most abused authoritarian institution was the decree-law, the 1988 Constitution deprives the president of the power to issue any. On the other hand, in recognition of the historic tendency of the executive to initiate legislation in Brazil, Article 62 authorizes the president to issue provisional measures with the force of law whenever he deems it urgent and relevant. The drafters copied the provisional measure from the Italian constitution under the assumption that Brazil was adopting a parliamentary system of government. When the form of government reverted from a parliamentary to a presidential system, the assembly committed a colossal blunder by failing to delete the provisional measure from Draft B.

The provisional measure quickly became a critical device for transferring substantial amounts of legislative power to the executive. Until 2001, Brazilian presidents could issue provisional measures with the force of law on any subject, thus expanding the breadth of their power to enact law by decree well beyond the military constitutions.[72] The only constraint on the president was that he had to submit provisional measures immediately to Congress; if not converted into law within thirty days, the measures were void ab initio. But Brazil is the land of the jeito, and Brazilian presidents quickly invented a technique for bypassing this constraint. The executive regularly reissued provisional measures, sometimes as many as eighty or ninety times, until Congress ultimately enacted them into law or rejected them. The executive also added a clause validating all acts performed in reliance on prior provisional measures.[73] Abuse of the provisional measure was substantially reduced by promulgation of Amendment 32 on September 11, 2001, which prohibits use of provisional measures in certain areas and permits provisional measures to be republished only once.[74] Nevertheless, Brazilian presidents continue to misuse the provisional measure to initiate ordinary rather than emergency legislation.

Conflict Resolution via Litigation

The 1988 Constitution augments judicial independence and makes the judiciary, particularly the Supreme Court, the primary guardian of constitutional rights. As a reaction against the twenty-one years of authoritarian military rule, the new constitution makes a very impressive effort to assure protection of an extensive list of individual, collective, and social rights. It also contains a number of procedural innovations designed to foster judicial protection of these rights. The 1934 Constitution had created a new summary remedy called a writ of security (*mandado de segurança*) to protect certain rights that habeas corpus did not protect from violation by public authorities. The 1988 Constitution creates a collective writ of security, a sensible expansion of Brazil's limited concept of a class action, to protect groups or classes against illegal or abusive governmental actions. It borrows from the Portuguese constitution a procedural device called *habeas data*, which allows anyone to discover any information the government has about him in its data banks and rectify that data if it is incorrect. The personal nature of this right, however, prevents its effective use to discover the fate of persons who disappeared or were killed during the period of military repression. The representation, an action to challenge the unconstitutionality of any law or decree directly before the Supreme Court, could be brought only by the procurator general during the time of military rule. The 1988 Constitution relabels the representation as a direct action of unconstitutionality and confers standing on a fairly large number of groups to secure an abstract determination of the constitutionality of any federal or state law or normative act.[75] To try to protect constitutional rights from congressional inertia, the constitution creates the mandate of injunction (*mandado de injunção*), which is to be granted whenever the absence of a regulatory or implementing rule makes impracticable the exercise of constitutional rights and liberties or the prerogatives inherent in nationality, citizenship, or sovereignty. It also imports from Portugal the action of unconstitutionality for omission, which is to be granted whenever the Supreme Court determines "the lack of measures to make a constitutional rule effective."[76]

Two additional constitutional remedies have been created since the adoption of the 1988 Constitution. The declaratory action of constitutionality, created by Amendment 3 in 1993, confers original jurisdiction on the Supreme Court to hear "actions declaring the constitutionality of federal laws or normative acts." This action, which can be brought only by the president, the executive committee of either house of Congress, or the procurator general, is essentially a mechanism for the federal government to bypass the lower courts and secure a speedy determination of the constitutionality of important and sensitive legislation. Disobedience of a fundamental precept, an action created by Law 9.882 in 1999, can be brought directly before the Supreme Court by anyone with standing to bring a direct action of unconstitutionality whenever there is no other effective remedy. This procedural device enables an absolute majority of the Supreme Court to suspend proceedings before any lower court; a two-thirds Supreme Court majority can declare unconstitutional any law or normative act.

The constitution also transforms the Public Ministry (*Ministério Público*) into an autonomous institution, assigning it a primary role in insuring that the laws are being faithfully executed and that collective and diffuse constitutional rights are being judicially protected. By instituting public actions against governmental authorities for misuse of public funds, class actions to protect the environment and consumers, and criminal prosecutions against corrupt politicians, the Public Ministry has become, in the opinion of several Brazilian scholars, a "fourth power."[77]

The result of this significant expansion of constitutional rights and remedies has been a flood of litigation, as the caseloads of the Brazilian courts have increased dramatically since the constitution was adopted.[78] Much of the litigation involves suits against the government, which stubbornly insists upon appealing every judgment against it, even if the issues have already been decided against it in Brazil's highest courts. As William Prillaman has observed, the 1988 Constitution was "so prescriptive and detailed that

it constitutionalized a staggering range of minor issues and flooded the courts—even the Supreme Court—with the most trivial cases." As a result, "a decade later, opinion was unanimous that unfettered access for everyone had produced, not surprisingly, access for no one."[79] On the other hand, the procedural innovations of the current constitution have forced the judiciary, particularly the Supreme Court, into the political arena on a regular basis. Consequently, the courts have become an active countermajoritarian political force.[80]

The Electoral System

Although Brazil has all the formal indicia of democracy,[81] the constitution enshrines one of the least democratic federal systems in the world. The Brazilian political system has long had a highly malapportioned system of representation in Congress. The military regime aggravated the malapportionment by fusing two heavily populated opposition states (Rio and Guanabara) and creating two new thinly populated states (Mato Grosso do Sul and Rondónia). The constituent assembly did nothing to rectify the situation. Instead, like the military regime, the assembly exacerbated the malapportionment by creating three new sparsely populated states and maintaining unique constitutional provisions that entitle every state to three senators and at least eight but no more than seventy deputies. Consequently, a vote for senator in the newly created state of Roraima has 144 times the weight of a vote for senator in São Paulo. If the Brazilian constitution had adopted the criterion of one person, one vote for the Chamber of Deputies, each of the three newly created states would have only one representative rather than eight, and São Paulo would have 114 rather than 70. In 1990, because of the new constitution, states from the north, northeast, and center-west, with only 43 percent of the population, controlled 74 percent of the seats in the Brazilian Senate.[82] This egregious overrepresentation gives enormous power to a minority to block any changes in the status quo.

The constituent assembly also did nothing to reform the malfunctioning of the political party system, which is one of the world's worst.[83] On the contrary, it imposed virtually no constraints on forming new political parties or allowing tiny splinter parties to be represented in Congress. The number of political parties in Brazil jumped from six in 1985 to thirty in 1990, seriously complicating the task of governance. Nor did it modify the open-list system of proportional representation, in which each state is a single, at-large multi-member district, a system that badly hinders party discipline.[84]

The Military

One of the pacts in the long transition from military to civilian rule was that no effort be made to try members of the military for human rights offenses committed during the period of authoritarian rule. The assembly constitutionalized this pact in Transitional Article 8, which confers broad amnesty for all acts motivated solely by political reasons between 1946 and 1988. The 1988 Constitution continues this ample protection of some of the military's interests, including its right to intervene in matters of national security, law, and order.[85] President Cardoso, however, pushed through Amendment 23 of September 2, 1999, which replaced the three military ministries and the joint chiefs of staff with the unified civilian-led Ministry of Defense. This amendment explicitly gives the president the power to appoint the commanders of the army, navy, and air force and makes them subject to the congressional impeachment process. Top military leaders are now subject to criminal trials before the Supreme Court, and civilian courts may now hear habeas corpus petitions against military orders.

The number of ministries that the military controls has dropped from six to zero. However, even though civilian control over the military has increased dramatically in recent years, the military still enjoys numerous privileges and special treatment in Brazil.[86]

Conclusion

The process by which Brazil's 1988 Constitution was adopted practically assured that the end product would be a hodgepodge of inconsistent and convoluted provisions. The decisions to designate the incoming Congress as the constituent assembly, to proceed without a draft, to entrust the initial drafting to all members of the assembly divided into twenty-four thematic subcommittees, and to invite as much participation by civil society as possible made it virtually impossible to produce a coherent document, particularly with a weak party system and president. The assembly's quixotic position that no topic was too trivial to be included on its agenda made the constitution-making process nearly unmanageable and wasted a large amount of time. The widespread belief that the new constitution would be a panacea for all Brazil's ills and the intense lobbying by popular groups made it difficult for the drafters to distinguish clearly between what belongs in a constitution and what belongs in ordinary legislation, or in no legislation. The intense lobbying and manner in which delegates were selected also made it difficult to resist efforts to embed in the constitutional text a plethora of political and economic entitlements without considering whether the country could afford them. Nor did the assembly adequately assess the risk of ungovernability that might result from its foolish decisions to lock in future generations by creating constitutional straitjackets.

Given the circumstances under which the assembly proceeded, the decision to make the constitution transitional and revisit it in five years was defensible. However, the badly needed top-to-bottom revision scheduled for 1993 never materialized. Instead, Congress has promulgated a constant stream of amendments. Some have made insignificant changes or contributed additional entitlements and complications, but others have eliminated or modified some of the ill-considered constitutional obstacles to governability and economic development. Many significant obstacles remain, and many proposed amendments are in the pipeline.

The 1988 Constitution does little to confront the major political, economic, and social problems confronting Brazil. Brazil's political institutions are still relatively weak, and the proliferation of undisciplined political parties in Congress makes governance a major problem. Brazil has long had one of the most unequal patterns of income distribution in the world. The new constitution has not improved this pattern; if anything, it has exacerbated it.

The return of democracy and the adoption of the 1988 Constitution has not appreciably reduced conflict in Brazil either; in many ways, conflict has been exacerbated. Brazil has been unable to deal effectively with the social problems resulting from the lack of effective agrarian reform. Landless peasants continue to invade privately owned farms, frequently provoking violent responses from rural landowners and the police. The formal legal system has done little to protect rural workers, lawyers, and Indians from violence stemming from land conflicts. Brazil also has significant problems with uncontrolled urban violence, some of which is attributable to arbitrary actions by the civil and military police, some to a malfunctioning criminal justice system, and some to police and prison officials' inability or unwillingness to control common criminals and drug traffickers. The wave of crime and violence afflicting Brazil has created a general climate of personal insecurity and mistrust of the legal system.[87]

Until 1994, many conflicts were shifted into the redistributive arena produced by galloping inflation. Since 1995, the Plano Real has virtually eliminated this cruel tax, which fell most heavily on the poor. Yet Brazil needs to find permanent solutions to its perennial fiscal crisis. In the past few years, important constitutional amendments have been adopted to facilitate the dismantling of Brazil's bloated governmental bureaucracy, rationalize the compensation and social security benefits of public employees, control state and municipal expenditures and indebtedness, and reform the judiciary. The Brazilian constitution impressively protects virtually all fundamental and human rights. Traditional first-generation rights, such as life, liberty, property, due process, free speech, equal protection, religious freedom, and freedom of association, are fully protected. Second-generation rights, such as the right to work, right to strike, maternity and paternity leave, housing, clothing, food, health, leisure, social security, and education, are also guaranteed, along with third-generation rights such as an ecologically balanced environment, self-determination, and cultural preservation. Amendment 45, of December 8, 2004, added what might be termed a fourth-generation right: "Everyone is assured that judicial and administrative proceedings will end within a reasonable time and the means to guarantee that they will be handled speedily." Unfortunately, many of these guarantees exist only on paper. Some very important guarantees are regularly violated with impunity, as a recent article by Augusto Zimmermann so vividly demonstrates.[88] Many important individual rights that the constitution created need strong enforcement to make them a reality. But the police and other law-enforcement officers function precariously, and the judiciary, which under normal conditions moves slowly, is swamped with cases. In 2005, the Supreme Court received 95,212 cases and decided 103,700 cases. Constitutional Amendment 45, adopted at the end of 2004, enables the Supreme Court to create binding precedents, provided they deal with constitutional issues and are adopted by a two-thirds vote. Thus far, this has done little to reduce the huge volume of cases. As of April 2009, the Supreme Court has adopted only fourteen binding precedents pursuant to this amendment. The court urgently needs a device like certiorari to allow it to hear only cases that address novel and important national issues.[89]

On the positive side, Brazil's constitution has provided a peaceful way of resolving many important conflicts. Rather than resort to a coup, Brazilians removed Collor de Mello, their first popularly elected president in three decades, by following the constitutionally prescribed procedure of impeachment. Elections are held regularly, peacefully, competently, and without claims of fraud. The electorate is one of the broadest in the world. All of the mechanisms of representative democracy, as well as those of direct democracy—such as the initiative, plebiscite, and referendum—are in place, though not much used. Political and fiscal power is substantially less concentrated in the federal executive and federal government by the strengthening of the powers of the states and local government, as well as the powers of the federal judiciary and legislature.

No longer do Brazilians talk of a coup d'état to resolve political problems.[90] The military did not threaten one in 1999, when a constitutional amendment created the Ministry of Defense and formally subordinated the military to civilian control. Nor did the military or other organized groups make such threats when Luis Inácio Lula da Silva, the first popularly elected leftist labor leader, assumed the presidency in January 2003.

Despite its many technical defects, the 1988 Constitution has enormous symbolic value. As Luís Roberto Barroso has pointed out, the constitution symbolizes the culmina-

tion of the process of the restoration of a democracy under a rule of law and the superseding of an authoritarian system characterized by intolerance, monopolization of power, and violence.[91]

Unfortunately, the 1988 Constitution has been more hindrance than help in working out democratic solutions to Brazil's most pressing economic and social problems. Ultimately, the legitimacy of the constitutional system has to survive a pragmatic test: Does it provide a substantial economic payoff for a substantial portion of its citizens?[92] Thus far, the answer has been negative. If persistent tinkering does not significantly change the answer, one can expect another round of constitution making from Brazil.

Notes

1. Kenneth P. Erickson, "Brazil: Corporative Authoritarianism, Democratization, and Dependency," in *Latin American Politics and Development*, 2nd ed., eds. Howard J. Wiarda and Harvey F. Kline (Boulder, CO: Westview Press, 1985), pp. 160, 169.

2. The amendment was Law 16 of August 12, 1834, called the Additional Act, which reduced the number of regents from three to one, abolished the Council of State, outlawed entailing of estates, and replaced the general councils with legislative assemblies that had powers to regulate local affairs. Four other laws arguably had the effect of constitutional amendments: Law 1 of October 1828 (creating municipal assemblies), Law 12 of October 1832 (ordering the provincial electors to confer upon the Chamber of Deputies powers to reform certain constitutional articles), Law 105 of May 12, 1840 (interpreting certain articles in the prior constitutional reform), and Law 234 of November 23, 1841 (reestablishing the Council of State).

3. The 1937 Constitution was called the *Polaca* because the Polish Constitution of 1935 declared that "the sole and individual authority of the State is concentrated in the person of the President of the Republic" (art. 2). Another reason was that in the argot of Rio de Janeiro, *polaca* meant any foreign prostitute. Walter Costa Porto, "A Constituição de 1937," in *As Constituições Brasileiras: Análise Histórica e Propostas de Mudança,* ed. Luiz Felipe D'Ávila (São Paulo: Editora Brasiliense, 1993), pp. 43, 50.

4. Alfred Stepan, *Rethinking Military Politics: Brazil and the Southern Cone* (Princeton, NJ: Princeton University Press, 1988), pp. 30–44. Scott Mainwaring offers a four-factor explanation: need for greater legitimacy, tensions between the military as government and as an institution, the success of the military in subjugating its opponents, and economic success. See Scott Mainwaring, "The Transition to Democracy in Brazil," *Journal of Interamerican Studies and World Affairs,* vol. 28, no. 1 (Spring 1986), pp. 149, 151–54.

5. The legal effects of acts based upon the Institutional Acts were maintained and excluded from judicial review. See Constitutional Amendment 11 of October 13, 1978, art. 3.

6. Law No. 6.683 of August 28, 1979.

7. Luís Roberto Barroso, "Dez Anos da Constituição de 1988 (Foi Bom Pra Você Também)," in *1988–1998: Uma Decada de Constituição,* ed. Margarida Maria Lacombe Camargo (Rio de Janeiro: Renovar, 1999), pp. 37, 40.

8. Constitutional Amendment 22 of June 29, 1982. The military government had reduced the voting requirement to an absolute majority of both houses of Congress by Constitutional Amendment 11 of October 13, 1978. The military's numerous manipulations of Brazil's electoral system are recounted in David Fleischer, "Manipulações Casuísticas do Sistema Eleitoral durante o Período Militar, ou Como Usualmente o Feitiço Se Voltava contra o Feiticeiro," in *21 Anos de Regime Militar: Balanços e Perspectivas,* eds. Gláucio Soares and Maria Celina D'Araujo (Rio de Janeiro: Fundação Getúlio Vargas, 1994), pp. 154–97.

9. Each state legislature selected three electors plus an additional elector for each one million inhabitants. Each state could choose at least four electors. Constitutional Amendment 8 of April 14, 1977.

10. State legislatures elected 138 out of the total of 686 electors in the Electoral College. The military government expected that even if it lost its majority in the Chamber of Deputies, it would keep its majority in the Senate and maintain a majority in the Electoral College by winning a majority of the state legislatures. David Fleischer, "Constitutional and Electoral Engineering in Brazil: A Double-Edged Sword," *Inter-American Economic Affairs,* vol. 37, no. 3 (Spring 1984), p. 29.

This system was blatantly unfair to the most populous states. São Paulo, with more than twenty-five million inhabitants, elected only sixty members of the Chamber of Deputies, while eight states, with a combined population of about ten million, each elected eight members. Each deputy from São Paulo represented 417,345 voters, while each deputy from Acre represented only 37,701 voters. See Superior Electoral Tribunal Resolution no. 11.355 of July 1, 1982. This egregious malapportionment was compounded by giving each state the right to elect the same number of additional members to the Electoral College.

11. Guimarães later explained that the only reason he did not dispute Sarney for the right to succeed Neves was because he was forced to follow the instructions of his jurist, General Leônidas Pires Gonçalves (the army minister in Sarney's cabinet), who insisted that Sarney assume the presidency. Jorge Zaverucha, *Frágil democracia: Collor, Itamar, FHC e os miltares: (1990–1998)* (Rio de Janeiro: Civilização Brasileira, 2000), pp. 38–39.

12. A number of groups, including the Brazilian Bar Association, the National Conference of Brazilian Bishops, the Brazilian Press Association, the Worker's Party, and the United Worker's Congress organized a movement to pressure Congress into calling a popular election for delegates to the constituent assembly under a new system of rules that would eliminate the disproportionate representation embodied in the existing electoral legislation. Their efforts were unsuccessful. Javier Martínez-Lara, *Building Democracy in Brazil: The Politics of Constitutional Change, 1985–95* (New York: St. Martin's Press, 1996), pp. 58–59.

13. Constitutional Amendment 26 of November 27, 1985.

14. Martínez-Lara, *Building Democracy in Brazil,* p. 57; David Fleischer, "The Constituent Assembly and the Transformation Strategy: Attempts to Shift Political Power from the Presidency to Congress," in *The Political Economy of Brazil: Public Policies in an Era of Transition,* eds. Lawrence Graham and Robert H. Wilson (Austin: University of Texas Press, 1990), pp. 210, 221. This was publicly confirmed (although later denied) by Fernando Henrique Cardoso. After his denial, the reporter published the tape of Cardoso's confirmation in the May 21, 1990, issue of the Folha de São Paulo. See Jorge Zaverucha, "The 1988 Constitution and its Authoritarian Legacy: Formalizing Democracy while Gutting its Essence," paper presented at the meeting of the Latin American Studies Association, Guadalajara, Mexico, April 17–19, 1997, pp. 6–7.

15. Barry Ames, *The Deadlock of Democracy in Brazil* (Ann Arbor: University of Michigan Press, 2001), pp. 54–55.

16. Decree-Law 1.543 of April 14, 1977, provided that one-third of each state's federal senators be elected by an electoral college composed of the members of the state and municipal legislatures. With a mandate of eight years, the term of these so-called bionic senators did not expire until 1990. At the assembly's second session, the PT challenged the right of these senators to participate in the constituent assembly. By a vote of 394 to 126, the assembly decided to permit the twenty-three senators to participate and to vote.

17. A decision of the Superior Electoral Tribunal of September 10, 1985, prohibited media interviews with the candidates during the three months prior to the election, making it very difficult to organize debates on the subject of the new constitution. The decision also prohibited party leaders who were not candidates from appearing on television and limited candidates' television appearances to states where they were running for office. Maria do Carmo Campello de Souza, "The Brazilian 'New Republic': Under the 'Sword of Damocles,'" in *Democratizing Brazil: Problems of Transition and Consolidation,* ed. Alfred Stepan (New York: Oxford University Press, 1989), pp. 351, 374.

18. Ames, *The Deadlock of Democracy in Brazil,* p. 273.

19. The history of the ill-fated Cruzado Plan is recounted in Hugo Presgrave de A. Faria, "Macroeconomic Policymaking in a Crisis Environment: Brazil's Cruzado Plan and Beyond," in *Brazil's Economic and Political Future,* eds. Julian Chacel, Pamela Falk, and David Fleischer (Boulder, CO: Westview Press, 1988), pp. 42–59; and Werner Baer and Paul Beckerman, "The Decline and Fall of Brazil's Cruzado," *Latin American Research Review,* vol. 24, no. 1 (1989), pp. 35–64.

20. See Campello de Souza, "The Brazilian 'New Republic,'" pp. 362, 373. In large part due to the strategic concealment of the disastrous results of the Cruzado Plan until after the 1986 election, the PMDB managed to elect 260 deputies and 36 senators. Adding the 7 senators it elected in 1982, the PMDB had a majority of 303 out of the 559 members to the constituent assembly. By August 30, 1988, party shifts caused the PMDB's representation in the assembly to fall to 235 members.

21. Thomas Jefferson took a contrary view, maintaining that the people should rewrite the constitution every generation because otherwise there would be too little citizen participation in governmental affairs. Geoffrey Stone, Louis Seidman, Cass Sunstein, and Mark Tushnet, *Constitutional Law,* 4th ed. (New York: Aspen Law & Business, 2001), p. 73.

22. Ames, *The Deadlock of Democracy in Brazil,* p. 28; Leonardo Avritzer, "The Conflict between Civil and Political Society in Postauthoritarian Brazil: An Analysis of the Impeachment of Fernando Collor de Mello," in *Corruption and Political Reform in Brazil: The Impact of Collor's Impeachment,* eds. Keith S. Rosenn and Richard Downes (Coral Gables, FL: University of Miami North-South Ctr. Press, 1999), pp. 119, 133.

23. David V. Fleischer, "Perfil Sócio-Econômico e Político da Constituinte," in *O Processo Constituinte 1987–1988,* ed. Milton Guran (Brasília: AGIL, 1988), pp. 29, 31.

24. Martínez-Lara, *Building Democracy in Brazil,* pp. 93–94.

25. Lucas Coelho, "O Processo Constituinte," in *O Processo Constituinte 1987–1988,* pp. 41, 43.

26. *Constituição Federal Anteprojeto da Comissão Afonso Arinos* (Rio de Janeiro: Forense, 1987). The committee included prominent businessmen, social scientists, and labor leaders, but jurists constituted the majority. Bolívar Lamounier, "Brazil: Toward Parliamentarism?" in *The Failure of Presidential Democracy,* eds. Juan J. Linz and Arturo Valenzuela (Baltimore, MD: Johns Hopkins University Press, 1994), pp. 253, 274. For an acerbic critique of the Arinos Committee's draft constitution, see Ney Prado, *Os notáveis erros dos notáveis da Comissão Provisória de Estudos Constitucionais* (Rio de Janeiro: Forense, 1987).

27. Abdo I. Baaklini, *The Brazilian Legislature and Political System* (Westport, CT: Greenwood Press, 1992), p. 164.

28. See Augusto Zimmermann, *Curso de Direito Constitucional* (Rio de Janeiro: Editora Lumen Juris, 2002), p. 182.

29. The rapporteurs drafted the initial proposals, screened amendments, integrated approved amendments into the text, and later integrated the final reports of the subcommittees into a single text.

30. Shortly before the vote on the leadership positions, PFL leaders threatened a boycott as a protest against Covas' stacking the leadership with liberal PMDB members, which they deemed a breach of an informal agreement that they had reached with Covas' predecessor, Luis Henrique. They ultimately backed down after receiving no support from the other parties. Martínez-Lara, *Building Democracy in Brazil,* p. 98.

31. Martínez-Lara, *Building Democracy in Brazil*, pp. 107–08.

32. For details about the project and insights into the popular suggestions, see *A Constituição Desejada; SAIC: As 72.719 Sugestões Enviadas Pelos Cidadãos Brasileiros a Assembléia Nacional Constituinte*, 2 vols., ed. Stéphane Monclaire (Brasília: Centro Gráfico, 1991).

33. Baaklini, *The Brazilian Legislature and Political System*, p. 172.

34. Lombardo, "A Constituição: Resultado de 613 dias de trabalho," *Gazeta Mercantil*, Octobert 6, 1988, at p. 1; *Jornal do Brasil*, September 3, 1988, 1st Caderno, p. 4.

35. Maria D'Alva G. Kinzo, "Transitions: Brazil," in *Democracy in Latin America: (Re)Constructing Political Society*, eds. Manuel Antonio Garretón M. and Edward Newman (New York: United Nations University Press, 2001), pp. 19, 31.

36. Margaret E. Keck, "The New Unionism in the Brazilian Transition," in Stepan, *Democratizing Brazil*, pp. 252, 284.

37. Article 492 of the Consolidated Labor Legislation created a system of job tenure by prohibiting employers from firing an employee with more than ten years of service except for "serious fault" or *force majeure*, criteria that were exceedingly difficult for employers to prove before the Labor Courts. Consequently, many employers routinely fired employees before they attained tenure. The military government pushed through Congress Law 5.107 of September 13, 1966, which "permitted" workers to opt for the FGTS regime, a compensation scheme for discharged workers, instead of the ten-year tenure system. As a practical matter, employers required virtually all workers without tenure to opt for the FGTS regime, thereby effectively preventing workers without tenure from acquiring it. See W. Gary Vause and Dulcina de Holanda Palhano, "Labor Law in Brazil and the United States—Statism and Classical Liberalism Compared," *Columbia Journal of Transnational Law*, vol. 33 (1995), pp. 583, 612–15.

38. Gary M. Reich, "The 1988 Constitution a Decade Later: Ugly Compromises Reconsidered," *Journal of Interamerican Studies and World Affairs*, vol. 40, no. 5 (Winter 1998), p. 15.

39. Juan J. Linz and Alfred Stepan, *Problems of Democratic Transition and Consolidation: Southern Europe, South America, And Post-Communist Europe* (Baltimore, MD: Johns Hopkins University Press, 1996), p. 169. For additional assessments of military domination of the constituent assembly, see Wolgran Junqueira Ferreira, *Comentários à Constituição de 1988*, vol. 1 (Campinas/São Paulo: Julex Livros Ltda., 1989), pp. 63–65; Stepan, *Rethinking Military Politics*, pp. 112–14; and Zaverucha, "The 1988 Constitution and its Authoritarian Legacy."

40. Kenneth P. Serbin, "The Catholic Church, Religious Pluralism, and Democracy in Brazil," in *Democratic Brazil: Actors, Institutions, and Processes*, eds. Peter R. Kingstone and Timothy J. Power (Pittsburgh, PA: University of Pittsburgh Press, 2000), pp. 144, 150–51.

41. See David Driesen, "Brazil's Transition to Democracy: Agrarian Reform and the New Constitution," *Wisconsin International Law Journal*, vol. 8, no. 1 (1989), pp. 66–81.

42. The systematization committee was supposed to have eighty-nine members, made up of all the presidents and rapporteurs of the committees and all the rapporteurs of the subcommittees, plus forty-nine members of the assembly chosen in proportion to party representation. Actually, the committee ended up having ninety-three members to ensure the presence of at least one member of each party. Coelho, "O Processo Constituinte," p. 44.

43. Cabral was assisted by three subrapporteurs, José Fragaça (PMDB), Adolfo de Oliveira (PL), and Antonio Carlos Konder Reis (PDS), all of whom were members of the systematization committee. Konder Reis had been the 1967 Constitution's rapporteur.

44. In his report accompanying Cabral Zero, the rapporteur explained that some of the incongruities and excesses in the draft resulted from ideological conflicts within the committees and subcommittees, as well as the tendencies of assembly members to introduce into the text "constitutional rules that turn its nature into a stew by dealing with subjects that fit better into ordinary legislation." Cited in Josaphat Marino, "Uma Perspectiva da Nova Constituição Brasileira," *Cadernos de Direito Constitucional e Ciência Política*, vol. 131, no. 2 (January–March 1993).

45. This account is largely drawn from Martínez-Lara, *Building Democracy in Brazil*, pp. 109–10.

46. The Centrão was made up of 152 delegates, 80 drawn from the PFL, 43 from the PMDB, 19 from the PDS, 6 from the PTB, 3 from the PDC and from the PL. DIAP, *Quem Foi Quem Na Constituinte Nas Questões de Interesse dos Trabalhadores* (São Paulo: Cortez/Obaré, 1988), cited in Maria D'Alva Gil Kinzo, "O Quadro Constituinte

Partidário e a Constituinte," in *De Geisel a Collor: O Balanço da Transição,* ed. Bolívar Lamounier (São Paulo: IDESP/Sumaré, 1990), pp. 105–34.

47. For an explanation of the eclectic nature of the PMDB and why it had great difficulty in taking coherent policy positions, see Frances Hagopian, "The Compromised Consolidation: The Political Class in the Brazilian Transition," in *Issues in Democratic Consolidation: The New South American Democracies in Comparative Perspective,* ed. Scott Mainwaring, Guillermo O'Donnell, and J. Samuel Valenzuela (South Bend, IN: University of Notre Dame Press, 1992), pp. 243, 265–71.

48. Ames, *The Deadlock of Democracy in Brazil,* p. 28.

49. Carlos Alberto Marques Novaes, "Dinâmica Institucional de Representação," *Novos Estudos Cebrap,* vol. 38 (March 1994), pp. 115, 117.

50. Martínez-Lara, *Building Democracy in Brazil,* pp. 116–17.

51. For an analysis of party voting patterns and coalitions on key votes on Drafts A and B, see Kinzo, "O Quadro Constituinte Partidário e a Constituinte," pp. 117–32.

52. The jeito is a commonly used device for bending legal norms to expediency. See Keith S. Rosenn, "Brazil's Legal Culture: The Jeito Revisited," *Florida International Law Journal,* vol. 1, no. 1 (1984), pp. 1–43.

53. Lydia Medeiros, "Constituição 15 Anos," *O Globo,* Oct. 5, 2003. At the time, Nelson Jobim was a PMDB leader in the constituent assembly.

54. Gilse Guedes, "Passarinho admite que inclui artigo não votado na Constituição," *O Estado de São Paulo,* Oct. 9, 2003. Passarinho, former minister of education and social security under the military governments, added a measure that eliminated a disparity in treatment for the military with respect to salary benefits.

55. Thélio Magalhães, "OAB recebe pedido de impeachment de Jobim," *O Estado de São Paulo,* Nov. 8, 2003.

56. Eduardo Kattah, "Jobim nega inclusão de artigos não-votadas na Constituição," *O Estado de São Paulo,* Nov. 10, 2003.

57. A study by an agency of the Justice Ministry found that the 1988 Constitution expressly required 256 complementary laws and implicitly required another 87. Paulo Gomes Pimentel Júnior, *Constituição e Ineficácia Social* (Curitiba: Juruá Editora, 2003), p. 42. Not surprisingly, Congress has failed to comply with many of these constitutional directives and deadlines. Even today, a substantial amount of implementing or regulatory legislation has yet to be enacted.

Thousands of existing laws were implicitly revoked or require modification to conform to the new constitution. Many still remain unmodified, leaving some areas of the law legally confused.

58. The argument that a provisional constitution is a useful technique for brokering the transition from military to civilian rule is made elegantly by Ruti Teitel, "Transitional Jurisprudence: The Role of Law in Political Transformation," *Yale Law Journal,* vol. 106 (1997), pp. 2009, 2057–63.

59. Transitional Constitutional Provisions Act, art. 2.

60. The reason for Bueno's amendment was that the first governmental decree after proclamation of the Old Republic in 1889 had promised, but never delivered, a plebiscite on whether Brazil should have a monarchy or a republican form of government. Martínez-Lara, *Building Democracy in Brazil,* pp. 144–45.

61. Luís Roberto Barroso, "Dez Anos da Constituição de 1988," pp. 37, 51; Cármen Lúcia Antunes Rocha, *República e Federação no Brasil: Traços Constitucionais da Organização Política Brasileira* (Belo Horizonte: Del Rey, 1997), p. 84.

62. Sanford Levinson, "Law as Literature," *Texas Law Review,* vol. 60 (1982), pp. 373, 376.

63. Albert O. Hirschman, *Journeys towards Progress: Studies of Economic Policy-Making in Latin America* (New York: Twentieth Century Fund, 1963), p. 222.

64. In 1985, the annual inflation rate was 235 percent. Although falling to 65 percent in 1986 as a result of the ill-fated Cruzado Plan, it rose to 416 percent the following year. By 1989, inflation had climbed to 1,783 percent. By March of 1990, when Collor de Mello assumed the presidency, the inflation rate was running at 84 percent per month. Between 1990 and 1994, the annual inflation rate averaged nearly 1,400 percent.

65. Peter Kingstone, "Muddling through Gridlock: Economic Policy Performance, Business Responses, and Democratic Sustainability," in *Democratic Brazil,* pp. 185, 191.

66. The only provisions that may not be amended are the federal system of government; direct, secret, universal, and periodic suffrage; separation of powers; and the individual rights and guaranties. See art. 60.

67. The emergency fund created by the First Revision Amendment lasted only until 1996. A second constitutional amendment, no. 10 of March 4, 1996, extended the fund until June 30, 1997, and a third amendment, no. 17 of November 22, 1997, extended it until December 31, 1999.

68. The most recent was Amendment 42 of December 19, 2003, which extended the tax until December 31, 2007, when it was finally allowed to expire.

69. Amendment 42 of December 19, 2003, art. 2, and Amendment 56 of December 20, 2007, reamending art. 76 of the Transitional Constitutional Provisions Act.

70. Amendments 20 of 1998 and 41 of 2003 made sweeping reforms in social security for both the public and private sectors. Amendments 1 of 1992 and 25 of 2000 imposed limits on compensation for state and local legislators. Amendment 19 of 1998 imposed salary ceilings and eliminated lavish benefits for civil servants, eliminated tenure for those who have not passed competitive exams, and permitted firing of tenured civil servants. Amendments 5 through 9 of 1995, Amendment 13 of 1996, and Amendment 36 of 2002 eliminated a number of obstacles to foreign investment and opened up several government monopolies.

71. Timothy J. Power, "Political Institutions in Democratic Brazil: Politics as a Permanent Constitutional Convention," in *Democratic Brazil,* pp. 17, 34.

72. The Supreme Court has held that the issue of whether a provisional measure is actually urgent and relevant is a nonjusticiable political question. ADIn 1.397-DF, Diário de Justiça, June 27, 1997. More recently, the Supreme Court has indicated its willingness, albeit exceptionally, to examine whether there really is the requisite urgency and relevancy to justify resorting to the provisional measure. ADI-MC 2213, Diário de Justiça, April 23, 2004.

Constitutional article 246, added by Amendments 6 to 9 of 1995, banned the use of provisional measures to regulate constitutional amendments promulgated after January 1, 1995. Amendment 32 of September 11, 2001, which substantially restricted the president's powers to issue provisional measures, modified article 246 to restore presidential power to regulate future constitutional amendments by decree.

73. The only limitation that the Supreme Court placed upon the power to reissue provisional measures was that the president could not reissue a measure that Congress had specifically rejected.

Ação Direta de Inconstitucionalidade 293, 146 R.T.J. 707 (Tribunal Pleno, June 6, 1990). As of September 11, 2001, when the executive's power to issue and reissue provisional measures was curbed by constitutional amendment, Brazilian presidents had issued 619 original provisional measures and 5,491 reissuances. During this entire period, Congress rejected only 22 provisional measures, enacting 473 into law. The rest were either revoked, became ineffective, or were merged into measures. See www.planalto.gov.br (accessed April 13, 2009).

74. Provisional measures may no longer be issued on certain matters, such as nationality, citizenship, political parties and rights, electoral law, criminal and procedural law, and budgets. To avoid another Plano Collor, no provisional measure may be used to seize or sequester any property or financial assets. Provisional measures are now valid for sixty instead of thirty days and may be extended only once for another sixty days. If rejected or invalid because of the passage of time, provisional measures may not be reissued in the same legislative session. A provisional measure that has lapsed is no longer void ab initio. Any legal relations constituted under it are to be regulated by legislative decree. If no such decree is issued within sixty days after lapse, legal relations constituted under the provisional measure remain in effect and are governed by it. Between September 11, 2001, and March 10, 2009, Brazilian presidents have issued an additional 458 original provisional measures. The overwhelming majority of these measures have been extended for an additional sixty and have been ultimately converted into law. Only thirty have been rejected, and another ten have been declared ineffective.

75. The constitution expanded standing to bring the direct action of unconstitutionality to include the president, executive committees of either house of Congress, state governors, the Federal Council of the Bar Association, any political party represented in Congress, and any national labor or business organization. Amendment 45 of 2004 expanded the category of persons with standing to bring a direct action of unconstitutionality to include the federal district's legislature, its executive committee, and its governor.

76. Constitution of 1988, art. 103 §2.

77. See Maria Tereza Sadek and Rosângela Batista Cavalcanti, "The New Brazilian Public Prosecution: An Agent of Accountability," in *Democratic Accountability in Latin America,* eds. Scott Mainwaring and Christopher Welna (New York: Oxford University Press, 2003), pp. 201, 207.

78. A striking result of the current constitution has been a phenomenal increase in the caseloads of the Brazilian courts. In the first eight years following the constitution's promulgation, the number of cases filed in Brazilian courts increased more than tenfold, from about 350,000 cases in 1988 to more than 3.7 million in 1996. The Supreme Court has been particularly overburdened; the number of cases it decided mushroomed from 17,432 in 1989 to 109,692 in 2001. Not all these cases involve constitutional questions, but Brazilians are increasingly resorting to litigation because of the enormous expansion in both substantive constitutional rights and procedural mechanisms to protect those rights.

79. William C. Prillaman, *The Judiciary and Democratic Decay in Latin America: Declining Confidence in the Rule of Law* (Westport: Praeger Publishers, 2000), pp. 6, 8.

80. See, generally, Matthew M. Taylor, *Judging Policy: Courts and Policy Reform in Democratic Brazil* (2008); Marcos Faro de Castro, "O Supremo Tribunal Federal e a Judicialicação da Política," *Revista Brasileira de Ciências Sociais* (No. 34, July 1997), pp. 147–56; Ernani Rodrigues de Carvalho, "Em Busca da Judicialização da Política no Brasil: Apontamentos para uma Nova Abordagem," 23 *Revista de Sociologia e Política* (No. 23, November 2004), pp. 115–26; Amandino Teixeira Nunes Junior, "A Constituição de 1988 e a Judicialização da Política no Brasil," *Revista de Informação Legislativa, Ano 45* (No. 178, April/June 2008), pp. 157–79; Rogério Bastos Arantes, "Constitutionalism, the Expansion of Justice and the Judicialization of Politics in Brazil," in *The Judicialization of Politics in Latin America,* eds. Rachel Sieder, Line Schjolden, and Alan Angell (New York, Basingstoke: Palgrave Macmillan, 2005), pp. 231–62.

81. Brazil has universal suffrage, with the exception of foreigners and military conscripts. Illiterates have been enfranchised since 1985, and the 1988 Constitution enfranchised those between the ages of sixteen and eighteen. Voting is compulsory for those between the ages of eighteen and seventy and optional for those over seventy or less than eighteen. Free and relatively honest elections are held regularly.

82. Alfred Stepan, "Brazil's Decentralized Federalism: Bringing Government Closer to the Citizens?" *Daedalus,* vol. 129, no. 2 (2000), pp. 145–69.

83. "Probably no country in the world currently is as anti-party, both in theory and practice, as is Brazil." Giovanni Sartori, *Comparative Constitutional Engineering: An Inquiry into Structures, Incentives, and Outcomes,* 2nd ed. (New York: New York University Press, 1996), p. 95.

84. Ames, *The Deadlock of Democracy in Brazil,* pp. 41–43.

85. The army, navy, and air force are declared to be permanent national institutions and military intervention is permitted to protect law and order at the request of any of the constitutional powers (art. 142). Military service is obligatory in terms of the law (art. 143). The rights and prerogatives of members of the military are amply protected (art. 42).

86. Compare the normalization view presented in Wendy Hunter, "Assessing Civil-Military Relations in Postauthoritarian Brazil," in *Democratic Brazil,* pp. 101, 106–07, with the much more critical view of military power and prerogatives in Zaverucha, *Frágil democracia,* pp. 35–56.

87. See Omar G. Encarnación, *The Myth of Civil Society: Social Capital and Democratic Consolidation in Spain and Brazil* (New York: Palgrave Macmillan, 2003), pp. 146–47.

88. Augusto Zimmermann, "Constitutional Rights in Brazil: A Legal Fiction?" *Murdoch University E-Law Journal,* vol. 14, no. 2 (2007), pp. 31–55.

89. Amendment 45 of December 8, 2004, took an important step in this direction by requiring a showing that constitutional questions presented in an extraordinary appeal have "general repercussions" for the Supreme Court to hear the appeal.

90. Perhaps a caveat should be made for the rant of Leonel Brizola, a leftist former governor of Rio de Janeiro, who was quoted in the *Jornal do Brasil* of May 18, 1995, saying that "if there is no civil reaction [against privatizations], there will be a military one." The next day *O Globo* published an article with the headline "Cardoso Criticizes Brizola for Defending a Military Coup." Cited in Richard Gunther, P. Nikiforos Diamandouros, and Hans-Jürgen Puhle, "O'Donnell's 'Illusions': A Rejoinder," in *The Global Divergence of Democracies,* ed. Larry Diamond and Marc F. Plattner (Baltimore, MD: Johns Hopkins University Press, 2001), pp. 131, 139.

91. Luís Roberto Barroso, *Temas De Direito Constitucional,* vol. 1 (Rio de Janeiro: Renovar, 2001), p. 10.

92. Seymour Martin Lipset, *The First New Nation: The United States in Historical and Comparative Perspective* (Garden City, NY: Doubleday, 1967), p. 52.

17

Lessons of the Colombian Constitutional Reform of 1991

Toward the Securing of Peace and Reconciliation?

Donald T. Fox, Gustavo Gallón-Giraldo, and Anne Stetson

The idea that a political constitution embodies a society's deepest level of consent is ancient in Western civilization. In *The Laws,* Plato defined a constitution as a framework that had to be built before a society's laws could be authoritatively drafted and promulgated.

The polestar of constitutionalism as a means of securing democratic government has guided Latin America since 1811, shortly after the wars of independence began. Simón Bolívar, creator of the short-lived Gran Colombia, convened a constitutional assembly in 1819 and later drafted a constitution of 151 articles for Bolivia. Some of his early ideas, such as a national chamber of civic virtue to direct morals and punish vice, were unfeasible, but his constitutional thoughts were presciently directed at curbing anarchy and violence among deeply antagonistic peoples and at developing a consensual framework for government. While dying in exile, he recognized the quixotic nature of his life's ambition; about the region that he had sought to unify, he prophesied that

The situation of America is so singular and so horrible that it is not possible for anyone to hope to conserve order for a long period, not even in a city. Never have I considered a danger so universal as now menaces the Americans; I express this badly; posterity never saw a scene as frightening as America offers, more for the future than for the present because where has anyone imagined an entire people to fall into a frenzy and devour its own race as cannibals?[1]

The history of Colombia tragically demonstrates Bolívar's fears, as the entire nineteenth century was marked by civil wars interrupted by sporadic periods of relative peace. That said, a gradual solidification of democracy also characterizes Colombia, which possesses one of the oldest democracies in Latin America. On a political level, the competing ideologies of liberal and conservative were embodied in parties fighting for control of the central government and regional economies. The military defeat of liberal forces in 1885 garnered conservative control and ushered in the nearly fifty-year period of so-called Conservative hegemony.

Among its first acts, the conservative government abolished the federal constitution of 1863, promulgated under the auspices of the Liberal Party, and adopted the authoritarian constitution of 1886. This iteration of the Colombian constitution placed the government under the firm control of the president, allowing him to suspend constitutional rules and rights by frequently declaring a state of emergency (*estado de sitio*), as would occur throughout the late nineteenth and twentieth centuries. Declaring a state of emergency was an exceptionally grave situation for the political and juridical order of the nation, as, apart from suspending constitutional rights, it permitted delegation of extraordinary faculties to the military. The constitution of 1991 would add the power to invoke *el estado de comoción interior*, a domestic uprising or situation of violent tumult.

The explosive growth of coffee cultivation led to the development of regional economies; growth of the oil industry and foreign investment led to prosperity, but the wealth was not shared with the majority of the population, nor were those who held it enlightened enough to invest in extending efficient government outside the major cities. As a result of discontent among the poor and of the weak state, the violence continued. Between 1899 and 1902, the Thousand Days' War became the longest and cruelest civil war the country had yet experienced. The conflict ended when the government defeated rebel forces and imposed an armistice.

In 1910, the first significant reform of the constitution of 1886 was adopted in response to the forced departure of President Rafael Reyes, who had assumed dictatorial powers. The constitutional assembly of 1910 introduced some moderating changes to the constitution of 1886, such as abolishing the death penalty and inserting the judicial power of the Supreme Court to review the constitutionality of laws.

Popular protest against the Conservative hegemony increased in the late 1920s, especially after armed forces in Bogotá killed two students and the Army massacred workers from the United Fruit Company in 1928. The Liberal Party won the 1930 elections and inaugurated a sixteen-year period known as the Liberal Republic. A second reform of the constitution of 1886, adopted in 1936, attempted to introduce some elements of a welfare state, such as government intervention in the economy, and diminished the constitutionally granted influence of the Catholic Church over public institutions and society.

In 1945, a third reform of the constitution of 1886 sought to modernize the state's administrative organization, though the Conservative Party recovered power with the 1946 presidential election of Mariano Ospina Pérez. Liberals had obtained more votes, but were divided between two candidates. One of them was Jorge Eliécer Gaitán, leader of a liberal faction called the Union of the Revolutionary Left. As he obtained the larger percentage of the vote between the two liberal candidates, he became the leader of the party and headed the opposition against the new Conservative government. Gaitán was murdered on April 9, 1948, and his death opened a new ten-year period of violence between Liberals and Conservatives known as *la violencia*, a bit of a misnomer, as the increase in political violence had begun some years before. Gaitán himself had addressed the growing violence in his most well-known speeches.

The year 1950 witnessed the inauguration of a new Conservative government, with Laureano Gómez as president. The Liberal Party did not participate in the elections in protest against the murder of its candidate, Camilo Echandía, during a parade. The country had in fact been under a state of emergency since November 9, 1949, when President Ospina

Pérez had closed down the Congress. New President Gómez organized a constitutional assembly to provide some legitimacy to his government and promote a new constitution based on a more authoritarian model, inspired by the regimes of Franco and Hitler.

In the face of growing violence, military chief Gustavo Rojas Pinilla declared that "the principles of Christ and Bolívar" required him to take charge, which he did in June 1953. The dictatorship lasted until the political parties, reacting to their exclusion from power, created a coalition that forced Rojas Pinilla from office in May 1957. The Liberal and Conservative parties forged a deal to reduce the political violence between them by rotating control of the presidency, thus establishing the parties' dual hegemony. This deal, the Covenant of the National Front, was approved for a twelve-year period as a constitutional reform by plebiscite on December 1, 1957. The system of shared hegemony proved so satisfactory to the principal parties that the system of alternating control and proportionate participation of each party was followed until President Virgilio Barco abandoned it in 1982.

However, new sources of violence arose that the political truce could not contain, as the disparities in economic and political power provided rich fodder for the explosive growth of the guerrilla movement. In 1963, student activists and Catholic radicals, including Camilo Torres, a priest, founded the National Liberation Army (ELN), hoping to emulate Castro's revolution in Cuba. The Popular Liberation Army (EPL) broke away from the traditional Communist Party and declared itself to be the armed faction of the Marxist-Leninist Party of Colombia. In 1964, the Revolutionary Armed Forces of Colombia (FARC) formed around a group of guerrillas formerly established by the Liberal Party that refused to abandon armed struggle in return for amnesty. To this nucleus were added groups of *campesinos* trying to organize protests against landowners.

In 1970, The Movement of April 19 (M-19), an urban guerilla group, was organized in reaction to alleged fraud in the May 19, 1970, elections. The presidential contest that year was won by the conservative representative of the National Front, Misael Pastrana, who ran against the former dictator, General Rojas Pinilla. General Pinilla had the support of a growing number of people who felt politically excluded by the National Front's institutions. Later, in 1984, the M-19 started a peace process with the conservative government of President Belisario Betancur; other guerrilla groups, such as the FARC and EPL, did so, as well. The government broke off the process in early 1985. That same year, the M-19 seized the Palace of Justice, which housed the Supreme Court, in an effort to force the government to reinitiate the peace process. Rather than negotiate, the Betancur government consented to a full-scale military attack that resulted in the destruction of the building and the deaths of about 100 people, including twelve judges.[2] Hostilities increased with the termination of the peace process. None of the armed groups would join in a common front, although some of them created the *Coordinadora Guerrillera Simón Bolívar* in the 1980s, a body that, in practice, did not act in a very coordinated way.

In addition to the violence spawned by the guerrilla groups, the United Self-Defense Force of Colombia (AUC), a loosely affiliated group of paramilitaries formed to oppose the guerrilla groups, directed their attacks largely against rural laborers. The AUC was protected by the Colombian army as an ally in the antiguerilla struggle. But the organization's brutality against peasants suspected of sympathizing with the guerillas and its practice of kidnapping civilians for ransom, even in neighboring Venezuela, led most Colombians to consider the paramilitaries as criminals. Meanwhile, narcotics traffickers, whose annual income since the mid-1980s is estimated at $2.5 billion to $3 billion, have paid both the guerilla groups and the AUC for protection and have invested in many sectors of the economy. The corruption, public and private, generated by these vast sums of money is a source of shame that many elements of society deprecate strongly.

Successive governments made limited efforts to end guerilla violence peaceably. Until the M-19 abandoned armed struggle to create a political party that participated in the 1991 constitutional assembly, however, there was no real effort to change the structures of power through the political process.[3]

Broadening Public Participation through a Constitutional Assembly

The movement to convene a constitutional assembly (*constituyente*) composed of the broadest range of social and political representation possible commenced in 1981 with the Second National Forum for Human Rights, attended by a diverse group representing a range of views across the political spectrum. The vision for the assembly sought to provide a constitutional means to overcome the political exclusion that had characterized Colombia's history. A National Commission for a constitutional assembly was created in 1987 and included representatives of the most powerful trade unions and non-governmental organizations, and some political leaders who formed a National Committee of Unity.

In December 1989, the National Commission proposed using the elections of March 11, 1990, to hold a referendum as to whether a constitutional assembly should be held. Notably, the newspaper *El Espectador* backed the initiative. A student-led movement, organized after the murder of Liberal leader and presidential candidate Luis Carlos Galán in August 1989, proposed a referendum text that became known as the *séptima papeleta*, or "seventh ballot," given that the election already involved six ballots. The students pledged to actively support democratic institutions and to bring about respect for human rights. Out of this effort grew the so-called *mesas de trabajo* (working groups) that functioned through December 1989 in an effort to analyze possibilities for judicial reform and promoting the séptima papeleta.

The "students' seventh vote" *(séptima papeleta de los estudiantes)* was so named by another periodical, *El Tiempo*, which also supported the text of the referendum. The six formal issues in the March 1990 elections dealt with the selection of mayors, senators, and representatives to the municipalities, regional chambers, and House of Representatives. As prevailing electoral rules prohibited the inclusion of an issue on the ballot by popular request, the authorities did not formally include the séptima papeleta in the March 11 elections. Instead, the séptima papeleta was distributed to voters through the newspapers. At the time, voting was not performed by filling in a printed ballot, but by depositing paper votes in the ballot box. This permitted the informal casting of votes on the proposal to convene a constitutional assembly. The overwhelming number of affirmative votes—five million—cast in the *séptima papeleta* led then-president Virgilio Barco to issue a decree, under state-of-emergency powers, to pose the issue formally in the presidential election on May 27, 1990.

Under the existing constitution and the traditional interpretation of it that had prevailed since 1957, Congress held the exclusive power to reform the constitution (Article 218). Accordingly, the constitutionality of President Barco's decree, issued as it was pursuant to his constitutionally granted state-of-emergency powers, was subject to review by the Supreme Court of Justice. Although the presidential state-of-emergency powers have been justly criticized for their undemocratic nature and potential for enabling repressive action by the executive branch, in this case President Barco sought to call for a democratic reform of the constitution for the very purpose of restoring public order to Colombia and strengthening the country's democratic institutions.[4] The Supreme Court ultimately upheld the decree principally on the grounds of popular sovereignty. The court considered that according to general principles of Colombian constitutional law, governance of the state derives from the people's will. Consequently, if the Colombian people decide to reform their constitution, they are free to do so without restraint. The court reasoned that popular demand for reforms was evidence that existing political organs were incapable of achieving them. When the Supreme Court boldly sidestepped the constitutional restriction of reform to legislative action, its jurisprudential and philosophical reasoning was based on the potential of the constitutional assembly to achieve peace.

The referendum demonstrated overwhelming support for constitutional reform: 88 percent of voters favored convening a constitutional assembly to "strengthen participatory democracy." To push the popularly mandated reform forward, César Gaviria, the new Liberal Party president, whose government was inaugurated on August 7, 1990, conferred with representatives of the other principal political parties, which had collectively received 96 percent of the popular vote in the May elections. These parties—including the Movement of National Salvation, a faction of the Conservative Party; the Democratic Alliance M-19, which had participated for the first time in the elections after signing a peace agreement with Barco's government; and the Social Conservative Party—entered into an agreement on the mechanics of the constitutional assembly. This agreement called for the assembly to meet for a limited number of days, pro-

vided for preparatory commissions representing diverse political, social, and regional interests, and set forth the necessary organizational details. In addition, the agreement called for the popular election of delegates to the assembly on December 8, 1990.

Under the agreement, seventy members of the constitutional assembly were to be elected nationally by means of electoral lists to assure representation of different political, social, and regional groups. In addition, two seats were reserved for guerrilla groups, which would agree to demobilize. The participation of the M-19, which received many votes in the presidential election of May 27, 1990, was considered very significant, as was the participation of the EPL, Partido Revolucionario de los Trabajadores (PRT; another guerrilla group), and Quintin Lame, an indigenous group. The FARC and ELN, however, refused all offers to participate in this process. The agreement provided further that sitting congressmen were ineligible to serve in the assembly. President Gaviria incorporated the details of the agreement into a decree, *Decreto numero 1926*, issued under his state-of-emergency powers on August 24, 1990, and upheld by the Supreme Court.

Decreto numero *1926* put careful limits on the constitutional assembly. It called for the assembly to begin work on February 5, 1990, and to meet for 150 days (Article 3). The assembly was mandated to approve a single text containing the constitutional reform within the duration of its sessions and was required to act within limits set not only by the decree incorporating the vote in the popular referendum but also by the Political Agreement of the constitutional assembly entered into by leaders of the principal political parties and the M-19.

The government set up 1,580 working groups throughout the country to receive proposals from diverse social and political groups, ranging from academics and lawyers to laborers and farmers. Over 100,000 proposals for constitutional reform were submitted for review by the working groups, with the logistical support of the faculty of the Escuela Superior of Public Administration.

Initially, the working groups were conducted by student leaders between September and November 1989 to analyze how to control the generalized violence through juridical means. *Decree numero 1926* promoted the preparatory work of such groups, representing social organizations throughout the country, universities, and indigenous communities. The groups' work was coordinated by the municipalities in which they were created, and they could call on the assistance of commissions of experts set up by the president. Thus, when the constitutional assembly was organized and established commissions to consider reform proposals, they had the benefit of significant preparatory work and the widespread public debate that the proposal had received.

Democratic Representation in the Constitution-Making Process

The campaign for seats in the assembly was largely waged by established political groups, with opportunities created through new electoral rules for independent groups to participate. The new electoral rules were designed to modernize and democratize the old electoral system, creating the most open and egalitarian process in Colombian history. Private voting booths were provided for the first time, and official ballots replaced the old system in which each candidate printed and distributed his or her own ballots. A national vote was taken to facilitate meaningful participation by new parties, minorities, and those unaffiliated with a political party. In the past, departmental votes had been taken to elect congressional representatives, giving rise to cronyism within the individual departments and favoring established parties. Significantly, the nationwide vote also assured that those elected

would have a national rather than a localized mandate. As a result, the constitution they would develop—which would require national rather than local consensus building—would have nationwide legitimacy. Given the task of developing a new constitution for the entire country, this was a significant step. Finally, for the first time in the history of Colombian elections, public finances supported the campaigns of the constituyente candidates. This, too, had a democratizing effect by improving the chances of election for a broader group of candidates than would otherwise have been possible. As a result, the election produced an assembly with a more democratic and nationally spirited character than had previously been true for the national legislature; over 35 percent of the votes went to groups other than the traditional parties (i.e., Liberals and Conservatives), an anomaly in the history of Colombian elections up to that point.

Perhaps the new electoral rules contributed to the relatively low turnout—26 percent—for the December 9, 1990, elections. Nevertheless, independent or new political movements obtained a significant percentage of the vote: The Democratic Alliance–M19 received 27.14 percent, followed by Indigenous with 2.85 percent, Patriotic Union with 2.85 percent, and Christians or Evangelists (non-Catholics) with 2.85 percent, for a total of 35.69 percent of the vote. Never before had independent forces obtained more than 4 percent of votes in congressional elections. Having one-third of the votes for the constitutional assembly, even if Liberals and Conservatives gained the majority of votes, indicated significant electoral support for independent political forces. Moreover, representatives of minority groups won seven seats in the constitutional assembly.[5] Of these seven, three were Colombian Indians, representing six hundred thousand of their people.[6]

By government decree issued pursuant to the agreement President Gaviria had estab-

Table 17.1   Final Composition of Constitutional Assembly in Colombia

Movement	Seats	Percent of total
Liberals	25	33.78
Democratic Alliance–M-19	19	25.67
National Salvation (faction of Conservative Party)	11	14.86
Social Conservative Party	5	6.75
Independent Conservatives	4	5.40
Indigenous	2	2.70
Patriotic Union	2	2.70
Christians	2	2.70
EPL (by decree)	2	2.70
PRT (by decree)	1	1.35
MAQL	1	1.35
Total	74	100

lished to govern the workings of the constituyente, seats were given to two EPL representatives, one PRT representative, and one representative (without vote) of the Quintín Lame Armed Movement (MAQL), an organization of indigenous people, after those guerilla organizations signed a peace accord with the government. The constitutional assembly also made new offers to the FARC and ELN later, but those groups refused to join. As a result of both the elections and the appointments made by decree, the final composition of the assembly was as follows in Table 17.1.

The multiparty character of the assembly marked was a bold departure from the entrenched bipartisanship of Colombian politics in distributing the greatest number of seats among three parties, as the recently demilitarized M-19 party stood side by side with the Liberal and Conservative parties.

Structure of the Process

The constitutional assembly convened on February 5, 1991, and elected a collective presidency composed of the leaders of the three principal groups: Antonio Navarro Wolf (Democratic Alliance M-19), Horacio Serpa Uribe (Liberal Party), and Alvaro Gómez Hurtado (Movement of National Salvation, a faction of the Conservative Party). After adopting regulations to govern its procedures and time limits, the assembly elected a Codification Committee of lawyers representing all political groups, with technical assistance provided by a Colombian institute, Instituto Caro y Cuervo.

The constituyente invited the government, Senate, House of Representatives, Supreme Court, and Council of State to submit reform proposals, and the Gaviria administration submitted a full reform proposal the day after the assembly convened. Nongovernmental organizations, universities, and guerrilla groups involved in the peace process also presented proposals, which did not carry the weight of official proposals, but were taken under serious consideration by the constituyente. In all, 131 official and 28 other proposals for reform were submitted.

Many of the proposals that the nongovernmental organizations generated reflected their particular mandates. For example, the Colombian Workers' Federation proposed reforms to the constitution's articulation of social and labor rights, and the Colombian Association of Retired Police Officers addressed the constitution's treatment of the national police force. Others, however, ranged more broadly in subject, such as the proposal submitted by the Foundation for the Future of Colombia and universities that participated in this step of the reform process.

To deal with diverse reform topics, the assembly organized five permanent commissions. The First Commission focused on the study of principles, rights, obligations, guarantees, and fundamental liberties; mechanisms and institutions of democratic participation, the electoral system, political parties, and the status of the opposition; and mechanisms for constitutional reform. The Second Commission was responsible for studying territorial regulation and regional and local autonomy. The Third Commission was dedicated to the study of reforms to the structure of the state, Congress, the police force, the state-of-emergency regime, and international relations. The Fourth Commission studied the administration of justice, principles of criminal law and due process, and the function of the Inspector General (Public Ministry). The Fifth Commission was mandated to study economic, social, ecological, and fiscal issues, as well as public services.

The commissions' decisions were not binding, but were brought to the full assembly for debate. The specific function of the commissions was to conduct a comparative study of the proposals within their respective areas of focus. For a proposed provision to gain approval as part of the new constitution, majority approval was required in both of two plenary debates. At the outset, the idea was to reform the existing constitution, but it became clear that the reform could best be accomplished not by amending the old constitution, but rather by proclaiming a new one. The commissions produced a collective 560 articles for such a new constitution, but in the first plenary debate, many of these were seen to be repetitive or inconsistent. Consequently, the number was reduced to about 400 articles, following which the Codification Commission produced a first draft of the new constitution. This draft was submitted for discussion at the second plenary debate. A final grammatical revision by a committee on style refined the constitution's text. The assembly adopted the new constitution on July 4, 1991.

The constituyente overcame two major obstacles in the course of its work. First, the Council of State, the principal administrative tribunal under the existing constitution, sought to impose its administrative authority on the assembly; to forestall this intervention, the assembly adopted a resolution declaring that the referendum had made provisions of the existing constitution relating to constitutional revision inapplicable, and that any regulations that the assembly adopted did not constitute administrative acts subject to Council of State review.

Second, as the Third Commission neared consensus on abolishing existing congressional subsidies and irregularities, members of Congress, fearful of their political future, undertook a campaign against the assembly. Years of abuse by the political class in Congress had led to public clamor for reform of the legislature, and to give these reforms the greatest chance for success, the constituyente, with President Gaviria's agreement, ordered Congress to be dissolved on July 5, 1991, the day after adopting the new constitution, and called for new congressional elections on October 27, 1991. The assembly established a special legislative commission, called *el Congresito* (the little Congress), proportionately representing the parties participating in the assembly. The assembly authorized el Congresito to promulgate laws related to implementing the new constitution. This commission of thirty-six leaders met between July 15 and October 4, and again from November 18 to November 30. Pursuant to the new constitution (transitional articles 6–8), el Congresito held the power to approve by majority presidential decrees issued during the interim, veto any decrees deemed overly broad, and propose legislation (*proyectos de ley*) to be submitted to the newly elected Congress that would enter office on December 1, 1991.

Unfortunately, the disqualification of members of the constitutional assembly to run in the new congressional elections led to a reelection of practically all of the old political class. The deal worked out with President Gaviria had the effect of marginalizing the Movement of National Salvation (MSN), a faction of the Conservative Party, and the M19, which had been most influential in the constitutional assembly. The victory of the old political class was probably due to the naïveté of their opponents. However, the new electoral rules did secure more seats for the new political parties than would have been achievable under the old rules, including seats for indigenous peoples.

The new constitution was never subjected to popular ratification. The preexisting constitution had not foreseen a successor or contemplated a mechanism for ratifying one. Rather, in accordance with President Gaviria's decree of August 24, 1990, concerning the powers of the constitutional assembly, the assembly itself was empowered to proclaim a new constitution, as it did on July 4, 1991, subject to affirmation by the Supreme Court of Justice that the reform had been conducted in conformity with the vote taken by the Colombian people on December 9, 1990, when the assembly's members had been elected. Upon proclaiming the new charter, Alvaro Gomez Hurtado, the elected president of the constitutional assembly, exhorted:

> We proclaim the Constitution of Colombia. It is the end of an effort.... We achieved it running risks. It is a text that seeks to represent Colombia, a new country that we wanted to find. Between remaining behind or pushing ahead, we preferred the vanguard.... Every Constitution is a beginning. Here, today something is born.... We hope that new generations will not live in a state of corruption as that we suffer today. We fulfilled our mandate to clean up the Congress.... We established bases on which justice can be restored.... Colombia is a young country that has to experiment. It must experiment. It cannot limit itself to opportunities that present no danger. Dangers have come upon us and to oppose them timorous measures will not suffice. We are not going to let the reform movement stagnate. This would be an injustice. We want it to be a living organism and not a document for the archives. This Constitution will have to be the source of all judicial and institutional organization. But we want it to be much more, that it be considered the navigational chart of our nationality.... The Constitutional transformation that we proclaim today has the objective of restoring our moral values. We intend that there be a rebirth of the essential

concepts of goodness, honesty and truth. And to complete our wishes—that we Colombians will value anew the meaning of peace and the spiritual condition of mankind. There, standing tall, are the possibilities of preserving human dignity forever.[7]

Timing of the Reforms

Gaviria seized the momentum of successful peace negotiations with the M-19 and a window of optimism throughout the country to carry forward a bold constitutional reform project to open the political process to a more inclusive group of participants and strengthen the state's capacity to secure democratic order. However, the absence of the FARC and ELN in the process has proven over time to be a definitive blow to the new constitution's capacity to achieve the peace that was among its goals. With impeccable timing, on December 9, 1990, the day of the elections for the constitutional assembly, the government carried out a military attack on the FARC's headquarters, Casaverde. Casaverde had hosted meetings between the FARC and many representatives of the government, political parties, and society over the prior months and years, all aimed at exploring the possibility of a negotiated peace. As a result, Casaverde symbolized the hope—but also the continued failure—of a negotiated peace. Although at that time a peace process was not formally open, the expectation, or perhaps merely the hope, prevailed that talks would be renewed and peace promoted through new avenues, including the FARC's participation in the constitutional assembly. The attack on Casaverde the same day that Colombians elected the members of the constitutional assembly closed the assembly's doors to the FARC. This mistake was deepened by the attitude of the FARC itself, which rejected the subsequent invitation by key members of the constitutional assembly to present their proposals. In any case, the actions of both the government and the FARC reduced the ability of the constitution of 1991 to secure peace in Colombia.

Had the government more vigorously negotiated with the FARC and ELN so that those groups could have been represented in the assembly, would it and the resulting constitution have been any more effective at establishing an enduring peace? The subsequent years of efforts to negotiate a peace with the guerrilla groups suggest that including FARC and ELN representation would have been impossible without serious compromises by the government, and that postponing the efforts to reform the state would only have reduced further its capacity to deal with the destructive forces that oppose it. Furthermore, given the depth and breadth of popular support for constitutional reform, the timing of the 1991 constitution was poised for success; to have gambled the moment away for the possibility of greater success at a later date would have carried risks and arguably diminishing returns.

Role of the International Community

The peace process that resulted in the proclamation of the 1991 constitution derived from the vision of Colombian leaders and the Colombian people, the negotiations held with the guerrilla groups during the 1980s, and a long constitutional tradition. No representatives of supportive countries or the United Nations were involved in the conversations leading up to the constitutional assembly, nor did they serve as guarantors of the peace accords. However, the international community did provide some financial support to the effort, and this went toward expanding the technical capabilities of the government, strengthening the proactive role of civil society, and disseminating information concerning the assembly's debates and the constitution itself.

To ensure the smooth running of the assembly, a UN-funded presidential agency operated as technical support in the preparation of the constitution and during the assembly's deliberations. The same agency contributed to elaborating the government draft of the constitution submitted for the assembly's consideration and, after the proclamation of the constitution, preparing bills for its legislative implementation. A final component of the program publicly promoted the new constitution, mainly to the legal community and government agencies. The dissemination of the constitution among the population, which included education about new constitutional rights and their guarantees, such as the new legal vehicle of *tutela* (discussed below), was developed only through a few short-term initiatives.

European agencies funded a pool of national non-governmental organizations that joined efforts and expertise around an initiative called *Viva la ciudadania*. This program was important to the process of creating the new constitution, as it provided a bridge between the assembly and those sectors of the population linked to social and political organizations. Through public debates around the country and the publication of a monthly paper, the project channeled proposals from citizens and popular organizations to the assembly, continuously updated the public on discussions in assembly sessions, and developed an education campaign after the constitution was proclaimed. However, the program's impact was limited because its publications did not use the mass media, and, therefore, did not reach the general public.

Although no foreign technical experts participated in or advised the assembly, several came to Colombia to observe the process. Several international non-governmental organizations participated in the debates, however, and thereby enriched the discussions with proposals inspired by international human rights law. For example, the secretary general of Amnesty International and the director of Human Rights Watch's

Americas program addressed the plenary of the assembly, describing their concerns about the human rights situation in Colombia and their views on how a modern human rights framework and checks on the public security forces could help to reduce the high number of human rights violations occurring in Colombia.

Role of International and Foreign Law

Undergirding the entire reform process—from parting of the judicial seas to permit a democratic movement to override the congressional lock on constitutional reform to electing the members of the constitutional assembly to formulating the provisions of the constitution itself—lie the principles of popular sovereignty and democratic participation. Although the process itself took its democratic course apart from international legal theory, de facto, the emerging international norm of self-governance prevailed in the Colombian constitutional reform experience.

International law, and international human rights law in particular, played an important and explicit role in the adoption of the 1991 constitution as the constituyente sought to secure a newly democratic and peaceful order in Colombia. While it would be impossible to identify any one international legal norm involved in the process that led to the peace settlement and the consensus around the new constitution, the international human rights instruments provided the basic standards considered by all parties at the time of debating the future bill of rights, as well as some aspects of the organization of state organs and their powers. The constitutional assembly looked also to foreign legal systems and procedures in deliberating on reforms to the Colombian constitution. For example, the common law injunction and habeus corpus actions were considered in the First Commission and in plenary session deliberations on the protection and application of rights.[8]

The 1886 constitution had been modeled on the Spanish constitution, which was in turn infused with French constitutional structures and principles. In addition, the rich intellectual tradition of legal scholarship in Colombia informed the research of the assembly's commissions. Among the commission members were some of the most respected legal scholars in the country, who were familiar with the importance of studying comparative legal systems. Legal experts in the Gaviria administration working on the constitutional-reform process brought their comparative legal knowledge and contacts with foreign administrations to the task of presenting reform proposals to the assembly.

Constitutional borrowing is evident in the separate treatment of a *carta de derechos*, or bill of rights, firmly set out in the first two sections of the new constitution, which echoes French and American legal traditions. Article 88, providing for citizens' rights for protection of collective interests, derives from constitutional provisions in Brazil, Spain, and Portugal. Establishing a human rights ombudsman, or *defensor del pueblo*, was borrowed from the successful experience of Scandinavian countries. The constituyente chose to adopt it with the objective of strengthening the protection of human rights in the country. The overhaul of the justice system to shift away from the European inquisitorial system to the American prosecutorial system of justice is notable in its establishing of a prosecutor general's office: A government prosecutor rather than a Colombian judge would be responsible for bringing charges against defendants. A separate constitutional court was also established, following the Spanish example (again, based on that of France) of charging a separate court with determining the constitutionality of laws and treaties issued or entered into by the other branches of government (Article 239).

Issues of Substance

In the effort to secure democracy and peace for all in Colombia, the constituyente embraced tenets of international law throughout the 1991 constitution, giving international human rights law superior status in cases of incompatibility with domestic law. Article 93 provides that ratified treaties that recognize human rights and prohibit their limitation in states of emergency must be recognized in domestic law. In this effort, the assembly drew on international human rights instruments as well as a number of contemporary constitutions, shown in the wording of some articles of the Bill of Rights and the adoption of new guarantees that were not present in the old constitution. In addition, as the international human rights treaties ratified by Colombia had been neglected, marginalized, or simply ignored, the constituyente confirmed and emphasized their validity in domestic law (Article 93).

The constituyente established protective procedures for those rights considered fundamental. The 1991 constitution prohibits the suspension of those rights protected by international treaties to which Colombia is party, including the norms of international humanitarian law, particularly in a state of emergency declared by the president.[9] International human rights law has also restrained the effects of the internal conflict in Colombia and promoted the peace efforts that followed the launch of the new constitution. By checking executive powers, particularly emergency powers, and those of the army and the police, the 1991 constitution's elaboration of human rights norms protected civilians from abuses by those in power. International humanitarian law has also served as a barrier to the abusive use of force in Colombia. It is true that as the hostilities have increased in scale, so have violations of human rights and humanitarian law. However, the constitutional restrictions on the power of the state and the new procedures for implementing

them have removed from the government the dubious distinction of being a primary cause of human rights violations.

The 1991 constitution also established new procedures for strengthening controls over executive powers, including the creation of the aforementioned human rights ombudsman (*Defensor del Pueblo*). The office of the *Defensoría del Pueblo* was established alongside the attorney general's office to focus on human rights protection and promotion. To this end, the *defensoría* works to denounce human rights violations, promote human rights by educating the public as to their rights and how to protect them, and defend those whose rights have been violated.

Article 86 of the 1991 constitution established the action of tutela, or writ of protection, one of the most important mechanisms for protecting fundamental rights. Through an action of tutela, every citizen has the right to seek immediate judicial judgment if one of that citizen's fundamental constitutional rights is threatened or violated by the act or omission of a public authority. The remedy of tutela has been widely used, and remains among the significant successes of the 1991 constitution.

A constitutional court was established to adjudicate the constitutionality of laws and treaties issued or entered into by the other branches of government; the court may be accessed not only by government officials but also by Colombian citizens. To prevent counterreforms that might endanger the basic pillars of the constitution and the viability of its efforts for peace, the assembly established particularly high requirements for adopting legislation regarding human rights, the judiciary, the political parties, the opposition, the mechanisms of participation (defined in Article 103 as elections, plebiscites, referendums, consultations of the people, open town meetings, legislative initiatives, and revocations of official powers), and states of exception that suspend the application of certain human rights under Article 152. Congressional legislation in these fields must be by *leyes estatuarias,* which have the seriousness of constitutional norms. The constitution also requires a referendum on constitutional amendments approved by Congress when those amendments affect norms regulating human rights and their guarantees or the procedures of popular participation in law-making activities (Article 377).

The 1991 constitution furthered the aim of achieving peace, both through provisions that specifically related to peace negotiations and by virtue of the constitutional reform itself. Given that the peace settlement achieved before the reform did not include the two largest guerrilla groups, and that the hostilities continued during the assembly's tenure, the constituyente included in the constitution a framework of provisions intended to foster continued peace efforts. At the same time, the assembly ensured that the new constitution would provide a helpful instrument for consolidating the peace accord already reached, and for the objective of securing a stable peace.

Regarding the provisions intended to facilitate new peace talks, the most significant of these sought to enable the government to support and advance peace talks. Transitional Article 30 authorized the national government to grant pardons and amnesty for acts committed by guerrilla groups before the constitutional assembly if they agreed to reincorporate into civil life. As approved on June 19, 1991, this article provided that these benefits would not apply to instances of atrocities, murders of defenseless persons, or acts committed outside of combat. In addition, according to Transitional Article 12, the president could designate new members of Congress from names presented by guerrilla groups engaged in a peace process. Transitional Articles 13 and 47 required the government to improve the economic and social conditions of areas where guer-

rillas operate and to organize a plan to assist those zones affected by acute violence. Although the peace process with the main guerrilla groups broke down in 1990, these powers were used to conclude negotiations with at least a faction of one of these groups. The impact of social programs born in this context, however, was very limited in terms of both efficacy and extent.

The constitutional process itself played an important role in the Colombian peace process thanks to these provisions, which helped to win the adhesion of several former guerrilla units and representatives of indigenous communities. Moreover, the constitutional reform as a whole was an attempt to resolve the armed conflict and its causes, and to ensure peace. Most notable among the causes of conflict are the exclusion of a majority of the population from political life and access to power, constant abuses committed by the military forces against the population, the neglect of the basic needs of the poorer sectors of the society, and the concentration of power in the hands of the executive branch.

After establishing peace as one of the main ends of the state and as a right and duty of all members of society (Preamble and Articles 2 and 22), the constitution attempted to open and democratize the political debate and access to power. In this regard, the constitution reformed the Congress, adopted a regime for political parties, called for legislation on the status of the opposition, and provided for a number of new mechanisms for popular participation in political life. Against a background of repeated and gross violations of basic liberties, the assembly adopted a very advanced bill of civil rights, including prohibitions of torture, disappearances, and the death penalty, the right not to be detained without judicial authorization, and the rights to habeas corpus and to a fair trial (Articles 11–41). A charter of social, economic, and cultural rights extended more power to individuals, associations, and members of certain groups—such as children, women, the elderly, disabled, indigenous peoples, and the black community—to claim attention to their needs in the areas of health, housing, work, land, education, and culture (Articles 42–77).

While state power in Colombia historically has been skewed toward a strong presidency and weak legislature and judiciary, the constituyente redressed this imbalance by significantly scaling back the expansive powers of the presidency in favor of the other two branches of a democratic government. The 1991 constitution particularly diminished the extent of the president's emergency powers, such that the legislature and constitutional court[10] now play a role in any declaration of a state of exception from human rights treaties. In addition, the constitution established stricter constraints on the duration and extent of all three forms of exception, which suspend the application of certain human rights when a state of emergency is declared.

Subsequent Developments

In the decade following promulgation of the 1991 constitution, the FARC escalated its campaign of terror, including kidnapping, extortion schemes, and an unofficial tax levied in rural areas for protection. The group is estimated to have an annual income ranging from $200 million to $400 million, at least half of which comes from the illegal drug trade. With a membership of 12,000 to 18,000, and between 9,000 and 12,000 armed combatants, it is the largest and richest insurgency in the world. In 1998, the Andrés Pastrana government launched peace negotiations with the FARC, ceding control of a 42,000-square-kilometer safe haven in Colombia's southeastern region. In February 2002, the negotiations collapsed with little result beyond deeply felt frustration. Much of the responsibility for this failure lies with the

FARC, which arrogantly abused the prerogatives accorded to them to facilitate the peace process. For its part, however, the government did not make an effective effort to avoid and punish human rights violations committed by state agents or demand of FARC a minimum respect for humanitarian law as a condition for maintaining a demilitarized zone. The government also failed to protect the civilian population against the many violent actions carried out by paramilitary groups, often with tolerance or complicity from public servants. After the peace process ended, the FARC increased its kidnapping of civilians, involvement in the drug business, and extortion. The FARC also launched a campaign of threats to eliminate elected mayors and destabilize every governmental authority.

With about 4,000 members, the ELN operates mainly in northeastern Colombia. Its income comes mainly from ransom or protection payments, but it also participates in the drug trade. The government attempted peace negotiations with the ELN, but refused to grant it a zone of control as it had granted the FARC. In May 2002, due to the failure to arrive at any agreement as to the procedural basis on which to structure negotiations, the Colombian government broke off the negotiations.

In the presidential election of 2002, President Álvaro Uribe, a dissident Liberal, garnered the support of 53 percent of the vote (though only 25 percent of the voting population turned out for the election). He maintained the confidence of other dissident Liberals as well as the Conservative Party, repeatedly declaiming the phrase of Bolívar that "order is the value on which liberty is based."

Four days after his inauguration, Uribe tested the constitutional limitations on his emergency powers. On August 11, 2002, he declared a state of internal unrest under the 1991 constitution's provisions affording him emergency powers for ninety days, with the possibility of two renewal periods. While declaring determination to guarantee respect for human rights, he emphasized the need to structure democratic authority to protect against illegal armed groups. To regain control over the country, the Uribe government committed to increasing the number of security troops from 250,000 to 850,000 over four years, while increasing defense expenditures from 3.6 percent of GDP to 6 percent of GDP by 2006. A program was established to provide human rights training to these troops and to establish offices to receive complaints by citizens of misconduct by military personnel. According to the U.S. State Department, the Colombian government's respect for human rights continued to improve and the majority of violations are committed by illegal armed groups. Although impunity for military personnel who collaborate with paramilitary forces remains a problem, the Office of Inspector General (Public Ministry) successfully charged 22 military persons with human rights violations and secured long prison terms for the offenders. Civilian courts adjudicate all serious violations of civilian human rights. Over a four-year period beginning on January 1, 2005, a new accusatory code of criminal procedures was set to replace the inquisitorial system traditional in Latin America, in jury trials open to the public.[11]

With substantial assistance from the United States, the Uribe administration established Plan Colombia to strengthen public institutions, reform the judicial system, combat corruption, and reduce the illegal drug trade. In part, the plan was implemented by destroying illegal coca crops while assisting poor farmers to replace the coca with legal crops. Nine hundred million dollars were allocated to building roads to the Putumayo region, increasing the government's presence there through schools, health clinics, and social services. This helped the negotiation of voluntary coca eradication agreements while the government employed Black Hawk helicopters and national police to destroy industrial coca plantations and laboratories.

Uribe has enjoyed strong public support for his authoritarian approach to governing. On October 19, 2005, the Colombian Congress amended the constitution to allow the president to serve two consecutive four-year terms. On May 25, 2006, Uribe was reelected by an overwhelming 62 percent of the votes cast. The electorate clearly approved of Uribe's pragmatic approach to further economic growth and achieve stability by cracking down on left-wing guerrillas and reaching an amnesty agreement with the paramilitary AUC. Although the crime rate has dropped, serious human rights issues remain. It remains to be seen whether the constitution's checks on executive authority are adequate, and whether the balance of power is flexible enough to enable the country to be governed well and democratically during this drive for stability.

Conclusion

The constitutional assembly's attempt to create a better framework for a functioning democracy represented an act of political will that, in the light of Colombia's history of violence, was nothing short of prodigious. Obviously, neither the assembly nor the constitution it created brought peace to Columbia, but it did as much as could be expected under the circumstances: It moved in the direction of consigning organized violence to the realm of outlaws, restricting the capacity of the government to exercise power illegally and creating new mechanisms and powers to protect individual rights against both the outlaws and the government.

However much the process of making the 1991 constitution diminished the duopoly of political power, fostered open dialogue and democratic cooperation, and strengthened the capacity of the legal system to protect the constitutional order, the ensuing decade demonstrated its inadequacy before the challenges presented to a weak state lacking the political will to address the root causes of violence. Despite the sincere effort in convening representatives from across the political spectrum and hammering out the consensual mandate that is the 1991 constitution, the potent cocktail of the internal conflict, narcotics trafficking, and a weak state unwilling to implement human rights norms defied the capacity of Colombia's democratic institutions to achieve peace and stability throughout the state, and particularly in rural areas.

In recent years, there has been progress in the effectiveness of government and an increase in stability. If the Uribe administration is to achieve lasting success, it will have to continue to reduce the violence that has plagued Colombia and promote a pattern of economic development that benefits the great majority of its citizens. The process that led to the adoption of the 1991 constitution is an example of political cooperation in the interest of the common good. Following the spirit of this *constituyente* would help secure peace and justice, along with order.

Notes

1. Vicente Lecuna Salboch, ed., *Cartas del Libertador*, vol. 9 (Caracas: Editorial Tip. del Comercio, 1929), p. 11; Augusto Mijares, *El Liberta-*

dor (Caracas: Fundación Eugenio Mendoza, 1967), p. 531. For a fictional depiction of Bolivar's state of mind, see Gabriel Garcia Marquez, *El general en su laberinto* (Bogotá: Editorial Oveja Negra, 1989).

2. See Joseph B. Treaster, "Colombia Siege Survivors are Bitter," *The New York Times*, November 11, 1985. Eleven judges were killed during the government's attack; one later died of a heart attack in a hospital.

3. See Comisión Andina de Juristas, *Violencia en Colombia* (Lima: Comisión Andina de Juristas, 1990).

4. This irony is well noted by Manuel José Cepeda, presidential counselor for the development of the constitution under President Gaviria, in his collection of addresses on the administration's success in securing a constitutional reform, *Introducción a la Constitución de 1991: hacia un nuevo constitucionalismo* (Bogota: Presidencia de la República, Consejería para el Desarrollo de la Constitución, 1993).

5. See "Colombia: Cooling It," *The Economist*, March 30, 1991, p. 4.

6. James Brook, "Door Opens a Crack for Colombia's Indians," *New York Times*, May 2, 1991, p. A10.

7. Gaceta Constitucional no. 114, p. 35.

8. Carlos Heras de la Fuente and Marcel Tangarife Torres, *Constitución Politica de Colombia*, vol. 1 (1996), pp. 332–44.

9. Arts. 93 and 214 (2).

10. The constitutional court has asserted its competence to judge the constitutionality of presidential decrees that declare states of exception under arts. 4, 213, 215, and 241 of the constitution.

11. U.S. Department of State, "Human Rights Practice in Colombia 2005," released March 8, 2006.

18

The Nicaraguan Constitutional Experience

Process, Conflict, Contradictions, and Change*

Lee Demetrius Walker and Philip J. Williams

The early literature on democratic transitions in Latin America paid scant attention to institutions; later, as scholars began to focus on the issue of democratic consolidation, emphasis shifted from process to institutions including parties and party systems, electoral systems, and parliamentary versus presidential forms of government. However, although scholars of democratization in Latin America have studied the institutions and institutional frameworks that constitutions have created, they generally have neglected constitution-making environments and processes and their relation to democratic consolidation.[1] Scholars of democratic transitions in Eastern Europe have paid more attention to constitutions and democracy, but generally empha-

size institutional choice and the substance of the constitutions themselves.[2]

In their comparative discussion of different constitution-making contexts and formulas, Linz and Stepan lay out six different scenarios ranging from the most to least confining conditions for democratic consolidation. Two of the scenarios include cases from Latin America. Chile is an example of the most confining case, characterized by the "retention of a constitution created by a non-democratic regime with reserve domains and difficult amendment procedures."[3] Argentina and Uruguay, on the other hand, provide more favorable contexts, in which the previous democratic constitution was restored "for reasons of speed, conflict avoidance, and the desire to call upon some legacies of historical legitimacy."[4] Linz and Stepan argue that the most favorable formula for democratic consolidation (Spain fits this pattern) includes a democratically elected constituent assembly that freely deliberates and drafts a new constitution appropriate for democratic

* The authors would like to thank John Booth, David Dye, Shelley McConnell, Kenneth Mijeski, and the members of the Constitution-Making Working Group for their invaluable comments on an earlier version of the paper.

consolidation. Ideally, the constituent assembly "should avoid a partisan constitution approved only by a 'temporary majority' that leads a large minority to put constitutional revisions on the agenda, thereby making consolidation of democratic institutions more difficult."[5] Potentially divisive issues should be resolved through consensus, and the constitution should be approved by popular referendum to enhance its legitimacy.

Linz and Stepan's emphasis on consensus recalls Przeworski's argument that the crucial step in any transition to democracy is to establish an institutional compromise among the country's principal political forces: Democracy "cannot be a result of a substantive compromise, but it can be a result of institutional compromise."[6] Groups enter into an institutional compromise as the most promising framework to achieve their interests. But institutional compromise is not always possible; in some cases of transition, not all the major political forces feel protected under democratic institutions. Groups on the right—either allied or opposed to the former authoritarian rulers—may be incapable of mobilizing support within civil society to defend their ideas and interests. Such historical conditions make institutional compromise difficult at best.

The Nicaraguan case does not fit neatly into any of the scenarios sketched out by Linz and Stepan. Moreover, the revolutionary nature of the Nicaraguan transition complicated the possibility of a Przeworskian institutional compromise. Unlike other transitions from authoritarian rule in Latin America, Nicaragua is the only recent example of a transition through armed struggle and the only case in which accommodating elite interests did not supercede the goals of social and economic democracy. Allies of the Anastasio Somoza Debayle dictatorship fled the country following the revolutionary takeover, while others on the right that participated in the antidictatorial movement were in no position to challenge the Sandinistas' leadership of the revolutionary government.

The constitutional process that followed the 1979 Nicaraguan revolution requires a somewhat different theoretical lens than the transition literature provides. McWhinney argues that "within an existing nation-state, a fundamental change in the existing social and economic base, effected by popular revolution or similar cataclysmic political event, usually means a corresponding change in the basic constitutional system and the postulation of a new legal starting point, or *Grundnorm*, as the basic premise of the new constitutional system."[7] In Nicaragua, the new legal starting point was the construction of a popular revolutionary democracy. For the Frente Sandinista de Liberación Nacional (FSLN) leadership, democracy consisted of more than simply contesting power through competitive elections; it meant transforming society, including fundamentally restructuring power and property relations as well as increasing popular participation in the country's political, economic, social, and cultural affairs.[8]

Hyden refers to constitution making that starts with the defeat or collapse of the previous regime as the "replacement model." The sponsors of the transition—in this case, the FSLN—"drawing on their rejection of past legacies, set very specific parameters for the direction of the constitution-making process."[9] The constitutional agenda is very much influenced by the precommitments that the victorious sponsors of the process have made. In Nicaragua, the FSLN rejected the historical legacy of pact making associated with previous constitutions. Any future constitution-making process would have to incorporate public input and produce a document that was relevant to ordinary citizens.

According to McWhinney, after the new legal starting point has been identified, "the primary and secondary principles of the resulting new legal order can be developed by a process of logical deduction and application as the basic norm progressively unfolds or concretizes itself."[10] That is to say, the basic norms become self-enforcing. McWhinney's logic is grounded in the notion that conflict has been resolved and the victorious group has the ability to search for consensus. In Nicaragua, conflict continued after the overthrow of the Somoza dictatorship, and the constitutional process was very much shaped by the context of an ongoing armed conflict. These conditions led to a more contradictory approach to constitution making than the replacement model suggests.[11]

The difficulty in assigning the 1987 Nicaraguan constitutional process to any one constitution-making typology[12] makes it important to understand its uniqueness, for it is in this uniqueness that the origins of the 1995 and 2000 reforms can be understood. McWhinney argues that the post–World War II wave of constitution making brought several tendencies to the forefront, notably the idea of popular democracy. The leadership of the revolutionary government in Nicaragua was clearly influenced by the popular democracy model. Jules Lobel terms the FSLN version of popular democracy "participatory democracy" and argues that it required "three interrelated efforts":

> First, it required developing structures and institutions such as the mass organizations, town hall meetings, and a broad-based militia which would encourage and permit popular participation in governmental affairs. Second, it involved dramatic social and economic restructuring of society and the guaranteeing of social, economic and cultural rights which would establish a socioeconomic base for popular democracy. Finally, the Nicaraguan government reconstituted key institutions such as the army and education system based explicitly on defending and extending the gains of the revolution.[13]

Even though the FSLN emerged as the dominant political force after the revolution and could have imposed a constitution based on the popular democracy model, the nation's ongoing conflict required consideration of other views.[14] External pressure from the United States and growing domestic opposition convinced the FSLN to make concessions during critical junctures. Between 1982 and 1984, the FSLN and other parties engaged in a series of negotiations to establish the ground rules for the 1984 elections. This process included both debate in the Council of State and bilateral talks between the FSLN and opposition parties. At several important points in the negotiations, the right-wing opposition alliance, Coordinadora Democrática Nicaragüense (CDN), withdrew from the council to force greater concessions from the FSLN. Although the FSLN did not incorporate all the CDN's demands, the resulting political parties law and electoral law contained responses to many of the opposition's key concerns.[15]

A second tendency in post–World War II constitution making is "'revived' or 'modernized' classical Western constitutionalism."[16] Concessions from advocates of the popular democracy approach primarily reflect this modernization tendency. Wilson argues that changes in revolutionary Nicaragua reflected modernization under the civil law model rather than "a wholesale conversion to the socialist model [McWhinney's popular democracy model]."[17] The 1984 elections for a national constituent assembly represented a shift away from corporatist structures and toward formally adopting liberal democratic political institutions. The Council of State, the previous legislature, was composed of representatives from various mass organizations, in addition to political parties. These mass organizations received twelve of the council's forty-seven seats. In the new National Assembly, mass organizations no longer enjoyed official representation.[18] Moreover, including the institutional structure of separation of powers tended to favor a liberal rather than a popular approach to democracy.[19]

The competing versions of democracy—one based on the concept of popular democracy and the other on the concept of Western liberal democracy—became a principal concern to the key actors in the Nicaraguan constitutional process. Shelley McConnell argues that "given the acute social polarization in Nicaragua, a remarkable high level of consensus was reached within the National Assembly."[20] On the other hand, the Nicaraguan constitution's unique nature and drafting during an ongoing conflict conform to the idea that the Nicaraguan constituent assembly understood that part of its job was to build consensus. At the same time, McConnell argues that "by combining principles of representative and participatory democracy, socialism and capitalism, and of international law and nationalism, the constitution appealed to a broad audience."[21] McConnell stresses that the conflicting principles of the constitution were left to be "worked out later through ordinary law."[22] The consensus that emerged thus was somewhat superficial: Instead of resolving key differences, the constitution contained much ambiguity, combining contradictory elements to provide something for everyone. While the Sandinistas were the dominant party in the revolutionary coalition, they refrained from resolving the most divisive issues in a majoritarian manner. These conditions suggest that previous examinations of the Nicaraguan constitution-writing process may have underemphasized the loyal opposition's role in the process.

While the new constitution was debated around the concept of democracy, the armed conflict was the driving force behind constitutional consensus. Chambliss argues that "every society, nation, economic system, and historical period contains contradictory elements which are the moving force of change."[23] These contradictions lead to conflicts and dilemmas that must be resolved through creating laws or changing institutional structures. In turn, such changes are temporary as new laws and institutional structures inevitably lead to new contradictions. Following Chambliss, the 1987 constitution and the constitution-making process contributed partially to resolving conflict in Nicaragua. Nevertheless, the end of the armed conflict in 1990 led to important constitutional contradictions that had been left unresolved in 1987. The chief dilemma facing the new government in 1990 was which version of democracy—popular or Western liberal—to institutionalize. The tools that the competing democracy proponents used were the formal institutions of government; in utilizing these tools, both sides eventually opted for the liberal model of democracy.[24]

The 1987 Constitution

The Sandinista-led revolution in 1979 succeeded in forging a broad-based coalition that overwhelmed the increasingly corrupt and repressive Somoza dictatorship. Given the widespread antipathy toward Somoza's regime, the 1974 Nicaraguan constitution—the product of a pact between Somoza and some opposition parties, intended to perpetuate his political control—was discredited beyond repair. As in other revolutionary contexts, constitutional continuity was out of the question. Following the replacement model, one of the first official acts of the new revolutionary government was to abolish the 1974 constitution through the Estatuto Fundamental (the Fundamental Statute) of July 20, 1979. This statute was quickly followed on August 21, 1979, by the Estatuto sobre Derechos y Garantías de los Nicaragüenses (Statute of Rights and Guarantees of the Nicaraguan People), which provided a basic bill of rights. These two documents were designed to provide a temporary framework for Nicaragua's government.

While the FSLN was the dominant party of the revolution, the Junta de Gobierno de Reconstrucción Nacional that formed after the overthrow was not strictly an FSLN government. Initially only three of the junta's seven members were affiliated with the FSLN.[25] The junta's composition represented the four main political blocs: the Sandinista bloc, the right opposition bloc, the moderate opposition bloc, and the left opposition bloc.[26]

The national unity that followed the 1979 revolution quickly evaporated.[27] Tension grew between the Sandinistas, who sought to create a state centered on the ideas of mass organization and popular participation, and others in the coalition, who desired a state centered on the ideas of private property and representative government.[28] By 1982, the FSLN fully controlled the government and was continuing to advance its ideas of popular democracy. Two members of the seven-member junta left the government to join the armed opposition; a third left the junta due to disagreements with its direction.[29] Also in 1982, the government reinstated a state of emergency, which had been lifted in April 1980. The state of emergency allowed the government to suspend a number of personal and political rights, including freedom of expression, the right of association and peaceful assembly, freedom of travel, and the right of habeus corpus.[30] The Sandinistas' 1982 decision to forcibly relocate thousands of Miskito Indians along the Atlantic coast exacerbated the conflict with indigenous groups who had taken up arms against the government.

Against the backdrop of armed conflict and governmental suspension of civil and political rights, the Council of the State approved a political parties law in 1983 that was an important step in initiating national elections. The law defined the rights, qualifications, and functions of parties and established the National Council on Parties to supervise party activities.[31] In addition, the council approved a new electoral law to prepare for the 1984 elections. Given that the old electoral law was created to preserve Somoza's political power, the council opted to draft a completely new law. A special commission visited the United States and several countries in Europe and Latin America to study their electoral laws and procedures. The new law instituted an electoral procedure that used proportional representation to elect the legislature and a plurality system to elect the president.[32] The country was divided into nine districts with ten assembly seats per district. The seats were allocated based on the percentage of votes each party received in each district.[33] Parties only needed to garner 1 percent of the vote nationally to receive representation in the assembly. The losing candidates from among the seven parties that ran for the presidency received the six remaining seats of the ninety-six-seat assembly. Finally, electoral law provided for the creation of an electoral commission, the Supreme Electoral Council (CSE), modeled after electoral tribunals in Costa Rica and Venezuela.[34] The CSE was charged with administering all aspects of the elections, including voter education and registration, receiving and verifying complaints, and ensuring a fair and transparent process.[35]

The elections for the national constituent assembly were held on November 4, 1984; 75 percent of eligible voters participated.[36] The election was declared valid by several international organizations, including Americas Watch, the Latin American Studies Association (LASA), and several foreign governmental delegations including Great Britain, Ireland, and Costa Rica.[37] The FSLN Party received 66.8 percent of the votes for the assembly and sixty-one of the ninety-six (63.5 percent) seats.[38] The opposition parties divided the other thirty-five seats. The assembly was inaugurated on January 9, 1985, and mandated to produce a constitution within two years.[39]

Structure of the Process

The Nicaraguan constitution-writing process employed the constituent assembly model as the chief structural mechanism to create the nation's new constitution. Nevertheless, the overall structure of the process was far more complex and in keeping with competing versions of democracy. Thus, while much of the work of drafting the constitution was entrusted to the representatives elected to the National Assembly, a number of mechanisms were designed to ensure public input at various stages of the process.

Following the elections, the national constituent assembly selected a twenty-two-member constitutional commission to prepare an initial draft constitution.[40] The commission solicited initial public input from groups in civil society by inviting these groups to appear before the commission.[41] The commission completed and presented the first draft of the constitution to the assembly in February 1986. The assembly then distributed approximately 150,000 copies of the first draft throughout the country.[42] Seventy-three *cabildos abiertos,* or town hall meetings, were held around the country to solicit further public input concerning the draft.[43] Following the cabildos abiertos, the assembly appointed a twenty-member Comisión Dictaminadora to review the public comments, prepare an advisory report, and write a second draft of the constitution. The Comisión Dictaminadora consisted primarily of the members of the constitutional commission, but there were a few replacements.[44] The Comisión then delivered the second draft to the full assembly for discussion and debate. Eighty-nine of the ninety-six assembly members approved the final draft of the constitution on November 19, 1986, and the constitution became effective on January 9,

1987. Electoral ratification was not used as a final mechanism of popular consultation.[45]

Public Participation

A major concession regarding public participation occurred in the elections for the national constituent assembly, the first instance of public participation in the constitution-making process. While the FSLN stressed a major role for mass organizations, the Council of the State's electoral law created an assembly constructed strictly on geographical zones with no provisions for mass organizations.[46] To compensate for this concession to the opposition, the FSLN allowed its mass organization supporters, who were not officially party members, to run on FSLN party ballots.[47] In addition, the government spent approximately $40 million to advertise the election and educate citizens concerning electoral procedures. At the same time, each political party was given free television and radio time to articulate their campaigns.[48]

However, other problems developed to undermine participation. First, former junta member Arturo Cruz and the Coordinadora decided to boycott the elections.[49] Because the Coordinadora represented the influential business sector of the country, an important voice was thus absent from the constitution-making process.[50] Next, the administration of U.S. President Ronald Reagan sought to dissuade opposition parties from participating in the election process and convince citizens that the electoral process was invalid.[51] U.S. pressure exacerbated divisions within the Partido Conservador Demócrata (PCD) and the Partido Liberal Independiente (PLI); some leaders urged a boycott on the eve of the elections. Despite these obstacles, voters were presented with a wide range of political options and opposition parties had ample opportunities to communicate their programs to the electorate. Even though voting was not obligatory, approximately

75 percent of registered voters cast ballots on election day.[52]

The second avenue of public participation in the constitution-writing process was through the special constitutional commission. This twenty-two-member commission was divided into three subcommittees, for which it established a two-stage process.[53] First, the leaders of civil-society organizations were invited to address the commission with the concerns of their respective groups. Morgan argues that women's groups were particularly active in this process and raised a large number of concerns of particular interest to women and children.[54] Second, between May and June 1986, seventy-three cabildos abiertos were held throughout the country after the first draft of the constitution had been circulated. Prior to the cabildos, the government distributed 150,000 copies of the draft, supplemented by twelve televised debates among representatives of opposing parties. Civil-society groups within each community assisted in organizing the cabildos. The meetings were broadcast live on radio, and highlights were published in newspapers and covered on television. Approximately 100,000 people attended the meetings; 2,500 citizens made presentations and 1,800 more submitted written comments.[55] The meetings took several different forms. Several of the cabildos allowed open discussion of any section of the draft constitution. Seven of the forums were specifically designed to address issues of particular importance to women.[56] These meetings were not only forums for FSLN-affiliated groups; cabildos also were held specifically for business and professional groups, which yielded serious concerns about private property protection and the rights of accused persons.[57]

Some opposition parties boycotted the cabildos, and critics of the government generally viewed them as well-controlled forums to permit only perfunctory modifications to the original draft constitution. Without a doubt, that citizens were presented with a draft potentially circumscribed the scope of debate and discussion at the cabildos. Most independent observers of the public forums agree, however, that the discussions were generally quite dynamic and freewheeling. Citizens often raised issues in the cabildos that did not appear in the draft constitution. Finally, the constitutional commission subsequently incorporated a number of changes to the second draft in response to issues and concerns raised in the cabildos. These changes included significantly strengthening women's rights, recognizing indigenous rights for the peoples of the Atlantic coast, protecting minors and the elderly, and recognizing the rights of prisoners.[58]

Democratic Representation

McWhinney argues that directly electing a constituent assembly gives it a direct political mandate and constitutional legitimacy, an idea that he grounds in the constitutional heritage of the 1789 French Revolution.[59] Certainly the FSLN-led government desired a strong mandate given the ongoing armed conflict, but the constituent assembly ultimately fulfilled the needs of both the FSLN and the loyal opposition groups, who wanted a more representative form of democratic governance. The revolutionary origins and populist nature of the constituent assembly made it appealing to FSLN supporters who wanted to include the poor and working classes in the constitution-writing process. On the other hand, the representative nature of the constituent assembly appealed to opposition party leaders, who desired to create a system that respected individual interests and property rights.[60] Meanwhile, the middle-class opposition clearly favored the constituent assembly over the popular initiative mechanism, which many perceived as overly favoring the FSLN because of the mass organizations that it mobilized in the first years after the revolution.[61]

The adoption of the proportional representation electoral format was a major decision in the structure of the constitution-writing process. This format tends to accentuate minority over majority interests and is generally the electoral system of choice in new democracies that emerge out of conditions of pronounced social and political divisions.[62] For the FSLN, the decision to employ proportional representation was a major concession. Unlike the Council of the State, which was based on a corporatist model and ensured representation for mass organizations, the new assembly was based on the principle of geographical representation, a key demand of opposition parties, the Catholic hierarchy, and indigenous groups on the Atlantic coast. Moreover, including defeated presidential candidates in the Assembly granted each minority party an additional representative.[63] These three FSLN concessions acknowledged the value of opposition voices in the process.[64] At the same time, the willingness of opposition parties to continue in the process while the FSLN advanced some elements of popular democracy indicated that the opposition parties were equally willing to compromise.

The national constituent assembly also appointed the special constitutional commission, which was even more favorable to the opposition parties than the assembly was itself: Ten of the twenty-two members were from parties other than the FSLN.[65] Nevertheless, tensions did develop within the commission between the Sandinistas and opposition parties. For the FSLN, a number of key issues were not negotiable: the revolutionary nature of the armed forces; presidential reelection; and the "popular orientation of the economy."[66] Whereas the opposition demanded that the armed forces be depoliticized, the FSLN insisted that it was legitimate for the armed forces to de-

fend the revolution. Second, the FSLN was unwilling to accept the opposition's demand for a ban on presidential reelection. Finally, whereas the conservative opposition demanded guarantees for private property and a market economy, the FSLN insisted on a significant role for the state in guaranteeing an economy that served the needs of poor Nicaraguans. Despite the FSLN's unwillingness to compromise on these issues, the second draft of the constitution accommodated a number of opposition concerns, including changes in the greater balance of power between the executive and legislative branches, additional provisions for autonomy of the judicial and electoral branches of government, and the easing of restrictions on reforming the constitution.[67]

Conflict over popular and representative versions of democracy also emerged. The PCD and PLI refused to participate in the cabildos and argued that because the national constituent assembly was elected, there was no need for further public input.[68] Nevertheless, both parties were involved in the discussion and debate processes of the second draft of the constitution, and at least one member from both parties voted for the final document.[69] More problematic from a representation standpoint was the boycott of the process by the Coordinadora members and the counterrevolutionary organizations that had taken up arms against the government. Consequently, a significant sector of society was not represented in the process and did not accept the new constitution as legitimate.

Finally, while women participated in the process at a high level, they were nonetheless underrepresented. Only fourteen of the ninety-six members of the national constituent assembly were women,[70] though the percentage of women elected to the assembly (14.6 percent) was slightly higher than the percentage of female candidates for office (13.2 percent).[71] While all seven parties had women among their candidates, the list system, which allowed parties to assign the order in which their candidates would receive seats in each of the nine districts, was not favorable to women, as they tended to be listed lower on the parties' lists.[72] Given the percentage of votes that parties other than the FSLN received in each district, female candidates from other parties were not high enough on the lists to receive assembly seats. When the assembly selected the special constitutional commission, only two women were appointed as members.[73] A third woman was added later to serve in place of her primary representative.[74]

Timing of the Process

The national constituent assembly was granted two years to complete the constitution-writing process. While the assembly used its time effectively, time was a factor in successfully completing the document. McWhinney argues that there are several requirements for an effective constituent assembly:

> A constituent assembly would seem to require to be elected against a background of an already existing, and continuing, societal consensus as to the nature and desired direction of fundamental political, social and economic—and hence constitutional—change. Either that, or the constituent assembly must itself be conceded enough time, within the definition of its mandate, to wait for such a societal consensus to develop or to get out itself and try to build it.[75]

McWhinney's points are relevant to the Nicaraguan case. At the beginning of the two-year period, the FSLN was well placed with its constituency and could count on a great deal of support in the process, whereas opposition parties had to convince their members and supporters that a FSLN-led process could produce a consensual document. This factor was particularly important given the existence of the armed counterrevolutionary forces. The national constituent assembly appointed the special constitutional com-

mission in April 1985. From August until October 1985, the commission held public hearings to gather public opinion about the constitution-making process.

On January 22, 1986, a month before the special constitutional commission released the first draft of the constitution, the armed opposition released a document entitled *United Nicaraguan Opposition Principles and Objectives for Provisional Government of National Reconciliation*.[76] Although this document did not greatly affect the constitution-writing process of the government, it was a reminder that alternatives existed to the current process. On February 21, 1986, the commission presented its first draft constitution to the assembly. Between May 18 and June 30, 1986, the commission gathered public opinion concerning the first draft document.[77] The Comisión Dictaminadora completed the second draft of the constitution by the end of August 1986 and presented it to the full assembly in early September. After ten weeks of debate, the constitution was approved on November 19, 1986.

International Community

While the constitution-writing process in Nicaragua was primarily domestically driven, the international community was important to completing the process. Officials in the Reagan administration and others argued that the FSLN agreed to the 1984 elections partly to gain international legitimacy.[78] There may be some truth to this argument. The revolutionary government badly damaged its international credibility during the resettlement of the indigenous groups on the Atlantic coast.[79] While the FSLN government attempted to correct the error, the successful elections did add to the legitimacy of the government and the constitution-writing process. International organizations (e.g., LASA and Americas Watch) and delegations from other nations validated the

1984 elections, which also facilitated the legitimacy of the constitutional process.[80] Nicaragua's signing of the Esquipulas Agreement on Regional Peace with four other Central American governments in 1987 exemplified the international community's positive influence. Although the agreement recognized existing constitutions and did not require any specific constitutional reforms, it did provide a framework for achieving national reconciliation, an end to hostilities, and advancement toward democratization.[81]

Several nations assisted in the Nicaraguan constitution-making process. First, in summer 1985, members of the Nicaraguan special constitutional commission traveled to several countries to study their respective constitutions.[82] The United States, however, refused to grant commission members visas to the United States.[83] Also during 1985, constitutional experts were invited to Nicaragua to consult with the commission on specific aspects of the constitution. Arthur Kinoy of Rutgers Law School was asked to address the National Assembly on the lessons of U.S. constitutional history. Other academics, such as Sylvia Law of New York University (NYU) Law School, visited Nicaragua to study the process. In October 1985, the Nicaraguan Supreme Court invited jurists from the United States, Cuba, Italy, France, the Soviet Union, and Spain to participate in a seminar focusing on the judiciary's function under the new constitution. In April 1986, Kinoy and Law organized a three-day workshop in New York at NYU Law School. The meeting was composed of small working groups that addressed specific issues, including the scope of judicial review, separation of powers, church and state relations, freedom of expression, private property, equality, prisons and the rights of the accused, and ethnic autonomy. Each of these working meetings included several members of the Nicaraguan constitutional commission,[84] constitutional scholars, and Latin American experts.

The U.S. consultation was one of several international consultations that the special constitutional commission conducted.[85] These consultations came after the release of the first draft of the constitution in February 1986 but before the cabildos abiertos in May and June 1986. Consequently, the input from international experts was helpful in highlighting problem areas in the draft and topics of discussion for the cabildos. In short, although domestically driven, the consultation process may have influenced the structure of the elicitation process of the open forums and possibly contributed to some of FSLN concessions.

The generally positive relations that the Nicaraguan government sustained with other nations somewhat mitigated its adversarial relationship with the United States. Nevertheless, the U.S. government's attempts to destabilize the Sandinista government complicated the constitution-making process. The Reagan administration persuaded several members of the opposition to boycott the 1984 elections in hopes of delegitimizing the process[86] and provided significant military assistance and training to the armed counterrevolutionary forces.[87] These U.S. attempts to subvert the process may have backfired; the historical pattern of U.S. interference in Nicaraguan domestic affairs may have unintentionally contributed to the successful completion of the constitution in that it strengthened the loyal opposition's resolve to see the process succeed. McDonald and Zatz identify two ideological orientations among the FSLN leadership—socialism and nationalism—that manifested themselves in opposition to U.S. intervention.[88] Similarly, Lobel argues that the Sandinista revolution, "is a nationalist revolution, in that it seeks to unite various sectors of the Nicaraguan society, including the anti-Somocista segments of the middle-class."[89] Valenta and Duran argue that many Nicaraguans, not just FSLN members, equated the United States' imperialist political and economic domination with control of the country by Somoza and the capitalist elite.[90] This may have encouraged the anti-Somocista middle class to give the constitution-making process and the transformation of society (within limits) a real chance to succeed.

International Law

The national constituent assembly adopted constitutional provisions that explicitly acknowledged the importance of international law in protecting human rights. In Article 46 of the 1987 constitution, the assembly incorporated the Universal Declaration of Human Rights; the American Declaration of the Rights and Duties of Man; the International Covenant on Economic, Social, and Cultural Rights; the International Covenant on Civil and Political Rights; and the American Convention on Human Rights as part of the Nicaraguan constitution.[91] The assembly approved this article by a single vote, which was not strictly along party lines. A coalition of PCD, Partido Popular Social Cristiano, and FSLN members supported incorporating the article.[92] Moreover, the assembly affirmed Nicaragua's existence as a multiethnic and secular state in articles 8 and 14.[93] This multiethnic stance is most vividly demonstrated in the articles that concern the indigenous people of the Atlantic coast.

The Autonomy Law

The government's efforts to draft an autonomy law for the Atlantic coast paralleled the 1985–87 constitution-making process. Similar to the 1987 constitution, the autonomy process was shaped by the context of the armed conflict on the Atlantic coast. Beginning in 1981, MISURA (Miskitos, Sumus, and Ramas), an organization representing indigenous communities on the Atlantic coast, launched armed attacks against

the Sandinista army from its bases in Honduras. Another indigenous organization, MISURASATA (Miskitos, Sumus, Ramas, and Sandinistas Working Together), staged attacks in the south from its base in Costa Rica. The Sandinista government combined a military strategy with negotiations to persuade the different armed groups to disarm. An important condition of the indigenous organizations was that the government recognize indigenous rights and the principle of self-determination. The government wanted to negotiate a ceasefire before discussing indigenous rights.[94] Despite these differences, in December 1984, the government named a national commission to draft an autonomy law. The commission produced a draft document that served as a basis for a series of workshops, educational sessions, and *consultas populares* similar to those organized for the constitution. Over six hundred local volunteers carried out the workshops and consultas throughout the Atlantic coastal region. The process in the south, where the armed conflict was winding down, was more successful, and the autonomy commission there produced a draft law in June 1986. In the north, the continuing armed conflict complicated the process.[95]

Despite the significant political and military tensions exacerbated by renewed U.S. assistance to the *contras* in April 1986, the Sandinistas' determined commitment to the autonomy process prevented these tensions from derailing it.[96] In April 1987, a joint draft was debated in Puerto Cabezas with 250 elected delegates from the north and south along with 2,000 observers. One of the most contentious issues had to do with the state's earnings from resource exploitation. Some delegates pushed for fixed percentages to be spelled out in the law, but the director of the national autonomy commission successfully argued that the law should be more flexible, allowing the percentages to be negotiated on a yearly basis. There was also disagreement over whether to divide the region permanently into two separate political entities, which would have reinforced geographical separation and weakened the future potential for regional autonomy. One autonomous region would create a single unified indigenous population, while two autonomous regions would dilute indigenous interests. In the end, the statute provided for the creation of the North and South Atlantic Autonomous Regions with directly elected assemblies.[97]

The National Assembly approved the autonomy law almost unanimously in September 1987. Key provisions of the law were incorporated into thirteen Atlantic coast-related articles in the new constitution. Especially important was Article 8, which defined the Nicaraguan state as multiethnic. Although the autonomy law provided for more than just cultural autonomy, it did not extend to the political autonomy that the armed indigenous groups demanded. The statute clearly recognized the principle of national unity and territorial sovereignty, and the central government reserved full control over foreign relations, national defense, and economic planning. Moreover, the powers of the regional assemblies were not very great: As Ortiz notes, "Other than the power to resolve differences among community land claims, the assemblies would mainly be adapting national laws to the particularities of regions."[98] Finally, natural resources not located on traditional communal lands were to be jointly administered by the central and regional governments.

While the autonomy process facilitated the pacification of the Atlantic coast and went a long way toward accommodating indigenous demands, it was less successful in creating widespread consensus. As Charles Hale argues, indigenous groups on the coast, especially the Miskitu, distinguished clearly between autonomy and the right of self-determination.[99] Autonomy was identified with the Sandinistas, while self-determination

was identified with the armed indigenous organizations. Since autonomy included many things that people wanted—bilingual education, rights to traditional communal lands, limited self-government, and resources for economic development—many Miskitu were inclined to test the waters: "Once Miskitu townspeople endorsed the distinction between *autonomía* and Miskitu rights, it made perfect sense to participate fully in the former, while viewing the latter as a desirable but presently unattainable ideal."[100]

The 1995 Constitutional Reforms[101]

The limited nature of the consensus underpinning the constitution was reflected in how quickly the opposition embraced constitutional reforms as central to its political platform.[102] As early as November 1987, fourteen opposition parties, including the loyal opposition, circulated a document calling for seventeen constitutional reforms.[103] Chief among the proposed reforms were prohibiting the reelection of the president, limiting presidential power, prohibiting family members of the president from succeeding him or her in office, and suppressing the preamble to the constitution.[104] Many of the reforms were aimed at the executive because it was through this branch that the FSLN had been able to advance its policies. The opposition parties conditioned their continuing participation in the National Dialogue—the talks initiated between the FSLN government and opposition under the auspices of the 1987 Central American peace accords—on the government's agreement to these reforms. Pressure by President Oscar Arias of Costa Rica and President Carlos Andrés Pérez of Venezuela, however, convinced opposition leaders to drop this key condition.

In August 1989, the government and opposition agreed on a series of changes to the electoral law in anticipation of the upcoming 1990 elections, leaving the issue of constitutional reforms for later. The Unión Nacional Opositora (UNO) coalition, comprising thirteen opposition parties and led by presidential candidate Violeta Chamorro and vice presidential candidate Virgilio Godoy, won a surprising victory in the February 1990 elections. The coalition won fifty-one of the ninety-two seats available in the assembly. The FSLN party won thirty-nine seats, sufficient to block constitutional reform, which required the approval of 60 percent of the legislature in two consecutive legislative sessions.

The UNO coalition, which ranged from the far left (Partido Comunista de Nicaragua) to the far right (Partido Conservador Nacional), had significant tensions stemming from fundamental ideological differences. These differences, which played out in conflicts between the executive and legislative branches, undermined the efforts to push through constitutional reforms. The growing rift between UNO's right wing and the executive developed into a full-blown constitutional crisis in September 1992, when assembly president Alfredo César attempted to elect new assembly officials without a legislative quorum. President Chamorro refused to recognize the new leadership; she was backed by the Supreme Court, which nullified the election. When César refused to accept the court's decision, the Chamorro government ordered the police to shut down the assembly and seize its assets until new elections could be held in January 1993.[105]

The constitutional crisis took place amid growing political violence and instability. Increasingly, many of the key political actors refused to accept the institutional framework established by the 1987 constitution, resorting to extraconstitutional means to address their demands. Demobilized *contras* and former Sandinista military took up arms to pressure the Chamorro government to implement the compensatory reinsertion programs promised to them after the war.[106] Sandinista base organizations and trade unions resorted to violent street demonstrations and strikes to challenge the government's neoliberal economic policies. Right-wing members of UNO appealed to allies in the U.S. administration to pressure the Chamorro government to return land taken from former property holders during the Sandinista land reform. And the Chamorro government turned to executive decrees to force through economic policies that the legislature rejected.[107]

The increasing intensity of the conflict convinced some political leaders to look to constitutional reforms to defuse the crisis. Ironically, a growing split between Sandinista legislators and the FSLN national directorate paved the way toward constitutional reforms.[108] Former vice president Sergio Ramírez and the majority of FSLN legislators supported constitutional reforms to empower the legislature, while ex-president Daniel Ortega sided with the Chamorro government in its efforts to block the reforms. The Ramírez faction was instrumental in forging a new legislative majority with moderate elements of the UNO coalition. The FSLN-Center Group coalition, as it was known, succeeded in electing centrist Gustravo Tablada as assembly president.[109]

During 1993, two opposing positions on constitutional reform emerged. One group supported amending the 1987 constitution; another demanded the establishment of a constituent assembly to produce a new constitution. In December 1993, FSLN assembly members signed accords with primarily centrist parties in favor of amendment.[110] The assembly appointed a special commission to study the proposed changes and present an opinion. Although some public forums were held to generate public discussion, the process was much less participatory than that of the 1987 constitution.[111] The special commission presented a revised reform bill to the assembly for approval by the required 60 percent in November 1994.

As the 1987 constitution required, the National Assembly voted a second time to approve the constitutional reforms in early 1995, and the reform package was sent to the president in February 1995 for promulgation. President Chamorro refused to sign off on the package, however, because she disagreed with amendments that weakened the executive's power.[112] On February 24, 1995, the new president of the National Assembly, Luis Guzmán, published the reforms in several newspapers. Because this action did not comply with constitutional provisions—the reforms could not take effect without the president's signature—another constitutional crisis ensued that lasted five months.

During the period of the "two national constitutions," international actors, including donor governments and multilateral lending agencies, were significant in breaking the impasse. They insisted that before initiating talks, the two sides come to an agreement on renegotiating Nicaragua's foreign debt.[113] After painstaking negotiations mediated by Cardinal Obando y Bravo, the two branches finally reached a compromise on the reforms in June 1995. In exchange for Chamorro's agreement to promulgate the reforms, the assembly agreed to pass the Framework Law, which modified important aspects of the reforms and delayed their implementation. For example, the assembly agreed to co-legislate taxes with the executive and committed itself not to alter the budget ceilings presented by the executive. In both cases, the assembly gave up power granted to it under the constitutional reforms. Consequently, as McConnell notes, "Chamorro managed to regain some of the lawmaking power that she was losing in the constitutional reform via the back door of the Framework Law."[114]

The reforms as a whole succeeded in reducing the intensity of political conflict, advancing the rules of liberal democracy, and shifting power from the executive to the legislative branch. Thirty-five of the sixty-five amendments concerned the organization of the national government and the nation's defense apparatus. Some important amendments included establishing two rounds of voting if no presidential candidate won at least 45 percent of the vote in the first round; prohibiting presidential succession in office (presidents had to wait out a term before running again and could only serve a total of two terms); reducing the presidential term from six years to five; expanding the Supreme Court from nine to twelve magistrates; and eliminating the military draft.[115] The reforms also spelled out more clearly the right to private property and limited the scope of future land expropriations, which helped lay the constitutional foundation for resolving the controversial property issue as a consequence of the Sandinista land reform. Nevertheless, it was somewhat surprising that the assembly did not go further in seeking to extract popular democracy elements from the constitution. It eschewed the opportunity to change or eliminate articles 98 and 101, which call, respectively, to abolish economic dependency and create "a more just distribution of wealth" and allow workers to participate in "the elaboration, execution, and control of economic plans." Clarifying the contradictory nature of the concept of democracy in the 1987 constitution would have to await subsequent reforms.

The 2000 Constitutional Reforms

Compared to the 1995 reforms, the process leading to the 2000 constitutional reforms lacked any mechanism for public input. During his successful campaign for president, Liberal Party (PLC) candidate Arnoldo Alemán called for a constituent assembly that would draft additional reforms subject to a referendum. Nevertheless, the 2000 reforms were the product of negotiations between the leadership of the two dominant parties, the PLC and FSLN. Conversations between the Alemán government and FSLN leaders began in 1998, but were put on hold in the wake of Hurricane Mitch. In June 1999, both parties named negotiating committees, although the most important agreements emerged out of closed-door meetings between Alemán and FSLN leader Daniel Ortega. In August 1999, the two sides announced a thirty-three-point agreement that covered a number of changes to the electoral law and a series of constitutional reforms. The National Assembly approved the constitutional reforms in January 2000.[116]

The reforms were yet another example of conflict resolution without widespread societal consensus. The Alemán government realized that it needed to reduce tensions with the FSLN to govern effectively. The Sandinistas, while no longer the dominant electoral force in the country, still could mobilize significant opposition to controversial government policies. The FSLN leadership, looking toward the 2001 elections, needed to reach some accommodation with the government if it was to have any chance of winning the elections. In a sense, both parties needed each other for survival.

Not surprisingly, the constitutional and electoral reforms represented an attempt to create a two-party monopoly of the political system and to share quotas of power between the PLC and FSLN. The number of Supreme Court justices was raised from twelve to sixteen (nine PLC and seven FSLN) and the Supreme Electoral Council magistrates from five to seven (four PLC and three FSLN). Also, the Office of Comptroller General was made into a collegial body with five members elected by the National Assembly. This was a blatant attempt by Alemán to remove from office the sitting comptroller general, Agustín Jarquín, who had been investigating the president's involvement in several corruption scandals.

Another reform, which required that any party participating in an alliance lose its of-

ficial standing if the alliance failed to win a minimum percentage of votes, also made it difficult to form electoral alliances that could challenge two-party dominance. An additional reform removed restrictions on presidential candidates who had renounced their Nicaraguan citizenship, which allowed the PLC to put forward as candidates some of their most important leaders who had become U.S. citizens during the 1980s. Particularly controversial was an agreement that the president, upon leaving office, would automatically assume a seat in the assembly. This guaranteed Alemán parliamentary immunity and would apply to Ortega if he should win in future elections.[117] Because both Alemán and Ortega feared being taken to court without immunity, another reform required a two-thirds assembly vote to suspend a legislator's immunity.

The latest constitutional reforms were the product of a pact in which an overriding concern with mutual elite accommodation trumped any effort to achieve broad societal consensus. The package of reforms sought to reduce the level of uncertainty and conflict between the PLC and FSLN, thereby freezing in place the political status quo. While the pact may have been a successful short-term mechanism for conflict resolution, it complicated the possibility for greater democratization by excluding other important social forces. Moreover, as Karl notes, elite pacts can deeply corrode state efficiency and productivity, since they are "based upon agreements that carve up the state through a complicated spoils system."[118]

Lessons from the Nicaraguan Case

The constitution-making process in Nicaragua resembles Hyden's replacement model, in that the process started with the defeat and collapse of the Somoza regime. Similarly, the process was shaped by the historical legacy of pact making and the absence of public input in political processes, as well as the FSLN's precommitments emphasizing the social and economic dimensions of democracy. Breaking with the past, the FSLN was committed to creating opportunities for public participation in crafting a constitution that was relevant to ordinary citizens. As the dominant political force in the country, the FSLN could have imposed a constitution that was completely unacceptable to the opposition. Instead, it reached out to diverse sectors and accommodated a number of key opposition concerns to defuse conflict. The result was that the loyal opposition was important in shaping a constitution that included both popular and liberal notions of democracy, but in an ambiguous and sometimes contradictory fashion. Unlike the replacement model, this creative ambiguity gave the process an open-ended dimension, meaning that some of the contradictions would have to be worked out subsequently through constitutional reforms.

Despite the significant level of inclusiveness, in the context of an armed conflict and U.S.-sponsored destabilization efforts, it was inevitable that some important political and social actors would be excluded in the process. The Coordinadora—linked to the business sector and the conservative Catholic hierarchy—boycotted the 1984 elections and thus was not represented in the constituent assembly that drafted the constitution. Groups that had taken up arms against the government also did not have a voice in the process. It is not surprising that the intensification of the armed conflict before 1985 significantly shaped the dynamics of the constitution-making process. Although the process contributed to reducing tensions somewhat, this was not so much the result of a genuinely broad-based consensus as it was a channeling of important divisions and disagreements into a constitutional framework. Increasingly, arguments over the form and substance of Nicaraguan democracy

took place within the political institutions that the 1987 constitution established. Even though by the end of 1987, a coalition of opposition parties made fundamental constitutional reforms central to their political platform, the liberal democratic content of the constitution provided important guarantees and protections for opposition groups. Moreover, the constitution's institutional framework supplied the means by which to remove the FSLN from power.

Beyond the constitution, the series of negotiations between the FSLN and opposition groups, both inside and outside the country, were essential to ending the conflict peacefully. These negotiations, which took place under the auspices of the Central American peace process,[119] succeeded in convincing the UNO coalition to participate in the 1990 elections and established the framework for demobilizing the armed opposition groups after the elections. Nevertheless, the peace accords that followed the opposition's victory in the 1990 elections could not prevent the violence that erupted in response to the Chamorro government's failure to deliver on its promises. Although the growing violence and instability threatened to undermine Nicaragua's fragile political institutions, the 1995 constitutional reforms helped defuse the conflict by convincing key political actors to recommit to the rules of the game. As with the 1987 constitution, the reforms did not resolve the social problems underlying the conflict, but they did help to structure a more effective political framework through which to address those problems.

While the 1985–87 constitution-writing process was primarily driven by domestic political concerns, the role of the international community was significant. At the same time, the Nicaraguan case offers few desirable lessons for other countries, in that the positive support from the international community was countered by U.S. destabilization efforts. On the one hand, various nations helped to legitimize the process by observing and sanctioning the election of the national constituent assembly and offering technical support in writing the first draft of the constitution. On the other hand, the United States persuaded Coordinadora members to boycott the 1984 elections and increased its funding of armed opposition groups to try to undermine the process. During the subsequent constitutional reform effort in 1995, the international community was more coordinated in facilitating the implementation of reforms. Both international donor governments and multilateral lending agencies combined their financial leverage to pressure the legislative and executive branches to come to a negotiated settlement. These efforts resulted in the Framework Law that ended the constitutional crisis of 1995.

The emphasis on public participation and inclusiveness that characterized the 1987 constitution-making process was part of a larger revolutionary process that aimed to mobilize civil-society groups politically. Nevertheless, the FSLN's belief that popular mobilization and empowerment contributed to more effective institutions progressively disappeared in subsequent constitutional reforms. While the 1995 reforms included some limited opportunities for public input, the 2000 reforms were notable for their exclusionary nature. Not unlike the 1974 constitution—the product of a pact between Somoza and the opposition Conservative Party—the 2000 reforms resulted from a pact between Alemán and Ortega to perpetuate the dominance of their two principal political parties. This reversion to the historical pattern of pact making raises important questions about the relationship between public participation and consensus. To the extent that consensus relies on mutual elite accommodation, high levels of public participation and inclusiveness may be detrimental to forging consensus. Consensus based on elite accommodation depends on both the

willingness of leaders to abide by the terms of agreements and their ability to control the demands of their rank and file.[120] A subservient rank and file affords leaders sufficient leeway to strike bargains and reduce competition and conflict. Considering this relationship between consensus and public participation in the Nicaraguan case, one could argue that the constitution-making process during 1985–87 achieved significant levels of citizen involvement, but only minimal elite consensus. Subsequent constitutional reforms, on the other hand, included low levels of public participation but greater success in achieving mutual elite accommodation.

Does the Nicaraguan case suggest an inherent contradiction between public participation and consensus? Certainly consensus based on mutual elite accommodation that seeks to reduce conflict and uncertainty is not easily compatible with high levels of citizen involvement. On the other hand, interelite agreements that fail to incorporate citizen input may be unlikely to endure. According to Levine, "The whole package works only if elites and popular groups are linked in mutually valued and enduring ways."[121] In a post-conflict setting, the challenge is to craft a constitutional process that is sensitive to the vital interests of elites and provides channels for the effective representation of citizen concerns. The Nicaraguan case highlights the difficulties in achieving the correct balance between these often conflicting yet necessary dimensions of peacebuilding.

Notes

1. Jon Elster, "Ways of Constitution-Making," in *Democracy's Victory and Crisis*, ed. Axel Hadenius (Cambridge: Cambridge University Press, 1997), p. 123.

2. A.E. Howard, ed., *Constitution Making in Eastern Europe* (Baltimore: John Hopkins University Press, 1993); and Andrew Arato, *Civil Society, Constitution, and Legitimacy* (Lanham, MD: Rowman and Littlefield Publishers, 2000).

3. Juan Linz and Alfred Stepan, *Problems of Democratic Transition and Consolidation* (Baltimore: John Hopkins University Press, 1996), p. 82.

4. Ibid., p. 83.

5. Ibid., p. 83.

6. Adam Przeworski, "Democracy as a Contingent Outcome of Conflicts," in *Constitutionalism and Democracy*, ed. Jon Elster and Runne Slagstad (Cambridge: Cambridge University Press, 1988), p. 64.

7. Edward McWhinney, *Constitution-Making Principles, Process, Practice* (Toronto: University of Toronto Press, 1981), p. 12. The term *Grundnorm*, which McWhinney defines as the "prior constitutional question," is found in Hans Kelsen, *General Theory of Law and State*, trans. Anders Wedberg (New York: Russell and Russell, 1961).

8. See Philip J. Williams, "Dual Transitions from Authoritarian Rule: Popular and Electoral Democracy in Nicaragua," *Comparative Politics*, vol. 26, no. 2 (1994), pp. 169–86.

9. Goran Hyden, *Constitution Making and Democratization in Africa* (Pretoria: Africa Century Publications, 1982), p. 204. Hyden contrasts the replacement model with the transformation model, which is a more open-ended process and characteristic of negotiated transitions that begin without the defeat or collapse of the previous regime.

10. McWhinney, *Constitution-Making Principles*, p. 13.

11. Hyden argues that given the new regime comes to power through a total rejection of the past, under the replacement model, the constitution-making process is likely to be more rigid and less inclusive than the transformation model. See Hyden, *Constitution Making*, pp. 204–05.

12. Gisbert H. Flanz, *Constitutions of the World: Republic of Nicaragua* (New York: Oceana Publications, 1996), p. 2.

13. Jules Lobel, "The Meaning of Democracy: Representative and Participatory Democracy in the New Nicaraguan Constitution," *University of Pittsburgh Law Review*, vol. 49 (1988), p. 858.

14. Indeed, the Marxist-Leninist Party believed that the FSLN approach to popular democracy did not go far enough and voted against the final version of the 1987 constitution.

15. Williams, "Dual Transitions," p. 172.

16. McWhinney, *Constitution-Making Principles*, p. 5.

17. Richard J. Wilson, "Criminal Justice in Revolutionary Nicaragua: Intimations of the Adversarial in Socialist and Civil Law Traditions," *University of Miami Inter-American Law Review*, vol. 23, no. 2 (1991), p. 280.

18. See Philip J. Williams, "Elections and Democratization in Nicaragua: The 1990 Elections in Perspective," *Journal of Interamerican Studies and World Affairs*, vol. 32, no. 4 (1990), pp. 13–34.

19. Wilson, "Criminal Justice in Revolutionary Nicaragua," p. 280; Lobel, "The Meaning of Democracy," p. 866.

20. Shelley McConnell, "Rules of the Game: Nicaragua's Contentious Constitutional Debate," *NACLA Report on the Americas*, vol. 27, no. 2 (1993), p. 21.

21. Ibid.

22. Ibid.

23. William J. Chambliss, "On Lawmaking," in *Making Law: The State, the Law, and Structural Contradictions*, ed. William J. Chambliss and Marjorie S. Zatz (Bloomington: Indiana University Press, 1993), p. 9.

24. McConnell, "Rules of the Game," p. 26.

25. Orlando Nuñez Soto, *Transición y lucha de clases en Nicaragua (1979–1986)* (Mexico: Siglo Veintiuno, 1987), p. 121. The three FSLN members were Daniel Ortega, Sergio Ramírez, and Moisés Hassan Morales. The other four members were Violeta Barrios Chamorro, widow of Pedro Joaquin Chamorro; Alfonso Robelo, president of the Democratic Movement of Nicaragua; Arturo Cruz; and Rafael Córdoba, director of the Partido Conservador Demócrata.

26. Nuñez Soto, *Transición y lucha*, p. 118.

27. For a more detailed discussion of the breakdown of the coalition and resulting conflict, see Thomas W. Walker, "Introduction," in *Reagan versus the Sandinistas: The Undeclared War in Nicaragua*, ed. Thomas W. Walker (Boulder, CO: Westview Press, 1987); and *Conflict in Nicaragua: A Multidimensional Perspective*, ed. Jiri Valenta and Esperanza Duran (Boston: Allen and Unwin, Inc., 1987).

28. Lobel, "The Meaning of Democracy," p. 841. For a further discussion of the FSLN's emphasis on popular participation, see C. Bendaña, "Reflexiones sobre la participación popular," *Revista Pensamiento Propio*, vol. 13 (1984), pp. 18–30; and Luis Serra, "Limitada por la guerra: pendiente del futuro: Participación y organización popular en Nicaragua," *Revista Nueva Sociedad*, vol. 104 (1989), pp. 134–43.

29. Alfonso Robelo left the government in 1980 when mass organizations were given seats on the Council of State. See J. Booth, "The National Governmental System," in *Nicaragua: The First Five Years*, ed. T. Walker (Westport, CT: Praeger Publishers, 1986), p. 32. He later joined the armed counterrevolutionary movement. Arturo Cruz left the process and joined the movement as well (Nuñez Soto, *Transición y lucha*, p. 121). Cruz considered running for president in the 1984 elections, but opted not to at the suggestion of some members of the Reagan administration (Lobel, "The Meaning of Democracy," p. 873). Chamorro left the junta but did not join the counterrevolutionary movement.

30. Williams, "Dual Transitions," p. 177.

31. Flanz, *Constitutions of the World*, p. 1.

32. The majority of democracies in Latin America combine the U.S. presidential system with the European system of proportional representation in the legislature.

33. See Latin American Studies Association, *Report of the Latin American Studies Association Delegation to Observe the Nicaraguan General Election of November 4, 1984*, LASA Forum, 1984.

34. Andrew Reding, "The Evolution of Governmental Institutions," in *Revolution and Counterrevolution in Nicaragua*, ed. Thomas Walker (Boulder, CO: Westview Press, 1991), p. 26.

35. The Swedish government provided technical assistance to the CSE.

36. David Close, *Nicaragua: Politics, Economics, and Society* (London: Pinter Publishers, 1988), p. 136.

37. Andrew Reding, "Nicaragua's New Constitution," *World Policy Journal*, vol. 4 (1987), p. 291.

38. Close, *Nicaragua*, p. 136.

39. Flanz, *Constitutions of the World*, p. 2.

40. Reding, "Nicaragua's New Constitution," p. 292.

41. See Asemblea Nacional de Nicaragua, *La Constitucion: Nuestro compromiso con el futuro* (Managua: Biblioteca de la Asamblea Nacional, 1989).

42. Andrew Reding, "By the People: Constitution Making in Nicaragua," *Christianity and Crisis*, vol. 46 (December 8, 1986), p. 435.

43. Reding, "By the People," p. 435.

44. Martha I. Morgan, "Founding Mothers: Women's Voices and Stories in the 1987 Nicaraguan Constitution," *Boston University Law Review*, vol. 70, no. 1 (1990), p. 25.

45. For a discussion of the merits of the referendum in the constitution-writing process, see Edward McWhinney and Muna Ndulo, "Constitution-Making in Africa: Assessing Both the Process and the Content," *Public Administration and Development*, vol. 21 (2001), pp. 101–17.

46. Lobel, "The Meaning of Democracy," p. 868.

47. Ibid.

48. Latin American Studies Association, *Report*, p. 15.

49. Morgan, "Founding Mothers," p. 20. See note 27.

50. McConnell, "Rules of the Game," p. 22.

51. Lobel, "The Meaning of Democracy," p. 873.

52. Williams, "Elections and Democratization in Nicaragua," p. 178.

53. The two other subcommittees were the drafting committee—which was charged to prepare a first draft document of the constitution, and the traveling committee—which was charged to study the constitutions of various countries (Asemblea Nacional, *La Constitucion*, p. 171).

54. Morgan, "Founding Mothers," p. 23. Morgan points out that the women's organization Asociación de Mujeres Nicaragüenses "Louisa Amanda Espinoza" (AMNLAE) raised the question of women's ability to control their own reproductive choices at these meetings and presented a ten-page document which outlined other issues of importance to Nicaraguan women. Nevertheless, the FSLN avoided the issue of abortion altogether given the certain opposition of Catholic Church officials.

55. Reding, "By the People," p. 435, and Morgan, "Founding Mothers," p. 24.

56. Morgan, "Founding Mothers," p. 24.

57. Lobel, "The Meaning of Democracy," p. 852. The State Department of the United States charged that the *cabildos* were only propaganda sessions for the Sandinistas. See Bureau of Inter-American Affairs, *The Sandinista Constitution*, publication no. 9523 (Washington, DC: United States Department of State, 1987).

58. Reding, "By the People," p. 437, and Morgan, "Founding Mothers," p. 26.

59. McWhinney, *Constitution-Making Principles*, p. 33.

60. Lobel, "The Meaning of Democracy," p. 873.

61. For a detailed discussion of mass organization development immediately after the 1979 Revolution, see Carlos Vilas, *The Sandinista Revolution: National Liberation and Social Transformation in Central America* (New York: Monthly Review Press, 1986) and G. Ruchwarger, *People in Power: Forging a Grassroots Democracy in Nicaragua* (South Hadley, MA: Bergin and Garvey Publishers, 1987).

62. For a discussion of the influence of proportional representation on party systems, see Giovanni Sartori, *Parties and Party Systems: A Framework for Analysis* (Cambridge: Cambridge University Press, 1976); Alan Ware, *Political Parties and Political Systems* (New York: Oxford University Press, 1996); and Arend Lijphart, *Democracies: Patterns of Majoritarian and Consensus Government in Twenty-One Countries* (New Haven, CT: Yale University Press, 1984).

63. Sixty-one of the ninety-six assembly members were FSLN. The party affiliation of other assembly members was fourteen for Partido Conservador Demócrata, nine for Partido Liberal Independiente, six for Partido Popular Social Christiano, two for Partido Comunista de Nicaragua, two for Partido Socialista Nicaragüense, and two for Movimiento de Acción Popular (Morgan, "Founding Mothers," p. 20).

64. Indeed, Carlos Chamorro, at the time the editor of the pro-FSLN newspaper *Barricada*, argued that "we (the FSLN) want to institutionalize dissent and opposition." See B. Nichols, "The Issue of Censorship," in *Nicaragua Unfinished Revolution: The New Nicaraguan Reader*, ed. P. Rosset and J. Vandermeer (New York: Grove Press, 1986), p. 115.

65. The committee had twelve FSLN members, three Partido Conservador Demócrata members, two Partido Liberal Independiente members, two Partido Popular Social Christiano members, one Partido Comunista de Nicaragua member, one Partido Socialista Nicaragüense member, and one Movimiento de Acción Popular member (Morgan, "Founding Mothers," p. 22, note 75).

66. Reding, "Nicaragua's New Constitution," p. 262.

67. Reding, "By the People," p. 440.

68. Ibid., p. 435, note 150.

69. Reding, "Nicaragua's New Constitution," p. 260, note 67.

70. Morgan, "Founding Mothers," pp. 20–21. Thirteen of the women assembly members were FSLN members, and the other female member served as a member of the Partido Conservador Demócrata.

71. Ibid.

72. Ibid.

73. Irela Prado and Benigna Mendiola, both FSLN party members, were the two woman members of the commission. See Morgan, "Founding Mothers," p. 22.

74. Angela Rosa Acevedo, also an FSLN member, was the woman added to the commission.

75. McWhinney, *Constitution-Making Principles*, p. 33.

76. Flanz, *Constitutions of the World*, p. 2.

77. See Asemblea Nacional, *La Constitucion*.

78. See Bureau of National Affairs, *Democracy in Latin America and the Caribbean* (Washington, DC: United States Department of State, 1987).

79. Martin Diskin, Thomas Bossert, Salomon Nahmad S., and Stefano Varese, *Peace and Autonomy on the Atlantic Coast of Nicaragua: A Report of the LASA Task Force on Human Rights and Academic Freedom* (Pittsburgh: Latin American Studies Association, 1986), p. 12.

80. Reding, "Nicaragua's New Constitution," and Americas Watch, *Human Rights in Nicaragua: Reagan, Rhetoric, and Reality* (New York: Americas Watch Committee, 1985).

81. Flanz, *Constitutions of the World*, p. 6. The agreement contained a number of provisions regarding democratization. It called for the lifting of states of emergency and the reinstitution of constitutional guarantees; free elections of municipal, legislative, and executive authorities in accordance with current constitutions; and national dialogues with opposition groups.

82. Nations that hosted the Nicaraguan commission included Argentina, Bulgaria, Colombia, Costa Rica, Cuba, East Germany, France, Hungary, Panama, Peru, Poland, the Soviet Union, Spain, Sweden, the United Kingdom, Venezuela, and West Germany. According to Reding in "The Evolution of Governmental Institutions," the choice of countries reflected the heterodox qualities of the FSLN and the multiplicity of political perspectives represented on the constitutional commission.

83. McConnell, "Rules of the Game," p. 21.

84. The members of the constitutional committee could enter the United States to participate in the conference as independent scholars, not as government officials. See Reding, "The Evolution of Governmental Institutions."

85. Laura Schulkind, "Cover Paper: Nicaragua Creates a New Constitution," in *Government, Constitutions, Laws and Codes: Miscellaneous Publications and Reports: 1985–1987,* Nicaragua file no. 38 (Nicaragua: NACLA Archive of Latin America, 1986), p. 2.

86. Lobel, "The Meaning of Democracy," p. 873.

87. Walker, "Introduction."

88. James H. McDonald and Marjorie S. Zatz, "Popular Justice in Revolutionary Nicaragua," *Social and Legal Studies,* vol. 1 (1992), p. 285.

89. Lobel, "The Meaning of Democracy," p. 841.

90. Valenta and Duran, *Conflict in Nicaragua,* p. 304.

91. Title IV, chap. I, Nicaraguan Constitution in *The Nicaraguan Constitution of 1987: English Translation and Commentary,* ed. Kenneth Mijeski (Athens: Ohio University for International Studies, 1991).

92. Reding, "Nicaragua's New Constitution," p. 262, note 102.

93. Title II, chap. I, Nicaraguan Constitution, in *The Nicaraguan Constitution of 1987.*

94. Charles Hale, *Resistance and Contradiction: Miskitu Indians and the Nicaraguan State, 1894–1987* (Stanford: Stanford University Press, 1994), p. 29.

95. Judy Butler, "The Peoples of the Atlantic Coast," in *Nicaragua without Illusions: Regime Transition and Structural Adjustment in the 1990s,* ed. Thomas Walker (Wilmington, DE: Scholarly Resources, 1997), p. 225.

96. Hale, *Resistance and Contradiction,* p. 186.

97. Butler, "The Peoples of the Atlantic Coast," p. 226.

98. Roxanne Dunbar Ortiz, *The Miskito Indians of Nicaragua* (London: The Minority Rights Group, 1988), p. 10.

99. Hale, *Resistance and Contradiction,* pp. 185–90.

100. Ibid., p. 193.

101. Throughout the chapter, *reform* refers to amendment or remaking of the constitution. We use the term in a politically neutral sense, reserving judgment as to whether reforms improve or correct defects in the constitution.

102. Moreover, as Shelley McConnell has observed, the very day that the new constitution was inaugurated, many of its articles were suspended by the government's renewal of the state of emergency.

103. Shelley McConnell, "Institutional Development," in *Nicaragua Without Illusions,* p. 50.

104. Other proposed reforms included changes to the electoral process, separation of the FSLN from the state and army, autonomy for universities, reform of the military, and autonomy for municipalities. See Antonio Esgueva Gómez, *Las constituciones políticas y sus reformas en la historia de Nicaragua* (Managua: Editorial IHNCA, 2000), p. 963.

105. Williams, "Dual Transitions," p. 181.

106. As part of the peace agreement worked out between the Chamorro government and the *contras* in 1990, demobilized combatants were to receive land and emergency assistance benefits. See David Dye, Judy Butler, Deena Abu-Lughod, and Jack Spence, *Contesting Everything, Winning Nothing: The Search for Consensus in Nicaragua, 1990–1995* (Cambridge, MA: Hemisphere Initiatives, 1995), p. 33.

107. For an in-depth account of the growing conflict between 1990 and 1995, see Dye, Butler, Abu-Lughod, and Spence, *Contesting Everything, Winning Nothing.*

108. McConnell, "Institutional Development," p. 50.

109. The FSLN-Center coalition totaled forty-seven members to the UNO right coalition's forty-five members. See McConnell, "Rules of the Game," p. 25.

110. Gómez, *Las constituciones políticas,* p. 964.

111. In addition to the public forums, the commission invited comments from fifty-nine social and political organizations and government institutions. See McConnell, "Institutional Development," p. 51.

112. Gómez, *Las constituciones políticas,* p. 965. Also contributing to Chamorro's opposition was an amendment that would prohibit her son-in-law, minister of the presidency Antonio Lacayo, from succeeding her in office.

113. "Nicaragua: Proceso Electoral: ¿las élites o la sociedad? *Envío* vol. 162 (1995), pp. 3–6.

114. McConnell, "Institutional Development," pp. 53–54.

115. "Nicaragua: Proceso Electoral," and McConnell, "Institutional Development."

116. President Alemán continued to insist on a constituent assembly even after the approval of the reforms. Many critics viewed Alemán's desire to convoke a constituent assembly as a blatant attempt to pave the way for his seeking a second consecutive term (prohibited under the existing constitution). Alemán's involvement in a huge corruption scandal and subsequent expulsion from the assembly and house arrest in December 2002 cast a pall over his political future and stalled further attempts to change the constitution. Nevertheless, in 2005, Ortega, with the support of the Alemán wing of the PLC, pushed through the assembly constitutional reforms aimed at reducing the powers of the presidency. The Bolaños administration's opposition to the reforms provoked a showdown between the executive and legislative branches. An agreement between Ortega and President Bolaños in October 2005 postponed implementation of the reforms until the end of Bolaños's term in January 2007. See Tim Rogers, "Nicaragua: Embattled President Negotiates Deal," *Miami Herald*, October 12, 2005.

117. "Nicaragua: ¿Juego cerrado? Preguntas y contradicticciones," *Envío,* vol. 210 (1999)—, pp. 4–6.

118. Terry Lynn Karl, "Petroleum and Political Pacts: The Transition to Democracy in Venezuela," in *Transitions from Authoritarian Rule: Latin America*, ed. Guillermo O'Donnell, Philippe Schmitter, and Laurence Whitehead (Baltimore: Johns Hopkins University Press, 1986), p. 219.

119. For an in-depth treatment of the Central American peace process, see Jack Child, *The Central American Peace Process, 1983–1991: Sheathing Swords, Building Confidence* (Boulder, CO: Lynne Rienner Publishers, 1992).

120. Alfred Stepan, "Paths toward Redemocratization: Theoretical and Comparative Considerations," in *Transitions from Authoritarian Rule*, p. 80.

121. Daniel Levine, "Paradigm Lost: Dependence to Democracy," *World Politics*, vol. 40 (1988), p. 390.

19

The 1999 Venezuelan Constitution-Making Process as an Instrument for Framing the Development of an Authoritarian Political Regime

Allan R. Brewer-Carías

In December 1999, a new constitution was approved in Venezuela as a result of a constitution-making process developed during that year. A national constituent assembly elected that same year sanctioned the new constitution, which was submitted to a referendum held on December 15, 1999, and approved.[1]

This author was an elected member of the national constituent assembly, participating in all its sessions and constitutional discussions. Nonetheless, eventually he opposed the sanctioning of the constitution and was one of the leaders of the political campaign against approving the constitution in the referendum. This position was based on his multiple dissenting and negative votes in the constituent assembly and on his publicly expressed fear that the new constitution,[2] despite its advanced civil and political rights regulations,[3] was an instrument framed to develop an authoritarian regime. This fear was based on the constitution's provisions allowing the possibility of concentration of state power, state centralization, extreme presidentialism, extensive state participation in the economy, general marginalization of civil society in public activities, exaggerated state social obligations reflecting state oil-income populism, and extreme militarism.[4]

Unfortunately, the warning signs of 1999–2000[5] have become reality. The political system that arose from the 1999 constitution-making process has turned out to be the current authoritarian regime, led by former lieutenant-general Hugo Chavez Frías, one of the leaders of the failed 1992 coup d'état.[6] Chavez was elected president of the republic in the general elections of December 1998[7] and was reelected in December 2006.[8] After nine years of consolidating the existing authoritarian regime, in August 2007 he proposed to the national assembly a radical reform to the constitution to formally consolidate a socialist, centralized, and militaristic police state.[9] The assembly sanctioned the reforms on November 2, 2007; the people, however, rejected them in a referendum held on December 2, 2007. In any event, these sorts of fundamental transformations of the state can only be sanctioned by a national constituent assembly,[10] and cannot be approved by a "constitutional reform" procedure under Article 342 of the constitution, as the president proposed in contravention of the constitution. In 2009, one of the rejected "constitutional" reforms proposals of 2007, seeking to establish the possibility for the continuous reelection of the president of the republic, was again submitted to referendum held on February 15, 2009, this time by means of a "constitutional amendment," which was finally approved.[11]

The 1999 constitution replaced the previous 1961 constitution,[12] becoming the twenty-sixth such document in the history of the country.[13] The 1999 constitution-making process was not the first of its kind in Venezuelan constitutional history. Originally, the independent and autonomous state of Venezuela was created through two initial constitution-making processes. The first one took place in 1811, after the declaration of independence (July 5, 1811) of the Spanish colonies that were integrated in 1777 into the General Captaincy of Venezuela, creating the Confederation of States of Venezuela (1811 constitution). The second process occurred in 1830, after the separation of the provinces of Venezuela from the Republic of Colombia that had been created nine years earlier, in 1821, by Simon Bolivar, when he managed to integrate the ancient Spanish colonies established in what is today the territories of Ecuador, Colombia, and Venezuela (1830 constitution).

Seven later constitution-making processes were carried out in 1858, 1863, 1893, 1901, 1914, 1946, and 1953 through constituent assemblies or congresses, with as many resulting constitutions. In each case, the constitution-making process was the consequence of a de facto rejection of the existing constitution, through a coup d'état, a revolution, or a civil war.[14]

The constitution-making process of 1999, in contrast, had a peculiarity that made it different from all the previous processes in Venezuelan history, and even from many similar processes that have occurred in other countries in the last decades: It was not the result of a de facto rejection of the previous constitution, through a revolution, a war, or a coup d'état. Rather, similar to the 1991 Colombian, 2006 Bolivian, and 2007 Ecuadorian[15] constitutional processes, the Venezuelan constitutional process of 1999 began as a democratic process that in its origins did not involve a rupture of the previous political regime.[16]

That said, the process did take place in the context of a severe political crisis[17] that was affecting the functioning of the democratic regime established in 1958.[18] The crisis had arisen from the lack of evolution from a system of overly centralized political parties,[19] which existed then and still exists to this day. The call for the referendum consulting the people on the establishment of the constituent national assembly, made by the then–newly elected Chavez through a decree issued on February 2, 1999, intended to ask the people their opinion on a constituent national assembly "aimed at transforming the State and creating a new legal order that allows the effective functioning of a social and participative democracy."[20] This formal raison d'etre of the constitutional process of 1999 is why, with few exceptions, it would have been difficult to find anyone in the country who opposed it. Few would argue against transforming the state and putting into practice a social, participative, and effective form of democracy. To accomplish this goal, undoubtedly, a political conciliation and participative process were necessary.

But unfortunately, Chavez did not formally conceive the constitutional process as an instrument of conciliation aimed at reconstructing the democratic system and assuring good governance. That would have required the political commitment of all components of society and the participation of all sectors of society in the design of a new functioning democracy, which did not occur.[21] Instead, the constitutional process of 1999 facilitated the total takeover of state power by a new political group that crushed all the others, including the then-existing political parties. Almost all opportunities for inclusion and public participation were squandered. Moreover, the constitution-making process became an endless coup d'etat[22] when the constituent assembly, elected in July 1999, began to violate the existing 1961 constitution by assuming powers it lacked under that text and under the terms of the April referendum that created it. As an independent nonpartisan candidate, this author was elected to the 1999 constituent assembly and participated in all its discussions; he dissented orally and in writing on all these unconstitutional and undemocratic decisions.[23]

The following sections trace the regime's seizure of power, beginning with the consultative referendum on the calling of a constituent assembly in April 1999, continuing through the election of the constituent assembly in July 1999 and the period from August 1999 to January 2000, during which the assembly exercised supraconstitutional power, and finally through the drafting, discussion, and approval of a new constitution by referendum in December 1999. The review shows that the 1999 constitution-making process failed as an instrument for political reconciliation and democratization.[24] With the benefit of hindsight, it is now clear that the stated democratic purposes of the process have not been accomplished. There also has not been an effective reform of the state, except for the purpose of authoritarian institution building, or the creation of a so-

cial and participative democracy, unless one can consider as democratic the election of a populist government that has concentrated all branches of government and crushed political pluralism. If political changes of great importance have been made, some of them have contributed to aggravating the factors that provoked the crisis in the first place. New political actors have assumed power, but far from implementing a democratic conciliation policy, they have accentuated the differences among Venezuelans, worsening political polarization and making conciliation increasingly difficult. The seizure of power that characterized the process has opened new wounds, making social and political rivalries worse than they have been for more than a century. Despite Venezuela's extraordinary oil wealth during the first years of the twenty-first century, the social problems of the country have increased.

The Political System, the Crisis of 1999, and the Need for Democratic Reconstruction

To understand the failure of Venezuela's 1999 constitution-making process as an instrument aimed at reinforcing democracy, it is essential to analyze its political background. As previously mentioned, the process began in the midst of a crisis facing the political system established in Venezuela at the end of the 1950s. That system was established as a consequence of the democratic (civil-military) revolution of 1958, during which then-president of the republic General Marcos Perez Jimenez, who had led a military government for almost a decade, fled the country.

The democratic revolution was led mainly by three political parties, the consolidation of which began in the 1940s: the social democratic Acción Democrática (AD), the Christian democratic Partido Social Cristiano (COPEI), and the liberal Unión Republicana Democrática (URD) parties. The parties agreed to establish democracy in Venezuela through a series of written agreements, the most famous of which was the so-called Pacto de Punto Fijo (1958). That document constitutes an exceptional example in the political history of Latin America of an agreement among political elites to assure the democratic governance of a country.[25] The democratic political system consolidated during the 1960s and 1970s under that agreement featured a democracy of parties, centralism of the state, and a system of presidential government subject to parliamentary control.

Party Domination and the Demand for Participation

The political parties increasingly monopolized the political regime established from the 1960s as a representative and pluralist democracy. Though they had established the democracy, they did not understand that the effects of the democratization process required the system of governance to become more representative and participatory.[26]

Democratic representation ended up being an issue exclusively for parties themselves. The d'Hondt method of electing party representatives constituted a system of proportional representation, in which party representatives felt more and more accountable to their party rather than to their constituents or community. In addition, public participation became a monopoly of the political parties, which progressively penetrated all of civil society, from trade unions and professional associations to neighborhood organizations.

The proportional representation system was established directly in the 1961 constitution and applied to all representative elections at the national, state, and municipal levels, allowing only the possible establish-

ment by statute of a different system at the local level, which partially occurred in the 1980s and the 1990s.[27] The absolute dominance of the congress by representatives of two or three political parties with no direct relationships to their supposed constituencies provoked the progressive popular rejection of the parties and the congress, which was seen as an exclusive partisan body and not as a house of representatives of the people. As a result, electoral support for the two main traditional parties, AD and COPEI, dropped from 92.83 percent in 1988 to 45.9 percent in 1993 to 36.1 percent in November 1998. In December 1998, when Chavez was elected president, support dwindled to 11.3 percent.[28]

At the beginning of the 1980s, the public began to make new and diverse demands for representation and political participation, but those demands were not met. Among other things, they called for a reform of the electoral system. In general, they wanted to make the democracy more participative. There was thus an urgent need for local government reform, as it was the only effective way to assure democratic participation. However, this was not generally understood.

Municipalities in Venezuela were and still are so disconnected from their citizens as to be of no benefit to them. They are not the primary political unit or the center of political participation, nor are they an effective instrument to manage local interests. They are accountable to no one; no one is interested in them except the political parties, and they have become a mechanism of political activism and unpunished corruption.[29]

Thus, while not eliminating political representation, the 1999 reforms should have created mechanisms that would have allowed people to participate on a daily basis in their local affairs. This should have been one of the purposes of the constitutional process of that year.[30]

State Centralism and the Crisis of Decentralization

Venezuela has been a federal state since the Constitution of the Confederation of the States of Venezuela, dated December 21, 1811. Just as federalism was the only constitutional force uniting the previously independent thirteen colonies of the United States, in 1811 in Venezuela, it was the only constitutional means of bringing together the dispersed and isolated seven provinces that comprised the General Captaincy of Venezuela. Subsequently, Venezuelan political history has been marked by swings of the pendulum between centralization and decentralization[31]: In the early stages of the republic, despite the centralist orientations of Simon Bolivar (1819–21),[32] regionalist pressure led in 1830 to the formation of a mixed central-federal form of state, which became definitively consolidated as a federal system in 1864 when the United States of Venezuela was established.

However, the federation as it existed in the nineteenth century was abandoned in 1901, and throughout the twentieth century, the country experienced a process of political centralization.[33] Centralized governance was autocratic in its first phase, but beginning in 1935, it evolved into the more democratic form of the past decades. At the end of the twentieth century, Venezuela remained a centralized federation, with power concentrated at the national level and illusory delegations of power to the federal states. At the same time, the centralism of the state led to the centralization of the political system, as the political parties became dominated by party leaders and party organizations governed from the center (i.e., from Caracas).

With the regional and local *caudillo* leadership of the nineteenth century long over and the twentieth-century consolidation of the national state, the call for increased democratization and decentralization in the modern era faced formidable challenges. Not only was it difficult to enhance the autonomy of local authorities, but there was resistance also to admit the need to devolve power even to intermediate levels of government. This state of affairs impeded the democratization of the country. Decentralization is a consequence of democracy and, at the same time, a necessary condition to its survival and improvement. It is an instrument to exercise power at the intermediate level in the territory, which should, in turn, link the activities of the center to regions and communities. There are no decentralized autocracies[34]; decentralization of power is only possible in a democracy. Consequently, the public outcry of 1989 called for the parties to accelerate state reforms related to political decentralization on the basis of provisions in the 1961 constitution. As a result of these demands, in 1989 state governors were directly elected for the first time in 100 years, and the introduction of direct elections of mayors superseded exclusive government by council on the local level.[35]

Without a doubt, the above democratic remedies breathed life into the system and allowed democracy to survive in the 1990s. Nevertheless, the decentralizing advances made as of 1993[36] were abandoned and the political system entered into a terminal crisis in the last years of that decade.[37] That crisis, as mentioned above, provoked the calling of a constituent assembly, the main objectives of which should have been to realize the decentralization of power and consolidate democracy.

The Demand for Reform

Latin American constitutionalism in recent decades has experienced an expansion of the traditional horizontal concept of separation of powers beyond the classic legislative, executive, and judicial powers. Many Latin

American states have introduced a series of constitutional and autonomous institutions outside of the three classical branches of government, such as general controllerships, defenders of the people or of human rights, judiciary councils, and public ministries (or public prosecutors). In addition, to increase the participation of citizens in the democratic order, they have introduced new remedies to protect citizens' rights. These measures have included judicial review of the constitutionality of legislation and judicial guarantees of constitutional rights, together with improvement in citizens' abilities to use the action of *amparo*—a specific judicial remedy for the protection of constitutional rights[38]—all of which have required more judicial independence and autonomy. The reforms have significantly transformed the system of checks and balances regulating the traditional powers in those states. There were demands to institute similar reforms in Venezuela in the late 1990s, which would have required a transformation of the balance and counterbalance among the traditional state powers; accomplishing these reforms should have been the purpose of the constitution-making process of 1999.

There was a particular need for reform in Venezuela. Although the Venezuelan system, like other Latin American systems, has been characterized by presidentialism, it was moderated by a series of parliamentary controls on the executive. Paradoxically, the crisis of the Venezuelan system stemmed not from excessive presidentialism, but from excessive parliamentarism, which took the form of a monopolistic control of power by the political parties.[39] Criticisms of this control in the late 1990s focused in particular on the congress's appointments of the heads of the nonelected organs of public power—the Supreme Court, judicial council, general controller of the republic, general prosecutor of the republic, and electoral supreme council. Blatant partisanship was shown in these ap-

pointments, which also lacked transparency and participation of civil society.[40] The demands for reform called for both increased checks and balances to break the monopoly of the political parties and reduce partisanship, as well as increased judicial guarantees of constitutional rights to ensure greater citizen participation in the democratic order.

Thus, the calling of a constituent assembly in 1999 should have been used as a vehicle to include and reconcile all political stakeholders beyond traditional political parties[41] in the redesign of the democratic system. The constituent assembly should have focused on establishing a system that would guarantee not only elections but also all the other essential elements of democracy, as were later set forth in the Inter-American Democratic Charter enacted by the general assembly of the Organization of American States on September 11, 2001. These elements include "the respect for human rights and fundamental freedoms, the access to power and its exercise subject to the rule of law, the making of periodic, free and fair elections based on universal and secret vote as an expression of the sovereignty of the people, the plural regime of parties and political organizations and the separation and independence of the public powers" (Article 3).

The Process and Its Deformation

The Choice of a National Constituent Assembly

Although the call for a constituent assembly materialized in 1999, the demand for such a body as a vehicle of conciliation or political reconstruction had actually arisen earlier: It had been proposed before and in the aftermath of the two attempted military coups of 1992,[42] which had been carried out, among others, by Chavez, then a lieutenant-colonel. The subject was publicly discussed from 1992 on,[43] but the leaders of the main political parties failed to appreciate the magnitude of the political crisis, and instead of attempting to democratize institutions, they tried to maintain the status quo. This response discredited the leaders and their political parties, creating a leadership vacuum in a regime that had been previously characterized by the hegemony of the political parties and their leaders.

In the middle of the political crisis, in 1998, Chavez as a presidential candidate raised the issue of the calling of a constituent assembly, only a few years after criminal charges against him stemming from his 1992 attempted military coup were withdrawn. The proposal was disputed by some of the traditional political parties and rejected by others; all political elements rejected the idea that the congress elected in December of 1998 could take the lead in the constitution-making process.[44] Consequently, the calling of the assembly became Chavez's exclusive project[45] and remained so after he was elected president in December 1998, with an overwhelming majority of 60 percent of the cast votes. However, the call for a constituent assembly posed a seemingly insurmountable constitutional problem: The text of the 1961 constitution did not provide for the institution of such an assembly as a mechanism of constitutional reform. That text set out only two procedures for revising the constitution, one that would apply in the case of a simple amendment, and another that would apply in the case of a larger "general reform."[46] Both procedures required the vote of both houses of congress, with additional approval by popular referendum or by the majority of the states' assemblies, without any provision for the creation of a separate constituent assembly.

Legitimacy and the Rule of Law

In December 1998 and January 1999, after Chavez's election and due to his commitment to the constituent assembly process, the political debate was not about whether or not to call an assembly, but about the way to do it.[47] The question was whether the election of the assembly required a previous constitutional amendment or whether the concept of popular sovereignty justified the election of an assembly in the absence of preexisting constitutional authority. In short, it was a conflict between constitutional supremacy and popular sovereignty.[48]

In hindsight, considerations of rule of law should have resolved the debate. Viewed from this perspective, there is no doubt that a constitutional amendment was required. It was the only way that the issue could have been resolved without violating the text of the existing constitution.[49] On the contrary, violating the constitution for a constitution-making process, giving preference to the supposed will of the people (popular sovereignty) over the rule of law (constitutional supremacy), always leaves an indelible imprint of political legitimacy doubts, which eventually can serve as an excuse to revert the situation.[50]

However, buoyed by his popularity of the moment, the president-elect publicly pressured the Supreme Court to decide the question. Members of civil society had brought the issue before the court through a request for interpretation, which was available under the statute governing the court. On January 19, 1999, almost two weeks before the president took office, the court issued two decisions that failed to resolve the issue in an express manner.[51] The decisions acknowledged the possibility of calling for a consultative referendum to seek popular opinion regarding the election of a constituent assembly and presented a theoretical summary of the constitutional doctrine of constituent power. However, they said nothing about whether a constitutional amendment was required,[52] which was the main purpose of the request for interpretation.

That decision emboldened the president, in his first official act after assuming office on February 2, 1999,[53] to issue a decree ordering a consultative referendum without constitutional authorization, in which he proposed to ask the people to authorize him, and him alone, not only to call the constituent assembly but also to define its composition, procedure, mission, and duration. Thus, he purported to hold a referendum on an assembly in which people would vote blindly without knowing the procedure for its election, its composition, or the nature or duration of its mission.

It is hardly surprising that the constitutionality of Chavez's decree was challenged before the Supreme Court,[54] which ruled in a series of judicial review decisions that the manner in which the president had acted in calling for the referendum on the assembly was unconstitutional.[55] It also declared that the composition, procedure, mission, and duration of the assembly would have to be submitted to the people. It further ruled that there was no authority under the 1961 constitution to endow an assembly with "original"[56] constituent power, as the president's proposal had purported to do.

The members of the Supreme Court had been elected years before by the party-controlled congress, and it was that same court which, under tremendous political pressure from president-elect Chavez, issued the aforementioned ambiguous decision of January 1999, by which it allowed, without expressly deciding it, the possibility of the election of a constituent assembly. After having freed the political constituent forces of society as a means for participation, when the Supreme Court tried to control them by ruling that the assembly to be elected had to observe and act according to the 1961 constitution,[57] it was too late to achieve that goal. After its election in July 1999, the assembly crushed all the constituted powers, including the Supreme Court itself, violating the 1961 constitution then in force.[58]

The Electoral Rule

Despite the Supreme Court's rulings and in the absence of any political negotiations among the various sectors of society, the president proceeded unilaterally with the consultative referendum on the calling of a constituent assembly on April 25, 1999. In a voting process in which only 38.7 percent of eligible voters cast their ballots—62.2 percent of eligible voters did not turn out to vote—the votes in favor obtained 81.9 percent of the vote and votes against captured 18.1 percent.[59] The approved proposal provided for the election of a 131-member constituent assembly: 104 members to be elected in 24 regional constituencies corresponding to the political subdivisions of the territory (states and the federal district); 24 members to be elected in a national constituency; and three members representing the Indian peoples, who comprise a very small portion of the Venezuelan population.

The referendum set up an electoral system in which candidates were to run individually. The 104 regional constituency seats were allotted according to the population of each state and the federal district. A list of all the candidates in each regional constituency was placed on the ballot in each constituency, and the voters had the right to vote for the number of candidates on their constituency's list corresponding to the number of seats allotted to their constituency. The elected candidates corresponding to the number of seats allotted were those receiving the highest number of votes. Voting proceeded in the same way on the national level for the 24 seats allotted, except that the voters were only allowed to choose 10 candidates from the list of those who were running.

The electoral system had no precedent in previous elections in Venezuela. It really amounted to a ruse by Chavez and his followers to assure their absolute control of the constituent assembly. In a campaign financed, among others, as it was later known, by Venezuelan insurance companies and foreign banks,[60] the president appeared personally in every state of the country proposing his list of candidates to be elected in each constituency. On the national level, he proposed only 20 candidates for the 24 seats allotted; dividing the country in two, he proposed a list of 10 candidates to the voters of the eastern states of the country and a separate list of 10 to the voters of the western states. This was rather unusual in Venezuelan political tradition. After more than a hundred years of a nonreelection constitutional rule, Venezuelans were not used to having presidents directly involved in electoral campaigns, and any governmental involvement in elections had been considered illegitimate.

The election was carried out on July 25, 1999. Only 46.3 percent of eligible voters cast their ballots; 53.7 percent of eligible voters did not turn out to vote.[61] The candidates that the president supported obtained 65.8 percent of the votes cast, but the election resulted in control by his followers of 94 percent of the seats in the constituent assembly. All the president's supported candidates except one were elected, for a total of 123. Of the 104 candidates elected at the regional (state) level, only one belonged to the traditional parties (AD), and of the 24 candidates elected at the national constituency, only 4 independent candidates who opposed the president were elected without his support, perhaps because the president only proposed 20 candidates at the national level out of the 24 to be elected. The three elected Indian representatives were all followers of the president and his party.

As a result of the electoral scheme, instead of contributing to democratic pluralism, the election established a constituent assembly totally controlled by the very newly established government party and by the president's followers, in which all traditional political parties were excluded. As mentioned, only one of the members out of 131 belonged to the traditional parties (one regional member), and four others were elected independently opposing the president.[62] Together, they instinctively became the opposition group in the assembly.

A constituent assembly formed by a majority of that nature was not a valid instrument for dialogue, political conciliation, or negotiation. It really was a political instrument to impose the ideas of a dominating group on the rest of society, totally excluding other groups.

Seizure of Constituted Powers

Before the election of the constituent assembly, not only Chavez but all the representatives to the national congress had been elected in December 1998, as per the provisions of the 1961 constitution. The governors of the twenty-three states, the representatives of the state legislative assemblies, and the mayors and members of the municipal councils of the 338 municipalities also had been elected in November 1998. That is to say, all the heads of the public powers set forth in the constitution had been popularly elected before the constitution-making process of 1999 began. In addition, the nonelected heads of the organs of state, such as the judges of the Supreme Court, the general prosecutor of the republic, the general controller of the republic, and the members of the supreme electoral council, had been appointed by the national congress, again in accordance with the 1961 constitution.

By the time the constituent assembly was elected on July 25, 1999, the constituted public powers elected and appointed only months before were functioning in parallel, with different missions. The constituent assembly was elected, according to the consultative referendum of April 1999 and to the

Supreme Court's interpretation, to design the reform of the state and establish a new legal framework institutionalizing a social and participative democracy, which was to be submitted to popular approval in a final referendum. It was not elected to govern or to substitute itself for or interfere with the constituted powers. Moreover, as the Supreme Court had declared, it had no original constituent authority.[63] However, in its first decision—adopting its own statute governing its functioning—the constituent assembly declared itself as "an original constituent power," granting itself the authority to "limit or abolish the power of the organs of state" and setting forth that "all the organs of the Public Power are subjected to the Constituent National Assembly" and are "obliged to comply with the juridical acts."[64] In short, the constituent assembly declared itself a state superpower, assuming powers that even the referendum of April 1999 had failed to grant. In this way, the constituent assembly, which functioned between July 1999 and January 2000, usurped public power, violated the 1961 constitution, and, in sum, accomplished a coup d'état.[65]

During the first months of the assembly's functioning, from August to September 1999, instead of conciliating and forming a new political pact for society, it usurped the role of the constituted powers elected in December 1998, which were functioning according to the 1961 constitution still in force. In August 1999, the assembly decreed the reorganization of all the public powers—that is, the three branches of government.[66] It encroached upon the judicial branch by creating a commission of judicial emergency to intervene in judicial matters, to the detriment of the autonomy and independence of existing judges.[67] It dissolved both the senates and the chambers of representatives of the national congress and the legislative assemblies of the states.[68] Finally, it suspended municipal elections.[69]

All the above actions were challenged before the Supreme Court, but in a decision of October 14, 1999, in contrast with its ruling in its earlier decision, the court upheld their constitutionality, recognizing the assembly as a supraconstitutional power.[70] This implied the attribution to the assembly of sovereign power, which it did not have, because the only sovereign power in a constitutional state is the people. However, the implication was the only way to justify the otherwise unconstitutional intervention of the constituted branches of governments, a confusion that was expressly pointed out by various magistrates' dissenting votes.[71] In issuing its decision, the court actually gave itself its own death sentence.[72]

The Supreme Court did not rule consistently with its previous decisions relating to the constituent assembly, even the ambiguous decision. The political pressure exercised upon it provoked this change, and the Supreme Court not only adopted a ruling in support of the constituent assembly's intervention in the judiciary but also appointed one of its magistrates as a member of the commission of judicial emergency. In this situation, only the president of the Supreme Court resigned.[73] The others, by action or omission, submitted themselves to the new power, but only for two months, until almost all were sacked by the same assembly, using its supraconstitutional power to replace the court.[74]

As a result, the initial period of the functioning of the constituent assembly was a period of confrontation and political conflict between the public power and the various political sectors of the country. The constituent process, in this initial phase, was not a vehicle for dialogue and consolidating peace or an instrument for avoiding conflict. On the contrary, it was a mechanism for confrontation, crushing all opposition or dissidence. The constituent assembly was thus subject to exclusive domination by one new political party—Movimiento V República (MVR)—which was the party of the government, answering to the president. In this way, the constitution-making process was used to abolish the political class and parties that had dominated the scene in previous decades.

The Drafting Phase: Haste and Exclusion

After the constituted powers had been either encroached upon or entirely usurped, the constituent assembly entered its second phase of work in September and October 1999. This involved the elaboration of the text of a draft constitution. The extreme brevity of this phase did not allow for any real public discussion or popular participation. The assembly rejected the method adopted in other constitutional processes whereby a broadly representative constitutional commission elaborates a draft that is later presented in a plenary session.[75]

Just before Chavez took office, he had informally created a constitutional council composed of independent political figures, but that council actually had devoted its time to the issues surrounding the election of the assembly. It never worked to develop a coherent constitutional draft, nor were its proceedings public or participative. It held no public meetings and met only with the president in the weeks before and after the installation of the Chavez government.

Thus, the constituent assembly began to work collectively without an initial draft. The president did submit to the assembly a document prepared with the assistance of the constitutional council he had appointed. Its intention was to propose ideas for the new constitution, but its contents were not completely coherent.[76] The assembly did not adopt the document as the draft constitution, but the drafting commission used parts of it, particularly because their members in general had no expertise in constitutional studies. Also, two constitution drafts were submit-

ted to the assembly, one by a tiny left-wing party and another by a non-governmental organization (NGO) named Primero Justicia, which in 2002 became a center-right political party. Neither of these were adopted as drafts for the discussions, and due to their origins, they had no particular influence in the drafting commissions.

After two months of functioning, the constituent assembly began the process of elaborating a draft by appointing twenty commissions that dealt with the essential subjects of any constitution. Each commission was charged with coming up with a proposed draft for its respective subject area. This all occurred during only a few days, between September 2 and September 28, 1999. During this very short period, each commission acted in an isolated manner, consulting only briefly with groups the commission considered appropriate.[77]

Once the assembly had usurped all public power, the president urged it to complete the constitution drafting quickly, to end the political instability provoked by the constituent process and use the new constitutional framework to relegitimize the public powers through new elections. The timetable to finish the drafting of the constitution was not established by the referendum of April 1999, nor by the constituent assembly, but by its board of directors in response to presidential pressure.

By the end of September 1999, the twenty commissions sent their drafts to an additional constitutional commission of the constituent assembly, in charge of integrating the texts received. Collectively, the commissions' submissions included almost eight hundred articles. The commission was charged with forming a single draft. Unfortunately, the board of directors of the constituent assembly gave the commission only two weeks to integrate all the isolated drafts. The hasty process of elaborating the draft left no room for public discussion or for the participation of civil society, whose input could have been incorporated into the discussions in plenary sessions.[78]

The draft that the constitutional commission submitted to the constituent assembly on October 18 turned out to be very unsatisfactory, as it was an aggregate or catalogue of wishes, petitions, and good intentions integrated into an excessively large text.[79] The draft followed many of the provisions of the 1961 constitution, with the addition of some portions of the president's proposed document. Some foreign constitutional provisions, particularly copied from the Colombian and Spanish constitutions,[80] were included in the draft constitutional text, and part of the text of the American Convention on Human Rights enriched the draft as well. Nevertheless, in the constituent assembly's process in general, no particular publicly known role was played by foreign experts[81] or governments, or by international or regional organizations. There was no time for that possibility.

The government imposed urgency in finishing the constitutional draft by requiring the constituent assembly to discuss and approve the draft in just one month, from October 19 to November 17, 1999, in order to submit the constitution for approval by referendum in December 1999. This schedule explains why only nineteen days were devoted to the first round of discussion sessions (October 20 to November 9) and three days to the second round (November 12 to 14), for a total of twenty-two days. During the discussions, this author intervened in all sessions, proposing drafts and expressing his opinions and dissenting votes,[82] and with the other opposition members of the assembly, led the political campaign for the vote against the constitution in the referendum because of its authoritarian content.[83] After one month of campaigning, the constitution was approved in the referendum of December 15, 1999.

Turnout was low: Only 44.3 percent of eligible voters cast their votes (57.7 percent of eligible voters did not turn out to vote), with 71.8 percent voting for the constitution and 28.2 percent against it.[84]

However, the text approved did not conform to the operational language of the consultative referendum of April 1999. It failed to provide the new democratic and pluralistic vision the society required, nor did it define the fundamental principles required to reorganize the country politically or create a decentralized state based on participative democracy. Despite some good intentions and brief attempts at public education, the hastiness of the process rendered any effective public and political participation impossible. One of the twenty commissions of the constituent assembly was a participatory commission, but it was totally controlled by the president's followers, who developed explanatory activities related to the drafting process and to the content of the other commissions' drafts, including television programs. The sessions of the constituent assembly were also directly broadcast on television, allowing the public to follow the daily discussions. But the great debate that should have taken place in the assembly, on such issues as the monopoly of the political parties, decentralization and the power of local government, the expansion of institutional protections of human rights, or the basic mission of the constitution, never took place. There was no program of public education to encourage civil-society groups and NGOs to submit proposals. The only minorities that can be said to have been offered an opportunity to participate were indigenous peoples, who, as mentioned above, were allowed three seats in the assembly. In the end, public participation was reduced to the votes cast by the public in the two referendums, in which the majority of eligible voters did not vote.

The Prologue

The ramifications of the departure from the rule of law entailed in the deformation of the constitutional process, described above, can be perceived not only in the events that immediately followed but also in the crisis that continues to plague the political system.

In the week following the adoption of the constitution by popular referendum, the constituent assembly, without questioning the duration of its authority, adopted a new decree establishing a transitory constitutional regime[85] on December 20, 1999, which was not approved by popular referendum and which violated the newly adopted constitution, including its transitional provisions.[86] The 1999 constitution gives a very important participatory role to diverse sectors of civil society in appointing the heads of the branches of government not elected by universal vote—the judges of the supreme tribunal of justice, the general prosecutor of the republic, the general controller of the republic, the defender of the people, and the members of the national electoral council (Articles 264, 279, 295). The proposal for the appointments of such officials by the legislative body was due to be submitted by various nominating committees, the membership of which would include representatives of civil society. Under the terms of the new constitution, the national assembly was to appoint persons to these posts only on the basis of proposals submitted by the nominating committees. This innovation in the constitution was an attempt to reduce the power of political parties in the national assembly, which, as described above, had been making those appointments on the basis of patronage, in the absence of transparency.

As part of the unconstitutional transition set forth in the transitory constitutional regime decree, the constituent assembly ratified the president in his post and, in violation of the new constitution and in the absence of any participation by civil society, directly appointed the members of the new supreme tribunal of justice, the members of the new national electoral council, the general prosecutor of the republic, the defender of the people, and the general controller of the republic, ending the tenure of those previously appointed. The constituent assembly, moreover, eliminated the congress definitively, and created and appointed a new legislative national commission that had not been provided for in the 1999 constitution; until the new national assembly was elected to supplant the dissolved congress, this new commission assumed legislative power. This unconstitutional transitional regime was challenged on judicial review before the new supreme judicial tribunal created as part of the very same regime. Deciding in its own cause, the tribunal upheld the transitional regime's constitutionality, justifying it on the basis of the constituent assembly's supraconstitutional powers.[87]

Once the new national assembly was elected in August 2000, it adopted a special statute[88] that granted to it almost the same appointment powers that the dissolved congress had held and that the constituent assembly had exercised unconstitutionally during the transitional period: the power to appoint the judges of the supreme tribunal of justice, the general prosecutor of the republic, the general controller of the republic, the defender of the people, and the national electoral council. Before the newly elected assembly had a chance to make appointments under that special statute, an action challenging it was brought before the transitional supreme tribunal by the people's defender. Several other judicial actions were brought before the supreme tribunal against other actions the transitional authorities had taken, but all of them were upheld as constitutional.[89]

Of all the decisions the supreme tribunal made, the response to the challenge of the people's defender was perhaps the most startling, as it called upon the tribunal to be a judge and party in its own cause. It was a ruling on the constitutionality of its own appointment. Even though the supreme tribunal did not finally decide the action regarding the constitutionality of the 2000 special statute, in a preliminary decision, it accepted that the newly elected national assembly was also exercising transitional constitutional authority, and that the constitutional conditions to be elected member of the supreme tribunal did not apply to those signing the preliminary decision, because they were not to be "appointed" but to be "ratified."[90]

The subsequent statutes regulating the other constitutional branches of government also failed to respect the new constitution. Instead of forming the constitutionally required nominating committees, integrating representatives of the various sectors of civil society, the new national assembly established as vehicles for making appointments parliamentary commissions, which included only scattered participation by some members of civil society.[91]

But the transitional constitutional regime set forth in 1999 by the constituent assembly without popular approval fixed the general framework for the subsequent process of concentration of powers and the consequent development of the current authoritarian political regime. This regime, which unfortunately has enjoyed the support of the constitutional chamber of the supreme judicial tribunal, has taken shape in Venezuela as President Chavez envisaged when he came to power in 1998. Under it, the president completely controls all branches of government.[92] In particular, control of the supreme tribunal has led to a judiciary composed of more than 90 percent provisional or temporary judges[93]; it is thus without any autonomy or independence.[94]

Process and Substance

The concept paper that forms the basis of this case study[95] refers to two substantive issues that are relevant to the 1999 constitution. One of those substantive issues relates to the so-called immutable principles found in many of the world's modern constitutions: Title I, Articles 1 and 3 of the 1961 constitution established the independence of the state and the republican and democratic form of government as immutable. Title I, Articles 1 and 6 of the 1999 constitution retain that feature. Apart from those very fundamental principles, no other immutable principles are to be found *expressis verbis* in either text.

Regarding the concept of the democratic form of government, however, the 1999 constitution, notwithstanding the immutable provision, breaks the essential democratic principles of separation of powers and of vertical distribution of state powers,[96] allowing the development of a centralized and plebiscitary system of government that is crushing democracy. This inconsistency within the text is a direct consequence of the successful effort by the president and his followers to use the constitution-making process to consolidate their power while at the same time maintaining a surface appearance of adherence to democratic norms.

The centralized and plebiscitary system that the 1999 constitution establishes is characterized, first, by the marginalization of the concept of political parties. In the constitutional text itself, even the expression *political parties* has disappeared. The 1999 constitution forbids public (i.e., state) financing of political organizations as well as the existence of party parliamentarian groups. It requires conscience voting by the members of the legislative assembly, forbidding any kind of voting instructions. Moreover, the constitution in principle limits the possibility of parties reaching agreement on the appointment of nonelected high public officials—such as justices of the supreme tribunal, general comptroller, public prosecutor, and members of the electoral council—by requiring the previously mentioned nominating committees to be formed only on the basis of representation of the various sectors of civic society.

However, not one of the above prescriptions is really in force. The president of the republic is the acting head of his own party, which completely controls the national assembly. He is the director of his party parliamentary group, in which he has imposed rigid party discipline. Through these mechanisms, he has intervened in the designation of the justices of the supreme tribunal and the members of the national electoral council, as well as the other nonelected high officials, disregarding the constitutional conception of the nominating committees, which have been converted effectively into extended parliamentary commissions firmly controlled by the government's party.[97]

Another aspect of such plebiscitary democracy that has been built under the new constitution is the progressive concentration of state powers, abrogating the principle of separation of powers among the branches of government. This has happened even though the 1999 constitution explicitly set forth a separation of powers among the executive, legislative, judicial, citizen,[98] and electoral branches of government. The constitution repeatedly specifies the independence of such branches of government, but in practice, this independence is undermined by the same text when it grants the national assembly (legislative branch) not only the power to appoint, but to remove the justices of the supreme judicial tribunal, the members of the national electoral council, the general comptroller, the public prosecutor, and the people's defender, in some cases by a simple majority vote.[99] That the heads of the nonelected branches of government can be removed from their offices by means of a parliamentary political vote—with no requirement of proof of misconduct or other objective grounds for removal, and

no procedural safeguards—is contrary to their independence, which has been corroborated in recent political practice.[100]

With the above provisions, the separation of powers framework has developed into a systemic concentration of powers, totally controlled by the president through the abovementioned control he exercises over the national assembly. In particular, the judiciary has lost its independence, confirmed by the fact that 90 percent of the judges are provisional or temporary judges and thus, by definition, political dependents. The mastermind of this system of concentration of powers has been the supreme tribunal itself—particularly its constitutional chamber, which by means of successive constitutional interpretation has cleared all the violations of the constitution committed by the other branches of government.[101]

Within this framework of concentration of powers, even more alarming is the unprecedented exaggeration of the power of the president that appears in the new constitution. As noted above, the excessive presidentialism that has characterized other Latin American systems has been traditionally checked in Venezuela by the powers of parliament. Nonetheless, several provisions of the new constitution reverse that tradition. First, the president continues to be elected by a relative majority, even though an absolute majority had long been recommended (Article 228).[102] Second, the president's term has been increased by five to six years (Article 230).[103] Third, for the first time in a century, the president could be elected for a consecutive additional term (Article 230),[104] a provision that in the 2009 "constitutional amendment" approved by referendum has been eliminated, allowing the possibility of the continuous and indefinite reelection of the president. Fourth, the national assembly may delegate lawmaking power to the president, and there is no limit on the powers that can be the subject of such a delegation (Articles 203 and

236.8).[105] Fifth, the president has the power to dissolve the national assembly after three votes of censure against the vice president (Article 236, Section 21), who nonetheless is conceived as an executive-branch official appointed by the president, with no parliamentary role. The parliamentary censure vote has a long tradition in Venezuela regarding cabinet ministers, but the provision concerning the vice president was an invention of the 1999 constitution.

Finally, and perhaps most significantly, the unprecedented increase in presidential power under the 1999 text has been accompanied by an equally unprecedented increase in the power of the military. For the first time in the history of Venezuelan constitutionalism, the new constitution exempts the military from all civilian control apart from that of the president himself.[106] The consequence has been the executive's progressive intervention in the armed forces, as well as the creation of militias (reserve forces)[107] tending toward the creation effectively of a military party.

The concept paper that guided preparation of this case study also refers to "certain fundamental issues, such as the power and status to be accorded to geographic subdivisions, and the centralization or devolution of power," and states that they "may be so integral to the construction of a stable peace as to be inseparable from an examination of the constitution-making process." This observation is particularly poignant in the Venezuelan case, as this is another area in which the deformation of the constitutional process described in the previous sections has resulted in an alarming incongruity between different portions of the text of the constitution. Article 4 of the 1999 Constitution defines the state as a "Federal decentralized State," and Article 158 defines decentralization as a national policy, but other sections of the constitution make possible an entirely different reality. Those sections allow the centralization of powers at the national level, progressively drowning any real possibility of political participation by the states of the federation and by the municipalities (local governments).[108]

Some historical analysis will help to underscore the incongruity. As noted above, before the establishment of the constituent assembly, there had been great public demand for reforms that would bring about the decentralization of the federal state. These reforms were to build upon those initiated in 1989, resulting in the direct election of state governors and the transfer of national powers to the states. However, in contrast to the general declaration of policy found in the text of Article 158, the new constitution has resulted in major setbacks to the prior reforms. First, Article 159 eliminates the senate and the bicameral nature of the legislature. This removes all possibility of equality among the federal states as a result of the unequal number of votes in the new single legislative chamber.[109] Second, the national government has been given authority in all tax matters not expressly delegated to the states and municipalities (Article 156, Section 12). Third, no tax power has been given to the states; even their power over sales tax has been eliminated (Article 156, Section 12). Fourth, Article 167, Section 5 provides that the states shall only have tax powers in matters expressly assigned by national law. Fifth, with the new text, powers that had previously been designated as exclusive to states have been subjected to the regulations of national legislation (Article 164). Sixth, even the exercise of concurrent powers has been made subject to the dictates of national law. Seventh, the autonomy of the states has been seriously limited by the constitutional provisions that allow the national assembly to regulate by means of statute, applicable throughout the federation by designation of the states' general comptrollers as well as the organization and functioning of the states' legislative councils or assemblies (Article 162).[110]

Clearly, despite the language of Article 158, the 1999 constitution has actually reversed the previous decentralizing reforms instead of building upon them.[111] This critical substantive development is a direct consequence of the manipulation of the constitution-making process by the president and his followers.

In particular, regarding the local governments (municipalities), in practice and in the constitutional text, they continue to be very far from citizens' reach, impeding any kind of real political participation.[112] Under the centralized and antiparticipatory democratic system of the 1999 constitution, the instruments for direct democracy have been deliberately confused with effective political participation. That is why local governments are gradually being replaced by newly created communal councils (2006) and citizens assemblies, all directed from the center, and without any electoral origin, creating the appearance that the people are participating.[113] In fact, to participate is to be part of, to appertain to, to be associated with, and that is only possible for the citizen when political power is decentralized and close to them. Thus, participative democracy, apart from elections, is only possible when effective decentralization of power exists. That is why only democracies can be decentralized.[114] Only with local governments established throughout the territory of a country can democracy be part of everyday life.[115] Nonetheless, in 2006 the national assembly sanctioned the Communal Council Law, creating such councils as "participatory" institutions directly attached to the Office of the President of the Republic, and whose members are not elected by popular vote, but appointed by Citizens Assemblies controlled by the government and the official party.[116]

It is certain is that the goal of participation cannot be achieved only by inserting instruments of direct democracy into a representative democratic framework, as has occurred in modern constitutionalism. Referenda can be useful instruments to perfect democracy, but by themselves cannot satisfy the aim of participation. This can be understood by studying the 2002–04 process concerning the Venezuelan presidential recall referendum, which was converted into a ratification referendum of a plebiscitary nature.[117] A recall referendum is a vote asking the people if the mandate of an elected official must be revoked or not; it is not a vote asking if the elected official must remain or not in office. But in the 2004 recall referendum, the National Electoral Council, in giving the voting results, converted it into a plebiscite ratifying the president.

The result of the implementation of the 1999 constitution is that the Venezuelan democracy has been transformed from a centralized representative democracy of more or less competitive and pluralist parties that alternated in government to a centralized plebiscite democracy, in which effectively all power is in the president's hands, supported by the military and by what amounts to a one-party system. The plebiscite democracy system has created an illusion of popular participation, particularly by means of the uncontrolled distribution of state oil income among the poor through governmental social programs that are not precisely tailored to promoting investment and generating employment.

Without a doubt, the plebiscite democracy is less representative and participatory than the traditional representative party democracy, which, notwithstanding all the warnings that were raised,[118] the traditional parties failed to preserve. All this is unfortunately contributing to the disappearance of democracy itself as a political system in Venezuela, which is much more than only elections and referendums, as has been made clear by the 2001 Inter-American Democratic Charter—a development that was intended to be furthered by the November 2, 2007, constitutional reforms, sanctioned by the national assembly but nonetheless rejected by popular vote in the December 2, 2007, referendum.

Conclusion

The Venezuelan constitution-making process of 1999 failed to achieve its stated mission regarding political conciliation and improving democracy. Contrary to the democratic principle, instead of offering the participation sought by so many, the process resulted in the imposition of the will of one political group upon the others and upon the rest of the population. As an instrument to develop a constitutional authoritarian government, it can be considered a success. Undoubtedly, the democratically elected constituent assembly conducted a coup d'état against the 1961 constitutional regime, facilitated the complete takeover of all the branches of government by one political group, crushing the other political parties, and drafted and approved a constitution with an authoritarian framework that has allowed the installment of a government that has concentrated and centralized all state powers.

As the constitution did not result from a political pact among all the main political factions of the country, but rather from one group's imposition upon all the others, the new document is likely to endure for as long as those who imposed it remain in control. True reforms of the political system, founded in the democratization and political decentralization of the country, remain as pending tasks that the constituent assembly of 1999 could not accomplish.

On August 15, 2007, the president presented to the national assembly a constitutional reform proposal intending to consolidate a socialist, centralized, and militaristic police state, minimizing democracy and limiting freedoms and liberties.[119] The main purpose of the proposals could be understood from the president's speech at the presentation of the draft constitutional reforms,[120] in which he said that the reforms' main objective is "the construction of a Bolivarian and Socialist Venezuela."[121] This was intended, as he explained, to sow "socialism in the political and economic realms,"[122] which the 1999 constitution did not do. When the document was sanctioned, said the president,

> We were not projecting the road of socialism.... Just as candidate Hugo Chavez repeated a million times in 1998, "Let us go to a Constituent [Assembly]," so candidate President Hugo Chavez said [in 2006]: "Let us go to Socialism" and, thus, everyone who voted for candidate Chavez then, voted to go to socialism.[123]

Thus, the draft constitutional reforms that Chavez presented, according to what he said in his speech, propose the construction of "Bolivarian Socialism, Venezuelan Socialism, our Socialism, and our socialist model."[124] It is a socialism the "basic and indivisible nucleus" of which is "the community," one "where common citizens shall have the power to construct their own geography and their own history."[125] This was all based on the premise that "real democracy is only possible in socialism."[126] However, the supposed "democracy" referred to was one which "is not born of suffrage or from any election, but rather is born from the condition of organized human groups as the base of the population," as the president suggests in his proposed reform to Article 136. Of course, this democracy is not democracy; there can be no democracy without the election of representatives.

The president in his speech summarized all the proposed reforms in this manner:

> on the political ground, deepen popular Bolivarian democracy; on the economic ground, create better conditions to sow and construct a socialist productive economic model, our model; the same in the political field: socialist democracy; on the economic, the productive socialist model; in the field of public administration: incorporate

new forms in order to lighten the load, to leave behind bureaucracy, corruption, and administrative inefficiency, which are heavy burdens of the past still upon us like weights, in the political, economic and social areas.[127]

All the 2007 constitutional reform proposals were sanctioned by the national assembly on November 2, 2007, and rejected in the December 2, 2007, popular referendum, increasing the extreme polarization the country has experienced since 1999. The president and the national assembly, nonetheless, announced that the rejected reforms were going to be implemented through legislation which, although in an unconstitutional way, has occurred.[128]

No one should discard the possibility that in the future, there will be a new demand for a new constituent assembly—a mechanism that the president and his supporters discarded in 2007—to be given the same challenge of serving as an agent of political conciliation and democratic reform. When the time comes, to succeed where the 1999 constituent assembly failed and reverse the tendency toward which the 2007 constitutional reforms were headed, in conceiving and electing such a body, Venezuela must bear in mind that it is always better to conciliate and achieve agreements before passing through the pain of civil strife than to arrive at the same agreements by means of a postconfrontation armistice, which never eliminates the wounds of civil conflict.

Notes

1. See Allan R. Brewer-Carías, *La Constitución de 1999* (Caracas: Editorial Jurídica Venezolana, 2000); and *La Constitución de 1999: Derecho Constitucional Venezolano*, 2 vols. (Caracas: Editorial Jurídica Venezolana, 2004). See also Hildegard Rondón de Sansó, *Análisis de la Constitución venezolana de 1999* (Caracas: Editorial Ex Libris, 2001); Ricardo Combellas, *Derecho Constitucional: una introducción al estudio de la Constitución de la República Bolivariana de Venezuela* (Caracas: McGraw Hill,

2001); and Alfonso Rivas Quintero, *Derecho Constitucional* (Valencia: Paredes Editores, 2002).

2. See the text of all this author's dissenting and negative votes in Brewer-Carías, *Debate constituyente (Aportes a la Asamblea Nacional Constituyente)*, vol. 3, October 18–November 30, 1999, Fundación de Derecho Público, Caracas, pp. 107–308ff.

3. See the proposal of this author in this matter in Brewer-Carías, *Debate constituyente (Aportes a la Asamblea Nacional Constituyente)*, vol. 2, September 9–October 17, 1999, pp. 76–155ff.

4. See Brewer-Carías, "Razones para 'No' firmar el proyecto" and "Razones para el voto 'No' en el Referéndum sobre la Constitución," in *Debate constituyente*, vol. 3, pp. 311ff.

5. See this author's critical comments regarding the new constitution expressed immediately after its approval, in "Reflexiones críticas y visión general de la Constitución de 1999," inaugural lecture on the Curso de Actualización en Derecho Constitucional, Aula Magna de la Universidad Católica Andrés Bello, Caracas, February 2, 2000; see also "La Constitución de 1999 y la reforma política," Colegio de Abogados del Distrito Federal, Caracas, February 9, 2000; "The Constitutional Reform in Venezuela and the 1999 Constitution," seminar on Challenges to Fragile Democracies in the Americas: Legitimacy and Accountability, organized by the Faculty of Law, University of Texas, Austin, February 25, 2000; "Reflexiones críticas sobre la Constitución de 1999," seminario internacional: El constitucionalismo latinoamericano del siglo XXI en el marco del LXXXIII aniversario de la promulgación de la Constitución Política de los Estados Unidos mexicanos, Cámara de Diputados e Instituto de Investigaciones Jurídicas UNAM, México, January 31, 2000; "La nueva Constitución de Venezuela del 2000," Centro Internationale per lo Studio del Diritto Comparato, Facoltà di Giurisprudenza, Facoltà de Scienze Politiche, Universita'degli Studi di Urbino, Urbino, Italia, March 3, 2000; and "Apreciación general sobre la Constitución de 1999," Ciclo de Conferencias sobre la Constitución de 1999, Academia de Ciencias Políticas y Sociales, Caracas, May 11, 2000. The text of these papers was published, respectively, in Diego Valadés, Miguel Carbonell, ed., *Constitucionalismo Iberoamericano del siglo XXI*, Cámara de Diputados, LVII Legislatura, Universidad Nacional Autónoma de México, México 2000, pp. 171–93; *Revista de Derecho Público*, no. 81 (January–March 2000), pp. 7–21; *Revista Facultad de Derecho, Derechos y Valores*, vol. 3, no. 5 (July 2000), pp. 9–26; and in *La Constitución de 1999,*

Biblioteca de la Academia de Ciencias Políticas y Sociales, Caracas 2000, pp. 63–88.

6. Regarding the February 4, 1992, coup d'état attempt, see H. Sonntag and T. Maingón, *Venezuela: 4-F 1992: Un análisis socio-político* (Caracas: Editorial Nueva Sociedad, 1992); and Gustavo Tarre Briceño, *4 de febrero–El espejo roto* (Caracas: Editorial Panapo, 1994).

7. In the 1998 presidential election, Hugo Chávez Frías obtained the 56.20 percent of the cast votes, followed by Henrique Salas Römer, who obtained 39.99 percent of the votes. Approximately, 35 percent of the eligible voters did not turn out to vote. See the references in *El Universal*, December 11, 1998, p. 1-1.

8. In the 2006 presidential election, Hugo Chávez Frías obtained 62.84 percent of the cast votes, and the opposition candidate, Manuel Rosales, obtained 36.9 percent of the votes. Approximately 25.3 percent of the eligible voters did not turn to vote.

9. See *Proyecto de reforma constitucional: Elaborado por el ciudadano Presidente de la República Bolivariana de Venezuela, Hugo Chávez Frías* (Caracas: Editorial Atenea, 2007). See the comments on the draft in Brewer-Carías, *Hacia la consolidación de un Estado Socialista, centralizado, policial y militarista: Comentarios sobre el alcance y sentido de la Reforma Constitucional 2007* (Caracas: Editorial Jurídica Venezolana, 2007); and *La Reforma Constitucional de 2007 (Sancionada inconstitucionalmente por la Asamblea Nacional el 2 de Noviembre de 2007)* (Caracas: Editorial Jurídica Venezolana, 2007). The reform was sanctioned by the national assembly on November 2, 2007, and was voted on in the referendum of December 2, 2007, where a majority of the people rejected it. The votes against comprised 51 percent (4.5 million) of the cast votes (9.2 million); approximately 44.11 percent of the eligible voters did not turn out to vote.

10. This is now expressly set forth in the 1999 constitution (art. 347). See Brewer-Carías, "El autoritarismo establecido en fraude a la Constitución y a la democracia y su formalización en Venezuela mediante la reforma constitucional. (De cómo en un país democrático se ha utilizado el sistema eleccionario para minar la democracia y establecer un régimen autoritario de supuesta 'dictadura de la democracia' que se pretende reg-ularizar mediante la reforma constitucional)," in *Temas constitucionales: Planteamientos ante una Reforma* (Caracas: Fundación de Estudios de Derecho Administrativo,

2007), pp. 13–74; and in Brewer-Carías, *Estudios sobre el Estado Constitucional 2005–2006* (Caracas: Editorial Jurídica Venezolana, 2007), pp. 79ff.

11. Brewer-Carías, Allan R., "Venezula 2009 Referendum on Continuous Reelection: Constitutional Implications." Paper written for panel discussion on Venezuela Referendum: Public Opinion, Economic Impact and Constitutional Implications (panelists: Luis Vicente León, Alejandro Grisanti, Allan R. Brewer-Carías; Moderator: Christopher Sabatini), Americas Society/Council of the Americas. New York, February 9, 2009. Available at www.allanbrewercarias.com/Content/449725d9-f1cb-474b-8ab2-41efb849fea2/Content/I,%201,%20984.%20VENEZUELA%202009%20REFERENDUM%20ON%20CONTINUOUS%20REELECTION.%20New%20York%20coa.pdf (accessed July 18, 2009).

12. See Brewer-Carías, *La Constitución y sus enmiendas* (Caracas: Editorial Jurídica Venezolana, 1991); and *Instituciones políticas y constitucionales, vol. 1 (Evolución histórica del Estado)*, (San Cristóbal-Caracas: Universidad Católica del Táchira and Editorial Jurídica Venezolana, 1996), pp. 455ff.

13. See the text of all the previous constitutions (1811–1961) in Brewer-Carías, *Las Constituciones de Venezuela* (Caracas: Biblioteca de la Academia de Ciencias Políticas y Sociales, 1997). Regarding the constitutional history behind those texts, see this author's "Estudio Preliminar" in the same book, pp. 11–256.

14. See Elena Plaza and Ricardo Combillas, eds., *Procesos constituyentes y reformas constitucionales en la historia de Venezuela; 1811–1999*, vols. 1 and 2 (Caracas: Universidad Central de Venezuela, 2005); Brewer-Carías, "Las asambleas constituyentes en la historia de Venezuela," *El Universal*, September 8, 1998, pp. 1–5; and Brewer-Carías, Historia Constitucional de Venezuela, Caracas: Editorial Alfa, 2 vols., 2008).

15. See Brewer-Carías, "El inicio del proceso constituyente en Ecuador en 2007 y las lecciones de la experiencia venezolana de 1999," in *Estudios sobre el Estado Constitucional 2005–2006* (Caracas: Editorial Jurídica Venezolana, 2007), pp. 766ff.

16. See Brewer-Carías, "Reflexiones sobre la crisis del sistema político, sus salidas democráticas y la convocatoria a una Constituyente," in *Los candidatos presidenciales ante la academia*, Ciclo de Exposiciones, Biblioteca de la Academia de Ciencias Políticas y Sociales, August 10–18, 1998, Caracas, pp. 9–66; also published in *Ciencias de*

Gobierno, no. 4 (July–December 1998), Gobernación del Estado Zulia, Instituto Zuliano de Estudios Políticos Económicos y Sociales (IZEPES), Maracaibo, Edo. Zulia, 1998, pp. 49–88; and in Brewer-Carías, *Asamblea Constituyente y ordenamiento constitucional* (Caracas: Biblioteca de la Academia de Ciencias Políticas y Sociales, 1999), pp. 13–77.

17. See Brewer-Carías, *La crisis de las instituciones: responsables y salidas,* Cátedra Pío Tamayo, Centro de Estudios de Historia Actual (mimeo) Facultad de Economía y Ciencias Sociales, Universidad Central de Venezuela, Caracas, 1985; published in *Revista del Centro de Estudios Superiores de las Fuerzas Armadas de Cooperación,* no. 11 (1985), pp. 57–83; and in *Revista de la Facultad de Ciencias Jurídicas y Políticas,* no. 64 (1985), pp. 129–55. See also Brewer-Carías, *Instituciones políticas,* vol 1, pp. 523–41.

18. Regarding the democratic political process after 1958, see Brewer-Carías, *Cambio político y reforma del Estado en Venezuela: Contribución al estudio sobre el Estado democrático y social de derecho* (Madrid: Editorial Tecnos, 1975).

19. See Brewer-Carías, *El Estado: Crisis y reforma* (Caracas: Biblioteca de la Academia de Ciencias Políticas y Sociales, 1982); *Problemas del Estado de partidos* (Caracas: Editorial Jurídica Venezolana, 1988).

20. See the text of the decree in *Gaceta Oficial* no. 36.634, February 2, 1999, and its modification in *Gaceta Oficial* no. 36.658, March 10, 1999. See the criticisms of the decree as a "constitutional fraud" in Brewer-Carías, *Asamblea Constituyente,* pp. 229ff.

21. See the 1998 political discussion regarding the necessarily inclusive character of the constitution-making process proposed, in Brewer-Carías, *Asamblea Constituyente,* pp. 38ff.

22. See Allan R. Brewer-Carías, *Golpe de Estado y proceso constituyente en Venezuela* (México: Universidad Nacional Autónoma de México, 2002), pp. 181ff.

23. See the author's dissenting votes in Brewer-Carías, *Debate Constituyente,* vols. 1 and 3, pp. 17ff and 109ff.

24. See Brewer-Carías, "El proceso constituyente y la fallida reforma del Estado en Venezuela," in *Estrategias y propuestas para la reforma del Estado* (México: Universidad Nacional Autónoma de México, 2001), pp. 25–48; also published in Brewer-Carías, *Reflexiones sobre el constitucionalismo en América* (Caracas: Editorial Jurídica Venezolana, 2001), pp. 243–53.

25. Regarding the Punto Fijo Pact, the origins of the 1961 constitution, and the political party system, see Juan Carlos Rey, "El sistema de partidos venezolano," in *Problemas socio políticos de América Latina* (Caracas: Ateneo de Caracas, 1980), pp. 255, 338; Brewer-Carías, *Instituciones Políticas y Constitucionales,* vol. 1, pp. 394ff.; Brewer-Carías, *Las Constituciones de Venezuela,* p. 201ff.; and Brewer-Carías, *La Constitución y sus enmiendas,* p. 13ff. The text of the pact was published in *El Nacional,* January 27, 1998, p. D-2.

26. See Brewer-Carías, *El Estado: Crisis y reforma,* pp. 7–89; and Brewer-Carías, *El Estado Incomprendido: Reflexiones sobre el sistema político y su reforma* (Caracas: Editorial Jurídica Venezolana, 1985).

27. See Brewer-Carías, "La reforma del sistema electoral," in *Revista Venezolana de Ciencias Políticas,* no. 1 (December 1987), pp. 55–75; Brewer-Carías, *Ley Orgánica del Sufragio* (Caracas: Editorial Jurídica Venezolana, 1993); J.G. Molina and C. Pérez Baralt, "Venezuela ¿un nuevo sistema de partidos? Las elecciones de 1993," *Cuestiones Políticas,* no. 13 (1994), pp. 63–99.

28. See the references in *El Universal,* December 11, 1998, p. 1-1.

29. See Brewer-Carías, "Municipio, democracia y participación: Aspectos de la crisis," *Revista Venezolana de Estudios Municipales,* no. 11 (1988), pp. 13–30; and "Democracia municipal, descentralización y desarrollo local," *Revista Iberoamericana de Administración Pública,* no. 11 (July–December 2003), pp. 11–34.

30. See in this regard one of the author's proposals to the 1999 constituent assembly in Brewer-Carías, *Debate Constituyente,* vol. 1, pp. 156ff.

31. Regarding the Venezuelan Federation evolution, see Brewer-Carías, *Instituciones Políticas y Constitucionales,* vol. 1, pp. 351 and ss.; and vol. 2, pp. 394ff.

32. See Brewer-Carías, "Ideas centrales sobre la organización el Estado en la Obra del Libertador y sus Proyecciones Contemporáneas," in *Boletín de la Academia de Ciencias Políticas y Sociales,* nos. 95–96 (1984), pp. 137–51.

33. See Allan R. Brewer-Carías, "El desarrollo institucional del Estado Centralizado en Venezuela (1899–1935) y sus proyecciones contemporáneas," en *Revista de Estudios de la Vida Local y Autonómica,* nos. 227 and 228 (1985), pp. 487–514 and 695–726; *Instituciones Políticas y Constitucionales,* vol. 1, pp. 351ff.; and "La reforma política del Estado: La descentralización política," in Brewer-Carías, *Estudios de Derecho Público (Labor en el Senado 1982),* vol. 1 (Caracas: Ediciones del Congreso Nacional, 1983), pp. 15–39.

34. See Brewer-Carías, *Reflexiones sobre la Organización Territorial del Estado en Venezuela y en la América Colonial* (Caracas: Editorial Jurídica Venezolana, 1997), pp. 108ff.

35. See Brewer-Carías, "Los problemas de la federación centralizada en Venezuela," *Revista Ius et Praxis,* no. 12 (1988), pp. 49–96; and "Bases legislativas para la descentralización política de la Federación Centralizada (1990: el inicio de una reforma)," in *Leyes y Reglamentos para la Descentralización política de la Federación* (Caracas: Editorial Jurídica Venezolana, 1994), pp. 7–53. See also Brewer-Carías, *Instituciones Políticas y Constitucionales,* vol. 2, pp. 394, ss.

36. See discussion of the 1993 last efforts to reinforce the decentralization process in Venezuela, in *Informe sobre la descentralización en Venezuela 1994,* Memoria del Dr. Allan R. Brewer-Carías, Ministro de Estado para la Descentralización, Caracas 1994.

37. See Pedro Guevara, *Estado vs. Democracia* (Caracas: Universidad Central de Venezuela, Facultad de Ciencias Jurídicas y Políticas, 1997); Miriam Kornblith, *Venezuela en los 90: Crisis de la Democracia* (Caracas: Ediciones IESA, Universidad central de Venezuela, 2002); Brewer-Carías, *Cinco siglos de historia y un país en crisis* (Caracas: Academia de Ciencias Políticas y Sociales y Comisión Presidencial del V Centenario de Venezuela, 1998), pp. 95–117; Brewer-Carías, "La crisis terminal del sistema político," in *Una evaluación a estos cuarenta años de democracia, El Globo,* November 24, 1997, pp. 12–13; Brewer-Carías, "La crisis terminal del sistema político venezolano y el reto democrático de la descentralización," in *Instituciones Políticas y Constitucionales,* vol. 3, pp. 655–78. See also Brewer-Carías, "Presentación," in *Los Candidatos Presidenciales ante la Academia,* pp. 9–66, and Brewer-Carías, *Asamblea Constituyente,* pp. 15–85.

38. See Brewer-Carías, *Judicial Protection of Human Rights in Latin America. A Comparative Constitutional Law study on the Latin American Injunction for the Protection of Constitutional rights ("Amparo" Proceeding).* Privately Printed for the Exclusive Use of Students at the Columbia University School of Law, New York, 2007, 383 pp.; *El amparo*

a los derechos y garantías constitucionales: Una aproximación comparativa (Caracas: Editorial Jurídica Venezolana, 1993); and in *Instituciones Políticas y Constitucionales,* vol. 5.

39. See Brewer-Carías, *Problemas del Estado de Partidos* (Caracas: Editorial Jurídica Venezolana, 1988), pp. 92ff.

40. Ibid.

41. See the author's proposal regarding the convening of the 1999 constituent assembly in Brewer-Carías, *Asamblea Constituyente,* pp. 56–60.

42. See, e.g., Frente Patriótico, *Por una Asamblea Constituyente para una nueva Venezuela* (Caracas: 1991).

43. Regarding the initial 1992 proposals, see Brewer-Carías, "La democracia venezolana ha perdido legitimidad," *El Nacional,* March 1, 1992, p. D-2, published in *Asamblea Constituyente,* pp. 30–34; Consejo Consultivo de la Presidencia de la República, *Recomendaciones del Consejo Consultivo al Presidente de la República* (Caracas: Presidencia de la República, 1992), p. 15; Oswaldo Alvarez Paz, *El Camino Constituyente* (Maracaibo: Gobernación del Estado Zulia, 1992); Ricardo Combellas, "Asamblea Constituyente: Estudio jurídico-político" and Angel Alvarez, "Análisis de la naturaleza de la crisis actual y la viabilidad política de la Asamblea Constituyente," in COPRE, *Asamblea Constituyente: Salida democrática a la crisis,* Folletos para la Discusión no. 18, Caracas, 1992; R. Escovar Salom, "Necesidad de una Asamblea Nacional Constituyente," *en Cuadernos Nuevo Sur,* no. 2–3 (July–December 1992), pp. 156–160; Frente Amplio Proconstituyente "¿Qué es la Constituyente?" *El Nacional,* June 30, 1994; Hermánn Escarrá Malavé, *Democracia, reforma constitucional y asamblea constituyente* (Caracas: 1995).

44. See this author's comments on November 1998 in Brewer-Carías, *Asamblea Constituyente,* pp. 78–85.

45. See his "Propuestas para transformar Venezuela" in Hugo Chávez Frías, *Una Revolución Democrática* (Caracas: 1998), p. 7.

46. See Brewer-Carías, "Los procedimientos de revisión constitucional en Venezuela," in *I Procedimenti di revisione costituzionale nel Diritto Comparato,* Atti del Convegno Internazionale organizzato dalla Facoltà di Giurisprudenza di Urbino, April 23–24, 1997, Università Degli Studi di Urbino, pubblicazioni della Facoltà di Giurisprudenza e della Facoltá di Scienze Politiche, Urbino, Italia, 1999, pp. 137–81; and in *Boletín de la Academia de Ciencias Políticas y Sociales,* no. 134 (1997), pp. 169–222. See also Brewer-Carías, *Asamblea Constituyente,* pp. 84–149.

47. See the author's 1998 proposal in Brewer-Carías, *Asamblea Nacional Constituyente,* pp. 56–69; see the position in contrary sense of Carlos M. Escarrá Malavé, *Proceso político y constituyente: Papeles constituyentes* (Maracaibo: 1999), pp. 33ff.

48. See Brewer-Carías, "El desequilibrio entre soberanía popular y supremacía constitucional y la salida constituyente en Venezuela en 1999," in *Revista Anuario Iberoamericano de Justicia Constitucional,* no. 3 (2000), pp. 31–56. See also Brewer-Carías, *Asamblea Constituyente,* pp. 152ff.

49. See Brewer-Carías, "Comentarios sobre la inconstitucional de la convocatoria a Referéndum sobre una Asamblea Nacional Constituyente, efectuada por el Consejo Nacional Electoral en febrero de 1999," in *Revista Política y Gobierno,* vol. 1, no. 1 (January–June 1999), pp. 29–92. See also Brewer-Carías, *Asamblea Constituyente,* pp. 229ff.

50. Among the authors who considered that the convening of the constituent assembly needed a prior constitutional provision establishing it was Ricardo Combellas, who in 1998 was head of the Presidential Commission on State Reforms. See Combellas, *¿Qué es la Constituyente? Voz para el futuro de Venezuela* (Caracas: Editorial Panapo, 1998), p. 38. The next year, after being appointed by President Chávez as a member of the Presidential Commission for the Constitutional Reform, he changed his opinion, admitting the possibility of electing the assembly even without constitutional support. See Combellas, *Poder Constituyente,* presentación, Hugo Chávez Frías, Caracas 1999, pp. 189ff. In 1999, Combellas was elected a member of the constituent assembly from the lists supported by Chávez, but a few years later, he withdrew his support for the president, becoming a critic of his antidemocratic government.

51. See the texts in *Revista de Derecho Público,* no. 77–80 (1999), pp. 56–73; and in Brewer-Carías, *Poder Constituyente Originario y Asamblea Nacional Constituyente* (Caracas: Editorial Jurídica Venezolana, 1999), pp. 25ff.

52. See comments on the decisions in Brewer-Carías, "La configuración judicial del proceso constituyente o de cómo el guardián de la Constitución abrió el camino para su violación y para su propia extinción," in *Revista de Derecho Público,* nos. 77–80 (1999), pp. 453–514; Brewer-Carías, *Asamblea Constituyente,* pp. 152–228; Brewer-Carías, *Golpe de Estado,* pp. 65ff; Lolymar Hernández Camargo, *La Teoría del Poder Constituyente: Un caso de estu-*dio: el proceso constituyente venezolano de 1999 (San Cristóbal: Universidad Católica del Táchira, 2000), pp. 53ff.; Claudia Nikken, *La Cour Suprême de Justice et la Constitution vénézuélienne du 23 Janvier 1961,* thèse docteur de l'Université Panthéon Assas (Paris II), Paris, 2001, pp. 366ff.

53. See the text in *Gaceta Oficial,* no. 36.634, February 2, 1999, and its modification in *Gaceta Oficial* no. 36.658, March 10, 1999. See the comments regarding the decree in Brewer-Carías, *Golpe de Estado,* pp. 113ff.; and in Brewer-Carías, *Asamblea Constituyente,* pp. 229ff.

54. See the text of the challenging action this author brought before the Supreme Court in Brewer-Carías, *Asamblea Constituyente,* pp. 255–321. Regarding the other challenging actions brought before the Supreme Court, see Carlos M. Escarrá Malavé, *Proceso político,* exhibit 4.

55. See the text of the 1999 Supreme Court decisions of March 18, March 23, April 13, June 3, June 17, and July 21 in *Revista de Derecho Público,* nos. 77–80 (1999), pp. 73–110; and in Brewer-Carías, *Poder Constituyente Originario,* pp. 169–98 and 223–51. See comments in Brewer-Carías, "Comentarios sobre la inconstitucional convocatoria a referendo sobre una Asamblea Nacional Constituyente efectuada por el Consejo Nacional Electoral en febrero de 1999," *Revista Política y Gobierno,* vol. 1, no. 1 (January–June 1999), pp. 29–92; and in Brewer-Carías, *Golpe de Estado,* pp. 160ff.

56. Venezuelan constitutional law distinguishes between derivative and original constituent authority, the latter being the unlimited authority such an institution would have at the very moment of a new state's conception. The constitutional convention of the United States would be considered original in this sense.

57. In particular, see the 1999 Supreme Court decisions of April 13, June 17, and July 21, in *Revista de Derecho Público,* nos. 77–80 (1999), pp. 85ff.

58. See the references to all those decisions in Brewer-Carías, *Debate Constituyente,* vol. 1, pp. 11–124.

59. See José E. Molina and Carmen Pérez Baralt, "Procesos Electorales: Venezuela, abril, julio y diciembre de 1999," *Boletín Electoral Latinoamericano,* no. 22 (July–December 1999), pp. 61ff.

60. For which a few high former officials of the Banco Bilbao Vizcaya of Spain were criminally indicted on Feb. 8, 2006, by the Juzgado Central de Instrucción no. 5, Audiencia Nacional, Madrid (Procedure no. 251/02-N).

61. Molina and Pérez Baralt, "Procesos Electorales," pp. 61ff.

62. Allan R. Brewer-Carías, Claudio Fermin, Alberto Franchesqui, and Jorge Olavarría.

63. See the decision of April 13, 1999, in *Revista de Derecho Público*, no. 77–80 (1999), pp. 85ff.; and in Brewer-Carías, *Poder Constituyente Originario*, pp. 169–98, 223–51.

64. See in *Gaceta Constituyente (Diario de Debates), Agosto–Septiembre 1999*, session of August 3, 1999, no. 1, p. 4. See the author's dissenting vote in *Gaceta Constituyente (Diario de Debates), Agosto–Septiembre 1999*, session of August 7, 1999, no. 4, pp. 6–13; and in Brewer-Carías, *Debate Constituyente*, vol. 1, pp. 15–39.

65. See Brewer-Carías, *Golpe de Estado*, pp. 181ff.

66. Decree of August, 12, 1999. See the text in *Gaceta Constituyente (Diario de Debates), Agosto–Septiembre de 1999*, session of August 12, no. 8, pp. 2–4, and in *Gaceta Oficial* no. 36.764 (August 13, 1999). See this author's dissenting vote in Brewer-Carías, *Debate Constituyente*, vol. 1, pp. 43–56.

67. Decree of August 19, 1999. See the text in *Gaceta Constituyente (Diario de Debates), Agosto–Septiembre de 1999*, session of August 18, 1999, no. 10, pp. 17–22, and in *Gaceta Oficial* no. 36.782 (September 8, 1999). See this author's dissenting vote in Brewer-Carías, *Debate Constituyente*, vol. 1, pp. 57–73. See the comments in Brewer-Carías, *Golpe de Estado*, pp. 184ff.; and in Brewer-Carías, "La progresiva y sistemática demolición institucional de la autonomía e independencia del Poder Judicial en Venezuela 1999–2004," in *XXX Jornadas J.M. Dominguez Escovar, Estado de derecho, Administración de justicia y derechos humanos*, Instituto de Estudios Jurídicos del Estado Lara, Barquisimeto 2005, pp. 33–174.

68. Decree of August 28, 1999. See the text in *Gaceta Constituyente (Diario de Debates), Agosto–Septiembre 1999*, session of August 25, 1999, no. 13. See this author's dissenting vote in Brewer-Carías, *Debate Constituyente*, vol. 1, pp. 75–113.

69. Decree of August 26, 1999. See the text in *Gaceta Constituyente (Diario de Debates), Agosto–Septiembre 1999*, session of August 26, 1999, no. 14, pp. 7–8, 11, 13, 14; and in *Gaceta Oficial* no. 36.776 (August 31, 1999). See the author's dissenting

vote in Brewer-Carías, *Debate Constituyente,* vol. 1, pp. 115–22.

70. See the decision of October 14, 1999 in *Revista de Derecho Público*, no. 77–80 (1999), pp. 111–32. See the comments in Brewer-Carías, "La configuración judicial del proceso constituyente," pp. 453ff.

71. Particularly by Magistrate Humberto J. La Roche, who was the one who rendered the opinion of the court in its initial decision of January 19, 1999. See Brewer-Carías, "Los procedimientos de revisión constituciónal."

72. As predicted by the resigning president of the Supreme Court. See the comments in Brewer-Carías, *Golpe de Estado*, pp. 218ff.

73. See the Decree of Judicial Emergency in *Gaceta Oficial* no. 36.772, August 25, 1999, and in *Gaceta Oficial* no. 36.782, September 9, 1999. The Supreme Court issued a formal act accepting the assembly's intervention of the judiciary, and later the new Supreme Tribunal upheld the decree in a decision of March 24, 2000, no. 659 (caso: Rosario Nouel), in *Revista de Derecho Público* no. 81 (2000), pp. 102–05. See the comments regarding the Supreme Court submission to the assembly's Hill and its consequences in Brewer-Carías, *Debate Constituyente*, vol. 1 (1999), pp. 141–52.

74. See the decree of December 22, 1999, on the transitory constitutional regime in *Gaceta Oficial* no. 36.859, December 29, 1999.

75. Such a method was used in developing the 1947 constitution. See *Anteproyecto de Constitución de 1947: Elección directa de Gobernadores y eliminación de Asambleas Legislativas*, Papeles de Archivo, no. 8 (Caracas: Ediciones Centauro, 1987).

76. See Hugo Chávez Frías, *Ideas Fundamentales para la Constitución Bolivariana de la V República* (Caracas: Presidencia de la República, 1999).

77. This author was president of the Commission on Nationality and Citizenship. See the report of the commission in Brewer-Carías, *Debate Constituyente*, vol. 2, pp. 45–74.

78. This author was also a member of the constitutional commission. See the difficulties of its participation in the drafting process in Brewer-Carías, *Debate Constituyente*, vol. 2, pp. 255–86.

79. See in *Gaceta Constituyente (Diario de Debates), Octubre–Noviembre 1999*, session of October 19, 1999, no. 23.

80. See for instance Brewer-Carías, "La Constitución Española de 1978 y la Constitución de la

República Bolivariana de Venezuela de 1999: algunas influencias y otras coincidencias," in *La Constitución de 1978 y el Constitucionalismo Iberoamericano*, ed. Francisco Fernández Segado (Madrid: Ministerio de la Presidencia, Secretaría General Técnica, Centro de Estudios Políticos y Constitucionales, 2003), pp. 765–86.

81. All the suggestions made by this author to the board of directors of the constituent assembly to invite the most distinguished constitutional lawyers of Latin America and Spain to advise the constitution-making process were systematically denied. Nonetheless, after the constitution was approved, it was known that some teaching members of the University of Valencia, Spain, helped the vice president of the assembly in the technical committee. See Roberto Viciano Pastor and Rubén Martínez Dalmau, *Cambio político y proceso constituyente en Venezuela (1998–2000)* (Valencia: Tirant lo Blanch, 2001).

82. See the text of all this author's 127 dissenting or negative votes in Brewer-Carías, *Debate Constituyente*, vol. 3, pp. 107–308.

83. See the arguments in Brewer-Carías, *Debate Constituyente*, vol. 3, pp. 309–40.

84. See Molina and Pérez Baralt, "Procesos Electorales," pp. 67–68.

85. See in *Gaceta Oficial* no. 36.859, December 29, 1999.

86. See the comments regarding this decree in Brewer-Carías, *Golpe de Estado*, pp. 354 ff.; and in *La Constitución de 1999: Derecho Constitucional Venezolano*, vol. 2 (Caracas: Editorial Jurídica Venezolana, 2004).

87. See the January 26, 2000, decision no. 4 (caso: Eduardo García), and the March 28, 2000, decision no. 180 (caso: Allan R. Brewer-Carías and others) in *Revista de Derecho Público*, no. 81 (2000), pp. 93ff., 86ff. See Brewer-Carías, *Golpe de Estado*, pp. 354ff.

88. Special statute for the ratification or appointment of the public officials of the citizen's power and of the justices of the Supreme Tribunal of Justice for the first constitutional term, in *Gaceta Oficial* no. 37.077, November 14, 2000.

89. See, e.g., the decision of March 28, 2000, no. 179 (caso: Pérez M. Gonzalo), in *Revista de Derecho Público*, no. 81 (2000), pp. 81ff.

90. Decision of December 12, 2000 (caso: People's Defender), in *Revista de Derecho Público*, no. 84 (2000), pp. 108ff.

91. Brewer-Carías, "La progresiva y sistemática demolición institucional," pp. 33–174; *La Sala Constitucional versus el Estado democrático de derecho: El secuestro del poder electoral y de la Sala Electoral del Tribunal Supremo y la confiscación del derecho a la participación política* (Caracas: Los Libros de El Nacional, Colección Ares, 2004); and "El secuestro del Poder Electoral y de la Sala Electoral del Tribunal Supremo y la confiscación del derecho a la participación política mediante el referendo revocatorio presidencial: Venezuela: 2000–2004," in *Revista Costarricense de Derecho Constitucional*, vol. 5 (2004), pp. 167–312; and in *Revista Jurídica del Perú*, vol. 54, no. 55 (March–April 2004), pp. 353–96.

92. This has led President Chavez to affirm since 2001 that "*La ley soy yo. El Estado soy yo*" [I am the law. I am the state]. See *El Universal*, Caracas, December 4, 2001, pp. 1.1 and 2.1; see also Brewer-Carías, Allan R., "Venezuela under Chavez: Blurring between Democracy and Dictatorship?" Lecture given at the University of Pennsylvania Law School, Philadelphia, April 16, 2009, available at http://allanbrewercarias.com/Content/449725d9-f1cb-474b-8ab2-41efb849fea2/Content/I,%201,%20989.%20VENEZUELA%20UNDER%20CHAVEZ.%20BLURRING%20BETWEEN%20DEMOCRACY%20AND%20DICTATORSHIP.%20Pennsylvania%20Law%20April%202009.%20l.pdf (accessed July 19, 2009).

93. Almost two years after the constituent assembly's intervention in the judiciary, some justices of the Supreme Tribunal acknowledged that more than 90 percent of the judges of the republic were provisional. See *El Universal*, August 15, 2001. In May 2001, other justices recognized that the so-called judicial emergency was a failure. See *El Universal*, May 30, 2001, pp. 1–4. See also *Informe sobre la Situación de los Derechos Humanos en Venezuela*, OAS/Ser.L/V/II.118. d.C. 4, rev. 2, December 29, 2003, para. 11, p. 3. It reads: "The Commission has been informed that only 250 judges have been appointed by opposition concurrence according to the constitutional text. From a total of 1772 positions of judges in Venezuela, the Supreme Court of Justice reports that only 183 are holders, 1331 are provisional and 258 are temporary."

94. See Brewer-Carías, "La progresiva y sistemática demolición institucional," pp. 33–174; and Rogelio Pérez Perdomo, "Judicialization in Venezuela," in *The Judicialization of Politics in Latin America*, ed. Rachel Sieder, Line Schjolden, and Alan Angell (New York: Palgrave Macmillan, 2005), pp. 145ff.

95. See introduction to this volume.

96. See Brewer-Carías, "La opción entre democracia y autoritarismo," in *Reflexiones sobre el constitucionalismo en América*, pp. 41–59; Brewer-Carías, *Constitución, Democracia y control del Poder* (Mérida, Centro Iberoamericano de Estudios Provinciales y Locales (CIEPROL), Universidad de Los Andes, Editorial Jurídica Venezolana, 2004).

97. See Brewer-Carías, "La progresiva y sistemática demolición institucional," pp. 33–174; Brewer-Carías, *La Sala Constitucional versus el Estado democrático de derecho*; Brewer-Carías et al., (Rozana Orihuela G., Maria Alejandra Correa, Gustavo Briceño V., José Ignacio Hernández) *Leyes Orgánicas del Poder Ciudadano* (Caracas: Editorial Jurídica Venezolana, 2004); and Brewer-Carías, *La crisis de la democracia en Venezuela (La Carta Democrática Interamericana y los sucesos de abril se 2002)* (Caracas: Ediciones Libros El Nacional, 2002).

98. The citizens branch is composed of the general comptroller, the public prosecutor and the people's defender.

99. This is also the case for the justices of the Supreme Tribunal. Article 23.4 of the Supreme Tribunal Organic Law refers to simple majority in the sense of more than 50 percent of those present and voting. See comments in Brewer-Carías, *Ley Orgánica del Tribunal Supremo de Justicia: Procesos y procedimientos constitucionales y contencioso administrativos* (Caracas: Editorial Jurídica Venezolana, 2004).

100. See the comments in Brewer-Carías, *Constitución, Democracia y control del Poder.*

101. See Brewer-Carías, *Crónica sobre la "In" Justicia Constitucional: La Sala Constitucional y el Autoritarismo* (Caracas: Editorial Jurídica Venezolana, 2007); in particular, "Quis custodiet ipsos custodes: de la interpretación constitucional a la inconstitucionalidad de la interpretación," paper submitted to the VIII Congreso Peruano de Derecho Constitucional, Colegio de Abogados de Arequipa, September 22–24, 2005, pp. 47ff.

102. See this author's dissenting vote in this regard in Brewer-Carías, *Debate Constituyente,* vol. 3, pp. 288ff.

103. In the 2007 constitutional reform draft proposals, the term is extended up to seven years. See *Proyecto de Reforma Constitucional. Elaborado por el ciudadano Presidente de la República Bolivariana de Venezuela, Hugo Chávez Frías* (Caracas: Editorial Atenea, 2007).

104. See this author's dissenting vote in this regard in Brewer-Carías, *Debate Constituyente,* vol. 3, pp. 289ff. In the 2007 constitutional reform draft proposals, the indefinite possible reelection of the president is established. See *Proyecto de Reforma Constitucional.*

105. See the comments regarding this provision in Brewer-Carías, "Régimen Constitucional de la delegación legislativa e inconstitucionalidad de los Decretos Leyes habilitados dictados en 2001," in *Revista Primicia,* Informe Especial, December 2001.

106. See this author's dissenting vote in this regard in Brewer-Carías, *Debate Constituyente,* vol. 3, pp. 303ff.

107. In the 2007 constitutional reform draft proposals, a new component of the armed forces is proposed: the Popular Bolivarian Militia. See *Proyecto de Reforma Constitucional.*

108. See Brewer-Carías, *Federalismo y Municipalismo en la Constitución de 1999 (Alcance de una reforma insuficiente y regresiva)* (Caracas-San Cristóbal: Editorial Jurídica Venezolana, 2001).

109. See this author's dissenting vote in this regard in Brewer-Carías, *Debate Constituyente,* vol. 3, pp. 286ff.

110. Brewer-Carías, "La 'Federación Descentralizada' en el marco de la centralización de la Federación en Venezuela: Situación y perspectivas de una contradicción constitucional," in *Constitución, Democracia y Control el Poder,* pp. 111–43. See the author's proposals to the constituent assembly regarding the political decentralization of the federation in Brewer-Carías, *Debate Constituyente,* vol. 1, pp. 155–70; and vol. 2, pp. 227–33.

111. In the 2007 constitutional reform draft proposals, Article 158 of the constitution and all the constitutional provisions referring to political decentralization are eliminated and changed to consolidate a centralized state. See *Proyecto de Reforma Constitucional.*

112. See Brewer-Carías et al., *Ley Orgánica del Poder Público Municipal;* and "El inicio de la desmunicipalización en Venezuela: La organización del Poder Popular para eliminar la descentralización, la democracia representativa y la participación a nivel local," en *AIDA, Opera Prima de Derecho Administrativo: Revista de la Asociación Internacional de Derecho Administrativo*, Asociación Internacional de Derecho Administrativo, UNAM, México, 2007, pp. 49–67.

113. In the 2007 constitutional reform draft proposals, a new branch of government was proposed, the Popular Power, seeking to consolidate the power of communal councils, with members not elected by popular vote and dependent on the office of the head of state. See the comments in Brewer-Carías, *Hacia la consolidación de un Estado Socialista*; and in *La Reforma Constitucional de 2007*.

114. See Brewer-Carías, "Democracia municipal, descentralización y desarrollo local," pp. 11–34.

115. See Brewer-Carías, "Democratización, descentralización política y reforma del Estado" and "El Municipio, la descentralización política y la democracia," in *Reflexiones sobre el constitucionalismo en América*, pp. 105–41, 243–53.

116. See Ley de Consejos Comunales, *Gaceta Oficial, no. 5806 Extra*, April 10, 2006. See also Allan R. Brewer-Carías, "El inicio de la desmunicipalización en Venezuela: La organización del Poder Popular para eliminar la descentralización, la democracia representativa y la participación a nivel local," in *Revista de la Asociación Internacional de Derecho Administrativo*, Universidad Nacional Autónoma de México, Mexico, 2007, pp. 49–67.

117. Brewer-Carías, "El secuestro del Poder Electoral," pp. 167–312.

118. See regarding this author's writings, Brewer-Carías, *El Estado: Crisis y reforma*.

119. See *Proyecto de Reforma Constitucional*. See the comments on the draft in Allan R. Brewer-Carías, *Hacia la consolidación de un Estado Socialista*.

120. "Discurso de Orden pronunciado por el ciudadano Comandante Hugo Chávez Frías, Presidente Constitucional de la República Bolivariana de Venezuela en la conmemoración del Ducentécimo Segundo Aniversario del Juramento del Libertador Simón Bolívar en el Monte Sacro y el Tercer Aniversario del Referendo Aprobatorio de su mandato constitucional," Special session of August 15, 2007, Asamblea Nacional, División de Servicio y Atención legislativa, Sección de Edición, Caracas 2007.

121. "Discurso de Orden," p. 4

122. Ibid., p. 33.

123. Ibid., p. 4.

124. See Brewer-Carías, "Reflexiones sobre la crisis del sistema político," p. 34

125. Ibid., p. 32.

126. Ibid., p. 35.

127. Ibid., p. 74.

128. See Lolymar Hernández Camargo, "Límites del poder ejecutivo en el ejercicio de la habilitación legislativa: Imposibilidad de establecer el contenido de la reforma constitucional rechazada vía habilitación legislativa," in *Revista de Derecho Público*, no. 115 (Estudios sobre los Decretos Leyes) (Caracas: Editorial Jurídica Venezolana, 2008), pp. 51ff.; Jorge Kiriakidis, "Breves reflexiones en torno a los 26 Decretos-Ley de Julio-Agosto de 2008, y la consulta popular refrendaría de diciembre de 2007," in *Revista de Derecho Público*, no. 115, pp. 57ff.; and José Vicente Haro García, "Los recientes intentos de reforma constitucional o de cómo se está tratando de establecer una dictadura socialista con apariencia de legalidad (A propósito del proyecto de reforma constitucional de 2007 y los 26 decretos leyes del 31 de julio de 2008 que tratan de imponerla)," in *Revista de Derecho Público*, no. 115, pp. 63 ff.

PART VI

MIDDLE EAST AND CENTRAL ASIA

20

Big Tent, Small Tent

The Making of a Constitution in Afghanistan[1]

J Alexander Thier

In late 2003, Afghanistan experienced a moment of hope for renewal and reconciliation after decades of turmoil and devastation. Thirty years earlier, a coup had upended a nascent democratic order, setting off a series of invasions, regime changes, and civil wars that would kill 10 percent of the population, send a third of Afghanistan's people into exile, and destroy the infrastructure and economy of this already least-developed nation. In December 2003, Afghanistan convened a *loya jirga*,[2] or grand national assembly, to revise and ratify a new constitution. The goal of this process and the document it would produce was to forge a new and lasting political compact that would end the cycle of destruction and create a foundation of rights and institutions to support the reemergence of Afghan nationhood and statehood.

Finding stability in Afghanistan requires its people and political leaders to overcome deep divisions that led to three decades of war and political turmoil.[3] There are numerous cleavages in Afghan society, including

those centered on urban-rural, modern-traditional, and ethnic distinctions, as well as on divergent views on the role of Islam in politics. These cleavages have fueled—and have been further exacerbated by—recent conflicts. Moreover, in the course of thirty years, Afghanistan changed from a constitutional monarchy to a republic, to a communist dictatorship under Soviet occupation, to a failed and fractured state engaged in devastating civil war, to the home of a fundamentalist and obscurantist theocracy which thrived, in part, upon the largesse of a global terrorist confederation's leaders and revenue from the world's largest opium crop. These cleavages and the legacy of political upheaval continue to manifest themselves in the ongoing peace process.[4]

The attacks on the World Trade Center and the Pentagon on September 11, 2001, marked the start of a new political situation for Afghanistan. A U.S.-led military campaign in the country led to the collapse of the Taliban regime that had provided safe haven to al Qaeda's leaders, the entry of Northern Alliance forces into Kabul, and eventually a transitional accord, the Bonn Agreement, signed in Bonn, Germany, in December 2001.[5] The political transition process that is still underway presents a great challenge and opportunity to the people of Afghanistan.

A key feature of the Bonn Agreement was a timetable for the creation of a new Afghan constitution. The culmination of the constitution-making process set in motion by that agreement was the December 2003 Constitutional Loya Jirga (CLJ).[6] For twenty-one days that December, over 500 Afghan men and women from every province, ethnic group, social class, political affiliation, and religious sect fought vigorously for their vision of Afghanistan's future. Elected leaders, human rights activists, and tribal leaders gathered in the vast white tent to negotiate compromises on power sharing, minority rights, and the role of Islam in the state. Meanwhile, much of the deal making went on among government officials, notorious warlords, and foreign power brokers in the small VIP tent off to the side. But unlike the struggles among the Taliban, warlords, drug traffickers, and international military forces still raging in many parts of the country, the Afghans in the tents were fighting over words, ideas, and amendments. By January 4, 2004, after several walkouts, a majority of delegates ratified the new constitution.[7]

The passage of a notionally democratic constitution was a triumph for war-ravaged Afghanistan. However, creating a new constitution for the country was a necessary but insufficient step in establishing democracy and the rule of law. Constitutions are little more than pieces of paper without a network of institutions and cultural values to support them. Post-Taliban Afghanistan lacks such a network. On paper, the new constitution creates a good foundation for political progress, but opportunities to build legitimacy for the future state were missed during the constitution-making process. A combination of secrecy, haste, insecurity, and intimidation made the process inaccessible to the public and also limited open, honest debate. The United States and United Nations could have fostered an environment of democratic openness; instead, much of their political influence on the process reinforced the tendency of Afghan power brokers to maneuver out of the public eye.

This chapter begins by examining Afghanistan's historical experience with constitution-making processes, focusing on Afghanistan's 1964 constitution, which served as the basis for today's constitution. The chapter then analyzes Afghanistan's constitution-making process from 2002 to 2004 and examines the key elements of the process—drafting the new constitution, consulting public opinion, choosing representatives for the CLJ, and ratifying the new constitution—as well as analyzing key substantive aspects of the new constitution. The chapter concludes by evaluating the prospects for implementation of the 2004 constitution and assessing the contribution of the constitution-making process to peace building and reconciliation in Afghanistan.

Afghan Constitutional History

The First Eighty Years

Afghanistan has had both too much and too little experience with constitutions in the past eighty years. Since 1923, when King Amanullah promulgated Afghanistan's first constitution, Afghanistan has had eight constitutions but little opportunity to actually implement some of the fundamental aspects of these documents.[8] The first two constitutions, in 1923 and 1931, were established by the monarchy after periods of turmoil—the final battle for independence from Great Britain and the revolt of 1929 that deposed King Amanullah, respectively.[9] These constitutions were created without a great deal of public participation, although tribal leaders were brought together to anoint their passage. Both constitutions kept almost all state power in the hands of the monarchy, with little room for democratic representation or popular participation in public affairs. They did include political reforms—especially the 1923 constitution—but the lack of popular involvement in and approval of a far-reaching reform process initiated in 1923 is a primary reason for the 1929 uprising that caused the fall of the monarch.[10]

In 1963, after over thirty years of relative stability and slow but steady economic and political development, King Zahir Shah, who had been on the throne for three decades, called for the drafting of a new constitution.[11] The preceding period of economic and social modernization, led by the prime minister and first cousin to the king, Mohammad Daoud, set the stage for political modernization in 1963, when Daoud stepped down amid a political crisis with Pakistan. The king, retaking the reins of power, mandated a constitutional process that would significantly alter Afghanistan's political system. The resulting constitution, which introduced a far greater degree of democratic participation, was drafted over an eighteen-month period after wide-ranging consultations with all sectors of society.[12] The constitution provided for a popularly elected and independent parliament, elected city councils, and provincial advisory councils. Once this constitution was ratified by a *loya jirga* in 1964, the era known as the new democracy began.[13] Two parliamentary elections were held, and the country began to experience democratic government.[14]

Between 1965 and 1973, however, the Afghan parliament, or Shura, suffered from inaction and deadlock. Although the new constitution allowed for the eventual creation of political parties, the law authorizing them was never passed, and so individual Shura members were elected independently in each district of the country.[15] This lack of parties meant that there was no hierarchy of leadership in the Shura, no one to organize delegates and bring them in line. Lack of organization, combined with the newness of authority in the hands of elected representatives, meant that the Shura struggled to accomplish anything. This fragile system could not withstand the intense political pressures and social conflict brought by the Cold War and modernization, and it collapsed.

The end of Afghanistan's short experiment with democracy came abruptly in 1973, when Mohammad Daoud, who had stepped aside in 1963, took power by a coup.[16] The 1964 constitution was suspended, and Afghanistan was declared a republic. A new constitution was prepared without wide consultation and promulgated in 1977. By this time, however, the government was in turmoil, and Daoud was overthrown in 1978 by a communist-led coup.[17] The constitution was once again suspended, and a new constitution was put in place in 1980 by Babrak Karmal, whom the Soviets installed upon their invasion in late 1979.[18] A brutal war ensued during the Soviet occupation, pitting an unpopular dictatorship and the Soviet military against rebel mujahideen forces. In an attempt to gain legitimacy after years of conflict, the government of President Mohammad Najibullah, who succeeded Babrak Karmal, introduced another constitution in 1987. This document was quickly replaced in 1990 after the Soviet withdrawal. In both the 1987 and 1990 processes, Najibullah convened *loya jirgas* of party loyalists to give the new documents the patina of widespread support and reliance on traditional Afghan political mechanisms. The Najibullah government then collapsed in early 1992, and the interim mujahideen government proposed a new constitution. However, fighting quickly broke out among the elements of the government in 1992, and the ensuing civil war destroyed the capital and the government. Afghanistan effectively broke into fiefdoms during this period, each ruled by clutches of competing warlords and commanders. The Taliban arose amidst the chaos of this failed state, slowly consolidating their hold on different regions: the west in 1995, Kabul and the east in 1996, and much of the north by 1998. The Taliban government did not create a new constitution per se, but did pass numerous laws and edicts concerning the structure of government and rights and duties of citizens.[19]

Overall, Afghanistan's record of legitimate constitution making and implementation is weak. The 1964 process was in many ways a model for its time, but a destabilizing backdrop of domestic intransigence and geopolitical competition obstructed the deep social and political changes the process was meant to catalyze. A constitution itself is but a piece of paper, reflecting decisions made by the political leadership. If that leadership does not have the power or the desire to implement the basic law, as has generally been the case in Afghanistan, then the constitution has little meaning. Afghans were promised many basic rights in their constitutions—freedom of speech, freedom of assembly, freedom from torture, freedom from discrimination—but when those freedoms were violated, the courts and police did not enforce them or punish the transgressors.[20] At the same time, when important changes are introduced, they require both some popular support and some time to take root. The legislators elected in 1965 played politics like buzkashi,[21] unable to act cohesively with allies and unwilling to make short-term sacrifices for long-term gains. The political representatives may have been able to work out these problems through practice, but they were not given the opportunity.

The 1964 Constitution

The 1964 constitution is the touchstone for the birth of democracy in Afghanistan. This constitution was intended to move Afghanistan into an era of greater citizen participation and more representative and accountable government. As the creation of the 2004 constitution followed the 1963–64 constitutional process quite closely in both substance and process, the key points of the latter are worth examining briefly here.

Upon retaking the reins of power in 1963, King Zahir Shah set out to modernize and democratize Afghanistan's political and legal system. He appointed a seven-man constitutional drafting committee, comprised of known reformers. For nearly a year, this committee met daily, developing and revising a draft document and seeking opinions from a wide range of Afghans and foreigners.[22] Following the input of a French adviser who the king had invited to Afghanistan, a joke circulated in the capital about the stability of the French model, with its fifteen constitutions since 1789.[23]

The committee presented its draft to the king in February 1964, and the king appointed a twenty-nine-member constitutional advisory commission to review the draft and make additional suggestions prior to the convening of the *loya jirga* that would ratify the constitution.[24] This advisory body broadened the political and ethnic representation in the drafting process and included two women.[25] The advisory body met with the drafting commission over a two-month period to hash through some of the most difficult questions in the draft, including the role of the king and the royal family in the political system.[26] The details of the revised draft approved by the constitutional advisory commission were made public and disseminated widely through government-controlled radio and print media.[27]

In the spring of 1964, the king issued a decree that called for a *loya jirga* to ratify the constitution and defined the composition of the body, including the parliament, the Supreme Court, the members of the constitutional commissions, and another 210 members to be selected by indirect elections and appointed by the king.[28] Although the existing parliament and the body of electors for indirect elections in no way represented universal suffrage, the outcome of this selection process produced a body with a broad range of social, religious, ethnic, cultural, and political diversity. Only 6 of the 452 delegates were women, but their inclusion was seen as progressive at the time for Afghanistan.[29]

On September 9, 1964, the king made the opening address to the assembled *loya jirga*, laying the responsibility for guiding the future of the republic at their feet, and departed.[30] The debate in the *loya jirga* proved far more in-depth than observers expected, producing wide-ranging discussions on controversial issues. Opposition on certain issues was well informed, and written dissents were submitted during the debate, making this Afghanistan's first "literate *Loya Jirga*."[31] In the course of debate, the king personally met with some of the dissenters, mostly conservatives who objected to what they perceived as the secular nature of many of the articles.[32] In the end, the *loya jirga* debated and passed 128 articles in eleven days, making few significant substantive changes to the original draft, but engendering a feeling of participation and ownership among the delegates.[33]

The 1964 constitution wrought several considerable substantive changes in the Afghan political and legal system, including the role of the monarchy, the parliament, and *loya jirga*; the creation of a unified and independent judiciary; and the role of Islam in the legal system. First, the 1964 constitution provided for a constitutional monarchy, whereby the king had ultimate executive authority, such as the power to declare war, sign treaties, and dissolve parliament.[34] The prime minister administered the executive authority. The parliament had broad legislative and executive oversight powers concerning the budget, the ratification of treaties, and the approval

and dissolution of the cabinet.[35] In practice, the prime minister was responsible for the daily operation of the government, and the king did not abuse his considerable constitutional powers. However, keeping these powers in the hands of one unelected official did not help to introduce a political culture in the country that respected peaceful and constitutional transfer of power from one leader to another. The Afghan state under the 1964 constitution was completely centralized,[36] with all subdivisions of the state (provinces and districts) merely administrative in nature; provincial governors were appointed by the minister of the interior.

The role of the parliament—the Shura—in Afghanistan was strengthened in the 1964 constitution as the preeminent law-making and representational body. The Shura was acknowledged in the constitution as manifesting the "will of the people."[37] The 1964 constitution envisioned a bicameral legislature with a directly elected lower house of 214 members, the Wolesi Jirga (House of the People), and a smaller upper house of 84 members, the Meshrano Jirga (House of Elders).[38] The two-house structure was a way of allowing people to vote for geographic representation while providing for representation of Afghanistan's diversity. Due to the model's extremely short trial period, the modalities of power sharing between the two houses of the legislature and between the executive and the legislature were never fully explored.[39]

For the first time, the 1964 constitution also institutionalized the *loya jirga*[40]; well known in Afghan history as an ad hoc body that brings together the nation for critical decisions in times of crisis or political transition, it was given a formal place in the structure of government. Under the 1964 constitution, the *loya jirga* was composed of both houses of the legislature as well as the chairmen of each provincial assembly.[41] It was something of a superparliament, capable of standing in for a government dissolved by the king and required to be formed to consider amendments to the constitution.[42]

The creation of a unified and independent judiciary was one of the most significant changes embodied in the 1964 constitution.[43] Previously, the judiciary had been divided between *sharia* courts, which were dominated by clerics, and state courts, which handled issues related to civil servants and government-owned lands. For the first time in Afghan history, unified government courts had jurisdiction over all subject matter. This unified judiciary was to be a fully independent and coequal branch of government, with the Supreme Court the highest judicial authority in the country.[44] The judiciary was charged with applying the laws and constitution of Afghanistan, and the court's jurisdiction was broadly worded, explicitly including litigation brought against the state.[45] The state was required to enforce all judgments, and the supremacy of the constitution and the laws of Afghanistan were made clear.

In reality, Afghanistan's judiciary, in the short time it had, achieved neither independence nor coherence. The judiciary faced four primary obstacles in its development. First, there were far too few qualified judges and lawyers to ensure the fair and even application of the law.[46] Second, local traditional practices for resolving disputes were entrenched, leaving little room for formal judicial power. In many cases, this meant that judges either supported the local practices, even when the practices were at odds with the law, or the judges became irrelevant. The third obstacle to independence was the preeminence of the king and the prime minister. The fourth obstacle was that the judiciary was made up principally of clerics who opposed the state's consolidation of the courts.

Finally, under the 1964 constitution, Islam was the state religion, and all laws the parliament passed were required not to contradict the basic principles of Islam.[47] In those cases not covered by any state law, judges were to apply the basic principles of jurisprudence of the Hanafi school of *sharia*, in accordance with the limitations of the constitution.[48] This system allowed the elected representatives of the people to decide how to ensure that the laws of Afghanistan accorded with the principles of Islam, and as the parliament adopted comprehensive legal codes, the need for judges to apply their own private Islamic legal interpretations became less necessary or acceptable. Removing religiously justified legal discretion from clerics had been one of the chief motivations of the constitution's founding reformers, and through these measures, they achieved their goal.

The Constitution-Making Process of 2002–04

The overall framework for Afghanistan's post-Taliban political transition, including interim government and legal arrangements and a timetable for constitution making, was agreed at a meeting among the main Afghan factions and international actors in Bonn, Germany, at the end of 2001. The subsequent process of creating a new constitution consisted of four distinct aspects: drafting the new constitution, conducting a public consultation process, choosing the representatives of the CLJ, and ratifying the new constitution at the CLJ. These several structural elements of the process are discussed below.

The Bonn Agreement

A scramble to organize Afghanistan's post-Taliban political leadership accompanied the fast-moving military campaign in the late months of 2001. Despite widespread insistence on a broadly representative transitional process given the polarizing civil war of the 1990s, the militia groups comprising the Northern Alliance were already dominating the political and security landscape, occupying Afghanistan's seat at the United Nations, and occupying Afghanistan's capital, Kabul, by November 2001. To help facilitate the process of forming a transitional government, UN secretary-general Kofi Annan reappointed Lakhdar Brahimi as his special representative to Afghanistan on October 3, 2001. Brahimi had served as special representative of the secretary-general (SRSG) to Afghanistan from 1997 to 1999 and was intimately familiar with the country's politics and players.

Representatives of the Northern Alliance and the former Afghan king held talks in Rome during this period, and on October 1, 2001, agreed to form a supreme council of national unity of Afghanistan. This council was supposed to meet to agree on convening a *loya jirga* to choose a new government. One critical faction, the non-Taliban Pushtun mujahideen, felt excluded from this agreement and held a gathering of 1,500 Pushtun tribal and religious leaders on October 24–25 to call for a *loya jirga* to establish the next government.

Events on the ground, however, quickly overtook the negotiations. The day after Kabul fell into the hands of the Northern Alliance, the UN Security Council passed Resolution 1378, affirming the United Nations' central role in supporting political transition efforts and calling for a new government that would be "broad-based, multi-ethnic and fully representative of all the Afghan people."[49] The resolution also encouraged member states to ensure the safety and security of the capital and an eventual transitional authority. This final appeal reflected a desire on the part of many Afghans and their international supporters to create an international security force that could provide the essential political space needed in Kabul to create a broad-based government.[50] The Northern Alliance quickly rejected proposals for a security force,

however, arguing that they would provide security themselves.

As the noose began to close on the Taliban in their home base of Kandahar, the intense diplomacy of the United Nations and United States persuaded key Afghan parties to meet to name an interim administration and chart the future political transition. The meeting began in Bonn on November 27 and included representatives of four main Afghan groupings: the Northern Alliance; the Rome Group, composed of family and supporters of the former king; the Peshawar Group, comprising Pushtun mujahideen, tribal, and religious leaders based in Pakistan; and the Cyprus Group, a mixture of factions with close ties to Iran. Numerous Afghan civil-society groups from inside and outside the country felt that these factions did not represent the Afghan people, and the Bonn Agreement itself acknowledges in its preamble that many groups were not "adequately represented" at the talks. Concerned Afghans outside the process organized a civil-society forum that took place near Bonn, in tandem with the political negotiations, to inject alternative voices into the process.

The official Bonn meeting initially evoked the failed peace talks held from 1992 to 1994 in places like Islamabad, Pakistan, and Ashkabad, Turkmenistan. Many of the same representatives had come together in that period with UN mediation, inking flowery agreements, and swearing on Korans to abide by them. Each of these efforts had dissolved almost instantly. In his opening remarks in Bonn, Lakhdar Brahimi, the conference chairman, warned the delegates that "you must not allow the mistakes of the past to be repeated, particularly those of 1992."[51] The situation in Afghanistan was quite different in 2001, however, and the international players with the power to twist arms to make agreements and keep them on track were again interested in the country, having seen what international abandonment of Afghanistan in the 1990s had wrought.

The Agreement on Provisional Arrangements in Afghanistan Pending the Re-Establishment of Permanent Government Institutions, otherwise known as the Bonn Agreement, was signed on December 5, 2001. In the end, the Bonn talks were dominated by the Panjshiri Tajik faction of the Northern Alliance, the Shura-i-Nizar. With undisputed control of the capital, the strongest military, and a strong battlefield alliance with the United States, they could successfully insist on key positions in the new government. In exchange, they agreed to a relatively unaffiliated Pushtun tribal leader, Hamid Karzai, as head of the interim administration; a limited international security force in Kabul; and a transition process that would lead to the creation of a new constitution and elections in just thirty months.

The scope and timetable of the Bonn Agreement were very ambitious. The agreement laid out the powers of an interim authority, which would be replaced by a transitional government selected by an Emergency Loya Jirga within six months. These successive administrations were to be responsible for shepherding the reconstruction process and unifying Afghanistan's political and military institutions. The agreement, however, did not detail how and when disarmament and integration of military forces must occur, or what the powers of the Emergency Loya Jirga should be. Nor did it clearly lay out or guarantee penalties for transgressions. The lack of detail was understandable in an agreement produced in a short time under intense pressure. The agreement represented a decision to push difficult questions into the transition process, rather than resolve them up front; it established a series of milestones to which the parties could eventually be held when the time was ripe. Thus, the Bonn Agreement set two simultaneous processes in motion: a state-building process and a peace process. The state-building process would be the vehicle for reconstruction, forming long-term security arrangements, and developing national unity. The peace process would aim to achieve order among the factions, allowing them to lessen their enmity while acknowledging, if implicitly, their de facto control of the country. The Bonn Agreement envisioned that the state and political processes, such as a constitutional process and elections, would slowly draw sovereign authority back to the government and people, and diminish the rule of the gun.

As part of the state-building process, the Bonn Agreement provided for the drafting of a new constitution, to be approved by the CLJ, which would convene just two years after Bonn.[52] Until the adoption of a new constitution, the 1964 constitution would be in force, but without a king or legislature, thus excluding a substantial portion of the meaningful provisions of that instrument.[53] The Bonn Agreement also allowed for the operation of existing laws that did not contradict the provisions of the agreement or the 1964 constitution. While sensible, this provision was practically unenforceable, due to both the enormous number of laws created by multiple, mutually antithetical regimes over thirty years and a general inability to enforce laws throughout the country. However, the chairman of the interim and transitional administrations was given the power to make law by decree with the agreement of his cabinet, which simplified the resolution of pressing legal issues.[54]

The final critical aspect of the Bonn Agreement was the selection of the interim cabinet. In Afghanistan, confidence in peaceful transitions of power was understandably low, and thus, the composition of the interim administration also defined, to many, the future composition of the Afghan government. The division of posts was widely viewed to be extremely lopsided, with the Panjshiri faction of the Northern Alliance claiming the three most powerful ministerial posts: defense, interior, and foreign affairs. The selection of Hamid Karzai, head of the Pushtun Popalzai tribe, as chairman, and the agreement to allow the return of the former king, were attempts to reduce Pushtun alienation from the interim administration. The potential power of the chairman and that of the former king were far less concrete, however, than the very real power that the Northern Alliance Panjshiri triumvirate exerted over Kabul and Afghanistan's foreign relations. Not only the less well represented non–Northern Alliance groups complained that "injustices have been committed in the distribution of ministries,"[55] powerful members of the Northern Alliance, such as Rashid Dostum and Ismael Khan, decried the outcome as unfair and even humiliating.[56] This sense of exclusion would undermine support for the transitional administration and foment widespread discontent.

Drafting a New Constitution[57]

Hamid Karzai, president of the Afghan transitional administration (ATA) anointed by the Emergency Loya Jirga, appointed a nine-member constitutional drafting commission by decree on October 5, 2002.[58] The commission was chaired by Vice-President Niamatullah Shahrani, an ethnic Uzbek and religious scholar from Badakhshan province. Shahrani's deputy was Professor Abdul Salam Azimi, former rector of Kabul University and a professor of the *sharia* faculty there.[59] Shahrani had been Azimi's student and they shared a close bond.[60] The remaining members were mostly lawyers and legal scholars, including two women, none of whom were powerful players in political or military affairs.[61] Although most of the members had a legal background in secular or religious law, none was a constitutional expert per se.

The ailing former king, Zahir Shah, who had been given the honorific title of Father of the Nation during the Emergency Loya Jirga in June 2002, officially inaugurated the drafting commission in November 2002. The commission struggled to compose itself, as it lacked organization and a competent secretariat, and suffered from considerable rancor among its members. This discord emerged from a mixture of tension over control of the commission's work and the draft of the constitution, and political disagreement about the roles of Islam and the king in the new draft.

The United Nations Assistance Mission for Afghanistan (UNAMA), which bore primary responsibility among international actors for aiding the commission, failed to direct sufficient resources toward the commission for months.[62] Six months after Karzai's decree, the commission was in disarray, and virtually no progress had been made on producing a decent draft of the constitution, or canvassing the political aims of the powerful or the population. Instead, the commission had broken into two camps, each creating a different draft. While these drafts had some substantive differences along liberal versus conservative lines, the primary disagreement was over the perceived exclusion of several commission members from the drafting process, which remained largely in the hands of Professor Azimi. Meanwhile, a French adviser, Guy Carcassone, provided to Karzai by the French government, created another separate draft. Other foreign advisers provided by the United States, the United Nations, and the Swiss government made trips to visit with the commission members to discuss various aspects of the constitution.[63] These three drafts were the subject of rumor and confusion, compounded by the government's failure to release the eventual draft constitution produced by the commission.

With the prospect of another national *loya jirga* looming, serious international pressure was placed on both the ATA and UNAMA to move the process forward. On

March 10, 2003, the secretariat of the constitutional drafting commission released a document, *The Constitution Making Process in Afghanistan*, outlining the proposed activities and timeline of a new, larger constitutional commission that would undertake a public consultation process, amend the draft constitution produced by the drafting commission, and prepare for the CLJ to ratify the document.

The drafting commission conducted an intensive series of meetings in March. Chairman Shahrani submitted a draft constitution to President Karzai in early April, intended to serve "as a set of recommendations . . . on constitutional arrangements" to the full constitutional commission.[64] This draft constitution was largely based on the 1964 constitution, but had not been subjected to a careful technical review. As a result, certain aspects of the document lacked internal coherence, or were simply unclear.

The Karzai government appointed a new constitutional commission on April 26, consisting of thirty-five members from a broader political and ethnic spectrum and including six members of the drafting commission.[65] The membership of this new body was a mix of politicians and experts. The decree establishing the new commission outlined a public consultation process, and determined that the CLJ would be held in October 2003.

The new commission received much more support from the United Nations and other international sources, and it extensively reworked the draft constitution, following both a public consultation process as well as more input from foreign experts. The constitutional commission was somewhat wary of the substantive input from foreign experts, fearing the appearance of foreign influence on a critical aspect of Afghanistan's political development. This meant that many of the most intensive substantive discussions involving foreign advisers happened in low-key gatherings, often outside the walls of the constitutional commission offices. This substantive foreign technical advice had a meaningful impact on narrow issues, but did not ultimately shape decisions on the most significant questions. The real foreign influence was not channeled through legal experts, but directly exerted by high-level diplomats upon the palace and other influential leaders.

Concerns about the appearance of foreign interference did not, however, extend to foreign support for designing the procedural aspects of the constitution-making process, including the public consultation process as well as the elections and rules of procedure for the CLJ. The U.S. Agency for International Development (USAID) funded the Asia Foundation to provide foreign experts and support staff, managed through UNAMA, to work with the constitutional commission secretariat on these issues. The staff was responsible for staging the delegate elections, conducting public outreach, organizing the CLJ, and drafting many of the key documents involved, including the rules of procedure.

Following a public consultation process during June and July (discussed below), the constitutional commission had one month—August 2003—to agree to changes to the draft constitution. They divided up into several committees, breaking down chapters of the constitution for different committees to consider. The commission's work took longer than the allotted month, and the enormous logistical undertaking required for the delegate selection process caused the government to delay the CLJ from October to December. Several issues were the subject of intensive debate within the constitutional commission, such as the choice between a presidential and a parliamentary system of government, the designation of national and official languages, and the question of whether there should be a constitutional court. The views of President Karzai and his inner circle were not yet clearly known on many of these issues, and so some critical political information was missing from the commission's deliberations. Eventually, the commission's committees came together, and the entire draft was discussed and voted on in plenary.

The constitutional commission did not deliver the draft constitution to President Karzai until late September 2003. At this point, it was expected that the draft document would be released to the public to allow for a few months of debate and scrutiny before the CLJ convened. However, the constitutional commission's independence had never been clarified, and the presidential palace took control of the draft, preventing its publication and undertaking an executive review. Anxious to secure greater power for President Karzai and limit the possibility of alternative power centers, members of Karzai's cabinet and national security council redrafted key aspects of the constitution. The most significant modifications were the change in government from a semipresidential system, which was designed to promote ethnic power sharing, to a presidential system, as well as the elimination of a constitutional court. Both changes reflected a desire to narrow government control, which was in line with Karzai's wish to wield power effectively, and with the interest of the international community and the United States in particular in limiting the number of key interlocutors in the Afghan government. Despite growing public outcry at delays and a secretive process,[66] President Karzai did not release the draft constitution until November 3, just five weeks before the CLJ.

The Public Consultation Process

From the very beginning, there were competing views about whether the constitutional process should be opened to public debate and wide participation within Afghan society. Some argued that the constitutional process had to be broadly inclusive to incorporate diverse views and allow for popular political participation. Such a process, it was argued, would be perceived as more legitimate when interested parties felt that they had their say, even if there were tight controls on the outcome of the debate. Others in government and the international community argued, however, that stoking confrontational issues through public debate could be destabilizing or undermine progress in resolving sensitive issues. There was a perception that open discussion of a few controversial issues, such as the role of Islam, could cause moderate forces to lose ground on a host of other matters. This camp preferred to keep debate on controversial issues out of the public sphere. The latter view was held in particular by Jean Arnault, deputy special representative of the secretary-general and head of the political pillar in UNAMA.[67]

Ultimately, a middle-of-the-road approach was taken. Although the constitutional commission refused to release a draft of the constitution for public debate, a public education and consultation process was conducted for two months starting in June. Eight regional offices in Afghanistan and two each in Pakistan and Iran were opened by the constitutional commission secretariat to support this process. Members of the constitutional commission traveled to provincial capitals and refugee populations in Iran and Pakistan, holding meetings with preselected groups of community leaders, religious leaders, women, businessmen, academics, and professionals.[68] These meetings, as well as questionnaires that were circulated to the general public through newspapers and an outreach campaign, generally kept discussions to vague principles rather than eliciting concrete views on key questions. The meetings throughout the country were useful, however, in exposing the Kabul and foreign-based Afghan elite on the constitutional commission to the opinions of Afghans around the country. Several of the commission members reported benefiting from these meetings, which demonstrated a greater appetite for accommodation and tolerance among the population than that which existed in elite political circles in Kabul.[69]

The constitutional commission also engaged in a public information effort that included television, radio, and print distribution of materials explaining the constitutional process and the Bonn Agreement, focusing on issues such as how a constitution could protect rights and prevent abuses of power. Independent civil-society networks held training sessions and consultations with a broad array of Afghans in an effort to contribute to the process from the outside.[70] Ultimately, tens of thousands of comments from the public were received and logged by the commission staff.

In the end, the public education and consultation process did more to advertise the process to the Afghan people and give the illusion of inclusion than to actually provide effective avenues for public input to the process. Most Afghans knew that a constitutional process was under way, but few knew what the substantive issues at stake were. Even those who submitted their opinions were unlikely to have been heard, for two reasons. First, as the results of these consultations were being collated and analyzed for a report, the power play among Afghan factions regarding the substance of the constitution was under way behind the scenes, unsullied by public involvement. Second, the report produced by the secretariat of the constitutional commission—which detailed the collection of 80,000 returned questionnaires and 6,000 additional written proposals, plus the results of 523 meetings—came too late to influence the drafting process and was not publicly distributed in advance of the CLJ, despite a decree requiring publication.[71] The report was eventually provided to the CLJ delegates, who were given copies only once the event was under way.[72] The constitutional commission and UNAMA had been reluctant from the start to engage in a meaningful public debate, as each felt it would compromise their agenda and interfere with their efforts to arrive at an elite compromise among existing power holders. The eventual public consultation process and its effectiveness reflected, and suffered from, this unease.

Delegate Selection

On July 15, 2003, a presidential decree was issued outlining the composition and selection process for the CLJ. There would be 500 delegates to the CLJ, as follows: 344 elected at the district level; 64 women elected by women at the provincial level; 42 delegates elected from refugee, internally displaced person (IDP), and minority communities; and 50 people (25 men, 25 women) appointed by President Karzai.[73] The composition of the body and the method of delegate selection were remarkably similar to the constitutional *loya jirga* called by King Zahir Shah in 1964.[74] Due to constraints imposed by funding, timing, security, and logistics, the delegates to the CLJ elected at the district level were not chosen in general elections, but rather were chosen by the roughly 15,000 community representatives who had elected the delegates to the Emergency Loya Jirga in 2002.[75] These community representatives, comprising forty to sixty persons from each of the approximately 360 districts in Afghanistan's thirty-two provinces, had come together as a result of an informal caucus process in 2002. Elections were held in Pakistan and Iran among Afghan refugee communities, and indirect elections in provinces and minority communities were held to select women and minorities. Similar to the 1964 process, the president was given about 10 percent of the seats to fill by appointment, to ensure that certain groups or individuals important to the process (in the government's eyes) were represented.

The elections proceeded through October and November without major security incidents. Gathering the 15,000 community representatives again in regional centers proved relatively easy. There were, however, reports of vote buying and intimidation in the election process.[76] Unlike the Emergency Loya Jirga elections in 2002, regional power brokers knew what to expect from the process and the importance of getting their representatives elected. Also, with fewer positions available compared to the 1,500 elected to the Emergency Loya Jirga, there was heightened competition for the seats. Ultimately, the CLJ delegate-selection process produced a highly diverse body of 502 delegates—two were added to account for the shifting number of provinces—representing every province and a wide range of views.[77]

The Constitutional Loya Jirga

On the morning of December 14, 2003, the former king of Afghanistan, the ninety-year-old Zahir Shah, opened the CLJ, telling the delegates that the new constitution was theirs to alter, improve, and approve. That the former monarch, no matter how feeble, was endorsing a process that would almost certainly lead to an end to Afghanistan's royalty was significant. President Karzai then made a speech introducing his draft constitution and exhorting the delegates to approve the presidential system he envisioned. Due to existing divisions, Karzai warned that "Afghanistan needs one source of power in government."[78] Karzai also threatened that he would not run for election unless his proposed system was approved.

The CLJ's first task, to elect a leadership, was critical, as debate needed both to flourish and be controlled. Since there was no formal party hierarchy among the delegates, most representatives considered themselves and their voices to be equal. The Emergency Loya Jirga in 2002 had been a disaster in part

due to poor leadership. With a weak chair and vague rules of procedure, a few warlords were able to control the agenda and debate through intimidation.[79]

Sebaghatullah Mojadeddi, a moderate mujahideen leader with a powerful religious pedigree and close ties to Karzai, quickly emerged as the front-runner for chairman of the CLJ. At the same time, another candidate, Abdul Hafiz Mansoor, editor of the newspaper *Voice of the Holy Warriors* and known for his fiery opposition to the Karzai government, made a concerted bid for the chairmanship. Mansoor made a speech arguing that Karzai was trying to rig the debate to ensure that he would become Afghanistan's president. His rhetoric roused many passions but fewer votes, and Mojadeddi won the election handily.

Overall, the CLJ was a well-organized and civil affair, in contrast to its rough-and-tumble emergency predecessor. With only one-third the number of delegates and an emphasis on literacy in the selection process, the CLJ had established rules of procedure (albeit often flouted), a respected chair, a library, and subcommittees that undertook intensive debate. The scene inside the tent, however, was no garden party. Among the 502 delegates were warlords, tribal leaders, communist poets, and mullahs, many of whom had limited formal education and had never read a constitution before. The constitution had already been drafted for them by the unelected constitutional commission, and the delegates would only have two to three weeks to debate and ratify it. This whole scene played out against a backdrop of foreign military domination and an ongoing war in the countryside.

In the first days of the CLJ, the tent pulsed with excitement. There were meandering floor speeches about the conditions in home provinces while the delegates met old friends, read the draft constitution, and began to adopt positions. The commission secretariat finished the rules of procedure just days before the meeting began, and no one really knew what the course of the debate would be. The rules—thirty-seven dense articles of parliamentary procedure—had been passed by presidential decree and gave tremendous authority to the CLJ chairman to control the debate, order of speakers, and other aspects of the process.[80] Karzai's people and representatives of the international community were openly saying that they expected the new constitution to be ratified within seven to ten days. But with 160 articles, a proposed new system of government, and 500-plus opinions in the tent, these expectations were misguided. Even if every delegate spoke only once, it would mean weeks of debate.

Outside input had been limited during the secretive drafting phase of the constitution, and many of the delegates were geared up for a full hearing. Some had ridden a donkey for days through snow-covered passes to be present. Others had risked murder by the Taliban for their participation. They had not come merely to smile and vote for the government's plan. Prior Afghan regimes had made (short) careers of underestimating rural leaders.

There was also a serious organized opposition to Karzai's last-minute modifications to the draft. The document was not the result of political consensus, and various groups were intent on fundamentally changing the structure envisioned by President Karzai and Zalmay Khalilzad, the powerful American ambassador to Kabul who wielded considerable influence over him. Khalilzad, an Afghan by birth, was a protégé of Paul Wolfowitz, then deputy secretary of defense; appeared to have the ear of U.S. Secretary of Defense Donald Rumsfeld as well; and had played an intensive behind-the-scenes role in Afghanistan since shortly after the U.S. invasion in October 2001. The Afghan government and the U.S. embassy both wanted power centered in a few hands in Kabul. A diverse opposition wanted power sharing both among ethnic and political factions in Kabul and between Kabul and the regions. The outcome of this struggle could define politics for generations. An attempt to rally support for the government draft and strongarm the opposition delayed the start of the CLJ, but to little effect.

On the third morning of the CLJ, a burst of rockets pounded Kabul in the early morning. Although they landed far from the tent, they were a stark reminder that the *loya jirga* was proceeding in a country still very much at war. As delegates geared up for the debate, the entity responsible for running the CLJ, the CLJ Secretariat, headed by Farooq Wardak, divulged the proposed format for the proceedings. The delegates would be broken up into ten subcommittees, each of which would debate the entire draft constitution. These subcommittees would elect representatives to a central committee, the reconciliation council, which would debate the views of the subcommittees and agree upon a draft by consensus. Ultimately, the draft would then be put to a vote. In the best light, this system would allow for each delegate to have a say and enable an in-depth debate unlikely in a plenary environment. One group of delegates, charging that this was a means for the government to suppress debate, wanted to vote on key issues in the plenary session first and threatened to boycott. By creating a hierarchy with a small committee deliberating in private at the top, this approach ultimately lent itself to control by a few powerful individuals.

The resulting power gambit was anything but subtle. Even though monitors and delegates believed that assignment to committees was supposed to be random, the head of the CLJ Secretariat agreed, at the suggestion of a mujahideen leader, to distribute the jihadi leadership (the heads of the mujahideen parties) and their supporters among the various committees. The die was cast. These men commanded their own private armies and would not hesitate to use intimidation to ensure that their point of view dominated.

The subcommittee facilitators had planned to have elections to choose the representatives to the reconciliation council. These were undermined, however, by the jihadi leaders in each committee. When former president Burhanuddin Rabbani appeared in his assigned committee, supporters immediately stood up and said that, of course, Rabbani would be chair. When it was suggested that a vote be held, one man asked, "Who would dare oppose the great jihadi leader President Rabbani?" In that small group, no one would.[81]

The situation heightened the already deep tension in the tent. Many mujahideen viewed Afghanistan's urban elites as communists and infidels, people divided from their own culture and traditions; they blamed them for bringing the Soviets into Afghanistan, killing nearly one million people, and sending millions more into refugee exile. The mujahideen believed that their blood saved Afghanistan from the communists and the Taliban. The royalists and "dog washers"[82] who left the country to live in comfort in the West, they argued, have no right to rule now. Others, in turn, blamed the mujahideen for years of war, their extremism and incompetence for the chaos that followed and then the Taliban. To them, the jihadi leaders were warlords.

On the fourth day of the CLJ, Malali Joya, a twenty-five-year-old woman from the remote western province of Farah, brought the confrontation to a head. Taking the microphone during an open debate session, Joya unleashed a torrent of vitriol against the jihadi leaders:

> Why do you not take all these criminals to one committee so that we see what they want for this nation? These were those who turned our country into the nucleus of national and international wars. . . . They should be taken to national and international court. If they are forgiven by our people, the barefooted Afghan people, our history will never forgive them.[83]

The room erupted in a mixture of applause and angry denunciations. In response, Abdul Rasool Sayyaf, a powerful, conservative mujahideen leader and militia commander, rose to say that impugning the reputation of the mujahideen, the true representatives of Islam, was criminal blasphemy. The CLJ chairman, Mojadeddi, called Joya an infidel and demanded that she be expelled from the proceedings, adding that, anyway, as a woman, her vote only counted for half of a man's. She received numerous death threats that day and had to remain under UN protection for the remainder of the convention, entering the tent with UN security guards.

On several occasions Mojadeddi ignored the rules of procedure to dispense with issues or viewpoints with which he disagreed. At one point, delegates collected more than 150 signatures for an amendment to remove the word *Islamic* from the proposed name of the country, Islamic Republic of Afghanistan. Although the petition accorded with the rules of procedure,[84] the chairman, a cleric, refused to allow a vote on the amendment, announcing that "people who suggest such things are infidels."[85]

Inside the subcommittees, a brave cadre of some of Afghanistan's most intelligent and active professionals facilitated the discussions. These men had to ensure that the warlords did not intimidate the participants and that the record would bear the true debate of the subcommittees. They made sure that delegates other than the subcommittee chairmen took minutes, so that the chair reflected rather than controlled the committee's message. Due to their deft and diplomatic facilitation, they managed to carry forward a meaningful debate, enforcing rules that allowed power brokers to be outvoted in their own subcommittees. However, despite these safeguards, several subcommittee leaders went into the reconciliation council attempting to push their own agendas. At one point, minutes of a subcommittee meeting were brought in to counter the assertions of Sayyaf that his subcommittee had agreed to a stricter version of Islamic law than, in fact, it had.

Many of the delegates refused to attend the subcommittee meetings, and most of the serious politicking went on outside of these meetings. The real bargaining took place in several VIP tents on the grounds of the CLJ. No one was in these tents more than the American envoy, Zalmay Khalilzad, and the UN envoy, Lakhdar Brahimi. These two men were determined to bring about an agreement within a brief period of time that would support their key Afghan allies (President Karzai), provide enough incentives to keep opposition figures engaged in the political process, and stand up to international scrutiny on issues of human rights, women's rights, and democratic governance. Together, they exerted a tremendous amount of pressure to complete the deliberations quickly, for two reasons. First, they were concerned that if the debate went on for too long, consensus might unravel and the whole constitutional process would collapse. Second, international donors were balking at contributing more funding to keep the already costly process afloat. Given the strong factional interests at play and President Karzai's relative weakness, the mediating roles of both Brahimi and Khalilzad were, in the end, essential to achieving agreement on controversial issues. This approach, however, perpetuated the dominance of Afghan politics by a few (usually armed) power holders rather than by a majority of the Afghan population, or even a majority of the CLJ delegates.

During the course of the CLJ, several blocs of delegates formed. The eighty-nine women delegates banded together to ensure that women would be granted complete equality in the constitution. Their unity was so striking that they could secure a quota of sixty-eight seats in the lower house of the parliament, or over 25 percent. This require-

ment would immediately catapult Afghanistan from a country where women were not allowed to show their faces in public to a country near the top of the list in women's political participation.

The most significant bloc of delegates to emerge, however, was that of the Pushtuns. After feeling divided, disenfranchised, and unfairly targeted by the war on terror for the previous two years, Pushtuns began to unite as a group behind Karzai's agenda. The hot-button issue of presidentialism divided the delegates along ethnic lines, with Pushtuns supporting a presidential system that they believed meant Pushtun rule. In turn, some Tajiks, Uzbeks, and Hazaras—but not a unified bloc—supported a parliamentary system.

There were strong arguments on both sides, backed by a good deal of self-interest among the parties. Afghanistan's fragile political situation suggested that the government should be designed to maximize representation and stability as well as reduce the tendency toward conflict and the risk of capture by illegitimate means. Power sharing among political and ethnic groups remained a critical aspect of the resolution of Afghanistan's conflicts and the consolidation of peace. The attempt on President Karzai's life in Kandahar in September 2002 and the killing of three ministers between July 2002 and March 2004 all too clearly highlighted how any structure had to account for not only Afghanistan's possible political evolution but also the possibility of political violence. At the same time, Afghanistan's atomized political system needed serious centripetal forces to forge a nation and a state from the fragments.

The proparliamentary camp argued that a consociational system of government would enshrine power sharing by creating coalition executives or establishing consultation mechanisms among representatives of major ethnic groups. There was also a concern about the accountability of the president. Trust in the electoral process is a fundamental feature underpinning a successful presidential system, because the authority of the executive over the government is tempered not so much by immediate obstacles—such as the need for legislative approval—but by the prospect of future losses at the polls. Bad policies or bad results elicit no immediate sanction, and so faith in future elections is essential to accountability. Given Afghans' limited experience with electoral politics and the fragility of the situation, this faith did not exist at the outset. The concentration of power in the hands of one person was also viewed as potentially dangerous in an unstable political situation, as it increased the rewards of illegitimate capture of the presidency, and thus increased the risk of this happening. Those supporting a presidential system countered that given the very atomized nature of Afghan political organization, it was likely that the legislature would be made up of multiple parties, with none gaining a clear majority. This could slow business in a presidential system and also lead to instability in a parliamentary system, which would likely be led by a fragile coalition.

The primary argument in favor of presidentialism, which resonated beyond Karzai's supporters, was the need for a strong executive to galvanize reconstruction and keep the military and various armed factions under control. The historical Afghan leaders who are revered, such as Abdul Rahman Khan—the country's monarch from 1880 to 1901, credited with creating the modern Afghan state—are lauded for their authoritarian use of state power to crush opposition and build the state apparatus, not for their inclusiveness and coalition building.[86] There was also a strong argument against a mixed system, based on fears that a president and prime minister from opposing camps would divide the government, making it ineffectual at best and potentially igniting armed conflict.[87]

In the end, the short-term interests in the consolidation of authority won out over long-term considerations of how to share power in a multiethnic divided society. It is not hard to see why this choice was made. The three sets of actors controlling the transition in Afghanistan—President Karzai and his supporters, the United Nations, and the United States—were all heavily invested in Karzai, and in the case of the latter two, were interested in managing their relations with Afghanistan through a single trusted figure. Their interests also dovetailed with those of a large number of delegates, whose interest in a diverse and representative government was somewhat curtailed by their fear of the factional politics and parties that had repeatedly torn Afghanistan asunder.

As the talks dragged on, the debate became more intense. Just as it seemed that a presidential system had a strong majority, ethnic leaders, such as Abdul Rashid Dostum, an Uzbek leader and militia commander, made strong statements in favor of a parliamentary system. Collateral issues, such as the designation of national languages, also began to roil the debate. At night, more rockets slammed into Kabul, and a UN guesthouse was bombed. Rumors abounded that these were not Taliban actions, but threats from disgruntled warlords; however, it was not publicly known who actually perpetrated the attacks. Meanwhile, the United Nations threatened to stop paying the bills if the CLJ did not conclude soon.

After the ten working committees completed their review, the reconciliation committee began meeting to produce a new draft, and backroom politics started to crescendo. As the jihadi leaders began to realize that the issue of a parliamentary system was a lost cause, they set their sights on increasing the Islamic content of the constitution. As one delegate quipped, they began to press for the addition of the word *Islam* into every article, calling for an Islamic state, an Islamic legal system, even an Islamic economy. Members of the international diplomatic corps became anxious, as their governments and organizations were concerned—perhaps above all else—that Afghanistan not have a fundamentalist Islamic government. For most Westerners, such an outcome would seem little different from the Taliban. So these diplomats, including Khalilzad, Brahimi, and the former UN official-turned-European Union ambassador Francesc Vendrell, privately laid out what they said were the red-lines that the constitution should not cross. The constitution could not enshrine *sharia* as the law of Afghanistan, though they could say that Afghanistan's laws should not be contrary to Islam. The jihadi leaders, exacting the price of their compromise from Karzai, pushed this to its limit.

Afghanistan is a firmly Islamic nation: Some 99 percent of its inhabitants are Muslim,[88] the legal system is heavily influenced by *sharia*,[89] and the political identity of a significant portion of the political leadership is rooted in Islam in some way. Moreover, Islam has had a prominent place in the constitutions of Afghanistan. In the 1964 constitution, Islam was the state religion, and state religious rites were to be performed according to the Hanafi school of Islamic interpretation. The king was required to be Muslim. The 1964 constitution also required that all laws passed by the parliament not contradict the basic principles of Islam.

In the new draft, the references to Islamic law were strengthened during the course of the CLJ. Rather than require that no law could be contrary to the principles of Islam, as in the 1964 constitution, the constitution as adopted by the CLJ requires that no law be contrary to the "beliefs and provisions" of Islam. The use of *provisions* in particular indicates something closer to reliance on the established Islamic *sharia*. This reliance on *sharia*, in turn, empowers the clergy.

In short, the CLJ produced a thoroughly Islamic constitution. References to Islam are incorporated into 14 of its 162 articles as well as the first line of the preamble. The first four articles clearly establish Islam as a fundamental political, legal, and religious basis for the state. The constitution creates an Islamic state, by, of, and for Muslims, with Islam as its official religion.[90] Political parties cannot have programs contrary to Islam, and the national education curriculum must be based, in part, on Islamic principles.[91] Despite clauses prohibiting discrimination, as well as accepting Afghanistan's international legal obligations, the president of the country must be Muslim. The constitution allows the practice of other religions, however, and shows greater tolerance toward Shia Islam than did previous constitutions.[92]

The question of who was to have the power to decide whether a law was sufficiently Islamic according to the standard of the constitution was a fundamental aspect of the debate over Islam in the CLJ. Article 121 of the constitution appears to give this power squarely to the Supreme Court, by providing that the "Supreme Court on the request of the Government or the Courts shall review the laws, legislative decrees, international treaties and international covenants for their compliance with the Constitution and provide their interpretation in accordance with the law." Thus, the character of the Supreme Court would be extremely important to the outcome of the cases referred to it. At the time of the CLJ, the Supreme Court was headed by a deeply conservative cleric, Fazl Hady Shinwari, who proclaimed the Koran as his constitution. Shinwari was an ally of the conservative militia leader Sayyaf, and his leadership of the Supreme Court created the possibility that a small unelected group of fundamentalists would use the court to short-circuit the political process with an Islamic trump card.

The reconciliation council produced a draft of the new constitution on December 30, sixteen days into the CLJ. But once the document was printed and released to the floor, several members of the council, including former president Rabbani, charged that the agreed text had been altered. As Chairman Mojadeddi attempted to move the draft toward a vote, an uproar ensued, and the vote was scuttled. Mojadeddi and Rabbani, both leaders of jihadi parties, had an infamous rivalry that began to affect the proceedings. Mojadeddi, recalling his claim that Rabbani tried to shoot down his airplane in 1992 over Kabul, said that Rabbani's efforts were "devilry" intended to destroy the entire CLJ.[93]

The increasingly heated rhetoric came to a head as over 100 delegates announced they were walking out of the proceedings. Chairman Mojadeddi was so incensed at the wrangling that he announced that he was quitting, promptly left the site, and went home. He only agreed to return after visits by the vice president and the foreign minister. Upon returning to the tent, he joked that "sometimes the *loya jirga* becomes so hot it is close to burning, and sometimes it is so cold that I must go home and get something warm to wear." After a day of cooling tempers and arm-twisting by the government and international diplomats close to the process, the delegates returned, along with the chairman.

In the final heat of the debate, several other issues also erupted. In a dig at the so-called neckties in Karzai's cabinet—the returned Afghans who had been living in comfort abroad—restrictions on cabinet ministers holding foreign passports and even on having foreign wives were proposed. In the end, dual passports for ministers of the government were prohibited (but not for foreign wives), unless the parliament explicitly approved them. The debates over which languages would be official as well as the tongue of the national anthem were also disconcertingly

fierce. Years of ethnic polarization had made these tense issues, as they went to the very identity of the future state and the nation. To complicate matters, the voting procedures in the CLJ were extremely confusing. Many delegates often did not know which articles they were approving in a vote. The rules of procedure were also routinely ignored.

On January 1, nearly half of the 231 delegates boycotted the CLJ out of dissatisfaction with the process and its outcomes. It seemed possible that the talks would collapse altogether. Brahimi and Khalilzad went into crisis mode, convening leaders to find a way to save the CLJ. As one delegate noted, it would take a while for tempers to cool: "When an Afghan feels provoked, even if you ask him to go to heaven with you he will say no."[94] But the frustrated leaders pushed ahead, even with few delegates in the tent. They called for votes on further amendments, which passed with a bare quorum of representatives.

While Khalilzad and Brahimi negotiated with the leaders of various blocs late into the night of January 3, the CLJ leadership engaged in brinksmanship. They said that the following day would be the last, regardless of the outcome. With little hope of securing significant changes and under enormous pressure, the boycotters gave up their final objections and returned to the tent. The last issue to be resolved was to grant language rights to people in their home provinces if their language was the majority language of the area. This would allow Uzbeks to speak their own language in courts and government offices in their region.

On the final day of the CLJ, the entire draft document was read out in Dari and Pashtu. The delegates were never given a chance for a formal ballot on the draft. The rules of procedure were unclear on final ratification of the document, calling for "every effort to adopt decisions by consensus" and failing that, a majority vote.[95] In the end, Chairman Mojadeddi simply asked the delegates to stand to show their support. Most in the tent stood, and the document was considered ratified.[96] Given the high level of tension in the process in the final days, the sudden end and failure to call for a final ballot appeared to be an attempt to force through final approval and disband the CLJ without further delay or dissent.

In classic Afghan fashion, Mojadeddi offered an emotional note, reciting a poem that included the words, "there is rain coming, and flowers are growing from my body."[97] President Karzai was triumphant, but noted that the constitution and the situation in the country were far from perfect. In a nod to his opponents, he said that the constitution could be amended, noting "the constitution is not the Quran. If five or ten years down the line we find that stability improves, proper political parties emerge, and we judge that a parliamentary system can function better, then a *loya jirga* can, at a time of our choosing, be convened to adopt a different system of government."[98] For its part, the U.S. government, seeking a triumph to balance the growing chaos of Iraq, lauded the constitutional process as a great leap forward. Ambassador Khalilzad called the document "one of the most enlightened constitutions in the Islamic world."[99]

UN special envoy Lakhdar Brahimi made a speech congratulating Afghanistan on adopting its new constitution, but he decried the ongoing control of Afghan politics by armed men in his address:

> Fear ... is in the heart of practically every Afghan because there is no rule of law yet in this country. The people of Afghanistan are afraid of the guns that are held by the wrong people and used not to defend them and not to wage a jihad ... but to frighten people, to terrorize people, to take advantages for their own.[100]

Some of the men whose conduct Brahimi was addressing had been at the center of the CLJ. They sat in the front rows, were the chairs of their subcommittees, and had access to the VIP tent where President Karzai, Ambassador Khalilzad, and Brahimi himself worked out political deals.

Conclusion

Only two years after the fall of the Taliban, Afghanistan's political and military leadership agreed on a new constitution, establishing the framework for the institutions of a new state. The new constitution will represent a significant achievement if it proves to be more than paper. At present, however, the constitution is aspirational. It seeks to create a modern, democratic Islamic state with a strong central government, a monopoly on the use of force, and the rule of law.

The constitution does not reflect the political realities of this physically and politically shattered nation. The country is replete with political and military factions pulling in different directions. There are fundamentalists inside and outside the tent whose visions for the country tend more toward theocracy than democracy. There are regional power brokers—the warlords and tribal leaders—who seek local autonomy to pursue ethnic-group interests and personal gain. Others seek control of national institutions for the same reasons. Although these groups participated in the constitutional process, it remains far from certain that they support the vision of the new constitution. Then there are total spoilers—the terrorists and drug traffickers, for whom the failure of the state is a means to their desired ends.

The constitutional process produced a clear victory for President Karzai and his domestic and international supporters. Afghanistan's new political system is a purely presidential system, with a directly elected president and two vice presidents, a bicameral legislature, and an independent judiciary. The president is both head of state and head of government, and is not subject to a no-confidence vote by the legislature (other than by impeachment). The president chooses his or her own cabinet, subject to approval by both houses of the legislature. The executive is represented and dominated by the powerful unitary figure of the president. Unfortunately, this outcome was not achieved through popular consensus building—which, research during the early phases of the constitution-making process suggests, was possible—but rather through backroom deal making.[101]

The constitution does, however, attempt to create a meaningful separation and balance of powers among the three branches of the central government. In the area of lawmaking, both the legislature and the executive can propose laws, which must be adopted by a majority of both houses of the legislature. The president can exercise a veto, which can be overridden by a two-thirds majority of the legislature. The Supreme Court has the power to review the constitutionality of laws and treaties, and may interpret those laws. The power to propose the budget lies with the executive, but the budget must be approved by the Wolesi Jirga, the 249-member lower house of parliament. There is also give and take with the appointments process. Cabinet officials must be approved by the legislature, and the Wolesi Jirga can both interpellate and dismiss cabinet officials, which had been a strong demand of those opposed to a presidential system. One-third of the Meshrano Jirga, the upper house of the parliament, is appointed by the president, and all Supreme Court justices are appointed by the president with the approval of the Wolesi Jirga. The president is the commander in chief of the military and has the right to declare war with the approval of the national assembly.

While there are important checks and balances in this constitutional setup, a political system that withstands actual confrontation among competing authorities is far harder to build. Ultimately, the system must be self-enforcing. If a citizen, group, or governmental body fails to obey the law, the executive must be willing and able to enforce the law. The court system must be willing to apply the law, regardless of the power of the parties before the court—and regardless of the personal beliefs of judges. Simply put, all the branches and their officials must be willing to submit to the rule of law and to apply it to others equally.

Since the creation of Afghanistan's 2004 constitution, none of these requirements has yet been met. The executive has not had the power to enforce the law throughout most of the country; it has been unable to control even its own officials. In early 2004, the forces of Governor Ismael Khan in Herat clashed with a central government–appointed military commander, and the forces of Presidential Special Advisor on Security and Military Affairs Rashid Dostum chased a Kabul-appointed governor out of Faryab province.[102] Ismael Khan was ultimately removed as governor, but was made minister of power in the Karzai cabinet.

For its part, the reach of the Supreme Court has been extremely circumscribed, yet it initially managed to abuse even its limited authority. Only ten days after the new constitution was ratified, the court announced that a video of a female singer shown on Kabul TV was un-Islamic and therefore illegal.[103] This pronouncement, with no case before the court nor any law to back the judgment, was itself blatantly unconstitutional. Furthermore, the court's decree was not enforced, demonstrating the shaky foundation on which the new constitution rests. A new reform-oriented Supreme Court was empaneled in 2006 following the seating of a newly elected parliament, which promptly rejected Karzai's attempt to reappoint the fundamentalist former chief justice, Maulavi Fazl Hady Shinwari. This new court, with its powers of judicial review, has already been called upon to referee constitutional disputes between the executive and an opposition-controlled parliament. In 2007, the lower house of parliament interpreted an ambiguous provision in the constitution to mean that they had the power to dismiss cabinet ministers through a vote of no confidence and attempted to remove the foreign minister. The president objected to the interpretation and the manner by which the vote was taken, and referred the question to the Supreme Court. The court ruled that the vote had indeed been problematic, annulling the minister's dismissal, without clearly addressing the question of the ultimate effect of a no-confidence vote. For its part, the leadership of the lower house claims that the Supreme Court did not have the jurisdiction to rule on this issue according to the constitution, and so refused to recognize the decision, producing a constitutional stalemate.[104]

Perhaps the greatest failing of the tightly controlled constitution-making process was its inability to address Afghanistan's greatest challenge as a nation and a state: balancing center-periphery issues. The new Afghan constitution creates a completely centralized state, with no political or administrative authority devolved to the provinces. Provincial governors and ministry officials stationed in the provinces are appointed by Kabul. The constitution does establish elected consultative bodies on the provincial and district (subprovincial) level. However, these councils are merely limited to "securing the development targets of the state" and giving "advice on important issues."[105] Elected mayors and city councils may be given more autonomous authority, to be determined by law.

The constitutional setup also could not be farther from the reality on the ground in Afghanistan. The territory, resources, and even government apparatus in most provinces remain in the hands of regional power brokers.[106] A true compromise on devolution of authority has yet to be reached, and thus, the extent to which governmental authority

will be centralized or decentralized remains a key question. This issue is critical in both a formal sense, as it will affect decisions in the institutional design process, and in a practical sense, as ideas of a strong central government confront the reality of strong regional autonomy created by the turmoil of the last few decades. Ethnic groups that were relatively disenfranchised in the past now have autonomous militia forces, and, to a lesser extent, political structures.[107]

Moreover, the historical reality is that power in Afghanistan has almost always operated through negotiation between the central authority and local power holders; tensions between these two levels have existed for as long as there has been a state. Even the Taliban, which exerted a greater measure of central control than its immediate predecessors, was forced to negotiate with local elites and accept a degree of local autonomy.[108] Most of Afghanistan has always been remote from the center, and the communications and transportation infrastructure is insufficient to impose high levels of central control. Strong local social organization and a tradition of independence mean that decisions imposed from outside are usually resented locally. Distrust of central government is also based on the experience of authoritarianism and brutality. The years of war opened up a gap between the local and the central structures, with little connecting them. Central government ceased to have anything to offer provinces, let alone districts. Part of the political challenge will be reestablishing that connection, and doing so in a legitimate way.

The disconnect between the constitution and the reality of the place that it is intended to govern is due to several factors. Due to the sense of entropy that emerged during the civil war in the 1990s, many Afghans became fearful that lack of a strong center leads to chaos or rule by predatory regional actors, tempering popular support for regional autonomy or federalism. Additionally, the four most powerful parties to the constitutional process—the Americans, the United Nations, the Karzai circle, and the Shura-i-Nizar (Panjshiri) branch of the Northern Alliance—all wanted a strong center in which to consolidate power. At the same time, the 1964 constitution, which also envisioned a completely unitary state without any devolution, was used as the model for the first draft of the 2004 constitution. Finally, Afghanistan's educated elite, who participated in disproportionate numbers in the constitutional drafting and ratification process, and many of whom had been outside Afghanistan since the 1970s, carried an outdated vision of the Afghan state at the height of its power. As a result, there was little public debate about the prospects for such a high degree of centralization, and local voices were neither well organized nor heard.

The test of the new constitution, as with any law, will be in its implementation. Dozens of new laws and regulations will have to be put into place. Institutions, such as the courts, the police, the ministry of justice, and the office of the prosecutor general, must be built, virtually from the ground up, and furnished with the fiscal and political resources to do their work. But the government must not only be built, but made credible and legitimate in the eyes of a wary population. This process is time and resource intensive and will be more easily undermined than accomplished in the next few years.

The extent to which the stabilization and state-building mission in Afghanistan depend upon the provisions of the new constitution remains to be seen. The 1964 constitution was to be a serious revamping of the Afghan political system, and ultimately failed due to internal and external pressures. It attempted to ease the way toward democracy by limiting the powers of the king and his family, but left them in place as a check on the developing system. The 2004 consti-

tution has little such potential recourse to tradition. The system is bounded by itself, not by an outside actor or institution of higher authority. This change at once maintains the integrity of the system and places immense pressure on its weakly grounded legitimacy to overcome political crises. There is still the potential under the new constitution to call a *loya jirga* in times of crises, but it is unclear whether such an institutionalized *loya jirga* can have the necessary effect.

The 2004 constitution has done much more than previous constitutions to ensure a diverse parliament, and new laws have paved the way for political parties to form and operate. The election law, however, does not allow for party lists in the context of electioneering, and so the first parliament was elected without a strong party structure to ensure discipline in the people's house. The 2004 constitution also does much more than previous constitutions for Afghan diversity as a whole, recognizing major languages other than Dari and Pashto and allowing for minority Shiite jurisprudence to be used in the courts in cases brought by Shia. It has also guaranteed a substantial portion of seats to women in the parliament, which already has added many more Afghan women to visible political life than ever before.

The vague yet powerful references to Islam and the legal system of the country in the 2004 constitution leave some cause for concern. In the wrong hands, the language ensuring that laws must adhere to the "beliefs and provisions" of Islam potentially takes away an important degree of discretion from Afghan's elected leaders and lawmakers and places it into the hands of those wielding clerical authority. This grant of power to the politically unaccountable threatens the democratic system and individual rights in a country that has decades of struggle ahead of it to consolidate the rule of law.

Ultimately, the new Afghan constitution was borne of haste. The rushed Bonn process laid out in a few days Afghanistan's transition on a tight timetable. Before the country was even nominally secured, it was agreed that a new constitution would be drafted, publicly vetted, and ratified within two years—following twenty-five years of devastation and disintegration. This timetable was largely imposed upon the disjointed Afghan factions by the United States, the United Nations, and other international actors leading the intervention, to ensure that the process would stay on track and that an exit strategy would remain in sight.

The combination of haste, lack of meaningful public debate, and outcomes at odds with powerful entrenched interests means that the constitution will have to overcome strong challenges to its legitimacy. A weak center that devolves no political authority will end up being defied by local de facto political authority not recognized within the constitutional framework. Additionally, there are early signs that the factions supporting a parliamentary system will continue to push that the constitution should be revised.[109]

It remains unclear whether the constitutional process of 2003 contributed to the goal of peacemaking and national reconciliation—or at least whether it could have been more effective in doing so. On one hand, the public spectacle of former enemies sitting in the same tent and producing an agreement (albeit with misgivings) strikes a dramatic contrast with the fratricidal conflict of the recent past. The use of the *loya jirga*, which strikes a chord of historical unity and national tradition for many Afghans, also contributed to the sense of progress toward peace. In addition, a framework for elections and division of powers, if followed, will hopefully channel conflict into the political system and away from more destructive pathologies.

However, the process also heightened tensions and highlighted deep fissures in the polity. The creation of a permanent constitution can be a high-stakes game, defining future winners and losers through structural means. In Afghanistan, a presidential system likely means a Pushtun president for the foreseeable future. Lack of clear elite consensus on the future, and deep lingering distrust between political and ethnic groups, made the CLJ a risky venture. It almost unraveled entirely during the process, and only intense international pressure kept it from doing so. This pressure forced an outcome, but not a consensus, while also laying bare the hand of foreign intervention in a delicate process and heightening the perception that Karzai's power flows from the Potomac rather than the Kabul or Helmand rivers.

Ultimately, the governmental structure that the constitution created is cognizable to most Afghans. But whether it will function, and overcome the struggles ahead, is far from assured. The most important lesson from the 1964 process, perhaps, is that the spirit of the document needs to be obeyed by those with the power to disobey it.

Notes

1. I would like to thank the constitutional and judicial reform commissions of Afghanistan, in particular Chief Justice Azimi, Justice Bahauddin Baha, and Ms. Fatema Gailani, for their extensive insights. I would also like to thank Toluwanimi Fadeyi for her research assistance. Portions of this chapter were previously published in J Alexander Thier, "The Making of a Constitution in Afghanistan," *New York Law School Law Review*, vol. 51, no. 3 (2006–07), pp. 557–79.

2. The *loya jirga* is an Afghan tradition with an august but vague history. The concept was extrapolated from the model of the tribal *jirga* or *shura*, an ad hoc, village-based institution that allows broad representation and, nominally, consensual decision making. The *loya jirga* is intended to be a national manifestation of community decision making. It has been used on average every twenty years to confirm the succession of monarchs, pass constitutions, and approve government policy. The last *loya jirga* deemed broadly legitimate was held in 1964 to approve a new reformist constitution.

3. For historical background on the conflicts, see William Maley, *The Afghanistan Wars* (New York: Palgrave Macmillan, 2002).

4. For insight into the cleavages within Afghan society, see Louis Dupree, *Afghanistan* (New Jersey: Princeton University Press, 1980); Larry P. Goodson, *Afghanistan's Endless War* (Seattle: University of Washington Press, 2001); Barnett R. Rubin, *The Fragmentation of Afghanistan: State Formation and Collapse in the International System*, 2nd ed. (New Haven, CT: Yale University Press, 2002).

5. Agreement on Provisional Arrangements in Afghanistan Pending the Re-establishment of Permanent Government Institutions, S/2001/1154, 2001 (hereinafter, the Bonn Agreement).

6. The constitutional loya jirga (CLJ) was the constituent national assembly mandated by the Bonn Agreement to ratify a new constitution for Afghanistan. The CLJ's legal framework was created by the Presidential Decree on the Convening of the Constitutional Loya Jirga, July 15, 2003, and augmented by the Presidential Decree on the Rules of Procedure of the Constitutional Loya Jirga, November 30, 2003.

7. Carlotta Gall, "Afghan Council Gives Approval to Constitution," *New York Times*, January 5, 2006, p. A1.

8. *The Constitutions of Afghanistan (1923–1996)* (Kabul: Shah M. Book Co., n.d.).

9. Vartan Gregorian, *The Emergence of Modern Afghanistan* (California: Stanford University Press, 1969), pp. 248–52 and 300–07.

10. Gregorian, *Emergence of Modern Afghanistan*, pp. 263–74. See also Louis Dupree, *Afghanistan* (New Jersey: Princeton University Press, 1980), pp. 441–57.

11. Richard S. Newell, "The Politics of Afghanistan," *South Asian Political Systems*, ed. Richard L. Park (Ithaca: Cornell University Press, 1972), pp. 95–116; Dupree, *Afghanistan*, pp. 559–65.

12. Newell, "Politics of Afghanistan."

13. The Constitution of Afghanistan (hereinafter, Afghanistan Constitution), 1964.

14. Newell, "Politics of Afghanistan."

15. Newell, "Politics of Afghanistan"; Marvin G. Weinbaum, "Afghanistan: Nonparty Parliamentary Democracy," *Journal of Developing Areas,* vol. 7, no. 1 (October 1972), pp. 57–74.

16. Dupree, *Afghanistan.*

17. Ibid.

18. *Constitutions of Afghanistan (1923–1996).*

19. Maley, *Afghanistan Wars*; Rubin, *Fragmentation of Afghanistan.*

20. UN Commission on Human Rights, Fifty-first Session, Item 12 of Provisional Agenda, *Final Report on the Situation of Human Rights in Afghanistan*, prepared by Felix Ermacora in accordance with UN High Commissioner for Human Rights, E/CN.4/1993/42, E/CN.4/1994/53, E/CN.4/1995/64, 1994.

21. See Whitney Azoy, *Buzkashi: Game and Power in Afghanistan* (Philadelphia: University of Pennsylvania Press, 1982). An Afghan game played on horseback, using a headless calf or goat as the ball. It is brutal, chaotic, and often played as every man for himself.

22. Dupree, *Afghanistan*, p. 566.

23. Dupree, *Afghanistan*, p. 566. In 2003, another Frenchman was sent to advise Karzai on the process and again inspired humor, this time about the potentially crippling competition between the president and prime minister embodied in the French constitution. In 1992, the Afghan prime minister in the interim government, Gulbuddin Hekmatyar, had famously shelled the presidential palace (and much of the city). And in 2003, Karzai's chief political rival, Younis Qanooni, made little secret of his desire for a weak president (Karzai) and a strong prime minister (himself). Cohabitation did not look promising to the Afghans.

24. Dupree, *Afghanistan*, p. 566.

25. Ibid., p. 566.

26. Ibid., p. 567.

27. Ibid., p. 567.

28. Ibid., pp. 567–78.

29. Ibid., pp. 567–78.

30. Ibid., at p. 571. The constitutional assembly convened in 1931 by King Zahir's father, Nadir Shah, had also begun on September 9, exactly thirty-three years earlier. Dupree, *Afghanistan*, p. 574.

31. Ibid., p. 573.

32. Ibid., p. 573.

33. Ibid., p. 585.

34. Afghanistan Constitution (1964), title 2, arts. 6–8.

35. Afghanistan Constitution (1964), title 4, art. 75.

36. Afghanistan Constitution (1964), title 8.

37. Afghanistan Constitution (1964), title 4, art. 41.

38. Afghanistan Constitution (1964), title 4, art. 42.

39. Weinbaum, "Afghanistan: Nonparty Parliamentary Democracy."

40. Afghanistan Constitution (1964), title 5, art. 84.

41. Afghanistan Constitution (1964), title 5, art. 78.

42. Afghanistan Constitution (1964), title 5, art. 78.

43. Afghanistan Constitution (1964), title 7.

44. Afghanistan Constitution (1964), title 7, arts. 97, 107.

45. Afghanistan Constitution (1964), title 7, art. 98.

46. Marvin G. Weinbaum, "Legal Elites in Afghan Society," *International Journal of Middle East Studies,* vol. 12, no. 1 (August 1980), pp. 39–57.

47. Afghanistan Constitution (1964), title 1, art. 2, and title 4, art. 64.

48. Afghanistan Constitution (1964), title 7, art. 102; see Colin Turner, *Islam: The Basics* (New York: Routledge, 1996). The Hanafi school is considered the oldest and most liberal of the four Sunni schools of law.

49. UN Security Council, UN Security Council Resolution 1378, S/RES/2001/1378, 2001.

50. Jarat Chopra, Jim McCallum, and J Alexander Thier, "Planning Considerations for International Involvement in Post-Taliban Afghanistan," *Brown Journal of World Affairs,* vol. 8, no. 2 (Winter 2002), pp. 2–4.

51. Ahmed Rashid, "Breaking the Cycle," *Far Eastern Economic Review,* December 6, 2001, p. 16.

52. The Bonn Agreement, art. I(6), available at www.uno.de/frieden/afghanistan/talks/agreement.htm (accessed April 10, 2009).

53. Bonn Agreement, art. II(1).

54. The power of decree was granted to the interim administration in the Bonn Agreement (art. III(C)(1)), but was never explicitly granted to the transitional administration through the Bonn Agreement or the emergency *loya jirga*. The transitional administration, however, continued to exercise this power. As of December 2002, Chairman Karzai had issued more than 150 decrees.

55. Reuters, "Uzbek Warlord Rejects Afghan Accord," December 6, 2001; quoting Sir Sayeed Gailani.

56. Reuters, "Uzbek Warlord Rejects Accord."

57. Much of the information in this section is based on the direct experience of the author.

58. Islamic Transitional State of Afghanistan, Presidential Decree Appointing Constitutional Commission, Afghan Transitional Administration, October 5, 2002.

59. Abdul Salam Azimi, interview by the author, December 2004.

60. Abdul Salam Azimi, interview by the author, December 2004.

61. They were Dr. Mohammad Qasim Fazili; Dr. Mohamad Rahim Sherzai; Sayed Musa Ashari; Professor Mohamad Musa Marufi; Asefa Kakar; Mukarama Akrami; and Mohammad Sarwar Danesh.

62. International Crisis Group, *Afghanistan's Flawed Constitutional Process,* ICG Asia Report no. 56, June 12, 2003, pp. 1–2.

63. USAID funded the Asia Foundation to hire a number of consultants to provide substantive input to the constitutional drafting process, including Yash Pal Ghai and this author. These inputs were transmitted through meetings and a series of options papers that were drawn up on specific subjects. Barnett Rubin of New York University also commissioned a series of options papers from constitutional experts.

64. Secretariat of the Constitutional Commission of Afghanistan, "The Constitution Making Process in Afghanistan," March 10, 2003, p. 2.

65. Islamic Transitional State of Afghanistan, Presidential Decree on the Constitutional Commission, April 26, 2003.

66. Masuda Sultan and Hannibal Travis, letter to the editor, *Boston Globe,* November 13, 2003, p. A19.

67. Abdul Salam Azimi, interview by the author, September 2003, Kabul, Afghanistan.

68. Secretariat, Constitutional Commission, "Public Consultation Strategy," n.d. (on file with author). See also Vanessa Gezari, "Mistrust Mars Drafting of Constitution; Afghans Mindful of Prior Failures," *Chicago Tribune,* July 9, 2003, p. 4; Elizabeth Sullivan, "Afghanistan's Constitution is a Local Creation," *Plain Dealer* (OH), January 8, 2004, p. B9.

69. Fatema Gailani, interview by the author, December 2004, Kabul, Afghanistan.

70. Azarbaijani-Moghaddam, *Technical Lessons Learned from the Afghan Civil Society Forum (ACSF)/Swisspeace Civic Education for the Constitution Project* (Sippi: ACSF-Swisspeace, 2003).

71. According to "The Constitution Making Process in Afghanistan" a report by the Constitutional Commission on March 10, 2003, which was formalized by decree on May 10, 2003, the responsibilities of the commission included "preparing a report analyzing the views of Afghans gathered during public consultations and making the report available to the public." For figures on the consultation process, see "UNAMA Draft Constitution Factsheet," available at www.unama-afg.org/docs/_ nonUN%20Docs/_Loya-Jirga/CLJ/Draft%20 Constitution%20Factsheet.doc (accessed April 10, 2009).

72. Constitutional Commission Secretariat, Transitional Islamic State of Afghanistan, *Analytical Report of the Views and Proposals Made by the People, for the Drafting of a New Constitution,* October 2003.

73. See Islamic Transitional State of Afghanistan, Presidential Decree on the Convening of the Constitutional Loya Jirga, July 15, 2003.

74. See Presidential Decree on the Constitutional Loya Jirga, July 15, 2003.

75. Presidential Decree on the Convening of the Constitutional Loya Jirga, July 15, 2003, art. 4.

76. Paul Watson, "Fears of Vote Buying Muddy Path to Loya Jirga; Such Allegations Are Undermining the Credibility of Upcoming Afghanistan Assembly Before It Even Begins to Debate a Draft Constitution." *Los Angeles Times,* December 12, 2003, p. A5; see also *Afghanistan: Hell of a Nation,* directed by Tamara Gould, Wide Angle PBS, 2004, the documentary film in which CLJ delegates provide firsthand accounts of intimidation and vote buying in the CLJ elections.

77. In the end, President Karzai exceeded his allotted appointments by two, which went unchallenged. This was deemed a minor overstep compared to the 150 delegates Karzai unexpectedly added to the Emergency Loya Jirga.

78. Reuters, "Karzai Seeks Strong Powers at Key Afghan Assembly," December 14, 2003.

79. International Crisis Group, *The Afghan Transitional Administration: Prospects and Perils,* Asia Briefing no. 19, July 30, 2002.

80. Rules of Procedure of the Constitutional Loya Jirga, Order of the President of the Islamic State of Afghanistan no. 4913, dated 16.09.1382 (November 2003).

81. Accounts from CLJ subcommittees were provided by delegates and facilitators in interviews with the author.

82. "Dog washers" is a derogatory term for Afghans who left to live in the West. They are called dog washers to suggest that in the rich and decadent West, the only jobs these Afghans could get was to wash people's dogs. It is an indictment of both the West and the Afghans who went there.

83. Malali Joya, speech from the floor of the Emergency Loya Jirga, December 17, 2003.

84. Order of the President of the Islamic Transitional State of Afghanistan on the Rules of Procedure of the Constitutional Loya Jirga, no. 4913, 2003, chap. XII, art. 37.

85. Waheedullah Massoud, "EU Envoy 'Disturbed' as Afghan Assembly Chairman Brands Delegates 'Infidels.'" Agence France-Presse, January 1, 2004.

86. Gregorian, *Emergence of Modern Afghanistan.*

87. As noted above in note 23, the former prime minister, Gulbuddin Hekmatyar, shelled the capital and presidential palace in 1992.

88. Dupree, *Afghanistan.*

89. Mohammad Hashim Kamali, *Law in Afghanistan: A Study of the Constitutions, Matrimonial Law, and the Judiciary* (Leiden: E.J. Brill, 1985).

90. Afghanistan Constitution (2004), arts. 1–3.

91. Afghanistan Constitution (2004), art. 45.

92. Afghanistan Constitution (2004), art. 131. Compare mention of Shia schools with the 1964 constitution, which solely relies on the Sunni Hanafi school.

93. Chairman Mojadeddi, interview by the author, December 2004, Kabul, Afghanistan.

94. Opinion of delegate, quoted in, Stephen Graham, "Parties Try to Save Afghan Charter Talks," Associated Press, January 2, 2004.

95. Rules of Procedure for the Constitutional Loya Jirga, Article 25, November 2003 (copy on file with the author).

96. Hamida Ghafour, "Afghans Agree to New Charter," *Los Angeles Times*, January 5, 2004, p. A1.

97. Gall, "Afghan Council Gives Approval to Constitution."

98. President Karzai, Closing Address to the Constitutional Loya Jirga, January 4, 2004.

99. Zalmay Khalilzad, letter to the editor, *Washington Post*, January 6, 2004. Khalilzad was the special presidential envoy and ambassador to Afghanistan.

100. UNAMA, Transcript of Impromtu Remarks by the Special Representative of the Secretary-General, Lakhdar Brahimi, at the Closing Ceremony of the Constitutional Loya Jirga, January 4, 2004, available at www.unama-afg.org/docs/Docs.htm (accessed April 10, 2009).

101. See Chris Johnson, William Maley, J Alexander Thier, and Ali Wardak, "Afghanistan's Political and Constitutional Development," Overseas Development Institute, 2003, describing widespread support for a strong executive in interviews conducted throughout the country in 2002.

102. Carlotta Gall, "Provincial Capital in Afghanistan Seized by a Warlord's Forces," *New York Times*, April 9, 2004, p. A5.

103. Nick Meo, "Afghan Court Revisits Days of the Taliban With Ban on Cable TV." *The Independent*, November 11, 2004, p. 33.

104. Author interview with Adbul Salam Azimi, chief justice of the Supreme Court of Af-ghanistan, October 2007; and author interview with Mohammad Younus Qanooni, speaker of the Wolesi Jirga (lower house) of Afghanistan, October 2007.

105. Afghanistan Constitution (2004), art. 139.

106. Barnett R. Rubin, "Afghanistan's Uncertain Transition from Turmoil to Normalcy," Council on Foreign Relations, March 2006, p. 26.

107. Conrad Schetter, "Ethnicity and the Political Reconstruction of Afghanistan," The Center for Development Research, Working Paper no. 3, 2004.

108. Maley, *Afghanistan Wars*.

109. Interview by the author with Mohammad Younis Qanooni, speaker of the Wolesi Jirga of Afghanistan, October 2007.

21

Deconstituting Mesopotamia

Cutting a Deal on the Regionalization of Iraq[1]

Jonathan Morrow

In the dust-ridden Baghdad summer of 2005, probably the most remarkable aspect of the drafting of the constitution for the Republic of Iraq was not the full-scale insurgency and incipient civil war raging a few hundred meters away on Haifa Street, outside the concrete blast walls of the Green Zone.[2] Nor was it the complexity of Iraq's competing ethnic and sectarian constitutional agendas, nor even the breathtakingly short timetable in which the document was produced, a little over a month. Rather, it was the scale of the mismatch between anticipation and reality. The process laid bare a vaulting expectation, defying all the evidence, of a transformative moment in which a new national truth about a post-Saddam Iraqi identity would be revealed. Instead, existing ethnic and sectarian differences prevailed, and the process was so mishandled that these differences were thrown, awkwardly, into even greater relief. The constitutional text was assembled hastily, by Iraqi political leaders who could barely stand each other's presence, under intense and public U.S. pressure, without popular involvement, and with the conspicuous absence of one of Iraq's major constituencies: the Sunni Arabs. Accounting for approximately 20 percent of Iraq's population,[3] Sunni Arabs had, before the U.S. intervention in 2003, dominated Iraq's political and economic life. By 2005, they were the main population base for an anti-U.S. and antigovernment insurgency. In the constitutional referendum of October 2005, Sunni Arab voters overwhelmingly rejected the new constitution,[4] though they failed to block its entry into force. Thus the new Iraq was born.

The world of politics—and not least Middle East politics—is defined by the distance between intentions and outcomes. Even so, the Iraqi constitution drafting process is worth pausing to consider. It was a constitution-making anticlimax that, far from marking the transformation of Iraqi social and political identities, and far from forging a new social contract around an Iraqi state, instead consecrated, in constitutional language, the already well-advanced breakup of the country into geographic regions that coincide with ethnicity and sect. The constitution-drafting process, inasmuch as it peremptorily confronted Sunni Arabs with a vision of Iraq they could not recognize, probably amplified the Sunni Arab insurgency and, in turn, steepened the slide to civil war. At the same time, this apparent failure carried the imprimatur of democratic legitimacy from beginning to end: The constitution drafters had been freely and fairly elected in January 2005 and the product of their work was duly ratified by the Iraqi people in an October 2005 referendum. Despite the Sunni Arab vote against it, nearly 80 percent of voters across Iraq approved the constitutional text in the referendum,[5] and soon afterward, in December 2005, reelected to the first Iraqi parliament the same politicians who had cut the deal for the constitutional carve-up of Iraq into two, and possibly three, separate regional entities. Confounding the lofty hopes of the constitutionalists, most Iraqis decided that they were not Iraqi at all. The resulting Iraqi state is, legally as well as practically, very weak: It has no power to tax if a region does not permit it[6]; it has management power over only a diminishing (albeit large) portion of Iraq's oil resources[7]; and beyond a small list of exclusive competencies, it is otherwise subject to regional paramountcy.[8] It is possibly the weakest federal government in the world. Why, one may ask in retrospect, would we have thought it might turn out differently?

Prelude to Constitution Making: A New Constitutionalism for Iraq?

From the beginning of the March 2003 occupation of Iraq by coalition forces, Iraqi political circles, the Iraqi media, the U.S. administration, and the United Nations all assumed that establishing a constitutional democracy would be the hallmark of success in post-Saddam Iraq. Well before Iraq's first national election on January 30, 2005, it was expected that writing a permanent constitution would be an important, perhaps crucial, turning point in Iraq's fortunes: It would be a moment of liberation, not only from Saddamism, but also from the congenital sense of arbitrariness from which Iraq, as a collection of ethnically and politically disparate Ottoman provinces and British colonial construct, had suffered. Iraq had seen constitutions before the Americans arrived; two of the most well-known examples were the Constitution for the Kingdom of Iraq, prepared in 1925 during the period of the British Mandate, and the interim constitution of 1990, which nominally governed the latter years of Baathist Iraq.[9] However, none of Iraq's previous constitutions were democratic, none satisfactorily acknowledged Iraq's regional and multiethnic nature, and the human rights protections expressed in these documents did little, in reality, to protect Iraqi citizens from abuse at public and private hands. Successive coups and atrocities by the autocratic rulers of Iraq through the twentieth century had eroded anything resembling constitutionalism and rule of law. From the very early days of the Coalition Provisional Authority (CPA)—the U.S.-led entity that the occupiers instituted in May 2003 as the governing body for Iraq—a new constitutional order for Iraq was a centerpiece of the occupation's promise of a new democratic future.

But a constitution drafted in what circumstances? Others have pointed out the irony that the CPA's early proposals for Iraq's constitution-drafting process hardly carried democratic credentials.[10] In the first two doomed iterations, the constitution was to be prepared by a CPA-appointed committee of Iraqi drafters, assisted in a somewhat public fashion by an American expert in Arab constitutions[11]; or, failing that, by a drafting body selected through a complicated system of caucuses, the members of which were, again, appointed (albeit indirectly) by the CPA. The U.S. motivation behind these undemocratic proposals was clearly a fear that *elected* drafters—drawn largely from the ranks of Iraq's religious Shia Arab majority—would be Islamist and pro-Iranian, and thus antipathetic to U.S. goals. Each of these proposals was, however, swiftly vetoed by Shia religious leader Grand Ayatollah Ali Al-Sistani, then at the height of his influence, who insisted in a *hukum sharii*, a religious ruling of greater strength than a *fatwa*, that Iraq's constitution be written by the elected representatives of the Iraqi people.[12] The force of his edict was felt well outside the community of the Shia faithful. Thus began a series of political negotiations that resulted in the CPA's promulgation of a March 2004 interim constitution that provided for a national election for a constituent body to prepare a new permanent constitution for Iraq.

The interim constitution—issued as a CPA edict[13] and known, somewhat euphemistically, as the Transitional Administrative Law (TAL)[14]—was itself far from a model of good constitutional or even good legislative process, as it was drafted by appointees of the occupier and there was very little citizen participation in its creation.[15] The CPA was to pay a heavy political price for its secretiveness.[16] However, at one remove, the TAL's treatment of the way in which the future permanent constitution was to be drafted arguably met the ideals of any "new constitutionalist" model for participatory constitution making. The relevant provisions of the TAL are as follows:

> Article 30. During the transitional period, the State of Iraq shall have a legislative authority known as the National Assembly . . . Elections for the National Assembly shall take place . . . no later than by 31 January 2005.
>
> . . .
>
> Article 60. The National Assembly shall write a draft of the permanent constitution of Iraq. *This Assembly shall carry out this responsibility in part*

by encouraging debate on the constitution through regular general public meetings in all parts of Iraq and through the media, and receiving proposals from the citizens of Iraq as it writes the constitution.

. . .

> Article 61. The National Assembly shall write the draft of the permanent constitution by no later than 15 August 2005. The draft permanent constitution shall be presented to the Iraqi people for approval to a general referendum to be held no later than 15 October 2005. *In the period leading up to the referendum, the draft constitution shall be published and widely distributed to encourage a public debate about it among the people.*[17]

There is some anecdotal evidence that the citizen-friendly emphasis of these TAL provisions was sponsored and authored not by the Iraqi negotiators but, ironically enough, by U.S. government officials who presided over the drafting. Those negotiators perhaps did so out of anxiety at the opacity of the protoconstitutional discussion in Iraq up to that point.[18] On the central issue in Iraq—the nature of Iraqi federalism—the TAL reflected a U.S. bias toward strong central government in Baghdad, qualified by an important and last-minute concession to the Kurdistan regional government that any permanent constitution could be vetoed by three governorates, including the three governorates that formed the bulk of the territory of the Kurdistan Region.[19]

The significance of the TAL's public-participation provisions was echoed a few months later, in June 2004, in the UN Security Council resolution that conferred international recognition on the coalition occupation of Iraq.[20] Though Resolution 1546 did not, in its terms, require popular participation in the making of the permanent constitution, it advocated the principle:

> The Security Council . . . *Decides* that . . . the Special Representative of the Secretary-General and the United Nations Assistance Mission for Iraq (UNAMI), as requested by the Government of Iraq, shall . . . play a leading role to . . . *promote national dialogue and consensus-building*

on the drafting of a national constitution by the people of Iraq.[21]

Where, precisely, did these expectations of good constitutional process come from? It is not difficult to identify external, non-Iraqi influences at work. Certainly among the lawyers at the U.S. State Department and in the United Nations, there was an appreciation of the post–Cold War new constitutionalism and the symbolic significance of popular constitution making in the democratization of countries such as South Africa. Those lawyers turned their attention to more recent post-conflict experiences in Afghanistan and East Timor, where international programs supporting peacekeeping and governance culminated, almost triumphantly, in the entry into force of newly minted constitutions. These comparative constitutional experiences have been well documented and sustained, for some in Iraq, the dream, if not the reality, of constitution making as a safe space in which true, unmediated, uncolonized visions for a country's future could be expressed by its citizens. The image of two million South Africans helping to draft their successful constitutional compact was especially influential.[22]

Moreover, the overwhelming U.S. political and cultural influence in the elite politics of post-2003 Iraq brought to bear the specific U.S. vision of a constitution as the centerpiece of stability and democratic independence. The constitutionalism of Philadelphia is at the heart of the U.S. vision of its own democratic identity; it should not be entirely surprising that this vision was rhetorically projected by the United States, unaccustomed to managing a garrison state, onto the democratization effort in Iraq. In a dynamic familiar to observers of transitional governments, the idea of a permanent constitution for Iraq became, over time, more and more closely linked, in U.S. policy plans, with a nation building success and a plausible exit strategy. "The only path to full Iraqi

sovereignty is through a written constitution, ratified and followed by free, democratic elections. Shortcutting the process would be dangerous," CPA administrator L. Paul Bremer had stated the previous September.[23] However, these enthusiasms and expectations were also echoed in drier prose outside the U.S. government, even by those otherwise critical of U.S. policy in Iraq. Take the International Crisis Group: "Iraqis are to get on with the creation of a document that truly reflects them and their complex society, that will set up a durable state structure protective of all religious and ethnic communities."[24]

The internal, domestic pressures for a new constitutionalism in Iraq were less obvious and perhaps less strong. Without question, in the dwindling ranks of the educated Arab Iraqi middle classes, there was a nationalist yearning for a level of juridical normality unknown in the Saddam Hussein period, which was characterized by conspicuously "interim" constitutions, frequently breached—in short, no social compact at all. As one young Baghdadi man put it in late 2004, "When we hear talk of a permanent constitution, our eyes light up."[25] In this nationalist vision, no particular constitutional outcome was the goal: It was enough to simply have a social compact, necessarily accompanied by a drafting process that would, somehow, engage the whole Iraqi population. The Iraqi Prospect Organization, a civil-society group with roots in the Shia south but following a liberal nonsectarian program, put it succinctly in December 2003: "This process in itself will help root democratic values and set Iraq on a course to freedom."[26] Never mind, for the time being, what "Iraq" actually was, and who in the end had a commitment to "Iraq" over other political entities.

The longing for a permanent social compact was powerful among Iraq's moderate Arab political elites as well. A senior independent Shia intellectual, Dr. Hussain Shahristani, sharing the popular desire for constitutionalism, recalled with a shudder one of Saddam Hussein's favorite bons mots: "A constitution is written by men so that another man can tear it up."[27] At the time, Dr. Shahristani was deputy speaker of the national assembly and, apparently, was determined that the new constitution should not be so partial and flimsy. Though Ayatollah Al-Sistani's earlier insistence on an elected constitutional drafting body was typically interpreted in the West as a demand that the constitution should be authored by Iraq's Shia majority, the ayatollah was also trying, with mixed results, to express the importance of the Iraqi people generally having a say in the founding document for the future stability of the country. This view of Sistani's motives is supported by the many instances in which he later encouraged Shia politicians to bring Sunni Arabs into the drafting process, and indeed, by the liberal views on public participation that those Shia politicians closest to Sistani espoused, including the chairman of the constitution committee, Sheikh Humam Hamoudi; former National Security Adviser Mowaffak Al-Rubaie; and Dr. Shahristani. Even if there was no strong Iraqi political identity, could not the act of drafting the constitution itself produce such an identity? Could not moderate, middle-class secularists, moderate Islamists, and moderate Arab nationalists come together and forge a new Iraqi state? Could not American constitutional idealism be harnessed to serve Iraqi ends?

Such was the more idealist constitutional narrative in Iraq. But within the complex frame of Iraqi politics, other less nationalistic, more pragmatic, and more powerful forces also worked to draw the public into the constitutional debate. Many Iraqis—particularly, but not exclusively, Iraqi Kurds—perceived that in a multisectarian, regionalized country, a permanent constitution would be desirable, if not necessary, less as a classic social compact between citizen and state, and more

as a kind of intercommunal, consociational peace treaty that might consolidate Kurdish independence from Baghdad.[28] Iraqi Kurds, having lived in de facto independence from Iraq and relative prosperity since the imposition of the no-fly zone at the end of the 1991 Gulf War, saw their own ethnic identity and the principles of their own regional constitution—in place, at least in draft form, from 1992—as the *grundnorms* of their largely secular and quasi-sovereign existence, not any Iraqi document. For Iraqi Kurds, who suffered years of Iraqi-sponsored genocide in the 1980s,[29] the posture toward a future permanent constitution for Iraq was essentially defensive; they wished to make sure that nothing agreed in Baghdad would erode their progress or qualify their autonomy.[30] To a lesser extent, the Shia Arab community replicated this approach in the south of Iraq, which had also enjoyed some protection against Saddam Hussein since 1991. This careful, pragmatic strain of constitutionalism was embodied in the unspectacular agreements among anti-Saddam oppositionists, including Kurdish and Shiite parties, at a 2002 meeting in London; these parties were united not by an Iraqi identity but by a common anti-Saddam agenda.

A constitution as treaty, then, would not be a principled document leading to the consolidation of Iraqi political identity; it would, more modestly, be a modus vivendi for the settlement of competing interests surrounding self-governance, resource management, and the role of religious law. As far as this last source of constitutionalism was concerned, the relevant analogies were less to the United States, or even Afghanistan and East Timor, and—though it was not spoken at the time—more to Bosnia and Herzegovina, Sri Lanka, and Sudan: countries where, if constitutional success was to be achieved, it would be in the absence of an overarching national identity. Even this pragmatic vision of an Iraq constitution, however, to some extent depended on popular support and engagement. In Iraqi Kurdistan, which prided itself on its fledgling democratic principles, elites realized that the argument for autonomy needed to be made with reference to popular support—hence the spontaneous poll organized by the Kurdistan Referendum Movement at the time of the January 2005 election, intended to demonstrate support for Kurdish independence. The results, overwhelmingly in favor of Kurdistan's independence,[31] were a useful negotiating instrument for Kurdish negotiators in Baghdad the following summer as they pressed for greater regional powers. Less sophisticated methods of demonstrating popular support for constitutional issues, most notably the mass rally, were used in the much less democratic Shia south. In the ideological vacuum left by the collapse of the Arabist, secular nationalism of Saddam Hussein's Baath Party, it was these narratives of non-Iraqi identity that became stronger and stronger. For those who cared to notice, the vision of the Iraqi citizen was almost completely unrecognizable to most Iraqis.

These were the idealist and realist impulses within Iraq that the U.S. drafters of the TAL drew upon, intentionally or not, when they included the mandatory language of public meetings, public debate, and citizen proposals on the constitution of Iraq. The language became important very quickly. After the TAL drafting in March 2004, the merits of a careful, open, truly organic public drafting process became increasingly obvious and urgent. By the end of 2004, the Sunni Arab insurgency, composed of both Baathist sympathizers and Islamist radicals, gathered force, wreaking violence and radicalizing the world of even peaceful Sunni politics.[32] The Sunni Arab political elite made it clear that they would, in protest at the occupation of Iraq, boycott the January 2005 elections for the national assembly, effectively forfeiting their right to coauthor the constitution with their

Shia and Kurdish compatriots. With one of Iraq's three major communities having thus denied itself an elected seat at the drafting table, it followed that the only way in which Sunni Arab citizens of Iraq would be able to express their views to the constitution committee would be by direct communication; no person within the committee purporting to be a Sunni Arab leader would have the democratic legitimacy to adopt positions on the constitution on behalf of the Sunni Arab people of Iraq. In short, it was clear that unelected Iraqis would need to participate in the drafting. Therefore, the public participation component of new constitutionalism, at least within the Sunni Arab parts of Iraq, began to look less like the icing on the cake of universal suffrage and more like an essential peacemaking instrument to prevent a full-scale civil war in the heart of the Middle East.[33] In the midst of a robust insurgency by the end of 2004, the secretly drafted TAL was already a failed document: Not a single substantive provision in it was implemented.[34] In particular, Kurdistan's regional government had not dismantled its irregular military forces, nor surrendered control of oil administration to Baghdad; human rights protections were in name only; provisions for the resolution of disputed internal boundaries were neglected; and the writ of the central government was barely enforceable in any part of Iraq. But, so the theory went, if Sunni Arabs could be persuaded to participate in and vote for a new, permanent constitution for a sovereign Iraq, then the alarming fractures that were opening up in Iraq could be narrowed and the coalition occupation of Iraq, apparently hated by the Sunni Arabs, could be brought to a close. Bromides about "inclusivity" and "public participation" by "civil society" began to get a foothold. This was a theory that was apparently shared across the country.[35] Secular, moderate, and Sunni idealists and Shia and Kurdish realists had much common ground on the question of constitutionalism, if not the constitution itself.

In these circumstances, one might have thought that by 2005, U.S. policy settings would have been fixed to maximize the benefits, within Iraq, that widespread commitment to a participatory process and a carefully drafted Iraqi constitution might deliver. Those policy settings might have consisted of some combination of the following seven strategies: first, maximizing the likelihood that Sunni Arab politicians would be elected to the national assembly (and thereby to the constitution committee); second, making sure that the Sunni Arab elites understood the constitutional implications of their own minority status; third, ensuring that the implications were also understood in the Sunni Arab heartland, as much of the Sunni Arab elite had boycotted the political process under pressure from the insurgency; fourth, ensuring that the national assembly and the constitution committee established by the assembly were fully resourced and staffed to conduct a major, intensive, comprehensive outreach campaign to all parts of Iraq, including the Sunni Arab areas, to show the benefits of federalism to national minorities; fifth, if necessary, encouraging the drafters to invoke the time extensions built into the constitutional timetable to allow the engagement with Sunni Arabs to take place; sixth, working with Shia and Kurdish leaders to determine what symbolic or substantive concessions could be made to a Sunni position; and seventh, at all costs, removing any reason that Iraqis, particularly the highly nationalistic Sunnis, may have to suspect that the constitution for Iraq would be imposed by the United States.

In fact, the United States did not adopt such a policy, and not one of the strategies was implemented. Lurching between the loftiness of Philadelphia-inspired idealism and a readiness to abandon Iraq's constitution

to the vagaries of the U.S. domestic political timetable, the U.S. administration was quite unable to find political solutions for Iraq. In fact, through the constitutional process in 2004 and 2005, U.S. policy worked to eliminate the possibility of a moderate, realistic, federal political agenda emerging from the Sunni heartland. Sunni exclusion from the constitutional talks was mishandled. What commitment existed in Iraq's Sunni, Shia, and Kurdish communities toward participatory constitution making was more or less wasted.

The Constitution-Making Process and Its Unraveling

Election Failure: Sunni Arab Boycott

The first concrete sign of Iraq's looming constitutional problem was the boycott announced by the bulk of the Sunni Arab leadership in advance of the January 31, 2005, election, required by Article 30 of the TAL. This boycott raised the specter of a constitution-drafting national assembly from which one of Iraq's major communities would exclude itself, massively undermining the status of any constitution that might ultimately emerge.

The scale of the problem was, as it turned out, compounded by the nature of the electoral law for Iraq—a law recommended by the Electoral Assistance Division of the Department of Political Affairs in the United Nations Secretariat. That law created for Iraq one single, nationwide electorate with proportional representation. The model was chosen in large part because it was easy to administer (the United Nations had implemented the same model in Afghanistan, East Timor, and elsewhere); because the model could, in theory, erode regionalism and sectarianism by forcing candidates to appeal to a nationwide electorate; and because it gave greater scope to independent candidates and smaller parties. However, the law was prepared before the fact of a Sunni Arab boycott, and in the face of the boycott, the results of such an electoral approach carried serious consequences for Iraq's constitution. The effect of the single electorate model—as opposed, say, to a model in which each of Iraq's eighteen provinces would constitute an electorate—was ultimately to eliminate Sunni Arab representation almost entirely in the national assembly.[36] An electoral system based on Iraq's provinces, which might guarantee a minimum number of elected candidates from each province regardless of a low turnout in the province, would have produced an elected Sunni leadership— from the overwhelmingly Sunni provinces of Anbar, Salahiddeen, and Ninevah—of a size proportionate to the Sunni share of the Iraqi population. That leadership would have had some claim to be able to represent the Sunni people of Iraq in the constitution drafting.[37] As it turned out, however, the electoral law threatened to reduce Sunni representation in the assembly to zero; seats forfeited by Sunni Arab boycotters would go, in their entirety, to Kurdish and Shiite candidates. Any subsequent constitution would, therefore, be unbalanced.

As the de facto decision maker in Iraq, the U.S. government did little more than ponder the question of whether to postpone the January election, in the hope that the Sunni parties would relax their boycott. Throughout this period, the agony of insurgent violence and the overwhelming question of Sunni participation prevented parties from developing substantive constitutional platforms for election, which was remarkable given that the overriding responsibility of the elected was to draft a constitution. Calls to postpone the election originated with Sunni politicians, who were by now openly hostile to the U.S.-led coalition and unimpressed with the results of the CPA's June 28 handover of sov-

ereignty. The calls were picked up by opinion makers in the United States.[38] The U.S. administration did not postpone the election, however, and the boycott took place. In November 2004, Sunni Arab leaders, including the umbrella Iraqi National Foundation Congress, rejected the election on the grounds that it was taking place under coalition "occupation" and was therefore illegitimate and likely, in the words of the Muslim Scholars Association leader Harith al-Dhari, to be "faked."[39] Even the more moderate Iraqi Islamic Party—moderate enough to have been part of the CPA's governing council—pulled out of the election, provoked by the October 2004 coalition military offensive against the predominantly Sunni town of Fallujah and the deteriorating security situation generally.[40] The boycotts and the simultaneous campaign of violent intimidation of Sunni Arab voters by insurgents resulted in only 17 Sunni Arabs being elected to the 275-member assembly, a very low number compared to the proportion of Sunni Arabs in Iraq. Moreover, none of these delegates was elected as part of an explicitly Sunni ticket. By contrast, the Kurdistan Coalition List, drawing support from an electorate about the same size as the pool of eligible Sunni Arab voters, won 75 seats. The predominantly Shia United Iraqi Alliance won 140 seats—an absolute majority that, in theory if not in fact, gave the party the ability to write a constitution without involving any other political grouping, as the TAL, surprisingly enough, had prescribed no special parliamentary majority for the approval of the constitutional text.[41]

The low Sunni Arab turnout at the January election raised the likelihood of a draft constitution that would exclude Sunni Arab views and that, in an already deteriorating security environment, would cement Sunni Arab opposition to the program of any elected government. This opposition presented immediate juridical problems for the United States. The first problem was the possibility that the constitution would be blocked at the referendum because of an overwhelming Sunni Arab vote against it in Anbar, Salahiddeen, and Ninevah.[42] This possibility was real, for the central functioning feature of the TAL was the provision, in Article 61(C), that gave any three of Iraq's eighteen provinces the ability to veto any constitutional draft by a two-thirds majority of votes.[43] Article 61(C) had been included in the TAL text as a modification of a demand from the Kurdish parties, who had strong support in at least three provinces and had perceived a threat to their de facto autonomy from an Arabist or nationalist Iraqi constitution; ironically enough, once included, an Article 61(C) veto posed the greatest threat to the Kurds, who were well-organized and therefore likely to do well in the constitutional negotiations. The Sunni Arabs, not the Kurds, were now the political outliers in Iraq, and the Kurds themselves would have a chance to write the permanent constitution, where they had no such chance with the TAL.

Sunni Arab opposition to the constitution also, however, presented a second, more grim problem that was not juridical but political in nature. Even if the constitution succeeded at the referendum, failed Sunni opposition to the text would signal a still more profound rupture in Iraq: a permanent sectarian cleavage in Arab Iraq between Sunni and Shia Muslims. This would spell the utter failure of Iraqi nationalist, new constitutionalist, and even pragmatist ambitions for a constitutional compact to include all three of Iraq's major groups. Once a permanent constitution for Iraq had been passed over Sunni Arab objections, that document would represent, indelibly, not only the absence of a shared Iraqi identity but also a failure to reach even a pragmatic treaty-like accommodation, with permanently destabilizing effects. The constitution would fail to deliver on the promise of Iraqi consensus and would be a permanent reminder of both Sunni Arab withdrawal of consent to the Iraq state and the constant threat of violence.

Process Failure: Time Pressures and the Exclusion of Sunni Arab Negotiators

It was of the utmost urgency and importance that popular, if unelected, Sunni leaders be able to put to one side the anti-American politics that led to the boycott and come forward with a serious constitutional position that, within a federal framework, truly served the interests of their constituents. However, at the beginning of 2005, U.S. policy was not directed at supporting the development of a Sunni position on federalism. By April, when the first formal constitution discussions began in Baghdad, the overriding U.S. policy objective continued to be speed. The United States clung to the view that the breakneck timetable of the transition should be met at all costs; in particular, Iraqis were reminded, the constitution had to be completed by August 15, 2005, the first deadline specified in the TAL. Statements from U.S. government officials ignored the power that the national assembly had, under the TAL, to extend the August 15 deadline by six months "if necessary."[44] Necessity, in the circumstances, presumably would encompass an extension to secure the support of one of Iraq's three main communities.[45]

There was some reason to expect that even in the short period between the January elections and the August deadline, Iraq's Sunni Arabs might regroup and engage in the constitution drafting. For one thing, the Sunni leaders themselves were saying so. A number of Sunni Arab leaders publicly indicated in November 2004 that notwithstanding the election boycott, they would be willing to engage in the postelection constitutional discussions. Statements of boycott often contained an implication that if future constitutional discussions for a democratic Iraq were relatively free from coalition influence, then unelected Sunni leaders could support those discussions as a sovereign Iraqi (and not foreign) process. In the weeks before the election, Shia and Kurdish party leaders reciprocated these Sunni Arab advances. As if to confirm the agreement, on January 27, Wamidh Nadhmi, a secular spokesman of the Iraq National Foundation Conference, echoing the views of the conservative Sunni fundamentalist Muslim Scholars Association, stated that despite the electoral boycott, "if we were invited by respectable committees [in the National Assembly] I don't see why we wouldn't say what we think of the constitution."[46]

Party leaders reaffirmed that this constitutional backup deal was on the table after the election results were announced in February, and their advisers acted accordingly. At that time, a group of Iraqi lawyers and political advisers discussed the question of Sunni Arab inclusion in detail in a cross-factional working session, convened by the United States Institute of Peace (USIP) and the American Bar Association near the Dead Sea, in Jordan. Senior UN officials attended the meeting. These discussions set the stage for a constitutional process that might have diminished the perception of illegitimacy among Sunni Arabs and other nationalists. Among other things, the cross-factional body recommended that Iraqis who were not elected to the assembly, including Sunni Arabs, should be appointed to any drafting committee or commission that the assembly created. These recommendations were apparently in line with Iraqi public expectation. The U.S.-based International Republican Institute's (IRI) polling conducted in April showed significant public will across Iraq to include Sunni Arabs in the constitutional process.[47]

As events transpired after the January 2005 elections, however, the fears of an exclusionary constitution-making process were realized. This was not immediately obvious.

The early weeks of the drafting process were promising in some respects. The national assembly leaders agreed that though the assembly was formally charged with responsibility to "write" the draft constitution under TAL Article 61(A), the 275-member assembly could appoint a smaller body to draft the document for later presentation to the larger assembly. This body—the constitution committee—was created, complete with thematic and functional subcommittees.[48] Moreover, with some U.S. and UN prodding, the leaders eventually agreed to the principle that nonmembers of the assembly could become members of the drafting committee. After some false starts,[49] Sunni Arab negotiators nominated fifteen[50] new representatives to join the assembly's fifty-five-member drafting committee in late June 2005, and the following weeks saw those representatives participate in the committee's activities.[51] The committee adopted the principle of consensus decision making[52] to provide some assurance that Sunni Arab members would not be sidelined in a committee on which, because they were not elected to the Assembly, they had no formal vote. In finalizing the committee composition in this way, the assembly implicitly rejected, without discussion, the earlier proposal developed at the February Dead Sea meeting that the constitution should, at least in the first instance, be drafted by a commission that would be independent of the government and the assembly, for later consideration by the assembly. The assembly also rejected the possibility raised at the Dead Sea meeting that the drafting body contain, as members, Iraqi civil-society representatives or constitutional experts.[53] Unelected members of the committee were added only to accommodate the most pressing constituency: Sunni Arab political figures.

Even so, the extent to which the committee could operate as a forum to express Sunni Arab constitutional positions was marginal at best. The real problem was that time was slipping away; the August 15 initial deadline was approaching. Prolonged negotiations over the formation of an Iraqi cabinet absorbed all political attention until April 28. Negotiations over committee membership continued until May 11. The chairman of the committee was not appointed until May 23. The result was that the period during which Sunni Arabs were able to take part in the committee's activities was incredibly short. It was late June before the fifteen Sunni Arab members were invited onto the committee, and it was later still, July 8, before they attended their first meeting. On July 13, the Sunni committee members arrived at the convention center and were shown texts of the sections of the constitution to which the subcommittees already had agreed, texts that settled almost all but the most important of constitutional questions, the respective powers of central and regional governments in the federation. Matters were complicated horrifically on July 19, when a Sunni Arab committee member, Sheikh Mijbil Issa, was assassinated, together with his adviser, in the Baghdad suburb of Karrada, presumably by Sunni Arab insurgents. Some Sunni Arabs on the committee suspended their membership until the government could assure them a higher level of security protection.

Meanwhile, the drumbeat from the United States on the immovability of the August 15 deadline continued. Committee leaders, having committed repeatedly and publicly to meeting the default TAL constitutional deadline of August 15, remained under intense time pressure from the United States to produce a draft. Public and private statements of senior U.S. officials, including the national security council senior director for Iraq, Meghan O'Sullivan,[54] Deputy Secretary of State Robert Zoellick,[55] Secretary of State Condoleezza Rice,[56] Secretary of Defense Donald Rumsfeld,[57] and the president himself,[58] dramatically increased this pressure. These statements made it clear that any move

to extend the constitutional deadline beyond August 15 would earn the displeasure of the U.S. government, on which, at that time, all politicians in Baghdad depended for their salaries and security. "The [United States] supports the Iraqi people in their desire to complete a constitution by August 15"[59] was the standard pronouncement, made in circumstances in which an expression of that desire was far from universal within Iraq. The desire was only ever expressed by pro-U.S. Iraqis after they had heard that the August 15 deadline was a demand of the United States government.[60]

Most of the Iraqis closest to the negotiations clearly favored a more extended timeline, including—though he never publicly announced as much—the chairman of the committee, Sheikh Humam Hamoudi, himself a quiet proponent of the southern federal region and particularly attuned to the fact that Iraq's Sunni Arabs were unprepared for such a structure. Under the terms of the TAL, if the assembly were to invoke the provisions to extend the constitutional process, it would have to do it before August 1, presumably on the committee's advice. On July 31, Sheikh Hamoudi indicated to the committee his wish to extend the process to September 15. In early June, he had already sought confidential independent advice from foreign consultants[61] on timeline extension options; the immense work needed to reach true consensus weighed heavily on his mind. This preference for an extension was shared by Mahmoud Othman[62] and other senior Kurdish negotiators, representatives of the group that was least dependent on U.S. protection and that, ironically, most benefited from the haste.[63] Foreign advisers to the Kurds, often suspected of encouraging Kurdish maximalism, also recognized the coming collision and supported extending the timeline or even abandoning the constitutional project altogether.[64] Senior Shia list officials on the committee, including Abbas Bayati, lent further support to extension,[65] as did—privately—senior independent Shia leaders in the assembly, such as committee member and chairman of the Council of Iraqi Minorities Dr. Hunain Al-Qaddo and Dr. Younadam Kanna, committee member and leader of an independent Chaldo-Assyrian Christian party.[66] The leaders of most, if not all, important civil-society organizations saw the problem and expressed their desire for an extension. Focus group research conducted in April 2005 by the U.S.-based National Democratic Institute (NDI) had already revealed strong reservations across Iraq regarding the value of a hasty constitutional process.[67] On August 1, the speaker of the assembly, moderate Sunni Islamist Hajim Al-Hassani, was clearly expecting to receive a request from Sheikh Hamoudi for an extension. Some outside observers, including the International Crisis Group, had noticed the wide interest in an extension and had publicly doubted the possibility and desirability of meeting the August 15 deadline. These outside views, picked up and echoed widely in the U.S. media,[68] in turn influenced the Iraqi political class.[69]

The United States, however, maintained its policy of haste, even when it was clear that no constitution was emerging from the committee, no public discussion had been conducted, and calls from Washington to accelerate the drafting process were increasingly heard as expressions of imperial power. In the days prior to August 1, U.S. ambassador Zalmay Khalilzad convened meetings with political party leaders to impress upon them the importance of meeting the August 15 deadline. He issued similar messages to members of the international community. The U.S. government's strong demarches stand out as the principal reason for the assembly ultimately declining to invoke the TAL extension provision on August 1. The rationale behind the rush to a deadline was sometimes explained by U.S. officials as the need to keep momentum in the Iraqi political process; what was

unstated, but widely assumed, was the desire of the George W. Bush administration to direct the attention of the U.S. public to some perceived—though, realistically, arbitrary—measure of success in Iraq.[70]

Under this pressure, the committee eventually snapped. By late July, the U.S. embassy was clearly unimpressed with the drafting progress the committee had made to that date and decided to move the discussions to a nonexpert, elite political level. The committee was effectively scrapped or rendered defunct by the closed-door meetings of political party leaders that began in the Baghdad International Zone on August 8, explicitly convened by the U.S. government. Scrapping the committee on August 8 meant that the Sunni Arab committee members, after no more than one month of halfhearted efforts to develop and assert a coherent constitutional position on Iraqi federalism, were retired en masse. The span of their entire life on the committee ran from July 8 to August 8.

After August 8, constitutional negotiations took place in a series of private, ad hoc meetings among Kurdish and Shia party leaders—the so-called Leadership Council, as it was termed by the international press, or more informally by committee members, the kitchen (*matbagh*).[71] In its basic form, the Leadership Council consisted of Supreme Council for the Islamic Revolution in Iraq (SCIRI) leader Abdul Aziz al-Hakim, Shia Dawa party leader and prime minister Ibrahim al-Jaafari, and Kurdish party leaders Jalal Talabani and Massoud Barzani.[72] No member of Iraq's Sunni Arab community was a member of the council. The meetings took place at irregular intervals at a number of private residences and compounds in the International Zone, and occasionally at the U.S. embassy. The U.S. ambassador was almost always present, but the Sunni committee members had no right of attendance and were not often invited, even though they frequently requested attendance. There were so few Arab nationalists in the room that much of the discussion was conducted not in Arabic, but in Farsi.[73] The U.S. ambassador, in his haste, would have consented to a Shia demand that clerics be appointed to the Supreme Federal Court, had certain secular negotiators not leaked this fact to the U.S. media. The expectation instigated by the U.S. embassy was quite clear: the Shia and Kurdish parties would agree to a constitutional text, which would then be presented as a fait accompli to the Sunni Arabs, who would be asked to take it or leave it.[74] Though the August 15 deadline was overshot—in legally dubious circumstances—this is exactly what happened: Instead of taking it, they left. This carried grim implications that the Sunni leaders pointed out immediately: "We warn of dire consequences of this situation."[75]

The problem was not the intrusion of elite politics upon some pristine expert constitutional drafting process. On the contrary, the sheer pace of the timetable made a farce of both idealist constitutionalism and any pragmatic form of intercommunal political bargaining.[76] The Kurdish and Shia members of the Leadership Council, though given license by an unwitting United States to dismantle the hitherto Sunni-dominated Iraqi state, were themselves distinctly uneasy with their instructions; the convening of the Leadership Council on August 8 had been delayed for weeks while the U.S. embassy strenuously pressured Kurdish national leader Massoud Barzani—the politician who most gained from the compressed timetable—to agree that a constitution for Iraq was worth the trip from the mountains. He came down from the mountains, spoke with Abdul Aziz Al-Hakim, and, to paraphrase Boris Yeltsin, they took as much sovereignty as they could swallow. The immediate result was a draft constitution that made petroleum production a regional power, stripped the federal government of taxation power, enshrined the ability of regions to maintain a regional guard,

and allowed new federal regions to be created by a unilateral electoral act. The Leadership Council summarily removed provisions establishing the powers of a federal human rights commission and the powers of an upper house of federal parliament and concentrated on bolstering the powers of regions. The future of Iraqi federalism now pivots around a uniquely short set of exclusive federal powers[77] and a provision that states that in all other matters—including by implication criminal process, personal status, and human rights—regional law takes priority in any conflict.[78]

Consequences of Rushing the Process: the Lost Sunni Arab Constitutional Agenda

Before the Leadership Council began meeting on August 8, would a more extended time period for constitutional deliberations within the committee have produced a better result? Would this have created the conditions for Sunni Arab engagement with Iraqi federalism? Given the committee's shortcomings, the proposition that an extension would have helped is, at first glance, doubtful. Through June and July, the committee lacked the ability to identify constitutional issues and reach common ground across factions. No agreement had been reached on the all-important questions of oil management and revenue, the role of religion in the state, or the status of federal regions. With some encouragement from the United States, the question of the very structure of the Iraqi state was frequently shrunk, in an exercise of rhetorical wishful thinking, to the issue of federalism—apparently just one of a number of issues, such as de-Baathification or the ethnic identity of Iraq. Committee drafting work was slow, and discussions at committee meetings were frequently abstract and academic. The discussions did not involve the practical bargaining and trading clearly necessary to produce the consensus that the committee had established rightly as its goal. Moreover, political party leaders did not provide their committee representatives with clear mandates, inhibiting true consensus. The short life of the committee was characterized by frequent resignations and walkouts by Sunni Arab, Kurdish, and other representatives. Committee meeting minutes were not taken, so that progress was not especially clear or transparent. Subcommittees produced draft chapters haphazardly, without consulting the committee in plenary.

The committee also did not adopt a set of rules and a work plan to clearly define, for all participants, the stages in the constitutional process. There was no protocol to address the fact that crucial off-line bilateral negotiations among the three major political blocs of Shia Arabs, Kurds, and Sunni Arabs would be needed at each step of the way. Nor was there a protocol for committee interaction with the Iraqi public. Occasional press conferences were held in the heavily guarded convention center in the International Zone to update the media on the committee's drafting work, but these did not involve serious dialogue on constitutional issues. In many respects, too, many viewed the committee's failures as specifically Sunni Arab failures. The Sunni Arab committee members were continually criticized for being drawn largely from the Baghdad political elite and insufficiently representing their constituency. Meanwhile, the Kurdish and Shia committee members wrestled interminably with their incompatible desires to exclude former Baathists and consolidate their gains or, in the face of the electoral boycott, to find truly representative Sunni Arabs with whom a durable constitutional order might be negotiated. Some on the committee felt that Sunni Arab civil-society leaders, including tribal leaders, had been largely overlooked to the peril of the final constitution but were unable or unwilling to make a serious effort to find Sunni Arab

pragmatists who might, in particular, accept a federal rather than a unitary state.[79]

Such a profound failure does not necessarily mean that representative, pragmatic Sunni leaders actually existed in Iraq at that time. Even with all the time in the world, the gap between the Sunni Arab and Shia constitutional positions on federalism may not have been reconcilable within the committee. Even if the Sunni Arabs had accommodated themselves to the reality of a legally distinct Kurdistan Region, there was arguably little chance that the Sunni Arabs would reach an accommodation with SCIRI, which, over the course of July, pressed for a constitutional right to create a new southern federal unit to mirror that of Kurdistan, a much greater threat to the Arab nationalist identity. The model of federalism the Kurdish and Shia kitchen finally offered to Sunni Arab negotiators at the end of August would not only consolidate a large degree of autonomy for the Kurdistan Region but would also allow for other future federal regions, including a southern, predominantly Shia, federal unit. In rejecting this model, the Sunni Arabs took a stance that bluntly and fundamentally contradicted the bilateral Kurd-Shia agreement on the terms of a regionalized Iraq, when that agreement was apparently not open to modification.[80] The central Sunni Arab objections as stated lay with the prospect that a southern federal unit would radically challenge a Sunni Arab conception of the integrity of the Iraqi nation and—so it was imagined—sandwich weak Sunni Arab nationalists between the two strong and oil-rich provincial powers of Iraqi Kurdistan and a new Iraqi "Shiastan."

The general sense of despair within the committee over its irreconcilable views turned into personal hostility. As constitutional rhetoric amplified toward the end of July, adherents of the Kurdistan and Shia parties alleged in public and private, and not without foundation, that the Sunni Arab negotiators had no intention of finding common ground. They stated a belief that the Sunni Arab negotiators had as their primary objective the assembly's failure to meet the August 15 deadline. Under the relevant TAL provisions, a failure to meet—or extend—the August 15 deadline would automatically precipitate the dissolution of the assembly and mandate elections for a new assembly, to which more Sunni Arabs would be presumably be elected.[81] In their darker moments, Kurdish and Shia negotiators apparently believed that this so-called nuclear option was the primary ambition of the Sunni Arabs, a belief that in turn strengthened the hands of Kurds and Shiites looking for pretexts to disband the committee and strike a bargain over the Sunnis' heads.[82] If Sunni Arabs had never intended to cooperate—if the Sunni leadership was conducting, in the negotiating room, a similar style of resistance to that of the armed insurgency then raging throughout Iraq's cities more fiercely than ever[83]—what hope was there for any constitutional process in Iraq? Why not just accept the U.S.-imposed timetable? Several indicators suggest, however, that Sunni Arab positions had not hardened against federalism and were not as intractable as some have suggested. An extended constitutional process very likely would have produced better results.

The Moderating Sunni Arab Position on Federalism

First, influential sections of the Sunni Arab community in June and July, in evolving discussions on the terms of Iraqi federalism, were beginning to produce more moderate constitutional positions—not out of any growing sense of fellow feeling with their Kurdish and Shia counterparts, but out of grim pragmatism. There were signs that some influential Sunni Arabs were coming to accept the possibility that federalism

might even work to their benefit.[84] Sunni Arab negotiators had already accepted a governorate-based federalism that would imply self-government in Sunni Arab areas of Iraq. As one Sunni Arab lawyer put it: "When you ask a Sunni if they want Anbar to rule Najaf they say no; if you ask if they want Najaf to rule Anbar, they say no. They want federalism without realizing it."[85]

Moreover, at no point was there a strong statement by Sunni Arab negotiators against the existence of a relatively autonomous Kurdistan Region. Rather, some Sunni Arab opinion makers were working with their constituents to bring about credible and acceptable Sunni Arab positions. Groups of secular Sunni Arab lawyers, including the National Constitutional Association, were working strenuously to modify the hard-line views of more extreme Sunni groups, including the Muslim Scholars Association.[86]

In the final days of August, some leading Sunni Arab negotiators were privately sympathetic to some models of Iraqi regional federalism but were unable to openly modify their positions because of the views of their constituent institutions and populations. Opinion data collected by NDI and others show that hostility in Sunni Arab society to the concept of federalism stemmed not from informed self-interest but rather from a misperception that federalism (*ittihadiyyah*) was some kind of code word for Kurdish separation and, more generally, the partition of Iraq.[87] There was scant recognition in the Sunni Arab heartland that federalism is an internationally recognized way to structure a state that can be mutually beneficial as to the respective interests of different regional and ethnic groups. Nationwide interviews conducted by the UN Office for Project Services between July 20 and July 25, 2005, showed that of the Sunni Arabs in the interview group, 51.7 percent believed federalism would lead to a divided Iraq and 46.8 percent believed federalism would lead to civil war; only the remaining 2.5 percent of the Sunni Arab interview group took the third choice, concluding that "federalism will ensure the rights of Kurds and other minorities."[88] By comparison, a year earlier Shia popular opinion reflected a similarly limited understanding of federalism, including a belief that federalism simply meant Kurdish separation. Over several months of Shia strategizing on constitutional matters, the position of popular Shia sentiment moved significantly—if not uniformly—toward accepting federal constitutional models, as evidenced by the August 11 show of support for a southern federal region. Similarly, if Sunni Arab constitutional negotiators were to accept the terms of a federal Iraq, their constituents would need to authorize them to do so. Getting Sunnis talking about federalism was clearly essential. By July, the dialogue had clearly begun, but the deadline of August 15 did not allow it to produce results. The Sunni Arab position as articulated in July and August was premature, emotional, and, most crucial, without the benefit of an informed debate among the broader Sunni Arab population.[89]

Imbalanced Negotiating Capacity

The highly compressed timeline for constitutional discussions also amplified the imbalance between the competence of the established Kurdistan and Shia parties on the one hand and the Sunni Arab representatives on the other. The August 8 dissolution of the committee apparatus and the beginning of a last-minute, unstructured three-way negotiation shifted great weight, very suddenly, onto the respective negotiating teams. The Sunni Arab team was, by far, the least organized, further radicalizing their position.

By August 2005, the Kurdistan Region parties were well prepared for ad hoc negotiations. They had developed constitutional positions and even draft Iraqi constitutional texts that, over time, became increasingly ambitious and firm. The Kurds had internally agreed on their nonnegotiable red-line positions, which committee members from the Kurdistan Coalition were not at liberty to modify.[90] During the January election, the Kurdish parties orchestrated a region-wide poll that predictably showed a popular preference for independence over integration into Iraq. This result sent the message to non-Kurdish parties that the Kurdish leaders had little room to retreat from maximalist constitutional positions. Similarly, in late July, the Kurdistan national parliament gave the Kurdistan parties a clear mandate on these red-line positions, which were made public.[91] Street demonstrations across the Kurdistan Region on August 15 also showed support for the Kurdish parties. Furthermore, the Kurdish parties were able to invite into the ad hoc meetings experienced non-Iraqi negotiators and constitutional lawyers to advance the Kurdish case.[92]

The Shia parties, for their part, did not have clear mandates from their constituencies and did not choose to deploy foreign experts or negotiators. The Shia Alliance position during the final days of the Shia-Kurd negotiations was subject to radical changes and reversals, frequently wavering on the basic terms of federalism, petroleum management, and the constitutional status of Shia clergy. Somewhat surprisingly, no Shia party tabled a ready-made draft constitution for Iraq. (An earlier, very Islamist-influenced draft, circulated in early 2005 by a branch of the Islamic Dawa Party of Iraq, did not arrive at the negotiating table.)[93] Strong factions within the Shia Alliance, however, clearly had resources to use as soon as their strategic interests became clear. On August 11, in the final days of negotiations, SCIRI leader Abdul Aziz al-Hakim mobilized the well-organized SCIRI base to stage large public demonstrations in Najaf and other southern Iraqi cities in favor of forming a southern federal region, a move even the Kurds declared to be surprising.[94] Anecdotal evidence suggests also that the government of Iran was channeling financial and in-kind support to bolster SCIRI's position.

The Sunni Arab negotiators, though not without institutional affiliation and support, lacked the ability to rally constituents and resources around a coherent constitutional strategy. Iraq's Arab neighbors had had little practical experience with constitutional matters and were of little help. At least until August, there was no clear Sunni Arab constitutional position at all beyond an outright rejection of the offered document. Again, Sunni Arab competence, negotiating mandates, and ability to organize the constituency could have coalesced with adequate time, but time was the resource least available to them.

The capacity imbalance further isolated and radicalized Sunni Arab negotiators; without an institutional means of developing a considered constitutional position, Sunni Arab negotiators resorted to emotional, rejectionist postures. The vehicle of the committee had perhaps been crucial in holding open the possibility of a rational Sunni engagement with the principles, and the merits, of federalism. Definitive Sunni Arab denunciation of regional federalism of the sort that the Kurds and SCIRI proposed came after, not before, the committee dissolution on August 8. As the July and August ad hoc discussions progressed, it became increasingly commonplace for Iraqi leaders to identify themselves and act according to ethnic and sectarian politics. The Sunni Arab participants, who typically (and misleadingly) saw themselves as simple nationalists,[95] were not well versed in these practices and did not succeed in pressing a coherent Sunni Arab constitutional position. As with any negotiation, all parties were hurt by the relative lack of competence of one side. Sunni Arab negotiators, in chaotic retreat, quickly moved away from the negotiating table and reverted to a strategy hinging on veiled and unveiled threats of nonparticipation, support for the armed insurgency, and opposition to the referendum. Constructive bargaining was finished almost before it began.

Lost Opportunities for International Mediation

The compressed time frame also undermined the ability of the United Nations and independent foreign constitutional experts to mediate among the parties to the negotiations and to help foster a realistic Sunni Arab agenda. The constitutional support team of the United Nations Assistance Mission in Iraq (UNAMI), led by South African lawyer Nicholas Haysom, arrived in Baghdad in May 2005 to begin the task of supporting the committee.[96] UN headquarters had been slow in starting to discharge its constitution-making mandate under Security Council Resolution 1546, waiting to formalize its role with the transitional Iraqi government and taking time to assemble its constitutional team. As in East Timor and Afghanistan, the United Nations in Iraq suffered from the lack of a ready roster of experts for rapid deployment to the field in support of post-conflict constitution making.

The Iraqi government did not issue a formal invitation to the United Nations to help with the constitution—required under the terms of Resolution 1546—until early June 2005. Further, committee chairman Sheikh Hamoudi was clearly skeptical of the value and propriety of any international involvement, however enlightened and unobtrusive, in the Iraq constitution-making process. Before this invitation was issued, Haysom, a veteran of the South African constitutional negotiations, worked behind the scenes to help the committee incorporate Sunni Arabs as members and offered assistance on community outreach. He developed a consensus model of decision making that would avoid the question of whether Sunni Arab appointees would have full voting rights. After the invitation was reluctantly issued to the United Nations, Haysom worked with the committee in designing the arrangement of thematic and technical subcommittees. On the substance, he explained to the committee a number of comparative federal models that might be sufficiently flexible to allow for the addition of future federal units and balance regional and national interests in natural resources. A paper he circulated on August 10, "A Framework for Decentralised Government in Iraq," set out a scheme of exclusive federal powers, a mechanism for the creation of new federal units, and joint federal-regional oil management. This paper would have carved out a clear, viable space for a central Iraqi government and thus would have been at least minimally sellable to Sunni Arabs. Kurdish and Shiite negotiators immediately accepted the paper, but the U.S. embassy rejected it as unsuitable on the grounds that it did not centralize petroleum power in Baghdad. The United Nations, in a move that it may now regret, withdrew the paper.[97]

Foreign experts brought to Iraq by the United Nations and USIP, including constitutionalism expert Professor Yash Ghai, had also made good early progress, working directly with Sheikh Hamoudi beginning in early June. With the sheikh's encouragement, they gave particular attention to the Sunni Arab committee members, spending much time illustrating the value of federalism in multiethnic states. Professor Ghai referred extensively to comparative constitutional models, explaining that federalism, far from precipitating the breakup of the state, in fact might hold Iraq together. "Iraq does not face a choice between a unitary or federal/autonomous system," he advised, "but between federalism/autonomy and bitter civil war (and ultimately no Iraq)."[98] During this time, committee members studied the Spanish constitution closely. Though it never

commanded the support of the Sunni representatives, more than any other model, the Spanish constitution provided the conceptual basis for the gradual process of creating new federal regions negotiated in the final Iraq text.

The colloquies with Sunni Arabs were broken, however, when the committee dissolved in August. Though Haysom had quite properly formalized a role for UNAMI in dealing with the committee, as of August 8 and the committee's de facto dissolution, the UNAMI role became unclear and informal. Haysom and other UN officials were sometimes called on to speak to party leaders and perform secretariat functions to the Leadership Council. The UN officials worked especially hard with Saleh Mutlaq of the National Dialogue Council, who had emerged as the most prominent, if not most reasonable, Sunni Arab negotiator, to reconcile his views with those of the Kurdish and Shia leadership. By this stage, however, there was no longer a negotiating table to which the United Nations had a standing invitation. The UN position was considerably weakened, especially by U.S. intervention in the negotiations. The UN role with respect to the Leadership Council was never clarified or assured.

Increased U.S. Visibility

The compressed timetable allowed, and inevitably required, a much heavier and more visible involvement of U.S. officials in the negotiations than would otherwise have been the case. August 15 was, after all, their deadline. The fingerprints of a foreign power in something so uniquely sovereign as the writing of a constitution is probably always regrettable, and not least in the heart of a Sunni Arab–dominated Middle East, in which national identity is almost by definition anticolonial. Even moderate Sunni Arab nationalists would frequently express the fear that the Iraq constitution would be written in Washington, DC, and, as one Baghdad University political science professor put it, only half-joking, "dropped from a helicopter onto Baghdad."[99] Prior to August 8, the U.S. embassy had kept some distance from the committee, referring to the need for the Iraqi constitution to be settled with Iraqi, not American, solutions. It was apparently not possible, however, to maintain this distance and at the same time to insist, as a matter of U.S. policy, that the August 15 deadline be met. From the time the Leadership Council was formed, U.S. Ambassador Khalilzad attended its meetings regularly, and U.S. embassy officials were engaged in less-than-subtle efforts to accelerate a final constitution. Several of the early meetings of the Leadership Council took place at the embassy. By August 10, the United States was expressing strong views on substantive constitutional issues to reach what they hoped would be fast compromises that resembled the terms of the TAL. The United States failed to centralize the petroleum sector, but its lumbering presence, with the suit pockets of embassy officials bulging with drafting suggestions, had been felt.

On August 12, in further efforts to accelerate the drafting process, the U.S. embassy circulated its own draft constitution in English. This took the form of a track-changes version proposing amendments to the committee's draft text and offering extensive U.S. views on the terms of federalism, the judiciary, human rights protections, de-Baathification, and other matters.[100] It is grimly ironic that the U.S. government, having urged an early Shia-Kurd deal on federalism to the exclusion of Sunni Arabs, expended a great deal of strenuous and ultimately futile effort in the final days of negotiations urging a speedy settlement of outstanding issues by pressing the Shia parties to accommodate Sunni Arab concerns. This effort included a telephone call from President Bush to SCIRI leader Abdul

Aziz Al-Hakim on August 25. The American press and the Baghdad-based *Al Sabah* newspaper reported this telephone call,[101] raising the U.S. profile in Iraq to a point that might be seen to confirm Sunni Arab suspicions that the constitution would be a U.S. or, worse, an Iranian product, as the president's call resulted in no observable softening of the SCIRI position. Finally, Ambassador Khalilzad took the unusual step of attending the national assembly's meeting on August 15, at which its leadership moved for a seven-day extension, and again on August 22, when a further extension was sought. Domestic Iraqi television channels broadcasted his attendance in the assembly, predictably attracting criticism from Iraqi nationalists and some Arab media.

* * *

All these factors amplified Sunni Arab hostility to the constitution at precisely the moment when Iraq was heading into civil war, a fact that eclipsed the other casualties of the constitutional process. Not one of the fifteen Sunni representatives in the constitution committee endorsed the constitution, and Iraq's Sunni Arabs voted overwhelmingly against the constitution in the October referendum,[102] setting the stage for a prolonged civil conflict with key constitutional issues—including federalism—at its heart.

Final Process Breakdown: Charges of Illegality

Beyond the impact on the Sunni Arab negotiating position, the headlong rush to August 15 led to grounds for worse criticism still, as the assembly overshot the deadline but chose to ignore the TAL provisions dealing with this eventuality. It was predictable from the outset of the process that even with the scrapping of the committee, the August 15 deadline was not likely to be met, given the ambitious goals, the complex and contentious political environment, and the delayed start. Not surprisingly, then, the unrealistic decision on August 1 not to extend the timetable beyond August 15 using TAL Article 61(F) led to a series of ad hoc assembly decisions after the deadline was missed. This exposed the assembly to reasonable accusations that it was operating illegally. Sections 61(E) and (G) of the TAL treated the eventuality of a missed August 15 deadline in the same way as a failed referendum. In both cases, the TAL prescribed that "the National Assembly shall be dissolved. Elections for a new National Assembly shall be held no later than 15 December 2005." Had the assembly behaved lawfully, the argument goes, it should have automatically dissolved, leaving the government to plan for new elections.

The precise nature of the assembly's proceedings on the evening of August 15 are unclear, though it seems arguable that the assembly, by a show of hands that exceeded the necessary 75 percent majority, effectively amended the TAL to change the deadline to August 22. In doing so, it seems that the assembly acted lawfully, albeit in a way that the TAL drafters may have thought eccentric. It is less clear, however, that the speaker's August 22 announcement allowing the assembly three additional days,[103] or an August 25 press conference purporting to grant the assembly still more time,[104] conformed to either the letter or the spirit of the TAL. The reading and adoption of the constitution by the assembly did not take place until August 28.[105] For its part, the U.S. embassy had always been somewhat vague as to the legal consequences of a failure to meet the August 15 deadline, being unwilling to discuss publicly the probable scenario that the deadline would not be met. Regardless, after August 15, the assembly did not formally amend the TAL deadline, and after August 1, formal amendment of the TAL deadline was the only legal mechanism by which to avoid the mandatory provisions of Article 61(E) and

(G). The Leadership Council was clearly unwilling to submit a series of rolling amendments of the TAL deadline to the assembly, in circumstances where the negotiating text of the constitution was being withheld even from assembly members. The Iraqi constitutional process was remarkable for the way in which assembly members, though legally charged with responsibility for writing the draft, were sidelined. Rank and file national assembly members had no access to constitutional drafts from August 8 to August 22, and the assembly leadership denied members' requests to address constitutional issues on the floor.[106]

Criticisms from the Sunni Arab community and elsewhere stating that the assembly acted contrary to the interim constitution continued to be aired after August 28, strengthening claims that the assembly and the document it later produced lacked legitimacy.[107] Worse, the version of the draft constitution that the assembly apparently endorsed on August 28 was later changed in negotiations before the United Nations printed and distributed five million copies throughout Iraq ahead of the referendum[108]; worse still, the distributed version was changed again, right up to October 12,[109] without formal public notification. In short, the assembly and the public were left in the dark, even up to the point of the referendum, as to the status and contents of the constitution. It is likely, of course, that had the United States allowed the assembly to adopt a more realistic deadline—a deadline that the assembly could reasonably meet—the constitution would not be exposed to claims of illegality and illegitimacy.

Collateral Damage: Exclusion of Civil Society

Sunni politics and the legality of the final document were not the only casualties of Iraq's constitutional process. Other casualties must be recorded if only because they confirm how far the Iraq constitutional process was from the ideal of new constitutionalism. The breakdown of the process worked against the interests of women, ethnic and religious minorities, and liberal and centrist political formations. From the time of the occupation, the continued rise of sectarian and ethnic political parties fragmented and marginalized these groups. It is thus doubtful whether any constitutional process, however inclusive, would have delivered to them the constitutional recognition they sought, such as strong statements of equality and human rights protections. Shia Muslim religious conservatives, clearly in the ascendancy by the time of the constitution-making process, contested those objectives at every step. Nevertheless, small and marginalized segments of Iraqi society had, by August 2005, hardly had the chance to group together under strong civil-society institutions to press their claims.

Some of the most promising initiatives in the postelection period came from nonpartisan leaders who wanted to form umbrella organizations to represent what remained of Iraqi civil society in constitutional discussions. From a centrist, relatively secular perspective, Dr. Ghassan Al-Atiyyah of the Iraq Foundation for Development and Democracy developed a proposal for an independent constitution commission (ICC). The ICC's stated purpose was to work alongside the official constitution committee and bombard it with civil-society constitutional views, under the oversight of a board composed of senior political party members. The ICC membership would consist of a large number of Iraqi non-governmental organizations (NGOs) that were active in canvassing popular views on the constitution through 2005.

Similarly, the Thaqalayn Research Institute, an independent Shia religious NGO, started up a civil constitutional forum of NGOs under the leadership of Dr. Sallama al-Khafaji and Sheikh Fateh al-Ghitta. The forum was designed to educate religious Shia communities on the value of constitutionalism and the separation between religious institutions and the state as well as bring consolidated civil-society views to the committee. Both the Iraq Foundation for Development and Democracy and the Thaqalayn Research Institute were, in the end, able to play a modest role in engaging the committee. Neither organization, however, realized its goal of creating the institutions necessary to strengthen civil society's influence on the draft. As the time-pressured Kurdish negotiators quickly withdrew their commitment to federal institutions in reaction to Sunni Arab centrism, the major axis of progressive secularism in northern and central Iraq was crippled: Kurds were no longer prepared to advocate humanitarian principles throughout Iraq, contenting themselves with consolidating the Kurdistan human rights regime.[110] Both Ghassan Al-Atiyyah and Sheikh Fateh al-Ghitta pointed to the lack of time as the primary reason for civil-society failure.[111] The effect of this failure was probably not trivial, as both civil-society organizations were well positioned to bypass sectarian lines and, in particular, cultivate serious discussions in the Sunni Arab heartland about ways in which federalism might work to everyone's benefit.

The truncated time frame also adversely affected women's groups in their efforts to reinstate the constitutional authority of a relatively secular 1959 Iraqi law on personal status. At meetings of such groups in late July, many participants identified an unmet need for a greater level of coordination if they were to successfully represent women's views to the committee. One proposed solution discussed at the meetings involved the creation of an Iraqi women's coordination committee. Again, it was clear that lack of time was the major constraint. Hanaa Edwar, leader of one very active women's group, the Iraqi Women's Network, met with the constitution committee briefly in late July but immediately expressed her anxiety that women had had no chance to interact with the committee and had generally been marginalized from any substantive discussion on the constitutional text.[112] She later resorted to a series of public demonstrations in Baghdad.

The committee composition may have represented a way of partially correcting the lack of minority and women's participation. The Kurdish and Shia blocs had taken some care to ensure that women were present on the committee, with a total of nine members, as well as representatives of the Assyrian, Shabak, and Yazidi communities. One of the committee members, Hunain Al-Qaddo, was also serving as chairman of the Council of Iraqi Minorities, a body formally established on July 2, 2005, by eight ethnic minority groups to advocate for their concerns in the constitutional discussions. However, the demise of the committee on August 8 dramatically reduced the ability of these groups to participate in negotiations. The post–August 8 ad hoc Leadership Council meetings included no women and no non-Kurdish minorities. Centrist party representatives, when they attended, played a minor role, having moved closer to Sunni Arab skepticism. As a result, the constitutional provisions that these groups were seeking in the text were frequently removed from the committee draft, diluted, or modified in ways that bore little relationship to the views of the groups concerned.

The removal of the drafting responsibility from the committee resulted in smaller groups, including Iraq's ethnic and religious minorities, turning immediately to international institutions for lobbying support and patronage. Previously they had been able to access Iraqi members of the committee directly. Hoping to influence the draft after August 8, these groups had an incentive to seek the backing of the U.S. embassy, and to a lesser extent the United Nations, as there were no longer accessible or sympathetic Iraqis close to the drafting action. The United States and the United Nations clearly welcomed this role. The UN special representative, Ashraf Ghazi, defined his own role as protecting human and minority rights in the constitution. The press releases he issued in August reveal a series of meetings with Iraqi supplicants looking for UN help when apparently none was available elsewhere.[113]

It is far from clear that the adopted roles of the United States and UNAMI as human rights lobbyists were successful. There is no doubt that some of the Iraqi minority groups found their meetings with the U.S. embassy and United Nations to be useful, if only to determine the status of the latest drafts of the constitution. By August, it became very difficult even for participants in the negotiations to follow the drafting work; at times, two or even three different drafts were being circulated by different negotiators as the "latest draft." Competing "authoritative" texts were variously claimed by Dr. Hajim Al-Hassani, the speaker of the assembly; Sheikh Humam Hamoudi; the U.S. embassy; and the United Nations. Although on two occasions certain drafts were leaked to the Iraqi press,[114] no drafts were officially released to the Iraqi public for comment. Very few, if any, were released to members of the committee or to the national assembly.

The absence of drafting and consultation protocols made it extremely difficult for nonexpert Iraqis to follow the process. This background of confusion and the desire for patronage by smaller Iraqi interests led, in turn, to the U.S. embassy gaining still greater publicly visible involvement in Iraqi constitutional politics. The embassy also became the most obvious agent for a range of non-Iraqi advocacy institutions, including the U.S. Commission for International Religious Freedom, Freedom House, and various U.S.-based Iraqi expatriate and women's groups.[115] Regardless of the value of these efforts to improve the constitution, the time pressure increased the likelihood that Iraqis would see foreigners as dominating their constitutional process, minimizing the popular legitimacy of the text.

Losing the Public

If relatively well-organized and well-connected women's and minority groups found it difficult to interact with the constitutional drafters, these difficulties were much greater for ordinary Iraqi citizens. Every meeting of the committee, the national assembly, and the Leadership Council took place behind the blast walls, barbed wire, and gun turrets of Baghdad's International Zone, to which Iraqi citizens could gain entry only after time-consuming and dangerous queuing and multiple body searches. Phone lines and Internet connections throughout the country were either bad or nonexistent. The opportunity for Iraqis to communicate, either formally or informally, with their constituent representatives was practically nil. The progress of the constitution-making process was covered extensively in Iraqi media, and there were indications that the Iraqi public was seized with the subject. However, and notwithstanding the efforts of committee staff, almost none of the popular debate on constitutional matters was formally presented to the committee in time for it to influence the constitutional text.

The Outreach Unit: A Missed Opportunity

In early June, under the management of Dr. Adnan Ali, Chairman Sheikh Hamoudi had established a skeleton secretariat for the committee. The secretariat was to include an outreach unit, responsible for disseminating constitutional information to the public and for receiving and analyzing the public response.[116] However, before June, neither the United States nor the United Nations had taken steps to prepare office space or other resources for the committee secretariat.[117]

As a result, it worked in an ad hoc fashion out of a cramped space in the International Zone's convention center through late July. Though the United Nations, NDI, and USIP each provided practical support to the unit, including funding and staffing, several weeks were lost recruiting the Iraqi staff. In late July, the outreach unit issued a one-page constitutional questionnaire, containing six questions designed to be disseminated throughout the country and returned for entry into a computer database.[118] The completed questionnaires could be placed in public submission boxes or emailed to a Yahoo address (dostorna@yahoo.com). By the end of July, when USIP officers visited the newly established outreach unit offices in downtown Baghdad, a staff of fifty was working around the clock in precarious security conditions to enter piles of public submissions into a computerized database and prepare a report to the committee.

Despite the professionalism and bravery of the outreach unit staff, the shortcomings of the process were striking. No written submissions reached the constitution committee before its demise on August 8. In the circumstances, this was perhaps unsurprising. From its inception in early June, the outreach unit had no more than eight weeks to complete its work. The attempt to conduct a serious national constitutional dialogue in such a short space of time was probably unprecedented; the East Timorese and Afghan constitutional processes, widely regarded as overly hasty, took around six and fifteen months, respectively. The effort in Iraq was all the more remarkable, given the poor and deteriorating security situation, not to mention the nationwide difficulties in delivering basic government services, including power and water. As there was no period of public education on constitutional issues, non-elite Iraqis had little chance to understand even the simple questionnaire. The outreach unit had no clear ability to receive substantial input from the Sunni Arab or even Kurdish regions of Iraq. By July 28, the outreach unit had received only 20,300 submissions. By August 10—after the committee was effectively disbanded—the outreach unit had received 126,000 submissions, but none from Kurdistan or the Sunni Arab regions. As of August 15, it had received around 150,000 submissions, of which only around 20,000 were from the Kurdistan Region and only around 10,000 from Sunni Arab areas (indeed, all 10,000 were from Fallujah). This was a politically volatile imbalance that the outreach unit was ultimately unable to correct.

The outreach unit staff was drawn mainly from religious Shia social networks, and the networks put in place to receive submissions were biased toward Shia areas of Baghdad and other cities. It is unclear whether there were any Sunni Arabs on the unit staff, though in early August, the unit attempted to recruit some Iraqis from smaller ethnic and religious minorities. The unit also distributed boxes in government buildings in Baghdad to allow citizens to submit completed questionnaires and written submissions for later collection; however, the distribution of these boxes was uneven at best.[119] Moreover, there was no ability to enter nonquestionnaire submissions—that is, open-ended submissions—into the database, obviously limiting the range of views that the public could express on constitutional issues. In addition, the results of the extensive constitutional awareness programs run throughout Iraq by international organizations, including NDI and IRI—again, largely in the form of questionnaires—were presented too late for the results to affect the draft constitution, if they were presented at all.

Most important, perhaps, the outreach unit could not circulate a report to the committee members until August 13, after the committee had already been sidelined. Interviews conducted with committee members in early August confirmed that they had not received reports from the outreach unit.[120] This was hardly surprising given the time constraints. As a result, there was little or no chance for the views of the public, as expressed to the committee via the unit, to be taken into account in the preparation of the constitution. By August 13, a mature negotiating draft had existed for some time with no will within the political blocs to reopen settled agreements within that draft. In short, any effort by an Iraqi citizen to communicate in writing to the committee was futile and had no effect on the draft constitution whatsoever. Later statements from the committee secretariat stated that they had received more than 400,000 submissions, but none of these reached the committee itself by the deadline; that fact alone suggests that even a modest deadline extension to allow the committee to digest the weight of the submissions would have offered a tremendous opportunity to interact with at least large parts of the Iraqi public, including Sunni Arabs. But this, of course, did not happen; the 400,000 submissions were wasted.[121] In very precise terms, the national assembly, under tremendous pressure, failed to meet the obligation imposed by Article 60 of the TAL to "receiv[e] proposals from the citizens of Iraq as it writes the constitution."[122]

Conclusion

The pressure-cooker approach that the United States foisted on Iraq's constitution-making process might conceivably have been effective if the central problem was that Iraqi parliamentarians were simply being slow in moving to consolidate their Iraqi identity in constitutional terms, though even in those circumstances, the U.S. haste would have been unwise and, probably, unethical.[123] The problem, however, was something much more profound: No strong Iraqi identity existed at all, and hasty constitution drafting prevented a clear recognition of this fact.[124] Kurds had never adopted an Iraqi identity in their history. Sunni and Shia Arabs, though they might have each expressed some form of Iraqi nationalism, were talking at cross purposes. Sunnis sought a centralized, secular Iraq under Sunni control that might be purged of Saddamism, but otherwise unchanged; those Shiites who rejected federalism (including the party of Moqtada Al Sadr) sought a new religious Iraq, over which they, as the majority, held sway. This clash of competing nationalisms—between those few Sunni and Shia Arabs who were nationalists—spurred the civil war that raged most strongly in 2006 and 2007 and has surely not yet run its course. The regionalist camps within the Shiite and Kurdish parties were relatively uninterested in battling for Baghdad, a capital that could not govern itself, much less the whole of Iraq, and were much more capable of reaching consensus. The superficial problem of Sunni Arab exclusion masked the more fundamental fact that Sunni Arabs could not, in the summer of 2005, reconcile themselves to a federal Iraq: Policy that was directed at making Sunni Arabs part of the central government should have instead encouraged them to regionalize.[125] The tragedy is that there was no time for Sunni regionalists to emerge.

The distance between expectations and reality need not have been so great. None of these political realities in Iraq were especially difficult for the U.S. government to identify, and they were indeed frequently identified by informed U.S. commentators.[126] It should have been clear from the outset that Iraqi constitution making would require a complex three-way treaty-like negotiation in circumstances where nothing could be taken for granted—certainly not a residual shared Iraqi identity. Conventional wisdom among U.S. policymakers presented Iraq as a centralized state undergoing a form of decentralization,[127] when the reality was almost diametrically opposite. Regionally based powers were, in effect, negotiating the terms

of a possible delegation of powers to the center. The three major negotiating blocs—Shia Arab, Kurd, and Sunni Arab—derived their authority (whether they would have admitted it or not) from de facto regional interests, and the power of any central government during the negotiating phase was marginal at best. No faction, not even the Sunni Arabs, saw any tactical reason to delegate power to the Baghdad government of the day, or even to commit wholeheartedly to constitutional negotiations. Any faction could walk out at any time. And the Sunni Arab walkout—the worst of the possible outcomes—not only accelerated the creation of Kurdish and Shiite ministates (probably inevitable) but also guaranteed a durable anger among Iraq's Sunni Arabs that would continue to feed the insurgency (nothing short of disastrous). The absence of the Sunni negotiators from the happy committee press conference of August 29, announcing the new draft, was well publicized and ominous.[128]

One can only assume that the U.S. government missed this fact. No amount of ex post facto fiddling by Ambassador Khalilzad could undo the damage.[129] Some eleventh-hour negotiations in September 2005 resulted in minor adjustments to the final text adopted by the national assembly before submitting the text to referendum. Those changes, designed to woo the Sunni Arab voters, included language stating that Iraq is "a founding and active member of the Arab League," moderating the language denigrating the Baath party; confirming the "unity" of Iraq; and adjusting provisions relating to international covenants and water resources. Immediately before the October referendum, yet another change was introduced to accommodate the Sunni Arab position, promising a process of "constitutional amendment" that would give the Sunni Arabs a theoretical chance to roll back Iraqi federalism if the constitution was approved in the referendum.[130] However, none of these efforts bore fruit: Sunni

Arabs almost universally opposed the constitution in the referendum, the constitution was passed,[131] and the civil war raged on.[132] Kurdistan political offices in the Green Zone were hit by Katyusha rockets in late August, and a rise in anti-Shiite sectarian violence culminated in the demolition of the Golden Mosque in Samarra, triggering a massive increase in sectarian violence. Four years later, by October 2009, no agreement had been reached on constitutional amendment, and the prospect of any substantive amendment, though it may be hoped for if only to secure a weak form of viability for the Iraq state,[133] is uncertain at best. By contrast, the Kurdistan and Shia parties pushed through legislation in October 2006—during yet another Sunni Arab boycott of Parliament—for the creation of a southern "Shiastan" that seems, sooner or later, to be inevitable. Efforts by current prime minister Nuri Al-Maliki to centralize power have been predictably sclerotic and are further alienating Kurdistan and Basra from Baghdad.

In a grim irony, the constitution as a substantive document is a fairly accurate representation of the views of most Iraqis regarding the fate of the Iraqi state. The constitution represents probably the only workable solution to competing interests of Arab nationalism, Kurdish nationalism, and Shia Islamism. Those critics of the constitution who blame the text itself for the poor governance in Iraq exaggerate the likelihood and desirability of a regionalized, heterogeneous Iraq being willing and able to resurrect a strong central government.[134] Those same critics also mistake the strength of regional entities in the Iraq constitution as a deficiency in drafting—an unfortunate ambiguity—rather than as a fairly unambiguous and deliberate dismantling of an excessively powerful central state.[135] As a model for a loose confederation, the constitution is adequate enough. However, this hardly obscures the fact that the procedure by which the Iraqi constitution was created was unacceptably poor. Though Iraq already was a chronically fragmented society, the rushed constitutional process amplified these fissures and squandered an opportunity to narrow them. Something that might have been organic looked very American and artificial. The prospect of a Sunni federalist or even regionalist political bloc emerging in 2005 was reduced to zero. Efforts by some in the United States to pretend that the 2005 process was successful should be seen, at best, as worthless.[136] Iraq in this sense marks a certain high point of neglect, and even cynicism, regarding the value of serious constitutionalism. The international community and the United States in particular promised—and required by law—if not an organic rebirth of the nation through constitutionalism, then at the very least a consensus-based, deliberative, treaty-like modus vivendi. For a moment, constitutionalism may have had a chance, more modestly, to produce a Sunni Arab negotiating position. Instead, the international community delivered to Iraq, and Iraq's leaders acquiesced in, a one-month charade from which not only fragmentation, but also civil war, was virtually guaranteed. It may be that over time, Iraq's Sunni Arabs will learn to live within Iraq's new regionalized federal structure,[137] but they will do so despite Iraq's constitutional process.

Notes

1. Portions of this chapter were originally published in two United States Institute of Peace reports by this author: Jonathan Morrow, "Iraq's Constitutional Process II: An Opportunity Lost," USIP Special Report 155 (Washington, D.C.: USIP, 2005), available at www.usip.org/pubs/special reports/sr155.html (accessed on April 19, 2009); and Jonathan Morrow, "Weak Viability: The Iraqi Federal State and the Constitution Amendment Process," USIP Special Report 168 (Washington, D.C.: USIP, 2006), available at www.usip.org/pubs/specialreports/sr168.html (accessed on April 19, 2009).

2. In August 2005, the month the bulk of the constitution was written, there were 70 attacks per day by "insurgents" throughout Iraq. There were 282 Iraqi military and police killed in that month, between 414 and 2,475 Iraqi civilians killed, and 81 members of the U.S. military killed in hostile incidents. There were 27 multiple fatality bombings, 23 kidnappings of non-Iraqis, and 3,000 insurgents detained or killed: see Iraq Index, Brookings Institution, September 26, 2005, available at www.brookings.edu/fp/saban/iraq/index20050926.pdf (accessed on April 19, 2009).

3. Iraq's other major communities include Shia Arabs (approximately 60 percent of the population) and Kurds (approximately 20 percent of the population). There are no accurate figures available, but these are the commonly accepted approximate numbers. This conventional breakdown of Iraq into three groups is an oversimplification of the many ethnic, religious, and political identities within Iraq's borders, but constitutional negotiations were characterized by this tripartite arrangement.

4. In the predominantly Sunni governorates of Anbar and Salahaddin, more than 96 and 81 percent of voters, respectively, rejected the constitution. See Independent Electoral Commission of Iraq, "Certification of the Constitutional Referendum Final Results," October 25, 2005, available at www.ieciraq.org/English/Frameset_english.htm (accessed on April 19, 2009).

5. More than 78 percent voted yes. Independent Electoral Commission of Iraq, "Certification of the Constitutional Referendum Final Results."

6. Article 110 of the constitution. I note Nathan Brown's argument that the federal government's exclusive power in relation to *wizarat al maliyya* (usually translated as finance) is, in fact, a reference to taxation. However, this is a minority view.

7. Article 112 of the constitution. For an analysis of these critical provisions, see Brendan O'Leary, "Federalizing Natural Resources," in *Iraq: Preventing a New Generation of Conflict,* ed. Markus E. Bouillon, David M. Malone, and Ben Rowswell (New York: International Peace Academy, 2007).

8. Article 115 of the constitution.

9. Phebe Marr narrates Iraq's twentieth-century history as a failure of constitutionalism, in particular the ineffectiveness of fundamental law and sporadic erasure of the distinction between executive and legislative authority: Phebe Marr, *The*

Modern History of Iraq (Boulder, CO: Westview Press, 2004).

10. See, e.g., Larry Diamond, *Squandered Victory: The American Occupation and the Bungled Effort to Bring Democracy to Iraq* (New York: Henry Holt and Company, 2005), p. 49; Noah Feldman, *What We Owe Iraq: War and the Ethics of Nation Building* (Princeton, NJ, and Oxford: Princeton University Press, 2004).

11. The committee's October 2003 report to the interim governing council presented no recommendations. A *New York Times* article had earlier announced the engagement of Noah Feldman, a New York University Law School professor and expert on Arab world constitutions, with the Iraq constitution. Jennifer Lee, "American Will Advise Iraqis on Writing New Constitution," *The New York Times,* May 11, 2003.

12. The approved English translation of the June edict rejected the appointment of constitution drafters and called for a "general election" to choose representatives to a "foundational constitution preparation assembly." For the full text, see www.juancole.com/2003_07_01_juanricole_archive.html (accessed on April 19, 2009) or Feldman, *What We Owe Iraq,* p. 146. For an analysis of the significance of Ayatollah Sistani's fatwas, see Reidar Visser, "Sistani, the United States and Politics in Iraq: From Quietism to Machiavellianism?" Norwegian Institute of International Affairs, 2006, available at http://historiae.org/documents/Sistani.pdf (accessed on April 19, 2009). At this point, the only governance issue in which Ayatollah Sistani expressed interest was constitution making.

13. See www.cpa-iraq.org/government/TAL.html (accessed on April 19, 2009). The TAL was issued in the name of the Iraqi people and formally approved by a group of Iraqi leaders known as the Iraqi Governing Council. After the transfer of sovereignty in June 2004 and the dissolution of the Governing Council, the TAL was published in Iraq's Official Gazette. However, as Andrew Arato notes, the reality was that the council "had no legal or factual independence" from the CPA. Andrew Arato, "From Interim to Permanent Constitution in Iraq?" paper dated October 2005, p. 2 (on file with the author).

14. The full name for this instrument is the Law of Administration for the State of Iraq for the Transitional Period.

15. See, e.g., Ghassan al-Atiyyah, "Memorandum to the Supreme Preparatory Committee for the National Conference," July 14, 2004 (on file with the author). Though the key provisions of the TAL were the subject of negotiation among the Iraqi political factions, the TAL was orchestrated by the U.S. government, drafted in English, and is clearly the product of Western-educated lawyers. One observer of the TAL process, a former adviser to the Kurdistan regional government, has stated that "all deliberations on the law were done in secret and probably fewer than one hundred Iraqis saw a copy of the [interim] constitution before it was promulgated. To write a major law in any democracy—much less a constitution—without public discussion should be unthinkable." Peter Galbraith, "How to Get Out of Iraq," *New York Review of Books,* vol. 15, no. 8, May 13, 2004. Sustained Iraqi engagement with the text was limited to expatriate lawyers Feisal Istrabadi and Salem Chalabi. See also the comment of Larry Diamond, former senior adviser to the Coalition Provisional Authority in Iraq: "The CPA had long been planning a campaign to sell the TAL to the Iraqi people once it was adopted. A British advertising agency with offices in the Middle East had been hired to produce a campaign of emotional and highly symbolic television and newspaper ads. Yet inexplicably, this campaign did not begin until several weeks after the TAL's signing." Larry Diamond, "What Went Wrong in Iraq," *Foreign Affairs,* vol. 83, no. 5 (September–October 2004), pp. 34–56.

16. See Diamond, *Squandered Victory,* p. 183 ff.

17. Transitional Administrative Law, www.cpa-iraq.org/government/TAL.html (accessed on April 19, 2009; emphasis added).

18. The International Crisis Group had noted in November 2003 that "the sense that Iraqis have no ownership of the political process and are blocked from participation in decisions critical to the future of their country is profound." International Crisis Group, *Iraq's Constitutional Challenge,* Middle East Report no. 19, November 13, 2003, p. 26.

19. Article 61(C).

20. Because the TAL was adopted neither by the Security Council nor by a sovereign Iraqi government, its legality remains doubtful.

21. United Nations Security Council Resolution 1546, S/RES/1546 (2004), June 8, 2004, para. 7 (emphasis added).

22. The comparative experience was more influential within the United Nations, which had borne direct responsibility for constitution making in East Timor and Afghanistan; this is evident in the papers circulated by Jamal Benomar, former adviser on Iraq to Ambassador Lakhdar Brahimi and senior official of the United Nations Development Program,

in 2004, including "Constitution-Making, Peace-Building and National Reconciliation: Lessons Learned from the Constitution-Making Processes of Post-Conflict Countries" and "Constitution-Making in Iraq: Framework and Options for an Effective, Participatory, Inclusive and Transparent Process" (copies on file with the author).

23. Statement by Ambassador Bremer before the House Armed Services Committee, U.S. House of Representatives, September 25, 2003. It was, notably, Bremer's primary (and unrealized) goal that he personally put in place a permanent constitution for Iraq—though not one that would reflect majoritarian Iraqi Islamist views. See generally L. Paul Bremer III and Malcolm McConnell, *My Year in Iraq* (New York: Simon and Schuster, 2006); and Rajiv Chandrasekaran, *Imperial Life in the Emerald City* (New York: Knopf, 2006).

24. International Crisis Group, *Iraq's Constitutional Challenge,* p. 2.

25. Author's conversation with a young Sunni Arab engineer, Baghdad, November 2004.

26. Iraqi Prospect Organisation, *Iraqi Constitution: Iraqi Thoughts,* December 2003, p. 8, available at www.iprospect.org.uk/rep8dec.html (accessed on April 19, 2009).

27. Conversation with the author, Baghdad, April 2005. Dr. Shahristani spent eleven years imprisoned by the Hussein regime, much of it in solitary confinement. At the time of this writing, he is the Iraqi minister of oil.

28. For an explanation of Iraq's recent political history as an example of liberal consociation, see John McGarry and Brendan O'Leary, "Iraq's Constitution of 2005: Liberal Consociation as Political Prescription," *International Journal of Constitutional Law,* vol. 5, no. 4 (2007), pp. 670–98.

29. For an account of that episode, see Samantha Power, *"A Problem from Hell": America and the Age of Genocide* (New York: Basic Books, 2002).

30. See, generally, Brendan O'Leary, John McGarry, Khaled Salih, eds., *The Future of Kurdistan in Iraq* (Philadelphia: University of Pennsylvania Press, 2005).

31. Polling centers were set up next to voting booths. The Kurdistan regional government claimed that more than 98 percent of those polled preferred Iraqi Kurdistan's independence to its continuation as part of Iraq. These claims seem plausible, and Western news outlets reported the strong preference. See, e.g., Ellen Knickmeyer, "Iraqi Kurds Call for Referendum," *Washington Post,* July 23, 2005.

32. For two accounts of the Sunni Arab insurgency, see Amatzia Baram, "Who Are the Insurgents? Iraq's Sunni Arab Rebels," USIP Special Report 134 (April 2004), available at www.usip.org/pubs/specialreports/sr134.html (accessed on April 20, 2009); and International Crisis Group, *In Their Own Words: Reading the Iraqi Insurgency*, Middle East Report no. 50, February 15, 2006.

33. The International Crisis Group in November 2003, aware of the problems earlier than most, said that "Iraq's constitutional process must begin to move forward, but at a deliberate pace and in a transparent and consultative manner." International Crisis Group, *Iraq's Constitutional Challenge*, Middle East Report no. 19, November 13, 2003, p. ii.

34. The only procedural provisions implemented, in the end, were those requiring an election by January 2005 (art. 30) and the establishment of a Federal Supreme Court (art. 44). Nor did the TAL provide, as Bremer had hoped (see Diamond, *Squandered Victory*, p. 16), a basis for the permanent constitution.

35. The U.S.-based National Democratic Institute for International Affairs (NDI) found that by April 2005, "almost every participant" in national, cross-sectarian focus group research "is of the opinion that the Iraqi citizens should be involved in the preparation of the constitution." David M. Dougherty, *Iraqi Voices: Public Attitudes and Political Opportunity in Transition; Findings from Focus Groups with Iraqi Men and Women (Conducted April 13–15, 2005)*, National Democratic Institute for International Affairs, p. 32, available at www.accessdemocracy.org/library/1921_iq_focusgroups_060105.pdf (accessed April 20, 2009).

36. For a contemporary argument in favor of a province-based electoral system, also citing the argument that a provincial system would have allowed for a delay in polling in the troubled Sunni Arab provinces, see Larry Diamond, "Getting to Elections in Iraq," unpublished paper, November 2004 (on file with the author).

37. This model was ultimately adopted for the December 2005 parliamentary elections in which fifty-five Sunni Arab legislators were elected.

38. See, e.g., *New York Times*, editorial, January 12, 2005.

39. Alissa Rubin, "46 Groups Will Boycott Iraq Vote," *New York Times*, November 19, 2004. See also "Statement by the Iraqi National Foundation Congress on the Elections," November 18, 2004, (copy on file with the author): "The illegitimacy of the occupation and the attacks on Iraqi cities, es-pecially the savage massacres in Falluja, categorically preclude sound participation in the political process under occupation and denial of sovereignty. How can a national dialogue and a political process proceed while crimes are being routinely committed against the people?"

40. See, e.g., Michael Howard, "Main Sunni Party Pulls Out of Election," *The Guardian*, December 28, 2004.

41. The omission of a special majority for parliamentary approval of the text was probably an oversight; none of the authors of the TAL have provided a reason for the unusually low threshold. In hindsight, the practical effect of such a mistake was negligible, however, given the three-governorate veto provision, which effectively required near unanimity of support in the parliamentary factions for any constitutional text.

42. In May 2005, the Muslim Scholars Association began to threaten to invoke the three-governorate veto. See Nancy Youssef, "Iraq Set to Take Major Step toward Drafting Constitution," Knight Ridder, May 14, 2005.

43. Article 61(C) states: "The general referendum will be successful and the draft constitution ratified if a majority of the voters in Iraq approve and if two-thirds of the voters in three or more governorates do not reject it." This provision gave great power to any organized region of Iraq—including Kurdistan—against an aspiring national government. Andrew Arato argues, persuasively, that the only "genuine bargaining" on the TAL was between the Kurdistan regional government and the United States on this and other key provisions: "The immediate reason . . . was that it was these two parties that held at the time something like state power in Iraq." Arato, "From Interim to Permanent Constitution in Iraq?" p. 6.

44. Article 61(F) of the TAL reads: "If necessary, the president of the National Assembly, with the agreement of a majority of the members' votes, may certify to the Presidency Council no later than 1 August 2005 *that there is a need for additional time to complete the writing of the draft constitution.* The Presidency Council shall then extend the deadline for writing the draft constitution for only six months" (emphasis added). Transitional Administrative Law, available at www.cpa-iraq.org/government/TAL.html (accessed on April 20, 2009).

45. Diamond notes that the reason for including the six-month extension in the TAL was because "we all worried that even six months might not be enough for the [constitutional] convention to complete its work in a manner that involved the Iraqi public." See *Squandered Victory,* p. 155.

46. Roula Khalaf, "Boycott Groups See Election as Just 'Small Step,'" *Financial Times,* January 27, 2005.

47. International Republican Institute, *Survey of Public Opinion,* April 11–April 20, 2005, available at www.iri.org/mena/iraq/pdfs/2005-05-05-Iraq%20Poll%20April%20April.pdf (accessed July 14, 2009). The press release accompanying the survey results stated: "Iraqis also want all groups to participate in the constitutional process. More than 35 percent strongly agree and another 35 percent generally agree that those who did not or could not participate in the January 30 election have a right to contribute to writing the constitution."

48. The subcommittees' themes included basic principles; system of government; federalism and local government; constitutional guarantees, rights, and duties; and transitional and amendment provisions.

49. In one early proposal of Deputy Speaker Hussain Shahristani and Committee Chairman Hamoudi, additional Sunni Arab participation was to be limited to providing subcommittees with advice. See e.g., National Public Radio (U.S.), Morning Edition, interview by Peter Kenyon with Sheikh Humam Hamoudi, May 23, 2005. In another proposal, the 55-member committee would be expanded to 101 members. See e.g., "Forty-Six New Members to Write the Iraqi Constitution," *Al-Taakhi* (Baghdad), May 24, 2005.

50. A number arrived at so as to maximize Sunni participation without exceeding the representation of the Kurdistan Alliance representation.

51. The fifteen additional Sunni Arab members were accompanied by ten Sunni Arab non-member experts. Of the original fifty-five members of the committee, three were Sunni Arabs who had been elected to the national assembly: the deputy chairman, Dr. Adnan al-Janabi; the former oil minister, Dr. Thamir Abbas Al-Ghadban; and Abd-al-Rahman Sa'id Husein al-Nu'aimi. The enlarged body was notionally renamed a commission (*hay'a 'ameh*) but was continually referred to in practice as "the committee" (*lajneh*).

52. As distinct from unanimous decision-making, thus permitting, at least in theory, the principle of "sufficient consensus" to permit decisions to be made over the objections of a small but unspecified number of members.

53. Assembly Speaker Hajim Al-Hassani, Deputy Speaker Hussein Shahristani, and Committee Chairman Sheikh Hamoudi each held the view that civil-society representatives should not be on the committee.

54. Meghan O'Sullivan traveled to Baghdad in the weeks prior to the drafting of the constitution to press Iraqi leaders to meet the initial August 15, 2005 deadline.

55. Interviews with NBC News and Al Arabiya television in Baghdad, April 13, 2005.

56. See, e.g., "Rice Makes Surprise Visit to Iraq: U.S. Secretary of State Urges Leaders to Get Constitution Done," CNN.com, May 16, 2005.

57 On July 26, Secretary Rumsfeld made an unannounced visit to Baghdad and told reporters, "We don't want any delays. Now's the time to get on with it." Eric Schmitt, "Rumsfeld Presses Iraqi Leaders on Constitution and Insurgency," *New York Times,* July 28, 2005.

58. He stated at a press conference at the White House on April 28, 2005, of then–prime minister of Iraq, Iyad Allawi, "He understands the need for a timely write of the constitution." See White House press release, April 28, 2005.

59. This was the standard talking point on the subject for U.S. officials in Baghdad. Robert Ford, the head of the U.S. embassy's political section, attempted to prevent the U.S. Institute of Peace, an independent federal institution, from even discussing the possibility of an extension of the August 15 deadline with Iraqis.

60. See, e.g., television interview with Deputy Secretary of State Robert Zoellick, conducted by Sawad Kazum of Al Arabiya, Baghdad, April 13, 2005: "Well, this is a topic that I discussed with all the Iraqi officials—Prime Minister Allawi, the President, Prime Minister-designate, the Speaker— and I get a sense that all of them want to stick to the timeframe that Iraqis have set to try to get that constitution done by August 15 … So, you know, constitutions—the U.S. Constitution was drafted in less time than that and so right now the Iraqi people have a start through the TAL."

61. Professor Yash Ghai and Mr. Scott Carlson, constitution process experts provided to the committee by USIP, provided this advice in "Constitutional Timetable Options with December 2005 Parliamentary Elections," a memorandum dated July 11, 2005 (on file with the author). The memorandum concluded that "to fulfill the TAL public participation mandate, some form of extension is needed" (p. 4).

62. Othman was quoted as saying, "If you're talking about a consensus, something on which we all agree, I certainly don't think it can be done on time. This is something too important to rush. We shouldn't be driven by America's domestic agenda." Liz Sly, "Iraqi Constitution Writers Find Time Is Running Out," *Chicago Tribune,* July 26, 2005.

63. See also Feryad Rawandozi, "Opinion: Constitution Deadline Should Have Been Delayed Earlier," *Al-Ittihad,* August 17, 2005. *Al-Ittihad* is the newspaper of the Patriotic Union of Kurdistan.

64. Ambassador Peter Galbraith, interview by Jim Lehrer, *The Newshour with Jim Lehrer,* PBS, May 4, 2005: "My sense is that if the constitutional process doesn't work, that Iraq would do well to set it aside. . . . There are many issues that can be handled practically, but which could make the situation in Iraq much worse, in fact contribute to the breakup of the country, if they are tried to be resolved in a constitutional process."

65. See, e.g., Hannah Allam and Alaa al Baldawy, "Shiite Cleric to Lead Panel Drafting Iraqi Constitution," Knight Ridder, May 24, 2005.

66. See also statements from former president Sheikh Ghazi al-Yawer, Iraqi Al-Sharqiyah television, May 2, 2005; and Dr. Bahaa Mayah, adviser to Prime Minister Jaafari, in Richard Beeston, "Squabbles as Iraq Prepares to Draw Up a Constitution," *The Times* (London), May 14, 2005.

67. National Democratic Institute for International Affairs, *Iraqi Voices: Public Attitudes and Political Opportunity in Transition, Findings from Focus Groups with Iraqi Men and Women (Conducted April 13–25, 2005),* available at www.accessdemocracy.org/library/1921_iq_focusgroups_060105.pdf (accessed on April 20, 2009), p. 31: "Iraqis are eager for stability and want the Constitutional Committee to draft a constitution as quickly as possible. However, many focus group participants expressed a desire for the Committee to take the necessary time to ensure the creation of a comprehensive and effective constitution and to sufficiently educate the Iraqi people on the constitutional process."

68. "An Iraqi Constitution," editorial, *New York Times,* August 12, 2005: "It would have been wiser to allow time for compromise and consensus." See also Charles Krauthammer, "Shelve this Deadline," *Washington Post,* July 1, 2005.

69. See International Crisis Group, "Iraq: Don't Rush the Constitution," Middle East Report no. 42, June 8, 2005; Nathan Brown, "Iraq's Constitution Process Plunges Ahead," Carnegie Endowment for International Peace, Policy Outlook, July

2005, available at www.carnegieendowment.org/files/PO19Brown.pdf (accessed on April 20, 2009).

70. For a discussion of this phenomenon in the U.S. handling of Iraq policy—including the constitution—see, e.g., Peter Baker and Robin Wright, "In Iraq, Bush Pushed for Deadline Democracy: Timeline Yields Order, Not Peace," *Washington Post*, December 11, 2005.

71. For an account of this drafting period from the perspective of two State Department lawyers then in the U.S. embassy in Baghdad, see Ashley S. Deeks and Matthew D. Burton, "Iraq's Constitution: A Drafting History," *Cornell International Law Journal,* vol. 40, no. 1 (2007), pp. 2–84.

72. Talabani was leader of the Patriotic Union of Kurdistan (PUK) and president of Iraq; Barzani was leader of the Kurdistan Democratic Party (KDP) and was president of the Kurdistan region.

73. Most of the Shia elites speak the language of their coreligionists in Persia, and the Kurds' native tongue is an Indo-European language closely related to Persian. In the Green Zone in the summer of 2005, it was often noted, wryly, that the Arabic word for constitution—*dustour*—is actually a Persian import. But by the time the text reached the *matbagh,* the drafting was done in English.

74. *Al-Sabah* paraphrased the sentiment in their headline of August 22, 2005: "US Embassy to Sunni Arabs: 'This Is an Iraqi Matter, and We Have Nothing to Do with It.'"

75. Sheikh Abd al-Nair al-Janabi, reported in Baghdad daily newspaper *Al-Sabah* on August 22, 2005. Former Baathist and lead Sunni constitutional negotiator Salih al-Mutlak was also quoted in the same report as saying: "We were not met, and both lists are trying to finish the draft without us. We contacted the American Embassy in order to get to know the situation, and we were notified that that was an Iraqi matter and the Embassy had nothing to do with it."

76. The proposal of one senior Kurdish member of the constitution committee, Dr. Saedi Barzinji, that Kurdish autonomy should be protected in the constitution by a set of international guarantees did not find its way into the final draft. That proposal will likely be proved to have been prescient.

77. Article 110 of the constitution.

78. Article 115 of the constitution.

79. In early June, Shia and Kurdish committee members—probably with U.S. embassy encouragement—rejected as too time-consuming a proposal to identify "grass roots" Sunni Arab constitutional drafters through a multiweek regional caucus. The Iraq Institute of Peace, a nongovernmental interfaith dialogue organization with strong Sunni Arab tribal connections, had tested the idea. As they were the only NGO able to open offices in the Sunni Arab heartland without being attacked, they convened a number of large Sunni meetings in May, including a May 2 conference of 800 Sunni Arab leaders, which elected ten representatives and formulated a set of precise constitutional recommendations—later overlooked.

80. The terms of that Kurd-Shia agreement gave to one or more of Iraq's eighteen provinces the right to "organize into a region" following a referendum in the respective province or provinces.

81. Article 61(G) of the TAL provided that "if the National Assembly does not complete writing the draft permanent constitution by 15 August 2005 and does not request extension of the deadline in Article 61(D) above, the provisions of Article 61(E), above, shall be applied." Article 61(E)—the provision dealing with the consequences of a failed referendum—stated that "the National Assembly shall be dissolved. Elections for a new National Assembly shall be held no later than 15 December 2005."

82. There can be little doubt that some Sunni negotiators, including Saleh Mutlaq, were attempting to precipitate this crisis; private comments of moderate assembly speaker Hajim Al-Hassani (April 2005) suggest that he too was entertaining this view.

83. Several of the fifteen Sunni Arab members of the committee were accused of being members of Saddam Hussein's Baath Party, including Sheikh Mijbal Issa (later assassinated) and Haseeb Arif. See, e.g., James Glanz, "Baathists May Be Joining Iraq's Constitution Drafters," *New York Times,* July 1, 2005. Some of the committee members, including Saleh Mutlaq, publicly aligned themselves with Baathism.

84. Although they do not conceive of themselves as a national minority, Iraq's Sunni Arabs have similar interests to other Iraqi ethnic and sectarian minority groups that are concentrated in particular areas and neighborhoods of the country. Far from having a real interest in a strong central government, they must look to the conventional political methods of preserving minority rights, including some of the minority and regional self-government and veto powers that the much-reviled Iraqi constitution provides. In particular, perhaps they should ensure that Iraq's Sunni Arab areas, oil-poor at least for the time being, receive from other regions their

constitutional entitlement of a share of Iraq's national oil revenues proportional to their share of the national population.

85. Author's conversation with Moamer Alkubesi, director, National Constitutional Society, Baghdad, August 2005. Alkubesi, a leading Sunni Arab lawyer from Fallujah and interlocutor with the hard-line Association of Muslim Scholars, had early seen the merits of federalism as the solution for Iraq—including power sharing on oil management and other sensitive matters—quite apart from Kurdish aspirations.

86. Those same lawyers were trying to address a major but clearly soluble grievance among Sunni Arab elites: that the Kurdish and Shia parties overlooked Sunni Arab technical constitutional expertise. The compressed timetable virtually eliminated any engagement with Iraqi technical experts of any sect or ethnicity. Iraq's federal judiciary had no opportunity to influence the draft; government ministries (such as the Ministry of Justice) were in the same situation.

87. Presentation by Leslie L. Campbell, senior associate and director of Middle East programs, National Democratic Institute, at U.S. Institute of Peace, Washington, D.C., October 2005.

88. *Constitutional Baseline Survey, Conducted on Behalf of the Transitional National Assembly, Constitution Drafting Committee,* copy on file with the author. If anything, these figures understate the degree of Sunni Arab distrust of federalism, as for security reasons, interviews could not be conducted in the overwhelmingly Sunni Arab Anbar governorate.

89. The results of a USIP-convened meeting of Iraq's Sunni Arab leaders in February 2006 suggested that, with time, incrementally more realistic positions could have been achieved: see Jonathan Morrow, "Weak Viability: The Iraqi Federal State and the Constitution Amendment Process," USIP Special Report 168 (July 2006), available at www. usip.org/pubs/specialreports/sr168.html (accessed on April 22, 2009).

90. One Kurdistan member of the committee, Dr. Saedi Barzinji, walked out of the committee over issues of regional autonomy.

91. On August 6, Massoud Barzani, Kurdistan region president, addressed the Kurdistan parliament on the negotiations, and Prime Minister Nerchivan Barzani articulated a set of "red lines" in "Why Kurdistan Insists on Kirkuk," *Financial Times*, August 15, 2005.

92. Those negotiators included former U.S. diplomat Peter Galbraith and University of Maryland professor Karol Soltan.

93. Copy on file with the author.

94. Hadi al-Amiri, head of the Badr Brigades, announced to the gathering: "Federalism has to be in all of Iraq. They are trying to prevent the Shi'ites from enjoying their own federalism. We have to persist in forming one region in the south or else we will regret it. What have we got from the central government except death?" See "Shi'ite Militia Calls for State in the South," Reuters, August 11, 2005. The August 11 declaration by SCIRI had been foreshadowed by smaller breakaway movements in Basra. See, e.g., Steven Vincent, "In the South, A Bid to Loosen Baghdad's Grip," *Christian Science Monitor*, June 28, 2005; Edward Wong, "Secular Shiites in Iraq Seek Autonomy in Oil-Rich South," *New York Times*, June 30, 2005. Similar regionalist initiatives were also made public in the central Iraqi cities of Kerbala (*Sharq Al-Awsat*, June 7, 2005) and Najaf (www.nahrain.com/d/news/05/06/16/nhr0616e.html; accessed April 22, 2009).

95. Nathan Brown observes that the fifteen-member Sunni Arab delegation on the constitution committee preferred to call themselves "representatives of those boycotting the election." Nathan Brown, "Iraq's Constitution Process Plunges Ahead," Carnegie Endowment for International Peace, Policy Outlook, July 2005, p. 7, available at www.carnegieendowment.org/files/PO19Brown.pdf (accessed April 22, 2009).

96. Haysom is a South African who served as Nelson Mandela's legal adviser during the South African constitutional negotiations and advised on many other constitutional problems, including those in Sudan, Burundi, East Timor, and Lebanon.

97. The goal of this strategy was probably questionable; the implementation certainly was. A few days after Ambassador Khalilzad did Washington's bidding by rejecting Haysom's oil provisions, new provisions emerged from the Kurdish-Shia negotiating table that gave oil powers almost entirely to the regions. By that stage, Ambassador Khalilzad had realized that a centralized oil sector was not on the table and consecrated the deal.

98. Yash Ghai, Jill Cottrell, and Bereket Selassie, "Paper on System of Autonomies in Iraq," August 6, 2005, copy on file with the author.

99. Interview with Dr. Saad Jawad Al-Saati, Baghdad, August 2005.

100. See Alissa Rubin, "Envoy Delivers U.S. Vision for Iraqi Constitution," *Los Angeles Times*, August 12, 2005. The U.S. version of the constitution removed an article that would have incorporated international human rights standards into Iraq domestic law.

101. See Ali Al-Basri, "The Telephone Call and Its Effect on Influencing the Draft Constitution," editorial, Iraq 4 All News, August 28, 2005, http://iraq4all.org ("Day after day U.S. interventions in the drafting of the Iraqi constitution reveal themselves.").

102. Shortly after the referendum, an ABC News poll conducted in November 2005 found that just 27 percent of people in Sunni Arab areas of Iraq approved of the constitution, compared with more than 80 percent in mixed, Kurdish, and Shiite areas. ABC News poll, "Where Things Stand in Iraq," December 12, 2005, available at abcnews.go.com/images/Politics/1000a1IraqWhereThingsStand.pdf (accessed on April 22, 2009).

103. See BBC News, "Iraq PM 'Confident of Agreement,'" August 23, 2005, available at news.bbc.co.uk/1/hi/world/middle_east/4176610.stm (accessed on April 22, 2009).

104. The parliament's announcement of a further delay did not set a date for a future session.

105. The adoption of the constitutional text by the assembly took place without a vote.

106. Interview with Dr. Sallama Al-Khafaji, member of the national assembly, Baghdad, August 2005.

107. The first such charge was voiced by Sunni hard-liner Saleh Mutlaq, who said when the August 15 deadline was not met that any subsequent extension "wouldn't be legal. . . . I think they may do it, but if they do, we [the Sunnis] will object to it in the strongest terms." Reuters, August 15, 2005.

108. On September 8, 2005, Nicholas Haysom of the United Nations stated that "we are awaiting a text certified by the National Assembly." See "UN Holds Presses on Iraq Constitution," Reuters, September 8, 2005.

109. October 12 was the date of an agreement to a schedule of "amendments" recorded in a letter from Sheikh Humam Hamoudi, "Amendments to the Constitution," letter dated October 13, 2005 (copy on file with the author).

110. Private conversation with Bakhtiar Amin, the Kurdish former minister for human rights in Iraq, May 2007, Erbil.

111. Private conversations with the author, July 2005, Baghdad.

112. Private email to the author, November 2005. See also Thalif Deen, "Iraqi Women May Lose Basic Rights Under the Constitution," Inter Press News Service, July 23, 2005.

113. See, e.g., "Special Representative of the Secretary-General for Iraq, Mr. Ashraf Qazi, Met with Sheikh Harith Al Dhari," June 29, 2005; "Special Representative of the Secretary-General for Iraq, Mr. Ashraf Qazi, Met with Representatives of the Turcoman Front," July 24, 2005; "Special Representative of the Secretary-General for Iraq, Mr. Ashraf Qazi, Met the President of the Council of Iraqi Minorities," August 4, 2005; and "The Special Representative of the Secretary-General for Iraq Recognizes Significant Public Participation in the Iraqi Constitution-Making Process," August 4, 2005. All press releases, UN Assistance Mission in Iraq, available at www.uniraq.org/newsroom/press releases.asp (accessed on April 22, 2009).

114. The Iraqi newspaper *Al-Hayat* published extracts from the draft on July 25; *Al-Sabah* published a draft on July 26. It is perhaps remarkable that public participation in constitution making has relied so much on leaks. A leaked draft was the beginning of public involvement in Spain in 1978, one of the most successful constitution-making processes in recent times. See Andrea Bonime-Blanc's chapter on Spain in this volume.

115. For a detailed criticism of this phenomenon, see Nathan Brown, "Constitution Drafting Update," Carnegie Endowment for International Peace, August 8, 2005, available at www.carnegie endowment.org/files/ConstitutionDraftingUpdate. pdf (accessed on April 22, 2009).

116. The outreach unit structure and mandate was prepared with the assistance of UN and USIP experts, including Scott Carlson, who had advised the Albanian constitutional commission.

117. The status of the outreach unit was somewhat complicated by the appearance of a proposal from the government that the minister for national assembly affairs, Dr. Safa al-Safi, would establish "a ministerial committee under the name of the Committee of Supporting and Encouraging National Dialogue on Popular Participation in Drafting the Constitution." See "Defense Department Briefing by Dr. Safa al-Safi," Combined Press Information Center, Baghdad, May 27, 2005. It is not clear that the ministerial committee conducted many constitutional dialogues.

118. The questions included the following, with multiple-choice options under each question: "Which form of government do you prefer?" (options including presidential, parliamentary, mixed); "What is the most suitable form for the distribution of power in Iraq?" (a range of federalist and unitary state options); "What is the role of Islam in legislation?" (a range of options from Islam as the only source for legislation to no mention of Islam or religion); "Who owns the natural wealth (such as oil, gas, etc.)? The public? What, in your view, is the ideal way to distribute it?"; "How can women's rights be protected in your view?"; "Which of the following issues needs to be mentioned in the constitution?" (options include de-Baathification, integrity commission, special court.) I am grateful to Dr. Yasin Al-Jibori for his assistance in translating this and other original documents.

119. USIP staff members in Baghdad, living in various neighborhoods, were unable over several weeks to locate a single box. The UNAMI note on July 24, 2005, on the collection of submissions from the boxes, stated that "except for Al Anbar, Salah Ad Din, Ninevah, At Tameem and Diyala governorates, regular collection takes place every couple of days." The named governorates are, of course, those with large Sunni Arab majorities and minorities.

120. Private conversations with Adnan Al-Janabi and Hunain Al-Qaddo, August 2005, Baghdad.

121. As of December 2006, it was unclear where the records of the constitution committee were being stored. The deputy chairman of the constitution review committee, Ayad Al-Samarraie, stated in a private conversation with the author on December 7, 2006, that he did not know what had happened to the committee's library.

122. The United Nations Office for Program Services interview study of July 20–25, 2005, showed, remarkably, that when asked, "Have you ever participated in a discussion, forum, or other event on the constitution?" 93 percent of Iraqis answered no. When asked, "How willing would you be to attend a live public forum on the constitution?" nearly 60 percent of Iraqis answered that they were either very willing or somewhat willing. *Constitutional Baseline Survey, Conducted on Behalf of the Transitional National Assembly, Constitution Drafting Committee,* copy on file with the author.

123. See, e.g., the third printing of Feldman, *What We Owe Iraq,* pp. 135–36, in which he makes this argument. Feldman's and other intelligent commentaries on U.S. policy toward Iraq's constitution making do not quite appreciate, however, the degree to which Iraqi identity was not capable of being expressed in constitutional language.

124. For one excellent dispassionate exposition of this fact from a longtime observer of Iraq, see Patrick Cockburn, *The Occupation: War and Resistance in Iraq* (London: Verso, 2006).

125. To this extent, the prescription of Larry Diamond that "Iraq needs . . . a political accommodation with the bulk of the Sunni population that feels marginalized from the emerging political order" (*Squandered Victory,* p. 316) addresses only part of the problem. Marina Ottaway of the Carnegie Endowment for International Peace was an early advocate for U.S. policy to work to create a "viable Sunni region," a policy that sadly was never implemented: see Marina Ottaway, "Back from the Brink: A Strategy for Iraq," Carnegie Endowment for International Peace Policy Brief 43, November 2005.

126. The views of advocates of the partition and regionalization of Iraq, including Leslie Gelb, Senator Joseph Biden, and Peter Galbraith, were dismissed out of hand by U.S. policymakers at least until the end of the George W. Bush administration.

127. It is ironic that many Sunni Arab Iraqis and their sympathizers since have accused the United States of adopting excessively consociational policies in Iraq, when in fact U.S. policy in the Bush administration ran in precisely the opposition direction.

128. "The 15 Boycotters Refuse to Sign the Draft Constitution," *Al-Sabah,* August 29, 2005, p. 2.

129. Even the strongest proponents of post-August renegotiation, including the International Crisis Group, acknowledged that a "last-ditch, determined effort to broker a true compromise" had doubtful chances of success. International Crisis Group, *Unmaking Iraq: A Constitutional Process Gone Awry,* Middle East Briefing no. 19, September 26, 2005, p. 1.

130. See Sheikh Humam Hamoudi, "Amendments to the Constitution," letter dated October 13, 2005, setting out the schedule of amendments (copy on file with the author). On October 12, after concluding the agreement, Ambassador Khalilzad announced in a Baghdad speech: "At the core of their agreement is a decision to mandate the next democratically elected Council of Representatives to review the constitution after its passage and recommend any amendments necessary to cement

it as a national compact. This constitution, the basis of Iraq's emerging democratic government and the road map to its future, will be a living document, as all enduring constitutions are." See Embassy of the United States, Baghdad, Iraq, "U.S. Envoy Welcomes Compromise on Iraq's Draft Constitution," available at iraq.usembassy.gov/iraq/101305_compromise.html (accessed on April 22, 2009).

131. A number of informed observers commented ahead of the referendum that notwithstanding any merits of the constitutional text, the politics of its production meant that it would be better if the constitution were rejected. See, e.g., Bernard Gwertzman, "Brown: Best Hope for Iraq Is Rejection of Draft Constitution and Reopening of Negotiations," Council on Foreign Relations, August 29, 2005, available at www.cfr.org/publication/8772/brown.html (accessed on April 22, 2009).

132. For a discussion of the connection between the constitution and Sunni Arab violence, see International Crisis Group, *In Their Own Words: Reading the Insurgency,* Middle East Report no. 50, February 15, 2006, p. 16 ("Armed groups condemn the constitution as a recipe for partition, a symptom of politicians' opportunism and selfishness and evidence of U.S. plans to break up the country"). For the role of the constitution and the civil war, see also International Crisis Group, *The Next Iraqi War? Sectarianism and Civil Conflict,* Middle East Report no. 52, February 27, 2006.

133. See, e.g., the Iraq Study Group report, which placed great hope for national reconciliation on the prospect of constitutional amendment, with little chance of a result. *The Iraq Study Group Report* (New York: Vintage Books, 2006), Recommendation 26, p. 65.

134. In this respect I disagree with the analyses of the International Crisis Group. See, e.g., International Crisis Group, *Unmaking Iraq: A Constitutional Process Gone Awry,* Middle East Briefing no. 19, September 26, 2005, p.1 ("The second casualty was the text itself. Key passages, such as those dealing with decentralization and with responsibility for the power of taxation, are ambiguous and so carry the seeds of future discord"). For variations on this theme from Iraqis who were ideologically committed to a future Iraqi nation-state of a unitary (non-federal) sort, see also Hatem Mukhlis, "Voting 'Yes' to Chaos," *The New York Times,* October 18, 2005; Kanan Makiya, "Present at the Disintegration," *The New York Times,* December 11, 2005.

135. This fact has attracted a historians' debate on the question of whether Iraq was, in the wake of World War I, an artificial construct, or whether there was some preexisting Iraqi identity that will be sufficiently durable to reemerge from the 2005 constitutional carve-up. See, e.g., Reidar Vissar, "Centralism and Unitary State Logic in Iraq from Midhat Pasha to Jawad al-Maliki: A Continuous Trend?" April 22, 2006, available at www.historiae.org (accessed April 22, 2009). It is not clear that this debate, and the contested historical trend lines to which the debate refers, will affect the juridical and political realities in a fragmented Iraq.

136. See, e.g., the National Security Council, National Strategy for Victory in Iraq, November 2005, pp. 15–16 ("In June, the national leg-islature formally invited non-elected Sunni Arab leaders to join constitutional negotiations, demonstrating that leaders from all communities understood the importance of a constitution with input from Iraq's major groups.... Signs of vibrant political life are sprouting. The constitutional drafting committee received more than 500,000 public comments on various provisions").

137. There are signs that a viable Sunni Arab Iraqi regionalist political leadership may now be emerging. See, e.g., "Tribes in the Western Region Form a Police Force, Fight al-Qaida," *Ad-Dustoor*, April 29, 2007.

PART VII

CONCLUSION

22

Designing Constitution-Making Processes

Lessons from the Past, Questions for the Future

Laurel E. Miller

This volume aims to inform the decisions of future constitution makers and experts advising them by offering an array of practical ideas, suggestions, and warnings about how to shape constitution-making processes. The volume uses a case study approach in order to draw lessons from the real-world experiences of past constitution makers. The case studies contain a wealth of information and analysis concerning the diverse procedural choices made by domestic and international actors responsible for organizing constitution-making processes—and the consequences of those choices—in a wide variety of circumstances.[1] As discussed below, the case studies also demonstrate the critical influence of context on process design choices, and on how well or poorly particular approaches to constitution making worked. Consequently, future constitution makers can benefit by using this volume to evaluate whether the circumstances in which they find themselves are more or less similar to those surrounding

particular past cases, and, thus, whether they would be well or ill advised to adopt similar approaches.[2]

The premise of this study is that the nature of a constitution-making process matters. The overarching objective of this concluding chapter is to explore what the nineteen case studies and two thematic chapters show about the ways in which process matters. To meet that objective, this chapter derives practical advice from comparisons among the case studies. Above all, these comparisons reveal that one-size-fits-all generalizations about good practice are hard to come by, and that attempting to synthesize the case studies into a model constitution-making process would be unrealistic. But they also reveal many insights into the procedural options available to constitution makers and into patterns of constitution-making practice. This chapter discusses both lessons concerning the key elements of constitution-making processes that surface in various groups of cases as well as themes that emerge from the study as a whole. In addition to the conclusions discussed here, the individual case studies stand on their own as sources of lessons, tied to the particular contexts of the constitution-making exercises they examine.

As the introduction to this volume indicates, recognition is growing that constitution-making processes merit attention just as the outcomes of those processes do.[3] The two thematic chapters in this volume provide legal and intellectual support for this view through an examination of international conventions and an expanding body of law. Though the case studies do not address the relative significance of constitutional substance and constitution-making process, work conducted under the auspices of the United States Institute of Peace's (USIP) Project on Constitution-Making, Peace Building, and National Reconciliation (described in the introduction)—including the material in this volume—demonstrates the importance of process and the increasing regard for process in the public and academic discourses on constitution making.[4] Indeed, one theme evident throughout this volume is that very many people involved in these constitution-making exercises—from citizens participating in public consultations to technical managers to autocrats resisting genuine democracy—behaved in a manner indicating that they believed the nature of the process mattered. That reality should be kept firmly in mind, even while grappling with the intellectual difficulties of determining precisely how process choices matter, and especially how they affect both lasting public sentiments and concrete outcomes. As one example of those difficulties, the thematic chapters and many of the case studies in this volume convey that public participation is a valuable means of democratizing the process of constitution making and legitimating the results, even as they raise complex questions concerning how to ensure the genuineness of

participation mechanisms and measure their effects.[5]

A particular challenge in producing procedural recommendations for future constitution makers is identifying which process choices in the past have led to successful results, against some specified set of criteria for success. The case studies demonstrate that this challenge is not easily met.[6] But among the contributions they make in the search for good practice, the case studies help to define a set of questions concerning assessment of concrete and perceptual outcomes, and the connections between process and outcomes, that merits further exploration. For instance, what are the appropriate criteria for judging success or failure in constitution making? Should such labels be applied on the basis of what the resulting constitutional text looks like (e.g., how well it protects human rights or meets some other widely accepted norms or qualitative standards), or whether the document and the process that produced it are well regarded among the citizenry, or how stable the political situation is sometime after the constitution making, or how prosperous the society becomes, or whether the process contributed to developing a culture of constitutionalism or to encouraging citizen involvement in public life? What if some of these or other possible criteria are met, but not others? And how proximate to the constitution making, as well as how long-lasting, must the relevant outcomes be in order to attribute them to specific process choices?

Moreover, how should we assess a constitution-making exercise in which there was broad representation, thorough deliberation, and popular participation—that is, a process that met plausible criteria for democraticness—and which produced a substantively respectable document, but after which the constitution was not implemented and opportunities for political competition were denied?[7] In such a situation, the influence of extra-constitutional factors—the power of an autocrat, civil conflict, or aggressive neighbors, for example—may especially complicate an analysis of the impact of a constitution-making process. Considering this dilemma from the opposite angle, how should we judge a process that was elite-driven and often secretive—in other words, not especially democratic or participatory—but which resulted in a durable constitution implemented by a largely peaceful and democratic society?[8]

To simplify, can a process be considered *good,* and therefore commended to future constitution makers, if the ultimate outcome experienced by the citizenry was *bad,* and vice versa? In addition, in trying to measure the contribution of a constitution-making process to whatever outcomes might be considered desirable, how can its effects be isolated from those of other variables, such as the broader state-building process and other contemporaneous political developments?[9] Comprehensive answers to these questions lie outside the scope of this volume, which offers neither a theoretical nor a social-science framework for analysis, but the case studies and the effort here to draw conclusions from them demonstrate the need to pursue such inquiries.

Others have suggested some criteria for success.[10] For example, Jennifer Widner uses three "'outcome' measures" in her analysis of data from an ongoing study of constitution writing in nearly 200 cases: the difference in violence between the five years prior to and the five years after ratification; the rate of suspension or replacement of the new constitution; and the degree of rights protection provided by the constitution's text.[11] She attempts to analyze empirically the claim that certain process choices produce more or less successful results, but cautions that it is very difficult to identify causal relationships between process and outcomes. She makes clear that a "number of very serious challenges bedevil the ability to give a social science answer" to questions concerning whether and how

certain process choices produce better and worse results; these include the difficulty of making comparisons, given that constitution making "embraces a bundle of procedures" that can be combined in many ways, and the complexity of distinguishing the impact of procedural choices from other influences.[12] One example of this empirical challenge concerns public consultation, an element of constitution-making processes on which this volume focuses. Indicating the difficulty of connecting even what many practitioners and academics regard as a desirable process choice to desirable outcomes, Widner finds no correlation between public consultation and stronger rights protection.[13] Similarly, among deeply divided societies, she finds that "the anticipated correlation of success with more representative features does not emerge."[14]

Unlike Widner's study, the present one is anecdotal, covering only a fraction of the constitution-making experiences relevant to its subject matter. This study therefore does not claim to establish a basis for determining whether certain process choices will predictably yield certain results. Moreover, given the themes on which the case study authors were asked to concentrate,[15] the material in this volume does not permit a comprehensive analysis of the outcomes of all the constitution-making processes covered. Even if it did, clear-cut judgments about the success or failure of a particular constitution-making exercise would likely remain elusive; in many cases, the picture is mixed.[16]

Aside from the uncertainty that surrounds measuring constitution-making success and the difficulty of reliably pinpointing causal links between process and results, drawing generalized prescriptive lessons from the case studies is problematic because process choices that seem to serve well in some circumstances do not in others. In certain respects, different cases seem to point to opposite lessons: For example, in looking at whether a deadline should be set for constitution making, the Hungary case study identifies the lack of one as a key process failure, while the Poland case study illustrates the value of not having one.[17]

The overarching conclusion that emerges most clearly from the case studies is that context is of paramount importance. The design of a constitution-making process must be matched to a country's particular political, economic, social, and other circumstances, and differences in circumstances at particular historical moments will require differences in approach. Context shapes constitution making in several ways: It determines the procedural options realistically available,[18] influences the process design choices leaders make, and affects whether those choices serve the desired objectives. This is not a groundbreaking observation, though this volume adds considerable texture to it; over a decade ago, Andrew Arato (coauthor of the Hungary case study) pointed out that "concrete models have a way of turning into something quite different when adopted under dramatically different circumstances. Thus, in a given situation, the circumstances must take priority in the analysis."[19] Drawing guidance from the case studies, therefore, entails identifying which contextual variables are relevant to understanding why certain process choices were made in a particular case, and with what results. Returning to an earlier example, determining what the case studies reveal about constitution-making timelines requires singling out the factors that made a deadline inappropriate for Poland but sorely missed in Hungary. The necessity of recognizing the high degree of particularity in constitution-making experiences, as well as the empirical challenges noted above, confirms the usefulness of a case study approach to examine constitution-making processes. By considering which procedures have worked well, or poorly, within the contexts of the various case studies, lessons can be drawn that will no doubt resonate for future constitution mak-

ers. Comparisons among the cases further illuminate the relevant contextual factors and their significance for procedural choices.

To facilitate comparing the cases, this chapter disaggregates the constitution-making processes into the components that surfaced as most important in the study. It examines how each of those components played out in various cases, referring wherever possible to outcomes that were shown to be relevant in those cases, such as whether the constitution was implemented, whether it is regarded as legitimate, and whether the constitution-making process seemed to affect political stability. In addition to presenting and analyzing procedural options, this conclusion addresses key issues with which future constitution makers will likely have to wrestle.

The chapter begins with an overview of the cases, followed by an examination of the main structural elements of the constitution-making processes. It then discusses a series of thematic topics: inclusiveness and representation; direct public participation; timelines and deadlines; external assistance and intervention; incorporation of constitution making in peacemaking processes; the impact of constitution making on conflict resolution; the relevance of international law and norms; and the question whether constitution making should adhere to existing law. The chapter ends by considering what the cases indicate about the importance of process, compiling common process pitfalls, and offering practical suggestions for assessing the contextual factors that should influence process design.

Overview of the Case Studies[20]

The nineteen cases examined in this volume concern selected constitution-making exercises carried out in diverse circumstances over a twenty-seven year period.[21] Table 22.1 lists the cases chronologically.

Table 22.1 Chronology of Case Studies

Year of Conclusion of Constitution-Making Process Discussed in Study	Country
1978	Spain
1987	Nicaragua
1988	Brazil
1989	Hungary
1990	Namibia
1991	Colombia
1993	Cambodia
1995	Bosnia and Herzegovina
1995	Uganda
1996 (signed)/1997 (effective date)	South Africa
1997	Eritrea
1997	Fiji
1997	Poland
1998	Albania
1980 (independence) and 1999	Zimbabwe
1999	Venezuela
2002	East Timor
2004	Afghanistan
2005	Iraq

While these cases vary greatly in terms of the events that led to the constitution-making exercise and the political and social environment in which the exercise was carried out, in all the cases, the making of a new constitution took place at an important moment in the country's state-building process.

The USIP project of which this volume is a product focuses especially on countries transitioning from conflict, and on the potential for constitution-making processes to contribute to building peaceful conditions and political stability in such countries. The material in this volume addresses the concerns of the project, but also explores constitution making in a wider variety of situations than those often labeled *post-conflict*.[22] This volume therefore provides ideas and lessons for countries pursuing constitution making in the context of many types of political and social turmoil, and the analysis in this con-

clusion applies to the full range of circumstances that the case studies cover.

Table 22.2 categorizes the case studies based on the general contexts in which the constitution-making exercises took place. Almost half of the cases involved circumstances in which the country was either emerging from conflict or still experiencing conflict. These two types of contexts are merged here, as often they are not clearly distinguishable. In Colombia and Iraq, violent conflicts persisted at the time of constitution making; in the other countries in this category, varying degrees of more limited open conflict or underlying tensions remained. In the other roughly half of the cases, the countries are evenly split between those that were undergoing a transition from nondemocratic forms of rule during the constitution-making period and those that were in the midst of some other period of institutional crisis or major reform of state structures. The particular circumstances in this latter category are spelled out briefly in the notes.

The categories in Table 22.2 are generalizations; each case study concerns a unique set of circumstances, and some of the cases are not amenable to precise and simple classification. Moreover, some cases exhibit characteristics of more than one category. For example, South Africa at the time of its constitution-making experience was emerging from both conflict and rule by a regime that oppressed a majority of the population. While violent conflict was a central feature of the conditions that led to the constitution making, and political violence in fact increased during the constitution-making process, the lengthy, multistage, negotiated transition with which that process was entwined was more similar to the circumstances of the cases in the second category than those in the first. Similarly, several countries in the first category have faced the double challenge of simultaneously managing a transition from conflict to peace and

Table 22.2   Categorization of Case Study Contexts

During conflict or transition from conflict, or at independence	Transition from nondemocratic regime	Other period of institutional crisis or major reform
Afghanistan	Albania	Brazil[1]
Bosnia and Herzegovina	Hungary	Fiji[2]
Cambodia	Poland	Uganda[3]
Colombia	South Africa	Venezuela[4]
East Timor	Spain	Zimbabwe[5]
Eritrea		
Iraq		
Namibia		
Nicaragua		

Notes: 1. The Brazilian constitution-making process was part of a long period of redemocratization initiated by the military in 1974. 2. A constitutional review provision in Fiji's 1990 constitution prompted the constitution-making process addressed in this volume. 3. The National Resistance Movement, led by President Yoweri Museveni, initiated the constitution-making process to signal a break with past regimes and to constitutionally implant the idea of "no-party democracy." 4. The Venezuelan process nominally was intended to restructure and improve the system of governance in a context of political crisis, but, in fact, was used to facilitate the consolidation of state power in the hands of President Hugo Chavez. 5. The 1980 process in Zimbabwe produced that country's independence constitution and would fit in the first category, but the 1999 process, which fits in the third category, is the major focus of the case study in this volume. Civil-society agitation for a new constitution to right the inequities of the 1980 constitution and displace subsequent amendments that eroded democracy prompted the 1999 process. The government responded to that agitation by launching a process that it controlled.

a transition from some form of authoritarian rule to democracy. Both transitions have deeply marked their experiences with constitution making and implementation. Bosnia and Herzegovina, for example, fits squarely in the first category, but the legacy of that country's communist period had a distinct impact on the shape of the 1995 constitution and has hampered the effort to establish a constitutional democracy there. Thus, the cases are sorted in Table 22.2 according to the category in which they fit best, but not necessarily exclusively.

Table 22.3 lays out the main structural elements of the constitution-making processes examined in this volume, showing which countries used each element.[23] It thus depicts the constitution-making process from a technical and functional perspective.[24] Across the cases, there are many variations in the combination of elements used, as well as significant variations in the details of how each element was designed and actually implemented. For instance, in some cases, an elected body (of one of the types indicated in the first column) managed the entire constitution-making process and genuinely deliberated on the substance of the constitutional text, while in others an elected body essentially rubber-stamped a text produced under executive or international control. As the chapters in this volume demonstrate, the structural fine details of the processes are extremely diverse, and those details matter greatly in assessing what happened in each country and with what results.

Structuring a Constitution-Making Process

The case studies contain a great quantity of descriptive information regarding the structures of the constitution-making processes examined. These descriptions will be useful to readers seeking a detailed understanding of the process choices made in those countries. This chapter offers some conclusions about the benefits and drawbacks of particular procedural choices in various circumstances. To that end, the discussion in this section is

Table 22.3 Structural Elements of Constitution-Making Processes Used in the Case Studies[1]

	Parliamentary process, constituent assembly, convention[2]	Appointed commission	Roundtable	Public participation process	Referendum (for ratification, unless noted otherwise)	Interim arrangement[3]	Judicial review
Afghanistan	X (Constitutional Loya Jirga, comparable to a constitutional convention, considered and amended draft)	X (35-member commission prepared draft modified by the executive)		X (weak/limited process)		X (transitional provisions in Bonn Agreement)	
Albania	X (parliamentary constitutional commission drafted text)			X	X	X (set of transitional laws termed Major Constitutional Provisions)	
Bosnia and Herzegovina	X (subnational parliamentary approval of negotiated document)						
Brazil	X (Congress acted as constituent assembly)[4]			X	X (plebiscite after five years to revisit form of government)		
Cambodia	X (constituent assembly, converted into National Assembly after adopting constitution)					X (transitional provisions in Paris Peace Agreements)	

continued

Table 22.3 Structural Elements of Constitution-Making Processes Used in the Case Studies[1] *continued*

	Parliamentary process, constituent assembly, convention[2]	Appointed commission	Roundtable	Public participation process	Referendum (for ratification, unless noted otherwise)	Interim arrangement[3]	Judicial review
Colombia	X (constitutional assembly prepared and adopted text)			X	X (on question whether to establish a constitutional assembly)		X
East Timor	X (constituent assembly, converted to National Assembly after adoption)			X (weak/limited process)			
Eritrea	X (National Assembly approved and constituent assembly ratified product of commission)	X (independent 50-member commission)		X		X (self-appointed provisional government and appointed transitional parliament)	
Fiji	X (changes to commission draft negotiated by parliamentary select committee, and adopted by parliament as amendment)[5]	X (3-person review commission)		X (weak/limited process)			
Hungary	X (parliamentary amendment process)		X		X (referendum on four substantive constitutional questions)		X

Iraq	X (National Assembly, with constitution committee responsible for drafting text)		X (weak/limited process)	X	X (Transitional Administrative Law promulgated by occupation authority)	
Namibia	X (constituent assembly, converted to National Assembly after adoption)				X (UN Security Council Resolution)	
Nicaragua	X (National Constituent Assembly, with special constitutional commission composed of political party representatives holding seats in the assembly responsible for preparing draft)		X		X (Fundamental Statute and Statute of Rights and Guarantees provided temporary framework after 1974 constitution abolished)	
Poland	X (National Assembly—the parliament of the outgoing regime; a transitional, partly democratic parliament; and a new, democratic parliament played roles at different stages)	X		X	X (several constitutional amendments including 1992 Small Constitution)	X
South Africa	X (constitutional assembly, double-hatted as ordinary parliament, drafted and adopted final constitution)		X		X (political parties negotiated Interim Constitution)	X

continued

Table 22.3 Structural Elements of Constitution-Making Processes Used in the Case Studies[1] *continued*

	Parliamentary process, constituent assembly, convention[2]	Appointed commission	Roundtable	Public participation process	Referendum (for ratification, unless noted otherwise)	Interim arrangement[3]	Judicial review
Spain	X (parliament)				X (for approval of transitional reform law and final constitution)	X (Eighth Fundamental Law, approved by referendum 1976, and "pre-autonomy laws")	
Uganda	X (constituent assembly, with elected and appointed members)	X (government-controlled commission)		X (extensive public engagement, but focus on civic education rather than consultation)			
Venezuela	X (constituent assembly)				X (on question whether to establish constituent assembly, and for ratification)		
Zimbabwe	X (parliamentary approval)	X (500-member government-controlled commission produced nonbinding draft)		X (1999: extensive process, but little impact)	X		

Notes: 1. With respect to the first three columns, the overlap is explained by the fact that use of an appointed commission independent of the legislature (for drafting and, in some cases, public consultation purposes) or roundtable (for negotiation and drafting) was accompanied in all the relevant cases by an elected body's control over other elements of the process. 2. This category includes parliamentary commissions or committees responsible for drafting or other aspects of constitution making where such a body was composed of members of the ordinary legislature or constituent assembly, and where the commission or committee therefore did not operate independently of the parliamentary process. The constitutional commission in Albania is one example of such a body. 3. Hungary is not included here, even though its substantially amended constitution technically remains interim. The 1996–97 effort there to create a wholly new constitution failed, and, as discussed in the Hungary chapter of this volume, momentum toward such an end has been lost. 4. The president of Brazil appointed a blue-ribbon committee to prepare a draft constitution for submission to the constituent assembly, but then refused to submit the draft because he disagreed with many of its provisions. Consequently, the constituent assembly drafted the 1988 constitution from scratch. 5. While technically an amendment of the 1990 constitution, the adopted changes, in fact, formed a new constitution of the Fiji Islands.

organized according to the structural elements identified in Table 22.3 (except for public participation, which will be addressed separately)—in other words, by the types of bodies and mechanisms used. Another useful way to consider structural questions is to identify the relevant functions undertaken, such as drafting, deliberation, and approval and ratification; thus, the discussion here highlights distinctions among the functions performed by the various types of mechanisms.[25]

The three tables above together reveal an absence of clear trends over the time period covered by the cases regarding the employment of particular elements of constitution making. For example, serious public consultation programs have been implemented intermittently; Nicaragua carried out a robust program in 1987, as did South Africa in the mid-1990s, but none of the countries that made new constitutions in the present decade—East Timor, Afghanistan, and Iraq—did so in a way that meaningfully brought public input into the process.[26] Similarly, independent commissions, used for drafting and other purposes, have been employed sporadically, while interim constitutional arrangements, used for transitional purposes during the creation of a final constitution, have been put in place fairly regularly.

Parliamentary Constitution-Making Processes and Constituent Assemblies

In all nineteen cases, an elected, partly elected, or indirectly elected body played some role in the constitution-making process, but the nature of both the body and its role varied widely.[27] In Brazil, the congress doubled as a constituent assembly, drafting the constitution from scratch and approving it with no further ratification procedure. In Bosnia and Herzegovina, the legislatures of the two subnational Entities rubber-stamped a constitution included in a peace treaty and already legally in effect. In some cases, an elected body was the lead actor in the process, responsible for drafting as well as deliberating on the text, as in South Africa, where the constitutional assembly drafted, debated, and adopted the final constitution, and Albania, where a parliamentary commission drafted the text. In others, an elected body's role was confined to ratifying the product of an independent commission, as occurred with the constituent assembly in Eritrea.

The case studies explore many, often idiosyncratic issues surrounding why certain types of elected bodies were used in a constitution-making process, how they were used, and how well they acquitted themselves. Elected bodies are political, and the political dynamics vary in the cases; overall, it is clear that the impact of those dynamics on the results often trumped the impact of the technical niceties of how the processes were structured.[28] Nevertheless, the case studies illustrate a useful variety of structural options. Some of the issues that transcend individual cases and merit consideration by future constitution makers are addressed below.

Use of Ordinary Legislature versus Extraordinary Constituent Assembly

Afghanistan is the only case considered here in which the main deliberative and decision-making body was neither a regular legislature nor an elected or mostly elected constituent assembly, but rather a *loya jirga,* a traditional Afghan grand national assembly composed of indirectly selected representatives of the various regions of Afghanistan, as well as some presidentially appointed delegates. The use of a traditional mechanism in Afghanistan may have enhanced the popular legitimacy of the outcome. Though the particular form of the *loya jirga* is not likely to be replicated in other contexts, the availability of local traditional procedures could usefully be explored elsewhere. All the other cases are split evenly between process choices more amenable to replication in their general forms: use of an ordinary legislature and use of a constituent assembly, for purposes of some combination of drafting, debating, and deciding on a constitutional text.[29]

The question of whether to employ an ordinary legislature or an extraordinary constituent assembly can be contentious, with conflicting positions generally centering on which option will serve whose interests. In Spain, it remained unclear in the period leading up to the 1977 elections which type of body those elections would produce because of a left versus right political dispute on the issue; in the end, the position of the center-right and right-leaning parties, which favored a regular parliament, prevailed. In Uganda, disagreement over what type of body would drive the constitution-making process was part of the broader struggle over the ruling National Resistance Movement's control of the process. The Movement originally intended to have the National Assembly serve as the relevant body, because of the large number of its followers holding seats there, but pressure from political parties to establish a constituent assembly, with delegates freely elected, successfully produced a different result. Other Movement efforts to keep the playing field uneven succeeded, however.

Use of a constituent assembly can have several advantages over the parliamentary approach. A constituent assembly may have greater popular legitimacy as a constitution maker, as its members are elected specifically to develop and adopt the new national charter. In addition, a constituent assembly—unless double-hatted as a parliament, as in South Africa—can devote itself full-time to constitution making without the distraction of day-to-day parliamentary business. As a consequence, it may be better able to focus on the broader questions of constitutional vision.

Brazil's experience illustrates a set of problems that can arise from using an ordinary legislature for the extraordinary task of constitution making. There, the congress served as the constituent assembly due to a condition secretly imposed by military authorities, which thought the congress would be more responsive to military demands than would a specially elected constituent assembly. Congress adopted, on President Sarney's proposal, a constitutional amendment empowering itself to double as the constituent assembly, even though the alternative had substantial popular support. Using the congress undermined the democratic character and legitimacy of the constitution-making process: Malapportionment badly underrepresented the most populous states, the 1986 congress that drafted the constitution included senators indirectly elected under the prior authoritarian electoral law, voters knew nothing about their representatives' views on the constitutional issues, and the congress had a "ravenous appetite for pork barrel benefits."[30] In addition, the approach forced the congress to divide its time between constitution making and regular legislative business.

A key consequence of the Brazilian approach was that the constitutional framers, as members of a highly politicized body elected primarily to represent state and local interests, operated with a short-term perspective. They injected numerous details that more appropriately belonged in legislation or regulations, while deferring for later a variety of questions of broad constitutional vision and governmental framework. Moreover, the congress had a clear conflict of interest; unsurprisingly, the final constitutional text aggrandized congressional power.[31] Though the Brazilian process was very open and public, the nature of the decision-making body made it vulnerable to active lobbying by special interest groups, which distorted the outcome. Moreover, military influence on the deliberations—in the form of a threat of a possible coup hanging over the delegates—was highly constraining. With complicated voting rules, multiple rounds, thousands of offered amendments to the draft, and protracted negotiations, ultimately the process was so unwieldy that it produced a very cumbersome text, which has been an obstacle to effective governance. The process was textbook in some formal respects, but the hodgepodge document that was its result has no coherent vision and is overly complex.[32] In recent years, key features of the 1988 constitution have been dismantled through a series of amendments.

Fiji, too, provides an example of problems that can arise when using a regular parliament instead of a constituent assembly. Parliament members there had vested personal and ethnic group interests in the constitutional status quo. A popular referendum might have helped to mitigate this problem, but the last word on the constitution was left entirely with the politicians in parliament, who in some ways undid the constructive work performed by an independent commission. In the end, though some tried to use the constitution-making process to improve ethnic relations, others used it to reinforce Fiji's ethnic divide.

Opposition elements in Hungary blocked use of a constituent assembly and promoted a roundtable approach (discussed below), as they feared that early elections for such a body organized by the government were likely to result in a communist majority, which could then enact a regime-conservative yet formally legitimate result.[33] Consequently, ordinary parliaments were significant in the process in Hungary, an approach inherited from the communist past, and, in the view of the case study authors, lacking the heightened legitimacy needed for democratic constitution making, in which voters should know that the delegates they elect will actually make a constitution. Ultimately, the parliaments failed to develop a final new constitution.

In Albania, a parliament-led constitution-making process succeeded for several reasons that stand in significant contrast to the above cases. The parliamentary mandate to undertake the drafting of a new constitution had been established a few years prior, foreclosing any legitimacy concerns of the sort noted in Hungary. Rather than assigning the task to the entire parliament, as in Brazil, the parliament established a small constitutional commission and ensured that it was broadly representative and inclusive of all parties, including minorities. And rather than starting from scratch, the Albanian parliament had a set of guiding constitutional principles as its starting point.

Of the cases in this volume, South Africa appears to have best combined the roles of an ordinary legislature and a constituent assembly in a single body. From a practical perspective, the roles were not always compatible because of conflicting time demands, but the procedure did not suffer from the legitimacy deficit noted above; at the time of the elections, voters were well aware of the dual function their representatives would perform. In addition, because the elected body was a new one, formed during the transition, the potential for vested interests to distort the process was minimized. Though the South African experience does not suggest that this is the best approach when other alternatives are available, it does show that some of the more serious problems can be avoided when, for practical or other reasons, there is no good alternative—in South Africa's case, because a wholly new parliament, operating under a new interim constitution, had to be created at the very same time as a democratically chosen constitution-making body.

In choosing between the parliamentary and constituent assembly options, sensitivity to the history and constitutional tradition of the country in question may be required, as these may be crucial to the popular legitimacy of the process. In Poland, there was no realistic alternative to using an ordinary legislature for constitution making, even though the procedure had practical downsides. Because the regular national assembly was responsible for drafting and deliberation, the process was repeatedly interrupted and delayed by parliamentary elections and various political crises that absorbed delegates' attention. These events lengthened the constitution-making process, which consumed almost eight years. Nevertheless, no alternate approach was seriously considered. Bypassing parliament would have contradicted Polish constitutional tradition; the case study authors observe that "because all Polish constitutions in the past had been drafted within the legislative branch, another way could hardly be regarded as legitimate." Moreover, another approach, such as establishing a constitutional convention, "would not have been practicable in the specific conditions of Polish political developments." It would have been premature at the outset of the process in 1989.[34] Later, once a new, democratically elected parliament was formed in 1991, "it had full legitimacy and competence to take care of the constitution writing." Furthermore, the lack of any major ethnic, religious, or regional divisions in Poland meant that it was reasonable to "link the constitution drafting process almost exclusively to the political preferences of Polish voters." Similarly, the Constitutional Loya Jirga, an approach similar to a constituent assembly, was viewed as the only acceptable option in Afghanistan, not only because the country lacked a functioning parliament at the time, but because the *loya jirga* had long been the default model to address major issues in the country, including the drafting of the well-respected 1964 constitution.

In several cases, constituent assemblies were converted into regular legislatures when their constitution-making work ended. This procedure poses a potential conflict of interest similar to that seen in using regular legislatures for constitution making. In East Timor, the regulation that laid out the legal basis for the constituent assembly gave it the option to transform itself into the nation's first parliament, which, as expected, it did. Consequently, the constituent assembly decided on the parameters of its own future powers. In Cambodia and Namibia, too, constituent assemblies were converted into regular national assemblies after adopting the constitutions. In Namibia, this was regarded as a practical necessity, to ensure that the major institutions would be in place on the day of independence. It was also considered harmless, because fresh elections would have yielded the same results as the very recent constituent assembly elections.

Namibia shows that despite the disadvantages in principle of using or converting to an ordinary legislature, actual harm depends on the political dynamics in the country. Similarly, South Africa and Poland show that even where some practical problems result, the benefits of using (or dual-hatting) an ordinary legislature can outweigh the drawbacks. Moreover, Colombia's experience illustrates that in certain circumstances, trying to avoid a conflict of interest can have unintended consequences: There, members of the constituent assembly were disqualified from running in the new congressional elections, but as a result, practically all the old political class was reelected, rather than the new and independent political formations that emerged in the constituent assembly under modernized electoral rules.

Overall, the cases suggest that using an ordinary legislature for constitution making can be a problematic choice when the legislature is not a broadly representative body in political, geographic, or other relevant terms; when giving the legislature a central role would likely undermine the legitimacy of the process (including when members have a vested interest in avoiding reforms); or where there may be reasons to suspect that legislative representatives are not those who would likely be chosen for a constitutional drafting job. But certain cases also suggest that under particular conditions, using an ordinary or convertible legislature can be regarded as fully legitimate, as in Poland and South Africa, or at least harmless, as in Namibia. Factors such as lack of resources or time to elect both an ordinary legislature and a constituent assembly—and, where still respected, a country's constitution-making tradition—must be considered in determining a suitable procedure.

Organization and Professional Support

Under either main approach discussed above, a variety of technical options are available for shaping the precise role and organizing the work of the elected body. Given the difficulty of having an entire elected body draft a constitution, some constituent assemblies and parliaments have created smaller drafting bodies from among their members, as discussed further below. Alternatively, or subsequent to this, both legislatures and constituent assemblies have created committee and subcommittee structures, generally arranged thematically to focus on different aspects of the constitution, for purposes of drafting and deliberation. Harmonization and editing or other technical committees also have been used to consolidate the work of thematic committees and finalize texts, as in the systemization and editing committees used in Brazil, or the systemization and harmonization committee in East Timor. Many of the chapters in this volume describe the specific committee structures used in the cases.

A process in which members of a parliament or constituent assembly may be offering and receiving potentially thousands of ideas, proposals, and amendments concerning, in some cases, hundreds of articles as they debate and draft a new constitution is an enormous challenge. To manage this challenge, the constitution-making body can benefit from the technical and administrative support of a professional, neutral, and well-resourced secretariat. Several variations appear in this volume. Depending on the particular case, the functions of such a professional staff unit may include conducting research for the constitution-making body and its committees, and providing information and analysis, for example, on how constitutions in different countries address particular issues; organizing, summarizing, and digesting suggestions and information received through public consultation; undertaking the technical drafting needed to form the substantive decisions made by the elected constitution makers into constitutional text; harmonizing the texts and decisions of various committees and identifying conflicts among them; developing reports for the assembly on the work of the various committees; and providing information on the assembly's work to the public. In Brazil, the Senate's informatics and data processing center filled many of these functions, in addition to its regular supporting role for the legislature. Albania employed a different model; it created a so-called quasi-non-governmental organization, with local and foreign staff, to perform several functions, including indexing and organizing all public comments for the parliamentary constitutional commission and its technical staff and coordinating foreign assistance to the commission. In Colombia, a UN-funded presidential agency provided technical support to the constituent assembly, organized some public promotion of the new constitution, and also prepared legislative bills needed for the constitution's implementation. A national academic institute also provided technical drafting assistance. Staff support for the constitution-making enterprise may involve more than a centralized secretariat, as in Eritrea, where the constitutional commission established and managed seven provincial offices to facilitate outreach.

Responsibility for Drafting

The case studies display a wide variety of choices regarding the assignment of drafting duties, including the use of neutral experts, drafting committees of constituent assemblies and legislatures, and appointed commissions (discussed later in this chapter).[35] The cases raise two key, interrelated questions about drafting procedures: first, whether to designate experts, as opposed to parliamentarians or delegates, to draft text; and, second, whether to commence constitutional negotiations with a provisional draft. Positive and negative experiences in several cases indicate the general utility of employing experts in the drafting process. Experiences with respect to the timing for introducing a draft are more idiosyncratic.

Namibia illustrates the effective use of experts in the drafting process; there, the constituent assembly appointed a three-member drafting panel of South African lawyers, charged with presenting a draft to the assembly. The choice of South Africans, two of whom were Afrikaners, lends insight into the conditions that the constituent assembly perceived to be relevant to its procedural choices. Though the assembly was offered an abundance of constitutional expertise from all parts of the globe, members were strongly suspicious of outside interference and felt that their constitution "should not be the product of some foreign experiment." On a practical level, the constitutional law and traditions of South Africa and Namibia were similar, their common law was the same, and assembly members knew that the future Namibian constitution would maintain its roots in the South African legal system. Assembly members also realized that appointing South African experts would help dispel mistrust in the constitution-making process, especially among the white population.

In Poland, the national assembly's drafting process initially was unworkable. In fall 1989, both chambers of parliament appointed their own constitutional committees, which produced two different drafts. These appeared irreconcilable, and no procedure was in place to mediate the differences. The drafting procedure was rectified when a joint committee was established in 1991. In addition to parliamentarians from both houses, the committee included nonvoting representatives of the president, cabinet, and constitutional court. The right to submit drafts to the committee was given to the committee itself, the president, and any group of at least fifty-six parliament members; at a later stage, provision was made for popular drafts, signed by at least 500,000 voters, to be submitted as well (one popular draft, sponsored by the Solidarity trade union, was submitted). Once the drafting process began in earnest, the joint committee appointed five law professors—all leading scholars in constitutional law, with no direct political involvement—as permanent experts who participated actively in the committee and its subcommittees, including assisting with writing the text.[36] A separate group of experts was engaged at the end to technically edit the text. Even among the committee members themselves, some were regarded as "'expert' politicians" (with the others regarded as "'pure' politicians").

In South Africa, domestic experts helped to draft text within the confines of the constitutional assembly's clear overall responsibility for preparing and approving the final constitution. After negotiations were already under way, and following a first stage of public outreach and consultation, the assembly's management committee appointed a team of experts, including law advisers, language experts, and members of a previously appointed panel of constitutional experts, to prepare the first working draft of the constitution as well as later versions of the draft as negotiations progressed. Aside from the experts, the constitutional assembly benefited from being able to draw on a deep well of talent among its own members. The timing of producing a draft roughly midway through the assembly's work allowed for a relatively open-ended phase of debate and public consultation during a period when, in any event, the parties were not yet prepared to make the necessary substantive compromises. This was followed by more focused negotiation and consultation once a first draft was produced. Delaying the use of drafting experts in this way perhaps reflected the strong sentiment in South Africa that elected representatives should lead the constitution-making process, and that any role for appointed experts should be minimized. In both Poland and South Africa, the timing for introducing expert assistance precluded any sense that outside experts were supplanting the role of the designated constitution makers and confirmed that the experts were in a supporting role, assisting and refining the drafting choices of those elected to create the constitution.

The manner in which experts and an appointed commission were used to support the drafting process in Fiji presents a more mixed picture. Some of the world's leading constitutional experts advised the appointed commission charged with launching the constitution-making process, and the commission, supported by a technical staff, prepared a very extensive report. However, that report provided drafting instructions for the new constitution, which, while framed in precise terms, were not, for the most part, actual textual formulations crafted to achieve the recommended result. This approach limited the utility of the commission's work.

In some countries, the constituent assembly members themselves assumed responsibility for drafting. In Venezuela, the constituent assembly organized twenty subject-specific committees to draft different parts of the constitution. Technically, this procedure was not problematic, though—as discussed elsewhere in this chapter—political manipulation distorted the constitution-making process overall. In Brazil, the drafting story is a distinctly unhappy one. The assembly considered whether to start the process with a draft prepared by constitutional scholars, but opted not to do so "on the theory that this would make the process as open and democratic as possible." The assembly "emphatically rejected the idea of commissioning a draft as a 'dangerous instrument of control'" over its work. As a result, the 1988 constitution was drafted "from scratch" by the entire 559-member assembly, divided into twenty-four thematic committees, though the drafters drew from previous Brazilian constitutions and proposals, and participated in seminars on constitution writing with foreign experts. This approach made it "virtually impossible to produce a coherent document, particularly with a weak party system and a weak president." In the case study author's view, had the assembly started its work with an experts' draft, it "probably would not have produced a document with such serious conceptual and organizational flaws."

As with other aspects of constitution-making processes, analysis of the drafting procedure requires distinguishing between the formal technique and the political reality of how a constitutional text is produced. In Cambodia, for instance, a twelve-member committee of the constituent assembly was charged with preparing a draft, and worked in secret for two and half months to do so; however, the two main political parties prepared their own competing drafts, one of which the constituent assembly adopted after only five days of debate. Somewhat similarly in Iraq, an elected constituent assembly was legally mandated to draft the text, a task it delegated to a committee of assembly members. But political party leaders pushed aside the assembly and its committee (which had been provided with foreign technical expertise), negotiated certain fundamental decisions, and completed the text behind closed doors.

As already noted, the cases suggest that in many instances future constitution makers would be well advised to employ constitutional experts in the drafting process and to bring them in from outside the country if domestic constitutional expertise is lacking. At least two cases demonstrate that expert advice is particularly helpful where it is neutral and not provided through political parties. In addition, these experiences illuminate the utility of a professional, well-organized structure to support the drafters and negotiators by facilitating expert input to the process and ensuring accurate revising of the text. Such a structure could take the form, for example, of a secretariat attached to the deliberative body, or a committee staff structure. As for timing, some cases indicate that preparing an experts' draft at the outset of the constitution-making process would be helpful to developing a coherent text, though South Africa in particular demonstrates the potential advantages of employing drafting experts after the decision-makers' and public's preferences have begun to take shape. Arguably, delaying the introduction of drafting experts, as was done in South Africa, could help to subordinate the experts' role to that of the democratically mandated constitution makers.[37]

Tabling of Drafts by Powerful Parties

In several cases, politically powerful parties strongly influenced the drafting process by tabling their own complete constitutional drafts. The positive and negative effects of powerful parties playing such a role are rather idiosyncratic. But it is clear that the issue merits close attention from those designing drafting procedures, and that past experiences will prove instructive.

East Timor offers a particularly negative example of this phenomenon. There, Fretilin's proposed text became the starting point of the drafting process in the constituent assembly because of the party's dominance in that body. Fretilin had created its draft at a 1998 conference of exiled party leaders in Sydney, Australia, but did not put the draft

before voters at the time of the constituent assembly elections in 2001.[38] Fretilin's dominance in the assembly precluded any real compromise or negotiation over the main issues addressed in the proposed text. Moreover, as the case study authors point out, by "taking the Fretilin draft as their point of departure, the committees [of the constituent assembly] failed to develop the constitution from the ground up, examining and discussing which options would be most suitable for East Timor." In the end, the constitution established a political system that capitalized on Fretilin's strengths.

Cambodia's experience is more ambiguous. Because of Prince Norodom Sihanouk's paramount influence on the constitution-making process, the draft constitution he favored—which, not incidentally, restored him to the throne—became the basis for the final constitution, rather than the work of the constituent assembly's drafting committee. This approach, which effectively precluded the possibility of an open-ended exploration of the constitutional options, was certainly undemocratic. In the case study author's view, however, it probably was unavoidable, given Sihanouk's central role in the transition, popular respect for his authority, and the cultural reluctance of assembly delegates to demonstrate significant independence. A more assertive UN mission in Cambodia may, perhaps, have been able to mitigate Sihanouk's dominance by laying down a clearer road map for the constitutional process.

On the positive side of the ledger, Namibia's experience shows the potential benefits of proceeding on the basis of a particular party's draft, if the decision to do so is based on a consensus view of the need to cement that party's support. The Namibian constituent assembly invited all parties that gained seats to submit constitutional proposals; all proffered more or less complete drafts. Once faced with the "seemingly insurmountable task of drawing up a constitution from a multitude of proposals," however, assembly members unanimously agreed to accept SWAPO's[39] proposal as a working document that would serve as the basis for drafting. Awareness of this move "produced a perception of credibility and legitimacy" for the work of the assembly among supporters of SWAPO, which had garnered 60 percent of the vote in the assembly elections. The panel of experts then produced a draft of the complete constitution (filling a number of lacunae) based on the SWAPO document. An important factor that helps explain Namibia's positive experience in starting with a political party draft is that political developments had caused SWAPO to abandon many of its own original ideas. The draft it tabled consolidated elements of most of the other parties' proposals, making it a sound basis on which to build consensus.

Appointed Constitutional Commissions

Five of the cases in this study involved the use of appointed commissions outside of the elected decision-making body to develop a draft constitution, and in some instances, to organize and conduct public consultation. In each of these cases, the commission's final product was submitted to an elected body for consideration. In theory, the commission approach enables the selection of a broadly representative group of citizens—perhaps even broader than a group of elected representatives, ideally with constitutional expertise, to prepare a draft.

Some experts see the constitutional commission approach as a possible way to circumvent the obstacles presented by domineering political forces in a more political elected forum. In East Timor, for example, Fretilin's political dominance undermined the extent to which the constituent assembly membership truly represented the variety of voices present in the country. The case study authors suggest that appointing a broad-based constitutional commission could have mitigated the problem and reduced the ef-

fect of Fretilin's dominance in the assembly, which was charged with deliberating on and approving the text. The arrangement for selecting the commissioners is key, however, to ensuring a commission's balance and inclusiveness. Where possible, appointment procedures that constrain the ability of domineering political forces to control the appointments are advisable. Uganda's experience illustrates the appointment dilemma: In that case, the president and the minister for constitutional affairs appointed a constitutional commission with a membership that was regionally balanced, but entirely made up of strong supporters of the Movement system that President Museveni used the constitution-making process to embed.

Where there is some commitment to an inclusive process, a commission can be useful for developing a draft constitution, though the cases in this study on the whole do not show that this approach produces a better result than using a constituent assembly or parliamentary drafting committees with expert assistance.[40] In Eritrea, an appointed commission was used to good effect, technically speaking (the outcome of the process as a whole has been an unhappy one, as the constitution has not been implemented). The national assembly appointed a fifty-member commission with a ten-member executive committee, and, in accordance with the provisional government's proclamation establishing the mandate for the commission, ensured full representation of a cross-section of Eritrean society. The commissioners included twenty-one women, members of each of the country's nine ethnic groups, and representatives of business and professional communities. Over a three-year period, the commission carried out a very extensive program of public education and consultation, and at the end presented the national assembly with a draft constitution for its approval and further public debate, after which the draft was submitted to a constituent assembly for ratification. Selassie highlights the importance of the commission's independence to its effectiveness: "The independence of a commission ensures the integrity of the process and consequent public confidence in the process and its outcomes, that is, the constitution itself."

Zimbabwe's experience runs counter to the ideal constitutional commission model, as President Mugabe appointed a 500-member constitutional commission filled with ruling party supporters. The commission undertook an "impressive and wide-ranging" public consultation exercise throughout the country, and formulated a draft that contained major substantive improvements over the 1980 independence constitution.[41] But in the end, given the legal procedure the president used to establish the commission, he was under no obligation to accept its recommendations; he rejected a number of them, including one prohibiting land seizures without compensation. In this way, the government used the commission ostensibly to consult with the public, while actually ensuring its own control over the process—at least up to the point of referendum, as discussed below. Control had been the government's objective from the start. It created the commission to thwart the ambitions of the NGO community in Zimbabwe, which began agitating for a new, more democratic constitution during the 1990s.

In Afghanistan, the question of the constitutional commission's independence was highly pertinent. The thirty-five commissioners, appointed by President Karzai, reflected a broad political and ethnic spectrum, including a mix of experts and politicians. However, after the commission produced a draft constitution, the presidential palace took control of the draft, prevented its anticipated publication, and undertook an executive review: "Anxious to secure greater power for President Karzai and limit the possibility of alternative power centers, members of President Karzai's cabinet and National Security Council redrafted key aspects of the constitution" before presenting it to the Constitutional Loya Jirga for debate and

approval. This maneuver undermined the value of vesting drafting responsibility in a commission.

Fiji's experience offers further cautionary lessons on how to structure and operate commissions. First, the small size of the three-person review commission appointed by parliament negated the possibility of wide representation. Although a constitutional commission's typically manageable size is a potential advantage, it should ideally be large enough to be broadly inclusive. Second, the composition of the commission—two local members, representing parties of competing ethnic groups, and one foreigner as chairman—was "not propitious to defining national goals and identity." Though the commissioners confounded critics by reaching consensus on many constructive recommendations, the case study authors still see the example as problematic. Third, at over 700 pages, the commission's final report was too long to be accessible to the public; due to its length, it was not even translated into local languages. Finally, the commission's report provided "drafting instructions" for the new constitution, but not an actual draft text of the new national charter, leaving that task to the legislature and reducing the utility of the commission's work.

Considering these five experiences, an appointed commission can potentially contribute positively to democratic constitution making; the commissioners can be appointed in a balanced way; an appropriate size and diversity of membership can be ensured; the commission has the necessary expertise; it can operate independently; and given its mandate and membership, the commission is adept enough to produce a draft that will be acceptable within the political context.

Roundtables

Negotiating forums referred to as *roundtables* were used most prominently in several East and Central European countries during their transitions from communism, as a means of bringing together elements of the outgoing regime and new democratic formations. This mechanism, which proved useful in the conditions of those negotiated transitions, is illustrated by two of the European case studies in this volume.

In Poland, the roundtable comprised the so-called semi-illegal opposition and representatives of the official regime. They spent six months secretly negotiating the organizational aspects of the roundtable, then reached a compromise agreement on Poland's transition path. The agreement became the basis for an amendment to the communist-era constitution that transformed the structure of both political branches of government and began a process of piecemeal amendment that continued until an entirely new constitution was written. The roundtable functioned for a relatively short time, but it played a crucial role in the first months of the transition process; it filled the legitimacy gap opened up by the discrediting of the existing parliament of the ancien regime. The case study authors point out that ultimately, however, "enacting the 1997 constitution was detached, in time and political context, from concluding the 'peace agreement' at the 1989 Round Table."

In Hungary's fully negotiated transition process, a national roundtable undertook the first of two main rounds of constitution making. The second round took the shape of a pact between the two largest parties in parliament that specified a set of amendments to the existing (1949) constitution. In both stages, the nature of the process excluded public participation (except through a referendum, discussed below). The main substantive negotiations in the first round took place in thematic committees of the roundtable that were not open to the media or the public. The pact-making process was even more opaque, involving secret talks among top political leaders.

The case study authors elucidate a number of benefits and detriments to the roundtable method Hungary employed. The approach had the "great strategic advantage of avoiding violence and civil strife" and prevented both the forces of the old regime and new revolutionary actors from imposing a constitutional solution. In addition, it solved the problem of how to begin the process democratically when there was no prior democracy, substituting "pluralist" legitimacy in the initial stage for democratic legitimacy "by including as many relevant actors as possible and having them come to agreement through consensus or fair compromise." The roundtable approach contributed significantly to maintaining legal continuity in the Hungarian transition and facilitated consensual decision-making, thus helping to keep the transition on a stable and nonviolent path. On the other hand, the roundtable's consensus was an elite one, and the lack of popular involvement in the process and the consequent absence of genuine political legitimacy "carried over from the Round Table to all its successors" during the twelve years of fragmented constitution making.

Though not generally characterized as a roundtable approach, the first stage of constitution making in South Africa was carried out using a forum named the Multi-Party Negotiating Process that in many respects resembled the roundtable negotiating forums described above. A broad spectrum of parties from both sides of the racial divide participated in the process, which formulated the interim constitution of 1993 (approved by the last white parliament), set a date for the country's first democratic elections, and defined the outlines of the final constitution-making process. This first stage was largely closed, involving both formal multiparty negotiations and informal bilateral and multilateral talks among political party leaders. But by producing consensus on a way forward for the transition to democracy and the creation of a new constitution, it formed the basis for the much more transparent and open final constitution-making process that followed. The first-stage process was a bridge between the structures of the apartheid regime and those of the new democratic system.

The Hungarian, Polish, and South African cases illustrate for future constitution makers the potential contributions of a negotiated transition with a two-stage constitution-making process—first elite, then more democratic—to building stability, consensus, and legitimacy.[42] The roundtable approach to constitution making makes particular sense in the context of a pacted transition in which the outgoing regime retains enough support or power to remain a relevant player, legal continuity is valued, and elite consensus-building is more important or more realistic, at least initially, than democratic decision-making on constitutional issues. Even if not precisely in the form of a roundtable, a mechanism that enables elite-level negotiation of key issues, as well as a more public constitution-making process, is warranted in a variety of transitional settings.

Referendums and Plebiscites

Almost half the constitution-making exercises examined here used referendums or plebiscites at various stages.[43] A variety of motivations prompted use of these procedures, and they were carried out with highly varying degrees of the type of civic education necessary to enable voters to make meaningful judgments. Vivien Hart, in her chapter in this volume, observes that a referendum "may seem as close as the process can come to direct democracy . . . but rather than the voicing of complex desires and criticisms, the voter is faced with an up or down vote." She also notes that partisan pressure may be exerted on voters, a dynamic evident in some of the case studies. Across the board, however, the case studies in this volume suggest that referendums can be valuable in constitution making, conferring a degree of legitimacy on the process and its outcome.

Some of a referendum's benefits and limitations as a device for democratizing the constitution-making process were evident in the Polish experience. Turnout for the ratification vote was only 42.86 percent,[44] and votes were influenced more by political sympathies than any careful study of the text. However, the prospect of the referendum appeared to have a salutary effect on the drafting process, as the constitution writers had to anticipate public acceptability of their work. In this sense, public opinion had an important passive impact on the formulation of the text.[45] Moreover, the referendum, in the case study authors' view, "legitimized the document and contributed to the public's accepting it."

While referendums have been used usually to ratify a final constitution, as in Poland, Widner's study finds that in rare instances, referendums are held at an interim stage to seek popular approval of decisions made during negotiations preceding the actual constitution-making process.[46] All three of the instances she cites are included among the case studies here. In Spain, voters were asked to approve a transitional reform law adopted by parliament. In South Africa, the apartheid government called a referendum of white voters to test acceptance of its efforts to negotiate with the African National Congress. And in Venezuela, a referendum was held to decide whether to create a constituent assembly. The chapter here on Colombia provides a fourth example: A referendum was held on the question whether to establish a constituent assembly. In each of these cases, the referendum served a context-specific purpose, though on a general level, it was used—as with any referendum—to provide some degree of democratic authorization for particular political choices.

The Iraq case presents an altogether different type of referendum, called for the purpose of crafting a bargaining chip in constitutional deliberations (a separate nationwide ratification referendum also was held, as discussed below). Elites in Iraqi Kurdistan realized that the argument for preserving their autonomy needed to be made with reference to popular support, "hence the spontaneous poll organized by the Kurdistan Referendum Movement at the time of the January 2005 election, intended to demonstrate support for Kurdish independence." The unsurprising result, which overwhelmingly favored Kurdistan's independence, became a useful instrument for Kurdish negotiators during the drafting negotiations the following summer, as they pressed for greater regional powers.

When referendums are used for their more common purpose, ratification, they occasionally have proven to be a valuable corrective measure, even at the end of an inferior constitution-making process. Zimbabwe is an outstanding example. The legitimacy of the 1999 constitution-making process was openly disputed, given tight government control over it. In the referendum, voters rejected the constitution by 54 percent, despite a vigorous government campaign in favor of the document. The rejection "sparked a furious reaction from the government," including large-scale invasions of white-owned farms by Mugabe loyalists. Ironically, though the electorate accurately perceived that the constitution-making process was seriously flawed, the text it rejected would have been a substantive improvement over the existing constitution. Similarly, in Albania, voters rejected a 1994 constitutional draft when it arguably was developed in violation of the interim constitutional arrangements; some voters saw it as favoring the governing coalition. In Venezuela, voters in December 2007 narrowly defeated constitutional amendments sought by the government of Hugo Chavez, despite the incentive of promises of a shorter workweek and even though President Chavez by then controlled all the major levers of power.

A crucial question for determining the utility of referendums is whether and to what extent they confer legitimacy on the constitution-making process and its outcome. In general, the case study authors take the view that they do bolster popular legitimacy. Vivien Hart is somewhat more skeptical, particularly where a referendum on a final text is the only opportunity for public participation in the constitution-making process: "The oft-cited function of legitimation of the text, essential if a culture of constitutionalism is to support its implementation, may not be achieved merely by casting a vote." Providing a simple up or down vote after all the key decisions have been made, she notes, "is not adequate participation in democratic governance, and the public knows this." Instead, Hart argues that a referendum can be a meaningful way of "holding representatives to account and creating legitimacy for the constitution, but only when it is embedded in a process of continuous and sustained participation." Some cases demonstrate that referendums, notwithstanding their potential value, are just one item on the menu of options for ensuring legitimacy. In South Africa and Eritrea, the constitution makers considered ratification referendums unnecessary given that the overall open and democratic nature of the constitution-making processes served the legitimation function.

In Hungary, however, a referendum held on four substantive questions provided the main source of the amended constitution's legitimacy, in Arato and Miklosi's view, as it was the *only* "popular moment" in the entire constitution-making process. But overall, they see the degree of legitimacy enjoyed by the Hungarian constitution as low—as a result of the failure to replace entirely the communist-era constitution, and the use of a gradualist amendment approach instead. This example raises the thorny question of how and why, precisely, legitimacy matters. The harm to the quality of Hungarian democracy may be real, but the practical manifestations of that harm are difficult to discern. Hungary is a stable country that since its constitution-making process concluded has been accepted into both the European Union and NATO. Hungary is thus one of those cases in which the question whether the constitution-making process was successful or not must be given a mixed response; the process unfortunately failed to generate democratic legitimacy for the new constitution, and yet, despite that, the country has become a stable constitutional democracy.

Regardless of the extent to which a referendum generates democratic legitimacy, its results, so long as the voting is basically free and fair, can serve as a useful means of gauging public regard for a new constitution at the moment of its adoption and public perception of the fairness of the constitution-making process. Such results can be an imperfect gauge, however, as propaganda, partisan pressure, and other factors may influence voting. Albania in 1998 illustrates such imperfections: A high percentage of cast votes (90 percent) approved the new constitution after a polarizing referendum campaign, but the opposition boycotted and turnout was low, disturbing the reliability of the referendum as a means of measuring public perceptions. But other cases permit some clearer observations. With respect to Iraq, for example, it may be reasonable to conclude that the constitution enjoys high regard among Shia and Kurds, who approved it in large numbers, but not among Sunnis, who saw the constitution-making process as ultimately unfair; they overwhelmingly voted against it, though not in great enough numbers to block adoption of the constitution.

Overall, the case studies suggest that referendums can be useful in many instances.[47] They may serve to validate, or repudiate, a constitution and the process of its develop-

ment. And if they are carried out under free and fair conditions—and preceded by opportunities for public input as well as public education to enable a vote on the constitution to be an informed one—they can help build a sense of public ownership and engagement with the new charter that is essential to healthy constitutionalism.

Interim Arrangements

Among the 194 constitution-writing exercises from 1975 to 2003 in Widner's study, one-third involved the preparation of an interim constitution, or a set of immutable principles or essential features intended to serve as required elements of the permanent constitution. These interim arrangements sometimes reinstated and selectively amended an earlier constitution.[48] Of the cases in this volume, more than half involved some type of interim arrangement (see Table 22.3 above).[49] The disproportionate representation of interim arrangements in this volume compared to Widner's data likely reflects their necessity in situations of regime change, conflict resolution, or other ruptures, where preexisting governance structures have either disintegrated or been discredited. Tables 22.2 and 22.3 above, considered together, show that all the cases in which interim arrangements were put in place were those involving periods of conflict, or transitions from conflict or authoritarian rule. None of the countries in the institutional crisis or reform category used interim arrangements; no regime rupture had occurred proximate to the constitution-making exercise.

Interim arrangements often are negotiated among political elites, generally in a closed or even secret manner—including through the use of a roundtable structure, as discussed above—though the case studies here also include arrangements specified in peace agreements or imposed by an occupation authority. Such arrangements may take a variety of forms, including a fully elaborated but explicitly temporary constitution, a statute that serves in place of a constitution, or a political agreement among conflicting parties who intend to engage in constitution making.[50] Whatever the form, two main aspects of such arrangements relevant to constitution-making processes are, first, the provision of operative transitional measures intended to serve as a constitutional placeholder, and second, the specification of fundamental principles to guide the future development of the state, including in some (but not all) instances to guide the development of a new constitution.

Operative Transitional Arrangements

To give just a few examples of the types of operative transitional arrangements adopted in the cases in this volume, in Spain, the 1976 "fundamental law" was effectively a transitional constitution sponsored by the king and the prime minister appointed by him, and approved by popular referendum.[51] In Nicaragua's revolutionary context, the 1974 constitution—discredited beyond repair—was promptly abolished and a "fundamental statute" as well as a "statute of rights and guarantees" were put in place to provide a temporary constitutional framework. Some transitional arrangements lay out requirements for the course of a constitution-making process, as in Eritrea. By contrast, the author of the Cambodia case study laments that the transitional provisions in the Paris Peace Agreement missed the opportunity to guide the constitution-making process, though the agreement did require certain substantive constitutional features.[52]

South Africa's experience provides an excellent example of a two-stage constitution-making process utilizing interim arrangements. There, in relatively closed and hard-fought negotiations, elites agreed upon a transitional constitution, followed by a two-year process of more open and participatory constitution making by an elected constitutional assembly that resulted in the adoption of a permanent constitution. The 1993 interim constitution, adopted in the first phase, put in place a power-sharing system that was used as a transitional device to achieve the objectives of immediate conflict resolution and peaceful coexistence. The national unity government formed at that stage, as well as other mechanisms intended to level the electoral playing field,[53] created political space for forming a new, integrative social contract and a majoritarian system (with protections for minorities) in the second stage. The interim constitution also outlined the procedures for making the final constitution, incorporating a set of principles with which the final text would have to comply. In effect, the interim constitution was a peace treaty, and while the need for it to serve that function resulted in some imperfections as a constitutional document, it created new facts on the ground that enabled the final constitution to be written in a more propitious atmosphere.[54]

The South African case illustrates the potential benefits of making intermediate reforms for a transitional period where there is a need for immediate compromises not suited for a constitution that is meant to endure, and where it is not feasible to craft those compromises in a democratic and transparent forum. (Similarly, the Bosnia case illustrates the harm of setting out in a permanent constitution the same sort of compromises agreed in closed negotiations, as discussed below.) The South African example also, however, raises a cautionary point for future cases: Once the interim constitution was agreed, it became a template for the final constitution. This may not have been problematic in South Africa, but it suggests the difficulty of revisiting the substance of interim agreements.[55] The Spanish experience also illustrates this phenomenon. A regionalization and devolution program put in place during the transition period was not supposed to prejudice the final constitutional dispensation on the key issue of regional autonomy, but, in the event, it became irreversible.[56]

Preconstitutional Principles

The extent to which the principles specified in some interim arrangements are consecrated in the permanent constitution varies. In South Africa, as discussed in the next section, judicial review by a constitutional court ensured that the final constitution was consistent with the thirty-two essential principles agreed by the parties that negotiated the interim constitution. In Cambodia, where there was no such enforcement mechanism and the UN Transitional Authority, in the case study author's view, was not as assertive on these points as it might have been, the constituent assembly did not hew closely to the principles in the 1991 peace agreement that were intended to be embodied in the constitution. Instead, the Cambodian assembly drew on two prior constitutions as the main substantive sources for the new constitution.

In Namibia, the constituent assembly effectively adopted the preconstitutional principles as its own, minimizing the need for judicial or other enforcement. The UN Security Council resolution that set the framework for the constitution-making process had failed to speak to the nature and content of the constitution to be created. The Namibian political parties regarded this as a serious shortcoming and consequently agreed to the so-called 1982 Constitutional Principles, brokered by international negotiators. The assembly formally adopted the principles as the basis for its work at its first meeting. Taken together, these examples suggest that the need for a mechanism to enforce compliance with preconstitutional principles depends entirely on the strength of the parties' will to adhere to them, or the need (as in South Africa) to back the principles with a guarantee as a means of securing agreement to proceed with constitution making.

With respect to both operative transitional arrangements and preconstitutional principles, the South Africa case in particular suggests that, in deeply divided societies, measures that safeguard the interests of all relevant groups appear to help in completing a transition without violence or process breakdown. However, the Iraq experience—in which the "transitional administrative law" served as an interim constitution and established basic requirements for the final constitution-making process—suggests that such measures may be insufficient in this regard. Perhaps the fact that an occupation authority imposed the law, following compressed negotiations among some of the parties rather than genuine negotiations among all key stakeholders, contributed to its inadequacy in ensuring a peaceful transition.

Judicial Roles

In a handful of cases, a constitutional or other court played a role in the constitution-making process. These cases illustrate a variety of ways in which the judiciary can provide legal interpretations that become part of the process or enforce political agreements in the unsettled conditions that usually accompany constitution making.

In South Africa—the most significant example—the interim constitution of 1993 both created a new Constitutional Court, and required it to review whether the final draft of the permanent constitution complied with thirty-two core principles laid out in the interim document. The court returned one draft to the constitutional assembly to revise eight points judged to be inconsistent with the principles; the assembly then modified the relevant provisions accordingly, and the court certified the amended document in a second decision. By assigning this task to the court, the political party leaders who crafted the interim constitution effectively substituted judicial affirmation of compliance with their political agreement for a more purely democratic validation of the final constitution.[57] In other words, the unelected court was given the authority to override the decisions of the democratically elected assembly on the basis of a comparatively undemocratically created constitutional pact.[58] The unprecedented role accorded to the court at least partly reflected South Africa's strong legal tradition, and lingering respect for the law as a means of dealing with conflict, both among those who were the oppressors and those who were oppressed during the apartheid period.[59]

The South African Constitutional Court exercised great care in formulating its certification decisions, its decisions were widely accepted, and, importantly, the invention of its certifying role broke a deadlock in the transition negotiations. But it would be difficult to recommend such an approach to other new or fragile democracies, which rarely have a supply of well-qualified, astute, independent judges comparable to South Africa and rarely enjoy the same level of respect for judicial institutions.[60] Where conditions similar to those in South Africa are found, however, judicial review may be useful in ensuring adherence to agreed-upon fundamental principles.

Among the case studies, other examples can be found of more limited, and more commonplace, roles for the judiciary in constitution-making processes. In Colombia, the Supreme Court ruled on a challenge to the presidential decree establishing the constituent assembly. Despite existing constitutional provisions authorizing only the congress to effect constitutional reforms, the court relied on the notion of popular sovereignty to uphold the decree, which was based on the results of a referendum that overwhelmingly supported the creation of a constituent assembly. Similarly, in Poland, the Supreme Court played a part in the process by examining 433 challenges to the validity of the referendum approving the constitution (it decided that the procedure had been valid).

Looking more broadly at constitutional formation during transition periods, Poland and Hungary provide additional examples of important judicial actions. Polish courts—in particular, the constitutional court—played a role during the long stretch of piecemeal amendment of the 1952 constitution that preceded the enactment of a new constitution. During that time, the courts declined to enforce some of the old constitutional provisions, relying on the newly introduced constitutional principles instead. Courts also rewrote some old constitutional provisions on the basis of both the new principles and provisions of the European Convention on Human Rights. The case study authors note that "in this way, the judicial branch civilized and modernized the old constitution and prepared a relatively smooth transition into the post-1997 constitutional order." In Hungary, the "air of temporariness" surrounding the constitution—the patchwork nature of the amendments to it, its shaky legitimacy, and the circumstances of the negotiated transition—enhanced the significance of the constitutional court's role as the constitution's guardian. In those unsettled conditions, the court, through its interpretations, effectively helped to make the constitution. As the consolidation of the new regime progressed and major interpretive rulings were made, the court's judicial activism diminished. These two examples demonstrate how capable judiciaries can strengthen constitutional democracy when performing their ordinary interpretive functions during extraordinary times.

Inclusiveness and Representation

The case studies indicate that the democratic representativeness of and degree of inclusiveness among constitution makers affect the perceived legitimacy of a constitution-making process, as well as the degree to which its outcome reflects a true social contract among all relevant groups.[61] A lack of inclusiveness may create a need for measures to avoid the disproportionate influence of a dominant political force. Moreover, the breadth of representation among decision makers of relevant groups and factions will likely determine whether the parties necessary to reach a durable constitutional bargain are at the table. The question of who needs to be included or represented depends entirely on the specific circumstances of the case, but generally, the cases show that consideration should be given, inter alia, to elite groups and other power holders; ethnic and minority groups; sectarian groups; civil-society organizations, especially those that are organized and active; and women. Particularly in deeply divided societies and those emerging from conflict, an inclusive approach can be vital to enabling conflicting parties to debate and negotiate the terms of the new national order and resolve important differences peacefully.

The most basic procedure for ensuring that the constitution makers are representative of the citizenry and include leaders of societal groups with varying interests is to elect the principal constitution-making body democratically, particularly through proportional representation.[62] An elected or partly elected body was a part of the process in all the case studies in this volume.[63] In Colombia, for example, the elections for the constituent assembly were based on new electoral rules that opened up the political process as never before to those outside traditional power structures, even though turnout was very low. Those traditional forces fought back later, but the constitution embodies very significant democratic reforms, no doubt affected by the assembly's composition.

Additional procedural techniques to ensure inclusiveness among constitution makers and enhance representativeness include appointing a broad-based constitutional com-

mission to play a key role in the process, as in Eritrea. Another technique involves supplementing an elected constituent assembly membership with some appointed members representing relevant groups in society, to ensure that a broad range of voices are present at the negotiating table. In Afghanistan, quotas for certain groups were established for the selection of members of the Constitutional Loya Jirga, and 10 percent of the seats were set aside for presidential appointment, "to ensure that certain groups or individuals important to the process (in the government's eyes) were represented." As with other aspects of constitution-making processes, the particular circumstances shape the particular procedural choices made to ensure representation: In Eritrea, for example, citizens living abroad were considered to have been crucial to the armed struggle in providing intellectual, diplomatic, and financial resources. Consequently, provision was made for their representation in the constituent assembly. In South Africa, although no seats were guaranteed for particular groups, inclusion and protection of the interests of minority groups were assured by constraining the substantive choices available to the constitutional assembly through prior negotiation of a set of binding constitutional principles.

In some cases, the formal promise of representation and inclusion is unfulfilled in reality. Overall, the cases demonstrate that fairly run elections are a valuable means of democratizing the constitution-making process. Several cases, however, illustrate that problematic elections can fail to fulfill their democratizing potential. For example, the constituent assembly in Venezuela was elected, but President Chavez manipulated the election to ensure that his followers controlled the assembly.

In the same vein, an appointment mechanism that is ostensibly established to broaden inclusion can be misused. In Uganda, both the electoral and appointment procedures were distorted, and the constituent assembly election process had a markedly negative impact on democratic representation even beyond constitution making. The election process gave every advantage to the National Resistance Movement and suppressed any other political party activity; consequently, the elections "became a turning point at which the Movement emerged as a de facto single ruling party." In addition, one-quarter of the seats in the constituent assembly were set aside supposedly to provide representation of various sectors. But the ruling National Resistance Movement's supporters filled nearly all the appointed slots, demonstrating that the nature and motivation of the appointing authority determine the extent to which an appointment procedure accomplishes its nominal objective.[64] As a result of all these maneuvers, the constitution-making process failed to achieve a genuine popular consensus on Uganda's political system.

Some cases also illustrate the problem of excluding key stakeholders, a dynamic that in some instances involved shutting the opposition out of constitution making,[65] and in others involved self-exclusion by boycotters.[66] In either situation, the depth and durability of any consensus achieved in the process can be harmed. In Nicaragua, for example, some opposition elements boycotted the process, thus limiting the consensus reached. As a result, though the constitution-making process was an important aspect of the transition, it cannot be said to have facilitated reconciliation.

In Iraq, too, electing the constitution drafters did not translate into real representation. This was due to the Sunni Arab boycott of the election and electoral rules that made Iraq a single district. Also, in the endgame where the real negotiating occurred, political party leaders excluded assembly members from the process, leaving them in the dark even as to the contents of the text. Iraq perhaps more than any other case dramatizes the need to have all key groups fully involved. The

constitution-making process had the potential to play a crucial role in preventing the country's slide into civil war, but the exclusion of Sunni representatives and Sunni interests from the process precluded this possibility.

Some cases demonstrate the paramount importance, in certain circumstances, of elite participation in the constitution-making process, so long as credible representatives of all key groups are included. In Spain, elite buy-in was regarded as essential, the negotiation process involved closed (at times secret) political party negotiations, and there was no public participation. Yet the outcome there, on the whole, can surely be considered a success.[67] In Namibia, too, strong elite ownership of the process provided excellent conditions for success. Based on that particular experience, the case study author comments that the "process of constitution making must be driven by elites . . . sustained by popular support." In South Africa, the success of the first stage of constitution making, which produced the negotiated interim constitution, hinged on the participation by and consensus reached among elites on both sides of the racial divide.

It is clear that regardless of the inclusiveness of a process, the support of the dominant political forces—sometimes certain political parties, sometimes individuals—is required for implementation of the constitution ultimately to occur. Spain, where the king and other political elites backed the constitution, is a positive example in this regard; Eritrea, where President Afwerki thwarted effectuation of the constitution, is a negative one.

Direct Public Participation

The manner and significance of providing opportunities for public participation in constitution-making processes emerged as a central topic in this study. The spectrum of citizen involvement in constitution making evident in the case studies runs from no involvement at all to direct consultation and substantive input, with tremendous variation among the cases in how participation was structured and whether and how public views influenced the result.[68] Where the constitution-making process featured public participation, the timing of this element varied as well: In most cases, it occurred during the drafting or approval phases, though in Colombia, public action fueled the start of the constitution-making process.

Election of representatives who will draft or deliberate on the content of a constitution—a form of indirect participation—was the most commonly utilized procedure in the cases for involving the public, and is discussed above. The use of referendums, a direct but limited form of participation, is addressed above as well. The discussion here is focused on direct public participation in the form of consultation procedures that solicit substantive citizen input and, in the best-managed cases, also educate the public about constitutional questions to be decided.[69] The East Timor chapter highlights the importance of distinguishing between civic education and popular consultation—sometimes conflated in both constitution-making practice and analysis of public participation. Though this point is not explored throughout the chapters, future constitution makers would be well advised to focus separate attention on both of these aspects of citizen outreach.

What does a serious program of public education and consultation look like? South Africa stands as perhaps the most elaborate and best-regarded example of such a program to date.[70] The outreach effort there was very wide-ranging and extensive, including public meetings, civil-society workshops, a newsletter published by the constitutional assembly, constitutional education television and radio programs, a telephone talk line, a Web site for the assembly, distribution of millions of copies of the draft constitution at various stages, posters, pamphlets, and advertising. The consultation process was conducted in two phases. In the first, more open-ended phase of consultation, the process elicited nearly two million submissions to the assembly, though the vast majority of these were signatures on petitions regarding a variety of issues. Of the submissions received, just over 11,000 contained substantive comments, some of which amounted to wish lists. The bulk of the substantive submissions reflected popular sentiment that the most important issues for inclusion in the constitution concerned immediate material needs, such as more jobs, more housing, better educational opportunities, crime prevention, and clean water. The petitions addressed issues including language rights (about half the petitions called for Afrikaans to be one of the official languages, an inevitable outcome of the process in any event), animal rights, abortion, the death penalty, and the seat of the parliament. Of less demonstrated concern were issues more typically associated with democratic constitutions, such as civil and political rights.[71]

In the second phase, the constitutional assembly invited comments on a working draft and received 1,438 submissions and almost 250,000 petitions concerning issues similar to those raised in the first phase. Much skepticism was expressed, including in some of the submissions and in responses to surveys, about the seriousness of the invitation for public comment, though the assembly was lauded for seeking to involve the public. However, while the submissions in both phases were mostly not directly translatable into constitutional text, they were carefully analyzed and summarized in reports presented to the constitutional assembly and certainly informed the constitution writers of the main trends in citizen interest in the substance of the constitution.

The emphasis on constitutional education, neglected in some other cases, was a hallmark of the South African consultation process. It was recognized at the outset that without empowering a population with no culture of constitutionalism, high levels of illiteracy, and low levels of access to media, the consultation process would be hollow. Thus, throughout the constitution-making process and interwoven with the consultation initiatives, interactive programs involving members of the constitutional assembly and the general public, media campaigns, advertising, and various types of printed matter were all used to create awareness of the constitutional process and opportunities to provide input, and to provide information about constitutional issues.

Moreover, the iterative nature of the public participation program—a more open-ended first phase, followed by a more focused second phase based on a draft—was a useful feature.[72] This approach allowed the constitutional assembly to begin consultation by broadly canvassing public opinion on constitutional priorities, and then to seek public comment on actual draft constitutional provisions and alternatives. As a result, opportunities were enhanced for meaningful popular participation in the constitutional design, as well as for a more extended—and in the second phase, more specific—civic education and consultation component.

Eritrea also conducted a very extensive public education and consultation process. Civic education organized by the constitutional commission reached more than 500,000 citizens. Seventy-three local committees and a series of provincial offices organized public education. In addition to commission members, over 400 specially trained instructors conducted public seminars in village and town meetings. In light of an 80 percent illiteracy rate in Eritrea, the commission organized songs, poetry, short stories, a comic book, mobile theater groups, and concerts dealing with constitutional themes, along with extensive use of radio programs. During the consultation phase, public meetings

on constitutional proposals in 157 locations involved 110,000 participants. An additional 11,000 Eritreans participated in consultations in sixteen locations outside the country. Rounds of public consultation occurred prior to drafting, on the commission's draft, and on the version approved by the legislature.

Even with respect to these exemplary consultation and education procedures, it must be acknowledged that their precise impact is exceedingly difficult to measure. In South Africa, the direct impact of public input on the text appears to have been slight, but the participation process is credited with having generated broad public awareness and positive popular perceptions of the constitution-making process. In Eritrea, the commissioners fully expected at the outset that public input would shape the constitution, but the concrete effect on the text was limited, as many of the public comments were not translatable into constitutional provisions. Nevertheless, the case study author (who chaired the commission) remarks that "it is beyond dispute that the public consultation and debates throughout the constitution-making process were important in instilling a sense of public ownership in the constitution. Whether and to what extent public input actually influenced the text of the constitution ultimately adopted is more difficult to discern." Some commissioners were clearly inspired by the depth and extent of public comment: "The spirit of such public input is reflected in the constitution." But the ideas that the public put forward were, for the most part, "not susceptible to being explicitly translated into the language of a modern constitution." In the end, the commission's hypothesis that public participation would critically influence the text "cannot be said to have been proven." But, as Selassie makes clear, the sense of public ownership the process created was certainly valuable in laying a foundation for constitutionalism, even though that value may have dissipated with the government's refusal to implement the new constitution and the passage of a long period of undemocratic rule.

The constitution-making experiences of Uganda and Zimbabwe suggest that invitations of public input may be little more than empty gestures unless accompanied by intentions to reflect seriously on that input. Both countries undertook extensive public consultation efforts, even though the constitutional commissions that conducted the consultations were effectively under the thumbs of the governments. The Uganda case study author observes that "rarely in Africa has one seen the level of popular engagement in education seminars, debates, media discussions, and submission of opinion memoranda that was evident in the Ugandan constitution-making process." In Zimbabwe, the commission held over 5,000 meetings in all fifty-seven districts, conducted a nationwide poll, and administered a questionnaire. And yet, in both of these two cases, the constitutional text was bent to the government's will. Indeed, the consultation process in Uganda "may have lent unwarranted legitimacy to the more undemocratic aspects of the process and the resulting constitution, giving the Movement more time to entrench itself."

Even where the motivations behind a participation program are positive, careful channeling of the results of a consultation process is critical to maximizing the program's potential benefits, as seen in Brazil. Public involvement in that case was very extensive: The constituent assembly's media center produced over 700 television programs and over 700 radio programs, and a weekly journal was broadly distributed; 182 public hearings were held; 5 million questionnaires were disseminated to citizens and civic groups; nearly 73,000 popular suggestions were received; and even though a popular amendment required 30,000 voter signatures for consideration, 122 such amendments were submitted, some with more than one million signatures. However, the intense public

participation contributed to an incoherent textual outcome, particularly because of the inability of a weak party system and weak president to channel the public input into a rational framework. Moreover, the highly politicized environment created by using the congress as a constituent assembly opened the door to undue influence by special interests, which lobbied forcefully. While the emphases on openness and democratic process in the Brazilian participation program were laudable, the execution of the program—in particular, the failure to define reasonable parameters for the issues to be considered and to impose reasonable constraints on the influence of organized pressure groups—led the process seriously astray.[73] Without such constraints, or any dominant party to exercise control over the process, "in principle and in final result, nothing was deemed too trivial for possible inclusion in the new constitutional text."

The Albania case study is the only one to quantify the impact of a public consultation process. Compared with some of the other cases, the process involved a relatively small number of participants—in the hundreds—but the program was well organized and conducted, involving several types of consultation procedures. Among the hundreds of suggestions from the public regarding changes to the draft constitution, the parliamentary constitutional drafting commission incorporated more than fifty proposed changes affecting 45 (of 183 total) articles into the revised text, which ultimately was submitted to a popular referendum. The nature of these changes varied widely, but some touched on high-profile subjects, such as property restitution. The sheer number of changes vividly demonstrated how seriously public input was taken. Ultimately, notwithstanding an opposition boycott, the constitution received the support of 90 percent of voters in a referendum, and the opposition eventually came to accept the document as well. While a public participation process could no doubt affect the general perspectives of constitution writers, and could produce public comments that mirror and bolster the priorities and formulations that the drafters already prefer, impact in these respects is difficult to identify. Including or modifying actual constitutional text in response to public input is, therefore, a helpful, though imperfect, indicator of the genuineness of a participation process. But a public consultation process can be genuine and have a legitimizing effect even if it cannot be tracked to specific identifiable textual modifications.

While most cases do not present dramatic evidence of public input resulting in textual change, Vivien Hart provides several examples of constitution-making experiences—including Canada, Colombia, Nicaragua, South Africa, and Sri Lanka—in which constitutional language was changed as a consequence of participation, the clearest evidence being the addition and development of women's rights and protection of the interests of indigenous peoples in various texts. She proposes that "a handful of examples is enough to indicate the potential of participatory processes to bring previously unconsidered people and issues into the constitutional arena." Regardless of how many words in a constitution can be traced directly to public input, the tabling of ideas, grievances, and goals by groups and individuals within society can inform the crafting of a national charter. From this perspective, Hart argues that an "increasing body of practical experience demonstrates that public participation can change the constitutional agenda."

Aside from the impact of public participation on constitutional legitimacy, ownership, and content, and regardless of the difficulty of measuring those effects, there appear to be practical benefits to public participation.[74] It is possible, for example, that opening the constitutional debate to groups previously excluded from, or underrepresented in, the political process helps to build social consensus. It is also possible that participation processes effectively demonstrate the practice of democracy, and that such processes build capacity in civil society.[75] This volume cannot claim such benefits definitively, particularly given the uneven implementation of participation programs among the cases, but arguments can be made for each. There is little doubt that widespread public education and debate over fundamental rights during a constitution-making process produce increased citizen awareness of those rights, which, in turn, can enable the expression of public demands that those rights be enforced. Vivien Hart cites evidence from a systematic study of Uganda that its legacy of education and participation in the constitution-making process was evident in a more informed, critical, and questioning public in subsequent politics. In Cambodia, where the United Nations and civil-society groups undertook a program of constitutional education—but popular participation was rejected by the drafters—the "process of reading and hearing about the constitution, and of learning that something so significant to their future was being decided in secret may well have influenced the population's long-term expectations." As a result, Cambodians have been "remarkably persistent in calling for greater transparency and accountability of government." The case study author speculates that "had the demands for participation by the vibrant civil society that took shape in the course of the process actually been met . . . perhaps the process itself would have been a capacity-building exercise, strengthening the role of civil society and the population at large in the political destiny of the country."

Furthermore, some of the case studies illustrate clear context-specific rationales for public participation. Several cases illuminate the importance of public expectations in determining the practical necessity of a public participation program. In Iraq, public participation was expected, desired, and promised in the interim constitution; the frustration of those expectations was one of the key flaws of the constitution-making process. In South Africa, a cultural "fetish with consultation" dictated the necessity of the strategy there.[76] And in Eritrea, the constitution-making process was part of a broader transition process that stressed public participation and popular authorization. A 1993 referendum on independence—intended to demonstrate the independence struggle's popular backing—set a precedent for popular participation: "Eritreans saw the constitution as fulfilling the goals of the liberation war, thus helping to vindicate their enormous sacrifice." Following a revolutionary armed struggle, "the Eritrean political and social context was marked by an anti-imperialist and anti-feudal bourgeois ideology that was suspicious of any event or process controlled by elites." Against the backdrop of these circumstances, the intensive public consultation process can easily be seen as crucial to ensuring popular acceptance of the outcome.

A dynamic similar to the Eritrean case was evident in Nicaragua. In the revolutionary context of the constitution-making exercise, and the consequent rejection of the legacy of pact making associated with prior constitutions, participation was needed to ensure popular acceptance of the result. Civil-society groups were invited to engage with the constitutional commission before an initial draft was prepared; following the drafting, 150,000 copies of the document were distributed. Twelve debates were televised, and seventy-three town hall meetings held around the country were broadcast live. Finally, a review committee reported on public input and prepared a second draft. In all, about 100,000 people attended the meetings, 2,500 citizens made presentations, and 1,800 more submitted written comments. Some questions were raised regarding the genuineness of the pro-

cess—government critics generally viewed the public meetings as "well-controlled forums to permit only perfunctory modifications to the original draft constitution"—but most independent observers found the discussions generally lively and freewheeling. The emphasis on participation "was part of a larger revolutionary process that aimed to mobilize civil society groups politically." Public input in this case had concrete effects; changes were made to strengthen women's rights, the rights of indigenous peoples, protection of minors and the elderly, and recognition of the rights of prisoners.

The Nicaraguan case also shows, however, that public participation is not the only necessary dimension of consensus building. Though this process "achieved significant levels of citizen involvement," minimal elite consensus was developed. Subsequent constitutional reforms, on the other hand, involved low levels of public participation, but—in a reversion to the historical pattern of pact making—were more successful in achieving mutual elite accommodation. There is generally a role for both public and elite participation at varying stages of the constitutional process.

Another context-based rationale for public participation was evident in East Timor. There, the political dominance in the constituent assembly of the Fretilin party constrained the debate, resulting in the party's own draft powerfully influencing the final text. A genuine sustained process of public participation might have helped to open up the debate and prevent an outcome in which one political party seemed to own the constitution.[77] Instead, the civic education and consultation process was poorly structured, rushed, and ultimately amounted to "window dressing."

The Iraq case presents an additional context-specific rationale for conducting a program of broad public participation. By boycotting the constituent assembly elections, the Sunni Arab community—one of three major communities in Iraq—denied itself an elected seat at the drafting table.

> It followed that the only way in which Sunni Arab citizens of Iraq would be able to express their views to the constitution committee [of the constituent assembly] would be by direct communication.... In other words, it was clear that unelected Iraqis would need to participate in the drafting. The public participation component of new constitutionalism, therefore, began to look less like the icing on the cake of universal suffrage and more like an essential peacemaking instrument to prevent a full-scale civil war in the heart of the Middle East.

In the event, however, the consultation process was unduly rushed and thus became utterly inconsequential. Furthermore, public access to participation opportunities, especially by Sunni Arabs, was uneven due to security issues and sectarian divisions. No results from the consultations were reported in time for drafters to consider them. Similarly, in Albania, the major opposition faction's boycott of the constitutional process heightened the importance of reaching out to the affected members of the public and engaging them directly in the constitutional discussion. However, Albania's consultation process was much better managed and, as a consequence, had greater impact than in Iraq.

The contrast between the Iraq and Albania experiences illustrates the importance of creating the institutional means to link participation to the actual drafting process. In Iraq, while some effort was made to create structures for receiving, digesting, and forwarding public input to the drafters, those efforts came too late, were distorted by sectarian divisions, and ultimately were ineffective. In Albania, by contrast, a professionally managed administrative body supported by foreign donors organized all the public comments received and assisted the parliamentary constitutional commission and its technical staff in the review process. As a result, the drafters actually considered citizens' and civil-society groups' proposals.

Fiji's experience powerfully illustrates the potential danger of failing to provide for public participation in particular circumstances. The constitutional commission there held some public hearings while developing its lengthy report. However, once the commission submitted its report, the remainder of the constitution-making process was conducted behind closed doors in parliament. The case study authors attribute the coup that occurred one year after the constitution came into effect partly to the secretiveness of the constitution-making process, as well as to the failure to engage in significant public consultation and education regarding the constitution.

A broadly applicable rationale for incorporating a program of public participation into the constitution-making process is the possible emergence of an international legal norm requiring states to do so. The examples of public participation in the present volume appear to have been driven more by evolving political norms and public expectations than by a sense of an obligation under international law. That said, Franck and Thiruvengadam (in this volume) conclude that while they do not yet find a specific requirement under international law for a particular form of participation in constitution making, there is a clear trend in practice and "growing acceptance of the norm that constitutions should be prepared through participatory processes with a high degree of transparency." This view tracks a decision of the UN Human Rights Committee, to which they refer, which found that under the International Covenant on Civil and Political Rights, a public right of participation extends to constitution making, though it is up to each state to choose "the modalities of such participation." Hart (also in this volume) more assertively argues the case for an emerging legal right to participation in constitution making. She notes that "no single authoritative set of standards has yet emerged in law or from organizational sources" to guide public participation, but affirms that the culture of constitution making has come to include the expectation of democratic practice.

As with other elements of constitution making, an overarching lesson from the case studies is that choices with respect to the degree and nature of direct public participation should be tailored to the particular circumstances. Cases such as South Africa, Eritrea, and Nicaragua illustrate the potential benefits of participation as well as the reality that certain political and social conditions effectively require openness and extensive participation if the results of a constitution-making process are to be regarded as legitimate. On the other hand, in Poland, which eschewed public participation, negative public sentiment with respect to the idea of participation was shaped by prior experience, as sham public discussions were typical in constitution-making processes in communist countries. In 1952, official data record that more than 11 million Polish citizens took part in more than 200,000 meetings within nine weeks, though as the case study author states, "needless to say, there was no room for any criticism, and the whole campaign had a purely decorative character. That was why, forty-five years later, any attempt to copy such a procedure would produce more distrust than support among the electorate." Although two of the earlier case studies—Spain and Namibia—show that excellent results can be achieved with elite-driven, mostly closed processes, more recent experience suggests that it is now far harder to claim legitimacy without at least some nod to public participation.

That said, while the case studies and thematic chapters on the whole regard public participation as valuable in terms of democ-ratizing the constitution-making process and legitimating the results, some cases in this volume raise a number of difficult questions still to be answered in theory and practice regarding how to structure and use the results of public participation to maximize its potential legitimating function.[78] Recognizing these questions should not discourage implementation of public participation processes; rather, it should encourage further exploration of their conduct and significance, and further development of effective participation procedures.

At the most basic level, the practical purposes of soliciting participation remain underspecified. Is the purpose to create the perception of legitimacy and the feeling of ownership among the population, or actually to shape the constitutional text? Is a public sense of participation all that is needed to create legitimacy and ownership, or must there be evidence that the constitution writers actually took into account popular views?[79] Is the purpose to develop a culture of constitutionalism, and if so, how does participation serve that purpose? Furthermore, what precisely does participation mean?[80] Should showing up and being counted among the attendees at a public hearing be regarded as participation, or must one actually express a view on a constitutional issue, and must that view be recorded and transmitted to the drafters? Must drafters seriously deliberate on public input for participation to serve plausible normative or instrumental purposes?[81] A program of public participation, regardless of whether outputs are recorded and utilized, might encourage dialogue among citizens about a country's future, contributing to reconciliation and a culture of respect for the constitution, but whether such a benefit actually is realized is difficult to discern.

The Eritrea case study author argues that "involving the public in the process empowers the public, giving its members a sense of ownership of the constitution and allowing them to air their views on a range of critical issues that affect their lives. Thus, public participation in the making of a constitution necessarily raises questions of substance." But is the public truly empowered if the views they express do not directly influence the substance of the constitution? The East Timor case study authors argue that drafters must at least consider the public's views for a consultation process to be meaningful.[82] Measuring such consideration is challenging, however. In most cases, the actual impact of public input on the text—the most tangible way to gauge the extent of the drafters' consideration—appears to be limited.[83] The case studies on the whole suggest that the purpose and effect of most consultation processes lie in the realm of conferring legitimacy and ownership rather than providing drafting guidance. And yet, without casting doubt on such aims, it should be noted that the extent to which participation *actually* produces legitimacy and ownership is difficult to assess, at least on the basis of information presented in this volume.[84]

A further set of issues concerns how input by individual citizens or civil-society groups should be treated when constitution writers wish to consider popular views. No clear methodological guidance emerges from the chapters on this point, but the development of such guidance would be useful, given growing interest in forms of participation. For example, what relevance and weight should be attached to individual citizen or interest group submissions, and based on what criteria, particularly where access to the process may be uneven throughout a society?[85] Reflecting public input in a text surely should not be a function of comparing tallies of submissions and comments for and against particular positions. What status should be accorded to public submissions compared to the positions of members of a demo-

cratically elected and soundly representative constitution-making body? Moreover, when many submissions are made, it is likely that different ones could be used to support quite varying textual provisions.[86] Is it reasonable for constitution writers to selectively adopt substantive positions offered by the public, or to selectively rely on submissions to support their own views—or does the invitation to comment imply some obligation to respect in the constitutional text at least dominant themes or requests among the popular views expressed?[87]

Though none of the case studies offers examples of rules applied to the process of review and consideration, in some instances, submissions have been summarized and digested for ease of review by constitution drafters. The common approach has been to allow the constitution makers to exercise their own discretion in determining whether and how to account for public input in crafting the text. This approach is reasonable, but it is apparent that even with the best of intentions, hundreds or thousands of public submissions cannot effectively inform the thinking of those negotiating and drafting the constitutional text unless they are organized into a usable form. Those designing future constitution-making processes would be well advised to make arrangements, and provide resources, for doing so. At the end of the consultations and debate, it is the responsibility of the members of a democratically selected constitution-making body to make choices, informed not only by the views received from members of the public but also by their own understanding of what is correct.

Finally, it must be acknowledged that it is difficult to distinguish the outcomes of the cases where serious efforts were made to involve the public from those where no space was made for participation, or where it amounted to little more than window dressing.[88] Future studies may usefully explore the question—not addressed in this volume—whether participation leads to substantively better or more durable and well-implemented constitutions.[89] Regardless of the results of such further inquiries, however, it is likely—and the impressions of some case study authors support the idea—that participation produces enhanced legitimacy, or popular perceptions of legitimacy, and supports the development of a culture of constitutionalism.[90] In cases where the public had opportunities to participate, the responses were generally enthusiastic and widespread, based on the numbers of participants in meetings and submissions of comments. Interested groups and the general public have seized chances to provide their input. These experiences demonstrate that in many contexts across a variety of cultures and regions, people want to participate; logically, where such desires are fulfilled, the citizenry's sense of ownership of the constitution is enhanced. And as the number of such experiences around the world increases, it is reasonable to assume that knowledge of those experiences will contribute to expectations on the part of the public in new cases that they should also be able to participate in their own constitutional reform exercises.

Timelines and Deadlines: When Is a Constitution-Making Process Too Long or Too Short?

The appropriate timeline for constitution making is one of the most idiosyncratic factors examined in this volume. The cases show that *long* and *short* have different meanings in different contexts, and that the value or harm of imposing deadlines cannot be generalized easily.[91] The most useful lessons from the case studies come from those in which timing was a central problem.[92]

In three such cases, external political forces set timelines that served their own needs and interests rather than those of the country in question.[93] In East Timor, the United Nations, anxious to conclude its work and rack up a success, set an agenda that rushed the process, thereby excluding the possibility of meaningful public consultation. In Zimbabwe, the three-month long constitutional negotiations in 1979, controlled by the British government, left key issues unresolved, including property rights and land reform, past human rights violations, and economic empowerment of the black majority. In Iraq, the severely rushed timetable, which weakened the process and its outcome, was driven by the demands and priorities of the United States, rather than by domestic needs. The extent to which rushing the process degraded its legitimacy was heightened by the fact that public hopes were otherwise. Focus-group research in April 2005 "revealed strong reservations across Iraq regarding the value of a hasty constitutional process." The actual process did not respect these public interests: "The sheer pace of the timetable made a farce of both idealist constitutionalism and any pragmatic form of intercommunal political bargaining." More specifically, the Iraq case indicates that constitution making should not be rushed when there is a need to develop popular authorization for unpopular positions, especially where leadership is new and weak. In other circumstances, bold and experienced leaders may be able to make bold and unpopular moves and bring their constituents along with them. Iraq's Sunni Arabs, however, without well-organized leadership and a clear vision of their own interests, needed time to develop their community's support for constitutional solutions such as federalism.

The self-interested agenda of an internal force can lead to a truncated process as well. In Venezuela, the short timeline—two-and-a-half months from the start of drafting to assembly approval, with the referendum one month later—was a manifestation of political manipulation by President Chavez, who pressed that timetable. But the suitability of a timetable cannot be judged by its length alone. Namibia's successful constitution-making exercise also was completed in two and a half months, from the first meeting of the constituent assembly to adoption. The appropriateness of a very short timeline and simple process may be explained by the high degree of consensus that existed before the constitution-making process started (for example, consensus on the importance of creating a unitary state). As all parties realized that creating a sovereign Namibia depended on the outcome of the process, they were "bent on making the process successful. SWAPO not only supported the constitution-making process wholeheartedly, but simultaneously pushed for its timely conclusion because it knew that an operating independence constitution was a prerequisite for SWAPO's entry into government." The process was, in the case study author's view, an "unqualified success," both in terms of the substance of the resulting document and the pride Namibians take in their constitution and the values it contains. In implementation, however, the constitution clearly was breached when the president obtained a third term of office, and power has become concentrated in the hands of the central government.

On the other extreme, Hungary's experience illustrates the potential danger of not having an agreed timetable at all. The process there was so drawn out that the window of political opportunity for crafting a completely new, more legitimate constitution closed before it could be done, and the 1996–97 effort to finally create a wholly new constitution consequently failed.[94] The Polish experience, on the other hand, demonstrates that a long, gradual process can, on balance, be valuable in a particular transitional setting. The eight years of constitution making there enabled the drafting of a text that reflected

new lessons from experience gained along the way. The need for significant institutional and procedural checks on the conduct of the political branches of government only became clear during the course of the process. Also, civil society developed considerably during the constitution-making period, so that it was fairly mature by the time the constitutional discussions entered their final stage. Contrary to the Hungary case study, the author of the Poland chapter concludes that setting time limits and target dates can be counterproductive, because it is impossible to predict the dynamics of a transition process at the outset.

South Africa stands out among the cases in the length of time devoted to negotiating the constitution-making procedures and substantive parameters—issues that were among those at the heart of the transition negotiations. More than three years of talks preceded agreement in June 1993 on a two-stage constitution-making process, with a negotiated interim constitution, a final constitution to be drafted by an elected body, and the use of binding constitutional principles to guide the drafters' work. The interim document was adopted in November 1993 and the final document at the end of 1996. The length of the entire process leading up to the final constitution's adoption was a consequence of many factors, including, perhaps most prominently, the main parties' commitment to achieving the maximum possible degree of consensus on both the procedures and substance of constitution making. Continuing violence stalled progress on many occasions as well, though crises sparked by particular violent episodes sometimes also helped to push the process forward. In the final two-year stage of constitution making, the complexity of the issues at hand, the assembly's undertaking to engage and consult the public, its dual-hatting as the regular parliament, and the decision not to begin by delegating preparation of a draft to a small group of experts were among the factors that contributed to the mad rush to the finish line as the deadline approached.

Aside from externally imposed (and damaging) constraints on timing, as in Iraq, as well as the impact on timing of political dynamics peculiar to the individual cases, the wide variation in time scales for the processes studied in this volume is partly explained by the varying assortments of procedural elements employed. Not surprisingly, a process that includes electing a constituent assembly, establishing an expert drafting body, meaningful civic education and public consultation, and a ratification referendum takes longer than one that utilizes an ordinary legislature, relies on a preexisting draft, and eschews public involvement. Given the variety of procedural choices to be made, as well as the varying complexity and contentiousness of the substantive constitutional issues to be decided in different countries, no optimal time frame can be calculated. But future constitution makers can be advised to ensure that sufficient time is set aside for all of the process elements that they choose to put in place. The case studies indicate that often the most time-consuming elements are elections for a constitution-making body, especially in countries emerging from conflict, where reliable voter rolls may not exist and electoral administration mechanisms may not be in place; establishing a constitutional commission or constituent assembly, including hiring of staff and development of rules of procedure; drafting, if starting more or less from scratch; and public education and consultation, if intended to be wide-ranging, and if drafters are to have an opportunity to consider public input.

External Assistance and Intervention

In assessing the role of foreign actors in the constitution-making exercises examined in this volume, a distinction must be drawn between, on one hand, advice and other technical or facilitative assistance provided by foreign experts, and, on the other hand, intervention in constitution-making processes on the part of foreign governments and international organizations.[95] The case studies show the former to have been quite helpful in a number of countries[96]; the latter has a more mixed history.

In Namibia, foreign experts played a significant role in the drafting process; as noted above, the constituent assembly appointed a three-member panel of South African lawyers to prepare a draft constitution. Foreign experts made useful contributions to the Polish constitution drafting process as well, particularly in the work of the 1989 parliament. But the limitations on their capacity to participate were similar to the limitations evident elsewhere with respect to foreign technical assistance: Few foreign experts spoke Polish well enough to take part in meetings, and, in this instance, few were truly experts in constitutional law. In addition, many of the experts were invited by the parliament's administration or political parties, and therefore were associated with particular political sympathies. In any event, there was a large supply of Polish scholars with expertise in comparative law and foreign constitutions, and thus, domestic experts played a significant role. Other cases in which foreign experts were particularly constructive include Eritrea, where an advisory body of foreigners assisted the constitutional commission, and Albania, where a body outside the national assembly—supported by the Organization for Security and Cooperation in Europe—effectively coordinated foreign advice provided to the assembly's drafters and were key to facilitating public participation. In these two cases, the expert advice had a neutral character, and was not provided through a political party.

However, that neutral foreign expert advice is provided does not necessarily mean that it is heeded; the degree of constitution drafters' receptivity varies across the cases.

In Cambodia, two foreign experts installed by the chair of the drafting committee helpfully provided a comparative perspective, drawing on various traditions, and were accessible to all members of the committee. However, they were quickly cut out of the process due to Prince Sihanouk's order to exclude foreigners from the constitution-making process. Instead, Sihanouk engaged a French law professor to prepare a draft to his liking, which became the basis for the final constitution. In Afghanistan, the drafters were wary of outside influence on their constitution; consequently, expert advice during the drafting phase had to be provided in a low-key manner. In Iraq, the case study author notes that the chair of the constitutional drafting committee was "skeptical of the value and propriety of any international involvement, however enlightened and unobtrusive." Nonetheless, some foreign experts provided by the United Nations and USIP did make progress in working with the committee to develop procedures and substantive proposals. But their opportunity to contribute to the process largely ended once the committee was effectively dissolved and the negotiations shifted to a small political circle working behind closed doors. On the whole, the case studies indicate that foreign expert advice on constitution making can contribute positively and constructively when it is respectful of domestic sovereignty, politics, culture, and history.

Foreign technical assistance can take a variety of forms in addition to offering advice. Practical assistance can include providing equipment and training, assisting (as in Albania) in the coordination of aspects of the process, designing participation mechanisms, and collecting and providing to constitution makers information about comparative models and options. In Afghanistan, for example, the United Nations played a significant role in organizing the logistical aspects of the Constitutional Loya Jirga. In Iraq, the UN mission and USIP each organized meetings for members of the drafting committee and other constitutional stakeholders, enabling them to explore options, develop proposals and, at times, find consensus on various issues. In addition, the UN constitutional support team assisted the drafting committee in designing thematic and technical subcommittees to organize its work.

While advice and other forms of technical assistance, sensitively delivered, are generally uncontroversial, the exertion of foreign pressure in the constitution-making process is another matter. The preceding section on timelines touches on the point that external agents will tend to pursue their own agendas. When the foreign actors are diplomats, dispatched to influence a constitution-making process, putting their own governments' priorities first is, in fact, their job. The problems posed by overbearing foreign interference are illuminated well in the Iraq case study. As the author notes, "in a dynamic familiar to observers of transitional governments, the idea of a permanent constitution for Iraq became, over time, more and more closely linked, in U.S. policy plans, with a nation-building success and a plausible exit strategy." U.S. heavy-handedness became more extreme as the process wore on. U.S. officials insisted on an unrealistic deadline; hosted Iraqi political leaders in the U.S. embassy for closed-door deal making; and expressed strong substantive views on the main issues, even circulating their own draft constitution in English. The U.S. ambassador personally played a visible role, including attending the national assembly meetings at which the deadline was extended.

In a similar, though perhaps less extreme, vein, UN and U.S. officials asserted themselves in Afghanistan's Constitutional Loya Jirga, not only mediating among various factions in an effort to overcome the final sticking points, but also laying on the table their own substantive "red lines" that the final constitutional text was not to cross. Moreover, as the case study author points out, "the United States and United Nations could have fostered an environment of democratic openness; instead, much of their political influence on the process reinforced the tendency of Afghan power brokers to maneuver out of the public eye." U.S. priorities in particular affected both the process and the result. During the negotiations, for example, the United States successfully supported the Karzai government's bid to centralize power in a few hands in Kabul. In the end, international pressure "forced an outcome, but not a consensus."

The Cambodian experience, on the other hand, suggests that in some circumstances, outside actors may be too stinting in their involvement. The United Nations applauded the conclusion of Cambodia's constitution-making process—even though the constitution was drafted in secret and the constituent assembly debated it for only five days—in no small part because of the United Nations' perceived need to end its mission successfully. The case study author argues that the United Nations should have exercised more control of the process to ensure better compliance with the peace agreement and deprive the political factions of control. He contends that the United Nations was "too sensitive" to Cambodian sovereignty. The United Nations paid close attention to the electoral process, but when it came to constitution making, bowed to Cambodian politics and Prince Sihanouk's preeminent role in the process.

Though Cambodia stands as an exception among the cases, generally foreign influence in a constitution-making process, for better or worse, will be strong—and difficult, if not impossible, for domestic players to avoid—in countries where foreign actors exercise control over the transition process. Such a situation can arise when foreign actors are responsible for ousting the previous regime (e.g., Afghanistan and Iraq)[97] or instrumen-

tal in resolving a conflict (e.g., Bosnia and East Timor). The burden rests on the outside players in such circumstances to gauge carefully the degree and nature of their involvement in constitution making that will contribute positively to the process and results.[98] In general, rather than demanding a particular end product or strengthening a particular party, the role of the United Nations or foreign powers is best focused on ensuring a good process—one that is broadly inclusive and has sufficient resources and staffing, adequate time, and neutral outside expert assistance. In addition, there may be circumstances, especially when constitution making takes place as part of a conflict resolution strategy, in which foreign actors may be seen as helpful or even essential as mediators or sponsors of a negotiation.[99]

Finally, even where the role of outsiders is confined to support for an essentially domestic process, the Ugandan experience provides a warning with respect to foreign involvement: "Many citizens interpreted international donor support for the constitution making process in Uganda as donor support for Museveni and his agenda." Donors, however, thought they were supporting a neutral process and "underestimated the extent to which the entire exercise was subject to political manipulation and the ways in which an unlevel playing field would influence the outcomes." A clear understanding of conditions in the recipient country is critical to avoiding such unintended consequences.

Incorporating Constitution Making in Peacemaking Processes

The few cases in which constitution making took place directly within the context of a peace process—as opposed to cases, such as Afghanistan and Cambodia, in which a peace negotiation laid the groundwork for a constitution-making exercise—reveal a special set of issues. Bosnia and Herzegovina is one such case, and it provides a cautionary tale. Unique among the cases examined here, the constitution was an integral part of the peace agreement. U.S. and European diplomats drafted the constitution, and while its main features were negotiated among the parties to the peace agreement, many of the details were not. Foreign analysts largely regard the constitution as lacking genuine democratic legitimacy, though it is, in effect, treated as legitimate. However, strong international pressure—and, in some instances, actual international control over political and legal decisions—has been required to implement the document.

Though at the time it seemed unavoidable to incorporate a complete new constitution (rather than interim constitutional arrangements) into the peace agreement, which was negotiated with the leaders of the wartime nationalist political parties, doing so institutionalized the stalemate that existed at the war's end. The decision also cemented a preeminent political role for Bosnia's ethnicity-based parties, because the peace agreement, including the constitution, divides the political spoils along ethnic lines. Bosnia illustrates that, in a peace negotiation, the driving imperative will be to make a constitutional deal that buys the warring parties' agreement to lay down arms, not necessarily one that is in the long-term public interest or that cloaks the document in democratic legitimacy.[100] Some process elements must be sacrificed in such a context; even actors who might in other circumstances agree on the importance of representativeness, inclusion, and popular participation will regard those to be of secondary concern when faced with the task of ending a war.

Bosnia's experience strongly suggests that when it is deemed necessary to incorporate a new constitution, or the main features of a constitution and new state structures, into a peace agreement, mechanisms should, if possible, be put in place, first, to ensure that the constitution does not perpetuate indefinitely the wartime political dynamics, and second, to encourage further constitutional development. Such an approach could include characterizing the constitution as explicitly interim, providing for a constitutional review procedure and timeline (whether or not the constitution is labeled interim), or creating a simplified adoption process for amendments within a limited time span. In general, however, it is preferable to include in a peace agreement rules and basic principles for a constitution-making process, rather than a complete new constitution, which should benefit from greater and more inclusive deliberation.

In Colombia, the constitution-making process, which took place during an ongoing conflict, was explicitly used to advance a peace process. The nature of the constitutional reforms responded directly to the sources of conflict, including human rights violations, excessive executive power, and improper use of judicial power. The guerilla groups FARC and ELN refused to participate, however, and their absence dealt a "definitive blow to the capacity of the new constitution to achieve the peace that was among its goals." Nevertheless, other guerilla groups were brought into the political process through the constitution-making exercise, including the M-19, suggesting that the strategy had merit even if it could not be fully implemented. This experience suggests that in some circumstances it may be better to seize the moment rather than wait for all potential spoilers to participate. In the outcome of the Colombian process, room was left open for FARC and ELN to join later in political life.

Zimbabwe's experience in 1979–80 similarly illustrates how the quality of a constitutional process and its outcome can be hostage to the constraints of a peace process. The British-mediated talks on Zimbabwe's independence constitution at Lancaster House in London involved tabling a draft constitution that was offered essentially on a nonnegotiable basis. Acceptance of all the terms of the proposed constitution became a condition for the transition to a black majority government, even though the document was not conducive to long-term resolution of conflicting interests. A central concession to the white minority included in the constitution dealt with land reform, which had been a stated objective of the war of liberation, and which presented a major challenge for transforming the country.[101] During the intense pressure of negotiations, and owing to the balance of power at the time, the Patriotic Front's leadership accepted the new constitution as the price for independence and the transfer of political authority. But the Lancaster House constitution failed to provide a framework for political and economic actors in Zimbabwe to negotiate the country's transformation from a colonial state with great economic disparities into a more equitable society. The constitution largely entrenched the economic status quo, particularly as it related to land ownership. As protests of the government's corruption and failure to improve the quality of life for most Zimbabweans increased, the government responded by becoming increasingly undemocratic and authoritarian. Many factors have contributed to the country's drastic economic decline and the tremendous political tensions that exist today, but the legacy of the Lancaster House process and the constitution it produced can be seen as one of those factors; certainly, a critical opportunity was missed to craft a basis for a more successful postcolonial transition and a constitutional order that could promote development, good governance, and protection of individual rights.

In Macedonia in 2001 (not among the case studies in this volume),[102] constitutional amendments were incorporated into the terms of a peace agreement with an agreed commitment to ensuring that parliament would adopt the amendments. Despite the intense involvement of the United States and European Union in forging the peace deal, including the amendment provisions, as well as foreign pressure to ensure their adoption by parliament, using a peace process to change the constitution does not seem to have had deleterious effects. This can perhaps be explained by Macedonia's circumstances as a small, weak state dependent on the goodwill of the international community. Perhaps, too, in contrast to Bosnia's experience, the use of constitutionally required parliamentary procedures to actually adopt the amendments mitigated the undemocratic aspects of the approach.

Impact of Constitution Making on Conflict Resolution

A central concern of this study has been whether and how constitution making can contribute to conflict resolution. In many of the cases in this volume, the act of constitution making was explicitly burdened with helping societies transition from conflict to peace. The possibility of recasting the terms of power sharing, rights, responsibilities, and foundational principles is a tremendous opportunity for a society in need of reconstitution and reconciliation. At the same time, the practical challenges of conducting any constitutional process—let alone a representative, deliberative, and participatory process—in the wake of violent conflict are great.

South Africa is perhaps the best example of a broadly inclusive, participatory process that was crucial to the transition from conflict to peace. Colombia, too, can be credited with having used its constitution-making process effectively to resolve conflict, though only with respect to some guerilla groups. And in Nicaragua, the fact that armed conflict was ongoing during the constitution-making process helped drive the search for consensus during that process. Even the dominant FSLN recognized the importance of considering others' views, though the resulting consensus proved somewhat superficial.[103] Although it is difficult, based on the material in this volume, to draw direct causal connections between the nature of a constitution-making process and positive outcomes with respect to peace building, these cases suggest that it is possible for countries to design constitution-making processes that contribute to conflict resolution. Hart points out that as a component of the high-stakes negotiations among competing powerful interests over the future exercise of power, constitution-making processes generally "have been seen as a means of creating trust: 'to clarify issues, grasp and articulate differences, let people speak in their own voice, and ultimately, build trust and recognition.'" The absence of such trust will undermine "the longer term legitimacy and sustainability of constitutionalism."

Positive outcomes in some cases, though, seem to have little relation to the nature of the constitution-making process. For instance, three of the European cases—Hungary, Poland, and Spain—involved elite processes far from the highly participatory one undertaken in South Africa. Yet, overall, these countries transitioned to democracy successfully. These outcomes suggest that the nature of a constitution-making process may be less important where conditions for conflict resolution and state building more broadly are propitious—such as the presence of democratic, prosperous neighbors interested in ensuring that a country becomes democratic and prosperous; relative economic strength; literacy and other benchmarks of human capital development; and, quite importantly, the peaceful nature of a transition.[104] These outcomes also highlight the extraordinary difficulty of measuring the relative importance of process compared to general social, political, economic, and security conditions.

Nevertheless, an important observation that emerges from the case studies is that flawed constitution-making processes can contribute to conflict perpetuation, worsening of conflict, or at least problems of governance. Such negative outcomes may result either from bad intentions on the part of those with the power to control the constitution-making exercise, or from poor execution of the exercise. Several case studies demonstrate the ways in which a constitution-making process may be abused—if not to create conflict, then certainly not to resolve it. Uganda shows how an undemocratic force seeking a patina of legitimacy can control and distort the process, particularly by creating an appearance of public participation. Venezuela shows how a constitutional reform process can be hijacked by political powers, even with the apparent consent of the people: A constitutionally suspect constituent-assembly process was approved by referendum; the constitution was overwhelmingly approved in a separate referendum; and President Chavez retained his popularity throughout. Chavez used the process to consolidate his own power and execute an effective coup. While the constitution-making exercise bore some hallmarks of democratic process, the reality was different.

In other cases, the constitution-making process itself may have exacerbated conflict. Iraq is the clearest example of this. To mitigate rising sectarian violence, some effort was made to draw the boycotting Iraqi Sunni Arabs into the constitution-drafting process, such as by adding appointed, nonvoting members to the constitutional drafting committee. This was a creditable strategy in principle, but it was not given time to work before the committee was pushed aside in favor of political negotiations that largely excluded Sunni representatives. As a result of such choices, the constitution-making process, though nominally democratic, deepened sectarian divisions, contributing to the descent into civil war. In the end, Sunni Arabs overwhelmingly rejected the constitution in the referendum, "setting the stage for a prolonged conflict with key constitutional issues—including federalism—at the heart of the conflict."

The Iraq case also illustrates the need to achieve consensus among all the conflicting parties for a constitution-making process to contribute to peace building.

> Even if the constitution succeeded at the referendum, failed Sunni opposition to the text would signal a still more profound rupture in Iraq: a permanent sectarian cleavage in Arab Iraq between Sunni and Shia Muslims. This would spell the utter failure of Iraqi nationalist, new constitutionalist, and even pragmatist ambitions for a constitutional compact to include all three of Iraq's major groups.

Failure to develop consensus among all groups on the terms of the text "would be a permanent reminder of Sunni Arab withdrawal of consent to the Iraqi state and the permanent threat of violence."

Zimbabwe offers another example of the dangers of a flawed process. As noted above, the government entirely controlled the 1999 process, despite some efforts to create the appearance of consultation and transparency, and mounted a vigorous campaign for the draft constitution's approval in a referendum. Voters' rejection of the document provoked a violent response by government loyalists, and "ushered in a rapid deterioration of the human rights situation." The case study author observes that "a defective process is unlikely to lead to a constitution that reflects the wishes of the people" and unlikely to gain sufficient popularity or legitimacy to endure.

In Fiji, the adoption of the constitution was followed a year later by a coup. While the case study authors do not draw a direct line between that event and the constitution-making process, the need to compromise in the constitutional process and the general

lack of understanding of what the constitution actually provided, due to the absence of any civic education component, seems to have helped ripen conditions for a coup. The authors observe that "both major [ethnic] communities were worried about the constitution at some level, and even harbored a sense that they had been betrayed." Consequently, it "was all too easy for those who wanted to stir up strife to portray the constitution to both sides as a sellout."

The Bosnian constitutional experience has a mixed legacy regarding conflict resolution. In the short term (but not at all unimportantly), adopting the constitution as part of the peace agreement helped to end the fighting. But the constitution itself—and perhaps its lack of democratic legitimacy—is problematic for the longer term, as it preserves the ethnic nationalist dynamics that helped fuel the conflict. Vested interests in the status quo have so far thwarted efforts to amend the constitution.

The Brazilian experience has a mixed legacy as well, though in a different sense. According to the case study author, the 1988 constitution can be credited with providing a peaceful means of conflict resolution, but it did little to improve governance and weak institutions, and it exacerbated political conflict. Because it sets out detailed rules instead of emphasizing fundamental principles, the constitution is a straitjacket, posing a serious obstacle to effective democratic governance and socioeconomic modernization, though some negative features have been dismantled in recent years.

Also related to the question of conflict resolution, though indirectly, Eritrea illustrates the potential limitations of constitution making as a means for political reconstruction and transition to democracy. In that case, the constitutional surgery was successful in that the process was well planned and executed, but the patient died anyway—the constitution still has not been implemented and the regime has failed to hold elections. The venal self-interest of those holding political power killed it: "a process that was participatory and earned general admiration has been defeated by a willful president who hijacked the democratic process."

To mitigate procedural flaws, in some circumstances, it may be possible to decide that a new constitution will be reviewed after a certain period of time, or will be relatively easily amendable during a certain period. This would create an opportunity for reflection on constitutional issues after passions have cooled, or for taking stock of how well a constitution has performed. Consideration should be given, however, to whether such provisions would create unwanted constitutional uncertainty. The case studies do not deeply explore this approach, but two touch on it briefly.

In Brazil, an opportunity to review and correct the constitution was provided, but not taken. The 1988 constitution permitted a plebiscite to be held five years after adoption on issues that had been central to the constitutional debate. A vote was held on two issues concerning the basic form of government, but the constitutional overhaul that was possible at that point was not undertaken. While the plebiscite provision left open the option (not exercised) for improving a flawed document, it also produced a five-year period of institutional uncertainty. During the Namibian constitution-making process, a proposal was considered that the constitution be subject to a periodic review. The constitutional committee rejected the idea because it "feared that such a procedure would create the impression that the constitution was a precarious document that needed to be amended and changed," and that such an impression "might encroach on the fundamental character of the text."

Relevance of International Law to Constitution-Making Process Requirements[105]

Franck and Thiruvengadam's chapter in this volume asks whether international law has anything to say about the nature of constitution-making processes. It concludes that there is a trend in practice toward involving the public in such processes, but that there are not, as yet, any specific international legal norms that must be followed. Their chapter identifies an apparent "growing acceptance of the norm that constitutions should be prepared through participatory processes with a high degree of transparency," but, again, no requirement. Hart's chapter more assertively argues the case for an emerging legal right to participation in constitution making, and observes the emergence of normative political criteria for participation. She contends that the culture of constitution making has come to include the expectation of democratic practice.

The case studies generally support the reflections of these two chapters on the nature of contemporary practice in constitution making (though in some of the most recent cases especially, the rhetoric of participation has exceeded the reality). Some also indicate an aspiration toward the culture of constitution making that Hart describes. But the case study chapters do not focus on the legal precedents that Hart in particular discusses, nor suggest that constitution makers in the cases considered the possible relevance of international law to their procedures. The sentiment that good form in constitution making requires public participation is evident in many of the cases, but, as this chapter earlier makes clear—and as Hart acknowledges—the genuineness of the solicitation of public input has been quite uneven.

The question at the heart of both conceptual chapters is whether there is or should be a legal basis for ensuring or ascertaining the legitimacy of a constitution. In discussing the deficit of democratic legitimacy in the Hungarian constitution-making experience, the case study authors suggest that whether or not a constitution is backed by a popular mandate is "an extralegal reality." They note that "there is no general rule that would furnish the criteria for deciding whether or not, in a particular case, a popular mandate is obtained." The particularities of the constitution-making experiences examined here and the contexts in which they unfolded have been highlighted throughout this chapter. It is not a difficult leap from the observation that the practical requirements of a constitution-making process depend very much on context to the conclusion that criteria for legitimacy must vary from place to place as well.[106]

Should Constitution Making Adhere to Existing Law?

While not explored widely throughout this volume, some of the case studies raise interesting questions regarding the benefits and detriments of adhering to existing constitutional and other domestic legal rules applicable to the constitution-making process. One aspect of this set of issues, touched on in some of the transition cases, concerns legal continuity—that is, the adherence to existing constitution making or amendment rules in a context of regime change. Is it important to ensure political stability? In principle, it can be argued that applying the existing rule of law is unnecessary because the whole point of drawing up a new constitution is to reconstitute the state and to create a new foundation for all subsidiary laws, as well as for procedures for instituting further constitutional modifications. On the other hand, proceeding with constitutional change in a way that respects the pertinent existing rules and treats them as valid has been helpful in a practical sense in some circumstances, including in Hungary, Poland, and South Africa.[107]

The Hungary case study authors note that a "remarkable feature of this process was the legalism of all the actors, who scrupulously adhered to the letter of the law even when it was to their disadvantage." They conclude that, "though legal continuity rested on the fiction of the rule of law under a lawless old regime, its value was considerable" because it helped to build consensus at the Round Table, and helped to keep the transition on a peaceful path.

Venezuela illustrates the potential costs of breaching existing legal rules in the constitution-making process. Following its election in 1999, the constituent assembly promptly violated the existing 1961 constitution by assuming wide powers it lacked under both that text and the terms of the referendum that created the constitution-making body. Instead of serving as a vehicle for dialogue, the assembly became "a mechanism for confrontation, crushing all opposition or dissidence" and effectuating President Chavez's bid to control all levers of power.

Colombia's experience, however, further complicates the question. As noted earlier, the existing constitution authorized only the congress to effect constitutional reforms, but a popular referendum, followed by a presidential decree, established a constituent assembly to perform that role instead. The Supreme Court then approved the procedural violation on the ground that it conformed to popular will. The referendum was a bottom-up initiative, and an overwhelming 88 percent of voters supported the creation of a constituent assembly. It is difficult to find fault with such a popularly mandated process. What distinguishes this case, in which a failure to adhere to the rule of law appears to have served a greater good, from the Venezuela case? The latter case study's author notes that the Colombian approach enjoyed wide support, including among the political parties, while in Venezuela the constituent assembly effectively executed a coup d'etat.[108] The distinction is not a principled one, but it offers the pragmatic lesson that the intentions that lay behind a decision to disregard the rule of law matter greatly.

Conclusion

The basic premise of this study is that process matters; its central project has been to show how process matters and to suggest ways to design processes that can be expected to achieve the most desirable outcomes. In the end, the case studies show more clearly that process failures can produce negative outcomes—perhaps especially in conflict-prone or weak state systems—than that well-designed processes necessarily produce positive outcomes. But the cases also show that constitution making is a moment of great opportunity to chart a positive course and to forge democratic practices, and, therefore, it is undoubtedly wise to make the most of it. Constitution makers in some cases—such as Eritrea, South Africa, and Albania—worked to seize that opportunity. In other cases—notably East Timor, Afghanistan, and Iraq—the opportunities for constitution making to help build state legitimacy and sustainable peace were missed.

Iraq in particular shows how serious the implications of bad process can be in unstable circumstances. The constitutional text that resulted from the process, in the case study author's view, is substantively acceptable to most Iraqis. But the way constitution making was carried out—the failure to use the process to develop consensus on the future of Iraq and the process's contribution to the alienation of Iraq's Sunni Arabs—had dire consequences. Measured by implementation, legitimacy, or contribution to stability, the Iraqi process, as of the writing of this volume, can be deemed a failure.

Other cases illustrate how factors outside the constitution-making process can affect the result more than do weaknesses in procedural form; such outside factors can also obscure those weaknesses. In Cambodia, for example, the process was flawed in many respects: It lacked transparency, the constituent assembly engaged in no genuine debate, monarchical provisions were grafted onto the text at the last moment, and the text only weakly incorporated international standards. But popular expectations of the process were not great, and therefore, the public generally was not disappointed, even though a vibrant civil society had demanded participation. The weaknesses of the process and the result must be judged, in the case study author's view, in light of Cambodia's very difficult political and physical conditions at the time. The process probably could not have been much different given the country's lack of experience with democracy, the autocratic and communist experiences of the recent past, time pressure due to continued military action, a limited window of opportunity, and the unavoidable role of a difficult character (Prince Sihanouk). The case study author observes that the constitution's long-term viability depends less on how the constitution was drafted than on the country's subsequent consolidation of democracy.

Bosnia and Herzegovina's experience also suggests that even where the process is problematic and the outcome substantively weak, the question must be asked whether the process and outcome could have been much different in the prevailing circumstances. In Iraq, the case study author points out, more time could very well have enabled a better process, and a better process could have been constructed if the U.S. government in particular had pursued a different strategy. But in Bosnia and Herzegovina, what were the real alternatives? The parties to the Dayton peace agreement wanted a constitution as part of the peace deal, a notion that the international negotiators did not push or resist. The parties also wanted a document with the security of a final—though obviously amendable—constitution.[109] A better course may have been to put in place an interim constitution, perhaps with a specific sunset provision, but whether that could have been achieved is uncertain. Unlike South Africa or Namibia, the contending parties in Bosnia and Herzegovina had not come to a basic consensus about the country's future before constitution making, and none were prepared to acknowledge that they might eventually need to cede some political ground to build a functioning state. In South Africa, such consensus, developed during lengthy preliminary negotiations, formed the basis of the parties' agreement to an interim power-sharing constitution, with the certain prospect of a more majoritarian permanent constitution to follow. The interim constitution was not simply a temporary compromise; rather, it confirmed the seismic shift in South African politics and, through the incorporation of binding principles and the parameters of the final constitution-making process, laid a definitive basis for the final constitutional dispensation. These examples illustrate the importance of context with respect to both the choices actually made and the process choices realistically available.

Clearly, what always matters to the outcome of a constitution-making process is the presence of political will to develop a genuine constitutional consensus and to implement the constitutional text.[110] The case studies routinely demonstrate the decisive negative impact of the absence of such political will (most clearly in Eritrea, Iraq, Uganda, Venezuela, and Zimbabwe), as well as the significance of its presence (e.g., Albania, Namibia, Poland, South Africa, and Spain). As the authors of the Fiji chapter observe, "experience shows that if politicians, who have a special purchase on state institutions, are not committed to a constitution, its prospects remain dim."[111]

A challenging question that arises from the case studies is whether constitutionally required mechanisms or procedures can be developed that would bolster the prospects for implementing a constitution.[112] But neither good procedural form nor technical implementation mechanisms can make up for lack of genuine political will. Some cases, notably Venezuela and Uganda, demonstrate that a constitution-making process can be used to cloak a regime in some of the trappings of constitutional democracy while actually enhancing or preserving the regime's powers and privileges. Political will to formulate and implement constitutional change is an ingredient that can be encouraged, as through international pressure, such as that applied to the apartheid regime in South Africa, or through domestic pressure, such as the student-led movement that contributed to sparking the constitution-making process in Colombia. But international actors or domestic reform advocates cannot create political will where powerful forces have other ideas in mind, as in Eritrea.[113] Practical advice, such as this volume offers, is a helpful resource for decision makers who seek to serve the public interest, but, ultimately, constitution-making—being about the allocation of political power—is a political, not a technical, process.

The question of political will is closely tied to the decisive role of individual leaders. While this is not a point explicitly addressed at length throughout the chapters, the value of the right leaders being in place at the right time is apparent. In South Africa, particularly given their personal histories, Nelson Mandela's and F.W. de Klerk's willingness to compromise and commit to consensus was nothing short of remarkable. The mature and effective leadership that they and other key figures exercised sustained momentum over the course of a long constitution-making process, overcoming numerous obstacles and crises along the transition path. In Spain, King Juan Carlos and Prime Minister Adolfo Suarez played pivotal—and, in the king's case, unexpected—roles in the transition to democracy. Franco had groomed Juan Carlos to be his successor as head of state, but the king "turned out to be the opposite of Franco's dreams—a man profoundly dedicated to democracy." Juan Carlos took the first critical step toward reform and democratization when he dismissed the initial post-Franco prime minister and appointed Suarez in his stead. Together, the king and Suarez became the "major engineers of Spain's transition to democracy." In Namibia, Dirk Mudge, a former member of the ruling white Nationalist Party who broke away to form an alliance of eleven ethnic political parties, played a major role in broadening the Namibian political elite, without which "the constitution-making process would not have had its successful outcome." The variation in circumstances that brought these leaders to the scene and the personal nature of the qualities they exhibited make clear that leadership, like political will, cannot be manufactured. But its significance should be recognized when assessing the prospects for a constitution-making process and identifying obstacles, such as the absence of effective leaders or presence of obstructionist leaders, that will have to be overcome.[114]

Common Pitfalls to Avoid

The process of making constitutions amid political transition, social upheaval, and conflict is enormously burdened by the challenges such environments pose for any serious undertaking that requires developing political and social consensus, let alone one of such potential significance. It is, therefore, hardly surprising that many such exercises fail to accomplish all the goals heaped upon them, including (re)creation of a social compact, nation building, protection of human rights, democratization, and national reconciliation. While these challenges are unavoidable, the case studies helpfully reveal several serious pitfalls that have marked the constitution-making experiences of multiple countries and that could be avoided in the future. Some of the more common ones evident in the cases are highlighted below.

First, several cases underscore the importance of devising a strategy for and devoting sufficient time to building broad consensus on a new constitutional arrangement. Afghanistan, Iraq, and East Timor are notable failures in this regard. South Africa provides a good example of deliberate and extensive consensus building, while the Namibia case suggests that drawn-out efforts to establish consensus may not be needed where considerable common ground has been achieved prior to constitution making.

Second, the problem of sometimes overbearing and detrimental involvement of foreign actors with their own agendas could be remedied if those actors adopted better policies and strategies for supporting constitution making. Iraq and East Timor are the preeminent examples of the problem; Albania, where a more light-handed and supportive approach was taken, provides a helpful contrast. Afghanistan presents a more mixed picture: There, foreign actors provided constructive and unintrusive logistical support and technical advice for the constitutional commission and Constitutional Loya Jirga, but the exceedingly high-profile role of the U.S. ambassador in the negotiations can be seen as troubling.[115] One specific aspect of the problem, which was central in Iraq and East Timor, and evident in Zimbabwe in 1979–80 as well, is the exertion by foreign actors of pressure on timetables for constitution making.

Third, several cases evince the phenomenon of using a constitution-making process to achieve ends other than developing genuine consensus on a new social contract. In Uganda, for example, the constitution-making process was driven by the government's interest in legitimating and embedding what is effectively a one-party system. In Iraq, the U.S. policy interest in racking up what could be billed as a success distorted the process. In Venezuela, President Chavez used the process to concentrate power in his own hands. In Bosnia, the motivations behind the process were not venal—the desired end of the process was to make peace—but the means required to achieve that end were not those best suited to crafting a durable, democratically sound constitution. The Uganda and Venezuela cases also indicate that foreign donors and international organizations should be wary of supporting or showing approval of constitution-making processes used as cover for other political purposes.

A fourth pitfall concerns drafting procedures. Several cases suggest that attempting to draft a constitution from scratch in a constituent assembly or parliament is problematic. Using as a starting point an expert's draft, a draft produced by an appointed commission (either independent or comprised of selected members of the assembly or parliament), or a political party draft that all the relevant parties accept (as in Namibia) is often a better course of action.[116]

Fifth, several cases illustrate the importance of ensuring that the deliberation and decision-making forum includes all parties whose agreement to constitutional terms is needed for conflict resolution or development of meaningful societal consensus. Both positive and negative examples are well represented.

Finally, the failure to design a public participation program that created meaningful opportunities for public input, and for constitution makers to account for that input, weakened the potential of the constitution-making process in several cases. In Afghanistan, East Timor, and Iraq, for example, participation opportunities were limited, and the results of consultation that did occur were not fed into the drafting process.

Contextual Factors to Consider for Future Cases

In examining the factors that have shaped the processes considered here and their outcomes, this chapter has emphasized the importance of context. Much work remains to be done to determine the precise contours of the ways in which context affects both pro-

cedural choices and how well those choices serve the public interest. It would be useful to build on the material in this volume by identifying more comprehensively the contextual variables that matter most and mapping those variables to the impact of specific procedural choices. Even without a definitive map, it is possible to draw some ideas from this volume regarding the aspects of context that should be assessed when preparing to design a constitution-making process.[117] Aside from the general political, social, cultural, and historical conditions to take into account, the case studies suggest a series of important questions that, if considered in advance, could help those engaged in the design and implementation of a constitution-making process make choices that will enhance the effectiveness of the process and its likelihood of success[118]:

- On popular and elite *expectations and attitudes*:
  - What is the nature and intensity of public expectations regarding how the constitution-making process will unfold?
  - Do particular procedural options, such as the use of referendums or provisional constitutions, carry negative historical associations?
  - What is the level of public trust in elites, including political parties, and what are cultural views more generally regarding respect for authority?
  - Is there a history of free and fair elections and, if so, does that history indicate public trust in the political process?
  - Is legal continuity valued or at least palatable in the circumstances, or is there a demand for a clean break with past constitutional arrangements?
  - What are popular and elite views concerning the legitimacy of international involvement, including the involvement of foreign experts?

- On available *resources and capacity* for designing and managing the constitution-making process:
  - How mature and cohesive are political parties? Would party leaderships in the assembly be able to organize and carry out a constitution-making process effectively, or should an independent commission be appointed?
  - Are domestic constitutional experts available to assist with the process?
  - Are there sufficient resources to conduct effective civic education and public consultation, and what level of financial and technical support is required from international organizations or foreign donors?
  - Are there sufficient resources to fund elections and referendums (which may in particular pertain to decisions on the question whether to elect a constituent assembly in addition to a regular parliament)?
- On *challenges to ensuring representation and inclusion* in the process:
  - What are the natures of the relevant cleavages (social, political, ethnic, sectarian, and other) in the country, and the significance of those cleavages for determining who should be included in the process and in what proportion?
  - What is the likelihood that all relevant social, ethnic, and other groups in society will be able and willing to participate in a constitution-making process and, consequently, what special measures or procedures may be needed to ensure their representation and participation?
  - Are political parties genuinely representative of the range of ideological views, and of ethnic, religious, geographic, or other relevant interests?
  - Are all political parties able and willing to participate in the process?
  - Is there an existing elected body that is broadly representative of relevant groups

and interests and could legitimately serve as a constitution-making forum, or will a new forum need to be created?
  - Do security conditions permit free and fair elections and referendums to be conducted?
  - Does a single figure, party, or faction dominate the political scene? Should that actor's power over the process be diluted?
- On *conduciveness of the environment* to public consultation and participation:
  - What is the extent of freedom of expression, and, thus, the prospect for genuine public participation?
  - How does the security environment affect access to information about the process and to opportunities for participation for all relevant groups throughout the country?
  - Are there representative groups within civil society with which to engage, consult, and partner?
  - What are the levels of development of print and broadcast media and the degree of media penetration throughout the country? Will parties to the process be able to rely on established media to transmit messages about the process, or will they need to create their own dissemination mechanisms?
  - How will the level of literacy affect the design of a public outreach campaign?
- On relevant *rules and precedents*:
  - Does an existing constitutional arrangement, peace agreement, or other relevant text provide guidance on the expected nature of the process? If not, is there a need for preliminary ground-rule negotiations on the constitution-making procedures and possibly on essential principles to bound the process?
  - What is the substantive quality and symbolic acceptability of the previous constitution? Does it provide a positive plat-

form on which to develop a new text, or is a clear break with the past required?

- Do any earlier constitutions provide helpful substantive or symbolic precedent?
- What is the degree of attachment, if any, to constitution-making traditions? What implications do any such traditions have for the choice of decision-making institution, appropriate techniques for ensuring inclusion, and other procedural mechanisms and rules?

The many trials and tribulations of the constitution-making processes explored in this volume fully support Elster's observation of "an inherent paradox" in constitution-making processes: "On the one hand, being written for the indefinite future, constitutions ought to be adopted in maximally calm and undisturbed conditions. On the other hand, the call for a new constitution usually arises in turbulent circumstances."[119] It is unavoidable that the constitutional moment is an exceedingly challenging one in which to make a lasting contribution to constitutionalism. Yet this challenge must be met, not only to foster democracy, stability, and the protection of rights, but to contribute to building lasting peace.

Notes

1. Commenting on the period 1987–2002, Jennifer Widner observes that there is "enormous variety in the procedures employed to make new constitutions. In the era of decolonization, processes were often remarkably similar to one another, but there is no longer a template—not surprising given the number of permutations and combinations of stages, delegate selection rules, decision rules, consultation processes, etc." Jennifer Widner, "Constitution Writing in Post-Conflict Settings: An Overview," *William and Mary Law Review,* vol. 49, no. 4 (2008), pp. 1513–41, p. 1525.

2. Donald Horowitz has pointed out that because constitutions "are made by people who have not made a constitution before and will not be likely to make a constitution again," there is "a great deal

of lost knowledge from one constitution-making process to another and a good deal of fumbling along the way." Donald L. Horowitz, "Conciliatory Institutions and Constitutional Processes in Post-Conflict States," *William and Mary Law Review,* vol. 49, no. 4, pp. 1213–1248, p. 1227. This volume is intended to help capture and disseminate such knowledge.

3. For example, the Commonwealth Human Rights Initiative has argued that the "process of constitution making is, and is seen to be, as important as the substantive content of the constitution itself," and a "credible" process is one that "constructively engages the largest majority of the population." "Recommendations to Commonwealth Heads of Government," in Hassen Ebrahim, Kayode Fayemi, and Stephanie Loomis, *Promoting a Culture of Constitutionalism and Democracy in Commonwealth Africa* (Pretoria: Commonwealth Human Rights Initiative, 1999), available at www.humanrightsinitiative.org/publications/const/constitutionalism_booklet_1999.pdf (accessed May 11, 2009). A background paper associated with these recommendations on best practices in constitution making advocates a "shift from juridical *constitutionality* to political *constitutionalism* by emphasising process as well as substance in the quest for constitutional and democratic governance." "Background Paper to Accompany CHRI's Recommendations to CHOGM '99," in *Promoting a Culture of Constitutionalism,* p. 10 (emphasis in original).

4. See, e.g., Yash Ghai and Guido Galli, "Constitution Building Processes and Democratization," (International Institute for Democracy and Electoral Assistance, 2006), available at www.idea.int/publications/cbp_democratization/index.cfm (accessed June 29, 2009), p. 9 ("The design of the process, that is, the *institutions* for the making of decisions and the *method* of making decisions, has a bearing on a number of factors such as which interests are articulated and which are excluded, how the views of participants are aggregated, and the congruence of the text with social realities.") Cf. Jennifer Widner's observation that "our instincts tell us that process makes a difference . . . [but] it is devilishly difficult to show, empirically, that procedures made the difference" in particular cases. Widner, "Constitution Writing in Post-Conflict Settings," p. 1514.

5. For a philosophical argument for a participatory style of constitutionalism, see James Tully, *Strange Multiplicity: Constitutionalism in an Age of Diversity* (Cambridge: Cambridge University Press,

1995). As explored in Vivien Hart's chapter, Tully argues that to achieve just and peaceful constitutional settlements in circumstances of cultural diversity, constitutions should be "seen as a form of activity, an inter-cultural dialogue in which the culturally diverse sovereign citizens of contemporary societies negotiate agreements on their forms of association over time in accordance with the three conventions of mutual recognition, consent and cultural continuity" (p. 30). In this view, "constitutions are not fixed and unchangeable agreements reached at some foundational moment, but chains of continual intercultural negotiations and agreements" (pp. 183–84).

6. Other literature on constitution-making processes highlights this gap in understanding the links between process and outcomes. See, e.g., Tom Ginsburg, Zachary Elkins, and Justin Blount, "Does the Process of Constitution-Making Matter?" *Annual Review of Law and Social Science* 2009 (forthcoming), version of January 15, 2009, manuscript on file with the author, p. 13 ("There is much speculation, but relatively little evidence, about the impact of these processes [of constitutional design and adoption] on different outcomes.")

7. This example is drawn from the Eritrea case, discussed further below.

8. Spain is a pertinent example here. It could be argued that public involvement could have made the process or result even better, but the argument would be difficult to substantiate.

9. Ginsburg, Elkins, and Blount, in their review of the literature on constitution-making processes, highlight the problem of endogeneity, which is "endemic in efforts to tie process to outcomes." It is likely that certain process choices and certain outcomes reflect the "common impact of an unobserved variable." Ginsburg, Elkins, and Blount, "Does the Process of Constitution-Making Matter?" p. 27.

10. For one list of suggested criteria for measuring success or failure in constitution making, and some of the attendant ambiguities, see Proceedings of the Workshop on Constitution Building Processes, Princeton University, May 17–20, 2007, Bobst Center for Peace and Justice, Princeton University, in conjunction with Interpeace and International IDEA, pp. 6–10, available at www.princeton.edu/bobst/program/program_archives/ (accessed June 26, 2009). Vicki Jackson proposes that "the goal of constitution-making should be understood, not as producing a written constitution, but as promoting constitutionalism." Focusing on post-conflict states, she suggests a variety of possible criteria for evaluating whether constitution making has advanced constitutionalism, including a more peaceful commitment to governance by law and politics, successful elections and changes in government, and the duration of the constitution and its success in protecting human rights. Vicki C. Jackson, "What's in a Name? Reflections on Timing, Naming, and Constitution-Making," *William and Mary Law Review,* vol. 49, no. 4 (2008), pp. 1249–1305, pp. 1254–1255. In an analysis based on twelve case studies, Kirsti Samuels adopts "democracy" and "peace" as the two criteria by which to assess the impact of constitutions. Without providing a detailed explanation, she finds that "the more representative and more inclusive constitution building processes resulted in constitutions favoring free and fair elections, greater political equality, more social justice provisions, human rights protections, and stronger accountability mechanisms." Kirsti Samuels, "Post-Conflict Peace-Building and Constitution-Making," *Chicago Journal of International Law,* vol. 6 (Winter 2006), pp. 665, 668. The quoted statement shows the problem of a limited sample, however, as some non-inclusive processes have also led to some of these results. In addition, cause-and-effect relationships are not explored here; for example, in some cases, the conditions that give rise to representativeness and inclusion certainly also generate such outcomes. See also Widner, "Constitution Writing in Post-Conflict Settings," pp. 1515–1517, for a discussion of some dimensions of "success."

11. Widner, "Constitution Writing in Post-Conflict Settings," p. 1526. Widner's study was supported by funding from the United States Institute of Peace. See also Ginsburg, et al., "Does the Process of Constitution-Making Matter?" p. 28 ("On the theoretical side, we found a broad consensus in the literature about the importance of public involvement as well as an apparent trend in practice. Yet many of the assumptions of proponents of participation remain untested, and the precise relationships between participation and desirable outcomes of interest remain underspecified.")

12. Jennifer Widner, "Constitution Writing and Conflict Resolution," *The Round Table,* vol. 94, no. 381 (September 2005), pp. 504–05. See also Widner, "Constitution Writing in Post-Conflict Settings," p. 1522.

13. Ibid., p. 1532.

14. Ibid., p. 1531. Widner remarks that based on the evidence in her study, "one might say that the choice of procedure does not really matter much.

More representative processes may yield better results in contexts where the level of violence is relatively low; the evidence is not overwhelming, however" (p. 1532).

15. See the introduction to this volume for a description of the concept paper that guided the chapter authors' work.

16. In Cambodia, for example, the constitution-making process was far from ideal: It was largely secretive and opaque, the constituent assembly failed to hew to constitutional principles specified in the 1991 peace agreement, expert advice was offered but not utilized, and both public and assembly debate were very limited. Nevertheless, the case study author characterizes the final product of the process as "reasonable." Moreover, no clear picture emerges regarding implementation of the text and its impact on political stability in Cambodia. The creation of constitutional structures has suffered delays, and the consolidation of democracy has proceeded problematically (including unstable power sharing, a coup in 1997, and election troubles). Yet there are some hopeful signs of good prospects for long-term democratization and stability, such as development of civil society. Given the difficult circumstances in which constitution making proceeded, and the multiplicity of variables affecting subsequent events in Cambodia, locating the case on a continuum between success and failure does not seem realistic or helpful.

17. With regard to the use of transitional constitutions, Vicki Jackson identifies many contextual factors that confound comparison of cases and generalization. Jackson, "What's in a Name?" pp. 1270–1271.

18. Context narrows not only the procedural options realistically available to constitution makers but the substantive options available as well. Donald Horowitz observes "there is no escaping the fact that process choices, like the choice of institutions to be incorporated in a constitution, are heavily colored by constraint." For example, civil or secessionist wars are likely to be resolved through negotiation, a process that is conducive to settling on consociational arrangements in a constitution. In these and other circumstances, "constitutional planning, with full scrutiny of available options, is unusual." Horowitz, "Conciliatory Institutions and Constitutional Processes in Post-Conflict States," p. 1247.

19. Andrew Arato, "Forms of Constitution Making and Theories of Democracy," *Cardozo Law Review*, vol. 17 (1995), p. 219.

20. The characterizations and analyses of the case studies in this chapter are the author's own, and should not be viewed as necessarily coinciding with the views of the individual case study authors.

21. See the introduction for an explanation of how the cases were selected.

22. The term *post-conflict*, while convenient shorthand, is generally a misnomer, as in many cases conflict does not abruptly and definitively end. It is usually more accurate to characterize countries as transitioning or emerging from conflict.

23. Some structural elements not included here have been used in cases other than those considered in this volume. For example, large national conferences have been held as part of the constitution-making processes of some countries, particularly in Africa.

24. Others have sorted cases according to generalized historical types of constitution-making processes. Jon Elster identifies eight historical modes of constitution making. See Jon Elster, "Ways of Constitution Making," in *Democracy's Victory and Crisis,* ed. Axel Hadenius (Cambridge: Cambridge University Press, 1997), pp. 125–31. Andrew Arato identifies five main types of constitution-making processes. See Arato, "Forms of Constitution Making," pp. 194–95. These approaches, while useful from a scholarly perspective, are less relevant to a pragmatically oriented study such as this one. Moreover, the cases here do not cover all the historical modes of constitution making. As all the cases are of relatively recent vintage, Table 22.3 supports the observation that most modern constitution-making processes, at least in form, fit among the more democratic of the historical types. Arato comments that "non-democratic procedures of constitution making cannot be justified today; the age-old figure of the 'law giver,' the non-participant architect of constitutions, can no longer be plausibly revived." Arato, "Forms of Constitution Making," p. 192. Elster notes that the widespread use of directly elected assemblies to make constitutions in the twentieth century "confirm[s] the general claim that as constitutions become more democratic so do the processes by which they are shaped." Elster, "Ways of Constitution Making," p. 130.

25. Another possibility is to consider structure in terms of general reform models. Widner's study of 194 cases during the period 1975–2003 identifies five main models: a commission or committee/elected constituent assembly model; a commission or committee/legislature model; a national conference; executive-directed constitution writing;

and peace negotiations. To this she adds "hybrid forms and unusual approaches." For some data on the frequency of use of each model and selected examples, see "Reform Models" at Princeton University's Constitution Writing and Conflict Resolution Web site, available at www.princeton.edu/~pcwcr/drafting/models.html (accessed May 11, 2009). Not all these approaches are represented in the case studies here; moreover, this chapter distinguishes the use of appointed commissions separate from an elected body from commissions or committees composed of members of an elected body.

26. At least in Afghanistan, however, the putative public consultation process seems to have had some educational benefit, as explained in the Afghanistan chapter.

27. Widner's study of 194 cases finds that "in most countries an elected or indirectly elected assembly has primary responsibility for debating, amending, and adopting the draft." See "Drafting Process" at Constitution Writing Web site, available at www.princeton.edu/~pcwcr/drafting/index.html (accessed May 11, 2009). The case studies in this volume are consistent with that pattern. South Africa's experience, though, indicates that using an elected body should not be considered a foregone conclusion. In that case, the question of whether an elected assembly would write and adopt the final constitution or whether that work would be done by a selected group of political party representatives was very hard fought during the transition negotiations. Ultimately, the African National Congress's view that purely democratic authorization for the agents of the constitution-making process was essential to secure the legitimacy of the final result won out, and a constitutional assembly was elected using proportional representation. South Africans elected 400 members of a national assembly (elected by proportional representation, using national and provincial candidate lists), and 90 members of a senate (10 from each of the nine provinces). A joint sitting of these parliamentary bodies made up the assembly.

28. In Uganda and Venezuela, elected bodies were, formally speaking, key to the constitution-making process, but in reality, members from the dominant political party in each case towed their party's line, delivering the result that the party sought from the outset. In Iraq, too, the constitution-making process accorded a central role to the national assembly, but in fact, political party leaders controlled the process in such a way that assembly members were marginalized and the party leaders' own backroom deals were ratified. In a separate example of how political imperatives can affect formal procedures, Widner has found that contrary to her initial expectations, voting rules for the deliberative bodies used in constitution-making processes "often display high levels of ambiguity. Why? In case after case, we encountered assemblies whose members were sensitive to the needs of the occasion—usually the desirability of higher thresholds for more sensitive items or for slightly less-than-perfect consensus in order to move forward to ratification." In addition, "cognizant of the need to save political face, yet also to adopt a new constitution, delegates in many settings made creative use of selective absences and abstentions." See "Voting Rules" at Constitution Writing Web site, available at www.princeton.edu/~pcwcr/drafting/voting.html (accessed May 11, 2009).

29. Colombia offers an interesting twist on the separation of the roles of a constituent assembly and ordinary legislature. Because the existing legislature could have been an obstacle, the constituent assembly dissolved the regular legislature and created an interim legislative commission to adopt laws and approve (or veto) executive decrees regarding implementation of the new constitution until new elections were held. Whether other countries could follow such an approach, if useful, would depend on the legal mandate of the constituent assembly.

30. Quotations in this chapter without citations are drawn from the chapters in this volume.

31. Ginsburg, Elkins, and Blount find, at least preliminarily, an absence of empirical support for the widely shared hypothesis that legislatures acting as constitution makers are likely to engage in institutional self-dealing. Ginsburg, et al., "Does the Process of Constitution-Making Matter?" pp. 15–18. Nonetheless, anecdotal evidence of self-dealing, such as that noted here, suggests constitution-making process designers should consider the potential risk of this phenomenon.

32. Fifteen years after the constitution's adoption, it was learned that three articles were slipped in at the last moment before the final vote, despite careful and detailed rules of procedure. The length of time it took to make this discovery perhaps illustrates the complexity of the document.

33. However, the authors of the Hungary chapter in this volume note that the later experiences of Bulgaria and South Africa showed that creating an interim constitution through a round-table process could be successfully combined with subsequent use of a constituent assembly.

34. The case study authors observe that there was no time to convene a constitutional convention when the April Amendment was drafted in 1989, and such a body could not be elected before the constitutional foundation for democratic elections was established.

35. Widner's study of 194 cases shows a similar variety: "In a little over half of all of the cases in this study, the development of a first draft rested with an appointed commission whose members were selected by the executive, the members of a round table, a legislature, or some other authority, such as a transitional legislature in tandem with a national conference. In about a quarter of all cases studied here, a sub-committee of the main deliberative body developed the first text. In eight percent of cases, an elected chamber wrote the initial text itself, in working groups that reported to a plenary. There are also instances in which political parties prepare and submit their own texts." See "Drafting Process" at Constitution Writing Web site available at www.princeton.edu/~pcwcr/drafting/voting.html. With the exception of the national conference, all of these modes of constitution drafting are represented in the case studies in this volume.

36. The experts were among twenty "outside" persons who actively participated (without voting) in the committee's work. The others represented trade unions, professional organizations, churches, and other religious groups.

37. In a related vein, Elster argues that "the role of experts should be kept to a minimum, because solutions tend to be more stable if dictated by political rather than technical considerations. Lawyers will tend to resist the technically flawed and deliberately ambiguous formulations that may be necessary to achieve consensus." Elster, "Ways of Constitution Making," p. 138.

38. Jim Della-Giacoma, "Ensuring the Well-Being of a Nation: Developing a Democratic Culture through Constitution Making in East Timor," conference paper, April 1, 2005, p. 8 (on file with the author). Della-Giacoma points out that the Fretilin draft was available only in Portuguese, and few voters would have understood it.

39. The South West African People's Organization (SWAPO) was the liberation force in Namibia that fought a low-intensity war almost to the end of the peace process.

40. Donald Horowitz argues that commissioning an expert or expertly informed body to engineer a draft constitution is especially important in ethnically divided post-conflict societies. Ordinary majoritarianism can produce ethnic exclusion rather than "arrangements that will enable conflicted ethnic groups to share power in a country that needs not only democratic government but a heavy dose of institutions for conflict resolution." An exception, he says, is where violent conflict requires urgent resolution, "usually on a heavily negotiated basis." Horowitz, "Conciliatory Institutions and Constitutional Processes in Post-Conflict States," pp. 1240–1241.

41. The case study author notes, however, that a large commission with a "broad and unregimented agenda," as was used in Zimbabwe, is inappropriate for elaborating a document as complex as a constitution.

42. In Hungary, the second stage was never achieved, however, due to the "mistake of Hungarian constitution makers, who postulated the interim nature of their constitution, but provided neither a democratically enhanced procedure for making the permanent constitution nor a timetable armed with relevant sanctions for the production of the definitive document."

43. Widner's study finds that for purposes of ratification, about half of the 194 cases in the study required a national referendum, and that this procedure was most common when the main deliberative body was appointed or indirectly elected. In most of the remaining countries, the assembly that developed the final draft was responsible for ratification, as occurred in the cases in this volume in which no referendum was held. See "Drafting Process" at Constitution Writing Web site. Specifically, 53.7 percent (of 195 cases in the first version of the study) used an assembly to ratify the final document, and 41.5 percent sponsored a national referendum. See "Adoption and Ratification" at Constitution Writing Web site, available at www.princeton.edu/~pcwcr/drafting/adoption.html (accessed May 11, 2009).

44. Similarly, in Venezuela, a majority of the voting public abstained from both the interim and ratification referendums held there.

45. Depending on the issues at stake and the sentiments of the majority of the population, the anticipation of public preferences to be expressed later in the process could have a positive or negative effect. See Ginsburg, et al., "Does the Process of Constitution-Making Matter?" p. 6, noting that ratification "can hamstring leaders in an earlier stage."

46. See "Ground Rules" at Constitution Writing Web site, available at www.princeton.edu/~pcwcr/drafting/rules.html (accessed on May 11, 2009).

47. One instance among the case studies in which a referendum was, in some respects, problematic was the all-white referendum held during the South African transition negotiations. While the result was an overwhelming victory for the National Party and confirmed that the majority of white people favored a negotiated settlement, it unfortunately also encouraged the National Party to overplay its hand and hold back for a time on some necessary compromises.

48. See "Drafting Process" at Constitution Writing Web site, available at www.princeton.edu/~pcwcr/drafting/rules.html (accessed May 11, 2009).

49. Preconstitutional arrangements that lay the groundwork for constitution making are not a recent innovation: "Although there has been much discussion of this role especially with regard to Hispanic and Latin American constitutions, almost every liberal-democratic constitution was preceded by some kind of pact or covenant that made constitution making possible." See "Conclusion," in *Constitution Makers on Constitution Making,* ed. Robert A. Goldwin and Art Kaufman (Washington, DC: American Enterprise Institute for Public Policy Research, 1988), p. 453 (comment of Daniel J. Elazar).

50. Vicki Jackson points out that distinguishing a category of "transitional" constitutions is difficult considering that "avowedly transitional constitutions" have sometimes become permanent, and "permanent" constitutions that endure must allow for "contest over changing understandings and new circumstances, whether through amendment or interpretation." Jackson, "What's in a Name?" p. 1281. In Bosnia, the Dayton constitution was not characterized as transitional, yet the international negotiators who helped craft it expected that it would be amended over time, and the text itself invited changes (such as the enhancement of central government powers) as political circumstances developed. This suggests that a constitution may be transitional in effect, even if not in form.

51. An additional set of transitional arrangements in Spain took the form of "preautonomy laws," adopted in 1977–78, which accelerated political regionalization. These were in response to the need to satisfy the demands of Catalonia and the Basque country before approving a constitution. While nominally the laws were not supposed to prejudice the terms of the constitution, they, in fact, "with some exceptions, determined the regional division of Spain without testing the popular support for autonomy in different parts of Spain. . . . The preau-

tonomy stage . . . illustrates something that those studying transitions from authoritarian regimes to democracy should never forget: decisions made during the transition period by a government that is either weak or not fully institutionalized become irreversible at a later stage." Juan J. Linz, "Spanish Democracy and the Estado de las Autonomías," in *Forging Unity Out of Diversity: The Approaches of Eight Nations,* ed. Robert A. Goldwin, Art Kaufman, and William A. Schambra (Washington, DC: American Enterprise Institute for Public Policy Research, 1989), pp. 272–73.

52. The Cambodia chapter notes: "With the benefit of hindsight and the knowledge of other constitution making processes that included comprehensive programs of public participation, it would have been preferable for the Paris Agreements to set out the basic structure of the process of citizen involvement and transparency. Without unduly extending the process, the agreements could have required transcription of the deliberations and some degree of popular consultation. Such requirements might have helped transform a closed and opaque process into a more open and democratic one."

53. Such as an independent electoral commission and an independent media commission.

54. See Cyril Ramaphosa, "Negotiating a New Nation: Reflections on the Development of South Africa's Constitution," in *The Post-Apartheid Constitutions: Perspectives on South Africa's Basic Law,* ed. Penelope Andrews and Stephen Ellmann (Johannessburg: Witwatersrand University Press, 2001), p. 80.

55. See Horowitz, "Conciliatory Institutions and Constitutional Processes in Post-Conflict States," p. 1247, focusing on post-conflict environments ("If interim arrangements have been put in place, political actors who benefit from them are unlikely to wish to start a wholly new constitutional process. Interests crystallize quickly in such settings.").

56. See note 51.

57. Vicki Jackson suggests that "although it is difficult to justify this court's creation through a theory of democratic consent, its independence from the prior regime and its high stature enabled it to perform the vital role of offering assurance to all parties that the rights and structures they negotiated would be carried forward." Jackson, "What's in a Name?" p. 1295.

58. At the insistence of the National Party, the interim constitution was adopted by the last apartheid-era parliament, but the democratic credentials of that body were obviously weak.

59. Comment of Nicholas (Fink) Haysom, Working Group Session on South Africa, Project on Constitution Making, Peace Building, and National Reconciliation, September 28, 2001, pp. 162–63 of transcript (on file with the U.S. Institute of Peace Rule of Law Program). Haysom, who was closely involved in the South African constitution-making process, commented further that the South African constitution frequently uses the constitutional court as a logjam breaker. He also has found that in other countries, it is not possible to replicate the role created for the South African constitutional court because of lack of public trust in the courts.

60. The Zimbabwe case study author explicitly notes that this approach would not have worked in that country because the judiciary is not perceived as independent.

61. It is not clear, however, whether inclusiveness affects other important outcomes. According to conclusions drawn from a set of constitution-making case studies commissioned by International IDEA, "there seems to be no concrete correlation between inclusiveness and successful implementation/sustainability." Guido Galli, "The Role of Constitution-Building Processes in Democratization," working paper, May 29, 2005, p. 9 (on file with the author).

62. Heinz Klug argues that modern constitution making calls for a democratically elected and representative constitution-making body because the precommitments entered into in the process "are presented as a form of self-binding, implying democratic participation in the constitution-making process." He adds that a body created on the basis of proportional representation "provides the greatest opportunity for including the voices of all those willing to enter into a compact of future self-restraint." Heinz Klug, "Participating in the Design: Constitution-Making in South Africa," *Review of Constitutional Studies,* vol. 3, no. 1 (1996), p. 56.

63. See note 27. In Afghanistan, the constitution-making body was indirectly elected.

64. In East Timor, Fretilin's political dominance undermined the extent to which the constituent assembly membership represented the variety of voices in the country. The case study authors suggest that appointing a broad-based constitutional commission could have mitigated the problem, though Fretilin's dominance would still be felt in the elected body needed to deliberate on and approve the text. Such an approach would have faced

the same challenges related to the appointing authority as in circumstances in which some assembly members are appointed.

65. In Ethiopia, not among the case studies in this volume, excluding the opposition-denied legitimacy to the constitutional commission; in the end, important issues were left unresolved, feeding secessionist trends. Jamal Benomar, "Constitution-Making after Conflict: Lessons for Iraq," *Journal of Democracy,* vol. 15, no. 2 (April 2004), p. 85.

66. There are several examples in the case studies of boycotts at various stages of the constitution-making process, including Albania, Iraq, and Uganda.

67. Spain has developed into a stable and prosperous democracy, though the country has suffered violence related to Basque separatism. With respect to the transition process, Juan Linz has observed that "the change from an authoritarian regime to democracy was basically peaceful and orderly, without the vengeance expected by those who feared a reenactment of the Civil War. This was one of the great achievements of the political elites, from the Communists to the heirs of the Franco regime." Linz, "Spanish Democracy," p. 263. Linz explains that the constitutional negotiations took place often behind closed doors, with many parliamentary leaders excluded and no public debate, because leaders during the transition found the Spanish democratic tradition based on majority rule ill-suited to resolving the issues of a multiethnic, multilingual, segmented society: "The actions of the Spanish leaders fitted both the style and the outcomes of consociational democracy, though they did not know it. . . . The context of consociational politics afforded no room for a great national debate" (pp. 268–69).

68. Ginsburg, Elkins, and Blount note their "sense is that actual constitutional design processes employ scattered and usually rather anemic forms of popular participation and oversight to substitute for actual consent." Ginsburg, et al., "Does the Process of Constitution-Making Matter?" p. 8.

69. Widner's study finds that some form of popular consultation was carried out in roughly 40 percent of the 194 cases. In just over 30 percent, more than one technique for soliciting views was used, and in 25 percent, consultation efforts extended to remote as well as urban locations. See "Participation" at Constitution Writing Web site, available at www.princeton.edu/~pcwcr/drafting/participation.html (accessed May 11, 2009).

70. A number of the case studies illustrate rather weak examples of public participation programs. In Fiji, for instance, a limited degree of public consultation was conducted through commission hearings and receipt of submissions, but no civic education was provided (except to some extent by civil society). The constitution draft was not even translated into local languages. The case study authors describe an absence of public understanding and ownership of the constitution. Interestingly, three of the weaker instances of public participation occurred in East Timor, Afghanistan, and Iraq, all situations in which the international community urged implementation of a public participation process (though at the same time failed adequately to facilitate participation). It may be that those processes were weak, in part, because, unlike South Africa, Eritrea, Brazil, and Nicaragua, for example, they were not organic.

71. See Heather Deegan, "A Critical Examination of the Democratic Transition in South Africa: The Question of Public Participation," *Commonwealth and Comparative Politics*, vol. 40, no. 1 (March 2002), pp. 49–50. See also Siri Gloppen, *South Africa: The Battle over the Constitution* (Aldershot: Dartmouth/Ashgate, 1997), pp. 257–58, 262.

72. Albania, Eritrea, and Nicaragua provide other examples of phased consultation processes.

73. See Ghai and Galli, "Constitution Building Processes and Democratization," p. 15 ("Public participation tends to lead to numerous demands and can greatly expand the scope of the constitution.").

74. See Ghai and Galli, "Constitution Building Processes and Democratization," pp. 10–15 for an exploration of the rationales for public participation.

75. But see Ghai and Galli, "Constitution Building Processes and Democratization," p. 16, noting that participatory processes are not automatically institutionalized, "so participation may fail to produce long-term change or create new social forces."

76. Ebrahim, Fayemi, and Loomis, *Promoting a Culture of Constitutionalism*, p. 17.

77. Some public meetings and discussions were held in East Timor, but the consultation process was very rushed and no civic education was offered to prepare for consultation. Two phases of consultation were conducted: prior to drafting (run by the UN mission), but with no impact on drafting; and after a draft was prepared (run by the constituent assembly). But the process was very ad hoc, based on no real plan; often participants had not seen the draft. In the case study authors' view, the lack of meaningful public consultation diminished the constitution's legitimacy.

78. For views questioning the value of public participation processes, at least in some circumstances, see Horowitz, "Conciliatory Institutions and Constitutional Processes in Post-Conflict States," p. 1232 ("To make participation and transparency the touchstones of the legitimacy of a constitution is to exaggerate the benefits and underestimate the costs of such a course. A single process model is unlikely to be apt for all situations, and over the long run the content of the institutions embodied in a constitution is likely to be more important for the democratic future of a state than is the presence of the highest levels of public participation and openness in the way in which the constitution is created."); and Mark Tushnet, "Some Skepticism about Normative Constitutional Advice," *William and Mary Law Review*, vol. 49, no. 4 (2008), pp. 1473–1495, p. 1492 ("These mechanisms do obtain some degree of public buy-in at relatively low cost. The consultative processes have, I believe, generally resulted in no more than cosmetic changes to the proposed constitution. And the up-or-down referenda have, I believe, basically rubber stamps.").

79. Questions such as this remain unsettled in the academic literature. For example, Vicki Jackson observes that "although there is arguably an emerging international consensus that 'legitimate' constitution-making requires public participation or ratification [citing Vivien Hart and Thomas Franck], history suggests that a fairly wide range of processes may, over time, create bonds of legitimacy between a constitutional instrument and a majority of the polity to which it applies.... Depending on existing social and political norms, constitutions negotiated by elite representatives of groups ... may prove sufficiently durable to move towards constitutionalism without having the added qualities of legitimately entrenched law that popular ratification may be thought to provide." Jackson, "What's in a Name?" pp. 1293–94.

80. The case studies employ rather varied implicit definitions of participation, as may be appropriate, given the varying circumstances.

81. See Angela M. Banks, "Expanding Participation in Constitution Making: Challenges and Opportunities," *William and Mary Law Review*, vol. 49, no. 4 (2008), pp. 1043–1069. Focusing on post-conflict contexts, Banks argues that inclusion in participatory constitution making requires "not only that individuals are physically present in the decision-making forums, but that they have an 'effective opportunity to influence the thinking of others'" (p. 1044). She argues further that "significant participation without power ... undermines the theoretical and legal justifications of participatory constitution making" (pp. 1045–46). Unless constitution makers engage with public input, citizen participants will lack the opportunity to exert influence (p. 1062).

82. See also Ghai and Galli, "Constitution Building Processes and Democratization," p. 16 ("Mere consultation is inadequate. The framers of the constitution must be obliged to take public views seriously into account and analyse and incorporate them into the constitution.").

83. Focusing on Rwanda as an example, Banks observes that elites will permit interest groups to influence constitution-making outcomes, so long as the general balance of political power is not affected. In Rwanda, gender equity advocates successfully gained access to the constitution-making process and influenced the content of the constitution, because their proposals "did not disrupt the governance system envisioned by Rwanda's political elites." Multiparty advocates, on the other hand, whose proposals "threatened the political elites' sense of certainty," were not similarly included in the process and "achieved little substantive success." Banks, "Expanding Participation in Constitution Making," pp. 1064–66.

84. In their review of the literature on constitution making, Ginsburg, Elkins, and Blount observe that "the claim that participatory design processes generate constitutions with higher levels of legitimacy and popular support has been subject to only limited study. We can find case studies that seem to support both the more optimistic and more pessimistic hypotheses." Ginsburg, et al., "Does the Process of Constitution-Making Matter?" p. 22.

85. See Gloppen, *Battle over the Constitution,* p. 259, pointing out that in the South African case, a disproportionate share of submissions appeared to come from the well educated, the middle class, former politicians, academics, professionals, and political activists. Gloppen asks, "Is it justified, on democratic grounds, to take into serious consideration the output of such a process?"

86. See John Hatchard, Muna Ndulo, and Peter Slinn, *Comparative Constitutionalism and Good Governance in the Commonwealth* (Cambridge: Cambridge University Press, 2004), p. 34, commenting on Zimbabwe.

87. A number of questions in addition to those identified above could provide fruitful lines of further inquiry. How can the actual impact of participation on legitimacy be measured? Can a generalized list be constructed of the types of issues for which it is most important to seek popular views? Are there certain types of issues on which popular views should not hold sway, particularly where public passions may be inflamed by recent conflict? And how, practically speaking, should public input be accounted for when there is interest in doing so?

88. Ghai and Galli make a similar point, citing successful cases without participation and failures with participation. Ghai and Galli, "Constitution Building Processes and Democratization," p. 14.

89. The IDEA study referenced earlier found that the "failure to adopt or implement a constitution developed by a participatory process has also resulted in increased dissatisfaction and societal tensions." Kirsti Samuels, "Constitution Building Processes and Democratization: A Discussion of Twelve Case Studies," paper prepared for International IDEA, available at www.idea.int/conflict/cbp/upload/IDEA%20CBP%20Comparative%20paper%20by%20Kirsti%20Samuels-2.pdf (accessed May 11, 2009), p. 23. That study further found that while use of participatory and inclusive processes tended to broaden the constitutional agenda, they also "tended to threaten the established power structures, which reacted by undermining the constitutions, amending them, preventing their adoption, or preventing their enforcement." In three of the four cases in that study—Kenya, Guatemala, and Colombia—a representative and participatory constitution-making process was employed, but "the constitution was not adopted, or adopted and not implemented, by the dominant power structures because it challenged their power" (p. 27).

90. Writing about South Africa, Siri Gloppen questions, however, whether there must be a real impact of participation on the text to reap the by-product—legitimacy—of the participation process. Gloppen, *Battle over the Constitution,* pp. 259–60.

91. One theory discussed in the working group meetings (see the introduction to this volume) is that longer processes might allow time for civil-society structures and political parties to develop more fully, thus enhancing possibilities for broad-based participation. Although the case studies do not address this point, it merits further exploration. As noted, idiosyncratic conditions seem to matter most in determining the appropriate length of a process.

92. The case studies focus more on timing questions concerning the length of the process than when a process should be initiated. As Vicki Jackson points out, "there may not be as much choice as might be imagined about whether and when to have a constitution-drafting process—any choice is often highly constrained." Jackson, "What's in a Name?" p. 1291.

93. This may reflect a more general dilemma of state building that is led or pushed by international intervention rather than by organic dynamics.

94. The constitutional reform efforts that were completed are technically "interim," in accordance with the Round Table Agreement, and, in form, substantially amend the 1949 constitution.

95. Ghai and Galli suggest that assessment of foreign engagement must disaggregate the kind of engagement, who is engaging, and the purpose and means of engagement. They propose that "the general principle should be that the foreign parties' role should be facilitative at all times, enabling local people and sometimes even empowering them to make their own decisions, assisting them with logistics, and making them familiar with the experience of other countries which have faced similar problems. As far as possible, intervention should be on a multilateral basis (with a key role for the UN)." Ghai and Galli, "Constitution Building Processes and Democratization," p. 10.

96. For a skeptical view of the value of normative advice-giving—on both the content of constitutions and the process of creating them—by experts outside the political process, see Tushnet, "Some Skepticism about Normative Constitutional Advice." Tushnet argues that "intensely local political considerations" primarily determine the content of constitutions, and therefore "normative recommendations about what 'should' be included in a constitution or constitution-making process are largely pointless" (p. 1474). He further argues that the procedural mechanisms for eliciting elite buy-in during a constitution-making process "will depend quite heavily on the array of political forces on the ground," and that "under some arrays of political power, almost anything will do" while "under others, perhaps only one or two mechanisms will produce sufficient buy-in" (p. 1489). Thus, the particular context in which constitution making takes place will outweigh any normative advice about how to design the process.

97. Kosovo (not among the case studies in this volume) provides another example. After NATO forces pushed Serbian forces out of the province in 1999, the UN Security Council established the United Nations Mission in Kosovo (UNMIK) effectively to govern the territory. In 2000, UNMIK adopted a provisional constitution for Kosovo. While the text was negotiated with Kosovar leaders, who influenced its terms, the United Nations controlled the negotiating process and its final outcome. (This author participated in those negotiations.)

98. One form of beneficial substantive external influence, addressed briefly in the Poland chapter, has been the demand placed on countries desiring to join the European Union to shape or modify their constitutions—as well as ordinary laws and regulations—to conform to EU norms and requirements. This demand has powerfully influenced postcommunist countries in Central and Eastern Europe.

99. The experience in Kosovo in 2000, described in note 96 above, is one example. A provisional constitution was important to Kosovo's political development, but Serb leaders in Kosovo were unwilling to negotiate directly with Kosovar Albanians. For this and other reasons it was essential that the United Nations sponsor the negotiations. Also see Tushnet, "Some Skepticism about Normative Constitutional Advice," p. 1491 ("Advisors who know something about negotiation, bargaining, and the like might be able to move negotiations forward, acting essentially as mediators do in nonjudicial dispute resolution processes.")

100. While not literally a peace negotiation, the roundtable process in Poland that produced the 1989 April Amendment had some of the characteristics of such a negotiation. The case study authors remark that "the connection between political agreement and constitutional amendment was so close that the constitution-writing process lost its authenticity." Parliamentary participation in the process was pro forma, and constitution writing was subordinated to political compromise. Nevertheless, the April Amendment played an important role during the first months of transition.

101. Section 16 of the constitution denied to the new government wide powers of land acquisition and redistribution or discretion in compensating landowners.

102. As a U.S. government official, this author was directly involved in the negotiation and drafting of the Ohrid Agreement in 2001. The discussion of this agreement is based on her personal observations.

103. The case study authors point out that "instead of resolving key differences, the constitution contained much ambiguity, combining contradictory elements to provide something for everyone." The constitution-making process thus "contributed partially to resolving conflict in Nicaragua."

104. The Hungary case study authors (in note 4) suggest that in such a case factors such as relatively successful economic performance and joining the European Union may have neutralized the impact of the legitimacy deficit that they regard as a critical failing of the Hungarian process.

105. The question whether international law speaks to the process of constitution making must be distinguished from questions concerning the impact of international and regional norms on the substance of constitutions, which in many cases has been profound.

106. If, instead, an international legal requirement of public participation was established, the difficult question would be raised whether a constitution that is *not* produced through a participatory process should truly be considered illegitimate or illegal—even if the process accorded with domestic law requirements, and even if the constitution is implemented and popularly respected.

107. In South Africa, legal continuity—which involved having the last apartheid-era parliament approve the interim constitution of 1993—was an important objective of the white political leadership during the transition negotiations. The ANC's willingness to compromise on this point facilitated consensus on the overall transition process.

108. Remark by Allan Brewer-Carías at Working Group Session on Colombia Project on Constitution Making, Peace Building, and National Reconciliation, p. 117 of transcript (on file with the U.S. Institute of Peace Rule of Law Program).

109. In Afghanistan, too, the clarity and security of a final rather than provisional document were sought. Political leaders were concerned that something less than a fully elaborated, permanent constitution would risk creating space for spoilers. But see note 50.

110. See Sam Moyo and Kayode Fayemi, "Zimbabwe's Constitution-Making Process of 1999/2000: A Multi-Dimensional Assessment," in *Constitutionalism in Transition: Africa and Eastern Europe*, ed. M. Serban-Rosen (Warsaw: The Helsinki Foundation for Human Rights, 2003), p. 329, in which the authors make the similar point that adoption of the principles and mechanics of new constitutionalism in Africa is "heavily dependent on the dominant political trends and social processes at play in the country in question." They note further

that "process and content issues are somewhat subordinated to wider political issues."

111. See also Ghai and Galli, "Constitution Building Processes and Democratization," p. 12 ("No way has yet been found to make constitutions politician-proof!").

112. As Ghai and Galli point out, "a constitution cannot guarantee its own protection. Its fate depends on forces outside itself." Ghai and Galli, "Constitution Building Processes and Democratization," p. 11. But it may be possible for a constitution to create arrangements that will encourage or facilitate its implementation. These may include a constitutional implementation commission, provisions for court review of implementation, public monitoring, and requirements for reporting on implementation or the lack thereof. In Colombia, for example, the United Nations funded a special presidential agency, the tasks of which included preparing draft legislation needed to implement the new constitution. Few good answers exist, and there is a need to develop more focused strategies to bolster the chances for effective implementation, particularly in countries without a strong history of constitutionalism.

113. See Horowitz, "Conciliatory Institutions and Constitutional Processes in Post-Conflict States," p. 1229, in which Donald Horowitz points out the impact of political will on decisions regarding the nature of institutions established in a new constitution: "In ethnically divided societies, there is a special, and especially pernicious, version of this problem [group and party interests posing an impediment to constitutional planning]. Politicians who benefit from hostile sentiment toward other groups and its concrete results in the political system are unlikely to transform the conflict-prone environment that supports their political careers. As a result, severely divided societies, which may be most in need of institutions to reduce conflict, may be least likely to adopt them."

114. Leaders can play a decisively negative role as well as a positive one. President Chavez's role in twisting the Venezuelan constitution-making process to his own ends is one example; Prince Sihanouk's unhelpful domination of the Cambodian process is another.

115. Ethiopia provides another example of problematic foreign intervention. The United States showed favoritism toward the dominant party, thus skewing the constitution-making process toward that party's interests.

116. As discussed earlier, East Timor and Cambodia illustrate the possible negative consequences of starting with a political party draft when that party is dominant. In both those cases, the tabling of a political party draft circumscribed the possibility of entertaining alternative proposals.

117. Andrew Arato observes that an analysis of the difficulty of imitating the U.S. constitutional model suggests that variables to consider include "the underlying political culture, the inherited institutional conditions, and the conditions for consensus." Arato, "Forms of Constitution Making," p. 231.

118. The Iraq case study provides a particularly clear example of the need for accurate assessment of the context: "It should have been clear from the outset that Iraqi constitution making would require a complex three-way negotiation in circumstances where nothing—and certainly not a residual shared Iraqi identity—could be taken for granted. Conventional wisdom among U.S. policy makers presented Iraq as a centralized state undergoing a form of decentralization, when the reality was almost diametrically opposite."

119. He continues: "On the one hand, the intrinsic importance of constitution-making demands procedures based on rational argument. On the other hand, the external circumstances of constitution-making invite procedures based on threat-based bargaining." Elster, "Ways of Constitution-Making," p. 138. Barnett Rubin, writing about Afghanistan's 2004 constitution, makes a similar point: The "central paradox of postconflict constitution making [is that] societies emerging from civil conflict need to agree on rules for national decisions that seem reasonably fair to all or most parts of the society. . . . Yet this historical moment when societies most need a constitution is also the one when they are least prepared to adopt it. Not only are their national capacities depleted by war and emigration, but it is uniquely difficult to draft for the ages when even the fairly immediate future is so uncertain." Barnett R. Rubin, "Crafting a Constitution for Afghanistan," *Journal of Democracy*, vol. 15, no. 3 (July 2004), p. 18.

Index

Contributors

Andrew Arato is the Dorothy Hart Hirshon Professor of Political and Social Theory in the Department of Sociology at the New School for Social Research in New York. He is the author of *Civil Society, Constitution and Legitimacy* (2000) and *Constitution Making Under Occupation: The Politics of Imposed Revolution in Iraq* (2009).

Louis Aucoin is an associate research professor at Tufts University's Fletcher School of Law and Diplomacy. Between 2001 and 2003, while a rule of law adviser at the United States Institute of Peace and then a U.S. Supreme Court Fellow, he advised the Rwandan Constitutional Commission on the development of that country's constitution-making process. In 2002, he served as an adviser in East Timor's constitution-making process, and in 1993, he worked for the Asia Foundation as an adviser to the Drafting Committee of the Cambodian Constituent Assembly that adopted Cambodia's Constitution that year.

Andrea Bonime-Blanc is general counsel, chief compliance officer, and corporate secretary at Daylight Forensic & Advisory LLC, an international compliance advisory firm. She was previously chief ethics and compliance officer at Bertelsmann AG and general counsel of PSEG Global, an international power company. Her publications include *Spain's Transition to Democracy: The Politics of Constitution-Making* (1987), *Hungarian Constitutional Reform and the Rule of Law* (1993), and numerous articles on compliance, ethics, and governance topics.

Michele Brandt is director of WSP International's Representation Office in New York City. She formerly was a program manager of East Timor's Constitutional Development Program while working with the Asia Foundation. She was also a full-time constitutional consultant to both the United Nations Transitional Administration in Afghanistan and the Constitutional Commission of Afghanistan.

Allan R. Brewer-Carías is emeritus professor of law at the Central University of Venezuela in Caracas and adjunct professor of law at Columbia Law School in New York. He was a member of the National Constituent Assembly of Venezuela in 1999, and has written extensively on constitutional law and constitutionalism in Venezuela.

Scott N. Carlson was a senior rule of law adviser at the United States Institute of Peace before joining the State Department in 2010. He was the director of the Democracy and Governance Practice Group at Chemonics International. From 1997 to 1998, Carlson was a director and legal adviser for the secretariat, supporting and organizing public participation in the Albanian constitution-making process. He has also served as a constitutional legal adviser for USIP in the Democratic Republic of the Congo (2004) and Iraq (2005).

Jill Cottrell retired recently after 40 years of teaching law at the university level. She worked in Nepal from 2006 to 2008 as a consultant with the United Nations Development Programme in the Constitution Advisory Support Unit. She has also advised on various other constitution-making processes.

Hassen Ebrahim was executive director of South Africa's Constitutional Assembly during its 1994–97 term. He previously served as a member of Parliament in the Gauteng Legislature, and as the national coordinator for the African National Congress's Negotiations Commission. He is the author of *The Soul of a Nation: Constitution-Making in South Africa* (1998).

Donald T. Fox is the senior partner of Fox, Horan & Camerini LLP in New York City. He is chairman of the American Association of the International Commission of Jurists, has conducted missions in a number of countries where the rule of law was imperiled, and has written widely on human rights and constitutionalism in Colombia and other countries.

Thomas M. Franck was the Murray and Ida Becker Professor of Law Emeritus at the New York University School of Law and was the director of the Center for International Studies there from 1965 to 2002. Franck served on the U.S. Department of State's Advisory Committee on International Law and served as director of research at the United Nations Institute for Training and Research (1980–82) and as director of the Carnegie

Endowment for International Peace's International Law Program (1973–79). Franck, a leading scholar of international law and a legal adviser to many foreign governments, passed away in 2009.

Gustavo Gallón-Giraldo has been the director of the Colombian Commission of Jurists in Bogotá, Colombia, since its creation in 1988. The author of many works on Colombia, he has been professor of constitutional law and human rights at several universities in Bogotá since 1979 and a visiting fellow at Notre Dame University's Kellogg Institute (1998–99). He was also special representative of the United Nations Human Rights Commission for Equatorial Guinea from 1999 to 2002.

Zofia A. Garlicka is currently an attorney with the law firm of Carmody MacDonald in Saint Louis. She is a member of the New York State Bar Association and the Missouri Bar Association. She graduated from the University of Warsaw School of Law (2000) and obtained her LLM degree from the Saint Louis University School of Law (2001). She was vice president of the European Law Students Association, Warsaw Chapter.

Lech Garlicki has been a judge of the European Court of Human Rights since 2002. He previously served as a judge of Poland's Constitutional Court (1993–2001) and as a member of the Legislative Council in the Office of the Prime Minister (1987–92 and 2001–02). Garlicki was a representative to the Polish parliament's constitutional commission, and is a former president of the Polish Association of Constitutional Law. He is the author of many publications in the field of human rights, and has served as an expert for the Venice Commission and for the Organization for Security and Cooperation in Europe.

Yash Ghai is professor emeritus at the University of Hong Kong, where he held the Sir Y. K. Pao Chair of Public Law from 1989 to 2006. Ghai chaired the Constitution of Kenya Review Commission and National Constitutional Conference (constituent assembly), and was adviser to the opposition parties during the constitution-making process in Fiji. His other consultancy work on constitution making has included Papua New Guinea (1973–75), Afghanistan (2002–03), Iraq (2005), and Nepal (2006–present).

Vivien Hart was a research professor in the School of Humanities at the University of Sussex in the United Kingdom. A comparative political scientist, she directed the Sussex Cunliffe Center for the Study of Constitutionalism for ten years and held visiting positions and fellowships in the United States and Canada, including as a senior fellow at the United States Institute of Peace. Hart, an innovator in examining how the process of making constitutions relates to the consolidation of democracy and human rights, passed away in 2009.

Stephen P. Marks is the François-Xavier Bagnoud Professor of Health and Human Rights at the Harvard School of Public Health and senior fellow at the University Committee on Human Rights Studies at Harvard University in Cambridge, Massachusetts. He previously directed the UN Studies Program and codirected the human rights and humanitarian affairs concentration at the School of International and Public Affairs at Columbia University. In 1992–93, he was head of human rights education, training, and information for the United Nations Transitional Authority in Cambodia.

Zoltán Miklósi is an assistant professor at the Central European University, Department of Political Science, where he teaches political philosophy.

Laurel E. Miller joined the RAND Corporation as a senior policy analyst in 2009. She has been an adjunct professor of law at Georgetown University and was a senior rule of law adviser at the United States Institute of Peace. She previously held several positions at the U.S. Department of State and the National Security Council. Miller was the deputy U.S. negotiator of a peace agreement for Macedonia, helped negotiate a provisional constitution for Kosovo, and was a member of the U.S. delegation at the Dayton peace conference for Bosnia and Herzegovina. Earlier, Miller practiced law in Washington, D.C., and Brussels.

Jonathan Morrow is international counsel at Hills Stern & Morley LLP, a Washington, DC, law firm, and currently advises the Kurdistan Regional Government of Iraq on constitutional and petroleum matters. He was a senior rule of law adviser at the United States Institute of Peace from 2004 to 2006, working on the constitution of Iraq. Previously, he advised the Asia Foundation and the government of Afghanistan on law reform. Morrow was a legal adviser to the UN Transitional Administration in East Timor, and subsequently to the World Bank, in the negotiation of East Timor's international petroleum treaties.

Muna Ndulo is professor of law and director of the Institute for African Development at Cornell University. He is also Honorary Professor of Law at Cape Town University. He has previously served as public prosecutor for the Zambian Ministry of Legal Affairs, dean of the University of Zambia Law School, Director of the Law Practice Institute in Zambia, political adviser to the United Nations Mission in South Africa

1992–94, Legal Adviser to the United Nations Assistance Mission in East Timor (1999), Legal Expert for the United Nations Mission in Kosovo (2000), and Legal Expert for the United Nations Assistance Mission in Afghanistan (2003).

James C. O'Brien is a principal in The Albright Group LLC, in Washington, DC. Previously, he was a lawyer in the negotiations on the Washington Agreement creating the Bosnian Federation, the Dayton Agreement for Bosnia and Herzegovina, and the Rambouillet negotiations for Kosovo. He was also the special presidential envoy for the Balkans during the Clinton administration.

Keith S. Rosenn teaches law at the University of Miami School of Law and has written widely on constitutional and other legal issues in Brazil. Prior to his academic career, Rosenn practiced law with a Brazilian law firm and worked as a project specialist with the Ford Foundation, helping to establish a graduate legal education program in Rio de Janeiro.

Bereket Habte Selassie is the William E. Leuchtenburg Distinguished Professor of African Studies and Professor of Law at the University of North Carolina at Chapel Hill. Selassie was the chairman of the Constitutional Commission of Eritrea, which led the process of constitution drafting from 1994 to 1997. He has also served as the attorney-general and associate justice of Ethiopia's Federal Supreme Court. Selassie is the author of *The Making of the Eritrean Constitution: The Dialectic of Process and Substance* (2003). Among his many consulting roles, Selassie acted as an external adviser in the Nigerian constitutional review process, September–December 2000.

Anne Stetson is an international lawyer and writer. She is a member of the New York Bar and has written on human rights and constitutional reform in Colombia and other countries.

J Alexander Thier is Director for Afghanistan and Pakistan at the United States Institute of Peace. Prior to joining USIP, he was director of the Project on Failed States at Stanford University's Center on Democracy, Development, and the Rule of Law. From 2002 to 2004, Thier was a legal adviser to Afghanistan's Constitutional and Judicial Reform Commissions in Kabul, where he assisted in the development of a new constitution and judicial system. He also served on an advisory board to the Southern Sudan constitutional process, and has organized expert support to the Constitutional Review Committee of the Iraqi Parliament.

Arun K. Thiruvengadam is an assistant professor in the Faculty of Law, National University of Singapore. His doctoral thesis focused on the area of comparative constitutional law, and studied developments—including those relating to constitution making—in six common law jurisdictions. He previously practiced law in Delhi and served as a law clerk to the chief justice of the Supreme Court of India.

Aili Mari Tripp is professor of political science and gender and women's studies at the University of Wisconsin-Madison. She is also director of the university's Center for Research on Gender and Women. Her publications include *Women and Politics in Uganda* (2000).

Lee Demetrius Walker is an assistant professor of political science at the University of

South Carolina in Columbia. His work has focused on democratization and the role of the justice system in Nicaragua. He is the author of the article "Gender and Attitudes toward Justice System Bias in Central America," *Latin American Research Review* (2008).

Marinus Wiechers is emeritus professor of constitutional and international law at the University of South Africa in Pretoria. He has had lengthy direct involvement in the legal issues surrounding the international status of Namibia. He participated in the Turnhalle Constitutional Conference as a constitutional and legal adviser and was later appointed as co-drafter of the Namibian constitution by the country's Constituent Assembly. He was also a member of the technical constitutional committee responsible for the drafting of the South African constitution.

Philip J. Williams is a professor in the Department of Political Science at the University of Florida. He is the author of many works on Latin America, including *The Catholic Church and Politics in Nicaragua and Costa Rica* (1989) and *Militarization and Demilitarization in El Salvador's Transition to Democracy* (1997).

United States Institute of Peace Press

Since its inception, the United States Institute of Peace Press has published over 150 books on the prevention, management, and peaceful resolution of international conflicts—among them such venerable titles as Raymond Cohen's *Negotiating Across Cultures; Herding Cats and Leashing the Dogs of War* by Chester A. Crocker, Fen Osler Hampson, and Pamela Aall; and I. William Zartman's *Peacemaking and International Conflict.* All our books arise from research and fieldwork sponsored by the Institute's many programs. In keeping with the best traditions of scholarly publishing, each volume undergoes both thorough internal review and blind peer review by external subject experts to ensure that the research, scholarship, and conclusions are balanced, relevant, and sound. As the Institute prepares to move to its new headquarters on the National Mall in Washington, D.C., the Press is committed to extending the reach of the Institute's work by continuing to publish significant and sustainable works for practitioners, scholars, diplomats, and students.

Valerie Norville
Director

About the
United States Institute of Peace

The United States Institute of Peace is an independent, nonpartisan institution established and funded by Congress. The Institute provides analysis, training, and tools to help prevent, manage, and end violent international conflicts, promote stability, and professionalize the field of peacebuilding.

Chairman of the Board: J. Robinson West
Vice Chairman: George E. Moose
President: Richard H. Solomon
Executive Vice President: Tara Sonenshine
Chief Financial Officer: Michael Graham